Annotated English Poets

GENERAL EDITOR: F. W. BATESON

THE POEMS OF

THOMAS GRAY
WILLIAM COLLINS
OLIVER GOLDSMITH

EDITED BY

ROGER LONSDALE

LONGMAN

NORTON

LONGMAN GROUP LIMITED
London
Associated companies, branches and representatives throughout the world

W. W. NORTON & COMPANY, INC.
New York

LONGMAN EDITION

First published 1969

ISBN 0 582 48444 8

NORTON EDITION

First published 1972

ISBN 393 04366 5

Library of Congress Catalog Card Number 74–178125

Printed in Great Britain by
William Clowes & Sons, Limited, London, Beccles and Colchester

Contents

THE POEMS

WILLIAM COLLINS

OLIVER GOLDSMITH

THE POEMS

Illustrations

Note by the General Editor

This series has been planned to apply to the major English poets the requirements, critical and scholarly, that a reading of their complete poetical works entails. Whereas the editorial emphasis recently has been on what may be called textual refinement, sometimes taken to grotesque extremes, the Annotated English Poets editions concern themselves as a series primarily with the *meaning* of the extant texts in their various contexts. In general, therefore, whenever there is a *textus receptus* we reprint it with only minor emendations. It is hoped that with the aids provided in the table of dates and the separate headnotes and footnotes the reader will have all, or almost all, that he needs to understand and appreciate the whole corpus of each poet represented.

Our ideal of combining comprehensibility with comprehensiveness has three technical consequences:

1. Since the essential clues to an author's intentions in any one poem are provided, on the one hand, by what he has already written (the stage reached in his literary evolution) and, on the other hand, by what he will write later (the direction of his progress), an editor will print the poems as far as possible in the order in which they were composed.

2. Since these poets wrote in English, they require elucidation of a different kind from that suitable to the poetry of a dead or foreign language; with occasional exceptions the vocabulary and syntax can be taken for granted or at most briefly paraphrased, but the sources, allusions, biographical implications and stylistic devices will usually need to be spelled out in some detail.

3. Since the modern reader in any English-speaking country will inevitably, even if incorrectly, pronounce English poets of the last five centuries as if they were his contemporaries, whatever impedes the immediate sympathetic response that is implicit in that fact must be regarded as undesirable. Obsolete or inconsistent systems of spelling, punctuation, capitalization and similar conventions of the original printing-house, including those of the author himself, have accordingly been modernized. A compromise has sometimes proved possible between standard modern usage and that of the first editions or the autograph MSS, the test being always that of immediate comprehensibility today.

F. W. BATESON

Preface

The general principles of the series to which this volume belongs will be found in a preliminary note by the General Editor. The following remarks are largely concerned with some effects of the application of those principles to the particular poets with whom I have been concerned. The texts of all poems (and related matter such as Prefaces and Dedications) have been modernized. Alterations to original texts have been kept to the minimum consistent with the aim of providing a text free of accidents of spelling or punctuation likely to obtrude between the modern reader and the poem. The amount of adjustment necessary has inevitably varied from poet to poet and from poem to poem, depending on the nature of the source of the text. Punctuation has normally been clarified by only small changes. Spelling has been modernized, although deliberate archaisms are of course retained. Various conventional contractions have been expanded ('prais'd' becomes 'praised'), as have some elisions ('th'art' becomes 'the art'). But no alterations have been made which would introduce an additional stressed syllable and so affect the metre. Eighteenth-century poets or their printers are not themselves consistent in their conventions in these matters and their variations often seem arbitrary. The word 'even' appears variously in this period as 'ev'n', 'e'en' and 'even', apparently with the same syllabic and metrical value. The word has normally been given in full in this edition.

The problem of the responsibility for accidentals of this kind in eighteenth-century printed texts is a complex and somewhat mysterious matter. The appearance of a poem as it was originally printed can undoubtedly have a typographical attraction and interest, but it would appear that much of the reverence currently felt for the original spelling, punctuation and capitalization of nouns is being paid in practice not to the poet but to his printer. As Bertrand H. Bronson has shown in his essay *Printing as an Index of Taste in Eighteenth Century England* (New York, 1958), the printer at this period usually considered such matters to be his own province and responsibility and considered any authorial interference to be eccentric and tiresome. The manuscripts of Collins and Goldsmith which survive (although Collins's were hardly prepared for the printer) are at best inconsistent and often suggest indifference on their part to such details: they presumably took it for granted that the printer would regularize the text according to his own principles. Gray was characteristically more careful in matters of punctuation and capitalization, but he too seems to have accepted the right of the printer to determine the final appearance of the poem in print, except when the sense was affected.

In the manuscripts which survive from the earlier part of his poetic career, Gray was inclined to capitalize the first letter of every noun, a practice corresponding to printing conventions in the first half of the century. In about 1750, as Bronson points out, printing conventions changed: the capitalization of nouns was suddenly abandoned or retained only for words of particular importance. Gray's practice in his manuscripts approximates to this change of convention. Much of Collins's poetry was published before the change, so that modernization has involved extensive decapitalization. Goldsmith's poetry was published only a decade or two later but after the change in convention, so that much less interference has been called for. Gray's poetic career spans the change: the earlier texts of his poems were heavily capitalized, whereas the later editions, like his own practice in manuscript, are much less so. There is no reason to suppose that he did not expect his printer to follow the new convention. As Bronson has remarked, the logic of modernizing a text in which all nouns are originally capitalized would be to capitalize none of them, since the original capitalization can have had no emphatic effect. The convention prevailing after 1750 has, however, been generally followed here, accepting occasional capitalization as a useful emphatic device, particularly in drawing the reader's attention to personifications. The presence of a personifying tendency has been the test I have normally applied in cases where the retention of a capital was in doubt. A few decisions proved difficult to make, but I hope that my practice has in general been consistent. It may be added that the use of italics as an additional emphatic device is found in early texts of Collins and proved a useful guide in many, though not all, marginal cases. Goldsmith, on the other hand, seems often to have been indifferent to capitalization; in the manuscript of *The Captivity*, for example, which was not printed in his lifetime, he does not at times capitalize what would appear to be obvious if unimportant personifications, and I have not imposed the convention on him in such cases. On the whole, my conclusion is that, while the appearance and particular details of original manuscript and printed texts will always retain a separate interest of their own, a discreet modernization of the text is only an equivalent to the regularization which these poets expected when their poetry was printed in their own lifetime.

It follows from the foregoing considerations that the textual notes do not record accidentals of spelling and punctuation from the early texts, although all substantive variants have been noted. When this edition was at an advanced stage of completion, two editions of poets in this volume were

published which deserve mention, although I was relieved to find that
their aims were basically different from my own: Arthur Friedman's edi-
tion of Goldsmith's *Works* (Oxford, 1965) and the edition of Gray's *Com-
plete Poems* (Oxford, 1967) by H. W. Starr and J. R. Hendrickson. The
emphasis in both these editions is primarily textual and, while I had already
covered much of the same ground, I am happy to acknowledge the advan-
tage I have enjoyed of checking my own textual findings by reference to
these editions. Goldsmith's poems occupy only a relatively small part of
Professor Friedman's edition, and his valuable index to the whole *Works*
would have saved me much labour in the less reliable editions of his pre-
decessors had it been available earlier. When I have derived information
from either of these editions I have tried to acknowledge the debt. In spite
of Professor Friedman's thoroughness, I have managed to use for the first
time one of the few manuscripts of Goldsmith's poetry known to survive,
The Haunch of Venison (by kind permission of the Berg Collection of the
New York Public Library). In the case of Gray, I have been able to correct
and expand the textual findings of the new Oxford edition in various small
ways. For Collins there has been no recent definitive edition and I have col-
lected for the first time the *Drafts and Fragments* (published in 1956), as well
as, at the very last minute, the newly discovered manuscript of the *Ode on
the Popular Superstitions of the Highlands*, much the most important Collins
manuscript to have survived. A few days before my manuscript went to
press, Professor Arthur Johnston's *Selected Poems of Gray and Collins* (1967)
was published, with an extensive interpretative commentary. In a few
cases I was able to refer to material in this edition, which I have in each case
acknowledged.

The present volume aims to go beyond these recent editions in the ex-
tent of the factual information and annotation it contains. In accordance
with the general principles of the series, the poems are arranged in their
order of composition so far as this can be established. In the headnotes I
have attempted to collect all the information—biographical, historical and
bibliographical—relevant to understanding each poem in its context; and
the annotation combines with the textual notes such elucidation of details
of the text as seems necessary. One feature of the annotation may need
justification, especially as the new Oxford edition of Gray explicitly shuns
virtually all the parallels with earlier poetry assiduously collected by his
editors up to the end of the nineteenth century.

The fact that Gray's poetry is often a remarkable tissue of the phrases of
other poets can hardly be ignored. Gray himself was conscious of this as-
pect of his verse: he wrote to Bedingfield on 27 August 1756, after admit-
ting to some borrowings in his Pindaric *Odes*, 'do not wonder therefore,
if some Magazine or Review call me Plagiary: I could shew them a

hundred more instances, wch they never will discover themselves'. Norton Nicholls recorded in his 'Reminiscences' of the poet that Gray 'congratulated himself on not having a good verbal memory; for, without it he said he had imitated too much; & if he had possessed such a memory all that he wrote would have been imitation, from his having read so much'. Perhaps disturbed by his friend Richard Hurd's discussions of the difference between legitimate 'imitation' and mere plagiarism—in the *Discourse concerning Poetical Imitation* (1751) and the *Letter to Mr. Mason on the Marks of Imitation* (1757)—Gray acknowledged some of his borrowings in his collected *Poems* in 1768 (the acknowledgement turning them into acceptable 'imitations'). After his death, successive editors and contributors to magazines steadily added to the number of such debts. Critics of Gray's poetry were thus able to point to a lack of originality or even to accuse him of plagiarism; his admirers, on the other hand, appealed to the older concept of legitimate imitation of earlier poets and emphasized Gray's skill in blending and improving what he borrowed. John Mitford was the most diligent of the nineteenth-century editors in this respect, but new 'sources' and parallels are still being produced at the present time. I have tracked down and examined all the parallels adduced in the past but have usually decided not to include those which seemed merely coincidental, as is frequently the case with the parallels with classical authors favoured in the nineteenth century, which seemed to Gray's admirers to be more proper for 'imitation' and more dignifying to his poetry. I have myself added a great many parallels to those already adduced, although I have concentrated—by no means exclusively, however—on the debts to earlier English verse.

In dealing with this aspect of Gray (which is a somewhat less striking aspect of Collins's poetry and considerably less so of Goldsmith's), I have been frequently surprised by the lack of caution and discrimination of those who produce or discuss the significance of such echoes or borrowings. The possibility of mere coincidence must always be borne in mind, and unless they are striking I have not usually recorded mere isolated parallels. Some parallels verge upon 'imitation', in the sense acceptable to the eighteenth century, where the reader was expected to cooperate by appreciating the parallel as a virtual allusion to another poet. (The headnote to Gray's *Ode on the Death of a Favourite Cat* may indicate, however, that it can be dangerous to identify a parallel as an allusion too facilely.) To a separate category belong such conscious borrowings as those which Gray was himself prepared to acknowledge in public (although he admitted that there were many others he was not owning): these, and others which, though genuine echoes, need not have been conscious, cannot be supposed to count as effective allusions affecting the meaning of the poem in which they occur in a precise way. Of the greatest interest are perhaps those sustained patterns of borrowing found in both Gray and Collins which have significance for the literary historian in indicating new and important areas of influence on this generation of poets. I have tried to record all borrowings from Spenser, Shakespeare and Milton, because the reorientation of much mid-eighteenth-century poetry towards the earlier English tradition is revealed by the way in which Gray and Collins not merely make these poets at times the explicit subject of their verse, but often imitate their diction, phrasing and imagery. Such parallels can significantly affect the local texture and meaning of a poem; consciously archaic effects aimed at by Gray and Collins can be missed without the specific parallels. When a particular parallel with one of these poets seems slight, it should be remembered that the cumulative debt is in some ways more relevant. It is worth recording that Gray once told Nicholls that 'he never sat down to compose poetry without reading Spencer for a considerable time previously'.

It would be misleading to give the impression that Gray and Collins borrowed consciously or unconsciously only from Spenser, Shakespeare and Milton. The minds and ears of mid-eighteenth century poets were still full of Dryden and Pope, as will be readily apparent. Other parallels indicate only that certain words and phrases were the common poetic property of the age and do not propose a particular source; parallels have often been triumphantly produced in the past which in fact embody phrases used by a dozen poets of the period. Certain parallels can emphasize new poetic vogues or preoccupations of the period. The influence of James Thomson on both Gray and Collins becomes more than ever clear, and other parallels emphasize Gray's relationship to the 'melancholy' poetry popular in the 1740s and the influence of the Warton brothers and Mark Akenside on Collins. The fact that such poets were contemporaries of our poets also affects the dating of certain poems when this is in doubt, although the possible ambiguity of such evidence must always be remembered. The final interest of the parallels is perhaps simply a matter of literary personality or the creative process. Goldsmith was much less of a borrower than Gray or Collins, his most striking thefts being from his own prose writings. Collins's debts are usually to those earlier poets whom he particularly and explicitly admired. In the case of Gray, one seems at times to be confronting a kind of literary kleptomania, such is his dependence on the phrasing and thoughts of other poets. For all these reasons—but with the caution that what is recorded may be either coincidence or purposeful allusion, common poetic diction of the age or furtive plagiarism, conscious or unconscious borrowing—the numerous parallels I have noted have seemed worth preserving, however they may have amplified the annotation.

Where possible, the texts I have cited have been standard editions, but in some cases I have had to rely on collections such as Anderson's and Chalmers's *British Poets*. In the case of Pope's translation of Homer, I was unable to use the recently published Twickenham edition and have not discriminated between Pope's own translation of the *Odyssey* and the books contributed by Broome and Fenton.

The three poets with whom I have been concerned were at the height of their reputation in the nineteenth century and it is inevitable that one should feel a particular debt to the editors of that period, whatever their limitations may now appear to be: in the case of Gray, to Mitford and Tovey; of Collins, to Dyce and W. C. Bronson; of Goldsmith, to Prior and Austin Dobson. Every student of the life and writings of Gray will have found himself deeply indebted to the magnificently annotated edition of his *Correspondence* (Oxford, 1935), edited by Paget Toynbee and Leonard Whibley. I hope that I have adequately indicated in the body of this work my many other debts to more recent scholarship.

I owe much to the courtesy and assistance of the staffs of the various libraries where I have worked or from which I have received answers to queries or permission to use material, in particular to the British Museum, the Bodleian Library and, at a late stage, the Alderman Library of the University of Virginia. I would also like to acknowledge the particular assistance of Dr Ian Jack, Librarian of Pembroke College, Cambridge; Mr J. M. G. Blakiston of Winchester College; Miss Ellen Shaffer of the Free Library of Philadelphia; Mr Herbert Cahoon of the Pierpont Morgan Library; the late Dr John Gordan of the Berg Collection of the New York Public Library; and Mr J. P. Cooper, the Librarian of Trinity College, Oxford. Mr E. V. Quinn, the Librarian of my own College, Balliol, has been invariably patient and helpful in dealing with many requests over the last five years.

For information and advice I would like to thank Mr Martin Dodsworth, Mr John Fuller, Mr Michael Gearin-Tosh, Miss C. Lamont, Mr T. J. Reed and Professor C. B. Ricks. Mr F. W. Bateson made many valuable suggestions in the course of reading through the entire manuscript before publication. Mr J. C. Maxwell, kindly read the page-proofs and drew my attention to a number of errors. My wife, who has had to live with these three poets for our entire married life, has given me moral and practical support in a task which at times seemed interminable: in particular with the translation of the Latin poems of Gray and with proof-reading. As for the errors and inaccuracies to which in a project of this sort one must resign oneself, I can only hope they are not indecently numerous.

R. H. L.

THE POEMS OF
THOMAS GRAY

THE POEMS

FRAGMENTARY AND
UNDATED POEMS

LATIN POETRY

GREEK POETRY

POEMS OF DOUBTFUL
AUTHENTICITY

Chronological Table of Thomas Gray's Life and Writings

1716   (*26 Dec.*) Born at the house of his father, Philip G., a scrivener, in Cornhill, where his mother, Dorothy, and her sister Mary Antrobus, also keep a milliner's shop. The only child of twelve to survive.

c. 1725–34 Educated at Eton, where his uncles, Robert and William Antrobus, are Assistants; becomes one of a group of friends (with Horace Walpole, Richard West and Thomas Ashton) known as the Quadruple Alliance. A few Latin exercises date from this period.

1734   (*4 July*) Entered as pensioner at Peterhouse, Cambridge. (*9 Oct.*) Admitted at Peterhouse. (Ashton has already been admitted a Scholar of King's, 11 Aug.; Walpole is to come up to King's on 11 March 1735; West matriculates at Christ Church, Oxford, 22 May 1735).
(*8 Dec.*) Sends his first extant poem in English, *Lines Spoken by John Dennis*, to Walpole.

1735   (*22 Nov.*) Admitted at the Inner Temple.

1736   (*12 Feb.*) His aunt Sarah Gray dies leaving him her small property.
(*April–May*) His *Hymeneal* on the marriage of the Prince of Wales published in the Cambridge *Gratulatio*.

1737   (*March*) Writes the Tripos Verses, *Luna habitabilis*.

1738   (*14 Sept.*) Leaves Cambridge and lives at his father's house, at first intending to embark on a legal career.

1739   (*29 March*) Begins his tour to France and Italy with Horace Walpole, staying principally at Paris, Rheims, Lyons, Florence and Rome. During this period sends several Latin poems to West and in the second half of 1740 begins *De Principiis Cogitandi*.

1741   (*c. 3 May*) Quarrels with Walpole at Reggio.
(*July–1 Sept.*) Travels back alone to England via Milan, Lyons

and Paris, visiting the Grande Chartreuse, where he writes an *Ode* in the album on 21 Aug.

(*6 Nov.*) Death of his father, leaving the family in an insecure financial position.

1742   During the winter and early spring intends to study law, corresponds regularly with West, sending him Latin verses and translations, and begins his tragedy *Agrippina*.

(*28 May*) Visits his uncle Jonathan Rogers at Stoke Poges, Bucks., staying there until the autumn, except for a month (mid-June to mid-July) in London.

(*1 June*) Death of Richard West; G. had just sent him his *Ode on the Spring*.

(*Aug.*) Writes *Sonnet on West, Eton Ode, Ode to Adversity*.

(*15 Oct.*) Returns to Peterhouse as a Fellow-commoner, remaining in Cambridge, with a few protracted absences, for the rest of his life; at some point in the months preceding his return writes the unfinished *Hymn to Ignorance*.

(*21 Oct.*) Death of Jonathan Rogers.

(*? Dec.*) G.'s mother and Mary Antrobus retire from Cornhill to Stoke Poges. G. accordingly divides his summers between Stoke and London in the following decade.

1743   (*Oct.*) Graduated as Bachelor of Laws.

1745   (*8 Nov.*) Reconciliation with Walpole.

1746   (*Autumn*) Shows Walpole some of his earlier poetry and probably the beginning of the *Elegy* which he has recently started.

1747   (*1 March*) Sends Walpole his *Ode on the Death of a Favourite Cat*.

(*30 May*) The *Eton Ode* published by Dodsley.

1748   (*15 Jan.*) Three of G.'s poems appear through Walpole in Dodsley's *Collection of Poems*.

(*Jan or Feb.*) Speaks of William Mason as a new acquaintance.

(*25 March*) His house in Cornhill burned down in a fire.

(*c. Aug.*) Begins writing *The Alliance of Education and Government*.

1749   (*5 Nov.*) Death of Mary Antrobus.

1750   (*12 June*) Sends *Elegy*, completed at Stoke Poges, to Walpole, through whom it passes into manuscript circulation.

(*? Aug.–Sept.*) Writes *A Long Story* for Lady Cobham.

1751   (*15 Feb.*) The *Elegy* published by Dodsley.

1752   Begins *Progress of Poesy*; projects a 'History of English Poetry' to be written in conjunction with William Mason.

1753   (*11 March*) Death of G.'s mother
(*29 March*) *Six Poems with Designs by Mr. Bentley* published by Dodsley.

1754   (*Dec.*) Has completed *Progress of Poesy* and is starting *The Bard* (and probably *Ode on Vicissitude*).

1755   Declines an offer of the position of Secretary to the Earl of Bristol in Lisbon.

1756   (*5 March*) Removes from Peterhouse to Pembroke Hall.

1757   (*8 Aug.*) *Odes* published, printed at the Strawberry Hill Press. This event marks the virtual end of G.'s creative career: his interests hereafter are primarily historical and botanical.
(*5 Dec.*) Declines the Poet Laureateship.

1758   (*c. Jan.*) Writes *Epitaph on Mrs. Clerke*.
(*c. June*) Writes *Epitaph on a Child* for Thomas Wharton.
(*Sept.*) Death of Mrs. Rogers; G.'s connection with Stoke Poges ends in the following year. Hereafter his summers usually include 'rambles' to visit friends in different parts of the country, only the more protracted of which are mentioned here.

1759   (*9 July*) Takes up residence in London, in Southampton Row, to read at the British Museum.

1760   (*28 June–21 July*) Stays at Shiplake with Mrs. Jennings and Miss Speed.
(*Summer*) Is excited by Macpherson's *Fragments of Ancient Poetry* and Evan Evans's discoveries of Welsh poetry.

1761   (*5 May*) By this date has written *The Fatal Sisters* and *The Descent of Odin* and probably his other imitations of Welsh and Norse poetry as well, with the intention of including them in his 'History of English Poetry'.
(*Aug.*) Writes *Epitaph on Sir W. Williams*.
(*Oct.*) Writes 'Song' for Miss Speed, who is married on 12 Nov.
(*19 Nov.*) Leaves London and returns to Cambridge.

1762   (*11 June*) Meets Norton Nicholls.
(*1 July–11 Nov.*) Visits Mason at York and Wharton at Old Park, Durham.

(*Nov.*) Fails to obtain the Regius Professorship of Modern History at Cambridge.

1764   (*Jan.–March*) During this period writes *The Candidate*.

1765   (*27 May–28 Oct.*) Visits York, Old Park, and the Highlands.

1766   (*16 May–4 July*) Visits Kent.

1766   (*15 June–2 Nov.*) Visits York, Old Park and the Lake District

1768   (*12 March*) Collected edition of his *Poems* published by Dodsley, including Norse and Welsh imitations.
(*4 May*) *Poems* published at Glasgow by Foulis.
(*7 April–15 July*) Visits Kent.
(*June*) Writes *On Lord Holland's Seat at Margate*.
(*28 July*) Appointed Regius Professor of Modern History at Cambridge.

1769   (*April*) Completes his *Ode for Music*.
(*1 July*) Performance of the *Ode for Music* at the Installation of the Chancellor of the University.
(*18 July–15 Oct.*) Visits York, Old Park and the Lake District.
(*Dec.*) Meets Charles-Victor Bonstetten, a young Swiss, and takes him to Cambridge.

1770   (*March*) Bonstetten leaves England.
(*2 July*) Makes his will.
(*2 July–3 Aug.*) Tour in West Country with Norton Nicholls.

1771   (*30 July*) Dies at Cambridge; is buried at Stoke Poges.

Abbreviations

EDITIONS AND MSS OF GRAY'S POEMS

Commonplace Book
: In 3 vols, at Pembroke College, Cambridge, containing G.'s transcripts of many of his poems (intermingled with a mass of other historical and literary material) and Mason's transcripts of other poems made after G.'s death.

1753
: *Designs by Mr. R. Bentley for Six Poems by Mr. T. Gray*, 1753.

1757
: *Odes, by Mr. Gray*, 1757.

1768
: *Poems by Mr. Gray*, 1768 (published by J. Dodsley in London; by Foulis in Glasgow).

1775
: *The Poems of Mr. Gray, to which are prefixed Memoirs of his Life and Writings by W. Mason*, York, 1775. (The *Memoirs* and *Poems* are separately paginated and the section in question has been cited explicitly when necessary.)

Wakefield
: *The Poems of Mr. Gray. With Notes by Gilbert Wakefield*, 1786.

Jones
: *The Poetical Works of Thomas Gray*, ed. Stephen Jones, 1799; 2nd edn enlarged, 1800.

Mitford
: *The Poems of Thomas Gray*, ed. John Mitford, 1814.
  The Works of Thomas Gray, ed. J. Mitford, 2 vols, 1816 (an expanded edn. in 4 vols was published in 1835–7).
  The Correspondence of Thomas Gray and William Mason, ed. J. Mitford, 1853.
  MS Notebooks of John Mitford (British Museum, Add. MS. 32561).

Mathias
: *The Works of Thomas Gray*, ed. T. J. Mathias, 2 vols, 1814.

Gosse
: *The Works of Thomas Gray, in Prose and Verse*, ed. Sir Edmund Gosse, 4 vols, 1884, (revised edn, 1902–06).

Tovey
: *Gray's English Poems*, ed. D. C. Tovey, Cambridge, 1898.

Corresp
: *The Correspondence of Thomas Gray*, ed. Paget Toynbee and Leonard Whibley, 3 vols, Oxford, 1935.

Starr and   *The Complete Poems of Thomas Gray, English, Latin and*
Hendrickson   *Greek*, ed. H. W. Starr and J. R. Hendrickson, Oxford,
                 1966.

OTHER WORKS

Dodsley's   *A Collection of Poems . . . By Several Hands*, published by
Collection   R. Dodsley (vols i-iii, 1748, 2nd edn, 1748; vol. iv, 1755;
                 vols. v-vi, 1758).

DNB   *The Dictionary of National Biography.*

Gentleman's   *The Gentleman's Magazine* (from 1731).
Mag.

Grose   Francis Grose, *A Classical Dictionary of the Vulgar Tongue*
                 (1785; 3rd edn, 1796), ed. Eric Partridge, 1931 (reprinted,
                 1963).

Johnson,   *A Dictionary of the English Language*, 1755 (cited from
Dictionary   4th edn, revised, 1773).

Johnson,   *Lives of the Most Eminent English Poets*, ed. G. Birkbeck
Lives   Hill, 3 vols, Oxford, 1905.

Ketton-   R. W. Ketton-Cremer, *Thomas Gray*, Cambridge, 1955.
Cremer

MLN   *Modern Language Notes.*

MLR   *Modern Language Review.*

MP   *Modern Philology.*

Northup   C. S. Northup, *A Bibliography of Thomas Gray*, New
                 Haven, 1917.

OED   *Oxford English Dictionary.*

PMLA   *Publications of the Modern Language Association of
                 America.*

Powell Jones   William Powell Jones, *Thomas Gray, Scholar*, Cambridge,
                 Mass., 1937.

RES   *Review of English Studies.*

Starr   H. W. Starr, *A Bibliography of Thomas Gray, 1917–1951*,
                 Philadelphia, 1953.

Times Lit.   *The Times Literary Supplement.*
Supp.

Walpole,   *Memoirs of the Reign of King George the Third*, ed. G. F. R.
Memoirs   Barker, 4 vols, 1894.

Walpole,   *Letters*, ed. Mrs Paget Toynbee, 16 vols, Oxford,
Letters   1903–05.

Walpole,   *Correspondence*, ed. Wilmarth S. Lewis and others, New
Correspondence Haven, (in progress), vols i–, 1937– .

Plate 1 Thomas Gray in 1747, painted at the request of
Horace Walpole. He is holding the MS. of the *Eton Ode*.
From the painting by John Giles Eckhardt.

1 [Lines Spoken by the Ghost of John Dennis at the Devil Tavern]

Written by 8 Dec. 1734, the day on which G., who had gone up to Peterhouse the previous Oct., sent it in a letter to Horace Walpole. First printed in 1915 by Toynbee, in the *Correspondence of Gray, Walpole, West and Ashton* 12–15. Walpole evidently refers to it in his 'Memoir of Gray', (*Corresp* iii 1287): 'One of his first pieces of poetry was an answer in English verse to an Epistle from H.W.'

G.'s letter introduces the poem as follows, (*Corresp* i 9): 'I (tho' I say it) had too much modesty to venture answering your dear, diverting Letter, in the Poetical Strain myself; but, when I was last at the DEVIL, meeting by chance with the deceased Mr Dennis there, he offer'd his Service, &, being tip'd with a Tester, wrought, what follows–'. John Dennis (1657–1734), dramatist and critic, often satirized by Pope, had died 6 Jan. 1734. An additional reason why G. considered him suitable to supply a message from the next world may have been that Dennis's last published work was a translation from the Latin of Thomas Burnet's *A Treatise Concerning the State of Departed Souls* (1733). The Devil Tavern, also mentioned more than once by Pope, was in Fleet Street.

In its literary affiliations G.'s poem belongs ultimately to the convention established in Lucian's *Mortuorum Dialogi* of short and grimly ironic conversations between famous characters in the underworld. Lucian had been imitated in France by Fontenelle in his *Dialogues des Morts* (1683) and by Fénelon (1712). The convention had been adapted in England in Thomas Brown's satirical *Letters from the Dead to the Living* (1702), where Brown acknowledges the relationship with Lucian and Fontenelle. The tone and some of the content of G.'s poem derive from Brown, in particular from such sections as 'A Letter of News from Mr. *Joseph Haines* of Merry Memory, to his Friends at *Will's* Coffee-House in *Covent-Garden*' and 'Beau *Norton* to his Brothers at *Hypollito's* in *Covent-Garden*' (written by John Ayloff). But G. seems also to have had in mind Elizabeth Rowe's entirely serious and very popular *Friendship in Death, in Twenty Letters from the Dead to the Living* (1728) of which a 3rd edn had been published in 1733. The ecstatic enthusiasm of most of Mrs Rowe's correspondents from the other world seems to be parodied in the opening lines. Mason suspected that G. was ridiculing Mrs Rowe in another letter written in Dec. 1736 (*Corresp* i 57 and *n*).

The text followed here is that of G.'s holograph letter in Pembroke College.

From purling streams and the Elysian scene,
From groves that smile with never-fading green,
I reascend: in Atropos' despite
Restored to Celadon and upper light.
5 Ye gods, that sway the regions under ground,
Reveal to mortal view your realms profound;
At his command admit the eye of day:
When Celadon commands, what god can disobey?
Nor seeks he your Tartarean fires to know,
10 The house of torture and the abyss of woe;
But happy fields and mansions free from pain,
Gay meads and springing flowers, best please the
    gentle swain.
That little, naked, melancholy thing.

¶ *1.1–3*. Mrs Rowe's correspondents from the other world often describe
its natural beauties and the 'happy mansions' in which they dwell, e.g.
'the happy Groves stood crown'd, with unfading Verdure; the lucid
Currents danc'd along, ov'r Sands of Gold; the charming Bowers dis-
play'd their ever-blooming Pride, and breathed *Ambrosia*', etc; and 'From
the fragrant Bowers, the ever-blooming Fields, and lightsome Regions
of the Morning Star, I wish Health, and every Blessing to the charming
Sylvia! the Blessing of the Earth', *Friendship in Death* (3rd edn, 1733)
pp. 23–5, 30. But G.'s phrasing was relatively common e.g., William
Broome, *On the Seat of the War in Flanders* 120–1: 'to gentler scenes, / To
shadowy bowers and never-fading greens!'
4. Dryden, *Flower and the Leaf* 484: 'Our Souls not yet prepar'd for upper
Light'.   *Celadon*] The name by which Walpole was known to the
members of the 'Quadruple Alliance'. At Eton. G. was 'Orosmades' (see
l. 41), Richard West 'Favonius' or 'Zephyrus' and Thomas Ashton
'Almanzor'. Celadon was the name of the amorous shepherd in
D'Urfé's pastoral romance, *Astrée*, and also of a lover in Dryden's *Secret
Love*.
7. eye of day] The sun. See *Education and Government* 67 (p. 97).
9. Par. Lost ii 69: 'Mixt with *Tartarean* Sulphur, and strange fire.'
11. Par Lost i 249–50: 'Farewell happy Fields / Where Joy for ever dwells';
and ii 461–2: 'the pain / Of this ill Mansion.'
13. Prior's *Imitation* of Hadrian's lines to his soul ll. 1, 3–4: 'Poor little,
pretty, flutt'ring Thing / ... / And dost Thou prune thy trembling Wing, / To
take thy Flight Thou know'st not whither!' In l. 6 he describes the soul as
'pensive, wav'ring, melancholy', but does not translate Hadrian's *nudula*
[naked]. Pope, *Iliad* xvi 1035 and xxii 458, have 'A naked, wandering,
melancholy ghost'.
13. Brown, *Letters from the Dead* pp. 2–3: 'When I shook hands with your
upper Hemisphere, I stumbled into a dark, uncouth dismal Lane . . . .'

My soul, when first she tried her flight to wing,
15 Began with speed new regions to explore,
And blundered through a narrow postern door.
First most devoutly having said its prayers,
It tumbled down a thousand pair of stairs,
Through entries long, through cellars vast and deep,
20 Where ghostly rats their habitations keep,
Where spiders spread their webs and owlish goblins
        sleep.
After so many chances had befell,
It came into a mead of asphodel:
Betwixt the confines of the light and dark
25 It lies, of 'Lysium the St. James's Park.
Here spirit-beaux flutter along the Mall,
And shadows in disguise skate o'er the iced Canal;
Here groves embowered and more sequestered shades,
Frequented by the ghosts of ancient maids,
30 Are seen to rise. The melancholy scene,
With gloomy haunts and twilight walks between,
Conceals the wayward band: here spend their time
Greensickness girls that died in youthful prime,
Virgins forlorn, all dressed in willow-green-i,

18. A piece of the letter has been cut out and 'Stairs' is supplied in pencil, apparently by Walpole.
23. Pope used this phrase several times: 'the flow'ry Meads of *Asphodill*', *Letter to Cromwell* 4; 'In yellow meads of asphodel', *Ode on St Cecilia's Day* 75; 'In ever-flowering meads of asphodel', *Odyssey* xxiv 20.
24. 'Betwixt the Confines of the Night and Day', Dryden, *Aeneid* vii 579.
25-6. One of Charles II's improvements of St James Park had been the addition of the Mall, the enclosed walk running parallel to the front of St James's Palace, which became a fashionable resort as soon as he made the Park public. Charles also added the Canal mentioned in l. 27.
28. 'In shadier Bower / More sacred and sequestered', *Par. Lost* iv 705-6.
29-34. G. may be alluding to the description of the underworld in Bk vi of the *Aeneid*, in which Virgil mentions *innuptae puellae* among the inhabitants, l. 307. But, more immediately, he was imitating *The Rape of the Lock* iv 27, 30-1, in which the two handmaids of the goddess in the Cave of Spleen are '*Ill-Nature* like an *ancient Maid*' and '*Affectation* with a sickly Mien', who 'Shows in her Cheek the Roses of Eighteen'.
31. 'To arched walks of twilight groves', Milton, *Il Penseroso* 133; 'echoing walks between', *Par. Lost* xi 1107.
33. *Green-sickness*] An anaemic disease affecting girls about the age of puberty.

35   With Queen Elizabeth and Nicolini.
    More to reveal, or many words to use,
Would tire alike your patience and my muse.
Believe that never was so faithful found
Queen Proserpine to Pluto under ground,
40   Or Cleopatra to her Mark Antony,
As Orozmades to his Celadony.
    P.S. Lucrece for half a crown will show you fun,
But Mrs. Oldfield is become a nun.
Nobles and cits, Prince Pluto and his spouse,
45   Flock to the ghost of Covent-Garden House:
Plays, which were hissed above, below revive,
When dead applauded that were damned alive.
The people, as in life, still keep their passions,
But differ something from the world in fashions.

35. Nicolini] Nicolino Grimaldi (b. *c.* 1673), an enormously popular Italian
opera-singer, who performed in London 1708–17. G. had mentioned him in
his previous letter to Walpole in Nov. 1734, *Corresp* i 8. Addison refers to
him frequently in *Spectator* Nos. 5, 13, 205, 235, 314, 323, 405. As a *castrato*
he parallels the Maiden Queen.
41. See l. *4n.* Orozmades or Orasmades is an alteration of Orosmasdes,
the principal Zoroastrian divinity, which is also found in Lee's *Rival
Queens* II i.
42–51. G. imitates Brown and Ayloff in this satiric reversal of roles which the
famous suffer in the underworld, e.g. *Letters from the Dead* pp. 254–5:
'Queen *Tamyris*, Proportions out the Offals for *Cerberus*; *Tarquin* Sweeps his
Den, and *Romulus* is a Turnspit in *Pluto's* Kitching; *Artaxerxes* is an under
Scullion, and *Pompy* the Magniffcent, a Rag-Man. *Mark Anthony*, that
disputed his *Mistress* at the price of the whole Universe, goes now about with
dancing Dogs, a Monkey and a Rope; *Cleopatra*, that cou'd swallow a
Province at one Draught, when it was to drink her *Lovers* Health, submits
now to the humble Employment of feeding Proserpina's Piggs.' Brown
also pays particular attention to Lucretia. Renowned in the upper world
for chastity, she is now reported to have been 'got with child upon a Hay-
cock by *Aesop* the Fabulist', *Letters from the Dead* p. 22. In the *Second Part*
of his *Letters* (1703), Brown reported on the collapse of her reputation in
greater detail.
42–3. Starr and Hendrickson suggest that *Lucrece* and *nun* were terms then
used of prostitutes but this meaning would tend to obscure rather than
reinforce G.'s point.
43. Mrs Oldfield] Anne Oldfield (1683–1730), a famous actress, who had
been the mistress successively of Arthur Mainwaring and Gen. Charles
Churchill.
44. cits] A shortened form of 'citizens'. Johnson defines a 'cit' as 'a pert low
townsman'.

50   Queen Artemisia breakfasts on bohea,
And Alexander wears a ramilie.

50. Artemisia] The heroine of Rowe's *Ambitious Stepmother*, was the wife and sister of Mausolus, King of Caria, to whose memory she erected the Mausoleum. As Starr and Hendrickson suggest, G.'s point is that Artemisia is supposed to have mixed ashes in her daily drink as a sign of grief at her husband's death.   *bohea*] 'A species of tea, of higher colour, and more astringent taste, than green tea' (Johnson). Cp. 'To pass her time 'twixt reading and Bohea', Pope, *Epistle to Miss Blount, on her leaving the Town* 15. *51. ramilie*] An elaborate wig, which had a long plait behind, tied with a bow at top and bottom.

2 [Translation from Statius, *Thebaid* VI 646–88, 704–24]

G. wrote to West from Cambridge on 8 May 1736: 'for this little while last past, I have been playing with Statius; we yesterday had a game at Quoits together, you'll easily forgive me for having broke his head, as you have a little Pique to him' (*Corresp* i 39). With the letter G. sent 59 ll. of his translation of the *Thebaid* vi 646–88. Before 24 May 1736 G. sent West a further 27 ll., translating *Thebaid* vi 704–24, which he introduced as follows: 'I send you my translation, which I did not engage in because I liked that part of the Poem, nor do I now send it to you because I think it deserves it, but merely to show you how I misspend my days' (*Corresp* i 41–2).

This second passage, and the letter which accompanied it, exist only in a garbled and composite form which Mason dated 8 May 1736 in *1775* (*Memoirs* pp. 7–10); it was undoubtedly sent later, but before 24 May when a letter from West referred to a line in the second passage. A note by Mason (*Memoirs* p. 8) states that G.'s translation consisted in all of 'about 110 lines'. If this is true, G.'s translation of *Thebaid* vi 689–703, which must have consisted of some 24 ll., has not survived. The first passage was first printed by Mitford, *Correspondence of Gray and Mason* pp. 2–4, in 1853; and the second passage, as stated above, by Mason in *Memoirs* pp. 9–10. The text of the first passage is that of the MS; Mason's text is the only authority for the second. The MS is damaged at ll. 55–6, where '[her]' and 'wi[th]' have been supplied.

Then thus the king: 'Whoe'er the quoit can wield,
And furthest send its weight athwart the field,

1. king] Adrastus. *G.'s marginal note.*

Let him stand forth his brawny arm to boast.'
Swift at the word, from out the gazing host
5   Young Pterelas with strength unequal drew,
Labouring the disc, and to small distance threw.
The band around admire the mighty mass,
A slippery weight and formed of polished brass.
The love of honour bade two youths advance,
10 Achaians born, to try the glorious chance;
A third arose, of Acarnania he,
Of Pisa one and three from Ephyre.
Nor more; for now Nesimachus's son,
By acclamations roused, came towering on.
15 Another orb upheaved his strong right hand,
Then thus: 'Ye Argive flower, ye warlike band,
Who trust your arms shall raze the Tyrian towers,
And batter Cadmus' walls with stony showers,
Receive a worthier load; yon puny ball
20 Let youngsters toss.'
He said, and scornful flung the unheeded weight
Aloof: the champions trembling at the sight
Prevent disgrace, the palm despaired resign. ⎫
All but two youths the enormous orb decline: ⎬
25 These conscious shame witheld and pride of noble line.⎭
As bright and huge the spacious circle lay,
With doubled light it beamed against the day:
So glittering shows the Thracian godhead's shield,
With such a gleam affrights Pangaea's field,
30 When blazing 'gainst the sun it shines from far,
And, clashed, rebellows with the din of war.
   Phlegyas the long-expected play began,
Summoned his strength and called forth all the man.
All eyes were bent on his experienced hand,
35 For oft in Pisa's sports his native land
Admired that arm; oft on Alpheus' shore
The ponderous brass in exercise he bore:
Where flowed the widest stream he took his stand;⎫
Sure flew the disc from his unerring hand, ⎬
40 Nor stopped till it had cut the further strand. ⎭
And now in dust the polished ball he rolled,
Then grasped its weight, elusive of his hold;
Now fitting to his grip and nervous arm,
Suspends the crowd with animation warm,
45 Nor tempts he yet the plain but, hurled upright,
Emits the mass, a prelude of his might.

13. *Nesimachus's son*] Hippomedon. *G.'s marginal note.*

Firmly he plants each knee and o'er his head,
Collecting all his force, the circle sped.
It towers to cut the clouds; now through the skies
50 Sings in its rapid way and strengthens as it flies;
Anon with slackened rage comes quivering down,
Heavy and huge, and cleaves the solid ground.
     So from the astonished stars, her nightly train,
The sun's pale sister, drawn by magic strain,
55 Deserts precipitant her darkened sphere.
In vain the nations with officious fear
Their cymbals toss and sounding brass explore:⎫
The Æmonian hag enjoys her dreadful hour, ⎬
And smiles malignant on the labouring power. ⎭

60 Third in the labours of the disc came on,
With sturdy step and slow, Hippomedon.
Artful and strong he poised the well-known weight,
By Phlegyas warned and fired by Mnestheus' fate,
That to avoid and this to emulate.
65 His vigorous arm he tried before he flung,
Braced all his nerves and every sinew strung;
Then, with a tempest's whirl and wary eye,
Pursued his cast and hurled the orb on high;
The orb on high tenacious of its course,
70 True to the mighty arm that gave it force,
Far overleaps all bound and joys to see
Its ancient lord secure of victory.
The theatre's green height and woody wall
Tremble ere it precipitates its fall;
75 The ponderous mass sinks in the cleaving ground,
While vales and woods and echoing hills rebound.
As when from Aetna's smoking summit broke,
The eyeless Cyclops heaved the craggy rock:
Where ocean frets beneath the dashing oar,
80 And parting surges round the vessel roar,
'Twas there he aimed the meditated harm,
And scarce Ulysses scaped his giant arm.
A tiger's pride the victor bore away,
With native spots and artful labour gay:
85 A shining border round the margin rolled,
And calmed the terrors of his claws in gold.

3 [Lines on Beech Trees]

Written by Aug. 1736, if the letter to Walpole in Pembroke College in which they appear is correctly dated by Toynbee and Whibley (*Corresp* i 47). First printed by Mason in *1775*, *Memoirs* p. 24. G. was staying at that time with his uncle Jonathan Rogers at Burnham and preceded these lines with a description of the famous beech trees: 'both Vale & Hill is cover'd over with the most venerable Beeches, & other very reverend Vegetables, that like most ancient People, are always dreaming out their old Stories to the Winds'. As G. goes on to say that he usually reads Virgil under the trees, he may have been imitating *Aeneid* vi 283–5, lines also imitated by Richard West in an exercise at Eton (*Correspondence of Gray, Walpole, West and Ashton* ed. Toynbee, ii 301): *In medio ramos annosaque bracchia pandit / ulmus opaca, ingens, quam sedem Somnia volgo / vana tenere ferunt, foliisque sub omnibus haerent* (In the midst an elm, shadowy and vast, spreads her boughs and aged arms, the home which, men say, false Dreams hold here and there, clinging under every leaf.)

G. may also echo Matthew Green's *The Spleen* 668–71: 'Here nymphs from hollow oaks relate / The dark decrees and will of fate, / And dreams beneath the spreading beech / Inspire, and docile fancy teach . . . .' As *The Spleen* was not published until Feb. 1737, the possibility of the echo has usually been rejected. But the Toynbee-Whibley dating of the letter can be questioned. Mason's date, Sept. 1737, is shown by the postmark to have the incorrect month, but there is no evidence that G. was *not* at Burnham again in the summer of 1737. He mentioned *The Spleen* enthusiastically in a letter to West on 22 May 1737, printed in *Times Lit. Supp.* 23 Sept. 1937, p. 776. In addition, in the letter containing these lines, G. stated that he had recently met Thomas Southerne the dramatist, adding that 'he is now 77 year old'. Too much weight should not be placed on such a statement, but Southerne was in fact born in the autumn of 1660 and in 1736 would have been only 75.

There are other parallels to G.'s lines, however, which make the similarity to Green less striking. See Dryden, *Conquest of Granada* IV ii 1: 'O could I read the dark decrees of Fate'; and Pope, *Iliad* xvi 290–1: 'Who hear, from rustling oaks, thy dark decrees; / And catch the fates, low-whispered in the breeze'; and see also G.'s Latin ode *Ad C. Favonium Zephyrinum* 33–4 (p. 311), written in 1740.

> And, as they bow their hoary tops, relate
> In murmuring sounds the dark decrees of fate;
> While visions, as poetic eyes avow,
> Cling to each leaf and swarm on every bough.

4 [Translation from Tasso, *Gerusalemme Liberata* Canto xiv 32–9]

G. wrote to West in a letter dated by Mason March 1737 (the editors of G.'s *Corresp* believed an earlier date was more likely): 'I learn Italian like any dragon, and in two months am got through the 16th book of Tasso, whom I hold in great admiration: I want you to learn too, that I may know your opinion of him; nothing can be easier than that language to any one who knows Latin and French already, and there are few so copious and expressive' (*Corresp* i 61). It was no doubt during his enthusiasm for Tasso that G. translated the following passage. His own transcript in his Commonplace Book (i 95–6), the text followed here, is dated '1738'. Mason, *Memoirs* p. 36 *n*, merely referred to its existence in 1775 and inaccurately described it as a translation from Canto iv. It was first printed by Mathias, ii 90–2, in 1814.

> *Preser commiato, e si'l desire gli sprona, &c:*
> Dismissed at length, they break through all delay
> To tempt the dangers of the doubtful way;
> And first to Ascalon their steps they bend,
> Whose walls along the neighbouring sea extend.
> 5 Nor yet in prospect rose the distant shore,
> Scarce the hoarse waves from far were heard to roar,
> When thwart the road a river rolled its flood
> Tempestuous, and all further course withstood:
> The torrent-stream his ancient bounds disdains,
> 10 Swoll'n with new force and late-descending rains.
> Irresolute they stand, when lo! appears
> The wondrous sage: vigorous he seemed in years,
> Awful his mien; low as his feet there flows
> A vestment unadorned, though white as new-fall'n
> snows;
> 15 Against the stream the waves secure he trod,
> His head a chaplet bore, his hand a rod.
> As on the Rhine when Boreas' fury reigns
> And winter binds the floods in icy chains,
> Swift shoots the village-maid in rustic play,
> 20 Smooth, without step, adown the shining way,
> Fearless in long excursion loves to glide,
> And sports and wantons o'er the frozen tide;
> So moved the seer, but on no hardened plain:

The river boiled beneath and rushed towards the
        main.
25   Where fixed in wonder stood the warlike pair
His course he turned and thus relieved their care:
    'Vast, O my friends, and difficult the toil
To seek your hero in a distant soil!
No common helps, no common guide, ye need,
30   Art it requires and more than winged speed.
What length of sea remains, what various lands,
Oceans unknown, inhospitable sands!
For adverse fate the captive chief has hurled
Beyond the confines of our narrow world.
35   Great things and full of wonder in your ears
I shall unfold; but first dismiss your fears,
Nor doubt with me to tread the downward road
That to the grotto leads, my dark abode.'
    Scarce had he said, before the warriors' eyes
40   When mountain-high the waves disparted rise:
The flood on either hand its billows rears,
And in the midst a spacious arch appears.
Their hands he seized and down the steep he led,
Beneath the obedient river's inmost bed.
45   The watery glimmerings of a fainter day
Discovered half, and half concealed, their way,
As when athwart the dusky woods by night
The uncertain crescent gleams a sickly light.
Through subterraneous passages they went,
50   Earth's inmost cells and caves of deep descent.
Of many a flood they viewed the secret source,
The birth of rivers, rising to their course;
Whate'er with copious train its channel fills,
Floats into lakes or bubbles into rills.
55   The Po was there to see, Danubius' bed,
Euphrates' fount and Nile's mysterious head.
Further they pass, where ripening minerals flow,
And embryon metals undigested glow;
Sulphureous veins and living silver shine,
60   Which soon the parent sun's warm powers refine,
In one rich mass unite the precious store,
The parts combine and harden into ore.
Here gems break through the night with glittering
        beam,
And paint the margin of the costly stream.
65   All stones of lustre shoot their vivid ray,
And mix attempered in a various day.
    Here the soft emerald smiles, of verdant hue,

> And rubies flame, with sapphires heavenly blue;
> The diamond there attracts the wondering sight,
> 70 Proud of its thousand dyes and luxury of light.

5 [Translation from Dante,
Inferno Canto xxxiii 1–78]

This translation may be ascribed to 1737–38, when G. was enthusiastically learning Italian and when he translated Tasso. G.'s original MS was apparently sold in 1845 and has since disappeared. 15 ll. were quoted in the *Gentleman's Mag.* xxxii New Series (1849) 343; and it was first printed in full by Gosse, *Works of G.* i 157–60, in 1884, 'from a MS., in the handwriting of Mitford, in the possession of Lord Houghton'. This copy was no doubt that sold at the 1851 sale of G.'s books and MSS, which bore the following note by Mitford: 'It is uncertain when Mr Gray translated the following story from Dante; but most probably very early, and when he was making himself Master of the Italian Language.' The text followed here is that in Mitford's Notebook (vol. iii ff. 70–73, 123), where an identical note appears and where the following variants are recorded: 'father' for 'felon' (l. 1); 'unbending' for 'unrelenting' (l. 82); and 'haply' for 'hasty' (l. 83). At the end of the poem Mitford has written: 'N.B. The above is not in Gray's Writing, but in a clear large hand. perhaps Mr Stonehewer's $\overset{+}{(}$yes,$\overset{+}{)}$'.

G.'s interest in and knowledge of Dante has been discussed at length by Paget Toynbee, *Dante in English Literature* (1909) i 230–8, who states that, with the exception of Thomas Tyrwhitt, G. was 'more intimately acquainted than any other Englishman of the eighteenth century' with Dante's poetry. For other comments see T. H. Warren, *Essays of Poets and Poetry Ancient and Modern* (1909) pp. 225–42, and F. A. Yates, 'Transformations of Dante's Ugolino', *Journal of the Warburg and Courtauld Institutes* xiv (1951) 94.

G.'s friend, Norton Nicholls, recalled in his 'Reminiscences' of the poet that it was his mentioning Dante which attracted G.'s attention to him when they met in June 1762: 'Mr Gray turned quickly round to me & said "Sir, do you read Dante?" & entered into conversation with me' (*Corresp* iii 1297). Norton Nicholls had given a fuller account in a letter to William Temple on 13 June 1762 (*Corresp* iii 1303): 'We had some Discourse about Dante and he seem'd very much astonished that I should have read any of it. He speaks of it in the highest Terms and particularly desir'd me to read one part of it the Story of Count Ugolino; as you may imagine, I read it the next morning, and found it what I expected one of the finest Things I had ever read in my Life.' The first complete translation of the *Divina Commedia*, by Henry Boyd, was not published until 1802.

From his dire food the grisly felon raised
His gore-dyed lips, which on the clottered locks
Of the half-devoured head he wiped, and thus
Began: 'Would'st thou revive the deep despair,
5   The anguish, that, unuttered, natheless wrings
My inmost heart? Yet if the telling may
Beget the traitor's infamy, whom thus
I ceaseless gnaw insatiate, thou shalt see me
At once give loose to utterance and to tears.
10   'I know not who thou art nor on what errand
Sent hither; but a Florentine my ear,
Won by thy tongue, declares thee. Know, thou see'st
In me Count Ugolino, and Ruggieri,
Pisa's perfidious prelate, this: now hear
15   My wrongs and from them judge of my revenge.
'That I did trust him, that I was betrayed
By trusting, and by treachery slain, it recks not
That I advise thee; that which yet remains
To thee and all unknown (a horrid tale),
20   The bitterness of death, I shall unfold.
Attend, and say if he have injured me.
'Through a small crevice opening, what scant light
That grim and antique tower admitted (since
Of me the Tower of Famine hight, and known
25   To many a wretch) already 'gan the dawn
To send. The whilst I slumbering lay, a sleep
Prophetic of my woes with direful hand
Oped the dark veil of fate. I saw methought
Toward Pisa's mount, that intercepts the view
30   Of Lucca, chased by hell-hounds gaunt and bloody
A wolf full-grown; with fleet and equal speed
His young ones ran beside him. Lanfranc there
And Sigismundo and Gualandi rode
Amain, my deadly foes, headed by this
35   The deadliest: he their chief, the foremost he
Flashed to pursue and cheer the eager cry.
Nor long endured the chase: the panting sire,
Of strength bereft, his helpless offspring soon
O'erta'en beheld, and in their trembling flanks
40   The hungry pack their sharp-set fangs embrued.
'The morn had scarce commenced when I awoke:
My children (they were with me) sleep as yet
Gave not to know their sum of misery,
But yet in low and uncompleted sounds
45   I heard 'em wail for bread. Oh! thou art cruel,
Or thou dost mourn to think what my poor heart

Foresaw, foreknew; oh! if thou weep not now,
Where are thy tears? Too soon they had aroused them,
Sad with the fears of sleep, and now the hour
50 Of timely food approached; when, at the gate
Below, I heard the dreadful clank of bars
And fastening bolts. Then on my children's eyes
Speechless my sight I fixed, nor wept, for all
Within was stone. They wept, unhappy boys,
55 They wept; and first my little dear Anselmo
Cried, 'Father, why do you gaze so sternly?
What would you have?' Yet wept I not or answered
All that whole day or the succeeding night,
Till a new sun arose with weakly gleam
60 And wan, such as mought entrance find within
That house of woe. But oh! when I beheld
My sons, and in four faces saw my own
Despair reflected, either hand I gnawed
For anguish, which they construed hunger. Straight
65 Arising all they cried, 'Far less shall be
Our sufferings, sir, if you resume your gift;
These miserable limbs with flesh you clothed;
Take back what once was yours.' I swallowed down
My struggling sorrow, nor to heighten theirs.
70 That day and yet another, mute we sat
And motionless. O earth, could'st thou not gape
Quick to devour me? Yet a fourth day came,
When Gaddo, at my feet outstretched, imploring
In vain my help, expired; ere the sixth morn
75 Had dawned, my other three before my eyes
Died one by one. I saw 'em fall; I heard
Their doleful cries. For three days more I groped
About among their cold remains (for then
Hunger had reft my eyesight), often calling
80 On their dear names, that heard me now no more;
The fourth, what sorrow could not, famine did.'
    He finished; then with unrelenting eye
Askance he turned him, hasty to renew
The hellish feast, and rent his trembling prey.

6 [Translation from Propertius, *Elegies* III v 1–2, 19–48]

Both passages are dated Dec. 1738 in G.'s Commonplace Book (i 96–7), the
text followed here. The first 4 ll. were first printed by Gosse, *Works of G.*

i 151, in 1884; the second passage had been printed by Mathias, ii 85-7, in 1814 (with the omission of ll. 57-8).

Love, gentle power, to peace was e'er a friend:
Before the goddess' shrine we too, love's votaries, bend.
Still may his bard in softer fights engage:
Wars hand to hand with Cynthia let me wage.

 5 Long as of youth the joyous hours remain,
Me may Castalia's sweet recess detain,
Fast by the umbrageous vale lulled to repose,
Where Aganippe warbles as it flows;
Or roused by sprightly sounds from out the trance,
10 I'd in the ring knit hands and join the Muses'
      dance.
Give me to send the laughing bowl around,
My soul in Bacchus' pleasing fetters bound;
Let on this head unfading flowers reside,
There bloom the vernal rose's earliest pride;
15 And when, our flames commissioned to destroy,
Age step 'twixt love and me, and intercept our joy;
When my changed head these locks no more shall
      know,
And all its jetty honours turn to snow;
Then let me rightly spell of nature's ways.
20 To Providence, to him my thoughts I'd raise,
Who taught this vast machine its steadfast laws,
That first, eternal, universal Cause;
Search to what regions yonder star retires,
Who monthly waning hides her paly fires,
25 And whence, anew revived, with silver light
Relumes her crescent orb to cheer the dreary night;
How rising winds the face of ocean sweep;
Where lie the eternal fountains of the deep;
And whence the cloudy magazines maintain
30 Their wintry war or pour the autumnal rain;
How flames perhaps, with dire confusion hurled,
Shall sink this beauteous fabric of the world;
What colours paint the vivid arch of Jove;
What wondrous force the solid earth can move,
35 When Pindus' self approaching ruin dreads,
Shakes all his pines and bows his hundred heads;
Why does yon orb, so exquisitely bright,
Obscure his radiance in a short-lived night;
Whence the Seven Sisters' congregated fires,

40 And what Bootes' lazy wagon tires;
How the rude surge its sandy bounds control;
Who measured out the year and bade the seasons roll;
If realms beneath those fabled torments know,
Pangs without respite, fires that ever glow;
45 Earth's monster-brood stretched on their iron bed;
The hissing terrors round Alecto's head;
Scarce to nine acres Tityus' bulk confined;
The triple dog that scares the shadowy kind;
All angry heaven inflicts or hell can feel,
50 The pendent rock, Ixion's whirling wheel,
Famine at feasts and thirst amid the stream.
Or are our fears the enthusiast's empty dream,
And all the scenes that hurt the grave's repose,
But pictured horror and poetic woes?
55   These soft, inglorious joys my hours engage;
Be love my youth's pursuit and science crown my
       age.
You, whose young bosoms feel a nobler flame,
Redeem what Crassus lost and vindicate his name.

7 Agrippina, a Tragedy

Begun in the winter of 1741–42 and abandoned by 23 April 1742. G. had been deeply impressed by a performance of Racine's *Britannicus* (in which Agrippina is an important character), which he saw in Paris on 21 May 1739 (*Corresp* i 108–9, 110–11). As Mason wrote in 1775, (*Memoirs* p. 124): 'The Britannicus of M. Racine, I know was one of Mr. Gray's most favourite plays; and the admirable manner in which I have heard him say that he saw it represented at Paris, seems to have led him to choose the death of Agrippina for this his first and only effort in the drama'. Norton Nicholls also remembered that G. 'admired Racine, particularly the Britannicus' (*Corresp* iii 1297).

Late in March or early in April 1742 G. sent Richard West 'a long speech of Agrippina; much too long, but I could be glad you would retrench it. Aceronia, you may remember, had been giving quiet counsels. I fancy, if it ever be finished, it will be in the nature of Nat. Lee's Bedlam Tragedy, which had twenty-five acts and some odd scenes' (*Corresp* i 189). This letter, like that from West which it answered, also discussed the *Annals* of Tacitus, which both of them were reading and which was the source for G.'s drama. G.'s letter indicates that West had already seen the opening of the play: according to Mason, *Memoirs* p. 124, G.'s letter included ll. 82–182 of the play, which Mason believed 'was begun the preceding winter'.

West, in his reply of 4 April 1742, thought the speech too long but did not see how to 'retrench' it. He also objected to G.'s 'antiquated' style and reminded him that Racine's 'language is the language of the times, and that of the purest sort'. West, who had himself begun a tragedy (*Pausanias*) in 1741, evidently thought that G. was imitating Shakespeare in style and suggested that Addison's *Cato* was a preferable model (*Corresp* i 189–90). G.'s letter of 8 April 1742 contains his well-known argument that 'the language of the age is never the language of poetry', which he expounded and illustrated at some length (*Corresp* i 192–3). G. believed that English poetry 'has a language peculiar to itself', that most poets have felt free to enrich it with words of foreign origin or of their own creation; and that they have often borrowed extensively from their predecessors, as he illustrated in detail from Dryden. Shakespeare seemed to G. the best model because 'Every word in him is a picture'. But he admitted, with reference to the speech he had already sent West, that 'the affectation of imitating Shakespear may doubtless be carried too far; and is no sort of excuse for sentiments ill-suited, or speeches ill-timed, which I believe is a little the case with me. I guess the most faulty expressions may be these:—*silken* son of *dalliance–drowsier* pretensions–wrinkled *beldams–arched* the hearer's brow and *riveted* his eyes in *fearful extasie* [see ll. 98, 103–4, 132, 164–5]. These are easily altered or omitted: and indeed if the thoughts be wrong or superfluous, there is nothing easier than to leave out the whole.'

G.'s generalization about the 'language of poetry', conveniently anti-thetical both to Restoration and to Wordsworth's views on poetic diction, is usually quoted out of context. Although it is not entirely uncharacteristic of G., it should at least be remembered that he was writing about dramatic verse (and his own first attempt at it) and that he had not yet started to write lyric poetry in English. His later remarks on diction show that he became more cautious about the use of 'antiquated' diction: see his letter to Walpole in Jan. 1747 quoted below.

While not agreeing entirely with West's criticism, G. was obviously discouraged by it, as he admitted on 23 April 1742: 'as to Agrippina, I begin to be of your opinion, & find myself (as Women are of their children) less enamour'd of my Productions the older they grow. she is laid up to sleep, till next Summer: so bid her Good night' (*Corresp* i 196). According to Mason, *Memoirs* p. 145 *n*, 'He never after awakened her; and I believe this was occasioned by the strictures which his friend had made on his dramatic style; which (though he did not think them well founded, as they certainly were not) had an effect which Mr. West, we may believe, did not intend them to have'.

But *Agrippina* was in fact to be 'awakened'. In Dec. 1746, at a time when he was showing most of his other poetry to Walpole, G. sent him 'a scene in a tragedy: if it don't make you cry, it will make you laugh; and so it moves some passion, that I take to be enough' (*Corresp* i 258). This 'scene' consisted of ll. 1–81, and in Jan. 1747 G. sent Walpole 'the remainder of Agrippina, that was lost in a wilderness of papers', adding (*Corresp* i 262): 'Certainly you do her too much honour: she seemed to me to talk like an *Oldboy* [a

character in a comic opera], all in figures and mere poetry, instead of nature
and the language of real passion . . . . However, you will find the remainder
here at the end in an outrageous long speech: it was begun above four years
ago (it is a misfortune you know my age, else I might have added), when I
was very young. Poor West put a stop to that tragic torrent he saw breaking
in upon him:—have a care, I warn you not to set open the flood-gate again,
lest it should drown you and me and the bishop [Ashton] and all.'

Although he was now conscious of the stylistic affectations of the play,
G. may have been hoping to be encouraged to continue it. But in Feb. 1747
he wrote to Walpole: 'I rejoyce to hear, there is such a Crowd of dramatical
Performances comeing upon the Stage. Agripp.^{na} can stay very well, she
thanks you; & be damn'd at Leisure: I hope in God you have not mention'd,
or shew'd to any Body that Scene (for trusting in it's Badness, I forgot
to caution you concerning it) but I heard the other Day, that I was writeing
a Play, & was told the Name of it, wch no body here could know, I'm
sure' (*Corresp* i 265). Tovey has suggested that, as a result of Walpole's
encouragement, G. may have written the 12 ll. of Scene ii at this time, since
in Jan. 1747 he had twice referred to Agrippina's long speech as 'the re-
mainder' of the play as it then stood. But G. need not have been speaking
precisely and the only other evidence cited by Tovey is ambiguous (see l. 186
n). The play was soon abandoned completely.

No MS has survived, the only text being that given by Mason, *Memoirs*
pp. 128–35. Mason admitted that he had put part of Agrippina's long speech
(ll. 82–182) 'into the mouth of Aceronia' and had broken it 'in a few other
places', in the belief that it 'was undoubtedly too long for the lungs of any
Actress', *Memoirs* p. 136 *n*. (Mason was obviously unaware that in G.'s
model, Racine's *Britannicus*, Agrippina has an even longer speech, IV ii
1–108.) The text followed here, with some misgiving, is that reconstructed
from Mason's version by Tovey and Bradshaw, who between them cut out
Mason's obvious interpolations and restored Aceronia's speeches to Agrip-
pina, with such minor grammatical changes as were necessary. Speculative
as such a text must be, it must still be closer to G.'s original intentions than
Mason's self-confessed revision. The 'Dramatis Personae' and 'Argument'
for the play as a whole are those given by Mason, *Memoirs* pp. 126–7, the
latter being conflated from 'Two detached papers' left by G.: 'The argu-
ment drawn out by him, in these two papers, under the idea of a plot and
underplot, I shall here unite; as it will tend to show that the action itself was
possest of sufficient unity.'

Most of G.'s historical material derives from Tacitus, *Annals* Bks xiii-xiv,
although he was also indebted to Racine's *Britannicus* (likewise based on
Tacitus) both for specific details and as a general model. The patent debts
to both are recorded in the notes. It may be added that *Britannicus* begins
with an expository dialogue between Agrippina and a confidante similar
to G.'s opening scene and that G.'s 'Argument' for the continuation of
the play suggests that his plot would have imitated Racine's.

Agrippina did not excite much interest after its publication in 1775.

Mason himself, *Memoirs* p. 128, believed that 'as such a fable could not possibly admit of any good character, it is terror only and not pity that could be excited by this tragedy, had it been completed. Yet it was surely capable of exciting this passion in a supreme degree'. But Johnson (*Lives of the Poets*, ed. G. B. Hill, iii 423) considered that 'It was certainly no loss to the English stage that *Agrippina* was never completed'; and even John Pinkerton ('Robert Heron'), a more sympathetic critic, in his *Letters of Literature* (1785) p. 42, regretted that G. 'admired the silly declamation of Racine so much as to begin a tragedy in his very manner; which however he was so fortunate as not to go thro with'.

DRAMATIS PERSONAE

Agrippina   *The Empress mother*
Nero   *The Emperor.*
Poppaea   *Believed to be in love with Otho.*
Otho   *A young man of quality, in love with Poppaea.*
Seneca   *The Emperor's preceptor.*
Anicetus   *Captain of the Guards.*
Demetrius   *The Cynic, friend to Seneca.*
Aceronia   *Confidante to Agrippina.*

Scene, the Emperor's villa at Baiae

THE ARGUMENT

The drama opens with the indignation of Agrippina, at receiving her son's orders from Anicetus to remove from Baiae, and to have her guard taken from her. At this time Otho having conveyed Poppaea from the house of her husband Rufus Crispinus, brings her to Baiae, where he means to conceal her among the croud; or, if his fraud is discovered, to have recourse to the Emperor's authority; but, knowing the lawless temper of Nero, he determines not to have recourse to that expedient, but on the utmost necessity. In the meantime he commits her to the care of Anicetus, whom he takes to be his friend, and in whose age he thinks he may safely confide. Nero is not yet come to Baiae: but Seneca, whom he sends before him, informs Agrippina of the accusation concerning Rubellius Plancus, and desires her to clear herself, which she does briefly; but demands to see her son, who, on his arrival, acquits her of all suspicion, and restores her to her honours. In the meanwhile Anicetus, to whose care Poppaea had been entrusted by Otho, contrives the following plot to ruin Agrippina: He betrays his trust to Otho, and brings Nero, as it were by chance, to the sight of the beautiful Poppaea; the Emperor is immediately struck with her charms, and she, by a feigned resistance, increases his passion; tho', in reality, she is from the first dazzled with the prospect of empire, and forgets Otho: She therefore joins with Anicetus in his design of ruining Agrippina, soon perceiving that it will be for her interest. Otho hearing that the Emperor had seen Poppaea, is much enraged; but not knowing that this interview was obtained thro' the treachery of Anicetus, is readily persuaded by him to see Agrippina in secret, and acquaint her with his fears that her son Nero would marry Poppaea. Agrippina, to support her own power, and to wean the Emperor from the love of Poppaea, gives Otho encouragement, and promises to support him. Anicetus secretly introduces Nero to hear their discourse; who resolves immediately on his mother's death, and, by Anicetus's means, to destroy her by drowning. A solemn feast, in honour of their reconciliation, is to be made; after which she being to go by sea to Bauli, the ship is so contrived as to sink or crush her; she escapes by accident, and returns to Baiae. In this interval Otho has an interview with Poppaea; and being duped a second time by Anicetus and her, determines to fly with her into Greece, by means of a vessel which is to be furnished by Anicetus; but he, pretending to remove Poppaea on board in the night, conveys her to Nero's apartment: She there encourages and determines Nero to banish Otho, and finish the horrid deed he had attempted on his mother. Anicetus undertakes to execute his resolves; and, under pretence of a plot upon the Emperor's life, is sent with a guard to murder Agrippina, who is still at Baiae in imminent fear, and irresolute how to conduct herself. The account of her death, and the Emperor's horrour and fruitless remorse, finishes the drama.

ACT I.

SCENE I.

[Agrippina. Aceronia]

AGRIPPINA

'Tis well, begone! your errand is performed.

[*Speaks as to* Anicetus *entering.*]

¶ 7.1. *Anicetus*] A freedman, formerly Nero's tutor, who commanded the fleet at Misenum. According to Tacitus, he was detested by Agrippina with a venom which he reciprocated. He was the author of a plot to have her murdered at sea (*Annals* xiv 3, 7–8).

Aceronia] First mentioned by Tacitus as a member of Agrippina's household in his account of Nero's attempt to have her drowned (*Annals* xiv 5). As a result of impersonating Agrippina on this occasion, Aceronia was killed by mistake.

The message needs no comment. Tell your master,
His mother shall obey him. Say you saw her
Yielding due reverence to his high command:
5 Alone, unguarded and without a lictor
As fits the daughter of Germanicus.
Say, she retired to Antium; there to tend
Her household cares, a woman's best employment.
What if you add, how she turned pale and trembled:
10 You think, you spied a tear stand in her eye,
And would have dropped, but that her pride
    restrained it?
(Go! you can paint it well) 'twill profit you,
And please the stripling. Yet 'twould dash his joy
To hear the spirit of Britannicus

5. *Annals* xiii 2: *Decreti et a senatu duo lictores* (The senate, too, accorded her a pair of lictors); and, after the murder of Britannicus, xiii 18: *Cognitum id Neroni, excubiasque militaris, quae ut coniugi imperatoris olim, tum ut matri servabantur, et Germanos nuper eundem in honorem custodes additos degredi iubet* (Nero knew it, and gave orders to withdraw the military watch, which she had received as the wife, and retained as the mother, of the sovereign, along with the Germans lately assigned to her as a bodyguard with the same complimentary motive). Cp. also Racine, *Britannicus* I i 3, where she is described *errant dans le palais sans suite et sans escorte*; and I i 85–6: *Néron devant sa mère a permis le premier / Qu'on portât les faisceaux couronnés de laurier.*
6. *Germanicus*] Germanicus Julius Caesar (15 B.C.–A.D. 19), commonly known as Germanicus, nephew and adopted son of Tiberius, the father of Agrippina. He was famous for his campaigns against Germanic tribes. See Tacitus, *Annals* ii 82, for an account of the sorrow of the Roman people at his death.
7–8. *Annals* xiv 3: *abscedentem in hortos aut Tusculanum vel Antiatem in agrum laudare quod otium capesseret* (when she left for her gardens or the estates at Tusculum and Antium, he commended her intention of resting).
8. 'for nothing lovelier can be found / In woman, than to studie household good', *Par. Lost* ix 232–3.
9. 'You that look pale and tremble at this chance', *Hamlet* V ii 345; and cp. *2 Henry VI* III ii 27.
12. 'He best can paint 'em, who shall feel 'em most', Pope, *Eloisa to Abelard* 366.
14–15. *Julius Caesar* V iii 95–6: 'O Julius Caesar, thou art mighty yet! / Thy spirit walks abroad . . .'
14. *Britannicus*] Tiberius Claudius Caesar Britannicus (A.D. 41–55), son of Claudius and Messalina. Agrippina had induced Claudius to adopt Nero and ensure his succession, rather than that of Britannicus, in A.D. 54. He was poisoned by Nero at a banquet; see l. 21 *n*.

15 Yet walks on earth: at least there are who know
    Without a spell to raise, and bid it fire
    A thousand haughty hearts, unused to shake
    When a boy frowns, nor to be lured with smiles
    To taste of hollow kindness, or partake
20 His hospitable board: they are aware
    Of the unpledged bowl, they love not aconite.

                    ACERONIA

    He's gone; and much I hope these walls alone
    And the mute air are privy to your passion.
    Forgive your servant's fears, who sees the danger
25 Which fierce resentment cannot fail to raise
    In haughty youth and irritated power.

                    AGRIPPINA

    And dost thou talk to me, to me, of danger,
    Of haughty youth and irritated power,
    To her that gave it being, her that armed
30 This painted Jove, and taught his novice hand
    To aim the forked bolt; while he stood trembling,
    Scared at the sound and dazzled with its brightness?
    'Tis like, thou hast forgot, when yet a stranger

18–20 Annals xiv 56: *His adicit complexum et oscula, factus natura et con-suetudine exercitus velare odium fallacibus blanditiis* (He followed his words with an embrace and kisses—nature had fashioned him and use had trained him to veil his hatred under insidious caresses). Cp. also *Britannicus* IV ii 1270–2: *Vous êtes un ingrat, vous le fûtes toujours. | Dès vos plus jeunes ans, mes soins et mes tendresses | N'ont arraché de vous que de feintes caresses.* G. may also have had in mind Nero's behaviour to his mother at a feast immediately before he attempted to murder her (*Annals* xiv 4).

21. the unpledged bowl] Perhaps a reference to the poisoning of Britannicus (*Annals* xiii 16; *Britannicus* V v). *aconite*] A poisonous plant, especially wolf's-bane. Cp. 'Though it do work as strong / As aconitum', *2 Henry IV* IV iv 47–8.

22–3. Britannicus II vi 712–13: *Vous êtes en des lieux tout pleins de sa puissance. | Ces murs mêmes, Seigneur, peuvent avoir des yeux* ... Cp. also, 'You think none but your sheets are privy to your wishes', *Antony and Cleopatra* I ii 42.

29–30. Albine to Agrippina, *Britannicus* I i 15–16: *Quoi? vous, à qui Néron doit le jour, qu'il respire, | Qui l'avez appelé de si loin a l'Empire?*

30–1. Dryden, *Annus Mirabilis* 155–6: 'And threatning *France*, plac'd like a painted *Jove*, / Kept idle thunder in his lifted hand.'

33–6. Britannicus I i 97–102: *Des volontés de Rome alors mal assuré, | Néron de sa grandeur n'étoit point enivré. | Ce jour, ce triste jour frappe encor ma mémoire, | Où Néron fut lui-même ébloui de sa gloire, | Quand les ambassadeurs de tant de rois divers | Vinrent le reconnoître au nom de l'univers.*

To adoration, to the grateful steam
35 Of flattery's incense and obsequious vows
From voluntary realms, a puny boy,
Decked with no other lustre than the blood
Of Agrippina's race, he lived unknown
To fame or fortune; haply eyed at distance
40 Some edileship, ambitious of the power
To judge of weights and measures; scarcely dared
On expectation's strongest wing to soar
High as the consulate, that empty shade
Of long-forgotten liberty: when I
45 Oped his young eye to bear the blaze of greatness;
Showed him where empire towered, and bade him
    strike
The noble quarry. Gods! then was the time
To shrink from danger; fear might then have worn
The mask of prudence; but a heart like mine,
50 A heart that glows with the pure Julian fire,

34–5. See *Elegy* 71–2 (p. 130).
34. 'Consum'd with nimble glance, and grateful steame,' *Par. Lost* xi 442.
38–9. See *Elegy* 118 (p. 139).
40–1. Juvenal, *Sat.* x 101–2: *et de mensura ius dicere, vasa minora / frangere pannosus vacuis aedilis Vlubris?* (adjudicating upon weights, or smashing vessels of short measure, as a thread-bare Aedile at deserted Ulabrae); and Persius, *Sat.* i 129–30: *sese aliquem credens, Italo quod honore supinus / fregerit heminas Arreti aedilis iniquas* (one puffed up with his dignity as a provincial aedile who deems himself somebody because he has broken up short pint measures at Arretum). Cp. Dryden's translations of these passages: 'To pound false Weights, and scanty Measures break', *Juvenal* x 165, and 'Whose Pow'r extends no farther than to speak / Big on the Bench, and scanty Weights to break', *Persius* i 269–70.
43. John Oldham, *Counterpart to the Satire against Virtue* st. vii: 'What art thou, Fame, for which so eagerly we strive? / What art thou but an empty Shade'; and Pope, *Essay on Man* iv 243: 'To all beside as much an empty shade'.
45–7. Cp. Agrippina in Seneca's *Octavia* 333–4, 336–8: *'haec' exclamat 'mihi pro tanto / munere reddis praemia, nate? / . . . quae te genui, quae tibi lucem / atque imperium nomenque dedi / Caesaris amens.'* (Such reward as this for my great boon, O son, dost thou return me? . . . who brought thee forth, who gave thee light and empire and the name of Caesar, fool that I was); and Nero to Agrippina, *Britannicus* IV ii 1223: *Je me souviens toujours que je vous dois l'Empire.*
50. Agrippina was descended from Julia, the sister of Julius Caesar and so of the blood of the great Julian House, which claimed descent from Iulus Ascanius) the son of Aeneas.

If bright ambition from her craggy seat
Display the radiant prize, will mount undaunted,
Gain the rough heights, and grasp the dangerous
    honour.

ACERONIA

Through various life I have pursued your steps,
55 Have seen your soul, and wondered at its daring:
Hence rise my fears. Nor am I yet to learn
How vast the debt of gratitude which Nero
To such a mother owes; the world you gave him
Suffices not to pay the obligation.
60   I well remember too (for I was present)
When in a secret and dead hour of night,
Due sacrifice performed with barbarous rites
Of muttered charms and solemn invocation,
You bade the Magi call the dreadful powers
65 That read futurity, to know the fate
Impending o'er your son: their answer was,
If the son reign, the mother perishes.
Perish (you cried) the mother! reign the son!
He reigns, the rest is heaven's; who oft has bade,
70 Even when its will seemed wrote in lines of blood,
The unthought event disclose a whiter meaning.
Think too how oft in weak and sickly minds

53. 'I like it better than a dangerous honour', *3 Henry VI* IV iii 17.
61. 'jump at this dead hour', *Hamlet* I i 65.
64–8. *Annals* xiv 9: *Hunc sui finem multos ante annos crediderat Agrippina contempseratque. Nam consulenti super Nerone responderunt Chaldaei fore ut imperaret matremque occideret; atque illa 'Occidat' inquit 'dum imperet'* (This was that ending to which, years before, Agrippina had given her credence, and her contempt. For to her inquiries as to the destiny of Nero the astrologers answered that he should reign, and slay his mother; and 'Let him slay,' she had said, 'so that he reign').
71. *whiter*] One meaning of 'white' given by Johnson is 'Having the colour appropriated to happiness and innocence.' It is also used to mean auspicious or propitious. Cp. 'And now time's whiter Series is begun', Dryden, *Astraea Redux* 292; cp. also 'The unthought-on accident', *Winter's Tale* IV v 549.
72. 'a weak and sickly guard', *Henry V* III vi 164; and 'sickly, weak and melancholy', *Richard III* I i 136.
72–6. G. may have had in mind in these lines his recent quarrel with Walpole, who undoubtedly patronized him at times. Cp. Johnson's remarks on the quarrel in his *Life of G.*: 'Men whose consciousness of their own merit sets them above the compliances of servility, are apt enough in their association with superiors to watch their own dignity with troublesome and punctilious

The sweets of kindness lavishly indulged
Rankle to gall; and benefits too great
75   To be repaid, sit heavy on the soul,
As unrequited wrongs. The willing homage
Of prostrate Rome, the senate's joint applause,
The riches of the earth, the train of pleasures
That wait on youth and arbitrary sway:
80   These were your gift, and with them you bestowed
The very power he has to be ungrateful.

AGRIPPINA

Thus ever grave and undisturbed reflection
Pours its cool dictates in the madding ear
Of rage, and thinks to quench the fire it feels not.
85   Sayest thou I must be cautious, must be silent,
And tremble at the phantom I have raised?
Carry to him thy timid counsels. He
Perchance may heed 'em: tell him too, that one
Who had such liberal power to give, may still
90   With equal power resume that gift, and raise
A tempest that shall shake her own creation
To its original atoms—tell me! say,
This mighty emperor, this dreaded hero,
Has he beheld the glittering front of war?
95   Knows his soft ear the trumpet's thrilling voice,
And outcry of the battle? Have his limbs

jealousy, and in the fervour of independence to exact that attention which
they refuse to pay', (*Lives*, ed. G. B. Hill III 422). Cp. also Agrippina to
Nero, *Britannicus* V vi 1678: *Tu voudras t'affranchir du joug de mes bienfaits.*
75. 'Let me sit heavy on thy soul tomorrow', *Richard III* V iii 118, 131, 139.
78. 'fair pleasure's smiling train', Pope, *Essay on Man* ii 117.
79. 'And haughty Britain yields to Arbitrary Sway', Prior, *Prologue, Spoken
at Court* 23; and ''Tis in the shade of Arbitrary Sway', Pope, *Dunciad* iv 182.
82. Of Agrippina's speech beginning here, G. wrote to West in April
1742 (*Corresp* i 192): 'The first ten or twelve lines are, I believe, the best;
and as for the rest, I was betrayed into a good deal of it by Tacitus; only
what he has said in five words, I imagine I have said in fifty lines: Such is
the misfortune of imitating the inimitable.'
82–3. 'To the cool Dictates of experienced Age', Dryden, *Iliad* i 388; and
'If modest Youth, with cool Reflection crown'd', Pope, *Epitaph on Duke
of Buckingham* 1.
83. *madding*] See *Elegy* 73 (p. 131).
90. 'And, weakling, Warwick takes his gift again', *3 Henry VI* V i 37.
91. Burrhus describes Nero as Agrippina's *ouvrage*, *Britannicus* IV i 1108.
94. Pope, *Iliad* i 299–300: 'When wert thou known in ambush'd fights to
dare, / Or nobly face the horrid front of war?'

Sweat under iron harness? Is he not
The silken son of dalliance, nursed in ease
And pleasure's flowery lap? Rubellius lives,
100 And Sylla has his friends, though schooled by fear
To bow the supple knee, and court the times
With shows of fair obeisance; and a call
Like mine might serve belike to wake pretensions
Drowsier than theirs, who boast the genuine blood
105 Of our imperial house. [Cannot my nod]
Rouse [up] eight hardy legions, wont to stem

98. *silken . . . dalliance*] One of the phrases admitted by G. to be an imitation
of Shakespeare. See headnote and cp. 'And silken dalliance in the wardrobe
lies', *Henry V* Chorus to Act II, 2. But see also 'Pours at great Bourbon's
feet her silken sons', Pope, *Dunciad* iv 298; 'numbers once in Fortune's
lap high-fed' and 'Ye silken sons of Pleasure', Young, *Night Thoughts*
i 298, 301.
99. 'flowery lap', Milton, *Vacation Exercise* 84 and *Par. Lost* iv 254.
99–100. Tacitus describes Agrippina's plotting against Nero in *Annals*
xiii 18: *tribunos et centuriones comiter excipere, nomina et virtutes nobilium, qui
etiam tum supererant, in honore habere, quasi quaereret ducem et partis* (Tribunes
and centurions she received with suavity; and for the names and virtues of
the nobility—there was a nobility still—she showed a respect which indi-
cated that she was in quest of a leader and a faction). *Annals* xiii 19–20 describe
the accusation against Agrippina that she was inciting Rubellius Plautus,
great-grandson of Tiberius, into revolution. (This had in fact happened some
four years before the rest of the events described by G.) Nero also suspected
that Cornelius Sulla, son-in-law of Claudius, the late emperor, was plotting
against him, *Annals* xiii 23. Both Plautus and Sulla were eventually murdered
on Nero's orders, *Annals* xiv 57–9; and cp. Seneca, *Octavia* 438–9. Racine
mentions them both as leaders of the nobles and potential supporters of
Agrippina, *Britannicus* III v 906–7.
101. 'And had the tribute of his supple knee', *Richard II* I iv 33; 'to bend /
The supple knee', *Par. Lost* v 784–5; 'And suffer scorn and bend the supple
knee', Pope, *Stanzas from Malherbe* 9.
103–4. *drowsier*] Admitted by G. to be an imitation of Shakespeare. See
headnote; and cp. 'a roisting challenge . . . / Will strike amazement to their
drowsy spirits', *Troilus and Cressida* II ii 208–10.
105–17. These lines are given by Mason to Aceronia (see headnote for Mason's
admitted interference with Agrippina's speech). Mason's version begins:
'Did I not wish to check this dangerous passion, / I might remind my mistress
that her nod / Can rouse . . .' Tovey conjecturally restored the passage to
Agrippina as in ll. 105–6 and also introduced the question mark into l. 108;
substituted 'me' for 'you' (110); 'mine' for 'yours' (112); 'my' for 'your'
(114). The lines are obviously inappropriate in the mouth of Aceronia.
106–7. *stem . . . the tide*] A fairly common formula in heroic poetry. Johnson

       With stubborn nerves the tide, and face the rigour
       Of bleak Germania's snows [?] Four, not less brave,
       That in Armenia quell the Parthian force
110   Under the warlike Corbulo, by [me]
       Marked for their leader: these, by ties confirmed
       Of old respect and gratitude, are [mine].
       Surely the Masians too, and those of Egypt,
       Have not forgot [my] sire: the eye of Rome
115   And the Praetorian camp have long revered,
       With customed awe, the daughter, sister, wife,

defines 'stem': 'to oppose a current; to pass cross or forward notwithstanding the stream'.

107–8. Annals xiii 35: *Retentusque omnis exercitus sub pellibus, quamvis hieme saeva adeo, ut obducta glacie nisi effossa humus tentoriis locum non praeberet* (The entire army was kept under canvas, notwithstanding a winter of such severity that the ice-covered ground had to be dug up before it could receive the tents); and Virgil, *Eclogues* x 66: *Sithoniasque nives hiemis subeamus aquosae* (and brave the Thracian snows and their wintry sleet).

108–11. Tacitus describes the campaign of Gneaeus Domitius Corbulo against the Parthians in A.D. 58, in *Annals* xiii 34–41, although he stresses the lethargy of the troops (*ignaviam militum*). Corbulo is also mentioned in *Britannicus* I ii 207. Nero made him commit suicide in A.D. 67.

112. Cp. 'old respect', *Samson Agonistes* 333.

113. Masians] This word is almost certainly a mistranscription by Mason. Tovey suggests that G. wrote 'Asians' (the error would then be caused by Mason's merging his own name with the word) but in the context this reference would seem to be too vague. More likely is 'Marsians', used of the legions in Germany but also of Roman soldiers in general. Their courage and fierceness are mentioned by Virgil, *Georgics* ii 167 and Horace, *Odes* II xx 18. Starr and Hendrickson prefer the explanation that G. wrote 'Moesians', on the grounds that he has already named the western and eastern extremes of the Roman empire (Germany and Armenia) and Egypt on the south. Moesia (on the Black Sea, corresponding to modern Serbia and Bulgaria) would complete the circle of border provinces.

114. Britannicus III i 768–70: *Agrippine, Seigneur, est toujours redoutable. / Rome et tous vos soldats révèrent ses aieux; / Germanicus son père est present à leurs yeux*.

115. The Praetorians, the imperial bodyguard, were placed in a camp outside the Colline gate, north-east of Rome.

116–17. Annals xii 42: *quam imperatore genitam, sororem eius, qui rerum potitus sit, et coniugem et matrem fuisse* (the daughter of an Imperator and the sister, the wife, and the mother of an emperor). Cp. also *Britannicus* I ii 155–6: *Et moi, qui sur le trône ai suivi mes ancêtres, / Moi, fille, femme, soeur, et mere de vos maitres!* Agrippina was daughter of Germanicus, sister of Caligula, wife of Claudius, and mother of Nero.

> And mother of their Caesars. Ha! by Juno,
> It bears a noble semblance. On this base
> My great revenge shall rise; or say we sound
> *120*   The trump of liberty; there will not want,
> Even in the servile senate, ears to own
> Her spirit-stirring voice; Soranus there,
> And Cassius; Veto too, and Thrasea,
> Minds of the antique cast, rough, stubborn souls,
> *125*   That struggle with the yoke. How shall the spark
> Unquenchable, that glows within their breasts,
> Blaze into freedom, when the idle herd
> (Slaves from the womb, created but to stare
> And bellow in the Circus) yet will start,
> *130*   And shake 'em at the name of liberty,
> Stung by a senseless word, a vain tradition,

117–18. Ha! by Juno . . . semblance] This sentence may be an interpolation by Mason, who had given the preceding 14 ll. to Aceronia. The metre would not be affected if it was omitted.

122. 'The spirit-stirring drum', *Othello* III iii 356; and 'the spirit-stirring form of Caesar', John Dyer, *Ruins of Rome* (1740) 102–3.

122–5. Marcius Barea Soranus was later accused of plotting revolution and of intimacy with Rubellius Plautus. Caius Cassius Longinus, governor of Syria *c.* A.D. 40, was a famous jurist. Cp. *Annals* xii 12: *Ea tempestate Cassius ceteros praeminebat peritia legum: nam militares artes per otium ignotas, industriosque aut ignavos pax in aequo tenet. Ac tamen quantum sine bello dabatur, revocare priscum morem* (In that period, Cassius stood unrivalled as a jurist: for the arts of war are lost in a quiet world, and peace maintains on a single level the man of action and the sluggard. Still, as far as was possible, he reintroduced the old code of discipline). For Cassius' *amor antiqui moris* (affection for ancient usage), see *Annals* xiv 43.

Lucius Antistius Vetus, father-in-law to Rubellius Plautus, was consul with Nero in the first year of his reign (A.D. 55). He commanded a Roman army in Germany in A.D. 58. Publius Clodius Thrasea Paetus, a Stoic, walked out when the Senate voted Nero honours on the death of Agrippina, *Annals* xiv 12.

125–30. Britannicus IV iii 1347–51: *Britannicus mourant excitera le zèle | De ses amis, tout prêts à prendre sa querelle. | Ces vengeurs trouveront de nouveaux défenseurs, | Qui, même après leur mort, auront des successeurs : | Vous allumez un feu qui ne pourra s'éteindre.*

126. 'Where flames refin'd in breasts seraphic glow', Pope, *Eloisa to Abelard* 320.

132–5. beldams] Admitted by G. to be an imitation of Shakespeare. See headnote and cf. 'Old men and beldams in the streets / Do prophesy upon it dangerously', *King John* IV ii 185; and 'old folk, time's doting chronicles', *2 Henry IV* IV iv 126.

As there were magic in it? Wrinkled beldams
Teach it their grandchildren, as somewhat rare
That anciently appeared, but when, extends
135   Beyond their chronicle–oh! 'tis a cause
To arm the hand of childhood, and rebrace
The slackened sinews of time-wearied age.
      Yes, we may meet, ungrateful boy, we may!
Again the buried Genius of old Rome
140   Shall from the dust uprear his reverend head,
Roused by the shout of millions: there before
His high tribunal thou and I appear.
Let majesty sit on thy awful brow
And lighten from thy eye: around thee call
145   The gilded swarm that wantons in the sunshine
Of thy full favour; Seneca be there
In gorgeous phrase of laboured eloquence
To dress thy plea, and Burrhus strengthen it
With his plain soldier's oath and honest seeming.
150   Against thee, liberty and Agrippina:

137. 'World-wearied flesh', *Romeo and Juliet* V iii 112.
139–40. Pope, *Essay on Criticism* 699–700: '*Rome's* ancient *Genius*, o'er its *Ruins* spread, / Shakes off the *Dust*, and rears his rev'rend *Head*!'
143. 'Thy awful brow', *Par. Lost* ix 537.
143–4. 'his eye / As bright as is the eagle's lightens forth / Controlling majesty', *Richard II* III iii 68–70.
145–6. See *Spring* 29 ff. esp. the lines from Henry Brooke quoted in ll. 29–30 *n*, and *Bard* 69 (pp. 52, 191).
146–9. Seneca . . . Burrhus] Cp. *Annals* xiii 2: *Hi rectores imperatoriae iuventae et (rarum in societate potentiae) concordes, diversa arte ex aequo pollebant, Burrus militaribus curis et severitate morum, Seneca praeceptis eloquentiae et comitate honesta* (Both guardians of the imperial youth, and–a rare occurrence where power is held in partnership–both in agreement, they exercised equal influence by contrasted methods; Burrus with his soldierly interests and austerity, and Seneca, with his lessons in eloquence and his self-respecting courtliness).
    Agrippina mentioned both men in *Britannicus* I i 113–14: *L'ombre seule m'en reste, et l'on n'implore, plus / Que le nom de Sénèque et l'appui de Burrhus.* Cp. also Burrhus's assertion to Agrippina, *Britannicus* I ii 141: *Burrhus pour le mensonge eut toujours trop d'honneur*; and I ii 173–4: *Je répondrai, Madame, avec la liberté, / D'un soldat qui sait mal farder la vérité.* Cp. also 'I speak to thee plain soldier', *Henry V* V ii 156; and 'He was wont to speak plain and to the purpose, like an honest man and a soldier', *Much Ado* II iii 20.
147. Cp. 'gorgeous tragedy', Milton, *Il Penseroso* 97.

The world, the prize; and fair befall the victors.
But soft! why do I waste the fruitless hours
In threats unexecuted? Haste thee, fly
These hated walls that seem to mock my shame,
155   And cast me forth in duty to their lord.
My thought aches at him; not the basilisk
More deadly to the sight than is to me
The cool injurious eye of frozen kindness.
I will not meet its poison. Let him feel
160   Before he sees me. Yes, I will be gone,
But not to Antium—all shall be confessed,

151. 'Now fair befall thee and thy noble house', *Richard III* I iii 283; and 'Now fair befall you! he deserved his death', *ibid*, III v 47; and many other examples.

152. soft] As in Shakespeare *passim.*

155. After this line Mason breaks Agrippina's speech with 2 ll. given to Aceronia:

'Tis time we go, the sun is high advanc'd
And, ere mid-day, Nero will come to Baiae.

156. Basilisks occur several times in Shakespeare's History Plays, e.g. 'Would they were basilisks to strike thee dead', *Richard III* I ii 151.

158. 'Injurious tribune! / Within thine eyes sat twenty thousand deaths', *Coriolanus* III iii 69–70.

160. me] After this word Mason again breaks the speech by giving to Aceronia:

Why then stays my sovereign,
Where he so soon may —

161–72. Annals xiii 14: *Non abnuere se, quin cuncta infelicis domus mala patefierent, suae in primis nuptiae, suum veneficium . . . Ituram cum illo in castra; audiretur hinc Germanici filia, inde debilis rursus Burrus et exul Seneca, trunca scilicet manu et professoria lingua generis humani regimen expostulantes. Simul intendere manus, adgerere probra, consecratum Claudium, infernos Silanorum manis invocare et tot inrita facinora* (She had no objection to the whole dark history of that unhappy house being published to the world, her own marriage first of all, and her own resort to poison . . . . She would go with [Brittanicus] to the camp. There, let the daughter of Germanicus be heard on the one side; on the other, the cripple Burrus and the exile Seneca, claiming, forsooth, by right of a maimed hand and a professorial tongue the regency of the human race. As she spoke she raised a threatening arm, and, heaping him with reproaches, invoked the deified Claudius, the shades of the dead Silani, and all the crimes committed to no effect). Racine had already paraphrased this passage in *Britannicus* III iii 839–54. Cp. especially ll. 849–54: *De nos crimes communs je veux qu'on soit instruit: / On saura les, chemins par où je l'ai conduit. / Pour rendre sa puissance et la vôtre odieuses, / J'avoûrai les rumeurs les plus injurieuses: / Je confesserai tout, exils, assassinats / Poison même . . .*

Whate'er the frivolous tongue of giddy fame
Has spread among the crowd; things that but
        whispered
Have arched the hearer's brow and riveted
165   His eyes in fearful ecstasy: no matter
What, so it be strange, and dreadful—sorceries,
Assassinations, poisonings; the deeper
My guilt, the blacker his ingratitude.
        And you, ye manes of ambition's victims,
170   Enshrined Claudius, with the pitied ghosts
Of the Syllani, doomed to early death
(Ye unavailing horrors, fruitless crimes!),
If from the realms of night my voice ye hear,
In lieu of penitence and vain remorse,
175   Accept my vengeance. Though by me ye bled,
He was the cause. My love, my fears for him,
Dried the soft springs of pity in my heart,
And froze them up with deadly cruelty.
        Yet if your injured shades demand my fate,
180   If murder cries for murder, blood for blood,

164. arched the hearer's brow] Admitted by G. to be an imitation of Shakespeare (see headnote); but Shakespeare does not use the phrase to describe surprise or horror. Cp. 'the right arched beauty of the brow', *Merry Wives of Windsor* III iii 59; 'His arched brows', *All's Well That Ends Well* I i 105; and see also 'Lost the arch'd eyebrow or *Parnassian* sneer', Pope, *Epistle to Arbuthnot* 96.

164–5. riveted . . . ecstasy] Also admitted by G. to be an imitation of Shakespeare (see headnote); and cp. 'I mine eyes will rivet to his face', *Hamlet* III ii 90; 'While he that hears makes fearful action, / With wrinkled brows, with nods, with rolling eyes', *King John* IV ii 191–2; and 'restless ecstasy', *Macbeth* III ii 22.

169–82. West wrote to G. in April 1742 (*Corresp* i 195): 'You think the ten or twelve first lines [of Agrippina's speech, ll. 82 ff.] the best, now I am for the fourteen last; add, that they contain not one word of antientry.'

169. manes] 'the shade of a departed person, as an object of reverence, or as demanding to be propitiated by vengeance' (*OED*).

171. Syllani] The Silani were brothers, great-great-grandsons of Augustus. Agrippina brought a false charge against the younger, who committed suicide, so that Octavia, his betrothed, might marry Nero. She had the elder poisoned lest he avenge his brother, *Annals* xii 3–4, 8; xiii. 1

180. This is a common formula. Cp. 'For life must life, and blood must blood repay', *Faerie Queene* I ix 43, 6; 'Here have we war for war, and blood for blood', *King John* I i 19; 'It will have blood; they say, blood will have blood', *Macbeth* III iv 122; 'But Blood for Blood, and Death for Death is fit', Dryden, *Meleager and Atalanta* 298.

Let me not fall alone; but crush his pride,
And sink the traitor in his mother's ruin.   [*Exeunt.*]

SCENE II.

[Otho, Poppaea]

OTHO

Thus far we're safe. Thanks to the rosy queen
Of amorous thefts: and had her wanton son
185   Lent us his wings, we could not have beguiled
With more elusive speed the dazzled sight
Of wakeful jealousy. Be gay securely;
Dispel, my fair, with smiles, the timorous cloud
That hangs on thy clear brow. So Helen looked,
190   So her white neck reclined, so was she borne
By the young Trojan to his gilded bark
With fond reluctance, yielding modesty,
And oft reverted eye, as if she knew not
Whether she feared or wished to be pursued.

---

183. Scene II] Marcus Salvius Otho became Emperor after Galba in A.D. 69.
G.'s 'Argument' shows that he intended to follow the account of his
relations with Poppaea given by Tacitus, *Annals* xiii 45–6, although he
would have had to postdate the story to fit it into his plot. Otho enticed
Poppaea away from her husband Rufius Crispinus and later married her.
He was exiled in A.D. 58 by Nero, who fell in love with Poppaea himself.
Tacitus wrote of her, *Annals* xiii 45: *Huic mulieri cuncta alia fuere praeter
honestum animum . . . . Sermo comis nec absurdam ingenium: modestiam prae-
ferre et lascivia uti* (She was a woman possessed of all advantages except an
honest heart . . . . Her conversation was engaging, her wit not without
point; she paraded modesty, and practised wantonness). She later urged
Nero to murder Agrippina and to divorce his wife Octavia. She is said to
have died in A.D. 65, after being kicked by Nero while pregnant.
   In *Britannicus* IV i 1205–6, Agrippina describes Otho to Nero as one of his
jeunes voluptueux, | Et de tous vos plaisirs flatteurs respectueux.
186. Cp. the text of the *Eton Ode* 29, in the Commonplace Book: 'To
chase the hoop's elusive speed', which was changed on publication in 1747
to 'the rolling circle's speed'. Tovey has suggested that G. wrote 12 ll. of
the second scene of *Agrippina* when his interest in the play revived in 1746–47.
It is at least conceivable that G. altered the phrase in the *Eton Ode* to avoid
the echo with *Agrippina*, which he may still have hoped to complete for
the stage.
192. Par. Lost iv 310–11: 'Yeilded with coy submission, modest pride, | And
sweet reluctant amorous delay.'
193. reverted] Directed backwards. This is the earliest example referring to
the eyes quoted in *OED.* Cp. *Vicissitude* 24 (p. 204 below).

8 [Translation] from Propertius, *Elegies* II i

To Maecenas

G. sent this translation to West on 23 April 1742 (*Corresp* ii 197–9). West, replying on 5 May, pointed out that G. had translated 2 ll. from another elegy by Propertius (II iii 45–6; see ll. 67–70 of G.'s translation) which he stated had been inserted in the text by the Dutch scholar Broekhuyzen in his edition of 1702. G. replied in a letter of 8 May that the lines had originally been transferred by Scaliger in 1577 (*Corresp* i 200, 202).

The translation, with the omission of ll. 1–30, was first printed by Mathias, ii 87–9, in 1814, from G.'s Commonplace Book (i 254–5). It was first published in full by Gosse, i 153–7, in 1884, who evidently believed that no part of it had previously been printed. The text followed here is that of the Commonplace Book (dated 'April 1742' by G.), with variants from G.'s letter to West, and Mitford's copy (Notebook, vol iii).

> You ask why thus my loves I still rehearse,
> Whence the soft strain and ever-melting verse:
> From Cynthia all that in my numbers shines;
> She is my genius, she inspires the lines;
> 5 No Phoebus else, no other muse I know;
> She tunes my easy rhyme and gives the lay to flow.
> If the loose curls around her forehead play,
> Or lawless o'er their ivory margin stray;
> If the thin Coan web her shape reveal,
> 10 And half disclose those limbs it should conceal;
> Of those loose curls, that ivory front, I write,
> Of the dear web whole volumes I indite.
> Or if to music she the lyre awake,
> That the soft subject of my song I make,
> 15 And sing with what a careless grace she flings
> Her artful hand across the sounding strings.
> If sinking into sleep she seem to close
> Her languid lids, I favour her repose
> With lulling notes, and thousand beauties see
> 20 That slumber brings to aid my poetry.
> When less averse and yielding to desires,
> She half accepts and half rejects my fires;
> While to retain the envious lawn she tries,
> And struggles to elude my longing eyes;

¶ 8.*10. those*] the *West, Mitford.*
18. lids] limbs *Mitford.*

25 The fruitful muse from that auspicious night
    Dates the long Iliad of the amorous fight.
    In brief, whate'er she do, or say, or look,
    'Tis ample matter for a lover's book;
    And many a copious narrative you'll see,
30 Big with important nothing's history.
        Yet would the tyrant Love permit me raise
    My feeble voice to sound the victor's praise,
    To paint the hero's toil, the ranks of war,
    The laurelled triumph and the sculptured car,
35 No giant-race, no tumult of the skies,
    No mountain-structures in my verse should rise;
    Nor tale of Thebes or Ilium there should be,
    Or how the Persian trod the indignant sea;
    Not Marius' Cimbrian wreaths would I relate,
40 Nor lofty Carthage struggling with her fate.
    Here should Augustus great in arms appear,
    And thou, Maecenas, be my second care;
    Here Mutina from flames and famine free,
    And there the ensanguined wave of Sicily,
45 And sceptred Alexandria's captive shore,
    And sad Philippi red with Roman gore.
    Then, while the vaulted skies loud Ios rend,
    In golden chains should loaded monarchs bend,
    And hoary Nile with pensive aspect seem
50 To mourn the glories of his sevenfold stream,
    While prows, that late in fierce encounter met,
    Move through the sacred way and vainly threat.
    Thee too the muse should consecrate to fame,
    And with his garlands weave thy ever-faithful name;
55 But nor Callimachus' enervate strain
    May tell of Jove and Phlegra's blasted plain,
    Nor I with unaccustomed vigour trace
    Back to its source divine the Julian race.
    Sailors to tell of winds and seas delight,

32. *sound*] sing *West.*
36. *structures*] Structure *West.*
37. *or*] not *Mitford.*
38. *Or*] Nor *West, Mitford.*
45–6. *Written in margin of Commonplace Book and marked for insertion.*
50. *After this line West has:*

> The long-contended World's old Discords cease,
> And Actium's Terrours grace the Pomp of Peace;

51. *prows*] Beaks *West.*
59. *winds and seas*] Seas & Winds *West.*

60   The shepherd of his flocks, the soldier of the fight;
      A milder warfare I in verse display;
      Each in his proper art should waste the day.
      Nor thou my gentle calling disapprove:
      To die is glorious in the bed of love.
65   Happy the youth, and not unknown to fame,
      Whose heart has never felt a second flame.
      Oh, might that envied happiness be mine!
      To Cynthia all my wishes I confine;
      Or if, alas! it be my fate to try
70   Another love, the quicker let me die.
      But she, the mistress of my faithful breast,
      Has oft the charms of constancy confessed,
      Condemns her fickle sex's fond mistake,
      And hates the tale of Troy for Helen's sake.
75   Me from myself the soft enchantress stole:
      Ah! let her ever my desires control.
      Or if I fall the victim of her scorn,
      From her loved door may my pale corse be borne.
      The power of herbs can other harms remove,
80   And find a cure for every ill but love.
      The Melian's hurt Machaon could repair,
      Heal the slow chief and send again to war;
      To Chiron Phoenix owed his long-lost sight,
      And Phoebus' son recalled Androgeon to the light.
85   Here arts are vain, even magic here must fail,
      The powerful mixture and the midnight spell.
      The hand that can my captive heart release
      And to this bosom give its wonted peace,
      May the long thirst of Tantalus allay,
90   Or drive the infernal vulture from his prey.
      For ills unseen what remedy is found,
      Or who can probe the undiscovered wound?
      The bed avails not or the leech's care,
      Nor changing skies can hurt nor sultry air.
95   'Tis hard the elusive symptoms to explore:
      Today the lover walks, tomorrow is no more;
      A train of mourning friends attend his pall,
      And wonder at the sudden funeral.

78. door] Doors *West.*
81. Melian's] Lemnian's *West, Mitford and Commonplace Book but* Melian's *is
substituted in margin of Commonplace Book.*
84. recalled] restored *West.*
85. arts are] Skill is *West.*
90. Or] And *West.*

When then my fates that breath they gave shall
  claim,
100 When the short marble but preserves a name,
A little verse, my all that shall remain,
Thy passing courser's slackened speed retain
(Thou envied honour of thy poet's days,
Of all our youth the ambition and the praise!);
105 Then to my quiet urn awhile draw near,
And say, while o'er the place you drop a tear,
Love and the fair were of his life the pride;
He lived while she was kind, and, when she frowned,
  he died.

100. but] shall *West* *preserves*] preserve *West, Mitford*.
102. retain] detain *West*; restrain *Mitford*.

9 Ode on the Spring

Written early in June 1742. G. entitled his transcript of this poem in his
Commonplace Book (i 275, 278), 'Noon-Tide, An Ode' and dated it
'at Stoke, the beginning of June, 1742. sent to Fav: not knowing he was
then Dead'. Richard West ('Favonius'), who was attempting to recover his
health at Hatfield in Hertfordshire, had sent G. his *Ode on May* on 5 May
1742 (*Corresp* i 200–01). It was in reply to this poem that G. wrote his own
Ode during a visit to his uncle and aunt, Mr and Mrs Rogers, at Stoke
Poges later in the month. West died on 1 June 1742 and G.'s letter containing
his poem was returned unopened. He did not learn of West's death until
17 June, when he saw Ashton's lines on West printed in a newspaper (*Corresp*
i 213 *n*).

  G. sent a copy of the poem to Walpole on 20 Oct. 1746 (*Corresp* i 250–2),
and it was evidently through Walpole that it was first printed anonymously
(entitled merely *Ode*) in Dodsley's *Collection* ii 265–7, in 1748. One alter-
ation to the text of the Commonplace Book had been made by the time
G. sent the poem to Walpole (l. 12) and a final change was made in *1753*
(ll. 19–20).

  G.'s original title suggested to Mason (*Poems* p. 75) that 'probably he
then meant to write two more, descriptive of Morning and Evening' and
he toyed with the idea that the opening of the *Ode on . . . Vicissitude* and of
the *Elegy* might at some stage have been part of some such plan. But there is
no external evidence to support this hypothesis, which may have been
suggested to Mason by the fact that such a sequence of three poems–'A
Morning Piece', 'A Noon-Piece' and 'A Night-Piece'–appears in Chris-
topher Smart's *Poems on Several Occasions* (1752) pp. 7–14, a collection to
which both G. and Mason subscribed.

  Johnson (*Lives of the Poets*, ed. G. B. Hill, iii 434) thought that the Ode 'has something poetical, both in the language and the thought; but the language is too luxuriant, and the thoughts have nothing new. . . . The morality is natural, but too stale; the conclusion is pretty.' The derivative nature of G.'s poem has often been pointed out and a number of new borrowings have been added here to those already recognized. In part the richness of effect at which G. was aiming was to be achieved by the deliberate echoing and evocation of earlier classical and native descriptions of the spring, both in details of phrasing and in the basic situation of the retired poet contemplating the frivolity of the world as represented by the 'insect youth'. It does not always seem to have been realized, however, that G.'s use of this 'stale' morality is self-conscious and ultimately dramatic in purpose. The point of the poem for G. lay in the final stanza, in which he moralizes on the moralistic pose he has adopted, undercutting with a characteristic touch of self-derision his own apparent complacency. The antithesis of the busy world and the contemplative life was to be dramatized again, more seriously and powerfully, in the *Elegy*, as was the poet's uneasiness about the choice he was attempting make between them.

The text is that in *1753* (from which the text in *1768* was reprinted); variants in a fragmentary draft at Yale, the Commonplace Book, the letter to Walpole, and Dodsley's *Collection* are recorded.

> Lo! where the rosy-bosomed Hours,
> Fair Venus' train, appear,
> Disclose the long-expecting flowers,

¶. *9.1–10.* This opening stanza is a deliberate attempt to evoke earlier descriptions of spring, particularly in classical literature. Mitford suggests that G. was imitating Horace, *Odes* I iv, and Anacreon's 'Ode on the Spring' and Ovid, *Fasti* v 183 ff. have also been cited as sources (see the article by A. Johnston mentioned in l. 4 *n*). But G. was aiming at a general richness of allusion rather than imitation of a particular model.

1–2. Hours] The Hours appear as attendants of Venus in the Homeric Hymns, *To Apollo* 194, and *To Venus* ii 5. Cp. *Comus* 986: 'The Graces, and the rosie-boosom'd Howres'; Thomson, *Spring* 1010: 'rosy-bosomed Spring'; and Milton, *Sonnet on the Nightingale* 4: 'While the jolly hours lead on propitious May'.

2. Venus] Venus Genetrix, the cause of all natural growth: see Lucretius i 10 ff, v 737–8, and Horace, *Odes* I iv 5, of the spring: *Iam Cytherea choros ducit Venus* (Already Cytherean Venus leads her dancing bands).

3. disclose] The first two meanings given by Johnson are 'To uncover; to produce from a state of latitancy to open view' and 'To hatch'. The word was often used of vegetable and plant life: e.g. of buds by Shakespeare, *Hamlet* I iii 40 and *Sonnets* liv 8; and Dryden, *Georgics* ii 23, 104, 446. See G. Tillotson, *Augustan Studies* (1961) p. 204.   *long-expecting*] Cp. Dryden, *Astraea Redux* 131–2: 'Frosts that constrain the ground, and birth deny / To flow'rs, that in its womb expecting lye'; and Pope, *Temple of Fame* 2: 'Call forth the Greens, and wake the rising Flowers'.

And wake the purple year!
5　　The Attic warbler pours her throat,
Responsive to the cuckoo's note,
The untaught harmony of spring:
While whispering pleasure as they fly,
Cool zephyrs through the clear blue sky
10　　Their gathered fragrance fling.

4. *purple year*] An imitation of the use of Latin *purpureus* in Virgil, *Eclogues* ix 40: *ver purpureum*; and *Pervigilium Veneris* 13: *ipsa gemmis purpurantem pingit annum floridis*, translated by Thomas Parnell, 'She paints the purple Year with vary'd show'. Dryden translated Virgil's phrase, *Eclogues* ii 62 and ix 52, as 'the Purple Spring', and was imitated by Pope, *Spring* 28, 'the Purple Year'. Warburton's note to this lines reads: 'Purple here used in the Latin sense of the brightest most vivid colouring in general, not of that peculiar tint so called'. Milton also used the word as a verb, *Lycidas* 141: 'And purple all the ground with vernal flowres'. See A. Johnston, ' "The Purple Year" in Pope and Gray', *RES* xiv (1963) 389–93, for a detailed discussion of the use of the word in both Latin and English poetry and for a defence of G.'s use of it to describe the brilliance of the flowers of an English spring. For G.'s own use of the phrase *Purpureum Veris gremium*, see *De Principiis Cogitandi* i 88 (p. 324).
5. *Attic warbler*] Cp. Propertius, *Elegies* II xx 5–6: *volucris . . . Attica*; and Milton, *Par. Regained* iv 245–6: 'the *Attic* Bird / Trills her thick-warbl'd notes'.　*pours her throat*] Cp. Lucretius i 39–40: *suavis ex ore loquellas / funde* (pour from thy lips sweet coaxings); Ovid, *Tristia* III xii 8: *indocilique loquax gutture vernat avis* (the chatty bird from unschooled throat utters a song of spring); and Pope, *Essay on Man* iii 33: 'the linnet pours his throat'.
6. Cp. *Par. Lost* iv 683: 'responsive each to others note'.
7. *untaught harmony*] Cp. Ovid's use of *indocilique* cited in l. 5 *n* above. Cowley has the 'untaught lays' of the birds, *Davideis* Bk i; and see also Thomson, *Spring* 578–80: 'while I deduce, / From the first note the hollow cuckoo sings, / The symphony of Spring'.
8–10. Lucretius v 738–40: *Zephyri vestigia propter / Flora quibus mater praespergens ante viai / cuncta coloribus egregiis et odoribus opplet* (Zephyr and mother Flora a pace behind him strewing the whole path in front with brilliant colours and filling it with scents). See also Milton, *Nativity Ode* 64, 66: 'The Windes . . . / Whispering new joyes'; *Comus* 989–91: 'And West winds, with musky wing / About the cedar'n alleys fling / Nard, and *Cassia's* balmy smells'; *Par. Lost* iv 156–9: 'now gentle gales / . . . dispense / Native perfumes, and whisper whence they stole / Those balmie spoiles'; *Par. Lost* viii 515–17: 'fresh Gales and gentle Aires / Whisper'd it to the Woods, and from their wings / Flung Rose flung Odours from the spicie Shrub'; and Matthew Green, *The Spleen* 79–80: 'And, mounting in loose robes the skies, / Shed light and fragrance as she flies'.

Where'er the oak's thick branches stretch
A broader browner shade;
Where'er the rude and moss-grown beech
O'er-canopies the glade,
15   Beside some water's rushy brink
With me the Muse shall sit, and think
(At ease reclined in rustic state)
How vain the ardour of the crowd,

11–14. Prior, *Solomon* i 57–8: 'I know not why the *Beach* delights the Glade /
With Boughs extended, and a rounder Shade'.

12. Their broadest brownest shade *Commonplace Book*.   *brown*] Used
of shadows in Fairfax's translation of Tasso (1600), XIV xxxvii 3 and XX
cxxiii 1, and frequently in English poetry thereafter: e.g. Milton, *Il Penseroso*
134–5: 'shadows brown that *Sylvan* loves / Of Pine or monumental Oake';
Par. Lost iv 245–6: 'the unpierc't shade / Imbround the noontide Bowrs';
Par. Lost ix 1087–8: 'umbrage broad, / And brown as Evening'; Dryden,
Theodore and Honoria 92: 'With deeper Brown the Grove was over spred';
Pope, *Eloisa to Abelard* 170: 'And breathes a browner horror on the woods';
and Mallet, *The Excursion* (1728) i 89–90: 'brown with woods / Of broadest
shade'.

13. Pope, *Eloisa to Abelard* 142: 'moss-grown domes'; and Parnell, *To
Mr Pope* 81: 'mossgrown trees'.

14. —— a bank [...] / [Quite] o'ercanopied with luscious woodbine.
Shakesp. Mids. Night's Dream [II i 249–51]. *G. 1768*.

G. had already acknowledged the imitation to Walpole in Oct. 1746,
Corresp i 251. Cp. also Phineas Fletcher, *Purple Island* I xxx: 'The beech
shall yield a cool safe canopy'; and *Comus* 543–4: 'a bank / With Ivy
canopied'.

15–17. The description of the poet reclining in the heat of mid-day beneath
a tree and beside a stream occurs frequently in classical poetry: e.g. Horace,
Odes I i 20–2 and II xi 14–16; Virgil, *Eclogues* i 1–2; Lucretius ii 29–33. Such
passages were widely imitated in Augustan poetry: e.g. Gay, *Rural Sports*
i 59–62, 65–6: 'Where the tall oak his spreading arms entwines, / And with
the beech a mutual shade combines; / Where flows the murmuring brook,
inviting dreams, / Where bordering hazel overhangs the streams . . . / Upon
the mossy couch my limbs I cast, / And e'en at noon the sweets of evening
taste.' See also David Mallet, *The Excursion* i 130–6; and Thomson, *Summer*
9–13, 284–6 (where the retreat to the shade at noon is followed as here by some
moralizing about insects) and 458–68 (where he who retires from the heat
in this way becomes an 'Emblem instructive of the virtuous man').

15. *Midsummer Night's Dream* II i 84: 'By paved fountain or by rushy brook';
Comus 890: 'the rushy-fringed bank'.

18. Horace, *Odes* III iii 2: *civium ardor* (the frenzy of fellow-citizens).

How low, how little are the proud,
20 How indigent the great!

Still is the toiling hand of Care;
The panting herds repose.
Yet hark, how through the peopled air
The busy murmur glows!
25 The insect youth are on the wing,
Eager to taste the honeyed spring,
And float amid the liquid noon:
Some lightly o'er the current skim,

19–20. Commonplace Book, letter to Walpole and Dodsley have:
> How low, how indigent the Proud,
> How little are the Great.

According to Mason, *Poems* p. 75, G. altered the lines 'on account of the point of *little* and *great*. It certainly had too much the appearance of a Concetto, though it expressed his meaning better than the present reading.' Cp. Henry Brooke, *Universal Beauty* (1735) iv 285: 'The little, low, fine follies of the great'.

22. Herds and flocks in the heat of day are a common classical topic: e.g. Virgil, *Eclogues* ii 8; Horace, *Odes* III xxix 21–2; Persius, *Satires* iii 6; and equally common in eighteenth-century pastoral: e.g. Pope, *Summer* 86–7: 'The lowing Herds to murm'ring Brooks retreat, / To closer Shades the panting Flocks remove.'

23. *peopled*] See *Spectator* No. 519: 'Every part of Matter is peopled: Every green Leaf swarms with Inhabitants'; and Pope, *Essay on Man* i 210: 'the peopled grass'.

24. *Par. Regained* iv 247–8: 'the sound / Of Bees industrious murmur'; Parnell, *The Flies* 22: 'A pleasing Murmur hums along the Plain'; and Pope, *Iliad* ii 552–3, 556–7: 'or thick as insects play, / The wandering nation of a summer's day, / ... with busy murmur run / The gilded legions, glittering in the sun'.   *glows*] An imitation of Virgil's *fervet*: e.g. *Georgics* iv 169 (of bees): *fervet opus*. See also *Aeneid* iv 407.

25. *youth*] Probably an imitation of Virgil's *iuventus*, used of bees, *Georgics* iv 22, also imitated by Milton, *Par. Lost* i 770: 'populous youth'. Thomson, *Spring* 729, has 'feathered youth'.

26. *honeyed*] Johnson objects in his *Life of G.* to this adjective, but G. had precedents for it in Milton (*Il Penseroso* 142; *Lycidas* 140; *Samson Agonistes* 1066), and other poets.

27. *Nare per aestatem liquidam* ——— *Virgil. Georg. lib. 4.* [59]. *G. 1768.*
He had already acknowledged the imitation to Walpole in Oct. 1746 (*Corresp* i 251). It means literally 'floating through the clear summer air'. For 'liquid', see also *Vicissitude* 16 (p. 203). Cp. also Gay, *Rural Sports* i 128, 130 (of fish): 'Float in the sun, and skim along the lake / ... / Their silver coats reflect the dazzling beams'.

Some show their gaily-gilded trim
30   Quick-glancing to the sun.

To Contemplation's sober eye
Such is the race of man:
And they that creep, and they that fly,
Shall end where they began.
35   Alike the busy and the gay
But flutter through life's little day,

29–30. —— sporting with quick glance / Shew to the sun their waved
coats drop'd with gold. *Milton's Paradise Lost*, book 7 [405–6]. *G. 1768.*

Milton was probably imitating Virgil, *Georgics* iv 98–9 and see also iv 27–
8: *et alas / pandere ad aestivum solem* (and spread their wings to the summer
sun). Mallet has 'quick-glancing', *Excursion* i 169. G. seems also indebted to
Henry Brooke, *Universal Beauty* v 166–9: 'the summer's glistering swarms, /
Ten thousand thousand gaily gilded forms, / In volant dance of mix'd
rotation play, / Bask in the beam, and beautify the day.'

31–40. Early in 1748 G. transcribed in a letter to Walpole part of Matthew
Green's *The Grotto* (1732), which he had seen in Dodsley's *Collection* and
added: 'The thought on which my second ode [*On the Spring*] turns is
manifestly stole from hence:–not that I knew it at the time, but, having seen
this many Years before, to be sure it imprinted itself on my Memory, &
forgetting the Author, I took it for my own' (*Corresp* i 299–300). G.
had ll. 57–64, 75–80 in mind, as he acknowledged by quoting them in *1768*:

> While Insects from the Threshold preach,
> And Minds disposed to Musing teach;
> Proud of strong Limbs & painted Hues
> They perish by the slightest Bruise
> Or Maladies begun within
> Destroy more slow Life's frail Machine:
> From Maggot-Youth thro' Change of State
> They feel like us the Turns of Fate . . . .
> Nor from their vigorous Schemes desist
> Till Death; & then are never mist.
> Some frolick, toil, marry, increase,
> Are sick & well, have War & Peace,
> And broke with Age in half a Day
> Yield to Successors, & away.

31–2. Cf. Richard West, 'Ad Amicos' 46–7, sent to G. in July 1737 (*Corresp*
i 63): 'How weak is Man to Reason's judging eye! / Born in this moment,
in the next we die . . . '

35–6. The comparison of frivolous pleasure-seekers to ephemeral summer
insects is common in eighteenth-century poetry: e.g. Pope, *To Mr John
Moore* 17–18: 'The Fops are painted Butterflies, / That flutter for a Day';
Thomson, *Summer* 346–51: 'Even so luxurious men, unheeding pass / An
idle summer life in fortune's shine, / A season's glitter! Thus they flutter on /

In fortune's varying colours dressed:
Brushed by the hand of rough Mischance,
Or chilled by age, their airy dance
40   They leave, in dust to rest.

Methinks I hear in accents low
The sportive kind reply:
Poor moralist! and what art thou?
A solitary fly!
45   Thy joys no glittering female meets,
No hive hast thou of hoarded sweets,
No painted plumage to display:
On hasty wings thy youth is flown;
Thy sun is set, thy spring is gone————
50   We frolic, while 'tis May.

From toy to toy, from vanity to vice; / Till, blown away by death, oblivion
comes / Behind and strikes them from the book of life'; and *Liberty* v 593–4:
'those vain insects fluttering in the blaze, / Of court and ball and play'.
38. Parnell describes a fly 'brush'd by careless Hands', *The Flies* 37.
39–40. Aeneid v 395–6: *sed enim gelidus tardante senecta / sanguis hebet* (but my
blood is chilled and dulled by sluggish age); Cowley, *The Grasshopper* 29–34:
'But when thou'st drunk, and danc'd and sung / Thy fill, the flowr'y leaves
among . . . / Sated with thy summer feast, / Thou retir'st to endless rest.'
42. Thomson, *Summer* 251–2, describes the insects which 'on the pool /
. . . sportive wheel'.
43–4. G. may have had in mind *Guardian* No. 70, which compares the
short-sighted philosopher to a fly in a large building; Thomson, *Summer*
324–8, imitating the passage, refers to man as a 'critic fly'.
45–6. Milton, *Par. Lost* iv 760, describes 'wedded Love' as a 'Perpetual
Fountain of Domestic sweets'. In 1761, Mason facetiously told G. that he
had found the source of these lines in Jeremy Taylor, (Sermon xvii, 'The
Marriage Ring': 'Celibate, like the fly in the heart of an apple, dwells in a
perpetual sweetness, but sits alone, and is confined and dies in singularity').
G.'s reply that he had not read Taylor (*Corresp* ii 719–20, 724).
47. plumage] Glories *Yale draft*. Perhaps an imitation of Virgil, *Georgics* iii
243: *pictaeque volucres*. See also *Par. Lost* vii 438 and Pope, *Windsor Forest*
118: 'painted wings'; and Dryden, *Flower and the Leaf* 107: and Thomson,
Spring 585.
48–50. In Yale draft these lines begin Thy Sun is set, thy . . . / Thy Youth on
hasty . . . / We wanton while . . .
49. Theocritus, *Idylls* i 102: 'Think'st thou my sun is set?'; and Fairfax's
Tasso XI lvii 8 (of warriors): 'Their sun was set, or else with clouds o'ercast'.
Nathan Drake, *The Gleaner* (1811) i 122–3, compares *The Free-Thinker*
No. 114 (24 April 1719), which elaborates a passage in Cicero, *Tusculan
Disputations* I xxxix 94, describing insects who live for a day, one of whom
philosophizes on the events of his lifetime.

10 Ode on a Distant Prospect of Eton College

G.'s transcript in his Commonplace Book (i 278–9, 284) is dated 'at Stoke Aug: 1742', and is entitled 'Ode, on a distant Prospect of Windsor, & the adjacent Country'. Another MS, now at Eton, (once in the possession of G.'s biographer William Mason, whose nephew, W. Dixon, gave it to Wordsworth), has the same title, but omits 'distant' and adds 'in 1743'. The mistake about the date was probably due to faulty memory, but it may indicate the date when G. made this transcript. There is a photograph of the Eton MS in the *Illustrated London News* cxxxii (20 June 1908) 896.

When G. sent Walpole his *Ode on the Spring* in Oct. 1746 (*Corresp* i 250), he referred to another *Ode* already in Walpole's possession, which is presumably the present poem. It was published anonymously by Dodsley in a folio pamphlet, price 6d, on 30 May 1747 and was the first of G.'s English poems to appear in print. Its publication was no doubt arranged by Walpole, to whom G. described its reception in Cambridge in mid-June 1747 (*Corresp* i 283): 'I promise you, few take to it here at all, which is a good sign (for I never knew anything liked here, that ever proved to be so any where else,) it is said to be mine, but I strenuously deny it, and so do all that are in the secret, so that nobody knows what to think; a few only of King's College gave me the lie, but I hope to demolish them; for if *I* don't know, who should?'

A type-facsimile of the original pamphlet was published at Oxford in 1924. Dodsley included the *Ode* in his *Collection* ii 261–4, in 1748, but without separating the stanzas. A few minor variants appear in the two MSS, but no changes to the text were made by G. after the first publication of the *Ode*. The motto from Menander is written beside ll. 41–55 in the Commonplace Book but was not printed with the poem until *1768*. It has been translated, 'I am a man; a sufficient excuse for being unhappy.' (See A. Meineke, *Quaestionum Menandrearum* (Berlin, 1818) p. 267; No. 263 in 'Incertarum Fabularum Fragmenta'.) Three footnotes were also added in *1768*. Three small variants have been noted in the Foulis edition of *1768*, which was supervised by James Beattie, who may have been responsible for them.

A letter from G. to West on 27 May 1742 (*Corresp* i 210) throws some light on his attitude to his contemporaries at Eton three months before he wrote this *Ode:* 'Is it not odd to consider one's Cotemporaries in the grave light of Husband and Father? There is my Lords [Sandwich] and [Halifax], they are Statesmen: Do not you remember them dirty boys playing at cricket? As for me, I am never a bit the older, nor the bigger, nor the wiser than I was then: No, not for having been beyond sea.' The distaste conveyed by G.'s reference to 'dirty boys playing at cricket' is explained at length in a letter from Jacob Bryant, a contemporary of G. at Eton, dated

24 Dec. 1798, first printed in *Gentleman's Mag.* xxv New Series (1846) 140–3. While still a schoolboy, it appears, G. already took a 'distant view' of the more robust amusements he describes in the poem: 'both Mr. Gray and his friend [Walpole] were looked upon as too delicate, upon which account they had few associates, and never engaged in any exercise, nor partook of any boyish amusement. Hence they seldom were in the fields, at least they took only a distant view of those who pursued their different diversions. Some, therefore, who were severe, treated them as feminine characters, on account of their too great delicacy, and sometimes a too fastidious behaviour. Mr. Walpole long time afterwards used to say that *Gray was never a boy*. . . . Mr. Gray was so averse to all rough exercise, that I am confident he was never on horseback.'

G.'s dislike of boyish games is betrayed by the self-conscious and ponderous diction he uses to describe them, which was intended to be gently humorous. But by Aug. 1742 Eton had acquired a more profound significance for G. than is apparent from the studied immaturity of his letter to West three months earlier. The death of West himself only a few days after the date of that letter had widened the gulf separating G. from his schooldays, which had been opened by his quarrel in Italy with Horace Walpole in the previous year. And, whatever his feelings about Walpole, he would not be able to help reflecting on the fall from power of his former friend's father, Sir Robert Walpole, the Prime Minister, early in 1742. His own father had died in November 1741 and G. himself was now financially insecure and uncertain about his future. All these considerations lie behind the poetry which he wrote in this uniquely prolific period in the summer of 1742, and in particular the *Ode* on Eton.

In this state of mind, G. could easily idealize his schooldays and the poem is built on a stark contrast between the joys of childhood and the evils which maturity will bring. Eton acquires a prelapsarian innocence, which is enforced by the echoes of Milton's description of Eden and other accounts of man in the Golden Age, before the onset of evil passions, by Pope and Thomson. Another member of the 'Quadruple Alliance', that defensive group of friends who had been too delicate or fastidious for the rougher pleasures of Eton, had described Eton as a state of lost innocence several years earlier, and G. may have remembered the 'Ode to Mary Magdalene' which Richard West, exiled to Oxford, had sent in Aug. 1736 to Walpole (*Walpole Correspondence* xiii 110–11), which includes the following stanzas:

> Lost and enwrapt in thought profound,
> Absent I tread Etonian ground;
> Then starting from the dear mistake,
>   As disenchanted, wake . . .
>
> Oh! how I long again with those,
> Whom first my boyish heart had chose,
> Together through the friendly shade
>   To stray, as once I strayed!

Their presence would the scene endear,
Like paradise would all appear,
More sweet around the flowers would blow,
More soft the waters flow.

In the letter quoted above, Jacob Bryant gives an implausible account of the composition of G.'s *Ode*, which describes G. crossing the playing-fields of Eton on his way to Windsor to visit Horace Walpole, who had sent him a letter of reconciliation. All the known facts contradict Bryant's story, but there is some basis to his general assertion that 'The poet saw and experimentally felt what he so masterly describes' in that G.'s title is no mere formula. The grounds of West End House at Stoke Poges, where he was staying with his uncle Jonathan Rogers, contained a summer-house overlooking the Thames valley, from which G. could see Eton and Windsor; see *Victoria County History of Buckinghamshire*, ed. W. Page, iii (1925) 303. Thus G. had a literal 'prospect' before him and he could literally feel the winds blowing from Eton, although part of the point is that the prospect was distant also in time with the winds blowing across the years which separated him from his schooldays. G.'s title also points to a relationship with the genre of the topographical poem, a number of features of which appear in miniature in it: according to R. A. Aubin, *Topographical Poetry in XVIII-Century England* (New York, 1936) p. 172, 'the opening address, very slight historical retrospection in the reference to the founder of Eton, the genre sketch of the children at play, the presence of abstractions and moralizing' are 'well-worn features' of this literary kind. The crucial innovation in G.'s poem is the development of the nostalgic associations of the landscape described. In effect, as G.'s title indicates, he was combining the topographical poem with the subjective ode to produce a new form, characterized by that interplay of the subjective and objective which distinguishes G.'s poetry.

The text is that of the 1747 pamphlet, with variants from the two MSS and the Foulis edition of *1768* at Glasgow.

Ἄνθρωπος· ἱκανὴ πρόφασις εἰς τὸ δυστυχεῖν.

Ye distant spires, ye antique towers,
That crown the watery glade,
Where grateful Science still adores

¶ 10.*1–2*. 'May thy lofty head be crown'd / With many a tower and terrass round', *Comus* 934–5; 'All up the silver *Thames*, or all a down; / Ne *Richmond's* self, from whose tall Front are ey'd / Vales, Spires, meandring Streams, and *Windsor's* tow'ry Pride', Pope, *Imitation of Spenser* 52–4; 'Where *Windsor*-Domes and pompous Turrets rise', Pope, *Windsor Forest* 352; 'And ancient towers crown his brow', John Dyer, *Grongar Hill* 71.
2. 'haunt the watry Glade', Pope, *Windsor Forest* 128.
3. *Science*] Knowledge in general, as in *Elegy* 119.

Her Henry's holy shade;
5 And ye that from the stately brow
Of Windsor's heights the expanse below
Of grove, of lawn, of mead survey,
Whose turf, whose shade, whose flowers among
Wanders the hoary Thames along
10 His silver-winding way.

    Ah, happy hills, ah, pleasing shade,
Ah, fields beloved in vain,
Where once my careless childhood strayed,
A stranger yet to pain!
15 I feel the gales, that from ye blow,
A momentary bliss bestow,
As waving fresh their gladsome wing,
My weary soul they seem to soothe,
And, redolent of joy and youth,
20 To breathe a second spring.

4. King Henry the Sixth, Founder of the College. *G. 1768.*

A bronze statue of Henry VI had been placed in the centre of School Yard at Eton not long before G. arrived there in 1725. G. makes other references to the sanctity of this monarch: see *Bard* 90 *n* and *Ode for Music* 46. Shakespeare called Henry 'holy', *Richard III* V i 4, and Pope referred to him as 'the Martyr-King', *Windsor Forest* 312.

7. Of Grove & Lawn & Mead survey *Commonplace Book.*

7–10. Cp. the first version of Pope, *Summer* 3–4: 'Where gentle *Thames* his winding Waters leads / Thro' verdant Forests, and thro' flow'ry Meads.'

9–10. *tardis ingens ubi flexibus errat / Mincius* (where great Mincius wanders in slow windings), Virgil, *Georgics* iii 14–15; and Pope, *Iliad* ii 623–4: 'From those rich regions where Cephisus leads / His silver current through the flowery meads'. 'Silver' is a frequent epithet for the Thames in Spenser, Dryden, Pope and Thomson.

11. Cp. Dryden, *Aeneid* iii 299, and *Flower and the Leaf* 314: 'pleasing Shade'; and Pope, *Autumn* 25: 'pleasing shades'.

11–14. Gay, *Rural Sports* ii 168, 170: 'Ye happy fields, unknown to noise and strife / . . . / Ye shady woods, where once I us'd to rove . . . '

12. *in vain*] See *Sonnet on West* 1, 14.

15–18. Aaron Hill, *Solitude* (a poem whose theme is close to G.'s at a number of points), 1–3: 'Welcome cool breeze, to fan my glowing mind, / Cinder'd with feverish cares and constant woe! / Welcome soft bliss, by gracious heav'n design'd . . . '

16. Cp. Dryden, *Juvenal* vi 279: 'The Momentary trembling Bliss'.

17. Cp. *Bard* 124 and *n* (p. 198).

19. And bees their honey redolent of spring. *Dryden's Fable on the Pythag. System* [110]. *G. 1768.*

Say, Father Thames, for thou hast seen
Full many a sprightly race
Disporting on thy margent green
The paths of pleasure trace,
25 Who foremost now delight to cleave
With pliant arm thy glassy wave?
The captive linnet which enthrall?
What idle progeny succeed
To chase the rolling circle's speed,
30 Or urge the flying ball?

While some on earnest business bent
Their murmuring labours ply
'Gainst graver hours, that bring constraint
To sweeten liberty:
35 Some bold adventurers disdain
The limits of their little reign,
And unknown regions dare descry:
Still as they run they look behind,

21. 'Father Thames' appears in Dryden, *Annus Mirabilis* 925, and Pope, *Windsor Forest* 197 and 330; but G. probably had in mind Matthew Green, *The Grotto* 5–7: 'Say, father Thames, whose gentle pace / Gives leave to view what beauties grace / Your flowery banks, if you have seen . . .' Cp. also, Pope, *Dunciad* iii 335: 'Till Thames see Eaton's sons for ever play'.
22. *sprightly*] smileing *Commonplace Book, Eton*.
23. 'By slow *Meander*'s margent green', *Comus* 232.
24. 'In the paths of Pleasure', Pope, *Essay on Man* iii 233.
25–6. Stephen Duck, *The Midsummer Wish* 17–18 (*Gent. Mag.* i (1731) 74), of bathing in the Thames at Windsor: 'Let me thy clear, thy yielding wave, / With naked arm once more divide . . .'
26. *arm*] arms *Foulis*.   Cp. 'Under the glassie, cool, translucent wave', *Comus* 861.
29. To chase the Hoop's elusive Speed *Commonplace Book*. (G. probably made the change to avoid an echo of 'elusive speed' in *Agrippina* 186.)
29–30. Ovid, *Tristia* III xii 19–20: *nunc luditur . . . / nunc pila, nunc celeri volvitur orbe trochus* (now there is play with the ball or the swift curling hoop).
30. Waller, *Of the Danger his Majesty Escaped* 41–2, 49–50: ' . . . the youths begin to sweep / Neptune's smooth face, and cleave the yielding deep. / . . . / They ply their feet, and still the restless ball, / Tost to and fro, is urged by them all'; and *On St James's Park* 65: 'No sooner had he touched the flying ball'; and Pope, *Dunciad* iv 592: 'The Senator at Cricket urge the Ball'.
32–3. 'They are supposed to be conning by heart and repeating aloud to themselves the tasks, 'saying lessons' &c. which they are to repeat in the 'graver hours,' i.e. when 'up' to their masters in school' (Tovey).
37. 'Till unknown regions it descries', Cowley, *To Mr Hobbes* 55.

They hear a voice in every wind,
40 And snatch a fearful joy.

Gay hope is theirs by fancy fed,
Less pleasing when possessed;
The tear forgot as soon as shed,
The sunshine of the breast:
45 Theirs buxom health of rosy hue,
Wild wit, invention ever-new,
And lively cheer of vigour born;
The thoughtless day, the easy night,
The spirits pure, the slumbers light,
50 That fly the approach of morn.

Alas, regardless of their doom,
The little victims play!
No sense have they of ills to come,
Nor care beyond today:

39. *nunc omnes terrent aurae, sonus excitat omnis* / *suspensum* (I am now affrighted by every breeze and startled by every sound), Virgil, *Aeneid* ii 728–9; and 'Sees God in clouds, or hears him in the wind', Pope, *Essay on Man* i 100.
40. *percussus* . . . / *laetitiaque metuque* (thrilled with joy and fear), *Aeneid* i 513–4; *laetoque pavore*, Silius Italicus, *Punica* xvi 431.
41–2. Lucretius iii 1082–3: *Sed dum abest quod avemus, id exsuperare videtur* / *cetera; post aliut, cum contigit illud, avemus* (But while we have not what we crave, that seems to surpass all else; afterwards when we have attained that, we crave something else). Cp. also Dryden's translation, iii 308–9: 'For still we think an absent blessing best; / Which cloys, and is no blessing when possest'.
44. 'Eternal sunshine of the spotless mind', Pope, *Eloisa to Abelard* 209; 'The soul's calm sunshine and the heartfelt joy', *Essay on Man* iv 168; 'True joy, the sunshine of the soul', Young, *Imperium Pelagi* IV xvi; 'friends, the sunshine of the soul', Thomson, *To the Memory of Lord Talbot* 244; 'It's all a Sunshine of the Soul', John Addison, *Works of Anacreon Translated* (1735) p. 91.
45. *buxom*] Lively, healthy. Cp. 'Celestial rosie red, Loves proper hue', *Par. Lost* viii 619.
47. 'In either cheeke depeincten liuely chere', Spenser, *Shepheardes Calender*, 'April' 69; and 'as lively vigour led', *Par. Lost* viii 269.
49–50. Cp. Adam waking in Eden: 'his sleep / Was Aerie light, from pure digestion bred', *Par. Lost* v 3–4; 'the Schoolboy's simple fare, / The temp'rate sleeps, and spirits light as air!', Pope, *Imitations of Horace*, *Sat.* II ii 73–4; and Thomson, *Spring* 244–5, of man in the Golden Age: 'For their light slumbers gently fumed away, / And up they rose as vigorous as the sun.'
50. 'the sweet approach of Ev'n or Morn' and 'th'approach of Morn', *Par. Lost* iii 42 and ix 191.
51. Dryden, *Astraea Redux* 13: 'And Heaven that seem'd regardless of our Fate!'

55　Yet see how all around 'em wait
　　The ministers of human fate,
　　And black Misfortune's baleful train!
　　Ah, show them where in ambush stand
　　To seize their prey the murtherous band!
60　Ah, tell them, they are men!
　　　These shall the fury Passions tear,
　　　The vultures of the mind,

55–6. 'ministers of fate', *The Tempest* III iii 61; 'minister of fate', Thomson, *Summer* 908; 'grim ministers of Fate', Otway, *Alcibiades* V ii; 'Behold the Fates Infernal Minister; / War, Death, Destruction, in my Hand I bear', Dryden, *Aeneid* vii 636–7; and 'While round, stern Ministers of Fate, / Pain, and Disease, and Sorrow wait', William Broome, *Melancholy: An Ode* 27–8, in *Poems on Several Occasions* (1727) p. 45.

55. *how*] where *Eton*.　　'*em*] them *Eton, Foulis*.

58–9. Spenser, *Faerie Queene* IV x 20,6–7: 'For hatred, murther, treason, and despight, / With many moe lay in ambushment there'; and Dryden, *Sigismunda and Guiscardo* 265–6: 'When these in secret Ambush ready lay, / And rushing on the sudden seiz'd the Prey.'

59. *murtherous*] griesly *underlined, with* murtherous *in margin, Commonplace Book.*

60. *them*] 'em *Commonplace Book, Eton, Foulis.*

61. 'The Fury-passions from that blood began', Pope, *Essay on Man* iii 167, after a description, corresponding to those of Thomson (see below) and G. himself, of man's original innocence.

61–90. The original source of most passages of this sort in English poetry is *Aeneid* vi 273–81: *vestibulum ante ipsum primisque in faucibus Orci / Luctus et ultrices posuere cubilia Curae, / pallentesque habitant Morbi tristique Senectus / et Metus et malesuada Fames ac turpis Egestas, / terribiles visu formae, Letumque Labosque; tum consanguineus Leti Sopor et mala mentis / Gaudia, mortiferumque adverso in limine Bellum / ferreique Eumenidum thalami et Discordia demens, / vipereum crinem vittis innexa cruentis* (Just before the entrance, even within the very jaws of Hell, Grief and avenging Cares have made their bed; there pale Diseases dwell, and sad Age, and Fear, and ill-counselling Famine, and loathly Want, shapes terrible to view; and Death and Distress; next, Death's own brother Sleep, and the soul's Guilty Joys, and, on the threshold opposite, the death-bearer War, and the Furies' iron cells, and savage Strife, her snaky locks entwined with bloody fillets).

See also the description of the Temple of Mars in Statius, *Thebaid* vii 47–50, which Chaucer imitated in his *Knight's Tale* and which G. would meet again in Dryden's *Palamon and Arcite* (see below): *primis salit Impetus amens / e foribus caecumque Nefas Iraeque rubentes / exsanguesque Metus, occultisque ensibus adstant / Insidiae geminumque tenens Discordia ferrum* etc. (From the outer gate wild Passion leaps, and blind Mischief and Angers flushing red and pallid Fear, and Treachery lurks with hidden sword, and Discord holding a two-edged blade.)

Disdainful Anger, pallid Fear,
And Shame that skulks behind;
65 Or pining Love shall waste their youth,
Or Jealousy with rankling tooth,
That inly gnaws the secret heart,
And Envy wan, and faded Care,
Grim-visaged comfortless Despair,
70 And Sorrow's piercing dart.

Ambition this shall tempt to rise,
Then whirl the wretch from high,

But G. was indebted to English poets for many of his details. Cp. Spenser, *Faerie Queene* II vii 22: 'On thother side in one consort there sate, / Cruell Reuenge, and rancorous Despight, / Disloyall Treason, and hart-burning Hate, / But gnawing Gealousie out of their sight / Sitting alone, his bitter lips did bight, / And trembling Feare still to and fro did fly, / And found no place, where safe he shroud him might, / Lamenting Sorrow did in darkness lye, / And Shame his vgly face did hide from liuing eye.' In the previous stanza Spenser had mentioned 'infernall Payne' and 'tumultuous Strife'; and in stanza 25 he described 'selfe-consuming Care'. Cp. also Dryden, *Palamon and Arcite* ii 480–7 and Pope, *Windsor Forest* 413–22. G. also appears to have had in mind a passage in Thomson's *Spring* 278–308, which describes the onset of the passions after man's early innocence in the Golden Age (version of 1730–38): '. . . the passions all / Have burst their bounds; and Reason, half extinct, / Or impotent, or else approving, sees / The foul disorder. Anger storms at large / Without an equal cause; and fell Revenge / Supports the falling Rage. Close Envy bites /With venomed tooth; while weak unmanly Fear, / Full of frail fancies, loosens every power. / Even Love itself is bitterness of soul, / A pleasing anguish pining at the heart. / Hope sickens with extravagance; and Grief, / Of life impatient, into madness swells, / Or in dead silence wastes the weeping hours. / These, and a thousand mixt emotions more, / From ever-changing views of good and ill, / Formed infinitely various, vex the mind / With endless storm: whence, deeply rankling, grows / The partial thought, a listless unconcern, / Cold, and averting from our neighbour's good; / The dark disgust and hatred, winding wiles, / Coward deceit, and ruffian violence.'
63. Cp. *exsanguesque Metus* in Statius quoted above; and 'There, the Red Anger dar'd the Pallid Fear', Dryden, *Palamon and Arcite* ii 563.
68. 'With praise enough for envy to look wan', Milton, *Sonnet to Lawes* 6; and 'care / Sat on his faded cheek', *Par. Lost* i 601–2.
69. 'Grim and comfortless despair', *Comedy of Errors* V i 80; and 'Grim-visaged war', *Richard III* I i 9. G. probably combined memories of these two phrases; but Mitford cites 'grim visadged dispaire', Robert Yarrington, *Two Lamentable Tragedies* (1601) sig. D 2 r.
71. *this*] that *Commonplace Book, Eton, Foulis.*

To bitter Scorn a sacrifice,
And grinning Infamy.
75 The stings of Falsehood those shall try,
And hard Unkindness' altered eye,
That mocks the tear it forced to flow;
And keen Remorse with blood defiled,
And moody Madness laughing wild
80 Amid severest woe.

Lo, in the vale of years beneath
A grisly troop are seen,
The painful family of Death,
More hideous than their Queen:
85 This racks the joints, this fires the veins,
That every labouring sinew strains,
Those in the deeper vitals rage:
Lo, Poverty, to fill the band,

75. *those*] These *Commonplace Book.*
76. 'Affected kindness with an alter'd face', Dryden, *Hind and the Panther* iii 79.
79. —Madness laughing in his ireful mood. *Dryden's Fable of Palamon and Arcite* [ii 582]. G. *1768.* Cp. also 'moody mad', *I Henry VI* IV ii 50.
81. 'The vale of years', *Othello* III iii 266.
82. 'With all the greisly legions that troop', *Comus* 603.
83. Dryden, *State of Innocence* V i: 'Immortal then; now Sickness, Care, and Age, / And War, and Luxury's more direful Rage, / Thy crimes have brought, to shorten mortal Breath, / With all the numerous Family of Death.' Cp. also 'With all the meager Family of Care', Dryden, *Lucretius* iv 127; Garth, *Dispensary* (1699) vi 138, 'the faded family of Care'; Pope, *Essay on Man* ii 118, 'Hate, Fear and Grief, the family of pain'.
84. Milton, *Elegies* ii 17, describes Death as *Magna sepulchrorum regina.*
85–90. Virgil, *Georgics* iii 457–9: *quin etiam, ima dolor balantum lapsus ad ossa / cum furit atque artus depascitur arida febris, / profuit incensos aestus avertere* (Nay more, when the pain runs to the very marrow of the bleating victims, there to rage, and when the parching fever preys on the limbs, it is well to turn aside the fiery heat). Cp. also 'grind their joints / With dry convulsions; shorten up their sinews / With aged cramps', *Tempest* IV i 259–61; 'unthred thy joynts, / And crumble all thy sinews', *Comus* 614–5; 'jointracking rheums', *Par. Lost* xi 485; 'And Rheumatisms I send to rack the joints', Dryden, *Palamon and Arcite* iii 407; 'The Gout's fierce Rack, the burning Feaver's Rage, / The sad experience of Decay; and Age, / Her self the sorest Ill', Prior, *Solomon* iii 142–4; and 'the Kinds / Of Maladies that lead to Death's grim Cave, / Wrought by Intemperance, joint racking Gout', John Philips, *Cyder* (1708) Bk. ii.
88–9. Cp. *Elegy* 51–2 (pp. 126–7).

That numbs the soul with icy hand,
90 And slow-consuming Age.

To each his sufferings: all are men,
Condemned alike to groan;
The tender for another's pain,
The unfeeling for his own.
95 Yet ah! why should they know their fate?
Since sorrow never comes too late,
And happiness too swiftly flies.
Thought would destroy their paradise.
No more; where ignorance is bliss,
100 'Tis folly to be wise.

90. 'So drooped the slow-consuming maid', Tickell, *Colin and Lucy* 11.
90-2. Sophocles, *Oedipus Coloneus* 1229-38: 'For when he hath seen youth go by, with its light follies, what troublous affliction is strange to his lot, what suffering is not therein?—envy, factions, strife, battles and slaughters; and, last of all, age claims him for her own,—age, dispraised, infirm, unsociable, unfriended, with whom all woe of woe abides'; and Prior, *Solomon* iii 240-1, 247-8: 'Who breathes, must suffer; and who thinks, must mourn / And He alone is bless'd, who ne'er was born / ... / I tell Thee, Life is but one common Care; / And Man was born to suffer, and to fear.'
95. *fate?*] fate, *Commonplace Book*.   Cp. *Comus* 362: 'What need a man forestall his date of grief'.
97. *flies.*] flies? *Commonplace Book*.
99-100. Many parallels with the thought of these two lines have been noted, although it is not clear that G. had any one of them in mind: e.g. Sophocles, *Ajax* 554-5: 'of woes thou knowest naught, for ignorance is life's extremest bliss'; Terence, *Hecyra* 286-7: *nam nos omnes quibus est alicunde aliquis obiectus labos, / omne quod est interea tempus prius quam id rescitumst lucrost* (If our path ahead is blocked with any trouble, all the time before we find it out is always pure gain); Davenant, *The Just Italian* V i Song: 'Since Knowledge is but sorrow's Spy, / It is not safe to know'; Prior, *To the Hon C. Montagu* 33-6: 'If We see right, We see our Woes: / Then what avails it to have Eyes? / From Ignorance our Comfort flows: / The only wretched are the Wise.' Edmund Blunden, in a pamphlet entitled *The Musical Miscellany* (Tokyo, 1949) p. 5, pointed out a close parallel with a song by Lewis Theobald, 'The Invitation' 10-11, in *The Musical Miscellany* ii (1729) 157: 'Then, like true Sons of Joy, Let's laugh at the Precise: / When Wisdom grows austere, 'tis Folly to be wise.' See also Pope, *Essay on Man* i 77-85 (showing that 'His happiness depends on his *Ignorance* to a certain degree') ; Cicero, *De Divinat.* II ix 22; *II Henry IV* III i 45, 53-6; and Izaak Walton, *Life of Wotton* (Wotton's reflections on his school-days at Winchester, noted in the *Gentleman's Mag.* lxviii (1798) 481). Other 'sources' have been discovered in Euripides, Martial, Montaigne and Robert Heath.

11 Sonnet [on the Death of Mr Richard West]

G.'s transcript of this poem, following the *Eton Ode*, in his Commonplace Book (i 284) is dated 'at Stoke, Aug: 1742'. A facsimile of this MS is given as the frontispiece to G.'s *Works*, ed. Gosse (1884), vol iv. Richard West, G.'s close friend at Eton and literary correspondent thereafter, had died on 1 June 1742 at the age of twenty-five. (See also headnote to *Ode on the Spring*, p. 47 above.) Norton Nicholls, a close friend of G. in the 1760s, wrote in his 'Reminiscences of Gray' (*Corresp* iii 1300): 'Whenever I mentioned Mr West he looked serious, & seemed to feel the affliction of a recent loss. He said the cause of the disorder, a consumption, which brought him to an early grave was the fatal discovery which he made of the treachery of a supposed friend, & the viciousness of a mother whom he tenderly loved; this man under the mask of friendship to him & his family intrigued with his mother; & robbed him of his peace of mind, his health, & his life.'

The *Sonnet* was not published in G.'s lifetime and what is presumably his only reference to it suggests that he did not think highly of it. In Jan. 1758 he wrote to Bedingfield, 'I will not send you the *Sonnet* you mention, but here is something else full as bad' (*Corresp* ii 560). It was first printed as 'Sonnet on the Death of Mr. Richard West' by Mason in *1775*, *Poems* p. 60. For G.'s other tribute in verse to West, see *De Principiis Cogitandi*, Bk ii (p. 328), which throws light on some elements in the *Sonnet*.

The nature and purpose of G.'s diction in this poem have been frequently discussed. Wordsworth quoted it in the Preface to the second edn of the *Lyrical Ballads* (1800) to show how G. 'attempted to widen the space of separation betwixt Prose and Metrical composition, and was more than any man curiously elaborate in the structure of his own poetic diction'. He asserted that only ll. 6–8 and 13–14 had 'any value'. Coleridge exposed the dubious assumptions underlying Wordsworth's argument in *Biographia Literaria*, ch. xviii, and another notable dissenter from Wordsworth's reproach was Gerard Manley Hopkins, *Correspondence of Hopkins and Richard Watson Dixon*, ed. C. C. Abbott (1955), p. 137. Hopkins praised the poem's 'rhythmical beauty, due partly to the accent being rather trochaic than iambic'; and he went on to describe Wordsworth's criticism of it as 'rude at best, since in a work of art having so strong a unity as a sonnet one part which singly is less beautiful than another part may be as necessary to the whole effect, like the plain shaft in a column and so on. But besides what he calls evident is not so, nor true.'

Hopkins's emphasis on the rhythmic control and larger organization of the poem is a useful antidote to criticism concerned solely with the diction, although two recent attempts to justify it deserve mention. J. Foldare, in

'Gray's "Frail Memorial" to West', *PMLA* lxxv (1960) 61–5, argues that
G.'s imitations of Milton in the poem, particularly of *Par. Lost* v 1–25,
make it 'a revelation in epithet and image of the kind of life West helped to
create, and consequently, a full measure of the desolation brought by his
death'. Although G. echoes the specific passages of Milton cited by Foldare
less consistently than he suggests, this characterization of the diction is
preferable to that of Professor G. Tillotson, *Augustan Studies* (1961) pp. 87–8,
who argues that it is deliberately artificial for a 'dramatic' purpose, G.
expressing his grief by rejecting 'the sights and sounds of the spring, which
poets less stricken have described in the stock terms he quotes'. G., according
to Tillotson, 'has no use for the things that his fellow poets, quite properly
on their less heavy occasions, have taken delight in and have described in
the sort of phrases he recalls.'

The influences acting on G. when he wrote the poem as well as his actual
diction in it suggest that this is a misreading of his aim. It is probable that
when writing it G. had in mind the poem, 'Ad Amicos', which Richard
West had sent him on 4 July 1737 (*Corresp* i 61–4). This poem, an imitation
of Tibullus, *Elegies* III v, also borrowed from a letter from Pope to Steele
on his ill-health, dated 15 July 1712 and printed by Steele as *Guardian* No.
132 in 1713. The passage which influenced West was Pope's prediction that,
'The morning after my Exit, the sun will rise as bright as ever, the flowers
smell as sweet, the plants spring as green, the world will proceed in its old
course, people will laugh as heartily, and marry as fast as they were us'd
to do.' West's melancholy poem ends:

> For me, whene'er all-conquering Death shall spread
> His wings around my unrepining head,
> I care not; though this face be seen no more,
> The world will pass as cheerful as before,
> Bright as before the day-star will appear,
> The fields as verdant, and the skies as clear . . .
> Unknown and silent will depart my breath,
> Nor nature e'er take notice of my death.
> Yet some there are (ere spent my vital days)
> Within whose breasts my tomb I wish to raise.
> Lov'd in my life, lamented in my end,
> Their praise would crown me as their precepts mend:
> To them may these fond lines my name endear,
> Not from the Poet but the Friend sincere.

West's prediction that nature would be indifferent to his death and his
hope that some friend would nevertheless remember him may well have
influenced the content and tone of G.'s poem, which describes the indifference
of nature to his own grief. Far from rejecting the activities and beauties
of nature, G. has been excluded by his friend's death from its cheerful and
fruitful life. The contrast of the joy of nature and the grief of the poet is
not uncommon in poetry, especially in love poetry, and the very form of

G.'s sonnet may indicate that he was also influenced by a model of this sort. In his 'Observations on English Metre', *Works*, ed. Gosse, i 349, G. describes the various rhyme schemes possible in the sonnet form. Two of them, the second of which he follows in his own *Sonnet*, he identifies as 'the true Sonnet of the Italians. Petrarch uses only these two measures.' There is other evidence to show that G. was familiar with Petrarch; the sonnet form itself was unusual in the eighteenth century, having been in effect abandoned since Milton. His use of it, then, virtually amounts in itself to an allusion to Petrarch, and he may well have had in mind one of the best known of Petrarch's sonnets on the death of Laura (No. 310 in modern editions of the *Canzoniere*). It was no doubt of G.'s *Sonnet* that Sir Egerton Brydges was thinking when he noted of Petrarch's *Zefiro torna, e'l bel tempo rimena* that 'Our Poet Gray had deeply studied the images, the sentiments, the language, and the tone of this beautiful Sonnet', *Res Literariae* (Naples, 1821) i 32 *n*. Literally translated Petrarch's sonnet reads: 'Zephyr returns and brings back the fine weather, and the flowers and the grass, its sweet progeny; and twittering Progne and mournful Philomena, and the white and red spring. The meadows smile and the sky is clear again. Jove rejoices to see his daughter. The air and the water and the earth are filled with love. Every creature turns again to love. But for me, wretched one, only heavier sighs return, which she, who has borne its key to heaven, tears from the depths of my heart. And the singing birds and the flowering slopes, and fair women, both courteous and gentle, are to me a desert, haunted by fierce and cruel beasts.'

Many other examples of the basic contrast on which this sonnet is constructed could be given, e.g. Guarini's *Pastor Fido* III i 1–12 (G. translated another part of this play into Latin in 1738, *Corresp* i 90); Cowley, *The Springtime*; Gay, *Panthea* 71–92; and Thomson, *To Amanda* 5–8, a short quotation from which may further indicate the relationship between G.'s poem and this convention of love poetry: 'Awakened by the genial year, / In vain the birds around me sing; / In vain the freshening fields appear, / Without my love there is no spring.'

Given that G.'s poem is organized around the contrast of a joyful, thriving nature and the poet's grief, a defence of the diction used to describe nature on the grounds that it is ironic is over-ingenious and distracting. Studied and occasionally stilted it may be, but there is no reason to suppose that G. was not serious in using it, and perhaps more purposeful than is usually allowed. In part the diction is intended to evoke a Miltonic richness which contrasts with the barer language (approved by Wordsworth) used to describe the poet's barren spiritual condition. This contrast, established in the octave, is re-explored in the sestet, in part through the diction itself. The anthropomorphic epithets used in the first quatrain – smiling, warm, amorous, cheerful – are re-examined and justified in the third, where fruitful nature, in contrast with the poet's sterile, friendless solitude, is shown as actively harmonious and benevolent, giving, serving, sharing and loving, all activities which emphasize the poet's condition and give added poignancy to the ironic paradox at the heart of the poem: that the poet is mourning the only friend who could have understood and shared such a grief.

As contributing to this development within the poem, the diction can in part be justified; but emphasis should also be placed on other features, such as the effect of the relentless rhyming (the sestet half-rhyming with the octave), the satisfying unity and balance of the poem's form (emphasized by the repetition of the opening phrase at the end of the poem, suggesting the fruitless circling of his sorrow), the restraint and dignity of its grief, and the simplicity with which the painful truth of the poet's loneliness is explored and defined.

The text followed here is that in the Commonplace Book, which is entitled merely 'Sonnet'. Mason gave it the expanded title but G.'s index to vol ii of the Commonplace Book had already listed it as 'West (Richard) Sonnet, on him'.

> In vain to me the smiling mornings shine,
> And reddening Phoebus lifts his golden fire:
> The birds in vain their amorous descant join,
> Or cheerful fields resume their green attire:
> 5 These ears, alas! for other notes repine,
> A different object do these eyes require.
> My lonely anguish melts no heart but mine;
> And in my breast the imperfect joys expire.

¶ 11.1. 'Awake, the morning shines, and the fresh field / Calls us', *Par. Lost* v 20–1; 'Then when fair Morning first smiles on the World', v 124; 'the smiling Morn', v 168; 'ere the Morning shine', vii 108; 'the Morn, / All unconcern'd with our unrest, begins / Her rosie progress smiling', xi 173–5. 2. *reddening*] cp. Virgil's use of *rubesco* with Aurora, *Aeneid* iii 521; Ovid, *Metamorphoses* iii 600; Lucretius iv 404–5: *iamque rubrum tremulis iubar ignibus erigere alte / cum coeptat natura* (even when nature begins to uplift on high her glow red with flickering fires); and vi 204–5: *mobilis ille / devolet in terram liquidi color aureus ignis* (that golden colour of flowing fire flies swiftly down to the earth). Pope has 'reddening dawn', *Odyssey* xvii 517. 3. 'amorous descant', *Par. Lost* iv 602. 4. 'Earth in her rich attire / Consummate lovely smiled', *Par. Lost* vii 501–2. 5. 'What if the head, the eye, the ear repin'd', *Essay on Man* i 261. 6. *require*] With the sense of both 'to need' and 'to seek for', as in Latin: cp. Ovid, *Metamorphoses* iv 128–9: *Ecce, metu nondum posito, ne fallat amantem, / Illa redit; iuvenemque oculis, animoque requirit* (Still trembling, but fearful also that her lover will miss her; she seeks for him both with eyes and soul). 8. 'And on her ear the imperfect accent dies', Dryden, *Ovid's Metamorphoses* i 710; 'And on her tongue imperfect accents die', Pope, *Odyssey* iv 937.

> Yet morning smiles the busy race to cheer,
> 10 And new-born pleasure brings to happier men:
> The fields to all their wonted tribute bear;
> To warm their little loves the birds complain.
> I fruitless mourn to him that cannot hear,
> And weep the more because I weep in vain.

9–12. 'No tuneful birds play with their wonted cheer', Cowley, *On the Death of William Hervey* 51.

14. Mitford cites Solon, according to Diogenes Laertes (*Lives of Eminent Philosophers* I lxiii): 'I weep for that very cause, that weeping will not avail'; 'therefore de we plaine, / And therefore weepe, because we weepe in vaine', Charles Fitzgeffrey, *Life and Death of Sir Francis Drake* (1596) st. 271, ll. 6–7; 'So must we weep, because we weep in vain', Colley Cibber's adaptation of *Richard III* (1700), II ii.

12 Ode to Adversity

G.'s transcript in his Commonplace Book (i 284–5) is dated 'at Stoke, Aug. 1742' and entitled 'Ode to Adversity'. He sent a copy of it (differing only in spelling and punctuation) to Walpole in a letter dated 8 Sept. 1751 (but redated 8 Oct. by the editors of *Walpole Correspondence* xiv 52), for inclusion in the collection of his poems illustrated by Richard Bentley, which Walpole was arranging. G. wrote (*Corresp* i 348): 'I send you this (as you desire) merely to make up half a dozen; tho' it will hardly answer your End in furnishing out either a Head or Tail-piece.' The poem duly appeared for the first time in 1753 in *Designs by Mr R. Bentley, for Six Poems by Mr T. Gray*. In 1755 Dodsley included it in the fourth volume of his *Collection* pp. 7–8.

In the Commonplace Book G. transcribed two quotations from Aeschylus as epigraphs: *Agamemnon* 176–7 (given here as the epigraph), 'Zeus, who leadeth mortals in the way of understanding, Zeus, who hath established as a fixed ordinance that wisdom comes by suffering'; and *Eumenides* 523: ξυμφέρει / σωφρονεῖν ὑπὸ στένει (It profiteth through sorrow to get discretion). The first of these quotations was prefixed to the poem in 1753 and retained for the Dodsley edn of 1768. But G. gave James Beattie, who was superintending the simultaneous Glasgow edn of 1768, a choice of the two and Beattie printed the quotation from the *Eumenides* (*Corresp* iii 1004 n).

Entitled an 'Ode' in the Commonplace Book, the poem was called 'Hymn' in the letter to Walpole in 1751, in 1753 and in Dodsley's *Collection* in 1755. But in his letters to Dodsley and Beattie in Feb. 1768, giving them instructions for the London and Glasgow edns of the *Poems* (*Corresp* iii 1000, 1004), G. twice lists the poem as 'Ode, to Adversity'. Beattie gave the poem this title, but Dodsley retained 'Hymn'. In 1775, Mason, *Poems* p. 77, changed the title back to *Ode to Adversity*, 'for the sake of uniformity in the page', adding that 'It is unquestionably as truly lyrical as any of his other Odes'. In making this change Mason seems to have been unaware that he was fulfilling G.'s own final wishes. Though *Hymn* was more appropriate for a poem addressed to a goddess, G. must have later decided that the distinction was immaterial.

The poem has been placed later than the *Eton Ode* here on the ground that it appears to have been intended as to some extent a reply to it. It was placed in this position in *1768*, the first collection which G. planned himself. To assume that *Adversity* was written first (as in Morris Golden, *Thomas Gray* (New York, 1964) pp. 57–61) entails a strained reading of the *Eton Ode*, which can hardly be shown to embody the attitudes adopted in *Adversity*. It is more natural to read *Adversity* as a mature and positive confrontation of the evils of adult life that are described with such unrelieved gloom in the *Eton Ode*. If the conclusion of the earlier poem is that man is doomed to suffer, the mottoes from Aeschylus which G. adopted for *Adversity* emphasize that suffering may lead to wisdom and various social virtues. In particular, adversity can lead to a deeper understanding of the suffering of others. The characteristic sense of alienation in G.'s poetry is here, intellectually at least, overcome by a willed self-dedication to that benevolence which his age accepted as the root of all virtue. The resolution undoubtedly represents an advance in G.'s thinking from the *Eton Ode*. The change of heart remains only an abstract proposition, but the stern discipline, both spiritual and technical, which it involves demands respect. G. was to repeat part of the content of the poem in a letter to John Chute, 12 Oct. 1746 (*Corresp* i 248): 'our Imperfections may at least excuse, & perhaps recommend us to one another: methinks I can readily pardon Sickness & Age & Vexation for all the Depredations they make within & without, when I think they make us better Friends & better Men, wch I am persuaded is often the Case. I am very sure, I have seen the best-temper'd generous tender young Creatures in the World, that would have been very glad to be sorry for People they liked, when under any Pain, and could not; merely for Want of knowing rightly, what it was, themselves.'

It is perhaps significant that Johnson much preferred this poem to the *Eton Ode*, the content of which he found obvious and the diction affected. The *Ode to Adversity* he praised as excelling Horace's *Ode* I xxxv, which Johnson took to be its source (see l. 7 *n*), 'by the variety of his sentiments, and by their moral application. Of this piece, at once poetical and rational, I will not by slight objections violate the dignity.' Its moral strenuousness has made it appear less personal than many of G.'s poems of this period, but it is not difficult to detect a strong personal feeling in the final stanza, where G. may have had his own broken friendship with Walpole in mind. If this is the case, then the fact that G. did not show the poem to Walpole until 1751 (several years after he had showed him the other early poems) can be understood.

The text is that printed with Bentley's *Designs* in *1753* (from the letter to Walpole), with variants from the Commonplace Book.

—Ζῆνα
Τὸν φρονεῖν βροτοὺς ὁδώ–
σαντα, τῷ πάθει μάθαν
θέντα κυρίως ἔχειν.

Daughter of Jove, relentless power,
Thou tamer of the human breast,
Whose iron scourge and torturing hour,
The bad affright, afflict the best!
5 Bound in thy adamantine chain

¶ *12.1. Daughter of Jove*] Mitford suggests that Adversity should be identified as Ate, 'blind Folly' in early Greek mythology and, in the tragedians, a curse avenging unrighteousness. See Pope, *Iliad* xix 92–8: 'Not by myself, but vengeful Ate driven; / She, Jove's dread daughter, fated to infest / The race of mortals, enter'd in my breast. / Not on the ground that haughty fury treads, / But prints her lofty footsteps on the heads / Of mighty men; inflicting as she goes / Long-festering wounds, inextricable woes!' But G. was not identifying Adversity with any particular goddess, although she has also some of the attributes of Athena. See also Pindar, *Olympics* xii 1 ff., where Fortune is personified as a daughter of Jove; and P. Fletcher, *Purple Island* VI xiii 1–2 (see also l. 38 *n* below): 'the just Dicaea full of rage / (The first born daughter of th'Almighty King)'.

2. 'Great Tamer of all human art!', Pope, *Dunciad* i 163.

3. 'Affliction's iron flail', Fletcher, *Purple Island* IX xxviii 5; 'To ease the anguish of a torturing hour', *Midsummer Night's Dream* V i 37; 'when the Scourge / Inexorably, and the torturing houre / Calls us to Penance', *Par. Lost* ii 90–2.

4. 'Heaven punishes the bad, and proves the best', Dryden, *Absalom and Achitophel* 44.

5. 'In Adamantine Chains', *Par. Lost* i 48; Pope, *Messiah* 47–8: 'In adamantine Chains shall Death be bound, / And Hell's grim Tyrant feel th'eternal Wound.' The original source may be Aeschylus, *Prometheus Bound* 6: 'shackles of binding adamant that cannot be broken'.

7. Johnson observed that 'the hint' of this poem 'was at first taken' from Horace, *Odes* I xxxv, addressed to *Fortuna*. G.'s first stanza certainly resembles Horace's *Ode* 17–20: *te semper anteit saeva Necessitas, / clavos trabales et cuneos manu / gestans aena, nec severus / uncus abest liquidumque plumbum* (Before thee ever stalks Necessity, grim goddess, with spikes and wedges in her brazen hands; the stout clamp and molten lead are there also).

In this line G. also echoes Horace, l. 12: *purpurei metuunt tyranni* (purple tyrants fear thee). (See also ll. 21–4 *n*.) 'Purple', the emblem of imperial power, is often linked with tyrants in eighteenth-century poetry: e.g. 'Till some new Tyrant lift his purple hand', Pope, *Chorus from Brutus* 23; 'the purple tyranny of Rome', Thomson, *Summer* 758; 'What purple tyrants quelled, and nations freed', Thomson, *Liberty* iii 256.

The proud are taught to taste of pain,
And purple tyrants vainly groan
With pangs unfelt before, unpitied and alone.

When first thy Sire to send on earth
10 Virtue, his darling child, designed,
To thee he gave the heavenly birth,
And bade to form her infant mind.
Stern rugged nurse! thy rigid lore
With patience many a year she bore:
15 What sorrow was, thou bad'st her know,
And from her own she learned to melt at others' woe.

Scared at thy frown terrific, fly
Self-pleasing Folly's idle brood,
Wild Laughter, Noise, and thoughtless Joy,
20 And leave us leisure to be good.
Light they disperse, and with them go

8. *unpitied and alone*] *written above* & Misery not their own *deleted, Common-place Book.* Cp. 'pangs unfelt before', *Par. Lost* ii 703; and *ibid* 182–5: '. . . for ever sunk / Under yon boyling Ocean, wrapt in Chains; / There to converse with everlasting groans, / Unrespited, unpitied, unrepreev'd'. Cp. also 'What pangs I feel, unpity'd and unheard', Dryden, *3rd Idyll of Theocritus* 53; 'Alike unheard, unpity'd, and forlorn', Pope, *Autumn* 22.

15–16. Virgil, *Aeneid* i 630: *non ignara mali miseris succurere disco* (Not ignorant of ill, do I learn to befriend the unhappy), and Dryden's translation, i 891: 'I learn to pity Woes, so like my own.' See also Pope, *Elegy to an Unfortunate Lady* 45–6: 'So perish all, whose breast ne'er learn'd to glow / For others' good, or melt at others' woe.' G. cites the line from Virgil in an entry entitled *Affectus* in his Commonplace Book (i 3): 'Grief inclines, & softens us to commiserate, & redress, if we be able, the Misfortunes of others in the like unhappy Circumstances; indeed we should be insensible to their Woes, [here G. quotes Virgil] had we not felt, what it was to be wretched; nor could we form any Idea of them, but by comparison of them with our own. . . . Compassion then, the Mother of so many generous actions, arises from this.' Earlier G. had written: 'Benevolence to our friends, & Charity to our Fellow-creatures, these are the very Links of Society, & foundations of the principal Virtues.'

18–19. 'Hence vain deluding joyes, / The brood of folly without father bred', Milton, *Il Penseroso* 1–2.

20. Oldham, *The Satyr against Vertue* st. v: 'And know, I have not yet the leisure to be good.'

21–4. Horace, *Odes* I xxxv 25–8: *At vulgus infidum et meretrix retro / periura cedit, diffugiunt cadis / cum faece siccatis amici, / ferre iugum pariter dolosi* (But the faithless rabble and the perjured harlot turn away; friends scatter so

          The summer friend, the flattering foe;
          By vain Prosperity received,
          To her they vow their truth and are again believed.

25   Wisdom in sable garb arrayed,
          Immersed in rapturous thought profound,
          And Melancholy, silent maid
          With leaden eye that loves the ground,
          Still on thy solemn steps attend:
30   Warm Charity, the general friend,
          With Justice to herself severe,
          And Pity, dropping soft the sadly-pleasing tear.

          Oh, gently on thy suppliant's head,
          Dread goddess, lay thy chastening hand!

soon as they have drained our winejars to the dregs, too treacherous to help us bear the yoke of trouble). Cp. also *Troilus and Cressida* III iii 76–9: '. . . what the declined is, / He shall as soon read in the eyes of others / As feel in his own fall: for men like butterflies, / Show not their mealy wings but to the summer'; *Timon of Athens* III vi 34: 'such summer-birds are men'; Herbert, *The Answer* 4–5: 'like summer friends, / Flies of estates and sunshine'; Quarles, *Sion's Elegies* I xix 4: 'Ah! summer friendship with the summer ends'.

25. 'Ore laid with black staid Wisdoms hue', Milton, *Il Penseroso* 16; 'And sable stole of *Cipres* Lawn', *ibid* 35; and 'Come, blissful Mourner, wisely sad, / In sorrow's Garb, in Sable clad', William Broome, *Melancholy: An Ode* 9–10, in *Poems* (1727) p. 44.

27–9. G. is again indebted to Milton's description of Melancholy, *Il Penseroso* 37–44: 'Come, but keep thy wonted state, / With ee'vn step, and musing gate, / And looks commercing with the skies, / Thy rapt soul sitting in thine eyes: / There held in holy passion still, / Forget thyself to Marble, till / With a sad Leaden downward cast, / Thou fix them on the earth as fast.'

28. *loves*] Used in the sense of Latin *amare*, 'to cling to, to be fastened to' (cp. Dryden, *Cymon and Iphigenia* 57: 'Eyes that ever lov'd the Ground').

31. Prior, *Solomon* iii 870: 'Perform, and Suffer: To Thy self severe.'

32. Opposite this line in the Commonplace Book G. wrote ἁ γλυκυδακρὺς (she who causes sweet tears), evidently as a parallel for his conception of Pity. Tovey pointed out that this word is found in Meleager, who in fact uses it three times, the only examples of it. In making the phrase feminine G. was no doubt merely adapting it to his female Pity. But see also Dryden, 'a sadly pleasing theam', *Hind and the Panther* iii 35, and 'a sadly pleasing Thought', *Aeneid* x 1167; Pope, 'sadly-pleasing Strain', *Ode on St Cecilia's Day* 5, and 'With ev'ry bead I drop too soft a tear', *Eloisa to Abelard* 270.

35 Not in thy Gorgon terrors clad,
   Nor circled with the vengeful band
   (As by the impious thou art seen)
   With thundering voice and threatening mien,
   With screaming Horror's funeral cry,
40 Despair and fell Disease and ghastly Poverty.

   Thy form benign, oh Goddess, wear,
   Thy milder influence impart,
   Thy philosophic train be there
   To soften, not to wound my heart.

35–7. Lucretius ii 621–3: *Telaque praeportant violenti signa furoris,* / *ingratos animos atque impia pectora volgi* / *conterrere metu quae possint numini' divae* (Martial arms show a front of violent fury, that they may amaze the ungrateful minds and impious hearts of the vulgar with fear of the goddess's majesty).

35. Gorgon terrors] This attribute is one of Athena's: e.g. Valerius Flaccus, *Argonautics* vi 173–6: *ipsaque Pallas* / *aegide terrifica ...* / *... horrentem colubris vultuque tremendam* / *Gorgoneo* (Pallas herself with terrifying aegis, bristling with snakes and fearful with Gorgon visage). See also Aeschylus, *Choephoroe* 1048–58; Ovid, *Metamorphoses* iv 801–2; and *Comus* 447–9: 'that snaky-headed *Gorgon* sheild / That wise *Minerva* wore, unconquer'd Virgin, / Wherwith she freez'd her foes to congeal'd stone'; and *Par. Lost* ii 611: '*Medusa* with *Gorgonian* terror'. For the phrasing see Pope, *Iliad* xviii 236: 'But, though unarm'd, yet, clad in terrors, go.'

36. vengeful band] Presumably the Furies or Eumenides.

38. Lucretius i 64–5: *quae caput a caeli regionibus ostendebat* / *horribili super aspectu mortalibus instans* (displayed her head in the regions of heaven, threatening mortals from on high with horrible aspect). Cp. also P. Fletcher, *Purple Island* VI xiii 3–4: 'Ah, sacred maid! thy kindled ire assuage; / Who dare abide thy dreadful thundering?'; and 'his dreadful voice no more / Would Thunder in my ears', *Par. Lost* x 779–80.

39. funeral] Ill-boding. Cp. Spenser, *Muiopotmos* 12: 'funerall complaints'. Cp. also the description of Horror, in Spenser, *Faerie Queene* II vii 23, accompanied by 'The hateful messengers of heauy things, / Of death and dolour telling sad tidings'.

40. 'perhaps in poverty / With sickness and disease thou bow'st them down, / Painful diseases and deform'd', Milton, *Samson Agonistes* 697–9. Cp. *Eton Ode* 69, 85–90 (pp. 61–2).

42. Thy milder Influence deign to impart, *Commonplace Book.*

43. 'Adversity's sweet milk, philosophy', *Romeo and Juliet* III iii 55.   *philosophic train*] Tovey suggests G. may mean ancient philosophers but he is surely contrasting with the 'vengeful band' (l. 36) the personified virtues described as resulting from Adversity in ll. 25–32.

45   The generous spark extinct revive,
      Teach me to love and to forgive,
      Exact my own defects to scan,
      What others are to feel, and know myself a man.

45–6. G. may have had in mind his recent quarrel with Horace Walpole
(see headnote).
47. 'The many hard consonants, which occur in this line, hurt the ear;
Mr. Gray perceived it himself, but did not alter it, as the words themselves
were those which best conveyed his idea, and therefore he did not chuse
to sacrifice sense to sound' (Mason, *Poems* p. 78).
47. 'Know then thyself, presume not God to scan', Pope, *Essay on Man* ii 1.
48. Cp. *Eton Ode* 60, 91 (pp. 60, 63); also Terence, *Heautontimorumenos* 77:
Homo sum; humani nihil a me alienum puto (I am a man, I count nothing human
indifferent to me); Sir John Davies, *Nosce Teipsum* 179–80: 'And, to con-
clude, I know myself a Man, / Which is a proud, and yet a wretched thing';
Otway, *Venice Preserved* I i: 'To see the sufferings of my fellow-creatures, /
And own myself a man.'

13 [Hymn to Ignorance.
   A Fragment]

Written between March and Oct. 1742. It would be natural to associate
this typically derisive address to the University in which he spent most of
the rest of his life with G.'s return to Peterhouse as a Fellow-Commoner to
read for a law degree on 15 Oct. 1742, but it may have been written earlier.
It seems to be influenced by Book iv of Pope's *Dunciad*, published in March
1742 and mentioned several times by G. in letters to West in March and
April (*Corresp* i 188–9, 191). If G. also imitates Young's *Night Thoughts*
(see ll. 14–22 *n*), the first part of which was published on 5 June 1742, the
date of composition can be narrowed further. The first reference to the plan
of returning to Cambridge occurs in a letter to Chute and Mann in July
1742 (*Corresp* i 215), when G. expected to be in Cambridge a fortnight later.
The statement in l. 11 that Hyperion has 'rolled his annual race' three times
since G. left Cambridge in Sept. 1738 is the main consideration pointing to
an earlier date than Oct. 1742, when four years had passed since G. left
Cambridge. But G.'s 'thrice' may have been dictated by metre and his
mock-heroic tone, and would in any case, if taken literally, only compel a
date earlier than Sept. 1742. The poem might appear to have been written
with a friend such as Richard West in mind as audience, but there is no
reference to it in G.'s letters to West, nor does he mention his plan of re-
turning to Cambridge before West's death on 1 June 1742. The lack of an
audience may have been the cause of G.'s failure to finish the poem.

Mason transcribed the lines in G.'s Commonplace Book (iii 1103–5), entitling it 'Fragment of an address or Hymn to Ignorance', and printed it in *1775* (*Memoirs* pp. 176–7). Mason introduced it as follows: 'It seems to have been intended as a Hymn or Address to Ignorance; and I presume, had he proceeded with it, would have contained much good Satire upon false Science and scholastic Pedantry. What he writ of it is purely introductory; yet many of the lines are so strong, and the general cast of the versification so musical, that I believe it will give the generality of Readers a higher opinion of his poetical Talents, than many of his Lyrical Productions have done. I speak of the Generality; because it is a certain fact, that their taste is founded upon the ten-syllable couplets of Dryden and Pope, and upon these only.' The text printed by Mason in *1775* has been followed here with variants from his transcript in G.'s Commonplace Book. For a couplet which may have been intended for this poem, see headnote to *Education and Government* (p. 87).

> Hail, horrors, hail! ye ever-gloomy bowers,
> Ye gothic fanes and antiquated towers,
> Where rushy Camus' slowly-winding flood
> Perpetual draws his humid train of mud:
> 5 Glad I revisit thy neglected reign;
> Oh, take me to thy peaceful shade again.
> But chiefly thee, whose influence breathed from high
> Augments the native darkness of the sky;
> Ah, Ignorance! soft salutary power!
> 10 Prostrate with filial reverence I adore.
> Thrice hath Hyperion rolled his annual race,
> Since weeping I forsook thy fond embrace.
> Oh say, successful dost thou still oppose

¶ 13.*1*. 'Hail, horrors! hail', *Par. Lost* i 250; and 'Welcome, kindred glooms! / Congenial horrors, hail!', Thomson, *Winter* 5–6.

3. Camus'] Camus *Commonplace Book.* Cp. *arundiferum . . . Carum* and *juncosas Cami . . . paludes,* Milton, *Elegies* i 11, 89, which G. may have had in mind.

4. 'where Rivers now / Stream, and perpetual draw thir humid traine', *Par. Lost* vii 305–6; and 'old *Vaga's* Stream, / . . . drew her humid Train aslope', John Philips, *Cyder* i 202, 204.

8. 'such Darkness blinds the Sky, / That the black Night receives a deeper Dye', Dryden, *Ceyx and Alcyone* 196–7.

11. After his transcript in the Commonplace Book, Mason noted of this line that it 'marks the time when this poem was written viz: on his return to the University after he came from abroad. about the year 1743'. G. had in fact left Cambridge in Sept. 1738 and finally returned there in 1742, by which time the sun had 'rolled his annual race' almost four times. 'Thrice' fits the metre better and G. may have wished to take advantage of the epic qualities of the number. See headnote.

Thy leaden aegis 'gainst our ancient foes?
15   Still stretch, tenacious of thy right divine,
The massy sceptre o'er thy slumbering line?
And dews Lethean through the land dispense
To steep in slumbers each benighted sense?
If any spark of wit's delusive ray
20   Break out, and flash a momentary day,
With damp, cold touch forbid it to aspire,
And huddle up in fogs the dangerous fire.
        Oh say – she hears me not, but, careless grown,
Lethargic nods upon her ebon throne.

14–22. Cp. the original text of *Dunciad* (1728) i 151–8: 'O ever gracious
to perplex'd mankind! / Who spread a healing mist before the mind, /
And, lest we err by Wit's wild, dancing light, / Secure us kindly in our native
night. / Ah! still o'er Britain stretch that peaceful wand, / Which lulls th'Hel-
vetian and Batavian land. / Where rebel to thy throne if Science rise, /
She does but shew her coward face and dies.' Cp. also Young, *Night Thoughts*
i 18–20: 'Night, sable goddess! from her ebon throne, / In rayless majesty,
now stretches forth / Her leaden sceptre o'er a slumbering world.'
14. aegis] A heavy shield, frequently used by Zeus, Apollo and Athene for
raising storms and causing general dismay. G.'s 'leaden' probably derives
from the *Dunciad* i 28, 'To hatch a new Saturnian age of Lead'; see also
iv 16.
15. 'Dulness o'er all possess'd her ancient right', *Dunciad* i 11.
16–18. Virgil, *Aeneid* v 854–6: *Ecce deus ramum Lethaeo rore madentem / vique
soporatum Stygia super utraque quassat / tempora, cunctantique natantia lumina
solvit* (But lo! the god, shaking over his temples a bough dripping with
Lethe's dew and steeped in the drowsy might of Styx, despite his efforts
relaxes his swimming eyes). Cp. also *Twelfth Night* IV i 66: 'Let Fancy still
my sense in Lethe steep.'
17. Oer all the land Lethaean showers dispense *Commonplace Book*
(*with present reading opposite*).
18. To] And *Commonplace Book.*
19–20. Dryden, *Macflecknoe* 21–2: 'Some Beams of Wit on other souls may
fall, / Strike through and make a lucid interval.' Cp. also 'a ray of Reason
stole / Half thro' the solid darkness of his soul', *Dunciad* iii 225–6, and 'Wit
shoots in vain its momentary fires', *ibid* iv 633.
21. 'And from his brows damps of oblivion shed', *Macflecknoe* 135.
22. 'His rising Fogs prevail upon the Day', *Macflecknoe* 24 and 'His Brows
thick fogs, instead of glories, grace', *ibid* 110; and 'Beholds thro' fogs, that
magnify the scene', *Dunciad* i 80 and 'A veil of fogs dilates her awful face',
ibid i 262.
24. 'Greet night's ascension to her ebon throne', William Browne, *Brit-
annia's Pastorals* II ii; Cotytto's 'cloudy Ebon chair', *Comus* 134. See also
Young, *Night Thoughts* i 18 quoted in l. *14–22 n.*

25   Goddess! awake, arise! alas, my fears!
      Can powers immortal feel the force of years?
      Not thus of old, with ensigns wide unfurled,
      She rode triumphant o'er the vanquished world;
      Fierce nations owned her unresisted might,
30   And all was Ignorance, and all was Night.
         Oh! sacred age! Oh! times for ever lost!
      (The schoolman's glory, and the churchman's boast.)
      For ever gone—yet still to Fancy new,
      Her rapid wings the transient scene pursue,
35   And bring the buried ages back to view.
         High on her car, behold the grandam ride
      Like old Sesostris with barbaric pride;
      . . . a team of harnessed monarchs bend . . . .

25. *Par. Lost* i 330: 'Awake, arise, or be for ever fallen.'

30. '*Art* after *Art* goes out, and all is Night', *Dunciad* iv 640.

31–5. *Dunciad* iii 63–6: 'Old scenes of glory, times long cast behind / Shall, first recall'd, rush forward to thy mind: / Then stretch thy sight o'er all her rising reign, / And let the past and future fire thy brain.'

32. 'The Young-men's Vision, and the Old men's Dream', Dryden, *Absalom and Achitophel* 239.

33–4. 'And now on Fancy's easy wings convey'd', *Dunciad* iii 13; and Time's 'rapid wing', *ibid* iv 6.

35. 'While Fancy brings the vanish'd piles to view', Pope, *Epistle to Jervas* 31.

37–8. The exploits of the Egyptian conqueror Sesostris are described by Herodotus, but the story of his yoking kings to his chariot probably came into English poetry from Lucan, *Pharsalia* x 276–7: *Venit ad occasus mundique extrema Sesostris / Et Pharios currus regum cervicibus egit* (Sesostris made his way to the West and to the limits of the world, and drove his Egyptian chariot with kings under his yoke). Cp. John Philips, *Blenheim* (1705) 16–17: 'As erst Sesostris, proud Egyptian king, / That monarchs harness'd to his chariots yok'd'; Pope, *Temple of Fame* 113–4: 'High on his Car *Sesostris* struck my View, / Whom sceptr'd Slaves in golden Harness drew'; Edward Young, *Busiris* (1719) I i 16–17: 'Have we not seen him shake his silver reins / O'er harnessed monarchs to his chariot yok'd'; Young, *Love of Fame* (1728) v 129–30: 'Sesostris-like such charioteers as *these* / May drive six harness'd monarchs, if they please.'

38. Mason added the following line to his transcript in the Commonplace Book, but did not print it in *1775*: 'The pondrous Waggon lumberd slowly on'.

14 Ode on the Death of a Favourite Cat, Drowned in a Tub of Gold Fishes

Written between 22 Feb. and 1 March 1747. In a letter of about 22 Feb. 1747 (*Corresp* i 271), G. replied to a request from Horace Walpole for an epitaph on one of his cats, which had been recently drowned in a goldfish bowl at his house in Arlington Street:

'As one ought to be particularly careful to avoid blunders in a compliment of condolence, it would be a sensible satisfaction to me (before I testify my sorrow, and the sincere part I take in your misfortune) to know for certain, who it is I lament. I knew Zara and Selima, (Selima, was it? or Fatima) or rather I knew them both together; for I cannot justly say which was which. Then as to your handsome Cat, the name you distinguish her by, I am no less at a loss, as well knowing one's handsome cat is always the cat one likes best; or, if one be alive and the other dead, it is usually the latter that is the handsomest. Besides, if the point were never so clear, I hope you do not think me so ill-bred or so imprudent as to forfeit all my interest in the surviver: Oh no! I would rather seem to mistake, and imagine to be sure it must be the tabby one that had met with this sad accident. Till this affair is a little better determined, you will excuse me if I do not begin to cry: 'Tempus inane peto, requiem, spatiumque doloris.'

G. here adapted *Aeneid* iv 433: *Tempus inane peto, requiem spatiumque furori* (For empty time I ask, for peace and reprieve for my frenzy). Instead of 'I knew Zara and Selima', as printed by Mason in 1775, G. actually wrote 'Zara I know & Selima I know', a parody of *Acts* xix 15, which Bedingfield persuaded Mason to alter (*Corresp* i 271 n).

G. sent the poem to Walpole on 1 March, having identified the cat in question, 'feüe Mademoiselle Selime, whom I am about to immortalise for one week or fortnight, as follows' (*Corresp* i 272). This text has not survived but, after giving it, G. added, 'There's a Poem for you, it is rather too long for an Epitaph.' On 17 March 1747 G. sent another copy of the poem to Thomas Wharton (*Corresp* i 277-8) entitled 'On a favourite Cat, call'd Selima, that fell into a China Tub with Gold-Fishes in it & was drown'd'. He introduced it by saying that 'the most noble of my Performances latterly is a Pôme on the uncommon Death of Mr W:s Cat'. The poem was first printed on 15 Jan. 1748, in Dodsley's *Collection of Poems* ii 267-9, no doubt as a result of Walpole's enthusiasm for it. This text, probably based on that originally sent to Walpole, appears to be the earliest. A number of changes were made in that sent to Wharton and in the transcript in G.'s Commonplace Book (i 381), which is entitled, 'On the Death of Selima, a favourite Cat, who fell into a China-Tub with Goldfishes in it, & was drown'd'. Final revisions were made for 1753. Two early printings of the poem are

noted by T.C.D. Eaves, in *Philological Quarterly* xxviii (1949) 512–5, and
xxx (1951) 91–4. The first was in the *Newcastle General Magazine* for Jan.
1748, p. 24, and the second in the *Scots Magazine* for June 1748, pp. 279–80.
These two texts are related, both being closer to the revised text sent to
Thomas Wharton than to that recently printed in Dodsley's *Collection*.
It is therefore possible that Wharton was responsible for these appearances
of the poem, or another revised MS of the poem may have been in
circulation before Dodsley's *Collection* appeared.

A minor misunderstanding about the poem should be cleared up. In a
discussion of Lord Lyttelton's celebrated *Monody* (1747) on the death of his
wife, in a letter dated 17 Sept. 1751, William Shenstone wrote: 'I heard,
once before, it was burlesqued under the title of "An Elegy on the Death of a
favourite Cat"' (*Letters*, ed. M. Williams, (Oxford, 1939) p. 319). It is natural
to assume that Shenstone was referring to G.'s poem, as Horace Walpole did,
who denied that G. had any such intention of burlesquing Lyttelton in
a letter to William Cole, *Walpole Correspondence* i 165. But Shenstone
was referring to another poem with a very similar title, published in
May 1748: *A Sorrowful Ditty; Or, the Lady's Lamentation for the Death of her
Favourite Cat. A Parody*, which parodies Lyttelton's *Monody* in detail and
imitates G.'s poem only in the title. (The parody has been claimed
for Smollett by some scholars: see *The Rothschild Library* (1954) ii 519.)
Professor William Scott has called to my attention an amusing allusion
to the poem ('a most elegant little ode') in Francis Coventry's *History of
Pompey the Little* (1751) p. 90. Another unusual tribute to the currency of
G.'s *Ode* was its appearance in Mary Masters's *Familiar Letters and Poems on
Several Occasions* (1755) pp. 248–50, where it is attributed to 'Mr De Grey'
and followed by a poem addressed by a lady to Selima's 'mistress' and further
verses in answer to a gentleman who had asked why Phoebus should have
rescued Selima. The text of G.'s *Ode* given by Mrs Masters contains several
unique if unimportant readings, which have not been recorded here, though,
together with the poems written in answer to it, they tend to confirm the
suggestion made above that it had been enjoying an independent circula-
tion in MS, perhaps in the form of 'album verses'.

On 29 July 1773 Walpole wrote to tell Mason that he was having a
pedestal made for the original tub in which the cat had been drowned, with
the first stanza of the *Ode* inscribed on it (*Walpole Correspondence* xxviii 101).
Mason (*Poems* p. 76) confirmed in 1775 that this had been done. The tub
(described as 'The celebrated large blue and white oriental china cistern, on
a Gothic carved pedestal, in which Horace Walpole's cat was drowned; this
gave occasion to Mr Gray, the poet, to write his beautiful ode') was sold
as Lot 32 at the Strawberry Hill Sale on 16 May 1842 and was bought by the
Earl of Derby for 40 guineas. It remained at Knowsley until its recent return
to Strawberry Hill, now St Mary's Training College for Teachers. Wal-
pole's letter concerning the tub mentioned above is illustrated in *Walpole
Correspondence* by John Carter's watercolour of the tub as it was placed by

Walpole in thc Little Cloister at the entrance to Strawberry Hill. It also appears as plate 71 in Randolph Churchill's *Fifteen Famous Houses* (1954).

The most detailed discussion of the *Ode* occurs in Geoffrey Tillotson's *Augustan Studies* (1961) pp. 216–23, but his conclusions about the poem are questionable. Tillotson is concerned to refute Johnson's criticism, *Lives of the Poets*, ed. G. B. Hill, iii 434: 'Selima, the Cat, is called a nymph [l. 19], with some violence both to language and sense; but there is good use made of it when it is done; for of the two lines [ll. 23–4], the first relates merely to the nymph, and second only to the cat.' Starting from a possible echo in ll. 4–5 of the *Ode* of Pope's description of Helen in his translation of the *Iliad*, Tillotson argues that the echoes of Pope are so frequent that we are obliged to bring Helen into the poem, to see her standing behind the cat throughout, her own disastrous career a parallel to that of Selima. Johnson's objections are irrelevant because the cat and the nymph were intended to remain distinct, while both of them remain actively in the poem. In fact the possible echoes of Pope's *Iliad* in G.'s poem are more scattered and du-bious than Tillotson suggests, many being merely stock heroic diction. Moreover, with a habitual borrower like G., it is never easy to prove that an echo of another poem is actually an allusion to it. Many young women could be imported into the poem on the same terms as those on which Tillotson admits Helen of Troy and the plurality of such identifications of Selima makes a single parallel impossible. At different points in the poem Selima resembles Milton's Eve (ll. 6–18), Camilla in Virgil's *Aeneid* Bk. xi (ll. 16–24), Lydia, the discarded mistress or 'favourite' in Gay's 'Town Eclogue', *The Toilette* (ll. 2–3, 4–5, 19) and Ovid's Daphne pursued by Apollo (ll. 32–5). The most striking resemblance is that to Virgil's Camilla (in Dryden's translation and Addison's account of her in the *Spectator* as well as the original), which may explain some of the diction used in the poem, although the parallel is not enforced so obtrusively that the fate of less heroic young ladies cannot be blended with it. Tillotson describes the poem as mock heroic *tout simple* and the parallel with Camilla certainly intro-duces such a note into the poem. But G. blends with it some elements of animal fable, which always concludes with a lightly moralistic application of the story to humanity, as well as of the kind of poem which moralizes ironically about women. Gay's *The Toilette* and Edward Moore's *Fables for the Female Sex* (1744) are examples of this minor genre which G. appears to echo. One of the fables in Moore's collection, 'The Female Seducers' (actually by Henry Brooke) enforces the moral that female honour once lost can never be retrieved and uses the image of drowning for the loss of that honour.

The text followed here is that printed in *1753* with Bentley's *Designs*, with variants from the letter to Wharton, the Commonplace Book, Dodsley's *Collection*, and the Foulis edition of *1768*. In addition, two minor variants have been noted from a hitherto unrecorded autograph MS (cited as *Pery*) sold at Sotheby's on 18 July 1967. A note on the MS signed 'Carolina Pery' states that the MS dates from 'about the year 1757'.

'Twas on a lofty vase's side,
Where China's gayest art had dyed
   The azure flowers, that blow;
Demurest of the tabby kind,

¶ 14.1. Perhaps a reminiscence of Dryden, *Alexander's Feast* 1–5: "'Twas at
the Royal Feast, for *Persia* won, / By *Philip's* Warlike Son: / Aloft in awful
State / The God-like Heroe sate / On his Imperial Throne.'
2–3. Gay, *The Toilette* 53–4: 'Where the tall jar erects his costly pride, /
With antic shapes in china's azure dy'd'; and Tickell, *Kensington Garden*
383–4: 'As some frail cup of China's purest mould, / With azure varnish'd
and bedropt with gold.'
3. *that blow*] Johnson (*Lives of the Poets*, ed. Hill, iii 434) thought that this
line showed 'how resolutely a rhyme is sometimes made when it cannot
easily be found'. 'Blow' itself means 'bloom' or 'blossom' and was a com-
mon enough word but it does seem unnecessarily emphatic. A writer in
the *Gentleman's Mag.* lii (Jan. 1782) 76, replied to Johnson's objection by
asserting that G. was actually making a definite distinction: 'China vessels
are generally ornamented with *fictitious* flowers; whereas those on the bowl
in question are not *imaginary*, but real ones; they are *azure flowers* THAT BLOW.'
Tillotson, *Augustan Studies* p. 219, suggests that 'redundancies of this
cheerful jingling sort are part of the method of a true ballad, and so a grace
in a mock-ballad'. G. may however have been influenced by *Comus*
993–4: 'Waters the odorous banks that blow / Flowers . . .' See also *Progress
of Poesy* 5 (p. 162 below).
4–5. These lines were transposed in *Dodsley*.
4. Tillotson, *Augustan Studies* p. 217 n, suggests that 'By Gray's time *demure*
had become a sort of Homeric epithet for a cat, whether male or female, but
more usually the latter'. Under 'demure' and 'demurely' Johnson's
Dictionary gives quotations from Bacon, L'Estrange and Dryden using these
words of cats.   *tabby*] Perhaps G. had now learned from Walpole that the
deceased cat was a tabby (see his caution in letter quoted in headnote);
the reference to 'tortoise' in l. 10 would then mean merely that Selima had
been as beautiful as the survivor. But Tovey has an involved reading of these
references, based on the assumption that G. was still in doubt about which
cat had died, while suspecting that it was in fact the tortoiseshell. His
praise of the tabby was aimed therefore, as he had stated in his letter, at
keeping an interest in the survivor.
4–5. J. C. Maxwell, *Notes and Queries* cxcvi (1951) 498, points out that these
lines echo Pope, *Iliad* iii 473–4: 'Meantime the brightest of the female kind, /
The matchless Helen o'er the walls reclined.' This echo was the basis of
Tillotson's case that G. is deliberately alluding to Helen's fate as parallel to
that of Selima. The second line is however a commonplace: cp. 'His pensive
Cheek upon his Hand reclin'd', Dryden, *Iliad* i 458; and 'Reclined upon her
arm she pensive sat', Gay, *The Toilette* 21.

5   The pensive Selima reclined,
     Gazed on the lake below.

     Her conscious tail her joy declared;
     The fair round face, the snowy beard,
     The velvet of her paws,
10   Her coat that with the tortoise vies,
     Her ears of jet and emerald eyes,
     She saw; and purred applause.

     Still had she gazed; but 'midst the tide
     Two angel forms were seen to glide,
15   The genii of the stream:
     Their scaly armour's Tyrian hue

5. Selima was the name of the heroine of Rowe's tragedy *Tamerlane* (1702).
6–18. Cp. Milton's description of Eve viewing herself with satisfaction in the 'Lake', until she sees a 'gleam' in the water, *Par. Lost* iv 456–66: 'I thither went / With unexperienc't thought, and laid me downe / On the green bank, to look into the cleer / Smooth Lake, that to me seemd another Skie. / As I bent down to look, just opposite, / A Shape within the watry gleam appeerd / Bending to look on me, I started back, / It started back, but pleasd I soon returnd, / Pleas'd it returnd as soon with answering looks / Of sympathie and love, there I had fixt / Mine eyes till now, and pin'd with vain desire'.
8. *The . . . the*] Her . . . her *Pery*. Cp. 'She licks her fair round Face' (of a cat), Pope, *Wife of Bath her Prologue* 146; and 'O'er her fair face a snowy veil she threw', Pope, *Iliad* iii 187.
10. *Her*] The *Dodsley, Foulis*.
13. *'midst*] 'mid *Commonplace Book*.
14. *angel*] beauteous *Commonplace Book, Dodsley, Foulis*.
15. *genii*] Guardian spirits. So 'th'unseen Genius of the Wood', Milton, *Il Penseroso* 154; and 'the genii of the place', Matthew Green, *The Grotto* 54.
16–24. Cp. the death of Camilla in *Aeneid* xi 768–82, 801–6, during the crucial battle between Aeneas and Turnus: *Forte sacer Cybele Chloreus olimque sacerdos / insignis longe Phrygiis fulgebat in armis / spumantemque agitabat equum, quem pellis aenis / in plumam squamis auro conserta tegebat. / ipse peregrina ferrugine clarus et ostro / spicula torquebat Lycio Gortynia cornu; / aureus ex umeris erat arcus et aurea vati / cassida; tum croceam chlamydemque sinusque crepantis / carbaseos fulvo in nodum collegerat auro, / pictus acu tunicas et barbara tegmina crurum. / hunc virgo, sive ut templis praefigeret arma / Troïa, captivo sive ut se ferret in auro, / venatrix unum ex omni certamine pugnae / caeca sequebatur totumque incauta per agmen / femineo praedae et spoliorum ardebat amore . . . / . . . nihil ipsa nec aurae / nec sonitus memor aut venientis ab aethere teli, / hasta sub exsertam donec perlata papillam / haesit, virgineumque alte bibit acta*

> Through richest purple to the view
> Betrayed a golden gleam.

> The hapless nymph with wonder saw:
> 20 A whisker first and then a claw,
>   With many an ardent wish,
>   She stretched in vain to reach the prize.

cruorem. / *concurrunt trepidae comites dominamque ruentem* / *suscipiunt.* (It chanced that Chloreus, sacred to Cybelus, and once a priest, glittered resplendent afar in Phrygian armour, and spurred his foaming charger, whose covering was a skin, plumed with brazen scales and clasped with gold. Himself ablaze in the deep hue of foreign purple, he launched Gortynian shafts from Lycian bow: golden was that bow upon his shoulders, and golden was the seer's helmet; his saffron scarf and its rustling linen folds were gathered into a knot by yellow gold; embroidered with the needle were his tunic and barbaric hose. Him, whether in hope to fasten on temple-gate Trojan arms, or to flaunt herself in golden spoil, the maiden, singling out from all the battle fray, blindly pursued in huntress fashion, and recklessly raged through all the ranks with a woman's passion for booty and for spoil. . . . She herself, neither of air, nor of sound, nor of weapon coming from the sky recked aught, till the spear, borne home, beneath the bare breast found lodging, and, driven deep, drank her maiden blood. In alarm, her comrades hurry around her, and catch their falling queen.) Addison had retold this episode in *Spectator* No. 15, in which his theme was the 'unaccountable Humour in Woman-kind, of being smitten with every thing that is showy and superficial; and . . . the numberless Evils that befall the Sex, from this light, fantastical Disposition.' The moral he drew from Camilla's fate is close to that of G.'s *Ode.* See ll. 37–42 *n*.
16. *Tyrian*] Dryden translates l. 772 of the passage from the *Aeneid* quoted above: 'A Robe of *Tyrian* Dye the Rider wore', *Aeneid* xi 1136; but cp. also Pope, *Windsor Forest* 142, 144: 'The bright-ey'd Perch with Fins of *Tyrian* Dye / . . .The yellow Carp, in Scales bedrop'd with Gold.'
17–18. Virgil, *Georgics* iv 274–5: *aureus ipse, sed in foliis, quae plurima circum* / *funduntur, violae sublucet purpura nigrae* (Golden is the disc, but in the petals, streaming profusely round, there is a crimson gleam amid the dark violet).
18. *Windsor Forest* 331–2: 'and o'er the Stream / His shining Horns diffus'd a golden Gleam'; see also *Temple of Fame* 253.
19–22. Dryden, *Aeneid* xi 1144–5, translating the passage about Camilla quoted above: 'Him, the fierce Maid beheld with ardent Eyes; / Fond and Ambitious of so Rich a Prize'; and 'He saw, he wish'd, and to the Prize aspir'd', *Rape of the Lock* ii 30, and Pope's explicit imitation of the Dryden couplet, *ibid* ii 43–4: 'and begs with ardent Eyes / Soon to obtain, and long possess the Prize'.
19. Gay, *The Toilette* 31: 'Ah, hapless nymph!'

What female heart can gold despise?
What cat's averse to fish?

25   Presumptuous maid! with looks intent
Again she stretched, again she bent,
    Nor knew the gulf between.
(Malignant Fate sat by and smiled)
The slippery verge her feet beguiled,
30   She tumbled headlong in.

Eight times emerging from the flood
She mewed to every watery god,
    Some speedy aid to send.
No dolphin came, no Nereid stirred:
35   Nor cruel Tom nor Susan heard.
    A favourite has no friend!

From hence, ye beauties, undeceived,
Know, one false step is ne'er retrieved,
    And be with caution bold.

24. averse to] a foe to *Dodsley*. Cp. 'A woman, and averse to praise!', Gay, *Fables* II xvi 8.

25. looks] eye *Commonplace Book*; eyes *Wharton*. Cp. 'Presumptuous Man!', Pope, *Essay on Man* i 35.

31. Eight times] An allusion to the nine lives ascribed to cats. Dryden has Thetis 'emerging from the deep', *Iliad* i 672.

32-5. The deities of the sea were Oceanus, Neptune, Nereus, Proteus and Triton. Dryden has 'wat'ry God', *Aeneid* vii 1081; cp. also his translation of *Ovid's Metamorphoses* i 739-40: 'Oh help, she cry'd, in this extreamest need. / If Water Gods are Deities indeed'; and Pope, *Windsor Forest* 197-8: 'In vain on Father *Thames* she calls for Aid, / Nor could *Diana* help her injur'd Maid.' See also the passages imitated here, Ovid, *Metamorphoses* i 545 and v 618.

34. dolphin] A reference to the story of Arion who was rescued from the sea by a dolphin; and see also *Comus* 833-5, of Sabrina: 'The water Nymphs that in the bottom play'd, / Held up their pearled wrists and took her in, / Bearing her straight to *Nereus* Hall.'

35. Tom] John *Pery*.   *Susan*] Harry *Wharton*, *Dodsley*.

36. What fav'rite has a friend? *Dodsley*.

37. E. Moore, *Fables for the Female Sex* vii 87: 'Learn hence, to study wisdom's rules'.

37-9. Gay, *The Tea-Table* 49-50: 'Laura learned caution at too dear a cost, / What fair could e'er retrieve her honour lost?'

40   Not all that tempts your wandering eyes
        And heedless hearts is lawful prize;
            Nor all that glisters gold.

40. tempts] strikes *Commonplace Book, Wharton.* (G. may have made the change to avoid too close an echo with 'They strike the soul and glitter in the eye', Lady M. W. Montagu, *The Basset-Table* 82.)
40–2. In his summary of the Camilla episode in *Spectator* No. 15, Addison emphasised Chloreus's gold and purple armour, on which Camilla so 'unfortunately cast her Eye. . . . being seized with a Woman's Longing for the pretty Trappings that he was adorned with'. Addison concluded: 'This heedless Pursuit after these glittering Trifles, the Poet (by a nice concealed Moral) represents to have been the Destruction of his Female Hero.'
40. Pope has 'wandring Eyes', *Essay on Criticism* 231.
41. Tillotson, *Augustan* Studies p. 223 *n*, suggests that G. is alluding in his 'moral' to the amorous sense of 'lawful prize' in a couplet in *Ovid's Art of Love . . . Translated by Several Eminent Hands* (1709) p. 223: 'But, that a Mistress may be Lawful Prize, / None, but her Keeper, I am sure, denies.'
42. This proverb appears frequently in English poetry: e.g. Chaucer, *Canon's Yeoman's Tale* 242–3; Spenser, *Faerie Queene* II viii 14, 5; Shakespeare, *Merchant of Venice* II vii 65 (where 'glisters' is used); Dryden, *Hind and the Panther* ii 215.

15 [The Alliance of Education and Government. A fragment]

Begun not later than mid-Aug. 1748 and probably abandoned by March 1749. G. sent ll. 1–57 of this fragment to Thomas Wharton on 19 Aug. 1748 (*Corresp* i 310–12), introducing them as 'the Beginning of a Sort of Essay. what Name to give it I know not, but the Subject is, the Alliance of Education & Government; I mean to shew that they must necessarily concur to produce great & useful Men.' G. added: 'I desire your Judgement upon so far, before I proceed any farther. . . . Pray shew it to no one (as it is a Fragment) except it be St[onhewe]r who has seen most of it already, I think.' Wharton evidently encouraged G. to continue the poem, as the MS of this letter in the British Museum is accompanied by Wharton's transcript of the rest of the fragment, ll. 58–107. G. himself also transcribed the whole of the fragment into his Commonplace Book (ii 619–20). But he wrote no more of the poem and did not refer to it again in his letters.
    In a footnote to his *Decline and Fall of the Roman Empire* (ed. J. B. Bury, 1896–1900, iii 332*n*), Gibbon, after quoting ll. 52–7, asked: 'Instead of compiling tables of chronology and natural history, why did not Mr. Gray apply the powers of his genius to finish the philosophic poem of which he has left

such an exquisite specimen?' Mason had already provided one answer to this question when he printed the fragment for the first time in *1775*. In his introductory remarks (*Memoirs* p. 192) he explained that G. 'was busily employed in it at the time when M. de Montesquieu's book [*L'Esprit des Loix*] was first published: On reading it, he said the Baron had forestalled some of his best thoughts; and yet the reader will find, from the small fragment he has left, that the two writers differ a little in one very material point, viz. the influence of soil and climate on national manners. Some time after he had thoughts of resuming his plan, and of dedicating it, by an introductory Ode, to M. de Montesquieu; but that great man's death, which happened in 1755, made him drop his design finally.'

There is no other evidence that G. contemplated resuming the poem, but the earlier part of Mason's statement is convincing. G. wrote enthusiastically to Wharton about *L'Esprit des Loix* on 9 March 1749 (*Corresp* i 317): 'he lays down the Principles on wch are founded the three Sorts of Government, Despotism, the limited Monarchic, & the Republican, & shews how from thence are deduced the Laws & Customs, by wch they are guided & maintained; the Education proper to each Form, the influences of Climate, Situation, Religion, &c: on the Minds of particular Nations, & on their Policy. the Subject (you see) is as extensive as Mankind; the Thoughts perfectly new, generally admirable, as they are just, sometimes a little too refined.' F. T. H. Fletcher, 'Montesquieu and British Education', *Modern Language Review* xxxviii (1943) 299–300, assumes that G. had read *L'Esprit des Loix* by Aug. 1748, when he sent the first section of his poem to Wharton. But G. cannot have read Montesquieu until he had written most of the fragment. *L'Esprit des Loix* was published at Geneva in Nov. 1748 and G.'s letter to Wharton in March 1749 indicates that he had only recently been reading the book. If Mason's theory that G. abandoned the poem on reading Montesquieu is correct, G. must have done so at about this time.

In his introductory remarks to the poem already quoted (*Memoirs* p. 192), Mason was confident that, if G. had completed this 'Ethical Essay', as he called it, 'it would have been one of the most capital Poems of the kind that ever appeared either in our own, or any language. I am not able to inform the reader how many Essays he meant to write upon the subject; nor do I believe that he had ever so far settled his plan as to determine that point: But since his theme was as extensive as human nature . . . it is plain the whole work would have been considerable in point of size.' The projected length of the poem, setting G. artistic and temperamental problems which he could not solve, provides another explanation of his failure to finish it. In the 1760s Norton Nicholls ('Reminiscences of Gray', *Corresp* iii 1291), 'asked him why he had not continued that beautiful fragment beginning 'As sickly plants betray a niggard earth' He said, because he could not; when I expressed surprise at this, he explained himself as follows; That he had been used to write only Lyric poetry in which the poems being short, he had accustomed himself, & was able to polish every part; that this having become habit, he could not write otherwise; & that the labour of this method in a long poem would be intolerable; besides which the poem would lose its effect for want of Chiaro-Oscuro; for that to produce effect it was absolutely necessary to have weak parts.—He instanced in Homer, & particularly in Milton, who he said in parts of his poem rolls on in sounding words that have but little meaning.'

This explanation is supported by the fact that G. expressed similar views in general terms in a letter to Mason in Jan. 1759 (*Corresp* ii 608): 'the true Lyric style with all its flights of fancy, ornaments & heightening of expression, & harmony of sound, is in its nature superior to every other style. wch is just the cause, why it could not be born in a work of great length, no more than the eye could bear to see all this scene, that we constantly gaze upon, the verdure of the fields & woods, the azure of the sea & skies, turn'd into one dazzling expanse of gems.'

A third and confused explanation of G.'s failure to complete this poem must be dealt with. After quoting a number of notes made by G. for the continuation of the poem (see below), Mason, *Memoirs* p. 203 *n*, added: 'I find also among these papers a single couplet much too beautiful to be lost, though the place where he meant to introduce it cannot be ascertained; it must, however, have made a part of some description of the effect which the reformation had on our national manners:

> When Love could teach a monarch to be wise,
> And Gospel-light first dawn'd from BULLEN's Eyes.'

Mason's assertion is the only evidence that this couplet is connected with *Education and Government*. On 25 March 1759 Horace Walpole wrote to Dalrymple (*Walpole Correspondence* xv 53): 'Of the "History of the Revival of Learning" I have not heard a word: Mr Gray a few years ago began a poem on that subject, but dropped it, thinking it would cross too much upon some parts of the *Dunciad*.' That Walpole was referring here to *Education and Government*, as has usually been assumed, seems to be clear from another reference in his 'Memoir of Gray' (*Corresp* iii 1287), in which he quotes one of the two lines cited by Mason: 'He began a poem on the Reformation of Learning, but soon dropped it, on finding his plan had too much resemblance to the Dunciad. It had this admirable line in it, "And Gospel-light first flash'd from Bullen's eyes".' But neither G.'s fragment nor his notes for its continuation resemble the *Dunciad* in any way. The poem by G., also unfinished, which most markedly resembles the *Dunciad* is his *Hymn to Ignorance*, which breaks off after a satirical account of medieval scholasticism and could well have proceeded to an account of 'the Reformation of Learning'. Mason's suggestion that the couplet on Anne Boleyn might have been part of an account of the Reformation of the Church may have been carelessly confused by Walpole with the Reformation of Learning. In any case, the matter as a whole does not throw any additional light on why G. abandoned *Education and Government*. It has been noted that the couplet on Anne Boleyn resembles Dryden, *Hind and the Panther* iii 203–5: 'Thus our eighth Henry's marriage they defame; / They say the schism of beds began the game, / Divorcing from the Church to wed the dame.'

One other possible reference to *Education and Government* may be noted. On 8 Dec. 1757 G. wrote to Wharton humorously protesting that, if he undertook to write an epic, he would not complete it until the age of seventy-four (*Corresp* ii 541–2). Toynbee and Whibley suggest that Wharton had been urging G. either to write an epic or to continue *Education and Government*. The second suggestion is unconvincing. G. was very unlikely to talk about *Education and Government* as an epic. He himself called it 'a sort of Essay' and Mason an 'Ethical Essay', and his model for this kind of didactic, philosophical poem in couplets would be Pope's *Essay on Man*, which he frequently echoes throughout his own fragment. G. has many other debts. One of the historical notes to the fragment provided by Edward Bedingfield for Mason in *1775*, observes that 'Mr. Gray's judgement, in what remains to us of this essay, is very remarkable. He borrows from poetry his imagery, his similes, and his expressions; but his thoughts are taken, as the nature of the Poem requires, from history and observation.' Bedingfield was correct in the first part of this statement for the poem is remarkably derivative in imagery, diction and phrasing. As for its content, apart from the knowledge of history which Bedingfield praises, G. seems also to have been familiar with earlier discussions of the relationship between environment, especially climate, and government and national character. G. may well have known Bodin's *Six Livres de la Republique* (1577) and Chardin's *Travels in the Orient* (1686 and 1711), both of which had drawn attention to the problem and contributed to Montesquieu's ambitious study of the effect of climate and soil on man and society in *L'Esprit des Loix*, Bk xiv. For some of the other numerous discussions of the subject, which go back to classical literature and continue at least until Goldsmith's *The Traveller* (1764), see René Wellek, *The Rise of English Literary History* (Chapel Hill, 1941) pp 32–3, 54–8. Three earlier works may be mentioned briefly. Bk II of the Abbé du Bos's *Reflexions Critiques sur la Poesie et sur la Peinture* (1719), translated into English by Thomas Nugent in 1748, the year G. was writing *Education and Government*, is an investigation into the nature of genius and several chapters discuss the effect of climate on the creative artist. Many passages in James Thomson's *The Seasons* and *Liberty*, dealing with the national characteristics of, in particular, the Italians and the Swiss, inevitably touch on the subject and more than once (e.g. ll. 94–9) G. seems directly indebted to him. But the most elaborate treatment of the problem in English poetry before G. appears to have been *The Nature of Man* (1711) by Sir Richard Blackmore. Although Blackmore's discussion is crude–his ultimate concern is a patriotic demonstration of the superiority of the English climate–G. more than once appears to echo passages dealing with the crippling effect on mankind of hot or cold climates. Some of the similarity, it must be admitted, lies merely in the pseudo-scientific poetic diction which the two poets share when dealing with a subject of this sort; but Blackmore's outline of the content of Bk I of his poem will indicate larger resemblances: 'The Design of this Poem, is to express how far the Disparity of the intellectual Faculties, Dispositions and Passions of Men is owing to the different Situation of their native Countries in Respect of the Sun; and to shew what Advantages those receive, who are born in a mild Air and temperate Climate; and what Disadvantages, in Respect of Understanding, Reason, and Moral Improvements, those Nations lye under, who suffer the Extream either of Cold or Heat.'

It has been suggested that other works which G. had recently been reading contributed to his poem. W. Powell Jones, *Thomas Gray, Scholar* (1937) pp. 58–61, has shown that between 26 Dec. 1747 and 1 March 1748 G. had been making notes on Isocrates's oration *On the Peace*, some of the themes of which–the ease with which luxury can lead to corruption and democracy become tyranny–recur in the poem which G. was writing a few months later. G.'s notes on Bk vi of Plato's *Republic*, which he greatly admired, also show his interest in the relations of education and government. At one point (Commonplace Book i 340) he uses an image which occurs in the poem; the passage also emphasises the similarity of the content of this fragment to parts of the *Elegy*, which G. had not yet completed: 'those Excellences & Endowments required to form a Mind susceptible of true Philosophy; as a quick & retentive Understanding, high Spirit, & a natural Greatness, & Simplicity of Soul (more particularly, if attended with what the World calls Blessings; Opulence, Birth, & Beauty of Person) are the most likely to draw off the Youth that possesses them, from that very Pursuit they were design'd for: and lighting (as he expresses it) in an improper Soil, that is, corrupted by a bad Education, & ill-regulated Government become the readier Instruments of Mischief to Mankind, by so much more, as Nature meant them for their Good. for every extraordinary Wickedness, every action superlatively unjust is the Product of a vigorous Spirit ill-nurtured; weak Minds are alike incapable of anything greatly good, or greatly ill.'

When Mason printed the poem in *1775, Memoirs* pp. 193–200, he gave 'a kind of commentary at the bottom of the pages', which he had formed from G.'s 'scattered papers in prose, which he writ, as hints for his own use in the prosecution of this work'. Mason believed that 'they will serve greatly to elucidate (as far as they go) the method of his reasoning'. This 'commentary' usefully indicates the way in which G. would have continued the poem:

'The Author's subject being (as we have seen) THE NECESSARY ALLIANCE BETWEEN A GOOD FORM OF GOVERNMENT AND A GOOD MODE OF EDUCATION, IN ORDER TO PRODUCE THE HAPPINESS OF MANKIND, the Poem opens with two similes; an uncommon kind of exordium: but which I suppose the Poet intentionally chose, to intimate the analogical method he meant to pursue in his subsequent reasonings. 1st, He asserts that men without education are like sickly plants in a cold or barren soil, (line 1 to 5, and 8 to 12;) and, 2dly, he compares them, when unblest with a just and well regulated government, to plants that will not blossom or bear fruit in an unkindly and inclement air (l. 5 to 9, and l. 13 to 22). Having thus laid down the two propositions he means to prove, he begins by examining into the characteristics which (taking a general view of mankind) all men have in common one with another (l. 22 to 39); they covet pleasure and avoid pain (l. 31); they feel gratitude for benefits (l. 34); they desire to avenge wrongs, which they effect either by force or cunning (l. 35); they are linked to each other by their common feelings, and participate in sorrow and in joy (l. 36, 37). If then all the human species agree in so many moral particulars, whence arises the diversity of national characters? This question the Poet puts at line 38, and dilates upon to l. 64. Why, says he, have some nations shewn a propensity to commerce and industry; others to war and rapine; others to ease and pleasure? (l. 42 to 46) Why have the Northern people overspread, in all ages, and prevailed over the Southern? (l. 46 to 58) Why has Asia been, time out of mind, the seat of despotism, and Europe that of freedom? (l. 59 to 64.) Are we from these instances to imagine men necessarily enslaved to the inconveniences of the climate where they were born? (l. 64 to 72) Or are we not rather to suppose there is a natural strength in the human mind, that is able to vanquish and break through them? (l. 72 to 84) It is confest, however, that men receive an early tincture from the situation they are placed in, and the climate which produces them (l. 84 to 88). Thus the inhabi-tants of the mountains, inured to labour and patience, are naturally trained to war (l. 88 to 96); while those of the plain are more open to any attack, and softened by ease and plenty (l. 96 to 99). Again, the Ægyptians, from the nature of their situation, might be the inventors of home-navigation, from a necessity of keeping up an intercourse between their towns during the inundation of the Nile (l. 99 to ****). Those persons would naturally have the first turn to commerce, who inhabited a barren coast like the Tyrians, and were persecuted by some neighbouring tyrant; or were drove to take refuge on some shoals, like the Venetian and Hollander; their discovery of some rich island, in the infancy of the world, described. The Tartar hardened to war by his rigorous climate and pastoral life, and by his disputes for water and herbage in a country without land-marks, as also by skirmishes between his rival clans, was consequently fitted to conquer his rich Southern neighbours, whom ease and luxury had enervated: Yet this is no proof that liberty and valour may not exist in Southern climes, since the Syrians and Carthaginians gave noble instances of both; and the Arabians carried their conquests as far as the Tartars. Rome also (for many centuries) repulsed those nations, which, when she grew weak, at length demolished her extensive Empire.'

Mason, *Memoirs* pp. 201–3n, also printed some 'other maxims on diff-erent papers, all apparently relating to the same subject, which are too excellent to be lost':

'Man is a creature not capable of cultivating his mind but in society, and in that only where he is not a slave to the necessities of life.

'Want is the mother of the inferior arts, but ease that of the finer; as eloquence, policy, morality, poetry, sculpture, painting, architecture, which are the improvements of the former.

'The climate inclines some nations to contemplation and pleasure; others to hardship, action, and war; but not so as to incapacitate the former for courage and discipline, or the latter for civility, politeness, and works of genius.

'It is the proper work of education and government united to redress the faults that arise from the soil and air.

'The principal drift of education should be to make men *think* in the Northern climates, and *act* in the Southern.

'The different steps and degrees of education may be compared to the artificer's operations upon marble; it is one thing to dig it out of the quarry, and another to square it; to give it gloss and lustre, call forth every beautiful spot and vein, shape it into a column, or animate it into a statue.

'To a native of free and happy governments his country is always dear:

"He loves his old hereditary trees." COWLEY

While the subject of a tyrant has no country; he is therefore selfish and base-minded; he has no family, no posterity, no desire of fame; or, if he has, of one that turns not on its proper object.

'Any nation that wants public spirit, neglects education, ridicules the desire of fame, and even of virtue and reason, must be ill governed.

'Commerce changes intirely the fate and genius of nations, by communicating arts and opinions, circulating money, and introducing the materials of luxury; she first opens and polishes the mind, then corrupts and enervates both that and the body.

'Those invasions of effeminate Southern nations by the warlike Northern people, seem (in spite of all the terror, mischief, and ignorance which they brought with them) to be necessary evils; in order to revive the spirit of mankind, softened and broken by the arts of commerce, to restore them to their native liberty and equality, and to give them again the power of supporting danger and hardship; so a comet, with all the horrors that attend it as it passes through our system, brings a supply of warmth and light to the sun, and of moisture to the air.

'The doctrine of Epicurus is ever ruinous to society: It had its rise when Greece was declining, and perhaps hastened its dissolution, as also that of Rome; it is now propagated in France and in England, and seems likely to produce the same effect in both.

'One principal characteristic of vice in the present age is the contempt of fame.

'Many are the uses of good fame to a generous mind: it extends our existence and example into future ages; continues and propagates virtue, which otherwise would be as short-lived as our frame; and prevents the prevalence of vice in a generation more corrupt than our own. It is impossible to conquer that natural desire we have of being remembered; even criminal ambition and avarice, the most selfish of all passions, would wish to leave a name behind them.'

The last sentence quoted here reveals another link between the material associated with *Education and Government* and the *Elegy*.

The epigraph chosen by G. for the fragment is from Theocritus, *Idylls* i 62–3: 'Begin, my friend, for to be sure thou canst in no wise carry thy song with thee to Hades, that puts all things out of mind.'

The text followed here is that of the Commonplace Book, with variants from G.'s letter to Wharton (ll. 1–57) and Wharton's transcript of the later part of the poem (ll. 58–107).

ESSAY I

... πόταγ', ὦ 'γαθέ· τὰν γὰρ ἀοιδάν
οὔτι πα εἰς 'Αΐδαν γε τὸν ἐκλελάθοντα φυλαξεῖς·

THEOC[RITUS].

As sickly plants betray a niggard earth,
Whose barren bosom starves her generous birth,
Nor genial warmth nor genial juice retains
Their roots to feed and fill their verdant veins;
5   And as in climes, where winter holds his reign,
The soil, though fertile, will not teem in vain,
Forbids her gems to swell, her shades to rise,
Nor trusts her blossoms to the churlish skies:
So draw mankind in vain the vital airs,

¶ 15.2. *barren*] flinty *Wharton.*

3. Such words as 'genial' and 'juice' and 'vital' (l. 9) occur regularly in descriptions of natural processes at this period; see J. Arthos, *The Language of Natural Description in the 18th Century* (Ann Arbor, 1949). Cp. Blackmore, *Nature of Man* (1711) p. 15: 'Soft Winds, their balmy Burden here unload, / And scatter genial Juices all abroad. / Prolific Heat fermenting Nature warms, / Exhilerates her Face, and calls forth all her Charms / ... / With gay Abundance, and with verdant Pride.'   *genial*] 'generative': cp. Pope, *Essay on Man* i 133: 'For me kind Nature wakes her genial power'.

7. gem] In this context, 'the first bud' (Johnson), especially the leaf-bud (derived from Latin *gemma*). Cp. Dryden, *Flower and the Leaf* 10–13: 'Till gentle Heat and soft repeated Rains, / Make the green Blood to dance within their Veins: / Then, at their Call, embolden'd out they come, / And swell the Gems, and burst the narrow Room.' Akenside, *Pleasures of Imagination* iii 587–8: 'and from the silken gem / Its lucid leaves unfolds'.

9. The phrase probably derives from Virgil, e.g. *auras / vitalis carpis, Aeneid* i 387–8; cp. 'That while my Nostrils draw this vital Air', Dryden, *Iliad* i 131; virtually reproduced by Pope, *Rape of the Lock* iv 137; and 'If yet he lives, and draws this vital Air', Dryden, *Aeneid* i 770; 'And drew Perfumes of more than vital Air', *Flower and the Leaf* 147.

9–21. Cp. for the thought and the language, Akenside, *Pleasures of Imagination* iii 535–44: 'But tho' heaven / In every breast hath sown these early seeds / Of love and admiration, yet in vain, / Without fair culture's kind parental aid, / Without inlivening suns, and genial show'rs, / And shelter from the blast, in vain we hope / The tender plant should rear its blooming head, / Or yield the harvest promis'd in its spring. / Nor yet will every soil with equal stores / Repay the tiller's labour.'

10 Unformed, unfriended, by those kindly cares
   That health and vigour to the soul impart,
   Spread the young thought and warm the opening
      heart.
   So fond Instruction on the growing powers
   Of nature idly lavishes her stores,
15 If equal Justice with unclouded face
   Smile not indulgent on the rising race,
   And scatter with a free though frugal hand
   Light golden showers of plenty o'er the land:
   But Tyranny has fixed her empire there, ⎫
20 To check their tender hopes with chilling fear, ⎬
   And blast the blooming promise of the year. ⎭
      This spacious animated scene survey
   From where the rolling orb, that gives the day,

11–12. Pope, *Essay on Man* ii 141–2: 'Whatever warms the heart, or fills
the head, / As the mind opens, and its functions spread'; Thomson, *Winter*
580: 'Would gradual open on our opening minds'; *Spring* 1152–3: 'to rear
the tender thought, / To teach the young idea how to shoot'. See also *Ode
for Music* 21 (p. 269).

14. 'And lavish Nature laughs, and strows her stores around', Dryden,
Pastorals vii 76.

15. 'unclouded ray', Pope, *Epistles to Several Persons* ii 257; Thomson,
Liberty v 612–3: 'Lo! justice, like the liberal light of heaven, / Unpurchased
shines on all.'

17–18. Cp. *Elegy* 63 (see p. 129).

19–21. Blackmore, *Nature of Man* p. 12: 'See, Cold extream clasps in its
rigid Arms / Dishonour'd Nature, of their Strength disarms / Her wither'd
Limbs, and blasts her blooming Charms', and *ibid* p. 78: 'Shelter'd by
Guardian Laws in this mild Seat / From nipping Frosts, fierce Winds, and
scorching Heat, / From blasting Plagues, and every various Death, / Which
spreads malignant from the Tyrants Breath, / The liberal Arts,
those tender Plants appear / Pleas'd with the Soil, and blooming Beauty
wear.'

19. *Tyranny has*] gloomy Sway have *Wharton*.

21. *blooming*] vernal *Wharton*.   Cp. Dryden, *Of the Pythagorean Philosophy*
179: 'The promise of the Year, a plenteous Crop'; Pope, *Vertumnus and
Pomona* 109: 'Destroy the Promise of the youthful Year'; and Prior, *Hymn
to the Spring* 16: 'The blooming promise of a fruitful Year'.

22. Blackmore, *Nature of Man* p. 5: 'Each *India*'s spacious Monarchys
survey'; Pope, *Essay on Man* i 5: 'Expatiate free o'er all this scene of Man.'

23. Pope, *Windsor Forest* 245–6: 'Now marks the Course of rolling Orbs on
high; / O'er figur'd Worlds now travels with his Eye.'

His sable sons with nearer course surrounds,
25 To either pole and life's remotest bounds.
How rude so e'er the exterior form we find,
Howe'er opinion tinge the varied mind,
Alike to all the kind impartial heaven
The sparks of truth and happiness has given:
30 With sense to feel, with memory to retain,
They follow pleasure and they fly from pain;
Their judgement mends the plan their fancy draws,
The event presages and explores the cause.
The soft returns of gratitude they know,

24. Pope, *Rape of the Lock* iii 82: 'Of *Asia*'s Troops and *Africk*'s Sable Sons';
Thomson, *Liberty* v 196: 'Afric's sable sons'.

27. 'Meanwhile Opinion gilds with varying rays', *Essay on Man* ii 283.

28-37. Dryden, *Sigismonda and Guiscardo* 505-11: 'The same Almighty
Pow'r inspired the Frame / With kindl'd Life, and form'd the Souls the
same: / The Faculties of Intellect, and Will, / Dispens'd with equal Hand,
dispos'd with equal Skill, / Like Liberty indulg'd with Choice of Good or
Ill. / Thus born alike, from Vertue first began / The Diff'rence that dis-
tinguish'd Man from Man.'

28-9. Pope, *Essay on Man* iv 53-4: 'Heav'n to Mankind impartial we con-
fess, / If all are equal in their Happiness.'

30-7. *Essay on Man* iii 131-8, 143-6: 'A longer love Man's helpless kind
demands; / That longer care contracts more lasting bands: / Reflection,
Reason, still the ties improve, / At once extend the int'rest and the love; /
With choice we fix, with sympathy we burn; / Each Virtue in each Passion
takes its turn; / And still new needs, new helps, new habits rise, / That
graft benevolence on charities / ... / Mem'ry and fore-cast just returns
engage, / That pointed back to youth, this on to age; / While pleasure,
gratitude, and hope, combin'd, / Still spread the int'rest and preserv'd the
kind.'

31. In his entry *Affectus* in his Commonplace Book (i 3), discussing Locke,
G. wrote: 'We should be in the state almost of mere Vegetables without
them [the passions], for why should we act, but to some End, & what end
can we have, but to gain the pleasure resulting from some Good, or avoid
the Pain accompanying, what we call Evil?' Cp. 'We Happiness pursue:
We fly from Pain', Prior, *Solomon* iii 627; 'Pain their aversion, Pleasure
their desire', Pope, *Essay on Man* ii 88.

32. Dryden's usual distinction between the functions of judgment and
fancy. Cp. Preface to *The Rival Ladies*: 'The fancy was yet in its first work,
moving the sleeping images of things towards the light, there to be dis-
tinguished, and then either chosen or rejected by the judgement' (*Of Dram-
atic Poesy and other Essays*, ed. G. Watson (1962) i 2).

33. *event*] Outcome, result.

35 By fraud elude, by force repel the foe;
    While mutual wishes, mutual woes, endear
    The social smile and sympathetic tear.
        Say then, through ages by what fate confined
    To different climes seem different souls assigned?
40 Here measured laws and philosophic ease
    Fix and improve the polished arts of peace.
    There Industry and Gain their vigils keep,
    Command the winds and tame the unwilling deep.
    Here force and hardy deeds of blood prevail;
45 There languid pleasure sighs in every gale.
    Oft o'er the trembling nations from afar

35. *fraud . . . force*] In his note to *Rape of the Lock* ii 32, 'By Force to ravish, or by Fraud betray', Tillotson shows that this is a common epic antithesis and cites Dryden, *Aeneid* i 942, ii 62; and Pope, *Odyssey* i 385, ii 235. Cp. also Dryden, *Aeneid* i 401, ii 527, viii 272, x 119.
36-7. G. wrote to West in July 1740: 'as mutual wants are the ties of general society, so are mutual weaknesses of private friendships' (*Corresp* i 168). Cp. Pope, *Essay on Man* ii 253-6: 'Wants, frailties, passions, closer still ally / The common int'rest, or endear the tie: / To these we owe true friendship, love sincere, / Each home-felt joy that life inherits here.' Cp. also 'On mutual Wants build mutual Happiness', 'But mutual wants this Happiness increase', *ibid* iii 112 and iv 55; 'But want for want with mutual aid supply', Thomson, *Liberty* iv 921.
37. 'The social tear would rise, the social sigh', Thomson, *Winter* 356.
38. Say] So used by Milton, *Par. Lost* i 26, and by Pope in the *Essay on Man* more than a dozen times.
39. different . . . different] A fairly common formula. Cp. Boileau's *Art of Poetry*, trans. Soames and Dryden 539-40: 'Of Countryes and of Times the humors know; / From diff'rent Climates, diff'ring Customs grow'; 'On diff'rent senses diff'rent objects strike', Pope, *Essay on Man* ii 128; 'Different minds / Incline to different objects', Akenside, *Pleasures of Imagination* iii 546-7; 'To different Objects different Souls incline', T. Warton Senior, *Poems* (1748) p. 18. Cp. especially Blackmore, *Nature of Man* p. 3: 'Tell . . . / What different Virtues, and as different Crimes, / Owe their Production to peculiar Climes.'
40. 'the calm abode / Of wisdom, virtue, philosophic ease', Thomson, *Liberty* ii 125-6; 'philosophic love of ease', Matthew Green, *The Spleen* 390.
41. 'Arts that polish Life', *Par. Lost* xi 606.
42. Blackmore, *Nature of Man* p. 36: 'Active, industrious, and intent on Gain, / *Gallia*, thy Sons incessant Toil sustain.'
43. 'Taught to command the fire, controul the flood', Pope, *Essay on Man* iii 220.
45. 'Diffusing languor in the panting gales', Pope, *Dunciad* iv 304.

Has Scythia breathed the living cloud of war;
And, where the deluge burst, with sweepy sway
Their arms, their kings, their gods were rolled away.
50 As oft have issued, host impelling host,
The blue-eyed myriads from the Baltic coast.
The prostrate south to the destroyer yields
Her boasted titles and her golden fields:
With grim delight the brood of winter view
55 A brighter day and heavens of azure hue,
Scent the new fragrance of the breathing rose,
And quaff the pendent vintage, as it grows.

47. Claudian, *Laus Serenae* 196: *bellica nubes* (cloud of war).

48. *deluge*] Cp. *Par. Lost* i 353–4: 'her barbarous Sons / Came like a Deluge on the South'; Pope, *Essay on Criticism* 691–2: 'A *second* Deluge Learning thus o'er-run, / And the *Monks* finish'd what the *Goths* begun.'   *sweepy*] Defined by Johnson as 'Passing with great speed and violence over a great compass at once'. Dryden used the phrase 'sweepy sway' on several occasions: *Georgics* i 651–2: 'And rolling onward, with a sweepy Sway, / Bore Houses, Herds, and lab'ring Hinds away.' A slightly modified version of this couplet appeared in his translation of *Ovid's Metamorphoses* i 395–6. Cp. also *Aeneid* vii 936–7: 'They rush along, the ratling Woods give way, / The Branches bend before their sweepy Sway'; Pope, *Odyssey* v 303: 'A wedge to drive with sweepy sway'.

50. *host impelling host*] The formula seems to begin with Dryden, *Of the Pythagorean Philosophy* 271: 'The Wave behind impels the Wave before', adapted by Pope to 'Heir urges Heir, like Wave impelling Wave', *Imitations of Horace, Ep.* II ii 253. Cp. Thomson, *Liberty* iv 802–3: 'Hence many a people, fierce with freedom, rushed / From the rude iron regions of the north, / To Libyan deserts swarm protruding swarm'; and *Winter* 840–2: 'Drove martial horde on horde, with dreadful sweep / Resistless rushing o'er the enfeebled south, / And gave the vanquished world another form.'

51. *A word perhaps* Nations, *has been deleted beneath* Myriads *in Wharton*. Cp. 'The North by myriads pours her mighty sons', *Dunciad* iii 89; *Caerula quis stupuit Germani lumina* (Who is amazed to see a German with blue eyes?), Juvenal, *Sat.* xiii 164; *nec fera caerulea domuit Germania pube* (nor wild Germany with its blue-eyed youth), Horace, *Epodes* xvi 7; 'the blue-eyed Saxon', Thomson, *Liberty* iv 670.

55. *heavens*] Skies *Wharton*.

56. *Scent*] Catch *Wharton*.   *breathing*] Emitting fragrance. Cp. 'Breathing Roses of the Wood', Milton, *Arcades* 32; and 'Here Western Winds on breathing Roses blow', Pope, *Spring* 32.

57. *pendent vintage*] Perhaps a memory of Virgil, *Georgics* ii 89: *pendet vindemia* (the vintage hangs). Tovey cites the words of an old warrior dissuading Alaric from further invasion of Italy in Claudius, *De Bello*

Proud of the yoke and pliant to the rod,
Why yet does Asia dread a monarch's nod,
60 While European freedom still withstands
The encroaching tide, that drowns her lessening lands,
And sees far off with an indignant groan
Her native plains and empires once her own?
Can opener skies and suns of fiercer flame
65 O'erpower the fire that animates our frame,
As lamps, that shed at even a cheerful ray,
Fade and expire beneath the eye of day?
Need we the influence of the northern star
To string our nerves and steel our hearts to war?
70 And, where the face of nature laughs around,

Gothico 504–6: *Quid palmitis uber Etrusci* / . . . *semper in ore geris* (Why dost thou ever have on thy lips the richness of Tuscan vineyards?).

58–9. Blackmore, *Nature of Man* p. 37: 'This mean ungenerous Race, for Thraldom fit, / Obsequious to the Yoke their passive Necks submit. / Their abject Minds ev'n Liberty disdain, / Pleas'd to be Slaves, they boast the Tyrant's reign, / And servile hug their ignominious Chain.'

59–63. As Tovey suggests, G. is probably thinking at first 'partly of the empire of Turkey in Asia but also of the progress of Mahommedan despotism further east, and notably in India'. G. then appears to refer to the Turks in Europe. Turkey's offensive power diminished after the peace of Karlowitz in 1699 but she continued to win and lose territory in Europe for several decades. She was victorious over the Austrians and Russians in 1738, crossed the Danube and at the peace of Belgrade in 1739 regained Belgrade and other places which she had lost earlier in the century.

60–1. 'Prescient, the tides or tempests to withstand', *Essay on Man* iii 101.

65. 'Each purer frame inform'd with purer fire', Pope, *Epistle to Jervas* 50.

66–7. Dryden was fond of a similar image referring to the stars, e.g.*Britannia Rediviva* 311–2: 'So lost, as Starlight is dissolv'd away, / And melts into the brightness of the day'; *Religio Laici* 8–9: 'as those nightly Tapers disappear / When Day's bright Lord ascends our Hemisphere'; cp. also 'And Stars grow paler at th'approach of Day', *Prologue to his Royal Highness* (1682) 6; and 'Like stars before the orb of day / Turn pale and fade', Gay, *Fables* II xvi 16–7.

67. eye of day] A poeticism for the sun found as early as Chaucer: cp. Milton, *Sonnets* i 5, and *Il Penseroso* 141; Pope, *Epilogue to Satires* ii 222.

69. According to Johnson, 'string' meant 'To make tense' and 'nerve' was 'used by the poets for sinew or tendon'. Cp. Dryden, *To my Kinsman, John Dryden* 89: 'Toil strung the Nerves, and purifi'd the Blood'; see also Gay, *Birth of the Squire* 27; Thomson, *Epistle to Dodington* 16; *Britannia* 249; *Autumn* (1730–38 text) 760; *Liberty* iv 1025.

Must sickening Virtue fly the tainted ground?
Unmanly thought! what seasons can control,
What fancied zone can circumscribe the Soul,
Who, conscious of the source from whence she springs,
75 By Reason's light on Resolution's wings,
Spite of her frail companion, dauntless goes
O'er Libya's deserts and through Zembla's snows?
She bids each slumbering energy awake,
Another touch, another temper take,
80 Suspends the inferior laws that rule our clay:
The stubborn elements confess her sway;
Their little wants, their low desires, refine,
And raise the mortal to a height divine.
    Not but the human fabric from the birth
85 Imbibes a flavour of its parent earth:
As various tracts enforce a various toil,
The manners speak the idiom of their soil.
An iron-race the mountain-cliffs maintain,
Foes to the gentler genius of the plain:
90 For where unwearied sinews must be found

71. 'And Guardian Virtue flys the hateful Ground', Blackmore, *Nature of Man* p. 98.

72–6. Prior, *On the Coronation of James II and Queen Mary* 1-7: 'What Limits can controul / The Rovings of my active Soul? / That Soul that scorns to be to Place confin'd, / But leaves its dull Companion *Earth* behind; / Whilst *Fancy* with unbounded flight, / Enjoys that Object of Delight, / Which envious distance would conceal from Sight'; Young, *Night Thoughts* i 98–101, of the soul: 'Her ceaseless Flight, tho' devious, speaks her Nature / Of subtler Essence than the trodden Clod; / Active, aerial, tow'ring, un-confin'd, / Unfetter'd with her gross Companion's fall.'

77. *Zembla*] Nova Zembla, a group of islands north of Russia in the Arctic Ocean. Referred to by Blackmore as a representatively frozen place in *Nature of Man* pp. 11, 29 (shortly before a reference to Libya).

79. *touch*] Quality.

83. Spenser, *Tears of the Muses* 459–60: 'That lowly thoughts lift up to heaven's hight, / And mortall men have powre to deifie.' Cp. also Dryden, *Alexander's Feast* 169–70: 'He rais'd a Mortal to the Skies; / She drew an Angel down'; Pope, *Essay on Man* iv 334: 'Joins heav'n and earth, and mortal and divine.'

88. *virumque / ferrea progenies* (man's iron race), Virgil, *Georgics* ii 340-1; 'An iron race', Thomson, *Autumn* 1294.

89. 'Or tames the Genius of the stubborn Plain', Pope, *Imitations of Horace*, Sat. II i 131.

With sidelong plough to quell the flinty ground,
To turn the torrent's swift-descending flood,
To brave the savage rushing from the wood,
What wonder if, to patient valour trained,
95   They guard with spirit what by strength they gained;
And while their rocky ramparts round they see,
The rough abode of want and liberty,
(As lawless force from confidence will grow)
Insult the plenty of the vales below?
100 What wonder in the sultry climes, that spread
Where Nile redundant o'er his summer-bed
From his broad bosom life and verdure flings,
And broods o'er Egypt with his watery wings,
If with adventurous oar and ready sail,

91. 'sidelong lays the glebe', Thomson, *Spring* 43. Thomson's adverbial
usage means 'to the side'. *OED* cites G.'s line under the meaning 'in a
sloping position; inclining to one side'.

93. *savage*] Wild beast. Cp. *Windsor Forest* 57, in which Pope revised 'Savages
or Subjects' to 'a Beast or Subject', on the grounds that 'the word Savages
is not so properly apply'd to beasts as to men'. But see Goldsmith, *Traveller*
190 and *n* (p. 642).

94–7. Several phrases in these lines derive from Thomson, *Liberty* iv 322–6,
335–42, on the Swiss: 'The mountains then, clad with eternal snow, / Con-
fessed my power. Deep as the rampart rocks / By nature thrown insuperable
round, / I planted there a league of friendly states, / And bade plain freedom
their ambition be / . . . / For valour, faith, and innocence of life / Renowned,
a rough laborious people there / Not only give the dreadful Alps to smile, /
And press their culture on retiring snows; / But, to firm order trained and
patient war, / They likewise know, beyond the nerve remiss / Of mercenary
force, how to defend / The tasteful little their hard toil has earned.'

99. Thomson, *Liberty* iv 327–9 (in the passage quoted above): 'There in
the vale, where rural plenty fills / From lakes and meads and furrowed
fields her horn.'

101. *Nile redundant*] Cp. *Nilus in aestatem crescit campisque redundat* (The
Nile towards summer-time swells and overflows on the fields), Lucretius
vi 712; and *Niloque redundat*, Claudian, *Nilus* 7. Young, *Busiris* V i, has
'The broad redundant Nile'.

102–3. Denham, *Cooper's Hill* 169–70, of the Thames: 'O'er which he
kindly spreads his spacious wing, / And hatches plenty for th'ensuing
spring'; and *Par. Lost* vii 234–5: 'on the watrie calme / His brooding wings
the Spirit of God outspred'.

104. 'with venturous oar', Thomson, *Autumn* 919.

104–5. 'Spread the thin oar, and catch the driving gale', Pope, *Essay on
Man* iii 178.

104–7. Virgil, *Georgics* iv 287–9: *qua Pellaei gens fortunata Canopi / accolit*

105 The dusky people drive before the gale,
        Or on frail floats to distant cities ride,
        That rise and glitter o'er the ambient tide.

effuso stagnantem flumine Nilum | et circum pictis vehitur sua rura phaselis
(where the favoured people of Pelaean Canopus dwell by the outspread
waters of the flooded Nile, and sail about their fields in painted skiffs).
Cp. also Dryden's translation of these lines, *Georgics* iv 409–12: 'For where
with sev'n-fold Horns mysterious *Nile* / Surrounds the Skirts of *Egypt*'s fruit-
ful Isle, / And where in Pomp the Sun-burnt People ride / On painted Barges,
o're the teeming Tide.'
105. dusky] 'G. has in mind the epithet *fuscus* so frequently applied by the
Latin poets to the Egyptians' (Tovey).
106. frail floats] *sic, cum tenet omnia Nilus, | Conseritur bibula Memphitis cumba
papyro* (And so, when Nile covers the land, the boats of Memphis are
framed of thirsty papyrus), Lucan, *Pharsalia* iv 135–6. Juvenal, *Satires* xv
127–8, writes scornfully of Egyptian boats in similar terms.   *distant*]
neighb'ring *Mason, 1775* (a substitution suggested by Bedingfield, *Corresp*
I xiii *n*).
107. ambient] 'Surrounding; encompassing; investing' (Johnson). A com-
mon word in natural descriptions: e.g. 'ambient Aire', *Par. Lost* vii 89;
'ambient sea', Dryden, *Prologue to The Unhappy Favourite* 19.

16 [Tophet]

Inscription on a Portrait

Written in about 1749. This epigram on the Rev. Henry Etough, Rector of
Therfield, Herts, from 1734, was first printed as 'On Mr E—'s being ordained'
in the *London Mag.* lii 296, in June 1783. When reprinted in the *Gentleman's
Mag.* lv 759, in Oct. 1785, it was introduced as follows by a letter signed
'Bion' (here corrected from errata noted in a later number of the magazine):

'Mr. Etoph, of Pembroke Hall, Cambridge, was, in his time, so very sin-
gular a person, that I imagine you will accept of any information which
relates to him. Of his private character, disposition, and attainments, you
have many correspondents better able than myself to relate many interesting
circumstances.

'But I understand that he received his education amongst the Dissenters,
and had imbibed all their strongest prejudices. Nevertheless, he was after-
wards ordained, though I know not by which of our bishops, a clergyman
of the established church.

'He was principally remarkable for the intimate knowledge he had ob-
tained of the private and domestic history of all the great families in the
kingdom.

'The various anecdotes of this nature which he possessed, and which he omitted no opportunity of communicating, made him, at the same time, an object of outward civilities and secret dislike. The eccentricities of his character were also extended to his personal appearance; and Mr. Tyson of Benet College, who, amongst other various and better attainments, successfully cultivated a taste for drawing, made an etching of his head, and presented it to Mr. Gray. Underneath, Mr. Gray wrote the following epigram, which I do not remember to have seen in print . . .'

Michael Tyson's etching of Etough can be dated 1769 (for a reproduction see *Corresp* i 302), but the original drawing upon which it was based, by G.'s friend William Mason, was made in about 1749. William Cole, the antiquarian, stated in a letter of 11 Dec. 1769 that Mason's drawing was made 'twenty years ago, and preserved by a friend, who let Mr. Tyson take a copy of it. The verses were also wrote at the same time; I do not think they should be shown much' (J. P. Malcolm, *Letters between the Rev. James Granger . . . and Many of the Most Eminent Literary Men of his Time* (1805) p. 331). Cole's account is more reliable and detailed than that of 'Bion' in the *Gentleman's Mag.* and his statement that Mason's drawing and G.'s epigram were both to be dated 1749 is supported by other evidence. Mason was 'a new acquaintance' of G. early in 1748 and he became a Fellow of Pembroke in March 1749. Their cooperation in an attack on Etough is most likely to have occurred after this date. The references to Etough in G.'s letters (*Corresp* i 302, 355, 365) are from approximately the same period. G. described him as a 'Fiend of a Parson' (as in the epigram) early in 1748 and as a 'Fiend' once more late in 1751. G. may have been referring to this epigram when he wrote to Walpole in July 1752: 'I desire you would not show that epigram I repeated to you, as mine. I have heard of it twice already as coming from you.'

G. particularly resented Etough's interference in university affairs (made possible by the closeness of his living to Cambridge), although the epigram refers primarily to his religious hypocrisy. Both aspects of Etough are discussed frankly and at length in William Cole's MS account of him (BM. Add MSS 5829 ff. 183–4; 5868 f. 48). Cole described him as 'a pimping, tale-bearing dissenting teacher, who by adulation and flattery, and an everlasting fund of news and scandal, made himself agreeable to many of prime fortune, particularly Sir Robert Walpole'. (According to some sources Etough officiated at Walpole's marriage to Maria Skerrett.) Cole added that Etough 'thought it more to the purpose to come over to the established Church, where better company, and better preferment were to be met with. He used to be much at Cambridge, when I resided there and was a busy, impertinent meddler in everyone's affairs.' Etough was not educated at a university, although a M.A. degree was conferred on him at Cambridge in 1717. He died in Aug. 1757 at the age of seventy. William Coxe, *Memoirs of Sir Robert Walpole* (1798) I xxvi–xxvii, described the 'Etough Papers' as a 'valuable mass of intelligence' about Walpole and other political affairs.

The publication of G.'s epigram in Oct. 1785 aroused some interest. In Jan. 1786, 'D.H.' sent a copy of Tyson's etching and some further infor-

mation about him to the *Gentleman's Mag.* lvi 25, but the editor, John
Nichols, did not publish the etching. Instead, he eventually passed it on to
Stephen Jones, in the 2nd edn of whose *Poems of G.* p. 182, it was
reproduced for the first time, and the epigram first collected. Also in Jan.
1786, John Duncombe contributed to the same magazine some derogatory
information about Etough's personal habits and career. This was countered
in April 1786 (lvi 281) by a letter from 'D.M.', which praised Etough's
cleanliness, hospitality and benevolence. These various accounts from the
Gentleman's Mag. were later collected by Nichols in *Literary Anecdotes* viii
261–4. For additional information see J. Beresford, *Times Lit. Supp.* 22
July 1926, p. 496.

   The text followed here is that transcribed by Mason into G.'s Common-
place Book (iii 1106). It contains the 6 ll. which are the basis of all versions,
but it is followed by a note indicating that ll. 3–4 are to be added after l. 2.
There are two other copies of the 6 ll. text, neither by G. himself. One
appears beneath a pen and ink copy of Tyson's etching in the Cole papers in
the British Museum (Add. MS. 5817 f. 191), inscribed on the back by Cole,
'Given to me by Mʳ Tyson in Nov. 1769'. Another copy of the same text,
also accompanied by the sketch, in Pembroke College MS. 85, describes
Etough as 'Rector of Therfeild in Hartfordshire, who had been a dissenting
Teacher in a Barn at Debden in Essex'. The Cole text, which has several
differences from Mason's, was followed when the poem was first printed in
the *London Mag.* (except for the misprint in l. 1). A few small variations appear
in the text in the *Gentleman's Mag.* in 1785. The Cole text is also basically that
which appears (with 'Affrighted' for 'While frighted' in l. 2 and 'the' for
'her' in l. 6) in a letter of 7 March 1788 from R. Greville to Richard Pol-
whele. Greville had obtained it from a 'Dr G.', a clergyman and former
friend of G.; see Richard Polwhele, *Traditions and Recollections* (1826) i
212–3.

> Such Tophet was; so looked the grinning fiend
> Whom many a frighted prelate called his friend;

¶ 16.1. Such Tophet was–so grin'd the bawling Fiend *Cole; and London
Mag. with* grum'd *for* grin'd; Thus Tophet look'd, so grinn'd the brawling
fiend *Gent. Mag.*   *Tophet*] A phonetic anagram of Etough, with the
connotations of the place near Jerusalem described by Tovey as 'infamous
for sacrifices to Moloch, and consequently regarded as a place of abomin-
ation, the very gate or pit of Hell'. It is mentioned in the opening pages
of *The Pilgrim's Progress*; and in *Par. Lost* i 403–5 Moloch 'made his Grove
/ The pleasant Vally of *Hinnom, Tophet* thence / And black *Gehenna* call'd,
the Type of Hell.'
2. While frighted Prelates bow'd and called him Friend *Cole; and Gent.
Mag. with* Whilst *for* While.   Satan, in *Par. Lost* ii 846, similarly 'Grinnd
horrible a ghastly smile'.

> I saw them bow and, while they wished him dead,
> With servile simper nod the mitred head.
> 5   Our Mother-Church with half-averted sight
> Blushed as she blessed her grisly proselyte:
> Hosannahs rung through Hell's tremendous borders,
> And Satan's self had thoughts of taking orders.

3–4. This couplet is found only after Mason's transcript of the other 6 ll. with a note that it was to be added to 'the first copy' after l. 2. *servile*] *written above* civil *in Commonplace Book.*

4. Pope, *Epistle to Arbuthnot* 140: 'Ev'n mitred *Rochester* would nod the head.'

6. grisly] grimly *Gent. Mag.*

7–8. Young, *Love of Fame* vi 35–6: 'When Ladies once are Proud of praying well, / SATAN himself will toll the Parish Bell.'

17 Elegy Written in a Country Churchyard

The date at which G. began writing his most celebrated poem has been the subject of frequent discussion and disagreement, and the scanty and unreliable nature of such evidence as there is makes it impossible to reach any definite conclusion. Writers on other aspects of the *Elegy* have so often adopted a dating merely to suit a particular argument that a full statement of the relevant considerations is perhaps still desirable.

The most precise single item of information that we have for the dating of the *Elegy* is that on 12 June 1750 G. wrote to Horace Walpole (*Corresp* i 326–7): 'I have been here at Stoke a few days (where I shall continue good part of the summer); and having put an end to a thing, whose beginning you have seen long ago, I immediately send it you. You will, I hope, look upon it in the light of a *thing with an end to it*; a merit that most of my writings have wanted, and are like to want . . .' At the end of the letter G. added: 'You are desired to tell me your opinion, if you can take the pains, of these lines.' It has never been doubted that these remarks refer to the *Elegy*, which was therefore completed early in June 1750 at Stoke.

The date at which G. began the *Elegy* constitutes the real problem. From his letter to Walpole it is clear that there was a considerable interval between his beginning and completing it. Walpole had seen the beginning 'long ago', but whether this had been at the time when G. began writing it or at a later date is not apparent: the distinction is important, as will be seen later. At this point it is as well to consider the evidence offered by what is clearly the earliest extant draft of the *Elegy*. The Eton MS, entitled 'Stanza's Wrote In A Country Church-Yard' (now in the Memorial Buildings, Eton College) originally belonged to Mason. After various appearances in the sale-room in the nineteenth century it was bequeathed by Sir William Fraser in 1898 to Eton College. The first eighteen stanzas of this MS, in spite of many small variants, appear substantially as in the form eventually published. The four following stanzas, marked by G. in the margin as if for omission, were either abandoned or reworked in the remaining seventeen stanzas which, like the opening eighteen, appear very much as in the final form of the poem.

The Eton MS was first discussed by Mason (*Memoirs* p. 157) in 1775. Writing of the poems which G. is known to have written in the summer of 1742, he added: 'I am inclined to believe that the Elegy in a Country Churchyard was begun, if not concluded, at this time also: Though I am aware that, as it stands at present, the conclusion is of a later date; how that was originally, I shall shew in my notes on the poem.' Accordingly, in his notes, Mason, *Poems* pp. 108–09, commented on the Eton MS: 'In the first manuscript copy of this exquisite Poem, I find the conclusion different from that which he afterwards composed'. Then, after quoting the four stanzas which G. eventually rejected, Mason added: 'And here the Poem was originally intended to conclude, before the happy idea of the hoary-headed Swain, &c. suggested itself to him.'

The Eton MS confirms at least part of Mason's account. The four 're-jected' stanzas do provide a perfectly coherent conclusion to the poem. It seems clear, moreover, that, after G. had transcribed the poem to this point, there was a definite interval of time before he added the new ending. In that interval the MS was folded and stained and the paper itself deterior-ated slightly. (I was kindly allowed to see an argument to this effect in an unpublished study of 'Gray's handwriting, and its value as evidence in the dating of his *Elegy*' by M. P. T. Leahy of Pennsylvania State University. That there was an interval cannot be doubted but neither the condition of the MS nor an examination of the handwriting itself throws any conclusive light on its length.)

Mason's tentative opinion that G. began the *Elegy* in 1742 was accepted by nineteenth-century editors and was also embellished: it was suggested, for example, that G. was inspired to begin the poem by the death of his uncle Jonathan Rogers in Oct. 1742; and this suggestion was balanced by the theory that he was inspired to take it up again after the death of his aunt Mary Antrobus in Nov. 1749. For neither suggestion is there any evidence. Apart from Mason's opinion, the only statement about the dating of the poem which can be thought to have any authority came in 1773, when Hor-ace Walpole was shown part of the *Memoirs* of G. on which Mason was then working. On 1 Dec. 1773 Walpole wrote to Mason: 'The *Churchyard* was, I am persuaded, posterior to West's death at least three or four years, as you will see by my note. At least I am sure that I had the twelve or more first lines from himself above three years after that period, and it was long before he finished it' (*Walpole Correspondence* xxviii 117–18). Unfortunately Mason's reply to this letter is not extant, but it contained his reasons for suggesting that the *Elegy* was begun in 1742. On 14 Dec. 1773 Walpole wrote again to Mason, accepting Mason's decision on another point he had raised about the *Memoirs* and adding briefly: 'Your account of the *Elegy* puts an end to my other criticism' (*ibid* 123).

In the absence of more definite evidence we cannot afford to abandon Walpole's objection as easily as he himself did. Admittedly, to convince Walpole, Mason must have produced a persuasive argument that he was right in believing G. began the *Elegy* in 1742. But just how persuasive must we assume it to have been? Mason did not meet G. until about 1747, so that his dating of the poem was not based on first-hand knowledge. If G. himself had told him that he began the poem in 1742, Mason would surely have said so. The very tentativeness with which he offers that opinion ('I am inclined to believe') appears to confirm its speculative character. It has not been noted, moreover, that this discussion in 1773 between Mason and Walpole as to the date of the *Elegy* was only incidental to a matter of much greater interest, at least to Walpole: namely, Mason's treatment in his *Memoirs* of Walpole's early friendship and eventual quarrel in Italy with G. Walpole was apprehensive about Mason's handling of this subject and undoubtedly offended Mason by some of his comments on it. In his letter of 14 Dec. 1773 he was therefore anxious to placate Mason and his decision in the same letter not to pursue further the matter of the dating should be seen in the context of the larger issue. At the best of times Walpole was given to 'agreeing' with correspondents with whom he obviously did not agree; and in this particular instance he had good reason for allowing himself to be persuaded.

In any case, Walpole retracted only the first part of his original assertion i.e. that G. began *writing* the *Elegy* three or four years after West's death, in 1745 or 1746. There is no reason to believe that he had not remembered correctly that G. had shown him twelve or more of the opening lines at that period. This memory fits easily enough with G.'s own statement in June 1750 that Walpole had seen the beginning of the *Elegy* 'long ago'. G. and Walpole had not become reconciled after their Italian quarrel until Nov. 1745, so that even if G. *had* begun the *Elegy* in 1742 he would not have shown it to Walpole any earlier. (This may have been the argument used by Mason against Walpole's objection to his dating.) The most likely period for G. to have shown Walpole the beginning of the poem is in the autumn of 1746, when Walpole was living at Windsor and when G. saw him regularly (*Corresp* i 239). It was also at this time that G. began showing his other poems to Walpole.

It may therefore be assumed that Walpole first saw the opening 12 ll. of the *Elegy* in the autumn of 1746. But a question at once arises. Why, if, as Mason and his adherents believe, G. had already written the whole of the first version of the poem, should he have shown Walpole only the 'twelve or more first lines' at this time? Is it not more likely that G. showed him only some twelve lines because he had written no more and more likely, in addition, that he had written them fairly recently? This problem was tackled ingeniously but unconvincingly by H. W. Garrod in 'A note on the composition of Gray's *Elegy*', in *Essays Presented to David Nichol Smith* (Oxford, 1945) pp. 111–16. Garrod pointed out that, without the four stanzas later rejected by G., the first version of the *Elegy* in the Eton MS contains 18 stanzas or 72 ll. Mitford's transcript of Walpole's letter of 1 Dec. 1773 provides the only text and Garrod argued that in making his copy of it Mitford had misread Walpole's '72' for '12'. In other words Walpole in fact told Mason that G. had shown him 'seventy-two or more first lines' of the *Elegy* some three or four years after West's death: i.e. almost the whole of the first version of the poem.

Garrod's argument is hardly tenable. It seems unlikely that G. in June 1750 would have referred to 72 or more lines as merely a 'beginning', when the whole poem contained only 128; and the manner in which G. asked for Walpole's opinion of 'these lines' does not suggest that Walpole had seen many of them before. As far as Walpole is concerned, it is unlikely that he would use such a phrase as 'seventy-two or more first lines': 72 is a very particular number to be vague about. Similarly, Walpole was always active in pressing G. to publish his poems and in 1747 and 1748 was responsible for the publication of three of them. His enthusiasm for the *Elegy* when he was shown it in 1750 makes it hard to believe that he had already seen its most memorable stanzas and had been content for some four years not to pester G. to finish and publish it. Finally, it is worth noting the authoritative opinion of the editors of Walpole's letters as to whether he wrote '12' or '72' and as to whether Mitford is likely to have mistranscribed the number: 'We believe [Walpole] wrote 12; HW's 1's and 7's are not at all similar, and it would have been unlike HW to count out the number of lines Gray sent him, or, if he had, to remember the total for a quarter of a century' (*Walpole Correspondence* xxviii 118 *n* 4).

The inconclusive nature of the main items of evidence as to the dating of the *Elegy* will be readily apparent. All that seems likely at this point is that the choice of dates is confined to two: the alternative to accepting Mason's tentative suggestion that G. at least began the poem in 1742 is to believe that when G. showed the twelve or more opening lines to Walpole in the autumn of 1746 he had only recently started it. In support of Mason's date is the fact that he managed to persuade Walpole that he was right, although the circumstances in which he did so must be taken into account. The other main fact in support of 1742 is that that year was by far the most creative of G.'s life: but there must obviously be a limit to this kind of argument, and it may be hard to believe that, in addition to the *Ode on Spring*, the *Sonnet on West*, the *Eton Ode*, the *Ode to Adversity* and the fragmentary *Hymn to Ignorance*, G. also found time and creative energy to write very much of the *Elegy*. It has also seemed natural to some scholars to connect the *Elegy* with the death of Richard West in June 1742, but once again there is no evidence to confirm such a theory. If West were to be involved in the poem at any point, it could only be in the description of the unhappy poet and in the epitaph at the end of the *Elegy*. Yet this section of the poem seems certainly to have been written in about 1750. The most elaborate of the theories involving

West, Odell Shepard's 'A youth to fortune and to fame unknown', *MP*, xx (1922–23) 347–73, argued that the 'Epitaph' had originally been a separate poem about West written in 1742, and that G. wrote his second conclusion to the *Elegy* so as to enable him to work the 'Epitaph' in. In this way the poem as a whole became 'a lament for a friend who died of a broken heart'. Shepard's theory consisted of sheer guesswork at almost every point, attractive as parts of it may seem. There is no evidence that the 'Epitaph' was ever a separate poem and it is noteworthy that in 1773 Walpole (a close friend of both G. and West) clearly saw no connection between the *Elegy* and West's death, being quite convinced, at least at first, that the poem was written several years later.

The case for dating the beginning of the *Elegy* in 1742 is not strong and must, in fact, rest almost entirely on whatever one supposes Mason's unknown arguments for that date to have been and on the faith one puts in his judgement. The case for dating the beginning of the poem in the summer or autumn of 1746 is more elaborate but not perhaps much more definite. Walpole's initial conviction that the poem had been started then must perhaps be ruled out in the light of his later withdrawal of it; but there is no reason to doubt that it was at this time that he saw the opening lines, and the question posed above has still not been answered. Why, if G. had already written at least the first version of the poem, did he show Walpole only some twelve lines of it? There are, moreover, two cryptic remarks by G. at this period which suggest that, for the first time since 1742, he was once more writing poetry. On 10 Aug. 1746 he told Wharton that 'the Muse, I doubt, is gone, & has left me in far worse Company: if she returns, you will hear of her' (*Corresp* i 238). He made a more significant statement in another letter to Wharton on 11 Sept. 1746: after mentioning that he had been reading Aristotle, he added, 'this & a few autumnal Verses are my Entertainments dureing the Fall of the Leaf' (*Corresp* i 241). There would appear to be no other poem than the *Elegy* to which G. could have been referring.

One argument on behalf of dating the beginning of the *Elegy* in 1742 is that it is known to have been, for G., a prolific creative period. But it can be argued on the other hand that the resumption of the friendship with Walpole, which was really re-established in the summer of 1746, marked the beginning of a renewal of G.'s literary activities. Since the death of West he had lacked an audience, but now he began showing what he had already written to Walpole and starting new poems. He wrote for Walpole his *Ode on the Death of a Favourite Cat*, considered continuing *Agrippina* and began *Education and Government*. It was at least as good a period as any for G. to have started and slowly worked on the *Elegy*. There are also circumstantial arguments for dating the beginning of the poem at this period, which can be described as at least no worse than some of those for 1742. Apparently the first such argument was a spirited but extravagant article by W. H. Newman, 'When curfew tolled the knell', *National Review*, cxxvii (1946) 244–8, which attempted to demonstrate that the *Elegy* was inspired by various events in Aug. 1746. G.'s reflections on the inevitability of death and the dangers of ambition and power are connected with his visits in that month to various royal homes, with a number of recent royal deaths, with the famous trial in Westminster Hall of three Jacobite peers involved in the '45 rebellion, and with the triumphant return of the Duke of Cumberland from quelling that rebellion in the previous July. By combining with these events a quantity of meteorological information, Newman demonstrated to his own satisfaction that he possessed an 'abundance of evidence' for identifying the moment at which G. began writing the Elegy as 8 p.m. on 18 Aug. 1746. A similar, but more restrained and detailed, argument for connecting the Elegy with the trial of the Scottish lords in Aug. 1746 was offered by F. H. Ellis, 'Gray's Elegy: The biographical problem in literary criticism', PMLA, lxvi (1951) 971–1008. The 'biographical problem' is, of course, whether or not such connections between the poet's life and contemporary events on the one hand, and the poem itself on the other, can or need to be made. As far as the poem is concerned, G.'s generalities on rich and poor and on life and death are obviously self-sufficient and in no way need to be related to specific events of Aug. 1746 or of any other particular period; and the very generality of G.'s themes in itself makes it impossible in the end to accept the arguments of Newman and Ellis, however plausible they may appear in parts. Nevertheless, they may be thought to add something to the argument for dating the Elegy in 1746.

There is another kind of internal evidence about the dating which is perhaps slightly more conclusive, although by its nature it can be used only with caution. G.'s use of the quatrain in the Elegy was to be greatly imitated by his contemporaries and later poets, but he was not of course the first English poet to have used it nor was he by any means solely responsible for its vogue in the later eighteenth-century. Very early in his Commonplace Book he transcribed part of Sir John Davies's Nosce Teipsum, a poem in quatrains which he admired. In his 'Observations on English Metre', Works, ed. Gosse, i 344, G. noted its use by Surrey, Spenser, Gascoigne and by Dryden in his Annus Mirabilis. Another notable use of the quatrain in the seventeenth-century was in Davenant's Gondibert; Thomas Hobbes employed it in his translation of Homer; and it occasionally appeared in the works of early eighteenth-century poets, such as William Walsh (The Retirement). G. had therefore no lack of models in the use of the quatrain but it is worth noting that this stanzaic form had been brought into some kind of fashion by a work published several years before the Elegy, James Hammond's Elegies, dated 1743 but published in Dec. 1742. Hammond's poems, largely imitations of Tibullus, were undoubtedly imitated by other poets and did much to establish the quatrain as 'elegiac'. It must of course be remembered that in the Eton MS G.'s poem is entitled 'Stanzas' and that it was Mason, according to his own story (Poems p. 108), who persuaded him to call it an Elegy. (For some discussion of the meaning of 'Elegy' at this period, see Joseph Trapp, Lectures on Poetry . . . Translated from the Latin (1742) pp. 163–71; William Shenstone, Works in Verse and Prose (1764) i 3–12: and the Annual Register for 1767, pt ii, pp. 220–2.) In addition, there is little to suggest, apart from the quatrain itself and the occasional echo, that G. was influenced by Hammond's *Elegies*. The possibility that he was, however, has been explored by J. Fisher,' James Hammond and the quatrain of Gray's *Elegy*', *MP* xxxii (1935) 301–10; and if G. was imitating Hammond, he could not have begun the *Elegy* in the summer of 1742. In a later article, 'Shenstone, Gray, and the "Moral Elegy"', *MP* xxxiv (1937) 273–94, Fisher argued that Shenstone's *Elegies*, which appear to contain many parallels with G.'s *Elegy* but which were not published until 1764, were in fact written between 1743 and 1749, most of them by 1745. At this period they were circulating in MS and Fisher suggested that they might even have reached G. This theory is unconvincing and it is much more probable that in revising his elegies after 1751 Shenstone imitated G.'s celebrated poem. Fisher's two articles, nevertheless, are of interest in that they show that G. cannot be regarded as the sole pioneer in the use of the quatrain and the popularity of the 'elegy'.

G.'s borrowings or echoes within the *Elegy* provide more evidence, although the possibility that any particular parallel may be no more than coincidental must always be borne in mind. It is surely significant, however, that consciously or unconsciously G. seems to have remembered phrases and longer passages from a number of poems written in the early 1740s: Blair's *The Grave* (1743), Akenside's *Epistle to Curio* and *The Pleasures of Imagination* (1744) and *Odes* (1745), the *Odes* of Collins and Joseph Warton (1746) and Thomas Warton's *Five Pastoral Eclogues* (1745) and *The Pleasures of Melancholy* (1747). G. could of course merely have shared common sources of inspiration with these poets and some of the echoes occur in the later part of the *Elegy*: but, considered as a whole and with the greatest caution, this evidence would certainly suggest that G. began the poem in 1746–47. The same conclusion would have to be reached if the *Elegy* is considered in relation to the vogue for 'graveyard' poetry and prose which emerged in the early 1740s. The *Elegy* could have been quite independent, but it must appear more likely that it came after rather than preceded such contemplations as Young's *Night Thoughts* (1742–45), Blair's *The Grave* (1743) and James Hervey's *Meditations among the Tombs* (1746).

Finally it may be noted that there would appear to be some relationship between the *Elegy* and the unfinished fragment on *Education and Government*, which G. probably wrote in 1747–48. Both poems deal with the subject of genius which circumstances have prevented from flourishing, and both may be related to Plato's discussion of education and its effect on 'virtue', which G. was reading at this time and commenting on in his Commonplace Book (see headnote to *Education and Government*, p. 89 above, and *Elegy* 65–6n). Once again, this evidence cannot be decisive and, although G.'s treatment of the theme is clearer in the *Elegy* than in *Education and Government*, it would be impossible to demonstrate from this fact which poem came first.

This discussion has tried to make clear that all of the evidence is ambiguous and nothing more confident than an assertion of likelihood can be achieved.

Even if it may appear that most of the poem was written in 1746 and later, it is still possible that G. began drafting it in 1742. Perhaps, like *The Progress of Poesy*, it was written 'by fits & starts at very distant intervals', although it may be pointed out here that G.'s method of working on his other poems suggests that he is unlikely to have taken eight years to complete a poem. Usually G. either abandoned a poem without finishing it, or took at most some two or three years, as was the case with his Pindaric *Odes*.

Whatever the date at which G. began the *Elegy*, it is certain that he sent the completed poem to Walpole on 12 June 1750. According to Mason, *Memoirs* p. 211, Walpole's 'good taste was too much charmed with it to suffer him to withold the sight of it from his acquaintance; accordingly it was shewn about for some time in manuscript . . . and received with all the applause it so justly merited'. The rapidity with which the poem had made its way in the fashionable world can be seen from the occasion for which, later in the summer, G. wrote his *Long Story* (see headnote, p. 142). G. himself described with mixed feelings the success of the MS circulation of the *Elegy* when he sent a copy to his friend Thomas Wharton on 18 Dec. 1750 (*Corresp* i 335): 'the Stanza's, wch I now enclose to you, have had the Misfortune by M^r W:^s Fault to be made still more publick, for wch they certainly were never meant, but it is too late to complain. they have been so applauded it is quite a Shame to repeat it. I mean not to be modest; but I mean, it is a shame for those, who have said such superlative Things about them, that I can't repeat them. I should have been glad, that you & two or three more People had liked them, wch would have satisfied my ambition on this Head amply.'

Widespread circulation of MS copies of the *Elegy* could have only one result and G. described it in a letter to Walpole on 11 Feb. 1751 (*Corresp* i 341–2): 'As you have brought me into a little Sort of Distress, you must assist me, I believe, to get out of it, as well as I can. yesterday I had the Misfortune of receiving a Letter from certain Gentlemen (as their Bookseller expresses it) who have taken the *Magazine of Magazines* into their Hands. they tell me, that an *ingenious* Poem, call'd, *Reflections* in a Country-Churchyard, has been communicated to them, wch they are printing forthwith: that they are inform'd, that the *excellent* Author of it is I by name, & that they beg not only his *Indulgence*, but the *Honor of his Correspondence*, &c: as I am not at all disposed to be either so indulgent, or so correspondent, as they desire; I have but one bad Way left to escape the Honour they would inflict upon me. & therefore am obliged to desire you would make Dodsley print it immediately (wch may be done in less than a Week's time) from your Copy, but without my Name, in what Form is most convenient for him, but in his best Paper & Character. he must correct the Press himself, & print it without any Interval between the Stanza's, because the Sense is in some Places continued beyond them; & the Title must be, *Elegy*, wrote in a Country Church-yard. if he would add a Line or two to say it came into his Hands by Accident, I should like it better.' After suggesting two improvements to the text he had sent Walpole the preceding June, G. continued:

'If you behold the Mag: of Mag:ˢ in the Light that I do, you will not refuse to give yourself this Trouble on my Account, wᶜʰ you have taken of your own Accord before now.' As a postscript he added: 'If Dodsley don't do this immediately, he may as well let it alone.'

G. was understandably reluctant that his new poem should be first published in *The Magazine of Magazines*, a recently established and undistinguished periodical edited by William Owen. Both Walpole and Dodsley responded to his demand for immediate publication and the *Elegy* appeared on 15 Feb. 1751, as a quarto pamphlet, price 6d. Considering the haste with which it had been printed, the first edn. was comparatively well produced, in spite of a number of *errata* which irritated G. The title-page was embellished by woodcuts of skulls, cross-bones and other symbols of mortality, commonly used for bourgeois funeral elegies since the 16th century. J. W. Draper has some interesting remarks on this matter in *The Funeral Elegy and the Rise of English Romanticism* (New York, 1929) pp. 309–11, although it may be doubted whether these decorations relate the *Elegy* very firmly to that particular genre. If G. did not choose them himself, he apparently did not object to them, for Dodsley retained them for the twelve quarto edns of the *Elegy* published up to 1763.

In accordance with G.'s wishes, Dodsley prefixed to the *Elegy* a short 'Advertisement' written by Walpole:

'The following POEM came into my hands by Accident, if the general Approbation with which this little Piece has been spread, may be call'd by so slight a term as Accident. It is this Approbation which makes it unnecessary for me to make any Apology but to the Author: As he cannot but feel some Satisfaction in having pleas'd so many Readers already, I flatter myself he will forgive my communicating that Pleasure to many more.
                                                              The EDITOR.'

Since the investigation of the relevant dates by R. Straus, *Robert Dodsley* (1910) p. 341, it has been assumed that Dodsley's edn of the *Elegy* won the race for publication by only one day. On 16 Feb. 1751 the *General Advertiser* announced that *The Magazine of Magazines* was 'This morning published. To be continued on the 16th of Every Month'. Another advertisement three days later listed among its contents 'Stanzas written in a Country Church-Yard. By Mr Gray, of Peter-House, Cambridge'. Whether the *Magazine* was actually published on 16 Feb. has, however, been questioned by M. Rothkrug in *Papers in Honour of Andrew Keogh* (New Haven, 1938) pp. 351–2, who pointed out that, although Owen habitually advertised his periodical on the 16th of each month, the last dated entries in each number indicate that it cannot have been published before the end of the month: e.g. in the Feb. number the last item in the Obituary and the 'Last Notice' are dated 28 Feb. Unless there were different issues of the *Magazine*, some containing later items of news, it must be assumed that the race for publication, whatever Owen's advertisements meant, was not as breathless as has been believed.

The advertisement in the *General Advertiser* of 19 Feb. meant that G. did did not retain the anonymity for which he hoped for long; otherwise he was satisfied that the best had been made of the situation. On 20 Feb. he wrote to thank Walpole for his part in the publication (*Corresp* i 342–3): 'You have indeed conducted with great decency my little *misfortune*: you have taken a paternal care of it, and expressed much more kindness than could have been expected from so near a relation. But we are all frail; and I hope to do as much for you another time. Nurse Dodsley has given it a pinch or two in the cradle, that (I doubt) it will bear the marks of as long as it lives. But no matter: we have ourselves suffered under her hands before now; and besides, it will only look the more careless, and by *accident* as it were. I thank you for your advertisement, which saves my honour, and in a manner *bien flatteuse pour moi*, who should be put to it even to make myself a compliment in good English.' G. informed Walpole of the 'chief errata' in the 1st edn in a letter of 3 March 1751 (*Corresp* i 344), and a number of corrections were made in the 3rd of Dodsley's quarto edns, published on 14 March. G. also inserted in this edn an additional stanza (usually known as the 'Redbreast' stanza; see l. 116 *n*) immediately before the 'Epitaph'. It was omitted once more in the 8th edn in 1753, when other corrections were made, and thereafter. G.'s original instructions that there should be no interval between the stanzas was followed in Dodsley's twelve quartos; but G. had decided to separate them as early as 1753 when the *Elegy* was published with Bentley's *Designs* and did not change his mind in the 1768 *Poems*. Mason duly separated the stanzas in 1775 but, oddly enough, in the 2nd edn of this work—having perhaps rediscovered G.'s original directions—printed the lines continuously.

The success of the *Elegy* was remarkable. *The Monthly Review* iv 309, for Feb. 1751 (published at the end of the month), commented that 'This excellent little piece is so much read, and so much admired by every body, that to say more of it would be superfluous'. John Hill, in the first of his series of contributions to the *Daily Advertiser* entitled 'The Inspector' on 5 March 1751 praised the *Elegy* enthusiastically, asserting that it 'comes nearer the manner of Milton than any thing that has been published since the time of that poet' and comparing it favourably with *Lycidas*. In 'The Inspector' No. 4 he printed a complimentary poem to the author of the *Elegy* by 'Musaphil'. The 4th quarto edn of G.'s poem had been published by 7 April and there was a 5th before the end of 1751. By 1763 twelve edns based on Dodsley's quarto had appeared. Inevitably the literary periodicals felt free to publish so celebrated a poem and, apart from the *Magazine of Magazines*, it had appeared in the *London Mag.*, the *True Briton* and the *Scots Mag.* by April 1751. M. Rothkrug, in the article mentioned above, pointed out that the *Elegy* also appeared in *Poems on Moral and Divine Subjects, by Several Celebrated English Poets* (Glasgow, 1751); and confirmed that, as had been suspected but not established, it had been published in the *Grand Magazine of Magazines* in April 1751. Apart from these two publications, the frequent appearances of the *Elegy* in G.'s lifetime are described in detail by F. G. Stokes

in his edn of the *Elegy* (Oxford, 1929). Stokes, *Times Lit. Supp.* 1937,
p. 92, made an addition to his bibliography of the poem when he noted the
inclusion of ll. 1–92 in the 4th edn of a volume of *Miscellaneous Pieces*,
apparently published in 1752 by R. Goadby and W. Owen, the publisher
of the *Magazine of Magazines*. See A. Anderson, *The Library*, 5th series, xx
(1965) 144–8, for a refutation of Stokes's argument for the importance of this
text, which was probably not printed in fact until late 1753.

In spite of, or perhaps because of, its popularity, G. rarely mentioned the
Elegy after its publication. He made a few comments on it in a letter to
Christopher Anstey, who published a Latin translation of the poem in
1762 (*Corresp* ii 748–9) but otherwise tended to be cynical about its celebrity.
During a visit to Scotland in 1765, he spoke to Dr John Gregory of the
Elegy: 'which he told me, with a good deal of acrimony, owed its pop-
ularity entirely to the subject, and that the public would have received it
as well if it had been written in prose' (Sir William Forbes, *Life of James
Beattie* (1806) i 83). Mason also believed this to be G.'s opinion, as he recalled
in his 'Memoirs of William Whitehead', in Whitehead's *Poems* iii (1788)
84: 'It spread, at first, on account of the affecting and pensive cast of
its subject, just like Hervey's Meditations on the Tombs. Soon after its
publication, I remember that, sitting with Mr. Gray in his College apart-
ment, he expressed to me his surprise at the rapidity of its sale. I replied:
"*Sunt Lachrymae rerum, mentem mortalia tangunt.*" He paused awhile, and
taking his pen, wrote the line on the title of a printed copy of it lying on
his table. "This," said he, "shall be its future motto." "Pity," cryed I, "that
Dr. Young's Night Thoughts have preoccupied it." "So," replied he,
"indeed, it is." He had still more reason to think I had hinted at the true
cause of its popularity, when he found how very different a reception his
two odes at first met with.'

Yet if G. at times disliked being a popular author, the 'affecting and pensive'
Mr Gray, he was not entirely indifferent to the *Elegy's* success. A marginal
note (apparently added to from time to time) in the transcript of the poem
in his Commonplace Book lists, with evident satisfaction, the various edns
it passed through, as well as the two Latin translations by Lloyd and Anstey.
And he can hardly have been unimpressed by the spate of imitations, paro-
dies and translations into other languages which was already in full flow in
his own lifetime; see Northup, *Bibliography of G.* (1917) pp. 123–45, H. W.
Starr's continuation (1953) pp. 33–8, and W. P. Jones, 'Imitations of G.'s
Elegy, 1751–1800', *Bulletin of Bibliography* xxiii (1963) 230–2. This aspect of
the *Elegy's* popularity and influence can be illustrated by John Langhorne's
remarks, in his review of *An Elegy, Written among the Tombs in Westminster
Abbey* (*Monthly Review* xxvi (1762) 356–8), on the number of G.'s imitators:
'An Undertaker was never followed by a more numerous or a more ridi-
culous tribe of mourners, than he has been; nor is the procession yet over,
for, behold, here is another Gentleman in black, with the same funereal
face, and mournful ditty; with the same cypress in his hand, and affecting
sentence in his mouth, viz. *that we must all die*! Hark! the Dirge begins.'

Langhorne's next review was of Edward Jerningham's *The Nunnery, an Elegy, in Imitation of the Elegy in a Churchyard.*

The first notable criticism of the *Elegy* did not appear until the 1780s. Johnson's brief but eloquent tribute in the *Lives of the Poets* (1781) was followed in more senses than one in 1783 by John Young's *Criticism of the Elegy* (2nd edn, 1810), a detailed discussion of the poem in a manner deliberately imitating Johnson's. There is also a chapter on the *Elegy* in John Scott's *Critical Essays* (1785) pp. 185–246. Discussion of the poem in the next century tended to be pre-occupied with such matters as G.'s sources, the location of the churchyard and G.'s relationship to the 'Age of Reason', and to attempt little more critically than general appreciation of G.'s eloquence, along the lines of Johnson's tribute. Some recent discussions of the poem, in addition to those mentioned above, which should be consulted are: Roger Martin, *Essai sur Thomas Gray* (Paris, 1934) pp. 409–36; William Empson, *Some Versions of Pastoral* (1935) p. 4; Cleanth Brooks. *The Well Wrought Urn* (1949) pp. 96–113; F. W. Bateson, *English Poetry: A Critical Introduction* (1950) pp. 181–93; and three essays by Ian Jack, B. H. Bronson and Frank Brady in *From Sensibility to Romanticism*, ed. F. W. Hilles and H. Bloom (1965) pp. 139–89. Amy L. Reed's *The Background to Gray's Elegy* (New York, 1924), investigates melancholy as a subject in earlier eighteenth-century poetry, but does not throw a great deal of light on the poem itself.

The crucial fact about the poem, of which by no means all discussions of the *Elegy* take account, is that we possess two distinct versions of it: the version which originally ended with the four rejected stanzas in the Eton MS, and the familiar, revised and expanded version. Many of the difficulties in the interpretation of the poem can be clarified if the two versions are examined in turn. As has been stated above, Mason's assertion that the first version of the poem ended with the rejected stanzas appears to be fully justified. In this form the *Elegy* is a well-constructed poem, in some ways more balanced and lucid than in its final version. The three opening stanzas brilliantly setting the poem and the poet in the churchyard, are followed by four balanced sections each of four stanzas, dealing in turn with the lives of the humble villagers; by contrast, with the lives of the great; with the way in which the villagers are deprived of the opportunities of greatness; and by contrast, with the crimes inextricably involved in success as the 'thoughtless world' knows it, from which the villagers are protected. The last three stanzas, balancing the opening three, return to the poet himself in the churchyard, making clear that the whole poem has been a debate within his mind as he meditates in the darkness, at the end of which he makes his own choice about the preferability of obscure innocence to the dangers of the 'great world'. (It is the personal involvement of the poet and his desire to share the obscure destiny of the villagers in this version of the poem which make Empson's ingenious remarks in *Some Versions of Pastoral* ultimately irrelevant and misleading.)

Underlying the whole structure of the first version of the *Elegy*, reinforcing the poet's rejection of the great world and supplying many details of thought and phrasing, are two celebrated classical poems in praise of rural retirement from the corruption of the court and city: the passage beginning *O fortunatos nimium* in Virgil's *Georgics* ii 458 ff and Horace's second *Epode*, (*Beatus ille* . . .). For a study of the pervasive influence of these poems on English poetry in the seventeenth- and eighteenth-centuries, see Maren-Sofie Røstvig, *The Happy Man* (2 vols, Oslo, 1954–58). In the concluding 'rejected' stanzas of the first version of the *Elegy* the classical praise of retirement is successfully blended with the Christian consolation that this world is nothing but vanity and that comfort for the afflicted will come in the next, although G.'s handling of the religious theme is very restrained. His tact and unobtrusiveness are all the more marked when his poem is compared with the emotional, even melodramatic, effects to which the other 'graveyard' practitioners–Young, Blair and Hervey–are prepared to resort when handling the same themes. The appendix to the poem (see p. 140), giving some parallels between these final stanzas and Hervey in particular, will suggest G.'s relationship to the religious meditators, but he shares none of their cemetery horrors and emotional over-indulgence. The classical or 'Augustan' restraint and balance which preserved him from such excesses is a strength which is manifested similarly in the balanced structure of the poem as a whole, as well as in the balancing effect of the basic quatrain unit.

The conclusion of the first version of the *Elegy* ultimately failed to satisfy G., partly perhaps because it was too explicitly personal for publication, but also no doubt because its very symmetry and order represented an over-simplification of his own predicament, of the way he saw his own life and wished it to be seen by society. A simple identification with the innocent but uneducated villagers was mere self-deception. G.'s continuation of the poem may lack some of the clarity, control and authority of the earlier stanzas, but it does represent a genuine attempt to redefine and justify his real relationship with society more accurately by merging it with a dramatisation of the social role played by poetry or the Poet. As G. starts to rewrite the poem, the simple antitheses of rich and poor, of vice and virtue, of life and death, which underlay the first version, are replaced by a preoccupation with the desire to be remembered after death, a concern which draws together both rich and poor, making the splendid monuments and the 'frail memorials' equally pathetic. This theme, which runs counter to the earlier resignation to obscurity and the expectation of 'eternal peace' hereafter, leads G. to contemplate the sort of ways in which he, or the Poet into whom he projects himself, may be remembered after his death, and the assessments he gives in the words of the 'hoary-headed swain' and of the 'Epitaph' (not necessarily meant to be identical) also evaluate the role of poetry in society. The figure of the Poet is no longer the urban, urbane, worldly, rational Augustan man among men, with his own place in society; what G. dramatises is the poet as outsider, with an uneasy consciousness of a sensibility and imagination at once unique and burdensome. The lack of social function so apparent in English poetry of the mid- and late eighteenth-century is constantly betrayed by its search for inspiration in the past. Significantly, G.'s description of the lonely, melancholy poet is riddled with phrases and diction borrowed from Spenser, Shakespeare and Milton. The texture of these stanzas is fanciful, consciously 'poetic', archaic in tone.

If the swain's picture of the lonely Poet is respectful but puzzled, emphasising the unique and somehow valuable sensibility which characterises him, the 'Epitaph', from a different standpoint, assesses that sensibility as the source of such social virtues as pity and benevolence (see l. 120n). G.'s Pindaric *Odes* of the 1750s were to show his continuing preoccupation with the subject of the function of poetry in society: for all his assertions of its value, the deliberate obscurity of the poems themselves betrays G.'s own conviction that poetry could not and perhaps should not any longer attempt to communicate with society as a whole. The central figure of *The Bard* himself is a not totally unpredictable development of the Poet at the end of the *Elegy*: more defiant in his belief that poetry and liberty in society are inseparably involved with each other and his awareness of the forces which are hostile to poetry; equally isolated and equally, if more spectacularly, doomed.

Two marginal problems associated with the *Elegy* may be mentioned in conclusion. The early nineteenth-century tradition that General Wolfe, on the night before the capture of Quebec from the French in 1759, declared, 'I would rather have been the author of that piece than beat the French tomorrow', is examined in detail by F. G. Stokes in an appendix to his edn of the *Elegy* (Oxford, 1929) pp. 83–8. Stokes also deals in another appendix (pp. 89–92), with the tiresome question of 'The Locality of the Churchyard'. Not surprisingly, no definite identification of the churchyard can be made, in spite of the number of candidates for the honour. (In his own lifetime, G. was already having to deny that he had been describing a churchyard he had never visited.) Anyone versed in the 'graveyard' poetry and prose of the mid-eighteenth-century will be satisfied that G. borrowed the traditional apparatus of his churchyard from no particular location.

Three MSS of the *Elegy* have survived. The earliest, the Eton MS, has already been described. (A facsimile of this MS and of the 1st edn of the *Elegy*, was published with an introduction by George Sherburn by the Augustan Reprint Society, Pub. No. 31, Los Angeles, 1951.) The MS sent to Walpole in June 1750 from which the 1st edn was presumably printed is not extant but it was probably based on the transcript of the poem in G.'s Commonplace Book (ii 617–18). The third MS, sent to Wharton on 18 Dec. 1750, is in the British Museum (Egerton MS 2400). This MS appears from its text to be later than that in the Commonplace Book. The text followed here is that printed in *1753*, which contains G.'s final revisions, the proofs of which he evidently corrected (*Corresp* i 364) and from which he directed the text in *1768* to be printed. Variants are given from the three MSS, the quarto edns printed by Dodsley (of which G. significantly 'corrected' the 3rd and 8th, although changes occur in other edns and

G.'s 'correction' did not remove all *errata*), Dodsley's *Collection* iv (1755), and the Foulis edn of the 1768 *Poems*.

> The curfew tolls the knell of parting day,
> The lowing herd wind slowly o'er the lea,
> The ploughman homeward plods his weary way,
> And leaves the world to darkness and to me.

¶ 17.1. In a letter to Bedingfield in Aug. 1756 (*Corresp* ii 477) and in *1768* G. acknowledged his debt to Dante, *Purgatorio* viii 5–6: *se ode squilla di lontano, | che paia il giorno pianger che si muore* (from afar he hears the chimes which seem to mourn for the dying day). He may have felt obliged to do so publicly as a result of Norton Nicholls's discovery of the debt: see *Corresp* iii 1297. Nicholls added: 'He acknowledged the imitation & said he had at first written "tolls the knell of *dying* day" but changed it to *parting* to avoid the *concetto*.' G.'s opening quatrain is also reminiscent of *Inferno* ii 1–3: *Lo giorno se n'andava, e l'aer bruno | toglieve gli animai, che sono in terra, | dalle fatiche loro; ed io sol uno* (The day was departing, and the brown air taking the animals, that are on earth, from their toils; and I, one alone ....); and see Petrarch, *Canzone 50* (*Ne lastagion che 'l ciel rapido inclina*).

curfew] Johnson (citing Cowel) described it as: 'An evening-peal, by which [William] the conqueror willed, that every man should rake up his fire, and put out his light; so that in many places, at this day, where a bell is customarily rung towards bed time, it is said to ring *curfew*.' Such a bell still rang in Cambridge at 9 p.m. G. probably remembered 'I hear the far-off *Curfeu* sound', *Il Penseroso* 73. But Shakespeare has 'To hear the solemn curfew', *Tempest* V i 40 and uses the word on three other occasions. It also occurs in Thomson, *Liberty* iv 755 and *n*; and in T. Warton, *Pleasures of Melancholy* (1747) 282–3: 'Where ever to the curfew's solemn sound / Listening thou sit'st.' Cp. also Collins's 'simple bell', *Ode to Evening* 38 (see p. 466). Shakespeare has 'A sullen bell / Remembered tolling a departing friend', *2 Henry IV* I i 102–3; Dryden, 'That tolls the knell for their departed sense', *Prologue to Troilus and Cressida* 22; and Young, 'It is the *Knell* of my departed Hours', *Night Thoughts* i 58.

2. *wind*] winds *edd* 1–7.   *lowing herd*] A common phrase: e.g. Pope, *Odyssey* x 485–7: 'As from fresh pastures and the dewy fields ... / The lowing herds return'; Cowley's imitation of *Horace*, *Epode II* 15 and of *Virgil*, *Georgic II* 20; Prior, *Solomon* ii 414 and Pope, *Spring* 86.   *lea*] In 1748 Thomson had felt it necessary to include this word ('a Piece of Land, or Meadow') in the list of 'obsolete Words' at the end of *The Castle of Indolence*.

3. Thomas Warton noted in Milton's *Poems on Several Occasions* (1785) p. 176 *n*, of *Comus* 291–2 ('what time the labour'd Oxe / In his loose traces from the furrow came'): 'This is classical. But the return of oxen or horses from the plough, is not a natural circumstance of an English evening. In England the ploughman always quits his work at noon. Gray, therefore, with Milton,

5   Now fades the glimmering landscape on the sight,
    And all the air a solemn stillness holds,

painted from books and not from the life, where in describing the departing
day-light he says . . .' This statement about the timetable of English plough-
men was challenged in the *Gentleman's Mag.* lvi (1786) 293–4 and 396–7.
The subject was reopened in *Notes and Queries* (1890) 7th series, ix 468
and x 18–19, 117; and again in 10th series, xii (1909) 309, 389–91. Although
the usual conclusion of these discussions was that the habits of ploughmen
varied in different parts of England, Warton was no doubt right in suggest-
ing that G. had classical sources in mind: for example, Virgil, *Eclogues* ii
66–7: *aspice, aratra iugo referunt suspensa iuvenci,* / *et sol crescentis decedens
duplicat umbras* (See, the bullocks drag home by the yoke the hanging plough,
and the retiring sun doubles the lengthening shadows); and Horace, *Odes*
III vi 41–3: *Sol ubi montium* / *mutaret umbras et iuga demeret* / *bobus fatigatis*
(When the sun shifted the shadows of the mountain sides and lifted the yoke
from the weary steers). Cp. Roscommon's imitation of this *Ode* 58–60,
which G. also seems to echo in ll. 25–8: 'And after the declining sun / Had
changed the shadows, and their task was done, / Home with their weary
team they took their way . . .' Cp. also Horace, *Epodes* ii 63, and for paral-
lels in earlier English poetry, see Pope, *Odyssey* xiii 39–42: 'As the tired
ploughman, spent with stubborn toil, / Whose oxen long have torn the fur-
rowed soil, / Sees with delight the sun's declining ray, / When home with
feeble knees he bends his way'; A. Philips, *Pastorals* ii 135–8: 'And now
behold the sun's departing ray, / O'er yonder hill, the sign of ebbing day: /
With songs the jovial hinds return from plough; / And unyok'd heifers,
loitering homeward, low'; Gay, *Rural Sports* i 91–2, 99–100, 105–6: 'Or
when the ploughman leaves the task of day, / And trudging homeward
whistles on the way . . . / Engaged in thought, to Neptune's bounds I stray,
/ To take my farewell of the parting day . . . / Here pensive I behold the
fading light, / And o'er the distant billow lose my sight.' See also Gay,
Shepherd's Week iii 19–22, 115–18, and J. Warton, *Ode to Evening* 2–4:
'Whose soft approach the weary woodman loves, / As homeward bent to
kiss his prattling babes, / He jocund whistles through the twilight groves.'
Spenser, *Faerie Queene* VI vii 39, 1, has 'And now she was uppon the weary
way'.

4. Petrarch, *Canzoniere* 223 1–2: *Quando 'l sol in mar l'aurato carro* / *E l'aer
nostro e la mia mente imbruna* (When the sun bathes his golden car in the ocean
and casts a shadow over our air and my mind).

5–8. The most striking parallel with this stanza occurs in Thomas Warton's
Five Pastoral Eclogues (1745) ii 20–3, 28–36: 'Then let me walk the twilight
meadows green, / Or breezy up-lands, near thick-branching elms, / While
the still landscape sooths my soul to rest, / And every care subsides to cal-
mest peace / . . . / The solitude that all around becalms / The peaceful air,
conspire[s] to wrap my soul / In musings mild, and nought the solemn
scene / And the still silence breaks; but distant sounds / Of bleating flocks,

> Save where the beetle wheels his droning flight,
> And drowsy tinklings lull the distant folds;
>
> Save that from yonder ivy-mantled tower

that to their destin'd fold / The shepherd drives; mean-time the shrill-tun'd bell / Of some lone ewe that wanders from the rest, / Tinkles far off, with solitary sound; / The lowing cows . . .' In ll. 47–8 a 'weary reaper' appears: 'along the vale, / Whistling he home returns to kiss his babes' (see l. 24 below). The 'silence . . . save where' formula, in this stanza and the passage from Warton above, had become relatively common in descriptions of evening by the 1740s: e.g. Akenside, *Ode to Sleep* (1744) 18–20: 'No wakeful sound the moonlight valley knows, / Save where the brook its liquid murmur pours, / And lulls the waving scene to more profound repose'; Collins, *Ode to Evening* 9–12; and T. Warton Senior, *Poems* (1748) p. 117: 'Here what a solemn Silence reigns, / Save the Tinklings of a Rill.' Further examples are given in ll. 9–12n below.

5. Addison, *Account of the Greatest English Poets* 30–1: 'But when we look too near, the shades decay, / And all the pleasing landscape fades away'; and David Mallet, *The Excursion* (1728) i 235–7: ' . . . th'aerial landscape fades. / Distinction fails: and in the darkening west, / The last light quivering, dimly dies away.'

6. *all*] now *Eton*. Cp. William Broome, *Paraphrase of Job* 40: 'A solemn stillness reigns o'er land and seas.' The subject of 'holds' is 'stillness', the object 'air'.

7–8. *Macbeth* III ii 41–3: 'ere to black Hecate's summons / The shard-borne beetle with his drowsy hums / Hath rung night's yawning peal . . .'; and Dryden, *Indian Emperor* I i 119: 'Which drowsily like humming beetles rise.' Dryden twice has 'wheeling Flight', *Georgics* iv 803 and *Aeneid* xii 699. Thomson, *Spring* 695–6, has 'the white-winged plover wheels / Her sounding flight'.

7. *droning*] drony *edd 9–12, Dodsley, Foulis*.

8. *And*] Or *Eton, Wharton, Commonplace Book, edd 3–7*. Cp. Addison, *The Vestal* 14: 'In drowsy murmurs lull'd the gentle maid'.

9–12. Mallet, *Excursion* i 272–5, in a description of a church, 'where ivy twines / Its fatal green around': 'All is dread silence here, and undisturbed, / Save what the wind sighs, and the wailing owl / Screams solitary to the mournful moon, / Glimmering her western ray through yonder aisle'; T. Warton, *Pleasures of Melancholy* 32–7: 'While sullen sacred silence reigns around, / Save the lone screech-owl's note, who builds his bower / Amid the mouldering caverns, dark and damp, / Or the calm breeze, that rustles in the leaves / Of flaunting ivy, that with mantle green / Invests some wasted tower.'

9. *ivy-mantled*] See T. Warton in previous note and cp. 'the mantling Vine', *Par. Lost* iv 258; and 'ivy . . . / That mantling crept aloft', Mallet, *Amynta and Theodora* (1747) i 285–6.

10   The moping owl does to the moon complain
Of such as, wandering near her secret bower,
Molest her ancient solitary reign.

Beneath those rugged elms, that yew-tree's shade,
Where heaves the turf in many a mouldering heap,
15   Each in his narrow cell for ever laid,
The rude forefathers of the hamlet sleep.

The breezy call of incense-breathing morn,

10. Virgil, *Aeneid* iv 462–3 : *solaque culminibus ferali carmine bubo / saepe queri et longas in fletum ducere voces* (And alone on the house-tops with ill-boding song the owl would often complain, drawing out its lingering notes into a wail).   *moping*] Perhaps in imitation of Ovid, *Metamorphoses* v 550: *ignavus bubo* (slothful owl). G. may also have remembered *Par. Lost* xi 485–6: 'moaping Melancholie / And Moon struck madness', and Rowe, *Jane Shore* II i 6, describing night: 'Care only wakes, and moping pensiveness'. See also T. Warton above ll. 9–12 *n*, and Gay, *Shepherd's Week* iii 118: 'And the hoarse owl his woeful dirges sings.'

11. *wandering*] stray too *written above in Eton.*   *secret*] sacred *edd 1–2, 4b–8* (*noted as erratum by* G., *Corresp* i *344*).   The owl is often given a 'bower' by the poets: e.g. Spenser, *Ruines of Time* 130: 'For the Shriche-owle to build her balefull bowre'; Pope, *Dunciad* iv 11: 'the Owl forsook his bow'r'; *Winter* 143–4: 'Assiduous, in his bower, the wailing owl / Plies his sad song'; and T. Warton above, ll. 9–12 *n*. Spenser has 'secret bowre', *Faerie Queene* IV v 5, 4.

12. *Molest her ancient*] & pry into *written above in Eton.*

13. 'Or 'gainst the rugged bark of some broad Elm', *Comus* 354. Blair's churchyard also provides a yew, 'Cheerless, unsocial plant'; and 'a row of reverend elms, / . . . all ragged show', *The Grave* 22, 46–7.

14–16. Thomas Parnell, *A Night-Piece on Death* 29–32: 'Those Graves, with bending Osier bound, / That nameless heave the crumbled Ground, / Quick to the glancing Thought disclose, / Where *Toil* and *Poverty* repose.' Parnell's churchyard, l. 53, also has a 'black and fun'ral Yew'.

16. *hamlet*] Village *Eton, deleted.*

17. For ever sleep. the breezy Call of Morn, *Eton.*   Cp. *Par. Lost* ix 193–4: 'the humid Flowrs that breathd / Thir morning Incense'; and Pope, *Messiah* 24: 'With all the incence of the breathing Spring'.

17–20. This is the first of several passages which resemble John Dart's poem *Westminster Abbey* (1721), reprinted in his *Westmonasterium* [1723], and again (significantly) in 1742. Cp. Dart's meditations among the tombs (I iii), 'Where Musick cheers no more the rising Morn, / The Lark high tow'ring, nor the Winding-Horn; / Nor Thickets ecchoing with the vocal Train, / Who hail the Day, and rouze the sleepy Swain . . .'

The swallow twittering from the straw-built shed,
The cock's shrill clarion or the echoing horn,
20   No more shall rouse them from their lowly bed.

For them no more the blazing hearth shall burn,

18. The swallow] Or Swallow *Eton.*   *twittering*] A frequent epithet for
the swallow, probably in imitation of Virgil's *garrula* . . . *hirundo, Georgics*
iv 307, translated by Dryden, iv 434: 'Or Swallows twitter on the Chimney
Tops'. The swallows 'twitter cheerful' in Thomson, *Autumn* 846.   *straw-
built*] A compound sanctioned by Milton: 'thir Straw-built Cittadel', *Par.
Lost* i 773. Cp. 'his little Straw-built Home' and 'Sudden he views some
Shepherd's straw-built Cell', T. Warton Senior, *Poems* (1748) pp. 106, 186.
18–19. Fletcher, *Faithful Shepherdess* IV iv: 'Dearer than swallows love the
early morn, / Or dogs of chase the sound of merry horn.'
19. The cock's . . . or the] Or Chaunticleer so shrill or *Eton.*   *or*] & *Com-
monplace Book, Wharton.* Cp. *L'Allegro* 49–50, 53–6: 'While the Cock with
lively din, / Scatters the rear of darknes thin / . . . / Oft list'ning how the
Hounds and horn / Chearly rouse the slumbring morn, / From the side of
some Hoar Hill, / Through the high wood echoing shrill'; 'the crested
Cock whose clarion sounds / The silent hours', *Par. Lost* vii 443–4; 'Chanti-
cleer with clarion shrill', J. Philips, *Cyder* i 753; 'the shrill horn's echoing
sounds', Gay, *Birth of the Squire* 17; 'This Midnight Centinel with Clarion
shrill', Young, *Night Thoughts* ii 3 (of the cock); 'The sounding Clarion and
the Sprightly Horn', Prior, *Colin's Mistakes* 13.
20. rouse] wake *edd 1–2, 4b, 6–7.*
21–4. Lucretius iii 894–6: *iam iam non domus accipiet te laeta, neque uxor /
optima nec dulces occurrent oscula nati / praeripere et tacita pectus dulcedine
tangent* (No longer now will your happy home give you welcome, no
longer will your best of wives and sweet children race to win the first kisses,
and thrill your heart to its depths with sweetness). Cp. Dryden's translation,
Latter Part of the 3rd Book of Lucretius 76–9: 'But to be snatch'd from all thy
household joys, / From thy Chast Wife, and thy dear prattling boys, /
Whose little arms about thy Legs are cast, / And climbing for a Kiss prevent
their Mothers hast'; and Thomson's imitation, *Winter* 311–6: 'In vain for
him the officious wife prepares / The fire fair-blazing and the vestment
warm; / In vain his little children, peeping out / Into the mingling storm,
demand their sire / With tears of artless innocence. Alas! / Nor wife nor
children more shall he behold.' Cp. also Horace, *Epodes* ii 39–40, 43–4:
*quod si pudica mulier in partem iuvet / domum atque dulces liberos . . . / sacrum
vestutis extruat lignis focum / lassi sub adventum viri* (But if a modest wife shall
do her part in tending home and children dear . . . piling the sacred hearth
with seasoned firewood against the coming of her weary husband). Cp. also
Dryden, *Georgics* ii 760–1 (translating Virgil, ii 523): 'His little Children
climbing for a Kiss, / Welcome their Father's late return at Night'; Thomson
adopted the first line of this couplet, *Liberty* iii 173; and see also J. Warton,
Ode to Evening 3 (quoted in l. *3n* above).

Or busy housewife ply her evening care:
No children run to lisp their sire's return,
Or climb his knees the envied kiss to share.

25 Oft did the harvest to their sickle yield,
Their furrow oft the stubborn glebe has broke;
How jocund did they drive their team afield!
How bowed the woods beneath their sturdy stroke!

Let not Ambition mock their useful toil,
30 Their homely joys and destiny obscure;

22. ply] Attend diligently to: cp. Milton, *Par. Lost* ix 201–2: 'Then commune how that day they best may ply / Their growing work.'   *care*] Responsibility, (domestic) duties, imitating Latin *cura*.
23. 'And stammering Babes are taught to lisp thy Name', Dryden, *Absalom and Achitophel* 243.
24. Or] Nor *Eton, Wharton, Commonplace Book.*   *envied*] coming *Eton, with* envied *written above, and* doubtful? *in margin.*
25. sickle] sickles *Wharton.*
26. stubborn glebe] Cp. Virgil, *Georgics* i 94: *glaebas qui frangit inertis.* The substance of the phrase is common in English poetry: cp. 'Commands / Th' unwilling Soil, and tames the stubborn Lands', Dryden, *Georgics* i 143–4; 'Or tames the Genius of the stubborn Plain', Pope, *Imitations of Horace, Sat.* II i 131; ''Tis mine to tame the stubborn plain, / Break the stiff soil', Gay, *Fables* II xv 89–90. See especially the earlier lines of the stanza by Roscommon quoted l. 3*n* above: 'Rough, hardy, season'd, manly, bold; / Either they dug the stubborn ground, / Or through hewn woods their weighty strokes did sound.'
27. they] they they *edd 1–2 (a misprint).*   Cp. 'Under the opening eye-lids of the morn, / We drove a field', *Lycidas* 26–7; and 'With me to drive a-Field the browzing Goats', Dryden, *Eclogues* ii 38. For 'their team', cp. the passage from Roscommon quoted in l. 3 *n* above.
28. 'pines bow low / Their heads', *Dunciad* ii 391–2; 'Low the woods / Bow their hoar head', Thomson, *Winter* 235–6; and cp. 'But to the roote bent his sturdy stroke', Spenser, *Shepheardes Calender,* 'Feb.' 201; Dryden, *Georgics* iii 638–9: 'Take, Shepherd take, a plant of stubborn Oak; / And labour him with many a sturdy stroke'; and 'And stood the sturdy Stroaks of lab'ring Hinds', Dryden, *Aeneid* ii 847.
29–32. Cp. Thomson, after describing 'laborious man' at work in the fields, *Spring* 52–4: 'Nor, ye who live / In luxury and ease, in pomp and pride, / Think these lost themes unworthy of your ear.' As Tovey argues, the rhymes in this quatrain were probably exact in G.'s time. Johnson rhymes *smile/toil* in *London* 222–3.
29. useful] *underlined in Eton with* homely *in margin.*
30. homely] rustic *Eton.*

Nor Grandeur hear, with a disdainful smile,
The short and simple annals of the poor.

The boast of heraldry, the pomp of power,
And all that beauty, all that wealth e'er gave,
35   Awaits alike the inevitable hour.

31-2. Cp. Pope's note to *Iliad* xiii 739, where he discusses 'Similes taken
from the Ideas of a rural Life': 'since these Arts are fallen from their ancient
Dignity, and become the Drudgery of the lowest People, the Images of
them are likewise sunk into Meanness.'

33-6. This quatrain seems to have been inspired by four lines in a *Monody
on the Death of Queen Caroline* by G.'s friend Richard West (reprinted in
Dodsley's *Collection* (1748) ii 269 ff.): 'Ah me! what boots us all our boasted
power, / Our golden treasure, and our purpled state, / They cannot ward
th'inevitable hour, / Nor stay the fearful violence of fate.' But the sentiment
occurs frequently in Horace, e.g. *Odes* I iv 13-4: *pallida Mors aequo pulsat pede
pauperum tabernas / regumque turres* (Pale Death with foot impartial knocks
at the poor man's cottage and at princes' palaces); I xxviii 15-6: *sed omnes
una manet nox, / et calcanda semel via leti* (But a common night awaiteth
every man, and Death's path must be trodden once for all); and II xvii
32-4: aequa tellus / pauperi recluditur / regumque pueris (For all alike doth Earth
unlock her bosom–for the poor man and for princes' sons). Cp. also
Cowley, translation of *Horace, Odes III i* 15-16, 21: 'Beauty, and strength,
and wit, and wealth, and pow'r, / Have their short flourishing hour / . . . /
Alas! Death mows down all with an impartial hand'; Mallet, *Excursion*
i 290-2 'Proud greatness, too, the tyranny of power, / The grace of beauty,
and the force of youth, / And name and place, are here–for ever lost!'; and
Dart, *Westminster Abbey* I xviii (see ll. 17–20 *n* above): 'To prove that *nor the
Beauteous*, nor the *Great*, / *Nor Form*, nor *Pow'r*, are *Wards secure from* Fate.'
G.'s lines have also been compared to Edward Phillips's Preface to *Theatrum
Poetarum* (1675), in J. E. Spingarn, *Critical Essays of the 17th Century* (1908–9)
ii 258 (and cp. l. *59n* below): 'no wonder if the memories of such Persons
as these sink with their Bodys into the earth, and lie buried in profound
obscurity and oblivion, when even among those that tread the paths of
Glory and Honour, those who have signaliz'd themselves either by great
actions in the field or by Noble Arts of Peace or by the Monuments of their
written Works more lasting sometimes than Brass or Marble, very many . . .
have fallen short of their deserved immortality of Name, and lie under a
total eclipse.'

33. Akenside, *Pleasures of Imagination* ii 729–30: 'the pomp / Of public
pow'r, the majesty of rule'.

35. This line has caused intermittent argument since John Young pointed
out in his *Criticism on the Elegy* (1783) pp. 27–8, that if the text reads 'Awaits'
the subject must be 'hour'; but that the reading 'Await' makes the two

> The paths of glory lead but to the grave.
>
> Nor you, ye Proud, impute to these the fault,
> If Memory o'er their tomb no trophies raise,
> Where through the long-drawn aisle and fretted vault
> *40* The pealing anthem swells the note of praise.

preceding lines the subject. G. undoubtedly intended 'Awaits', with 'hour' as the subject, in spite of the fact that 'await' appears in *edd 9–12*, in Dodsley's *Collection* in 1755, and in *1775*. For some discussion see *Notes and Queries* clxxxiv (1943) 102–3, 174, 204, 237–8.

36. paths . . . lead] path . . . leads *Foulis.* Cp. 'With equal steps the paths of glory trace', Pope, *Odyssey* i 392; 'once trod the ways of glory', *Henry VIII* III ii 435 (see l. 44 *n*).

37–8. Eton, Wharton, Commonplace Book and edd 1–7 have: Forgive, ye Proud, th'involuntary Fault / If Memory to These no Trophies raise, *The present reading is underlined in the margin of the Commonplace Book.*

37–40. The scene is still the churchyard, contrasting the humble graves with the splendid tombs and memorials inside the church itself or, perhaps more probably, inside a larger church elsewhere. Cp. Parnell's *Night-Piece on Death* 29–46, which describes in turn the 'nameless' graves; the 'flat smooth stones that bear a name' belonging to 'A middle race of mortals'; and (in this case, also in the churchyard) 'The marble tombs that rose on high, / Whose dead in vaulted arches lie, / Whose pillars swell with sculptured stones . . .'

37. Dryden, *Sigismonda and Guiscardo* 490–2: 'I wonder thou shouldst oversee / Superior Causes, or impute to me / The Fault of Fortune, or the Fates Decree.'

38. 'Till we with trophies do adorn thy tomb', *Titus Andronicus* I i 388.

39. fretted] Decorated with carved work in patterns. Cp. 'This majestical roof fretted with golden fire', *Hamlet* II ii 293; 'The Roof was fretted Gold', *Par. Lost* i 717; 'Wide Vaults appear, and Roofs of fretted Gold', Pope, *Temple of Fame* 137. G.'s spelling of 'aisle' ('isle') is also found in Pope: e.g. 'And Arches widen, and long Iles extend', *Temple of Fame* 265, and 'Long-sounding isles, and intermingled graves', *Eloisa to Abelard* 164. Cp. also Dart, *Westminster Abbey* I iv, xii (see ll. 17–20 *n*): 'The long resounding Isle, and hallow'd Choir' and 'the long Isles and vaulted Roofs resound'.

40. Cp. Milton, *Il Penseroso* 161, 163: 'There let the pealing Organ blow / . . . / In Service high, and Anthems cleer.' G.'s letter to Anstey, the translator of the *Elegy* into Latin, in 1761 (*Corresp* ii 749) makes it clear that he had organ music in mind. Cp. also Pope, *Eloisa to Abelard* 272: 'And swelling organs lift the rising soul'; and T. Warton, *Pleasures of Melancholy* 198–9: 'The many sounding organ peals on high, / The clear slow-dittied chaunt, or varied hymn'.

Can storied urn or animated bust
Back to its mansion call the fleeting breath?
Can Honour's voice provoke the silent dust,
Or Flattery soothe the dull cold ear of Death?

45   Perhaps in this neglected spot is laid
Some heart once pregnant with celestial fire;

41. J. Young, in his *Criticism on the Elegy* (1783) p. 31, complained that 'storied' needed explaining as meaning 'having stories figured upon it' i.e. inscribed. Cp. 'And storied Windows richly dight', *Il Penseroso* 159; 'The trophy'd arches, story'd halls', Pope, *Essay on Man* iv 303; 'the awful bust / And storied arch', Akenside, *Pleasures of Imagination* ii 735–6. *animated*] As if alive or breathing. Cp. Virgil, *Georgics* iii 34: *Stabunt et Parii lapides, spirantia signa* (Here too shall stand Parian marbles, statues that breathe); and *Aeneid* vi 847–8: *excudent alii spirantia mollius aera, / (credo equidem), vivos ducent de marmore voltus* (Others, I doubt not, shall beat out the breathing bronze with softer lines; shall from marble draw forth the features of life); and Pope, *Temple of Fame* 73: 'Heroes in animated Marble frown'. G. uses the conventional epithet ironically.

41–4. Richard Blackmore, 'On Fame', *Poems on Various Subjects* (1718) p. 307: 'Do's *Maro* smile, when we extol his Lays? / Or *Tully* listen in his Urn to Praise? / Do shouts of triumph sooth great *Caesar's* ear? / Or Fame, young *Ammon,* thy cold Ashes cheer?'

42. Il Penseroso 91–2: 'The immortal mind that hath forsook / Her mansion in this fleshly nook . . .'; Prior, *Ode to the Memory of Col. Villiers* 41, has 'fleeting breath'; and cp. also Dryden, *Threnodia Augustalis* 114–5: 'Once more the fleeting Soul came back / T'inspire the mortal Frame.'

43–4. Honour . . . Flattery] The contents of the epitaphs on the tombs of the great.

43. provoke] awake *Eton, with* provoke *in margin.* The sense is 'arouse to action, call forth', as Latin *provoco.* Cp. Pope, *Ode on St Cecilia's Day* 36: 'But when our Country's Cause provokes to Arms'.

44. Henry VIII III ii 434–4: 'When I am forgotten, as I shall be, / And sleep in dull cold marble.'

45–60. In *Eton* ll. 57–60 follow l. 48, but the figures 1 to 4 in the margin indicate the present order of the stanzas. Tovey cites Addison, *Spectator* No. 215: 'The Philosopher, the Saint, or the Hero, the Wise, the Good, or the Great Man, very often lie hid and concealed in a Plebean, which a proper Education might have disenterred, and have brought to Light.'

46. Par. Lost vi 483: 'pregnant with infernal flame'. Spenser, *Tears of the Muses* 391, and *Hymn in Honour of Love* 186, has 'celestiall fire'; and cp. Young, *Night Thoughts* vi 378–9: 'a soul, / Which boasts her lineage from celestial fire'.

Hands that the rod of empire might have swayed,
Or waked to ecstasy the living lyre.

But Knowledge to their eyes her ample page
50   Rich with the spoils of time did ne'er unroll;
Chill Penury repressed their noble rage,

47. *rod*] reins *Eton, Wharton, Commonplace Book,* edd 1–7. *Commonplace Book* has rod *in the margin.*   G. may have decided that there was something ludicrous about 'swaying' reins or have wished to avoid echoing 'Proud names who once the reins of empire held', Tickell, *On the Death of Mr Addison* 37, or 'command / The Reins of Empire with a steady Hand', Blackmore, *Nature of Man* (1711) p. 100.

48. *ecstasy*] Cp. 'Dissolve me into extasies', Milton, *Il Penseroso* 165, and 'hearken even to extasie', *Comus* 625; 'Till all my soul is bath'd in ecstasies', T. Warton, *Pleasures of Melancholy* 200 (after the lines cited in l. 40 *n* above). *waked . . . the living lyre*] Cp. Lucretius ii 412–3: *ac musaea mele, per chordas organici quae / mobilibus digitis expergefacta figurant* (melodies of music which harpers awaken and shape on the strings with nimble fingers); Cowley, *The Resurrection* 13: 'Begin the song and strike the living lyre'; Prior, *Carmen Seculare* 463: 'They strike the living Lyre'; Pope, *Windsor Forest* 279–80: 'where *Cowley* strung / His living Harp'.

49–52. Tovey compares Waller, *To Zelinda* 19–26, and points out that G.'s Cromwell (l. 60) was originally Caesar. Waller's lines deal with Caesar and Alexander: 'Great Julius, on the mountains bred, / A flock perhaps, or herd, had led: / He, that the world subdued, had been / But the best wrestler on the green. / 'Tis art, and knowledge, which draw forth / The hidden seeds of native worth'. See also Fourdrinier's frontispiece to Robert Dodsley's *A Muse in Livery* (1732) which depicts the poet reaching vainly up towards Happiness, Virtue and Knowledge, one hand being chained by Poverty to Misery, Folly and Ignorance, and one foot weighted down with Despair.

50. *unroll*] The image is of a scroll. Cp. 'Rich with the spoils of nature', Browne, *Religio Medici* I xiii; and 'For, rich with Spoils of many a conquer'd Land', Dryden, *Palamon and Arcite* ii 452.

51. *repressed*] had damp'd *Eton, with* depress'd repress'd *written above. repressed their rage*] Dryden was fond of the phrase: cp. *Hind and the Panther* 305; *Ovid's Metamorphoses* i 1055; and *Aeneid* x 970; but by 'rage' he meant anger. G. means rapture, ardour, inspiration (equivalent to the favourable sense of Latin *furor*). Cowley has 'noble rage' in *Davideis* Bk iv; and see Pope, *Windsor Forest* 291: 'Here noble *Surrey* felt the sacred Rage'; and *Prologue to Cato* 43: 'Be justly warm'd with your own native rage'; and Collins, *The Passions* 111. Thomson, *Winter* 597–601, has a passage which is close to G.'s meaning here and in the following stanzas: 'if doomed / In powerless humble fortune to repress / These ardent risings of the kindling soul, / Then, even superior to ambition, we / Would learn the private virtues'.

And froze the genial current of the soul.

Full many a gem of purest ray serene
The dark unfathomed caves of ocean bear:
55 Full many a flower is born to blush unseen
And waste its sweetness on the desert air.

Some village-Hampden that with dauntless breast

---

52. *genial*] Warm, creative. Ian Jack (see headnote) compares Virgil, *Georgics* ii 484: *frigidus obstiterit circum praecordia sanguis*, translated by Thomson, Preface to 2nd edn of *Winter*: 'If the cold current freezes round my heart'; see also *Agrippina* 177–8 (p. 42 above).

53. Cp. 'There is many a rich stone laid up in the bowels of the earth, many a fair pearl in the bosom of the sea, that never was seen, nor never shall be', Joseph Hall, *Works*, ed. P. Wynter, 1863, i 137.

54. Blackmore, *Alfred. An Epick Poem* (1723) p. 97: 'Thou mak'st the secret Chambers of the Deep / Thy Walks, where peaceful ancient Waters sleep, / And searchest dark unfathom'd Caves beneath.'

55–6. Many sources for this famous image have been suggested: W. Chamberlayne, *Pharonnida* (1659) IV v: 'Like beauteous flowers which vainly waste the scent / Of odours in unhaunted deserts'; Ambrose Philips, *Fable of Thule* 39–40: 'Like woodland flowers, which paint the desert glades, / And waste their sweets in unfrequented shades'; Pope, *Rape of the Lock* iv 157–8: 'There kept my Charms conceal'd from mortal Eye, / Like Roses that in Deserts bloom and die'; Young, *Universal Passion* v 229–32: 'In distant wilds, by human eyes unseen, / She rears her flowers and spreads her velvet green. / Pure gurgling rills the lonely desert trace, / And waste their music on the savage race'; Thomson, *Autumn* 211–13: 'A myrtle rises, far from human eye, / And breathes its balmy fragrance o'er the wild–/ So flourished blooming, and unseen by all'; Thomson, *Liberty* i 167–8: 'In vain, forlorn in wilds, the citron blows; / And flowering plants perfume the desert gale.' Cp. also Waller's *Go, Lovely Rose* 6–15; Racine, *Athalie* II ix 778–85; J. Armstrong, *The Oeconomy of Love* 120–1, suggested by J. D. Short, *Notes and Queries*, ccx (1965) 454. Images of both the gem and the flower occur in a canzone, *Chi di lagrime un fiume a gli occhi presta*, by Celio Magno, a minor sixteenth-century Italian poet. For other suggested parallels with his poetry in G., see *European Mag.* l (1806) 295.

56. 'The desert air', *Macbeth* IV iii 194.

57. *Hampden*] Cato *Eton*. Dryden has: 'with dauntless breast / Contemn the bad, and Emulate the best', *To Kneller* 79–80; and 'Stems a wild Deluge with a dauntless brest', *Eleonora* 362.

57–60. These lines on unfulfilled greatness among the villagers have been compared to Dryden, *Annus Mirabilis* 849–54: 'As when some dire Usurper Heav'n provides, / To scourge his Country with a lawless sway: / His birth, perhaps, some petty Village hides, / And sets his Cradle out of Fortune's

> The little tyrant of his fields withstood;
> Some mute inglorious Milton here may rest,
> 60   Some Cromwell guiltless of his country's blood.

way: // Till fully ripe his swelling fate breaks out, / And hurries him to mighty mischief on'; and Shenstone, *The Schoolmistress* (1745) st. xxvii–xxix, in which 'The firm fixed breast which fit and right requires, / Like Vernon's patriot soul', a potential Milton, and other great men are seen in embryo among the schoolchildren. Thomson's panegyric of England's 'sons of glory' in *Summer* 1488–91, 1493, includes: 'a steady More, / Who, with a generous though mistaken zeal, / Withstood a brutal tyrant's useful rage; / Like Cato firm . . . / A dauntless soul erect, who smiled on death.' Thomson goes on to mention in this passage (not expanded to this form until 1744) Hampden, l. 1515: 'Wise, strenuous, firm, of unsubmitting soul'; and Milton, ll. 1567–71. As is shown below, G.'s instances of greatness were originally classical in the Eton MS. The alteration to Hampden, Milton and Cromwell corresponds to the fact that the continuation of the poem after the original ending is markedly less classical and more English in character. But G. also wanted examples of greatness which had proved dangerous to society (as opposed to the innocence of the villagers) and the Civil War, 100 years earlier, provided him with three convenient examples. For all their individual qualities, these three men had been responsible in one way or another for bringing turmoil to their country. Without assenting to the identification of the churchyard with Stoke Poges, it is possible to accept Tovey's suggestion that G. may also have been influenced to some extent by the Buckinghamshire connections of Milton, who spent several early years at Horton, and Hampden, whose family home was at Great Hampden, where he was often visited by Cromwell.

58. *fields*] *written above* Lands *deleted in Commonplace Book.* G.'s meaning is best explained by a passage in Blair's *The Grave* 219–23: 'Here too the petty tyrant, / Whose scant domains geographer ne'er noticed, / And, well for neighbouring grounds, of arm as short, / Who fixed his iron talons on the poor, / And gripped them like some lordly beast of prey . . .'

59. *Milton*] Tully *Eton.* Cp. Virgil, *Aeneid* xii 397: *et mutas agitare inglorius artis* (and to ply, inglorious, the silent arts); *inglorius* also occurs in *Georgics* ii 486, in the passage (*O fortunatos nimium*) which underlies this central section of the poem (see ll. 67–72): *flumina amem silvasque inglorius* (may I love the waters and the woods, though fame be lost). (See l. 75 n.) See also E. Phillips, Preface to *Theatrum Poetarum* (see ll. 33–6 n): 'there is something of compassion due to extinguisht vertue, and the loss of many ingenuous, elaborate, and useful Works, and even the very names of some, who having perhaps been comparable to *Homer* for Heroic Poesy, or to *Euripides* for Tragedy, yet nevertheless sleep inglorious in the croud of the forgotten vulgar.'

60. *Cromwell*] Caesar *Eton.*

The applause of listening senates to command,
The threats of pain and ruin to despise,
To scatter plenty o'er a smiling land,
And read their history in a nation's eyes,

65   Their lot forbade: nor circumscribed alone
Their growing virtues, but their crimes confined;
Forbade to wade through slaughter to a throne,

61. Cp. *Agrippina* 77 (p. 36); and 'While listening senates hang upon thy tongue', Thomson, *Autumn* 15, and 'the listening senate', *Winter* 680; and Akenside, *To Sleep* 34–7: 'The rescued people's glad applause, / The listening senate and the laws / Bent on the dictates of Timoleon's tongue, / Are scenes too grand for fortune's private ways.'

62. Cp. Horace's description of *iustum et tenacem propositi virum* (the man tenacious of his purpose in a righteous cause), *Odes* III iii 7–8: *si fractus inlabatur orbis, / impavidum ferient ruinae* (Were the vault of heaven to break and fall upon him, its ruins would smite him undismayed).

63. Cp. *Education and Government* 17–18 (p. 93).

64. *read*] G. uses the word to mean 'discern', as in Shakespeare: e.g. 'Let not my sister read it in your eye' and 'let her read it in thy looks', *Comedy of Errors* III ii 9, 18. But the combination with 'history' makes it hard to exclude the more common modern sense.

65–6. Cp. G.'s comments on Plato's *Republic* Bk vi in his Commonplace Book i 340, quoted in headnote to *Education and Government* (p. 89), probably made in about 1748, especially the last sentence: 'every extraordinary Wickedness, every action superlatively unjust is the Product of a vigorous Spirit ill-nurtured; weak Minds are alike incapable of anything greatly good, or greatly ill.'

65. *lot*] Fate *Eton, with* Lot *written above.*

66. *growing*] struggling *Eton, with* growing *written above.*

67–72. Cp. Virgil's contrast of the 'happy husbandmen' with the ambitious citizen, *Georgics* ii 503–10: *sollicitant alii remis freta caeca, ruuntque / in ferrum, penetrant aulas et limina regum; / hic petit excidiis urbem miserosque penates, / ut gemma bibat et Sarrano dormiat ostro; / condit opes alius defossoque incubat auro; / hic stupet attonitus rostris; hunc plausus hiantem / per cuneos geminatus enim plebisque patrumque / corripuit; gaudent perfusi sanguine fratrum* (Others vex with oars seas unknown, dash upon the sword, or press into courts and the portals of kings. One wreaks ruin on a city and its hapless homes, that he may drink from a jewelled cup and sleep on Tyrian purple; another hoards up wealth and broods over buried gold; one is dazed and astounded by the Rostra; another, open-mouthed, is carried away by the plaudits of princes and of people, rolling again and again on the benches. Gleefully they steep themselves in their brothers' blood).

67. *wade through slaughter*] For the image see *Richard II* I iii 138; *King John* II i 42; *Macbeth* III iv 137; Pope, *Temple of Fame* 346–7: 'For thee whole

And shut the gates of mercy on mankind,

The struggling pangs of conscious truth to hide,
70 To quench the blushes of ingenuous shame,
Or heap the shrine of Luxury and Pride
With incense kindled at the Muse's flame.

Nations fill'd with Flames and Blood, / And swam to Empire thro' the
purple Flood'; Blair, *The Grave* 209–10: 'the mighty troublers of the
earth, / Who swam to sovereign rule through seas of blood'; and 631–2:
'Whilst deep-mouth'd slaughter . . . / Wades deep in blood new-spilt'.
68. And] Or Wharton, *Commonplace Book*. Cp. *III Henry VI* I iv 177:
'Open thy gate of mercy', and cp. *Henry V* III iii 10: 'The gates of mercy
shall be all shut up'; and Congreve, *Mourning Bride* III i: 'So did it tear the
ears of Mercy, from / His Voice, shutting the Gates of Pray'r against him.'
69–72. Young, *Ocean, An Ode* st. lvii–lviii: 'The public Scene / Of harden'd
Men / Teach me, O teach me to despise! / The *World* few know, / But to their
Woe, / Our *Crimes* with our *Experience* rise; // All tender Sense / Is banish'd
thence, / All maiden Nature's first Alarms; / What shock'd before, / Dis-
gusts no more, / And what disgusted has its Charms.'
69–70. 'And to suppress reluctant Conscience strive', Blackmore, *Poems*
(1718) p. 295.
70. Winter's Tale IV iv 67: 'Quench your blushes.'   *ingenuous shame*]
Neither word has its modern meaning. Cp. *ingenuus pudor,* Catullus lxi
79, and *puer ingenuique pudoris,* Juvenal, *Sat* xi 154. Johnson's definitions
confirm that G.'s meaning was close to the Latin *ingenuus*: natural, or noble
('Freeborn; not of servile extraction'–Johnson) or, combining these senses,
innately noble or honourable. Cp. also Johnson's definition of 'shame':
'The passion felt when reputation is supposed to be lost; the passion expres-
sed sometimes by blushes.'
71. Or heap] And at *Eton, with* crown *written above* at.   *shrine*] Shrines
Wharton.
72. With] Burn *Eton, deleted.   incense kindled at*] Incense hallowd in
Eton, with kindled at *written below.*
*72. After this line Eton has the following four stanzas, with an irregular vertical
line beside them in the margin:*

> The thoughtless World to Majesty may bow
> Exalt the brave, & idolize Success
> But more to Innocence their Safety owe
> Than Power & Genius e'er conspired to bless

> And thou, who mindful of the unhonour'd Dead
> Dost in these Notes thy [*corr to* their] artless Tale relate
> By Night & lonely Contemplation led
> To linger in the gloomy Walks of Fate

> Hark how the sacred Calm, that broods around
> Bids ev'ry fierce tumultuous Passion cease

Far from the madding crowd's ignoble strife
Their sober wishes never learned to stray;
75   Along the cool sequestered vale of life
They kept the noiseless tenor of their way.

In still small Accents whisp'ring from the Ground
A grateful Earnest of eternal Peace

No more with Reason & thyself at strife;
Give anxious Cares & endless Wishes room
But thro' the cool sequester'd Vale of Life
Pursue the silent Tenour of thy Doom.

Mason (*Poems* p. 109) states: 'And here the Poem was originally intended
to conclude, before the happy idea of the hoary-headed Swain, &c. sug-
gested itself to him. I cannot help hinting to the reader, that I think the third
of these rejected stanzas equal to any in the whole Elegy.' See also headnote,
p. 104, and for parallels with these stanzas, the Appendix (p. 140).

73–6. Cp. G.'s *Alcaic Ode* 17–20 (p. 317).

73. madding] Cp. William Drummond, *Sonnet xlix* 11: 'Far from the madding
worldling's hoarse discords'. Milton uses the word, *Par. Lost* vi 210. The
madding/cool antithesis also occurs in *Agrippina* 83 (p. 36). Cp. also Dryden,
Aeneid i 213–4: 'As when in Tumults rise th'ignoble Crowd, / Mad are their
Motions, and their Tongues are loud', and xii 1359: ''tis mean ignoble
Strife'; Dart, *Westminster Abbey* I viii (see ll. 17–20 n above): 'By thee secure,
we leave the Road of Strife, / And tread the pleasing silent Path of Life: /
Where unconcern'd we hear the Noise afar / Of wrangling Traveller's,
and the Din of War.'

74. learned] knew *Eton.* Cp. 'His soul proud Science never taught to stray',
Pope, *Essay on Man* i 102.

75. Cowley, *Imitation of Virgil, Georgics* II *458ff* 45–7: 'let woods and rivers
be / My quiet, though inglorious destiny: / In life's cool vale let my low
scene be laid.' Cp. also 'In life's low vale', Pope, *Epistles to Several Persons*
i 95; and 'O may I steal / Along the vale / Of humble life, secure from foes',
Young, *Ocean* st. lxi.

76. noiseless] silent *Eton, with* noiseless *written above.* Cp. Dryden (cited by
Johnson under 'noiseless'): 'So noiseless would I live, such death to find, /
Like timely fruit, not shaken by the wind, / But ripely dropping from the
sapless bough'; and Pope, *Temple of Fame* 330: 'The constant Tenour of
whose well-spent Days'. There may also be a curious reminiscence of
Essay on Criticism 240–1: 'Correctly cold, and regularly low, / That shunning
Faults, one quiet Tenour keep'. It seems more likely that G. was remembering
these passages than the parallel in Tacitus, *Agricola* vi 4, noted by J. C.
Maxwell, *Notes and Queries* cxcvi (1951) 262: *idem praeturae tenor et silentium*
(his praetorship followed the same quiet course). G. himself uses the phrase
serventque tenorem in his *Latin Verses at Eton* (p. 290). For the sense see also
Horace, *Epistles* I xviii 102–3: *Quid pure tranquillet, honos an dulce lucellum,* /

Yet even these bones from insult to protect
Some frail memorial still erected nigh,
With uncouth rhymes and shapeless sculpture decked,
80 Implores the passing tribute of a sigh.

Their name, their years, spelt by the unlettered muse,
The place of fame and elegy supply:
And many a holy text around she strews,
That teach the rustic moralist to die.

85 For who to dumb Forgetfulness a prey,
This pleasing anxious being e'er resigned,

an secretum iter et fallentis semita vitae (What gives you unruffled calm–honour,
or the sweets of dear gain, or a secluded journey along the pathway of a life
unnoticed?). Pope inscribed the second of these lines over his grotto.

77–84. Arthur Johnston, *Selected Poems of Gray and Collins* (1967) p. 44, cites
Swift's *Thoughts on Various Subjects* (*Works* (1735) vol i): 'There is in most
people a reluctance and unwillingness to be forgotten. We observe even
among the vulgar, how fond they are to have an inscription over their
grave. It requires but little philosophy to discover and observe that there is no
intrinsic value in all this; however, if it be founded in our nature, as an incite-
ment to virtue, it ought not to be ridiculed.'

79. With] *Written above a deletion in Eton, perhaps* In. Cp. Spenser, *Faerie
Queene* V v 37, 1: 'uncouth speach', and VI viii 18, 4: 'uncouth words';
and Philips, *Cyder* Bk ii: 'uncouth Rhythms'.

80. Pope, *Odyssey* xi 89–90: 'The tribute of a tear is all I crave, / And the
possession of a peaceful grave.'

81. Milton, *Comus* 174: 'unleter'd Hinds'.

82. elegy] Epitaph *Eton, Commonplace Book.*

84. Tickell, *On the Death of Mr Addison* 81–2: 'There taught us how to live;
and (oh! too high / The price for knowledge) taught us how to die.'

85–6. For] The link in G.'s thought is not clear, since the causal connection
implied could be with either the memorials or the texts in the previous stanza:
man's reluctance to be forgotten after death could have caused either the
inscriptions on the graves or the need to have texts on the graves to teach
those still living how to consider death. But these two lines are ambiguous
in themselves and could be read in three ways: 'For who, about to become a
prey to dumb forgetfulness (= oblivion)'; 'For who ever resigned this
being to dumb forgetfulness (= oblivion)'; and 'For who was already so
much the prey of forgetfulness (= insensibility) as to resign' etc. The first
of these readings seems most likely: for 'forgetfulness' as 'oblivion' see
Spenser, *Ruins of Time* 377–8: 'And them immortal make, which els would
die / In foule forgetfulnesse'; and *Visions of Bellay* i 3: 'the forgetfulnes of
sleepe'. See also *Par. Lost* ii 146–51: 'for who would loose, / Though full
of pain, this intellectual being, / Those thoughts that wander through

Left the warm precincts of the cheerful day,
Nor cast one longing lingering look behind?

On some fond breast the parting soul relies,
90   Some pious drops the closing eye requires;

Eternity, / To perish rather, swallowd up and lost / In the wide womb of uncreated night, / Devoid of sense and motion?'
87. Lucretius i 23: *dias in luminis oras* (the shining borders of light i.e. the created world); and *Par. Lost* iii 88: 'the Precincts of light'.   *day*] Equivalent to 'life', like Latin *lux*: e.g. Virgil, *Aeneid* iv 631: *invisam . . . lucem* (hateful life); and Lucretius v 989: *dulcia linquebant labentis lumina vitae* (they left the sweet light of lapsing life). Spenser has 'chearfull day', *Faerie Queene* I iii 27, 7 and II vii 29, 4; and *Colin Clout* 856; and Pope, *Odyssey* xi 116 and 570.
88. Rowe, *Fair Penitent* II i Song: 'Nor casts one pitying look behind'; and Blair, *The Grave* 358–61: 'How wishfully she [the soul] looks / On all she's leaving, now no longer her's! / A little longer, yet a little longer, / Oh! might she stay . . .'
89–90. Mitford cites Drayton, *Moses's Birth and Miracles* Bk i: 'It is some comfort to a wretch to die, / (If there be comfort in the way of death) / To have some friend or kind alliance by, / To be officious at the parting breath'. Cp. also C. Hopkins, 'Leander to Nero', *The Art of Love* (1709) p. 444: 'While on thy Lips I pour my parting Breath, / Look thee all o'er, and clasp thee close in Death; / Sigh out my Soul upon thy panting Breast.'
90. pious] 'Careful of the duties of a near relation' (Johnson). Cp. Latin *pius*: e.g. Ovid, *Tristia* IV iii 41–4: *spiritus hic per te patrias exisset in auras / sparsissent lacrimae pectora nostra piae, / supremoque die notum spectantia caelum / texissent digiti lumina nostra tui* (This spirit of mine through thy aid would have gone forth to its native air, pious tears would have wet my breast, my eyes upon the last day gazing at a familiar sky would have been closed by thy fingers). Dryden has 'pious tears', *Annus Mirabilis* 958; *Aeneid* vi 641; and *Sigismonda and Guiscardo* 669. See also Pope, *Elegy to an Unfortunate Lady* 49–51, where the 'pious' acts are done by 'foreign hands'.   *closing eye*] Cp. Pope, *Elegy to an Unfortunate Lady* 77–9: 'Ev'n he whose soul now melts in mournful lays, / Shall shortly want the gen'rous tear he pays; / Then from his closing eyes thy form shall part . . .'   *requires*] See *Sonnet on West* 6 and *n*, for this sense of both needing and seeking; and cp. *Annus Mirabilis* 1021–4, a quatrain which G. seems unconsciously to have recalled: 'Those who have none sit round where once it was, / And with full eyes each wonted room require: / Haunting the yet warm ashes of the place, / As murder'd men walk where they did expire.'

Ev'n from the tomb the voice of nature cries,
Ev'n in our ashes live their wonted fires.

91. Prior, *Solomon* iii 319–20: 'can Nature's Voice / Plaintive be drown'd';
Thomson, *Liberty* iii 122: 'The voice of pleading nature'; Akenside,
Pleasures of Imagination ii 357–8: 'the faithful voice of nature'. Lucretius has
vocem rerum natura . . . / mittat, iii 931–2. Cp. also Dart, *Westminster Abbey*
I xxvii: 'Thus Learning blossoms ev'n in the Tomb.'

92. And buried Ashes glow with social Fires *Eton*; And in our Ashes glow
their wonted Fires *Wharton, with* Even in our ashes lives &c *noted, and
Commonplace Book, with* Ev'n *amd* live *in margin*; Awake, & faithful to her
wonted Fires G. *to Walpole, 11 Feb 1751 (Corresp i 341), edd 1–7*. G. wrote to
Walpole, 3 March 1751 (*Corresp* i 344): 'I humbly propose, for the benefit
of Mr. Dodsley and his matrons, that take *awake* for a verb, that they should
read *asleep*, and all will be right.' If G. was referring to the comma which
appeared after 'Awake', the fault was his own (see his letter to Walpole of
11 Feb. above). It was removed in *ed 3*.

In *1768* G. acknowledged as the source of this line Petrarch's *Sonnet 169*
(more usually numbered 170), which he himself had earlier translated into
Latin (see p. 309): *Ch'i veggio nel pensier, dolce mio fuoco, / Fredda una lingua,
& due begli occhi chiusi / Rimaner doppa noi pien di faville* (For I see in my
thoughts, my sweet fire, one cold tongue and two beautiful closed eyes will
remain full of sparks after our death). But there are other parallels with G.'s
image and thought: e.g. Lucretius iv 925–6: *Quippe ubi nulla latens animai
pars remaneret / in membris, cinere ut multa latet obrutus ignis* (Since, if no part of
the spirit were left hidden in the limbs, like fire covered in a heap of ashes);
Ovid, *Tristia* III iii 81–4: *Tu tamen extincto feralia munera semper / deque tuis
lacrimis umida serta dato. / quamvis in cineres corpus mutaverit ignis, / sentiet
officium maesta favilla pium* (Yet do you ever give to the dead the funeral
offerings and garlands moist with your own tears. Although the fire change
my body to ashes, the sorrowing dust shall feel the pious care); Propertius,
Elegies II xiii 42: *Non nihil ad verum conscia terra sapit* (Not at all unconscious
and witless of the truth are the ashes of man: i.e. of the way his memory
is regarded after death); Ausonius, *Parentalia*, Praefatio 11–12: *Gaudent
compositi cineres sua nomina dici: / frontibus hoc scriptis et monumenta iubent* (Our
dead ones laid to rest rejoice to hear their names: and thus even the lettered
stones above their graves would have us do). Arthur Johnston, *Selected
Poems of Gray and Collins* (1967) p. 46, cites the translation of Euripides,
Bacchae 8, in the life of Solon in *Plutarch's Lives* (1683) vol i: 'Still in their
embers living the strong fire'. See also Young, *Night Thoughts* i 105–7:
'Why wanders wretched Thought their tombs around, / In infidel Distress?
Are *Angels* there? / Slumbers, rak'd up in dust, Etherial fire?' The version
of the line which appeared in *edd 1–7* echoes Pope, *Eloisa to Abelard* 54:
'Warm from the soul, and faithful to its fires'.

> For thee who, mindful of the unhonoured dead,
> Dost in these lines their artless tale relate;
95   If chance, by lonely Contemplation led,
> Some kindred spirit shall inquire thy fate,
>
> Haply some hoary-headed swain may say,
> 'Oft have we seen him at the peep of dawn

93–6. At this point Eton has:

> For Thee, who mindful &c: as above.
>
> If chance that e'er some pensive Spirit more,
> By sympathetic Musings here delay'd,
> With vain, tho' kind, Enquiry shall explore
> Thy once-loved Haunt, this long-deserted Shade.

The first of these lines refers back to the second of the rejected stanzas (see l. 72 *n*). These two repetitive stanzas, which G. was to compress into one, are close to T. Warton, *Pleasures of Melancholy* 17–21, where Contemplation is invoked as follows: 'O lead me, queen sublime, to solemn glooms / Congenial with my soul; to cheerless shades, / To ruin's seats, to twilight cells and bow'rs, / Where thoughtful melancholy loves to muse, / Her fav'rite midnight haunts.'

93. thee] In *Eton* the poet clearly addresses himself, in spite of the shift to the second person (cp. l. 4), and there is no reason to suppose that G. refers to anyone else in his revised version of these lines. But the view has recently been fashionable that G. was referring either to a 'village poet' other than himself or, specifically, to the village stonecutter responsible for the rhymes and inscriptions on the gravestones mentioned in ll. 79–84. No stonecutter is actually mentioned (only a female Muse) and it is unlikely that 'these lines' (l. 94) can refer back as far as l. 79. For discussion of the 'stonecutter' theory still held in some quarters, see F. H. Ellis, *PMLA* lvi (1951) 992–1004; M. Peckham, *MLN* lxxi (1956) 409–11; J. H. Sutherland, *MP* lv (1957) 11–13 (a cogent refutation of the theory).

95. If chance] If by chance or if it should chance that: so used by Spenser, *Faerie Queene* III ii 16, 4; and Milton, *Par. Lost* ix 452. Cp. Rowe, *Jane Grey* II i: 'Where lonely contemplation keeps her cave'.

96. kindred] hidden *ed 1*, noted as erratum by G. (*Corresp i 344*).

97. may] shall *Eton*. Shakespeare has 'hoary-headed frosts', *Midsummer Night's Dream* II i 107; and 'his hoary head' is common in Spenser and Dryden. But G.'s source was probably Blair, *The Grave* 453–4, 458–60: 'See yonder maker of the dead man's bed, / The sexton, hoary-headed chronicle . . . / . . . Scarce a skull's cast up, / But well he knew its owner and can tell / Some passage of his life.'

98. Fairfax's *Tasso* XIV lxxix 4 and XIX lxvi 3: 'by Peep of springing Day'; and Milton, *Comus* 139–40: 'Morn . . . / From her cabin'd loop hole peep'. Spenser also uses 'peep' as a verb of the dawn, *Faerie Queene* I i 39, 5 and IV v 45, 4.

'Brushing with hasty steps the dews away
100 'To meet the sun upon the upland lawn.

'There at the foot of yonder nodding beech
'That wreathes its old fantastic roots so high,
'His listless length at noontide would he stretch,

99–100. Eton has:

> With hasty Footsteps brush the dews away
> On the high Brow of yonder hanging Lawn.

Cp. *Par. Lost* v 428–9: 'though from off the boughs each Morn / We brush
mellifluous Dewes'; Thomson, *Spring* 103–6: 'Oft let me wander o'er the
dewy fields / Where freshness breathes, and dash the trembling drops /
From the bent bush, as through the verdant maze / Of sweet-briar hedges I
pursue my walk'; and J. Warton, *To a Lady who hates the Country* (1746)
13–14: 'By health awoke at early morn, / We'll brush sweet dews from
every thorn.' Spenser, *Faerie Queene* II i 34, 9, has 'hasty steps'.
100. Lycidas 25–6: 'ere the high Lawns appear'd / Under the opening eye-lids
of the morn'; and *L'Allegro* 92: 'up-land Hamlets'.
After this line Eton has an additional stanza:

> Him have we seen the Green-wood Side along,
> While o'er the Heath we hied, our Labours done,
> Oft as the Woodlark piped her farewell Song
> With whistful Eyes pursue the setting Sun.

Mason (*Poems* p. 110) wrote: 'I rather wonder that he rejected this stanza,
as it not only has the same sort of Doric delicacy, which charms us peculiarly
in this part of the Poem, but also compleats the account of his whole day:
whereas, this Evening scene being omitted, we have only his Morning
walk, and his Noon-tide repose.' But G. may have felt that he had already
described 'the poet' at evening in the opening lines of the poem as a whole.
With l. 3 of this rejected stanza cp. G.'s impromptu *Couplet about Birds*
(p. 280). Spenser twice has 'green woods syde', *Faerie Queene* II iii 3, 6 and
VI iv 39, 2.
101–4. Cp. *Ode on the Spring* 13–17 and *nn* (p. 50); and the *Lines on Beech
Trees* (p. 20) from which G. seems at first to have taken 'hoary' (see below).
101. There] Oft *Eton.*   *nodding*] hoary *Eton, with* spreading *written above
and* nodding *in margin.*
102. Cp. Spenser's description of an oak, *Ruins of Rome* 381–2, 384: 'Lifting
to heaven her aged hoarie head, / Whose foote in ground hath left but feeble
holde . . . / Shewing her wreathed rootes, and naked armes'; and *As You
Like It* II i 30–2 (of Jacques): 'he lay along / Under an oak whose antique
root peeps out / Upon the brook that brawls along this wood.' Mason, in a
note to his own *Elegy in a Churchyard in South Wales* (1787) refers to Jacques
as 'a character to which in its best parts Mr. Gray's was not dissimilar',
Works (1811) i 115 *n.*

'And pore upon the brook that babbles by.

105 'Hard by yon wood, now smiling as in scorn,
'Muttering his wayward fancies he would rove,
'Now drooping, woeful wan, like one forlorn,
'Or crazed with care, or crossed in hopeless love.

'One morn I missed him on the customed hill,
110 'Along the heath and near his favourite tree;
'Another came; nor yet beside the rill,
'Nor up the lawn, nor at the wood was he;

'The next with dirges due in sad array
'Slow through the church-way path we saw him borne.

104. Horace, *Odes* III xiii 15–16: *unde loquaces / lymphae desiliunt tuae* (whence thy babbling waters leap). Cp. also 'divided by a babbling brook', Thomson, *Spring* 646.
105. Hard by yon wood] With Gestures quaint *Eton*.   *smiling*] frowning *edd 1–2, 6–7, (noted as an erratum by G., Corresp i 344).*   G. was probably obliged to make the first alteration by his decision to drop the stanza after l. 100, which refers to the wood. Some mention of the wood was necessary because of l. 112. Cp. 'hard by a forests side', *Faerie Queene* I i xxxiv, 2; and 'Hard by, a Cottage chimney smokes', *L'Allegro* 81. Cp. also 'To love a cheek that smiles at thee in scorn', *Venus and Adonis* 252.
106. wayward fancies] fond Conceits *Eton, with* wayward fancies *written above.   he would*] he wont to *Eton, with* wont to *and then* loved *above deleted and* would he *written above;* would he *Wharton, Commonplace Book.* Cp. Spenser, *Faerie Queene* I i 42, 7–8: 'whose dryer braine / Is tost with troubled sights and fancies weake'; and III iv 54, 4: 'And thousand fancies bet his idle braine'.
107–8. Cp. Spenser, *Shepheardes Calender*, 'Jan'. 8–9: 'For pale and wanne he was, (alas the while,) / May seeme he lovd, or els some care he tooke'; and 47: 'Thou weake, I wanne; thou leane, I quite forlorne'. See also Collins, *The Passions* 25. G.'s 'woeful wan' probably imitates Spenser's 'solemne sad', *Faerie Queene* I i 2, 8; II vi 37, 5.
107. Now woeful wan, he droop'd, as one forlorn *Eton, with* he droop'd *deleted and* drooping, *written above* woeful wan.
109. I] we *Eton.   on*] from *Commonplace Book.   customed*] accustom'd *Eton.*   Cp. 'th'accustom'd Oke', *Il Penseroso* 60.
110. Along . . . near] By the Heath-side, & at *Eton, with* Along the *written above* By the, side *deleted, and* near *written above* at.
112. After this line Eton has There scatter'd oft, the earliest *deleted; see 116 n below.*
113. due] meet *Eton.*
114. through] thro *Eton, with* by *written above.* Cp. *Midsummer Night's Dream* V ii 391: 'In the church-way paths to glide'.

115 'Approach and read (for thou can'st read) the lay,
    'Graved on the stone beneath yon aged thorn.'

THE EPITAPH

Here rests his head upon the lap of earth
A youth to fortune and to fame unknown.

115. Cp. Pope, *Essay on Man* iv 260: 'Tell (for You can) what is it to be wise?'
116. *Graved*] Wrote Eton, *with* Graved carved *written above.*   *the*] his
Foulis.   *you*] that Eton, *with* you *written above.*   *aged*] ancient Eton;
aged *Commonplace Book, with* ancient *deleted. G. told Walpole of the change,*
11 *Feb.* 1751 *(Corresp* i 342).   *thorn*] 'The thorn in Glastonbury church-
yard is known to have suggested to Gray, in the Elegy, the idea of that thorn,
under which he supposes himself to be buried', John Young, *Criticism on the*
Elegy (1783) p. 82. Whether or not the Glastonbury thorn suggested the
idea to G., it is not obvious that he would want to refer to its miraculous
powers as part of the meaning of the poem.
116. *After this line in Eton appears an additional stanza, also added at the foot of*
the page in Commonplace Book, with the note Omitted in 1753, *and printed in*
edd 3–7 as follows:

> There scatter'd oft, the earliest of the Year,
> By Hands unseen, are show'rs of Violets found;
> The Red-breast loves to build and warble there,
> And little Footsteps lightly print the Ground.

Eton has the following variants: Year] Spring *deleted with* year *written above.*
show'rs of] frequent *with* Showers of *written above.*   *Red-breast*] Robin
with Redbreast *written above.*
    Mason, *Poems* pp. 110–11, wrote of this 'very beautiful stanza' that G.
eventually omitted it 'because he thought (and in my opinion very justly)
that it was too long a parenthesis in this place. The lines however are, in
themselves, exquisitely fine, and demand preservation.' G. also may have felt
that he was echoing too closely Collins's *Ode, Written in the Beginning of*
1746 and *Song from Cymbeline* 3–4, 13–16 (see pp. 401–2, 437 below).
116f. *The Epitaph*] *Written in the margin in Eton; Wharton and Commonplace*
Book omit The.
117–28. The 'Epitaph' was perhaps inspired by the inscription in the church
in Mallet, *The Excursion* i 299–311: 'Lamented shade! whom every gift
of heaven / Profusely blest: all learning was his own. / Pleasing his speech,
by nature taught to flow, / Persuasive sense and strong, sincere and clear. /
His manners greatly plain; a noble grace, / Self-taught, beyond the reach of
mimic art, / Adorn'd him: his calmer temper winning mild; / Nor pity
softer, nor was truth more bright. / Constant in doing well, he neither sought /
Nor shunned applause. No bashful merit sighed / Near him neglected:
sympathising he / Wiped off the tear from sorrow's clouded eye / With
kindly hand, and taught her heart to smile.' Cp. also the epitaph at the end

> *Fair Science frowned not on his humble birth,*
> *And Melancholy marked him for her own.*
120

> *Large was his bounty and his soul sincere,*
> *Heaven did a recompence as largely send:*

of Hammond's *Elegy* ix 41–4: 'Here lies a youth, borne down with love and care, / He could not long his Delia's loss abide, / Joy left his bosom with the parting fair, / And when he durst no longer hope, he died.'

117. *Aeneid* iii 509: *gremio telluris* (lap of earth), borrowed by G. for his *Latin Verses at Eton* 10 (p. 290); *Faerie Queene* V vii 9, 2: 'mother Earths deare lap', the same phrase occurring in *Par. Lost* x 777 and xi 536; Dryden, *Of the Pythagorean Philosophy* 373: 'Lies on the lap of Earth'. See also *Progress of Poesy* 84 *n* (p. 172).

118. Richard West, *Monody on Queen Caroline* st. viii: 'A muse as yet unheeded and unknown'; and G.'s translation from Propertius II i 65, and *Agrippina* 38–9 (pp. 34, 46).

119. *Science*] Knowledge or learning in general, described as 'fair' because conceived by G. as one of the Muses: cp. Horace, *Odes* IV iii 1–2: *Quem tu, Melpomene, semel / nascentem placido lumine videris* (Whom thou, Melpomene, hast once beheld with favouring gaze at his natal hour).

120. *Melancholy*] The meaning of this word is crucial to the 'Epitaph'. G. does not mean simply that the poet has been made melancholy (=gloomy) because his education made him aware of abilities which he has been unable to fulfil; if that had been the case the 'And' of this line would have logically been a 'But'. The favourable sense of 'melancholy', implying a valuable kind of sensibility, though not found in Johnson's *Dictionary*, was becoming fashionable at this time. The heightened sensibility of the melancholy man ideally expresses itself in benevolence and other social virtues, rather than merely in solitary wandering, although that usually precedes it. Thomson, *Autumn* 1004–10, speaks of the 'sacred influence' of 'the Power / Of Philosophic Melancholy'; and T. Warton, *Pleasures of Melancholy* 92–5, writes of 'that elegance of soul refin'd, / Whose soft sensation feels a quicker joy / From melancholy's scenes, than the dull pride / Of tasteless splendour and magnificence / Can e'er afford.' See also *Ode to Adversity* 25–32 (p. 72), where Melancholy is associated with Wisdom, Charity, Justice and Pity. Thus the melancholy which marks the young man explains not merely his solitary wanderings and sad wisdom about life, but the social virtues described in the next stanza.

121. *soul*] Heart *Eton*.   *Large*] Abundant, as Latin *largus*. Cp. Cowley, *On the Death of William Hervey* 73–80: 'Large was his *Soul*; as large a *Soul* as ere / Submitted to *inform* a *Body* here. / High as the Place 'twas shortly in *Heaven* to have, / But low, and humble as his *Grave*. / So *high* that all the *Virtues* there did come / As to their chiefest seat / Conspicuous, and great; / So *low* that for *Me* too it made a room.' G. may also have remembered Dryden, *Eleonora* 25: 'Heav'n, that had largely giv'n, was largely pay'd';

> *He gave to Misery all he had, a tear,*
> *He gained from Heaven ('twas all he wished) a friend.*

> *125   No farther seek his merits to disclose,*
> *Or draw his frailties from their dread abode,*
> *(There they alike in trembling hope repose)*
> *The bosom of his Father and his God.*

and John Pomfret, *The Choice* 39–42: 'And all that objects of true pity were, / Should be reliev'd with what my wants could spare; / For that our Maker has too largely given, / Should be return'd in gratitude to Heaven.'
123. See G.'s *De Principiis Cogitandi* ii 27–8 (p. 328).
124. Cp. Matthew Green, *The Spleen* 642–3: 'May Heaven (it's all I wish for) send / One genial room to treat a friend.'
126. Or . . . frailties] Nor seek to draw them *Eton, with* think *written above* seek.   Cp. Pope, *Eloisa to Abelard* 174–5: 'And here ev'n then, shall my cold dust remain, / Here all its frailties, all its flames resign'; and 316: 'For God, not man, absolves our frailties here.'
127. There they alike] His Frailties there *Eton.   trembling hope*] G.'s acknowledged source is Petrarch, *Sonnet* 114 (more usually 115): *paventosa speme* (fearful hope). Lucan, *Pharsalia* vii 297, has *spe trepido* (I tremble with hope); and J. Young, *Criticism on the Elegy* (1783) p. 85, cites Pope, *Dying Christian to his Soul* 3: 'Trembling, hoping, ling'ring, flying'.

APPENDIX

The following representative parallels to the four rejected stanzas in the Eton MS (see l. 72 *n*) are intended to stress the mood of Christian Stoicism which underlies the first conclusion to the *Elegy* and which G. almost entirely removed in his revision of the poem. Most of the parallels are drawn from James Hervey's popular *Meditations among the Tombs* (1746) and his other *Meditations and Contemplations* (references here are to the 4th collected edn of 1748 in 2 vols), a work which acknowledged the influence of Young's slightly earlier *Night Thoughts* (1742–5). Certain features of the *Elegy*, in particular the churchyard setting, the silent darkness, the graves, the bell and the owl, although found in other writers, are exploited with sensational effect by Hervey, but the following parallels are confined to the four rejected stanzas:
1–2. Hervey i 72: 'Let Others, if they please, pay their obsequious Court to your wealthy Sons; and ignobly fawn, or anxiously sue, for Preferments; my Thoughts shall often resort, in pensive Contemplation, to the Sepulchres of their Sires; and learn, from their sleeping Dust, – to *moderate* my Expectations from Mortals: – to stand *disengaged* from every undue Attachment, to the little Interests of Time: – to get above the delusive *Amusements* of Honour; the gaudy *Tinsels* of Wealth; and all the empty *Shadows* of a perishing World.'

This passage is followed immediately, i 73, by a description of the bell:
'Hark! What *Sound* is That!–In such a Situation, every Noise alarms.–
Solemn and slow, it breaks again upon the silent Air.–'Tis the *Striking
of the Clock*: Designed, one would imagine, to ratify all my serious Medi-
tations . . .'

3–4. Young, *Night Thoughts* v 253–4: 'Grief! more proficients in thy school
are made / Than genius or proud learning e'er could boast'; Hervey ii 12:
'Our Innocence, is of so *tender* a *Constitution*, that it suffers in the promiscuous
Croud; our Purity of so *delicate* a *Complexion*, that it scarce touches on the
World, without contracting a Stain. We see, we hear, with *Peril*. But here
Safety dwells. Every meddling and intrusive Avocation is secluded. Silence
holds the Door against the Strife of Tongues, and all the Impertinencies of
idle Conversation. The busy Swarm of vain Images, and cajoling Tempt-
ations; that beset Us, with a buzzing Importunity, amidst the Gaieties of
Life; are chased by these thickening Shades.'
5–8. See *Elegy* 93–6 *n* (p. 135) for a parallel to this stanza from Thomas War-
ton's *Pleasures of Melancholy* (1747).
9–12. Young, *Night Thoughts* v 195–200: 'auspicious midnight! hail! /
The world excluded, every passion hushed, / And opened a calm intercourse
with heaven, / Here the soul sits in council; ponders past, / Predestines future
action; sees, not feels, / Tumultuous life, and reasons with the storm';
and *ibid* ix at end: 'Thus, darkness aiding intellectual light, / And sacred
silence whisp'ring truths divine, / And truths divine converting peace to
pain'; Joseph Warton, *Ode to Evening* 21–4: 'Now ev'ry Passion sleeps;
desponding Love, / And pining Envy, ever-restless Pride; / An holy Calm
creeps o'er my peaceful Soul, / Anger and mad Ambition's storms subside';
Hervey i 3: 'The deep *Silence*, added to the gloomy Aspect, and both
heightened by the Loneliness of the Place, greatly increased the *Solemnity*
of the *Scene*.–A sort of *religious Dread* stole insensibly on my Mind, as I
advanced, all pensive and thoughtful, along the inmost Isle. Such as
hushed every *ruder Passion*, and dissipated all the *gay Images* of an alluring
World'; *ibid* i 11: 'Drowned is this gentle *Whisper*, amidst the Noise of
mortal affairs; but speaks distinctly, in the *Retirements* of serious *Contem-
plation*'; *ibid* i 13–14: 'Oh! that we might learn from these friendly Ashes,
not to perpetuate the *Memory* of *Injuries*; not to foment the *Fever* of *Resent-
ment*; nor cherish the *Turbulence* of *Passion*; that there may be as little Ani-
mosity and Disagreement in the Land of the Living, as there is in the Con-
gregation of the Dead!'; *ibid* ii xvi: 'The *Evening*, drawing her Sables over
the World, and gently darkening into *Night*, is a Season peculiarly proper
for sedate Consideration. All Circumstances concur, to hush our Passions,
and sooth our Cares; to tempt our Steps abroad, and prompt our Thoughts to
serious Reflection.'
13–14. Dryden, *Lucretius, Latter Part of Book III, Against the Fear of Death*
267–70: 'Eternal troubles haunt thy anxious mind, / Whose cause and cure
thou never hop'st to find; / But still uncertain, with thyself at strife, / Thou
wander'st in the *Labyrinth* of Life.'

18 A Long Story

Written between Aug. and Oct. 1750. Mason, *Memoirs* pp. 211–12, describes the occasion of the poem in detail. G., who was staying at Stoke Poges, had sent the completed *Elegy* to Walpole on 12 June 1750 and it rapidly passed into MS circulation:

'Amongst the rest of the fashionable world, for to these only it was at present communicated, Lady Cobham, who now lived at the mansion-house at Stoke-Pogis, had read and admired it. She wished to be acquainted with the author; accordingly her relation Miss Speed and Lady Schaub, then at her house, undertook to bring this about by making him the first visit. He happened to be from home, when the Ladies arrived at his Aunt's solitary mansion; and, when he returned, was surprized to find, written on one of his papers in the parlour where he usually read, the following note: "Lady Schaub's compliments to Mr. Gray; she is sorry not to have found him at home, to tell him that Lady Brown is very well." This necessarily obliged him to return the visit, and soon after induced him to compose a ludicrous account of this little adventure for the amusement of the Ladies in question.'

Lady Cobham, the widow of Sir Richard Temple, 1st Viscount Cobham (d. 1749), was the daughter of Edmund Halsey of Stoke Poges, who had purchased the Manor House in about 1720. Lady Cobham lived there after her husband's death with her niece Henrietta Speed (1728–83), to whom she left a considerable fortune at her death in 1760. Miss Speed disappointed the contemporary rumour that she would marry G. (*Corresp* ii 704) by marrying in 1761 Joseph de Viry, the Sardinian Minister in London. (For further information, see *Corresp* i 331 *n* 1). Lady Schaub (d. 1793) was French and had married Sir Luke Schaub (d. 1758), a naturalized Swiss, who had been secretary to Lord Cobham when he was ambassador at Vienna in 1715. Lady Brown, whose acquaintance with G. gave the ladies the formal excuse for the visit, was the daughter of the Hon. Robert Cecil and wife of Sir Robert Brown, a merchant who had at one time been Paymaster of the Works.

G. dated the poem 'Aug: 1750' in his Commonplace Book (ii 651–2), but there is a reference in l. 120 to the trial of the highwayman James Macleane on 13 Sept. 1750 and G.'s note about Macleane–'A famous Highwayman hang'd the week before'–has also been taken to prove that the poem could not have been completed before 10 Oct. 1750, a week after Macleane's execution on 3 Oct. (see l. 120 *n*). But G.'s own dating of the poem may not have been as erroneous as has been suggested. The visits to and from the Manor House may well have taken place in Aug. 1750, G. beginning the poem then and adding the reference to Macleane in l. 120 in mid-Sept., when his trial excited much interest. The reference in the poem itself is only to the trial and not to the execution on 3 Oct., which is mentioned only in G.'s footnote. In a MS of the poem (now in the J. W. Garrett Library of

Johns Hopkins University) described by L. Whibley in 'Notes on two manuscripts of Gray', *Essays and Studies* xxiii (1937) 55–7, G.'s note to l. 120 describes Macleane as 'hanged last Week'–which proves only that the note and MS, and not necessarily the poem, can be dated *c.* 10 Oct. 1750. This MS cannot be the original sent to the ladies at the Manor House, as G.'s footnotes refer to them in the third-person and explain domestic matters which would be immediately obvious to them. G. clearly made this copy, and annotated it, for some friend, possibly Walpole. G. had changed the wording of his original note to 'hang'd the week before' by the time of the transcription into his Commonplace Book, apparently without realizing that this would now appear to affect the date of the whole poem. It seems most probable, then, that the poem was written between Aug. and mid–Sept. 1750.

A Long Story quickly followed the *Elegy* into MS circulation, although some of the admirers of the earlier poem were evidently puzzled by the contrast offered by this metrical tale in the manner of Prior. Such a confusion may even be detected in Miss Speed's undated first acknowledgement of the poem (*Corresp* i 331–4; the dating of the poem proposed here will alter that of this letter suggested by G.'s editors): 'I am as much at a loss to bestow the Commendation due to your performance as any of our modern Poets would be to imitate them; Every body that has seen it, is charm'd and Lady Cobham was the first, tho' not the last that regretted the loss of the 400 stanzas' (see l. 140 *n*). In Dec. 1750 G. was stating defensively that these 'Verses . . . were wrote to divert that particular Family, & succeeded accordingly, but, being shew'd about in Town, are not liked there at all' (*Corresp* i 335). Mason, *Memoirs* p. 211, recalled that, when the poem was 'handed about in manuscript, nothing could be more various than the opinions concerning it; by some it was thought a master-piece of original humour, by others a wild and fantastic farrago; and when it was published, the sentiments of good judges were equally divided about it.'

The poem was published only once in G.'s lifetime with his approval, in *Designs by Mr R. Bentley, for Six Poems by Mr T. Gray* in March 1753. Mason, *Memoirs* p. 227, states that G. allowed it to be published, 'not without clearly foreseeing that he risked somewhat by the publication of it . . . and indeed the event shewed his judgement to be true in this particular, as it proved the least popular of all his productions.' In 1767, when Dodsley was planning the collected edn of G.'s *Poems* published in the following year, G. was anxious that *A Long Story* should be omitted. As he wrote to Beattie (*Corresp* iii 982), G. had told Dodsley that 'if he would omitt entirely the *Long Story* (wch was never meant for the publick, & only suffer'd to appear in that pompous edition because of Mr Bentley's designs, wch were not intelligible without it) I promised to send him some thing else to print instead of it'. Accordingly, he allowed Dodsley to print three of his translations from the Norse and Welsh and *A Long Story* was dropped. It had, however, been appearing in various unauthorized collections of his verse in Ireland, as well as in later edns of the *Designs* in 1765 and 1766, and it was reprinted in

1768 in edns of his poems at Dublin and Cork. Mason did not include it in the
Poems in *1775*, but printed it instead in the *Memoirs* pp. 214–20.

There is some interesting information about the history of the Manor
House at Stoke, and about the Cobhams and Miss Speed's relations with G.,
in John Penn's *Historical and Descriptive Account of Stoke Park* (1813). Penn
also prints his own sequel to *A Long Story* and there is another sequel to it in
Henry Pye, *Verses on Several Occasions* (1801).

The text is that of *1753*, with variants from the Commonplace Book and
the Garrett MS. G.'s notes from the two MSS have been given when they
differ significantly from those in *1753*.

> In Britain's isle, no matter where,
> An ancient pile of building stands:
> The Huntingdons and Hattons there
> Employed the power of fairy hands
>
> 5 To raise the ceiling's fretted height,
> Each panel in achievements clothing,

¶ 18.*1*. G. aimed at a ballad-like opening. Cp. 'Lord Henry and Katherine' in
The Tea-Table Miscellany (10th edn, 1740) iv 409, which begins 'In ancient
times, in *Britain's* isle'; and Parnell, *A Fairy Tale in the Ancient English Style*,
beginning 'In Britain's isle and Arthur's days'. G. seems also to have re-
membered two lines in Henry Brooke's 'The Female Seducers' in
Edward Moore's *Fables for the Female Sex* (1744): 'Within this sublunary
sphere, / A country lies–no matter where'.

2. pile] The Manor House at Stoke Poges.

3. N:B: the House was built by the Earls of Huntingdon, & came from them
to Sᵣ Christopher afterwards Lᵈ Keeper, Hatton, prefer'd by Q: Elizabeth
for his graceful Person & fine Dancing. *Garrett. Commonplace Book has a
shorter version of this note.*

According to John Penn, *Historical and Descriptive Account of Stoke Park*
(1813) pp. 14–15, Henry Hastings, Earl of Huntingdon (1535–95), rebuilt
the Manor House in about 1555. Financial difficulties later forced
him to mortgage it (in about 1580), 'during which time it was occupied
by Lord Chancellor Sir Christopher Hatton, the celebrated favourite
of Queen Elizabeth'. The evidence for this tradition is uncertain but
it seems to correspond to G.'s allusion. It may have arisen from the fact the
Lord Chief Justice Coke, who later held it as lessee under the crown and
entertained Queen Elizabeth there in 1601, married the relict of Sir William
Hatton, nephew of the Lord Chancellor.

5. Cp. 'fretted vault', *Elegy* 39 *n.*

5–8. Omitted in *Garrett; written in margin for insertion in Commonplace Book.*

6. achievements] Escutcheons or heraldic representations of arms granted for
great actions. Cp. Dryden, *Palamon and Arcite* iii 932, where Arcite's horse
is 'cover'd with th'Atchievements of the Knight'. According to Daniel

Rich windows that exclude the light,
And passages that lead to nothing.

Full oft within the spacious walls,
10 When he had fifty winters o'er him,
My grave Lord-Keeper led the brawls;
The Seal and Maces danced before him.

His bushy beard and shoe-strings green,
His high-crowned hat and satin-doublet,
15 Moved the stout heart of England's Queen,
Though Pope and Spaniard could not trouble it.

What, in the very first beginning!
Shame of the versifying tribe!
Your history whither are you spinning?
20 Can you do nothing but describe?

and Samuel Lysons, *Magna Britannia* (1806) i 635–6, the windows of the
Manor House 'were filled with the arms of the family of Hastings and its
alliances, those of Sir Edward Coke, and many of his great contemporaries
in the law'.
7. Milton, *Il Penseroso* 159–60: 'And storied Windows richly dight / Casting
a dimm religious light'; Pope, *Eloisa to Abelard* 144: 'And the dim windows
shed a solemn light'.
11. *Lord-Keeper*] Hatton, prefer'd by Queen Elizabeth for his graceful Person
and fine Dancing. *G. 1753. In Garrett this information appears as a note to l. 3
and in Commonplace Book the note begins* Sr Christ. Hatton, promoted by
Queen Elizabeth *etc. and refers to l. 10.*
Hatton was born in 1540 and was Lord Chancellor, not Lord Keeper,
the two offices not being united until 1757. Sir Robert Naunton, *Fragmenta
Regalia* (1641), ed. E. Arber (1870) p. 44, mentions 'the graces of his person,
and dancing'. G. may have been referring to an incident at the marriage of
Hatton's nephew in June 1589: 'At the festivities which followed, Hatton
divested himself of his gown, and, placing it in his chair with 'Lie thou
there, chancellor,' joined the dancers' (*DNB*).
brawls] an old fashion'd Dance. *Garrett*. The word derives from
French *bransles*. Cotgrave (1611) defines it as a dance 'wherein many [men
and women] holding by the hands sometimes in a ring, and otherwhiles at
length move altogether'. Cp. Jonson, *The Vision of Delight* 228–9: 'And
thence did *Venus* learne to tread / Th'Idalian Braules.' In Peter Whalley's
edn of Jonson, 1756, vi 27, 'tread' is replaced by 'lead' and a note com-
ments: '*To lead a Brawl* would be odd English now.'
12. The officials who bore the Great Seal and the Maces, the insignia of the
Lord Chancellor.
16. No doubt a reference to the Armada and perhaps to the fact that Elizabeth
was excommunicated by Pope Pius V in 1570.
20. *you*] ye *Garrett*.

A house there is (and that's enough)
From whence one fatal morning issues
A brace of warriors, not in buff,
But rustling in their silks and tissues.

25 The first came cap-a-pee from France
Her conquering destiny fulfilling,
Whom meaner beauties eye askance,
And vainly ape her art of killing.

The other Amazon kind heaven
30 Had armed with spirit, wit, and satire:
But Cobham had the polish given,
And tipped her arrows with good-nature.

To celebrate her eyes, her air——
Coarse panegyrics would but tease her.
35 Melissa is her nom de guerre.
Alas, who would not wish to please her!

With bonnet blue and capucine,
And aprons long they hid their armour,
And veiled their weapons bright and keen
40 In pity to the country-farmer.

Fame in the shape of Mr. P— t
(By this time all the parish know it)

23 *buff*] 'A military coat made of thick leather, so that a blow cannot easily pierce it' (Johnson). But the sense of *buff* as 'stark naked' may also be entailed.

25. *The first*] Lady Schaub (see headnote). 'Cap-a-pee' means literally from head to foot; G. perhaps refers to her fashionable French clothes. Cp. *Hamlet* I ii 200 and Dryden, *Palamon and Arcite* iii 489: 'Arm'd *Cap-a-pe*, with Rev'rence low they bent.'

27. 'You meaner beauties of the night', Wotton, *On the Queen of Bohemia* 1.

29. *The other*] Miss Speed (see headnote).

31. *Cobham*] For Lady Cobham, see headnote.

33. *eyes*] Looks *Garrett*.

35. *Melissa*] She had been call'd by that Name in Verse before. *Garrett*.
  Cp. '*Fair Rosamond* was but her *Nom de Guerre*', Dryden, *Epilogue to Henry II* 6.

37. *capucine*] Capuchin: 'a female garment of a cloak and hood, made in imitation of the dress of *capuchin* monks' (Johnson).

41. *P—t*] Purt *Commonplace Book, Garrett*. Robert Purt, Fellow of King's College, Cambridge 1738. He had taught at Eton and in 1749 had accepted a living at Settrington in Yorkshire. He died in April 1752. A note in *Garrett* describes him as 'a Clergyman, Tutor to the Duke of Bridgewater, who had first mentioned me to them [i.e. the ladies].' Mason later wrote,

Had told that thereabouts there lurked
A wicked imp they call a poet,

45 Who prowled the country far and near,
Bewitched the children of the peasants,
Dried up the cows and lamed the deer,
And sucked the eggs and killed the pheasants.

My lady heard their joint petition,
50 Swore by her coronet and ermine,
She'd issue out her high commission
To rid the manor of such vermin.

The heroines undertook the task;
Through lanes unknown, o'er stiles they ventured,
55 Rapped at the door nor stayed to ask,
But bounce into the parlour entered.

The trembling family they daunt,
They flirt, they sing, they laugh, they tattle,

Memoirs p. 215 *n*: 'I have been told that this Gentleman, a neighbour and acquaintance of Mr. Gray's in the country, was much displeased at the liberty here taken with his name; yet, surely, without any great reason.' Bentley depicted him as Fame blowing a trumpet in one of his designs in *1753*.

44. *Dunciad* ii 123–4: 'Three wicked imps, of her own Grubstreet choir, / She deck'd like Congreve, Addison, and Prior.'

45–8. G. was probably imitating such passages as *Midsummer Night's Dream* II i 34–9: 'are not you he / That frights the maidens of the villagery; / Skim milk, and sometimes labour in the quern, / And bootless make the breathless housewife churn; / And sometime make the drink to bear no barm; / Mislead night-wanderers, laughing at their harm?' See also ll. 123–4. Cp. Jonson, *Entertainment at Althrope* 53–70; and Dryden, *The Wife of Bath her Tale* 1–45, which describes the victory of the parson over the 'wicked elves' of the parish and which G. apparently imitates later in the poem.

51–2. As in fifteenth- and sixteenth-century edicts against minstrels and vagabonds.

54. *ventured/entered*. For the rhyme, Tovey compares Goldsmith, *Letter to Mrs Bunbury* 3–4 (see p. 737 below).

55–68. Cp. Prior, *The Dove* 33–6, 97–100, 105–8: 'With one great Peal They rap the Door, / Like Footmen on a Visiting-Day. / Folks at Her House at such an Hour! / Lord! what will all the Neighbours say // ... / Her keys he takes; her Doors unlocks: / Thro' Wardrobe, and thro' Closet bounces; / Peeps into ev'ry Chest and Box; / Turns all her Furbeloes and Flounces // ... / I marvel much, She smiling said, / Your Poultry cannot yet be found: / Lies he in yonder Slipper dead, / Or, may be, in the Tea-pot drown'd?'

Rummage his mother, pinch his aunt,
60   And up stairs in a whirlwind rattle.

Each hole and cupboard they explore,
Each creek and cranny of his chamber,
Run hurry-skurry round the floor,
And o'er the bed and tester clamber,

65   Into the drawers and china pry,
Papers and books, a huge imbroglio!
Under a tea-cup he might lie,
Or creased, like dogs-ears, in a folio.

On the first marching of the troops
70   The Muses, hopeless of his pardon,
Conveyed him underneath their hoops
To a small closet in the garden.

So Rumour says (who will, believe)
But that they left the door ajar,
75   Where, safe and laughing in his sleeve,
He heard the distant din of war.

Short was his joy. He little knew
The power of magic was no fable.
Out of the window, whisk, they flew,
80   But left a spell upon the table.

The words too eager to unriddle,
The poet felt a strange disorder:

59. G.'s mother was living at Stoke with Mrs Rogers, the widow of his uncle, Jonathan Rogers.
72. *in*] near *Garrett.*   *closet*] Bentley's illustration to the poem makes the nature of the closet unambiguous.
73. (*who will, believe*)] who will, may believe *Commonplace Book, Garrett.*
75. *laughing in his sleeve*] Johnson and *OED* give examples of this phrase for secret amusement from the sixteenth century.
76. 'the din of war', *Par. Lost* i 668 and vi 408; and 'all the distant din the world can keep', Pope, *Imitations of Horace, Sat.* II i 123.
77. 'Short is his Joy! he feels the fiery Wound', Pope, *Windsor Forest* 113.
79. *whisk*] This is the first adverbial use cited by *OED*, meaning 'With a whisk, or sudden light movement'.
80. *spell*] The note left by Lady Schaub (see headnote).
81–8. Mason, *Memoirs* p. 217, has a long note defending the blend of fancy and humour which has made these stanzas 'amongst those which are the least relished by the generality'. G. needed 'something like machinery' to enliven the simple situation his poem describes and Mason expounds its

> Transparent birdlime formed the middle,
> And chains invisible the border.
>
> 85 So cunning was the apparatus,
> The powerful pothooks did so move him,
> That, will he, nill he, to the Great-House
> He went, as if the Devil drove him.
>
> Yet no his way (no sign of grace,
> 90 For folks in fear are apt to pray)
> To Phoebus he preferred his case,
> And begged his aid that dreadful day.
>
> The godhead would have backed his quarrel,
> But, with a blush on recollection,
> 95 Owned that his quiver and his laurel
> 'Gainst four such eyes were no protection.
>
> The court was sate, the culprit there,
> Forth from their gloomy mansions creeping

consistency in its own terms: 'the author chose, with propriety enough, to employ for that purpose those notions of witchcraft, ghosts, and enchantment, which prevailed at the time when the mansion-house was built. He describes himself as a daemon of the lowest class, *a wicked imp who lamed the deer*, &c. against whose malevolent power Lady Cobham (the Gloriana of the piece) employs two superior enchantresses. Congruity of imagery, therefore, required the card they left upon the table to be converted into a spell. Now all the old writers on these subjects, are very minute in describing the materials of such talismans. Hence, therefore, his grotesque idea of a composition of transparent bird-lime, edged with invisible chains in order to catch and draw him to the tribunal.' Mason then quotes serious instances of this kind of imagery from *The Bard* and *The Fatal Sisters* but concludes, 'no person can fully relish this burlesque, who is not much conversant with the old romance-writers, and with the Poets who formed themselves on their model.'

83. Cp. a play by Dryden, cited by Johnson; 'I'm ensnared, / Heaven's birdlime wraps me round, and glues my wings'.

87. Great-House] So the Country People call it. *Garrett.*

89. 'a tear (portentous sign of Grace)', *Dunciad* i 243.

91. preferred] explain'd *Commonplace Book, Garrett.*

95. Owned that] He own'd *Garrett.*

97. culprit] Prisoner *Garrett.* In Dryden's *The Wife of Bath Her Tale* a knight is similarly tried by a court of ladies. Cp. ll. 268–73: 'The Female Senate was assembled soon, / With all the Mob of Women in the Town: / The Queen sat Lord Chief Justice of the Hall, / And bad the Cryer cite the Criminal. / The Knight appear'd; and Silence they proclaim, / Then first

The Lady Janes and Joans repair,
100   And from the gallery stand peeping:

Such as in silence of the night
Come (sweep) along some winding entry
(Styack has often seen the sight)
Or at the chapel-door stand sentry;

105   In peaked hoods and mantles tarnished,
Sour visages, enough to scare ye,
High dames of honour once, that garnished
The drawing-room of fierce Queen Mary!

The peeress comes. The audience stare,
110   And doff their hats with due submission:
She curtsies, as she takes her chair,
To all the people of condition.

The bard with many an artful fib
Had in imagination fenced him,
115   Disproved the arguments of Squib,
And all that Groom could urge against him.

But soon his rhetoric forsook him,
When he the solemn hall had seen;
A sudden fit of ague shook him,
120   He stood as mute as poor Macleane.

the *Culprit* answer'd to his Name.'
98–100. These are the ghosts of the Manor House; G. may also have had
particular portraits in mind.
100. from] in *Garrett.*
103. Styack] The House-Keeper. G. *1753.*
    John Penn, *Historical and Descriptive Account of Stoke Park* (1813) p. 30 *n*,
stated that her name was Tyack: 'Her name, which has hitherto been
written Styack, is corrected from her gravestone, in the church-yard.' This
information was repeated in Sharpe's edn of G. in 1826, where it was
pointed out that G.'s error was an understandable aural slip.
115. Squib] Groom of the Chambers. G. *1753.*
    James Squibb (d. 1762), son of Dr Arthur Squibb, chaplain to Col.
Bellasis's regiment *c.* 1685, had been in the service of Lord Cobham for
many years.
116. Groom] The Steward. G. *1753.*
    Penn notes, p. 31 *n*, that 'His grave-stone is close to that of Tyack, in the
south-west corner of the churchyard'.
could] might *Commonplace Book, Garrett.*
120. Macleane] A famous Highwayman hang'd the week before. *Common-
place Book and 1753. Garrett reads* hanged last week.
    For the effect of this note on the dating of the poem see headnote. G. was

Yet something he was heard to mutter,
'How in the park beneath an old-tree
'(Without design to hurt the butter,
'Or any malice to the poultry,)

125 'He once or twice had penned a sonnet;
'Yet hoped that he might save his bacon:
'Numbers would give their oaths upon it,
'He ne'er was for a conjurer taken.'

The ghostly prudes with hagged face
130 Already had condemned the sinner.
My lady rose and with a grace——
She smiled, and bid him come to dinner.

'Jesu-Maria! Madam Bridget,
'Why, what can the Viscountess mean?'
135 (Cried the square hoods in woeful fidget)
'The times are altered quite and clean!

no doubt interested in James Macleane because in Nov. 1749 he had robbed Horace Walpole in Hyde Park and a pistol had accidentally exploded during the hold-up (*Corresp* i 325–6). He was arrested on 27 July 1750 and immediately became an important topic in 'the conversation of the town' because of the 'gentlemanly' manner in which he was living: he 'had handsome lodgings in St *James's-street* . . . and passed for an *Irish* gentleman of 700 *l.* a year', *Gentleman's Mag.* xx (Sept. 1750) 391; and *Walpole Correspondence* xx 168–9. On 1 Aug. he confessed to the robbery of Walpole and to other crimes and was tried on 13 Sept. He made a speech in his own defence but was found guilty: 'when he was called to receive sentence, he attempted to make an apology, but only said, *My Lord, I cannot speak*', *ibid* 392. It was clearly to this incident in mid-Sept. 1750 that G. was referring although his note in *1753* gives the impression that he was referring to Macleane's execution on 3 Oct.

123. hurt] spoil *Garrett*.
126. Yet] but *Commonplace Book.*
128. conjurer] Enchanter. Tovey notes that G. elsewhere used the phrase 'no conjurer' in the sense of 'not over wise'. Johnson notes this meaning: 'By way of irony, a man of shrewd conjecture; a man of sagacity'.
129. hagged] 'i.e. the face of a witch or Hag; the epithet Haggard has been sometimes mistaken, as conveying the same idea; but it means a very different thing, viz. wild and farouche, and is taken from an unreclaimed Hawk, called an Hagard; in which its proper sense the Poet uses it finely on a sublime occasion [*Bard* 17–18]', Mason, *Memoirs* p. 220 *n.*
132. 'Here the story finishes; the exclamation of the Ghosts which follows is characteristic of the Spanish manners of the age, when they are supposed to have lived; and the 500 stanzas, said to be lost, may be imagined to contain the remainder of their long-winded expostulation', Mason, *Memoirs* p. 220 *n.*

'Decorum's turned to mere civility;
'Her air and all her manners show it.
'Commend me to her affability!
140   'Speak to a commoner and poet!'

(*Here 500 stanzas are lost.*)

And so God save our noble King,
And guard us from long-winded lubbers,
That to eternity would sing,
And keep my lady from her rubbers.

140. Miss Speed in her note to G. (*Corresp* i 333) refers to 'the loss of the 400 stanzas'. This may be her mistake or could indicate the number in the first draft of the poem.
142. lubbers] Johnson defines a 'lubber' as 'A sturdy drone; an idle, fat, bulky losel; a booby'.
*144.*ˌ*rubbers*] Games of whist, cribbage, backgammon, etc.

19 Stanzas to Mr Bentley

Written between 1751 and 1753, most probably in the second half of 1752. There is no extant reference to it by G. and no MS has survived. Mason, who first printed it in 1775 from G.'s MS, says (*Memoirs* pp. 227–8) that it was written while Walpole was supervising the publication (on 29 March 1753) of *Designs by Mr R. Bentley for Six Poems by Mr T. Gray*. Bentley's drawings for G.'s poems are first mentioned by Walpole in a letter dated 13 June 1751 and he describes them as almost complete in a letter of 6 June 1752. On 28 Aug. 1752, he referred to G.'s admiration for one of Bentley's designs, the figure of Melancholy which was to appear at the end of the *Ode to Adversity*, (*Walpole Correspondence* ix 116, 134, 143–4). It was probably about then that G. wrote this poem.

While working on his drawings to illustrate G.'s poems, Richard Bentley (1708–81), son of the celebrated classical scholar and Master of Trinity College, Cambridge, was also engaged in advising Walpole about his elaborate 'Gothic' alterations to Strawberry Hill, completed in 1753. The *Designs* can be considered as a byproduct to some extent of this activity. G. himself modestly told Dodsley, the publisher of the expensive volume, that it 'could never sell but from the notion the Town may entertain of the Merit of the Drawings, wᶜʰ they will be instructed in by some, that understand such things,' and he wished it to be clear that 'the Verses are only subordinate, & explanatory to the Drawings' (*Corresp* i 371).

The admiration for Bentley's whimsical and grotesque drawings which the poem expresses even more forcibly was thought excessive by some readers when it was first published in 1775. John Langhorne, reviewing Mason's *Memoirs* in the *Monthly Review* liii 6–7, asked his readers to compare the second stanza of G.'s poem with one of Bentley's designs 'and bid defiance to risibility if you can.' As R. W. Ketton-Cremer has pointed out (*Thomas Gray* pp. 113–14) opinions as to the merits of the illustrations still vary considerably. Sir Kenneth Clark, *The Gothic Revival* (1929) p. 67, has called the book 'the most graceful monument to Gothic Rococo'; while C. F. Bell, 'Thomas Gray and the fine arts', *Essays and Studies* xxx (1945) 80, described it as 'a barbaric, amateurish curiosity'. Mason himself, *Memoirs* p. 226, admitted that G.'s praise of Bentley had at first seemed excessive to him, while claiming that the original drawings (now in the possession of W. S. Lewis at Farmington, Connecticut) 'are so infinitely superior to the published engravings of them' that they cannot be fairly judged. In any case, Mason believed such 'grotesque fancy' could not be expected at the best of times 'to please universally'. G. may eventually have realized that his praise of Bentley was exaggerated–the fact that he did not publish the poem would support this view–but it is probable that he was tempted into eulogy by the genre he was using, represented by such poems as Dryden's *Epistle to Kneller* and Pope's *Epistle to Jervas*. Of the relation of G.'s *Stanzas* to these earlier poems, J. H. Hagstrum, *The Sister Arts* (Chicago, 1958) p. 289, has written: 'The reference to Dryden and Pope [ll. 15–6] is happy, for Gray, like them, is using the occasion of addressing a painter-friend to interpret the relations of the sister arts and, by implication at least, to identify himself with the tradition of their association. . . . Gray's view of painting is revealed to be the traditional one: it possesses the power of *energeia* in even greater measure than poetry–the power of rendering the animation and lustre of life itself.' The text (and title) given here is that in *1775*. Mason also transcribed the poem into G.'s Commonplace Book. G.'s MS was torn and the final words of the last three lines were missing: Mason's attempt to supply them has been confined to the notes (see ll. 26–8 *n*).

> In silent gaze the tuneful choir among,
> Half pleased, half blushing, let the Muse admire,
> While Bentley leads her sister-art along,
> And bids the pencil answer to the lyre.

¶ 19. *1.* Dryden, *Alexander's Feast* 20–2: ' *Timotheus* plac'd on high / Amid the tuneful Quire, / With flying Fingers touch'd the Lyre'; 'tuneful quire', Pope, *Ode on St Cecilia's Day* 126 and Tickell, *To Mr Addison* 51.

3. sister-art] Painting. There are many examples of the compound: 'Long time the Sister Arts in Iron sleep' (cp. also 'Our Arts are Sisters'), Dryden, *Epistle to Kneller* 57, 89; 'Ye sister arts of paint and verse', Isaac Watts, *Epitaph on William III* 17; and see Pope, *Epistle to Jervas* 13 and *Essay on Criticism* 701; Parnell, *Death of Viner* 7; Thomson, *Liberty* v 683. See also Collins, *Epistle to Hanmer* 134 (p. 399 below).

4. 'One dip the pencil, and one string the lyre', Pope, *Epistle to Jervas* 70. Pencil, from Latin *penicillum*, means 'A small brush of hair which painters dip in their colours' (Johnson), although the lead pencil was already common.

5   See, in their course, each transitory thought
      Fixed by his touch a lasting essence take;
      Each dream, in fancy's airy colouring wrought,
      To local symmetry and life awake!
      The tardy rhymes that used to linger on,
10   To censure cold and negligent of fame,
      In swifter measures animated run,
      And catch a lustre from his genuine flame.
      Ah! could they catch his strength, his easy grace,
      His quick creation, his unerring line;
15   The energy of Pope they might efface,
      And Dryden's harmony submit to mine.
      But not to one in this benighted age

7. Prior, *Solomon* ii 788: 'In borrow'd Shapes, and airy Colors wrought';
and Pope, *Imitations of Horace, Odes* IV i 41–2: 'Thee, dressed in Fancy's
airy beam, / Absent I follow thro' th'extended dream.'

8. *Midsummer Night's Dream* V i 14–7: 'And as imagination bodies forth /
The forms of things unknown, the poet's pen / Turns them to shapes, and
gives to airy nothing / A local habitation and a name.' Cp. also 'Where
life awakes and dawns at ev'ry line', Pope, *Epistle to Jervas* 4.

10. Dryden, *Religio Laici* 452: 'Yet neither Praise expect, nor Censure fear';
and Pope, *Essay on Criticism* 741: 'Careless of *Censure*, nor too fond of
Fame'.

13–16. The model for this quatrain is an often imitated passage in Addison,
A Letter from Italy 51–4: 'Oh could the Muse my ravished breast inspire /
With warmth like yours, and raise an equal fire, / Unnumbered beauties in
my verse should shine, / And Virgil's Italy should yield to mine.' Cp. Robert
Vansittart, 'The Pleasure of Poetry' st. xviii, in Dodsley's *Collection* (1748)
iii 231: 'O could I catch one ray divine / From thy intolerable blaze! / To
pour strong lustre on my line, / And my aspiring song to raise; / Then should
the Muse her choicest influence shed, / And with eternal wreaths entwine
my lofty head.' See also Collins, *Epistle to Hanmer* 107–10, and the lines from
W. Harte quoted in note (p. 397 below).

13–14. Pope, *Epistle to Jervas* 36–7: 'Match *Raphael's* grace, with thy lov'd
Guido's air, / *Caracci's* strength, *Correggio's* softer line.'

14. Pope, *Epistles to Several Persons* ii 151–2: 'Pictures like these, dear Madam,
to design, / Asks no firm hand, and no unerring line.'

15. Pope had himself praised Dryden's 'energy divine', *Imitations of Horace,
Ep.* II i 269. See G.'s note to *Progress of Poesy* 105 (p. 175).

17–20. G. wrote to Walpole, 8 Feb. 1747 (*Corresp* i 265): 'Litterature (to
take it in its most comprehensive Sense, & include every Thing, that re-

THE PROGRESS OF POESY. A PINDARIC ODE

> Is that diviner inspiration given,
> That burns in Shakespeare's or in Milton's page,
> 20   The pomp and prodigality of heaven.
> As when, conspiring in the diamond's blaze,
> The meaner gems, that singly charm the sight,
> Together dart their intermingled rays,
> And dazzle with a luxury of light.
> 25   Enough for me, if to some feeling breast
> My lines a secret sympathy [   ]
> And as their pleasing influence [   ]
> A sigh of soft reflection [   ].

quires Invention, or Judgement, or barely Application & Industry) seems indeed drawing apace to its Dissolution . . .'

20. Dryden, *To my Dear Friend Mr Congreve* 62–3: 'Heav'n that but once was Prodigal before, / To *Shakespeare* gave as much; she cou'd not give him more.'

21–4. G.'s translation of Tasso, *Gerusalemme Liberata* xiv 32–3: 'The diamond then attracts the wondering sight, / Proud of its thousand charms and luxury of light.'

21. 'In the bright *Muse* tho' thousand *Charms* conspire', Pope, *Essay on Criticism* 339; 'Tho' the same Sun with all-diffusive rays / Blush in the Rose and in the Diamond blaze', *Epistles to Several Persons* i 97–8.

26–8. The corner of G.'s MS copied by Mason had been torn away, so that the last words of these lines were missing. Mason supplied them in 1775 as follows: 'impart / flows confest / heave the heart'. Reviewing Mason's *Memoirs,* Langhorne, *Monthly Review* liii (1775) 7, suggested these alternatives: 'convey / there shall rest / steal away'. The *European Mag.* xliv (1803) 21, suggested 'convey / imprest / heave for Gray'. A writer in *Notes and Queries* i (1850) 416–17, commenting on this suggestion, thought that it might explain why G. had torn off the corner of the MS in 'some peculiar fit of modesty'. Mitford at first accepted Mason's suggestions but later provided his own words for the *lacunae*, on the grounds that 'Gray had in his mind Dryden's Epistle to Kneller, from which he partly took his expressions'. Mitford suggested 'convey / is exprest / dies away'. The last couplet of Dryden's poem rhymes 'convey / takes away' and 'exprest' is the rhyme word 6 ll. earlier (ll. 174, 180–1).

20 The Progress of Poesy.
A Pindaric Ode

Written between Sept. 1751 and Dec. 1754. In the late summer of 1751 Walpole asked G. about the truth of a rumour that he had promised a poem for the fourth volume of Dodsley's *Collection of Poems*, which the publisher was planning at this time. In a letter dated 8 Sept. 1751 (corrected by the editors of the *Walpole Correspondence* xiv 52, to 8 Oct.) G. denied the rumour: 'I have nothing more, either nocturnal or diurnal, to deck his Miscellany with' (*Corresp* i 348). But he kept the proposed volume in mind and, in a letter to Walpole in July 1752 which discussed the forthcoming publication by Dodsley of his *Six Poems . . . With Designs by Mr R. Bentley*, he revealed that he might yet contribute to the continuation of Dodsley's anthology (*Corresp* i 364): 'I don't know but I may send him very soon (by your hands) an ode to his own tooth, a high Pindarick upon stilts, which one must be a better scholar than he is to understand a line of, and the very best scholars will understand but a little matter here and there. It wants but seventeen lines of having an end, I don't say of being finished. As it is so unfortunate to come too late for Mr. Bentley, it may appear in the fourth volume of the Miscellanies, provided you don't think it execrable, and suppress it.'

Although the poem lacked only 17 ll. G. no doubt also revised this first draft extensively and it was not completed until 1754. In April 1756 he described it as being written 'by fits & starts at very distant intervals' (*Corresp* ii 462). In 1775 William Mason admitted, *Memoirs* p. 145 *n*, to having been 'the innocent cause of his delaying to finish his fine ode on the progress of Poetry. I told him, on reading the part he shewed me, that "though I admired it greatly, and thought that it breathed the very spirit of Pindar, yet I suspected it would by no means hit the public taste." Finding afterwards that he did not proceed in finishing it, I often expostulated with him on the subject; but he always replied "No, you have thrown cold water upon it." I mention this little anecdote, to shew how much the opinion of a friend, even when it did not convince his judgement, affected his inclination.'

G.'s transcript of the poem in his Commonplace Book (ii 727–8) is entitled 'Ode in the Greek Manner' and described as 'Finish'd in 1754'. All the marginal corrections in this text were followed in a MS of the poem (still entitled 'Ode in the Greek Manner') which G. sent to Wharton on 26 Dec. 1754 (*Corresp* i 412–6), so that it may have been completed some months earlier. This possibility is perhaps confirmed by G.'s remark in his covering letter to Wharton: 'If this be as tedious to You, as it is grown to me, I shall be sorry that I sent it you.' No doubt remembering his experience with the *Elegy*, he instructed Wharton to use great caution in circulating the poem: 'I desire you would by no means suffer this to be copied; nor even shew it, unless to very few, & especially not to mere Scholars, that can scan all the measures in Pindar, & say the Scholia by heart.'

That G. was now troubled about the form in which his new poem should be published is clear from another letter to Wharton of 9 March 1755 (*Corresp* i 420). He had finished it too late for inclusion in the new volume of Dodsley's *Collection*, published this year, but in any case he obviously now viewed that anthology with some distaste. On the other hand, he was not enthusiastic about the prospect of publishing the poem and others which he had in mind (*The Bard* and probably the fragment entitled by Mason *Ode on the Pleasure*

Arising from Vicissitude) in separate, pretentious pamphlets: 'in truth I am not so much against publishing, as against publishing *this alone*. I have two or three Ideas more in my head. what is to come of them? must they too come out in the shape of little six-penny flams, dropping one after another, till Mʳ Dodsley thinks fit to collect them with Mʳ this's Song, and Mʳ t'other's epigram, into a pretty Volume?'

The solution to the problem which probably occurred to G. was to withhold his 'Ode in the Greek Manner' until he had written enough other poems to justify publication in book form. By the summer of 1755 he had made good progress with what was to become *The Bard* and the earlier ode was laid aside in the meantime. In a letter to Bedingfield of 29 April 1756 G. referred to it under a new title, 'the *Powers of Poetry*' (*Corresp* ii 462), adding: 'I have been already threaten'd with publication, tho' there are no more than three copies of it in the world. to abate your curiosity I assure you it is very incorrect, & being wrote by fits & starts at very distant intervals is so unequal that it will hardly admit of particular corrections. . . . you call it *celebrated*, but its celebrity is only owing to its being yet unpublish'd.' Another letter from G. to Bedingfield of 27 Aug. 1756 (*Corresp* ii 475) gives the impression that the latter had by then seen a large part of the poem, perhaps as much as from l. 23 to the end. On 29 Dec. 1756, G. sent Bedingfield ll. 1–23 of the poem (which he described as 'no favourite of mine'), adding that 'the end you have already' (*Corresp* ii 491–2).

Since G. did not complete *The Bard* until the summer of 1757, the earlier poem remained unpublished for some three years after its completion. The two *Odes* were eventually published by Dodsley on 8 Aug. 1757, having been printed at Horace Walpole's newly established press at Strawberry Hill. (For a more detailed account of the publication and reception of the *Odes*, see the headnote to *The Bard*, pp. 179–80). Dodsley paid G. 40 guineas for the copyright and in G.'s receipt for this sum, dated 29 June 1757, the first of the two poems is still referred to as *The Powers of Poetry* (*Corresp* ii 513 *n*). When published it was entitled merely *Ode* and it was not until *1768* that it received its full title, *The Progress of Poesy. A Pindaric Ode*. Shortly before its publication in *1757* Horace Walpole had referred to it as an ode 'on the power and progress of Poetry' (in his *Journal of the Printing-Office at Strawberry Hill*, ed. Toynbee (1923) p. 3); but in a letter to Lyttelton, *Letters*, ed. Toynbee (1903) iv 85, he wrote that G. had decided to give the poem no title, because 'Mr. Cooke published an ode with such a title.' Thomas Cooke's *Ode on the Powers of Poetry* was published in 1751.

In *1757* G. did not provide notes to *The Progress of Poesy*. Perhaps embarrassed by the great popularity of the *Elegy*, he seems to have been determined to puzzle all but the most learned of his readers, as is clear from the brief motto from Pindar's *Olympian Odes* ii 85, which he himself translated '*vocal to the Intelligent alone*' (*Corresp* ii 797), prefixed to the *Odes*. G. amplified the quotation in *1768* as an early reviewer, *Critical Review* iv (1757) 167, had recommended. Walpole tried to persuade G. to help his readers, as he told Horace Mann in a letter of 4 Aug. 1757 (*Walpole Correspondence* xxi 120), when he sent him 'two amazing odes of Mr Gray–they are Greek, they are Pindaric, they are sublime–consequently I fear a little obscure. . . . I could not persuade him to add more notes; he says whatever wants to be explained, don't deserve to be.' G. had told Walpole in July, 'I do not love notes. . . . They are signs of weakness and obscurity. If a thing cannot be understood without them, it had better be not understood at all' (*Corresp* ii 508). Although G. restated this conviction in Sept. 1757–'I would not have put another note to save the souls of all the *Owls* in London' (*Corresp* ii 522)– he was undoubtedly hurt by the misunderstandings and confusion the *Odes* caused, derisive as he may have been about their readers. A writer in the *Critical Review* made a conspicuous blunder about the opening of the *The Progress of Poesy* (see l. 1 *n*); and 'a lady of quality, a friend of Mason's' was baffled by ll. 83–106: 'She knew there was a compliment to Dryden, but never suspected there was anything said about Shakspeare or Milton, till it was explained to her; and wishes that there had been titles prefixed to tell what they were about' (*Corresp* ii 520). Bedingfield wrote to tell him in Oct. (*Corresp* ii 532), 'that at York-races he overheard three People, whom by their dress & manner he takes for Lords, say, that I was impene-trable & inexplicable, and they wish'd, I had told them in prose, what I meant in verse'.

In *1768* G. virtually submitted to the wishes of the racegoers by providing an extensive prose commentary on the poem, albeit with a somewhat derisive 'Advertisement' : 'When the Author first published this and the following Ode, he was advised, even by his Friends, to subjoin some few explanatory Notes; but had too much respect for the understanding of his Readers to take that liberty.' G. had written virtually the same words in his own copy of the 1757 *Odes* (now in the Pierpont Morgan Library), but had added: 'The words of Pindar prefixed to them . . . were prophetic of their fate: Very few understood them; the multitude of all ranks call'd them unintelligible.' The *Odes* were, however, to become, after the *Elegy*, the most admired of G.'s poems, as is clear from the indignation aroused by Johnson's severe criticism of them in his *Life* of the poet. In any case, some of the first readers of the *Odes* were much more discerning and appreciative than G. admitted. For a detailed account of their reception see W. Powell Jones, 'The contemporary reception of Gray's *Odes*', *MP* xxviii (1930–1) 61–82.

Like *The Bard*, *The Progress of Poesy* is a 'Pindaric Ode'. The effective introduction of the form into English poetry has usually been attributed to Cowley, whose *Pindarique Odes* were published in 1656. Cowley was un-aware of the metrical and structural principles of Pindar's poetry, and the irregular stanzaic forms of his imitations did much to promulgate what rapidly became a common misconception of Pindar as an impassioned poet, whose genius was unfettered by normal rules. This misconception, as well as the popularity of the Pindaric Ode itself, was fostered by Dryden's effective use of the irregular stanza in his *Song for St Cecilia's Day* and *Alexander's Feast*. As a vehicle for 'enthusiastic' religious and patriotic poetry, the Pindaric

Ode became a popular form, permitting (as it was supposed to do) virtually any kind of metrical and thematic inconsequentiality and providing an attractively emancipated alternative to the logical and metrical demands of stricter verse forms.

A vigorous protest against this misconception of Pindar was made by William Congreve in 1706, in the preface to his *Pindarique Ode to the Queen*. Congreve objected that most supposed imitations of Pindar were merely 'a Bundle of rambling incoherent Thoughts, express'd in a like parcel of irregular Stanza's, which also consist of such another Complication of disproportion'd, uncertain and perplex'd Verses and Rhimes'. Congreve went on to expound the true principles of Pindar's odes and to show that 'there is nothing more regular than the Odes of *Pindar*, both as to the exact Observation of the Measures and Numbers of his Stanza's and Verses, and the perpetual Coherence of his Thoughts'. As Congreve explained, the ode usually (but by no means invariably) consisted of three stanzas, the strophe, antistrophe and epode. The poet fixed the metre and stanzaic form of the strophe (which varied from ode to ode), which had to be duplicated precisely in the antistrophe. In the epode the poet devised another, usually contrasting, stanzaic form. The ode could consist of several sets of three stanzas, but the stanzaic forms established in the first tripartite set had to be duplicated exactly thereafter. Pindar himself varies this basic form, which is however that followed meticulously by G. Although it gave considerable scope for metrical variation within the symmetrical pattern, it was never irregular.

Congreve's protest did not immediately dispose of the misconception of Pindar as an artless genius or halt the flow of the irregular ode. But Collins's *Odes* represent an attempt to compromise more closely with Greek principles and the argument for the regularity of Pindar was firmly repeated by Gilbert West in the Preface to his *Odes of Pindar. Translated from the Greek* in 1749. In any case, G. had already investigated the principles of Pindar's odes for himself. A letter to Wharton of 17 March 1747 (*Corresp* i 277) shows that he was studying Pindar at that time; and a notebook now in the British Museum (Add. MS 36817 ff 4–5) contains his notes on the poet, dated 20 March 1747. G. transcribed several of the passages from Pindar which he was to imitate in *The Progress of Poesy* and carefully analysed the metre. It is not surprising, therefore, that G. observed the principles of Pindar's verse in his imitations more faithfully than any earlier English poet. In addition, G. attempted to capture the manner of Pindar's odes by imitating the highly allusive and concise narrative technique and the swift transitions from one topic to another which characterize them. G.'s repeated emphasis on the learned character of his Pindaric poems (reinforced in the MSS by the fact that the divisions of the poem are labelled Strophe, Antistrophe and Epode) points to his desire to dissociate himself from the debased, irregular form, which had, in any case, lost much of its popularity by the mid-century. (Johnson more than once speaks of 'our Pindarick infatuation' as lasting only into the first decade or two of the century; *Lives of the Poets*, ed. G. B. Hill, ii 210, 234, iii 303.) Mason, *Memoirs* p. 233*n*, states explicitly that 'there was nothing which [G.] more disliked than that chain of irregular stanzas which Cowley introduced, and falsely called Pindaric; and which from the extreme facility of execution produced a number of miserable imitators'. These remarks were made in a note to a letter from G. to Wharton, 9 March 1755 (*Corresp* i 420–1), in which G. discusses the length of stanza desirable in the strophe and antistrophe. If it is too great, he believed, 'it has little or no effect upon the ear, wch scarce perceives the regular return of Metres at so great a distance from one another. to make it succeed, I am persuaded the Stanza's must not consist of above 9 lines each at the most.' Ironically, it was precisely on these grounds that Johnson was to criticise the stanzas of *The Bard*: 'the ode is finished before the ear has learned its measures, and consequently before it can receive pleasure from their consonance and recurrence' (*Lives of the Poets* iii 439).

The first of G.'s 'Pindaric Odes' is a 'progress poem', as the title on which he eventually settled makes clear. It therefore belongs to one of the most popular poetic genres of the seventeenth and eighteenth centuries, a genre which flourished as the Augustans developed a historical perspective that established them as the heirs in a direct line of succession from the civilizations of ancient Greece and Rome. The purpose of the progress poem was to expound this genealogy, tracing back their arts and virtues to Greece and then describing the continuous historical and geographical progress westward to Britain. The route could show minor variations, but usually proceeded through Rome and medieval Italy. The reason for the steady progress of the arts to Britain was usually – as in *The Progress of Poesy* 77–82 – the decline of liberty in the former cultural centres of the world. Only in Britain was true liberty to be found, according to the Augustans, so that the arts had inevitably settled there. The route followed by Liberty herself to Britain is explicitly described in such progress poems as Thomson's *Liberty* and Collins's *Ode to Liberty*. A number of Collins's other odes belong to the genre. Nevertheless, by the mid-eighteenth century the patriotic conviction that the classical arts and virtues had not merely been transmitted to Britain but had thrived there as never before was losing some of its confidence. That the sense of the past out of which the progress poem sprang could induce in this new generation a sense of inferiority rather than simple complacency is clear from the conclusion of G.'s *Progress of Poesy* and from Collins's *Ode on the Poetical Character*. For further information about the progress poem, see R. H. Griffith, 'The progress pieces of the eighteenth century', *Texas Review* v (1919–20) 218–33; Mattie Swayn, 'The progress piece of the seventeenth century', *Univ. of Texas Bulletin* (*Studies in English*) xvi (1936) 84–92; and Aubrey L. Williams, *Pope's Dunciad* (1955) pp. 42–8. Two earlier poems have virtually the same title and framework as G.'s: the section 'The Progress of Poetry' in *Of Poetry*, in Samuel Cobb's *Poems on Several Occasions* (1707); and Judith Madan's *Progress of Poetry* (1721).

The Progress of Poesy, like *The Bard*, has received relatively little critical attention: there are some perceptive comments on both poems in F. Doherty,

'The two voices of Gray', *Essays in Criticism* xiii (1963) 222–30 and P. M. Spacks, ' "Artful strife": Conflict in Gray's poetry', *PMLA* lxxxi (1966) 63–9.

The text followed here is that of *1768*, which G. directed Dodsley to print from *1757* (*Corresp* iii 1000), but to which he added explanatory notes. Variants are given from the Commonplace Book and the passages contained in the letters to Wharton and Bedingfield. Horace Walpole's MS notes in his copy of the *Odes* are cited from *The Rothschild Library* (1954) i 266–8.

φωνᾶντα συνετοῖσιν ·ἐς
δὲ τὸ πᾶν ἑρμηνέων χατίζει.

PINDAR, *Olymp*[*ian Odes*] *II.*

I. I

Awake, Aeolian lyre, awake,
And give to rapture all thy trembling strings.
From Helicon's harmonious springs

¶ 20.*1*. Awake, my Lyre, my Glory, wake *Commonplace Book, with present reading in margin.*

G. added the following note in *1768*:

'Awake, my glory; awake, lute and harp. *David's Psalms* [lvii 9].

Pindar styles his own poetry with its musical accompanyments, Ἀιολὴὶς μολπή, Ἀιολίδης χόρδαί, Ἀιολίδων πνοαὶ αὐλῶν Aeolian song, Aeolian strings, the breath of the Aeolian flute [*Olympian Odes* i 102; *Pythian Odes* ii 69; *Nemean Odes* iii 79]'.

Mason, *Poems* p. 86, explained that this note was not 'the mere parade of Greek quotation': he believed that G. included it because a writer in the *Critical Review* iv 167, reviewing the *Odes* in Aug. 1757, assumed that 'Aeolian' referred to the Harp of Aeolus, or wind-harp, instead of a mode in Greek music (*Corresp* ii 523 and *n*).

Cp. also Cowley, *Davideis* Bk iii: 'Awake, awake, my lyre'; Pope, *Ode on St Cecilia's Day* 3–4: 'Wake into Voice each silent String, / And sweep the sounding Lyre'.

2. rapture] transport *Commonplace Book, Wharton.* Cp. Dryden, *Ovid's Amours* I i 15: 'As well may *Phoebus* quit the trembling String'; but see also the passage from Pindar quoted in l. 25 *n*.

3. The subject and simile, as usual with Pindar, are united. The various sources of poetry, which gives life and lustre to all it touches, are here described; its quiet majestic progress enriching every subject (otherwise dry and barren) with a pomp of diction and luxuriant harmony of numbers; and its more rapid and irresistible course, when swoln and hurried away by the conflict of tumultuous passions. *G. 1768.*

Helicon] A mountain in Boeotia, sacred to the Muses. The springs on it were Hippocrene and Aganippe.

A thousand rills their mazy progress take:
5   The laughing flowers, that round them blow,
Drink life and fragrance as they flow.
Now the rich stream of music winds along,
Deep, majestic, smooth, and strong,
Through verdant vales and Ceres' golden reign:

4. Milton has 'mazie error', *Par. Lost* iv 239. Cp. also Pope, *Odyssey* v 91–2:
'And every fountain pours a several rill, / In mazy windings wandering down
the hill.'

5. *laughing*] Johnson gives one meaning of 'laugh' as 'To appear gay,
favourable, pleasant, or fertile'. Cp. Latin *ridens*, e.g. *ridenti acantho* (with
the laughing acanthus), Virgil, *Eclogues* iv 20.

6. Virgil, *Georgics* iv 32: *bibant violaria fontem*, translated by Dryden, iv 46,
'And let the purple Vi'lets drink the Stream'. G.'s phrasing may echo
Matthew Green, *The Spleen* 80: 'Shed light and fragrance as she flies.'

7–12. See Pope's 'Postscript' to the *Odyssey*, 12mo edn, v (1726) 236, for a
similar contrast as a metaphor for poetic effects, particularly the 'sublime'.
Like Pope, G. probably had in mind two much imitated passages in Horace,
Odes III xxix 33–41: *cetera fluminis / ritu feruntur, nunc medio alveo / cum
pace delabentis Etruscum / in mare, nunc lapides adesos // stirpesque raptas et pecus
et domos / volventis una non sine montium / clamore vicinaeque silvae, / cum fera
diluvies quietos // inritat amnes* (All else is borne along like some river, now
gliding peacefully in mid-channel into the Tuscan Sea, now rolling polished
stones, uprooted trees, and flocks and homes together, with echoing of the
hills and neighbouring woods, while the wild deluge stirs up the peaceful
streams); and *Odes* IV ii 5–8: *monte decurrens velut amnis, imbres / quem super
notas aluere ripas, / fervet immensusque ruit profundo / Pindarus ore* (Like a river
from the mountain rushing down, which the rains have swollen above its
wonted banks, so does Pindar seethe and, brooking no restraint, rush on
with deep-toned voice).

7–8. A couplet of Pope, *Imitations of Horace*, Ep. II ii 171–2, is often quoted
as G.'s source: 'Pour the full Tide of Eloquence along, / Serenely pure, and
yet divinely strong'; but there are closer passages in Thomson, cp. *Winter*
688–90: 'through the varied maze / Of eloquence, now smooth, now quick,
now strong, / Profound and clear, you roll the copious flood'; and *Liberty*
ii 257–60: 'In thy full language, speaking mighty things, / Like a clear torrent
close, or else diffused / A broad majestic stream, and rolling on / Through all
the winding harmony of sound'. See also Pope, *Ode on St Cecilia's Day*
11: 'The deep, majestic, solemn Organs blow'; Thomson, 'Winds in pro-
gressive majesty along', *Summer* 815, and 'Large, gentle, deep, majestic yet
sedate', *Autumn* 122. Prior, *Carmen Seculare* 276–83, has similar ideas and
diction, as has Young, *To the King* st.v: 'The Roman ode / Majestic flowed;
/ Its stream divinely clear, and strong; / In sense, and sound, / Thebes rolled
profound; / The torrent roared, and foamed along.'

10   Now rolling down the steep amain,
       Headlong, impetuous, see it pour:
       The rocks and nodding groves rebellow to the roar.

I. 2

Oh! Sovereign of the willing soul,
Parent of sweet and solemn-breathing airs,

10–12. Most such descriptions contain 'headlong' and/or 'impetuous', as
well as echoing rocks: 'The headlong torrents foaming down the hills',
Thomson, *Spring* 817, and *Summer* 590–3, 596: 'Smooth to the shelving brink
a copious flood / Rolls fair and placid; where, collected all / In one impetuous
torrent, down the steep / It thundering shoots, and shakes the country
round / . . . / And from the loud-resounding rocks below'; etc. Johnson
defines 'rebellow' as 'to echo back a loud noise'. It occurs in Spenser (*Faerie
Queene* I viii 11, 4; IV x 46, 4; V xii 41, 6) and is frequently used by Dryden
and Pope in their heroic verse: Dryden, *Aeneid* v 1127–8: 'Th'impetuous
Ocean roars; / And Rocks rebellow from the sounding Shores'; Pope,
Iliad xvii 315: 'And distant rocks rebellow from the shore'; Thomson,
Liberty iii 284–5: 'On every hand rebellowed to their joy / The swelling
sea, the rocks and vocal hills'. It is equivalent to Latin *reboare*, as used by
Virgil, etc.
10. rowling] rushing *Bedingfield.*   *amain*] 'With vehemence; with vigour;
fiercely; violently. It is used of any action performed with precipitation'
(Johnson). It is frequently used by Dryden: e.g. *Georgics* i 155–6: 'And calls
the floods from high, to rush amain / With pregnant streams.'
11. Headlong, impetuous] With torrent-rapture *Commonplace Book*, *Wharton*;
Impetuous, headlong, *Bedingfield.*
12. The rocks] While rocks *Bedingfield.*
13. Power of harmony to calm the turbulent sallies of the soul. The thoughts
are borrowed from the first Pythian of Pindar. *G. 1768.*
        G. was imitating *Pythian Odes* i 5–12, which celebrates the power of the
lyre: 'Thou abatest even the warring thunderbolt of everlasting flame;
and the eagle, king of birds, sleepeth on the sceptre of Zeus, while his swift
pinions twain are drooping, and a darksome mist is shed over his bending
head, sweetly sealing his eyelids; and the bird, as he slumbereth, heaveth his
buxom back beneath the spell of thy throbbing tones. For even the stern
god of war setteth aside his rude spears so keen, and warmeth his heart in
deep repose; and thy shafts of music soothe even the minds of the deities,
by grace of the skill of Leto's son and the deep-zoned Muses.' See also l. 25 *n.*
13. Richard II IV i 108: 'with willing soul'; and Dryden, *The Fair Stranger* 8:
'The mighty Soveraign of my Soul'.
14. Comus 555: 'A soft and solemn breathing sound'.

15   Enchanting shell! the sullen Cares
And frantic Passions hear thy soft control.
On Thracia's hills the Lord of War
Has curbed the fury of his car,
And dropped his thirsty lance at thy command.
20   Perching on the sceptered hand
Of Jove, thy magic lulls the feathered king
With ruffled plumes and flagging wing:
Quenched in dark clouds of slumber lie
The terror of his beak and lightnings of his eye.

15–16. Cp. Collins, *The Passions* 3–4 (p. 480 below).

15. shell] Lyre, in imitation of Latin *testudo*. The first lyre was traditionally supposed to have been invented by Hermes from strings stretched across a tortoise shell. Cp. Spenser, *Prothalamion* 5: 'sullen care'; Dryden, *Aeneid* vi 385: 'Revengeful Cares, and sullen Sorrows dwell'; and *Ceyx and Alcyone* 312: 'Care shuns thy soft approach, and sullen flies away'.

16. Faerie Queene V viii 48, 7: 'With franticke passion and with furie fraught'.

17–19. Cp. Collins, *Ode to Mercy* 4–6 (p. 439 below), and *Ode to Peace* 4–5 (p. 468 below).

17. Mars is repeatedly associated with Thrace in classical literature: e.g. Homer, *Odyssey* viii 361; Ovid, *Art of Love* ii 588; Statius, *Achilleid* i 201: *studiis multum Mavortia Thrace* (Thrace, steeped in the passionate love of war); and Claudian, *In Rufinum* ii, 'Praefatio', 17–20: *fertur et indomitus tandem post proelia Mavors / lassa per Odrysias fundere membra nives / oblitusque sui posita clementior hasta / Pieriis aures pacificare modis* (Even unwearying Mars is said to have stretched his tired limbs in the snowy Thracian plain when at last the battle was ended, and, unmindful of his wonted fierceness, to have laid aside his spear in gentler mood, soothing his ear with the Muses' melody).

19. Spenser, *Faerie Queene* I v 15, 2: 'his thirstie blade'.

20–4. This is a weak imitation of some incomparable lines in the same Ode. G. *1768.* (See l. 13 *n* above.)

20. The writer in the *Critical Review* (see l. 1 *n*) observed that 'perching' appears strictly to refer to the lyre's 'magic' rather than the eagle.

21–3. Faerie Queene I i 41, 1: 'The more to lulle him in his slumber soft'.

21. Cp. Shakespeare, *Phoenix and Turtle* 11: 'the eagle, feathered king'.

22. Pope, *Satires of Donne* iv 186: 'Where Contemplation prunes her ruffled Wings'; A. Philips, *Pastorals* v 119: 'She droops, she hangs her flagging wing'; Prior, *Solomon* ii 341: 'Tir'd may'st Thou pant, and hang thy flagging Wing'.

23. dark] black *Commonplace Book, Wharton and Bedingfield.*

23–4. Faerie Queene I v 14, 4–5: 'Let us now abate the terror of your might, / And quench the flame of furious despight . . .'

24. Dryden, *Epilogue to Calisto* 8: 'The force of any lightning but the eye';

I. 3

25   Thee the voice, the dance, obey,
       Tempered to thy warbled lay.
       O'er Idalia's velvet-green
       The rosy-crowned Loves are seen
       On Cytherea's day
30   With antic Sports and blue-eyed Pleasures,
       Frisking light in frolic measures;
       Now pursuing, now retreating,

and *Fable of Acis, Polyphemus and Galatea* 172: 'And only fear the lightning of your eyes'.
25ff. Power of harmony to produce all the graces of motion in the body. G. *1768.*

  Cp. Pindar, *Pythian Odes* i 1–4: 'O golden lyre, that are owned alike by Apollo and by the violet-tressed Muses! thou, lyre, which the foot-step heareth as it beginneth the glad dance; lyre, whose notes the singers obey, whenever, with thy quivering strings, thou preparest to strike up the prelude of the choir-leading overture!' Walpole noted in his copy of the *Odes*: 'Mrs Garrick formerly the Violette, a famous Dancer, sd, nobody had ever understood dancing like Mr. Gray in this description' (*Rothschild Library* (1954) i 267).
26. Cp. 'Their notes unto the voice attempred sweet', *Faerie Queene* II xii 71, 2; 'Tempering their sweetest notes unto thy lay', P. Fletcher, *Purple Island* IX iii 6; 'With eager thought warbling his Dorick lay', *Lycidas* 189, and 'Temper'd to th'Oaten Flute', *ibid* 33.
27–9. Aphrodite was said to have landed on Cythera, an island off the south coast of Laconia, after her birth in the sea and so was often called the Cytherean. Idalia was a town in Crete where she was worshipped. Cp. Juno's words to Venus, in Virgil, *Aeneid* x 86: *est Paphus Idaliumque tibi, sunt alta Cythera* (Paphus is thine, Idalium, and high Cythera).
27. 'She rears her flowers and spreads her velvet green', Young, *Universal Passion* v 230. G. probably had this passage in mind (cp. *Elegy* 55–6 *n*) but Fairfax, in his translation of Tasso, XIII xxxviii 1–2, has 'a fair and spacious green . . . / . . . like velvet, soft'; and Matthew Green, *The Spleen* 650: 'a green like velvet neat'.
28–30. Faerie Queene IV x 42, 2–3: 'A flocke of little loues, and sports, and ioyes, / With nimble wings of gold and purple hew'.
30. antic] Quaint, fantastic.
31. 'In friskful glee / Their frolics play', Thomson, *Spring* 837–8.
32–41. Mitford cites the following lines from an 'Ode. On Mira Dancing' in *Memoirs of Barton Booth. To which are added Several Poetical Pieces*, ed. Benjamin Victor (1733) pp. 49–50: 'Now to a slow and melting Air she moves; / Her Eyes their Softness steal from *Venus*' Doves: / So like in Shape in Air, and Mien, / She passes for the *Paphian* Queen; / The Graces all around

Now in circling troops they meet:
To brisk notes in cadence beating
35 Glance their many-twinkling feet.
Slow melting strains their queen's approach declare:
Where'er she turns the Graces homage pay.
With arms sublime, that float upon the air,
In gliding state she wins her easy way:
40 O'er her warm cheek and rising bosom move
The bloom of young desire and purple light of love.

her play; / The wondering Gazers die away. // Whether her easy Body bend, /
Or her fair Bosom heave with Sighs; / Whether her graceful Arms extend, /
Or gently fall, or slowly rise; / Or returning, or advancing; / Swimming
round, or sidelong glancing. // . . . // Strange Force of Motion! that subdues
the Soul . . .'
33. 'The gladsome Ghosts, in circling Troops, attend', Dryden, *Aeneid* vi 655.
34. in] the *Commonplace Book, Wharton.*
35. In *1768* G. acknowledged as his source Homer, *Odyssey* viii 265:
Μαρμαρυγὰς θηεῖτο ποδῶν· θαύμαζε δὲ θυμῷ (with feet that seemed
to twinkle as they moved). But cp. 'many-twinkling leaves', Thomson,
Spring 158.   *glance*] 'To shoot a sudden ray of splendour' (Johnson). Cp.
in Pope's translation of the passage cited by G., *Odyssey* viii 306: 'The
glancing splendours as their sandals play'.
36. their] the *Wharton.*   Cp. 'melting strains', Dryden, *To his Sacred Majesty*
55.
37. The Graces or Charites were the personification of loveliness or grace,
usually attendants of some greater goddess. They are attendants of Venus, as
here, in Homer, *Odyssey* viii 364; in Pope's translation, viii 400. Cp.
Tibullus, *Elegies* III viii 7–8: *Illam, quidquid agit, quoquo vestigia movit,* / *com-
ponit furtim subsequiturque Decor* (Whatsoever she does, whithersoever she
turns her steps, Grace follows her unseen to order all aright); and the 'Queen'
in Dryden, *Flower and the Leaf* 178–81, 190–1: 'She in the midst began with
sober Grace; / Her Servants Eyes were fix'd upon her Face: / And as she
mov'd or turn'd her Motions view'd, / Her Measures kept, and Step by
Step pursu'd / . . . / Admir'd, ador'd by all the circling Crowd, / For
wheresoe'er she turn'd her Face, they bow'd.'
39. 'on all sides round / Environ'd wins his way', *Par. Lost* ii 1015–16.
41. In *1768* G. gives a typically recondite source *Phrynicus, apud Athenaeum*
[*Deipnosophistae* xiii 604a]: Λάμπει δ'ἐπὶ πορφυρέῃσι / Παρείῃσι φῶς
ἔρωτος (and on his roseate cheeks there gleams the light of love). But see
also Virgil, *Aeneid* i 590–1: *lumenque iuventae* / *purpureum et laetos oculis
adflarat honores* (with youth's ruddy bloom, and on his eyes a joyous lustre);
imitated by Dryden, *Britannia Rediviva* 132–3: 'For She her self had made his
Count'nance bright, / Breath'd honour on his eyes, and her own Purple
Light.' See also *lumine* . . . / *purpureo, Aeneid* vi 640–1; and *Purpureus* . . .
Amor, Ovid, *Ars Amatoria* i 232, and *Amores* II i 38 and ix 34. Cp. also Pope,

II. 1

Man's feeble race what ills await,
Labour, and penury, the racks of pain,
Disease, and sorrow's weeping train,
45 And death, sad refuge from the storms of fate!
The fond complaint, my song, disprove,
And justify the laws of Jove.
Say, has he given in vain the heavenly Muse?
Night and all her sickly dews,
50 Her spectres wan and birds of boding cry,
He gives to range the dreary sky:
Till down the eastern cliffs afar

Imitations of Horace, Odes IV i 26: 'the smiling Loves and young Desires';
and Akenside's description of Venus's birth in the sea, *Pleasures of Imagination*
i 334–8: 'With fond acclaim attend her o'er the waves, / To seek th'Idalian
bower. Ye smiling band / Of youths and virgins, who thro' all the maze /
Of young desire with rival-steps pursue / This charm of beauty . . .'
42 ff. To compensate the real and imaginary ills of life, the Muse was given
to Mankind by the same Providence that sends the Day by its chearful
presence to dispel the gloom and terrors of the Night. G. *1768.*
42–5. Cp. *Eton Ode* 61–90 (pp. 60–3), and *Adversity* 39–40 (p. 73). Cp. also
William Broome, *Melancholy: An Ode* 27–8 (in *Poems*, 1727, p. 45): 'While
round, stern Ministers of Fate, / Pain, and Disease, and Sorrow wait.'
46. 'fond complaints', Addison, *Cato* I vi 53.
47. 'And justifie the wayes of God to men', *Par. Lost* i 26.
49–50. R. Hurd, *Select Works of Cowley*, 1772, i 199, believed that G. was
alluding to Cowley's *Hymn to Light* 37–40: 'Night, and her ugly subjects,
then dost fright, / And sleep, the lazy owl of night; / Asham'd and fearful
to appear / They screen their horrid shapes with the black hemisphere.'
50. 'as wan / As the pale Spectre of a murder'd Man', Dryden, *Palamon
and Arcite* i 528–9. Cp. Virgil, *Georgics* i 470: *importunaeque volucres* (ominous
birds): and *Aeneid* xii 861–3: *alitis in parvae subitam collecta figuram, / quae
quondam in bustis aut culminibus desertis / nocte sedens serum canit importuna
per umbras* (suddenly shrinking to the shape of the small bird which oft,
perched at night on tombs or deserted roofs, chants her late, ill-omened lay
amid the shadows). Cp. also 'boding screech-owls', *II Henry VI* III ii 327;
and 'the boding night-birds', Matthew Green, *The Grotto* 126.
51. gives] Permits.
52–3. Commonplace Book has:
    Till o'er the eastern cliffs from far
    Hyperion hurls around his glittering shafts of war.
These lines have been struck out and written in the margin is:
    Till fierce Hyperion from afar
    Hurls at their flying rear his glitt'ring shafts of war.
In the second line G. has then substituted on *for* at *and* scatter'd, *followed by*

Hyperion's march they spy and glittering shafts of war.

shadowy, *for* flying. *In Wharton this line reads:* Pours on their scatter'd rear his glitt'ring shafts of war.

G. gives as his source Cowley, *Brutus, an Ode* st. iv: 'Or seen the Morning's well-appointed Star / Come marching up the eastern hills afar', a misquotation of 'Or seen her well-appointed *Star* / Come marching up the *Eastern Hill* afar.' For the *afar/war* rhyme, see *Education and Government* 46–7 (p. 95–6), and G.'s translation of Statius (vi 646–88) 30–1 (p. 18).

52. Par. Lost v 275: 'th'Eastern cliff of Paradise'.

53. Hyperion] One of the Titans, either the father of the Sun or the Sun itself. Cp. Euripides, *Phoenissae* 168–9: 'Lo, how he flasheth in armour golden, like the morning shafts of the sun bright-blazing'; and Lucretius i 146–8: *Hunc igitur terrorem animi tenebrasque necessest / non radii solis neque lucida tela diei / discutiant, sed naturae species ratioque* (This terror of mind therefore and this gloom must be dispelled, not by the sun's rays or the bright shafts of day, but by the aspect and law of nature). See also *Agrippina* 94 (p. 36).

54ff. Extensive influence of poetic Genius over the remotest and most uncivilized nations: its connection with liberty, and the virtues that naturally attend on it. [See the Erse, Norwegian, and Welch Fragments, the Lapland and American songs.] G. *1768.*

A reference to the works of James Macpherson and Evan Evans discussed in the headnote to *The Fatal Sisters* and no doubt to his own translations of fragments of Norse and Welsh poetry. South American poetry had been discussed by various travellers, since Montaigne's essay *On the Cannibals*, which quotes from two songs. T. Warton Senior imitated the second of these in his *American Love-Ode* (*Poems* (1748) pp. 139–40). The 'Lapland songs' were no doubt the specimens of Lapp lyric poetry printed in John Scheffer's *Lapponia* (Frankfurt, 1673; Oxford, 1674), which became well known after translations had appeared in *Spectator* Nos. 366 and 404. See F. E. Farley, 'Three "Lapland Songs"', *PMLA* xxi (1906) 1–39. The growing interest in primitive poetry at this period can be illustrated by a letter from Thomas Percy to Evan Evans, 14 Aug. 1762, suggesting that Evans publish a collection entitled *Specimens of the ancient Poetry of different nations*. Percy himself had collected Erse, Runic, Peruvian, Lapland and Greenland poetry, as well as that of other nations: see *Correspondence of Percy and Evans*, ed. A. Lewis, 1957, p. 31. See also Sir William Temple, *Of Poetry* (1690), on the 'Antiquity' of poetry: 'It is, I think, generally agreed to have been the first sort of Writing that has been used in the World, and in several Nations to have preceded the very Invention or Usage of Letters. This last is certain in *America*, where the first *Spaniards* met with many strains of Poetry, and left several of them Translated into their Language, which seem to have flowed from a true Poetick Vein before any Letters were known in those Regions' (*Critical Essays of the 17th Century*, ed. J. E. Spingarn (1908–9) iii 85).

II.   2

In climes beyond the solar road,
55   Where shaggy forms o'er ice-built mountains roam,
The Muse has broke the twilight-gloom
To cheer the shivering native's dull abode.
And oft, beneath the odorous shade
Of Chile's boundless forests laid,
60   She deigns to hear the savage youth repeat
In loose numbers wildly sweet

54. In *1768* G. gave as his sources Virgil, *Aeneid* vi 796: *extra anni solisque vias* (beyond the paths of the year and the sun); and Petrarch, *Canzoniere* ii 48: *Tutta lontana dal camin del sole* (all remote from the solar road). Petrarch was no doubt imitating Virgil, as many English poets had done: e.g. Dryden, 'Beyond the Year, and out of Heav'ns high-way', *Annus Mirabilis* 639; 'Out of the *Solar* walk and Heav'ns high-way', *Threnodia Augustalis* 353; 'Beyond the Sunny walks, and circling Year', *Britannia Rediviva* 306; 'Far as the solar walk', Pope, *Essay on Man* i 102.

55-7. Tovey suggests that the first of these lines is an epitome of Virgil, *Georgics* iii 354-5, 366, 383: *sed iacet aggeribus niveis informis et alto | terra gelu late septemque adsurgit in ulnas | . . . | stiriaque impexis induruit horrida barbis | . . . | et pecudum fulvis velatur corpora saetis* (But far and wide earth lies shapeless under mounds of snow and piles of ice, rising seven cubits in height . . . and the rough icicle hardens on the unkempt beard . . . their bodies clothed in the tawny furs of beasts). But, as Walpole noted in his copy of the *Odes*, G. must also have remembered Dryden's *Prologue to his Royal Highness* (1682) 1-7: 'In those cold Regions which no Summers cheer, / When brooding darkness covers half the year, / To hollow Caves the shivering Natives go; / Bears range abroad, and hunt in tracks of Snow: / But when the tedious Twilight wears away, / And Stars grow paler at th'approach of Day, / The longing Crowds to frozen Mountains run.'

56. 'twilight shade', Milton, *Nativity Ode* 188.

57. *shivering*] buried   *dull*] chill *Commonplace Book, with the present readings in the margins*. 'Chili' in l. 59 no doubt forced G. to abandon 'chill'. Cp. 'Mean time in dark Abodes the Natives mourn', Blackmore, *The Nature of Man* (1711) p. 11 (on the Arctic).

59-61. Thomson, *Castle of Indolence* II xiv 6-8: 'Earth was till then a boundless Forest wild; / Nought to be seen but savage Woods and Skies; / No Cities nourished Arts, no Culture smiled . . .'

60. *youth*] Young man, as Latin *iuventus*.

61. *loose numbers*] See Horace on Pindar, *Odes* IV ii 11-12: *numerisque . . . | lege solutis* (in measures freed from rule). Cp. also Milton, *L'Allegro* 133-4: 'Or sweetest *Shakespear* fancies childe, / Warble his native Wood-notes wilde.'

Their feather-cinctured chiefs and dusky loves.
Her track, where'er the goddess roves,
Glory pursue and generous Shame,
65 The unconquerable Mind and Freedom's holy flame.

II. 3

Woods that wave o'er Delphi's steep,

62. 'girt / With feather'd Cincture', *Par. Lost* ix 1116; and Pope, *Windsor Forest* 404–5, 409–10: 'And Feather'd People crowd my wealthy Side, / And naked Youths and painted Chiefs admire / . . . / Till the freed *Indians* in their native Groves / Reap their own Fruits, and woo their Sable Loves.'
63–5. For the association of poetry and liberty, see ll. 77–82 below and *The Bard* (p. 178 below); Collins, *Ode to Simplicity* 31–6 (p. 426 below); Goldsmith, *Deserted Village* 407–16 (pp. 693–4 below).   *track*] The object of 'pursue', which in turn is plural because governed by all the nouns which follow as well as 'Glory'. G. is imitating classical practice.
63. *Goddess*] The Muse of Poetry.
64. *Shame*] As used here, fear of disgrace or loss of reputation, see *Elegy* 70 (p. 130 above).
65. 'the unconquerable Will', *Par. Lost* i 106; and 'Love's holy flame', Akenside, *Pleasures of Imagination* i 468.
66ff. Progress of Poetry from Greece to Italy, and from Italy to England. Chaucer was not unacquainted with the writings of Dante or of Petrarch. The Earl of Surrey and Sir Tho. Wyatt had travelled in Italy, and formed their taste there; Spenser imitated the Italian writers; Milton improved on them: but this School expired soon after the Restoration, and a new one arose on the French model, which has subsisted ever since. *G. 1768.*
See his plan for a history of English poetry, sent to Thomas Warton, 15 April 1770 (*Corresp* iii 1123–4), for an exposition of similar ideas.
66–9. Richard Chandler, in his *Travels in Greece* (1776) p. 79, attacked this passage, although he did not mention G. by name: 'And here it may be remarked, that the poets who celebrate the Ilissus as a stream laving the fields, cool, lucid, and the like, have both conceived and conveyed a false idea of this renowned water-course. They may bestow a willow fringe on its naked banks, amber waves on the muddy Meander, and hanging woods on the bare steeps of Delphi, if they please; but the foundation in nature will be wanting.' Walpole believed that 'amber' was merely poetic diction for 'muddy' (*Walpole Correspondence* xxviii 257); but see l. 69 *n*.
66. 'the steep of *Delphos*', Milton, *Nativity Ode* 178. Delphi was an ancient oracular shrine and precinct of Apollo, the God of poetry, on Mt Parnassus. This allusion suitably introduces G.'s references to the kinds of Greek poetry: the lyric poets, Sappho, Alcaeus and Simonides, associated with the Aegean islands; the tragic drama of Athens; and epic poetry associated with Asia Minor (see Maeander, l. 69), on the coast of which the *Iliad* and *Odyssey*

Isles that crown the Aegean deep,
Fields that cool Ilissus laves,
Or where Maeander's amber waves
70   In lingering lab'rinths creep,
How do your tuneful echoes languish,
Mute but to the voice of anguish?
Where each old poetic mountain
Inspiration breathed around:
75   Every shade and hallowed fountain
Murmured deep a solemn sound:
Till the sad Nine in Greece's evil hour
Left their Parnassus for the Latian plains.
Alike they scorn the pomp of tyrant-power,

may have originated. There are notes on Delphi and Parnassus, and many
Greek islands, in G.'s Commonplace Book (vol. i).

68. Ilissus] A stream originating on Mt Hymettus and running past Athens.
Cp. Collins, *Pity* 14 (see p. 416 below).

69. Or] And *Commonplace Book.*   *amber*] Probably derived, as Tovey
suggests, from Virgil's *electrum*: e.g. *non . . . / purior electro . . .. amnis* (no
stream purer than amber), *Georgics* iii 521–2. Milton has 'amber stream',
Par. Lost iii 359 and *Par. Regained* iii 288. The Maeander is in fact a muddy
river but, as Tovey points out, G. does not necessarily use the word to con-
note purity, as Virgil and Milton evidently do.

69–70. There are many classical references to the Maeander's tortuous course,
but G. is probably remembering the description of it in Ovid, *Metamorphoses*
viii 162–6, where Daedalus's labyrinth is compared to it. See also Fairfax's
Tasso XVI viii.

70–1. 1757 has 'Lab'rinth's' and 'Echo's' in these lines, as though they were
both genitive singular (see G. to Walpole, 10 Aug. 1757, *Corresp* ii 513).
Only the first error was corrected in *1768*.

70. Virgil, *Georgics* iii 14–15: *tardis ingens ubi flexibus errat / Mincius* (where
great Mincius wanders in slow windings).

71. Milton, *Comus* 230–2, describes 'Sweet Echo' as living by 'Slow *Mean-
der's* margent green'.

71–6. Milton, *Nativity Ode* 181–3: 'The lonely mountain o're, / And the
resounding shore, / A voice of weeping heard, and loud lament.'

73. 'Like that poetic mountain to be hight', G. West,*Education* (1751) I xvi 6.

75. Virgil, *Eclogues* i 51–2: *hic inter flumina nota / et fontis sacros frigus captabis
opacum* (Here, amid familiar streams and sacred springs, you shall court the
cooling shade).

76. deep a solemn] a celestial *Commonplace Book, with present reading in margin.*

77. sad Nine] The Muses.

78. Latian] Roman.

79. Parnassus] The mountain near Delphi associated with the worship of the
Muses.

80   And coward Vice that revels in her chains.
When Latium had her lofty spirit lost,
They sought, oh Albion! next thy sea-encircled coast.

III.   I

Far from the sun and summer-gale,
In thy green lap was Nature's darling laid,
85   What time, where lucid Avon strayed,
To him the mighty Mother did unveil
Her awful face: the dauntless child
Stretched forth his little arms and smiled.

80. Cp. *Ode for Music* 6 (p. 628).
82. J. Warton, *Ode to Liberty* 60, refers to Britain's 'sea-encircled land'.
84–8. J. Warton, *The Enthusiast* 168–72: 'What are the lays of artful Addison, /
Coldly correct, to Shakespeare's warblings wild? / Whom on the winding
Avon's willowed banks / Fair Fancy found, and bore the smiling babe /
To a close cavern . . .'
84. Nature's darling] Shakespear. G. *1768.*
    Mitford notes the phrase in Cleveland. Cf. Statius, *Thebaid* iv 786: *At
puer in gremio vernae telluris* (But the child, lying in the lap of the vernal
earth); 'The fresh green lap of fair King Richard's land', *Richard II* III iii 47,
and 'the green lap of the new come spring', *ibid* V ii 47; 'her green lap',
Milton, *Sonnet on May Morning* 3, and J. Warton, *Ode to Fancy* 80. See
also *Elegy* 117 (p. 138).
85. What time] Latin *quo tempore.*   *lucid*] Also a Latinism: e.g. Seneca,
Thyestes 129–30: *lucidus / Alpheos.*
86. mighty Mother] Cybele, the goddess of the powers of nature, known as
magna mater. Cp. Dryden, *Ovid's Metamorphoses* i 528: 'This Earth our
Mighty Mother is'; and *Georgics* i 465–6: 'On the green Turf thy careless
Limbs display, / And celebrate the mighty Mother's day'. There is an odd
echo in G.'s lines of *Dunciad* i 1: 'The Mighty Mother and her Son' and i
262: 'A veil of fogs dilates her awful face'. A writer in the *Gentleman's
Mag.* in 1781 (li 569) regretted that the reader was so 'forcibly reminded' of
Pope, and Gilbert Wakefield remarked in 1786 that 'Wicked memory
brings into the mind the *Queen* of the *Dunces*, and destroys all the pleasure
of the description by an unlucky contrast' (*Poems of Mr Gray* p. 88).
87–8. Virgil, *Eclogues* iv 60: *incipe, parve puer, risu cognoscere matrem* (Begin,
baby boy, to know thy mother with a smile); Horace, *Odes* III iv 20: *non
sine dis animosus infans* (with the gods' help a fearless child); Catullus, lxi
213–5: *matris e gremio suae / porrigens teneras manus / dulce rideat* (stretching his
baby hands from his mother's lap, smile a sweet smile); *Dunciad* iv 284: 'A
dauntless infant' (imitating Horace above).

'This pencil take,' (she said) 'whose colours clear
90   Richly paint the vernal year:
Thine too these golden keys, immortal boy!
This can unlock the gates of joy;
Of horror that and thrilling fears,
Or ope the sacred source of sympathetic tears.'

III.   2

95   Nor second he, that rode sublime
Upon the seraph-wings of Ecstasy,
The secrets of the abyss to spy.

89–90. pencil] See *Stanzas to Bentley* 4 (p. 154); and cp. *Pervigilium Veneris* 13: *ipsa gemmis purpurantem pingit annum floridis* (she herself paints the crimsoning year with flowery jewels), and G.'s *Latin Verses at Eton* 9–10 (p. 290); *Par. Lost* v 24: 'How Nature paints her colours'; Dryden, *Palamon and Arcite* ii 56: 'And Nature's ready Pencil paints the Flow'rs'; Thomson, *To the Memory of Lord Talbot* 204: 'The silent treasures of the vernal year'.

91–4. See G. to Wharton, 7 Sept. 1757 (*Corresp* ii 526): 'Dr. Akenside criticises opening *a source* with *a key*.'

91. Milton, *Comus* 13–14: 'that Golden Key / That ope's the Palace of Eternity'. G. has 'ope' in l. 94.

93. Horror] Terror *margin of Commonplace Book, Wharton.*   Cf. *Romeo and Juliet* IV iii 15: 'I have a faint cold fear thrills through my veins'.

94. See G.'s *O lacrimarum fons* (p. 380).

95. he] Milton. G. 1768.

sublime] G. combines with the eighteenth-century meaning of 'lofty' in style or theme, Milton's usual meaning 'aloft': cp. *Par. Lost* vi 771: 'Hee on the wings of Cherub rode sublime.'

95–100. G. may be alluding to Milton's Invocation to Urania, *Par. Lost* vii 12–14: 'Up led by thee / Into the Heav'n of Heav'ns I have presum'd, / An Earthlie Guest, and drawn Empyreal Aire.' See also his *Lines at a Vacation Exercise* 33 ff. But there are several characterizations of Milton in earlier poetry which resemble G.'s: e.g. Addison, *An Account of the Greatest English Poets* 56 ff.; Samuel Cobb, *Of Poetry* in *Poems on Several Occasions* (1707) 195; and Isaac Watts, *The Adventurous Muse* st. iv: 'There Milton dwells: the mortal sung / Themes not presumed by mortal tongue / . . . / Behold his Muse sent out t'explore / The unapparent deep where waves of chaos roar, / And realms of night unknown before. / She traced a glorious path unknown'.

96. ecstasy] Cowley's *The Ecstasy* describes a flight of the Muse similar to that G. attributes to Milton.

97. 'To wing the desolate Abyss, and spie / This new created World', *Par. Lost* iv 936; 'To trace the secrets of the dark abyss', Thomson, *Autumn* 778.

He passed the flaming bounds of place and time:
The living throne, the sapphire-blaze,
100   Where angels tremble while they gaze,
He saw; but blasted with excess of light,
Closed his eyes in endless night.
Behold, where Dryden's less presumptuous car,
Wide o'er the fields of glory, bear

98. G. gave as his source Lucretius i 73. See also its context, esp. i 72–4: *ergo vivida vis animi pervicit, et extra / processit longe flammantia moenia mundi / atque omne immensum peragravit mente animoque* (Therefore the lively power of his mind prevailed, and forth he marched far beyond the flaming walls of the heavens, as he traversed the immeasurable universe in thought and imagination).

99. G.'s note quotes *Ezekiel* i 20, 26, 28: 'For the spirit of the living creature was in the wheels–And above the firmament, that was over their heads, was the likeness of a throne, as the appearance of a saphire-stone.–This was the appearance of the glory of the Lord.' Milton himself imitated this passage in *Par. Lost* vi 750–9. For the sapphire throne see also *At a Solemn Music* 7; *Par. Lost* vi 772; and the 'fiery-wheeled throne', *Il Penseroso* 53.

101. Cp. *Par. Lost* iii 380: 'Dark with excessive bright'; and Pope, *Odyssey* xix 52: 'Celestials, mantled in excess of light'.

102. In *1768* G. gives as his source Homer, *Odyssey* viii 64 (of Demodocus, a ministrel of Alcinous): Ὀφθαλμῶν μὲν ἄμερσε ˙δίδου δ᾽ἡδεῖαν ἀοιδήν. ([the Muse] took away his sight, but she gave him [the power of] sweet song). Cp. also Virgil, *Aeneid* x 746: *in aeternam clauduntur lumina noctem* (his eyes closed in everlasting night); and Dryden, *Aeneid* iv 992: 'And clos'd her Lids at last, in endless Night'. Several writers have compared the account of Homer's blindness in Hermias: having decided to write about Achilles, Homer prayed that he might be allowed to see him. His request was granted but the poet was blinded by the splendour of the hero's armour. Mason denied that G. would have known such an obscure story; but, as a writer in the *Monthly Mag.* ix (1800) 258, pointed out, it is quoted by Pope, in the 'Essay on Homer' prefixed to his translation of the *Iliad*. Walpole, in his notes on the *Odes*, also cites Warburton, *Critical and Philosophical Enquiry into the Causes of Prodigies and Miracles* (1727) p. 61 *n*, where Hobbes is said to have 'broke thro'' the entangling Darkness, but dazled with the sudden Effusion of too much Light, in a little Time became stark blind'.

103. See James Beattie, *On Poetry and Music*, in *Essays* (Edinburgh, 1776) p. 360 *n*: 'One of the greatest poets of this century, the late and much-lamented Mr Gray of Cambridge, modestly declared to me, that if there was in his own numbers any thing that deserved approbation, he had learned it all from Dryden.'

105 Two coursers of ethereal race,
With necks in thunder clothed, and long-resounding
pace.

III. 3

Hark, his hands the lyre explore!
Bright-eyed Fancy hovering o'er
Scatters from her pictured urn
110 Thoughts that breathe and words that burn.
But ah! 'tis heard no more————

105. Meant to express the stately march and sounding energy of Dryden's rhimes. G. *1768.* (By 'rhimes' G. means Dryden's couplets.)

105. Virgil, *Aeneid* vii 280–1: *currum, geminosque iugales / semine ab aetherio, spirantes naribus ignem* (a car and two coursers of etherial seed, with nostrils breathing flame). Cp. also Dryden, *Aeneid* viii 51: 'Undoubted Off-spring of Etherial Race'; xii 175: 'Th'Etherial Coursers bounding from the Sea'; Pope, *Iliad* xvii 80: 'Achilles' coursers of etherial race'.

106. G. cites *Job* xxxix 19: 'Hast thou cloathed his neck with thunder?' Cp. Pope, *Imitations of Horace, Ep.* II i 267–9: 'Dryden taught to join / The varying verse, the full resounding line, / The long majestic march, and energy divine.' Cp. also 'long-resounding course', Thomson, *Winter* 775, and 'long-resounding voice', *Hymn on the Seasons* 77. G. had facetiously quoted the sentence from *Job* in a letter to West in July 1740: 'Have you learned to say Ha! ha! and is your neck clothed with thunder?' (*Corresp* i 173).

107. G. now turns to Dryden's lyric poetry from his heroic couplets (ll. 105–6). Dryden's irregular odes were particularly admired in the eighteenth century.

108. Bright-eyed] Full-plumed *Commonplace Book, Wharton.*

108. Comus 213–4: 'pure-ey'd Faith ,white-handed Hope, / Thou hovering angel'.

110. G. gave as his source (in a letter to Bedingfield in Aug. 1756, *Corresp* ii 477, and in *1768*) Cowley's *The Prophet* 20: 'Words, that weep, and tears, that speak'. Gosse and Tovey believed that G. had misquoted 'Tears which shall understand and speak', which is how the line first appeared in *The Mistress* in 1647. But G. was in fact quoting the 2nd edn of 1656, in which Cowley revised the poem. Cp. also David Mallet, 'With words that weep, and strains that agonise', *Amyntor and Theodora* (1747) ii 320.

111. We have had in our language no other odes of the sublime kind, than that of Dryden on St. Cecilia's day; for Cowley (who had his merit) yet wanted judgment, style and harmony, for such a task. That of Pope is not worthy of so great a man. Mr. Mason indeed of late days has touched the true chords, and with a masterly hand, in some of his Choruses,–above all in the last of Caractacus, 'Hark! heard ye not yon footstep dread? *&c.*' G. *1768.*

Mason's *Caractacus*, which G. had criticized in MS, had been published

Oh! lyre divine, what daring spirit
Wakes thee now? Though he inherit
Nor the pride nor ample pinion,
115   That the Theban eagle bear
Sailing with supreme dominion
Through the azure deep of air:
Yet oft before his infant eyes would run

in May 1759. G. wrote to James Brown at the time (*Corresp* ii 622): 'the last Chorus, & the lines that introduce it, are to me one of the best things I ever read, & surely superior to any thing he ever wrote.'

112–13. Cp. Collins's *Ode on the Poetical Character* 51–4 (p. 433 below), and *Elegy* 48 *n* (p. 126).

113–17. Horace, *Odes* IV ii 25–32: *multa Dircaeum levat aura cycnum / tendit, Antoni, quotiens in altos / nubium tractus. ego apis Matinae / more modoque // grata carpentis thyma per laborem / plurimum circa nemus uvidique / Tiburis ripas operosa parvus / carmina fingo* (A mighty breeze uplifts the Dircaean swan, Antonius, as oft as he essays a flight to the lofty regions of the clouds. I, after the way and manner of the Matinian bee, that gathers the pleasant thyme laboriously around full many a grove and the banks of well-watered Tibur, I, a humble bard, fashion my verses with incessant toil). Hurd, *Select Works of Cowley* (1772) i 161 *n*, notes the resemblance between Cowley's imitation of these lines, *The Praise of Pindar* st. iv, and G.'s lines. Cowley calls Pindar 'The Theban Swan'. Cp. also *Faerie Queene* V iv 42, 1–3: 'Like to an Eagle in his Kingly pride, / Soring through his wide Empire of the aire, / To weather his brode sailes . . .'

113. he] G. himself.

114. 'His ample pinions', Young, *Night Thoughts* ii 223.

115. In *1768* G. cites Pindar, *Olympian Odes* ii 88, Διὸς πρὸς ὄρνιχα θεῖον (against the godlike bird of Zeus); and adds: 'Pindar compares himself to that bird, and his enemies to ravens that croak and clamour in vain below, while it pursues its flight, regardless of their noise.' G.'s epigraph to the poem comes from the same passage: cp. ll. 81–8: 'Full many a swift arrow have I beneath mine arm, within my quiver, many an arrow that is vocal to the wise; but for the crowd they need interpreters. The true poet is he who knoweth much by gift of nature, but they that have only learnt the lore of song, and are turbulent and intemperate of tongue, like a pair of crows, chatter in vain against the godlike bird of Zeus.'

117. deep of air] Cp. Lucretius v 276: *aeris in magnum . . . mare* (into the great sea of air); and Euripides, *Medea* 1297: 'Or lift on wings her frames to heaven's far depths'.

118–22. Commonplace Book has:

> Yet, when they first were open'd on the day,
> Before his visionary eyes would run
> Such Forms, as glitter in the Muse's ray

Such forms as glitter in the Muse's ray
120 With orient hues, unborrowed of the sun:
Yet shall he mount and keep his distant way
Beyond the limits of a vulgar fate,
Beneath the Good how far – but far above the Great.

With orient hues unborrow'd of the Sun:
Yet never can he fear a vulgar fate

In the third of these lines Shapes *is written in the margin to replace* forms. *The final version of this passage is written below.*

118–120. A writer in the *Gentleman's Mag.* lxi (1791) 981, suggests that G. had in mind a passage in Sir William Temple's essay, *Of Poetry (Critical Essays of the 17th Century*, ed. Spingarn, iii 81): 'There must be a spritely Imagination or Fancy, fertile in a thousand Productions, ranging over infinite Ground, piercing into every Corner, and by the Light of that true Poetical Fire discovering a thousand little Bodies or Images in the World, and Similitudes among them, unseen to common Eyes, and which could not be discovered without the Rays of that Sun.'

120. orient] Bright, shining. Cp. 'Which are arayd with much more orient hew', Spenser, *Hymne in Honour of Beautie* 79, and 'With Orient Colours', *Par. Lost* i 545. Cp. also Virgil, *Georgics* i 396: *nec fratris radiis obnoxia surgere Luna* (and the moon rises under no debt to her brother's rays). Dryden translates, i 542, 'As with unborrow'd Beams'. Cp. also Dryden, *Eclogues* iv 53: 'With native Purple, or unborrow'd Gold'.

121–3. Horace, *Odes* III ii 21–4: *Virtus, recludens immeritis mori / caelum, negata temptat iter via, / coetusque vulgares et udam / spernit humum fugiente pinna* (True worth, opening Heaven wide for those deserving not to die, essays its course by a path denied to others, and spurns the vulgar crowd and damp earth on fleeting pinion). Cp. also Pope, *Epitaph On Mr Fenton* 3–4: 'A Poet blest beyond the Poet's fate, / Whom Heav'n kept sacred from the Proud and Great'; and *Imitations of Horace, Odes* IV ix 3–4: 'Taught on the Wings of Truth, to fly / Above the reach of vulgar Song'; Jean Baptiste Louis de Gresset, *La Mediocrité (Oeuvres*, 1748, i 361–2): *Sourd aux censures populaires, / Il ne craint point les yeux vulgaires, / Son oeil perce au-delà de leur foible horison; / Quelques bruits que la foule en sème, / Il est satisfait de lui-même, / S'il a su mériter l'aveu de sa raison.*

123. Cp. Katherine Philips, *To the Countess of Thanet* 33, in *Poems* (1667) p. 133: 'Still shew how much the Good outshine the Great'.

21 The Bard. A Pindaric Ode

Written between 1755 and May 1757. G. told Thomas Wharton in a letter dated 9 March 1755 that, in addition to *The Progress of Poesy* completed in the previous year, he had 'two or three Ideas more in my head' (*Corresp* i

420). According to Mason. 'One of these was the BARD, the exordium of which [presumably ll. 1–22] was at this time finished' (*Memoirs* p. 233). G. worked hard on the poem during the summer. On 6 Aug. 1755 he asked Wharton's opinion of the '*Morceau*' he had sent him, evidently ll. 1–56 of the poem (*Corresp* i 428). On 21 Aug. he wrote to Stonhewer: 'As you have the politeness to pretend impatience, and desire I would communicate, and all that, I annex a piece of the Prophecy; which must be true at least, as it was wrote so many hundred years after the events' (*Corresp* i 432–3). The extract from *The Bard* which accompanied this letter has not survived, but Mason described it as 'The second Antistrophe and Epode, with a few lines of the third Strophe' i.e. ll. 63–*c*. 100 (*Memoirs* p. 241 *n*). This extract was to be sent on to Wharton, to whom G. also wrote on the same day, describing it as 'very rough & unpolish'd at present' and discussing Wharton's comments on what he had already seen of the poem (*Corresp* i 434).

At this point, with more than two-thirds of the poem in draft, G.'s creative energy suddenly flagged. In mid-Oct. 1755 he admitted to Wharton that he had 'not done a word more of *Bard*, having been in a very listless, unpleasant, & inutile state of Mind for this long while'; and another letter to Wharton of 9 Jan. 1756 shows that he had still added nothing to what he had written in the previous summer (*Corresp* i 442–3, ii 457). Late in April 1756, after discussing the *Progress of Poesy*, he explained to Bedingfield that, 'I have written part of another, wch intends to be much better, but my Inspiration is very apt to fail me before I come to a conclusion' (*Corresp* ii 462). Another letter to Bedingfield of 27 Aug. 1756 shows that he had already sent his friend ll. 1–22 of *The Bard* and he now sent ll. 23–56, discussing his sources and borrowings in some detail (*Corresp* ii 475–8). By the end of 1756, however, he had still made no further progress with the poem (*Corresp* ii 486, 488).

One reason for G.'s inability to finish the poem, according to Mason, *Poems* pp. 91–2, lay in the 'original argument' which he quoted from G.'s Commonplace Book. It is notable that in this version there is no mention of the chorus of bards:

'The army of Edward I. as they march through a deep valley, are suddenly stopped by the appearance of a venerable figure seated on the summit of an inaccessible rock, who, with a voice more than human, reproaches the King with all the misery and desolation which he had brought on his country; foretells the misfortunes of the Norman race, and with prophetic spirit declares, that all his cruelty shall never extinguish the noble ardour of poetic genius in this island; and that men shall never be wanting to celebrate true virtue and valour in immortal strains, to expose vice and infamous pleasure, and boldly censure tyranny and oppression. His song ended, he precipitates himself from the mountain, and is swallowed up by the river that rolls at its foot.'

Unfortunately, Mason believed, G. was unable in practice to persuade himself that the English poets from Spenser to Addison had been preoccupied with the celebration of 'true virtue and valour'; and Mason remembered

that 'the Ode lay unfinished by him for a year or two on this very account'.
G. did not in fact complete *The Bard* until May 1757. At the end of that
month he sent a draft of the conclusion (ll. 111–44) to Mason and described
the event which had provided him with the inspiration to finish the poem
(*Corresp* ii 501–3). This had been a visit to Cambridge by John Parry, a
blind musician of Ruabon in Wales, harper to Sir Watkin Williams Wynne,
and the joint editor of some of the earliest collections of Welsh music: 'Mr
Parry has been here, & scratch'd out such ravishing blind Harmony, such
tunes of a thousand year old with names enough to choak you, as have set
all this learned body a'dancing, & inspired them with due reverence for
Odikle, whenever it shall appear. Mr Parry (you must know) it was, that
has put Odikle in motion again, & with much exercise it has got a *tender
Tail* grown . . .' This draft of the conclusion had been extensively revised
by the time G. wrote again to Mason on 11 June 1757 (*Corresp* ii 503–4)
when he discussed objections that his friends had been making to it and ex-
plained other alterations. A copy of ll. 57–144 of the poem in G.'s
hand, now with the Wharton MSS (*Corresp* i 434–7), seems to embody the
changes G. made between his letter to Mason at the end of May and that of
11 June. G. may well have given this corrected version to Wharton in
mid-June 1757, when they met in London.

G. was now anxious that his two Pindaric Odes should be published
together without delay. On 29 June 1757 he signed a receipt for 40 guineas
for the copyright from Dodsley, reserving to himself only 'the right of
reprinting them in any one Edition I may hereafter print of my Works'
(*Corresp* ii 513 *n*). At this point, Horace Walpole, somewhat to G.'s dismay,
interfered by asking that he should be allowed to print them for Dodsley at
his newly established press at Strawberry Hill. Walpole himself said in a
letter to Chute, 12 July 1757 (*Letters*, ed. Toynbee, iv 73) that he had 'snatched'
the *Odes* 'out of Dodsley's hands'; and G. told Mason on 1 Aug. (*Corresp* ii
512): 'they had been out three weeks ago, but Mr W:, having taken it into
his head to set up a Press of his own at Twickenham, was so earnest to handsel
it with this new pamphlet, that it was impossible to find a pretence for
refusing such a trifle. you will dislike this, as much as I do, but there is
no help. you understand, it is he, that prints them not for me, but for
Dodsley.'

Walpole's new press was 'erected' on 25 June 1757 and began to print the
Odes, its first book, on 16 July. By 3 Aug. 1000 copies had been printed and
on 8 August 2000 copies were published by Dodsley (Paget Toynbee,
Journal of the Printing-Office at Strawberry Hill (1923) p. 3). The existence of
copies of the *Odes* on both thick and thin paper, with minor textual variants,
caused at one time a considerable amount of bibliographical speculation.
It is now established that the copies on thick paper belong to an independent
small edn of perhaps 100 copies, printed by Thomas Kirgate at the Straw-
berry Hill press in about 1790. For a full discussion see A. T. Hazen, *Biblio-
graphy of the Strawberry Hill Press* (New Haven, 1942) pp. 23–31. In spite of
G.'s uneasiness about Walpole's printing the *Odes* and the fact that he detected

a number of *errata*, he admitted that the book was 'very pleasant to the eye, & will do no dishonour to your Press' (*Corresp* ii 513).

For all his defiant awareness that the *Odes* would perplex many of his readers, G. had never hitherto been so anxious to learn the opinions of his friends and the world at large. He had told Bedingfield in Aug. 1756 that he expected that few female readers would be able to understand 'this kind of composition', but the reasons he gave would obviously also apply to many of his male readers (*Corresp* ii 478): 'there is a certain measure of learning necessary, & a long acquaintance with the good Writers ancient & modern . . . and without this they can only catch here & there a florid expression, or a musical rhyme, while the Whole appears to them a wild obscure unedifying jumble.' G.'s reluctance to annotate the *Odes* has been described in the headnote to the *Progress of Poesy*, which had no notes in *1757*. Walpole persuaded G. to provide an Advertisement and four short notes for *The Bard*, but they did not prevent a considerable amount of confusion in his readers, which G. reported to his friends with grim relish. The 'intelligent' to whom he had expected the *Odes* to be 'vocal' turned out to be 'still fewer, than even I expected'. In Sept. 1757 he told Mason that 'nobody understands me, & I am perfectly satisfied' (*Corresp* ii 518, 522). Neither statement was entirely true, for there were enthusiastic readers (see W. Powell Jones, 'The Contemporary Readers of Gray's *Odes*', *MP* xxviii (1930–1) 61–82, and R. W. Ketton-Cremer, *Thomas Gray* pp. 153–7); and G. was by no means satisfied about some of the misunderstandings. As he told Wharton in mid-Aug. (*Corresp* ii 518): 'the great objection is obscurity, no body knows what we would be at. one Man (a Peer) I have been told of, that thinks the last Stanza of [*The Bard*] relates to Charles the first & Oliver Cromwell.' In *1768* G. at last provided his readers with full historical notes to *The Bard*, but his last comment was as defiant as ever, when he explained his concession to James Beattie (*Corresp* iii 1002): 'as to the notes I do it out of spite, because the Publick did not understand the two odes (wch I have call'd Pindaric) tho' the first was not very dark, & the second alluded to a few common facts to be found in any six-penny History of England by way of question & answer for the use of children. the parallel passages I insert out of justice to those writers, from whom I happen'd to take the hint of any line, as far as I can recollect.'

G.'s 'Advertisement' in *1757* read: 'The following Ode is founded on a Tradition current in Wales, that EDWARD THE FIRST, when he completed the Conquest of that country, ordered all the Bards, that fell into his hands, to be put to death.' G.'s source for the tradition was a passage in Thomas Carte's *General History of England* ii (1750) 196, concerning Edward I's campaigns in Wales:

'The onely set of men among the *Welsh*, that had reason to complain of *Edward*'s severity, were the *Bards*, who used to put those remains of the antient *Britains* in mind of the valiant deeds of their ancestors: he ordered them all to be hanged, as inciters of the people to sedition. Politicks in this

point got the better of the king's natural lenity: and those, who were after-
wards entrusted with the government of the country, following his example,
the profession becoming dangerous, gradually declined, and, in a little time,
that sort of men was utterly destroyed.'

Carte's acknowledged source for this information was 'Sir J. Wynne's
Hist. of the Gwedir Family, p. 31'. G. seems to have come across the passage
in Carte in 1755, for he made a note on the fly-leaf of his pocketbook for
that year of 'J. Wynne's Account of the Gwedir Family', presumably
intending to consult it. Wynne's History was in fact still in MS and was not
published until 1770.

The passage in Carte provided G. with a sufficient source for The Bard,
but his interest in the tradition did not cease with the publication of the
poem nor did he accept it as necessarily authentic. At some date before
1759, in the course of the historical review of Anglo-Welsh relations in
the long article 'Cambri' in his Commonplace Book, G. wrote of Edward
I: 'he is said to have hanged up all their Bards, because they encouraged the
Nation to rebellion, but their works (we see), still remain, the Language (tho'
decaying) still lives, & the art of their versification is known, and practised
to this day among them.' Later in the essay G. prefaced quotations from
records and documents of the reign of Edward I from William Wotton's
edition of Leges Wallicae (1730), with another qualification of Carte's story:
'Whatever severity Edward the first might exercise at the time, when he
reduced that Country, on some of the Welch Bards; yet it appears, he pro-
ceeded no farther against them in general, than to order that they should not
travel (as usual) about Wales, nor ask any rewards from the Inhabitants.'

G. thus arrived at the modern conclusion about the tradition preserved
by Carte: that Edward I did not in fact suppress the bards but merely issued
an edict against vagrancy. Nevertheless, it is not surprising that G. welcomed
evidence to suggest that his poem had some historical basis, as is clear from
the correspondence between Thomas Percy and Evan Evans, the Welsh
scholar. Percy wrote to Evans on 21 July 1761, mentioning that he had been
told that Evans was 'acquainted with Mr Gray the Poet', and asking whether
there was any truth in the tradition that Edward I hanged the Welsh bards,
as G. had asserted in his poem.

Evans replied on 8 Aug. 1761 that he did not know G., but that the tradition
about the bards was 'very true' and quoted as evidence the passage from
Wynne's MS History of the Gwedir Family (in the Mostyn Library) which
had been Thomas Carte's source. On 15 Oct. 1761 Percy wrote to tell
Evans that he had recently visited Cambridge and that early in Sept. he had
spent an afternoon with G.: 'Our discourse turned on you and the Welsh
Poetry: I shewed him your Letter, and he desired leave to transcribe the
passage relating to K. Edwd's massacre of the Welsh bards. – All the authority
he had before, it seems, was only a short hint in Carte's History. He seemed
very glad of this authentic extract.' See The Correspondence of Thomas Percy
and Evan Evans, ed. Aneirin Lewis (Baton Rouge, 1957) pp. 5, 11-12, 14-15;

and for further discussion, E. D. Snyder, *The Celtic Revival 1760–1800* (1923) pp. 42–5; W. Powell Jones, *Thomas Gray, Scholar* (1937) pp. 95–8; and *Corresp* ii 746–7 and *n*.

A few minor points in connection with *The Bard* may be mentioned in conclusion. On several occasions it was stated that G.'s model was Nereus's prophecy of the destruction of Troy, in Horace's *Odes* I xv. The suggestion was first made by Goldsmith in the *Monthly Review* xvii (1757) 242, and the resemblance was again noted by Algarotti in a letter to William Taylor How dated 26 Dec. 1762, printed by Mason in *1775, Poems* p. 85. Johnson also stated in his *Life of G.* (*Lives of the Poets*, ed. G. B. Hill, iii 438) that 'The Bard appears, at the first view, to be . . . an imitation of the prophecy of Nereus'. In a letter to Wharton in Oct. 1757, G. stated that he particularly admired Goldsmith's suggestion of his indebtedness to Horace, which might appear to be an acknowledgement of this source; but in Dec. 1758 he described the imitation of Horace as 'falsely laid to my charge' (*Corresp* ii 532, 602). It is likely that the idea of the Bard's prophecy was in fact suggested to G. by some such work as Thomas Pugh's *British and Out-landish Prophesies: Most Of above a 1000 years Antiquity, the rest very Antient: Fore-telling The several Revolutions which hath and shall befall the Scepter of ENG-LAND . . published in Welsh and English for the satisfaction of the Intelligent in either* TONGUE, 1658. This work purported to show that English history had been prophesied by the ancient Welch poets. Rose M. Davis, *Stephen Duck*, Univ. of Maine Studies, 1926, pp. 170–1, points out that, although there is no verbal resemblance between *The Bard* and Duck's *Caesar's Camp* (1755), in each of them occurs 'an ancient seer of Celtic race, who censures a victorious conqueror of his native land and then beholds the future unroll'd in a vision, which he uses as a weapon of reproach against the warrior'.

From G.'s writings on Welsh poetry in his Commonplace Book it is clear that he understood at least some its principles. How far they can be assumed to have affected the versification of *The Bard* has not been settled and would not be easy to establish. G. himself admitted to attempting to imitate 'a peculiar measure in the Welch Prosody' by a recurring 'double cadence' (see l. 43 *n*) and this may support suggestions that to some extent he also tried to reproduce the alliterative patterns of the Welsh *cynghanedd* in *The Bard*. See E. D. Snyder, 'Thomas Gray's interest in Celtic', *MP* xi (1914) 562; and W. Powell Jones, *Thomas Gray, Scholar* pp. 92–3. The idea is rejected, however, by Roger Martin, *Essai sur Thomas Gray* p. 453, on the grounds that the *Elegy* can be shown to contain alliteration as frequent and complex as any in *The Bard*. Arthur Johnston, 'Gray's use of the Gorchest y Beirdd in *The Bard*', *MLR* lix (1964) 335–8, discusses the relationship of ll. 43–6 to Welsh metrical practice and examines earlier and closer example of the metre in English poetry. He points out that the 'Gorchest y Beirdd' was not in use at the time of Edward's supposed massacre of the Welsh bards: it was first used in the mid-fifteenth century.

Mason, *Poems* p. 92, gives an account of a plan for a setting of *The Bard* by the composer John Christopher Smith, the pupil of Handel, with which

G. himself assisted. Mason quotes G.'s 'sentiments . . . concerning the over-ture' in full. These instructions to the composer are of interest; but, soon after the publication of Mason's book, Thomas Twining, a former friend of G. at Cambridge, wrote to Charles Burney on 9 June 1775 (British Museum, Add. MS 39933 ff. 136–7), asserting that the plan for the overture to *The Bard* was partly his own and written in his own words: 'I have the original paper which Mr G. wrote.' Although Twining was anxious for Mason to rectify this error, no change was made in the passage in later edns of the *Memoirs*.

The text followed here is that of *1768*, to which G. added extensive notes. Variants are given from passages contained in letters to Wharton, Beding-field and Mason as described above. Horace Walpole's MS notes in his copy of the *Odes* (1757) are cited from *The Rothschild Library* (1954) i 266–8.

I. I

'Ruin seize thee, ruthless king!
'Confusion on thy banners wait,
'Though fanned by Conquest's crimson wing
'They mock the air with idle state.
5 'Helm nor hauberk's twisted mail,
'Nor even thy virtues, tyrant, shall avail
'To save thy secret soul from nightly fears,

¶21.*1*. 'Ruin seize thee / And swift perdition overtake thy treachery', Nicholas Rowe, *Jane Shore* II i.

1–2. 'There comes the ruin, there begins confusion', *I Henry VI* IV i 194; and 'vast confusion waits / . . . The imminent decay of wrested pomp', *King John* IV iii 152, 154.

3. '. . . murder's crimson badge', *II Henry VI* III ii 200.

3–4. 'Where the Norweyan banners flout the sky / And fan our people cold', *Macbeth* I ii 49–50; and 'With silken streamers the young Phoebus fanning', *Henry V* III Prol. 6.

4. G. acknowledged a debt (to Bedingfield in Aug. 1756, *Corresp* ii 477 and in *1768*) to *King John* V i 72: 'Mocking the air with colours idly spread'; cp. also 'melts the thoughtless hours in idle state', Thomson, *Autumn* 1252.

5. The Hauberk was a texture of steel ringlets, or rings interwoven, forming a coat of mail, that sate close to the body, and adapted itself to every motion. G. *1768*.

Cp. Dryden, *Palamon and Arcite* iii 603: 'Hauberks and Helms are hew'd with many a Wound'. Mitford notes that Fairfax often combines the words in his translation of Tasso; e.g. VII xxxviii, 7: 'Now at his helm, now at his hauberk bright'; and XI xxi 4; XVII xviii 6, etc.

7. secret soul] A phrase used by Dryden, *Annus Mirabilis* 31; *Cinyras and Myrrha* 34; *Cymon and Iphegenia* 422. Cp. also 'nightly feare', *Faerie Queene* I iv 28, 8; 'these terrible dreams / That shake us nightly', *Macbeth* III ii 18–9.

'From Cambria's curse, from Cambria's tears!'
Such were the sounds, that o'er the crested pride
10   Of the first Edward scattered wild dismay,
As down the steep of Snowdon's shaggy side
He wound with toilsome march his long array.
Stout Gloucester stood aghast in speechless trance:
'To arms!', cried Mortimer and couched his quivering
    lance.

9. G.'s note in *1768* cites 'The crested adder's pride', Dryden, *Indian Queen*
III i. Cp. also 'And Crested Morions, with their Plumy Pride', Dryden,
Palamon and Arcite iii 452; and 'I begin to bear my Crest aloft when I hear
of your pride', G. to Walpole, Feb. 1735 (*Corresp* i 25).

11. *Snowdon* was a name given by the Saxons to that mountainous tract,
which the Welch themselves call *Craigian-eryri*: it included all the highlands
of Caernarvonshire and Merionethshire, as far east as the river Conway.
R. Hygden speaking of the castle of Conway built by King Edward the
first, says 'Ad ortum amnis Conway ad clivum montis Erery;' and Matthew
of Westminster, (ad ann. 1283,) 'Apud Aberconway ad pedes montis
Snowdoniae fecit erigi castrum ferri.' *G. 1768.*

shaggy] As an adjective for a mountain probably derived from Milton:
e.g. 'the shaggy top of *Mona* high', *Lycidas* 54 (after a reference to 'bards');
and see also *Par. Lost* iv 224 and vi 645. John Dyer, *Ruins of Rome* 315,
has 'Snowdon's rugged side'.

12–14. toilsome ... array ... aghast ... trance ... couched] G.'s diction is mar-
kedly Spenserian at this point in the poem.

12. 'in long array his Vessels show', Dryden, *Annus Mirabilis* 263; and 'are
led / In long Array', Dryden, *Aeneid* xi 113–4.

13–14. Gloucester ... Mortimer] Gilbert de Clare, surnamed the Red, Earl
of Gloucester and Hertford, son-in-law to King Edward.

Edmond de Mortimer, Lord of Wigmore.

They both were *Lords-Marchers*, whose lands lay on the borders of
Wales, and probably accompanied the King in this expedition. *G. 1768.*

Gilbert de Clare (1243–95), 7th Earl of Hertford, 9th Earl of Clare and
8th Earl of Gloucester, fought against the Welsh in 1276–83. He married
Edward I's daughter Joan in 1290 and was driven out of Wales by a native
uprising in 1294. G. was mistaken in referring to Edmond de Mortimer: he
seems almost certainly to have intended Roger de Mortimer (1231?–1282),
6th Baron Wigmore, who was conspicuous in Edward I's struggles against
the Welsh in 1276–9.

14. Virgil, *Aeneid* ii 175: *hastamque trementem* (quivering spear) and xii
94–5; Marlowe, *I Tamburlaine* II iii 18: 'our quivering lances'; *I Henry VI*
III ii 134: 'A braver soldier never couched lance'.

I. 2

15   On a rock, whose haughty brow
Frowns o'er old Conway's foaming flood,
Robed in the sable garb of woe,
With haggard eyes the poet stood;
(Loose his beard and hoary hair

15–16. Pope, *Odyssey* iii 374–5: 'There stands a rock, high eminent and steep, / Whose shaggy brow o'erhangs the shady deep'; and Thomson, *Spring* 755–7: 'High from the summit of a craggy cliff, / Hung o'er the deep, such as amazing frowns / On utmost Kilda's shore.'

16. old Conway] Perhaps an imitation of 'old Euphrates', *Par. Lost* i 420. Cp. 'the foaming Flood', Dryden, *Aeneid* ii 677.

17–18. G. wrote to Wharton in Aug. 1755 (*Corresp* i 434): 'you may alter that *Robed in the Sable*, &c, almost in your own words, thus

With fury pale, & pale with woe,
Secure of fate, the Poet stood &c:

Tho' *haggard*, wch conveys to you the Idea of a *Witch*, is indeed only a metaphor taken from an unreclaim'd Hawk, wch is call'd a *Haggard*, & looks wild & *farouche* & jealous of its liberty.' Dryden frequently uses 'haggard' of eyes: e.g. 'His Hands and hagger'd Eyes to Heav'n he cast', *Aeneid* x 942; and see *Georgics* iv 370, *Aeneid* ii 86.

17. 'In Sorrow's Garb, in Sable clad', William Broome, *Melancholy: An Ode* 10, in *Poems* (1727) p. 44.

18. stood] The Bard was seated in the original 'argument': see headnote.

19–20. The image was taken from a well-known picture of Raphaël, representing the Supreme Being in the vision of Ezekiel: there are two of these paintings (both believed original), one at Florence, the other at Paris. *G. 1768*.

    G. had admitted to this source of inspiration in a letter to Bedingfield in Aug. 1756: 'the thought . . . is borrow'd from painting. Rafael in his Vision of Ezekiel (in the Duke of Orleans' Collection) has given the air of head, wch I tried to express, to God the Father; or (if you have been at Parma) you may remember Moses breaking the Tables by the Parmeggiano, wch comes still nearer to my meaning' (*Corresp* ii 476–7). In 1765 G. urged his friend Palgrave, who was visiting Italy, to see this painting by Mazzuola, known as 'il Parmigiano' (*Corresp* ii 867). Mason mentioned this second painting after quoting G.'s own note in *Poems* p. 93. The works in question are Raphael's *Vision of Ezekiel* (in the Pitti Gallery, Florence) and Parmigiano's *Moses* (a fresco in the Chiesa della Steccata, Parma). G.'s references to these paintings emphasise the visual effect for which he is striving in these lines. G.'s note on the *Moses*, made when he saw it in Italy, is in the Mitford MSS in the British Museum (Add. MS 32561 f. 140).

19. Faerie Queene II xi 23, 3: 'With hoarie lockes all loose'; and IV v 34, 8: 'With rugged beard, and hoarie shagged heare'.

20   Streamed, like a meteor, to the troubled air)
      And, with a master's hand and prophet's fire,
      Struck the deep sorrows of his lyre.
      'Hark, how each giant-oak and desert cave
      'Sighs to the torrent's awful voice beneath!
25   'O'er thee, oh king! their hundred arms they wave,
      'Revenge on thee in hoarser murmurs breathe;
      'Vocal no more, since Cambria's fatal day,
      'To high-born Hoel's harp or soft Llewellyn's lay.

                           I.   3
            'Cold is Cadwallo's tongue,
      30   'That hushed the stormy main:

20. G. admitted to Bedingfield in 1756 that this line was 'almost stoln'
from *Par. Lost* i 537 (*Corresp* ii 477), and acknowledged the debt in 1768:
'Shone like a Meteor streaming to the Wind'. Cp. also Cowley, *Davideis*
Bk. ii, of Gabriel: 'An harmless flaming meteor shone for hair'. A distracting
parallel from *Hudibras*, I i 247–8, has frequently been noted. Butler wrote of
Hudibras's beard: 'This hairy meteor did denounce / The fall of sceptres and
of crowns'. Cp. also 'Like the meteors of a troubled heaven', *I Henry IV* I i
10; 'the troubled air' is a fairly common poetic phrase: e.g. Fairfax's
Tasso XII lxxvii 3 and XVIII lxxxviii 3; Dryden, *Ovid's Metamorphoses* xii
81; Thomson, *Winter* 82.
21. Cp. Collins, *Poetical Character* 21 (p. 429 below) and *Liberty* 127 (p. 453
below).
23. 'the Woods, and desert Caves', *Lycidas* 39.
26. 'the Tides with their hoarse murmurs', Dryden, *Eclogues* ix 52.
27–8. Par. Lost v 203–4: 'To Hill, or Valley, Fountain, or fresh shade /
Made vocal by my Song.'
28–33. There is no reason to suppose that G. wished to refer to actual bards
when he chose these names for the supposed victims of Edward I. But he was
careful to use real Welsh names which had been borne by earlier (in some
cases much earlier) poets and princes. The exception is 'Modred', perhaps
adapted from the name of King Arthur's nephew Mordred, often mentioned
in early histories of Wales. It must be admitted that 'Highborn Hoel' has
the effect of an allusion to the famous poet-prince Hywel ab Owein (d.
1170).
28. 'high-born Howard', Pope, *Dunciad* i 297.
29. Cadwallo's] Caswallo's *Bedingfield.*   *cold . . . tongue*] Cp. *fredda . . .
lingua* in Petrarch, quoted in *Elegy* 92 *n* (p. 134).
30. stormy] roaring *Bedingfield.* Cp. *Midsummer Night's Dream* II i 151–2:
'Uttering such dulcet and harmonious breath, / That the rude sea grew civil
at her song'; and *Comus* 88: 'hush the waving Woods'. Dryden has 'stormy
main', *Aeneid* x 966; *Palamon and Arcite* iii 1081; and on three other occasions.

     'Brave Urien sleeps upon his craggy bed:
     'Mountains, ye mourn in vain
     'Modred, whose magic song
     'Made huge Plinlimmon bow his cloud-topped head.
35   'On dreary Arvon's shore they lie,
     'Smeared with gore and ghastly pale:
     'Far, far aloof the affrighted ravens sail;
     'The famished eagle screams and passes by.

31. Brave] Great *Bedingfield.* According to Walpole's MS notes on the *Odes,*
Brave 'originally was *Stern* which was much better'.
33–4. Henry VIII III i 3–5: 'Orpheus with his lute made trees / And the
mountain tops that freeze / Bow themselves when he did sing.'
34. Plinlimmon] A mountain on the border of Cardigan and Glamorgan.
Cp. John Philips, *Cyder* i 105–6: 'that Cloud-piercing Hill, / *Plinlimmon*';
Pope, *Essay on Man* i 104: 'Behind the cloud-topt hill'.
35. Arvon] The shores of Caernarvonshire opposite to the isle of Anglesey.
G. *1768.*
   Cp. 'dreery Shore', Dryden, *Aeneid* ix 121.
36. Par. Lost i 392: 'Moloch, horrid King besmear'd with blood'; Dryden,
Aeneid v 433: 'besmear'd with Filth, and Holy Gore'; *Cymon and Iphiginia*
607–8: 'the sprinkled Gore / Besmears the Walls'; *Cock and Fox* 244: 'Pale,
naked, pierc'd with Wounds, with Blood besmeared'; *Aeneid* vi 648: 'And
pale *Adrastus* with his ghastly Face'; Pope, *Temple of Fame* 125–7: 'There, on
rude Iron Columns smear'd with Blood, / The horrid Forms of *Scythian*
Heroes stood, / *Druids* and *Bards* (their once loud Harps unstrung)'.
37–8. G. may be indebted to the following passages cited by Mitford,
although, as Tovey pointed out, the circumstances are not exactly similar,
since G. is describing Nature's revulsion from Edward's crime: Lucretius
vi 1215–8: *Multaque humi cum inhumata iacerent corpora supra / corporibus,
tamen alituum genus atque ferarum / aut procul apsiliebat, ut acrem exeiret odorem, /
aut, ubi gustarat, languebat morte propinqua* (And although bodies on bodies
lay unburied upon the ground in heaps, yet the tribes of winged creatures
and wild beasts would either leap away to escape the rank smell, or having
tasted would faint in a speedy death); Statius, *Thebaid* i 624–5: *illam et
nocturno circum stridore volantes / impastae fugistis aves* (Her did ye flee unfed, ye
birds, wheeling round with nocturnal clamour). Similar descriptions are in
Ovid, *Metamorphoses* vii 549–50; Lucan, *Pharsalia* vi 627–8. Cp. also Dryden,
Palamon and Arcite ii 532–3: 'The Fowl, that scent afar, the Borders fly, /
And shun the bitter Blast and wheel about the Sky.'
38. Cambden and others observe, that eagles used annually to build their
aerie among the rocks of Snowdon, which from thence (as some think) were
named by the Welch *Craigian-eryri,* or the crags of the eagles. At this day (I
am told) the highest point of Snowdon is called *the eagle's nest.* That bird is
certainly no stranger to this island, as the Scots, and the people of Cumber-

'Dear lost companions of my tuneful art,
40 'Dear as the light that visits these sad eyes,
'Dear as the ruddy drops that warm my heart,
'Ye died amidst your dying country's cries—
'No more I weep. They do not sleep.
'On yonder cliffs, a grisly band,
45 'I see them sit, they linger yet,
'Avengers of their native land;

land, Westmoreland, &c. can testify: it even has built its nest in the Peak of
Derbyshire. [See Willoughby's *Ornithol.* published by Ray.] G. *1768*.

G. refers to *The Ornithology of Francis Willoughby, Translated into English,
and enlarged*, by John Ray (1678) p. 21.

39–45. Virgil, *Aeneid* xi 271–4: *Nunc etiam horribili visu portenta sequuntur, /
et socii amissi petierunt aethera pinnis / fluminibusque vagantur aves (heu dira
meorum / supplicia!) et scopulos lacrimosis vocibus implent* (Even now, portents
of dreadful view pursue me; my lost comrades have winged their way to the
sky or haunt the streams as birds—alas! the dire punishment of my people!—
and fill the cliffs with their tearful cries). In his version of these lines, Dryden
translates *socii amissi* as 'lost Companions'.

39. tuneful art] Cp. Congreve, *Ode to the Queen* 5: 'Thy lyre, thy voice, and
tuneful art'.

40–1. G. gave as his source (in his letter to Bedingfield in Aug. 1756, *Corresp*
ii 477 and in *1768*) *Julius Caesar* II i 289–90: 'As dear to me as are the ruddy
drops, / That visit my sad heart.' Cp. also Virgil, *Aeneid* iv 31: *O luce magis
dilecta sorori* (O dearer to thy sister than the light); Milton's invocation
to Light, *Par. Lost* iii 22–3: 'thou / Revisit'st not these eyes'; Otway,
Venice Preserved V i: 'Dear as the vital warmth that feeds my life, / Dear as
these eyes that weep in fondness o'er thee.'

42. 'And greatly falling with a falling state', Pope, *Prologue to Cato* 22.

43. They] ye *Bedingfield.*   G. wrote against this line in his own copy of the
Odes (Pierpont Morgan Library): 'The double cadence is introduced here
not only to give a wild spirit and variety to the Epode; but because it bears
some affinity to a peculiar measure in the Welch Prosody, called Gorchest-
Beirdh, i.e. the *Excellent of the Bards*.' See W. Powell Jones, *Thomas Gray,
Scholar* p. 93, and the article by Arthur Johnston cited in the headnote.
For a 'double cadence', see also ll. 45, 91, 93, 139, 141. Cp. Milton, *Lycidas*
165–6: 'Weep no more, woful Shepherds weep no more, / For *Lycidas*
your sorrow is not dead.'

44–6. Statius, *Thebaid* xi 422–3: *Montibus insidunt patriis tristique corona /
infecere diem* (Seated upon their native hills [the Ogygian ghosts] pollute the
day with grisly band). In June 1756 (*Corresp* ii 465), G. had written to Mason
concerning his use of the spirits of Snowdon in his *Caractacus*: 'I am of your
opinion, that the Ghosts will spoil the Picture, unless they are thrown at a
huge distance, & extremely *kept down*.'

'With me in dreadful harmony they join,
'And weave with bloody hands the tissue of thy line.'

II. 1

"Weave the warp and weave the woof,
50   "The winding-sheet of Edward's race.
"Give ample room and verge enough
"The characters of hell to trace.
"Mark the year and mark the night,
"When Severn shall re-echo with affright
55   "The shrieks of death, through Berkeley's roofs that
       ring,

47–8. See the Norwegian Ode, that follows. G. *1768*.

In his own copy of the *Odes*, G. wrote: 'The image is taken from an ancient Scaldic Ode, written in the old-Norwegian tongue about A :D :1029.' This poem was *The Fatal Sisters* (see the headnote to it, p. 210 below). A number of commentators have objected to G.'s introduction of Norse mythology into a poem about Welsh bards. Cf. *Gentleman's Mag.* lviii (1788) 24: 'The poet might, with equal propriety, and only the same violation, have had recourse to Mahometan, or Grecian, or Indian, or any other Mythology.' For G.'s views on 'that scarcity of Celtic Ideas we labour under' and the need for tactful adoption of 'foreign whimsies' to blend with them, see his letter to Mason, 13 Jan. 1758 (*Corresp* ii 550–1).

49. Johnson objected in his *Life of G.* (*Lives of the Poets*, ed. G. B. Hill, iii 439–40): 'They are then called upon to "weave the warp, and weave the woof," perhaps with no great propriety; for it is by crossing the *woof* with the *warp* that men *weave* the *web* or piece'. The 'warp' is the fixed thread, which may have been Johnson's point; but by the repetition of 'weave' G. clearly meant no more than 'interweave' or 'weave together'. It is at this point that the chorus of bards begin their prophecy, which continues until l. 100.

51. Dryden, *Don Sebastian* I i: 'I have a soul that, like an ample shield, / Can take in all, and verge enough for more'; Pope, *Iliad* xvii 670: 'Beneath its ample verge'.

52. *characters*] Johnson defines 'character' in this sense as 'A mark; a stamp; a representation'.

54–6. Edward the Second, cruelly butchered in Berkley-Castle [1327]. G. *1768*.

Cp. Drayton, *The Barons' Wars* V lxvi 1–4, lxvii 1–3: 'When those (i'th' depth and dead time of the night) / Poor simple people, that then dwelled near, / Whom that strange noise did wond'rously affright, / That his last shriek did in his parting hear / . . . // Berkely, whose fair seat hath been famous long, / Let thy sad echoes shriek a deadly sound, / To the vast air . . .'

"Shrieks of an agonizing King!
"She-wolf of France, with unrelenting fangs,
"That tear'st the bowels of thy mangled mate,
"From thee be born who o'er thy country hangs
60   "The scourge of heaven. What terrors round him wait!
"Amazement in his van, with Flight combined,
"And Sorrow's faded form, and Solitude behind.

II. 2

"Mighty victor, mighty lord,
"Low on his funeral couch he lies!
65   "No pitying heart, no eye, afford
"A tear to grace his obsequies.

56. agonizing] Johnson defines *agonize* as 'To feel agonies; to be in excessive pain'; but *OED* gives also 'to be in the throes of death'.
57. She-wolf] Isabel of France, Edward the Second's adulterous Queen. *G. 1768.*
She is supposed to have procured his murder and formed a connection with Roger Mortimer, Earl of March. Shakespeare calls Margaret of Anjou 'She-wolf of France', *III Henry VI* I iv iii.
58. who] This Latinate compression of 'him who' is in the manner of Milton, e.g. *Par. Lost* iv 792–3.
59. Triumphs of Edward the Third in France. *G. 1768.*
60. Attila was called *flagella Dei*; and Marlowe's Tamburlaine frequently claims to be the 'scourge of God'.
60–2. Virgil, *Aeneid* xii 335–6: *circumque atrae Formidinis ora | Iraeque Insidiaeque, dei comitatus, aguntur* (Around him speed black Terror's forms, and Anger, and Ambush, attendants on the god). Cp. also Cowley, *Davideis* Bk iv: 'Ruin behind and terror marched before'; Oldham, *The Praise of Homer* st. iii: 'Horror stalks in the Van, and Slaughter in the Rear.'
62. G. told Walpole, 10 Aug. 1757 (*Corresp* i 513), that 'sorrow' and 'solitude' should have had capital letters in *1757*; but the correction was not made in *1768*.
63–4. Oldham, *David's Lamentations* st. iv: 'Lo! there the mighty Warriour lies, / With all his Lawrels, all his Victories.'
64. Death of that King [1377], abandoned by his Children, and even robbed in his last moments by his Courtiers and his Mistress [Alice Perrers]. *G. 1768.*
63. Victor] Conqueror *Wharton, deleted.*
64. his] the *Wharton, deleted.*
65. No . . . no] What . . . what *Wharton, deleted.*   *afford*] The plural verb is governed by both singular nouns. Cp. Dryden, *The Despairing Lover* 98: 'Nor wept his fate, nor cast a pitying eye'.
66. III Henry VI I iv 147: 'These tears are my sweet Rutland's obsequies'; *Titus Andronicus* I i 159–60: 'My tributary tears / I render for my brethren's obsequies'.

"Is the sable warrior fled?
"Thy son is gone. He rests among the dead.
"The swarm that in thy noon-tide beam were born?
70 "Gone to salute the rising morn.
"Fair laughs the morn and soft the zephyr blows,
"While proudly riding o'er the azure realm

67. *sable warrior*] Edward, the Black Prince, dead some time before his
Father [1376]. *G. 1768.*
69. *in thy . . . born*] hover'd in thy noontide ray *Wharton deleted.* Cp.
'summer's noontide air', *Par. Lost* ii 309; 'their noontide ray', Pope, *Essay
on Man* iv 305; 'noontide rays', Dryden, *Persius* iii 3; 'noontide beam',
Young, *Night Thoughts* vii 207; and see also *Ode on the Spring* 25–30 (pp. 51-2)
and *Agrippina* 144–6 (p. 40).
70. *Morn*] day *Wharton, deleted.* Cp. 'As when the golden sun salutes the
morn', *Titus Andronicus* II i 5; and 'Saluted in her Song the Morning gray',
Dryden, *Palamon and Arcite* ii 38. Dryden also has 'the rising morn' in
Aeneid iii 682 and *Ovid's Metamorphoses* i 73.
71. Magnificence of Richard the Second's reign. See Froissard, and other
contemporary Writers. *G. 1768.*
71–6. *Wharton reads as follows, with the present text written on the back of the MS,
but in for on (l.74):*

Mirrors of Saxon truth & loyalty,
Your helpless old expiring Master view
They hear not. scarce Religion dares supply
Her mutter'd Requiems, & her holy Dew.
Yet thou, proud Boy, from Pomfret's walls shalt send
A sigh, & envy oft thy happy Grandsire's end.

Cp. Dryden, *Aeneid* vi 1214–5: 'Mirror of ancient Faith in early Youth! /
Undaunted Worth, Inviolable Truth!'
With the final version Mitford compares Petrarch, *Canzone XLII*
st. ii; and Spenser's translation, *The Visions of Petrarch* 15–24: 'after at sea a
tall ship did appeare, / Made all of Heben and white Yvorie, / The sailes of
golde, of silke the tackle were, / Milde was the winde, calme seem'd the sea
to bee, / The skie eachwhere did show full bright and faire; / With rich
treasures this gay ship fraighted was: / But sudden storme did so turmoyle the
aire, / And tumbled up the sea, that she (alas) / Strake on a rock, that under
water lay, / And perished past all recoverie.' Coleridge, *Biographia Literaria*
ch. i (where he criticizes G.'s lines), thought G. was indebted to *Merchant of
Venice* II vi 14–9, but the resemblance is not verbal. Cp. also *Rape of the Lock*
ii 47–8, 50: 'But now secure the painted Vessel glides, / The Sun-beams
trembling on the floating Tydes / . . . / Smooth flow the Waves, the Zephyrs
gently play'; and 'the gilded Mast', *ibid* ii 69.
72. Virgil, *Ciris* 483: *caeruleo pollens coniunx Neptunia regno* (Neptune's
spouse, queen of the azure realm).
72–3. Dryden, *Annus Mirabilis* 601, 603–4: 'The goodly *London* in her gallant

"In gallant trim the gilded vessel goes;
"Youth on the prow and Pleasure at the helm;
75   "Regardless of the sweeping whirlwind's sway,
"That, hushed in grim repose, expects his evening-
prey.

II.   3

"Fill high the sparkling bowl,
"The rich repast prepare,

trim / . . . / Like a rich Bride does to the Ocean swim, / And on her shadow
rides in floating gold.'
74. Ovid, *Heroides* xv 215: *ipse gubernabit residens in puppe Cupido* (Cupid him-
self will be helmsman, sitting upon the stern); Prior (cited by Johnson under
'helm'): 'Fair occasion shows the springing gale, / And interest guides the
helm, and honour swells the sail.' Ian Jack, *From Sensibility to Romanticism*
(ed. F. W. Hilles and H. Bloom, 1965), p. 169, compares Rochester, *Letter
from Artemisia in the Town to Chloe in the Country* 196: 'Youth in her Looks,
and Pleasure in her Bed.'
75. Cp. *Education and Government* 48 and *n* (p. 96); Pope, *Epistles to Several
Persons* iii 353–4: 'the whirlwinds sweep / The surge'.
76. Walpole's MS note states that 'This image of the whirlwind, like a
Lion in ambush, is very like a passage in Dr. Young's fine paraphrase of
Job,

But fiercer still the Lordly Lion stalks . . .'
Walpole quotes three more lines. The resemblance is only general and it is
the lion's 'tawny brood' which 'couch'd in dreadful Ambush pant for
Blood'. See Edward Young, *Poetical Works* (1741) i 133.
77. Richard the Second, (as we are told by Archbishop Scroop and the
confederate Lords in their manifesto, by Thomas of Walsingham, and all
the older Writers,) was starved to death [1400]. The story of his assassination
by Sir Piers of Exon, is of much later date. G. *1757, except for* and the
confederate . . . manifesto, *added in 1768.*
Cp. Dryden, *Aeneid* viii 363: 'Fill high the Goblets with a sparkling
Flood'; and *Persius* v 264: 'when sparkling bouls go round'.
77–82. Virgil, *Aeneid* vi 603–6: *lucent genialibus altis / aurea fulcra toris, epulae-
que ante ora paratae / regifico luxu; Furiarum maxima iuxta / accubat et manibus
prohibet contingere mensas* (High festal couches gleam with frames of gold, and
before their eyes is spread a banquet in royal splendour. Yet, reclining hard
by, the eldest Fury stays their hand from touch of the table). See also
Dryden's translation, *Aeneid* vi 818–21: 'They lye below, on Golden Beds
display'd; / And genial Feasts, with Regal Pomps, are made. / The Queen
of Furies by their sides is set; / And snatches from their Mouths th'untasted
Meat'.
78. 'And frequent Cups prolong the rich Repast', Pope, *Rape of the Lock* iii
112.

"Reft of a crown, he yet may share the feast:
80 "Close by the regal chair
"Fell Thirst and Famine scowl
"A baleful smile upon their baffled guest.
"Heard ye the din of battle bray,
"Lance to lance and horse to horse?
85 "Long years of havoc urge their destined course,
"And through the kindred squadrons mow their way.

79. 'When death has reft their crown', David Mallet, *William and Margaret* 12.

80. Dryden has 'the regal chair', *Hind and the Panther* iii 732.

81–2. Cp. Satan's 'baleful eyes', *Par. Lost* i 56, and *ibid* ii 845–7: 'Death / Grinnd horrible a gastly smile, to hear / His famine should be fill'd.'

82. *baleful smile upon*] smile of horror on *Wharton*.

Walpole's MS note reads: 'In the life of Gower in the 4th vol. of the Biographies p. 224–5 [*sic*] it is sd that some of our historians affirm that *Richard was served in a royal manner but was restrained from eating or drinking anything set before him* which exactly answers to this picture.' See *Biographia Britannica* (1757) iv 2245 *n*, which goes on to mention the alternative theory that Richard was murdered by Sir Peter of Exeter.

83. Ruinous civil wars of York and Lancaster. G. *1768*.

Cp. 'Arms on Armour clashing bray'd / Horrible discord', *Par. Lost* vi 209–10. Pope added the following note to his use of 'bray' in the *Dunciad* ii 260: 'Sir R[ichard] B[lackmore] delighted much in the word *Bray*, which he endeavour'd to ennoble by applying it to the sound of *Armour, War,* &c.'

84. The pattern of this line is common in heroic poetry, e.g. Statius, *Thebaid* viii 398–9: *Iam clipeus clipeis, umbone repellitur umbo, / ense minax ensis, pede pes et cuspide cuspis* (Then shield thrusts against shield, boss upon boss, threatening sword on sword, foot against foot and lance on lance). Ovid, *Metamorphoses* ix 44 and Lucan, *Pharsalia* iii 573 are similar. English equivalents are frequent: 'Harry to Harry shall, hot horse to horse, / Meet', *I Henry IV* IV i 122–3; 'Shield 'gainst shield, and helm 'gainst helm they crush', Fairfax's *Tasso* IX lii 8; 'And Chief to Chief, and Troop to Troop oppos'd', Dryden, *Palamon and Arcite* iii 577; 'and Man to Man, / And Steed to Steed oppos'd', Dryden, *Flower and the Leaf* 290–1; 'To armour armour, lance to lance opposed', Pope, *Iliad* iv 509 (cp. also Pope, *Iliad* xiii 80–2 and xvi 260–1). Pope parodied the formula in *Rape of the Lock* i 101–2.

85. Dryden, *Aeneid* i 778–9: 'renew / Our destin'd Course'.   *urge*] 'To labour vehemently; to do with eagerness or violence' (Johnson).

86. *kindred squadrons*] Cp. Lucan, *Pharsalia* i 4: *cognatasque acies*; 6–7 following describe war in the pattern indicated in l. 84 *n* above. Cp. also Dryden, *All for Love* I i: 'mow 'em out a passage, / And entering where the foremost squadrons yield'.

"Ye towers of Julius, London's lasting shame,
"With many a foul and midnight murther fed,
"Revere his consort's faith, his father's fame,
90 "And spare the meek usurper's holy head.
"Above, below, the rose of snow,
"Twined with her blushing foe, we spread:
"The bristled Boar in infant-gore
"Wallows beneath the thorny shade.
95 "Now, brothers, bending o'er the accursed loom,
"Stamp we our vengeance deep and ratify his doom.

87. Ye] Grim *Wharton, deleted.*

Henry the Sixth, George Duke of Clarence, Edward the Fifth, Richard Duke of York, believed to be murthered secretly in the Tower of London. The oldest part of that structure is vulgarly attributed to Julius Caesar. G. *1768.*

Cp. *Richard III* III i 68–9: 'I do not like the Tower, of any place. Did Julius Caesar build that place?' Shakespeare frequently uses 'foul' of murder.

89. consort's] Margaret of Anjou, a woman of heroic spirit, who struggled hard to save her Husband and her Crown. G. *1768.*

father's] Henry the Fifth. G. *1768.*

90. holy] hallow'd *Wharton.*

meek usurper] Henry the Sixth very near being canonized. The line of Lancaster had no right of inheritance to the Crown. G. *1768.*

Henry VI is called 'usurper' in *II Henry VI* I iii 188 and IV iv 30; and *III Henry VI* I i 114. He was revered after his death as a saint and martyr in certain parts of the country and his formal canonization was sought for by Henry VII. See G.'s other references to him, *Eton Ode* 4 (p. 57) and *Ode to Music* 46 (p. 271).

91–2. The white and red roses, devices of York and Lancaster. G. *1768.* (See *I Henry VI* II iv.)

93–4. bristled Boar] The silver Boar was the badge of Richard the Third; whence he was usually known in his own time by the name of *the Boar.* G. *1768.*

Richard III is supposed to have been responsible for the deaths of Edward, the young Prince of Wales, at Tewkesbury; and of Edward V and his brother, the Duke of York, in 1483. Shakespeare often calls him the 'Boar' in *Richard III.* Cp. 'boar with bristled hair', *Midsummer Night's Dream* II ii 31; 'bristled Boar', Dryden, *Georgics* iii 397, *Aeneid* vii 20, xi 303, and *Hind and the Panther* i 43.

96. 'This ratifies th'irrevocable doom', Dryden, *Iliad* i 707; 'I seal your Doom, and ratify the Deed', Dryden, *Palamon and Arcite* ii 307; 'Assents to fate, and ratifies the doom' Pope, *Iliad* xvi 558.

III.   1

"Edward, lo! to sudden fate
"(Weave we the woof. The thread is spun)
"Half of thy heart we consecrate.
100   "(The web is wove. The work is done.)"
'Stay, oh stay! nor thus forlorn
'Leave me unblessed, unpitied, here to mourn:
'In yon bright track, that fires the western skies,
'They melt, they vanish from my eyes.
105   'But oh! what solemn scenes on Snowdon's height
'Descending slow their glittering skirts unroll?

97. 'sudden fate', Spenser, *Ruins of Time* 573.

99. *Half of thy heart*] Eleanor of Castile died a few years after the conquest
of Wales. The heroic proof she gave of her affection for her Lord is well
known. The monuments of his regret, and sorrow for the loss of her, are
still to be seen at Northampton, Geddington, Waltham, and other places.
G. *1768*.

When this note first appeared in *1757*, it ended 'seen in several parts
of England'. Edward's queen is supposed to have saved his life by sucking a
poisoned wound. After her death in 1290, Edward marked the route taken
by her funeral procession from Nottinghamshire to London with crosses at
its halting-places. The second sentence of G.'s note may refer to James
Thomson's tragedy, *Edward and Eleonora* (1739).

Cp. Horace, *Odes* I iii 8: *animae dimidium meae* (half of my own soul)
and II xvii 5: *te meae si partem animae*.

100. Cp. *Fatal Sisters* 51–2 (p. 220).

101. *thus*] here *Wharton, deleted.*   The Bard now resumes his monologue.

101–2. Pope, *Autumn* 21–2: 'I mourn, / Alike unheard, unpity'd, and forlorn';
and see *Ode to Adversity* 8 (p. 71).

102. *me . . . here*] your despairing Caradoc *Wharton, deleted.* Walpole believed
that this change was for the worse. G. explained to him on 11 July 1757
(*Corresp* ii 508): 'Caradoc I have private reasons against; and besides it is in
reality Carãdoc, and will not stand in the verse.' Tovey suggests that G.
wished to avoid confusion with Mason's *Caractacus*.

103. *track*] clouds *Wharton, deleted.*   Describing the sun, Shakespeare refers
to 'the bright track of his fiery car', *Richard III* V iii 20, and 'the track / Of
his bright passage to the occident', *Richard II* III iii 66–7. Cp. also 'The sun
begins to gild the western skies', *Two Gentlemen of Verona* V i 1.

104. *melt*] sink *Wharton, deleted.*   Cp. *Macbeth* I iii 80–2: 'Whither are they
vanished? / Into the air, and what seemed corporal melted / As breath into
the wind.' See l. 110 *n* below where *Macbeth* again seems to be in G.'s mind.

105. *oh*] ah *Wharton.*   *solemn scenes*] scenes of heav'n *Wharton, deleted with
present reading inserted.*

'Visions of glory, spare my aching sight,
'Ye unborn ages, crowd not on my soul!
'No more our long-lost Arthur we bewail.
110   'All-hail, ye genuine kings, Britannia's issue, hail!

III.   2
'Girt with many a baron bold

106. glittering] golden *Wharton, deleted.   skirts*] See Collins, *Ode to Evening* 6 and *n* (p. 463).
107. Dryden, *State of Innocence* IV i 7: 'Their glory shoots upon my aching sense.'
108. Pope, *Imitations of Horace, Ep.* II i 228: 'Ages yet unborn'; and see *Ode for Music* 17 and *n* (p. 269).
109. It was the common belief of the Welch nation, that King Arthur was still alive in Fairy-Land, and should return again to reign over Britain. G. *1768.*

G. mentions this tradition in his essay 'On the Poems of Lydgate', *Works*, ed. Gosse, i 389: 'We may remark too the notion then current in Britain, that King Arthur was not dead, but translated to Fairy-Land, and should come again to restore the Round Table.' G. then quotes Lydgate's *Fall of Princes* VIII xxiv: 'This errour abideth yet among Britons, / Which founded is upon the prophesie / Of old Merlin, like their opinion; / He as a king is crowned in faërie, / With scepter and sworde, and with his regalie / Shall resort as lord and soveraine / Out of faerie, and reigne in Britaine,' etc. G. has another reference to the belief in Peter of Blois's *Epistles* 57 (*c.* 1170). This tradition, like the supposed descent of the Britons from the Trojan prince Brutus and the prophesied return of a British (not Saxon) line of monarchs, was preserved by Geoffrey of Monmouth, and revived under the Tudors in whom the prophesy was held to be fulfilled. It occurs in Spenser's *Faerie Queene* (e.g. III iii 48) and other Elizabethan works.
109–10. Wharton, with present reading above:
    From Cambria's thousand hills a thousand strains
    Triumphant tell aloud, another Arthur reigns.
110. Both Merlin and Taliessin had prophesied, that the Welch should regain their sovereignty over this island; which seemed to be accomplished in the House of Tudor. G. *1768.*

In *1757* G. noted merely: 'Ascension of the Line of Tudor.' As Tovey pointed out, the prophecies belong to a much later period than that of these bards. The Bard's 'All hail' seems to echo again Macbeth's confrontation with the witches, in which the phrase is repeated: e.g. 'All hail, Macbeth! that shalt be king hereafter' (I iii 50).
111–12. Mason has:
    Haughty Knights, and Barons bold
    With dazzling helm & horrent spear
Wharton first reproduces this, with Youthful *for* Haughty, *then gives present*

'Sublime their starry fronts they rear;
'And gorgeous dames, and statesmen old
'In bearded majesty, appear.
115   'In the midst a form divine!
'Her eye proclaims her of the Briton-line;
'Her lion-port, her awe-commanding face,
'Attempered sweet to virgin-grace.
'What strings symphonious tremble in the air,
120   'What strains of vocal transport round her play!

reading above. Cp. Milton, *L'Allegro* 119: 'throngs of knights and barons
bold'. Fairfax's *Tasso* III xiii 2, XI lxxvi 1, and XIV xix 3, has 'Baron bold'
and 'Barons bold'.

112. Milton, *The Passion* 18: 'his starry front'; and *Par. Lost* iv 300: 'His fair
large Front and Eye sublime'. Mitford cites a number of classical parallels:
e.g. Statius, *Thebaid* v 613: *siderei vultus* (star-bright face). Tovey adds
further examples: e.g. Valerius Flaccus, *Argonautica* iv 331: *siderea de fronte*.

114. In] Of *Mason*. (G. made the change 'only because the next line begins
with *In* the midst &c.' (*Corresp* ii 504), but it does not appear elsewhere.)

A writer in the *Gentleman's Mag.* xlix (1779) 23–4, objected that
'the short and curled beards' of Elizabeth's reign 'could not be thought
strikingly expressive of dignity' by the Bard, who himself possessed so
fine a specimen (see ll. 19–20). Cp. 'bearded wisdom', Rowe, *Jane Shore* I i.

115. Dryden uses the phrase 'form divine' twice in the description of Aeneas's
vision of the future leaders of Rome in the underworld. See *Aeneid* vi
1077–8: 'But next behold the Youth of Form Divine, / *Caesar* himself,
exalted in his Line'; and *Aeneid* v 722 and vi 1188.

116–18. Statius, *Silvae* IV ii 41–4: *tranquillum vultus et maiestate serena /
mulcentem radios summittentemque modeste / fortunae vexilla suae; tamen ore
nitebat / dissimulatus honos* (Calm-visaged and in majesty serene tempering his
rays and gently veiling the glory of his state; yet the splendour that he would
fain conceal shone in his countenance).

116. of the Briton-line] born of Arthur's line *Mason.*   *proclaims*] As used by
Shakespeare: 'Thine eye and cheek proclaim / A matter from thee', *Tempest*
II i 220–1; 'the apparel oft proclaims the man', *Hamlet* I iii 72.

117. Her . . . her] A . . . an *Wharton, deleted.*

Speed relating an audience given by Queen Elizabeth to Paul Dzialinski,
Ambassadour of Poland, says, 'And thus she, lion-like rising, daunted the
malapert Orator no less with her stately port and majestical deporture,
than with the tartnesse of her princelie checkes.' G. *1768.*

See John Speed, *The History of Great Britaine* (1611) p. 871, which reads
'departure' for 'deporture'.

118. See *Progress of Poesy* 26 and *n* (p. 165).

119. Par. Lost vii 558–60: 'the sound / Symphonious of ten thousand Harpes
that tun'd / Angelic harmonies'; and see also *Progress of Poesy* 2 (p. 161 above)
and *Ode for Music* 88 (p. 274).

'Hear from the grave, great Taliessin, hear;
'They breathe a soul to animate thy clay.
'Bright Rapture calls and, soaring as she sings,
'Waves in the eye of heaven her many-coloured wings.

III.   3

125   'The verse adorn again
'Fierce war and faithful love,
'And truth severe, by fairy fiction dressed.
'In buskined measures move

121. Taliessin, Chief of the Bards, flourished in the VIth Century. His works
are still preserved, and his memory held in high veneration among his
Countrymen. G. *1768.* In his 'Observations on the Pseudo-Rhythmus',
Works, ed. Gosse, i 365 *n*, G. qualifies a remark on Welsh poetry with 'if the
remains of Taliessin . . . be not fictitious'. It is not certain that all the poems
attributed to him in the thirteenth-century MS which survives are his.

122. 'Dead things with inbreath'd sense able to pierce', Milton, *At a Solemn
Music* 4; 'strains that might create a soul / Under the ribs of Death', *Comus*
561–2.

123. calls] wakes *Mason.*   Cp. Waller, *Of the Queen* 7–8: 'Singing she mounts,
her airy wings are stretched / Towards heaven, as if from heaven her note
she fetched'; Congreve, *Ode to Lord Godolphin* 56: 'And soars with rapture
while she sings'; Richard West, *Monody on Queen Caroline* st. ii: 'Sublime
in air he spreads his dappled wings, / Mounts the blue aether, and in
mounting sings'.

124. eye of heaven] A phrase for the sun used by many poets: e.g. *King John*
IV ii 15; *Richard II* III ii 37; *Faerie Queene* I iii 4, 7; Phineas Fletcher, *Purple
Island* VI xviii 7. Cp. also 'here Love . . . / . . . waves his purple wings',
Par. Lost iv 763–4; 'Colours that change whene'er they wave their Wings',
Pope, *Rape of the Lock* ii 68.

125. G. told Mason, 11 June 1757 (*Corresp* ii 504): 'I understand what you
mean about the *Verse* adorn again, but do not think it signifies much, for
there is no mistaking the sense, when one attends to it.' (Mason had no doubt
objected to G.'s inverted word order, with 'verse' the object of 'adorn'.)
After 'adorn again' in his letter G. wrote, and then deleted: 'you may read
Fierce War and faithful Love / Resume their'.

126. G.'s note in *1768* acknowledges a debt to *Faerie Queene*, Proem i 9:
'Fierce warres and faithfull loves shall moralize my song.'

127. truth severe] Cp. 'Truth, Wisdom, Sanctitude severe and pure', *Par.
Lost* iv 293; 'the severe Delights of Truth', Dryden, *Religio Laici* 233.
fairy fiction] Cp. 'No fairy field of fiction all on flower', Young, *Night
Thoughts* v 70.

128. buskined] mystic *Mason.*   'buskined' means tragic, alluding to the boot
('cothurnus') worn in Athenian tragedy. Cp. Milton, *Il Penseroso* 101–2:
'Or what (though rare) of later age, / Ennobled hath the Buskind stage.'
G.'s note in *1768* shows that he was referring to 'Shakespear'.

      'Pale Grief and pleasing Pain,
130   'With Horror, tyrant of the throbbing breast.
      'A voice as of the cherub-choir
      'Gales from blooming Eden bear;
      'And distant warblings lessen on my ear,
      'That lost in long futurity expire.
135   'Fond impious man, think'st thou yon sanguine cloud,

129. Cp. 'pleasing paine', *Faerie Queene* III x 60, 4; VI iii 32, 4 and ix 10, 3; 'pleasing pains', Dryden, *Lucretius* i 48; *Eclogues* iii 170; 'Song' from *Tyrannic Love* 3. Pope has 'pleasing pain', *Dunciad* ii 211.

130. With horror wild, that chills the throbbing breast *Mason.*   G. told Mason, 11 June 1757 (*Corresp* ii 504): ' *That chills the throbbing* &c: I dislike, as much as you can do. Horror *wild* I am forced to strike out, because of *wild* dismay in the first Stanza.' He then suggested the present reading. Cp. 'my throbbing breast', *II Henry VI* IV iv 5; 'Tyrant Passion preying on his breast', Dryden, *Lucretius* iii 198; 'And reign'd the short-liv'd Tyrant of his Breast', Pope, *January and May* 231; 'Thou gloomy Tyrant of the frighted Breast', Prior, *Solomon* ii 775.

131. A voice] Milton. G. *1768.*

    Cp. 'the Cherubick host in thousand quires', Milton, *At a Solemn Music* 12; and 'the quires of cherubim', *Par. Lost* iii 666.

132. 'blooming Eden', Young, *Night Thoughts* iii.

133. The succession of Poets after Milton's time. G. *1768.*

134. G. wrote to Mason on 11 June 1757 (*Corresp* ii 504): 'why you would alter *lost* in long futurity I do not see, unless because you think *lost* & *expire* are tautologous, or because it looks as if the end of the prophecy were disappointed by it, & that people may think Poetry in Britain was some time or other really to expire: whereas the meaning is only, that it was lost to his ear from the immense distance. I can not give up *lost*, for it begins with an L.' Cp. 'Th'Event of things in dark Futurity', Dryden, *Aeneid* vi 101; and 'Tho' skill'd in Fate and dark Futurity', Pope, *Statius His Thebais* 552.

135–8. Mitford compares a passage from Hieronymus Vida, *Hymnus xv. Divo Andreae Apostolo* 99–106, in his *Poemata* (1732) ii 111–12. Tovey considered the resemblance 'probably only coincidence', but it seems too close to be accidental: *Impie, quid furis? | . . . | Tene putas posse illustres abscondere caeli | Auricomi flammas, ipsumque extinguere solem | . . . | Forsitan humentem nebulam proflare, brevemque | Obsessis poteris radiis obtendere nubem: | Erumpet lux, erumpet rutilantibus auris | Lampas, et auriflua face nubila differet omnia* (Impious man, why dost thou rage? . . . Thinkest thou that thou canst hide the splendid flames of the golden-tressed heaven, and quench the sun himself? Thou wilt, perhaps, avail to raise by thy breath a dark mist, and curtain with a momentary cloud his encumbered rays. Yet his light shall burst forth; forth with reddening gleam his torch shall burst, and scatter all the rack with a flood of golden fire.)

'Raised by thy breath, has quenched the orb of day?
'Tomorrow he repairs the golden flood,
'And warms the nations with redoubled ray.
'Enough for me: with joy I see
140 'The different doom our fates assign.
'Be thine despair and sceptered care;
'To triumph, and to die, are mine.'
He spoke, and headlong from the mountain's height
Deep in the roaring tide he plunged to endless night.

136. 'The lamp of day is quenched beneath the deep', Pope, *Odyssey* iii 427.
137. repairs] Restores, renews. Cp. Milton's *Lycidas* 167–9: 'Sunk though he
be beneath the watry floar, / So sinks the day-star in the Ocean bed, / And yet
anon repairs his drooping head.' *Reparare* is used of the moon by Horace,
Odes IV vii 13, and Lucretius, v 734. Cp. also P. Fletcher, *Purple Island* VI
lxiv 7: 'So soon repairs her light, trebling her new born rays'; and for 'repair',
ibid lxx 7, and lxxi 1. Young, *Night Thoughts* iv 204–5, has 'a golden flood /
Of endless day'; and Thomson, *Summer* 609, 'the flood of day' (of the sun's
light).
140. Dryden, *Aeneid* xi 197: 'the City which your Fates assign'; and *Ovid's
Art of Love* i 786: 'The same the Fates for *Hector*'s Thread assign.'
142. Mitford compares Statius, *Thebaid* iii 85–6, in which a bard who has
survived his companions commits suicide in front of the tyrant: *vado
equidem exultans ereptaque fata / insequor et comites feror exspectatus ad umbras*
(I go, yea exultant, and meet the fate whereof [Tydeus] robbed me; I am
borne to the shades of my expectant comrades). G. told Mason on 11 June
1757 (*Corresp* ii 504) that some of his friends 'dislike the conclusion of the
Bard, & mutter something about Antithesis & Conceit in *To triumph, to
die*, wch I do not comprehend, & am sure, it is alterd for the better. it was
before
                    Lo! to be free, to die, are mine.
if you like it better so, so let it be. it is more abrupt, & perhaps may mark the
action better. or it may be, *Lo! Liberty & Death are mine*, wch ever you please
. . . pray, think a little about this conclusion, for all depends upon it.'
143. Dryden, *Aeneid* x 758: 'the Mountains Height'.
144. plunged] sunk *Mason, Wharton*. In his copy of the *Odes* Walpole wrote:
'It was originally *sunk*; Mr Garrick advised *plung'd* as a more emphatic word
on such an occasion'. Cp. a line in Richard West's *Ad Amicos*, sent to G. in
July 1737 (*Corresp* i 64 *n*): 'Yet some there are (ere sunk in endless night)'. See
also *Progress of Poesy* 102 and *n*; and 'sunk in endless night', Young, *Night
Thoughts* iii 216. Cp. also Virgil, *Eclogues* iii 59–60: *Praeceps aerii specula
de montis in undas / deferar; extremum hoc munus morientis habeto* (Headlong from
some towering mountain-crag I will plunge into the waves; this take thou
as my last dying gift); *King John* II i 24: 'the ocean's roaring tides'; Dryden,
Aeneid iii 529: 'the roaring Tides'; and Dryden, *Ovid's Metamorphoses* xii
456: 'Leapt headlong from the Hill of steepy height'.

22 [Ode on the Pleasure Arising from Vicissitude]

Probably written in 1754 or 1755. Mason copied a note from G.'s pocketbook for 1754 into the Commonplace Book (iii 1110): 'Contrast between the Winter past & coming spring   Joy owing to that vicissitude. many that never feel that delight. Sloth envy Ambition. how much happier the rustic that feels it tho he knows not how.' Mason printed this note in 1775, *Memoirs* p. 235. In the Commonplace Book he had added: 'Then follow a few lines of the Ode now the golden Morn &c so that the note above appears to be a kind of argument to the fragment. Four lines also, as follow, are among the others.' Mason then quoted the lines discussed below and given in l. 17 *n*. G.'s note clearly contains the germ of this poem. G. may also have had it in mind when he told Wharton in a letter dated 9 March 1755 that, having completed *The Progress of Poesy*, he had 'two or three Ideas more in my head' (*Corresp* i 420).

G. did not complete the poem. It was transcribed by Mason into G.'s Commonplace Book (iii 1097–1100) and entitled, 'Fragment of an Ode found amongst Mr. Grays papers after his decease and here transcribed from the corrected Copy.' Mason also recorded a number of 'Variations in the 1st copy'. He printed the completed stanzas, entitled merely 'Ode', for the first time in 1775 in *Memoirs* pp. 236–7; but he also printed, in *Poems* pp. 78–81, a version of 96 ll. which contains his own extensive additions. In this form the poem was given its present title; 4 ll. not found in Mason's transcript in the Commonplace Book or in the text in the *Memoirs*, but transcribed from G.'s pocketbook for 1754 into the Commonplace Book separately (see above and l. 17 *n*), were made the basis of a third stanza; and the fragmentary ll. 49–59, which do not appear in his first transcript in the Commonplace Book, but are written on the opposite leaf, were also reconstructed. Mason consulted a number of his friends before deciding to publish this composite version (see *Walpole Correspondence* xxviii 133, 136–7; *Correspondence of Hurd and Mason*, ed. E. H. Pearce and L. Whibley (Cambridge, 1932) pp. 90–4); and he also circulated an offprint of it before the *Memoirs* were published. Only one copy, that in the Clark Library, Los Angeles, appears to have survived: it was edited by L. Whibley in 1933.

Mason noted in 1775, *Poems* p. 82, that 'I have heard Mr. Gray say, that M. Gresset's "Epitre a ma Soeur" (see his works in the Amsterdam edition, 1748, p. 180) gave him the first idea of this Ode: and whoever compares it with the French Poem, will find some slight traits of resemblance, but chiefly in our Author's seventh stanza' (ll. 41–8). G. wrote enthusiastically about Gresset's poetry in two letters to Wharton in June and Aug. 1748 (*Corresp* i 304–9). Gresset's *Oeuvres* had been published at Amsterdam in 2 vols in 1747. G. called him 'a great master' and especially praised the *Epitre à ma Soeur* and the ode *La Médiocrité*, both of which he seems to have

remembered when writing the present poem. The text followed here is
that of Mason's transcript in the Commonplace Book, with the addition at
the end of the poem of the fragmentary continuation written on the opposite
page.

Now the golden Morn aloft
Waves her dew-bespangled wing;
With vermeil cheek and whisper soft
She wooes the tardy spring,
5   Till April starts, and calls around
The sleeping fragrance from the ground;
And lightly o'er the living scene
Scatters his freshest, tenderest green.

New-born flocks in rustic dance
10   Frisking ply their feeble feet;
Forgetful of their wintry trance

¶ 22.*1–12*. Lucretius i 10–14: *Nam simul ac species patefactast verna diei* |
et reserata viget genitabilis aura favoni, | *aeriae primum volucres te, diva, tuumque* |
significant initum perculsae corda tua vi. | *inde ferae pecudes persultant pabula*
laeta (For as soon as the vernal face of day is made manifest, and the breeze
of the teeming south wind blows fresh and free, thee first the fowls of the air
proclaim, thee divine one, and thy advent, pierced to the heart by thy might:
next the herds go wild and dance over the rich pastures); Seneca, *Phaedra*
10–12: *Qua prata iacent* | *quae rorifera mulcens aura* | *Zephyrus vernas evocat*
herbas (Where meadows lie which Zephyr soothes with his dewladen breath
and calls forth the herbage of the spring).
1. 'Then with expanded wings he stears his flight / Aloft', *Par. Lost* i 225–6.
2. Cp. Milton's 'dew-besprent', *Comus* 542; 'the Dew with Spangles
deck'd the Ground', Dryden, *Flower and Leaf* 92; 'When falling Dews with
Spangles deck'd the Glade', Pope, *Autumn* 99.
3. 'her vermil Cheeks', Fairfax's *Tasso* II xliii 2; 'That did thy cheek enver-
meil', Milton, *On the Death of a Fair Infant* 6; 'a vermeil-tinctured lip',
Comus 752; and 'that on a green / Stood whispering soft', *Par. Lost* iv
326–7.
4. 'provoke the tardy Day', Dryden, *Cymon and Iphiginia* 539.
5, 8. Cp. Dryden, *Georgics* iii 500–1: 'But when the Western Winds with
vital pow'r / Call forth the tender Grass, and budding Flower'; 'Call forth
the Greens, and wake the rising Flowers', Pope, *Temple of Fame* 2.
9–10. Lucretius i 259–61: *hinc nova proles* | *artubus infirmis teneras lasciva per*
herbas | *ludit* (hence the young ones gambol in merry play over the delicate
grass on their weakly limbs). Cp. also Thomson, *Spring* 836–8: 'his sportive
lambs / This way and that convolved in friskful glee, / Their frolics play.'
10. Frisking] Quaintly *Mason variant.*
11. Forgetful . . . their] Rousd from their long & *Mason variant.*

The birds his presence greet:
But chief the sky-lark warbles high
His trembling thrilling ecstasy
15   And, lessening from the dazzled sight,
Melts into air and liquid light.

Yesterday the sullen year
Saw the snowy whirlwind fly;
Mute was the music of the air,
20   The herd stood drooping by:

13–16. Similarly in Thomson, *Spring* 590–4, 'Up springs the lark, / Shrill-voiced and loud, the messenger of morn', and 'from their haunts / Calls up the tuneful nations'.
15–16. Cp. Waller, *To Mr Killigrew* 11–12: 'Whilst nobler fancies make a flight too high / For common view, and lessen as they fly.'
15. lessening] towering *Mason variant.*   Cp. 'All mists that dazzle sense', Fletcher, *Faithful Shepherd* III i.
16. liquid] clear, transparent. Cp. Lucretius v 281: *Largus item liquidi fons luminis, aetherius sol* (The generous fountain of clear light, the ethereal sun); and 'the liquid Light', *Par. Lost* vii 362. Cp. also 'Are melted into air, into thin air', *Tempest* IV i 150; and 'She melted into air', *Winter's Tale* III iii 37.
17. At this point in his expanded version of the poem in *1775* Mason printed the following 4 ll., together with 4 ll. of his own to complete the stanza:

Rise, my Soul! on wings of fire,
Rise the rapt'rous Choir among;
Hark! 'tis Nature strikes the Lyre,
And leads the general song:

Mason had transcribed these lines from G.'s pocketbook for 1754 into the Commonplace Book (iii 1110), a few pages after the main text of the poem. Although his placing of them appears to be purely conjectural, many editors have printed the lines at this point in the poem. There is no evidence to suggest that G. intended them to be placed here, at a point where they interrupt the flow of the poem, nor even that he intended to use them at all. For this reason they do not appear here in the main body of the poem. One link with the rest of the poem may be an echo of Gresset, *La Mediocrité*, in *Oeuvres* (1748) i 359: *Sur des ailes de feu je me sens enlevé.* Cp. also Dryden, *Flower and the Leaf* 18–19: 'Joy spreads the Heart, and with a general Song, / Spring issues out, and leads the jolly Months along.'
sullen] darken'd *Mason variant.*
18. snowy whirlwind] *Mason noted two variants,* scowling tempest *and* snow in whirlwind.
20. 'The drooping cattle dread the impending skies', Pope, *Iliad* xvii 620; 'The cattle droop' and 'Drooping, the labourer-ox / Stands cover'd o'er with snow', Thomson, *Winter* 63, 240–1.

Their raptures now that wildly flow,
No yesterday nor morrow know;
'Tis man alone that joy descries
With forward and reverted eyes.

25   Smiles on past Misfortune's brow
Soft Reflection's hand can trace;
And o'er the cheek of Sorrow throw
A melancholy grace;

21–6. Par. Lost ii 490–5: 'the lowring Element / Scowls ore the dark'ned lantskip Snow, or showre; / If chance the radiant Sun with farewell sweet / Extend his ev'ning beam, the fields revive, / The birds thir notes renew, and bleating herds / Attest thir joy, that hill and valley rings.' And cp. the imitation by Thomson, *Spring* 198–200.

21–4. Virgil, *Georgics* i 415–23, of rooks after a storm: *Haud equidem credo, quia sit divinitus illis / ingenium aut rerum Fato prudentia maior; / verum ubi tempestas et caeli mobilis umor / mutavere vias et Iuppiter uvidus Austris / denset erant quae rara modo, et quae densa relaxat, / vertuntur species animorum, et pectora motus / nunc alios, alios dum nubila ventus agebat, / concipiunt: hinc ille avium concentus in agris / et laetae pecudes et ovantes gutture corvi.* Dryden's translation of this passage runs: 'Not that I think their Breasts with Heav'nly Souls / Inspir'd, as Man, who Destiny controls. / But with the changeful Temper of the Skies, / As Rains condense, and Sunshine rarifies; / So turn the Species in their alter'd Minds, / Compos'd by Calms, and discompos'd by Winds. / From hence proceeds the Birds harmonious Voice: / From hence the Crows exult, and frisking Lambs rejoice.' Cp. also the Song, 'Ah fading joy', from Dryden, *Indian Emperor:* 'See how on every bough the Birds express / In their sweet notes their happiness. / They all enjoy, and nothing spare; / But on their Mother Nature lay their care: / Why then should Man, the Lord of all below / Such troubles chuse to know / As none of all his Subjects undergo?' G. may have remembered *Hamlet* IV iv 36–7: 'He that made us with such large discourse, / Looking before and after'; and Young, *Night Thoughts* vii 744–5, distinguishing man from animals: ''Tis man alone expostulates with Heav'n; / His all the pow'r and all the cause to mourn.'

25–40. Cp. a passage from G.'s notes on Plato, printed from his Commonplace Book by Gosse, *Works* iv 126: 'If we had no memory nor reflection, we could have no enjoyment of past pleasure, nor hope of future, and scarcely any perception of the present, which would be much like the life of an oyster: on the other hand, a life of thought and reflection, without any sense of pleasure or of pain, seems no desirable state. Neither contemplation, therefore, nor pleasure, are the good we seek after, but probably a life composed of both.'

25. past] black *Mason variant.*

While Hope prolongs our happier hour,
30 Or deepest shades, that dimly lower
And blacken round our weary way,
Gilds with a gleam of distant day.

Still, where rosy Pleasure leads,
See a kindred Grief pursue;
35 Behind the steps that Misery treads,
Approaching Comfort view:
The hues of bliss more brightly glow,
Chastised by sabler tints of woe;
And blended form, with artful strife,
40 The strength and harmony of life.

See the wretch, that long has tossed
On the thorny bed of pain,

29–32. Pope, *Essay on Man* ii 283–5: 'Meanwhile Opinion gilds with varying rays / Those painted clouds that beautify our days; / Each want of happiness by Hope supply'd'; and *ibid* iv 341–2, 345–6: 'For him alone, Hope leads from goal to goal, / And opens still, and opens on his soul / . . . / He sees, why Nature plants in Man alone / Hope of known bliss, and Faith in bliss unknown.'
29. 'Seen him I have, but in his happier hour', Pope, *Epilogue to Satires* i 29.
31. 'While the long fun'rals blacken all the way', Pope, *Elegy to an Unfortunate Lady* 40.
33–40. *Essay on Man* ii 117–22: 'Love, Hope, and Joy, fair pleasure's smiling train, / Hate, Fear, and Grief, the family of pain; / These mixed with art and to due bounds confin'd, / Make and maintain the balance of the mind: / The lights and shades, whose well-accorded strife / Gives all the strength and colour of our life'; and Young, *The Force of Religion* Bk ii, in *Poetical Works* (1741) i 99: 'But there's a sure Vicissitude below / Of Light and Darkness, Happiness and Woe; / The Dawn of Day is an Approach to Night, / And Grief is the Conclusion of Delight.'
35–6. *Essay on Man* ii 271, 273: 'See some strange comfort ev'ry state attend / . . . / Hope travels thro', nor quits us when we die.'
39–40. Augustan theories of painting commonly described the 'strife' between light and shade. Cp. the passage from *Essay on Man* ii 117–22 above; Raphael's 'mingled strength of shade and light', Addison, *Letter from Italy* 95; and 'As in thy pictures light contends with shade, / And each to other is subservient made', Congreve, *To Sir Godfrey Kneller* 25–6. For a similar strife in human personality, as here, see *Essay on Man* i 169–70: 'But ALL subsists by elemental strife; / And Passions are the elements of Life.'
41–8. G. no doubt had in mind the following passage from Gresset, *Epitre A Ma Soeur* in *Oeuvres* (1748) i 189–90: *O jours de la Convalescence! / Jours d'une pure volupté! / C'est une nouvelle naissance, / Un rayon d'immortalité. / Quel feu! tous les plaisirs ont volé dans mon ame, / J'adore avec*

At length repair his vigour lost,
And breathe and walk again:
45   The meanest flowret of the vale,
The simplest note that swells the gale,
The common sun, the air and skies,
To him are opening Paradise.

Humble Quiet builds her cell

transport le céleste flambeau; | Tout m'intéresse, tout m'enflame, | Pour moi
l'Univers est nouveau. | Sans doute que le Dieu qui nous rend l'existence, |
A l'heureuse Convalescence | Pour de nouveaux plaisirs donne de nouveaux
sens; | A ses regards impatiens | Le cahos fuit; tout nait; la lumière com-
mence; | Tout brille des feux du Printems; | Les plus simples objets, le
chant d'une Fauvette, | Le matin d'un beau Jour, la verdure des Bois, |
La fraîcheur d'une Violette, | Mille spectacles, qu'autrefois | On voyoit
avec nonchalance, | Transportent aujourd'hui, présentent des apas | In-
connus à l'indifférence, | Et que la foule ne voit pas. But G. seems also to
be indebted to similar sentiments already expressed in English, e.g. Young,
Epistle to Lord Lansdowne, in *Works* (1741) i vi: 'The Patient thus, when on
his bed of pain, / No longer he invokes the Gods in vain, / But rises to new
life; in every field / He finds Elysium, rivers nectar yield; / Nothing so cheap
and vulgar but can please, / And borrow beauties from his late disease'; and
Akenside, *Pleasures of Imagination* (1744) ii 88–96: 'Fair the face of spring, /
When rural songs and odours wake the morn, / To every eye; but how much
more to his, / Round whom the bed of sickness long diffus'd / Its melan-
choly gloom! how doubly fair, / When first with fresh-born vigour *he*
inhales / The balmy breeze, and feels the blessed sun / Warm at his bosom,
from the springs of life / Chasing oppressive damps and languid pain!'
45–6. Akenside, *Hymn to Chearfulness* in *Odes*, 1745, p. 29: 'Till fields and
shades their sweets exhale, / And music swells each opening gale.'
45. Young, *Night Thoughts* vi 197: 'As the mead's meanest flowret to the
sun'.
47. Cp. Ovid, *Metamorphoses* i 135: *communemque prius ceu lumina solis*
et auras (a common possession like the sunlight and the air); *ibid* vi 350:
nec solem proprium natura nec aera fecit (Nature has not made the sun private
to any, nor the air); and 'Shut from the common air and common use /
Of their own limbs', Thomson, *Winter* 333–4; 'The common benefit of
vital air', Dryden, *Hind and Panther* i 298.
48. 'And breatheth balm from opened paradise', Fairfax's *Tasso* IV lxxv 6;
'And *Paradise* was open'd in his face', Dryden, *Absalom and Achitophel* 30;
'And Paradise was open'd in the Wild', Pope, *Eloisa to Abelard* 134.
49 *ff.* Mason's transcript of the poem in the Commonplace Book omits
these lines, but they are written on the opposite page. In *1775* Mason
attempted to reconstruct these stanzas, which are here given only in the
fragmentary form of his original transcription.
49–50. Dryden, *Epilogue to the King at Oxford, 1681* 11–12: 'This Place the

50 Near the source whence Pleasure flows;
    She eyes the clear crystalline well
    And tastes it as it goes.
    Far below   the crowd.
    Broad and turbulent it grows
55   with resistless sweep
    They perish in the boundless deep

    Mark where Indolence and Pride,
    Softly rolling side by side,
    Their dull but daily round.

seat of Peace, the quiet Cell / Where Arts remov'd from noisy business
dwell'; Dyer, *Grongar Hill* 15–16: 'Grongar, in whose mossy cells / Sweetly-
musing Quiet dwells.' But G. also remembered Gresset's ode *La Mediocrité*
(*Oeuvres*, 1748, i 359–60): *Aux bords d'une mer furieuse, / Où la Fortune
impérieuse / Porte et brise à son gré de superbes vaisseaux, / Il est un port
sûr et tranquile / Qui maintient dans un doux asile / Des barques à l'abri du
caprice des eaux. / Sur ces solitaires rivages / D'où l'oeil, spectateur des
naufrages, / S'aplaudit en secret de sa sécurité, / Dans un Temple simple et
rustique, / De la Nature ouvrage antique, / Ce Climat voit règner la
Médiocrité. / Là, conduite par la sagesse, / Tu te fixas, humble Déesse, /
Loin des Palais bruyans du fastueux Plutus: / Là sous tes loix et sous ton
culte, / Tu rassemblas, loin du tumulte, / Le vrai, les plaisirs purs, les sincères
vertus. / Séduits par d'aveugles idoles, / Du bonheur, fantômes frivoles, /
Le Vulgaire et les Grands ne te suivirent pas.*
51. G. followed Milton in stressing the second syllable of 'crystalline':
e.g. 'And that Crystalline Sphear' and 'On the Crystallin Skie', *Par. Lost*
iii 482 and vi 772; and 'from the cool Crystalline stream', *Samson Agonistes*
546.
56. 'the vast and boundless Deep', *Par. Lost* i 177.
57–9. G. seems to have intended to imitate in this fragment the passage in
Gresset's *Epitre A Ma Soeur* in *Oeuvres* (1748) i 190, which followed the lines
on convalescence: *Las des mêmes plaisirs, las de leur multitude, / Le senti-
ment n'est plus flaté; / Dans le fracas des jeux, dans la plus vive Orgie, /
L'Esprit sans force et sans clarté / Ne trouve que la létargie / De l'insipide
oisiveté. / Cléon depuis dix ans de fêtes et d'ivresse, / Frais, brillant d'embon-
point, ramené chaque jour, / Entre la Jeunesse et l'Amour, / Dans le néant de
la mollesse / Dort et végète tour à tour.*

23 [Epitaph on Mrs Clerke]

Written not long before 31 Jan. 1758, when G. sent it in a letter to Edward
Bedingfield (*Corresp* ii 560): 'I will not send you the *Sonnet* you mention

[presumably that on Richard West], but here is something else full as bad, only as it is just wrote, I send it you. it is an epitaph on the Wife of a Friend of mine.' John Clerke (1717-90) had been a contemporary of G. at Peterhouse, became a Fellow in 1740 and practised as a physician for many years at Epsom. His father had been Rector of Beckenham in Kent and G.'s epitaph was duly inscribed on a mural tablet of slate and stone in St George's Church, Beckenham. Mrs Clerke had died in childbirth at the age of 31 on 27 April 1757.

The first printing of the poem has not hitherto been noted. It appeared in the *Gentleman's Mag.* xxix 485, for Oct. 1759, entitled (not accurately), 'An Epitaph, copied from a Tomb-stone in a Country Church Yard'. (This text contains one variant: 'thus' for 'yet' in l. 11.) It was accompanied by a Latin translation, which has not otherwise been traced in print, although it may be connected with a copy of the epitaph, with an unfinished Latin translation, in an unidentified hand found among Richard Hurd's papers (see *Correspondence of Hurd and Mason*, ed. Pearce and Whibley, 1932, p. 168). The only other occasion on which the poem was printed in G.'s lifetime was in the *Poetical Calendar* (2nd edn, 1763) viii 121. It was reprinted in the *New Foundling Hospital for Wit* (1772) vi 76-7, and in the *Gentleman's Mag.* xliv (1774) 487, before Mason collected it in the *Poems* p. 61, in 1775. Wordsworth, *Prose Works*, ed. A. B. Grosart (1876) ii 66-7, thought its first 6 lines 'vague and languid' but praised the 'latter part' as 'almost the only instance among the metrical epitaphs in our language of the last century, which I remember, of affecting thoughts rising naturally and keeping themselves pure from vicious diction; and therefore retaining their appropriate power over the mind'.

The text printed here is that of the tablet in Beckenham Church, with variants from the letter to Bedingfield.

> Lo! where this silent marble weeps,
> A friend, a wife, a mother sleeps:

¶ 23.1. *silent*] little *Bedingfield.*   *marble weeps*] Commenting on the phrase 'weeping Vaults' in Pope, *Windsor Forest* 302, Gilbert Wakefield described it as 'A puerile conceit, from the dew, which runs down stone and metals in damp weather', and cited Virgil, *Georgics* i 480: *et maestum inlacrimat templis ebur aeraque sudant* (in temples the ivory weeps in sorrow, and bronzes sweat). Cp. Congreve, *The Mourning Muse of Alexis* 85: 'The marble weeps'; Pope, *Epitaph on Duke of Buckingham* 5: 'this weeping marble', and 'Here o'er the Martyr-King the Marble weeps', *Windsor Forest* 313; and 'While o'er her Grave the Marble Statue weeps', John Dart, *Westminster Abbey* (1723) I xx.
2. 'The virgin's part, the mother and the wife', Waller, *Thyrsis and Galatea* 25; 'A wife, a mistress and a friend in one', Dryden, *Epitaph on Lady Whitmore* 2; 'The tender sister, daughter, friend and wife', Pope, *Epistle to Jervas* 52.

A heart, within whose sacred cell
The peaceful virtues loved to dwell.
5   Affection warm, and faith sincere,
And soft humanity were there.
In agony, in death, resigned,
She felt the wound she left behind.
Her infant image, here below,
10 Sits smiling on a father's woe:
Whom what awaits, while yet he strays
Along the lonely vale of days?
A pang, to secret sorrow dear;
A sigh; an unavailing tear;
15 Till time shall every grief remove,
With life, with memory, and with love.

4. *The peaceful virtues*] Each peaceful Virtue *Bedingfield.*
6. *soft humanity*] Used by Dryden, *Threnodia Augustalis* 350 and *All for Love*
II i; Pope, *Epitaph on General Withers* 4.
7–10. *In place of these lines, Bedingfield has*:

> To hide her Cares her only art,
> Her pleasure pleasures to impart.
> In ling'ring pain, in death resign'd,
> Her latest agony of mind
> Was felt for him, who could not save
> His All from an untimely grave:

This variant is also recorded by Mason in 1775.

Toynbee and Whibley, *Corresp* ii 560 *n* 7, mention John Clerke's copy of
G.'s 1768 *Poems*, in which he had transcribed this poem, as 'Epitaph on Mrs
—— who died in Childbirth, by Mr Gray'. G. may not at first have known
the manner of Mrs Clerke's death and have decided later to introduce a
reference to the child in his revised version of these lines.
11–12. Cp. *Elegy* 74–5 (p. 131).
13. *secret*] silent *Bedingfield.*

24 [Epitaph on a Child]

Written not earlier than mid-June 1758 and probably not much later. It is
generally assumed that the subject of this epitaph was Robert (familiarly
known as Robin) Wharton, eldest son of G.'s friend Dr Thomas Wharton,
Fellow of Pembroke in 1739, later a physician in London until 1758, when
he went to live on his estate at Old Park, near Durham. Robin Wharton,
born in 1753, apparently died in April 1758 (*Corresp* ii 569). Mason, *Memoirs*
p. 270, explained the following passage in a letter from G. to Wharton on

18 June 1758 (*Corresp* ii 571), with the statement that 'His friend had re-
quested him to write an Epitaph on the child': 'You flatter me in thinking,
than any thing, I can do, could at all alleviate the just concern your late loss
has given you: but I can not flatter myself so far, & know how little qualified
I am at present to give any satisfaction to myself on this head, & in this way,
much less to you. I by no means pretend to inspiration, but yet I affirm,
that the faculty in question is by no means voluntary. it is the result (I
suppose) of a certain disposition of mind, wch does not depend on oneself &
wch I have not felt this long time. you that are a witness, how seldom this
spirit has moved me in my life, may easily give credit to what I say.'

The epitaph was first printed by Gosse, *Works* i 126–7, from a copy made
by Alexander Dyce (now in the Dyce Collection at South Kensington),
when G.'s MS was sold in 1854. There are also two copies in the Mitford MSS
(British Museum, Add. MS 32561 ff. 74, 121), one of them from G.'s MS,
which appeared in the three sales of G.'s books and papers between 1845 and
1854. The second has two small variants: 'free' for 'freed' (l. 1) and 'the
night' for 'his night' (l. 6). The present text is taken from G.'s MS, now in
the Pierpont Morgan Library, New York.

> Here, freed from pain, secure from misery, lies
> A child, the darling of his parents' eyes:
> A gentler lamb ne'er sported on the plain,
> A fairer flower will never bloom again.
> Few were the days allotted to his breath;
> Now let him sleep in peace his night of death.

¶ 24.3–4. G. seems to echo two phrases from Shakespeare: *Richard II*
II i 174: 'In peace was never gentle lamb more mild'; and the phrasing and
rhythm of *I Henry VI* III ii 134–5: 'A braver soldier never couched lance, /
A gentler heart did never sway in court.'
6. *Here*] Now *Gosse*.

25 The Fatal Sisters. An Ode

Written in 1761, not later than the beginning of May. Since G.'s translations
from Norse and Welsh poetry were associated with his plans to write a
'History of English Poetry', some account of that abortive project must be
given. In July 1752 William Warburton sent Mason a sketch for a history
of English poetry which he had found among Pope's papers (*Letters from a
Late Eminent Prelate to one of his Friends* (1808) p. 89). According to Mason,
Memoirs p. 337:

'Mr. Gray was greatly struck with the method which Mr. Pope had traced
out in this little sketch; and on my proposal of engaging with him in com-
piling such a history, he examined the plan more accurately, enlarged it

considerably, and formed an idea for an introduction to it. In this was to be ascertained the origin of Rhyme; and specimens given, not only of the Provençal Poetry, (to which alone Mr. Pope seemed to have adverted) but of the Scaldic, British, and Saxon; as, from all these different sources united, English Poetry had its original. . . .'

G.'s transcript of Pope's MS is in the Commonplace Book (ii 707). The elaborate scholarly projects with which G. had been occupied since 1746– a survey of ancient Greek civilization, the study of classical literature and of travel books–were replaced, at about the time that Mason suggested a collaboration on the 'History', by research into the historical background of English poetry. G.'s borrowings from Pembroke College Library and the entries in his pocketbooks and Commonplace Book show that from 1753 onwards he was engaged on a systematic study of Romance, Germanic and Celtic poetics and philology, as well as of medieval English poetry. A series of articles in his Commonplace Book illustrates the scale on which he was working. An annotated catalogue of English poets before 1600 is followed by various essays: 'Lydgate', 'Metrum', 'Pseudo-Rhythmus', 'Gothi', 'Additional Observations on the Use of Rhyme' and 'Cambri'. These essays were printed in part by Mathias in 1814 and by Gosse in 1884. The important article 'Cambri' has been printed in full by Roger Martin, *Chronologie de la vie et de l'oeuvre de Thomas Gray* (Toulouse, 1931) pp. 170–99. For a detailed account of G.'s achievement as a literary historian, see W. Powell Jones, *Thomas Gray, Scholar* (1937) pp. 84–107.

G.'s historical labours were followed with interest by his literary friends. Richard Hurd wrote encouragingly on 16 Aug. 1757 (*Corresp* ii 517): 'I hope you don't forget, among your other amusements this summer, your design for a history of the English poetry. You might be regulating your plan, and digesting the materials you have by you. I shall teaze you perpetually, till you set about the project in good earnest.' Nevertheless, G.'s interest in the 'History' gradually waned and by 1758, stimulated by Horace Walpole, he had turned instead to the study of English history and antiquities. When the British Museum opened in 1759, G. took up residence in London so that he could pursue his interests in the new library. As he explained to Mason in Oct. 1759 (*Corresp* ii 646): 'My only employment & amusement in Town . . . has been the Musaeum: but I have been rather historically than poetically given. with a little of your encouragement perhaps I may return to my old Lydgate & Occleve, whose works are there in abundance.'

The stimulus to return to the 'History' duly came in 1760, but not from Mason. In Jan. 1760 Sir David Dalrymple sent Walpole, with the intention that they should be passed on to G., two specimens of James Macpherson's supposed translations from Gaelic poetry (*Corresp* iii 1223). Although he had doubts about their authenticity, G. was greatly excited by them. In June 1760 Macpherson published his *Fragments of Ancient Poetry, collected in the Highlands of Scotland and translated from the Galic or Erse Language* at Edinburgh, and G. admitted to Wharton that he had 'gone mad about them'

and that he was '*extasié* with their infinite beauty'. Whether or not they
were genuine, he was enthusiastic: 'in short this Man is the very Demon of
Poetry, or he has lighted on a treasure hid for ages.' Almost simultaneously
he was shown the MS of the *De Bardis Dissertatio* by the Welsh antiquary
Evan Evans, which was to be published in 1764 (*Corresp* ii 680).

The specimens of ancient Erse and Welsh poetry produced by Macpherson
and Evans inspired G. to return to his 'History of English Poetry'. When he
printed his translations from Norse and Welsh poetry in *1768* he prefixed an
'Advertisement' in which he explained that the plan for the 'History' had
been abandoned, but that: 'In the Introduction to it he meant to have
produced some specimens of the Style that reigned in ancient times among
the neighbouring nations, or those who had subdued the greater part of
this Island, and were our Progenitors: the following three Imitations made a
part of them.' Further detail is given in the sketch of his plan for the 'History'
which he sent to Thomas Warton in April 1770 (*Corresp* iii 1123). The Intro-
duction was to deal with 'the poetry of the *Galic* (or Celtic) nations, as far
back as it can be traced', as well as 'that of the Goths: its introduction into
these islands by the Saxons & Danes, & its duration.'

G. may always have intended therefore to include some verse translations
in his 'History'. There is no way of dating precisely a list of works dealing
with Scandinavian history and antiquities at the front of vol. ii of his Com-
monplace Book, which is followed by a list of 'Gothic', 'Erse' and 'Welch'
poems, although the 'Erse' and 'Welch' entries seem to have been added
later and to have been inspired by the collections of Macpherson and Evan
Evans. Both the poems which G. translated as *The Fatal Sisters* and *The
Descent of Odin* appear in the list of 'Gothic' poems and both are checked
off, as if G. had intended at one stage to translate the others. Both had been
translated by 5 May 1761, when Walpole wrote to George Montagu
(*Walpole Correspondence* ix 364): 'Gray has translated two noble incantations
from the Lord knows who, a Danish Gray, who lived the Lord knows when.
They are to be enchased in a history of English bards, which Mason and
he are writing, but of which the former has not writ a word yet, and of
which the latter, if he rides Pegasus at his usual foot-pace, will finish the first
page two years hence.' Walpole knew G.'s character all too well, for after
this sudden return of enthusiasm in 1760–61, nothing is heard of the 'History'
until 1768, when G. stated in his 'Advertisement' to *The Fatal Sisters* (see
above) that 'He has long since drop'd his design, especially after he had heard,
that it was already in the hands of a Person well qualified to do it justice,
both by his taste, and his researches into antiquity'. G. may have abandoned
it as early as 1762, when Thomas Warton was already planning his own
History (*Corresp* iii 1092 *n*). In April 1770 G. surrendered to Warton the
'sketches' of his design (*Corresp* iii 1122–5). Warton's unfinished *History*
appeared in three volumes between 1774 and 1781. Mason appears to have
completed for the projected 'History' only a translation from Bartholinus,
'Song of Harold the Valiant': see his *Works* (1811) i 196–8.

The Fatal Sisters, together with *The Descent of Odin* and *The Triumphs of*

Owen, was first printed in *1768*. G. included these translations to replace *A Long Story*, which had appeared in *1753* with Bentley's illustrations and which he was now determined to omit. To James Beattie, who supervised the Glasgow edn of *1768*, he explained that this was 'the sole reason I have to publish these few additions' (*Corresp* iii 1001–2); and he told Walpole (*Corresp* iii 1017–18) that 'The *Long Story* was to be totally omitted, as its only use (that of explaining [Bentley's] prints) was gone: but to supply the place of it in bulk, lest *my works* should be mistaken for the works of a flea, or a pismire, I promised to send [Dodsley] an equal weight of poetry or prose: so, since my return hither, I put up about two ounces of stuff; viz. The Fatal Sisters, The Descent of Odin (of both which you have copies), a bit of something from the Welch, and certain little notes.' The notes to which G. referred here were taken from the critical apparatus which he supplied for the Latin texts of the poems in the article 'Gothi' in his Commonplace Book (see below). Others, which G. did not include in *1768*, were printed by Mason in *1775*.

In the list of 'Gothic' poems at the front of his Commonplace Book vol. ii, *The Fatal Sisters* is entitled 'The Song of the Weïrd Sisters, or Valkyries–after A:D: 1029. In Tormodus Torfaeus. (Orcad[es] & Bartholin).' G.'s transcript of the poem in his Commonplace Book, where it is dated 1761, is entitled merely 'The Song of the Valkyries'. A transcript by Wharton in the British Museum is entitled 'The Song of the Weird Sisters, translated from the Norwegian about 1029'. The present title first appears in *1768* where it is followed by the explanation: '(From the Norse-Tongue,) In the Orcades of Thormodus Torfaeus; Hafniae, 1697, Folio: and also in Bartholinus.' G. then quoted the first line of the Norse original: 'Vitt er orpit fyrir valfalli, &c.' The sources of the poem mentioned by G. are Thomas Bartholin's *Antiquitatum Danicarum De Causis Contemptae A Danis Adhuc Gentilibus Mortis* (Copenhagen, 1689) in which many extracts from Norse poetry and the sagas were first published, including Norse and Latin texts of the original of *The Fatal Sisters* on pp. 617–24; and Thormodus Torfaeus's *Orcades Seu Rerum Orcadensium Historiae* (Copenhagen, 1697), which reproduces Bartholin's text on pp. 36–8. In 1760 or 1761, G. made a second entry in his Commonplace Book with the title 'Gothi' (iii 1041–3), in which he copied out part of the Norse and the entire Latin text of the poem from the Danish antiquaries and added elaborate notes.

The question of how much Old Norse G. actually knew has inevitably been raised: the evidence suggests that he depended almost entirely on the Latin translations (by Arni Magnússon) for his understanding of the poems and on the Latin commentaries of Bartholin and Torfaeus for his annotation. It has been pointed out that, while he transcribed the Latin texts of the poems in full, he omitted much of the original Norse, and that he reproduced errors which occur in the Latin. It is possible, however, that, whether or not he understood it, G. may have tried to imitate the characteristic rhythms of the original Norse verse. For further discussion of this problem see G. L. Kittredge's appendix, 'Gray's knowledge of Old Norse' in W. L. Phelps,

Selections from Thomas Gray (Boston, 1894) pp. xli–l; F. E. Farley, *Scandinavian Influences in the English Romantic Movement* (Boston, 1903) p. 35 and *n*; and W. Powell Jones, *Thomas Gray, Scholar* p. 101. Farley also discusses G.'s place in the growth of Scandinavian studies in the eighteenth century and the particular influence of his translations.

The original poem, known in its separate form as *Darraðar Ljóð*, was probably written not long after the Battle of Clontarf, fought on Good Friday 1014, of which it purports to be a prophetic account. At a later stage it was absorbed into the late 13th century *Njáls Saga*, ch. 157. In the Battle of Clontarf a number of characters of the *Njáls Saga* fight on the side of Sictryg (or Sihtric), King of Dublin, and Sigurd, Earl of the Orkneys, against Brian, King of Munster. Although Brian himself was killed, his forces were victorious and the invaders retreated leaving Sigurd dead. See L. M. Hollander, *Old Norse Poems* (New York, 1936) pp. 72–5; and, for the full context of the poem, the translation of the *Njáls Saga* by C. F. Bayerschmidt (1955) pp. 355–60. The title of the poem has been the subject of some speculation. When the poem was absorbed into the saga, the name of the man who saw the vision in Caithness (see G.'s Preface), given as Dorruðr in the saga, was probably formed from a misunderstanding of the kenning 'vef darraðar' ('web of the dart' = 'battle'), which occurs three times in the original (ll. 30, 38, 46). For the Latin mistranslation of the phrase, see l. 25 *n*. When the poem was once more reproduced separately, its title may have been intended (as Starr and Hendrickson, p. 211, suggest) merely to mean 'The Song of Dorruðr'. Tovey has argued, however, that *Darraðar Ljóð* means 'Lay of the Darts' and that the name of the man who saw the vision was mistakenly formed from the title of the poem rather than the reverse. The evidence suggests that the separate title of the poem came later than its inclusion in the saga.

A literal translation of the Latin used by G., as given by Mason in *1775*, follows:

Wide is scattered
Before the coming slaughter
The cloud of arrows:
Down rains the blood:
Already to the spears is tied
The deadly-pale
Warp of warriors,
Which the Sisters weave
With the red woof
Of Randver's death.
  This web is woven
With human entrails
And to the warp-thread are tightly
    bound
Human heads,
There are blood-spattered
Spears as treadles,
The weaving-tools are of iron
With arrows in the place of shuttles:

We will beat close with swords
This web of victory.
  There come to the weaving Hilda
And Hiorthrimula,
Sangrida and Swipula;
With drawn swords
The lance shall be shivered,
The shield split asunder
And the sword
Broken on the shield.
  Let us weave, let us weave
The web of Darrad!
This sword the youthful king
Once possessed.
Let us go forth
And join the battle-lines,
Where our friends
Contend with weapons.
  Let us weave, let us weave

The web of Darrad;
And to the King then,
Then let us cling.
There they saw
Shields dewed with blood,
Gunna and Gondula
Who stood guard over the King.
  Let us weave, let us weave
The web of Darrad!
When the weapons clang together
Of the warlike men
We will not allow him
To be deprived of life:
The Valkyries possess
Power over death.
  Those peoples shall rule the land,
Who on desolate headlands
Dwelled before.
I foretell that over the powerful King
Death impends.
Already the Earl has fallen to the
  arrows;
  And to the Hibernians
A grief shall come,
Which will never
Among men be ended.

Now the web is woven.
In truth the plain is dewed (with
  blood);
Over the lands shall sweep
The strife of soldiers.
  Now it is dreadful
To look around,
For a cloud of blood
Flies through the air:
The air will be stained
With the blood of warriors
Before our prophecies
Shall fall to the ground.
  Well do we sing
About the young King
Many songs of victory:
May it be well for us, the singers,
And may that man learn
Who is listening
Many songs of war
And make them known among men.
  Let us ride off on horses
Since we are bearing forth drawn
  swords
From this place.

The text followed here is that in G.'s letter to James Dodsley in early Feb. 1768 (British Museum, Add. MS 38511 ff. 5–6), from which that in *1768* was printed, except for changes in punctuation and capitalization, and the separation of stanzas to which G. did not apparently object. Variants are given from the Commonplace Book (iii 1067–8) and Wharton's transcript.

PREFACE

In the eleventh century Sigurd, Earl of the Orkney Islands, went with a fleet of ships and a considerable body of troops into Ireland, to the assistance of Sictryg with the silken beard, who was then making war on his
5   father-in-law Brian, King of Dublin: the Earl and all his forces were cut to pieces, and Sictryg was in danger of a total defeat; but the enemy had a greater loss by the death of Brian, their King, who fell in the action. On Christmas-day (the day of the battle), a native of

¶ 25 *Preface 9. Christmas-day*] Torfaeus makes it clear that the battle actually occurred on Good Friday (*eodem die passionis dominicae*), 23 April 1014. With reference to Christmas Day, G. noted in the Commonplace Book (printed by Mason in *1775, Poems* p. 100): 'The People of these Islands were Christians, yet did not become so till after A:D:966. probably it happen'd in 995. but tho' they & the other Gothic Nations no longer worship'd their

10 Caithness in Scotland saw at a distance a number of
persons on horseback riding full speed towards a hill,
and seeming to enter into it. Curiosity led him to follow
them, till looking through an opening in the rocks he
saw twelve gigantic figures resembling women: they
15 were all employed about a loom; and as they wove,
they sung the following dreadful song; which when they
had finished, they tore the web into twelve pieces, and
(each taking her portion) galloped six to the north and
as many to the south.

Now the storm begins to lower,
(Haste, the loom of hell prepare,)

old Divinities, yet they never doubted of their existence, or forgot their
ancient mythology, as appears from the History of Olaus Tryggueson
(see Bartholin: L. 3. c:i. pag: 615.)'.

p9–10. native of Caithness] Named Dorruðr in the *Njáls Saga*, where he
sees twelve people ride to a 'dyngja' or women's room, where such work as
weaving was done, often partly underground.

p15. loom] The draft of the 'Preface' in the Commonplace Book adds:
'The threads, that formed the texture, were the entrails of Men, the shuttles
were so many swords, the weights were human heads, the warp was all of
bloody spears. as they wove, they sung the following magic song.'

1. Note. The *Valkyriur* were female Divinities, Servants of *Odin* (or *Woden*)
in the Gothic mythology. Their name signifies *Chusers of the slain*. They
were mounted on swift horses, with drawn swords in their hands; and in
the throng of battle selected such as were destined to slaughter, and conduct-
ed them to *Valkalla*, the hall of *Odin*, or paradise of the Brave; where they at-
tended the banquet, and served the departed Heroes with horns of mead
and ale. *G. 1768.* ('*Valkalla*' was a printer's error for '*Valhalla*'.)

A similar note in the Commonplace Book adds: 'Gunna, Gondula, &
Hilda, are the names of three such divinities mention'd in the Edda (Gunnr,
Gaundol, Hilldr). there were also Skaugol, Geirskaugol, Skulld, Sigrun, &
others. they are often described as spinning, or flying thro' the air, dress'd
in the skin of a swan: some of them were married to mortal Men, (as
Svanhvitr, Aulrunr, & Alvitrar) with whom they cohabited for a few years.
they also are call'd *Disir* (see Bartholin, L: 3. cap: i, & L: 2. cap: ii) there
were a great number more of these Valkyriur, as Hrist, Mist, Skeggiold,
Thrudr, Hlokk, Herfiotur, Gaull, Geira, Hod, Ranngrid, Radgrid, Regin-
leif, &c: whose office it was to serve the departed Heroes with horns of
Mead & Ale.'

1–4. Par. Lost ii 490–1: 'the lowring Element / Scowls ore the dark'ned
lantskip Snow, or showre.'

Iron-sleet of arrowy shower
Hurtles in the darkened air.

5   Glittering lances are the loom,
    Where the dusky warp we strain,
    Weaving many a soldier's doom,
    Orkney's woe, and Randver's bane.

    See the grisly texture grow,
10 ('Tis of human entrails made,)
    And the weights that play below,
    Each a gasping warrior's head.

    Shafts for shuttles, dipped in gore,
    Shoot the trembling cords along.
15 Sword, that once a monarch bore,
    Keep the tissue close and strong!

3. *arrowy shower*] G. follows the Latin *nubes sagittarum*, a mistranslation (or simplification) of the rather obscure kenning in the original, *rifs rei sky*, which Bayerschmidt and Hollander translate 'the weaver's-beam's-web' = the interweaving of darts and arrows in the air, a kenning for battle.

G.'s note acknowledges a debt to *Par. Regained* iii 323–4: 'How quick they wheel'd, and flying behind them shot / Sharp sleet of arrowie showers.' Cp. also Virgil, *Aeneid* xii 283–4: *it toto turbida caelo / tempestas telorum ac ferreus ingruit imber* (through the whole sky flies a thickening storm of javelins and the iron rain falls fast); and Statius, *Thebaid* viii 412–3: *exclusere diem telis, stant ferrea caelo / nubila* (Their darts shut out the day, a steely cloud hangs athwart the sky). William Browne, *Britannia's Pastorals* II iv 56, has 'iron shower' for spears.

4. G.'s note in *1768* acknowledges a debt to *Julius Caesar* II ii 22: 'The noise of battle hurtled in the air.'

8. *Orkney*] Earl Sigurd.   *Randver's bane*] The Latin *Randveri mortis* evades the obscurity of the original. G. Vigfusson and F. York Powell, *Corpus Poeticum Boreale* (Oxford, 1883) i 281, translate the original as 'the web which we the friends of Woden are filling with red weft', taking *Randvéss bana* to be Woden or Odin (the slayer of Randver) and the 'friends of Woden' to be the Valkyries. Bayerschmidt and Hollander translate 'which valkyries fill with the red warp-of-Randver's banesman', taking the last phrase as a probable kenning for blood.

12. 'The gasping Head flies off', Dryden, *Aeneid* ix 446.

13. 'And dip'd his Arrows in *Lernaean* Gore', Dryden, *Aeneid* vi 1096.

15. *Sword*] Blade *Wharton*.

16. This line in particular reveals the general influence on the poem of the witches in *Macbeth*: see IV i, especially l. 32.

Mista black, terrific maid,
Sangrida and Hilda see,
Join the wayward work to aid:
20   'Tis the woof of victory.

Ere the ruddy sun be set,
Pikes must shiver, javelins sing,
Blade with clattering buckler meet,
Hauberk crash and helmet ring.

25   (Weave the crimson web of war)
Let us go and let us fly,
Where our friends the conflict share,
Where they triumph, where they die.

As the paths of fate we tread,
30   Wading through the ensanguined field:

17–18. Sangrida, terrific Maid, / Mista black, and Hilda see, *Wharton*.
17–18, 31. G. took three of these names of the Valkyries– Sangrida, Hilda
and Gondula–from the Latin text; but for Hriorthrimula, Swipula and
Gunna he substituted Mista and Geira, names which he found in another
list of the Valkyries in Bartholin's Latin translation of part of the *Griminsval*
from the *Poetic Edda*, p. 554. See his note on the Valkyries in the Common-
place Book quoted above.
19. wayward] Perverse. But G. no doubt had in mind the witches in *Macbeth*,
the Weird Sisters, spelt 'weyward' in the Folio edns of Shakespeare and
in G.'s MS. In this sense it means 'Having the power to control the fate of
men'.
21. Cp. the witches in *Macbeth* I i 5: 'That will be ere the set of sun'.
23. Blade] Sword *Wharton*.   Cp. Dryden's 'clatt'ring shields', *Aeneid*
vii 1084, ix 960, and *Palamon and Arcite* iii 996.
24. Cp. *The Bard* 5 and *n* (p. 183); 'his Helmet rung', Dryden, *Aeneid* x 1089.
25. web of war] The Latin translation of the phrase 'vef darraðar' ('web of
the dart'), which occurs three times in the original, is *telam Darradi* (once)
or *telam Darradar* (twice). The translator was probably misled into taking
'darraðar' as a proper name by the context of the poem in the saga or by the
title (see headnote). G. corrected the error in a note, based on Bartholin
p. 624, in his Commonplace Book, printed by Mason, *Poems* p. 99 *n*: 'So
Tormodus interprets it, as tho' *Daradr* were the name of the Person, who saw
this vision, but in reality it signifies a *range of spears*, from *Daur*, hasta, &
Radir, ordo', etc.
28. triumph] conquer *Commonplace Book, written above* triumph *deleted*.   Cp.
The Bard 142 (p. 200 above); Pope, *Iliad* iv 636–7: 'So fought each host,
with thirst of glory fired, / And crowds on crowds triumphantly expired.'
30. Cp. *Elegy* 67 (p. 129); and 'th'ensanguind Field', *Par. Lost* xi 650; John
Philips, *Blenheim* 155, and many other instances.

Gondula and Geira, spread
O'er the youthful King your shield.

We the reins to slaughter give,
Ours to kill and ours to spare:
35   Spite of danger he shall live.
(Weave the crimson web of war.)

They, whom once the desert-beach
Pent within its bleak domain,
Soon their ample sway shall stretch
40   O'er the plenty of the plain.

Low the dauntless Earl is laid,
Gored with many a gaping wound:
Fate demands a nobler head;
Soon a King shall bite the ground.

45   Long his loss shall Eirin weep,
Ne'er again his likeness see;

31. Gunna and Gondula, spread *Commonplace Book, Wharton.*
32. youthful king] Sictryg.
33. slaughter] havock *Commonplace Book.*   Cp. *Par. Lost* vi 695–6: 'Warr
wearied hath perform'd what War can do, / And to disorder'd rage let
loose the reines.'
37–40. G. evidently understood the poem to be a celebration of Sictryg
(see ll. 32, 56) and probably intended these lines to refer to his forces and
their future in Ireland. In fact, Sictryg was virtually defeated in the battle
and the lines corresponding to these in the original have more commonly
been taken to refer to the Vikings from the north.
39. 'And o're *Campania* stretch'd his ample Sway', Dryden, *Aeneid* vii 1018.
40. Cp. *Education and Government* 99 (p. 99).
41. Earl] G. obviously had Sigurd in mind, although some editors of the
original poem believe that it may refer to Brian's son. Cp. 'Now low on
Earth the lofty Chief is laid', Dryden, *Aeneid* xii 1346.
42. Cp. *Faerie Queene* II iv 3, 8 and vii 13, 7: 'gor'd with many a wound';
I viii 16, 6: 'the gaping wound'. Shakespeare parodied this kind of diction
in *II Henry IV* II iv 213–3: 'Why, then, let grievous, ghastly, gaping wounds /
Untwine the Sisters Three!' Dryden has 'gaping Wound', *Aeneid* ix 1017,
x 1117.
44. shall] must *Commonplace Book, Wharton.*
King] Brian.   Cp. Dryden, *Aeneid* xi 528: 'So many Valiant Heroes bite the
Ground'; also *Georgics* iv 117; *Aeneid* xii 928; Pope, *Iliad* xvi 853.
45. his] her *Commonplace Book.*
46. Hamlet I ii 188: 'I shall not look upon his like again.'

> Long her strains in sorrow steep,
> Strains of immortality!
>
> Horror covers all the heath,
> 50 Clouds of carnage blot the sun.
> Sisters, weave the web of death;
> Sisters, cease. The work is done.
>
> Hail the task, and hail the hands!
> Songs of joy and triumph sing!
> 55 Joy to the victorious bands;
> Triumph to the younger King.
>
> Mortal, thou that hear'st the tale,
> Learn the tenor of our song.
> Scotland, through each winding vale
> 60 Far and wide the notes prolong.
>
> Sisters, hence with spurs of speed:
> Each her thundering faulchion wield;
> Each bestride her sable steed.
> Hurry, hurry to the field.

50. blot] veil *Wharton.*   Cp. *The Bard* 135 (p. 199 above).
57. G. evidently refers to Dorruðr, the eavesdropper named in the *Njáls Saga* and mentioned in his 'Preface'. The corresponding passage in the original poem may have been addressed to listeners in general.
58. Cp. Spenser, *Colin Clout* 100; 'Heare then (quoth he) the tenor of my tale.'
59. winding] echoing *Wharton.*   Cp. 'winding Vale', Dryden, *Aeneid* viii 809; Pope, *Summer* 26.
61–3. Wharton has:
> Sisters, hence! 'tis time to ride:
> Now your thund'ring faulchion wield;
> Now your sable steed bestride,
and so Commonplace Book with faulchions *and* steeds.
61. 'Spurring at speed', Dryden, *Aeneid* xi 923.
63. 'bestride our foaming steeds', *III Henry VI* II i 183; 'his Sable Steed he spurr'd', Dryden, *Theodore and Honoria* 335.

26 The Descent of Odin. An Ode

Written in 1761, not later than the beginning of May; for the date of composition, the background to this translation and its publication in *1768*, see headnote to *The Fatal Sisters*. In the list of 'Gothic' poems in G.'s Commonplace Book, it is entitled 'Incantation of Woden (call'd Vegtams Kvitha) in Bartholin p. 632. very ancient.' G.'s transcript in the Commonplace Book (iii 1069–70) has the present title and is dated 1761. There is also a transcript by Wharton (British Museum, Egerton MS 2400 ff. 230–1), entitled 'The Vegtams Kwitha from Bartholinus.' In *1768* the title is followed by the explanation: '(From the Norse-Tongue,) In Bartholinus, de causis contemnendae mortis; Hafniae, 1689, Quarto'. G. then quotes the first line of the original Norse: 'Upreis Odinn allda gautr, &c.'

G. found the original text and a Latin translation in Bartholin, pp. 632–40. The Norse text and an English translation are given in G. Vigfusson and F. York Powell, *Corpus Poeticum Boreale* (1883) i 181–3. Known in its earliest source as *Baldrs Draumar* ('Balder's Dream'), the poem was later entitled *Vegtamskviða* ('Lay of the Wayfarer'; see ll. 37–8 *n*). It purports to be a supplement to the *Voluspa*, elaborating the episode of Balder's death. In the *Voluspa*, the prophetess foretells the fall of the gods, as she here prophesies what was to be the first incident of that fall. Scholarly opinion has been divided as to whether it belongs to the tenth century or is merely a skilful twelfth century imitation of the older manner. See L. M. Hollander, *The Poetic Edda* (Austin, 1928) pp. 136–9.

According to the legend, Balder, son of Odin, chief of the gods of Northern mythology, dreamed that his life was in danger. Frigga, his mother, exacted an oath from all things that they would not harm him, but omitted to make the mistletoe do so. Lok, the evil deity, placed a bough of mistletoe in the hand of the blind Hoder and directed his arm so that it struck Balder, who accordingly died. The poem concerns the visit by Odin, before Balder's death, to the underworld to learn his son's fate. The prophetess identifies Hoder as the murderer and Vali, son of Odin and Rinda, as the avenger of Balder.

G. followed Bartholin in omitting the first stanza of the poem, translated by Vigfusson and Powell, i 181: 'At once the Anses all went into council, and all the goddesses to a parley. The mighty gods took counsel together that they might find out why dreams of evil haunted Balder.' These editors also mention a short preliminary section to the poem, supplied between 1643 and 1670, probably by Paul Hallson, to elucidate the earlier part of the story.

G.'s notes have three sources: the Commonplace Book, *1775*, where some of G.'s notes from it were printed, and *1768*. The English translation of the Latin used by G., as given by Mason, is as follows:

Odin arose	Breast in front
Greatest among men	His muzzle eager to bite
And on Sleipner	And his lower jaw:
Laid the saddle.	He barked
He rode downwards	And bared his teeth
Towards Nifhel.	At the Father of Spells,
On his way he met the Whelp	And long he barked.
Coming from the abodes of Hela.	Odin rode on
Spattered with blood were his	(The earth beneath trembled)

Until he came to the deep
Abode of Hela.
Then Odin rode
To the east side of the portal
Where the Prophetess's
Grave he knew to be.
    To the Wise Woman charms
Which raise the dead he chanted.
He looked to the North Wind
He placed letters (on the grave)
He began to address her
And demanded answers
Until she arose, all unwilling,
And spoke the language of the dead.
Prophetess. Who among men
Has dared to make my
Soul sad?
Upon me snow
And clouds have been shed
I have been bedewed with rain
Long I have lain dead.
Odin. I am called Traveller
I am the Son of Warrior.
Tell me what things are done in
    Hela's dwelling:
I will (tell) what is done on earth.
For whom are these seats strewn with
    gold,
Beautiful couches
Adorned with gold?
Prophetess. Here for Balder mead
Ready prepared is put out.
A pure draught,
With a shield laid over it.
For certain will the son of the gods
Be stricken with pain.
I have said these things against my
    will,
And now I will be silent.
Odin. Do not be silent, Prophetess.
I want to question you
Until I shall have learned all.
Still I wish to know
Who it is that on Balder
Will inflict death
And the son of Odin
Deprive of life.
Prophetess. Hoder bears aloft
His honoured brother to this place.
It is he who on Balder

Will inflict death,
And the son of Odin
Deprive of life.
I have said these things against my
    will,
And now I will be silent.
Odin. Do not be silent, Prophetess.
Still I want to question you
Until I shall have learned all.
I still wish to know
Who it is that to Hoder
Will pay back hatred
Or the killer of Balder
Will fit for the pyre by slaying him.
Prophetess. Rinda will bear a son
In the dwellings of the West:
He, the son of Odin,
Only one night born, will take arms;
He will not wash his hand
Nor comb his hair
Until he has placed on the pyre
The enemy of Balder.
I have said these things against my
    will,
And now I will be silent.
Odin. Do not be silent, Prophetess.
Still I want to question you
Who the Virgins are
Who weep because of their thoughts
And toss into the sky
The garments from their shoulders.
You must tell me this one thing,
For you will not sleep before you do.
Prophetess. You are no Traveller,
As I believed before;
But rather Odin,
Greatest among men.
Odin. You are no Prophetess,
Nor a wise-woman,
But rather of three
Giants the mother.
Prophetess. Ride home, Odin,
And glory in this deed:
For no one shall come in such a way
Seeking knowledge
Until the time when Lok
Is freed from his bonds
And at the Twilight of the Gods
The Destroyers shall come.

    The text followed here is that in G.'s letter to James Dodsley early in
Feb. 1768 (British Museum, Add. MS 38511 ff. 5–6), from which that in
1768 was printed, except for the occasional intervals between lines introduced
by Dodsley to which G. did not apparently object. Variants are given from
the Commonplace Book and Wharton's transcript.

Uprose the King of Men with speed,
And saddled straight his coal-black steed;
Down the yawning steep he rode,
That leads to Hela's drear abode.
5   Him the dog of darkness spied,
His shaggy throat he opened wide,
While from his jaws, with carnage filled,
Foam and human gore distilled:
Hoarse he bays with hideous din,
10   Eyes that glow and fangs that grin;
And long pursues with fruitless yell
The father of the powerful spell.
Onward still his way he takes,
(The groaning earth beneath him shakes,)
15   Till full before his fearless eyes
The portals nine of hell arise.

¶ 26. *1. uprose*] G. deliberately imitates 'Upreis', the first word of the original as quoted after the title to the poem.

2. steed] *Sleipner* was the Horse of Odin, wch had eight legs. *Commonplace Book.* (Starr and Hendrickson incorrectly state that G. wrote '*Shipner*'.) Sleipner, the offspring of Loki and the stallion Svathilfari, was traditionally grey.

Cp. 'coleblacke steeds yborne of hellish brood', Spenser, *Faerie Queene* I v 20, 8; and 'High on a Coal-black steed', Dryden, *Theodore and Honoria* 120.

3. 'Hell at last / Yawning receavd them', *Par. Lost* vi 875.

4. Niflheimr, the hell of the Gothic nations, consisted of nine worlds, to which were devoted all such as died of sickness, old-age, or by any other means than in battle: Over it presided HELA, the Goddess of Death. *G. 1768.* *Commonplace Book* adds, '*Hela* is described with a dreadful countenance, & her body half flesh-colour & half blew.' G.'s source for this note was Bartholin, p. 585.

5. dog] Garm, guardian of the gate of the underworld.

7. 'His ample maw, with human carnage fill'd', Pope, *Odyssey* ix 352.

8. 'he gan fret and fome out bloudy gore', *Faerie Queene* VI xii 31, 3; and 'Their Heads distilling Gore', Dryden, *Aeneid* xii 743.

9. 'The Hounds at nearer distance hoarsly bay'd', Dryden, *Theodore and Honoria* 279.

11. fruitless] ceaseless *Wharton.*

14. shakes] quakes *Wharton.* Cp. 'Groans the sad Earth', Dryden, *Aeneid* xii 504.

16. portals nine] The phrase is G.'s own, referring to the nine worlds of Hell (see l. 4 n above) among which Hela distributed the dead.

Right against the eastern gate,
By the moss-grown pile he sate,
Where long of yore to sleep was laid
20   The dust of the prophetic maid.
Facing to the northern clime,
Thrice he traced the runic rhyme;
Thrice pronounced, in accents dread,
The thrilling verse that wakes the dead;
25   Till from out the hollow ground
Slowly breathed a sullen sound.

Pr. What call unknown, what charms, presume
To break the quiet of the tomb?
Who thus afflicts my troubled sprite,
30   And drags me from the realms of night?
Long on these mouldering bones have beat
The winter's snow, the summer's heat,
The drenching dews, and driving rain!

17. Cp. Milton, *L'Allegro* 59: 'Right against the Eastern gate'.
20. 'the Prophetic Maid', Dryden, *Aeneid* ii 464.
22. 'Prophesying with accents terrible', *Macbeth* II iii 55.
22-3. The emphatic 'thrice' is introduced by G.
23. accents] murmurs *Wharton.*
24. The original word is *Vallgaldr*; from *Valr* mortuus, & *Galdr* incantatio.
G. *1775.*
25. 'the hollow ground', Spenser, *Faerie Queene* II vii 20, 8 and VI x 10, 4;
Richard II III ii 140; *Romeo and Juliet* V iii 4; Dryden, *Aeneid* viii 324.
26. 'a sullen sound', Dryden, *Palamon and Arcite* iii 371.
27-30. G. here, as later in the poem (see 34, 82-3 below), echoes a song from
Dryden's *King Arthur*, in which Cupid confronts the Genius of Winter.
(G. described with great enthusiasm a performance of *King Arthur* in a
letter to Walpole in Jan. 1736, *Corresp* i 37. He thought the 'Frost Scene', in
which this song occurs, 'excessive fine'.) Cp. the 'Song' 5-7: 'What Power
art thou, who from below, / Hast made me Rise, unwillingly, and slow, /
From Beds of Everlasting Snow!'
27. call] voice *Wharton.*
29. my troubled] a weary *Wharton.*   Cp. *Faerie Queene* V viii 45, 5: 'it
much appall her troubled spright'.
30. Cp. 'the Realm of night', *Par. Lost* ii 133; Dryden, *Aeneid* vi 529, 1136.
32-3. 'In winter's cold and summer's parching heat', *II Henry VI* I i 76; 'The
scorching Sun had born, and beating Rain', Dryden, *Flower and the Leaf*
408; 'To scorn the Summer Suns and Winter snows', Prior, *Ode to the
Memory of Col. Villiers* 11. Cp. also 'driving Rain', Dryden, *Georgics* i 301,
and Collins, *Ode to Evening* 33 (p. 466 below); 'drenches with *Elysian* dew',

Let me, let me sleep again.
35 Who is he, with voice unblest,
That calls me from the bed of rest?

O. A Traveller, to thee unknown,
Is he that calls, a Warrior's son.
Thou the deeds of light shalt know;
40 Tell me what is done below,
For whom yon glittering board is spread,
Dressed for whom yon golden bed.

Pr. Mantling in the goblet see
The pure beverage of the bee,
45 O'er it hangs the shield of gold;
'Tis the drink of Balder bold:
Balder's head to death is given.
Pain can reach the sons of Heaven!
Unwilling I my lips unclose:
50 Leave me, leave me to repose.

O. Once again my call obey.

Milton, *Comus* 996; and 'drenching rains', Nahum Tate, *Absalom and Achitophel* pt ii 1118.
34. Cp. 'Song' from *King Arthur* 11 (see ll. 27–30 *n*): 'Let me, let me, Freeze again to Death'.
35. *he*] this *Wharton.*
37–8. In the original Odin gives his name as Vegtam ('The Wayfarer'), the son of Valtam ('The Warrior').
41–6. These are the usual preparations for the arrival of an honoured guest: in this case, the doomed Balder.
41. *yon*] the *Wharton.*
42. *yon*] the *Wharton.*
43. 'the mantling bowl', Pope, *Imitations of Horace, Sat.* II ii 8.
44. 'dewy Bev'rage for the Bees', Dryden, *Georgics* ii 294.
48. *reach*] touch *Wharton.*
51–2. Women were look'd upon, as having a particular insight into futurity; & some there were, that made profession of magic arts & of divination: these travel'd round the country, & were received in every house with great respect & honour. such a Woman bore the name of *Volva, Seidkona,* or *Spakona.* the dress of Thorbiorga, one of these Prophetesses, is described at large in *Eiriks Rauda Sogu* (apud Bartholinum, L:3. cap:4. p: 688) she had on a blew vest spangled all over with stones, a necklace of glass beads, a cap made of the skin of a black lamb, lined with white cat-skin; she lent on a staff adorn'd with brass with a round head set with stones, & was girt with a Hunlandish belt, at wch hung her pouch full of magical instruments. her

Prophetess, arise and say,
What dangers Odin's child await,
Who the author of his fate.

55   *Pr*. In Hoder's hand the hero's doom:
His brother sends him to the tomb.
Now my weary lips I close:
Leave me, leave me to repose.

O. Prophetess, my spell obey,
60   Once again arise and say,
Who the avenger of his guilt,
By whom shall Hoder's blood be spilt.

Pr. In the caverns of the west,
By Odin's fierce embrace compressed,
65   A wondrous boy shall Rinda bear,
Who ne'er shall comb his raven-hair,
Nor wash his visage in the stream,
Nor see the sun's departing beam:
Till he on Hoder's corse shall smile
70   Flaming on the funeral pile.
Now my weary lips I close:
Leave me, leave me to repose.

O. Yet a while my call obey.
Prophetess, awake and say,

buskins were of rough calves-skin bound on with thongs adorn'd with
knobs of brass; & her gloves of white cat, the fur turn'd inwards. &c: they
were also call'd Fiolkynga or fiol-kunnug i:e: Multiscia, & Visind-kona,
i:e: Oraculorum mulier, Nornir, i:e: Parcae. *Commonplace Book*.
    Mason printed a version of this note in *1775*.
51, 60. Once again] Prophetess *Wharton*.
52, 59. Prophetess] Once again *Wharton*.
61–2. Transposed in Wharton.
63–70. Rinda's son, Vali, was begotten by Odin for the express purpose of
avenging Balder's death. Vali slew Hoder on the day after his birth.
64. Dryden, *Aeneid* xii 213–4: 'E're to the Lust of lawless *Jove* betray'd: /
Compress'd by Force'; Pope, *Odyssey* vii 78: 'by Neptune's amorous power
compress'd'.
65. wondrous] giant *Wharton*.
68. Dryden, *Ovid's Metamorphoses* i 78: 'the remnants of departing light';
Pope, *Autumn* 98: 'The Skies yet blushing with departing Light.'
74. awake] arise *Wharton*.

75   What virgins these, in speechless woe,
That bend to earth their solemn brow,
That their flaxen tresses tear,
And snowy veils, that float in air.
Tell me whence their sorrows rose:
80   Then I leave thee to repose.

Pr. Ha! no Traveller art thou,
King of Men, I know thee now,
Mightiest of a mighty line——

O. No boding maid of skill divine
85   Art thou, nor prophetess of good;
But mother of the giant-brood!

Pr. Hie thee hence and boast at home,
That never shall enquirer come
To break my iron-sleep again,

75–8. Mason suggests that the virgins are the Nornir or Fates, normally invisible to mortals: 'therefore when Odin asks this question on seeing them, he betrays himself to be a God; which elucidates the next speech of the Prophetess.' Although G. may also have had some such idea, these lines, probably corrupt, are thought to refer to the waves. Vigfusson and Powell, i 499, state: 'Here should follow some wanton query, whereby the Sibyl sees that she had to deal with the wrong man. As it stands, the verse, taken from some riddle poem such as Heiðrek's, is a mere conundrum, of which the answer is "the waves".' L. M. Hollander, *The Poetic Edda* p. 138, states that the maidens are the daughters of the sea-god, Aegir: i.e. the waves. He translates the phrase corresponding to G.'s 'snowy veils' as 'their kerchief corners', suggesting that there is a pun, since the phrase could also mean 'corners of the sail'. The lines could refer to the sail of the ship bearing Balder's corpse, which dips into the sea.

77. That . . . flaxen] Who . . . flowing *Wharton*.

78. 'snowy veil', Pope, *Iliad* iii 187.

79. Tell me] Say from *Wharton*.   *sorrows*] sorrow *Commonplace Book*.

82–3. Cp. 'Song' from *King Arthur* 20–1 (see ll. 27–30 *n* above): 'Great Love, I know thee now; / Eldest of the Gods art Thou.'

83. The Mightiest of the mighty line *Wharton*.

86. 'the giant-brood', Spenser, *Faerie Queene* III ix 49, 8; *Par. Lost* i 576, and *Samson Agonistes* 1247; Dryden, *Hind and the Panther* ii 535, and *Britannia Rediviva* 237.

87. hence, and] Odin *Wharton*.

89. iron] 'Unbroken; indissoluble' (Johnson). Cp. Virgil, *Aeneid* xii 309–10: *ferreus . . . somnus*; 'Iron sleep', Dryden, *To Sir Godfrey Kneller* 57; *Aeneid* v 1095, xii 467; and 'Death's Iron-Sleep', John Philips, *Cyder* Bk ii.

90   Till Lok has burst his tenfold chain;
       Never, till substantial Night
       Has reassumed her ancient right;
       Till wrapped in flames, in ruin hurled,
       Sinks the fabric of the world.

90. has] have *Wharton.*

Lok is the evil Being, who continues in chains till the *Twilight of the Gods*
approaches, when he shall break his bonds; the human race, the stars, and
sun, shall disappear; the earth sink in the seas, and fire consume the skies;
even Odin himself and his kindred-deities shall perish. For a farther explan-
ation of this mythology, see Mallet's Introduction to the History of
Denmark, 1755, Quarto. *G. 1768.*

Lok had not yet been chained. It was after the death of Balder that the
gods bound him to a rock with the bowels of his son Narfi. There is a
longer note on the 'Twilight of the Gods' in G.'s Commonplace Book,
quoted in W. Powell Jones, *Thomas Gray, Scholar* p. 102 *n.*

92. Has reassum'd] Reassumes *Wharton.*   Cp. 'Dulness o'er all possess'd her
ancient right, / Daughter of Chaos and eternal Night', Pope, *Dunciad* i
11-12, and 'And laughing Ceres reassume the land', *Epistles to Several
Persons* iv 176.

93. 'Hurld headlong flaming from th'Ethereal Skie / With hideous ruine',
Par. Lost i 45-6; 'Atoms or systems into ruin hurl'd', Pope, *Essay on Man* i 89.

94. Cp. G.'s translation of Propertius III v 31-2 (p. 26): 'How flames perhaps,
with dire confusion hurled, / Shall sink this beauteous fabric of the world.'

27 The Triumphs of Owen.
A Fragment

Written in 1760 or 1761. G.'s research for his proposed 'History of English
Poetry' (see headnote to *The Fatal Sisters*) had soon brought him to the study
of early Welsh literature. Some knowledge of Welsh history and literature
is implicit in *The Bard* (1755-57) and the essays in G.'s Commonplace Book
indicate that he had at least attempted to investigate the subject with his
characteristic thoroughness. In the essay 'Pseudo-Rhythmus' he speculated
about the connections between Welsh and Anglo-Saxon poetry, and by
1758 he had written the elaborate entries on the metre and technique of
Welsh poetry, entitled 'Cambri'. Although he did not understand Welsh,
he could grasp some of the prosodic principles involved, many of which he
found discussed in J. D. Rhys's *Cambrobrytannicae Cymraecaeve Linguae
Institutiones et Rudimenta* (1592). From Rhys he transcribed not only notes
on prosody but also texts of medieval Welsh poetry.

By Sept. 1758 Evan Evans, the most distinguished Welsh scholar of the period, had given to Daines Barrington, a friend of G., literal Latin translations of three Welsh poems. One of them was 'Arwyain Owain Gwynnedd' by Gwalchmai ap Meilyr (fl. 1130–80), upon which G. was to base *The Triumphs of Owen* (*Letters of Lewis, Richard, William and John Morris 1728–65* ed. J. H. Davies, Aberystwyth, 1906–9, ii 86). When G. received the translations from Barrington is uncertain, but it is unlikely that they were in his possession by 'the summer of 1758', as has been stated by Arthur Johnston in the article cited below. All that is certain is that he had seen them by April 1760 and the evidence suggests that he had then seen them only recently. It is likely that he was shown them by Barrington at some time after July 1759, when he was living in London. Nor is it true that G.'s interest in his 'History' was 'at its height' between 1758 and 1761: in 1758 G. turned from the study of the origins of English poetry to English history and antiquities, so that it is unlikely that, even if he had received Evans's translations in 1758, he would have thought of translating them into English at this period.

By the end of 1759 Evan Evans had completed a Latin dissertation on the Welsh Bards and was being encouraged to publish it, together with additional translations into Latin of Welsh poetry. On 23 April 1760 Evans (*Additional Letters of the Morrises*, ed. Hugh Owen, (1947–9) p. 453) wrote to Richard Morris, another Welsh scholar, that Daines Barrington had told him 'that Mr Grey of Cambridge admires *Gwalchmai's* Ode to *Owain Gwynnedd*, and I think deservedly. He says he will shew the Dissertation to Mr Grey, to have his judgement of it, and to correct it where necessary; so that I hope it will be fit for the press when I have it.'

G. mentioned that he had seen the MS of Evans's *De Bardis Dissertatio* in a letter of about 20 June 1760 to Wharton (*Corresp* ii 679–80). After admitting that he had 'gone mad' about Macpherson's supposed translations of Erse poetry, he continued: 'the Welch Poets are also coming to light: I have seen a Discourse in MSS. about them (by one Mr Evans, a Clergyman) with specimens of their writings. This is in Latin, & tho' it don't approach the other, there are fine scraps among it.' It was no doubt at about this time that G. added to the list of 'Gothic' poems in his Commonplace Book (see headnote to *The Fatal Sisters*), which he intended to translate as illustrations to the Introduction to his 'History', the titles of five 'Erse' ('Very ancient (if genuine)') and five 'Welsh' poems. The Welsh poems include 'End of Aneurin's Gododin . . . about A:D: 570' and 'Gwalchmai's Triumph of Owen . . . about 1260'. It can be assumed that G. made his translations from the Welsh not long after he had seen Evans's *Dissertatio* and almost certainly not later than 1761. He copied them into his Commonplace Book (iii 1068–70) at the same point as *The Fatal Sisters* and *The Descent of Odin*, which had been written by May 1761.

Of the Welsh translations only *The Triumphs of Owen* was included in *1768* (for the reason for the inclusion of the translations see headnote to *The Fatal Sisters*). G. described it there as 'From Mr. EVANS'S Specimens of the Welch Poetry; LONDON, 1764, Quarto.' Evans's *Some Specimens of the Poetry of the Antient Welsh Bards. Translated into English*, which incorporated the Latin *De Bardis Dissertatio*, was not G.'s actual source, although this acknowledgement of it has misled scholars into the assumption that his translations were based on Evans's English translations. As has been shown, G. had Evans's Latin translation of 'Arwyain Owain Gwynnedd' in his possession by April 1760 at the latest and by the following June had seen Latin translations in the *Dissertatio* of the fragments of the *Gododdin* which he also translated. In Oct. 1761, by which time G. had probably completed his translations, Evans had not yet decided to include English versions in his book; see *The Correspondence of Thomas Percy and Evan Evans*, ed. A. Lewis (Baton Rouge, 1957) p. 20. G.'s use of Evans's original Latin translation of Gwalchmai's poem, a copy of which was preserved by Percy, and the elements in the poem which suggest that he attempted to imitate techniques of the original Welsh, have been discussed in detail by Arthur Johnston, who also examines G.'s technique as a translator, in 'Gray's "The Triumphs of Owen"', *RES* xi (1960) 275–85. See also the appendix 'Gray's Studies of Welsh Poetry', in *Corresp* iii 1229–31; and W. Powell Jones, *Thomas Gray, Scholar* pp. 90–9. The *Percy-Evans Correspondence* referred to above gives a good picture of Welsh scholarship in the mid-eighteenth century; for a more general discussion, which places G.'s contribution to Welsh studies in a larger context, see E. D. Snyder, *The Celtic Revival in English Literature 1760–1800* (Cambridge, Mass., 1923).

G. prefixed the following 'Advertisement' to *The Triumphs of Owen* in *1768*: 'Owen succeeded his Father Griffin in the Principality of North-Wales, A.D. 1120. This battle was fought near forty years afterwards.' Owen was in fact Prince of North Wales from 1137 to 1170. Gwalchmai's *Ode* probably celebrates his victory over the three fleets sent against him by Henry II in 1157, at Tal y Moelfre on the north-east coast of Wales, where the islanders defeated a number of marauding knights. For further information and discussion of the location of the battle, see J. E. Lloyd, *A History of Wales* (1938) ii 498–9 and *n*.

A modern literal translation of the Welsh is given by K. H. Jackson, *A Celtic Miscellany* (1951) p. 254. Although Evan Evans's English translation in his *Specimens* pp. 25–6 (the Welsh text appears on pp. 127–8) was not G.'s source and although both his Latin and English versions are no longer considered satisfactory, it is not irrelevant to an appreciation of G.'s translation:

'A Panegyric upon Owain Gwynnedd, Prince of North Wales, by Gwalchmai, the Son of Meilir, in the Year 1157.

'I will extol the generous hero descended from the race of Roderic, the bulwark of his country, a prince eminent for his good qualities, the glory of Britain, Owain the brave and expert in arms, a prince that neither hoardeth nor coveteth riches. – Three fleets arrived, vessels of the main, three powerful fleets of the first rate, furiously to attack him on a sudden. One from Iwerddon, the other full of well-armed Lochlynians, making a grand appearance on the floods, the third from the transmarine Normans, which was attended with an immense, though successless toil.

'The Dragon of Mona's sons were so brave in action, that there was a great tumult on their furious attack, and before the prince himself, there was vast confusion, havock, conflict, honourable death, bloody battle, horrible consternation, and upon Tal Moelvre a thousand banners. There was an outrageous carnage, and the rage of spears, and hasty signs of violent indignation. Blood raised the tide of the Menai, and the crimson of human gore stained the brine. There were glittering cuirasses, and the agony of gashing wounds, and the mangled warriors prostrate before the chief, distinguished by his crimson lance. Lloegria was put into confusion, the contest and confusion was great, and the glory of our prince's wide-wasting sword shall be celebrated in an hundred languages to give him his merited praise.'

It will be seen that G. did not translate the whole poem, which was no doubt why he described it as 'A Fragment'. For the four lines omitted by G. in *1768*, see l. 36 *n*. The text followed here is that in G.'s letter to James Dodsley in early Feb. 1768 (British Museum, Add. MS 38511 ff. 5–6) from which that in *1768* was printed, except for two intervals apparently introduced by Dodsley to which G. seems not to have objected. Variants are given from the Commonplace Book.

> Owen's praise demands my song,
> Owen swift, and Owen strong;
> Fairest flower of Roderic's stem,
> Gwyneth's shield and Britain's gem.
> 5 He nor heaps his brooded stores,
> Nor on all profusely pours;
> Lord of every regal art,
> Liberal hand and open heart.
>
> Big with hosts of mighty name,
> 10 Squadrons three against him came;
> This the force of Eirin hiding;
> Side by side as proudly riding,

¶ 27.3. See Evans's note to his English translation: 'Owain Gwynnedd . . . was descended in a direct line from Roderic the Great, prince of all Wales, who divided his principality amongst his three sons.' Roderick, or Rhodri Maur, was King of Gwynedd 844–78.

4. *Gwyneth*] North-Wales. G. *1768*.

5. One meaning of 'brood' given by Johnson is 'to cherish by care'. Cp. 'But the base Miser starves amidst his Store, / Broods on his Gold', Dryden, *Wife of Bath* 468–9.

6. 'Powrd forth profuse', *Par. Lost* iv 243; 'Or pours profuse on earth', Pope, *Essay on Man* iii 117; 'Profusely pours', Thomson, *Summer* 738.

10. Cp. Fairfax's *Tasso* XVIII xcvi 5: 'A battle round of squadrons three'.

12–13. 'And on her shadow rides in floating gold', Dryden, *Annus Mirabilis* 604, and *Bard* 72 (p. 191 above).

On her shadow long and gay
Lochlin ploughs the watery way;
15   There the Norman sails afar
Catch the winds and join the war:
Black and huge along they sweep,
Burthens of the angry deep.

Dauntless on his native sands
20   The Dragon-son of Mona stands;
In glittering arms and glory dressed,
High he rears his ruby crest.
There the thundering strokes begin,
There the press and there the din;
25   Talymalfra's rocky shore
Echoing to the battle's roar.
Where his glowing eye-balls turn,
Thousand banners round him burn.
Where he points his purple spear,

14. Lochlin] Denmark. *G. 1768.* 'To plough the watery way' is a common
epic formula. Cp. Dryden, *Aeneid* ix 118; Pope, *Iliad* ii 685, viii 655;
Odyssey xiii 363.

15. Norman] Norwegian, not French.

16. 'their Sails / . . . catch the Gales', Dryden, *Ceyx and Alcyone* 93–4;
'catch the driving gale', Pope, *Essay on Man* iii 178.

17–18. 'my navy, at whose burthen / The angered ocean foams', *Antony
and Cleopatra* II vi 20; and 'the angry flood', *Julius Caesar* I ii 103.

20. The red Dragon is the device of Cadwallader, which all his descendants
bore on their banners. *G. 1768.*

Mona] Cp. G. to Mason, 23 July 1756 (*Corresp* ii 467): 'I can only tell you
not to go & take the Mona for the Isle of Man. it is Anglesey, a tract of
plain country, very fertile, but picturesque only from the view it has of
Caernarvonshire, from wch it is separated by the Menai, a narrow arm of
the Sea.' See Collins, *Ode to Liberty* 82 *n* (p. 450 below).

21. 'glitt'ring Arms', Dryden, *Aeneid* ii 640, vi 312, x 749, xi 1132; *Palamon
and Arcite* iii 450.

22. 'his rough crest he rears', Dryden, *Hind and the Panther* i 164.

25. Talymalfra] Bradshaw describes Moelfre as 'a small bay on the north-
east coast of Anglesey'.

27. 'glowing eye-balls', Dryden, *Hind and the Panther* ii 223; 'Like fiery
meteors his red eyeballs glow', Pope, *Iliad* xv 731.

29–32. Cp. Fairfax's *Tasso* VIII xix 7–8: 'And whereso'er he turn'd his fatal
Brand, / Dread in his Looks, and Death sat in his Hand'; Oldham, *The
Praise of Homer* st. iii: 'Where-e'er he does his dreadful Standards bear, /
Horror stalks in the Van, and Slaughter in the Rear'; and Prior, *Seeing the
Duke of Ormond's Picture* 6–9: 'Let His keen Sabre, Comet-like, appear, /

30   Hasty, hasty Rout is there,
      Marking with indignant eye
      Fear to stop and shame to fly.
      There Confusion, Terror's child,
      Conflict fierce and Ruin wild,
35   Agony that pants for breath,
      Despair and honourable Death.

Where-e'er it points, denouncing Death: below / Draw routed Squadrons,
and the num'rous Foe / Falling beneath, or flying from His Blow.'
31–2. Pope, *Iliad* xvii 119–20: 'He flies indeed, but threatens as he flies, /
With heart indignant and retorted eyes.'
33–6. Waller, *Instructions to a Painter* (1665) 59–60: 'There paint confusion in
a various shape: / Some sink, some yield, and flying some escape'; Dryden,
Aeneid xii 505, 507: 'Wrath, Terror, Treason, Tumult, and Despair / ... /
Friends of the God, and Followers of the War'; Pope, *Iliad* xx 170: 'And
these, in ruin and confusion hurled.'
*36. The following lines appear at the end of the fragment in G.'s Commonplace
Book:*

> Check'd by the torrent-tide of blood
> Backward Meinai rolls his flood:
> While heap'd his Master's feet around
> Prostrate Warriors gnaw the ground.

Mason inserted these lines after l. 26 in *1775* (*Poems* p. 57). But G. treats
Evans's Latin freely in this part of the poem and the lines could be placed
equally well after l. 28. In any case, G. himself evidently thought them un-
satisfactory and omitted them in *1768*.

28 [The Death of Hoel]

Written in 1760 or 1761. For the background to this translation, and to the
two which follow, see the headnote to *The Triumphs of Owen*. G. tran-
scribed them into his Commonplace Book together with the Norse trans-
lations. *The Death of Hoel* was first printed by Mason in *1775*, *Poems* pp.
58–9. In his Commonplace Book (iii 1070) G. had entitled it merely: 'From
Aneurin, Monarch of the Bards, extracted from the Gododin.'
   The Welsh poem, the *Gododdin*, the nucleus of which is ascribed to
Aneirin, the sixth century poet, had been discovered by Evan Evans, in
the MS of whose *De Bardis Dissertatio* G. first saw fragments in the Latin
translation in 1760. The Gododdin were a tribe of North Britain. Their
lord Mynyddawg Mwynfawr of Caereidyn (near Edinburgh) sent three
hundred chosen warriors to recapture Catraeth (Catterick in N. Yorkshire)
from the Saxon invaders in about A.D. 603. All except one of the three

hundred were killed in the battle. Aneirin's *Gododdin* consists of lyrical elegies lamenting the warriors and extolling their courage and loyalty.

G.'s translation was based on the following Latin text in Evans's *Dissertatio* pp. 71, 73: *Si mihi liceret sententiam de* Deirorum *populo ferre,* / *Aeque ac diluvium omnes una strage prostrarem;* / *Amicum enim amisi incautus,* / *Qui in resistendo firmus erat* / *Non petiit magnanimus dotem a socero,* / *Filius* CIANI *ex strenuo* GWYNGWN *ortus.* / *...* // *Viri ibant ad* CATTRAETH, *et fuere insignes,* / *Vinum et mulsum ex aureis poculis erat eorum potus.* / *...* / *Trecenti et sexaginta tres aureis torquibus insigniti erant,* / *Ex iis autem qui nimio potu madidi ad bellum properabant,* / *Non evasere nisi tres, qui sibi gladiis viam muniebant,* / *Sc. bellator de* Aeron *et* CONANUS DAEARAWD, / *Et egomet ipse* (*sc. Bardus Aneurinus*) *sanguine rubens,* / *Aliter ad hoc carmen compingendum non superstes fuissem.* (If I were allowed to judge the Deirans, I would strike them all down like a flood in one massacre; for heedlessly I have lost a friend, who was strong in resistance. Magnanimous, he sought no dowry from his father-in-law, he, the son of Cian, sprung from vigorous Gwyngwn. ... The warriors went to Cattraeth; they were renowned; wine and mead from golden horns was their drink. ... Three hundred and sixty three were adorned with golden torques; but of those who hastened to battle soaked with excess of liquor, only three escaped, who with their swords secured themselves a passage: the warrior of Aeron and Conan Daearawd, and I myself (the bard Aneurin) red with blood; otherwise I would not have survived to make this song.)

Evans's translation is inaccurate. For a literal translation of this and the following passages see *The Gododin of Aneurin Gwawdrydd*, trans. T. Stephens (ed. T. Powell, 1881–86) pp. 159–61, 191–3, 211–3, 293.

The text is that of Commonplace Book.

> Had I but the torrent's might,
> With headlong rage and wild affright
> Upon Deïra's squadrons hurled,
> To rush and sweep them from the world!
> 5   Too, too secure in youthful pride,
> By them my friend, my Hoël, died,
> Great Cian's son: of Madoc old
> He asked no heaps of hoarded gold;
> Alone in nature's wealth arrayed,
> 10   He asked and had the lovely maid.
> To Cattraeth's vale in glittering row

¶ 28.*1–2*. Dryden, *Juvenal* x 246–7: 'Then, like a Torrent, rowling from on high, / He pours his head-long Rage on *Italy*.'

2. 'wild amazement, and affright', Milton, *Comus* 356.

3. Deïra] A Saxon Kingdom in N. E. Yorkshire.

6–7, 21. None of these persons has been identified.

Twice two hundred warriors go;
Every warrior's manly neck
Chains of regal honour deck,
15   Wreathed in many a golden link:
From the golden cup they drink
Nectar, that the bees produce,
Or the grape's ecstatic juice.
Flushed with mirth and hope they burn:
20   But none from Cattraeth's vale return,
Save Aeron brave and Conan strong,
(Bursting through the bloody throng)
And I, the meanest of them all,
That live to weep and sing their fall.

12. Twice two hundred] Evans's figure was 363. Many editors since Mitford
have printed 'Thrice' for 'Twice'.

29 [Caradoc]

First printed by Mason in 1775, in the notes to *The Death of Hoel* (*Poems*
p. 106). There is no MS. G.'s source for this fragment from the *Gododdin*
was Evans's *Dissertatio* p. 73: *Quando ad bellum properabat* CARADOCUS, /
*Filius apri sylvestris qui truncando mutilavit hostes, / Taurus aciei in pugnae
conflictu, / Is lignum (i.e. hastam) ex manu contorsit* (When Caradoc hastened
to the battle, like the son of the forest boar who maimed and rended the
enemy, like the bull in the clash of the sharpness of battle, so did he hurl
the spear from his hand). Evans's translation of the third line is obscure.
Stephens's translation of the Welsh, 'he was the bull of battle in the cutting
down of conflict', is not much clearer.

Have ye seen the tusky boar,
Or the bull, with sullen roar,
On surrounding foes advance?
So Caradoc bore his lance.

¶ 29.1. 'tusky Boar', Dryden, *2nd Epode of Horace* 48; *Eclogues* vii 41, x 89;
Aeneid i 448, iv 229, vii 424; Thomson, *Autumn* 59.
2. 'sullen roar', Milton, *Il Penseroso* 76.

30 [Conan]

First printed by Mason in 1775, in the notes to *The Death of Hoel* (*Poems*
pp. 106–7). There is no MS. G.'s source was Evans's *Dissertatio* p. 75:

Debitus est tibi cantus, qui honorem assecutus ses [sic] maximum, | Qui eras instar ignis, tonitrui et tempestatis, | Viribus eximie, eques bellicose | RHUDD FEDEL, bellum meditaris (The song is due to you, who have obtained the greatest honour; you, who were like fire, thunder and tempest; exceptional in strength, O warlike knight, Rhudd Fedel, who meditated the war).

> Conan's name, my lay, rehearse,
> Build to him the lofty verse,
> Sacred tribute of the bard,
> Verse, the hero's sole reward.
> 5 As the flame's devouring force;
> As the whirlwind in its course;
> As the thunder's fiery stroke,
> Glancing on the shivered oak;
> Did the sword of Conan mow
> 10 The crimson harvest of the foe.

¶ 30.2. 'build the lofty rhyme', *Lycidas* 11.
9–10. Horace, *Odes* IV xiv 29–32: *ut barbarorum Claudius agmina | ferrata vasto diruit impetu | primosque et extremos metendo | stravit humum sine clade victor* (even as Claudius overwhelmed with destructive onslaught the mail-clad hosts of savages, and strewed the ground, mowing down van and rear, victorious without loss).

31 [Sketch of his Own Character]

Written in 1761, almost certainly after mid-April, and first printed by Mason in 1775, in a note to his introduction to G.'s so-called 'Essay on the Philosophy of Lord Bolingbroke' (*Memoirs* p. 264 *n*). Mason observed of G.'s essay that it proved that he was not 'so great a wit as to disbelieve the existence of a Deity' and added in the footnote: 'In one of his pocket-books I find a slight sketch in verse of his own character, which may, on account of one line in it, come into a note here with sufficient propriety. It was written in 1761.' Mason had transcribed it from G.'s pocketbook for 1761 into the Commonplace Book (iii 1111). Since the appointments of Townshend and Squire to which G. refers in l. 6 occurred in March and April 1761 respectively, it may be assumed that he wrote these lines not long afterwards. The text is that in *1775*, with variants from Mason's transcript.

> Too poor for a bribe and too proud to importune,
> He had not the method of making a fortune:

¶ 31.1. G. may have remembered Swift's statement, in a letter to Gay, 8 Jan. 1722–23, that poets are 'too poor to bribe Porters and Footmen, and too proud to cringe to Second hand Favorites in a Great Family'

Could love and could hate, so was thought somewhat
    odd;
No very great wit, he believed in a God.
5 A post or a pension he did not desire,
But left church and state to Charles Townshend and
    Squire.

(*Correspondence*, ed. H. Williams, 1963, ii 443). Pope, *Epilogue to the Satires* ii 205, 207 describes himself as: 'So proud, I am no Slave: / . . . So odd, my Country's Ruin makes me grave.' Both poets may have had in mind Horace, *Odes* II xviii 9–13: *at fides et ingeni / benigna vena est, pauperemque dives / me petit: nihil supra / deos lacesso nec potentem amicum / largiora flagito* (But I have loyalty and a kindly vein of genius, and me, though poor, the rich man courts. I importune the gods for nothing more, and of my friend in power I crave no larger boon).

4. wit, he] Wit: for he *Mason transcript.* Cp. Pope, *Epistle to Arbuthnot* 265–8: 'Above a Patron, tho' I condescend / Sometimes to call a Minister my Friend: / I was not born for Courts or great Affairs, / I pay my Debts, believe, and say my Pray'rs.'

5. post] In the margin of his transcript Mason added an obscure note: 'first word *Place* wch authenticates these lines'. G. declined the Poet Laureateship in Dec. 1757 on the death of Colley Cibber (*Corresp* ii 543–4); but tried unsuccessfully for the Professorship of History at Cambridge in 1762. When he obtained it in 1768, he wrote to the Duke of Grafton, the Prime Minister: 'Your Grace has dealt nobly with me; and the same delicacy of mind that induced you to confer this favour on me, unsolicited and unexpected, may perhaps make you averse to receive my sincerest thanks and grateful acknowledgements' (*Corresp* iii 1034).

G.'s feelings were close to those of Pope and may have consciously imitated them. Cp. Pope to Lord Carteret, 16 Feb. 1722–23 (*Correspondence*, ed. Sherburn, ii 160): 'I take my self to be the only Scribler of my Time, of any degree of distinction, who never receiv'd any Places from the Establishment, any Pension from a Court, or any Presents from a Ministry. I desire to preserve this Honour untainted to my Grave.' Cp. also 'Un-plac'd, un-pension'd, no Man's Heir, or Slave', *Imitations of Horace, Sat.* II i 116; 'Expect a Place, or Pension from the Crown', *Ep.* II i 371; 'I bought no Benefice, I begg'd no Place', *Imitations of Donne* iv 12.

6. Charles Townshend (1725–1767), best known as Chancellor of the Exchequer 1766–7, had been appointed Secretary at War on 24 Mar. 1761 (*Gentleman's Mag.* xxxi 141). Walpole, *Memoirs* iii 72, wrote of him: 'he must have been the greatest man of this age, and perhaps inferior to no man in any age, had his faults been only in a moderate proportion [to his talent] – in short, if he had had but common truth, common sincerity, common honesty, common modesty, common steadiness, common courage, and common sense.' Dr Samuel Squire (1713–66) had been Fellow of St John's, Cambridge 1735–44; Chaplain to the Duke of Newcastle 1748–1761;

Dean of Bristol 1760–1; and became Bishop of St David's on 14 Apr. 1761 (*Gentleman's Mag.* xxxi 189). G. had expressed interest in this impending appointment in a letter to Mason in Jan. 1761 (*Corresp* ii 720–1); and in May 1761 wrote to Wharton, 'I wish you joy of Dr Squire's Bishoprick: he keeps both his livings, & is the happiest of Devils' (*Corresp* ii 737). Squire was widely disliked for his servility and ambition.

church and state] the phrase occurs several times in Pope: 'He dies, sad outcast of each church and state', *Epistles to Several Persons* i 204; 'Now all for Pleasure, now for Church and State', *Imitations of Horace, Ep.* II i 158; 'These Madmen never hurt the Church or State', *ibid* 190; and *Epistle to Arbuthnot* 229–30: 'But sick of Fops, and Poetry, and Prate, / To *Bufo* left the whole *Castalian* state.'

32 [Epitaph on Sir William Williams]

Written between May and Aug. 1761. Sir William Williams (*c.* 1730–61), 2nd Baronet (1758), of Clapton, Northants, graduated M.A. from Clare Hall, Cambridge, in 1759, and became M.P. for Shoreham and a Captain in Burgoyne's Regiment of Dragoons. G. met him early in Oct. 1760, when he learned of the impending British expedition against France, although the exact target was not yet known: 'In my way to Town I met with the first news of the expedition from Sr Wm Williams, who makes a part of it, & perhaps may lay his fine Vandyke-Head in the dust' (*Corresp* ii 706–7). That Williams had some kind of death-wish seems to have been widely felt. William Cole described him as 'one of the prettiest figures of a man that could be seen. He was wild and extravagant, and not having an estate equal to the greatness of his condition, it is said that he went in the expedition to Bellisle, with a formed design not to return home again', (Sir Egerton Brydges, *Restituta* (1814–16) iii 53).

The expedition against Belle Isle (west of the Loire off the southern coast of Brittany) landed successfully on 22 Apr. 1761. The citadel fell on 8 June and the whole operation succeeded in diverting French forces from the Rhine. But Williams had already been killed on 27 Apr. According to the *Gentleman's Mag.* xxxi (1761) 234, '250 *l.* in bank notes were found in his pockets, which, together with the body, were returned by the *French* governor.' Walpole, writing to George Montagu on 5 May 1761 (*Walpole Correspondence* ix 364), considered his death quite unnecessary: 'We have lost a young genius, Sir William Williams; an express from Belleisle, arrived this morning, brings nothing but his death. He was shot very unnecessarily, riding too near a battery. In sum, he is a sacrifice to his own rashness,—and to ours—for what are we taking Belleisle?' Walpole wrote similarly to Mann on 14 May 1761 (*Walpole Correspondence* xxi 505), describing Williams–'a young man much talked of for his exceeding ambition, enterprising spirit, and some parts in Parliament'– as poor exchange for 'such a trumpery island'.

During May 1761 G. met in London Frederick Montagu, a barrister whom he had known as a Cambridge undergraduate. Montagu was 'in real affliction for the loss of S^r W: Williams, who has left him one of his executors' (*Corresp* ii 738). (Walpole described Montagu as merely 'heir to his debts.') In Aug. 1761 G. wrote to Mason (*Corresp* ii 746): 'Montagu (as I guess, at your instigation) has earnestly desired me to write some lines to be put on a Monument, wch he means to erect at Bellisle. it is a task I do not love, knowing S^r W: W: so slightly as I did: but he is so friendly a Person, & his affliction seem'd to me so real, that I could not refuse him. I have sent him the following verses, wch I neither like myself, nor will he, I doubt. however I have shew'd him, that I wish'd to oblige him.'

According to Mason, who first printed the epitaph in *1775*, *Poems* p. 62, the plan of inscribing it on a monument was eventually abandoned 'from some difficulty attending the erection of it'. In addition to the text in the letter to Mason, followed here, there is a transcript by Mason in G.'s Commonplace Book (iii 1108), which differs from both G.'s text and from that which Mason printed in *1775*. G. had asked Mason for his 'real opinion' of the epitaph and his friend's criticism may be reflected in the later versions. Mason's transcript is accompanied by some variants and others are recorded by Mitford (Add. MS 32562 f. 119).

> Here, foremost in the dangerous paths of fame,
> Young Williams fought for England's fair renown;
> His mind each Muse, each Grace adorned his frame,
> Nor Envy dared to view him with a frown.
> 5   At Aix uncalled his maiden sword he drew,
> (There first in blood his infant glory sealed);
> From fortune, pleasure, science, love, he flew,
> And scorned repose when Britain took the field.
>   With eyes of flame and cool intrepid breast,
> 10 Victor he stood on Belle Isle's rocky steeps;

¶ 32.3. Dryden, *To Mr Congreve* 70: 'But You, whom ev'ry Muse and Grace adorn'; Pope, *Imitations of Horace, Odes* IV i 27: 'There, every Grace and Muse shall throng.'
5. *uncalled his maiden*] his voluntary *Mason transcript and 1775*.   *Aix*] 'Sir William Williams, in the expedition to Aix [in Sept. 1757] was on board the Magnanime with Lord Howe; and was deputed to receive the capitulation' (Mason, *Poems* p. 108). Cp. *I Henry IV* V iv 133–4: 'Bravely hast thou fleshed / Thy maiden sword.'
6. *infant*] maiden *Mitford*.   *glory*] honour *Mason transcript and 1775*.
8. *And scorned*] Nor brooked *variant in Mason's transcript.*
9. *intrepid*] undaunted *Mason transcript and 1775*.
10. The citadel did not in fact fall until 8 June: see headnote.

> Ah gallant youth! this marble tells the rest,
> Where melancholy Friendship bends and weeps.

12. Mason's transcript gives two variants:
> Where bleeding Friendship oer her altar weeps
> Where Montagu & bleeding Friendship weep

and three lines of a 'Rejected Stanza':
> Warrior, that readst the melancholly line
> x   x   x   x
> Oh be his Genius be his spirit thine
> And share his Virtues with a happier fate

33 Song I ('Midst beauty and pleasure's gay triumphs to languish')

Written before Oct. 1761. Much of the extant information about this and the following poem has been attributed to the anonymous editor of an edn of G.'s *Poems* published by Sharpe in 1826. These statements had originally been published, however, in *An Historical and Descriptive Account of Stoke Park* (1813) by John Penn, then the owner of Stoke Manor House. Writing of G.'s former friend Henrietta Speed, later the Comtesse de Viry (see headnote to *A Long Story*, p. 142 above), Penn (p. 50) states that 'It was in ... 1780, that this lady enabled the lover of poetry to see in print the *Rondeau*, and another small amatory poem of Gray, called *Thyrsis*, by presenting them to the Rev. Mr. Leman, of Suffolk, while on a visit at her Castle in Savoy.' That Penn meant by the *Rondeau* the poem given below is clear from his references to its publication with G.'s other works. Earlier (pp. 38–40) Penn had quoted some reminiscences of G. and Miss Speed by Admiral Sir John Duckworth, who remembered seeing them at Stoke during his childhood. Rejecting suggestions that G. and Miss Speed had been seriously interested in each other, Penn continued: 'Another erroneous surmise of the same nature, might be formed, on hearing (what nevertheless is true) that the beautiful *rondeau*, which appears in the latter editions of his works, was inspired by "*the wish to please*" this lady. The fact is, however, that it was produced (and probably about this time) on a request she made to the poet one day, when he was in company with Mr. Walpole, that she might possess something from his pen, written on the subject of *love*.' Since John Penn was born in 1760, this information can hardly be firsthand and must be treated cautiously. From his remarks it has been assumed, perhaps rightly, that it was through 'the Rev. Mr. Leman' that these two poems were eventually published, although it can be shown that, by that time, they were already in MS circulation, possibly from another source. If, as Duckworth states, G. wrote 'Midst beauty and pleasure's gay triumphs' so that Miss Speed 'might possess something from his pen ... on the subject of *love*', this poem must have been written before the second *Song*, which also concerns 'love', and which can be dated Oct. 1761. It was probably written at about the same time, however: R. W. Ketton-Cremer, *Thomas Gray* p. 175, suggests that it dates from G.'s visit to Ship-lake, Oxfordshire, in June and July 1760, when he stayed with a Mrs Jennings, her daughter and Miss Speed.

Song I was first published in a footnote in Joseph Warton's edn of the *Works of Pope* (1797) ii 285, but it had been in MS circulation for some years. Mrs Thrale-Piozzi copied it into her journal in July 1790, having obtained it from Norton Nicholls (*Thraliana*, ed. K. C. Balderston, 2nd edn, 1951, ii 774). Tovey, *Gray's English Poems* (1898) p. 262, stated that: 'Dr Glynn, Gray's friend and physician at Cambridge, sent this and the following poem to a friend, G. S. Calcott, at Bristol, July 1, 1791. From his letter I find that it was headed "A song without a tune," and the "Thyrsis &c." was called "The Inconstant".' *Song I* was entitled 'Amatory Lines' by Mitford and some later editors, but it was merely called 'Song' in Mason's transcript of the poem into G.'s Commonplace Book (iii 1105) from 'an interlined & Corrected copy'. Mason's text is followed here and variants are given from Warton, with whose text Mrs Piozzi's agrees, except where indicated.

> 'Midst beauty and pleasure's gay triumphs, to
>   languish
> And droop without knowing the source of my anguish;
> To start from short slumbers and look for the
>   morning—
> Yet close my dull eyes when I see it returning;
>
> 5   Sighs sudden and frequent, looks ever dejected,
> Sounds that steal from my tongue, by no meaning
>   connected!
> Ah say, fellow-swains, how these symptoms befell me?
> They smile, but reply not. Sure Delia will tell me!

¶ 33.1. *'Midst ... triumphs*] With Beauty, with Pleasure surrounded, *Warton*.
2. *And droop*] To weep *Warton.   source*] cause *Warton.   my*] one's *Piozzi*.
3. *look*] wish *Warton*.
4. *Yet*] to *Warton*.
6. *Sounds*] Words *Warton*.
8. *but ... will*] and ... can *Piozzi*.

34 Song II ('Thyrsis, when we parted, swore')

Written in Oct. 1761. Walpole sent this song to the Countess of Ailesbury on
28 Nov. 1761 (*Letters*, ed. Toynbee, v 147): 'You will like . . . to see
some words which Mr. Gray has writ at Miss Speed's request, to an air of
Geminiani: the thought is from the French.' He repeated this information
in his 'Memoir of Gray' (*Corresp* iii 1288), where he dated the song Oct.
1761. (For further background information see headnote to *Song I*.) Mrs
Piozzi obtained a copy of it from Norton Nicholls in July 1790 and copied
it into *Thraliana* ii 773–4. It was first published a few months later in the
European Mag. xix 152, for Feb. 1791. The text in Walpole's letter was printed
in his *Works* v 561, in 1798. The text followed here is that of G.'s holograph
MS in the Pierpont Morgan Library, New York, which has no title. Mason
entitled the poem 'Song' when he copied it into G.'s Commonplace Book
(iii 1106), together with variants described as 'First Expressions'. Further
variants were recorded by Mitford.

Although the French source mentioned by Walpole has not been identi-
fied with certainty, Tovey drew attention to the following 'Air' by Mlle
Deshoulières, which may have provided G. with the 'thought' of his poem
(*Oeuvres de Madame et de Mlle. Deshoulières* (1753) ii 245): *Pourquoi revenez-
vous, Printems? qui vous rapelle? | Le chant des Rossignols & leurs tendres
amours | Redoublent ma douleur mortelle. | Que le cruel Hyver ne duroit-il
toujours! | Tirsis, helas! Tirsis est-il infidéle. | Hé! qu'ai-je affaire de beaux
jours?* But E. E. Kellett, in *Times Lit. Supp.* (1932) p. 95, claimed that G.'s
song is 'almost word for word identical' with a song by J. N. Goetz (1721–
1781), entitled 'Thamire an die Rosen'.

    Thyrsis, when we parted, swore
    Ere the spring he would return.
    Ah, what means yon violet flower,
    And the buds that deck the thorn?
5   'Twas the lark that upward sprung!
    'Twas the nightingale that sung!

¶ 34.*1. we parted*] he left me *Piozzi, European Mag.*
2. Ere] In *European Mag.*
3. What then means yon op'ning Flowr? *Piozzi*; Ah! what means the opening
flower! *European Mag.*
4. buds . . . deck] bud . . . decks *Piozzi, European Mag., Walpole.   that*]
which *Piozzi.*
5–6. Transposed in *European Mag.*

        Idle notes, untimely green,
        Why such unavailing haste?
        Western gales and skies serene
   10   Prove not always winter past.
        Cease my doubts, my fears to move;
        Spare the honour of my love.

7. green] bloom *deleted by G., noted by Mitford.*
8. such] this *Walpole.*
9. Western] Warmer *deleted by G., noted by Mason and Mitford.*   skies] sky
European Mag.
10. G. first wrote Can not prove, that Winter's past?, *later changed to* Can ye
etc. Mason and Mitford note these variants. Walpole has Speak not always *etc.*
12. Spare the honour] Dare not to reproach *deleted by G., noted by Mason and*
Mitford as a variant. Mitford notes as a further variant, Dare you to reproach your
love

35 The Candidate

Written between Jan. and 30 March 1764. The remarkable contest for the
High Stewardship of Cambridge in 1764, which occasioned this poem, has
been described in great detail by D. A. Winstanley, *The University of
Cambridge in the Eighteenth Century* (1922) pp. 55–139; and a summary of
this account is given in *Corresp* iii 1236–42. The episode illustrates the close
involvement of the University in national politics. The Duke of Newcastle,
elected Chancellor in 1749, had used his position, with the aid of the patron-
age at his disposal, to establish the Whig influence in the University. In
addition, at his wish his friend and political associate, Lord Chancellor
Hardwicke, had been appointed High Steward in 1749, to prevent any
political rivalry within the University.
    Newcastle fell from political power in May 1762. As the leader of a dis-
credited opposition party and deprived of the royal patronage which had
ensured the obedience of Cambridge, his influence diminished. When Lord
Hardwicke fell ill in the autumn of 1763, the King and the Grenville ministry
wished to reduce that influence even further by ensuring that his successor
as High Steward was a member of the Government. The man who even-
tually proposed himself as the Government candidate late in Nov. 1763
was John Montagu (1718–92), fourth Earl of Sandwich, First Lord of the
Admiralty and one of the principal Secretaries of State, who successfully
secured the support of the King and Grenville, in spite of their misgivings
about the suitability of this notorious profligate for a high academic post.
Public outrage at Sandwich's licentious character had recently become
acute, when he hypocritically attacked his former friend John Wilkes in
the House of Lords on 15 Nov. 1763 for his obscene *Essay on Woman* (see
l. 1 *n*).

Although Hardwicke was still alive, Sandwich began a highly organized canvassing campaign for support in Cambridge before the end of 1763 and Newcastle, anxious to retain his influence in the University, was forced to follow his lead by pressing the claims of his candidate, Lord Royston, the retiring and unattractive son of Lord Hardwicke. So began what Winstanley calls 'one of the fiercest and most hardly fought contests that either university has ever known'. Repugnance in Cambridge at Sandwich's character was qualified by the promise of royal and ministerial patronage which he carried. As much of this patronage was ecclesiastical, he was well supported by those likely to benefit from it, and the ironic point of G.'s poem is the fact that much of his support came from the Faculty of Divinity.

G. had always disliked Newcastle, but he was even more strongly opposed to his former school-fellow Sandwich. As a Bachelor of Laws he was not entitled to vote in the election, but he followed the machinations of both parties with mingled interest and disgust. Norton Nicholls recalled in his 'Reminiscences of Gray' (*Corresp* iii 1289–90): 'In the contest for the High Stewardship at Cambridge between Lord Hardwick [as Royston became after his father's death] & Lord Sandwich Mr Gray took a warm, & eager part, for no other reason, I believe, than because he thought the licentious character of the latter candidate rendered him improper for a post of such dignity in the University. His zeal in this cause inspired the verses full of pleasantry & wit which have been published since his death.'

Joseph Cradock wrote in his *Literary Memoirs* (1828) iv 223: 'From recollection I am sure Lord Sandwich was aware of [G.'s opposition]; for, about the time he offered himself as High Steward, contrary to his usual maxim of not seeing an enemy on public occasions, he once said to me, I have my private reasons for knowing of his absolute inveteracy.' So well organized were Sandwich's agents in Cambridge that it is not improbable that they knew that G. was actively opposed to their candidate. He wrote to Walpole on 27 Jan. 1764 (*Corresp* ii 830) of Sandwich's canvassing: 'who can damn the Devil? he continues his temptations here with so much assiduity, that I conclude he is not absolutely sure of success yet. his leading Partisans, tho' not ashamed of themselves, are yet heartily ashamed of him, & would give their ears, it were any other devil, but he. yet he would be chose at present, I have little doubt, tho' with strong opposition, & in a dishonourable way for him.'

Hardwicke did not die until 6 March 1764, by which time the campaign for his successor had been running for some months. The election took place on 30 March but it ended in indecision and disorder, after a misunderstanding about the counting of the votes, which were almost exactly even. Eventually, after a lawsuit and protracted intrigue and negotiation, the new Lord Hardwicke was elected High Steward in April 1765.

G.'s lines on Sandwich were most probably written between Jan. and March 1764, i.e. while the canvassing for support was at its height and before the abortive election on 30 March. C. C. Walcutt, in 'Jemmy Twitcher's Ghost', *Notes and Queries* clxxiii (1937) 56–62, attempted to demonstrate that this nickname was not given to Sandwich until mid-Feb. 1764, so that G.'s use of it in the first line of his poem would further limit the date of composition to the six weeks before 30 March. Walcutt also concluded that 'lovers of Gray may have the satisfaction of thinking that his verses on Lord Sandwich contain one of the earliest uses of the nickname and were perhaps rather the cause than the result of "Jemmy Twitcher's" enduring notoriety'. Walcutt was, however, mistaken. It is reasonable to assume that the nickname (from *The Beggar's Opera*) was applied to Sandwich almost immediately after his denunciation of Wilkes in mid-Nov. 1763; and in fact a cursory search reveals that it was used of him in the *St James's Chronicle* as early as the issue for 17–20 Dec. 1763 and again in that for 24–26 Jan. 1764. The nickname cannot therefore be used to date the poem and G.'s poem may not have been influential.

A few copies of a fly-sheet containing the poem, entitled 'The Candidate: By Mr. Gray', have survived and it was at first thought that it was circulated in this form during the election. It is more likely that G. merely passed the poem round in MS to a few friends and that the fly-sheet, as suggested below, was printed much later. Although Mason never saw the poem in G.'s lifetime, but merely heard him repeat it (possibly during a three-week visit to Cambridge in Feb. 1764, *Corresp* ii 831), Walpole received a MS of it from G., the rediscovery of which he triumphantly announced to Mason, in a letter of 16 Sept. 1774, (*Walpole Correspondence* xxviii 168):

'Why what should I have found, but the thing in the world that was most worth finding? . . . I tell you it is, what I have searched for a thousand times, and had rather have found than the longitude, if it was a thousand times longer—oh! you do guess, do you! I thought I never lost anything in my life; I was sure I had them, and so I had, and now am I not a good soul, to sit down and send you a copy incontinently. . . . I am in a panic till there are more copies than mine, and as the post does not go till tomorrow, I am in terror lest the house should be burnt tonight. I have a mind to go and bury a transcript in the field – but then if I should be burnt too! nobody would know where to look for it; well here it is! I think your decorum will not hold it proper to be printed in the life [Mason's *Memoirs of Gray*], nor would I have it. We will preserve copies, and the devil is in it, if some time or other it don't find its way to the press. My copy is in his own handwriting . . .'

At the end of his letter Walpole expressed his uneasiness about the final couplet of the poem and suggested a drastic alteration to it. Mason also attempted to provide an alternative; see ll. 33–4 *n*.

Mason did not print the poem in *1775* and Walpole's remark – 'the devil is in it, if some time or other it don't find its way to the press'—led some scholars to believe that he himself had the fly-sheet bearing the poem printed at his press at Strawberry Hill; see L. Whibley, *Times Lit. Supp.* 21 Aug. 1930, pp. 667–8 and A. T. Hazen, *Bibliography of the Strawberry Hill Press* (New Haven, 1942) pp. 212–4. Dr Hazen has more recently abandoned this theory and now suggests that Walpole merely made a number of MS copies of the poem in 1774 (*Walpole Correspondence* xxix 377). G.'s holograph MS, which was then in Walpole's possession, has disappeared but copies in Walpole's hand are in the Pierpont Morgan Library and the collection of W. S. Lewis. The poem was first printed without a title in the *London Evening Post* in Feb. 1777, introduced by the following letter:

The following verses are said to be the production of the late celebrated Mr. Gray. They were written on the occasion of Jemmy Twitcher's standing a candidate for the ———, at ———, and in whose favour the gentlemen of the gown took a very active part. As they are in but a few hands, and I think them too good to be lost, you are at liberty to print them, if you shall think them worth a corner of your paper.

Anti-Twitcher.

The poem was reprinted, entitled 'Jemmy Twitcher, or The Cambridge Courtship', with a letter from 'Adurfi', in the *Gentleman's Mag.* lii 39–40, in Jan. 1782; in the *London Mag.* lii 296 in 1783; and again in the *New Foundling Hospital for Wit* iv 106–7, in 1784. These texts are closely related and show a number of common differences from the text of Walpole's MS copies, from which they may not derive. The fly-sheet mentioned above, however, is close to Walpole's text and it is likely that he or some agent of his was responsible for it. Dr Hazen now believes that the fly-sheet, in which the poem is entitled *The Candidate* as in Walpole's MSS, may have been printed in London as late as 1787. A MS note on the copy in the Forster Collection at South Kensington reads: 'Published anno 1787, dedicated to the Rt. Hon. Earl of Sandwich 1788.' The final couplet, omitted in the other printings of the poem, was now added for the first time, except for the last word. The poem was first collected by Stephen Jones in his expanded 2nd edn of G.'s *Poems*, 1800, pp. 185–7, the final couplet being again omitted and replaced by asterisks.

John Wooll, *Memoirs of Joseph Warton* (1806) p. 83 *n*, objected to the in-clusion of this 'vulgar and indecent copy of verses' in the works of a poet 'through whose whole volume was not, ere this, one line which could raise the slightest blush on the cheek of virginity'. Mitford, who included the poem in his edns of G., omitted the final couplet as 'too gross to give', as it continued to be until A. L. Poole printed the text of the fly-sheet in 1917. (Bradshaw had confined the last couplet to a note in 1891 and Tovey had quietly omitted the whole poem in 1898.) The complete text of the poem, including the last word, was first printed from Walpole's copy in the Pierpont Morgan Library in the *Walpole Correspondence* xxviii 169–70, in 1955.

Although it is much more effective, G.'s attack on Sandwich closely resembles in tone and content much of the satirical opposition to Sandwich's candidacy for the High Stewardship which appeared in the press early in 1764. Poems and facetious reports on the progress of the contest appeared in almost every issue of the *St James's Chronicle* from mid-Jan. to mid-March 1764. Sandwich's lecherous reputation was a popular topic in both verse and prose and the University was frequently represented as an elderly

woman (in G.'s version three elderly women, representing the three
Faculties) being wooed by the profligate Sandwich. One example may be
given from the *St James's Chronicle* for 10–12 Jan. 1764, in a letter from
Cambridge, dated 3 Jan.:

'We hear, a certain *elderly Gentlewoman*, of some Figure and Character
in the World, who has long been settled in this Neighbourhood, and has in
her time been honoured with the Addresses of many Persons of the first
Rank and Reputation, has lately given her Friends and Relations the most
alarming Apprehensions, by seeming to listen to some Overtures of a Match,
every way unsuitable to a Person of her Years and Discretion; and this too
at a Time, when the Man, to whom she is bound by the strongest Bonds
[Hardwicke], is yet alive. Such an Instance of Levity and Weakness they
cannot help considering a Symptom of an approaching Decay, since they
are very sure, if the old Lady's Intellects had not been greatly on the Decline,
she never would have dreamt of entering into so preposterous and disrepu-
table an Alliance, much less at a time, when common Decency should have
made her reject any Offers of the Kind . . . .
. . . What is most surprising is, that a Man of his Turn, who has been re-
markable for his tender Intercourse with the younger Part of the Sex,
should think of bestowing so much of his Time and Attention on an old
Woman! In Answer to this some pretend to say, that the softer Passions,
for the Indulgence of which he has been so remarkable, are in this In-
stance to be sacrificed to that of Ambition. The old Lady, it seems, has the
Disposal of a Borough in her Power, on which it is said, he has long had his
Eye.'

An epigram in the issue of 28 Feb.–1 March described Sandwich as
'*essaying*, it's said, to debauch his *old Mother*'. The 'Intelligence Extra-
ordinary' in the same issue reported that 'Poor *Jemmy Twitcher's* greatest
Failing was always an *ungovernable* Passion for the Fair Sex'. The sprightly
metre and deliberately 'low' vocabulary of G.'s poem suggest that he may
have been consciously imitating this sort of journalistic satire. He had
undoubtedly read Charles Churchill's frequent attacks on Sandwich,
notably in *The Author* (Dec. 1763) and *The Duellist* (Jan. 1764), since he
annotated these and other poems and identified the references to Sandwich
in them; see E. Gosse, 'Gray's notes on Churchill', *Transactions of the Royal
Society of Literature* xxxvi (1918) 161–79. Churchill's poem on the election,
The Candidate, which may have suggested the title later given to G.'s poem,
was not published until May 1764, by which time G.'s lines had probably
been written. Another poem attacking Sandwich, also entitled *The Candi-
date*, had appeared in the *St James's Chronicle* for 8–10 March 1764.

The text followed here is that of the fly-sheet, except that 'G--' (l. 30) and
'D--n' (l.33) have been spelt in full and the last word supplied, as in Wal-
pole's MS copy in the Pierpont Morgan Library. Variants are recorded from
Walpole's other copy (*Lewis MS*), the *London Evening Post*, the *Gentleman's
Mag.* and the *London Mag* lii 296, where the poem was reprinted in June

1783, entitled 'On Lord Sandwich's canvass for the High Stewardship of
the University of Cambridge'. Notes attributed to Walpole are from his
copy in the possession of W. S. Lewis, as printed in *Walpole Correspondence*
xxviii 169–70.

> When sly Jemmy Twitcher had smugged up his face
> With a lick of court whitewash and pious grimace,
> A-wooing he went, where three sisters of old
> In harmless society guttle and scold.
> 5   'Lord! Sister,' says Physic to Law, 'I declare
> Such a sheep-biting look, such a pick-pocket air,

¶ *35.1. Jemmy Twitcher*] On 15 Nov. 1763 Sandwich denounced his former
friend John Wilkes in the House of Lords for his *Essay on Woman* (an obscene
parody of Pope's *Essay on Man*) 'in strains of more hypocrisy than would
have been tolerable even in a professed Methodist', Walpole, *Memoirs of
the Reign of George III*, ed. G. F. R. Barker (1894) i 247. Walpole added that
this betrayal so disgusted the public, 'that the *Beggar's Opera* being performed
at Covent Garden Theatre soon after this event, the whole audience, when
Macheath says, *That Jemmy Twitcher should peach me, I own surprises me*,
burst out into an applause of application; and the nick-name of *Jemmy
Twitcher* stuck by the Earl so as almost to occasion the disuse of his title'
(*ibid* i 249). For the date of this 'application', see headnote.
    smugged] Smartened or spruced. *OED* cites Francis Coventry, *History of
Pompey the Little* (1751) I ix: 'Your ... master ... has been smugging up
his pretty face.'
    2. *pious*] serious *London Mag.*   *lick*] Francis Grose, *Classical Dictionary of
the Vulgar Tongue*, ed. E. Partridge (1963) p. 218, gives as a meaning of the
verb 'to paint slightly over'.   *whitewash*] 'A cosmetic formerly used for
imparting a light colour to the skin' (*OED*).   *grimace*] Used contemptu-
ously of 'any affected or exaggerated attitude or gesture of politeness' (*OED*).
    3. *three sisters*] The three Faculties at Cambridge of Medicine, Jurisprudence
and Divinity.
    4. *harmless*] Mason wrote to Walpole, 2 Oct. 1774, about this poem: 'I
remember when [G.] repeated them to me (for I never before saw them in
writing) that the epithet in the fourth line was *awkward* society, which I
think better than *harmless*' (*Walpole Correspondence* xxviii 171).   *guttle*]
'To feed luxuriously; to gormandise. A low word' (Johnson). Cp. 'Quaffs,
Crams, and Guttles, in his own defence', Dryden, *Persius* vi 51. Churchill
has 'Ere Luxury sat guttling at the helm', *The Times* 14, not published till
Sept. 1764.   *scold*] 'To quarrel clamorously and rudely' (Johnson).
    6. *sheep-biting*] A sheep-biter was 'A shifty, sneaking, or thievish fellow'
(*OED*). Johnson cites L'Estrange, *Fables* (1692) p. 288, which G. may have
remembered: 'There are *Political Sheep-biters* as well as *Pastoral*; *Betrayers of
Publick Trusts*, as well as of *Private*'.
    6–8. Cp. Churchill's description of Sandwich, *The Duellist* (Jan. 1764

Not I, for the Indies! you know I'm no prude;
But his nose is a shame and his eyes are so lewd!
Then he shambles and straddles so oddly, I fear—
10   No; at our time of life, 'twould be silly, my dear.'
    'I don't know,' says Law, 'now methinks, for his look,
'Tis just like the picture in Rochester's book.
But his character, Phyzzy, his morals, his life;
When she died, I can't tell, but he once had a wife.

897–904: 'Consult his person, dress, and air, / He seems, which strangers well
might swear, / The master, or by courtesy, / The captain of a colliery. /
Look at his visage, and agree / Half-hanged he seems, just from the tree /
Escaped; a rope may sometimes break, / Or men be cut down by mistake.'
G.'s mention of Sandwich's nose may be intended to hint at damage caused
by venereal disease.
8. nose] name *Gentleman's Mag.* (*an obvious misprint*).   *shame*] sham
London Mag.
9. Then he] He *Lewis MS.*   Johnson defines shambling: 'Moving aukwardly
and irregularly. A low bad word.' Sandwich's peculiar gait was notorious;
see Joseph Cradock, *Literary Memoirs* (1828) iv 165–6: 'he had an awkward,
careless gait. Two gentlemen observing him when at Leicester, one of them
remarked, "I think it is Lord Sandwich coming;" the other replied that he
thought he was mistaken. "Nay," says the gentleman, "I am sure it is
Lord Sandwich; for, if you observe, he is walking down both sides of the
street at once." But Lord Sandwich gave a better anecdote of himself:
"When I was at Paris I had a dancing-master; the man was very civil, and
on taking leave of him I offered him any service in London. 'Then,' said the
man, bowing, 'I should take it as a particular favour if your Lordship would
never tell any one of whom you learned to dance.'" Mason may have
remembered this line in his *Heroic Epistle* (1773) 125: 'See Jemmy Twitcher
shambles; stop! stop thief!'
10. my dear] I swear *London Mag.*
11. now] but *London Post, Gentleman's Mag., London Mag.*
12. 'Lord Sandwich was [great-] grandson of Lord Rochester and resembled
his portraits' (Walpole). John Wilmot (1647–80), second Earl of Rochester,
had also been a notorious libertine, which is G.'s point.
13. But] Then *London Post, Gentleman's Mag.   But . . . Phyzzy,*] The
character! phiz!–then *London Mag.   his life*] and life *London Mag.*
14. can't tell] don't know *London Mag.   but*] *omitted in London Post,
Gentleman's Mag.   wife*] 'Lady Sandwich was confined for lunacy, but
Lord S.'s enemies said she was still shut up after she recovered her senses–at
least she never appeared again in the world' (Walpole). Sandwich married
Judith, daughter of Viscount Fane in 1741. They separated in 1755 and she
became insane, but lived until 1797. Sandwich's mistress, Martha Ray, was
murdered in 1779. Cp. a line in a poem in the *St James's Chronicle* 13–15
March 1764: 'Jem turns away his wife and takes a whore.'

15   'They say he's no Christian, loves drinking and
             whoring,
        And all the town rings of his swearing and roaring,
        His lying and filching, and Newgate-bird tricks:—
        Not I,—for a coronet, chariot and six.'
        Divinity heard, between waking and dozing,
20   Her sisters denying and Jemmy proposing;
        From dinner she rose with her bumper in hand,
        She stroked up her belly and stroked down her band.

15–17. G. appears to have in mind Churchill's bitter attack on Sandwich in
The Duellist 905–48, esp. 909–12, 917–23, 927–30: 'His life is a continued
scene / Of all that's infamous and mean; / He knows not change, unless,
grown nice / And delicate, from vice to vice / . . . / To run a horse, to make
a match, / To revel deep, to roar a catch, / To knock a tottering watchman
down, / To sweat a woman of the town, / By fits to keep the peace, or
break it, / In turn to give a pox, or take it, / He is in, in faith, most excellent /
. . . / Hear him but talk, and you would swear / Obscenity herself was
there; / And that Profaneness had made choice, / By way of trump, to
use his voice.'
16. roaring] Being riotous.
17. His lying and filching] And filching and lying *London Post, Gentleman's
Mag.*, *London Mag.*   *filching*] 'When this genius presided at the [Admir-
alty], in 1763, about three months only, he —— every appointment that
then became vacant; which example, *famous* as it was, was strictly followed
by his compeer, his successor in office, to the injury of merit and faithful
services' (note to *filching* in *London Post*).   *Newgate-bird*] Newgate bad
London Mag.   *Newgate-bird*] 'A thief or sharper, frequently caged at
Newgate', Grose, *Classical Dictionary of the Vulgar Tongue*, ed. E. Partridge,
p. 242.
19. between] betwixt *Lewis MS, London Mag.*   Sandwich was conspicuously
supported by prominent clergymen in Cambridge, who might have been
expected to take most offence at his reputation. The 'Intelligence Extra-
ordinary' from Cambridge in the *St James's Chronicle* for 1–3 March 1764
reported: 'It is whispered here, that a Set of *Reverends* (we suppose in Comp-
liment to a certain Candidate) have Thoughts of forming themselves into a
Society, to be called the *Beef-Stake-Club*.' The 'Intelligence Extraordinary'
from Cambridge in the following issue of 3–6 March commented on the
'remarkable Species of *Deafness* and *Blindness*' (to Sandwich's reputation)
which had seized the University, although its members 'can hear very
distinctly and perfectly the Words *Preferment, Prebend, Deanery, Bishoprick*,
&c.'
21. dinner] table *London Post, Gentleman's Mag.*; the table *London Mag.*   *with
her*] with a *London Post, London Mag., Lewis MS*; and with *Gentleman's Mag.*
22. She] And *London Post*; First *London Mag.*   *and*] then *London Mag.*

'What a pother is here about wenching and roaring!
Why David loved catches and Solomon whoring.
25 Did not Israel filch from the Egyptians of old
Their jewels of silver and jewels of gold?
The prophet of Bethel, we read, told a lie;
He drinks: so did Noah; he swears: so do I.
To refuse him for such peccadillos were odd;
30 Besides, he repents, and he talks about God.
'Never hang down your head, you poor penitent elf!
Come, buss me, I'll be Mrs Twitcher myself.
Damn ye both for a couple of Puritan bitches!
He's Christian enough that repents and that stitches.'

23. *wenching*] drinking *Lewis MS*.
24. *David*] The Psalmist. 'Lord S. instituted the Catch Club' (Walpole).
Sandwich was an important figure in London musical life and his establish-
ment of the Noblemen and Gentlemen's Catch Club in 1761 was only one of
his activities. The Club met weekly and dined, and toasts by the members
alternated with songs, catches and glees. Charles Burney praised its activities
warmly in his *History of Music* (1789) iv 683. The 'Intelligence Extraordinary'
from Cambridge in the *St James's Chronicle* for 1–3 March 1764, suggested
that the university prize for an essay on morality would soon be replaced by
one for 'those who shall produce the most approved *Catch* or Canon, after
the Manner of the famous Society at *Almack's*'. For further information
about Sandwich's love of catches, see Cradock, *Literary Memoirs* i 117, 122,
iv 172, 185.
25–6. *Exodus* xii 35–6: 'And the children of Israel did according to the word
of Moses; and they borrowed of the Egyptians jewels of silver, and jewels
of gold, and raiment: And the Lord gave the people favour in the sight of
the Egyptians, so that they lent unto them such things as they required. And
they spoiled the Egyptians.'
25. *Did not*] Didn't *London Post, London Mag*.
27–8. Printed in reverse order in *London Mag*.
27. *read*] Know *Lewis MS*.   *prophet of Bethel*] For this episode, see *I Kings*
xiii 11–19.
28. For Noah's drunkenness, see *Genesis* ix 21.
29. *refuse*] reject *London Post, Gentleman's Mag., London Mag*.
30. *and*] for *London Post, Gentleman's Mag., London Mag*.   *about*] much of
London Mag. After l. 30 Speaking to Jemmy *London Post;* To Jemmy *Gentle-
man's Mag*.
31. *elf*] A diminutive, mischievous being.
33–4. For the embarrassment this couplet has caused G.'s editors, see head-
note. The last word of the poem is found only in the MS copy by Walpole
in the Pierpont Morgan Library, and even there it has been crossed out.
According to Grose, *Classical Dictionary of the Vulgar Tongue*, 'stitch' is 'a

term for lying with a woman'. In his letter to Mason of 16 Sept. 1774, Walpole wrote about the poem (*Walpole Correspondence* xxviii 170):

'Methinks I wish you could alter the end of the last line, which is too gross to be read by any females, but such cock bawds as the three dames in the verses – and that single word is the only one that could possibly be minded. P.S. Might it not do thus?

Damn you both! I know each for a Puritan punk.
He is Christian enough that repents when he's drunk.'

Mason wrote on the letter another alternative:

Damn ye both for a couple of Puritan saints,
He's Christian enough that both whores and repents.

Under 'whores' Mason added 'drinks'. Mason sent a slightly altered version of this couplet to Walpole on 2 Oct. 1774 (*Walpole Correspondence* xxviii 171):

'The couplet which you wish me to alter is one of those that can only be altered, not improved; the utmost one can hope is a passable alteration. However I think with you (and always did) that the lines ought to be altered. I read (somewhat nearer his idea than yours)

Damn ye both for two prim puritanical saints!
He's Christian enough that both whores and repents!
(or) that drinks, whores and repents.

The rhymes here are not quite perfect, yet in this sort of verse I believe they are permissible.'

Eventually Walpole and Mason seem to have abandoned their attempt to provide a substitute couplet. It was simply omitted from all texts intended for the general public and the last offending word omitted by Walpole from the flysheet and one of his MS copies. Starr and Hendrickson p. 239, raise the possibility that even 'stitches' may have been merely a euphemistic substitute by Walpole or Mason for some other word, but such caution seems unjustified. The fact that 'stitches' itself could not be printed and was deleted by some hand in Walpole's MS copy indicates that it was hardly felt to be euphemistic; and some stronger evidence for the exact meaning of such alternatives as 'switches' and 'twitches' is needed before they can be considered.

36 William Shakespeare to Mrs Anne, Regular Servant to the Revd Mr Precentor of York

Written early in July 1765. G. sent these lines to William Mason, who had been Canon Residentiary and Precentor of York since 1762, in a letter

¶ 36. *Title:* Mitford notes deleted variants of 'Meg' for 'Anne, Regular' and 'Mason' for 'Precentor'.

of about 8 July 1765 (*Corresp* ii 879–80). G. had just been staying with Mason at York and wrote from the home of his friend Dr Thomas Wharton at Old Park, near Durham. His only comment on the poem was: 'Tell me, if you don't like this, & I will send you a worse.' Mason replied on 22 July: 'As bad as Your Verses were, they are Yours, & therefore when I get back to York Ill paste them carefully in the first page of My Shakespeare to inhance its Value for I intend it to be put in My Marriage Settlement as a Provision for my Younger Daughters' (*Corresp* ii 881). Mason had apparently been annotating an interleaved Shakespeare, though he did not publish his observations; see J. W. Draper, *William Mason* (New York, 1924) pp. 64–5.

The poem was first printed in the *Gray-Mason Correspondence* pp 339–340, by Mitford in 1853. There is an earlier draft in a notebook in the possession of Lt-Col. Sir John Murray, described in detail by Paget Toynbee, *MLR* xxv (1930) 83–5. There is also a copy among the Mitford MSS in the British Museum. Both texts have variants from that in G.'s letter, which is followed here.

> A moment's patience, gentle Mistress Anne!
> (But stint your clack for sweet St Charitie)
> 'Tis Willy begs, once a right proper man,
> Though now a book and interleaved, you see.
> 5   Much have I borne from cankered critic's spite,
> From fumbling baronets and poets small,

1. 'Have patience, gentle Julia', *Two Gentlemen of Verona* II ii 1; and 'patience, gentle Audrey', *As You Like It* V i 1.
2. *But*] And *Murray.*   *your*] thy *Murray, Mitford.*   *sweet*] dear *Murray.* Cp. 'It stinted and said "Ay". / – And stint thou too, I pray thee', *Romeo and Juliet* I iii 58; 'But still his tongue ran on, / And with its everlasting clack . . .', Butler, *Hudibras* III ii 444–5. Cp. also 'Ah, dear Lord, and sweet Saint Charitee', Spenser, *Shepheardes Calender*, 'May' 247; 'By Gis and by Saint Charitie', *Hamlet* IV v 59; 'Yet for the sake of sweet Saint Charity', Dryden, *Cock and the Fox* 648; 'At least, kind Sir, for Charity's sweet sake', Pope, *January and May* 732; 'write to me then for *sweet S*ᵗ *Charity*', G. to Wharton 17 Aug. 1757 (*Corresp* ii 519).
3. 'As proper a man as ever went on four legs', *Tempest* II ii 63, and many other instances in Shakespeare.
5. *cankered*] crabbed *Mitford.* Cp. 'envious jealousy and cankered spite', Prior, *Henry and Emma* 536. Tovey suggests that G. may have had in mind Thomas Rymer's *Short View of Tragedy* (1693).
6. *baronets and poets*] e.g. Sir Thomas Pope Blount, who included remarks on Shakespeare in *De Re Poetica* (1694), and Sir Thomas Hanmer, editor of Shakespeare 1743–44 (see Collins, *Epistle to Hanmer*); Nicholas Rowe, who published an edn of Shakespeare 1709–10; and Lewis Theobald, whose 7 vol. edn appeared in 1733 (G. owned and annotated a copy of the 2nd edn

Pert barristers and parsons nothing bright:
But what awaits me now is worst of all.
'Tis true, our master's temper natural
10 Was fashioned fair in meek and dovelike guise;
But may not honey's self be turned to gall
By residence, by marriage, and sore eyes?
If then he wreak on me his wicked will,

of 1740). Pope, who would hardly seem to G. a 'poet small', published his edn in 6 vols in 1725. Samuel Johnson's edn was to appear a few months after the date of this poem.

7. barristers] Baronets *Mitford.*   *barristers and parsons*] e.g. Thomas Edwards of Lincoln's Inn, who attacked William Warburton's edn of Shakespeare (1747) in his *Canons of Criticism* (1748); John Holt, 'formerly of Gray's Inn', *Attempte to rescue . . . Maister Williaume Shakespere from the Maney Errours faulsely charged on him* (1749); John Upton, *Critical Observations on Shakespeare* (1746) and Zachary Grey, *Critical, Historical, and Explanatory Notes on Shakespeare* (2 vols, 1754).

8. worst of] worse than *Mitford.*

9–10. In June 1748, not long after making his acquaintance, G. described Mason as 'a good & well-meaning Creature; but then he is really *in Simplicity a Child*'; and in Aug. 1749 referred again to his 'great Good-Nature & Simplicity . . . so sincere & undisguised, that no Mind with a Spark of Generosity would ever think of hurting him, he lies so open to Injury' (*Corresp* i 307, 323). Mason's meekness later seems to have become something of a joke: in a letter in Dec. 1756 G. calls him 'Dove'. The *Monthly Review*, in an article on the *Odes* of Colman and Lloyd which parodied those of G. and Mason, observed of the latter pair that 'one at least of these Writers hath borne his faculties meekly'. This sentence provoked a facetious protest to Mason by G. in Aug. 1760: 'I leave you to guess, wᶜʰ that is: I think, I know. you Oaf you, you must be meek, must you? & see, what you get by it!' (*Corresp* ii 488, 690). In these lines G. may be referring specifically to this incident.

9. 'Tis . . . master's] True, the Precentor's *Murray.*

10. fashioned fair] moulded soft *Murray.*   *dove-like*] lowly *Murray with alternative* dovelike.

11. 'Thy honey turns to gall, thy joy to grief', *Rape of Lucrece* 889.

12. sore eyes] Mince Pies *Mitford.*   G. refers to Mason's duties as a Residentiary Canon of York and to his marriage to Mary Sherman, which occurred two months later, on 25 Sept. 1765. Mason's eyes caused him trouble in 1758 and G. mentioned that they were 'very bad' again in a letter to Wharton in June 1765. In the letter which contained this poem, G. wrote, 'I rejoice to hear, your eyes are better as much as if they were my own' (*Corresp* ii 597, 599, 878, 880–1).

13. 'A wicked will: / A woman's will; a canker'd grandam's will', *King John* II i 193–4.

Steal to his closet at the hour of prayer,
15   And (when thou hear'st the organ piping shrill)
Grease his best pen, and all he scribbles, tear.
   Better to bottom tarts and cheesecakes nice,
Better the roast meat from the fire to save,
Better be twisted into caps for spice,
20   Than thus be patched and cobbled in one's grave.
   So York shall taste what Clouët never knew,
So from *our* works sublimer fumes shall rise:
While Nancy earns the praise to Shakespeare due
For glorious puddings and immortal pies.

14. i.e. when Mason would be at service in the Minster.   *at*] in *Mitford.*
16. Grease] i.e. make it impossible for him to write.
17–20. These lines precede ll. 13–16 in Mitford.
17–24. The use of the works of forgotten authors for various culinary purposes was one of the most popular jokes of the preceding hundred years: e.g. 'From dusty shops neglected Authors come, / Martyrs of Pies . . . ', Dryden, *Macflecknoe* 100–1; 'Hither, retrieved from Cooks and Grocers, come / M------ works entire . . . .', Garth, *Dispensary* iv 133–4; 'But now are damned to wrapping drugs and wares', Oldham, *A Satyr* 101; 'There, sav'd by spice, like Mummies, many a year, / Dry Bodies of Divinity appear', Pope, *Dunciad* i 151–2; 'Redeemed from tapers and defrauded pies', *ibid* i 156; etc.
17. cheesecakes] puddings *Murray, altered to* biscuits. *17 and 19 are transposed in Murray.*
20. one's] my *Murray.*
21. De St Clouet was the Duke of Newcastle's famous French cook, who had been celebrated in Verral's *System of Cookery* (1759), a copy of which, now in the British Museum, G. owned and annotated. See R. Fukuhara, *Bibliographical Study of Thomas Gray* (Tokyo, 1933) pp. 61–8, and *The Cook's Paradise, being William Verral's 'Complete System of Cookery' published in 1759 with Thomas Gray's Cookery Notes in holograph*, ed. R. L. Mégroz, (1948).
22. our] thy *Murray altered to* our.   *works*] work *Mitford.*
23. earns] reaps *Murray.*   Cp. 'And *Betty*'s praised for Labours not her own', Pope, *Rape of the Lock* i 148.
24. For . . . puddings] To . . . Cheese cakes *Mitford.*

37 [Epitaph on Mrs Mason]

Written between 27 March and 23 May 1767. Norton Nicholls, in his 'Reminiscences of Gray' (*Corresp* iii 1294), first published by Mitford in 1843, revealed that 'The last four lines of Mason's epitaph on his wife were written by Gray, I saw them in his hand-writing interlined in the Mss which he showed me. . . . I do not now remember the lines of Mason which were effaced & replaced by these which have the genuine sound of the lyre of Gray. I remember that they were weak, with a languid repetition of some preceding expressions. Mᵣ Gray said "That will never do for an ending, I have altered them thus."' Mrs Mason, to whom Mason had been married for only 18 months, died on 27 March 1767 at the age of 28. The epitaph, an apostrophe calling on her to speak from the grave an exhortation to the reader, was eventually inscribed on a tablet in Bristol Cathedral. There is a copy in G.'s hand of the epitaph among the papers of Richard Hurd (*Correspondence of Hurd and Mason*, ed. Pearce and Whibley, 1932, p. 168) which G. must have sent him during May 1767. On 23 May G. wrote to Mason, 'I have shew'd the Epitaph to no one but Hurd, who entirely approves it. he made no objection, but to one line (& that was mine) *Heav'n lifts* &c [l. 3 of Gray's quatrain]: so if you please to make another, you may: for my part I rather like it still' (*Corresp* iii 957).

The epitaph was first published in *The New Foundling Hospital for Wit* (new edn, 1784) vi 45; and was reprinted in the *Gentleman's Mag.* lxiv (1794) 64. The text printed here is that on the monument in Bristol Cathedral.

Tell them, though 'tis an awful thing to die,
('Twas e'en to thee) yet the dread path once trod,
Heaven lifts its everlasting portals high,
And bids the pure in heart behold their God.

38 [Parody on an Epitaph]

Written *c.* 3 Sept. 1767. G. visited Brough, and presumably Appleton, in the first week of Sept. 1767, during a short tour of the Lake District with Thomas Wharton (*Corresp* iii 976). It must have been on this occasion that he wrote what Wharton described as an 'Extempore Epitaph on Ann Countess of Dorset, Pembroke, and Montgomery, made by Mᵣ Gray on reading the Epitaph on her mothers tomb in the Church at Appleby, composed by the Countess in the same manner'. G.'s holograph MS, with this inscription, is in the British Museum (Egerton MS 2400 f. 181).

The object of G.'s parody was an epitaph, written in 1617, by Anne Clifford (1590–1676) on her mother, Margaret, widow of George Clifford, third Earl of Cumberland: 'Who Faith, Love, Mercy, noble Constancy / To God, to Virtue, to Distress, to Right / Observed, expressed, showed, held religiously / Hath here this monument thou seest in sight, / The cover of her earthly part, but passenger / Know Heaven and Fame contains the best of her.' G. did not merely parody the involved syntax of these lines. The Countess resided consecutively at each one of her six castles, Skipton, Appleby, Brougham, Brough, Pendragon and Bardon Tower, four of which G. mentions. In the first two lines of his parody he plays on these names.

G. visited Brough again with Wharton during another tour in the Lake District in Oct. 1769, but Wharton had to return home because of asthma (*Corresp* iii 1074). The parody may have been written during this later expedition, but in the journal which he began to send to Wharton describing his travels, G. referred to Skipton Castle as 'one of our good Countesse's buildings', as though she had been a long-standing joke between them (*Corresp* iii 1108–9).
The parody was first printed in G.'s *Works*, ed. Gosse, i 140, in 1884.

Now clean, now hideous, mellow now, now gruff,
She swept, she hissed, she ripened and grew rough,
At Broom, Pendragon, Appleby and Brough.

39 [Invitation to Mason]

G. sent these lines to Mason from Cambridge in a letter dated 8 Jan. 1768, (first printed by Mitford in the *Gray-Mason Correspondence* pp. 411–4, in 1853). He introduced them as follows: 'Here are, or have been, or will be all your old & new Friends in constant expectation of you at Cambridge, yet Christmas is past, & no Scroddles appears!' ('Scroddles' was a nickname for Mason used occasionally in their correspondence.) All these friends were not in fact in Cambridge at the time, as G. explained after giving his poem (*Corresp* iii 993–4): 'it is true, of the two Archdeacons [Hurd and Balguy], the latter is now here, but goes on Monday: the former comes to take his degree in February. the Rector [Palgrave] writes to ask, whether you are come, that he may do the same. as to Johnny [Stonhewer], here he is, divided between the thoughts of fornication & marriage. Delaval only waits for a little intreaty. the Masters [Powell and Marriott], the Doctor [Glynn], the Poet [Nevile], & the President [Brown], are very pressing & warm; but none so warm as the Coffee-house and I.' Mason duly came to Cambridge on 20 Jan. 1768.
The text is that of G.'s original letter, with variants in a copy by Mitford recorded in the notes.

Prim Hurd attends your call and Palgrave proud,
Stonhewer the lewd and Delaval the loud.

¶ *39.1.* The names of Hurd, Stonhewer (l. 2) and Balguy (l. 8) are scored through in the original letter. Mitford printed 'Weddell' for 'Prim Hurd', and this reading occurs in a transcript in one of his note-books, although the correct reading occurs in another copy by him. He may have been unable to decipher the name at first. Richard Hurd (1720–1808), Fellow of Emmanuel College 1742, became Archdeacon of Gloucester in 1767, D.D. in 1768, Bishop of Lichfield and Coventry in 1774 and Bishop of Worcester 1781–1808. His literary works include an edn of Horace's *Ars Poetica* (1749) and *Letters on Chivalry and Romance* (1762). Richard Palgrave (*c.* 1735–99),

For thee does Powell squeeze and Marriott sputter,
And Glynn cut phizzes and Tom Nevile stutter.
5   Brown sees thee sitting on his nose's tip,
The Widow feels thee in her aching hip,
For thee fat Nanny sighs and handy Nelly,
And Balguy with a bishop in his belly!

Scholar of Pembroke College 1753, Fellow-Commoner 1757, Fellow 1764, became Rector of Thrandeston, Suffolk in 1759, and Rector of Palgrave in 1766. Mason also calls him 'Proud Palgrave' in a letter to G. in Aug. 1768 (*Corresp* iii 1044).

2. Richard Stonhewer (*c.* 1728–1809), Fellow of Peterhouse 1751, Historiographer to the King 1755, private secretary to the Duke of Grafton 1766. G. obtained the Regius Professorship of Modern History in 1768 through Stonhewer's influence with the Duke of Grafton, who was then Prime Minister. Edward Hussey Delaval (1729–1814), Fellow of Pembroke 1751, was a scientist, classical scholar and linguist. G. mentioned in April 1769 that he 'talks as loud as ever' (*Corresp* iii 1058).

3. William Samuel Powell (1717–75), Master of St John's College 1765–75; James Marriott (*c.* 1730–1803), Master of Trinity Hall 1764. In Oct. 1766 G. referred to Marriott as one 'whose follies let us pardon, because he has some feeling & means us well' (*Corresp* iii 941).

4. Robert Glynn (1719–1800), Fellow of King's College 1740–1800. The leading physician in Cambridge, he attended G. in his last illness. He was also a minor poet.   *cut phizzes*] Probably to grimace. Glynn was notoriously ugly. Thomas Nevile (*c.* 1720–81), Fellow of Jesus College 1746. He published imitations of Horace (1758), Virgil (1767) and Juvenal and Persius (1769). William Cole mentions that he 'has an impediment in his speech' (*Corresp* ii 501 *n*).

5. James Brown (1709–84), Fellow of Pembroke 1735; President (i.e. Vice-Master) 1749–70, Master 1770–84. He was a close friend of G. throughout his life, and joint-executor with Mason of his will.

6–7. *Widow . . . Nanny . . . Nelly*] From G.'s remarks on his poem quoted in the headnote it appears that these women were employed at the Coffeehouse he frequented.

8. Thomas Balguy (1716–95), Fellow of St John's College 1741–48; Archdeacon of Winchester 1759–95. He was offered the Bishopric of Gloucester in 1781, on the death of Warburton, but declined it.   *bishop in his belly*] Toynbee and Whibley note that this is an adaptation of a seventeenth-century phrase used of suspected Papists and they cite from *OED*: 'Some shallow-pated puritan . . . will . . . cry me up to have a Pope in my belly', James Howell, *Letters* (1650) i 472. Tovey also cites Macaulay's *History* vol II ch viii: 'When Cartwright, the Popish Bishop of Chester, passed through Westminster Hall, after the acquittal of the seven Bishops (1688), one in the the crowd shouted: "Make room for the man with the Pope in his belly."'

40 On L[or]d H[olland']s Seat near M[argat]e, K[en]t

Written in June 1768. The dating is discussed at length by Whibley (*Corresp* iii 1259–62). Sir Egerton Brydges told Mitford (*Works of Gray*, 1835–43, I ciii) that G. wrote these lines during a visit to his friend William Robinson of Denton Court, Kent (one of whose daughters became Brydges's second wife), and that they were 'found in the drawer of Gray's dressing table after he was gone. They were restored to him; for he had no other copy, and had forgotten them.' The poem has usually been dated 1766, probably, as Whibley suggested, because the only letter by G. in Mason's *Memoirs* which mentions a visit to Kent was written in that year. But a letter from G. to Norton Nicholls, dated 26 Aug. 1766, specifically states that 'I did *not* go to Kingsgate, because it belong'd to my L⁴ Holland' (*Corresp* iii 927). G. did visit Robinson at Denton again in June 1768 and Whibley argues that G. wrote the poem on that occasion.

The suggestion is supported by the fact that G.'s poem almost certainly alludes to a poem by Lord Holland himself, *Lord Holland returning from Italy 1767*, which was privately printed in a broadsheet in that year. G. had heard a line of this poem by June 1767 (*Corresp* iii 962), and eventually saw the whole poem: ll. 17–20 of his own poem refer directly, it may be assumed, to the following passage by Holland, quoted from J. H. Jesse, *George Selwyn and his Contemporaries* (1843) ii 162–3: 'But, Rigby, what did I for thee endure! / Thy serpent's tooth admitted of no cure; / Lost converse, never thought of without tears; / Lost promised hope of my declining years! / O! what a heavy task 'tis to remove / Th'accustomed ties of confidence and love! / Friendship in anguish turn'd away her face, / While cunning Interest sneer'd at her disgrace. / And what has he, mistaken man! obtain'd / For broken faith?–for truth and honour stain'd? / Shelburne and Calcraft,–O!, the holy band, / See, see, with Gower caballing where they stand.'

Henry Fox (1705–74) had been Secretary of State in the Newcastle ministry in 1755–56. At this period he had been friendly with Horace Walpole, through whom G. had in fact sought Fox's support for a friend in an election to the Mastership of Pembroke College. In a letter, dated 31 July 1756 (*Walpole Correspondence* xxx 127), which was never sent, Walpole wrote to Fox: 'Great poets have a right to command and none are so much their subjects as great men. I know you think Mr G[ray] the greatest poet we have and I know he thinks you the greatest man we have; judge if you can disobey him.' G.'s attitude to Fox soon changed. In 1757 Fox became Paymaster-General and proceeded to amass a huge fortune. In 1762 he became a member of Bute's cabinet and Leader of the House of Commons, playing an important rôle in ensuring that Parliament accepted the Peace of Paris in 1763. This success was attributed for many years to gross bribery and intimidation by Fox, partly because of the exaggerated accounts of Horace

Walpole, who was of course G.'s main informant about politics. But, even if later historians have modified this familiar image of Fox, he was undoubtedly widely mistrusted by his contemporaries as an unscrupulous and self-interested schemer and between 1763 and 1765 many of his political allies abandoned or, as he believed, betrayed him. His political career virtually ended in 1763, when he was created Baron Holland of Foxley, but, after quarrelling with Bute and Shelburne, he managed to retain his lucrative post as Paymaster until he was forced to resign it in 1765. G. followed political events at this period with keen interest. In Sept. 1763 he wrote to Walpole: 'the present times are so little like any thing I remember, that you may excuse my curiosity: besides I really interest myself in these transactions, & can not persuade myself, that Quae supra nos, nihil ad nos' (*Corresp* ii 817).

After 1763 Holland, in poor health, travelled on the Continent and constructed the strange residence at Kingsgate, near Margate, which inspired G.'s poem. According to James Dallaway, *Anecdotes of the Arts in England* (1800) p. 385, the house itself was 'a correct imitation of Cicero's Formian villa, at Baiae'; and another account (*Letters from Mrs Carter to Mrs Montagu*, ed. M. Pennington (1817) iii 89) states that 'scattered around it [were] many fanciful representations of antique and ruined buildings'. William Cowper saw the estate at an early stage in its development in 1763, and was impressed by 'a fine piece of ruins, built by . . . Lord Holland, at a great expense, which, the day after I saw it, tumbled down for nothing' (*Correspondence*, ed. T. Wright (1904) i 155). Horace Walpole described Kingsgate in a letter to Lady Ossory, 19 Aug. 1784 (*Walpole Correspondence* xxxiii 437): 'The situation is uncommon and cheerful, and the buildings and erections so odd, and so little resembling any one ever saw, that a view might to those who were never there, be passed for a prospect in some half-civilized island discovered by Capt. Cook'. In a letter to Mary Berry, 28 Sept. 1796 (*Walpole Correspondence* xii 110), Walpole described once more how Holland had 'scattered buildings of all sorts, but in no style of architecture that ever appeared before or has since, and with no connection with or to one another, and in all directions–and yet the oddity and number made that naked, though fertile soil, smile and look cheerful–Do you remember Gray's bitter lines on him and his vagaries and history?'

In a letter of 29 Dec. 1768, G. had complained to Mason that he had 'gone & told my *Arcanum Arcanorum* to that leaky Mortal Palgrave, who never conceals any thing he is trusted with' (*Corresp* iii 1052). Mitford and later editors have assumed that G. was referring to the present poem. If so, his anxiety was justified, for it was published without G.'s permission a few months later in the *New Foundling Hospital for Wit* (1769) iii 34–5, entitled 'Inscription for the Villa of a Decayed Statesman on the Sea Coast'. According to Joseph Cradock, the poem 'was at first denied to be [Gray's]', *Literary Memoirs* (1828) iv 225, and no one it may be assumed was more active in doing so than Horace Walpole. He wrote to Lady Ossory, 19 Aug. 1784 (*Walpole Correspondence* xxxiii 438): 'I was very sorry that he wrote them, and ever gave a copy of them. You may be sure I did not recommend their being printed in his works; nor were they.' Walpole had in fact written to Mason on 1 Dec. 1773 (*Walpole Correspondence* xxviii 118) for this purpose: 'I think you determined not to reprint the lines on Lord H[olland]. I hope it is now a resolution. He is in so deplorable a state, that they would aggravate the misery of his last hours, and you yourself would be censured . . . . As Gray too seems to have condemned all his own satirical works, that single one would not [?give] a high idea of his powers, though they were great in that walk; you and I know they were not inferior to his other styles.' Mason evidently agreed, but the poem could not be permanently suppressed. Lord Holland died on 1 July 1774. On 17 June 1775, soon after the publication of his *Memoirs* of G., Mason wrote to Walpole (*Walpole Correspondence* xxviii 209): 'A man who styles himself Philo-Gray of Salisbury has twitted me in the newspaper for not publishing a complete edition of Gray, because I have omitted the stanzas on a decayed statesman. You must take this sin of mine upon your own back. I suspect it is Almon in order to sell his own *Foundling Hospital for Wit* where those verses are printed.' The newspaper item to which Mason referred has not been found.

The text printed in the *New Foundling Hospital* in 1769 is closely related to a copy of the poem in the hand of G.'s friend Thomas Wharton (British Museum, Egerton MS 2400 f. 232), and it is likely that it was through one of the friends such as Wharton or Palgrave to whom it had been shown that the poem first reached the press. There is another copy in the papers of William Cole (British Museum, Add. MS 5821 f. 55), entitled 'On seeing the Seat of a decayed Nobleman in Kent'. Coles noted: 'These *Verses* on *Lord Holland* are said to have been *composed* by *Mr Gray*: *Dr Glynn* dictated them to me at *Milton May 1. 1777*.' (For Richard Glynn see p. 258 above.) A text with a number of distinctive variants was printed in two parts in the *Gentleman's Mag.* in Dec. 1777 and Jan. 1778 (xlvii 624 and xlviii 88), with the avowed purpose in the first instance of showing that G. had been 'a lover of his country, and an abhorrer of its intestine foes.' (Misprints in this text were corrected in the *Gentleman's Mag.* lii 39 and 75, in 1782.) This text was followed by John Nichols in his *Select Collection of Poems* (1781) vii 350–1, where, however, he attempts to supply the names omitted in l. 18 of the *Gentleman's Mag.* text and introduces one other variant. The poem was first collected by Stephen Jones in his edn of G. in 1799, where the poem is entitled 'Stanzas, suggested by a View, in 1766, of the Seat and Ruins of a deceased Nobleman, at Kingsgate, Kent'. Jones followed the *Gentleman's Mag.* text but in his revised 2nd edn in 1800, the poem was retitled 'Impromptu [etc.]' and a number of changes were made to the text: readings were adopted from the *New Foundling Hospital* and in several cases readings without earlier authority are introduced (including a new set of identifications in l. 18). This text was followed by Mitford and was invariably reprinted throughout the rest of the century. The text followed here is that of Wharton's copy, with variants from the *New Foundling Hospital*, Cole's copy, the *Gentleman's Mag.* (with which Nichols agrees except as noted) and the 2nd edn of Jones's *Poems* (1800).

Old and abandoned by each venal friend,
  Here H[olland] took the pious resolution
To smuggle some few years and strive to mend
  A broken character and constitution.
5 On this congenial spot he fixed his choice;
  Earl Godwin trembled for his neighbouring sand;
Here sea-gulls scream and cormorants rejoice,
  And mariners, though shipwrecked, dread to land.
Here reign the blustering North and blighting East,
10 No tree is heard to whisper, bird to sing:
Yet nature cannot furnish out the feast,
  Art he invokes new horrors still to bring.
Now mouldering fanes and battlements arise,

¶ 40.*1. each*] its Cole.
2. took] form'd *New Foundling Hospital, Cole (with* framed *in margin), Jones.*
3. some] a *Gentleman's Mag., Jones.   smuggle*] G. adds to the sense of con-
veying in a stealthy manner, the connotations of *smug,* 'to smarten up';
cf. *Candidate* 2 (p. 248 above).
5. congenial] Used ironically in both the modern weakened sense of 'agree-
able'and the stronger sense of 'kindred, suited in disposition to'.
6. Godwin] Goodwin *all other texts.* The Goodwin Sands are a dangerous
line of sandbanks about 6 miles off the Kent coast. According to tradition
they are the remains of an island called Lomea, which belonged to Earl God-
wine in the 11th century.
7. Cp. Spenser's description of the 'Rocke of vile Reproach', *Faerie Queene*
II xii 8, 2–5: 'A daungerous and detestable place, / To which nor fish nor
fowle did once approach, / But yelling Meawes, with Seagulls hoarse and
base, / And Cormoyrants, with birds of rauenous race.'
8. dread] fear *Gentleman's Mag.*
9. reign] reigns *New Foundling Hospital, Gentleman's Mag.*; reign'd *Cole.*
Cp. Pope, *Rape of the Lock* iv 19–20: 'No cheerful Breeze this sullen Region
knows, / The dreaded *East* is all the Wind that blows.'
11. cannot] could not *Gentleman's Mag., Jones.*   Cp. 'Your own provisions
furnish out our Feasts', Dryden, *Prologue to Wit without Money* 11, after an
account of 'shipwrack't Passengers' coming ashore.
12. horrors] terrors *Gentleman's Mag.   still*] *written above a deleted word,
perhaps* here, *in Cole.*
13. Now] Here *Jones*
13–16. This quatrain repeatedly echoes the opening of Pope's *To Mr Addison,*
a description of the ruins of ancient Rome, especially 3, 7, 9, 11: 'With
nodding arches, broken temples spread! / ... / Huge Theatres, that now
unpeopled Woods / ... / Fanes, which admiring Gods with pride survey /
... / Some felt the silent stroke of mould'ring age.'

Arches and turrets nodding to their fall,
15   Unpeopled palaces delude his eyes,
And mimic desolation covers all.
'Ah', said the sighing peer, 'had Bute been true,
Nor Shelburne's, Rigby's, Calcraft's friendship vain,

14. Arches and turrets] Turrets and arches *Gentleman's Mag., Jones.*   Cp. 'the Wall / Of tottering *Troy*, now nodding to her fall', Dryden, *Ovid's Metamorphoses* xii 774–5; 'Or some old temple nodding to its fall', Pope, *Essay on Man* iv 129.

15. palaces . . . his] monasteries . . . our *Gentleman's Mag., Jones.*

17–18. See the verses by Holland quoted in the headnote.   *Bute*] John Stuart (1713–92), 3rd Earl of Bute, was in effect Prime Minister from the accession of George III in 1760 until his resignation in 1763. Holland had been a member of his Cabinet and, as Leader of the House of Commons, had served Bute significantly by securing an easy passage for the Peace of Paris in 1763.   *Shelburne*] William Petty (1737–1805), 2nd Earl of Shelburne, President of the Board of Trade 1763, and Secretary of State under Pitt 1766, informed Bute that Holland would resign his post as Paymaster-General when he was raised to the Lords. An unpleasant quarrel took place when Holland refused to do this, alleging that Shelburne was guilty of fraud and deception.   *Rigby*] Richard Rigby (1722–88) was the manager of the Duke of Bedford's parliamentary group, Vice-Treasurer for Ireland 1765, and Paymaster of the Forces 1768. He died extremely rich. He originally attached himself to Holland, before abandoning him for Bedford.   *Calcraft*] John Calcraft (1726–72) had been appointed a regimental agent in the Pay Office by Holland when he was Paymaster and had made a fortune in the post. Eventually he deserted Holland for Pitt. G. made two notes on Calcraft in his copy of Churchill's *Poems*, described by Gosse, *Trans. Royal Soc. Lit.* xxxvi (1918) 171–3. Against Churchill's *Epistle to Hogarth* 205, he wrote 'CALCRAFT, he quarrelld with Lord Holland, whose creature, & (as was said) natural son he was'; similarly G. annotated *The Conference* 294; 'Mʳ CALCRAFT, agent to a hundred Regiments, a Creature of Lord Holland's'.

18. Nor Shelburne's . . . vain] Nor Shelburne's, Calcraft's, Rigby's friendship vain *New Foundling Hospital*; Nor *Calcraft's, Shelburne's, Rigby's* Friendship vain *Cole*; Nor ——, ——, ——'s friendship vain *Gentleman's Mag.*; Nor G——'s, nor B——d's promises been vain *Nichols*; Nor M——'s, R——'s, B——'s friendship vain *Jones 1800, having printed dashes in 1799*. Nichols and Jones, faced with the dashes in the *Gentleman's Mag.*, evidently felt free to fill them as they pleased. Mitford, following Jones, explained the names as Mungo, Rigby and Bradshaw, comparing Mason, *Heroic Epistle* (1773) 95, where these names also occur. Jones no doubt found them there, but this is no argument for adopting them; and the identifications in *Wharton, New Foundling Hospital* and *Cole* are preferable, especially in the light of Holland's verses, where these names are mentioned.

Far other scenes than these had blessed our view
20   And realised the ruins that we feign.
Purged by the sword and beautified by fire,
Then had we seen proud London's hated walls:
Owls might have hooted in St Peter's choir,
And foxes stunk and littered in St Paul's.'

19. *other*] better *Jones*.   *these*] this *Gentleman's Mag.*   *blessed*] crown'd
New Foundling Hospital, Cole; grac'd *Gentleman's Mag.*
Cp. 'Far other dreams my erring soul employ', Pope, *Eloisa to Abelard*
223; 'Far other scenes and palaces arise,' Thomson, *Liberty* iii 550.
20. *ruins that*] glories which *Gentleman's Mag.*; horrors which *Nichols*;
beauties which *Cole, Jones*.   *realised*] Brought into actual being.
21. *beautified*] purify'd *Gentleman's Mag., Jones, and also as an alternative in
the margin of Cole.*   Cf. 'Go, purified by flames ascend the sky', Pope,
Dunciad i 227.
21–4. Dryden, *Annus Mirabilis* 1101–4:

The dareing flames peep't in and saw from far,
The awful beauties of the Sacred Quire:
But, since it was prophan'd by Civil War,
Heav'n thought it fit to have it purg'd by fire.

23–4. Cp. *Isaiah* xiii 21, xxxiv 15 (quoted in part by G. in a letter to West
in Dec. 1736, *Corresp* i 56): 'But the wild beasts of the desert shall lie there;
and their houses shall be full of doleful creatures; and owls shall dwell there,
and satyrs shall dance there. And the wild beasts of the islands shall cry in
their desolate houses, and dragons in their pleasant palaces . . . There shall
the great owl make her nest, and lay, and hatch, and gather under her sha-
dow; there shall the vultures also be gathered, every one with her mate.'
Cp. also Virgil, *Georgics* i 470–1: *obscenaeque canes importunaeque volucres
/ signa dabant* (ill-boding dogs and ominous birds gave their tokens); *Geor-
gics* i 485–6: *altae / per noctem resonare lupis ululantibus urbes* (or lofty cities to
echo all the night with the howl of wolves); Horace, *Epodes* xvi 19–20:
habitandaque fana / apris reliquit et rapacibus lupis (and left their shrines to
be the dwelling-place of boars and ravening wolves); and Pope, *Windsor
Forest* 70–1: 'The Fox obscene to gaping Tombs retires, / And savage
Howlings fill the sacred Quires.'
23. *might*] should *Gentlemen's Mag.*; would *Jones*.   *St Peter's*] Westmin-
ster Abbey.

41 Ode for Music

Written between 6 Feb. and 20 April 1769. The Duke of Grafton, who as
Prime Minister had been directly responsible for G.'s appointment as
Regius Professor of History at Cambridge in July 1768, was elected Chan-

cellor of the University on 29 Nov. 1768. As in 1749, when the Duke of
Newcastle became Chancellor, a special ode, set to music by a well-known
composer, was to be performed at the Installation ceremony on 1 July 1769.
G. explained to James Beattie, not long after the ceremony: 'I thought
myself bound in gratitude to his Grace unasked to take upon me the task
of writing those verses that are usually set to musick on this occasion'
(*Corresp* iii 1070). Norton Nicholls, in his 'Reminiscences of Gray', recalled
the mingled distaste and sense of duty with which G. set about the task
(*Corresp* iii 1300–1):

'After I had quitted the University I always paid Mr Gray an annual visit;
during one of these visits it was he determined as he said to offer with a
good grace what he could not have refused if it had been asked of him viz.,
to write the Installation Ode for the Duke of Grafton. This however he
considered as a sort of task to which he submitted with great reluctance; &
it was long after he first mentioned it to me, before he could prevail with
himself to begin the composition. One morning when I went to him as
usual after breakfast, I knocked at his door, which he threw open, & ex-
claimed with a loud voice
                "Hence! avaunt, 'tis holy ground."
I was so astonished, that I almost feared he was out of his senses; but this
was the beginning of the Ode which he had just composed.'

The composer of the ode's setting was originally to have been Charles
Burney, who was later better known as a historian of music. Burney wrote
to William Mason, who was then in Cambridge, early in 1769 to find out
whether G. had made any progress and also the kind of setting he favoured.
Mason, who had himself written the Installation Ode in 1749, replied on
6 Feb. that he had seen G. but that 'I do not find that he has yet begun to
write the Ode tho he seems to intend it, but all that I can learn from him
about it is that he wishes even the intention should be, at present, kept a
secret & therefore I think you will oblige him if you keep it such'. Mason
added that Burney had rightly assumed that G. would have preferred a
setting in the Italian rather than the German musical style: 'yet I would not
advise you to endeavour to please him, but the University, therefore the
Councel is: Out roar Old Handel if you can.' Eventually, however, there
was an altercation between Burney and the Duke of Grafton over the
expense of bringing London musicians to Cambridge for the performance
and a new composer was appointed, John Randall, Professor of Music at
Cambridge. For a full account, see R. Lonsdale, *Dr Burney* (1965) pp. 77–8.

G. had completed the *Ode* by 20 April 1769, when he wrote to Wharton,
'I must comfort myself with the intention: for I know it will bring abuse
enough on me. however it is done, & given to the V:Chancellor, & there
is an end' (*Corresp* iii 1057). As he wrote at about the same time to James
Brown, his friend Delaval had recently 'told me of the obloquy that waits
for me; and said everything to deter me from doing a thing that is already
done' (*Corresp* iii 1058). The abuse of his poetical flattery of Grafton duly

came from the Duke's political enemies. G. anticipated it in a letter to his friend Stonhewer, Grafton's secretary, on 12 June 1769, when he sent the *Ode* for the Duke's perusal (*Corresp* iii 1062):

'I did not intend the Duke should have heard me till he could not help it. You are desired to make the best excuses you can to his Grace for the liberty I have taken of praising him to his face; but as somebody was necessarily to do this, I did not see why Gratitude should sit silent and leave it to Expectation to sing, who certainly would have sung, and that *à gorge deployée* upon such an occasion.'

G. was never anything but deprecating about the *Ode*. On 24 June he told Nichols (*Corresp* iii 1065): '*Odicle* has been rehearsed again & again, & the boys have got scraps by heart: I expect to see it torn piece-meal in the North-Briton, before it is born. the musick is as good as the words: the former might be taken for mine, & the latter for Dr. Randal's.' Joseph Cradock, in his *Literary Memoirs* (1828) i 107–8, recalled accompanying G. to one of these rehearsals:

'The pleasantest morning that I passed then at Cambridge, was in company with Mr. Gray and some critics, at the rehearsal of the musick for his own Ode, previous to its grand performance in the Senate-house; and I thought, that as he had so many directions to give, and such nice distinctions to make, it was well he had to deal with the pliant Dr. Randall, rather than with some of the very able Composers or Professors that I could have named in the Metropolis. Mr. Gray was not much more comfortable at this time than the Chancellor himself; for the press was teeming with abuse, and a very satirical parody was then preparing, which soon afterwards appeared. His own delicious Ode, indeed, must always be admired, yet this envenomed shaft was so pointedly levelled at him, though he affected in his letter to Mason to disregard it, that, with his fine feelings, he was not only annoyed, but very seriously hurt by it.'

There is a long description of Grafton's installation as Chancellor in a letter from Richard Gough to Benjamin Foster, in J. Nichols, *Literary Illustrations of the Eighteenth Century* v 315–16. Gough thought the *Ode* 'well set and performed, but charged with obscurity'; but the company departed cheerfully enough to 'dinner, in Trinity College Hall, where were seven turtles and a number of haunches, with plenty of Claret, Champagne, and Burgundy.' Nichols (v 797) also quotes another immediate reaction, by Joseph Cockfield, who considered the *Ode* 'a recent instance of flattery bestowed indiscriminately on the great' and that it would 'do no credit to that celebrated writer.' The fact that G.'s name did not appear on the title-page when the *Ode* was published was owing less, perhaps, to any hope he might still have of retaining his anonymity, than to a wish to indicate that he was not particularly proud of what he had always regarded as essentially a duty. When Norton Nicholls told him in June 1769 that he had been approached by Woodyer, a Cambridge bookseller, who was hoping to 'be admitted to a share in the sale of the Ode', G. replied that 'I do not publish at all, but Alma Mater prints 5 or 600 for the company' (*Corresp* iii 1063, 1068). The *Ode* was in fact printed for the University by Archdeacon, the University printer, in eight pages quarto. Later in the year a 2nd edn was issued.

Writing to James Beattie about 'those verses' in mid-July 1769, G. told him, 'I do not think them worth sending you, because they are by nature doom'd to live but a single day, or if their existence is prolong'd beyond that date, it is only by means of news-paper parodies, & witless criticism. this sort of abuse I had reason to expect, but did not think it worth while to avoid it' (*Corresp* iii 1070). One parody of the *Ode* had appeared almost immediately in the *St James's Chronicle*, 1–4 July 1769, beginning 'Hence! avaunt! 'tis venal ground'; and a second followed in the *London Chronicle* 14–16 Sept. beginning 'Hence! avaunt! 'tis sacred ground, / Let pallid Freedom ever fly'. The *Ode* itself and these two parodies were reprinted together in the *New Foundling Hospital for Wit* (1771) iv 8–22. The *London Chronicle* for 27–9 July 1769 also published a parody of the epitaph of the *Elegy*, which contained such lines as 'And smooth-tongued flatt'ry mark'd him for her own.' Junius, in his fifth letter to the Duke of Grafton, dated 8 July 1769, had described the time when Grafton would be dismissed from office and would retire to a Cambridge which would then ignore him: 'The learned dulness of declamation will be silent; and even the venal Muse, though happiest in fiction, will forget your virtues.'

As Cradock realized, G. was much more sensitive to this sort of abuse than he would admit; it is also unlikely that the *Ode* received much praise on purely literary grounds. Beattie assured him that it was 'the finest pane-gyrical poem in the world' (*Corresp* iii 1082), but a more typical comment may have been George Montagu's reference to it in a letter to Walpole as 'Grey's copy of himself' (*Walpole Correspondence* x 284). Mason, when he printed it in *1775*, considered that the fact that it was 'irregular' was a serious defect, but otherwise thought it, 'in point of lyrical arrangement and ex-pression, to be equal to most of his other Odes'. He added some explanatory notes for the benefit of the general public, 'who may be reasonably supposed to know little of the particular founders of different Colleges and their history here alluded to' (*Poems* pp. 37–43, 97–8). One rather unexpected admirer of the poem was Coleridge, who thought that 'there is something very majestic in Gray's Installation Ode; but as to *The Bard* and the rest of his lyrics, I must say I think them frigid and artificial', *Specimens of the Table Talk of Samuel Taylor Coleridge* (1835) ii 271.

For some useful background to the genre in which G. was writing, see R. M. Myers, 'Neo-classical criticism of the Ode for Music', *PMLA* lxii (1947) 399–421.

The text is that of the original edn, which G. did not alter. It was entitled: 'Ode performed in the Senate-House at Cambridge, July 1, 1769, at the installation of His Grace Augustus-Henry Fitzroy, Duke of Grafton, Chancellor of the University. Set to music by Dr. Randal, Professor of Music.' It is entitled merely 'Ode for Music' on the first page of text.

Air

'Hence, avaunt, ('tis holy ground)
'Comus and his midnight-crew,
'And Ignorance with looks profound,
'And dreaming Sloth of pallid hue,
5   'Mad Sedition's cry profane,
'Servitude that hugs her chain,
'Nor in these consecrated bowers
'Let painted Flattery hide her serpent-train in flowers.

Chorus

'Nor Envy base nor creeping Gain
10   'Dare the Muse's walk to stain,
'While bright-eyed Science watches round:
'Hence, away, 'tis holy ground!'

Recitative

From yonder realms of empyrean day
Bursts on my ear the indignant lay:
15   There sit the sainted sage, the bard divine,
The few whom genius gave to shine

¶ 41.*1*. Virgil, *Aeneid* vi 258: *Procul o, procul este, profani* (Away! away! unhallowed ones!); Statius, *Sylvae* III iii 13: *procul hinc, procul ite nocentes* (Begone, begone, ye wicked). Shakespeare has 'hence, avaunt', *II Henry IV* I ii 103 and *Othello* IV i 271.

2. 'Midnight shout, and revelry' and 'he and his curst crew', Milton, *Comus* 103, 653.

4. Cp. 'pallid hew', *Faerie Queene* III ii 28, 1; VI viii 40, 6.

6. Cp. *Progress of Poesy* 80 (p. 172); and 'If, like a fool, thou dost not hug thy chain', Dryden, *Lucretius* iv 135.

7. 'Near to her close and consecrated bower', *Midsummer Night's Dream* III ii 7.

8. 'as the snake roll'd in a flowering bank', *II Henry VI* III i 228; and 'Look like the innocent flower, / But be the serpent under't', *Macbeth* I v 66–7. The image may derive from Virgil, *Eclogues* iii 92–3.

11. 'With Science bright-eyed as the morn', Joseph Warton, *Ode to Liberty* 6, and 'bright-eyed fancy', *Progress of Poesy* 108.

13. 'the vast ocean of unbounded day / In th'empyrean heaven does stay', Cowley, *Hymn to Light* st. xxvi.

14. indignant lay] The preceding verses.

15–17. Pope, *Essay on Criticism* 189, 193–4: 'Hail *Bards Triumphant*! born in *happier Days* / . . . / Nations *unborn* your mighty *Names* shall sound, / And Worlds applaud that must not yet be *found*!' Cp. also 'Like them to shine thro' long succeeding age', Pope, *Epistle to Jervas* 11; 'In awful sages and in noble bards', Thomson, *Summer* 1532.

Through every unborn age and undiscovered clime.
Rapt in celestial transport they,   (*accomp.*)
Yet hither oft a glance from high
20   They send of tender sympathy
To bless the place, where on their opening soul
First the genuine ardour stole.
'Twas Milton struck the deep-toned shell,
And, as the choral warblings round him swell,
25   Meek Newton's self bends from his state sublime,
And nods his hoary head and listens to the rhyme.

Air
'Ye brown o'er-arching groves,
'That Contemplation loves,
'Where willowy Camus lingers with delight!
30   'Oft at the blush of dawn

21. *place*] Cambridge.   *opening soul*] Cp. *Education and Government* 12 and *n* (p. 93).

23. *Milton*] An undergraduate at Christ's College.   *shell*] Lyre. See *Progress of Poesy* 15 and *n*. (p. 164).   Cp. 'When Jubal struck the chorded shell', Dryden, *Song for St Cecilia's Day* 17.

25. *Newton*] Sir Isaac Newton (1642–1727), Scholar and later Fellow of Trinity College, Cambridge.   *state*] Perhaps intended to convey only a general idea of lofty dignity; or a throne (cp. 'sit', l. 15), or more particularly, the canopy over a throne, as in *Par. Lost* x 445–6: 'his high Throne, which under state / Of richest texture spred'.

27–34. 'This stanza spoken by *Milton* is judiciously distributed into the same measure, as that in which the great poet composed his sublime *Hymn* on the *Nativity*; except that the last verse but one in *Mr. Gray's* sonnet is longer by two syllables than the corresponding verse in his original' (Wakefield, 1786, pp. 149–50, expanding an observation of Mason, *Poems* p. 98).

27. 'To arched walks of twilight groves, / And shadows brown that *Sylvan* loves', Milton, *Il Penseroso* 133–4; 'Where th'*Etrurian* shades / High over-arch't imbowr' and 'A Pillard shade / High overarch't', *Par. Lost* i 304, ix 1106–7; and 'Brown with o'erarching shades', Pope, *Odyssey* iii 97.

28. 'The Cherub Contemplation', Milton, *Il Penseroso* 54.

29. Joseph Hall, *Satires* I i 31, refers to the Cam's 'willow-shaded shore'; and cp. 'Or where the *Cam* thro' Willows winds its way', John Dart, *Westminster Abbey* (1723) I xl.

30–4. These lines are a deliberate pastiche of Milton, *Il Penseroso* 61–7: 'Sweet Bird that shunn'st the noise of folly, / Most musicall, most melancholy! / Thee Chauntress oft the Woods among, / I woo to hear thy eeven-Song; / And missing thee, I walk unseen / On the dry smooth-shaven Green, / To behold the wandring Moon.' But there are other Miltonic echoes: e.g.

'I trod your level lawn,
'Oft wooed the gleam of Cynthia silver-bright
'In cloisters dim, far from the haunts of Folly,
'With Freedom by my side, and soft-eyed Melancholy.'

Recitative

35   But hark! the portals sound and, pacing forth
With solemn steps and slow,
High potentates and dames of royal birth
And mitred fathers in long order go:
Great Edward with the lilies on his brow

'After short blush of Morn', *Par. Lost* xi 184; 'The Shepherds on the
Lawn, / Or ere the point of dawn', *Nativity Ode* 85–6; 'there does a sable
cloud / Turn forth her silver lining on the night, / And casts a gleam over
this tufted Grove', *Comus* 223–5; 'ere the high Lawns appear'd / Under the
opening eye-lids of the morn', *Lycidas* 25–6.

32. 'Their armours that marched hence so silver-bright', *King John* II i 315;
William Drummond, *Sonnet xiii* 7–8: 'with silver bright / Who moon
enamels'.

33. 'the studious Cloysters pale', Milton, *Il Penseroso* 156, and 'Far from
the cheerfull haunt of men', *Comus* 388; 'Hence from the haunts / Of vice
and folly, vanity and man', David Mallet, *The Excursion* i 11–2.

34. 'Or from the soft-ey'd Virgin steal a tear', Pope, *Epistle to Arbuthnot*
286; and 'sensible soft Melancholy', Pope, *On a Certain Lady at Court* 8.

36. 'With wandring steps and slow', *Par. Lost* xii 648; 'with solemn pace
and slow', Pope, *Odyssey* xi 397; 'with pensive steps and slow', *ibid* x 286;
'By timid steps, and slow', *Dunciad* iv 465.

37–8. Benefactors of the University.

38. long order] Cp. *Unde omnis longo ordine posset / adversos legere* (whence,
face to face, he might scan all the long array), *Aeneid* vi 754–5. The phrase
is a common formula in heroic poetry: e.g. Fairfax's *Tasso* XII xcv 1;
Dryden, *Aeneid* i 984, ii 1043, iii 533, v 133; Pope, *Iliad* i 643, and *Imitations
of Horace, Ep.* II i 316.

39. Edward] Edward the Third [1312–77]; who added the fleur de lys of France
to the arms of England. He founded Trinity College. *Mason.*

Trinity was actually founded by Henry VIII from other foundations,
including King's Hall, established by Edward III in 1337. Edward proclaim-
ed himself King of France in 1340 and thereafter 'quartered the lilies of
France with the leopards of England' (*DNB*). The lilies were frequently
associated with him by the poets: cf. Denham, *Cooper's Hill* 77–8: 'But
thee (great Edward) and thy greater son, / (The lillies which his father wore,
he won)'; Pope, *Windsor Forest* 303–6, describing Edward III, mentions
'The Lillies blazing on the Regal Shield'; John Dart, *Westminster Abbey*
(1723) I xvi: 'Draw mighty *Edward* as he conq'ring stood, / The Lillies on his
Shield stain'd red with *Gallick* Blood.' Cp. also Thomson, *Summer* 1484–6:

40 From haughty Gallia torn,
      And sad Chatillon, on her bridal morn
      That wept her bleeding love, and princely Clare,
      And Anjou's heroine, and the paler rose,
      The rival of her crown and of her woes,
45 And either Henry there,
      The murthered saint and the majestic lord,
      That broke the bonds of Rome,
      (Their tears, their little triumphs o'er,   (*accomp.*)
      Their human passions now no more,
50 Save charity, that glows beyond the tomb).

'With him thy Edwards and thy Henrys shine, / Names dear to fame; the first who deep impressed / On haughty Gaul the terror of thy arms.'

41. Chatillon] Mary de Valentia, Countess of Pembroke, daughter of Guy de Chatillon Comte de St. Paul in France: of whom tradition says, that her husband Audemar de Valentia, Earl of Pembroke, was slain at a Tournament on the day of his nuptials. She was the Foundress of Pembroke College or Hall, under the name of Aula Mariae de Valentia. *Mason.*

The tradition is hardly supported by the facts. Aymer de Valence, Earl of Pembroke, married Marie de Castillon, daughter of Guy IV, Count de St Pol, in July 1321, and did not die until June 1324, during an embassy to Charles IV at Paris. His wife founded Pembroke Hall in 1343.

42. Clare] Elizabeth de Burg, Countess of Clare, was Wife of John de Burg, son and heir of the Earl of Ulster, and daughter of Gilbert de Clare, Earl of Gloucester, by Joan of Acres, daughter of Edward the First. Hence the Poet gives her the epithet of 'Princely'. She founded Clare Hall. *Mason.*

Clare Hall had been founded by Dr Richard Badew in 1326 as University Hall, but it was rebuilt and renamed by Elizabeth de Burg in about 1342.

43. Anjou's heroine] Margaret of Anjou, wife of Henry the Fifth, foundress of Queen's College. The Poet has celebrated her conjugal fidelity in the former Ode:V: Epode 2d, Line 13th [i.e. *The Bard* 89]. *Mason.*

Margaret of Anjou was actually Queen Consort of Henry VI. She founded Queen's College in 1448.

paler rose] Elizabeth Widville, wife of Edward the Fourth (hence called the paler rose, as being of the House of York.) She added to the foundation of Margaret of Anjou. *Mason.*

Cp. Shakespeare's reference to the emblem of the House of York as 'this pale and angry rose', *I Henry VI* II iv 107. Elizabeth Woodville refounded and endowed Queen's College in 1465.

44. Tovey compares *Richard III* IV iv, where Margaret of Anjou and Queen Elizabeth balance their 'woes', especially ll. 40–6.

45. Henry the Sixth and Eighth. The former the founder of King's [1441], the latter the greatest benefactor to Trinity College. *Mason.*

46. saint] For G.'s other references to Henry VI, see *Eton Ode* 4 (p. 57); and *Bard* 90 (p. 194).

All that on Granta's fruitful plain
Rich streams of regal bounty poured,
And bade these awful fanes and turrets rise,
To hail their Fitzroy's festal morning come;
55 And thus they speak in soft accord
The liquid language of the skies.

Quartetto
'What is grandeur, what is power?
'Heavier toil, superior pain.
'What the bright reward we gain?
60 'The grateful memory of the good.
'Sweet is the breath of vernal shower,
'The bee's collected treasures sweet,
'Sweet music's melting fall, but sweeter yet
'The still small voice of gratitude.'

Recitative
65 Foremost and leaning from her golden cloud
The venerable Margaret see!
'Welcome, my noble son,' (she cries aloud)
'To this, thy kindred train, and me:
'Pleased in thy lineaments we trace

54. *Fitzroy*] Augustus Henry Fitzroy, Duke of Grafton.

56. Cp. *liquidas avium voces* (the liquid notes of the birds), Lucretius v 1379; 'the language of the sky', Dryden, *Hind and Panther* iii 821.

57–8. William Broome, *Epistle to Fenton* 103–4: 'None are completely wretched but the great, / Superior woes, superior stations bring.'

61. Milton, *Epitaph on Marchioness of Winchester* 40: 'New shot up from vernall showr'; and *Par. Lost* iv 641, 645–6: 'Sweet is the breath of morn, her rising sweet / ... / ... fragrant the fertil earth / After soft showers.' Cp. also 'A soft Retreat from sudden vernal Show'rs', Pope, *Spring* 98.

63. 'That strain again! it had a dying fall', *Twelfth Night* I i 4; 'While melting Musick steals upon the Sky', Pope, *Rape of the Lock* ii 49; and 'And melt away / In a dying, dying Fall', *Ode on St. Cecilia's Day* 20–1.

64. 'and after the fire a still small voice', *I Kings* xix 12; 'now in a still small tone / Your dying accents fell', Dryden, *Oedipus* II i; 'The world can't hear the small still voice', Matthew Green, *On Barclay's Apology for the Quakers* 29. Cf. also the lines omitted from the *Elegy*: 'In still small Accents whisp'ring from the Ground' etc. (see p. 131).

65. 'from whence a voice / From midst a Golden Cloud thus milde was heard', *Par. Lost* vi 27–8.

66. *Margaret*] Countess of Richmond and Derby; the Mother of Henry the Seventh, foundress of St John's [1508] and Christ's [1505] Colleges. *Mason*.

69. 'The old lineaments of his fathers grace', Spenser, *Shepheardes Calender*, 'May' 212 (quoted by G. in his 'Observations on English Metre', ed.

70   'A Tudor's fire, a Beaufort's grace.

Air
'Thy liberal heart, thy judging eye,
'The flower unheeded shall descry,
'And bid it round heaven's altars shed
'The fragrance of its blushing head:
75   'Shall raise from earth the latent gem
'To glitter on the diadem.

Recitative
'Lo, Granta waits to lead her blooming band,
'Not obvious, not obtrusive, she
'No vulgar praise, no venal incense flings;
80   'Nor dares with courtly tongue refined
'Profane thy inborn royalty of mind:
'She reveres herself and thee.

Gosse, i 340); 'What Lineaments divine we trace', Swift, *On Poetry: A Rhapsody* 417; 'Nor hope the British lineaments to trace', Johnson, *London* 101

70. The Countess was a Beaufort, and married to a Tudor [Edmund, Earl of Richmond]: hence the application of this line to the Duke of Grafton, who claims descent from both these families. *Mason.*

The pedigree was traced through Henry Fitzroy, First Duke of Grafton, an illegitimate son of Charles II. G.'s compliment contrasts sharply with Junius' comment on the same matter in his letter to Grafton, dated 30 May 1769: 'The character of the reputed ancestors of some men has made it possible for their descendants to be vicious in the extreme without being degenerate. Those of your Grace, for instance, left no distressing examples of virtue even to their legitimate posterity, and you may look back with pleasure to an illustrious pedigree in which heraldry has not left a single good quality upon record to insult or upbraid you. You have better proofs of your descent, my Lord, than the register of a marriage, or any troublesome inheritance of reputation.'

71. 'A Face untaught to feign! a judging Eye', Pope, *Epistle to Craggs* 5; and '*Dryden* alone escap'd this judging eye', *Epistle to Arbuthnot* 246.

72–6. Cp. *Elegy* 53–6 (p. 127).

77. blooming] i.e. in 'the state of anything improving and ripening to higher perfection' (Johnson).

78. 'Not obvious, not obtrusive, but retir'd', *Par. Lost* viii 504.

79. Cp. Pope on the Muse, 'No Hireling she, no Prostitute to Praise', *Epistle to Oxford* 36; 'All see 'tis Vice, and itch of vulgar praise', *Epistles to Several Persons* i 119; and 'This, from no venal or ungrateful Muse', *Epistle to Jervas* 2.

80. Pope, *Satires of Donne* iv 47–8: 'Of whose best Phrase and courtly Accent join'd, / He forms one Tongue exotic and refin'd.'

'With modest pride to grace thy youthful brow
'The laureate wreath, that Cecil wore, she brings,
85   'And to thy just, thy gentle hand
'Submits the fasces of her sway,
'While spirits blest above and men below
'Join with glad voice the loud symphonious lay.

Grand Chorus
'Through the wild waves as they roar
90   'With watchful eye and dauntless mien
'Thy steady course of honour keep,
'Nor fear the rocks nor seek the shore:
'The star of Brunswick smiles serene,
'And gilds the horrors of the deep.'

83. youthful] Grafton was born in 1735. Cp. 'Yeilded with coy submission, modest pride', *Par. Lost* iv 310.

84. [William Cecil,] Lord Treasurer Burleigh was Chancellor of the University, in the reign of Q. Elizabeth [1559]. *Mason.*

Cp. 'And Worcester's laureate wreath', Milton, *Sonnet to Cromwell* 9.

86. fasces] The rods which symbolized consular authority in ancient Rome. Cp. Dryden, *Astraea Redux* 248–9: 'Proud her returning Prince to entertain / With the submitted fasces of the main', and *Threnodia Augustalis* 516–7: 'And with a willing hand restores / The fasces of the main.' G. again echoes a passage in *Par. Lost* iv 307–9 (cp. l. 83): 'which impli'd / Subjection, but requir'd with gentle sway, / And by her yeilded, by him best received.'

87–8. See *Bard* 119 and *n.* (p. 197).

89. 'Well knows to still the wild winds when they roar', Milton, *Comus* 87.

92. Horace, *Odes* II x 1–4: *neque altum / semper urgendo neque, dum procellas / cautis horrescis, nimium premendo / litus iniquum* (neither always pressing out to sea nor too closely hugging the dangerous shore in cautious fear of storms).

94. star of Brunswick] 'The guiding star of George III. and the House of Brunswick generally. George I. was son of the Duke of Brunswick-Luneburg, who became Elector of Hanover' (Tovey).

FRAGMENTARY AND UNDATED
POEMS

42 [Translation from Statius, *Thebaid* IX 319–27]

These lines were first printed by Paget Toynbee, *Correspondence of Gray, Walpole, West and Ashton* ii 299–300, in 1915, from the MS in G.'s handwriting now at Pembroke College, with a facsimile. Walpole wrote G.'s name at the top of the MS and added at the end, 'This written when he was very young'. The boyish handwriting suggests that it was an early exercise at Eton, where G. was educated from about 1725. The MS contains a rough draft (see facsimile mentioned above), with many corrections not noted here, of the first 13 ll., a fair copy of the same passage, the original Latin, and then 3 ll. of further translation in draft.

Crenaeus, whom the nymph Ismenis bore
To Faunus on the Theban river's shore,
With new-born heat amidst his native stream
Exults in arms, which cast an iron gleam.
5 In this clear wave he first beheld the day;
On the green bank first taught his steps to stray,
To skim the parent flood and on the margin play:
Fear he disdains and scorns the power of fate,
Secure within his mother's watery state.
10 The youth exulting stems the bloody tide,
Visits each bank and stalks with martial pride,
While old Ismenus' gently-rolling wave
Delights the favourite youth within its flood to lave.
Whether the youth obliquely steers his course
15 Or cuts the downward stream with equal force,
The indulgent river strives his steps to aid.

43 [Verse Fragments]

Copied from G.'s pocketbook for 1754 by Mason into the Commonplace Book (iii 1110). First printed by Tovey, *Gray and his Friends* (1890) pp. 269–70.

Gratitude
The Joy that trembles in her eye
She bows her meek & humble head
in silent praise
beyond the power of Sound.

(Mr Pope dead)
and smart beneath the visionary scourge

–'tis Ridicule & not reproach that wounds
Their vanity & not their conscience feels

A few shall
The cadence of my song repeat
& hail thee in my words.

44 [Impromptus]

These spontaneous epigrams were preserved by Thomas Wharton and are
among his papers in the British Museum, (Egerton MS 2400, ff. 233–4).
All but the second were printed for the first time by Gosse, *Works of G.* i
140–1, in 1884. The second had been printed by Joseph Cradock, *Literary
Memoirs* (1828) iv 224, in the course of a description of the offence given by
G.'s derisive remarks on Cambridge University as printed by Mason in
1775:
'Being desirous of ascertaining who had dared to speak with high dis-
pleasure, [Mason] was informed, that the Right Reverend Dr. Keene had
give his decided opinion against them. "Has he?" replied Mason, hastily;
"I wish I had been aware of that sooner, for I purposely suppressed Gray's
Epitaph on his Lordship:

Here lies Dr. Keene, the good Bishop of Chester,
Who eat up a fat goose, but could not digest her."'

The fact that the epigrams are written consecutively in Wharton's MS
suggests that they have a common date, although this cannot be fixed with
accuracy. Edmund Keene (1714–81), Master of Peterhouse 1749–54,
became Bishop of Chester in 1752 and in May 1753 married the daughter of
a wealthy London linen draper. All the epigrams may have been written
after this last event. From 1740 to 1770 Keene also held the rich living of
Stanhope in Co. Durham, not far from Wharton's home at Old Park.
G. may have repeated the epigrams on Keene, if he did not actually compose
them then, during a visit to Wharton. Such a visit occurred in the summer of
1753, but there were later ones in 1762, 1765, 1767 and 1769. The reference
to 'Harry Vane' could be either to Henry Vane (*c.* 1705–58), who became
Baron Barnard in 1753 and Earl of Darlington in 1754, and who was
alive only during the first of these visits (shortly before his visit in
1753, G. referred to Vane in a letter to Wharton as 'your friend',
Corresp i 377); or to Henry Vane (1726–92), 2nd Earl of Darlington, whom
G. described as 'your noble Friend at Raby' in July 1764 (*Corresp* ii 839).
Raby Castle, seat of the Vanes, was not far from Old Park. Starr and Hend-
rickson suggest a date in the later 1760s for these *Impromptus* on the grounds
that most of the references to Keene in G.'s letters occur at that period; but,
as the index to G.'s *Corresp* reveals, there are almost as many in the period
1748–52 and this consideration cannot materially affect the dating.

Extempore by Mr Gr[ay] on Dr K[eene], B[ishop] of C[hester]:

> The Bishop of Chester
> Though wiser than Nestor
> And fairer than Esther,
> If you scratch him will fester.

One day the Bishop having offered to give a gentleman a goose, Mr Gr[ay] composed his epitaph thus:

> Here lies Edmund Keene Lord Bishop of Chester,
> He eat a fat goose and could not digest her—

And this upon his lady:

> Here lies Mrs Keene, the Bishop of Chester,
> She had a bad face which did sadly molest her.

Impromptu by Mr Gray, going out of Raby Castle:

> Here lives Harry Vane,
> Very good claret and fine champagne.

A couplet by Mr Gray:

> When you rise from your dinner as light as before,
> 'Tis a sign you have eat just enough and no more.

45 [Couplet about Birds]

Written after 11 June 1762. This couplet was preserved by Norton Nicholls, who recalled in his 'Reminiscences of Gray' that it was 'made by Mʳ Gray as we were walking in the spring in the neighbourhood of Cambridge' (*Corresp* iii 1290). G. first met Nicholls on 11 June 1762, when Nicholls (*c.* 1742–1809) was a pensioner of Trinity Hall; he graduated Ll.B. in 1766 and was ordained in 1767. During this period he became a close friend of G. and visited the poet annually after he left Cambridge. G. could therefore have uttered this extempore couplet in the spring of virtually any year from 1762 until his death, although 1763–67, when Nicholls was resident in Cambridge, is most likely.

In spite of the apparent spontaneity of the couplet, G. was characteristically echoing another poet, Thomson, *Spring* 24–5: 'The plovers . . . scatter o'er the heath, / And sing their wild notes to the listening waste.' *Spring* 598–601 runs: 'The thrush / And wood-lark . . . / . . . run through the sweetest length of notes'; and a line in a stanza in the Eton MS of the *Elegy*, later rejected, is 'Oft as the Woodlark piped her farewell Song'.

Mrs Piozzi copied the couplet (with minor variants) into *Thraliana* ii 925, in May 1793: 'These are two Lines of Gray the great Poet it seems; Mr Nicholls . . . repeated them to me; they stand alone–but one sees & feels they are Gray's.' Nicholls also communicated the lines to T. J. Matthias, who printed them for the first time in his edn of G.'s *Works*, ii 596, in 1814.

There pipes the woodlark, and the song-thrush there
Scatters his loose notes in the waste of air.

46 [Lines on Dr Robert Smith]

Written between 1742 and 1768. The first known reference to these lines occurs in the *Gentleman's Mag.* xxii New Series (1844) 164. In a review of Tooke's edition of the *Life and Poems of Churchill*, a note mentions the *Compleat System of Opticks* (1738) by Dr Robert Smith (1689–1768), Master of Trinity College, Cambridge, 1740–68. The reviewer adds that 'In allusion to this work Gray wrote his severe and caustic epigram on him, beginning, "What's the reason old Fobus has cut down yon tree," &c.' No earlier publication of the lines has been discovered and there was no response to a request by a contributor to *Notes and Queries*, 3rd series, iv (1863) 268, who asked for the remaining lines of the epigram. They were first printed by Gosse, *Works of G.*, revised edn, i 142, in 1902, from a MS in the possession of Professor Adam Sedgewick. Gosse added cryptically, 'There was a second stanza'. 'Fobus' in the earlier quotation was clearly incorrect, for G. invariably used that nickname for the Duke of Newcastle. Dr Smith was sometimes called 'Old Focus', because of his *System of Opticks*.

The epigram can not be dated with any precision. Its occasion was presumably a proposal by Dr Smith to cut down the Chestnut Walk at Trinity, which cannot, however, be dated. The epigram could have been written at any time between 1742 (when G. returned to Cambridge) and 1768, when Smith died.

Do you ask why old Focus Silvanus defies,
    And leaves not a chestnut in being?
'Tis not that old Focus himself has got eyes,
    But because he has writ about seeing.

47 Satire on the Heads of Houses;

or, Never a Barrel the Better Herring

First printed by Gosse, *Works of G.* i 134–5, in 1884, from the holograph MS owned by Lord Houghton. This text is followed here; variants from a copy

by Mitford are also given. Since the point of the poem is merely the ingenuity
with which G. rhymes the names of Cambridge colleges with phrases
describing the ovine lack of originality of the heads of the colleges, there is
no personal evidence within the poem for dating it; nor it is obvious that
G.'s mockery of the heads of houses was the result of any more specific
occasion than a challenge to his ingenuity. The second part of G.'s title is a
variant of a common saying meaning 'all equally bad': see Francis Grose,
Classical Dictionary of the Vulgar Tongue, ed. E. Partridge (1963) p. 185.

> O Cambridge, attend
> To the satire I've penned
> On the heads of thy Houses,
> Thou seat of the Muses!
> 5   Know the Master of Jesus
> Does hugely displease us;
> The Master of Maudlin
> In the same dirt is dawdling;
> The Master of Sidney
> 10 Is of the same kidney;
> The Master of Trinity
> To him bears affinity;
> As the Master of Keys
> Is as like as two peas,
> 15 So the Master of Queen's
> Is as like as two beans;
> The Master of King's
> Copies them in all things;
> The Master of Catherine
> 20 Takes them all for his pattern;
> The Master of Clare
> Hits them all to a hair;
> The Master of Christ
> By the rest is enticed;
> 25 But the Master of Emmanuel
> Follows them like a spaniel;

¶ 47. *Title.* Lines on the Heads of Houses. Never a barrell better Herring.
Mitford.
2. *I've*] I *Mitford.*
3. *thy*] the *Mitford.*
6. *hugely*] largely *Mitford.*
12. *him*] these *Mitford.*
13. *As the Master*] The Master *Mitford.*
15. *So the Master*] The Master *Mitford.*
20. *his*] a *Mitford.*
25. *But the Master*] The Master *Mitford.*

The Master of Benet
Is of the like tenet;
The Master of Pembroke
30 Has from them his system took;
The Master of Peter's
Has all the same features;
The Master of St John's
Like the rest of the dons.

P.S.—As to Trinity Hall
We say nothing at all.

LATIN POETRY

Note

The main aim of the following section is not to edit G.'s Latin poems on the same principles as his English poems, but to provide reliable texts and literal translations. G.'s original spelling has been modernized, his inconsistent accentuation ignored and his punctuation slightly emended on occasion in the interests of clarity. Unmetrical and ungrammatical lines have not normally been noted, unless the sense is affected. No attempt has been made to provide explanatory notes nor have G.'s numerous borrowings from classical poetry been recorded. Textual notes concern only substantive variants in holograph MSS or the earliest texts. Emendations or errors reproduced by G.'s nineteenth-century editors have normally been ignored.

48 [Latin Exercise from The Tatler]

Written at Eton and preserved by Norton Nicholls, who wrote in his 'Reminiscences' of G. (*Corresp* iii 1290) that he had asked Jacob Bryant (1715–1804), 'who was next boy to him at Eton, what sort of a scholar Gray was he said a very good one & added that he thought he could remember part of an exercise of his on the subject of the freezing & thawing of words, taken from the Spectator, the fragment is as follows'. Jacob Bryant himself, in a letter printed in the 'Life' of G. by Mitford in John Moultrie's edn of G. (1847) p. lxi, tells the same story, adding that G. wrote the lines when he was 'rather low in the fifth form'. Tovey, *Gray and His Friends*, 1890, p. 272, pointed out that they are based on *Tatler* No. 254, and not the *Spectator*, as stated by Nicholls.

> . . . pluviaeque loquaces
> Descendere iugis, et garrulus ingruit imber.

and the babbling rains came down from the hills, and the shower of language fell heavily.

49 [Paraphrase of Psalm lxxxiv]

Preserved in Mitford's transcript in his Notebook (vol iii ff. 67–69), with the following comment at the end:
'N.B. The above Ode is written in Mr Grays Hand: but evidently when young, the hand being unformed, & like a Schoolboys, tho' very plain & careful. The Leaf on which it is written, apparently torn from a Copy-book. Some of the expressions resemble those in the Gr. Chartreuse Ode.'
A similar passage introduced the first 5 stanzas of the poem when they were printed in the *Gentleman's Mag.* xxxii New Series (Oct. 1849) 343, no doubt by Mitford. The paraphrase was first published in full by Tovey, *Gray and his Friends* pp. 300–01, in 1890.

> Oh! Tecta, mentis dulcis amor meae!
> Oh! Summa Sancti religio loci!
>   Quae me laborantem perurit
>   Sacra fames, et amoenus ardor?
>
> 5 Praeceps volentem quo rapit impetus!
>   Ad limen altum tendo avidas manus,
>   Dum lingua frustratur precantem,
>   Cor tacitum mihi clamat intus.

Illic loquacem composuit domum
10 Laresque parvos Numinis in fidem
Praesentioris credit ales
Veris amans, vetus hospes arae:

Beatus ales! sed magis incola
Quem vidit aedes ante focos [Dei]
15   Cultu ministrantem perenni
Quique sacra requievit umbra.

Bis terque felix qui melius Deo
Templum sub imo pectore consecrat;
Huic vivida affulget voluptas
20   Et liquidi sine nube Soles.

Integriori fonte fluentia
Mentem piorum gaudia recreant,
Quod si datur lugere, quiddam
Dulce ferens venit ipse luctus.

25 Virtute virtus firmior evenit
Nascente semper, semper amabili
Aeterna crescit, seque in horas
Subiciit per aperta Caeli.

Me, dedicatum qui genus, et tuae
30 Iudaeae habenas tempero, regio
Madens olivo, dexter audi
Nec libeat repulisse regem.

Lux una sanctis quae foribus dedit
Haerere amatae limine ianuae,
35   Lux inter extremas columnas
Candidius mihi ridet una,

Quam Saeculorum Saecula barbaros
Inter penates sub trabe gemmea
Fastus tyrannorum, brevesque
40   Delicias, et amoena regni:

Feliciori flumine copiam
Pronaque dextra Caelicolum Pater
Elargietur, porrigetque
Divitias diuturniores.

¶ 49.14. focos Dei] focos Mitford, Gentleman's Mag. The insertion of Dei to
complete the metrical requirements follows Tovey.

O dwellings, the dear love of my soul! O supreme sanctity of this holy place!
What is this sacred hunger, this kindly flame that burns me in my toils?
Where does this headlong impulse take me, willing as I am? I stretch out

eager hands to the threshold high above. While my tongue makes me falter as I pray, my silent heart shouts within me. There the bird who loves the spring, long a guest of the altar, has set up his noisy house and entrusted his tiny Lares to the care of a more potent God. Blessed is the bird, but even more the dweller therein whom the temple sees before the altars of God, serving them with a continual ministry, and who goes to his rest within the holy shade. Twice, three times happy he who sets up a better temple to God deep in his heart; a living joy shall shine on him, and clear suns without a cloud. Delights flowing from a purer spring shall refresh the souls of the pious, but if it is allotted them to mourn, then even the grief itself brings a certain sweetness with it. From strength a greater strength comes forth; continually born anew, continually lovely, it grows eternally and soars aloft hour by hour through the clear realms of Heaven. As for me, who rule this chosen people and hold the reins of thy Judaea, anointed with the olive of kingship, hear me favourably, and may it not please thee to have rejected a king. One day permitted to linger at the holy portals, on the threshold of the loved door, one day among the outermost columns, smiles on me more brightly than all eternity among alien gods beneath jewelled beams, amid the pride of tyrants, the brief delights and pleasures of kingship. From a more blessed river, the Father of the dwellers in Heaven will pour out his abundance with an open hand, and will hold out more lasting riches.

50 [Translation of 'Away, Let Nought to Love Displeasing']

Presumably written at Eton. Mitford transcribed the poem into his Notebook (vol iii ff. 86–7) from G.'s MS, describing it as 'written with ink by Mason over Gray's pencil'. A holograph MS, presumably the same one, was sold at Sotheby's on 29 Feb. 1960 and printed by Starr and Hendrickson, who state: 'The hand seems definitely to be Gray's, although somewhat sprawling and ill formed as compared with his mature hand.' The poem had been printed by Tovey, *Gray and his Friends* pp. 298–9, in 1890. Mitford's transcript notes that it is a 'free translation of Gilbert Cooper's Ode Away let Nought to Love displeasing. See Essay on Taste p. 97'. Starr and Hendrickson, p. 250, reject this attribution to Cooper of the original poem. It does, however, occur in John Gilbert Cooper's *Letters Concerning Taste* (1755) pp. 97–8, where Cooper does not claim that the poem is his own. Although he states that it was written 'above a hundred Years ago' and has been 'as yet introduced into no modern Collection', it had in fact appeared in David Lewis's *Miscellaneous Poems by Several Hands* (1726) pp. 53–5, as follows:

Translation from the Antient British.

I

Away; let nought to Love displeasing,
My *Winifreda*, move your Care;

Let nought delay the Heav'nly Blessing,
　　Nor squeamish Pride, nor gloomy Fear.

II

What tho' no Grants of Royal Donors
　　With pompous Titles grace our Blood?
We'll shine in more substantial Honours,
　　And, to be Noble, we'll be Good.

III

Our Name, while Virtue thus we tender,
　　Will sweetly sound where-e'er 'tis spoke:
And all the Great ones, They shall wonder,
　　How they respect such little Folk.

IV

What tho', from Fortune's lavish Bounty,
　　No mighty Treasures we possess?
We'll find, within our Pittance, Plenty,
　　And be content without Excess.

V

Still shall each kind returning Season
　　Sufficient for our Wishes give:
For we will live a Life of Reason,
　　And that's the only Life to live.

VI

Through Youth and Age, in Love excelling,
　　We'll Hand in Hand together tread;
Sweet-smiling Peace shall crown our Dwelling,
　　And Babes, sweet-smiling Babes, our Bed.

VII

How should I love the pretty Creatures,
　　While round my Knees they fondly clung,
To see them look their Mother's Features,
　　To hear them lisp their Mother's Tongue.

VIII

And, when with Envy Time transported
　　Shall think to rob us of our Joys;
You'll, in your Girls, again be courted,
　　And I'll go wooing in my Boys.

Vah, tenero quodcunque potest obsistere amori,
　　exulet ex animo et Delia cara, tuo;
Ne timor infelix, mala ne fastidia sancti
　　gaudia distineant, Delia cara, tori.
5　Quid si nulla olim regalia munera nostras
　　ornarunt titulis divitiisque domos?
At nobis proprioque et honesto lumine claris
　　ex meritis ortum nobile nomen erit.

Dum tanto colimus virtutem ardore volabit
10   gloria dulce sonans nostra per ora virum.
Interea nostram mirata superbia famam
   tales splendoris tantum habuisse gemet.
Quid si Diva potens nummorum divitis auri
   haud largo nostros proluit imbre lares?
15 At nobis erit ex humili bona copia censu;
   vitaque non luxu splendida, laeta tamen.
Sic horas per quisque suas revolubilis annus
   nostra quod expleret vota precesque dabit.
Nam duce natura peragemus, Delia, vitam:
20   vita ea vitalis dicier una potest.
Et iuvenes et amore senes florebimus aequo.
   Et vitae una alacres conficiemus iter.
Nostros interea ornabit pax alma Penates,
   iucundum pueri, pignora cara, torum.
25 Oh quanta aspicerem lepidam dulcedine gentem
   luderet ad patrium dum pia turba genu
Maternos vultu ridenti effingere vultus,
   Balbo maternos ore referre sonos.
Iamque senescentes cum nos inviderit aetas
30   nostraque se credet surripuisse bona,
In vestris tu rursus amabere pulchra puellis,
   rursus ego in pueris, Delia, amabo meis.

¶ *50.12. Tales*] *In the MS G. seems first to have written* Talis *and then changed the* i *to* e.

Ah, let whatever can stand in the way of tender love be exiled from your mind, dear Delia; may no unlucky fear, nor misplaced prudery delay the joys of the holy marriage-bed, dear Delia. What does it matter if no royal gifts in times past have embellished my house with titles and wealth? We will derive a noble name for ourselves from praiseworthy deeds, with a deserved lustre all our own. As long as we cultivate virtue with such fervour, our fame will fly abroad, sounding sweetly on the lips of men. Meanwhile, Pride, astonished at our reputation, will bewail that two such have gained so great a glory. What matter if the goddess who has power over the coins of wealth-giving gold has poured upon our house no lavish shower? Still we will have a comfortable plenty for our humble station, and our life, though not striking in its luxury, will nevertheless be happy. Thus each returning year, from hour to hour, will grant the fulfilment of our prayers and vows. For let us spend our life, Delia, with Nature as our guide; for that life alone can be called true living. In youth and age we will enjoy an unaltered love, and together we will come to the end of life's road with unflagging energy. Meanwhile, kindly Peace will adorn our house, and sons, dear pledges, our happy bed. O with what rapture would I look on the charming creatures while, a loving band, they play at their father's knee, displaying their mother's looks in their own smiling faces and echoing their mother's accents in their stammering voices. And when at last, as we grow old, age blights us and believes it has snatched away our joys, then you will be loved again, beautiful as you are, in your daughters and I, Delia, will love again in my sons.

51 [Latin Verses at Eton]

The text of these verses is in the Commonplace Book (i 50–1), where they are entitled 'Play-Exercise at Eton' in the margin at the end. In the index they are called 'Knowledge of Himself, Latin Verses at Eton'. First published by Gosse in 1884, i 163–4. An article by C. W. Brodribb in *Notes and Queries*, 12th series, viii (1921) 101–2, pointed out the many parallels with Pope's *Essay on Man* Bk i, which fixes the date of these verses between Feb. 1733 and Sept. 1734, when G. left Eton. A note in *The Correspondence of Gray, Walpole, West and Ashton*, ed. Paget Toynbee, (1915) i 137, states that 'A "sent-up for Play" exercise is an exercise especially honoured by being made the occasion of a holiday. The more ordinary type of sent-up exercise is called "sent-up for good".'

> — quem te Deus esse
> Iussit et humana qua parte locatus es in re
> Disce—   Persius, *Satires* iii 71–73

Pendet homo incertus gemini ad confinia mundi
Cui parti accedat dubius; consurgere stellis
An socius velit, an terris ingloria moles
Reptare, ac muto se cum grege credere campis:
5   Inseruisse choro divum hic se iactat, et audet
Telluremque vocare suam, fluctusque polumque,
Et quodcunque videt, proprios assumit in usus.
'Me propter iam vere expergefacta virescit
'Natura in flores, herbisque illudit, amatque
10   'Pingere telluris gremium, mihi vinea foetu
'Purpureo turget, dulcique rubescit honore;
'Me rosa, me propter liquidos exhalat odores;
'Luna mihi pallet, mihi Olympum Phoebus inaurat,
'Sidera mi lucent, volvunturque aequora ponti.'
15   Sic secum insistit, tantumque haec astra decores
Aestimat esse suae sedis, convexaque caeli
Ingentes scenas, vastique aulaea theatri.
At tibi per deserta fremit, tibi tigris acerbum
Succenset, nemorum fulmen, Gangeticus horror?
20   Te propter mare se tollit, surgitque tumultu?
Hic ubi rimari, atque impallescere libris
Perstitit, anne valet qua vi connexa per aevum
Conspirent elementa sibi, serventque tenorem;

Sufficiant scatebrae unde mari, fontesque perennes
25 Iugis aquae fluviis, unde aether sidera pascat,
Pandere? nequaquam: secreta per avia mundi
Debile carpit iter, vix, et sub luce maligna
Pergit, et incertam tendit trepidare per umbram.
Fata obstant; metam Parcae posuere sciendi,
30 Et dixere: veni huc, Doctrina, hic terminus esto.
Non super aethereas errare licentius auras
Humanum est, at scire hominem; breve limite votum
Exiguo claudat, nec se quaesiverit extra.
Errat, qui cupit oppositos transcendere fines,
35 Extenditque manus ripae ulterioris amore;
Illic gurges late hiat, illic saeva vorago,
Et caligantes longis ambagibus umbrae.
    Oceani fontes, et regna sonantia fluctu,
Machina stellantis caeli, terraeque cavernae
40 Nullis laxantur mortalibus, isque aperiret
Haec qui arcana poli, magnumque recluderet aequor,
Frangeret aeternos nexus, mundique catenam.
    Plurimus (hic error, demensque libido lacessit)
In superos, caelumque ruit, sedesque relinquit,
45 Quas natura dedit proprias, iussitque tueri.
Humani sortem generis pars altera luget
Invidet armento, et campi sibi vindicat herbam.
'O quis me in pecoris felicia transferet arva,
'In loca pastorum deserta, atque otia dia?
50 'Cur mihi non lyncisve oculi, vel odora canum vis
'Additur, aut gressus cursu glomerare potestas?
'Aspice, ubi, tenues dum texit aranea casses,
'Funditur in telam et late per stamina vivit!
'Quid mihi non tactus eadem exquisita facultas,
55 'Taurorumve tori solidi, pennaeve volucrum.'
    Pertaesos sortis doceant responsa silere.
Si tanto valeas contendere acumine visus,
Et graciles penetrare atomos; non aethera possis
Suspicere, aut lati spatium comprendere ponti.
60 Vis si adsit maior naris; quam, vane, doleres,
Extinctus fragranti aura, dulcique veneno!
Si tactus, tremat hoc corpus, solidoque dolore
Ardeat in membris, nervoque laboret in omni;
Sive auris, fragor exanimet, cum rumpitur igne
65 Fulmineo caelum, totusque admurmurat aether:
Quam demum humanas, priscasque requirere dotes
Attonitus nimium cuperes, nimiumque reverti
In solitam speciem, veterique senescere forma.
    Nubila seu tentes, vetitumque per aera surgas,

70   Sive rudes poscas sylvas, et lustra ferarum;
      Falleris; in medio solium Sapientia fixit.
      Desine sectari maiora, minorave sorte,
      Quam Deus, et rerum attribuit natura creatrix.

Learn what God has commanded you to be, and in what station you are placed in human affairs.

PERSIUS.

Man is suspended in doubt on the borders of two worlds, not knowing to which side he should tend; whether he should wish to rise to join the stars, or, an ignoble hulk, to crawl over the earth and trust himself to the fields with the dumb flock. He boasts that he has taken his place in the chorus of the gods and dares to call the earth, the waters and the sky his own, possessing for himself whatever he sees. 'It is on my account that in the spring renewed nature blossoms into flower, lavishes her plants and loves to colour the lap of earth; for me the vine swells with its purple fruit, and grows red with its sweet adornment. It is on my account, mine alone, that the rose breathes out her pure scents; for me the moon shines pale, and for me Phoebus gilds Olympus; for me the stars shine and the waters of the sea roll on.'

So he persuades himself and imagines these stars to be simply the ornaments of his dwelling and the vaults of heaven a vast stage, and the curtains of an immense theatre.

But is it for you that the tiger ranges through the wilderness, is it for you that he burns with a fierce rage, the dire thunderbolt of the forests, the terror of the Ganges? Is it for your sake that the sea boils up and rises in tumult?

Does man, when he pursues knowledge and grows pale over his books, gain the power to disclose by what force the elements, joined together through eternity, retain their harmony and maintain their course unchanged? Or to disclose whence the gushing springs fill up the sea and the unceasing streams the rivers of fresh water, and how the ether nourishes the stars?

By no means! He takes his feeble way across the remote and lonely regions of the world, scarcely advancing through the half-light and moving fearfully through the uncertain shadows. Destiny opposes him; the Fates have put a limit to knowledge and said, 'Come this far, Learning, but let this be your boundary. It is not given to man to wander more freely above the upper air, but to know Man. He should confine his little desires within narrow bounds and not search beyond himself. He errs who wishes to pass the limits set for him, and reaches out his hands in longing for the farther shore. There the raging torrent stretches wide and the fearsome whirlpool, and the shadows darkening in endless obscurities.' The springs of ocean and the regions thunderous with the flood, the workings of the starry heavens and the caverns of the earth are not revealed to any mortal, and the man who would lay bare the secrets of the sky and uncover the great waters would break the eternal bonds and the chain of the universe. Most men (so this folly and mad desire spurs them on) rush upwards to the heavens and the sky, and abandon the dwellings which Nature gave to be their own and bade them keep. Another group bewails the lot of the human race, envies the dumb beasts and claims for itself the grass of the field. 'O who will remove me to the happy pastures of the herd, to the unfrequented haunts of shepherds, and to blessed idleness? Why have I not been endowed with the eyes of the lynx or the keen scent of dogs, or the power to gallop with rapid tread? See where the spider weaves her slender snares, takes her place in the web, and spends her life now here, now there, among the threads! Why have I not the same delicate sense of touch or the powerful frame of bulls or the wings of birds?' May these answers teach those who are dissatisfied with their lot to be silent. If you were able to compete with such a sharpness of vision, and make out the minute atoms, you would not be able to look up at the sky or take in the extent of the broad sea. And if you were to have a more acute power of smell, what pain you would feel, foolish man, dying of a fragrant breeze, a sweet poison! If a more sensitive touch, the body would tremble and burn in all its limbs with unrelieved pain, and suffer in every nerve. If keener hearing, the crash would leave you senseless when the sky explodes in thunderous fire and all the heavens re-echo. In short, driven out of your mind, how you would long to recover the human attributes you once had, return to your accustomed nature and grow old in your original form!

If you aim for the clouds or try to soar through the forbidden air, or if you demand untrodden forests and the lairs of beasts, you will be wrong. Wisdom has set up her throne in the middle way. Cease from trying to pursue a lot greater or lesser than that which God and Nature, the mother of all things, has bestowed.

52 [Hymeneal]

First published in *Gratulatio Academiae Cantabrigiensis Auspicatissimus Frederici Walliae Principis & Augustae Principissae Saxo-Gothae Nuptias Celebrantis*, printed by the Cambridge University Press in 1736. The marriage of Frederick, Prince of Wales and Princess Augusta of Saxe-Gotha took place on 27 April 1736. Walpole and Ashton also contributed to the collection in Latin, as did G.'s future friend, Thomas Wharton, in Greek. Richard West wrote a Latin poem for the Oxford *Gratulatio*. Ashton referred to G.'s poem in a letter to West on 11 April 1736 ('Master Gray seems to touch upon the Manner of Claudian'), *Correspondence of Gray, Walpole, West and Ashton*, ed. Toynbee, i 68; and on 24 May 1736 West told G. (*Corresp* i 43): 'Your Hymenêal I was told was the best in the Cambridge Collection before I saw it, and indeed, it is no great compliment to tell you I thought it so when I had seen it, but sincerely it pleased me best.' The poem is not titled in the *Gratulatio*, which provides the only text. Mason referred derisively to the poem in 1775 (*Memoirs* p. 10n), saying that 'adulatory verses of this kind ... are usually buried, as they ought to be, in the trash with which they are surrounded. Every person, who feels himself a poet, ought to be above prostituting his powers on such occasions, and extreme youth (as was the case with Mr. Gray) is the only thing that can apologize for having done it.' The poem was first reprinted by Stephen Jones in 1799.

> Ignarae nostrum mentes, et inertia corda,
> Dum curas regum, et sortem miseramur iniquam,

Quae solio affixit, vetuitque calescere flamma
Dulci, quae dono Divum, gratissima serpit
5　Viscera per, mollesque animis lene implicat aestus;
Nec teneros sensus, Veneris nec praemia norunt,
Eloquiumve oculi, aut facunda silentia linguae:

Scilicet ignorant lacrimas, saevosque dolores,
Dura rudimenta, et violentae exordia flammae;
10　Scilicet ignorant quae flumine tinxit amaro
Tela Venus, caecique armamentaria Divi,
Irasque, insidiasque, et tacitum sub pectore vulnus;
Namque sub ingressu, primoque in limine Amoris
Luctus et ultrices posuere cubilia Curae;
15　Intus habent dulces Risus, et Gratia sedem,
Et roseis resupina toris, roseo ore Voluptas:
Regibus huc faciles aditus; communia spernunt
Ostia, iamque expers duris custodibus istis
Panditur accessus, penetraliaque intima templi.

20　Tuque Oh! Angliacis, Princeps, spes optima regnis,
Ne tantum, ne finge metum; quid imagine captus
Haeres, et mentem pictura pascis inani?
Umbram miraris: nec longum tempus, et Ipsa
Ibit in amplexus, thalamosque ornabit ovantes.
25　Ille tamen tabulis inhians longum haurit amorem,
Affatu fruitur tacito, auscultatque tacentem
Immemor artificis calami, risumque ruboremque
Aspicit in fucis, pictaeque in virginis ore:
Tanta Venus potuit; tantus tenet error amantes.

30　Nascere, magna Dies, qua sese AUGUSTA Britanno
Committat Pelago, patriamque relinquat amoenam;
Cuius in adventum iam nunc tria regna secundos
Attolli in plausus, dulcique accensa furore
Incipiunt agitare modos, et carmina dicunt:
35　Ipse animo sedenim iuvenis comitatur euntem,
Explorat ventos, atque auribus aëra captat,
Atque auras, atque astra vocat crudelia; pectus
Intentum exultat, surgitque arrecta cupido;
Incusat spes aegra fretum, solitoque videtur
40　Latior effundi pontus, fluctusque morantes.

Nascere, Lux maior, qua sese AUGUSTA Britanno
Committat iuveni totam, propriamque dicabit;
At citius (precor) Oh! cedas melioribus astris:
Nox finem pompae, finemque imponere curis
45　Possit, et in thalamos furtim deducere nuptam;
Sufficiat requiemque viris, et amantibus umbras:

Adsit Hymen, et subridens cum matre Cupido
Accedant, sternantque toros, ignemque ministrent;
Ilicet haud pictae incandescit imagine formae
50 Ulterius iuvenis, verumque agnoscit amorem.

Sculptile sicut ebur, faciemque arsisse venustam
Pygmaliona canunt; ante hanc suspiria ducit,
Alloquiturque amens, flammamque et vulnera narrat;
Implorata Venus iussit cum vivere signum,
55 Femineam inspirans animam; quae gaudia surgunt,
Audiit ut primae nascentia murmura linguae,
Luctari in vitam, et paulatim volvere ocellos
Sedulus, aspexitque nova splendescere flamma;
Corripit amplexu vivam, iamque oscula iungit
60 Acria confestim, recipitque rapitque; prioris
Immemor ardoris, Nymphaeque oblitus eburneae.

Ignorant are our minds and unknowing our hearts, when we pity the cares of kings and that inequitable fate which ties them to the throne and forbids them to grow ardent with that sweet flame which, by the gift of the gods, glides so pleasingly through our inmost parts and gently twines its soothing warmth about our spirits. They know (we imagine) neither those tender sensations nor the rewards of Venus, neither the eloquence of the eye nor the expressive silence of the tongue. In truth, it is only tears and bitter sorrows of which they are ignorant, the harsh beginnings and the kindling of the fierce flame. In truth, it is only the darts which Venus dips in the bitter river and the armoury of the blind god of which they are ignorant, the quarrels and treacheries and the unspoken wound in the heart. For indeed it is true that, at the entrance and on the first threshold of Love, weeping and vengeful cares have chosen out their resting-places. Within, sweet Laughter and Affection have their abode and Pleasure, rosy-lipped, lying on rose-strewn couches. For kings, the entrance to this place is easy; they disdain the common door and already, untroubled by those stern guards, the way lies open and even the inmost recesses of the temple. And you, O Prince, the brightest hope of the British realms, must not so much as imagine fear. Why do you hesitate, rapt by her image, and feast your thought on an insubstantial picture? Now you marvel at a shadow—just a little while and the woman herself will come to your embraces and adorn the joyful bridal chambers. But still, poring over the picture, he drinks a great draught of love, enjoys a wordless converse and, forgetful of the painter's brush, listens to her though she says nothing, detecting a smile and a blush in the rosy pigment and on the lips of the painted maiden. So powerful is Venus, and such fantasy seizes lovers.

Begin, great Day on which Augusta entrusts herself to the English Channel and leaves behind her pleasant fatherland. Already, against her arrival, three kingdoms, fired by a happy ardour, are beginning to stir themselves to welcoming applause, to strike up music and declaim poems. But the young Prince himself accompanies her in imagination as she approaches; he makes trial of the winds and listens to every gust, calling the breezes and the stars cruel. His eager heart exults and excited desire arises. Fevered with longing he curses the ocean, and the sea seems to be wider spread than its wont, and the

waves also that delay her. Begin, thou greater Day on which Augusta will give
herself entirely to the British prince and call herself his. But quickly, I beg you,
give place to the stars, for they are better. Let Night have power to put an
end to the ceremonial and to their care and let it lead the bride in secret to
the bridal chamber. Let it provide rest for men and shadows for lovers.
May Hymen be there, and may smiling Cupid and his mother approach,
strew the couch and keep watch over the fire. From this time on, the Prince
will glow with ardour at a figure which is certainly not painted and will
recognize true Love.

So, the poets tell, did Pygmalion burn for the lovely form of the sculptured
ivory. Before it he breathed sighs and addressed it wildly, telling of his
burning passion and the wounds of love. But when Venus at his entreaty
ordered the statue to live, imbuing it with a woman's soul, what joys surged
up as he heard the nascent sounds of her first utterances and eagerly watched
her struggle to life and little by little roll her eyes and grow bright with a
new radiance. He seizes the living creature in his embrace and at once presses
his burning lips to hers, giving and taking kisses, oblivious of his former love
and forgetful of the ivory nymph.

53 In D[iem]: 29ᵃᵐ Maii

G.'s holograph MS is Pembroke College MS. LC. II. 86. First printed by
Gosse, i 166, in 1884. There is no evidence for dating the poem but, like the
following exercise, it may be related to a statement in a letter from Walpole
to West, 9 Nov. 1735 (*Correspondence of Gray, Walpole, West and Ashton*,
ed. Toynbee, i 50): 'We have not the least poetry stirring here; for I can't
call verses on the 5th of November and 30th of January by that name, more
than four lines on a chapter in the New Testament is an epigram.' The anni-
versary of Guy Fawkes's attempt to blow up Parliament in 1605, of Charles
II's birthday and the day of his return to London at his Restoration in 1660
(the subject of the present verses), and the anniversary of the execution of
Charles I on 30 Jan. 1649 (referred to in Walpole's letter) were often the
themes of undergraduate exercises. (See Milton's *In Quintum Novembris*
written at Cambridge when he was seventeen.) For ceremonies at Cambridge
on these days, see Adam Wall, *Account of the Different Ceremonies Observed
in . . . the University of Cambridge* (1798) pp. 36, 51–2.

The first line of the present exercise echoes, no doubt deliberately, the
first line of Lucan's *Pharsalia*.

> Bella per Angliacos plusquam civilia campos
> Praeteritae videre dies: desaevit Enyo,
> Tempestasque iacet; circum vestigia flammae
> Delentur, pacisque iterum consurgit imago:
> 5 Litore, quo nuper Martis fremuere procellae,
> Alcyone tutum struit imperterrita nidum.
> Reddita spes solii regno, regemque vagantem

Patria cara tenet, dictisque affatur amicis.
Quas ego te terras, quot per discrimina vectum
10 Accipio, quantis iactatum, Nate, periclis?
Quam metui, nequid tibi Gallia regna nocerent,
Belgarumque plagae, periuraque Scotia patri!
Quam tremui, cum laeva tuas Vigornia turmas
Fudit praecipites, hostemque remisit ovantem!
15 Tuque, Arbor, nostrae felix tutela coronae,
Gloria camporum, et luci regina vocare:
Tota tibi silva assurget, quae fronde dedisti
Securas latebras, nemorosa palatia regi;
Sacra Iovi Latio quondam, nunc sacra Britanno.
20 Olim factus honos, illi velasse capillos,
Qui leto civem abripuit, salvumque reduxit;
Iam potes ipsa tribus populis praestare salutem.

On the twenty-ninth day of May

Days that are past have seen the worst of civil wars on the English plains; Enyo [Goddess of War] has spent her rage and the storm has died away; all around, the signs of the conflagration are smoothed away and the image of peace rises once more. On the shore where recently the gusty winds of Mars raged, the halcyon, unmolested, now builds her nest securely. The hope of the throne has been restored to the kingdom and the beloved fatherland receives its wandering king and addresses him with kindly words.

'After you have travelled over so many lands and through so many hazards, threatened by such great dangers, my son, I now welcome you home. How afraid I was that the Gallic kingdoms would do you some harm and the regions of the Belgians, and Scotland which forswore your father! How I trembled when the ill-omened field of Worcester scattered your squadrons in headlong flight and sent back the enemy in triumph! And thou, O Tree, the happy preserver of our Crown, shall be called the glory of the plains and the queen of the wood. To you the whole forest shall rise, you who yielded a safe hiding-place in your branches, a shady palace for a king! Once you were sacred to Jove in Latium and now you will be sacred in Britain. Of old, the honour was conferred of crowning [with oak] the head of the man who rescued a fellow-citizen from death and brought him back in safety; now you yourself can claim to have been the salvation of three peoples.'

54 In 5ᵗᵃᵐ Novembris

G.'s holograph MS is Pembroke College MS L.C.II.86. First printed by Gosse, i 167–8, in 1884. See headnote to previous poem. In l. 32, apparently for metrical reasons, G. has 'haud' where 'non' would be less awkward; the line has been translated in the only way possible.

Lis anceps, multosque diu protracta per annos,
  iudice nec facile dissoluenda fuit;
Cui tribuenda modo sceleratae praemia palmae?
  quem merito tantus nobilitaret honos?
5 Multa sibi Romae saevi ascivere tyranni,
  multa sibi primus, posteriorque Nero:
Qui retulit praedam nostro de litore conchas:
  quem dedit ex pura Flavia stirpe domus:
Multa sibi Phalaris petiit, Trinacria pestis;
10   diraque causa tui, magna Diana, rogi:
Quaeque referre mora est, portenta replentia famae
  invitae annales, crimine nota suo
At demum innumeris belli Anglia clara triumphis
  militis ostentat parta tropaea manu;
15 Nec satis est, gemina palma insignita nitere
  artibus et bellis, orbis et esse decus;
Accedat nactae sceleris nisi gloria famae,
  et laudis numeros impleat illa suae:
Ex natis surgit mens aspernata priores,
20   et tentare novas ingeniosa vias,
Quae caecis novit Martem sepelire latebris,
  tectosque a visu Solis habere dolos;
Scilicet, ut fallat, non ire in viscera terrae,
  non dubitat simili clade vel ipse mori.
25 Iamque incepit opus: careat successibus, opto;
  et vetet inceptum Fors, precor, istud opus:
Nec frustra; effulget subito lux aurea caeli,
  (aspice) rimanti dum domus atra patet;
Reclusamque vides fraudem, letique labores,
30   antraque miraris sulphure foeta suo:
Quod si venturi haec armamentaria fati
  panderat haud sacri gratia dia poli;
Iure scelus se iactaret, procerumque ruina
  tantum una gentem perdomuisse manu.

On the fifth day of November

There has been a dispute, evenly-balanced and protracted for many years,
not easily to be settled by an arbitrator: to whom should the prize for out-
standing wickedness be awarded? Whom would such a distinction deservedly
make notorious? Many were the claims which cruel tyrants made for them-
selves at Rome—many did the first and many the later one, Nero; and he who
took shells back as booty from our shores and he whom the Flavian house
produced from untarnished stock. Much did Phalaris claim for himself, the
terror of Sicily, and the grim cause, great Diana, of your funeral pyre. It
would take too long to relate all the deeds which fill up the histories of in-
voluntary notoriety, each distinguished for its own crime.

But at last England, famous for innumerable triumphs in war, displays trophies won by the soldier's hand. And yet it is not enough to shine conspicuous for a double prize, in the Arts and in War, and to be the glory of the world, unless the splendour of a reputation won by wickedness is added and thus fulfils the measure of her own praise. Among her sons arises a spirit which despises all predecessors and is full of invention in testing new paths, which knows how to bury Mars in secret ambushes and keep its cunning devices hidden from the eye of the sun. Indeed, in order to escape detection, it does not hesitate to go down to the bowels of the earth, or even to perish itself in the same disaster. Already the deed has begun; my wish is that it may meet with no success; and may Fortune, I pray, forbid that deed which has already been begun. Nor do I pray in vain; behold, suddenly the golden light of Heaven shines forth until the black vault lies open to the searcher. And you may see the plot revealed and the works of death, and marvel at the caverns filled with their own sulphur. But if the blessed grace of the sacred Heaven had not revealed this armoury of coming doom, then he could rightly boast of his wickedness and that single-handed, by the destruction of its leaders, he had overwhelmed such a nation.

55 Luna habitabilis

Written between 29 Dec. 1736 and 17 March 1737. On the first of these dates G. wrote to Walpole (*Corresp* i 59): 'the Moderatour has asked me to make the Tripos-Verses this year'. The 'Tripos-Verses' were Latin verses written by an undergraduate and distributed with the lists of successful Tripos candidates each year. They would have had to be produced at a Congregation on the Thursday after Mid-Lent, which in 1737 would be 17 March. See Whibley's appendix (*Corresp* iii 1198–9). Whibley mentions that a printed copy of *Luna habitabilis* was sold by Sotheby's at a sale of G.'s books and MSS on 4 Aug. 1854, and this was no doubt one of the original copies for distribution, none of which are otherwise known to have survived. The poem was reprinted in *Musae Etonenses* ii 107–12, in 1755, the only authority for the text. There are a few comments on the poem in a letter from West to Walpole, 18 April 1737 (*Correspondence of Gray, Walpole, West and Ashton* i 132–5). Mason referred only in passing to this poem, *Memoirs* p. 36 *n*, in 1775, and it was apparently not printed again after 1755 until it appeared in the *Gentleman's Mag.* xci (Oct. 1821) pt ii 315–6. Two misprints in *Musae Etonenses* – 'ossa' for 'Ossa' (l. 44) and 'propriori' for 'propiori' (l. 73) – were corrected by later editors.

> Dum nox rorantes non incomitata per auras
> Urget equos, tacitoque inducit sidera lapsu;
> Ultima, sed nulli soror infitienda sororum,
> Huc mihi, Musa: tibi patet alti ianua caeli,
> 5 Astra vides, nec te numeri, nec nomina fallunt.
> Huc mihi, Diva veni: dulce est per aperta serena
> Vere frui liquido, campoque errare silenti;

Vere frui dulce est; modo tu dignata petentem
Sis comes, et mecum gelida spatiare sub umbra.
10   Scilicet hos orbes, caeli haec decora alta putandum
          est,
Noctis opes, nobis tantum lucere; virumque
Ostentari oculis, nostrae laquearia terrae,
Ingentes scenas, vastique aulaea theatri?
Oh! quis me pennis aethrae super ardua sistet
15   Mirantem, propiusque dabit convexa tueri;
Teque adeo, unde fluens reficit lux mollior arva,
Pallidiorque dies, tristes solata tenebras?
Sic ego, subridens Dea sic ingressa vicissim:
Non pennis opus hic, supera ut simul illa petamus:
20   Disce Puer potius caelo deducere Lunam;
Neu crede ad magicas te invitum accingier artes,
Thessalicosve modos: ipsam descendere Phoeben
Conspicies novus Endymion; seque offeret ultro
Visa tibi ante oculos, et nota maior imago.
25   Quin tete admoveas (tumuli super aggere spectas
Compositum) tubulo; simul imum invade canalem
Sic intenta acie, caeli simul alta patescent
Atria; iamque, ausus Lunaria visere regna,
Ingrediere solo, et caput inter nubila condes.
30   Ecce autem! vitri se in vertice sistere Phoeben
Cernis, et Oceanum, et crebris freta consita terris;
Panditur ille atram faciem caligine condens
Sublustri, refugitque oculos, fallitque tuentem;
Integram Solis lucem quippe haurit aperto
35   Fluctu avidus radiorum, et longos imbibit ignes:
Verum his, quae, maculis variata nitentibus, auro
Caerula discernunt, celso sese insula dorso
Plurima protrudit, praetentaque litora saxis;
Liberior datur his quoniam natura, minusque
40   Lumen depascunt liquidum; sed tela diei
Detorquent, retroque docent se vertere flammas.
Hinc longos videas tractus, terrasque iacentes
Ordine candenti, et claros se attollere montes;
Montes queis Rhodope assurgat, quibus Ossa nivali
45   Vertice: tum scopulis infra pendentibus antra
Nigrescunt clivorum umbra, nemorumque tenebris.
Non rores illi, aut desunt sua nubila mundo;
Non frigus gelidum, atque herbis gratissimus imber:
His quoque nota ardet picto Thaumantias arcu,

¶ *55.13.* Taken over from *Latin Exercise at Eton* 17.
21. accingier] *all editors*; accingere *1755.*

50   Os roseum Aurorae, propriique crepuscula caeli.
     Et dubitas tantum certis cultoribus orbem
     Destitui? exercent agros, sua moenia condunt
     Hi quoque, vel Martem invadunt, curantque triumphos
     Victores: sunt hic sua praemia laudi;
55   His metus, atque amor, et mentem mortalia tangunt.
        Quin, uti nos oculis iam nunc iuvat ire per arva,
     Lucentesque plagas Lunae, pontumque profundum:
     Idem illos etiam ardor agit, cum se aureus effert
     Sub sudum globus, et Terrarum ingentior orbis;
60   Scilicet omne aequor tum lustrant, scilicet omnem
     Tellurem, gentesque polo sub utroque iacentes:
     Et quidam aestivi indefessus ad aetheris ignes
     Pervigilat, noctem exercens, caelumque fatigat;
     Iam Galli apparent, iam se Germania late
65   Tollit, et albescens pater Apenninus ad auras:
     Iam tandem in Borean, en! parvulus Anglia naevus
     (Quanquam aliis longe fulgentior) extulit oras:
     Formosum extemplo lumen, maculamque nitentem
     Invisunt crebri proceres, serumque tuendo
70   Haerent, certatimque suo cognomine signant:
     Forsitan et Lunae longinquus in orbe tyrannus
     Se dominum vocat, et nostra se iactat in aula.
        Terras possim alias propriori Sole calentes
     Narrare; atque alias, iubaris queis parcior usus,
75   Lunarum chorus, et tenuis penuria Phoebi:
     Ni, meditans eadem haec audaci evolvere cantu,
     Iam pulsat citharam Soror, et praeludia tentet.
        Non tamen has proprias laudes, nec facta silebo
     Iampridem in fatis, patriaeque oracula famae.
80   Tempus erit, sursum totos contendere coetus
     Quo cernes longo excursu, primosque colonos
     Migrare in lunam, et notos mutare Penates:
     Dum stupet obtutu tacito vetus incola, longeque
     Insolitas explorat aves, classemque volantem.
85   Ut quondam ignotum marmor, camposque natantes
     Tranavit Zephyros visens, nova regna, Columbus;
     Litora mirantur circum, mirantur et undae
     Inclusas acies ferro, turmasque biformes,
     Monstraque feta armis, et non imitabile fulmen.
90   Foedera mox icta, et gemini commercia mundi,
     Agminaque assueto glomerata sub aethere cerno.
     Anglia, quae pelagi iamdudum torquet habenas,
     Exercetque frequens ventos, atque imperat undae;
     Aeris attollet fasces, veteresque triumphos
95   Huc etiam feret, et victis dominabitur auris.

That the Moon is habitable

While Night, not unaccompanied, drives her horses on through the dew-laden air and draws on the stars in their silent course; come hither to me, Muse, youngest of all, but not to be disowned by any of your sisters. To you the doors of the lofty sky lie open, you see the stars and neither their numbers nor their names escape you. Come hither to assist me, Muse; it is sweet to enjoy the clear spring under an open sky and to wander on the silent plain; sweet indeed to enjoy the spring, if only you, responsive to my prayers, would be my companion and walk with me in the cool darkness. Surely we are not to think that these spheres and these lofty ornaments of the heavens, the riches of the Night, shine only on us; that they are displayed only to the sight of men, the decorated ceilings of our world, the vast stage and the curtains of a huge theatre. O who will convey me marvelling as I fly above the heights of the upper air and allow me to look at the vault more closely, even as far as you, from whom a milder light flows, discovering the fields again, a paler daylight which cheers the gloomy shades.

Thus I spoke, and the goddess with a smile thus began in turn: There is no need for wings to enable us to seek the upper regions together. Learn, my son, rather to bring the moon down from the sky. And do not think that you must employ magic arts, however reluctantly, or Thessalian incantations: you, a second Endymion, will see Phoebe herself descend; and of her own free will she will present herself to your view, before your very eyes, greater in appearance than you have ever known her.

Merely set yourself at the end of a small tube (you see it set up on the top of a high mound), and as soon as you put your watchful eye to the tube the lofty habitations of Heaven will lie revealed. And at once, even as you dare to gaze upon the lunar regions, you will tread the earth and yet place your head among the clouds.

But look! You can see Phoebe taking her place at the upper end of the glass, and an ocean and straits strewn with many lands. This part (the ocean) is displayed even as it hides its darkened face in a twilight mist; it evades the sight and cheats the spectator, for it draws the pure light of the sun into its open flood, greedy for the rays, and drinks in the far-travelled fires. As for these (straits) speckled with shining spots, which divide the deep blue tracts with gold, many an island protrudes itself with a high ridge and shores lying in front of rocks. For to these regions is granted a more generous nature and they do not consume the pure light so completely, but deflect the shafts of sunlight and teach the flames to run back on themselves.

From this place you may see vast regions and lands disposed in glistening ranks, and bright mountains rising up, to which Rhodope would look up and Ossa with its snowy peak. Then, below, caves in overhanging crags look black in the shade of the hills and the shadow of the woods. This world does not lack dew or its own clouds, neither the chilling cold nor the rain so welcome to the plants. In these regions, too, the famous daughter of Thaumas glows with her many-coloured bow, and the rosy face of Aurora and the twilight of its own sky.

And can you believe that a sphere such as this lacks some kind of inhabitants? These too work the fields, and found their own cities; and perhaps they go to war and the victors celebrate triumphs; for here too renown has its own rewards. Fear and love and mortal feelings touch their hearts.

Moreover, just as at this moment it pleases us to let our eyes wander over the fields and glowing plains of the Moon and its deep sea, the very same desire excites them when the golden ball, the greater sphere of the Earth, presents itself in the clear sky. Then, no doubt, they examine every ocean and all the Earth and the peoples living at either pole. And some watcher spends the whole night gazing, untired, at the fires of the summer sky and wearies the heavens. Now the Gauls appear, and far-extending Germany presents itself, and white-capped Appenninus rises high into the air. And now, at last, see! towards the north, tiny England, a mere spot (though more brightly shining than all the rest), displays its shores. At once, a throng of nobles comes to see this lovely light, this gleaming dot, and stays watching late into the night, as each vies with another to give it his own name. And perhaps some far-off tyrant on the Moon's sphere calls himself our master and lords it in our palaces.

I could tell of other worlds warmed by the nearer sun, and of others where the sun's rays are more weakly felt – with a throng of moons but a dearth of even that feeble sunlight – if my sister Muse, intending to unfold these same things in her daring song, was not already striking the lyre and beginning the prelude.

But I will not be silent about those praises which are mine by right, nor the deeds already predestined, prophecies of our country's renown. The time will come when you will see whole crowds hastening aloft in a great procession, and the first colonists emigrating to the moon, giving up their familiar hearths; meanwhile, the old inhabitant gazes in astonished silence and from afar descries strange new birds, a flying fleet.

As once Columbus sailed across the watery plains of an unknown sea to see the lands of Zephyr, new realms; so the shores around and the waves look on in wonder at the iron-clad ranks, the regiments of monsters, and gigantic beasts full of armed men, and the inimitable lightning. Soon I see treaties made and traffic between the two worlds, and troops of men gathered under a sky with which they have grown familiar. England, which for so long has held sway over the sea and so often set the winds to work and ruled the waves, will assume the symbols of power in the sky, will bring her wonted triumphs even here and have dominion over the conquered air.

56 'Gratia magna'

This poem was first printed by Tovey, *Gray and his Friends* pp. 296–8, in 1890, on the assumption that it was by G., although it lacked any 'description or designation', from a transcript in Mitford's Notebook (vol iii ff. 83–5). Tovey pointed out its resemblance to an English poem by Richard West (*Gray and his Friends* pp. 108–9) and admitted the possibility that the Latin was also the work of West. G.'s authorship of the poem would appear to have been confirmed by the recent discovery of a MS of the poem in his hand, now in the possession of Mr Gordon N. Ray of New York, first described by Starr and Hendrickson, 'Supplementary note on Thomas Gray's *Gratia Magna*', *Notes and Queries* ccxii (1967) 412. This is the text followed here.

Gratia magna tuae fraudi quod pectore, Nice,
non geret hoc ultra regna superba Venus:
Respirare licet tandem misero mihi; tandem
appensa in sacro pariete vincla vides.
5   Numquam ... urar; liber sum: crede doloso
suppositus cineri non latet ullus amor:
Praesto non ira est, cuius se celet amictu;
sera, sed et rediit vix mihi nota quies.
Nec nomen si forte tuum pervenit ad aures,
10   pallor, et alternus surgit in ore rubor,
Corda nec incerto trepidant salientia pulsu
irrigat aut furtim lacrima fusa genas.
Non tua per somnos crebra obversatur imago
non animo ante omnes tu mihi mane redis.
15   Te loquor; at tener ille silet sub pectore sensus,
nec, quod ades, laetor; nec quod abes, doleo.
Rivalem tacitus patior; securus eburnea
quin ego colla simul laudo, manusque tuas.
Longa nec indignans refero periuria: prodis
20   obvia, mens certa sede colorque manet.
Quin faciles risus, vultusve assume superbos,
spernentem sperno, nec cupio facilem.
Nescit ocellorum, ut quondam, penetrabile fulgur
ah! nimium molles pectoris ire vias;
25   Non tam dulce rubent illi, mea cura, labelli
iuris ut immemores, imperiique sui.
Laetari possum, possum et maerere; sed a te
gaudia nec veniunt, nec veniunt lacrimae.
Tecum etiam nimii soles, et frigora laedunt
30   vere suo sine te prata nemusque placent.
Pulchra quidem facies, sed non tua sola videtur.
(forsitan offendam rusticitate mea)
Sed quiddam invenio culpandum, qua mihi nuper
parte est praecipue visus inesse lepos.
35   Cum primum evulsi fatale ex vulnere telum
credebam, ut fatear, viscera et ipsa trahi.
Luctanti rupere (pudor) suspiria pectus,
tinxit et invitas plurima gutta genas.
Aspera difficilem vicit medicina furorem;
40   ille dolor saevus, sed magis asper amor.
Aucupis insidiis, et arundine capta tenaci
sic multo nisu vincula rupit avis:
Plumarum laceros reparat breve tempus honores,
nec cadit in similes cautior inde dolos.
45   Tu tamen usque illam tibi fingis vivere flammam,
et male me veteres dissimulare faces.

Quod libertatem ostento, fractamque catenam,
tantus et insolitae pacis in ore sonus.
Praeteritos meminisse iubet natura dolores;
50   quae quisque est passus, dulce pericla loqui:
Enumerat miles sua vulnera; navita ventos
narrat, et incautae saxa inimica rati.
Sic ego servitium durum, et tua regna. Laborant
Nice, nullam a te quaerere dicta fidem;
55 Nil nimium haec mandata student tibi velle placere,
nec rogito, quali perlegis ore notas.

Many thanks to your treachery, Nice, that Venus will no longer hold her haughty sway in this heart. At last I, poor wretch, am granted a breathing space; at last you can see my chains hung up on the wall of the shrine. No more . . . will I burn; I am free: believe me, no fire of love lies hidden in the deceitful ashes; no anger is there in whose cloak it may conceal itself. It has been a long time, but that peace of mind with which I had grown unfamiliar has really returned to me. And if by chance your name comes to my ears pallor and blushing do not rise in turn in my face; nor does my leaping heart palpitate with uncertain pulse nor a flowing tear water my cheeks in secret. Your image does not confront me constantly in my sleep, nor do you return before all else to my mind in the morning. I talk of you but that tender feeling slumbers in my heart, and I am not happy because you are there, nor sad because you are absent. I endure a rival without a word; indeed, I can praise your ivory neck and your hands, unmoved. I do not recite your endless treacheries, in bitterness; when we come face to face, my mind remains unmoved in its seat, and my expression unchanged. By all means, put on your winning smiles, your haughty looks; I despise you when you despise me, and I do not desire you when you are making advances. The piercing lightning of your eyes no longer knows how to travel, as once it did, the paths of my heart, alas! too yielding as they were. Nor are those lips, that I once loved, so sweetly red, as if they were forgetful of their dictates and their rule. I can feel pleasure and I can grieve, but my joys do not derive from you, nor do my tears. In your presence, moreover, the sun can be excessive and cold can hurt me; away from you, the fields and woods are pleasing as in springtime. Your face seems pretty enough, but not yours alone. (Perhaps I will offend you by my crudeness.) But I find something displeasing in that very part in which, not long ago, your charm essentially seemed to lie. When I first tore out the deadly dart from the wound, I confess I thought that my bowels themselves were drawn out, too. And (the shame of it!) sighs rent my heart as I struggled and many a tear stained my unwilling cheeks. But the harsh cure overcame the obstinate frenzy; the pain was cruel, but love was even more bitter. Just so, when the bird, caught in the traps and the clinging reeds of the fowler, has broken its fetters with many a struggle, it repairs, in a short time, the torn finery of its feathers, nor, having learnt its lesson, does it fall again into similar traps. But you go on imagining that that flame still burns, and that I am making a poor attempt to hide the old fires, because I am making this display of my freedom and my broken chain, and there is such a sound of unaccustomed peace on my tongue. Nature loves to recall troubles that are past, and each finds it sweet to tell of the perils he has endured. The soldier counts over all his wounds, the sailor tells of the storms and rocks which threatened the unwary ship: so do I my harsh slavery and your power. My words, Nice, take no pains to gain your credence. This message is by no means eager to seek to please you, nor do I inquire with what expression you read through my rebukes.

57 Ad C: Favonium Aristium

Sent by G. to West in a letter dated June 1738 (*Corresp* i 85–6), which was first printed by Mason (*Memoirs* pp. 30–2) with the comment that 'this delicate Sapphic Ode' was 'the first original production of Mr. Gray's Muse; for verses imposed either by schoolmasters or tutors ought not, I think, to be taken into the consideration'. G. also transcribed it into his Commonplace Book (i 53 and 90), where it has the present title, a facetious elaboration of the name 'Favonius' by which West was known to the Quadruple Alliance, and is dated 'Cambridge. June 1738'. West had gone down from Oxford early in 1738 and, as the son of a distinguished lawyer, was also expected to embark on a legal career. G., about to leave Cambridge, was intending to do likewise, and to share rooms with West in the Temple; but this poem expresses their shared dislike of the profession they were entering.

> Barbaras aedes aditure mecum,
> Quas Eris semper fovet inquieta,
> Lis ubi late sonat, et togatum
>   Aestuat agmen!
>
> 5 Dulcius quanto, patulis sub ulmi
> Hospitae ramis temere iacentem
> Sic libris horas, tenuique inertes
>   Fallere Musa?
>
> Saepe enim curis vagor expedita
> 10 Mente; dum, blandam meditans Camenam,
> Vix malo rori, meminive serae
>   Cedere nocti;
>
> Et, pedes quo me rapiunt, in omni
> Colle Parnassum videor videre
> 15 Fertilem silvae, gelidamque in omni
>   Fonte Aganippen.
>
> Risit et Ver me, facilesque Nymphae
> Nare captantem, nec ineleganti,
> Mane quicquid de violis eundo
> 20   Surripit aura:

Me reclinatum teneram per herbam;
Qua leves cursus aqua cunque ducit,
Et moras dulci strepitu lapillo
          Nectit in omni.

25 Hae novo nostrum fere pectus anno
Simplices curae tenuere, caelum
Quamdiu sudum explicuit Favoni
          Purior hora:

Otia et campos nec adhuc relinquo,
30 Nec magis Phoebo Clytie fidelis;
(Ingruant venti licet, et senescat
          Mollior aestas).

Namque, seu, laetos hominum labores
Prataque et montes recreante curru,
35 Purpura tractus oriens Eoos
          Vestit, et auro;

Sedulus servo, veneratus orbem
Prodigum splendoris: amoeniori
Sive dilectam meditatur igne
40   Pingere Calpen;

Usque dum, fulgore magis, magis iam
Languido circum, variata nubes
Labitur furtim, viridisque in umbras
          Scena recessit.

45 O ego felix, vice si (nec unquam
Surgerem rursus) simili cadentem
Parca me lenis sineret quieto
          Fallere letho!

Multa flagranti, radiisque cincto
50 Integris ah! quam nihil inviderem,
Cum Dei ardentes medius quadrigas
          Sentit Olympus?

To C. Favonius Aristius

O thou, about to approach with me the barbarous dwelling which unquiet Strife ever haunts, where legal dispute sounds far and wide, and the civilian army throngs; how much sweeter, lying at ease under the spreading boughs of a sheltering elm, to while away the idle hours with books and the humble Muse? For I often roam, my mind unburdened with cares, and while I contemplate the sweet Italian Muse, I hardly remember to shun the baneful dew or the lateness of the night; and, wherever my feet bear me, I seem to see Parnassus, richly wooded, in every hill, and cool Aganippe in every fountain. The spring smiles on me, and the kindly Nymphs, as I catch with no undiscriminating nostrils whatever the morning breeze steals from the violets as it passes; and lie back on the soft grass, wherever the stream makes its rippling way, and dallies at every pebble with a pleasing murmur. These innocent cares absorbed my heart at about the time when the year was new, as long as the fresher season of Favonius provided clear skies; nor do I yet renounce idleness and the fields, nor is Clytie more faithful to Phoebus, (even if the winds are rising and the balmier summer grows old).

For I serve him diligently, worshipping the orb so lavish of its splendour, whether, while his chariot gives life again to the pleasant toils of men and the meadows and hills, he clothes the lands of the East as he rises with purple and gold, or whether he is about to tint his beloved Calpe with a more delicate fire; even until, as the gleam grows dimmer and ever dimmer, the many-coloured cloud sinks imperceptibly away and the landscape recedes into green shadows. Oh how blessed would I be (even though I never rose again), if a gentle fate would let me, sinking in just such a way, pass from sight in quiet death! Ah how little would I envy the god blazing fiercely, and clothed in his rays at their full power, when Heaven at its midpoint feels his burning chariot.

58 Alcaic Fragment

Sent by G. to West in a letter dated June 1738 (*Corresp* i 85–6), first printed by Mason in *1775* (*Memoirs* p. 33). Mason believed that 'no poet of the Augustan age ever produced four more perfect lines, or what would sooner impose upon the best critic, as being a genuine antient composition'. G. also transcribed it into his Commonplace Book (i 90): in the index it is entitled 'Tears (Latin Alcaic) fragment on them'. For the possible sources and influence of the stanza, see John Sparrow, *RES* xiv (1963) 58–61, and C. B. Ricks, *Times Lit. Supp.* 21 June 1963, p. 468.

> O lacrimarum fons, tenero sacros
> Ducentium ortus ex animo; quater
>   Felix! in imo qui scatentem
>   Pectore te, pia Nympha, sensit!

O fount of tears, that have their sacred sources in the tender spirit; four times blessed is he who has felt you, holy Nymph, gushing forth from the depths of his heart!

59 From Petrarch, Lib: I: Sonnet: 170

Transcribed by G. into his Commonplace Book (i 139) and first printed by Mathias, *Works* (1814) ii 93. In the absence of definite evidence as to its date, it may be attributed to 1737–8, when G. was translating Tasso and

Dante. See *Elegy* 92 *n* (p. 134 above), where G. acknowledged his debt to the last 3 ll. of this sonnet. In the title G. first wrote 169, which has been underlined and 170 (the normal numbering of the sonnet) written in brackets.

> Uror io! veros at nemo credidit ignes:
>   quin credunt omnes; dura sed illa negat.
> Illa negat, soli volumus cui posse probare:
>   quin videt, et visos improba dissimulat.
> 5 Ah durissima mi, sed et ah pulcherrima rerum!
>   nonne animam in misera, Cynthia, fronte vides?
> Omnibus illa pia est, et, si non fata vetassent,
>   tam longas mentem flecteret ad lacrimas.
> Sed tamen has lacrimas, hunc tu, quem spreveris, ignem,
> 10 carminaque auctori non bene culta suo
> Turba futurorum non ignorabit amantum:
>   nos duo, cumque erimus parvus uterque cinis,
> Iamque faces, eheu! oculorum, et frigida lingua
>   hae sine luce iacent, immemor illa loqui:
> 15 Infelix Musa aeternos spirabit amores,
>   ardebitque urna multa favilla mea.

Alas, I am on fire; but no one believed that the fires are real: or rather, they all believe–it is just she, hard as she is, that denies it. She denies it, whom alone I long to convince. In fact, she sees them, and, wicked woman, pretends that she has not. Ah, most cruel to me! but also, alas, the most beautiful of creatures! Do you not see my soul in my wretched face, Cynthia? She is gracious to all, and if the fates had not forbidden it, she would have softened her heart in the face of such prolonged weeping. But yet the throng of future lovers will not be ignorant of these tears, the fire which you disdain, and the songs that have brought no profit to their poet; even when we two will each be no more than a handful of ashes, then alas, the flames of my eyes will lie deprived of light, and my cold tongue forget how to speak: but the ill-starred Muse will breathe out eternal love and many a spark will glow in my urn.

60 'Horridos tractus'

Sent by G. to West in a letter from Genoa, dated 21 Nov. 1739 (*Corresp* i 129) and first printed by Mason, *Memoirs* p. 68, in 1775. If the poem can be taken literally, G. had written it during his journey to Genoa from Turin, which he had left on 18 Nov.

> Horridos tractus, Boreaeque linquens
> Regna Taurini fera, molliorem
> Advehor brumam, Genuaeque amantes
>   Litora soles.

Leaving behind the rugged passes and the wild realms of the Taurine Boreas,
I am conveyed towards a milder winter and the suns which love the shores of
Genoa.

61 [Elegiac Verses]

Sent by G. to West from Florence, in a letter dated 15 Jan. 1740 (*Corresp*
i 137), first printed by Mason, *Memoirs* p. 75, in *1775*. The poem continues
a sentence begun by G. in English: 'Secondly, how we passed the famous
plains'. The river Trebbia, which falls into the Po near Piacenza, was the
scene of Hannibal's defeat of the Romans in 218 B.C.

> Qua Trebiae glaucas salices intersecat unda,
>   arvaque Romanis nobilitata malis.
> Visus adhuc amnis veteri de clade rubere,
>   et suspirantes ducere maestus aquas;
> 5 Maurorumque ala, et nigrae increbescere turmae,
>   et pulsa Ausonidum ripa sonare fuga.

. . . where the stream of Trebia cuts through the grey-green willows and fields
made famous by Roman woes. The current, even now, seems to run red from
the ancient slaughter, and to bear down in grief its sighing waters; the
Moorish cavalry, the dark-skinned battalions, to prevail, and the trampled
bank to resound with the flight of the sons of Ausonia.

62 Ad C: Favonium Zephyrinum

Sent by G. to West from Rome in a letter dated May 1740 (*Corresp* i 158–9),
first printed by Mason, *Memoirs* pp. 87–8, in *1775*. G. transcribed the poem
into his Commonplace Book (i 128), with the following note at the end:
'Wrote at Rome, the latter end of the Spring, 1740. after a journey to
Frescati, & the Cascades of Tivoli.' G.'s title is another facetious elaboration
of the name by which West had been known to the Quadruple Alliance at
Eton. There is another holograph MS (entitled 'Alcaïca') in Pembroke
College MS L.C.II.123, no. 107, in which ll. 22–4 read as follows: *qua niveas
lavit | Tam saepe plumas rore puro | Et gelido* (where the bird of Venusia so
often bathes its snowy feathers with pure, cool dew).

> Mater rosarum, cui tenerae vigent
> Aurae Favoni, cui Venus it comes
>   Lasciva, Nympharum choreis
>   Et volucrum celebrata cantu!

5 Dic, non inertem fallere qua diem
   Amat sub umbra, seu sinit aureum
       Dormire plectrum, seu retentat
       Pierio Zephyrinus antro,
   Furore dulci plenus, et immemor
10 Reptantis inter frigora Tusculi
       Umbrosa, vel colles amici
       Palladiae superantis Albae.
   Dilecta Fauno, et capripedum choris
   Pineta, testor vos, Anio minax
15   Quaecumque per clivos volutus
       Praecipiti tremefecit amne,
   Illius altum Tibur, et Aesulae
   Audisse silvas nomen amabiles,
       Illius et gratas Latinis
20   Naiasin ingeminasse rupes.
   Nam me Latinae Naiades uvida
   Videre ripa, qua niveas levi
       Tam saepe lavit rore plumas
       Dulce canens Venusinus ales:
25 Mirum! canenti conticuit nemus,
   Sacrique fontes, et retinent adhuc
       (Sic Musa iussit) saxa molles
       Docta modos, veteresque lauri.
   Mirare nec tu me citharae rudem
30 Claudis laborantem numeris: loca
       Amoena, iucundumque ver in-
       Compositum docuere carmen.
   Haerent sub omni nam folio nigri
   Phoebea luci (credite) somnia;
35   Arguitiusque et lympha, et aurae
       Nescio quid solito loquuntur.

To C. Favonius Zephyrinus

Mother of roses, for whom the gentle breezes of Favonius rise, and whose
companion is pleasure-loving Venus, honoured in the dances of the Nymphs
and the songs of the birds! tell me in what shady place Zephyrinus loves to
beguile the busy day, whether he lets the golden plectrum sleep, or, filled
with sweet inspiration, reawakens it in the Pierian cave, forgetful of his friend
wandering among the cool shades of Tusculum or climbing the hills of Pall-
adian Alba. Pinewoods, dear to Faunus and the chorus of goat-footed satyrs,
I call you to witness, whichever of you impetuous Anio with his headlong
current has caused to tremble as he tumbles over the slopes, that lofty Tibur
and the delightful woods of Aesula have heard his name, and that it is his name
that the crags dear to the Latin Naiads have re-echoed. For the Latin Naiads
saw me on the moist bank where so often the sweet-singing bird of Venusia
bathed its snowy feathers with a sprinkling of dew. Marvellous! that, as he

sang, the grove and sacred springs fell silent and, to this day (for so the Muse
commanded), the stones skilled in song and the ancient laurels prolong the
soothing strains. Do not therefore wonder at me, ignorant as I am of the
lyre, struggling along with faltering notes: these delightful places and the
cheerful spring have taught me my ill-composed song; for, believe me, be-
neath every leaf of the dark grove cling visions from Phoebus, and the streams
and breezes speak with something more than usual eloquence.

63 [The Gaurus]

Sent by G. to West from Florence in a letter dated 25 Sept. 1740 (*Corresp* i
176–7), first printed by Mason, *Memoirs* pp. 105–9, in 1775. It was evidently
written towards the end of June or early in July 1740, since the transcript in
the Commonplace Book (i 115, 128) is dated 'Rome–July, 1740. just
return'd from Naples' and the other holograph MS (Pembroke College
MS L.C.II.123, no. 108) 'Rome . . June 1740'. G. left Rome for Florence
on 4 July. G.'s letter to West introduces the poem as follows: 'What I send
you now, as long as it is, is but a piece of a poem. It has the advantage of all
fragments, to need neither introduction nor conclusion: Besides, if you do not
like it, it is but imagining that which went before, and came after, to be
infinitely better. Look in Sandy's Travels for the history of Monte Barbaro,
and Monte Nuovo.' G. was referring to George Sandys, *The Relation of a
Journey begun an. Dom. 1610, in Four Books* (1615) iv 275, 277–8, (quoted
by Mason, pp. 105–6). The Gaurus, known in modern times as Monte
Barbaro, is a mountain between Cumae and Naples. Monte Nuovo was a
mountain which rose out of the Lucrine Lake during a volcanic eruption
in Sept. 1538, described in the passage in Sandys. Variants have been recorded
from the Pembroke College MS.

> Nec procul infelix se tollit in aethera Gaurus,
> Prospiciens vitreum lugenti vertice pontum.
> Tristior ille diu, et veteri desuetus oliva
> Gaurus, pampineaeque eheu iam nescius umbrae:
> 5   Horrendi tam saeva premit vicinia montis,
> Attonitumque urget latus, exuritque ferentem.
>   Nam fama est, olim, media dum rura silebant
> Nocte deo victa, et molli perfusa quiete;
> Infremuisse aequor ponti, auditamque per omnes
> 10   Late tellurem surdum immugire cavernas:
> Quo sonitu nemora alta tremunt, tremit excita tuto
> Parthenopaea sinu, flammantisque ora Vesevi.
> At subito se aperire solum, vastosque recessus
> Pandere sub pedibus, nigraque voragine fauces:

¶ 63.10. *Late tellurem*] Tellurem late *Pembroke.* *immugire*] mugire
Pembroke.

15 Tum piceas cinerum glomerare sub aethere nubes
Vorticibus rapidis, ardentique imbre procellam.
Praecipites fugere ferae, perque avia longe
Silvarum fugit pastor, iuga per deserta,
Ah, 'miser! increpitans saepe alta voce per umbram
20 Nequicquam natos, creditque audire sequentes:
Atque ille excelso rupis de vertice solus
Respectans notasque domos, et dulcia regna,
Nil usquam videt infelix praeter mare tristi
Lumine percussum, et pallentes sulphure campos,
25 Fumumque, flammasque, rotataque turbine saxa.
   Quin ubi detonuit fragor, et lux reddita caelo:
Maestos confluere agricolas, passuque videres
Tandem iterum timido deserta requirere tecta;
Sperantes, si forte oculis, si forte darentur
30 Uxorum cineres, miserorumve ossa parentum
(Tenuia, sed tanti saltem solacia luctus)
Una colligere, et iusta componere in urna.
Uxorum nusquam cineres, nusquam ossa parentum
(Spem miseram) assuetosve Lares, aut rura videbunt;
35 Quippe ubi planities campi diffusa iacebat,
Mons novus: ille supercilium, frontemque favilla
Incanum ostentans, ambustis cautibus, aequor
Subiectum, stragemque suam, maesta arva, minaci
Despicit imperio, soloque in litore regnat.
40   Hinc infame loci nomen, multosque per annos
Immemor antiquae laudis nescire labores
Vomeris, et nullo tellus revirescere cultu:
Non avium colles, non carmine matutino
Pastorum resonare; adeo undique dirus habebat
45 Informes late horror agros, saltusque vacantes.
Saepius et longe detorquens navita proram
Monstrabat digito litus, saevaeque revolvens
Funera narrabat noctis, veteremque ruinam.
   Montis adhuc facies manet hirta atque aspera saxis
50 Sed furor extinctus iamdudum, et flamma quievit,
Quae nascenti aderat; seu forte bituminis atri
Defluxere olim rivi, atque effeta lacuna
Pabula sufficere ardori, viresque recusat:
Sive in visceribus meditans incendia iam nunc,

15. *Tum*] Et *Pembroke*.
44. *adeo undique*] informes tam *Pembroke*.
45. *Informes late horror agros*] Horror agros late circum *Pembroke*.
46. *et*] hoc *Pembroke*.
54. *meditans*] meditata *Pembroke*.

55   Horrendum! arcanis glomerat genti esse futurae
      Exitio, sparsos tacitusque recolligit ignes.
         Raro per clivos haud secius ordine vidi
      Canescentem oleam. Longum post tempus amicti
      Vite virent tumuli, patriamque revisere gaudens
60   Bacchus in assuetis tenerum caput exerit arvis
      Vix tandem, infidoque audet se credere caelo.

57. *Raro per clivos haud*] Per clivos raro nec *Pembroke.*
59. *virent*] *Followed by a deletion in Pembroke, perhaps* colles.

And not far off, the ill-fated Gaurus rose to the sky, looking out over the glassy
sea from its grieving crest. For long now the Gaurus has been a mournful place,
long unaccustomed to its ancient olive tree and now, alas, knowing no more
the shade of the vine. For the awful closeness of that dreaded mountain
oppresses it and threatens its blasted sides, burning up what it brings forth.
For the story goes that once, while the countryside lay still at dead of night,
overcome by the God and drenched in soothing rest, the surface of the ocean
roared and far and wide the dumb earth was heard to bellow through all its
caverns. At this sound, the lofty forests tremble and awakened Parthenope
shivers in her secure bay, and the shore of flaming Vesuvius. Then, suddenly,
the earth opened and immense gulfs lay revealed beneath the feet and the
gaping jaws of a black abyss. Then pitch-black clouds of ashes collected in the
air in rapid whirlwinds, a storm of fiery rain. The wild beasts fled headlong,
and the herdsman fled across the pathless tracts of the forest and over wild
ridges, calling loudly on his children through the gloom, but in vain, wretched
man, believing that he heard them following. And then, when, all alone, he
looks back at the familiar dwellings and well-loved fields from the lofty
summit of a crag, nothing does he see anywhere, unhappy man, but the sea
bathed in a gloomy light and plains white with sulphur, and smoke, flames
and rocks tossed in the whirlwind. Then, when the uproar had spent itself,
and daylight returned to the sky, you might have seen the stricken farmers
gathering, and at last, with nervous steps, seeking out their deserted homes
again; hoping, if by chance they were allowed to come upon the ashes of their
wives or the bones of their wretched parents, to collect them together and inter
them in a decent urn: small solace, but at least some consolation for so great
a grief. But nowhere would they see the ashes of their wives, nowhere the bones
of their parents (vain hope!), nor their accustomed hearths and fields. For in
fact, where once the level extent of the plain lay stretched out, there is a new
mountain: displaying a brow and face white with warm ashes and strewn
with scorched rocks, it looks down in threatening tyranny over the sea lying
at its feet, over the destruction it has wrought, the desolated fields, and rules
over the deserted shore. Hence the evil repute of the place, and for many
years, forgetful of its ancient renown, the soil knew nothing of the labours of
the plough and would not grow green again with any cultivation. The hills
did not re-echo with the morning song of birds or shepherds; everywhere,
indeed, a grim horror possessed the hideous fields and abandoned pastures.
Often a sailor, turning his ship far out at sea, would point at the shore with his
finger and, repeating the story, tell of the deaths of that dreadful night and
the destruction of long ago. Even now, the appearance of the mountain

remains bristling and rough with rocks; but the violence has long since been stilled, and the flames which assisted at its birth have died away. It may be that the streams of black bitumen ran dry long ago, and the spent crater refuses fuel and strength to feed the fires; or even now (appalling thought!) it is brooding, hoarding flames in its secret depths for the destruction of some future race, and is amassing its scattered fires. Nevertheless, I have seen the hoary olive tree in a thin line across the slopes; after a long time, the vineclad hillocks grow green; and Bacchus, glad to revisit his old home, is raising his delicate head once more, though with difficulty, in the accustomed fields, and dares to entrust himself to that treacherous sky.

64 [Farewell to Florence]

Sent by G. to West from Florence in a letter dated 21 April 1741 (*Corresp* i 182), first printed by Mason (*Memoirs* p. 115) in 1775. G. transcribed it into his Commonplace Book (i 139), where it has no title and is dated 1741. (Starr and Hendrickson, p. 149 *n*, incorrectly state that the date is blurred, 'apparently 1740'.) G.'s letter to West introduces the poem as follows: 'Eleven months, at different times, have I passed at Florence; and yet (God help me) know not either people or language. Yet the place and the charming prospects demand a poetical farewell, and here it is.' The poem describes the 'prospect' of Fiesole, some four miles north-east of Florence. In line 1, G.'s own comma, making 'Faesulae' vocative plural, has been retained in preference to Mason's removal of the comma, followed by Starr and Hendrickson, making it genitive singular. (Cp. 'Oh ubi colles' 1, p. 318).

    . . . oh Faesulae, amoena
    Frigoribus iuga, nec nimium spirantibus auris!
    Alma quibus Tusci Pallas decus Apennini
    Esse dedit, glaucaque sua canescere silva.
5   Non ego vos posthac Arni de valle videbo
    Porticibus circum, et candenti cincta corona
    Villarum longe nitido consurgere dorso,
    Antiquamve aedem, et veteres praeferre cupressus
    Mirabor, tectisque super pendentia tecta.

O Fiesole, hills lovely for your coolness and the breezes which do not blow too strongly! To which gracious Pallas granted that they should be the pride of the Tuscan Appennines, and grow hoary with her own grey-green trees. Henceforward, I shall see you no more from the valley of the Arno, rising up far away, with your gleaming ridge encircled all about with porticoes and a shining crown of villas; no more shall I gaze in wonder at the ancient church and the aged cypresses before it, and the roofs overhanging roofs.

65 Imitated [from Buondelmonte]

Sent by G. to West from Florence in a letter dated 21 April 1741 (*Corresp* i 183), first printed by Mason, *Memoirs* p. 115, in *1775*. G. also sent West the original Italian by Giuseppe Maria Buondelmonte (1713–57), whom he and Walpole had met some months previously. Walpole had in fact already sent West G.'s imitation, with his own translation into English and the original Italian, in a letter of 2 Oct. 1740 (*Walpole Correspondence* xiii 231–2), introduced as follows: 'Bondelmonti . . . is a low mimic; the brightest cast of his parts attains to the composition of a sonnet: he talks irreligion with English boys, sentiments with my sister, and bad French with any one that will hear him. I will transcribe you a little song that he made t'other day; 'tis pretty enough; Gray turned it into Latin, and I into English; you will honour him highly by putting it into French, and Ashton into Greek.' Walpole's text of G.'s Latin has 'Risit' for 'Lusit' (l. 1) and 'Sudentem' for 'Ludentem' (l. 5), perhaps due to mistranscription by the editor of his *Works* (1797), the only source for his letter. G. also transcribed the poem and the original Italian into his Commonplace Book (i 139), where it is clearly dated 1741 (in spite of Starr and Hendrickson's assertion that it is blurred). The Italian text as he gives it is as follows:

> Spesso Amor sotto la forma
> D'amistá ride, e s'asconde:
> Poi si mischia, e si confonde
> Con lo sdegno, e col rancor.
> In pietade ei si transforma;
> Par trastullo, e par dispetto:
> Má nel suo diverso aspetto
> Sempr' egli é l'istesso Amor.

Walpole's translation is: 'Love often in the comely mien / Of friendship fancies to be seen; / Soon again he shifts his dress, / And wears disdain and rancour's face. // To gentle pity then he changes; / Through wantonness, through piques he ranges; / But in whatever shape he move, / He's still himself, and still is love.'

> Lusit amicitiae interdum velatus amictu,
>   et bene composita veste fefellit Amor.
> Mox irae assumpsit cultus, faciemque minantem,
>   inque odium versus, versus et in lacrimas:
> 5 Ludentem fuge, nec lacrimanti, aut crede furenti:
>   idem est dissimili semper in ore Deus.

Sometimes Love jested, concealed in the cloak of friendship, and disguised himself in seemly attire. Next, he assumed the mask of anger and a threatening visage; turned now to hate and now again to tears. Flee him when he sports nor trust him whether he weeps or rages. For all his different faces, he is always the same god.

66 [Alcaic Ode]

In the Book at the Grande Chartreuse among the Mountains of Dauphiné

G. wrote this poem in the album of the monastery of the Grande Chartreuse on 21 Aug. 1741, during his journey from Turin to Lyons, on his way back to England. The album was destroyed during the French Revolution; see *Notes and Queries* i (1850) 416. G. had previously visited the monastery in 1739; see *Corresp* i 122–3 for the striking impression it made on him. He transcribed the poem into his Commonplace Book (i 129), dating it 'August –1741'. It was first printed by Mason, *Memoirs* pp. 117–8, in *1775*, and became one of the most frequently translated of G.'s Latin poems.

> O Tu, severi religio loci,
> Quocumque gaudes nomine (non leve
>   Nativa nam certe fluenta
>   Numen habet, veteresque silvas;
>
> 5 Praesentiorem et conspicimus Deum
> Per invias rupes, fera per iuga,
>   Clivosque praeruptos, sonantes
>   Inter aquas, nemorumque noctem;
>
> Quam si repostus sub trabe citrea
> 10 Fulgeret auro, et Phidiaca manu)
>   Salve vocanti rite, fesso et
>   Da placidam iuveni quietem.
>
> Quod si invidendis sedibus, et frui
> Fortuna sacra lege silentii
> 15   Vetat volentem, me resorbens
>   In medios violenta fluctus:
>
> Saltem remoto des, Pater, angulo
> Horas senectae ducere liberas;
>   Tutumque vulgari tumultu
> 20   Surripias, hominumque curis.

O Thou, divine spirit of this forbidding place, by whatever title pleases Thee (for certainly no mean power rules over these native streams and ancient forests; and we perceive God closer to us among pathless rocks, wild ridges and precipitous ravines, and in the thundering of waters and the darkness of the woods, than if, kept under a roof of citrus-wood, He glowed with gold even from the hand of Phidias): Hail! And if I invoke Thee rightly, grant a calm repose to this weary youth.

But if Fortune forbids me, in spite of my wish, to enjoy this enviable dwelling and the sacred rule of silence, sucking me back violently into the midst of the waves, then at least grant, Father, that I may pass the untroubled hours of old age in some secluded corner; and bear me off unharmed from the tumult of the crowd and the cares of men.

67 'Oh ubi colles'

Transcribed by G. into his Commonplace Book (i 381) without a title or date; first printed by Tovey, *Gray and His Friends* p. 296, in 1890, who comments that it was 'obviously written after his return from the continent in [Sept.] 1741'. Tovey also notes that it echoes the stanza 'Horridos tractus' in G.'s letter to West, 21 Nov. 1739 (p. 315 above).

> Oh ubi colles, ubi Faesularum,
> Palladis curae, plaga, Formiaeque
> Prodigae florum, Genuaeque amantes
>   Litora soles?
>
> 5   Abstulit campos oculis amoenos
> Montium quantus, nemorumque tractus?
> Quot natant eheu! medii profundo
>   Marmore fluctus?

O where are the hills, where the region of Fiesole, dear to Pallas, and Formiae, rich in flowers, and the suns which love the shores of Genoa? How huge a tract of mountains and forests has hidden those pleasant plains from my sight? How many waves, alas, roll over the vast, shining ocean between?

68 Sophonisba Masinissae. Epistola

Sent by G. to West in a letter first printed by Mason in *1775*, *Memoirs* pp. 153–5, and dated by him 27 May 1742, although it is probably a conflation of two or more letters written between about 15 May and 27 May 1742 (see *Corresp* i 209–13, esp. 209 *n*). G. introduces the poem as follows: 'Here follows also the beginning of an Heroic Epistle; but you must give me leave to tell my own story first, because Historians differ. Massinissa was the son of Gala King of the Massyli; and, when very young at the head of his father's army, gave a most signal overthrow to Syphax, King of the Masaesylians, then an ally of the Romans. Soon after Asdrubal, son of Gisgo the Carthaginian General, gave the beautiful Sophonisba, his daughter, in marriage to the young prince. But this marriage was not consummated on account of Massinissa's being obliged to hasten into Spain, there to command his father's troops, who were auxiliaries of the Carthaginians. Their affairs at this time began to be in a bad condition; and they thought it might be greatly for their interest, if they could bring over Syphax to themselves. This in time they actually effected; and to strengthen their new alliance, commanded Asdrubal to give his daughter to Syphax. (It is probable their ingratitude to Massinissa arose from the great change of affairs, which had happened among the Massylians during his absence; for his father and uncle were dead, and a distant relation of the royal family had usurped the throne.) Sophonisba was accordingly married to Syphax: and Massinissa, enraged at the affront, became a friend to the Romans. They drove the Carthaginians before them out of Spain, and carried the war into Africa, defeated Syphax, and took him prisoner; upon which Cirtha (his capital) opened her gates to Laelius and Massinissa. The rest of the affair, the marriage, and the sending of poison, every body knows. This is partly taken from Livy [xxix 23; xxx 3–15], and partly from Appian [*Punic Wars* 10, 27–8].' Whibley and Toynbee summarize the 'rest of the affair' as follows: 'Masinissa married Sophonisba, but the Romans demanded her surrender; whereupon Masinissa, to spare her the humiliation of captivity, sent her a bowl of poison with which she put an end to her life.'

Egregium accipio promissi munus amoris,
　　inque manu mortem iam fruitura fero:
Atque utinam citius mandasses, luce vel una;
　　transieram Stygios non inhonesta lacus.
5　Victoris nec passa toros, nova nupta, mariti,
　　nec fueram fastus, Roma superba, tuos.
Scilicet haec partem tibi, Massinissa, triumphi
　　detractam, haec pompae iura minora suae
Imputat, atque uxor quod non tua pressa catenis,
10　　obiecta et saevae plausibus urbis eo:
Quin tu pro tantis cepisti praemia factis,
　　magnum Romanae pignus amicitiae!
Scipiadae excuses, oro, si tardius utar
　　munere. Non nimium vivere, crede, velim.
15　Parva mora est, breve sed tempus mea fama requirit:
　　detinet haec animam cura suprema meam.
Quae patriae prodesse meae regina ferebar,
　　inter Elisaeas gloria prima nurus,
Ne videar flammae nimis indulsisse secundae,
20　　vel nimis hostiles extimuisse manus.
Fortunam atque annos liceat revocare priores,
　　gaudiaque heu! quantis nostra repensa malis.
Primitiasne tuas meministi atque arma Syphacis
　　fusa, et per Tyrias ducta trophaea vias?
25　(Laudis at antiquae forsan meminisse pigebit,
　　quodque decus quondam causa ruboris erit.)
Tempus ego certe memini, felicia Poenis
　　quo te non puduit solvere vota deis;

Moeniaque intrantem vidi: longo agmine duxit
30   turba salutantum, purpureique patres.
Feminea ante omnes longe admiratur euntem
        haeret et aspectu tota caterva tuo.
Iam flexi, regale decus, per colla capilli,
        iam decet ardenti fuscus in ore color!
35   Commendat frontis generosa modestia formam,
        seque cupit laudi surripuisse suae.
Prima genas tenui signat vix flore iuventas,
        et dextrae soli credimus esse virum.
Dum faciles gradiens oculos per singula iactas,
40   (seu rexit casus lumina, sive Venus)
In me (vel certe visum est) conversa morari
        sensi; virgineus perculit ora pudor.
Nescio quid vultum molle spirare tuendo,
        credideramque tuos lentius ire pedes.
45   Quaerebam, iuxta aequalis si dignior esset,
        quae poterat visus detinuisse tuos:
Nulla fuit circum aequalis quae dignior esset,
        asseruitque decus conscia forma suum.
Pompae finis erat. Tota vix nocte quievi:
50   sin premat invitae lumina victa sopor,
Somnus habet pompas, eademque recursat imago;
        atque iterum hesterno munere victor ades.

Sophonisba to Masinissa. An Epistle

Admirable indeed is the reward I now receive of plighted love, and, even as I
am about to enjoy it, I hold death in my hand; but would that you had given it
to me sooner even by one day: then I would have crossed the Stygian pools
without dishonour. I would not, then, a newly wedded bride, have endured
the bed of a conqueror-husband, nor your arrogance, haughty Rome. For
sure, Masinissa, Rome will charge it to you that part of her triumph has been
snatched away, some of the perquisites of her triumphal procession, in that
your wife will not march weighed down with chains and exposed to the shouts
of the cruel mob. What a reward you have won for such mighty deeds!
What an impressive pledge of Roman friendship! You will make my excuses
to Scipio, I beg, if I make use of your gift rather too slowly. Believe me, I am
not so eager to stay alive. The delay is a short one, but my reputation demands
a little time; it is this last care alone that detains my soul. I, who was said to
have been of benefit to my country when I was queen, and the most renowned
of the daughters of Elissa, would not be thought to have indulged too readily
a second passion, or to have been too terrified by enemy force. Let me recall
the good fortune of past years and my joys, paid for, alas, with so much evil.
Do you remember your first success, the troops of Syphax routed and your
trophies borne through the Tyrian streets? (But perhaps you will be loth to
recall your former praises and what was once a glory to you will now be a source
of shame.) I, at least, remember the time when you were not ashamed to fulfil

those fortunate vows you made to the Carthaginian gods; I saw you entering the city and the crowd of people came to acclaim you, stretching in a long line, and the purple-clad elders also. As you advanced, a throng of women admired you more than all the rest, and hung on every detail of your appearance: now your locks curling over your shoulders, the mark of kings, and now so pleasing the swarthy colour of your glowing face! A becoming diffidence enhances the beauty of your appearance and longs to steal away from the praise it excites. First manhood has hardly set its mark on your cheeks with its fine bloom and it is only by the deeds of your hand that we believe you a man. As you walked along, you cast casual glances at every object (whether chance directed your gaze, or Venus), and I felt your eyes linger as they turned on me (or so, at least, it seemed); and maiden shame suffused my face. I felt sure that your expression softened a little as you gazed and that your feet went forward more slowly. I looked to see whether there was one of my companions around me who could have been more worthy of engaging your attention. But there was not one of them around me who could have been more worthy and conscious beauty claimed the honour for itself. The procession came to an end. All night I hardly rested; or, if drowsiness overcame me and closed my eyes against my will, then sleep held its own procession and the same image recurred; and once more you, the conqueror, were there, as in the spectacle of the previous day.

69 De Principiis Cogitandi

Begun not earlier than July 1740 and probably left unfinished not long after June 1742. G.'s transcript of Bk i in his Commonplace Book (i 129, 138, 289, 438) has a marginal note at the beginning: 'Begun at Florence. in 1740'. G. was in Florence between 7 July 1740 and 27 April 1741. Shortly before leaving, in a letter dated 21 April 1741 (*Corresp* i 183), G. sent West 'the beginning not of an Epic Poem, but of a Metaphysic one. Poems and Metaphysics (say you, with your spectacles on) are inconsistent things. A metaphysical poem is a contradiction in terms. It is true, but I will go on. It is Latin too to increase the absurdity. It will, I suppose, put you in mind of the man who wrote a treatise of Canon Law in Hexameters. Pray help me to the description of a mixt mode, and a little Episode about Space.' Mason, *Memoirs* p. 116 *n*, explained that G. was referring to 'The beginning of the first book of a didactic Poem, "De Principiis Cogitandi." The fragment which he now sent contained the first 53 lines.'

G.'s next reference to the poem occurs in a letter to Wharton, 26 April 1744 (*Corresp* i 225), in which he states: 'Master Tommy Lucretius (since you are so good to enquire after the Child) is but a puleing Chitt yet, not a bit grown to speak off, I believe, poor Thing! it has got the Worms, that will carry it off at last.' Finally G. sent Walpole the 29 lines of Book ii (or iv) in a letter of 8 Feb. 1747 (*Corresp* i 267): 'I send you a few Lines, tho' Latin (wch you don't like) for the sake of the Subject. it makes Part of a large Design, & is the Beginning of the fourth Book, wch was intended to treat of the

Passions. excuse the 3 first Verses: you know Vanity (with the Romans) is a poetical License.' These lines in fact constitute an elegy on Richard West, who had died on 1 June 1742 and a marginal note to his transcript in G.'s Commonplace Book (i 286) states that they were 'Begun at Stoke, June, 1742'. Although G.'s letter to Walpole says that they were intended for Bk iv of the poem, his transcript in the Commonplace Book (i 286) is headed 'Liber Secundus', the numbering adopted here. The MS of the lines sent to Walpole in 1747 is now Pembroke College MS. L.C.II.90.

The incomplete poem was first printed by Mason, *Memoirs* pp. 160–9, preceded by some discussion of G.'s plan. Mason stated that 'It is clear . . . from the Exordium itself, that he meant to make the same use of Mr Locke's Essay on the human Understanding, which Lucretius did of the Dogmas of Epicurus. And the first six lines plainly intimate, that his general design was to be comprized in four books.' The text is that of the Commonplace Book, with variants from the letter to Walpole. In the Index to the Commonplace Book the poem is listed as: 'Thinking (the Principles of) a Latin Poem, unfinish'd'.

G.'s subheadings, written in the margin of the Commonplace Book, are recorded in the footnotes below.

LIBER PRIMUS: AD FAVONIUM

Unde Animus scire incipiat: quibus incohet orsa
Principiis seriem rerum, tenuemque catenam
Mnemosyne: Ratio unde rudi sub pectore tardum
Augeat imperium; et primum mortalibus aegris
5   Ira, Dolor, Metus, et Curae nascantur inanes,
Hinc canere aggredior. Nec dedignare canentem,
Oh decus! Angliacae certe oh lux altera gentis!
Si qua primus iter monstras, vestigia conor
Signare incerta, tremulaque insistere planta.
10   Quin potius duc ipse (potes namque omnia) sanctum
Ad limen (si rite adeo, si pectore puro)
Obscurae reserans Naturae ingentia claustra.
Tu caecas rerum causas, fontemque severum
Pande, Pater; tibi enim, tibi, veri magne Sacerdos,
15   Corda patent hominum, atque altae penetralia
      Mentis.
     Tuque aures adhibe vacuas, facilesque, Favoni,
(Quod tibi crescit opus) simplex nec despice carmen,
Nec vatem: non illa leves primordia motus,

¶ 69.i *1*. Plan of the Poem. *G.*
i *6*. Invocation to Mr Lock. *G.*
i *17*. Use & Extent of the Subject. *G.*

Quanquam parva, dabunt. Laetum vel amabile
    quicquid
20 Usquam oritur, trahit hinc ortum; nec surgit ad auras,
Quin ea conspirent simul, eventusque secundent:
Hinc variae vitaï artes, ac mollior usus,
Dulce et amicitiae vinclum: Sapientia dia
Hinc roseum accendit lumen, vultuque sereno
25 Humanas aperit mentes, nova gaudia monstrans,
Deformesque fugat curas, vanosque timores:
Scilicet et rerum crescit pulcherrima Virtus.
Illa etiam, quae te (mirum) noctesque diesque
Assidue fovet inspirans, linguamque sequentem
30 Temperat in numeros, atque horas mulcet inertes;
Aurea non alia se iactat origine Musa.
Principio, ut magnum foedus Natura creatrix
Firmavit, tardis iussitque inolescere membris
Sublimes animas; tenebroso in carcere partem
35 Noluit aetheream longo torpere veterno:
Nec per se proprium passa exercere vigorem est,
Ne sociae molis coniunctos sperneret artus,
Ponderis oblita, et caelestis conscia flammae.
Idcirco innumero ductu tremere undique fibras
40 Nervorum instituit: tum toto corpore miscens
Implicuit late ramos, et sensile textum,
Implevitque umore suo (seu lympha vocanda,
Sive aura est); tenuis certe, atque levissima quaedam
Vis versatur agens, parvosque infusa canales
45 Perfluit; assidue externis quae concita plagis,
Mobilis, incussique fidelis nuntia motus,
Hinc inde accensa contage relabitur usque
Ad superas hominis sedes, arcemque cerebri.
Namque illic posuit solium, et sua templa sacravit
50 Mens animi: hanc circum coëunt, densoque feruntur
Agmine notitiae, simulacraque tenuia rerum:
Ecce autem naturae ingens aperitur imago
Immensae, variique patent commercia mundi.
    Ac uti longinquis descendunt montibus amnes

i 32. Union of the Soul & Body. G.

i 39. Office of the nervous System. G.

i 43. *Sive aura est); tenuis certe,*] *The semi-colon has been inserted, otherwise this is G.'s punctuation in the Commonplace Book, preferred here to Starr and Hendrickson's alteration to* Sive aura est; tenuis certe),

i 44. *versatur agens*] *In margin of the Commonplace Book to replace* agitat late *in text.*

i 50. Sensation, the Origin of our Ideas. G.

55 Velivolus Tamisis, flaventisque Indus arenae,
Euphratesque, Tagusque, et opimo flumine Ganges;
Undas quisque suas volvens, cursuque sonoro
In mare prorumpunt: hos magno acclinis in antro
Excipit Oceanus, natorumque ordine longo
60 Dona recognoscit venientum, ultroque serenat
Caeruleam faciem, et diffuso marmore ridet.
Haud aliter species properant se inferre novellae
Certatim menti, atque aditus quino agmine complent.
    Primas tactus agit partes, primusque minutae
65 Laxat iter caecum turbae, recipitque ruentem.
Non idem huic modus est, qui fratribus: amplius ille
Imperium affectat senior, penitusque medullis,
Visceribusque habitat totis, pellisque recentem
Funditur in telam, et late per stamina vivit.
70 Necdum etiam matris puer eluctatus ab alvo
Multiplices solvit tunicas, et vincula rupit;
Sopitus molli somno, tepidoque liquore
Circumfusus adhuc: tactus tamen aura lacessit
Iamdudum levior sensus, animamque reclusit.
75 Idque magis simul ac solitum blandumque calorem
Frigore mutavit caeli, quod verberat acri
Impete inassuetos artus: tum saevior adstat,
Humanaeque comes vitae Dolor excipit; ille
Cunctantem frustra, et tremulo multa ore querentem
80 Corripit invadens, ferreisque amplectitur ulnis.
Tum species primum patefacta est candida Lucis
(Usque vices adeo Natura bonique, malique,
Exaequat, iustaque manu sua damna rependit)
Tum primum, ignotosque bibunt nova lumina soles.
85   Carmine quo, Dea, te dicam, gratissima caeli
Progenies, ortumque tuum; gemmantia rore
Ut per prata levi lustras, et floribus halans
Purpureum Veris gremium, scenamque virentem
Pingis, et umbriferos colles, et caerula regna?

i 58. magno . . . antro] In margin of Commonplace Book to replace magna . . .
urna in text.
i 61. In margin of Commonplace Book: ποντίων τέ [sic] κυμάτων/'Ανήριθμον
γέλασμα [And the unnumbered smiles of the ocean waves] — Prometheus
[Vinctus] ap. Aeschylum [89–90].
i 64. The Touch, our first & most extensive Sense. G.
i 69. Taken over from Latin Verses at Eton 53 (p. 291).
i 74. levior] In margin of Commonplace Book to replace teneros in text.
i 81. Sight, our second Sense. G.
i 85. Digression on Light. G.

90 Gratia te, Venerisque lepos, et mille colorum,
Formarumque chorus sequitur, motusque decentes.
At caput invisum Stygiis Nox atra tenebris
Abdidit, horrendaeque simul formidinis ora,
Pervigilesque aestus curarum, atque anxius angor:
95 Undique laetitia florent mortalia corda,
Purus et arridet largis fulgoribus aether.
Omnia nec tu ideo invalidae se pandere Menti
(Quippe nimis teneros posset vis tanta diei
Perturbare, et inexpertos confundere visus)
100 Nec capere infantes animos, neu cernere credas
Tam variam molem, et mirae spectacula Lucis:
Nescio qua tamen haec oculos dulcedine parvos
Splendida percussit novitas, traxitque sequentes;
Nonne videmus enim, latis inserta fenestris
105 Sicubi se Phoebi dispergant aurea tela,
Sive lucernarum rutilus colluxerit ardor,
Extemplo huc obverti aciem, quae fixa repertos
Haurit inexpletum radios, fruiturque tuendo.
Altior huic vero sensu, maiorque videtur
110 Addita, Iudicioque arte connexa potestas,
Quod simul atque aetas volventibus auxerit annis,
Haec simul, assiduo depascens omnia visu,
Perspiciet, vis quanta loci, quid polleat ordo,
Iuncturae quis honos, ut res accendere rebus
115 Lumina coniurant inter se, et mutua fulgent.
Nec minor in geminis viget auribus insita virtus,
Nec tantum in curvis quae pervigil excubet antris
Hinc atque hinc (ubi Vox tremefecerit ostia pulsu
Aeriis invecta rotis) longeque recurset:
120 Scilicet Eloquio haec sonitus, haec fulminis alas,
Et mulcere dedit dictis et tollere corda,
Verbaque metiri numeris, versuque ligare
Reperit, et quicquid discant Libethrides undae,
Calliope quoties, quoties Pater ipse canendi
125 Evolvat liquidum carmen, calamove loquenti
Inspiret dulces animas, digitisque figuret.
At medias fauces, et linguae umentia templa
Gustus habet, qua se insinuet iucunda saporum

---

i *96. largis fulgoribus*] *In margin of Commonplace Book to replace two words
deleted, the first perhaps* liquidis.

i *102.* Sight, imperfect at first, gradually improves. G.

i *112.* Ideas of Beauty, Proportion & Order. G.

i *116.* Hearing, also improveable by the Judgement. G.

i *126.* Taste. G.

Luxuries, dona Autumni, Bacchique voluptas.
130   Naribus interea consedit odora hominum vis,
Docta leves captare auras, Panchaia quales
Vere novo exhalat, Floraeve quod oscula fragrant
Roscida, cum Zephyri furtim sub vesperis hora
Respondet votis, mollemque aspirat amorem.
135   Tot portas altae capitis circumdedit arci
Alma Parens, sensusque vias per membra reclusit;
Haud solas: namque intus agit vivata facultas,
Qua sese explorat, contemplatusque repente
Ipse suas animus vires, momentaque cernit.
140   Quid velit, aut possit, capiat, fugiatque, vicissim
Percipit imperio gaudens; neque corpora fallunt
Morigera ad celeres actus, ac numina mentis.
    Qualis Hamadryadum quondam si forte sororum
Una, novos peragrans saltus, et devia rura;
145   (Atque illam in viridi suadet procumbere ripa
Fontis pura quies, et opaci frigoris umbra)
Dum prona in latices speculi de margine pendet,
Mirata est subitam venienti occurrere Nympham:
Mox eosdem, quos ipsa, artus, eadem ora gerentem
150   Una inferre gradus, una succedere silvae
Aspicit alludens; seseque agnoscit in undis.
Sic sensu interno rerum simulacra suarum
Mens ciet, et proprios observat conscia vultus.
Nec vero simplex ratio, aut ius omnibus unum
155   Constat imaginibus. Sunt quae bina ostia norunt;
Hae privos servant aditus; sine legibus illae
Passim, qua data porta, ruunt, animoque propinquant.
Respice, cui a cunis tristes extinxit ocellos,
Saeva et in aeternas mersit natura tenebras:
160   Illi ignota dies lucet, vernusque colorum
Offusus nitor est, et vivae gratia formae.
Corporis at filum, et motus, spatiumque, locique
Intervalla datur certo dignoscere tactu:
Quandoquidem his iter ambiguum est, et ianua
        duplex,
165   Exclusaeque oculis species irrumpere tendunt
Per digitos. Atqui solis concessa potestas

i *130*. Smell. G.
i *135*. Reflection, the other Source of our Ideas. G.
i *154*. Ideas approach the Soul, some by single Avenues, some by two, others by every Sense. G.
i *158*. Illustration. Light, an Example of the first. G.
i *162*. Figure, Motion, Extension, of the second. G.

Luminibus blandae est radios immittere lucis.
   Undique proporro sociis, quacunque patescit
Notitiae campus, mixtae lasciva feruntur
170 Turba voluptatis comites, formaeque dolorum
Terribiles visu, et porta glomerantur in omni.
Nec vario minus introitu magnum ingruit Illud,
Quo facere et fungi, quo res existere circum
Quamque sibi proprio cum corpore scimus, et ire
175 Ordine, perpetuoque per aevum flumine labi.
   Nunc age quo valeat pacto, qua sensilis arte
Affectare viam, atque animi tentare latebras
Materies (dictis aures adverte faventes)
Exsequar. In primis spatii quam multa per aequor
180 Millia multigenis pandant se corpora saeclis,
Expende. Haud unum invenies, quod mente licebit
Amplecti, nedum proprius deprendere sensu,
Molis egens certae, aut solido sine robore, cuius
Denique mobilitas linquit, texturave partes,
185 Ulla nec orarum circumcaesura coercet.
Haec coniuncta adeo tota compage fatetur
Mundus, et extremo clamant in limine rerum,
(Si rebus datur extremum) primordia. Firmat
Haec eadem tactus (tactum quis dicere falsum
190 Audeat?) haec oculi nec lucidus arguit orbis.
   Inde potestatum enasci densissima proles
Nam quodcunque ferit visum, tangive laborat
Quicquid nare bibis, vel concava concipit auris,
Quicquid lingua sapit, credas hoc omne, necesse est
195 Ponderibus, textu, discursu, mole, figura
Particulas praestare leves, et semina rerum.
Nunc oculos igitur pascunt, et luce ministra
Fulgere cuncta vides, spargique coloribus orbem
Dum de sole trahunt alias, aliasque superne
200 Detorquent, retroque docent se vertere flammas.
Nunc trepido inter se fervent corpuscula pulsu,
Ut tremor aethera per magnum, lateque natantes
Aurarum fluctus avidi vibrantia claustra
Auditus queat allabi, sonitumque propaget.
205 Comminus interdum non ullo interprete per se

i *168*. Pleasure, Pain, of yᵉ 3ᵈ. G.
i *172*. Also Power, Existence, Unity, Succession, Duration. G.
i *177*. Primary Qualities of Bodies. G.
i *183*. Magnitude, Solidity, Mobility, Texture, Figure. G.
i *200*. Taken over from *Luna habitabilis* 41 (see p. 300).

Nervorum invadunt teneras quatientia fibras,
Sensiferumque urgent ultro per viscera motum.

LIBER SECUNDUS

Hactenus haud segnis Naturae arcana retexi
Musarum interpres, primusque Britanna per arva
Romano liquidum deduxi flumine rivum.
    Cum Tu opere in medio, spes tanti et causa laboris,
5 Linquis, et aeternam fati te condis in umbram!
Vidi egomet duro graviter concussa dolore
Pectora, in alterius non unquam lenta dolorem;
Et languere oculos vidi et pallescere amantem
Vultum, quo nunquam Pietas nisi rara, Fidesque,
10 Altus amor Veri, et purum spirabat Honestum.
Visa tamen tardi demum inclementia morbi
Cessare est, reducemque iterum roseo ore Salutem
Speravi, atque una tecum, dilecte Favoni!
Credulus heu longos, ut quondam, fallere soles:
15 Heu spes nequicquam dulces, atque irrita vota!
Heu maestos soles, sine te quos ducere flendo
Per desideria, et questus iam cogor inanes!
    At Tu, sancta anima, et nostri non indiga luctus,
Stellanti templo, sincerique aetheris igne,
20 Unde orta es, fruere; atque oh si secura, nec ultra
Mortalis, notos olim miserata labores
Respectes, tenuesque vacet cognoscere curas;
Humanam si forte alta de sede procellam
Contemplere, metus stimulosque cupidinis acres,
25 Gaudiaque et gemitus, parvoque in corde tumultum
Irarum ingentem, et saevos sub pectore fluctus:
Respice, et has lacrimas, memori quas ictus amore
Fundo; quod possum, iuxta lugere sepulcrum
Dum iuvat, et mutae vana haec iactare favillae.

ii *3. flumine*] flumina *Walpole.*
ii *22. tenues*] *In margin of Commonplace Book to replace* parvas *in text.*
ii *23. In margin of Commonplace Book:* ὁ τῆς ψυχῆς χειμών (the storm of
the soul) Epicurus ad Menoeceum [128.5].
ii *28. iuxta*] propter *Walpole.*

The Principles of Thinking.
Book I. To Favonius

From what origins the Mind begins to have knowledge; from what beginnings
Memory arises and sets in order the sequence of events and her slender
chain; whence Reason spreads its gradual mastery in the savage breast; and

whence anger, grief, fear, and insubstantial cares are first born to wretched mortals; it is of these matters that I begin my song. Do not disdain the singer, thou glory! thou second sun of the English race! Wherever thou first point the way, I am trying to mark thy faint footprints and to follow, albeit with hesitant tread. Better still (for thou art able to do all things), thyself lead the way to the holy threshold (if I approach with reverence and a pure heart) and throw open the mighty portals of secret Nature. Disclose, father, the unseen causes of things and their awful source; for to thee, thou great priest of truth, the hearts of men and the innermost places of the lofty mind lie open. And you, Favonius, lend me an attentive and sympathetic ear (for the work is produced for you) and do not despise the simple poem nor the poet; for these beginnings, though small, will give rise to no trivial activities. Wherever anything delightful or attractive comes into being, it is to these that it owes its origin, nor does it rise to the light unless they unite and favour the outcome. Hence derive the different arts of life, and gentler conduct, and the sweet bonds of friendship; here divine Wisdom lights her rosy flame and with serene countenance enlarges the minds of men, pointing out new joys and putting to flight monstrous anxieties and baseless fears; hence, indeed, grows Virtue, the most beautiful of all things. She also (wonderful indeed), who assiduously fosters you night and day with her inspiration, fits the willing language to metre and sweetens hours of leisure: she, the Golden Muse herself, boasts of no other origin.

In the beginning, when all-creating Nature confirmed the great covenant and ordered divine souls to grow in sluggish bodies, she did not wish that ethereal part to grow dull with long imprisonment in a shadowy cell; nor did she allow it to exercise its special powers in isolation, lest it despise the jointed limbs of the mass to which it was bound, forgetful of their weight and aware only of its celestial flame. Therefore, she arranged that the fibres of the nerves should tremble in every part in innumerable ducts; and, distributing them throughout the body, she interwove the branches everywhere, a sensitive network, and filled them with their own fluid (whether we call it lymph or air). Certainly, a delicate and almost imperceptible driving-force circulates it, and flows through the tiny channels once it is admitted. Constantly excited by external stimuli and rapid in motion, acting as a faithful messenger of the impulse which strikes it, it flows back from the impact to the upper regions of man, the citadel of the brain. For there the reasoning element of the soul has placed its throne and consecrated its temples. Round this, throng the sensations and fleeting impressions of things, borne along in a dense rank. Then, behold, a vast image of boundless Nature is disclosed, and the activities of the varied world are laid open.

And just as the rivers descend from the distant mountains – sail-studded Thames and the tawny-sanded Indus, the Euphrates, the Tagus and the Ganges with its fertile stream, each rolling down its waters – and burst into the sea with thunderous torrent; and Ocean, reclining in his great cavern, welcomes them and acknowledges the gifts of his children as they approach him in extended line, and willingly calms his sky-blue visage, smiling with many a ripple: just so do novel sensations hurry emulously to present themselves to the Mind and crowd round the entrances in a five-fold rank.

Touch takes the leading part and first lays open the dark route for the tiny throng, and absorbs the force of their onrush. This sense does not have the same limitations as its brothers: as the eldest, it claims wider sway, and has its abode deep in the marrow and the vitals, spreading into the outermost web of the skin, and has its being everywhere among the threads. Even before the child has struggled from his mother's womb and broken through his many layers of covering and burst his bonds; while he is still drugged with soft sleep and bathed in warm fluid, a slight breath has already stimulated his sense of touch and released his soul. This happens all the more at the moment when he exchanges the familiar soothing warmth for the cold of the atmosphere, which strikes at his unaccustomed limbs with a bitter onslaught. Then, yet more cruelly, Pain, the companion of human life, is waiting to receive him and tears out with violent hands the child who in vain delays and utters many querulous cries, clasping him in its iron embrace.

Then, for the first time, the bright face of Light is revealed (in such a way does Nature balance good and evil by turns and with just hand make amends for the harm she inflicts); and then it is that the newborn eyes first drink in the sunlight unknown before.

With what song, Goddess, shall I speak of you, the dearest offspring of Heaven, and of your origin; as you traverse the meadows bejewelled with light dew, making the purple lap of spring fragrant with flowery breath, and as you paint the verdant landscape, the shady hills and the azure heaven?

Grace and the charm of Venus and the train of myriad colours, forms and pleasing motions, follows after you. But black Night hides away her hated head in Stygian shadows and, with it, the face of terrible fears and a raging torrent of sleepless cares and uneasy torment; while everywhere the hearts of men are filled with joy, and the clear sky smiles with abundant rays.

But you do not fully reveal yourself to the Mind in its infant weakness (for daylight so powerful can harm the sight that is too tender and upset it while it is still unpractised); for you do not believe that infant minds can take in such a diverse crowd of impressions and the sights revealed by the miracle of light. And yet this brilliant novelty strikes infant eyes with remarkable sweetness and draws their attention. For have we not seen that, wherever the golden shafts of Phoebus scatter through broad windows, or the golden glow of lamps shines out, there at once the gaze is turned and stays drinking in insatiably the new-found beams and taking pleasure in watching.

A more sublime and important power, indeed, seems to be connected with this sense and closely allied to Judgement. As soon as age increases Judgement with the turning years, so this power, gaining nourishment from everything by gazing continually, perceives the importance of position, what force order has and what value should be placed in combination, as the eyes agree between them to illuminate things by things and shine in unison.

No less a power flourishes, dwelling in the twin ears, a force which not only stands watchfully on guard in these winding caverns on this side and on that (where the voice, carried on aerial wheels, makes its gates tremble with its knock) and runs far back; it is, in fact, this power which has also given to Eloquence the sounds and the wings of the thunderbolt, and to words the power of soothing and arousing the heart, and discovered how to fit words to metres and join them in verse, and all that the Libethridaean waters have learned, as often as Calliope, or the Father of Singing himself, unfold a pure song or breathe sweet airs from the vocal reed, forming them with the fingers.

Taste holds sway between the jaws, the moist home of the tongue, where the pleasing profusion of flavours makes its way in, the gifts of autumn and the pleasures of Bacchus.

Meanwhile, the power of smell resides in the nostrils of men, skilled to pick up delicate breezes, such as Panchaea breathes out in early spring, or the dewy lips of Flora sweetly emit, when, towards evening, she complies in secret with the prayers of Zephyrus and sighs with yielding love.

With so many portals did the kindly Mother surround the lofty citadel of the head and concealed the paths of sense throughout the body; but not these alone, for a lively faculty operates within, by which the mind explores itself and, having made the examination, at once comprehends its own powers and impulses. It perceives, in turn, what it wishes for or is capable of, what it desires or shuns, and it rejoices in its power; and neither the parts of the body, responsive to swift actions, nor the dictates of the Mind elude its notice.

It is just as if one of the sister Hamadryads of old was wandering through unknown glens and trackless country (and utter stillness and the shade's dark chill moved her to lie down on the green bank of a stream). As she lay hanging from the bank over the mirroring water, she was amazed that a Nymph at once came to meet her. Soon she noticed, while she sported, that, with the same limbs and features as her own, it moved forward as she did and, as she did, withdrew to the wood: and she recognized herself in the waters.

Thus it is that the mind stirs up by some inner sense images of its own functions and consciously examines its own features. But there is no one master-plan, nor does a single law regulate all images. There are some which know two gateways while others make use of a single entrance; others, which are liable to no rules, rush in wherever an entrance is offered and gather to the soul. Consider the man whose wretched eyes cruel Nature has extinguished in the cradle, plunging him into never-ending darkness. To him the daylight shines unknown, and unknown to him the spring-time glory of colours and the grace of living forms is poured forth. But it is granted that he should distinguish with sure touch the shape of a body, movements, space and the distance between places: since for these sensations there is a two-fold path and a double gateway, and, although shut out by the eyes, these impressions strive to break in through the fingers. Nevertheless, to the eyes alone is given the power of admitting the rays of soothing light.

Moreover, on every side, wherever the field of awareness extends, the companions of diverse pleasures, an idle crowd, are borne along, and the forms of pain, terrible to behold, which darken every doorway. And by no less varied entrances that great power forces its way in, whereby we know that we act and are acted upon, and that objects exist around us, each with its individual form, and progress in due order, borne along on the endless stream through the ages.

Now I shall explain by what means and what art sensible matter takes its way to and penetrates the secret places of the mind (give my words a favourable hearing). First of all, consider how many myriads of bodies through so many ages have appeared in the tracts of space. You will not come upon a single one which can be comprehended by the mind, let alone grasped by the senses, which lacks definite mass or is without solid substance, or in which mobility or texture have left the parts, or which is not confined by some limitation of shape. The world in its whole structure manifests that these bodies are conjoined and, as elements, they clamour at the outermost threshold of things (if we posit such a bound). Touch confirms the existence of these things (and who would dare to say Touch lies?), and the shining orb of the eye does not disprove it.

Thence is born a multitudinous offspring of powers; for whatever strikes the eyesight or struggles to be felt, whatever you absorb through the nostrils or the hollow ear receives, whatever the tongue tastes: you must believe that fragile particles, the seeds of things, furnish all this with weight, texture, motion, mass, and shape. Thus, they feed the eyes and by the mediation of light you see everything shine and the world spangled with colours, while they draw some rays down from the sun and others from above they bend aside, teaching them to return on their path. Thus, again, these tiny bodies seethe together with quivering beat, so that the vibration through the vast aether – the waves of air flowing far and wide – is able to slip in through the pulsating door of the greedy sense of hearing and begets sound. Meanwhile, with no intermediary, they themselves attack at close quarters, battering on the delicate fibres of the nerves spontaneously, and driving the sense-carrying impulse throughout the vitals.

Book II

So far had I, interpreter of the Muses, assiduously uncovered the secrets o Nature and first led a lucid stream from the Roman river through British fields. But now you, the inspiration and cause of so great a task, have deserted me in the midst of it and have hidden yourself in the eternal shadow of Death! I myself watched your breast cruelly racked by bitter suffering, a breast never slow to respond to another's pain; I watched your eyes grow dull and your loving face grow pale, a face in which only the most exalted affection, and loyalty, and deep love of truth, and unsullied integrity were expressed. At last the harshness of your lingering sickness seemed to be abating, and I hoped for the return of Health, with rosy cheeks, and you yourself with it, my dear Favonius! Foolishly trusting, alas, that we might spend the long, sunny days as before. Alas, the hopes, sweet but vain, and the ineffectual prayers! Alas, the sunny days, now spent in mourning, which I am forced to pass without you, in weeping because you are not there, and in vain complaints.

But you, blessed spirit, who do not need my grief, rejoice in the starry circuit of the heavens and the fire of the pure ether whence you sprang. But, if, released from cares as you are, but not beyond mortal concerns, you look back with pity on once-familiar toils and are free to perceive our trivial anxieties; if, by chance, you look down from your lofty seat on the storm of human passion, the fears, the fierce promptings of desire, the joys and sorrows and the tumult of rage so huge in our tiny hearts, the furious surges of the breast; then look back on these tears, also, which, stricken with love, I pour out in memory of you; this is all I can do, while my only wish is to mourn at your tomb and address these empty words to your silent ashes.

70 [Translations from the Greek Anthology]

These translations are found in G.'s Commonplace Book (i 287–8). Eleven of them were first published by Mathias (ii 94–7) in 1814, and I and XII were first published by Tovey, *Gray and His Friends* p. 295, in 1890. Bradshaw (pp. 168–72) printed them in G.'s order for the first time in 1891. G.'s own copy of the *Anthology* was the edn by H. Stephanus, Paris, 1566. There is no way of dating these translations. They have usually been assigned to a period later than 1742.

The numbering of the epigrams (in the present order) in the Loeb edn of the *Greek Anthology* is as follows: xi 365, xvi 136, xvi 57, xvi 119, xvi 129, xvi 164, xvi 211, xvi 210, ix 627, xi 391, v 215, v 125, v 74.

I. FROM THE GREEK

Fertur Aristophanis fatorum arcana rogatum,
  tempore sementis, rusticus isse domum;
(Sideris an felix tempestas, messis an esset
  magna, vel agricolam falleret ustus ager.)
5 Ille supercilio adducto multa anxius arte
  disposuit sortes, consuluitque Deos;
Tum responsa dedit: vernus suffecerit imber
  si modo, nec fruges laeserit herba nocens;
Si mala robigo, si grando pepercerit arvis,
10 attulerit subitum pigra nec aura gelu;
Caprea si nulla, aut culmos attriverit haedus;
  nec fuerit caelum, nec tibi terra gravis:
Largas polliceor segetes, atque horrea plena.
  tu tamen, ut veniat sera locusta, cave.

It is said that a countryman came to Aristophanes' house at sowing time to ask the secret decrees of Fate; (whether the constellations were in a lucky phase, whether it would be a good harvest or whether the parched fields would fail the farmer). He, with furrowed brow, carefully laid out the lots with great skill and consulted the gods; then he gave the response: If only the spring rains are adequate and no harmful weed injures the crop; if evil blight and hail spare the fields and no numbing wind brings on a sudden frost; if no goat nor kid eats away the shoots and neither the sky nor the earth is unkind to you–then I promise a bountiful harvest and full granaries. You must keep watch, however, in case the locust comes, later in the year.

II. FROM THE GREEK OF ANTIPHILUS BYZANTIUS.

In Medeae imaginem, nobile Timomachi opus

En ubi Medeae varius dolor aestuat ore,
  iamque animum nati, iamque maritus, habent!
Succenset; miseret; medio exardescit amore
  dum furor, inque oculo gutta minante tremit.
5 Cernis adhuc dubiam: quid enim? licet impia matris
  Colchidos, at non sit dextera Timomachi.

On a Depiction of Medea, the Noble Work of Timomachus

See where the changing passions seethe in Medea's face, as now her children,
now her husband hold her attention! She grows angry; feels pity; rage blazes
out even in the midst of love, and the teardrop trembles in her threatening
eye. You see her still irresolute: why is this? The hand of the Colchian mother
may have been wicked, but that of Timomachus would not (depict wicked-
ness).

III. IMITATION OF THE GREEK
OF PAUL SILENTIARIUS

In Bacchae furentis statuam

Credite, non viva est Maenas; non spirat imago.
artificis rabiem miscuit aere manus.

On the Statue of a Frenzied Bacchante

Believe me, the Maenad is not alive; the statue does not breathe. The hand
of the craftsman mingled madness with the bronze.

IV. FROM THE GREEK OF POSIDIPPUS

In Alexandrum, aere effictum

Quantum audet, Lysippe, manus tua! surgit in aere
spiritus, atque oculis bellicus ignis adest.
Spectate hos vultus, miserisque ignoscite Persis:
quid mirum, imbelles si leo sparsit oves?

On Alexander, depicted in Bronze

How bold is your hand, Lysippus! The breath surges in the bronze and there
is a warlike fire present in the eyes. Look on these features and pity the
wretched Persians: what wonder if the lion scatters the unwarlike sheep?

V. FROM THE GREEK

In Niobes statuam

Fecerat e viva lapidem me Iupiter: at me
Praxiteles vivam reddidit e lapide.

On the Statue of Niobe

From a living woman, Jupiter had turned me to stone; Praxiteles has re-
stored me from stone to life again.

VI.   FROM THE GREEK OF LUCIAN

Offering a Statue of herself to Venus

En tibi te, Cytherea, fero: formosius ipsa
cum tibi, quod ferrem, te, Dea, nil habui.

Lo, I offer thee to thyself, Cytherea; for I had nothing more beautiful than thyself, Goddess, that I could offer thee.

¶ *70*.vi 1 *En . . . fero*] *In margin of Commonplace Book to replace* Te tibi, sancta, fero nudam *in text.*

VII.   FROM THE GREEK OF STATYLLIUS FLACCUS

In Amorem dormientem

Docte Puer vigiles mortalibus addere curas!
 anne potest in te somnus habere locum?
Laxi iuxta arcus, et fax suspensa quiescit,
 dormit et in pharetra clausa sagitta sua:
5 Longe mater abest, longe Cythereïa turba.
 verum ausint alii te prope ferre pedem;
Non ego: nam metuo valde; mihi, perfide, quiddam
 forsan et in somnis ne mediteris mali.

On Cupid Sleeping

Boy, so skilled at heaping wakeful cares on mortals, can sleep find a place in you? Your unstrung bow lies still beside you, your torch is hung up and your arrow slumbers, shut in its quiver: your mother is far off and far off the Cytherean throng. Others, doubtless, may dare to tread near you, but not I; for I am too much afraid that even in sleep, treacherous boy, you may be plotting some harm for me.

VIII.   FROM A FRAGMENT OF PLATO

Itur in Idalios tractus, felicia regna,
 fundit ubi densam myrtea silva comam:
Intus Amor teneram visus spirare quietem,
 dum roseo roseos imprimit ore toros.
Sublimem procul a ramis pendere pharetram,
 et de languidula spicula lapsa manu
Vidimus, et risu molli diducta labella,
 murmure quae assiduo pervolitabat apes.

I went to the regions of Idalium, happy realms, where the myrtle woods spread their thick foliage: within, I saw Love, breathing softly in sleep, as he pressed the rose-strewn couch with his rosy face. At a distance, I saw his quiver hung on high from the branches and the arrow fallen from his hand as

it grew languid; his lips parted in a gentle smile, while a bee hovered about
them with a continual murmur.

IX. FROM THE GREEK OF MARIANUS

In Fontem aquae calidae

Sub platanis puer Idalius prope fluminis undam
    dormiit, in ripa deposuitque facem.
Tempus adest, sociae! Nympharum audentior una,
    tempus adest: ultra quid dubitamus? ait.
5 Ilicet incurrit, pestem ut divumque, hominumque,
    lampada collectis exanimaret aquis.
Demens! nam nequit saevam restinguere flammam
    Nympha, sed ipsa ignes traxit, et inde calet.

On a Spring of Warm Water

The Idalian boy was sleeping under the plane-trees, by the waters of a
river, and had laid down his torch on the bank. 'The time is come, comrades,'
says one of the Nymphs more daring than the rest; 'the time is come; why
do we hesitate any longer?' Instantly, she runs forward to extinguish the torch,
that bane of gods and men, in the gathered waters. Madness! for the Nymph
is unable to put out the fierce flame, but herself has caught fire and there-
after glows warm.

X. FROM LUCILLIUS

Irrepsisse suas murem videt Argus in aedes,
    atque ait, heus! a me numquid, amice, velis?
Ille autem ridens, metuas nihil; inquit, apud te,
    O bone, non epulas, hospitium petimus.

Argus saw that a mouse had crept into his house, and said, 'Ho there, friend!
Is there something you want from me?' But the mouse, smiling, said, 'Fear
nothing; for at your house, my good man, I am not looking for a banquet,
just a roof over my head.'

XI. IMITATED FROM THE GREEK OF POSIDIPPUS

Ad Amorem

Paulisper vigiles, oro, compesce dolores,
    respue nec Musae supplicis aure preces:
Oro brevem lacrimis veniam, requiemque furori.
    ah, ego non possum vulnera tanta pati!
5 Intima flamma, vides, miseros depascitur artus,
    surgit et extremis spiritus in labiis.
Quod si tam tenuem cordi est exsolvere vitam;

stabit in opprobrium sculpta querela tuum:
(Iuro perque faces istas, arcumque sonantem,
10   spiculaque hoc unum figere docta iecur)
Heu fuge crudelem puerum, saevasque sagittas!
huic fuit exitii causa, viator, amor.

To Cupid

For just a little while, pray, set at rest my wakeful cares, and do not refuse to
listen to the prayers of the suppliant Muse: I ask a brief respite from tears, a
relief from frenzy. Alas, I cannot endure such wounds! You see how the flames
deep within me consume my wretched limbs and my soul rises to the very
edge of my lips. But if you have resolved to put an end to a life which hangs by
such a thread, then this complaint will remain graven in stone, to your
shame (I swear by that notorious torch of yours, and your sounding bow, and
the darts taught to pierce these vitals alone): Alas, flee the pitiless boy and
his cruel arrows! It was Love, traveller, who caused the death of him who lies
beneath.

XII. [FROM THE GREEK] OF BASSUS

Non ego, cum malus urit amor, Iovis induor arma.
Nil mihi cum plumis, nil mihi cum corio:
Non ego per tegulas mittor liquefactus in aurum.
Promo duo obolos: sponte venit Danaë.

I do not assume the armour of Jove when wicked Love fires me; I have
nothing to do with feathers or with bulls' hides; I do not cast myself over the
roof-tiles melted into gold; I just take out two obols and Danae comes wil-
lingly.

XIII. [FROM THE GREEK] OF RUFINUS

Hanc tibi Rufinus mittit, Rodoclea, coronam.
has tibi decerpens texerat ipse rosas.
Est viola, est anemone, est suave rubens hyacinthus,
mixtaque Narcisso lutea caltha suo.
5   Sume: sed aspiciens ah fidere desine formae!
qui pingit, brevis est, sertaque teque, color.

Rufinus sends you, Rhodoclea, this garland. He picked the roses for you
himself and wove them together. There are violets and anemones and softly-
blushing hyacinths and the yellow marigold, mixed with its narcissus. Take
it: but when you look on it, ah then give up trusting to your beauty! The hue is
short-lived which colours both the garland and you.

71 [Orders of Insects]

G. transcribed these verses into his annotated and interleaved copy of Linn-
aeus's *Systema Natura* (10th edn, 1758–9), now in the Library of Harvard

College. They were first printed by Mathias (ii 570–3) in 1814, as 'Generick Characters of the Orders of Insects, and of the Genera of the first six Orders, named Coleoptera, Hemiptera, Lepidoptera, Neuroptera, Hymenoptera, and Diptera; expressed in Technical Verses.' It can no doubt be assumed that these verses were not written before G. acquired his copy of Linnaeus, which he bought soon after his arrival in London on 15 Oct. 1759; see W. Powell Jones, *Thomas Gray, Scholar* (1937) p. 128. The existence of the 'Additional Lines on Insects', a rough draft with corrections which was apparently abandoned, in the Pierpont Morgan Library, New York, was first noted by W. Powell Jones, *Thomas Gray, Scholar* p. 181; they were first printed by Starr and Hendrickson, p. 185. Since they evidently represent a draft of the incomplete section vii, 'Aptera', of the 'Orders of Insects', it is possible that G. was working on it at the time of his last illness in 1771. For facsimiles of some of G.'s notes and drawings in his interleaved Linnaeus, see Charles E. Norton, *The Poet Gray as a Naturalist* (Boston, 1903). G. himself numbered all but the first and last sections; the names of the orders and the sub-headings in the first section are those given by Linnaeus.

[I. COLEOPTERA]

Alas lorica tectas Coleoptera iactant.

*[Antennis clavatis]

Serra pedum prodit Scarabeum et fissile cornu.
Dermesti antennae circum ambit lamina caulem,
Qui caput incurvum timidus sub corpore celat.
5   In pectus retrahens caput abdit claviger Hister.
Occiput Attelabi in posticum vergit acumen.
Curculio ingenti protendit cornua rostro.
Silpha leves peltae atque elytrorum exporrigit oras.
Truncus apex clavae, atque antennula Coccionellae.

**[Antennis filiformibus]

10 Cassida sub clipei totam se margine condit.
Chrys'mela inflexa loricae stringitur ora.
Gibba caput Meloë incurvat, thorace rotundo.
Oblongus frontem et tenues clipei exerit oras
Tenebrio. Abdomen Mordellae lamina vestit.
15 Curta elytra ostentat Staphylis, caudamque recurvam.

***[Antennis setaceis]

Tubere cervicis valet, antennisque Cerambyx.
Pectore Leptura est tereti, corpusque coartat.
Flexile Cantharidis tegmen, laterumque papillae.
Ast Elater resilit sterni mucrone supinus.

20 Maxilla exerta est, oculoque Cicindela grandi.
Bupresti antennae graciles, cervice retracta.
Nec Dytiscus iners saetosa remige planta.
Effigiem cordis Carabus dat pectore trunco.
Necydalis curto ex elytro nudam explicat alam.
25 Curtum at Forficulae tegit hanc, cum forcipe caudae.
Depressum Blattae corpus, venterque bicornis.
Dente vorax Gryllus deflexis saltitat alis.

[HEMIPTERA]

II. (Dimidiam rostrata gerunt Hemiptera crustam.
Femina serpit humi interdum: volat aethere coniunx.)

30 Rostro Nepa rapax pollet, chelisque. Cicada
Fastigio alarum et rostrato pectore saltat.
Tela Cimex inflexa gerit, cruce complicat alas.
Notonecta crucem quoque fert, remosque pedales;
Cornua Aphis caudae et rostrum: saepe erigit alas;
35 Deprimit has Chermes, dum saltat, pectore gibbo.
Coccus iners caudæ saetas, volitante marito;
Thrips alas angusta gerit, caudamque recurvam.

[LEPIDOPTERA]

III. (Squamam alae, linguae spiram Lepidoptera iactant.)

Papilio clavam et squamosas subrigit alas.
40 Prismaticas Sphinx antennas, medioque tumentes;
At conicas gravis extendit sub nocte Phalaena.

[NEUROPTERA]

IV. (Rete alae nudum, atque hamos Neuroptera caudae.)

Dente alisque potens, secat aethera longa Libella.
Cauda saetigera, erectis stat Ephemera pennis.
45 Phryganea elinguis rugosas deprimit alas;
Hemerinusque bidens: planas tamen explicat ille.
Et rostro longo et cauda Panorpa minatur.
Raphidia extento collo saetam trahit unam.

[HYMENOPTERA]

V. (At vitreas alas, iaculumque Hymenoptera caudae,
Femineo data tela gregi, maribusque negata.) 50

Telum abdit spirale Cynips, morsuque minatur.
Maxillas Tenthredo movet, serramque bivalvem;
Ichneumon gracili triplex abdomine telum.

Haurit Apis lingua incurva, quod vindicat ense.
55 Sphex alam expandit laevem, gladiumque recondit.
Alae ruga notat Vespam, caudaeque venenum;
Squamula Formicam tergi, telumque pedestrem,
Dum minor alata volitat cum coniuge coniunx.
Mutilla impennis, sed cauda spicula vibrat.

[DIPTERA]

VI. (Diptera sub geminis alis se pondere librant.)   60

Os Oestro nullum est, caudaque timetur inermi.
Longa caput Tipula est, labiisque et praedita palpis.
Palpis Musca caret, retrahitque proboscida labris;
Qua Tabanus gaudet pariter, palpis sub acutis.
65 Os Culicis molli e pharetra sua spicula vibrat;
Rostrum Empis durum et longum sub pectore curvat;
Porrigit articuli de cardine noxia Conops;
Porrigit (at rectum et conicum) sitibundus Asilus;
Longum et Bombylius, qui surgit mella volando.
70 Unguibus Hippobosca valet: vibrat breve telum.

[VII. APTERA]

(Aptera se pedibus pennarum nescia iactant.)

I. Coleoptera

The Coleoptera boast wings that are covered with leathern armour.

With Club-shaped Antennae

A serration on the legs and a divided horn mark out the Scarabeus. Plating surrounds the stem of the Dermestes' antenna, and it fearfully hides its head bowed beneath its body. The club-bearing Hister conceals its head, withdrawing it into its body. The occiput of the Attelabus comes to a sharp point at the back. The Curculio extends horns from a vast beak. The Silpha protrudes fine edges of a shield and sheaths. The Coccionella has a truncated top to its club and small antennae.

With Thread-like Antennae

Cassida hides itself completely beneath the rim of its shield. Chrysomela is drawn in tightly by the inflexible edge of its leathern armour. Hunch-backed Meloë bends in its head, with a rounded thorax. Oblong Tenebrio juts out its head and the thin margins of its shield. Plating covers the abdomen of Mordella. Staphylis displays shortened sheaths and a backward-curving tail.

With Bristly Antennae

The Cerambyx is strong in the girth of its neck and its antennae. The thorax of the Leptura is smooth and its body tapers. The covering of the Cantharis is flexible and it has papillae on its sides. The Elater, when supine, leaps back on its feet by means of the spike on its breast. The jaw is thrust forth in the Cicindela and it has large eyes. The antennae of Buprestis are slender and its neck retracted. Dytiscus is not inactive by virtue of the rowing motions of its bristle-covered feet. The Carabus presents the picture of a heart with its shortened thorax. The Necydalis unfolds bare wings from a shortened sheath; but a shortened one covers this part on the Forficula also, and its tail is forked. The body of the Blatta is flattened and the abdomen has two horns. The fierce-toothed Gryllus jumps with close-folded wings.

II. Hemiptera

(The beaked Hemiptera bear a shell divided in half. The female creeps on the ground at other times, but when mating flies in the air.)

The voracious Nepa is powerful with beak and claws. The Cicada jumps by means of its wing-tips and hooked breast. The Cimex bears in-curving darts and folds its wings in the shape of a cross. The Notonecta also forms a cross and has oar-like feet. The Aphis has a spiny tail and a beak and often spreads its wings. The Chermes depresses these on its hump-backed body when it jumps. The slow Coccus has bristles on its tail and the male flies when mating. The slender Thrips bears wings and a tail which bends backwards.

III. Lepidoptera

(The Lepidoptera boast scale-clad wings and a spiral tongue.)

Papilio lifts a club and scaly wings. The Sphinx has prism-like antennae which swell in the middle; but the heavy Phalaena extends conical ones in the night.

IV. Neuroptera

(The Neuroptera have bare, mesh-like wings and hooks on the tail.) The long Libella, powerful in teeth and wings, cuts through the air. With a bristling tail the Ephemera stands with wings erect. The tongueless Phryganea presses down its wings in ridges, as does the Hemerinus with two teeth: but when it unfurls them they are smooth. The Panorpa menaces with long beak and tail. The Raphidia, with neck outstretched, bears a single bristle.

V. Hymenoptera

(But the Hymenoptera have transparent wings and a dart in the tail. The weapons are given to the female species and denied to the males.)

The Cynips conceals a spiral dart and menaces with its bite. The Tenthredo moves its jaws and a double-plated saw. The Ichneumon has a three-fold dart in its slender abdomen. The Apis drinks with its in-curving tongue what it claims by the sword. The Sphex spreads open a smooth wing and hides away its weapon. The creases on its wings denote the Vespa, as also the poison in its tail. There are small scales and a weapon on the back of the Formica which moves on foot. The smaller mate flutters with the winged female. The Mutilla is wingless but brandishes darts with its tail.

VI. Diptera

(The Diptera poise themselves by a balance beneath their two wings.)

The Oestrus has no mouth and is feared in spite of its unarmed tail. The Tipula has a long head and is endowed with lips and palpi. The Musca lacks palpi and draws its proboscis under its lips, [a proboscis which] Tabanus equally enjoys beneath its pointed mouth. The Culex' mouth brandishes darts from a soft quiver; the beak of the Empis is hard and curves a long way beneath the breast. The noxious Conops extends its beak by a hinged joint. The thirsty Asilus extends it also (but it is straight and conical). The Bombylius has a long beak which sucks up honey in flight. The Hippobosca is powerful in its talons and brandishes a short weapon.

VII. Aptera

(The Aptera boast of their feet, having no acquaintance with wings.)

[ADDITIONAL LINES ON INSECTS]

> Palpos ore duos, triplexque Lepisma flagellum
> Pone gerit: cauda saltatque Podura bifurca.
> Maxillis Termes, at lingua pollet acuta
> Phthir laterumque lobis. Compresso abdomine Pulex
> 5   Inflexoque minax rostro salit.

The Lepisma bears two palpi on its mouth and a threefold whip behind: the Podura jumps by means of a forked tail. The Termes is powerful in the jaws, Phthir in its pointed tongue and the lobes on its sides. The Pulex has a compressed abdomen and jumps menacing with in-curving beak.

GREEK POETRY

72 Inscription for a Wood in a Park

G. sent this epigram to West in a letter first printed by Mason, *Memoirs* p. 152, although Whibley and Toynbee suspect that his date of 27 May 1742 covers a conflation of two or more letters between 15 and 27 May (see *Corresp* i 209 *n*). G. introduces the epigram as follows: 'I send you an inscription for a wood joining to a park of mine; (it is on the confines of Mount Cithaeron, on the left hand as you go to Thebes) you know I am no friend to hunters, and hate to be disturbed by their noise.' G. transcribed it into his Commonplace Book (i 278), where it is dated at the end 'May: 1742'.

> Ἁζόμενος πολύθηρον ἑκηβόλου ἄλσος Ἀνάσσας,
> Τᾶς δεινᾶς τεμένη λεῖπε, κυναγὲ, θεᾶς·
> Μοῦνοι ἄρ᾽ ἔνθα κύνων ζαθέων κλαγγεῦσιν ὑλαγμοὶ,
> ἀνταχεῖς Νυμφᾶν ἀγροτερᾶν κελάδῳ.

In reverence, huntsman, leave the game-filled grove of the far-darting Lady, the precinct of the awe-inspiring Goddess; for there only the baying of the sacred hounds re-echoes, answering the cry of the huntress nymphs.

POEMS OF DOUBTFUL AUTHENTICITY

73 The Characters of the Christ-Cross Row, By a Critic, To M^{rs}—

G. sent this poem to Walpole in mid-June 1747 (*Corresp* i 284–6), in a letter which first discusses the reception in Cambridge of his *Eton Ode*:

'it is said to be mine, but I strenuously deny it, and so do all that are in the secret, so that nobody knows what to think; a few only of King's College gave me the lie, but I hope to demolish them; for if *I* don't know, who should? .... I send you a Poem that I am sure they will read (as well as they can) a masterpiece–it is said, being an admirable improvement on that beautiful piece called Pugna Porcorum, which begins

Plangite porcelli Porcorum pigra propago;

but that is in Latin, and not for their reading, but indeed, this is worth a thousand of it, and unfortunately it is not perfect, and it is not mine.'

G. refers here to *Pugna Porcorum per P. Porcium Poetam* (1530) by Joannes Leo Placentius (*c.* 1500–*c.* 1530), a poem consisting of 249 ll., each word of which begins with the letter 'p'. (The first word is in fact 'Plaudite', not 'Plangite'.)

The poem was discussed by Walpole and Mason, while the latter was writing his *Memoirs* of G. In a letter of 20 March 1773 (*Walpole Correspondence* xxviii 74), Mason stated that William Trollope (*c.* 1707–49), Fellow of Pembroke 1731–49, was 'the author of the poem on the alphabet, from which and from Gray's a more perfect copy might be taken of that whimsical yet clever production'. Walpole replied on 27 March (*ibid* 79): 'I return you Mr Trollop's verses, of which many are excellent, and yet I cannot help thinking the best were Gray's, not only as they appear in his writing, but as they are more nervous and less diffuse than the others; when we meet, why should not we select the best, and make a complete poem?' From this exchange it would appear either that G. had merely revised Trollope's MS (as most recent editors assume) or that there were two distinct poems, attempting the same humorous use of the alphabet, one by Trollope and one in G.'s handwriting, though not admitted by him to be his. The second of these would no doubt be that in G.'s letter to Walpole. (G.'s denial of his authorship of the poem on that occasion, in a letter in which he described his efforts to deny authorship of the *Eton Ode*, could be ironic.) Walpole certainly believed that G. had written it himself. When Mitford first printed the poem in the *Correspondence of Gray and Nicholls* (1843) pp. 217–21, he quoted Walpole's note on G.'s holograph MS: 'Gray would never allow the foregoing Poem to be his, but it has too much merit, and the humour and versification are so much in his style, that I cannot believe it to be written by any other hand.' Mitford gave more information about the MS in the *Correspondence of Walpole and Mason* (1851) i 412. He had printed it originally from 'Gray's autograph in the Strawberry Hill Collection', although he admitted that 'a few omissions deemed necessary were made in printing the poem' (presumably on the grounds of obscenity). Mitford added that 'Gray's MS copy was destroyed by the gentleman who bought it at Strawberry Hill; and the transcript which I made, and from which I printed the poem, is probably the only one existing'. There is no conclusive evidence for an attribution to G., but there is clearer evidence than recent editors have acknowledged for the existence of a poem, other than Trollope's, in G.'s hand, which may have been his own composition.

'Christ-Cross Row' was a sixteenth-century name for the alphabet, so called from the figure of a cross prefixed to it in the hornbooks.

> Great D draws near – the Duchess sure is come,
> Open the doors of the withdrawing-room:
> Her daughters decked most daintily I see,
> The dowager grows a perfect double D.
> 5 E enters next and with her Eve appears.
> Not like yon dowager depressed with years:
> What ease and elegance her person grace,
> Bright beaming as the evening-star her face.
> Queen Esther next – how fair e'en after death;
> 10 Then one faint glimpse of Queen Elizabeth;
> No more, our Esthers now are nought but Hetties,
> Elizabeths all dwindled into Betties.
> In vain you think to find them under E,
> They're all diverted into H and B.
> 15 F follows fast the fair – and in his rear
> See folly, fashion, foppery straight appear,
> All with fantastic clues, fantastic clothes,
> With fans and flounces, fringe and furbelows.
> Here Grub-street geese presume to joke and jeer,
> 20 All, all but Grannam Osborne's *Gazetteer*.
> High heaves his hugeness H: methinks we see
> Henry the Eighth's most monstrous majesty.
> But why on such *mock* grandeur should we dwell?
> H mounts to heaven and H descends to hell.
> 25 As H the Hebrew found, so I the Jew:
> See Isaac, Joseph, Jacob pass in view.
> The walls of old Jerusalem appear,
> See Israel and all Judah thronging there.
>
> *   *   *   *
>
> P pokes his head out, yet has not a pain:

¶ 73.20. *Grannam Osborne's Gazetteer*] The *Daily Gazetteer* was conducted by James Pitt (1679–1763) under the name of Francis Osborne. He was often called 'Mother Osborne' after being so nicknamed by the *Craftsman* in 1742. See Pope, *Dunciad* ii 312.

30 Like Punch he peeps, but soon pops in again.
    Pleased with his pranks, the pisgys calls him Puck,
    Mortals he loves to prick and pinch and pluck.
    Now a pert prig, he perks upon your face;
    Now peers, pores, ponders with profound grimace;
35 Now a proud prince, in pompous purple dressed,
    And now a player, a peer, a pimp or priest,
    A pea, a pin, in a perpetual round,
    Now seems a penny, and now shows a pound.
    Like perch or pike in pond you see him come;
40 He in plantations hangs like pear or plum,
    Pippin or peach, then perches on the spray,
    In form of parrot, pye or popinjay.
    P, Proteus-like, all tricks, all shapes can show,
    The pleasantest person in the Christ-cross Row.

                *   *   *   *

45 As K a king, Q represents a queen,
    And seems small difference the sounds between.
    K as a man with hoarser accent speaks;
    In shriller notes Q like a female squeaks.
    Behold, K struts as might a king become;
50 Q draws her train along the drawing-room.
    Slow follow all the quality of state:
    Queer Queensberry only does refuse to wait.

                *   *   *   *

    Thus great R reigns in town, while different far,
    Rests in retirement *little* rural R;
55 Remote from cities lives in lone retreat,
    With rooks and rabbit-burrows round his seat.
    S sails the swan slow down the silver stream.

                *   *   *   *

    So, big with weddings, waddles W,
    And brings all womankind before your view:
60 A wench, a wife, a widow and a w[hor]e,
    With woe behind and wantonness before.

31. *pisgys*] A dialect form of 'pixies'.
52. *Queer Queensbury*] The beautiful and eccentric Lady Catherine Hyde
(1701–77) married the Duke of Queensberry in 1720 and became the
patroness of John Gay.

74 Lines on the Accession of George III

The only reference to these lines occurs in Joseph Cradock's *Literary Memoirs* (1828) iv 224. They have never been considered seriously to be G.'s: 'Many light satires perhaps have since been given to him that he did not write, but certainly very like him: take that for instance on the Cambridge Condolence and Congratulation on the Death of King George II. and the Accession of George III.'

> The Old One's dead,
> And in his stead,
>   The New One takes his place;
> Then sing and sigh,
> And laugh and cry,
>   With dismal cheerful face.

Note.

As there is so little evidence for the attribution of the following poems, Nos. 75 to 77, to G., the texts are not given, though the poems are listed for completeness.

75 Translation of Philips's *The Splendid Shilling*, ll. 1-12

Tovey, *Gray and His Friends* (1890) p. 298, introduces these lines as follows: 'After some Latin Alcaics signed 'Antrobus' comes in the 3rd volume of Mitford's Excerpts [ff. 110–11] a Latin translation of Philip's 'Splendid Shilling,' to which he does not assign the authorship.' There is no other reason for believing that this translation of the first 12 ll. of John Philips's *Splendid Shilling* (1701) is by G.

76 Paraphrase of Martial, Book X, Epigram 23

The MS of this poem, which had been among the collection of papers owned by descendants of John Nichols (1745–1826) where it was attributed to G., was sold as a holograph at Sotheby's on 6 Nov. 1951 (ll. 1–8 being printed in the sale catalogue). It is now in the Bibliothèque Martin Bodmer at Geneva. The poem was first printed in full by H. W. Starr in *Notes and Queries*, cxcix(1954) 435–6. There is no evidence to suggest that the MS is in G.'s hand or in that of any of his circle, nor is there any internal evidence to support the attribution of the poem to him. The title in the MS incorrectly states that the poem is 'Martials Lib. 10. Epig. 13. paraphrased.'

77 Imitation of Martial

First printed in the *Gentleman's Mag.* lxxi 591, in July 1801 and included by Starr and Hendrickson, p. 197, among 'Poems of Doubtful Authenticity.' A letter from Sheffield signed by Edmund C. Mason sent the magazine 'a paper lately found in the possession of my late most highly-honoured relative and namesake'. The 'Anecdote' he enclosed is as follows: 'Mr. Gray, after having proceeded to the degree of A.B. at Cambridge, was supposed to have contracted an affection for Miss D----me; at the same time that Mr. M. was said to have felt the tender passion for Miss C--t-y, afterwards Mrs. H--g--m. On Mr. M's commending the superiority of his mistress, Mr. Gray penned the following lines, a very masterly imitation of Martial.' The 6 ll. of the Latin 'imitation' follow, 'which afterwards Mr. West, on his return from the grand tour, thus elegantly, though perhaps somewhat inaccurately, translated'. A Greek translation is then given.

G. never received the degree of A.B. nor did West ever go on the Grand Tour. In any case, as E. J. Kenney in *Notes and Queries* ccxii (1966) 464, has pointed out, this poem was in fact written by Catullus (poem 86): only a few slight verbal changes and alteration of the proper names mentioned were made in the text attributed to G. in 1801.

THE POEMS OF
WILLIAM COLLINS

Chronological Table of William Collins's Life and Publications

1721   (*25 Dec.*) Born at Chichester, son of William C., a hatter, Mayor of the town in 1714 and 1721.

1725–33   Educated probably at a Prebendal School.

1734   (*23 Feb.*) Admitted as Scholar at Winchester School. Contemporaries include Joseph Warton, James Hampton and John Mulso.

1739   (*Oct.*) His *Sonnet* published in the *Gentleman's Mag.* Writes his *Persian Eclogues* at this period.

1740   Placed first on list of Scholars for New College, but no vacancy occurs.
(*22 March*) Matriculates at Queen's College, Oxford.

1741   (*29 July*) Elected Demy of Magdalen College, where his cousin William Payne is a Fellow.

1742   (*Jan.*) His *Persian Eclogues* published by J. Roberts.

1743   (*18 Nov.*) Graduates B.A.
(*Dec.*) His *Verses . . . to Sir Thomas Hanmer* published by M. Cooper.

1744   (*9 May*) Revised edn of the *Epistle to Hanmer* published by M. Cooper and R. Dodsley, including the *Song from Cymbeline*. Probably in London by this date.
(*6 July*) Death of his mother. Her will leaving her property to her three children not proved until 12 Aug. 1745.
(*18 July*) Letter from Mulso to Gilbert White describes C. in London as 'entirely an Author' and refers to his 'Subscriptions' (see *Dec.*).
(*17 Sept.*) By this date has applied to the Duke of Richmond for a living and has been offered a curacy at Birdham. Dissuaded from accepting it by John Hardham, tobacconist and under-treasurer at Drury Lane Theatre.
(*8 Oct.*) By this date is lodging with Miss Bundy at the corner of King's Square Court, Soho.

(*Dec.*) His proposed *History of the Revival of Learning* mentioned in *A Literary Journal* in Dublin.

1745   At this period his friends include Johnson, Armstrong, and the actors Quin, Garrick, Foote and Davies. Plans a tragedy, undertakes a translation of Aristotle's *Poetics* with commentary and engages to supply articles for the *Biographia Britannica*: none of these projects is known to have been executed. Gilbert White describes him at this period as 'spending his time in all the dissipation of Ranelagh, Vauxhall, and the playhouses'.

(*13 March*) Will of his uncle, Charles C., proved, leaving him property in Chichester.

(*11 May*) Battle of Fontenoy. Writes his *Ode to a Lady* before the end of the month.

(*17 Sept.*) Mulso tells White that C. 'has been some Time return'd from Flanders', is intending to take orders and wants an army chaplaincy. C. may have been motivated by the landing of the Young Pretender in Scotland in July to visit his uncle Col. Martin, then in Flanders, for advice about his career.

1746   (*16 April*) Battle of Culloden.

(*23 April*) Letter from John Gilbert Cooper to Dodsley refers to C. as 'that wandering Knight'.

(*c. 20 May*) Meets Joseph Warton at Guildford Races and plans a joint volume of their *Odes*, eventually abandoned.

(*28 May*) His encounter with a bailiff mentioned by Mulso. At some point during the next few months probably removes to Richmond.

(*7 June*) His *Ode to a Lady* published in *The Museum*, ed. Mark Akenside and published by Dodsley.

(*1 Aug.*) Mulso has received a letter from C. in Antwerp, describing his travels through Holland and his plan to 'set out for the army', presumably to meet Col. Martin once more, who has left Scotland for Flanders at about this time.

(*10 Oct.*) Sells property at Chichester, on which he had raised money by a mortgage in April.

(*4 Dec.*) Joseph Warton's *Odes on Various Subjects* published by Dodsley.

(*20 Dec.*) C.'s *Odes on Several Descriptive and Allegoric Subjects*, dated 1747, published by A. Millar. Later destroys the unsold copies.

1747   By this period living at Richmond and friendly with James Thomson and John Ragsdale.

(*1 May*) Joins with his sisters to sell his father's old premises and other property in Chichester.

(*10 Nov.*) Writes to J. G. Cooper about their projected *Clarendon Review*, never published.

1748   (*7 April*) Johnson's Preface to *The Preceptor* refers to a commentary on Aristotle's *Poetics*, presumably C.'s, as 'soon to be published'.

(*27 Aug.*) Death of James Thomson at Richmond.

(*Dec.*) Three poems published in 2nd edn of Dodsley's *Collection*.

1749   (*19 April*) C.'s uncle, Col. Martin, makes his will and dies a week later, leaving C. one-third of his property, estimated by some sources as £2000.

(*June*) His *Ode Occasioned By the Death of Mr. Thomson* published by R. Manby and H. S. Cox.

(*Oct.*) His *Song from Cymbeline* reprinted in the *Gentleman's Mag.* as *Elegiac Song*.

1749–50   (*c. Dec.–Jan.*) Writes his *Ode Addressed to a Friend*, presented to John Home (published in 1788 as *Ode on the Popular Superstitions of the Highlands*).

1750   Seen in London at this period by Thomas Warton, still planning his *History of the Revival of Learning* (of which only the preliminary dissertation was ever written) and the *Clarendon Review*.

(*Feb.–March*) His *Epistle to the Editor of Fairfax his Translation of Tasso* advertised but not published by Manby and Cox.

(*2 July*) *The Passions*, set to music by William Hayes, performed at Encaenia at Oxford and printed as a pamphlet.

(*8 Nov.*) Writes to William Hayes from Chichester (where he may have been living permanently for some time), referring to a revised version of *The Passions* and an *Ode on the Music of the Grecian Theatre*.

1751   (*Easter*) Seriously ill, according to Thomas Warton.

(*9 June*) Missing letter from Chichester mentioned by Warton.

1751–54   According to Ragsdale, travels in France and visits Bath in an attempt to regain health. Johnson mentions meeting him at Islington after his return to England.

1753   (*May*) *The Union*, ed. T. Warton, published at Oxford, contains *Ode to Evening* and *Ode on Thomson*.

1754   According to Ragsdale is removed by his sister from McDonald's madhouse at Chelsea. Visits Oxford for a month, lodging opposite Christ Church and is seen there by Gilbert White.

(*Sept.*) Visited by the Wartons at Chichester, where he is living in the Cathedral Cloisters with his sister Anne. Shows them several fragmentary MS. poems.

1755   (*28 Jan.*) His younger sister Anne marries Lieut. Hugh Sempill; after his death she will marry Thomas Durnford, Rector of Bramdean and Vicar of Harting.

(*March*) His *Epistle to Hanmer* printed in Dodsley's *Collection of Poems*, vol iv.

1757   His *Oriental Eclogues* reprinted by J. Payne.

1759   (*12 June*) Dies at Chichester and is buried in St Andrew's Church three days later.

Abbreviations

EDITIONS OF COLLINS'S POEMS

1746 *Odes on Several Descriptive and Allegoric Subjects*, 1747 (published Dec. 1746).

1765 *The Poetical Works . . . With Memoirs of the Author; and Observations on his Genius and Writings*, ed. John Langhorne, 1765 (later edns 1771, 1776, 1781).

Strutt *Eclogues and Miscellaneous Pieces*, ed. Benjamin Strutt, Colchester, 1796.

Barbauld *The Poetical Works . . . With a Prefatory Essay*, ed. Mrs A. L. Barbauld, 1797.

Dyce *The Poetical Works*, ed. Alexander Dyce, 1827 (including 'Various Notes' by John Mitford).

Crowe *The Poetical Works*, ed. William Crowe, Bath, 1828.

Brydges *The Poetical Works*, ed. Sir S. E. Brydges, 1830 (Aldine edn, reprinted 1853; containing 'Essay' by Brydges and 'Memoir' by Sir N. H. Nicolas).

Wilmott *The Poetical Works*, ed. R. A. Wilmott (with Gray, Parnell, Green and T. Warton), 1854.

Thomas *The Poetical Works*, ed. W. Moy Thomas, 1858 (Aldine edn, reprinted 1866, 1894).

Bronson *The Poems*, ed. W. C. Bronson, Boston, 1898.

Poole *The Poetical Works* (with Gray), ed. C. Stone and A. L. Poole, Oxford, 1917; revised by F. Page, 1937.

Blunden *The Poems*, ed. Edmund Blunden, 1929.

Cunningham *Drafts and Fragments of Verse*, ed. J. S. Cunningham, Oxford, 1956.

OTHER WORKS

Ainsworth E. G. Ainsworth, *Poor Collins: His Life, his Art and his Influence*, Ithaca, 1937.

Boswell, *Life of Johnson* James Boswell, *The Life of Johnson*, ed. G. B. Hill and L. F. Powell, 6 vols, Oxford, 1934–50.

Carver P. L. Carver, *William Collins: The Life of a Poet*, 1967; based on 'Notes on the Life of William Collins', *Notes and Queries* clxxvii (Aug.–Oct. 1939).

Garrod H. W. Garrod, *Collins*, Oxford, 1928.

Nichols John Nichols, *Literary Anecdotes of the Eighteenth Century*, 9 vols, 1812–15.

PMLA *Publications of the Modern Language Association.*

The Reaper *The Reaper* No. 26 (in the *York Chronicle* for 16 Feb. 1797, one of a series of essays contributed by Thomas Maude in 1796–97) containing letters about C. by Thomas Warton and John Ragsdale; reprinted by Nathan Drake, *The Gleaner: A Series of Periodical Essays; Selected and Arranged from Scarce or Neglected Volumes*, 1811, iv 474–84. (A slightly fuller text of Ragsdale's letter also appeared in the *Monthly Magazine*, xxi (1806) 494.)

Salmon Thomas Salmon, *Modern History: or, The Present State of All Nations*, 3rd edn, 3 vols, 1739.

Times Lit. Supp. *The Times Literary Supplement.*

Plate 2   William Collins at the age of 14.
Engraved for the European Magazine from an
Original Drawing in the possession of the late
William Seward Esqr.
Published in September 1811 in the
European Magazine vol. lx, facing page 208

1 Sonnet

First printed in the *Gentleman's Mag.* ix 545, in Oct. 1739, signed 'Delicatulus', and preceded by two poems entitled 'Sappho's Advice' and 'Beauty and Innocence', According to an editorial note all three poems 'were sent us in one letter'. John Wooll, *Memoirs of Joseph Warton* (1806) p. 107 *n*, quotes a 'memorandum, in Dr. Warton's handwriting', which he had found on p. 545 of an unnamed magazine (obviously the *Gentleman's Mag.*): 'Sappho's Advice was written by me, then at Winchester school; the next by Tomkyns; and the sonnet by Collins.' In Nov. 1739, a letter to the editor of the *Gentleman's Mag.* ix 601, praises the three poems, adding that 'The least, which is a Favourite of mine, carries a *Force* mix'd with *Tenderness*, and an uncommon *Elevation*'. Wooll, p. 109 *n*, attributes this 'unqualified eulogium' to Samuel Johnson, but this ascription was confidently denied in 1810 by Alexander Chalmers, *Works of the English Poets* xviii 145, where the poem was first collected.

C.'s title meant simply 'A small poem', the second meaning given by Johnson.

> When Phoebe formed a wanton smile,
>   My soul, it reached not here!
> Strange that thy peace, thou trembler, flies
>   Before a rising tear!
>
> 5 From midst the drops my love is born,
>   That o'er those eyelids rove:
> Thus issued from a teeming wave
>   The fabled queen of love.

2 Persian Eclogues

Probably written in 1739 and certainly not later than 1740 when C. went to Oxford, although they may well have been revised for publication in 1742. On the title-page of a copy of the 1742 edn in the Dyce Library, South Kensington, which contains C.'s own alterations and corrections, Joseph Warton has noted, 'By Mr Collins. (written at Winchester School)'. Warton expanded this statement in his edn of the *Works of Alexander Pope* (1797) i 61 *n*: 'Mr. Collins wrote his Eclogues when he was about seventeen years old, at Winchester School, and, as I well remember, had been just reading that volume of Salmon's Modern History, which described Persia; which determined him to lay the scene of these pieces[there], as being productive of new images and sentiments.'

If Warton's memory can be trusted, the *Eclogues* were presumably written sometime between C.'s seventeenth birthday on 25 Dec. 1738 and March 1740. Thomas Salmon's *Modern History: or, The Present State of All Nations*, which is named by Warton as C.'s source and is referred to in C.'s own notes, was originally published in 31 vols between 1725 and 1738 and republished in 3 vols quarto in 1739. (References in the notes are to the 1739 edn.) It is possible that C.'s poems were connected with the appearance of this much more accessible collected edn in April 1739 (*Gentleman's Mag.* ix 220), which would further limit the date of composition.

C. was at Oxford when the *Eclogues* were published in Jan. 1742 (*Gentleman's Mag.* xii 56), by J. Roberts, price 6d. A ledger kept by Henry Woodfall the printer records that they were printed on 10 Dec. 1741: 'Persian Eclogues, $1\frac{1}{2}$ shts., No. 500. Reprinting $\frac{1}{2}$ sht.', *Notes and Queries*, 1st series, xi (1855) 419. The *Eclogues* were reprinted with the new title *Oriental Eclogues* in Jan. 1757 by J. Payne (*Gentleman's Mag.* xxvii 47). The copy of the 1742 edn in the Dyce Library, mentioned above, contains C.'s own autograph alterations and corrections, most of which appear in 1757. On the verso of the title-page, Joseph Warton has written: 'Mr Collins gave me this Copy with his own Hands when I & my Brother visited Him for the Last Time at Chichester.' This visit took place in Sept. 1754. In the *Works of Pope* (1797) i 61 *n*, Warton refers to this copy when describing C.'s later opinion of the *Eclogues*. a detail he had already communicated to Johnson for his biography of C. in 1781 (*Lives of the Poets*, ed. G. B. Hill, iii 340):
'In his maturer years he was accustomed to speak very contemptuously of them, calling them his Irish Eclogues, and saying they had not in them one spark of Orientalism; and desiring me to erase a motto he had prefixed to them in a copy he gave me;

–quos primus equis oriens afflavit anhelis. Virg.

He was greatly mortified that they found more readers and admirers than his Odes.'
The original motto on the title-page of the 1742 edn had been from Cicero, *Pro Archia Poeta* vii 16: *Quod si non hic tantas fructus ostenderetur, et si ex his studiis delectatis sola peteretur; tamen, ut opinor, hanc animi remissionem humanissimam ac liberalissimam judicaretis.* (But let us for the moment waive these solid advantages; let us assume that entertainment is the sole end of reading; even so I think you would hold that no mental relaxation is so broadening to the sympathies or so enlightening to the understanding.) On the copy he gave Warton in 1754 C. substituted for this motto the line, slightly adapted from Virgil, *Georgics* i 250, to which Warton refers above. It reads in full *nosque ubi primus equis Oriens adflavit anhelis* (and when on us the rising sun first breathed with panting steeds). In this form but without the first word the new motto appeared on the title-page of the 1757 edn. Although this edn thus carries a number of changes called for by C. in the copy he gave to Warton, its authority cannot be considered unquestionable. In addition to those alterations, some lines are extensively revised and

a new couplet is inserted. It is possible, but not at all certain, that C. was responsible for these changes and additions which do not appear in the copy he gave Warton when they met for the last time in 1754. If, as seems likely, Joseph Warton superintended the 1757 edn, he may well have made these well-meaning 'improvements' himself, on behalf of his friend who was now thought to be insane. For this reason, the text printed here is that of the 1742 edn, as corrected in the Dyce copy by C. himself. Other changes made in 1757 are recorded in the notes. C.'s own notes are cited as *C.1742*.

As C. himself seems to have been resentfully aware, his *Eclogues* were for some time more popular than his later poetry. Their republication in Jan. 1757 marks the beginning of C.'s gradual emergence, as a poet if not as a man, from the obscurity of his last unhappy years. Extracts from all four *Eclogues* were printed in the *London Chronicle*, 13–15 January 1757, and *Eclogue IV* appeared in the *Gentleman's Mag.* xxvii (Feb. 1757) 81. The poet James Grainger, writing about the *Eclogues* in the *Monthly Review* xvi (June 1757) 486–9, believed that they contained many of 'the bold figures with which the poetry of the East abounds'. He observed that 'the thoughts are appropriated, the images wild and local, the language correct, and the versification harmonious'. Another remark by Grainger indicates that this new edn of the *Eclogues* did also serve to remind readers of the existence of the 1746 *Odes*: 'We are much mistaken if, in this little performance, we do not discover the elegance and the picturesque genius of the too much neglected Author of *Odes on several Subjects, descriptive and allegorical*.' Two years later Oliver Goldsmith wrote in his *Enquiry into the Present State of Polite Learning* (1759) p. 143: 'The neglected author of the Persian eclogues, which, however inaccurate, excel any in our language, is still alive. Happy, if *insensible* of our neglect, not *raging* at our ingratitude.' Later in the same year they were praised as 'exquisite' by an anonymous writer in the *Critical Review* viii (Nov. 1759) 414.

Some contemporary readers of the *Eclogues* echoed C.'s own sense, as reported by Warton, of their perfunctorily 'oriental' character, which relied for superficial local colour entirely on Salmon's *Modern History*. William Shenstone wrote to Thomas Percy in Feb. 1760, a few months after C.'s death: 'The Orientals afforded a new, & very fertile subject for eclogues. Poor Collins did not wholly satisfy me; having by no means sufficiently availd himself of their many local peculiarities', *Letters*, ed. Marjorie Williams (Oxford, 1939) p. 552. But, especially after Langhorne's edn of C.'s poems in 1765, the *Eclogues* were at least reprinted and imitated. A so-called 'Second Edition' had been published by Thomas Hope in 1760, but this consists only of the sheets of the 1757 edn with a new title-page. They also appeared in *The Weekly Amusement* i (30 June and 15 Sept. 1764) 447–8, 623–4; ii (9 March 1765) 159–60; and iv (5 July 1766) 451–2. Goldsmith included them in his *Poems for Young Ladies* (1767) pp. 228–41, and again in his *Beauties of English Poesy* (1767) i 239–53, introducing them there as 'very pretty', while admitting that the 'images . . . are not very local' and repeating that the 'great variety of poetical imagery' provided by 'Asiatic magnificence and manners' had not yet been properly explored. The *Eclogues* were reprinted in Pearch's *Collection of Poems* (1768) ii 1–14, and in *A Collection of the Most Esteemed Pieces of Poetry* (1767) pp. 11–23, both collections enjoying more than one edn, and there were German translations in 1767 and 1770; see A. S. P. Woodhouse, *Times Lit. Supp.*, 1930, p. 838. Imitations include: Chatterton's *African Eclogues* (1770); Eyles Irwin, *Eastern Eclogues* (1780); John Scott, 'Oriental Eclogues', in his *Poetical Works* (1782); Harriet Chilcot, *Ormar and Zabria . . . an Oriental Eclogue* (1783). John Scott of Amwell also gave the *Eclogues* detailed attention in his *Critical Essays* (1785) pp. 153–84, praising them for 'description, incident, sentiment, and moral; they have simplicity of thought, and melody of language.'

Retrospectively C.'s achievement in his *Eclogues* has been seen as the extension of the subject matter of the pastoral by the introduction of exotic elements into English poetry; cp. R. F. Jones, 'Eclogue Types in English Poetry of the Eighteenth Century', *Journal of English and Germanic Philology* xxiv (1925) 51–7; and Marion K. Bragg, *The Formal Eclogue in Eighteenth-Century England* (Orono, Maine, 1926) p. 76. But C. was probably attracted not merely by the opportunity of exploiting exotic, 'pseudo-oriental' material. The supposed character of Middle-Eastern poetry also appealed to him by apparently sanctioning an escape from the inhibiting rationality and omnipresent social tone of much Augustan poetry. Moralizing remains, but C., however tentatively, was seeking licence for more extravagant imagery and more emotional stimulation for its own sake than the accepted genres offered. From the beginning of the century there had been an increasing interest in and acceptance of the distinctive features of Oriental poetry. Characteristics condemned by neo-classical critics were becoming attractive to the immediately post-Augustan generation. Writing about 'Arabian' poetry in 1674 (Preface to Rapin's *Reflections on Aristotle's Treatise of Poetry*, in *Critical Essays of the Seventeenth Century*, ed. J. E. Spingarn (1908–9) ii 165), Thomas Rymer asserted that: '*Fancy* with them is predominant, is wild, vast, and unbridled, o're which their *judgement* has little command or authority: hence their conceptions are monstrous, and have nothing of exactness, nothing of resemblance or proportion.' Fifty years later, fancy, wildness and sublimity (all attributed to Oriental poetry) were becoming more appreciated. The Bible provided an influential example of Oriental poetry, which was at once exotic, sublime and yet, because sacred, profoundly important. Qualities attributed to Hebrew poetry could be seen in that of neighbouring nations. As early as April 1717, Lady Mary Wortley Montagu was writing to Pope from Turkey that Turkish poetry has 'the *sublime*, that is, a stile proper for poetry, and which is the exact Scripture stile', *Correspondence of Pope*, ed. G. Sherburn (1956) i 399. Pope himself once thought of writing a 'very wild' Persian Fable, 'in which I should have given a full loose to description and imagination' (Joseph Spence, *Observations, Anecdotes and Characters of Books and Men*, ed. J. M. Osborn (1966) i 151; see also *Correspondence*, ed. Sherburn, ii 202). The prefatory note purporting to be addressed by 'The Publisher to the Bookseller' in Lord Lyttelton's *Letters from a Persian in England, to his Friend at Ispahan* (1735) p. iv, acknowledges the supposed qualities of Persian writing as well as the difficulty of capturing them in English in a manner that anticipates C.'s own 'Preface': 'I must acknowledge my Translation far inferior to the *Eastern Sublimity* of the Original, which no *English* Expression can come up to, and which no English Reader wou'd admire.'

C.'s pretence that he was translating Persian poetry therefore allowed him to attempt, however feebly, the 'rich and figurative' style, the 'elegancy and wildness of thought', which he opposes in his Preface to the established 'strong and nervous' English (or Augustan) manner. Thomas Salmon's *Modern History* (1739), his main factual source, no doubt also provided C. with his rather vague conception of the nature of Persian poetry. The following (Salmon, i 398) is a typical passage:

'According to the Persians, the antient philosophers in the east were all poets, and their wise lessons were delivered in verse, to render them the more amiable and venerable, and that the people might readily retain them in their memories. It is the same thing in effect at this day in Persia. The subject of their poems is generally some piece of morality, or philosophy.

'Poetry seems to be a talent peculiar to the Persians, and in which they excel more than in any other part of literature. Their invention is fruitful and lively, their manner sweet, their temper amorous, and their language has a softness proper for verse: one who did not understand a word of Persian would be charmed with hearing their verse recited, the very tone and cadence are so affecting . . . .

' . . . the thoughts are noble and elevated, their expressions soft, and their terms always the most proper that can be hit upon: their allusions are delicate, and abundance of hyperbole you must expect in all their figures. Love is sometimes the subject of their poems, as well as morality and history; but nothing immodest, or that countenances debauchery of any kind, is ever the subject of their verse.'

Only for the third *Eclogue* has a specific narrative source been suggested. John Mitford, in *The Poems of Thomas Gray* (1814) p. 36, stated that C.'s source was a story in *The Free-Thinker* (a periodical conducted and largely written by Ambrose Philips) Nos. 128–9, which originally appeared on 12 and 15 June 1719. Collected edns of the periodical appeared in 1733 and 1739 (in which the story appears in iii 114–22), so that it is not unlikely that C. could have seen it. Dyce in 1827 rejected this source but not convincingly and it deserves at least summary consideration. *The Free-Thinker* No. 128 describes how '*CHA-ABBAS*, King of *Persia*, making a Progress through his Dominions' was 'led by his Curiosity to see the simple, natural Life of the Peasants'. He told the courtier who accompanied him: 'I am weary of being perpetually surrounded by Courtiers, who watch my Looks and my Words, to ensnare me with Flattery. Be not surprized then, that I have determined to lay aside the King, for a Time; that I may converse, freely and unknown, with Husbandmen and Shepherds.' His heart was duly 'ravished with delight, upon discovering the cheap, innocent, peacable Pleasures, which are not to be found but at a distance from Courts'. Cha-Abbas eventually meets Alibez, a shepherd, whose beauty and virtue so impress him that he decides to take him back to court. Alibez was 'at first, dazled with the Splendour of the Court. . . . The Sheep-hook, the Pipe, and the Shepherd's Garb, were laid aside; he was now cloathed in a Purple Robe, and a Turban sparkling with Jewels.'

The Free Thinker No. 129 describes Alibez's eventual longing for the rural life he has left: 'O, blessed Days! would he say to himself; Days of Innocence; Days, in which I relished uninterrupted Joys, not mixed with Fears: O Days, such as I have never since enjoy'd! And, am I, never, to see the like again? . . . He grew impatient to revisit his native Village: And his Heart beat with Emotions of Tenderness, as he viewed the Places, where (in his Youth) he used to dance, to pipe, and to sing, with his Companions.' On the death of Abbas, the new king inspects Alibez's strong-room to discover the extent of the treasure he had amassed as a royal favourite. It contained only 'a Sheep-Hook, a Pipe, and a Shepherd's Habit . . . all which, he often took a pleasure in visiting privately, to remind him of his former Condition'.

E. G. Ainsworth also refers to Salmon's 'Present State of Proper India', *Modern History* (1739) i 242–4, for an account of the Emperor Cha Selim, which has some general resemblance to C.'s narrative, but not enough to suggest that it was his source.

As C. himself readily admitted, there was little that is genuinely oriental about his *Eclogues*. In diction and style they obey most of the conventions of the eighteenth-century pastoral. According to Joseph Warton, *Works of Pope* (1797) i 61 *n*, James Thomson told C. that the 'first hint and idea' of his *Seasons* had come from Pope's four *Pastorals*, and obviously C. himself was influenced considerably by the same work. Not only is he indebted for specific phrases and much of his diction to Pope, but he seems also to have been imitating their dramatic structure, varying as does Pope the setting of each eclogue and following the same sequence of morning, noon, evening and night in the four episodes. (This scheme is stressed at the head of each eclogue, perhaps in direct imitation of Pope's practice in the notes he added to the 1736 edn of his *Pastorals*.) What was new in C. was the combination of pastoral convention and 'oriental' setting. For the growing 'pseudo-orientalism' of the eighteenth century, which spread from France around 1700 and which was already common in prose, see Martha P. Conant, *The Oriental Tale in England in the Eighteenth Century* (New York, 1908). Some qualifications and some additional information can be found in André Parreaux, *William Beckford* (Paris, 1960) pp. 301–35.

The Preface

It is with the writings of mankind, in some measure, as with their complexions or their dress, each nation hath a peculiarity in all these, to distinguish it from the rest of the world.

5 The gravity of the Spaniard and the levity of the Frenchman are as evident in all their productions as in their persons themselves; and the style of my country-men is as naturally strong and nervous as that of an Arabian or Persian is rich and figurative.

10 There is an elegancy and wildness of thought which recommends all their compositions; and our geniuses are as much too cold for the entertainment of such sentiments as our climate is for their fruits and spices. If any of these beauties are to be found in the following

15 Eclogues, I hope my reader will consider them as an argument of their being original. I received them at the hands of a merchant, who had made it his business to enrich himself with the learning, as well as the silks and carpets, of the Persians. The little information I

20 could gather concerning their author was that his name was Mahamed and that he was a native of Tauris.

It was in that city that he died of a distemper fatal in those parts, whilst he was engaged in celebrating the victories of his favourite monarch, the great Abbas. As

25 to the Eclogues themselves, they give a very just view of the miseries and inconveniencies, as well as the felicities, that attend one of the finest countries in the East.

The time of the writing them was probably in the

¶ 2. Preface 21. Mahamed] ABDALLAH 1757.   Tauris] Salmon (1739) i 367 and 375, describes Tauris in the province of Adirbeitzan as 'populous, and a place of very great trade', noted for its 'exchanges, where abundance of rich merchandize is exposed to sale'.

P 24. Abbas] 1757 adds a note: 'In the Persian tongue, ABBAS signifieth "the father of the people".'   Salmon, i 405, describes the achievements of 'the great Shaw ABBAS', both civil and military. Abbas, 'having reigned about forty years, died anno 1628'. Salmon, i 375, also explains why C.'s supposed poet would be celebrating Abbas's victories. The city of Tauris had often changed hands, 'but the great SHAW ABBAS, somewhat above a hundred years ago, drove the Turks out of this part of Persia'.

P 29. the writing] writing 1757.

30 beginning of Sha Sultan Hosseyn's reign, the successor
      of Sefi or Solyman the Second.
         Whatever defects, as, I doubt not, there will be many,
      fall under the reader's observation, I hope his candour
      will incline him to make the following reflections:
35   That the works of Orientals contain many peculi-
      arities, and that through defect of language few Euro-
      pean translators can do them justice.

ECLOGUE THE FIRST
SELIM; OR, THE SHEPHERD'S MORAL

SCENE, *a Valley near Bagdat*
TIME, *the Morning*

'Ye Persian maids, attend your poet's lays,
And hear how shepherds pass their golden days:
Not all are blest, whom fortune's hand sustains
With wealth in courts, nor all that haunt the plains:
5 Well may your hearts believe the truths I tell;
'Tis virtue makes the bliss, where'er we dwell.'

Thus Selim sung, by sacred Truth inspired;
No praise the youth, but hers alone, desired.
Wise in himself, his meaning songs conveyed
10 Informing morals to the shepherd maid,
Or taught the swains that surest bliss to find,
What groves nor streams bestow, a virtuous mind.

When sweet and odorous, like an eastern bride,

P *30-1.* Cp. Salmon, i 406: Shaw Sefi II succeeded to the throne in 1664;
'The Prince changed his name, and took that of SOLYMAN instead of SEFI . . .
he died on the 29th of July 1694, and was succeeded by his son Shaw Sultan
HOSSEIN.'
P *34. reflections*] reflection *1757.*
P *35. Orientals*] Orientals *1742, corrected in 1757.*
i 6. Pope, *Essay on Man* iv 310: 'Virtue alone is Happiness below'; and iv 397:
'That VIRTUE only makes our Bliss below'.
i *8.* Nor praise, but such as Truth bestow'd, desir'd: *1757.*
i *13. odorous . . . an Eastern*] blushing . . . a virgin *1757.*
   (Cp. 'eastern' at l. 69, also removed in *1757,* as implying an inappropriate
European viewpoint.)
   C. was imitating Dryden, *Alexander's Feast* 9-11: 'The Lovely *Thais*
by his side, / Sate like a blooming *Eastern* Bride / In Flow'r of Youth and
Beauty's Pride.'

The radiant morn resumed her orient pride,
15 When wanton gales along the valleys play,
Breathe on each flower, and bear their sweets away:
By Tigris' wandering waves he sat, and sung
This useful lesson for the fair and young.

'Ye Persian dames,' he said, 'to you belong,
20 Well may they please, the morals of my song;
No fairer maids, I trust, than you are found,
Graced with soft arts, the peopled world around!
The morn that lights you to your loves supplies
Each gentler ray delicious to your eyes:
25 For you those flowers her fragrant hands bestow,
And yours the love that kings delight to know.
Yet think not these, all beauteous as they are,
The best kind blessings heaven can grant the fair!
Who trust alone in beauty's feeble ray,
30 Balsora's pearls have more of worth than they;
Drawn from the deep, they sparkle to the sight,
And all-unconscious shoot a lustrous light:
Such are the maids and such the charms they boast,
By sense unaided or to virtue lost.

i 14. 'Orient' and 'morn' are often associated by Milton. Cp. *Par. Lost* vi 524:
'Now when fair Morn Orient in Heav'n appeerd' and elsewhere.
i 17. *wandering*] Wand'rer *1742*. (The correction is made by C. himself in
the Dyce copy, and in *1757*.)
i 19, 21, 25. *you*] ye *1742*. (The alteration is made by C. himself in the Dyce
copy, and in *1757*.)
i 19–42. This passage as a whole is reminiscent of Clarissa's speech in *Rape of
the Lock* v 9–34. Cp. especially with ll. 33–4, *Rape of the Lock* v 15–18: 'How
vain are all these Glories, all our Pains, / Unless good Sense preserve what
Beauty gains: / That Men may say, when we the Front-box grace, / Behold
the first in Virtue, as in Face!'
i 30–2. *1757 has:*

Boast but the worth Balsora's pearls display;
Drawn from the deep we own their surface bright,
But, dark within, they drink no lust'rous light:

This revision may seem too clear and pointed to have been made by C. him-
self.
i 30. *Balsora*] The Gulph of that Name, famous for the Pearl-fishery. *C. 1742.*
Cp. Salmon (1739) i 369, who describes the pearl-fishery 'in the gulph of
Bossora [i.e. the Persian Gulf] . . . of which they are very jealous, it being
reckoned the best in the world. . . . The pearl fishery lyes near the island of
Baharem'. There is more about the fishery in Salmon, i 396.

35   Self-flattering sex! your hearts believe in vain
    That love shall blind when once he fires the swain,
    Or hope a lover by your faults to win,
    As spots on ermine beautify the skin.
    Who seeks secure to rule, be first her care
40   Each softer virtue that adorns the fair,
    Each tender passion man delights to find,
    The loved perfections of a female mind.

    'Blest were the days when Wisdom held her reign,
    And shepherds sought her on the silent plain;
45   With Truth she wedded in the secret grove,
    The fair-eyed Truth, and daughters blessed their love.

    'O haste, fair maids, ye Virtues, come away,
    Sweet Peace and Plenty lead you on your way!
    The balmy shrub for you shall love our shore,
50   By Ind excelled or Araby no more.

i *37–8*. Pope, *Epistles to Several Persons* ii 43–4, of women: 'Their happy
Spots the nice admirer take, / Fine by defect, and delicately weak.' Johnson
in his *Dictionary* under 'Ermine' quotes Trevoux: 'The fellmongers and
furriers put upon it little bits of Lombardy lambskin, which is noted for its
shining black colour, the better to set off the whiteness of the ermine.'
i *39–42*. *Faerie Queene* VI viii 2, 1–6, addressed to 'Ye gentle Ladies': 'And
as ye soft and tender are by kynde, / Adornd with goodly gifts of beauties
grace, / So be ye soft and tender eeke in mynde; / But cruelty and hardnesse
from you chace, / That all your other praises will deface, / And from you
turn the loue of men to hate.'
i *45*. Milton, *Il Penseroso* 28–9: 'in secret shades / Of woody *Ida's* inmost
grove'.
i *46. The fair-eyed*] Immortal *1757* (perhaps considered more suitable for
Truth personified as male).
i *49–50*. C. may be recalling Virgil, *Georgics* ii 114–19, as translated by
Dryden, ii 160–6: 'Regard th'extremest cultivated Coast, / From hot
Arabia to the *Scythian* Frost: / All sorts of Trees their sev'ral Countries
know; / Black Ebon only will in *India* grow: / And od'rous Frankincense
on the *Sabaean* Bough. / Balm slowly trickles through the bleeding Veins /
Of happy Shrubs, in *Idumaean* Plains.' Cp. also Pope, *Windsor Forest* 29–30:
'Let *India* boast her Plants, nor envy we / The weeping Amber or the
balmy Tree . . .' Line 48 may echo *Windsor Forest* 42: 'And Peace and Plenty
tell, a STUART reigns.'
i *49. you*] ye *1742*. (This change made in *1757* is similar to those made in ll.
19, 21, 25 by C. himself.)

'Lost to our fields, for so the fates ordain,
The dear deserters shall return again.
O come thou, Modesty, as they decree,
The rose may then improve her blush by thee.
55 Here make thy court amidst our rural scene,
And shepherd-girls shall own thee for their queen.
With thee be Chastity, of all afraid,
Distrusting all, a wise suspicious maid,
But man the most—not more the mountain doe
60 Holds the swift falcon for her deadly foe.
Cold is her breast, like flowers that drink the dew;
A silken veil conceals her from the view.
No wild desires amidst thy train be known,
But Faith, whose heart is fixed on one alone;
65 Desponding Meekness with her down-cast eyes,
And friendly Pity full of tender sighs;
And Love the last: by these your hearts approve,
These are the Virtues that must lead to love.'

Thus sung the swain, and eastern legends say
70 The maids of Bagdat verified the lay:
Dear to the plains, the Virtues came along,
The shepherds loved, and Selim blessed his song.

i 51–68. Cp. the 'trains' of personified qualities led by Mirth and Melancholy in Milton's *L'Allegro* and *Il Penseroso*.
i 51. *so the fates ordain*] A phrase common in Dryden (e.g. *Aeneid* i 780, ii 468, iii 215, iv 878), a version of the classical formula *Sic fata ferebant*, *Aeneid* ii 34, etc.
i 53–4. *1757 has:*

Come thou whose thoughts as limpid springs are clear,
To lead the train, sweet MODESTY appear:

i 58–9. *Rape of the Lock* i 114: 'Beware of all, but most beware of Man!'
i 61–2. A reminiscence of Milton, *Samson Agonistes* 728, 730: 'Like a fair flower surcharg'd with dew, she weeps / ... / Wetting the borders of her silk'n veil'. But cp. also *Il Penseroso* 172: 'And every Herb that sips the dew'; Pope, *Summer* 32: 'And ev'ry Plant that drinks the Morning Dew'; and Pope, *Iliad* xi 877: 'And ev'ry herb that drinks the morning dew'.
i 65. Cp. Spenser's description of 'Shamefastnesse', *Faerie Queene* IV x 50, 2: 'Ne euer durst her eyes from ground upreare'; and *Il Penseroso* 43: 'With a sad Leaden downward cast'.
i 69 *eastern*] ancient *1757*. (Cp. l. 13 n.)

ECLOGUE THE SECOND
HASSAN; OR, THE CAMEL-DRIVER

SCENE, *the Desert*
TIME, *Mid-day*

In silent horror o'er the desert-waste
The driver Hassan with his camels passed.
One cruse of water on his back he bore,
And his light scrip contained a scanty store;
5 A fan of painted feathers in his hand,
To guard his shaded face from scorching sand.
The sultry sun had gained the middle sky,
And not a tree and not an herb was nigh.
The beasts with pain their dusty way pursue,
10 Shrill roared the winds and dreary was the view!
With desperate sorrow wild, the affrighted man
Thrice sighed, thrice struck his breast, and thus began:

ii *1 ff.* C.'s starting-point was no doubt the description in Salmon (1739) i 368, of the desert area of South Persia: 'The winds blow over large sandy deserts, heated like an oven, and especially between the mountains, which reflect the heat from one side to the other, and there are no refreshing breezes or showers to cool the air, as there generally are near the line.' Salmon goes on to describe a kind of 'pestilential blast' which can suffocate instantly those exposed to it. For dramatic purposes C. ignores Salmon's later observation on desert travel, i 381: 'People usually travel in this country with the caravan, consisting of four or five hundred camels... and there is no place where they travel with greater security... a traveller seldom meets with any difficulties but what are easily surmounted.' Thomson's *Summer* 961–79, has sometimes been suggested as a source but these lines were not added until the 1744 edn of *The Seasons*.
ii *1. desert-waste*] boundless waste *1757* (perhaps to avoid tautology). But cp. Spenser, *Faerie Queene* I ii 42, 6: 'Then brought she me into this desert waste': and II vii 2, 9 'desert wildernesse'; and Fairfax's *Tasso* VIII xii 6, XIX vi 3, and lxxxvi 1.
ii *4–6.* C. may have remembered Spenser's description, *Faerie Queene* I vi 35, of Archimago disguised as a pilgrim, with 'face all tand with scorching sunny ray, / As he had traueild many a sommers day, / Through boyling sands of *Arabie* and *Ynde*', with his 'scrip' hanging behind.
ii *5.* Marlowe, *Hero and Leander* ii 11: 'Her painted fan of curled plumes let fall.'
i *7. the middle sky*] A classical formula, cp. *Iliad* viii 68; *Odyssey* iv 400; xvi 777 etc.
ii *12. struck*] The spelling in *1742* is 'strook': 'The preterite of *strike*, used in poetry for *struck*' (Johnson). It is found in Milton, Waller and Dryden etc.

'Sad was the hour and luckless was the day,
When first from Schiraz' walls I bent my way.

15   'Ah! little thought I of the blasting wind,
The thirst or pinching hunger that I find!
Bethink thee, Hassan, where shall thirst assuage,
When fails this cruse, his unrelenting rage?
Soon shall this scrip its precious load resign,
20   Then what but tears and hunger shall be thine?

'Ye mute companions of my toils, that bear
In all my griefs a more than equal share!
Here, where no springs in murmurs break away,
Or moss-crowned fountains mitigate the day,
25   In vain ye hope the green delights to know,
Which plains more blest or verdant vales bestow.
Here rocks alone and tasteless sands are found,
And faint and sickly winds for ever howl around.
Sad was the hour and luckless was the day,
30   When first from Schiraz' walls I bent my way.

ii *13*. Henry Headley, *Select Beauties of Ancient English Poetry* (1787) ii 190, compares a passage in William Browne's *Britannia's Pastorals* (1613–16) II iii 763–6: 'Faire was the day, but fayrer was the maide / Who that day's morne into the green-woods straid. / Sweet was the ayre, but sweeter was her breathing, / Such rare perfumes the roses are bequeathing.'

ii *14*. Salmon, i 373: 'Schiras, or Sheraz, as we pronounce it ... is usually reckoned the second city of the kingdom. It is the capital of the province of Fars, or the antient Persia.' Unfortunately for C., 'There are no walls about the place. ... what Sheraz is most remarkable for, is the fine gardens and vineyards about it.'

ii *16*. *Par. Lost* x 691: 'Avoided pinching cold and scorching heate', which may have suggested 'scorching' in l. 6.

ii *24*. *moss-crowned fountains*] Cp. Virgil, *Eclogues* vii 45: *muscosi fontes*, translated 'mossy Fountains', Dryden, *Eclogues* vii 67; and Pope, *Summer* 72; *Messiah* 3. See also J. Philips, *Cyder* Bk ii: 'whence thou artificial Wines shalt drain / Of icy taste, that ... / ... mitigate the Day'.

ii *25–6*. Langhorne in *1765*, pp. 120–1, pointed out that 'there is a verbal pleonasm where the poet speaks of the *green* delights of *verdant* vales'. C. was remembering Thomson, *Summer*, 1738 edn, 794–5: 'Disdainful of *Campania's* gentle Plains, / And all the green Delights of *Italy*'. (The second line was revised in 1744.)

ii *29–30*. *1742 from this point on gives only the first 4 words of the refrain, which is given in full here.*

'Cursed be the gold and silver which persuade
Weak men to follow far-fatiguing trade.
The Lily-Peace outshines the silver store,
And life is dearer than the golden ore.
35   Yet money tempts us o'er the desert brown,
To every distant mart and wealthy town:
Full oft we tempt the land and oft the sea;
And are we only yet repaid by thee?
Ah! why was ruin so attractive made,
40   Or why fond man so easily betrayed?
Why heed we not, whilst mad we haste along,
The gentle voice of Peace or Pleasure's song?
Or wherefore think the flowery mountain's side,
The fountain's murmurs and the valley's pride,
45   Why think we these less pleasing to behold
Than dreary deserts, if they lead to gold?
Sad was the hour and luckless was the day,
When first from Schiraz' walls I bent my way.

'O cease, my fears! all frantic as I go,
50   When thought creates unnumbered scenes of woe,
What if the lion in his rage I meet!
Oft in the dust I view his printed feet:
And fearful! oft, when Day's declining light
Yields her pale empire to the mourner Night,

ii *31–40*. Reminiscent of Pope's treatment of avarice in his *Imitations of Horace, Ep.* I i 69–80 and *Ep.* I vi 69 ff, and cp. also Phineas Fletcher, *The Purple Island* I xxxvi.

ii *37. tempt*] Used in this line with its classical meaning of 'To try; to attempt; to venture on' (Johnson). Cp. Horace, *Odes* III iv 29–31: *libens / insanientem navita Bosphorum / temptabo* (gladly I will as a mariner essay the raging Bosphorus). The phrase or its equivalents are found in Spenser (*Faerie Queene* III ix 45, 5; IV x 46, 5) and are common in Augustan heroic verse: cp. 'tempt the watry Plains', Dryden, *Iliad* i 86; 'tempt the stormy Main', Dryden, *Cymon and Iphigenia* 386; 'Tempt Icy Seas', Pope, *Windsor Forest* 389. C. uses 'tempt' again in this sense in l. 67 but typically introduced its more normal sense in l. 35, apparently without any sense of inappropriateness.

ii *51–8*. Salmon, i 394: 'In Hyrcania and Curdistan, the woody parts of the country, wild beasts abound, such as lions, tygers, leopards, wild-hogs, jackalls, &c.' Such animals did not frequent deserts.

ii *51*. Catullus, xlv 6–7: *solus in Libya Indiaque tosta / caesio veniam obvius leoni* (may I in Libya or sunburnt India meet a green-eyed lion alone).

55 By hunger roused, he scours the groaning plain,
    Gaunt wolves and sullen tigers in his train:
    Before them death with shrieks directs their way,
    Fills the wild yell and leads them to their prey.
    Sad was the hour and luckless was the day,
60 When first from Schiraz' walls I bent my way!

    'At that dead hour the silent asp shall creep,
    If aught of rest I find, upon my sleep;
    Or some swoll'n serpent twist his scales around,
    And wake to anguish with a burning wound.
65 Thrice happy they, the wise contented poor,
    From lust of wealth and dread of death secure.
    They tempt no deserts and no griefs they find;
    Peace rules the day, where reason rules the mind.
    Sad was the hour and luckless was the day,
70 When first from Schiraz' walls I bent my way.

    'O hapless youth! for she thy love hath won,
    The tender Zara, will be most undone!
    Big swelled my heart and owned the powerful maid,
    When fast she dropped her tears, as thus she said:
75 "Farewell the youth whom sighs could not detain,
    "Whom Zara's breaking heart implored in vain;
    "Yet as thou goest, may every blast arise,
    "Weak and unfelt as these rejected sighs!
    "Safe o'er the wild, no perils mayst thou see,
80 "No griefs endure, nor weep, false youth, like me."
    O let me safely to the fair return,
    Say with a kiss, she must not, shall not mourn.

ii 55. *scours the . . . plain*] Another formula in Augustan translations from the classics. Cp. Dryden, *Georgics* iii 381–2: ''Tis with this rage, the Mother Lion stung, / Scours o're the Plain; regardless of her young.' Cp. also Dryden, *Georgics* i 691; *Aeneid* iv 221; and Pope, *Essay on Criticism* 372.

ii 56. *sullen*] A word of which C. is fond, using it to describe objects of a vaguely dismal or threatening character. Cp. *Il Penseroso* 76.

ii 61–4. Cp. Salmon, i 394: 'That part of the country which lyes upon the Caspian or Hyrcanian sea is full of serpents, toads, scorpions, and other venomous insects. . . . Scorpions particularly there are of an immoderate size, whose sting is mortal, it is said, if proper remedies be not immediately applied, and at best a person stung by one of them is in such torture, that he becomes raving mad for some time.'

ii 65. *Thrice happy*] A classical expression; cp. *Aeneid* i 94: *O terque quaterque beati* (O thrice and four times blest).

ii 66. Pope, *Epistle to Oxford* 26: 'The Lust of Lucre, and the Dread of Death'.

Go teach my heart to lose its painful fears,
Recalled by Wisdom's voice and Zara's tears.'

85   He said, and called on heaven to bless the day,
When back to Schiraz' walls he bent his way.

ECLOGUE THE THIRD
ABRA; OR, THE GEORGIAN SULTANA

SCENE, *a forest*
TIME, *the Evening*

In Georgia's land, where Tefflis' towers are seen,
In distant view along the level green,
While evening dews enrich the glittering glade,
And the tall forests cast a longer shade,
5   Amidst the maids of Zagen's peaceful grove,
Emyra sung the pleasing cares of love.

Of Abra first began the tender strain,
Who led her youth with flocks upon the plain.
At morn she came those willing flocks to lead,
10   Where lilies rear them in the watery mead;
From early dawn the livelong hours she told,
Till late at silent ev'n she penned the fold.

ii *83*. O! let me teach my heart to lose its fears, *1757*.
iii *1*. Salmon, i 367 and 376, describes Tefflis as the capital of Eastern
Georgia and mentions its fourteen Christian churches, its cathedral and
castle, to which C.'s 'towers' may refer specifically.
iii *2*. *Rape of the Lock* iii 80: 'the level Green'.
iii *3–4*. Pope, *Autumn* 99–100: 'When falling Dews with Spangles deck'd
the Glade, / And the low Sun had lengthen'd ev'ry Shade.' In l. 4 C. may
also have had in mind Virgil, *Eclogues* i 83: *maioresque cadunt altis de montibus
umbrae* (and longer shadows fall from the mountain-heights).
iii *4. After this line 1757 has a new couplet:*
What time 'tis sweet o'er fields of rice to stray,
Or scent the breathing maze at setting day;
A writer in the *Quarterly Review* xxxii (1826) 15–16 observed that: 'Had
Collins been better informed . . . [he] would have been sensible that to
wade through a rice-field is a most laborious and wearisome occupation, at
whatever period of the day.'
iii *9–10*. Gay, *Dione* III iii: 'what time my flock to lead / To sunny moun-
tains, or the watery mead'.
iii *12. Par. Lost*, iv 185–6: 'Watching where Shepherds pen thir Flocks at
eve / In hurdl'd Cotes amid the field secure'.

Deep in the grove beneath the secret shade,
A various wreath of odorous flowers she made.
15 Gay-motleyed pinks and sweet jonquils she chose,
The violet-blue that on the moss-bank grows;
All-sweet to sense, the flaunting rose was there;
The finished chaplet well-adorned her hair.

Great Abbas chanced that fated morn to stray,
20 By love conducted from the chase away;
Among the vocal vales he heard her song,
And sought the vales and echoing groves among.
At length he found and wooed the rural maid:
She knew the monarch, and with fear obeyed.
25 Be every youth like royal Abbas moved,
And every Georgian maid like Abra loved.

The royal lover bore her from the plain,
Yet still her crook and bleating flock remain:
Oft as she went, she backward turned her view,
30 And bade that crook and bleating flock adieu.
Fair happy maid! to other scenes remove,
To richer scenes of golden power and love!

iii *13. secret shade*] Spenser is fond of this phrase, cp. *Faerie Queene* I v 15, 4;
II vii 3, 3; II xii 72, 6 etc; and Milton, *Il Penseroso* 28–9: 'in secret shades /
Of woody *Ida's* inmost grove'. Cp. also *Eclogue I* 45 *n* above, and Dryden,
Flower and the Leaf 204.
iii *15–18*. That these Flowers are found in very great Abundance in some of
the Provinces of *Persia*; see the *Modern History* of the ingenious Mr. *Salmon*.
C. 1742.
This note is cut through in the Dyce copy but not omitted in *1757*.
Cp. Salmon, i 392: 'About Ispahan and some other towns jonquils grow
wild: they have also daffodils, lilies, violets and pinks in their season,
and some flowers which last all the year round; but what they have the
greatest quantity of are lilies and roses.' Thomson, *Spring* 548–52, includes
jonquils, 'gay-spotted pinks', and roses, and may have influenced C.
iii *17. flaunting*] Perhaps a reminiscence of *Comus* 545: 'flaunting Hony-
suckle'. C.'s 'All-sweet' and 'all-rural' (l. 46) no doubt imitate Milton's
fondness for 'all-' compounds.
iii *29–32. Faerie Queene* I ix 21, 5: 'Still as he fled, his eye was backward
cast'; Marlowe, *Hero and Leander* ii 5: 'Yet as she went, full often looked
behind'; Dryden, *Iliad* i 484: 'She wept, and often cast her Eyes behind';
and Cowley, *Country Life* 17–22: 'Unwillingly, and slow, and discontent, /
From his lov'd cottage to a throne he went; / And oft he stopped in his
triumphant way, / And oft looked back and oft was heard to say, / Not
without sighs, Alas! I there forsake / A happier kingdom than I go to take.'

Go leave the simple pipe and shepherd's strain,
With love delight thee, and with Abbas reign.
35   Be every youth like royal Abbas moved,
And every Georgian maid like Abra loved.

Yet midst the blaze of courts she fixed her love
On the cool fountain or the shady grove;
Still with the shepherd's innocence her mind
40   To the sweet vale and flowery mead inclined,
And oft as spring renewed the plains with flowers,
Breathed his soft gales and led the fragrant hours,
With sure return she sought the sylvan scene,
The breezy mountains and the forests green.
45   Her maids around her moved, a duteous band!
Each bore a crook all-rural in her hand.
Some simple lay of flocks and herds they sung;
With joy the mountain and the forest rung.
Be every youth like royal Abbas moved,
50   And every Georgian maid like Abra loved.

And oft the royal lover left the care
And thorns of state, attendant on the fair:
Oft to the shades and low-roofed cots retired,
Or sought the vale where first his heart was fired;
55   A russet mantle, like a swain, he wore,
And thought of crowns and busy courts no more.
Be every youth like royal Abbas moved,
And every Georgian maid like Abra loved.

iii *35–6*. 1742 *from this point on gives only the first 3 words of the refrain, which is here given in full.*
iii *37*. Pope, *Epistles to Several Persons* iii 281: 'Blush, Grandeur, blush! proud Courts, withdraw your blaze!'
iii *38–44*. These lines are a tissue of conventional pastoral phrases: e.g. Pope, *Vertumnus and Pomona* 5–6: 'To her the shady Grove, the flow'ry Field, / The Streams and Fountains, no Delights cou'd yield;' cp. also 'the shady grove', Spenser, *Faerie Queene* I i 7, 2 and IV xi 42, 5, *Par. Lost* iii 28 and Pope, *Spring* 78; 'And flowry Meads, and Vales of chearful green', Dryden, *Song from Tyrannic Love* ii 10; 'Thro' verdant Forests, and thro' flow'ry Meads', Pope, *Summer* (1st version) 4; '*Sylvan* Scenes', Dryden, *To Mrs Anne Killigrew* 108, and Pope, *Summer* 59 and *Windsor Forest* 285.
iii *51–3*. C.'s diction is again conventional: cp. 'Not all in shades and humble cots delight', Gay, *Birth of the Squire* 2; and 'The court he quits, to fly from care, / And seeks the peace of rural air', Gay, *Fables* I xxxi. 'Low-roofed' probably derives from 'the low-rooft house', *Par. Regained* iv 273.
iii *55*. 'russet mantle', *Hamlet* I i 166.

Blest was the life that royal Abbas led:
60 Sweet was his love and innocent his bed.
What if in wealth the noble maid excel;
The simple shepherd girl can love as well.
Let those who rule on Persia's jewelled throne,
Be famed for love and gentlest love alone:
65 Or wreathe, like Abbas, full of fair renown,
The lover's myrtle with the warrior's crown.

Oh happy days! the maids around her say,
Oh haste, profuse of blessings, haste away!
Be every youth like royal Abbas moved,
70 And every Georgian maid like Abra loved.

ECLOGUE THE FOURTH
AGIB AND SECANDER; OR, THE FUGITIVES

SCENE, *a Mountain in Circassia*
TIME, *Midnight*

In fair Circassia, where, to love inclined,
Each swain was blest, for every maid was kind!
At that still hour, when awful midnight reigns,
And none but wretches haunt the twilight plains;
5   What time the moon had hung her lamp on high,
And passed in radiance through the cloudless sky:
Sad o'er the dews two brother shepherds fled,
Where wildering fear and desperate sorrow led.
Fast as they pressed their flight, behind them lay
10 Wide ravaged plains and valleys stole away.
Along the mountain's bending sides they ran,
Till faint and weak Secander thus began.

SECANDER
O stay thee, Agib, for my feet deny,
No longer friendly to my life, to fly.
15 Friend of my heart, O turn thee and survey,
Trace our sad flight through all its length of way!
And first review that long-extended plain,
And yon wide groves, already passed with pain!
Yon ragged cliff whose dangerous path we tried,
20 And last this lofty mountain's weary side!

iv 19. *Faerie Queene* I v 38, 6: 'His goodly corps on ragged cliffs yrent'; and
L'Allegro 9–10: 'There under *Ebon* shades, and low-brow'd Rocks, / As
ragged as thy Locks'.

AGIB

Weak as thou art, yet hapless must thou know
The toils of flight, or some severer woe!
Still as I haste, the Tartar shouts behind,
And shrieks and sorrows load the saddening wind:
25   In rage of heart, with ruin in his hand,
He blasts our harvests and deforms our land.
Yon citron grove, whence first in fear we came,
Droops its fair honours to the conquering flame:
Far fly the swains, like us, in deep despair,
30   And leave to ruffian bands their fleecy care.

SECANDER

Unhappy land, whose blessings tempt the sword,
In vain, unheard, thou call'st thy Persian Lord!
In vain thou court'st him, helpless to thine aid,
To shield the shepherd and protect the maid.
35   Far off in thoughtless indolence resigned,
Soft dreams of love and pleasure soothe his mind:
Midst fair sultanas lost in idle joy,
No wars alarm him and no fears annoy.

iv 26. It is not clear why the invading Tartars should 'blast' the harvests.
Salmon, i 424, actually describes the Persian custom of destroying their own
countryside as they retreat, in the hope of starving invaders.

iv 28. honours] 'that is, Beauties, which make things Honoured; in which
sense Virgil often uses the word, and delights in it' (Cowley, Davideis ii n 1,
cited by Tillotson, Rape of the Lock iv 140 n). Cp. Virgil, Georgics ii 404:
frigidus et silvis Aquilo decussit honorem (the cold North-wind has shaken their
glory from the woods), translated by Dryden, ii 558–9: 'when Storms have
shed / From Vines the hairy Honours of their Head'.

iv 30. 'fleecy Care', Pope, Spring 19, and Messiah 49; and Gay, Dione III iv.

iv 31–8. Cp. Salmon, i 381: 'The late Sophi, Shaw Sultan HOSSEIN,
succeeded his Father Sultan SOLYMAN, anno 1694. This Prince chose to
live an indolent unactive life among his women in the haram, leaving the
administration of the government entirely to his ministers, who placed
and displaced whom they saw fit, oppressed the subjects with taxes and
impositions', etc. Salmon, i 381–9, goes on to describe the subsequent civil
war in Persia and simultaneous invasions by Turks, Tartars and Arabs. C.
may also have been influenced by a later passage in Salmon, i 421: 'The
Persians Kings have given themselves up to a luxurious indolent life, and so
neglected the discipline of their troops, as well as the government of the
state, that we have seen a little despicable rebel undertake a march from the
borders of the Usbeck Tartary, six or seven hundred miles, with no more
than five or six thousand men, depose the King, and make himself master
of the capital city of the kingdom . . . and the Turk and Muscovite have
seized those towns on the frontiers which lay next them.'

AGIB
Yet these green hills, in summer's sultry heat,
40 Have lent the monarch oft a cool retreat.
Sweet to the sight is Zabran's flowery plain,
And once by maids and shepherds loved in vain!
No more the virgins shall delight to rove
By Sargis' banks or Irwan's shady grove:
45 On Tarkie's mountain catch the cooling gale,
Or breathe the sweets of Aly's flowery vale:
Fair scenes! but ah! no more with peace possessed,
With ease alluring and with plenty blest.
No more the shepherds' whitening tents appear,
50 Nor the kind products of a bounteous year;
No more the date with snowy blossoms crowned,
But Ruin spreads her baleful fires around.

SECANDER
In vain Circassia boasts her spicy groves,
For ever famed for pure and happy loves;
55 In vain she boasts her fairest of the fair,

iv *41.* 'flow'ry Plains', Pope, *Autumn* 86 and *Windsor Forest* 428. Langhorne in *1765*, p. 131, complained that 'there is no distinction between the plain of *Zabran* and the vale of *Aly* [l. 46]; they are both *flowery*, and consequently undiversified. This could not proceed from the poet's want of judgement, but from inattention'.

iv *44. shady grove*] Cp. iii 38 and *n* above.

iv *44–6.* C. found most of these place-names in Salmon, i 367. 'Ervan, or Irvan' is in the province of Shirvan, 'upon the river Sargi, near the borders of Armenia'; Tarku is the capital of Dagistan. Aly appears not to be mentioned but is marked on the map of Persia on the opposite page.

iv *45.* Pope, *Essay on Man* iii 178: 'catch the driving gale'.

iv *46. Par. Lost* iii 569: 'flourie Vales'.

iv *48.* Pope, *Windsor Forest* 107: 'Some thoughtless Town, with Ease and Plenty blest'.

iv *49. tents*] seats *1742.* (The change is made by C. in the Dyce copy, and in *1757*.) Cp. Pope, *Spring* 19: 'Pour'd o'er the whitening Vale their fleecy Care'.

iv *50.* Dryden, *Britannia Rediviva* 266: 'The timely product of the bounteous Year'; and 'the Bounteous Year', *Satires of Juvenal* vi 25.

iv *51. date*] dale *1742.* (The correction is made by C. in the Dyce copy, and in *1757*.) Cp. Salmon, i 391: 'Dates are reckoned one of the most delicious fruits in this country: they are no where so good as in Persia'.

iv *52. Par. Lost* i 56: 'round he throws his baleful eyes'.

Their eyes' blue languish and their golden hair!
Those eyes in tears their fruitless grief must send;
Those hairs the Tartar's cruel hand shall rend.

AGIB

Ye Georgian swains that piteous learn from far
60   Circassia's ruin and the waste of war:
Some weightier arms than crooks and staves prepare,
To shield your harvests and defend your fair:
The Turk and Tartar like designs pursue,
Fixed to destroy and steadfast to undo.
65   Wild as his land, in native deserts bred,
By lust incited or by malice led,
The villain-Arab, as he prowls for prey,
Oft marks with blood and wasting flames the way;
Yet none so cruel as the Tartar foe,
70   To death inured and nursed in scenes of woe.

He said, when loud along the vale was heard
A shriller shriek and nearer fires appeared:
The affrighted shepherds through the dews of night,
Wide o'er the moonlight hills, renewed their flight.

iv 56. Pope, *Iliad* xviii 50: 'And the blue languish of soft Alia's eye.'
iv 71-2. Virgil, *Aeneid* ii 705-6: *Dixerat ille, etiam per moenia clarior ignis* / *auditur, propiusque aestas incendia volvunt* (He ceased, and now through the city more loudly is heard the blaze, and nearer the flames roll their fiery flood).
iv 72. *shriller shriek*] The diction is Spenserian, e.g. 'With shrilling shriekes', *Faerie Queene* III viii 29, 8.
iv 73-4. Pope, *First Book of Statius* 557-8: 'And seiz'd with Horror, in the Shades of Night, / Thro' the thick Desarts headlong urg'd his Flight . . .'

3 An Epistle: Addressed to Sir Thomas Hanmer, on his Edition of Shakespeare's Works

The first version of this poem was probably written during the autumn of 1743. C. himself dated it 'Oxford, Dec. 3, 1743', when it was published in London in that month, anonymously, by Mary Cooper, price sixpence (*Gentleman's Mag.* xiii 672). Its original title was *Verses Humbly Address'd to Sir Thomas Hanmer. On his Edition of Shakespear's Works. By a Gentleman of*

Oxford. The publication of the handsome edn of Shakespeare by Sir Thomas Hanmer in 6 vols quarto at the Clarendon Press, Oxford, which occasioned the poem, is not easily datable and does not therefore assist with dating the composition of the poem. The edn of Shakespeare was for subscribers only and, as Hanmer himself stated in Dec. 1742, 'none are to go into the hands of booksellers', J. Nichols, *Literary Anecdotes of the 18th Century* (1812) v 589. For this reason, no doubt, details of publication are scanty. The individual plays in vols i–iv are dated 1743, those in vols v–vi 1744. The general title-page to each volume is dated 1744 and the Imprimatur, signed by the Vice-Chancellor of the University, is dated 26 March 1744. The edn was obviously being printed throughout much of 1743. Hanmer had delivered copy to the press by the end of 1742 (Nichols, *loc. cit.*); Alexander Pope had heard details of the subscription by Jan. 1743 and saw sheets of the edn in the printing-house in Oct. 1743, *Correspondence*, ed. Sherburn (1956) iv 438–9, 475.

C.'s poem was therefore presumably published in immediate anticipation of Hanmer's edn rather than to celebrate its appearance. C. was apparently still in Oxford, having graduated as B.A. only a few weeks earlier, on 18 Nov. 1743. If, as has been suggested, C. was about to leave Oxford and was anxious to obtain Hanmer's patronage, there is no evidence to show that he succeeded. It is also possible that, as Ragsdale later supposed (see headnote to *The Manners*, p. 469), C. was counting on a Fellowship in Oxford; and, in that case, he may have been hoping that his poem on this important Oxford literary event (see below) would help to establish his claims. Again, he was unsuccessful.

Sir Thomas Hanmer (1677–1746) had been Speaker of the House of Commons 1714–15. After helping to secure the Protestant succession on the death of Queen Anne, he had joined the Tory opposition but retired on the accession of George II in 1727 to his seat at Mildenhall near Newmarket. Here, his edn of Shakespeare eventually became a consuming interest, although he himself always claimed that he undertook it for his own satisfaction and was indifferent as to its publication. As he wrote in Oct. 1742: 'As to my own particular, I have no aim to pursue in this affair: I propose neither honour, reward, or thanks, and should be very well pleased to have the books continue upon their shelf, in my own private closet. If it is thought they may be of use or pleasure to the publick, I am willing to part with them out of my hands, and to add, for the honour of Shakespeare, some decorations and embellishments at my own expence', Nichols, *Literary Anecdotes* v 589. In spite of some happy conjectures and a useful glossary, Hanmer's edn was undistinguished and was marred by his failure to collate early texts, his excessively free emendations and his attempts to 'regularize' Shakespeare's metre. Thus although Johnson in 1765, while criticizing Hanmer's weaknesses as an editor, praised him as 'a man . . . eminently qualified by nature for such studies' ('Preface to Shakespeare' in *18th Century Essays on Shakespeare*, ed. D. Nichol Smith, (2nd edn, 1963) pp. 135–6), C.'s praise of the edn is extravagant and uninformed. For

Hanmer's quarrel with William Warburton, the next editor of Shakespeare (1747), which helped to earn him a place, as Montalto, in the *Dunciad* iv 105–18, see Nichol Smith, *op. cit.*, pp. li–lvi.

The first version of C.'s poem celebrates the edn not merely, however, as a personal achievement by Hanmer but as an important Oxford event, perhaps, as suggested above, for interested reasons. It was a notable local event because the actual printing of the edn in Oxford was supervised by Joseph Smith, Provost of Queen's College and Robert Shippen, Principal of Brasenose, and because it was supported by subscriptions from the colleges and members of the University. Hanmer's 'Oxford edition', as it was known, was the only edn of Shakespeare between Rowe's of 1709 and Johnson's of 1765, not to be published by the firms of Tonson and Wellington, who owned the copyright of Shakespeare and who regarded this 1744 edn as a piracy. See Giles E. Dawson, 'Warburton, Hanmer and the 1745 Edition of Shakespeare', *Studies in Bibliography* ii (1949–50) 47–8.

A second and extensively revised edn of C.'s poem was published on 9 May 1744, the name of R. Dodsley being now added to that of M. Cooper as publisher (R. Straus, *Robert Dodsley* (1910) p. 327). C.'s name now appeared on the title-page for the first time, which identified him as of '*Magdalene*-College in Oxford'. His 'Song from *Cymbeline*' (q.v.) was added and the price doubled to one shilling. The poem had been shortened from 160 to 148 ll., at least 42 ll. having been extensively revised, and two notes added. The most noticeable alterations occur at the beginning of the poem, where Oxford's part in the edn is now unmentioned and the compliments to Hanmer reduced to a minimum. Presumably C. had left Oxford in disgust and no longer had any hope of Hanmer's patronage. The main purposes of the poem are now more easily visible. In part C. has produced a 'progress poem', describing the progress of drama from Ancient Greece to Britain, although the climax is reached with Shakespeare and not, as in most Augustan exercises in the genre, in the early eighteenth century; see John R. Crider, 'Structure and Effect in Collins' Progress Poems', *Studies in Philology* lx (1963) 57–72. C.'s other interest, which often affected his own practice as a poet, was in the relationship between poetry and painting, in this case the inspiration which Shakespeare's plays might give to the painter. (C. could have been influenced in this respect by Pope's praise of Homer's pictorial effects: see, for example, the notes to his translation of the *Iliad* vi 595 and xxi 41.) C. recommends to the artist two scenes in particular, from *Julius Caesar* (ll. 115–20) and *Coriolanus* (ll. 121–32); and he also evokes in some detail scenes from *Richard III* (ll. 87–92) and *A Midsummer Night's Dream* (ll. 95–8). J. H. Hagstrum, *The Sister Arts* (Chicago, 1958) p. 281, has described these lines as 'iconic in a special way. They do not describe pictures that have been painted; they describe pictures that it is hoped will be painted. Collins is, as it were, instructing a painter how to improve *Julius Caesar* and *Coriolanus* into fashionable pictorialism.' This view needs some qualification. It is true that the scenes described by C. do not correspond to those depicted in Gravelot's engravings from drawings by himself and Francis Hayman in Hanmer's edn nor to those in Theobald's 1740 edn. But it seems not to have been noticed before that all four scenes evoked in C.'s poem appear in the frontispieces to the respective plays in Rowe's edn of Shakespeare in 1709, reprinted in 1714 with a number of new engravings by Du Guernier, though of the same scenes in almost every case. The detailed correspondences seem to be too close for coincidence, so that, while C. is recommending these scenes to the painter of the future, it must appear that he was also remembering the engravings he had seen (perhaps as a child) in the earliest illustrated edn of Shakespeare.

Not surprisingly in a work of this character in couplets, C. was still strongly influenced by Pope, particularly by the *Essay on Criticism* in both detail and, to some extent, organization. When dealing with the relations of poetry and painting, he also predictably echoed two famous Augustan poems addressed to painters, Dryden's *To Sir Godfrey Kneller* and Pope's *Epistle to Jervas*.

The *Epistle to Hanmer* was never to be one of C.'s most popular poems, but it was included in Dodsley's *Collection* iv 64–70, in 1755; and ll. 93–100 were printed in Samuel Derrick's *Poetical Dictionary; or, The Beauties of the English Poets* (1761) ii 23. G. Birkbeck Hill, *Letters of Samuel Johnson* (1892) ii 131 *n*, refers to an entry in *The Orders of the Delegates of the Clarendon Press*: 'February 8, 1769. Mr. Collins's Copy of Verses to Sir Thos. Hanmer to be inserted after the Preface.' This refers to the so-called 'Second Edition' of Hanmer's *Shakespeare*, edited by Thomas Hawkins, published at Oxford in 1770–1, in which the revised text of the *Epistle* appears in vol i as instructed.

The text followed here is that of the revised 2nd edn of 1744, with variants from the 1st edn, referred to as *1743*.

> Sir,
> While born to bring the Muse's happier days,
> A patriot's hand protects a poet's lays:
> While nursed by you she sees her myrtles bloom,
> Green and unwithered o'er his honoured tomb:

¶ 3.1–6. *1743 has:*

> While, own'd by you, with Smiles the Muse surveys,
> Th'expected Triumph of her sweetest Lays:
> While, stretch'd at Ease, she boasts your Guardian Aid,
> Secure, and happy in her sylvan Shade:
> Excuse her Fears, who scarce a Verse bestows,
> In just Remembrance of the Debt she owes;

C. attempted in *1744* to clarify his use of the Muse of Poetry. Hanmer is the guardian of the Muse (as manifested in Shakespeare) but the Muse (as manifested in C. himself) is diffident about expressing her gratitude. In *1743* the Muse is simultaneously relaxed and worried.

5   Excuse her doubts, if yet she fears to tell
     What secret transports in her bosom swell:
     With conscious awe she hears the critic's fame,
     And blushing hides her wreath at Shakespeare's name.
     Hard was the lot those injured strains endured,
10 Unowned by Science and by years obscured:
     Fair Fancy wept; and echoing sighs confessed
     A fixed despair in every tuneful breast.
     Not with more grief the afflicted swains appear,
     When wintry winds deform the plenteous year;
15 When lingering frosts the ruined seats invade
     Where Peace resorted and the Graces played.

6. Pope, *Windsor Forest* 90: 'And secret Transport touch'd the conscious Swain'.

9–16. *1743 has:*

> Long slighted *Fancy*, with a Mother's Care,
> Wept o'er his Works, and felt the last Despair.
> Torn from her Head, she saw the Roses fall,
> By all deserted, tho' admir'd by all.
> "And oh! she cry'd, shall Science still resign
> "Whate'er is Nature's, and whate'er is mine?
> "Shall *Taste* and *Art*, but shew a cold Regard,
> "And scornful Pride reject th'unletter'd Bard?
> "Ye myrtled Nymphs, who own my gentle Reign,
> "Tune the sweet Lyre, and grace my airy Train!
> "If, where ye rove, your searching Eyes have known
> "One perfect Mind, which Judgment calls its own:
> "There ev'ry Breast its fondest Hopes must bend,
> "And ev'ry Muse with Tears await her Friend.
>
> 'Twas then fair *Isis* from her Stream arose,
> In kind Compassion of her Sister's Woes.
> 'Twas then she promis'd to the mourning Maid
> Th'immortal Honours, which thy Hands have paid:
> "My best-lov'd Son (she said) shall yet restore
> "Thy ruin'd Sweets, and Fancy weep no more.

10. C. exaggerates the neglect of Shakespeare. Whatever their scholarly shortcomings, there had been three notable edns already in the century: those by Rowe, 6 vols, 1709; by Pope, 6 vols, 1725; and by Theobald, 7 vols, 1733.

11. Pope, *Eloisa to Abelard* 41–2: 'join / Griefs to thy griefs, and eccho sighs to thine.'

Each rising art by just gradation moves,
Toil builds on toil and age on age improves:
The Muse alone unequal dealt her rage,
20   And graced with noblest pomp her earliest stage.
Preserved through time, the speaking scenes impart
Each changeful wish of Phaedra's tortured heart;
Or paint the curse that marked the Theban's reign,
A bed incestuous and a father slain.
25   With kind concern our pitying eyes o'erflow,
Trace the sad tale and own another's woe.

To Rome removed, with wit secure to please,
The comic Sisters kept their native ease.
With jealous fear declining Greece beheld
30   Her own Menander's art almost excelled!
But every muse essayed to raise in vain
Some laboured rival of her tragic strain;

17. *just*] slow *1743*. Cp. Dryden, *To Sir Godfrey Kneller* 35: 'By slow degrees, the Godlike Art advanc'd'; W. Harte, 'Essay on Painting', in *Poems on Several Occasions* (1727) p. 7: 'Painful and slow, to noble arts we rise, / And long, long labours wait the general prize'; Pope, *Essay on Man* iii 169: 'See him from Nature rising slow to Art!'. C.'s revision kept him close to the *Essay on Man*: cp. 'Gradations just' and 'this just gradation', i 31 and 229.
19. *rage*] Inspiration.
22. Phaedra's love for her stepson Hippolytus is depicted in Euripides' play of that name. C. would also know Racine's *Phèdre* (1671) and Edmund Smith's adaptation, *Phaedra and Hippolitus* (1707).
23. The *Oedipus* of Sophocles. C. *1743*.
    In *Oedipus Tyrannus*, Sophocles depicts Oedipus' discovery that he has unwittingly murdered his father and married his mother.
25. *With kind concern*] Line after line *1743*. (This revision shows C. trying to reduce the extent of his echo of Pope, *Eloisa to Abelard* 35-6: 'Line after line my gushing eyes o'erflow, / Led thro' a sad variety of woe . . .')
26. Pope, *Elegy to an Unfortunate Lady* 46: 'melt at others' woe'; and *Universal Prayer* 37: 'feel another's Woe'. See also Gray, *Ode to Adversity* 16 and *n* (p. 71 above).
27. *wit secure*] equal Pow'r *1743*.
28. Cp. Pope (of comedy), *Epistle to Miss Blount with Voiture* 27: 'a native Ease and Grace'.
30-4. Menander (c. 342-292 B.C.) was the most famous of the writers of the Athenian 'New Comedy'. Plautus and Terence were the most notable writers of Roman comedy. C.'s point is that Rome produced no tragic poet who could similarly rival the Greeks.

Ilissus' laurels, though transferred with toil,
Drooped their fair leaves nor knew the unfriendly soil.

35   As arts expired, resistless dulness rose;
Goths, priests or Vandals,–all were learning's foes.
Till Julius first recalled each exiled Maid,
And Cosmo owned them in the Etrurian shade.

33. Ilissus] A river flowing past Athens, the home of Greek tragedy.
35–41. 1743 has:

> When *Rome* herself, her envy'd Glories dead,
> No more Imperial, stoop'd her conquer'd Head:
> Luxuriant *Florence* chose a softer Theme,
> While all was Peace, by *Arno's* silver Stream.
> With sweeter Notes th'*Etrurian* Vales complain'd,
> And Arts reviving told—a *Cosmo* reign'd.
> Their wanton Lyres the Bards of *Provence* strung,

C. may have been trying to escape from some of the prominent echoes of
Pope in these lines by revision: e.g. *Essay on Criticism* 703, describing the
same period: 'With *sweeter Notes* each *rising Temple* rung'; *Windsor Forest*
42: 'And Peace and Plenty tell, a STUART reigns'.
35. C. is remembering Pope's vision of the triumph of Dulness, *Dunciad* iv
640: '*Art* after *Art* goes out, and all is Night' and iv 650: 'And unawares
Morality expires'.
35–6. This was the standard Augustan view of the Middle Ages. Cp. Dryden,
To the Earl of Roscommon 15–16: 'But *Italy*, reviving from the trance, / Of
Vandal, Goth, and *Monkish* ignorance'; *To Sir Godfrey Kneller* 45–9:
'*Rome* rais'd not Art, but barely kept alive; / And with Old *Greece,* unequally
did strive: / Till *Goths* and *Vandals,* a rude *Northern* Race, / Did all the
matchless Monuments deface. / Then all the Muses in one ruine lye'; and
Pope, *Essay on Criticism* 692: 'And the *Monks* finish'd what the *Goths* begun.'
37. Julius the Second, the immediate Predecessor of *Leo* the Tenth. *C., added
in 1744.*
Julius was Pope 1503–13, laid the foundation stone of St Peter's in
Rome, and was the friend and admirer of Raphael and Michaelangelo. C.
was particularly interested in this period: in Dec. 1744, *A Literary Journal,*
Dublin, I (Pt i) 226, mentioned his projected *Review of the Advancement of
Learning from 1300 to 1521,* one of his many abortive enterprises. James
Hampton, in the *Poetical Calendar* (1763) xii 109, referred to this work as a
projected 'history of the revival of learning in Italy, under the pontificates
of Julius II. and Leo X.', adding that it was abandoned because of a lack of
subscribers. Thomas Warton in *The Reaper,* reprinted in *The Gleaner* (1811)
iv 479, stated that C. completed a 'Preliminary Dissertation' for it, which he
had been told, 'was written with great judgment, precision, and knowledge
of the subject.'   *each exiled Maid*] The Muses.
38. Cosmo] Cosimo de Medici (1389–1464), the first great patron in his
family at Florence, which is in the ancient Etruria and on the river Arno (l. 40).

Then deeply skilled in love's engaging theme,
40 The soft Provencial passed to Arno's stream:
With graceful ease the wanton lyre he strung,
Sweet flowed the lays – but love was all he sung.
The gay description could not fail to move;
For, led by nature, all are friends to love.

45 But heaven, still various in its works, decreed
The perfect boast of time should last succeed.
The beauteous union must appear at length,
Of Tuscan fancy and Athenian strength:
One greater muse Eliza's reign adorn,
50 And even a Shakespeare to her fame be born!

Yet ah! so bright her morning's opening ray,
In vain our Britain hoped an equal day!
No second growth the western isle could bear,
At once exhausted with too rich a year.
55 Too nicely Jonson knew the critic's part;
Nature in him was almost lost in art.
Of softer mould the gentle Fletcher came,
The next in order as the next in name.
With pleased attention midst his scenes we find
60 Each glowing thought that warms the female mind;

40–2. C.'s chronology is very vague. Provençal troubadors flourished in Italy in the 13th century and they dealt not merely with love, but with military, didactic and heroic themes. Cp. *Ode to Simplicity* 37–42 (p. 426).

41. he] they *1743*.

43. Pope, *Dunciad* i 73: 'Here gay Description Ægypt glads with show'rs'.

45. various] rising *1743*. Cp. Pope, *Essay on Man* iii 1–2: 'The Universal Cause / Acts to one end, but acts by various laws'.

47–50. Dryden, *To the Earl of Roscommon* 26–9: 'The Wit of *Greece*, the Gravity of *Rome* / Appear exalted in the *Brittish Loome*; / The Muses Empire is restor'd agen, / In *Charles* his Reign . . .'

55–6. Dunciad ii 224: 'With Shakespear's nature, or with Johnson's art'. This is the conventional contrast. Pope's 'Preface to Shakespeare' (1725) asserted that Jonson 'brought critical learning into vogue'. Theobald, 1733, contrasted Shakespeare's 'prodigious natural genius' with Jonson's 'art and learning'. Cp. *Eighteenth Century Essays on Shakespeare*, ed. D. Nichol Smith (2nd edn, 1963) pp. 47, 71. There is some evidence that C. admired Ben Jonson: Tom Davies, *Dramatic Miscellanies* (1783) ii 77, stated that the beauties of the conclusion to *Every Man Out of His Humour* as acted before Queen Elizabeth were pointed out to him by C.

57. John Fletcher (1579–1625) usually collaborated with Francis Beaumont (1585?–1616). He began writing for the stage about a decade later than Jonson.

Each melting sigh, and every tender tear,
The lover's wishes and the virgin's fear.
His every strain the Smiles and Graces own;
But stronger Shakespeare felt for man alone:
65   Drawn by his pen, our ruder passions stand
The unrivalled picture of his early hand.

With gradual steps and slow, exacter France
Saw Art's fair empire o'er her shores advance:
By length of toil a bright perfection knew,
70   Correctly bold and just in all she drew.
Till late Corneille, with Lucan's spirit fired,

62. Pope, *Eloisa to Abelard* 55: 'The virgin's wish without her fears impart'
63. Their Characters are thus distinguish'd by Mr. *Dryden. C. 1743.*

Cp. Dryden's 'Preface' to *Troilus and Cressida*, in *Of Dramatic Poesy and Other Critical Essays*, ed. G. Watson (1962) i 260: 'The excellency of that poet [Shakespeare] was . . . in the more manly passions; Fletcher's in the softer: Shakespeare writ better betwixt man and man; Fletcher, betwixt man and woman: consequently, the one described friendship better; the other love: yet Shakespeare taught Fletcher to write love . . . . Shakespeare had an universal mind, which comprehended all characters and passions; Fletcher a more confined and limited.'

Smiles] Loves *1743.* Cp. Pope, *To Miss Blount with Voiture* 1: 'In these gay Thoughts the Loves and Graces shine'.
67. About the Time of *Shakespear*, the Poet *Hardy* was in great Repute in *France.* He wrote, according to *Fontenelle,* six hundred Plays. The *French* Poets after him applied themselves in general to the correct Improvement of the Stage, which was almost totally disregarded by those of our own Country, *Johnson* excepted. C., added in *1744.*

C. had evidently been reading Fontenelle's *Vie de P. Corneille avec l'histoire du théatre François jusqu'à lui*, in vol iii of his *Oeuvres* (Paris, 1742). Alexandre Hardy (*c.* 1569/75–1632) was a prolific playwright who wrote or arranged several hundred plays. He is usually considered to have been an important agent in the transition from Renaissance tragedy to the French classical drama of the following period.

Cp. *Par. Lost* xii 648: 'with wandring steps and slow', a frequently imitated phrase. Cp. 'pensive steps and slow' and 'solemn pace and slow', Pope, *Odyssey* x 286 and xi 397; and 'timid steps, and slow', *Dunciad* iv 465. Cp. also Gray, *Ode for Music* 36 and *n* (p. 270 above).
67–8. Pope, *Essay on Criticism* 711–12: 'Thence Arts o'er all the *Northern World* advance; / But *Critic Learning* flourish'd most in *France.*'
70. Pope, *Essay on Criticism* 240: '*Correctly cold,* and *regularly low*'.
71–2. *1743* has:

Till late *Corneille* from Epick *Lucan* brought
The full Expression, and the *Roman* Thought;

> Breathed the free strain, as Rome and he inspired:
> And classic judgment gained to sweet Racine
> The temperate strength of Maro's chaster line.
> 75 But wilder far the British laurel spread,
> And wreaths less artful crown our poet's head.
> Yet he alone to every scene could give
> The historian's truth, and bid the manners live.
> Waked at his call I view, with glad surprise,
> 80 Majestic forms of mighty monarchs rise.
> There Henry's trumpets spread their loud alarms,
> And laurelled Conquest waits her hero's arms.
> Here gentler Edward claims a pitying sigh,
> Scarce born to honours and so soon to die.
> 85 Yet shall thy throne, unhappy infant, bring
> No beam of comfort to the guilty king?
> The time shall come when Gloucester's heart shall
>   bleed
> In life's last hours, with horror of the deed:
> When dreary visions shall at last present
> 90 Thy vengeful image in the midnight tent:
> Thy hand unseen the secret death shall bear,
> Blunt the weak sword and break the oppressive spear.

72. *Lucan*] The favourite Author of the Elder *Corneille*. C. *1743*.

Pierre Corneille (1606–84) was strongly influenced by the *Pharsalia* of Lucan (A.D. 39–65), an epic of the wars between Caesar and Pompey.

74. Pope, *Epistle to Jervas* 37: '*Caracci's* strength, *Correggio's* softer line'. *Maro*] The cognomen of Virgil.

78. Pope, *Essay on Man* i 14: 'And catch the Manners living as they rise'; and cp. C.'s own *The Manners*. Dryden, *Of Dramatic Poesy and Other Essays* (ed. G. Watson, 1962) ii 278, defines the 'manners' as 'the passions and, in a larger sense, the descriptions of persons, and their very habits'.

81–2. A reference to *Henry V*, which describes the English victory at Agincourt.

83–92. The reference is to *Richard III*, in which the boy king, Edward V, is murdered in the Tower soon after Richard's accession to the throne. In Act V Scene iii Richard dreams that the ghosts of all those he has murdered in his progress to the crown appear before him and promise him defeat in the Battle of Bosworth Field on the following day. This scene is depicted in the frontispiece to the play in Rowe's Shakespeare, vol iv (1709 edn); vol v (1714 edn).

87. Tempus erit Turno, magno cum optaverit emptum / Intactum Pallanta, &c. C. *1743*.

These lines (which should read *Turno tempus erit* etc) are from *Aeneid* x 503–4: 'To Turnus shall come the hour when for a great price will he long to have bought an unscathed Pallas'.

> Where'er we turn, by Fancy charmed, we find
> Some sweet illusion of the cheated mind.
> 95 Oft, wild of wing, she calls the soul to rove
> With humbler nature in the rural grove;
> Where swains contented own the quiet scene,
> And twilight fairies tread the circled green:
> Dressed by her hand, the woods and valleys smile,
> 100 And spring diffusive decks the *enchanted isle*.
>
> O more than all in powerful genius blest,
> Come, take thine empire o'er the willing breast!
> Whate'er the wounds this youthful heart shall feel,
> Thy songs support me and thy morals heal!

93–4. Pope, *Eloisa to Abelard* 263: 'What scenes appear where-e'er I turn my view!', and 239–40: 'To dream once more I close my willing eyes; / Ye soft illusions, dear deceits, arise!'; Milton, *Comus* 155: 'Of power to cheat the eye with blear illusion'; Roscommon, 'The Dream', *Poems* (1717) p. 125: 'Once more present the vision to my view, / The sweet illusion, gentle fate, renew'.

95. *Par. Lost* viii 188–9: 'But apte the Mind or Fancie is to roave / Uncheckt, and of her roaving is no end.'

97–8. Pope, *Rape of the Lock* i 31–2: 'Of airy Elves by Moonlight Shadows seen, / The silver Token, and the circled Green.' Shakespeare's fairies and the 'circled green' are clearly depicted in the frontispiece to *A Midsummer Night's Dream* in Rowe's Shakespeare, vol ii (1709 and 1714 edns).

99. Pope, *Imitations of Horace, Odes* IV i 41: 'drest in Fancy's airy beam'.

100. The Tempest, or the Enchanted Island was the full title of the adaptation (staged 1667) of Shakespeare's play by Davenant and Dryden. Cp. Pope, *Spring* 100: 'While opening Blooms diffuse their Sweets around'.

101–10. 1743 has:

> O blest in all that Genius gives to charm,
> Whose Morals mend us, and whose Passions warm!
> Oft let my Youth attend thy various Page,
> Where rich Invention rules th'unbounded Stage.
> There ev'ry Scene the Poet's Warmth may raise,
> And melting Music find the softest Lays.
> O might the Muse with equal Ease persuade
> Expressive Picture. to adopt thine Aid!
> Some pow'rful *Raphael* shou'd again appear,
> And Arts consenting fix their Empire here.

Cp. with l. 6 of this passage, 'melting Musick', *Rape of the Lock* ii 49. The last line was no doubt changed in *1744* because of its echo of l. 68 above.

104. Pope, *Imitations of Horace, Ep.* II i 262: 'And heals with Morals what it hurts with Wit.'

105 There every thought the poet's warmth may raise,
There native music dwells in all the lays.
O might some verse with happiest skill persuade
Expressive Picture to adopt thine aid!
What wondrous drafts might rise from every page!
110 What other Raphaels charm a distant age!

Methinks even now I view some free design,
Where breathing nature lives in every line:
Chaste and subdued the modest lights decay,
Steal into shade and mildly melt away.

105. Pope, *Epistles to Several Persons* ii 250: 'To raise the Thought and touch the Heart, be thine!'

107–10. For the pattern of this quatrain, cp. Gray, *Stanzas to Bentley* 13–16 n (p. 154 above). Cp. W. Harte, 'An Essay on Painting', in *Poems on Several Occasions* (1727) p. 38: 'Ah, thus, for ever may my numbers shine, / Bold as your thoughts, but easy as your line! / Then might the muse to distant ages live, / Contract new beauty, and new praise receive'.

111. free] fair *1743*. (By this point in *1743* C. had already used 'fair' three times and it now appeared twice in 4 ll., both of which were removed in *1744*. But the first revision brought him even closer to Pope's *Epistle to Jervas*.)

111–14. Pope, *Epistle to Jervas* 3–4: 'Whether thy hand strike out some free design, / Where life awakes, and dawns at ev'ry line'; cp. also *To Miss Blount with Voiture* 2: 'And all the Writer lives in ev'ry Line'; and W. Harte, 'An Essay on Painting', in his *Poems on Several Occasions* (1727) p. 10: 'Whoever meditates some great design, / Where strength and nature dawn at ev'ry line; / Where art and fancy full perfection give, / And each bold figure glows, and seems to live: / Where lights and shades in sweet disunion play, / Rise by degrees, or by degrees decay . . .' Harte's and C.'s lines are typical of the Augustan conception of painting as composed 'tensions' of light and shade and echo earlier versifications of it. Cp. Dryden, *To Sir Godfrey Kneller* 69–70: 'Where Light to Shades descending, plays, not strives; / Dyes by degrees, and by degrees revives.' And Pope, on the 'well accorded strife' of light and shade, *Essay on Man* ii 121–2; and *Essay on Criticism* 488–9: 'When the ripe Colours *soften* and *unite*, / And sweetly *melt* into just Shade and Light.'

113–6. 1743 has:

> Chaste, and subdu'd, the modest Colours lie,
> In fair Proportion to th'approving Eye.—
> And see, where *Antony* lamenting stands
> In fixt Distress, and spreads his pleading Hands!

115 — And see, where Antony in tears approved,
  Guards the pale relics of the chief he loved:
  O'er the cold corse the warrior seems to bend,
  Deep sunk in grief, and mourns his murthered friend!
  Still as they press, he calls on all around,
120 Lifts the torn robe and points the bleeding wound.

  But who is he, whose brows exalted bear
  A wrath impatient and a fiercer air?
  Awake to all that injured worth can feel,

115. See the Tragedy of *Julius Caesar* [Act III Sc ii]. *C. 1743.*
  This scene is depicted in the frontispiece to the play in Rowe's Shakespeare, vol v (1709 edn); vol vi (1714 edn).
117. cold] pale *1743.*
121. Coriolanus [V iii]. See Mr. *Spence*'s Dialogues on the *Odyssey. C. 1743.*
  Cp. Joseph Spence, *An Essay on Pope's Odyssey* (1726) p. 84: 'And certainly what makes so beautiful a Figure in the finest Poets, might deserve the imitation of the best Painters. ... If our *Shakespear* can give us the struggle of Passions in the Breast of *Coriolanus, Thornhill* might trace the same, and speak them as well with his Pencil.' Spence was referring to Sir James Thornhill (1675–1734), the painter. In the 2nd edn (1737) after Thornhill's death, he substituted the name 'Wall': no doubt John Wall (1708–83), physician and amateur painter. This scene from *Coriolanus* was invariably chosen to illustrate the play in edns of Shakespeare: but only in Rowe's edn of 1709, vol iv, has Coriolanus his sword in hand as his mother and wife plead with him.
122. wrath] Rage *1743.* (The revision was no doubt made because 'Rage' recurs at l. 132.)
123–30. 1743 has:

  Ev'n now, his Thoughts with eager Vengeance doom
  The last sad Ruin of ungrateful *Rome.*
  Till, slow-advancing o'er the tented Plain,
  In sable Weeds, appear the Kindred-train:
  The frantic Mother leads their wild Despair,
  Beats her swoln Breast, and rends her silver Hair.
  And see he yields! — the Tears unbidden start,
  And conscious Nature claims th'unwilling Heart!

Cp. with l. 2 of this passage, 'the last sad office', Pope, *Eloisa to Abelard* 321; with l. 3, 'the tented field', *Othello* I iii 85; with l. 4, 'What tho' no friends in sable weeds appear', Pope, *Elegy to an Unfortunate Lady* 55. C. no doubt revised this passage because of its excessively emotional misrepresentation of the scene in the play.
123. Pope, *Imitations of Horace, Ep.* II i 227: 'Proud Vice to brand, or injur'd Worth adorn'.

On his own Rome he turns the avenging steel.
125 Yet shall not war's insatiate fury fall
(So heaven ordains it) on the destined wall.
See the fond mother midst the plaintive train
Hung on his knees and prostrate on the plain!
Touched to the soul, in vain he strives to hide
130 The son's affection in the Roman's pride:
O'er all the man conflicting passions rise,
Rage grasps the sword, while Pity melts the eyes.

Thus, generous critic, as thy bard inspires,
The sister arts shall nurse their drooping fires;
135 Each from his scenes her stores alternate bring,
Blend the fair tints or wake the vocal string:
Those Sibyl-leaves, the sport of every wind,
(For poets ever were a careless kind),
By thee disposed, no farther toil demand,
140 But, just to nature, own thy forming hand.

So spread o'er Greece, the harmonious whole
      unknown,
Even Homer's numbers charmed by parts alone.
Their own Ulysses scarce had wandered more,
By winds and water cast on every shore:
145 When, raised by fate, some former Hanmer joined

133–4. Pope, *Essay on Criticism* 100, praising ancient critics: 'The gen'rous Critick *fann'd* the *Poet's Fire*'; and Dryden, *Threnodia Augustalis* 348: 'Reviv'd the drooping Arts again'. For the 'Sister Arts', cf. Dryden, *Epistle to Kneller* 57, 89; and Pope, *Epistle to Jervas* 13, 69; see also Gray, *Stanzas to Bentley* 3 and *n* (p. 153 above).

136.*Blend*] Spread *1743*. Cp. Pope, *Epistle to Jervas* 5: 'Or blend in beauteous tints the colour'd mass'; and *Ode on St Cecilia's Day* 3: 'Wake into Voice each silent String'.

137. C. is referring to Virgil's Sybil, who wrote her oracular verses on leaves which were then disordered by the wind. Cp. *Aeneid* iii 445–51; and vi 75: *rapidis ludibria ventis*, translated by Dryden, *Aeneid* vi 117, 'the sport of ev'ry Wind'.

139–40. This optimistic compliment reflects Hanmer's own claim in the Preface to his edn that he had produced 'a true and correct Edition of *Shakespear's* works cleared from the corruptions with which they have abounded'.

145. Several ancient authors, including Cicero, *De Oratore* iii 137, state that Pisistratus, the tyrant of Athens in the 6th century B.C., was responsible for collecting and arranging the disordered and scattered books of Homer. But C. could have had in mind another 'former Hanmer'; cp. Sir William Temple, 'Of Poetry', in *Critical Essays of the 17th Century*, ed. J. E. Spingarn

Each beauteous image of the boundless mind;
And bade, like thee, his Athens ever claim
A fond alliance with the poet's name.

(1908–9) iii 107, where he states that Lycurgus 'was so great a Lover of [poetry], That to his Care and Industry we are said by some Authors to owe the Collection and Preservation of the loose and scattered Pieces of *Homer* in the Order wherein they have since appeared'.
146. boundless] tuneful *1743.* Cp. 'the tuneful mind', Pope, *Imitations of Horace, Ep.* II i 192.

4 A Song from Shakespeare's Cymbeline

Sung by Guiderus and Arviragus over Fidele,
supposed to be dead

See page 278 of the 7th Vol of Theobald's Edition of Shakespeare.

This song was written by 9 May 1744, when it was published in the 2nd edn of C.'s *Epistle to Hanmer* (q.v.). There is no other evidence for dating it. The fact that C. refers to the 2nd edn of Theobald's Shakespeare (1740) in his subtitle does not necessarily mean that he must therefore have written this song before the publication of Hanmer's edn, as C. seems to have written his *Epistle to Hanmer* before the latter was published and did not necessarily possess a copy of the expensive volumes himself. But it is curious that he should not cite Hanmer, after a long poem purporting to celebrate his merits. C. may have written this imitation of Shakespeare between the two edns of his poem to Hanmer i.e. between Dec. 1743 and May 1744 but there is no evidence to support this suggestion.

The *Song* was reprinted as *Elegiac Song*, with a number of changes, in the *Gentleman's Mag.* (Oct. 1749) xix 466–7. In his *Life of Johnson* (1787) pp. 48–9, Sir John Hawkins recalled a visit to Edward Cave, editor of the magazine, which he made at this time: 'I remember that, calling in on him once, he gave me to read the beautiful poem of Collins, written for Shakespeare's Cymbeline, 'To fair Fidele's grassy tomb,' which, though adapted to a particular circumstance in the play, Cave was for inserting in his Magazine, without any reference to the subject: I told him it would lose of its beauty if it were so published: this he could not see; nor could he be convinced of the propriety of the name Fidele: he thought Pastora a better, and so printed it.' It seems likely therefore that Cave was responsible for a number of other small changes in the text which he printed: 'swains' for 'lads' (l. 7); 'But' for 'The' (l.11); 'bed' for 'grave' (l. 12); 'chiding' for 'howling' (l. 17);

'tempest' for 'tempests' (l. 18); 'flocks' for 'chase' (l. 19); 'lovely' for
'lonely' (l. 21); 'can' for 'could' (l. 23). Dodsley restored the original
readings when he included the poem in his *Collection* (1755) iv 71–2. Another
early, anonymous printing (noted by A. S. P. Woodhouse, *Times Lit. Supp.*
1930, p. 838) was in *The Second Volume of Lyric Harmony* [? 1746], with a
setting by Thomas Arne.

The context of the poem to which C.'s title directs the reader is *Cymbeline*
IV ii, in particular the well-known dirge over Imogen, the supposed Fidele,
'Fear no more the heat of the sun'. At this point in his edn of Shakespeare
(1765) vii 358 *n*, Samuel Johnson remarked: 'For the obsequies of *Fidele*,
a song was written by my unhappy friend, Mr. *William Collins* of *Chichester*,
a man of uncommon learning and abilities. I shall give it a place at the end in
honour of his memory.' Johnson accordingly printed the *Song* (vii 403–4).
Later editors of Shakespeare for a time followed his example: e.g. Malone
(1790) viii 482. Alexander Dyce, in his edn of Collins (1827) p. 194,
stated that 'All succeeding editors of Shakespeare have followed [Johnson's]
example in subjoining it to the tragedy'. A Latin translation of the *Song* was
published in the *Gentleman's Mag.* lxxiii (Sept. 1803) 860. For discussion of
eighteenth-century imitators of Shakespeare's lyrics, of whom C. is one of
the first, see E. R. Wasserman, *Elizabethan Poetry in the Eighteenth Century*
(Urbana, 1947) pp. 187–91.

To fair Fidele's grassy tomb
    Soft maids and village hinds shall bring
Each opening sweet of earliest bloom,
    And rifle all the breathing spring.
5   No wailing ghost shall dare appear
    To vex with shrieks this quiet grove;

¶ *4.2.* The 'maids' and 'hinds' have a similar function in *Ode to a Lady*
16–17, and *Ode on the Death of Mr. Thomson* 39–40 (see pp. 458, 491 below).
They may derive from Tickell, *Colin and Lucy* 65–8 (one of the best-
known ballad-imitations of the early 18th century): 'Oft at his grave, the
constant hind / And plighted maid are seen; / With garlands gay and
true-love knots, / They deck the sacred green'.
3–4. C.'s starting-point was *Cymbeline* IV ii 218–20: 'With fairest flowers, /
Whilst summer lasts, and I live here, Fidele, / I'll sweeten thy sad grave.' Cp.
also Addison, *Virgil's Georgic IV* 133–4: 'they bring / Their gathered sweets,
and rifle all the spring'; Pope, *Spring* 100: 'While opening Blooms diffuse
their Sweets around'; and *Messiah* 23–4: 'See Nature hasts her earliest
Wreaths to bring, / With all the Incence of the breathing Spring'.
5–6, 9–10. Cp. Shakespeare's dirge for Fidele, *Cymbeline* IV ii 276–9: 'No
exorciser harm thee! / Nor no witchcraft charm thee! / Ghost unlaid forbear
thee! / Nothing ill come near thee!'
5–6. Julius Caesar II ii 24: 'And ghosts did shriek and squeal about the
streets.'

But shepherd lads assemble here,
    And melting virgins own their love.

No withered witch shall here be seen,
10   No goblins lead their nightly crew;
The female fays shall haunt the green,
    And dress thy grave with pearly dew!

The red-breast oft at evening hours
    Shall kindly lend his little aid:
15   With hoary moss and gathered flowers,
    To deck the ground where thou art laid.

When howling winds and beating rain
    In tempests shake the sylvan cell,
Or midst the chase on every plain,
20   The tender thought on thee shall dwell.

Each lonely scene shall thee restore,
    For thee the tear be duly shed:

8. 'melting Maids', Pope, *Rape of the Lock* i 71.

9. 'Wither'd hag', *Richard III* I iii 214. The witches in *Macbeth* I iii 40, were also 'wither'd'.

11. Cymbeline IV ii 217: 'With female fairies will his tomb be haunted.'

12. Spenser has 'perly deaw', *Faerie Queene* III x 46, 6 and IV v 45, 5; and Dryden, 'Pearly Dews', *Songs from King Arthur* iii 27 and vi 11. Cp. also *Midsummer Night's Dream* I i 211, 'Decking with liquid pearl the bladed grass'; and Pope, *Elegy to an Unfortunate Lady* 63: 'Yet shall thy grave with rising flow'rs be drest.'

13–16. Cymbeline IV ii 224–5, 227–9: 'The ruddock would / With charitable bill . . . / . . . bring thee all this; / Yea and furr'd moss besides, when flowers are none, / To winter-ground thy corse.' 'Ruddock' is another name for the robin. Webster, *The White Devil* V iv 89–92, has been compared: 'Call for the robin redbreast and the wren / Since o'er shady groves they hover, / And with leaves and flowers do cover / The friendless bodies of unburied men.' But C. is more likely to have derived his use of the robin from *Spectator* No. 85 (7 June 1711).

15. Spenser, *Faerie Queene* VI iv 14, 4: 'the bare ground with hoarie moss bestrowed'.

16. Spenser frequently uses 'deck' and 'decked' for the adornment of graves and tombs with flowers, as does C.: cp. *Ode, Written in the beginning of 1746* 4; *Ode to Mercy* 13; *Ode on the Death of Mr. Thomson* 4 (pp. 437, 439, 489).

17. Cymbeline III iii 36–7: 'we shall hear / The rain and wind beat dark December'; and *Othello* II i 68, 'howling winds'.

18. cell] 'Any small place of residence; a cottage' (Johnson), so used by Milton, *Il Penseroso* 169 and *Comus* 387. Cp. 'Silvan Lodge', *Par. Lost* v 377.

Beloved, till life could charm no more,
And mourned, till Pity's self be dead.

23–4. Henry Headley, *Select Beauties of Ancient English Poetry* (1787) ii 154,
compares the last two lines of Lovelace's *On the Death of Mrs. Elizabeth
Filmer* 43–4: 'And her eternal fame be read, / When all but very Virtue's
dead.' But the echo is probably coincidental. See also Pope, *Elegy to an
Unfortunate Lady* 77–8, 81–2: 'Ev'n he, whose soul now melts in mournful
lays, / Shall shortly want the gen'rous tear he pays / . . . / Life's idle business
at one gasp be o'er, / The Muse forgot, and thou belov'd no more!'

5 Song. The Sentiments Borrowed from Shakespeare

First published in the *Gentleman's Mag.* lviii (pt. i) 155, in Feb. 1788, intro-
duced by a letter to the editor:

MR. URBAN,   *Feb. 2.*
    In turning over your Magazine, for May, 1765, I observed a copy of most
elegant verses by Collins, which are not to be found in any edition of his
poems. The following lines are to the best of my knowledge in the same
predicament, and I believe have never yet appeared in print.
                    Yours, &c.   C—T—O.

The poem was reprinted a few days later in the *Public Advertiser*, 7 March
1788. (The lines *On a Piece of Bride Cake*, to which the letter begins by
referring, had in fact been collected in Johnson's *English Poets* xlix 283–4).
    The *Song* was added to C.'s poems in the 1790 edn of Johnson's *English
Poets* lviii 66, and in all edns of C. thereafter, although its authenticity
has been questioned. William Beloe, *The Sexagenarian* i (1817) 178–9,
attributed the *Song* to his friend Henry Headley, the poet and critic, who
had died in his early twenties in the year of its publication. In 1810, however,
another friend of Headley, Henry Kett, had stated in his edn of Headley's
Select Beauties of Ancient English Poetry I viii, that 'C—T—O' was the sig-
nature under which Headley contributed to the *Gentleman's Mag.*: this would
suggest that Headley had not actually written the *Song* but had been respon-
sible for its publication. Alternatively, Beloe's assertion can be accepted,
which would mean that Headley's attribution of the poem to C. was
merely a device for ensuring the poem's publication. This theory has been
ingeniously but unconvincingly argued by P. L. Carver, *Notes and Queries*
clxxvii (1939) 272–4 and clxxx (1941) 407–8, repeated in *The Life of a Poet*
(1967) pp. 183–5; see E. R. Wasserman's reply, clxxviii (1940) 193–4.
    Although the evidence is not conclusive, the attribution to C. may be
cautiously accepted. Headley was a friend and admirer of Thomas Warton

(see Henry Kett, *op. cit.* I iv) from whom he could have obtained a copy of the *Song*. For all his youth, he was a reliable scholar and it is not easy to see why he should have resorted to such a subterfuge for publishing a poem of his own, when he had already published a book of verse in 1785 (reissued in 1786), in addition to his *Select Beauties* and some poems with his usual signature of 'C—T—O' in the *Gentleman's Mag.* It must be assumed that William Beloe, never the most reliable of authorities, mistook Headley's interest in the poem for his authorship of it.

W. Moy Thomas, in the Aldine edn of C. (1858) p. 101, refers to a MS of this poem (not C.'s holograph), formerly in the possession of William Upcott and then in the British Museum, which was inscribed: 'Written by Collins when at Winchester School. From a Manuscript.' This copy has not been traced since. A. D. McKillop, *Philological Quarterly* xxxvi (1957) 353, on the other hand links the *Song* with the other 'Damon' pastoral lyric found among the drafts and fragments in Trinity College, Oxford ('No longer ask me, gentle friends', *c.* 1745–46), which he believes helps to authenticate this *Song*. The poem is certainly extremely derivative, not merely from Ophelia's mad-scene in *Hamlet* IV v, the main source, but from David Mallet's popular 'ballad', *William and Margaret* (?1723), and this may point to an early date of composition. In any case, in the absence of more definite evidence, the poem may be associated with C.'s other, datable imitation of Shakespeare.

> Young Damon of the vale is dead,
>   Ye lowland hamlets moan:
> A dewy turf lies o'er his head,
>   And at his feet a stone.
>
> 5   His shroud, which death's cold damps destroy,
>   Of snow-white threads was made:
> All mourned to see so sweet a boy
>   In earth for ever laid.
>
> Pale pansies o'er his corpse were placed,
> 10   Which, plucked before their time,

¶ 5.2. *lowland*] lowly *Dyce*. But C. was probably imitating Milton, *L'Allegro* 92: 'up-land Hamlets'.

3–4. *Hamlet* IV v 29–32: 'He is dead and gone, lady, / He is dead and gone; / At his head a grass-green turf, / At his heels a stone.'

5–6. *Hamlet* IV v 35: 'White his shroud as the mountain snow'; and *Par. Lost* x 848: 'damps and dreadful gloom'.

9–12. Mallet, *William and Margaret* 17–20: 'But love had, like the canker-worm, / Consum'd her early prime; / The rose grew pale and left her cheek; / She died before her time.' C. may also have remembered *Hamlet* IV v 176, 'There is pansies, that's for thoughts', and 185, 'I would give you some

Bestrewed the boy, like him to waste
And wither in their prime.

But will he ne'er return, whose tongue
Could tune the rural lay?
15   Ah, no! his bell of peace is rung,
His lips are cold as clay.

They bore him out at twilight hour,
The youth who loved so well:
Ah, me! how many a true-love shower
20   Of kind remembrance fell!

Each maid was woe – but Lucy chief,
Her grief o'er all was tried;
Within his grave she dropped in grief,
And o'er her loved-one died.

violets, but they withered all when my father died'; and *Pericles* IV iv 34–5:
'The fairest, sweetest, and best lies here, / Who withered in her spring of
year'.

10. Cp. *Lycidas* 3–8.

13. will he] According to A. L. Poole's Oxford edn, p. 316, the *Gentleman's
Mag.* in 1788, misprinted 'he will' but this is untrue.

13–16. Hamlet IV v 191–5: 'And will a' not come again? / And will a' not
come again? / No, no, he is dead, / Go to thy death-bed, / He never will
come again.'

14. 'Rural Lay', Pope, *Spring* 6; 'Rural Lays', Pope, *Autumn* 2 and 6;
Winter 90; and 'let me tune my Lays', *Summer* 37.

16. Mallet, *William and Margaret* 7: 'And clay-cold was her lily hand.'

17. Hamlet IV v 164: 'They bore him barefaced on the bier.'

18. who loved] beloved *Public Advertiser*. Poole's Oxford edn, p. 310, has a
confused textual note giving the impression that its own text reads 'belov'd',
which it does not.

19. Hamlet IV v 39: 'Which bewept to the grave did not go / With true-
love showers'; and 166: 'And in his grave rain'd many a tear.'

20. Hamlet IV v 175: 'There's rosemary, that's for remembrance.'

21–4. This final stanza seems too facile to have been written by C. but may
be an imitation of Mallet, *William and Margaret* 61–8: 'He hied him to the
fatal place, / Where Margaret's body lay; / And stretched him on the green-
grass turf, / That wrapped her breathless clay. // And thrice he called on
Margaret's name, / And thrice he wept full sore, / Then laid his cheek to her
cold grave, / And word spoke never more.'

6 Written on a Paper which Contained a Piece of Bride Cake given to the Author by a Lady

This poem, attributed to 'the late Mr Collins' and with no other explanation of its provenance, was published in the *Gentleman's Mag.* xxxv 231, in May 1765. Whoever possessed the MS was no doubt stimulated to publish it by the appearance of Langhorne's edn of C. in March 1765. It was reprinted in Pearch's *Collection of Poems* (1768) ii 46–7, and collected in Johnson's *Works of the English Poets* xlix 283–4. Its authenticity was not thereafter questioned, in spite of the fact that nothing whatever was known of its source or its occasion, until P. L. Carver, *Notes and Queries* clxxvii (1939) 274, declined to accept it as C.'s, on the grounds that there was insufficient evidence for doing so. But its traditional inclusion in C.'s works makes an outright rejection impossible and there is no internal evidence to suggest that C. could not have written it. The testimony of John Ragsdale (see headnote to *On a Quack Doctor*, p. 563) makes clear that a certain amount of C.'s poetry, 'written on particular occasions', had got into circulation and this poem may well be an example. In addition, C. was not famous in 1765 and there would be no motive for forgery at this early date. Carver, *The Life of a Poet* (1967) pp. 166–7, has recently retracted his original view and accepts the attribution to C., connecting the poem with the marriage of his friend Thomas Barrow (see p. 502) in 1753. There is no evidence for such a hypothesis.

The idea underlying the poem is the popular custom, according to which young people placed a piece of bride-cake (i.e. wedding-cake) under their pillows at night, in the belief that it would make them dream of their lover: cp. John Brand, *Observations on Popular Antiquities* (Newcastle, 1777) p. 335 n.

There is no evidence for dating the poem, unless its amorous character points to the same period as 'No longer ask me, gentle friends' (c. 1745–46). The echoes of Pope may also indicate an early date and for these reasons it has been placed in its present position.

> Ye curious hands, that, hid from vulgar eyes,
>   By search profane shall find this hallowed cake,
> With virtue's awe forbear the sacred prize,
>   Nor dare a theft for love and pity's sake!

¶ 6.1. Pope, *Dunciad* i 33: 'One Cell there is, conceal'd from vulgar eye'.

5   This precious relic, formed by magic power,
      Beneath her shepherd's haunted pillow laid,
    Was meant by love to charm the silent hour,
      The secret present of a matchless maid.

    The Cyprian queen, at Hymen's fond request,
10   Each nice ingredient chose with happiest art;
    Fears, sighs and wishes of the enamoured breast,
      And pains that please, are mixed in every part.

    With rosy hand the spicy fruit she brought,
      From Paphian hills and fair Cythera's isle;
15 And tempered sweet with these the melting thought,
      The kiss ambrosial and the yielding smile;

    Ambiguous looks, that scorn and yet relent,
      Denials mild and firm unaltered truth,
    Reluctant pride and amorous faint consent,
20   And meeting ardours and exulting youth.

    Sleep, wayward god! hath sworn, while these remain,
      With flattering dreams to dry his nightly tear,
    And cheerful Hope, so oft invoked in vain,
      With fairy songs shall soothe his pensive ear.

25 If, bound by vows to friendship's gentle side,
      And fond of soul, thou hop'st an equal grace,
    If youth or maid thy joys and griefs divide,
      O much intreated, leave this fatal place.

6. *shepherd*] i.e. the poet.

8. 'the matchless Maid', Pope, *Spring* 67.

9. *Cyprian queen*] Venus: cp. l. 14 *n* below.

10–12. These lines recall the manifestations of female temperament collected by the goddess Spleen in Pope, *Rape of the Lock* iv 84–6: 'Sighs, Sobs, and Passions, and the War of Tongues. / A Vial next she fills with fainting Fears, / Soft Sorrows, melting Griefs, and flowing Tears.' Cp. also 'pleasing pain', *Dunciad* ii 211.

13. 'with rosie hand', *Par. Lost* vi 3.

14. *Paphian*] Venus was supposed to have landed at Paphos in Cyprus, when she emerged from the sea. According to another version of the legend she landed on the same occasion on the island of Cythera. Both places are accordingly frequently associated with her.

17–20. *Par. Lost* iv 310–11: 'with coy submission, modest pride, / And sweet reluctant amorous delay'.

24. 'a fairy song', *Midsummer Night's Dream* II ii 1; and *Eloisa to Abelard* 365: 'The well-sung woes will sooth my pensive ghost.'

27. Cp. Pope, *Epitaph on Harcourt* 3: 'Who ne'er knew Joy, but Friendship might divide'.

Sweet Peace, who long hath shunned my plaintive day,
30   Consents at length to bring me short delight:
Thy careless steps may scare her doves away,
And grief with raven note usurp the night.

32. *II Henry VI* III ii 40–1: 'A raven's note, / Whose dismal tune bereft my vital powers'; and *Hamlet* I i 46: 'What art thou that usurp'st this time of night'.

Odes on Several Descriptive
and Allegoric Subjects

The only one of his various literary projects after his arrival in London in 1744 to reach fulfilment, C.'s *Odes* were published in Dec. 1746. Even this project did not end as originally planned. C. had at first intended to publish his odes in one volume with those of his Winchester and Oxford friend Joseph Warton, who described the scheme in a letter to his brother Thomas, which is quoted by John Wooll, *Memoirs of Joseph Warton* (1806) pp. 14–15n:

'Dear Tom,

You will wonder to see my name in an advertisement next week, so I thought I would apprize you of it. The case was this. Collins met me in Surrey, at Guildford Races, when I wrote out for him my Odes, and he likewise communicated some of his to me: and being both in very high spirits we took courage, resolved to join our forces, and to publish them immediately. I flatter myself that I shall lose no honour by this publication, because I believe these Odes, as they now stand, are infinitely the best things I ever wrote. You will see a very pretty one of Collins's, on the death of Colonel Ross before Tournay. It is addressed to a lady who was Ross's intimate acquaintance, and who by the way is Miss Bett Goddard. Collins is not to publish the Odes unless he gets ten guineas for them.

I returned from Milford last night, where I left Collins with my mother and sister, and he sets out to-day for London. I must now tell you that I have sent him your imitation of Horace's Blandusian [*sic*] Fountain, to be printed amongst ours, and which you shall own or not as you think proper. I would not have done this without your consent, but because I think it very poetically and correctly done, and will get you honour.

— — — — —

You will let me know what the Oxford critics say.'

Wooll noted that the letter was 'Without a date of time or place'.

The letter can be dated late May or early June 1746 with some confidence. Guildford Races occurred each Whitsun (*History and Description of Guildford* (1777) p. 4); and the *General Evening Post* (20–22 May 1746) mentions that the meeting's most notable race, for the King's Plate, had been run there on the previous Tuesday, 20 May. That the letter was written in 1746 and not in 1745 seems clear from the impatience of the two young poets, who could surely not have waited for 18 months before publication. As it was, they seem to have expected publication in the near future, but it seems likely that they were dissuaded from summer publication by the booksellers. The advertisement mentioned by Warton has not been identified, a fact which may indicate that the project of joint publication had soon fallen through, although whether this was a result of disagreement between the poets or of the insistence or the taste of the bookseller is not known. All that is clear is that Dodsley agreed to print Warton's *Odes* and not C.'s. One explanation may be C.'s insistence that he be paid for his *Odes*, mentioned by Warton. The tone of a letter from Dodsley to Thomas Warton on 29 Jan. [1747] (British Museum, Add. MS 42560 f. 13), a few weeks after publishing Joseph's *Odes* and shortly before publishing Thomas's *Pleasures of Melancholy*, suggests that he was not usually prepared to pay in advance for poetry: 'As to the Terms, I believe I shall rather chuse to print as I did your Brothers, for so very few Poems sell, that it is very hazardous purchasing almost any thing.'

C. may have tried to insist on a fixed sum for his *Odes* or Dodsley may have perceived that C.'s bolder and obscurer poetry would not sell so well as Warton's, with which it in any case overlapped to some extent in subject matter (Warton had also written odes *To Evening* and *To Liberty*, as well as *To Fancy*, constantly referred to by C.). Whatever the reason, Warton's *Odes on Various Subjects* were published on 4 Dec. 1746 in quarto, and C.'s *Odes on Several Descriptive and Allegoric Subjects* by A. Millar in octavo on 20 Dec. 1746, according to an advertisement in the *General Advertiser* on that day. An entry in the ledger of the printer Henry Woodfall reads: 'Mr. Andrew Millar, Dr. / Dec. 15, 1746. Mr. Collins's Odes, 8vo., No. 1000, 3½ shts.' (*Notes and Queries*, 1st series (1855) xi 419). Although published in Dec. 1746, the *Odes* are dated 1747 on the title-page, a common practice for books published shortly before the end of the year at this period as later.

After C.'s death, the terms on which Millar published the *Odes* were the subject of some argument. John Langhorne, in his important edn of C.'s *Poems* (1765) p. xi, described Millar as 'a favourer of genius, *when once it has made its way to fame*' and stated that he had agreed to publish C.'s volume only 'on the author's account'. Langhorne then told for the first time the story of C.'s burning the unsold copies of the *Odes* in anger and disappointment at their failure to sell. Langhorne's account of C.'s transactions with Millar, who did not die until 1768, was rejected by Ralph Griffiths, the publisher and editor of the *Monthly Review*, when he himself reviewed Langhorne's edn of C. there, xxxii (1765) 294. According to Griffiths, Millar 'actually *purchased* the copy, at a *very handsome price* (for those times) and, at his own expence and risk, did all in his power to introduce Mr. Collins to the notice of the Public. . . . The *sequel* of this little anecdote, is greatly to the honour of our Poet's memory. –At the time when he sold his

Odes to Mr. Millar, his circumstances were too narrow to have allowed him
to print them at his own expence; and the copy-money was then, to him,
a considerable object. Afterwards, when he came to the possession of an
easy fortune, by the death of his uncle, Colonel Martin, –he recollected that
the publisher of his poems was a *loser* by them. His spirit was too great to
submit to this circumstance, when he found himself enabled to do justice
to his own delicacy; and therefore he desired his bookseller to balance the
account of that unfortunate publication, declaring he himself would make
good the deficiency; the bookseller readily acquiesced in the proposal, and
gave up to Mr. Collins the remainder of the impression, which the generous,
resentful Bard immediately consigned to the flames.' Langhorne, who was in
fact one of Griffith's leading reviewers, dropped the remarks about Millar
in later edns. It may be added that the great rarity of the book lends
some weight to the story that C. destroyed all the unsold copies. (The one
known presentation copy, inscribed 'From the Author' but without any
indication of the identity of the recipient, was sold at Sotheby's on 8 Nov.
1965 for £500.)

Although the *Odes* of C. and Warton were eventually published sep-
arately, the short 'Advertisement' which Warton prefixed to his volume
is worth quoting because it expresses views with which C. almost certainly
sympathised (cp. the epigraph to the *Persian Eclogues* p. 366 above):

'The Public has been so much accustom'd of late to didactic Poetry alone,
and Essays on moral Subjects, that any work where the imagination is
much indulged, will perhaps not be relished or regarded. The author there-
fore of these pieces is in some pain least certain austere critics should think
them too fanciful and descriptive. But as he is convinced that the fashion of
moralizing in verse has been carried too far, and as he looks upon Inven-
tion and Imagination to be the chief faculties of a Poet, so he will be happy
if the following Odes may be look'd upon as an attempt to bring back
Poetry into its right channel.'

The almost simultaneous publication of the two volumes of verse invited
comparison and received it from a notable source, which is remarkable as
the only extended discussion of C.'s *Odes* in his lifetime. On 27 Dec. 1746,
Thomas Gray (*Correspondence*, ed. Toynbee and Whibley, i 261) wrote to a
friend: 'Have you seen the Works of two young Authors, a Mr Warton
& a Mr Collins, both Writers of Odes? it is odd enough, but each is the half
of a considerable Man, & one the Counter-Part of the other. the first has
but little Invention, very poetical choice of Expression, & a good Ear. the
second, a fine Fancy, model'd upon the Antique, a bad Ear, great Variety of
Words, & Images with no Choice at all. they both deserve to last some
Years, but will not.' Gray accurately predicted the resounding failure of C.'s
Odes in his own lifetime. He was less accurate about the more accessible
Warton, and C.'s distress at the failure of his own volume was no doubt
increased by the fact that on 9 Jan. 1747 Dodsley published a 2nd edn of his
friend's book.

In spite of the lack of success of the book as a whole, C. may have found some consolation in the fact that four of the poems were reprinted more than once in his lifetime. Three are in Dodsley's *Collection* (2nd edn 1748) i 327–32. The *Ode to Evening* also appeared in Thomas Warton's anthology *The Union* (1753; 2nd edn 1759); *The Passions* was set to music by William Hayes and reprinted three times in 1750; and the *Ode, Written in the Beginning of 1746* was absorbed into a musical entertainment in 1753. (See headnotes of the individual poems for details; for other musical settings of several of the *Odes* up to 1800, see A. S. P. Woodhouse, *Times Lit. Supp.* 1930, p. 838.) Before C.'s death there were at least two protests at the neglect of his *Odes*. Arthur Murphy in the *Gray's Inn Journal* No. 62 (23 Dec. 1753) complained that 'A treatise on Cribbidge, or a calculation of the Chances at Whist, is sure of being better receiv'd at present, than the Odes of a Collins or any other performance of distinguished Genius.' And John Gilbert Cooper protested in similar terms in his *Letters Concerning Taste* (1755) p. 50 *n* (see headnote to *Ode to Evening*). A rather different tribute came in *The Student* ii (1751) 313–15, which contained an *Ode to Horror: In the Allegoric, Descriptive, Alliterative, Epithetical, Fantastic, Hyperbolical, and Diabolical Style of our Modern Ode-Wrights and Monody-Mongers*, an obvious enough parody of C. and the Wartons, even if there is some evidence to suggest that it was written by Thomas Warton himself, who included it in his *Oxford Sausage* (1764) pp. 61–4. Joseph Warton quoted it (as by 'a descriptive poet of the first class') in his edn of Pope's *Works* (1797) ii 345–6, where he stated that 'Mr. William Collins thought himself aimed at by this piece of ridicule. His odes had been just published; and the last lines seemed to refer to a particular passage in them.'

More reverent imitation of C.'s *Odes* was to come after his death, the way being pointed by the title of Richard Shepherd's *Odes Descriptive and Allegorical* (1761). The first reprint of all C.'s *Odes*, together with the *Eclogues*, *Epistle to Hanmer* and some shorter poems, came in November 1763 in *The Poetical Calendar* xi 17–75, edited by Francis Fawkes and William Woty. A critical turning-point came with John Langhorne's notice of this collection in the *Monthly Review* xxx 20–6, in January 1764. Langhorne expressed unbounded enthusiasm for C.'s 'luxuriance of imagination, a wild sublimity of fancy, and a felicity of expression so extraordinary, that it might be supposed to be suggested by some superior power, rather than to be the effect of human judgment, or capacity.' The publication of Langhorne's edn, with his ecstatic commentary on the *Odes*, in 1765 marked the real beginning, however, of the reputation of C.'s shorter poems as opposed to the *Eclogues*. (Langhorne made a few silent emendations to the text of the *Odes*, which have no independent authority but which have been recorded here since they are usually thoughtful and emphasize difficulties met in C.'s poetry by his earliest readers.) One other curious tribute to C.'s *Odes*–and a very early one–deserves special attention. In Feb. 1747, three months after the publication of the *Odes*, two poems appeared in *The British Magazine: Or the London and Edinburgh Intelligencer* (which ran from Jan. 1747 to Dec. 1748; not to be confused with *The British Magazine*, ed. John Hill, 1746–51): 'An

Ode, To the Memory of Colonel Gardiner, In Imitation of Milton' and
'An Ode to Evening', both of which strikingly resemble passages in C.'s
Ode, Written in the Beginning of 1746, Ode to a Lady and *Ode to Evening*. P. L.
Carver, 'Collins and Alexander Carlyle', *Review of English Studies* xv
(1939) 34–44, has plausibly argued for the attribution of these poems to
Alexander Carlyle, a Scottish clergyman, who knew many of C.'s friends
and who could have met C. in London early in 1746. But there are no grounds
for accepting Carver's thesis that these blatant exercises in plagiarism repre-
sent joint efforts by Carlyle and C. from which C. later distilled the *Odes*
which they so remarkably resemble. Carver repeated his theory in *The Life
of a Poet* (1967) pp. 77–86.

Some scraps of information about the way in which C. wrote his *Odes*
have survived and may be thought worth preserving. A letter from Thomas
Warton in *The Reaper* No. 26, reprinted in *The Gleaner*, ed. Nathan Drake
(1811) iv 477, states: 'I have seen all his Odes already published in his own
hand-writing; they had the marks of repeated correction; he was perpetually
changing his epithets.' The recently discovered MSS confirm this account
of C.'s practice. Variants mentioned by Warton as examples are given in
the notes to *Ode to a Lady*. Drake also reprinted from *The Reaper* No. 26, in
The Gleaner iv 483, a letter concerning C. by John Ragsdale (also printed
in full in the *Monthly Magazine* xxi (1806) 494, and there dated July 1783),
who recollected: 'To raise a present subsistence, he set about writing his
Odes; and, having a general invitation to my home, he frequently passed
whole days there, which he employed in writing them, and as frequently
burning what he had written, after reading them to me. Many of them
which pleased me I struggled to preserve, but without effect; for, pretending
he would alter them, he got them from me and thrust them into the fire.'

Such evidence as there is for dating the individual poems (for which see
headnotes) is usually very tenuous, arising at best from allusions to public
events but often depending merely on possible echoes of the works of other
poets. (In the case of suggested echoes of Joseph Warton's *Odes*, it should be
admitted that influences could have worked in both directions, although it
would appear that Warton had completed his *Odes* before seeing any of
C.'s.) On the other hand, it does seem clear that all the *Odes* were written
between 1744 and 1746, i.e. after C.'s arrival in London in 1744, and most
of them were probably written in 1746. This conclusion finds some con-
firmation in C.'s impatient, experimental character as a poet: he is always
likely to have been best pleased with his most recent work. The *Ode to a
Lady* can be definitely dated May 1745; and C.'s own original dating of the
Ode, Written in the Beginning of 1746 can perhaps be accepted at face value.
The *Ode on the Poetical Character, The Manners* and *The Passions* belong to
1745 or 1746, the first and third most probably coming late in this period.
The *Odes* to *Pity, Fear* and *Simplicity* may belong to the spring or summer of
1746. The *Ode to Mercy* seems clearly to have been written in July or August
1746; *Liberty* alludes to events in the autumn of 1746 and the *Ode to Evening*
was probably written no earlier than May 1746. Because the dating of the

ODES

ON SEVERAL

Descriptive and *Allegoric*

SUBJECTS.

By WILLIAM COLLINS.

————Ειην
Ευρησιεπης αναγεισθαι
Προσφορος εν Μοισαν Διφρω ·
Τολμα δε και αμφιλαφης Δυναμις
Εσποιτο.———   Πινδαρ. Ολυμπ. Θ.

LONDON:
Printed for A. MILLAR, in the *Strand.*
M.DCC.XLVII.
(Price One Shilling.)

Plate 3 The titlepage of Collins's *Odes*, dated 1747,
although the volume was published in December, 1746

individual poems remains at best tentative in many cases, it has not seemed reasonable to change the order in which C. himself published them, presumably with some specific scheme in mind.

The possibility of such a scheme has inevitably been involved in studies of the themes and aims of the *Odes* taken as a whole. S. Musgrove, 'The Theme of Collins's *Odes*', *Notes and Queries* clxxxv (1943) 214–7, 253–5, has argued that 'what the book, taken as a whole, is about, is the nature of the True Poet, as Collins conceived it, and that each Ode is descriptive of one of the qualities or circumstances essential to the attainment of the poet's true stature'. A similar, if more sophisticated, approach is provided by Ricardo Quintana, 'The Scheme of Collins's *Odes on Several* . . . *Subjects*', in *Restoration and Eighteenth-Century Literature*, ed. Carroll Camden (Chicago, 1963) pp. 371–80. Quintana distinguishes two main groups within the *Odes*: those dealing with the different 'kinds' of poetry and aspects of creative art and those dealing with themes of patriotic citizenship. Quintana perhaps presses his argument too far, but his approach is useful. The outstanding discussion of the *Odes*, as well as of C.'s literary context and relationships as a whole, is A. S. P. Woodhouse, 'The Poetry of Collins Reconsidered', in *From Sensibility to Romanticism: Essays Presented to F. A. Pottle*, ed. F. W. Hilles and H. Bloom (New York, 1965) pp. 93–137, which supersedes Woodhouse's earlier essay, 'Collins and the Creative Imagination', in *Studies in English by Members of University College, Toronto* (Toronto, 1931) pp. 59–130, though this still remains useful.

So far as the order of the *Odes* is concerned, it has usually been noted that the first four and last two are concerned with the nature of poetry (or music in *The Passions*) and the poet, and that the middle group deals with political and patriotic themes, with the exception of *Evening*, the ninth. It seems likely that C. did plan his *Odes* in these two main groups and that he decided to begin and end the volume with a pair of poems on related subjects. But another organizing principle has usually been overlooked: using a variety of forms, C. arranges his *Odes* so that no two poems with the same metrical form are juxtaposed. This may explain the otherwise puzzling insertion of *Evening* into the 'patriotic' group. The nearest C. comes to a repetition of forms is in the sixth and seventh poems, *Mercy* and *Liberty*, which however exploit the 'Pindaric' structure in contrasting ways. For comments on the Pindaric Ode in England and its basic principles of construction, see the headnote to Gray's *Progress of Poesy* (p. 158 above). C.'s contribution to the form was to vary the usual formula of identically patterned strophe and antistrophe, followed by a relatively restrained and regular epode, by moving the epode to a position between the strophe and antistrophe. As a result, the characteristic movement of C.'s Pindaric Odes is from tension to tension via an interlude of comparative repose. (In this central position, the epode is more accurately described as the mesode.) In spite of these general principles, C. in practice is more variable. In *Mercy*, for example, there is no epode, and in *Liberty* there are two; and the metrical correspondence of strophe and antistrophe is not always maintained. For further discussion of C.'s formal practice, see G. N. Shuster, *The English Ode from Milton to Keats* (New York, 1940); Norman Maclean, 'From Action to Image: Theories of the Lyric in the Eighteenth Century', *Critics and Criticism*, ed. R. S. Crane (1952) pp. 408–60; and A. S. P. Woodhouse's recent essay, mentioned above, especially pp. 118–20. Other structural principles, mainly of a visual character, are described by J. H. Hagstrum, *The Sister Arts* (Chicago, 1958) pp. 268–86.

The epigraph chosen by C. for his title-page is from Pindar, *Olympian Odes* ix 80–3:

—————"Εἴην
῾Ευρησιεπὴς ἀναγεῖσθαι
Πρόσφορος ἐν Μοισᾶν Δίφρῳ·
Τόλμα δὲ καὶ ἀμφιλαφὴς Δύναμις
"Εσποιτο.—————

(Would I could find me words, as I move onward as a bearer of good gifts in the Muses'car; would I might be attended by Daring and by all-embracing Power). The emblem, engraved by Van der Gucht, on the title-page had been used for several earlier edns of Thomson's *The Seasons*: see *The Book Collector* i (1952) 195, ii (1953) 157. A facsimile of the original edn was published in 1926 in the series of Noel Douglas Replicas.

7 Ode to Pity

The dating of this ode and the following *Ode to Fear* may connect with C.'s projected translation and commentary on Aristotle's *Poetics*. The two odes are devoted to the two emotions which, according to Aristotle, are aroused and purged by the process of *catharsis* in tragedy. That C. linked them in such a way seems clear from *Fear* 42–5. Johnson, in his biography of C. (*Lives of the Poets*, ed. G. B. Hill (1905) iii 336) describes how he helped the poet to escape immurement by a bailiff by obtaining money from a bookseller on the strength of C.'s engaging to undertake a translation of the *Poetics*, 'with a large commentary'. This incident may be that referred to in a letter written by a friend of C., John Mulso, dated 28 May 1746, which similarly links Aristotle and a bailiff, *Letters to Gilbert White of Selborne from . . . the Rev. John Mulso*, ed. R. Holt-White, [1907], p. 14. Mulso states that C. had recently been visited by the bailiff and, after describing the incident, adds that 'The ἀναγνώρισις (a word He is fond of) was quite striking & ye catastrophe quite poetical & interesting'. C.'s allusion was to Aristotle's description of 'recognition' scenes in tragedy. In spite of some vagueness in Johnson's account, it seems likely (i) that he and Mulso were describing the same episode in May 1746 (ii) that it was at this time that C. was engaged on his translation of Aristotle and (iii) that this is the most likely period for him to have written the odes to *Pity*, *Fear* and *Simplicity*, all of which deal with

Greek tragedy to some extent. It must be acknowledged here, however, that C.'s biographers have usually dated his undertaking the translation of Aristotle somewhat earlier, in 1745. John Ragsdale, *The Gleaner* (1811) iv 482–3, records that C. made some progress with his translation of the *Poetics*, but the work never reached publication. The evidence for dating the three odes is obviously slender but *c.* May 1746 seems as plausible as any. Mulso's letter quoted above, it will be noted, was written only a few days after C.'s meeting with Joseph Warton at the Guildford Races, when the two friends agreed to publish their *Odes* jointly.

Thomas Warton's letter quoted by Nathan Drake in *The Gleaner* iv 478, states that: 'In the Ode to Pity [ll. 24–30], the idea of a Temple of Pity, of its situation, construction, and groupes of painting with which its walls were decorated, was borrowed from a poem, now lost, entitled the Temple of Pity, written by my brother, while he and Collins were school-fellows at Winchester College.' This statement is confirmed by notes in Thomas Warton's papers described by J. S. Cunningham, 'Thomas Warton and William Collins: a Footnote', *Durham University Journal* xlvi (1953) 22–4. But Joseph Warton's lost poem, as described by Thomas, bears a suspicious resemblance to a fragment of a poem quoted by John Wooll, in his *Memoirs of Joseph Warton* (1806) pp. 91–5, describing the 'Temple of Love', which may well have been the work Thomas had in mind and which, in a general way, probably did influence C.

O thou, the friend of man assigned,
With balmy hands his wounds to bind,
And charm his frantic woe:
When first Distress with dagger keen
5   Broke forth to waste his destined scene,
His wild unsated foe!

2.
By Pella's bard, a magic name,
By all the griefs his thought could frame,
Receive my humble rite:
10 Long, Pity, let the nations view

¶ 7.7. *Pella's bard*] *Euripides*, of whom *Aristotle* pronounces, on a Comparison of him with *Sophocles*, That he was the greater Master of the tender Passions, ἦν τραγικώτερος. C.
Euripides died at Pella, the capital of the Macedonian kings, in 406 B.C., at the court of Archelaus. Aristotle states, in the *Poetics* xiii 10, that Euripides 'is certainly the most tragic of the poets'. It has been objected against C.'s note that Aristotle made this statement without specific reference to Sophocles; but, as he discusses Sophocles shortly before and after making it, the 'Comparison' is certainly implicit.

>   Thy sky-worn robes of tenderest blue,
>   And eyes of dewy light!
>
>   3.
>   But wherefore need I wander wide
>   To old Ilissus' distant side,
> 15   Deserted stream and mute?
>   Wild Arun too has heard thy strains,
>   And Echo, midst my native plains,
>   Been soothed by Pity's lute.
>
>   4.
>   There first the wren thy myrtles shed
> 20   On gentlest Otway's infant head,
>   To him thy cell was shown;

11. Phineas Fletcher, *Purple Island* IX xxii 1: 'His sky-like arms, dy'd all in blue and white' and IX xxx 1: 'clad in sky-like blue'; and Milton, *Comus* 83: 'These my skie robes'.

14. Ilissus] The river flowing to the south of Athens, where Euripides spent most of his life and where his tragedies, like those of Aeschylus and Sophocles, were performed.

16–18. The River *Arun* runs by the Village in *Sussex*, where Otway had his Birth. *C.*

Thomas Otway (1652–85), playwright and poet, was, like C., a native of Sussex (born at Trotton, he spent his childhood three miles away at Woolbedding, where his father became Vicar), a Wykehamist and an Oxonian. There is a marble memorial to Otway in the Sixth Chamber at Winchester, erected by 'W.C.' and 'J.W.', presumably C. and Joseph Warton. C. refers twice to him in fragments: 'Lines on Restoration Drama' 15–16 *n* and 'No longer ask me, gentle friends', 27–30 *n* (see pp. 525, 550 below). C.'s early editors enjoyed pointing out that the parallels between the two poets extended to the fact that they both died in unfortunate circumstances at an early age, although there is now some disagreement as to Otway's supposed destitution and starvation. Cp. Langhorne, *1765* p. 149: 'Both these poets, unhappily, became the objects of that pity by which their writings are distinguished.' Otway owed his reputation in the eighteenth century to his tragedies *Venice Preserved* and *The Orphan*, both notable for the treatment of love and the 'pathetic'. *Biographia Dramatica*, ed. Isaac Reed (1782) i 344, thought 'perhaps none ever excelled him in touching the passions, particularly that of love. . . . The heart that does not melt at the distresses of his *Orphan*, must be hard indeed!'

19. It is not clear why C. associates the wren with Pity, although he may have felt there was precedent for it in Shakespeare, *Cymbeline* IV ii 303–5: 'If there be / Yet left in heaven as small a drop of pity / As a wren's eye'; and Webster, *White Devil* V iv 89 ff. (Cp. C.'s 'Song from Cymbeline' 13–16 *n*.) *myrtles*] Traditionally sacred to the goddess of love and used for wreaths

And while he sung the female heart,
With youth's soft notes unspoiled by art,
   Thy turtles mixed their own.

5.

25 Come, Pity, come, by Fancy's aid,
Even now my thoughts, relenting maid,
   Thy temple's pride design:
Its southern site, its truth complete,
Shall raise a wild enthusiast heat
30   In all who view the shrine.

6.

There Picture's toils shall well relate
How chance or hard involving fate
   O'er mortal bliss prevail:
The buskined Muse shall near her stand,
35 And sighing prompt her tender hand
   With each disastrous tale.

7.

There let me oft, retired by day,
In dreams of passion melt away,
   Allowed with thee to dwell:

for bloodless victors. Cp. Horace, *Odes* III iv 11–13, 18–20: *ludo fatigatumque somno | fronde nova puerum palumbes | texere* ... *||* ... *ut premerer sacra | lauroque conlataque myrto, | non sine dis animosus infans* (When I was tired with play and overcome with sleep, the doves of story covered me over with freshly fallen leaves. ... I was overspread with sacred bay and gathered myrtle, with the gods' help a fearless child). Pope alludes to the lines in *Temple of Fame* 230–1: 'The Doves that round the Infant Poet spread / Myrtles and Bays, hung hov'ring o'er his Head.'

24. 'The turtle dove, the bird of Venus by reason of its talent in courtship, may also be claimed by Pity for its gentleness. Collins is creating a new Pantheon in these odes, and his deified abstractions perforce filch from the old gods' (Bronson, p. 97).

25–36. These are the lines said by Thomas Warton to have been inspired by a poem by his brother Joseph (see headnote). If this can be identified as the fragment quoted in Wooll's *Memoirs of Warton* pp. 91–5, it may be admitted that the 'disastrous' tales depicted in C.'s temple do recall those of Ariadne, Phaedra, Eloise, Tancred and Desdemona portrayed in Warton's 'Temple of Love'.

31. *toils*] toil Langhorne, 1765.

34. *buskined Muse*] The Muse of Tragedy, probably an imitation of Milton, *Il Penseroso* 102: 'the Buskind stage'.

37. *Il Penseroso* 141: 'Hide me from Day's garish eie'.

40   There waste the mournful lamp of night,
       Till, virgin, thou again delight
        To hear a British shell!

37–8. Pope, *Eloisa to Abelard* 221–2: 'To sounds of heav'nly harps, she dies away, / And melts in visions of eternal day.'
39. Cp. the conclusion to *Il Penseroso* 175–6: 'These pleasures *Melancholy* give, / And I with thee will choose to live.' And cp. *L'Allegro* 151–2, for a similar conclusion.
40. Cp. *Il Penseroso* 85, for Milton's 'Lamp at midnight hour'; and *Eloisa to Abelard* 267: 'I waste the Matin lamp in sighs for thee'.
42. shell] A poeticism for a lyre, in accordance with the tradition that the first lyre was a tortoise-shell stringed. Cp. Dryden, *Song for St Cecilia's Day* 17: 'When *Jubal* struck the corded Shell'.

8 Ode to Fear

For an argument that this poem should be dated in the spring or summer of 1746, see headnote to *Pity*. Possible echoes in ll. 10–12 and l. 24 of *Odes* by Joseph Warton, of which C. was given the MS at Guildford in May 1746 (see general headnote to *Odes*), would confirm this dating.

The *Ode to Fear* may have been C.'s first adaptation of the form of the Greek ode. Bronson, pp. lxix–lxx, notes that 'The epode should have been called a mesode, as it comes between strophe and antistrophe instead of after the latter. In the extant odes of Pindar there are no mesodes, but they sometimes occur in the choral odes of the Greek dramas.' C. obviously preferred to use the calmer epode as a temporary relief of tension rather than as a final resolution. While the structure of the poem is consciously Greek, the diction is equally consciously Spenserian. Apart from specific debts recorded in the notes, the following words used by C. recur frequently in Spenser: 'shadowy, appalled, frantic, disordered, fixed (of the eyes), hideous, accursed, brood, ghastly, awful, amazement, disdained, a-while, trembling, trace, baleful, mournful, devoutly, fury, meed'.

       Thou, to whom the world unknown
       With all its shadowy shapes is shown;
       Who see'st appalled the unreal scene,
       While Fancy lifts the veil between:
5   Ah Fear! Ah frantic Fear!
          I see, I see thee near.
       I know thy hurried step, thy haggard eye!
       Like thee I start, like thee disordered fly.
       For lo, what monsters in thy train appear!

10   Danger, whose limbs of giant mould
       What mortal eye can fixed behold?
       Who stalks his round, an hideous form,
       Howling amidst the midnight storm,
       Or throws him on the ridgy steep
15   Of some loose hanging rock to sleep;
       And with him thousand phantoms joined,
       Who prompt to deeds accursed the mind;
       And those, the fiends who, near allied,
       O'er nature's wounds and wrecks preside;
20   Whilst Vengeance in the lurid air
       Lifts her red arm, exposed and bare,

¶ *10–12*. Spenser describes 'Daunger' and 'Feare' in the Masque of Cupid, *Faerie Queene* III xii 11–12; and 'Daunger' again in the Temple of Venus, IV x 16–20, where Daunger is 'An hideous Giant', in whose 'hindparts' 'hatred, murther, treason, and despight, / . . . lay in ambushment'. C. seems also to have remembered another of Spenser's giants, I vii 8, 3–4: 'With sturdie steps came stalking in his sight, / An hideous Geant horrible and hye'. Cp. also Pope, *Rape of the Lock* iii 72: 'His Giant Limbs in State unwieldy spread'; J. Philips, *Cyder* i 218: 'Horror stalks around'; and J. Warton, *Ode to Fancy* 65: 'Where giant Terror stalks around'.

13–14. Pope, *Imitations of Horace, Ep.* II i 328–9: 'Loud as the Wolves on Orcas' stormy steep, / Howl to the roarings of the Northern deep.'

16–19. A. S. P. Woodhouse, 'Collins and the Creative Imagination', in *Studies in English by Members of University College, Toronto* (1931) p. 105 *n* 31, suggested as a source for these lines the spirits who 'dwell in the elements and preside over storm and earthquake as well as over human violence', in Thomas Nashe's *Pierce Penniless his Supplication to the Devil*, in *Works*, ed. R. B. McKerrow (1904–8) i 230–1. Nashe describes both the evil spirits who incite men to violence and iniquity, coupling with them the Spirit of Revenge (cp.l.20); and the class of fiends who operate in nature itself through storm and earthquake. It may appear unlikely that C. would know this pamphlet, but, in view of his interest in Elizabethan literature, the possibility cannot be ruled out.

20. Pope, *Windsor Forest* 417: 'There purple *Vengeance* bath'd in Gore retires.'

21. Horace, *Odes* I ii 2–3: *Pater . . . rubente / dextera sacras iaculatus arces* (the Father smiting with his red right hand the sacred hill-tops). There are several examples of the phrase in English: Milton's Satan fears that 'intermitted vengeance' might 'Arme again / [God's] red right hand to plague us', *Par. Lost* ii 173–4; Dryden, *Aeneid* vi 800–1: 'the King of Heav'n, obscure on high, / Bar'd his red Arm'; there are references to Jove's 'red arm' in Pope, *Odyssey* xii 456, xxiv 623; and William Broome, *Battle of the Gods and Titans* 24: 'Bares his red arm and wields the forky brand'.

On whom that ravening brood of fate,
Who lap the blood of sorrow, wait;
Who, Fear, this ghastly train can see,
25   And look not madly wild like thee?

EPODE

In earliest Greece to thee with partial choice
    The grief-full Muse addressed her infant tongue;
The maids and matrons on her awful voice,
    Silent and pale, in wild amazement hung.

30   Yet he, the bard who first invoked thy name,
    Disdained in Marathon its power to feel:
For not alone he nursed the poet's flame,
    But reached from Virtue's hand the patriot's steel.

But who is he whom later garlands grace,
35   Who left awhile o'er Hybla's dews to rove,
With trembling eyes thy dreary steps to trace,
    Where thou and Furies shared the baleful grove?

22. Alluding to the κύνας ἀφύκτους of *Sophocles*. See the ELECTRA. *C.*
    C. refers to the chorus in *Electra* 1385–8: 'Breathing out blood and venge-ance, lo! stalks Ares, sure though slow. E'en now the hounds are on the trail; within, the sinners at their coming quail.' C. probably changed the case and order of the phrase he quotes to adapt it to the grammar of his English sentence. Cp. also *Richard III* IV iv 48, 50: 'A hell-hound that doth hunt us all to death / . . . / To worry lambs and lap their gentle blood.'
24. J. Warton, *Ode on Superstition* 24: 'ghastly train of terrors'.
27. *grief-full*] C. probably adopted the epithet from Spenser, *Faerie Queene* IV i 16, 4; and VI viii 40, 5.
29. Cp. Milton, *Comus* 356: 'in wild amazement, and affright'; and Dryden, *Palamon and Arcite* iii 302: 'wild Amazement'.
30. *the bard*] *Æschylus. C.*
    The dramatist (525–456 B.C.) fought against the Persians at Marathon in 490 B.C. and probably at Salamis in 479 B.C. as well.
34. *he*] Sophocles (496–406 B.C.) was 29 years younger than Aeschylus.
35. *Hybla*] A city in Sicily famous for its honey (see *Simplicity* 14, p. 425 below). Sophocles was often described as 'the Attic bee', because of the sweetness of his verse. C. is merely referring to a supposed change of tone in *Oedipus Coloneus*; but see l. 37 *n*.
37. *baleful grove*] The setting of Sophocles's *Oedipus Coloneus* is a grove dedicated to the Eumenides or Furies. C. appears to be suggesting that this play is grimmer than was normal in Sophocles, whereas it is on the whole markedly less stern than *Oedipus Tyrannus* which C. may in fact be absorbing into his allusion.

Wrapped in thy cloudy veil the incestuous queen
Sighed the sad call her son and husband heard,
40   When once alone it broke the silent scene,
And he, the wretch of Thebes, no more appeared.

O Fear, I know thee by my throbbing heart,
Thy withering power inspired each mournful line,
Though gentle Pity claim her mingled part,
45   Yet all the thunders of the scene are thine!

ANTISTROPHE

Thou who such weary lengths hast passed,
Where wilt thou rest, mad nymph, at last?
Say, wilt thou shroud in haunted cell,
Where gloomy Rape and Murder dwell?

38. incestuous queen] Jocasta. C.
In *Oedipus Tyrannus* she was shown to have unwittingly married her
own son, Oedipus, who had become King of Thebes. Cp. 'cloudy vele',
Faerie Queene III iii 19, 6.
39–41. the sad call] C. *himself quotes Oedipus Coloneus* 1622–5: οὐδ' ἔτ'
ὀρώρει βοή, / Ἦν μὲν σιωπή, φθέγμα δ'ἐξαίφνης τινὸς / Θώϋξεν
αὐτόν, ὥστε πάντας ὀρθίας / Στῆσαι φόβῳ δείσαντας ἐξαίφνης
τρίχας / (But when they had made an end of wailing, and the sound went
up no more, there was a stillness; and suddenly a voice of one who cried
aloud to him, so that the hair of all stood up on their heads for sudden fear,
and they were afraid). C. seems to think that Jocasta 'sighed the sad call',
whereas she is not mentioned by Sophocles at this point: the voice is that
of the god, who called Oedipus, not 'once alone' but 'with many callings
and manifold'.
42. throbbing heart] The phrase is Spenserian: cp. 'With hart then throbbing',
Faerie Queene II iv 17, 1 and IV x 53, 1.
42–5. See headnote to *Pity* for the two emotions purged by tragedy in
Aristotle's theory of catharsis, here explicitly linked.
45. There may be a curious unconscious echo in this line of Pope, *Prologue for
Mr. Dennis* 16: 'And shook the Stage with Thunders all his own'. Pope was
referring to Dennis's invention of an improved method of making stage-
thunder, a meaning C. would hardly wish to include, if he was aware of it.
46–8. Strutt, in the Colchester edn of C., 1796, suggested that 'The
wanderings of Io, and her miseries' in Aeschylus, *Prometheus Bound* 561–8
provided the prototype '. . . of this fugitive nymph.' There are general
resemblances; but C. also remembered Spenser's *Faerie Queene* II vii 22,
6–7: 'And trembling Feare still to and fro did fly, / And found no place,
where safe he shroud him might.'   *shroud*] Shelter or hide, used also by
Milton, *Comus* 316: 'shroud within these limits'.

50   Or in some hollowed seat,
      'Gainst which the big waves beat,
      Hear drowning seamen's cries in tempests brought!
      Dark power, with shuddering meek submitted thought
      Be mine to read the visions old,
55   Which thy awakening bards have told:
      And, lest thou meet my blasted view,
      Hold each strange tale devoutly true;
      Ne'er be I found, by thee o'erawed,
      In that thrice-hallowed eve abroad,
60   When ghosts, as cottage-maids believe,

50–1. Fairfax's *Tasso* (1600) III vi 5–6: 'Such noise their passions make, as when one hears / The hoarse sea waves roar, hollow rocks betwixt', and IV vi 5: 'The rocks, on which the salt-sea billows beat'; and J. Warton, *The Enthusiast* (1744) 185–6: 'Or wand'ring near the sea, attend the sounds / Of hollow winds, and ever-beating waves.'

53. 'meek submission', *Par. Lost* xii 597.

55. awakening] Exciting a response (in the reader).

56. blasted] Cp. *OED*, 'blast', *v*, 8d: 'To strike (the eyes or vision) with dimness or horror'; and cp. Gray, *Progress of Poesy* 101 (p. 174 above).

58–63. Without echoing particular phrases, C. may have had in mind such descriptions of ghosts and goblins as *Midsummer Night's Dream* III ii 381–4 and V i 374–81; *Hamlet* I i 152–5 and I v 11; and Milton, *L'Allegro* 100–16.

59. Although early editors did not find this obvious, it seems clear that by the 'thrice-hallowed eve' C. meant Hallowe'en, the last night of the year according to the old Celtic Calendar, when ghosts and witches were traditionally most likely to wander abroad. The Church 'hallowed' this date by transforming it into the Eve of All Saints. Langhorne, *1765* p. 154, however, recounted 'an old traditionary superstition' that on St Mark's Eve (April 24) the spirits of those who were to die during the following year appeared in the churches of their respective parishes; and Mrs Barbauld, 1797, p. xxi and Dyce, 1827, p. 173 tell of a similar superstition which apparently obtained with reference to Midsummer Eve or St John's Eve (June 23). Crowe, 1828, p. 23, complicates the matter further by asserting that C. was referring to Christmas Eve. For information about these various dates, see R. Chambers, *The Book of Days* (1881) i 549–50, 814–17; ii 519–20. Arthur Johnston, *Selected Poems of Thomas Gray and William Collins* (1967) p. 158 *n*, suggests that 31 October is 'thrice-hallowed' because 'it is the day of three saints, St Quintin, St Foillan and St Wolfgang.'

60–3. Milton, *Comus* 432–6: 'Som say no evil thing that walks by night / In fog, or fire, by lake, or moorish fen, / Blew meager Hag, or stubborn unlaid ghost, / That breaks his magick chains at *curfeu* time, / No goblin, or swart faëry of the mine . . .'; and *Il Penseroso* 93–4: 'those *Daemons* that are found / In fire, air, flood, or under ground'.

Their pebbled beds permitted leave,
And goblins haunt, from fire or fen
Or mine or flood, the walks of men!
O thou whose spirit most possessed
65 The sacred seat of Shakespeare's breast!
By all that from thy prophet broke,
In thy divine emotions spoke,
Hither again thy fury deal,
Teach me but once like him to feel:
70 His cypress wreath my meed decree,
And I, O Fear, will dwell with thee!

61. Cp. Ophelia's burial, *Hamlet* V i 252–4: 'She should in ground unsancti-
fied have lodged / Till the last trumpet; for charitable prayers, / Shards,
flints and pebbles should be thrown on her.'
70. *cypress wreath*] The crown appropriate to the tragic poet.
71. Cp. *Pity* 39 and *n* (p. 418).

9 Ode to Simplicity

Apart from the fact of its publication in Dec. 1746, there is little evidence for
dating this poem. The reference to Sophocles (l. 18) suggests a connection
with the *Odes* to *Pity* and *Fear*, which would make the spring or summer of
1746 the most likely date of composition. Internal evidence is of slight value:
the possible echo of Akenside (ll. 13–21) would merely indicate a date after
Jan. 1744 and the possibility of the echo of Thomas Warton (l. 9), which
would necessitate a date of 1745 or later, is too slight to be reliable. C.'s use of
the word 'unboastful' (l. 12) may be more significant. The first recorded
appearance of the word is in a passage in Thomson's *Summer*, added in the
edn published in July 1744. C. also used the word twice in the draft
poem, *To Simplicity*, ll. 29 and 31, which was presumably earlier than the
present poem and which anticipates it in a number of ways.

For the varying meanings and implications in different contexts of 'sim-
plicity', see R. D. Havens, 'Simplicity, a Changing Concept', *Journal of
the History of Ideas* xiv (1953) 3–32. The features repeatedly attributed to
'simplicity' in its literary manifestations were unity, clarity and universality
and it was often associated with classical literature and with 'Nature'. For
an analysis of the concept as it appears in C.'s poem, see John R. Crider,
'Structure and Effect in Collins' Progress Poems', *Studies in Philology* lx
(1963) 62–9.

I

O thou by Nature taught
To breathe her genuine thought,
In numbers warmly pure and sweetly strong:

Who first on mountains wild
5   In Fancy, loveliest child,
Thy babe or Pleasure's, nursed the powers of song!

2

Thou, who with hermit heart
Disdain'st the wealth of art,
And gauds and pageant weeds and trailing pall:
10   But com'st a decent maid
In Attic robe arrayed,
O chaste unboastful nymph, to thee I call!

3
By all the honeyed store

¶ 9.6. or] and 1765. C.'s uncertainty as to whether Fancy was the child of Simplicity or Pleasure is curious but does not justify Langhorne's emendation. J. R. Crider (see headnote) cites *The Guardian* No. 22 (6 April 1713), on the first ages of the world: 'It was a State of Ease, Innocence and Contentment; where Plenty begot Pleasure, and Pleasure begot Singing, and Singing begot Poetry, and Poetry begot Pleasure again.'
9. *gauds*] Showy ornaments. The word occurs in Shakespeare (e.g. *Midsummer Night's Dream* I i 33) and Dryden, *Annus Mirabilis* 822. C. seems to remember *Il Penseroso* 97–8: 'let Gorgeous Tragedy / In Scepter'd Pall com sweeping by'. T. Warton, *Pleasures of Melancholy* (published 1747, but written in 1745 and no doubt accessible to C.) 214, 226–7 may be echoed: 'Queen of the stately step and flowing pall / . . . / What are the splendours of the gaudy court, / Its tinsel trappings and its pageant pomps . . .' Crider cites Steele, *The Tatler* No. 68 (15 Sept. 1709):'We see in tragical representations, it is not the pomp of language, nor the magnificence of dress in which passion is wrought, that touches sensible spirits; but something of a plain and simple nature, which breaks in upon our souls.'
10. *decent*] Beautiful but modest and seemly (rather than the modern sense of tolerable or respectable), e.g. *Il Penseroso* 35–6: 'And sable stole of *Cipres* Lawn, / Over thy decent shoulders drawn.'
11. *In . . . robe arrayed*] A Spenserian phrase e.g. *Faerie Queene* I x 30, 9: 'in yellow robes arayed still'.
12. *unboastful*] OED gives the first usage as Thomson, *Summer* 683–4: 'Oft in humble station dwells / Unboastful worth, above fastidious pomp', dating these lines 1727. But the passage in which they occur was not added until the edn of *The Seasons* published in July 1744.
13–21. Thomson, *Liberty* ii 138–42, describes the 'thymy treasures' of Hymettus and mentions Ilissus and Cephisus. Thomson's model was *Par. Regained* iv 245–50, where the nightingale is the 'Attic bird'. But C. echoes most consistently Akenside, *Pleasures of Imagination* (1744) i 591–6:

On Hybla's thymy shore,
15 By all her blooms and mingled murmurs dear;
By her, whose love-lorn woe
In evening musings slow
Soothed sweetly sad Electra's poet's ear:

4

By old Cephisus deep,
20 Who spread his wavy sweep
In warbled wanderings round thy green retreat,
On whose enamelled side
When holy Freedom died
No equal haunt allured thy future feet.

'the green retreats / Of Academus and the thymy vale, / Where oft en-
chanted with Socratic sounds, / Illissus pure devolved his tuneful stream /
In gentler murmurs. From the blooming store / Of these auspicious fields
. . . .' See also l. 16 n.

14. *Hybla*] See *Fear* 35 and *n* (p. 420).

16. *Her*] The ἀηδών, or Nightingale, for which *Sophocles* seems to have
entertain'd a peculiar Fondness. *C.*

With ll. 13–21 of this poem cp. a passage which C. no doubt had in mind,
from *Oedipus Coloneus* 668–93, in which the nightingale, 'a constant guest,
trills her clear note in the covert of green glades . . . . Nor fail the sleepless
founts whence the waters of Cephisus wander, but each day with stainless
tide he moves over the plains of the land's swelling bosom'.

love-lorn] love-born *1746, corrected in the errata.* Cp. *Comus* 234: 'the
lovelorn nightingale'; and the 'Song from *Midsummer Night's Dream*',
attributed to C. but more probably by Thomas Warton, 13 (see 'Lost
and Doubtful Poems', p. 564 below).

16–18. Pope, *Eloisa to Abelard* 365: 'The well-sung woes will sooth my pen-
sive ghost'.

18. *Electra's poet*] Both Sophocles and Euripides wrote tragedies on Electra.
Milton describes Euripides as 'sad *Electra*'s poet', *Sonnet viii* 13, but C. clearly
refers to Sophocles. He may have misunderstood Milton or merely have
reapplied the phrase rather confusingly. C. probably had in mind another
description of the nightingale by Sophocles, *Electra* 147–9: ἀλλ' ἐμὲ γ'
ἁ στονόεσσ' ἄραρεν φρένας, / ἃ Ἴτυν, αἰὲν Ἴτυν ὀλοφύρεται, / ὄρνις
ἀτυζομένα Διὸς ἄγγελος (O bird of Zeus, to thine I'll set my note, who
with full throat for Itys, Itys griev'st from eve till morn).

19. *Cephisus*] The chief river in the Athenian plain, flowing a mile to the
west of Athens.

21. Pope, *Summer* 72 and *Windsor Forest* 1: 'Green Retreats'; the phrase also
occurs in the passage from Akenside quoted in ll. 13–21 *n.*

22. *enamelled*] 'Beautified with various colours' (*OED*). Cp. 'the smooth
enameld green', Milton, *Arcades* 84.

5

25   O sister meek of Truth,
      To my admiring youth
Thy sober aid and native charms infuse!
      The flowers that sweetest breathe,
      Though Beauty culled the wreath,
30   Still ask thy hand to range their ordered hues.

6

      While Rome could none esteem
      But Virtue's patriot theme,
You loved her hills and led her laureate band:
      But stayed to sing alone
35   To one distinguished throne,
And turned thy face, and fled her altered land.

7

      No more, in hall or bower,
      The passions own thy power,
Love, only love, her forceless numbers mean:
      For thou hast left her shrine,
40   Nor olive more nor vine
Shall gain thy feet to bless the servile scene.

27. native] Unadorned, artless. Cp. *L'Allegro* 134: 'Warble his native Wood-notes wilde'.

31. While] As long as.

33. You] Only here does C., no doubt absent-mindedly, alter the number from 'Thou'.

35. Cp. Sir William Temple, 'Of Poetry' (1690), in *Critical Essays of the Seventeenth Century*, ed. J. E. Spingarn (1908–9) iii 107–8: '*Augustus* was not only a Patron, but a Friend and Companion of *Virgil* and *Horace*, and was himself both an Admirer of Poetry and a pretender too, as far as his Genius would reach or his busy Scene allow. 'Tis true, since his Age we have few such Examples of great Princes favouring or affecting Poetry, and as few perhaps of great Poets deserving it.'

37. hall or bower] Cp. Milton, *Comus* 44–5: 'What never yet was heard in Tale or Song / From old, or modern Bard in Hall, or Bowr.' The phrase is found in medieval literature; and Spenser several times has 'bowre or hall': e.g. *Faerie Queene* I iv 43,6; I viii 29, 9; IV vi 39, 7; VI ix 32, 4.

39. her] C. evidently continues to refer to Rome or Italy, though now to the character of its poetry in medieval and modern times.

8

Though taste, though genius bless
To some divine excess,
45   Faints the cold work till thou inspire the whole;
What each, what all supply
May court, may charm our eye,
Thou, only thou can'st raise the meeting soul!

9

Of these let others ask
50   To aid some mighty task:
I only seek to find thy temperate vale,
Where oft my reed might sound
To maids and shepherds round,
And all thy sons, O Nature, learn my tale.

43–5. T. Tickell, *To Sir Godfrey Kneller* 27–30: 'Vain care of parts; if, impo-
tent of soul, / Th'industrious workman fails to warm the whole, / Each theft
betrays the marble whence it came, / And a cool statue stiffens in the frame.'
C.'s use of 'eye' in l. 47 (Garrod p. 65, objected that it ought to be 'ear')
suggests that like Tickell he has sculpture in mind.
45. Faints] Faint's *1765*. (Langhorne's emendation (= Faint is) seems more
awkward than the original reading.)
48. L'Allegro 137–8: 'immortal verse / Such as the meeting soul may pierce'.

10 Ode on the Poetical Character

Apart from its imaginative boldness, which in itself suggests a date no earlier
than 1746, the only evidence for dating this poem before its publication in
Dec. 1746 is that of echoes of other poets, notably Akenside. The reminis-
cences of *The Pleasures of Imagination* (Jan. 1744) seem too consistent to be
coincidental and there are also three possible echoes of Akenside's *Odes*
(March 1745), which would serve to narrow the dating a little (ll. 21, 51–4,
60).

This is the most controversial of C.'s poems: the areas of disagreement
and the main protagonists are described in the notes to ll. 23–54 and 39.

As once, if not with light regard
I read aright that gifted bard,

¶ *10.1–2.* C. begins by adopting two phrases from Spenser, the poet he is
praising: *Faerie Queene* III viii 14, 6: 'But she thereto would lend but light

(Him whose school above the rest
His loveliest Elfin Queen has blessed)
5   One, only one, unrivalled fair
Might hope the magic girdle wear,
At solemn tourney hung on high,
The wish of each love-darting eye;

regard'; and I ix 6, 6: 'Full hard it is (quoth he) to read aright'. The second
phrase recurs at III iii 16, 7; III viii 23, 7; IV vi 35, 3; and V xi 49, 9. It was
probably an easily recognized archaism: cp. Prior, *An Imitation of Chaucer* 3:
'Now, and I read aright that Auncient Song'.
3. school] C. has in mind such imitators of Spenser as William Browne,
Edward Fairfax, Giles and Phineas Fletcher and Michael Drayton and may
also include Milton (see ll. 55–76).
4. Faerie Queene II i 1, 6: 'To serue againe his soueraine Elfin Queene'.
5–16. C.'s note to l. 5 reads: '*Florimel*. See *Spenser Leg.* 4th.' Florimel's
loss of her girdle and its discovery by Satyrane is described in *Faerie Queene*
III vii 31 and III viii 2 and 49. The competition for it is first mentioned in IV
ii 25–7 and the girdle itself is described at IV iv 15–16. C.'s main reference is
to the competition between the various ladies for which the girdle was offered
as a prize, which is described at length in IV v 1–20. C.'s summary of the
situation is confusing but his main point is clear. See Spenser, IV v 3, 1–5:
'That girdle gaue the virtue of chaste loue, / And wiuehood true, to all that
did it beare; / But whosoeuer contrarie doth proue, / Might not the same
about her middle weare, / But it would loose, or else a sunder teare.' Flori-
mel, the true owner of the girdle, was not present at the competition. The
False Florimel won the competition but could not fasten the girdle (IV v 16,
6–9): 'For euer as they fastned it, it loos'd / And fell away, as feeling secret
blame. / Full oft about her wast she it enclos'd, / And it as oft was from
about her wast disclos'd.' The girdle did in fact fit Amoret but the False
Florimel, as the winner of the competition, duly bore it away. It was finally
restored to the true Florimel, V iii 27–8. Spenser's account at this point,
apparently ignoring Amoret, perhaps explains C.'s over-simplification of
the story: 'Full many Ladies often had assayd, / About their middles that
faire belt to knit; / And many a one suppos'd to be a mayd: / Yet it to none
of all their loynes would fit, / Till *Florimell* about her fastned it.'
7. The competition for the girdle took place at 'A solemne feast, with pub-
like turneying', *Faerie Queene* IV ii 26, 8, at which Satyrane produced
the girdle, IV iv 16, 1–2: 'That same aloft he hong in open vew, / To be the
prize of beautie and of might.' *Il Penseroso* 116–18 is also echoed: 'great
Bards beside, / In sage and solemn tunes have sung, / Of Turneys and of
Trophies hung . . .'
8. The 'Love-darting eyes' of *Comus* 753 had been echoed by Pope, *Elegy
to the Memory of an Unfortunate Lady* 34.
8–9. 1746 has a slight gap between these lines, which seems to have no
formal significance and may have originated in the printing-house. There

Lo! to each other nymph in turn applied,
10   As if, in air unseen, some hovering hand,
Some chaste and angel-friend to virgin-fame,
    With whispered spell had burst the starting band,
It left unblest her loathed, dishonoured side;
      Happier hopeless fair, if never
15   Her baffled hand with vain endeavour
Had touched that fatal zone to her denied!
Young Fancy thus, to me divinest name,
    To whom, prepared and bathed in heaven,
    The cest of amplest power is given,
20   To few the godlike gift assigns
    To gird their blest prophetic loins,
And gaze her visions wild, and feel unmixed her flame!

2

The band, as fairy legends say,

is no way of knowing whether a similar gap was intended at the corresponding point in the third section of the poem (the antistrophe), which occurs at the bottom of a page. But C., or his printer, was not careful to emphasize formal correspondences of this kind.

9. *applied*] Brought into contact.

10–11. *Comus* 214–15: 'Thou hovering Angel girt with golden wings, / And thou unblemish't form of Chastity', and *Par. Lost* iv 677–8: 'Millions of spiritual Creatures walk the earth / Unseen'. With 'Angel-Friend', cp. 'Angel guest', *Par. Lost* v 328. With these echoes of Milton, C. has combined a memory of Pope's sylphs, *Rape of the Lock* iii 113: 'Strait hover round the Fair her Airy Band'.

12. 'breathed spell', Milton, *Nativity Ode* 179.

13. Cp. the Squire of Dames on the girdle, *Faerie Queene* IV v 18, 6–7: 'Fie on the man, that did it first inuent / To shame vs all with this, *Vngirt vnblest*.'

16. *zone*] Belt or girdle, common poetic diction e.g. Pope, *Iliad* xiv 210.

19. *Faerie Queene* IV v 6, 1: 'That goodly belt was *Cestus* hight by name'. The word was often used for Venus' or Aphrodite's girdle: e.g. Fairfax's *Tasso* XVI xxiv 8, and Pope, *Iliad* xiv 256. Cp. 'our amplest pow'rs', Pope, *Dunciad* ii 375.

20. *godlike*] Cp. the passage from Cowley quoted in ll. 23–54 *n.*

21. Cp. Akenside, *Odes* (1745) vi 5–6: 'Where is the bold prophetic heat, / With which my bosom wont to beat.'

23–54. C. combines three basic concepts in this difficult–and frequently misunderstood–passage. In ll. 17–22 he has already described the true poetical character in religious terms, as 'godlike'. In the following section he pursues this idea by describing God's creation of the world as analogous to the poet's act of imaginative creation: God was the original and type of all poets because of the sublime act of imagination with which he created the

Was wove on that creating day
25 When He, who called with thought to birth
Yon tented sky, this laughing earth,
And dressed with springs and forests tall,

world and, correspondingly, the poet, however faintly, imitates that divine power. This analogy was first elaborated in Italy in the 15th century and there are several examples in English before C.'s audacious use of it here, e.g. Cowley, *Davideis* (1656) i 446–56: 'As first a various unform'd *Hint* we find / Rise in some god-like *Poets* fertile *Mind*, / Till all the parts and words their places take, / And with just marches *verse* and *musick* make; / Such was *Gods Poem*, this *Worlds* new *Essay*; / So wild and rude in its first draught it lay; / Th'ungovern'd parts no *Correspondence* knew, / An artless *war* from thwarting *Motions* grew; / Till they to *Number* and fixt Rules were brought / By the *eternal Minds Poetique Thought*.' See also Shaftesbury, *Characteristicks* (5th edn, 1732) i 207 and Akenside, *Pleasures of Imagination* (1744) i 56–78; ii 309–15; iii 380–405, 419–24. Akenside exploits the analogy in both directions, describing God as poet and poet as godlike. See also the essay, 'Of the Essential Excellencies in Poetry' in *The Museum* (4 July 1747) iii 281–6, which has been attributed to C. by F. Page (*Times Lit. Supp.* 1935, p. 448; but see pp. 477, 501), but which might just as plausibly have been written by the editor, Akenside, who shared so many ideas with C. Here again the parallel between the divine and the poetic 'Power of Creating' is asserted. For further information about the development of this concept, see A. S. P. Woodhouse's two essays mentioned in the headnote to the *Odes*; and M. H. Abrams, *The Mirror and the Lamp* (1953) pp. 42–3, 272–85.

C. complicates this basic analogy between God and the poet by adding two further layers of allegory. Fancy, already introduced into the poem as female (l. 22), although essentially only an attribute of God, is represented as separate from him (ll. 29–40). For C.'s models, see l. 29 *n*, and for the confused interpretations resulting from a misunderstanding of his intentions, see l. 39 *n*. C.'s third concept, carried over from the first section of the poem, is that of the metaphor of the girdle of true poetic imagination, which rather confusingly reintroduces as an additional means of describing the first manifestation of the genuine poetical character. Simply summarized, this passage asserts that: 'God created the world (ll. 23–8) by an act of Fancy (ll. 29–40) and in this way the poetic imagination was born (ll. 41–50)'.

24. *creating day*] Strictly, the fourth in the Creation.
25. Prior, *Solomon* iii 665–6: 'Father of Heav'n! I said, and Judge of Earth! / Whose Word call'd out this Universe to Birth.'
26. *tented*] Tent-like. Cp. Sir John Davies, *Orchestra* 55: 'Jove's blue tent'.
laughing] 'In poetry. To appear gay, favourable, pleasant, or fertile' (Johnson, *s.v.* 'laugh').
27. *dressed*] Adorned. Cp. Dryden, *Lucretius* i 9: 'For thee the Land in fragrant Flow'rs is drest'.

And poured the main engirting all,
Long by the loved Enthusiast wooed,
30 Himself in some diviner mood,
Retiring, sat with her alone,
And placed her on his sapphire throne,

28. Cp. William Browne, *Britannia's Pastorals* II i 984–5: 'the wat'ry zone /
Ingirting Albion'.
29. The 'Enthusiast' is Fancy (from l. 17). Cp. Dryden's description of
St Cecilia as 'The sweet Enthusiast', *Alexander's Feast* 163. The word means
'one who is possessed by a God or who possesses divine communications'.
Barbauld, 1797, p. xxiv, objected that: 'It is difficult to reduce to any thing
like a meaning this strange and by no means reverential fiction concerning
the Divine Being.' But C. had respectable precedents for the personification
of divine attributes as female companions, in particular Spenser, *Hymne of
Heavenly Beautie* 172–266, who describes Sapience sitting in God's bosom,
'The soueraine dearling of the *Deity*'; and Milton (following *Proverbs* viii
23–30), *Par. Lost* vii 8–12, in his invocation to Urania, the Muse of Sacred
Song: 'Before the Hills appeerd, or Fountain flow'd, / Thou with Eternal
wisdom didst converse, / Wisdom thy Sister, and with her didst play / In
presence of th'Almightie Father, pleas'd / With thy Celestial Song.' See
P. Legouis, 'Les Amours de Dieu Chez Collins et Milton', *Revue Anglo-
Américaine* viii (1930) 136–8.
30. Crowe, 1828, pp. 29–30, while trying to defend C. against Mrs Barbauld's
charge of irreverence, admitted that 'to say of the Deity, that he is at any
time, or upon any occasion, in a *diviner mood*, is an unguarded expression,
and neither reverend or true. The works of his creation may be more or less
divine; but He himself is the same in all his perfections, whether creating the
soul of a man, or the body of a worm.' C. may have been imitating *mens
divinior*, Horace, *Satires* I iv 43.
31. *retiring*] Akenside, *Pleasures of Imagination* i 59–78, in a passage which C.
may well have had in mind, describes how God, 'then deep-retir'd / In his
unfathom'd essence, view'd at large / The uncreated images of things; /
... till in time compleat, / What he admir'd and lov'd, his vital smile /
Unfolded into being'. Akenside then goes on to describe the creation of the
earth.
32–4. *Ezekiel* i 26, 28: 'And above the firmament that was over their heads
was the likeness of a throne, as the appearance of a sapphire stone. ... As
the appearance of the bow that is in the cloud in the day of rain, so was the
appearance of the brightness round about. This was the appearance of the
likeness of the glory of the Lord.' Milton imitates this passage closely,
Par. Lost vi 758, where he mentions the 'Saphir Throne'. But C. seems also
to have had in mind *At a Solemn Music* 6–13: 'That undisturbed Song of
pure content, / Ay sung before the saphire-colour'd throne / To him that
sits thereon ... / Where the bright Seraphim in burning row / Their loud

The whiles, the vaulted shrine around,
Seraphic wires were heard to sound,
35   Now sublimest triumph swelling,
Now on love and mercy dwelling;
And she, from out the veiling cloud,
Breathed her magic notes aloud:
And thou, thou rich-haired youth of morn,
40   And all thy subject life was born!
The dangerous Passions kept aloof,
Far from the sainted growing woof;
But near it sat ecstatic Wonder,

up-lifted Angel trumpets blow, / And the Cherubick host in thousand quires / Touch their immortal Harps of golden wires . . .'

33. *The whiles*] A common Spenserian phrase.

35. Pope, *Ode for St Cecilia's Day* 16: 'Exulting in Triumph now swell the bold Notes.'

37. Cp. the 'cloudy veil' in *Fear* 38 and *n* (p. 421 above). God has 'a cloud / Drawn round about [him] like a radiant Shrine' in *Par. Lost* iii 378–9 and is surrounded by a 'Golden Cloud' at vi 28.

39–40. youth of morn] The correct interpretation seems to be that of C.'s first commentator, Langhorne, followed by Barbauld, Bronson and Woodhouse, who agree that C. is referring to the sun. Notable dissenters from this view are Garrod, Blunden and Ainsworth: their belief that the 'youth' is the Poet, the child of some kind of quasi-sexual union of God and Fancy, has been elaborated by two critics determined to see in C. a forerunner of Blake: Northrop Frye, *Fearful Symmetry* (1947) pp. 169–70, and Harold Bloom, *The Visionary Company* (1962) pp. 3–10. But C. is referring to the creation of the sun as a climactic moment in God's creation of the world, which he has been describing. He is not describing the birth of the Poet as the result of a marriage between God and Fancy, but the imaginative act of creation by which God, through the embodiment of his 'Fancy', himself became the supreme type of the Poet. Line 40 is much easier to explain if the 'youth' is identified as the sun (all the life dependent on the sun on earth) and this is true of the whole third section of the poem, as both Garrod and Bloom admit. Cp. also with 'rich-haired youth', Spenser, *Faerie Queene* I v 2, 3–4: 'And *Phoebus* fresh . . . / Came dauncing forth, shaking his deawie haire'; and C.'s own phrase, 'bright-haired sun', *Evening* 5. Strutt, 1796, p. 7, explains the 'subject life' thus: 'The golden-tressed Apollo, and his subject divinities, the inferior orbs that encircle him.'

41. *kept aloof*] A Spenserian phrase, *Faerie Queene* IV vii 37, 4 and VI vii 3, 3.

42. *sainted*] Sacred. Cp. 'Sainted seats', *Comus* 11.

43. Akenside, *Pleasures of Imagination* i 222–70, describes 'novelty or wonderfulness' as one of the three main sources of imaginative pleasure, following Addison, *Spectator* No. 412 (23 June 1712).

Listening the deep applauding thunder;
45 And Truth, in sunny vest arrayed,
By whose the tarsel's eyes were made;
All the shadowy tribes of Mind
In braided dance their murmurs joined,
And all the bright uncounted powers,
50 Who feed on heaven's ambrosial flowers.
Where is the bard, whose soul can now
Its high presuming hopes avow?
Where he who thinks, with rapture blind,
This hallowed work for him designed?

3
55 High on some cliff to Heaven up-piled,

44. 'thunder deep', Milton, *Psalm lxxxi* 29.
45. Akenside, *Pleasures of Imagination* i 21–3, describes 'Majestic TRUTH' as 'The guide, the guardian' of the 'lovely sports' of the personified qualities associated with imaginative pleasure.
46. tarsel] Tercel, a male hawk.
47–50. C. probably had in mind some such passage as that in Akenside's description of the creative process, *Pleasures of the Imagination* iii 385–95: 'Anon ten thousand shapes, / Like spectres trooping to the wisard's call, / Fleet swift before him. From the womb of earth, / From ocean's bed they come: th'eternal heav'ns / Disclose their splendors, and the dark abyss / Pours out her births unknown. With fixed gaze / He marks the rising phantoms. Now compares / Their diff'rent forms; now blends them, now divides; / Inlarges and extenuates by turns; / Opposes, ranges in fantastic bands, / And infinitely varies.' Cp. also the passage from Sir William Temple, quoted in note to Gray, *Progress of Poesy* 118–20 (p. 177 above).
48. braided] Woven, intertwined. Cp. *Par. Lost* iv 349: 'breaded train'.
50. 'Ambrosial Flowers', *Par. Lost* ii 245.
51–4. Akenside, *On Lyric Poetry*, in *Odes* (1745) p. 50: 'But, O Melpomene, for whom / Awakes thy golden shell again? / What mortal breath shall e'er presume / To ccho that unbounded strain?'
55. Fairfax's *Tasso* XIX xxx 3 has 'up-piled'.
55–61. C. deliberately imitates in these lines Milton's descriptions of the hill on which Eden was situated, as seen from the outside by Satan. C. is trying to evoke Milton's Eden in order to convey his sense of Milton's, as it were, pre-lapsarian poetic imagination. His use of this material is complex and rich: in his imaginative recreation of Eden in *Par. Lost*, Milton imitated God's creative powers (as described in the epode of this poem) both literally and metaphorically. Milton's poem about Eden reveals an imaginative power as difficult of access and imitation as was Eden itself. Cp. *Par. Lost* iv 132–8: 'delicious Paradise, / Now nearer, Crowns with her enclosure green, / As with a rural mound the champain head / Of a steep wilderness, whose hairie

Of rude access, of prospect wild,
Where, tangled round the jealous steep,
Strange shades o'erbrow the valleys deep,
And holy genii guard the rock,
60   Its glooms embrown, its springs unlock,
While on its rich ambitious head,
An Eden, like his own, lies spread;
I view that oak, the fancied glades among,
By which as Milton lay, his evening ear,

sides / With thicket overgrown, grottesque and wilde, / Access deni'd;
and over head up grew / Insuperable highth of loftiest shade', and iv 172–7:
'Now to th'ascent of that steep savage Hill / Satan had journied on,
pensive and slow; / But further way found none, so thick entwin'd, / As
one continu'd brake, the undergrowth / Of shrubs and tangling bushes had
perplext / All path of Man or Beast that past that way'. Cp. also the descrip-
tion of 'the eastern gate of Paradise', iv 543–50: 'it was a Rock / Of Alablas-
ter, pil'd up to the Clouds, / Conspicuous farr, winding with one ascent /
Accessible from Earth, one entrance high; / The rest was craggie cliff, that
overhung / Still as it rose, impossible to climbe. / Betwixt these rockie
Pillars Gabriel sat / Chief of th'Angelic Guards, awaiting night . . .' Cp. also
Akenside's description of a similar scene, which C. may have had in mind,
Pleasures of Imagination ii 274–92. For a discussion of C.'s use of the Creation
and Fall in this poem, cp. E. L. Brooks, 'William Collins's "Ode on the
Poetical Character"', College English xvii (1956) 403–4.

57. Cp. the 'jealous wings' of darkness, L'Allegro 6.

60. embrown] Darken or shadow. Cp. Par. Lost iv 245–6: 'the unpierc't shade
/ Imbround the noontide Bowrs'. Cp. also Dryden, Georgics ii 245: 'Once
more unlock for thee the sacred Spring' and Aeneid x 241: 'Now sacred
Sisters open all your Spring'. Pope imitates the formula, Windsor Forest 4:
'Unlock your Springs, and open all your Shades'; but C. may have picked
it up from Akenside, On Lyric Poetry in Odes (1745) p. 51: 'Propitious Muse, /
While I so late unlock thy hallowed springs'.

61. Pope, Epistles to Several Persons iv 59: 'Or helps th' ambitious Hill the
heav'n to scale'.

63. Milton, Il Penseroso 59–60, describes himself listening to Philomel's
'even-song', 'While Cynthia checks her Dragon yoke, / Gently o're th'accus-
tom'd Oke . . .' It is not impossible that C. intended the oak to have a
further association. The oak-tree was considered sacred by the Druids, in
whom C. was demonstrably, if vaguely, interested; and it has also been
pointed out that there was an oak tree at the oracle at Dodona, whose rust-
ling leaves were supposed to be of prophetic significance. There seems to be
an unconscious echo in these two lines of Pope, Epistle to Miss Blount on her
leaving Town 31, 33: 'In some fair evening, on your elbow laid . . . / In
pensive thought recall the fancy'd scene.'

64. 'ev'ning wings', Dryden, Hind and the Panther i 322.

65   From many a cloud that dropped ethereal dew,
     Nigh sphered in heaven its native strains could hear:
     On which that ancient trump he reached was hung;
          Thither oft his glory greeting,
          From Waller's myrtle shades retreating,
70   With many a vow from hope's aspiring tongue,
     My trembling feet his guiding steps pursue:
          In vain—such bliss to one alone
          Of all the sons of soul was known,
          And Heaven and Fancy, kindred powers,
75   Have now o'erturned the inspiring bowers,
     Or curtained close such scene from every future view.

65. Cp. Thomson, *Spring* 1–2: 'ethereal mildness, come; / And from the bosom of yon dropping cloud' etc; and Akenside, *Pleasures of Imagination* ii 436–8: 'celestial rounds were heard, / And thro' the fragrant air aetherial dews / Distill'd around them.'
66. C. may have had in mind the celestial music which Adam and Eve could hear in Paradise, *Par. Lost* iv 680–8; or the 'Angelic harps' and 'seraphic strain' granted to the 'hallow'd ear' of the poet when close to Nature, described by Thomson, *Summer* 556–63. Cp. also 'Sphear'd in a radiant Cloud', *Par. Lost* vii 247.   *its*] Garrod, 1928, p. 66, states that this refers back to Milton's 'ear', l. 64; but 'its' could just as well refer to 'Heaven'.
67. 'The wakefull trump', Milton, *Nativity Ode* 156. C. seems to have had in mind only the characteristic quality of Milton's verse.
69. The myrtle was sacred to Venus and emblematic of love. C. is in fact announcing his allegiance to the poetic line of Spenser and Milton and dissociating himself from the Augustan mode initiated by Waller, the first 'correct' English poet, much of whose verse was amorous in character. C. was almost certainly imitating and making more extreme a contrast between Shakespeare and Waller made by Akenside, *Pleasures of Imagination* iii 550–67. Akenside quotes in a note three lines from Waller's *Battle of the Summer-Islands* i 62–4, which C. may have had in mind: 'O! how I long my careless limbs to lay / Under the plantane's shade; and all the day / With am'rous airs my fancy entertain'.
71. Pope, *Essay on Criticism* 195–8: 'Oh may some Spark of *your* Celestial Fire / The last, the meanest of your Sons inspire, / (That on weak Wings, from far, pursues your Flights; / *Glows* while he *reads*, but *trembles* as he *writes*)', and *Essay on Man* i 91: 'Hope humbly then; with trembling pinions soar'. Cp. also Tickell, *On the Prospect of Peace*, *ad fin*: 'See that bold swain to heaven sublimely soar, / Pursue at distance and his steps adore.'
75. C.'s allusion to the Fall is reinforced by Guyon's destruction of the Bower of Bliss, *Faerie Queene* II xii 83, 1–2: 'But all those pleasant bowres and Palace braue, / *Guyon* broke downe, with rigour pittilesse.'
76. 'close-curtain'd sleep', *Comus* 554; and Pope, *Dunciad* iii 3: 'Him close she curtains round with Vapours blue'. Cp. 'future views', Pope, *Essay on Man* iv 72.

11 Ode, Written in the Beginning of the Year 1746

C.'s title might seem to date this poem and it would be natural to relate such a celebration of national heroes to the Battle of Falkirk, fought on 17 Jan. 1746, in spite of the fact that the English forces were defeated by the Young Pretender. But when the poem was reprinted in the 2nd edn of Dodsley's *Collection* (1748) i 330, it followed C.'s *Ode to a Lady*, 'Written May, 1745', and was described as having been 'Written in the same Year' as the preceding poem. C. may conceivably not have been responsible for the title in Dodsley's *Collection* and it must be safer to accept the date given in the *Odes*. Even if C. were responsible for the date in Dodsley, it is possible that he was being deliberately misleading, preferring in 1748 to give the impression that this poem, like the *Ode to a Lady*, was written to celebrate British heroes who died fighting the French, rather than English heroes who died fighting the Scots. Such an alteration would be natural once the anxiety caused by the Jacobite invasion had receded; and, in any case, by 1748 C. was friendly with a group of expatriate Scotsmen centred round James Thomson whom he would be anxious not to offend.

Many critics have assumed that this poem grew directly out of the earlier *Ode to a Lady*, which Middleton Murry, *Countries of the Mind* (1922) p. 94, for example, describes as 'a diffuse preliminary version' of the present poem. The true relation of the two poems is, however, more complicated. The present poem certainly contains a reworking of ll. 7–20 of the *Ode to a Lady* as they appeared in its original form, but when C. came to revise the earlier poem for the *Odes* he appears to have taken a number of details in turn from the *Ode Written in 1746*: cp. *Ode to a Lady* 19–24 and n (p. 458 below).

Ainsworth, 1938, p. 69, accepting C.'s earlier date, suggests that ll. 3–4 refer to the '*next*' spring and imply a dating early in the year 1746. This in fact adds little to C.'s title but, in any case, C.'s 'When' almost certainly means 'Whenever'.

For eighteenth-century musical settings of this poem, see A. S. P. Woodhouse, *Times Lit. Supp.* 1930, p. 838: the first was an unacknowledged use as 'a new funeral elegy in honour of the heroes who die in the service of their country' at the end of Act II of *Alfred the Great, A Drama for Music* .... *New-Compos'd by Mr. Arne* (1753; another edn, 1754). The poem was put to another rather curious use in C.'s lifetime by his friend Samuel Johnson, who misquotes ll. 5–6 in his *Dictionary* (1755) under 'Sod', reading 'Here fame' for 'She there'. This was apparently C.'s only appearance in the *Dictionary*.

How sleep the brave, who sink to rest
By all their country's wishes blest!
When Spring, with dewy fingers cold,
Returns to deck their hallowed mould,
5 She there shall dress a sweeter sod
Than Fancy's feet have ever trod.

2

By fairy hands their knell is rung,
By forms unseen their dirge is sung;
There Honour comes, a pilgrim grey,
10 To bless the turf that wraps their clay,
And Freedom shall awhile repair
To dwell a weeping hermit there!

¶ 11.*1–12*. C. is indebted for the attractively delicate elegiac mood of this poem, as well as for details of diction, to Pope's *Elegy to the Memory of an Unfortunate Lady* 51–4, 61–8: 'By foreign hands thy dying eyes were clos'd, / By foreign hands thy decent limbs compos'd, / By foreign hands thy humble grave adorn'd, / By strangers honour'd, and by strangers mourn'd! / . . . / What tho' no sacred earth allow thee room, / Nor hallow'd dirge be mutter'd o'er thy tomb? / Yet shall thy grave with rising flow'rs be drest, / And the green turf lie lightly on thy breast: / There shall the morn her earliest tears bestow, / There the first roses of the year shall blow; / While Angels with their silver wings o'ershade / The ground, now sacred by thy reliques made.'
3. Cymbeline IV ii 284–5: 'The herbs that have on them cold dew o' the night / Are strewings fitt'st for graves.' Cp. also *Evening* 39 and *n*.
4. 'earths hallowd mould', *Par. Lost* v 321 and 'hallow'd mould', Tickell, *On the Death of Mr. Addison* 36. Cp. also *Song from Cymbeline* 16 *n* (p. 402 above).
5. Spenser, *Ruins of Time* 195–6: 'Scarce anie left vpon his lips to laie / The sacred sod.'
7. Merchant of Venice III ii 70: 'Let us all ring Fancy's knell'; and *Tempest* I ii 402: 'Sea-nymphs hourly ring his knell.'
8. unseen] Cp. *Poetical Character* 10–11 and *n* (p. 429).
9. Par. Regained iv 427: 'with Pilgrim steps in amice gray'.
10. wraps] Perhaps a memory of Spenser's elegiac 'wrapt in lead', *Shepheardes Calender*, 'June' 89; 'Oct.' 63; 'Nov.' 59.
11. 'to repair awhile', *Faerie Queene* II ii 33, 4.

12 Ode to Mercy

The most likely date is July or Aug. 1746. C.'s earliest editor, Langhorne, *1765* p. 161, gives the crucial clue to the dating which has not usually been taken seriously: 'The ode written in 1746, and the ode to Mercy, seem to have been written on the same occasion, viz. the late rebellion; the former in memory of those heroes who fell in the defence of their country, the latter to excite sentiments of compassion in favour of those unhappy and deluded wretches who became a sacrifice to public justice.' Langhorne's suggestion has usually been accepted to the point of admitting that ll. 14–22 probably refer to the Young Pretender's invasion of England, although C.'s method of treating this matter is not very direct. The 'Fiend of Nature' is *not* the Young Pretender personally but war in general, or more precisely, the threat of catastrophic civil war which the Young Pretender brought but which was suppressed at Culloden in April 1746. C. is ostensibly not taking sides, since he is recommending Mercy.

Langhorne's claim that the poem can be more precisely associated with specific rebels is more plausible than has been realized. The 'unhappy and deluded wretches' to whom he refers are undoubtedly the three rebel noblemen, the Earls of Kilmarnock and Cromartie and Lord Balmerino, who were tried for high treason on 28 July 1746, and sentenced to death on 1 Aug. All three pleaded guilty and sought the King's mercy. The trial aroused enormous interest, the three lords attracted a great deal of sympathy and there was almost unremitting discussion of the nature of the proper punishment for their alleged 'crimes' in the press. The key word in this discussion was that of the title of C.'s poem: Mercy. C.'s attitude was clearly enough the normal liberal one, urging that justice be tempered with mercy and recommending this to the King, in whose hands the fate of the rebels ultimately lay (l. 26). Cromartie was eventually pardoned but Kilmarnock and Balmerino were executed on 18 Aug. 1746. Discussion of the proper use of mercy, which had begun in the press at least by July, continued throughout the summer. The *General Evening Post* (16–19 Aug. 1746) stated that: 'Since the Defeat of the Rebels at Culloden, but more especially since the Commencement of their Trials, their Partisans and Wellwishers have been very industrious in composing and publishing large Panegyricks on Mercy.' The same paper, for 19–21 Aug. 1746, reported that: 'Mercy and Pardon to the subdued Rebels are the repeated Themes of their Friends.' This is the context in which C.'s poem should be seen: the last line of the poem, referring to the King's role, points clearly to the particular trial of the rebel lords, during which the King's powers were repeatedly discussed. But C. obviously had sympathy with the plight of the Highlanders as a whole. For examples of the 'Mercy' debate in the summer of 1746, see the *General Evening Post* for July and Aug. *passim*. The *Gentleman's Mag.* also printed discussions of the topic from various papers: see xvi (1746) 261–2, 266–7, 412–17, 424–6, 488, 546–7 (this last reference shows the discussion continuing as late as Oct. 1746, which indicates why C.'s poem could still be considered topical when it was published in Dec. 1746).

A painting, inspired by this poem, of 'Mercy stopping Wrath', by William Artaud, was shown at the exhibition of paintings by British artists,

'Illustrative of the British Poets', organized in 1788 and succeeding years
by Thomas Macklin: cp. *St James's Chronicle* 17–19 April 1788.

STROPHE

O thou, who sitt'st a smiling bride
By Valour's armed and awful side,
Gentlest of sky-born forms and best adored:
Who oft with songs, divine to hear,
5   Winn'st from his fatal grasp the spear,
And hid'st in wreaths of flowers his bloodless sword!
Thou who, amidst the deathful field,
By godlike chiefs alone beheld,
Oft with thy bosom bare art found,
10   Pleading for him the youth who sinks to ground:
See, Mercy, see, with pure and loaded hands,
Before thy shrine my country's Genius stands,
And decks thy altar still, though pierced with many a
    wound!

¶ *12.1–13.* Cp. Mercy as described by Phineas Fletcher, *Purple Island* VI
xvi: 'But see, how 'twixt her sister and her sire, / Soft-hearted Mercy sweetly
interposing, / Settles her panting breast against his fire, / Pleading for grace,
and chains of death unloosing: / Hark! from her lips the melting honey
flows; / The striking Thunderer recalls his blows / And every armed soldier
down his weapon throws'. *Faerie Queene* V XI also refers to Mercy's
heavenly origins.

3. Edward Young, *Night Thoughts* (1744) vi 418: 'Sky-born, sky-guided,
sky-returning race'. Spenser has such formations as 'earth-born, hell-born,
wood-born'.

4–5. Cp. Pindar's invocation to his lyre, *Pythian Odes* i 10–12: 'For ever the
stern god of war setteth aside his rude spears so keen and warmeth his heart
in deep repose'.

5. fatal] Deadly, sure to result in death. Cp. 'fatall hand', *Faerie Queene* VI
xii 25, 8.

6. Pope, *Dunciad* i 87: 'Pomps without guilt, of bloodless swords and maces'.

7. Milton, *Samson Agonistes* 1513: 'Blood, death and deathful deeds are in
that noise'; and Pope's *Homer* (cited by Johnson): 'These eyes behold /
The deathful scene: princes on princes rolled.'

8. 'Under thir God-like Leaders', *Par. Lost* vi 67.

12–13. Pope, *Epilogue to the Satires* i 152: 'Old *England's* Genius, rough with
many a Scar'.

13. 'though pierc'd with wound', *Par. Lost* vi 435.

When he whom even our joys provoke,

14–22. C. must be alluding to the recent invasion of England by the forces of the Young Pretender (see headnote), though it is not as clear as it might be why Mercy was responsible for its failure, unless C. is rather confusingly using his personified figure in these lines for 'God's mercy to us, the English'. C. was perhaps distracted from any exact meaning by the memory of earlier poetic treatments of the theme of disarmed cruelty. C.'s Mercy is thus related to Venus in Lucretius i 31–40: *nam tu sola potes tranquilla pace iuvare / mortalis, quoniam belli fera moenera Mavors / armipotens regit, in gremium qui saepe tuum se / reicit aeterno devictus vulnere amoris, / atque ita suspiciens tereti cervice reposta / pascit amore avidos inhians in te, dea, visus, / eque tuo pendet resupini spiritus ore. / hunc, tu, diva, tuo recubantem corpore sancto / circumfusa super, suavis ex ore loquellas / funde petens placidam Romanis, incluta, pacem* (Cause meanwhile the savage works of war to sleep and be still over every sea and land. For thou alone canst delight mortals with quiet peace, since Mars mighty in battle rules the savage works of war, who often casts himself upon thy lap wholly vanquished by the everliving wound of love, and thus looking upward with shapely neck thrown back feeds his eager eyes with love, gaping upon thee, goddess, and as he lies back his breath hangs upon thy lips. There as he reclines, goddess, upon thy sacred body, do thou, bending around him from above, pour from thy lips sweet coaxings, and for thy Romans, illustrious one, crave quiet peace). Cp. also Statius, *Thebaid* iii 263–70: *cum Venus ante ipsos nulla formidine gressum / figit equos; cessare retro iamiamque rigentes / suppliciter posuere iubas. tunc pectora summo / adclinata iugo voltumque obliqua madentem / incipit – interea dominae vestigia iuxta / spumantem proni mandunt adamanta iugales–: / 'bella etiam in Thebas, socer o pulcherrime, bella / ipse paras ferroque tuos abolere nepotes?'* (Venus unafraid stood in his horses' very path; backward they gave place, and e'en now have dropped their thick manes in suppliant wise to the earth. Then leaning her bosom on the yoke, and with sidelong tearful glance she begins– meanwhile bowed at their mistress' feet the horses champ the foaming steel: 'War even against Thebes, O noble father, war dost thou thyself prepare, and the sword's destruction for all thy race?') As the first of these passages in particular suggests, C. seems to have meant by 'the Fiend of Nature' the recent war in a general sense, rather than in terms of a particular invader. Cp. *Fear* 18–22 and *n* (p. 419): Woodhouse's suggestion that C. was indebted there to Nashe's demonology is equally relevant here, where C. may well be merging with the classical God of War Nashe's spirits who preside over 'massacres, murder, fury, and all manner of cruelties', such as are attendant on civil war. Cp. Woodhouse p. 105 *n*. Two other sources seem to have contributed to this passage. Cp. Spenser's description of the lion which threatened Una (alluded to in *Peace* 16–18) in *Faerie Queene* I iii 5–6, which was tamed by the sight of her. From these lines C. may have acquired

15   The Fiend of Nature, joined his yoke,
     And rushed in wrath to make our isle his prey,
       Thy form, from out thy sweet abode,
       O'ertook him on his blasted road,
     And stopped his wheels, and looked his rage away.
20   I see recoil his sable steeds,
       That bore him swift to salvage deeds;
     Thy tender melting eyes they own.
     O maid, for all thy love to Britain shown,
       Where Justice bars her iron tower,
25   To thee we build a roseate bower,
     Thou, thou shalt rule our Queen and share our
       Monarch's throne!

such words as 'rushed, salvage, prey, rage'. Ainsworth, p. 139, argues that
C. has in mind Milton's Satan, envious of the joys of Eden and eventually
turned away by Gabriel, in *Par. Lost* IV; but the resemblance of the two
situations is limited.

14–15. Spenser, *Hymn in Honour of Love* 234–5: 'And *Orpheus* daring to
prouoke the yre / Of damned fiends'.

15. joined his yoke] Yoked his horses to his chariot. Cp. Pindar, *Pythian Odes*
ii 10–12: 'He yokes the strength of his steeds to his polished car, and to the
wheels that obey the bit.'

17. Faerie Queene III vi 42, 8: 'Emongst the shadie leaues, their sweet
abode'.

19–20. 1746 has a slight gap between these lines, which seems to have no
formal significance and has not been retained.

21. salvage] Archaic form of 'savage' and the spelling used by Spenser.
Johnson states 'It is now spoken and written *savage*' and Langhorne, 1765,
emended the spelling accordingly, ignoring C.'s consciously archaic
intention. Cp. Dryden, *Iliad* i 382: 'When salvage Beasts and Men's more
salvage Bands'.

22. 'melting eyes', Spenser, *Shepheardes Calender*, 'May' 207; *Ruins of
Time* 532; *Faerie Queene* III v 30, 4 and VI 24, 3.

25. 'I come, I come! prepare your roseate bow'rs', Pope, *Eloisa to Abelard*
317.

26. C. evidently means 'rule *as* our Queen', although he goes on to refer
literally to George II (see headnote).

13 Ode to Liberty

Written in the autumn of 1746, in Sept. or Oct., after C.'s return from Hol-
land in Aug.: this dating is made possible by the reference to Genoa's
'bleeding state' (l. 49), an allusion to the allied attack on Genoa in the course

of the campaign against the French in Italy. See l. 49 *n* for evidence of popular interest in Genoa's fate and the arrival of news of its humiliation in Oct. 1746. Similarly, the concluding lines (129–44) express the hope that Liberty will be joined by Concord on 'Britain's ravaged shore', an obvious allusion to the war with France and the widespread desire for peace (see headnote to *Peace*, p. 467).

STROPHE

Who shall awake the Spartan fife,
And call in solemn sounds to life
The youths, whose locks divinely spreading,
 Like vernal hyacinths in sullen hue,
5 At once the breath of fear and virtue shedding,
 Applauding Freedom loved of old to view?
What new Alcaeus, Fancy-blest,

¶ 13.*1–6*. C. may have had in mind the 'exhortations' of Tyrtaeus (*c.* 640 B.C.) to the Spartans at the time of the Second Messenian War, urging them to fight for their country, praising courage and stressing the disgrace and disadvantages of cowardice. His poems, half a dozen of which are extant, became a kind of sacred literature memorized by young Spartans. C. could have read about him in Athenaus (see l. 7 *n*), *Deipnosophistae* xiv 630, where the Spartans are said to have recited the poems of Tyrtaeus as they marched forward in time to music and to have sung them in competition after dining. Cp. also Sir William Temple, 'Of Poetry', *Critical Essays of the Seventeenth Century*, ed. J. E. Spingarn (1908–9) iii 77: 'I easily believe, That the disheartened *Spartans* were new animated, and recovered their lost Courage, by the Songs of *Tyrtæus*'.
3–4. C. evidently alludes to the Spartan custom of combing their hair before battle, as described before Thermopylae by Herodotus vii 208–9.
4. Cp. 'Hyacinthin Locks', *Par. Lost* iv 301. This adjective, frequently used in poetry for hair, derives from Homer, *Odyssey* vi 231: ... κόμας ὑακινθίνῳ ἄνθει ὁμοίας (locks like the hyacinth flower). It is perhaps only coincidental that the mythical Hyacinthus, who was unwittingly killed by Apollo at a game of quoits and from whose blood the flower of the same name was supposed to spring, was the son of the King of Sparta. Cp. 'Young Hyacinth the pride of *Spartan* land', Milton, *Death of a Fair Infant* 26.
7–12. *C.'s note to l. 7 reads*: Alluding to that beautiful Fragment of *Alcaeus*. *He then quotes 10 ll. of Greek verse* (C.'s text):

ἐν μύρτου κλαδὶ τὸ ξίφος φορήσω, | Ὥσπερ Ἁρμόδιος καὶ Ἀριστο-
γείτων. | Φίλταθ' Ἁρμόδι', οὔπω τέθνηκας, | Νήσοις δ' ἐν Μακάρων σε
φασὶν εἶναι. | Ἐν μύρτου κλαδὶ τὸ ξίφος φορήσω | Ὥσπερ Ἁρμόδιος
καὶ Ἀριστογείτων, | Ὅτ' Ἀθηναίης 'εν θυσίαις | Ἄνδρα τύραννον
Ἵππαρχον 'εκαινέτην. | Ἀεὶ σφῶν κλέος 'εσσεται κατ' αἶαν, |
Φίλταθ' Ἁρμόδι', καὶ Ἀριστογείτων.

The poem to which C. refers is a well-known scolion or drinking-song

Shall sing the sword in myrtles dressed,
   At Wisdom's shrine awhile its flame concealing,
10   (What place so fit to seal a deed renowned?)
   Till she her brightest lightnings round revealing,
It leaped in glory forth and dealt her prompted
      wound!
   O goddess, in that feeling hour,
   When most its sounds would court thy ears,

preserved in Athenaeus, *Deipnosophistae* xv 695, described by some scholars
as a kind of 'national hymn of Athens'. C.'s attribution of it to Alcaeus of
Lesbos, a lyric poet of the seventh–eighth century B.C. is mistaken, as he
could not have celebrated an event which took place in 514 B.C. Part of it
at least has been ascribed to Callistratus. The error, which is found in other
eighteenth-century writers, may have been caused by the fact that in the
folio edns of Athenaus by Casaubon, published at Lyons in 1612 and
1657, which C. may well have used, the following sentence from Aris-
tophanes is quoted in italic on the opposite page at the same level as this
poem: 'Take the myrtle branch and sing me a glee from Alcaeus or
Anacreon'. C. may have accepted the misattribution all the more readily
because of a note to Akenside's *On Lyric Poetry* in *Odes* (1745) p.49, explaining
an allusion to Alcaeus of Mitylene, 'the Lesbian patriot', 'who fled from
his native city to escape the oppression of those who had inslav'd it, and
wrote against them in his exile those noble invectives which were so much
applauded by the ancient critics.'
   C. omits six ll. from the poem, which fully translated reads as follows:
   'In a myrtle-branch I will carry my sword, as did Harmodius and
Aristogeiton, when they slew the tyrant and made Athens a city of equal
rights.
   'Dearest Harmodius, thou art not dead, I ween, but they say that thou art
in the Islands of the Blest, where swift-footed Achilles lives, and, they say,
the brave son of Tydeus, Diomed.
   'In a myrtle-branch I will carry my sword, as did Harmodius and
Aristogeiton, when at the Feast of Athena they slew the tyrant Hipparchus.
   'Ever shall your fame live in the earth, dearest Harmodius and Aristo-
geiton, for that ye slew the tyrant, and made Athens a city of equal rights.'
   Harmodius and Aristogeiton conspired to assassinate Hippias and Hippar-
chus, the tyrants of Athens. Their plot miscarried and only Hipparchus
died. Harmodius was immediately killed and Aristogeiton tortured and
put to death. They were revered at Athens as champions of liberty. See
Herodotus v 55 and vi 123; Thucydides i 20, vi 53–4 and 56–8; Aristotle,
Politics 1311 a 34.
9. As the song to which C. refers explains, the assassination occurred at the
Panathenea, a festival in honour of Pallas Athene, Goddess of Wisdom.

15   Let not my shell's misguided power
            E'er draw thy sad, thy mindful tears.
        No, Freedom, no, I will not tell
        How Rome, before thy weeping face,
        With heaviest sound, a giant-statue, fell,
20   Pushed by a wild and artless race
        From off its wide ambitious base,
        When Time his northern sons of spoil awoke,
            And all the blended work of strength and grace,
            With many a rude repeated stroke
25   And many a barbarous yell, to thousand fragments
            broke.

                        EPODE
                          2
        Yet even, where'er the least appeared,
        The admiring world thy hand revered;
        Still midst the scattered states around
        Some remnants of her strength were found;
30   They saw by what escaped the storm
        How wondrous rose her perfect form;
        How in the great, the laboured whole,
        Each mighty master poured his soul!
        For sunny Florence, seat of art,

15. *In a note C. quotes Callimachus, Hymn to Demeter* 17: Μὴ μὴ ταῦτα
λέγωμες, ἃ δάκρυον ἤγαγε Δηοῖ. (Nay, nay, let us not speak of that
which brought the tear to Demeter).

16. *mindful*] Keeping remembrance of something.

20–23. Dryden, *To Sir Godfrey Kneller* 47–8: 'Till *Goths* and *Vandals*, a rude
Northern Race, / Did all the matchless *Monuments* deface', and Akenside,
Pleasures of Imagination ii 743–5: 'When ruthless rapine from the hand of time
/ Tears the destroying scythe, with surer blow / To sweep the works of
glory from their base'. Cp. also Thomson, *Liberty* ii 246: 'the solid base of
Liberty' and *ibid* iii 14–15: 'And from its base / The broad republic tore'.

23. According to Thomson, *Liberty* i 102–3, Rome's architecture exemplified
'All that to Roman strength the softer touch / Of Grecian art can join'.

24. *Il Penseroso* 136: 'the rude Ax with heaved stroke'.

26. *the least*] i.e. of the 'thousand fragments' into which, in C.'s image, the
'giant-statue' of Rome (l. 19) had been broken. The image disappears after
l. 38.

34–55. Cp. Thomson, *Liberty* iv 266–382, where, after alluding to Florence,
he deals in turn with the virtue's manifestations in Genoa, Venice and
Switzerland. For the political reflections aroused by the free states of Italy
and the republic of Switzerland in various eighteenth century travellers,

35 Beneath her vines preserved a part,
    Till they, whom Science loved to name,
    (O who could fear it?) quenched her flame.
    And lo, an humbler relic laid
    In jealous Pisa's olive shade!
40 See small Marino joins the theme,
    Though least, not last in thy esteem;
    Strike, louder strike the ennobling strings
    To those whose merchant sons were kings;

who influenced Thomson and may thus have been mediated by him to C.,
cp. A. D. McKillop, *The Background of Thomson's Liberty* (Houston, Texas,
1951) pp. 34–40.
36. they] The Family of the *Medici. C.*

By the mid-fourteenth century Florence had become a democratic and
commercial republic but, after 1434, was dominated by the Medici family,
except for two brief periods when they were expelled and the republic
restored. The Medicis were, of course, renowned for their patronage of the
arts and letters. By 'Science' C. means knowledge or learning in general,
not a specific branch.
37. Pope, *Eloisa to Abelard* 39: 'There stern religion quench'd th' unwilling
flame'.
38–9. Pisa attained independence even earlier than Florence and the two
cities were inevitable rivals. Pisa was annexed to Florence in 1406 and, after
efforts to assert its independence in the 1490s, was crushed again in 1509.
40. The little Republic of *San Marino. C.*

Cp. Addison, *Remarks on Several Parts of Italy* (1705) in *Misc. Works*, ed.
A. C. Guthkelch (1914) ii 76, on San Marino: 'Nothing indeed can be a
greater instance of the natural love that mankind has for liberty, and of their
aversion to an arbitrary government, than such a savage mountain covered
with people, and the *Campania* of *Rome*, which lyes in the same country,
almost destitute of inhabitants.' The tiny republic (24 square miles) in N. Italy
was founded, according to tradition, by Marinus probably after the middle
of the fourth century. Its independence had been threatened in 1739 but was
restored in 1740.
42. Milton, *Lycidas* 17: 'Begin, and somwhat loudly sweep the string', and
Dryden, *Alexander's Feast* 123–4: 'Now strike the Golden Lyre again: /
A lowder yet, and yet a lowder Strain.'
43. those] The *Venetians. C.*

Salmon, 'The Present State of Italy', *Modern History* (1739) (used by C. as
a source for the *Persian Eclogues*), ii 364, describes the decline of the power
of the Doges, as 'the sovereign power became vested in the most substantial
citizens' of Venice and their families, the 'Noble Venetians'. Cp. E.
Young, *Imperium Pelagi* II iii 6, of 'Old Tyre': 'Her Merchants, Princes!
every Deck, a Throne!'.

     To him who, decked with pearly pride,
45 In Adria weds his green-haired bride;
     Hail, port of glory, wealth and pleasure,
     Ne'er let me change this Lydian measure:
     Nor e'er her former pride relate
     To sad Liguria's bleeding state.
50 Ah no! more pleased thy haunts I seek
     On wild Helvetia's mountains bleak
     (Where, when the favoured of thy choice,
     The daring archer, heard thy voice,
     Forth from his eyrie roused in dread,
55 The ravening Eagle northward fled);

44. him] The Doge of *Venice. C.*

Salmon, *Modern History* ii 369, concludes his account of Venice by describing 'the ceremony of the Doge's espousing the sea annually, every Ascension-day'. After embarking on 'the Bucentaur, a noble galeasse finely carved and gilded', at the appropriate place in the Adriatic 'the Doge receives a gold-ring from the master of the ceremonies, which he throws into the sea, over the stern, saying at the same time, *We espouse thee, O Sea, as a mark of our true and perpetual dominion over thee.*'

47. The Lydian mode in Greek music was supposedly plaintive, soft and even effeminate. Cp. *L'Allegro* 136: 'Lap me in soft *Lydian* Aires.' C. seems to use Lydian as sweet or pleasing; perhaps following Dryden, *Alexander's Feast* 97–8: 'Softly sweet, in *Lydian* Measures, / Soon He sooth'd his Soul to Pleasures.'

49. Liguria] Genoa. *C.*

Salmon describes the republic of Genoa, 'the antient Liguria', in his *Modern History* ii 324–30. Genoa had been taken by the French in 1684 and was again recaptured by the Austrians in the autumn of 1746. The *Gentleman's Mag.* in Sept. 1746, xvi 471, observed that 'the public is at present very attentive to the critical situation of the *Genoese* republick'; and in Oct. 1746, xvi 498, it reported the 'thorough humiliation of that proud city, which has been forc'd to submit on very hard terms to the conqueror'. A footnote added that, of the 'distinguishing epithets' used by the Italians for their chief cities, that used of Genoa was 'the *Proud*'.

51–5. Helvetia] *Switzerland. C.*

Cp. Salmon, *Modern History* ii 286–7, who describes William Tell's refusal to respect the Austrian Governor, his shooting of the apple off his son's head to save both their lives, his killing of the Governor and the Swiss insurrection against the Austrians under the leadership of three 'substantial yeomen'. Thus was 'the foundation of the Helvetick liberty laid by three plain countrymen, without the advantages of birth or riches'. The 'Eagle' (l. 55) was the Austrian ensign.

Or dwell in willowed meads more near,
With those to whom thy stork is dear:
Those whom the rod of Alva bruised,
Whose crown a British queen refused!
60 The magic works, thou feel'st the strains,
One holier name alone remains;
The perfect spell shall then avail.
Hail nymph, adored by Britain, hail!

ANTISTROPHE
Beyond the measure vast of thought,

56. *willowed*] The first example of this word in the sense of 'Bordered or grown with willows' given by the *OED* is in T. Warton's *Ode to Morning* 14: 'The willowed marge of murmuring brook'. This poem was written in 1745 but not printed until 1750.

57. *those*] The *Dutch*, amongst whom there are very severe Penalties for those who are convicted of killing this Bird. They are kept tame in almost all their Towns, and particularly at the *Hague*, of the Arms of which they make a Part. The common People of *Holland* are said to entertain a superstitious Sentiment, That if the whole Species of them should become extinct, they should lose their Liberties. *C.*

Salmon mentions the 'national superstition' in favour of the stork in his 'Present State of the Netherlands', *Modern History* ii 234. C. himself had twice been in the Netherlands, in the summers of 1745 and 1746, and could have encountered the belief personally. Sir Thomas Browne, *Pseudodoxia Epidemica* (1646) p. 173, mentions the 'pretty conceit' that 'Storkes are to be found and will onely live in Republikes or free States'; and the storks in the Netherlands are described by Thomson, *Autumn* 849–61, his source being Richard Bradley's *Philosophical Account of the Works of Nature* (1721) pp. 84–5.

59. *British queen*] Queen *Elizabeth*. *C.*

Salmon, *Modern History* ii 151–4, describes the attempt by the Duke of Alva, the Spanish general sent by Philip II, to crush the Protestant revolt in the Netherlands in 1567, and also Queen Elizabeth's refusal to accept the crown of the United Provinces in 1575 and 1585.

58. Cp. *Par. Lost* v 884–5: 'an Iron Rod to bruise and breake / Thy disobedience'.

63. Augustan poets frequently claim Liberty as a peculiarly British possession. Pope refers to 'Fair *Liberty, Britannia's* Goddess', *Windsor Forest* 91; and Thomson, *Liberty* i 29, 33–4, characterized the Goddess of Liberty as 'British Liberty': 'her bright temples bound with British oak / . . . and her high care / The queen of isles, the mistress of the main'. The 'Hails' probably derive from *Il Penseroso* 11–12.

64–5. *Par. Lost* vii 602–3: 'Great are thy works, *Jehovah*, infinite / Thy power; what thought can measure thee . . .'

65   The works the wizard Time has wrought!
     The Gaul, 'tis held of antique story,
     Saw Britain linked to his now adverse strand,
     No sea between nor cliff sublime and hoary:
     He passed with unwet feet through all our land.
70   To the blown Baltic then, they say,
         The wild waves found another way,
     Where Orcas howls, his wolfish mountains rounding;

66. 'as antique stories tellen vs', *Faerie Queene* IV ii 32, 1; and 'antique history', *ibid* II x 56, 3.

67. This Tradition is mention'd by several of our old Historians. Some Naturalists too have endeavour'd to support the Probability of the Fact, by Arguments drawn from the correspondent Disposition of the two opposite Coasts. I don't remember that any Poetical Use has been hitherto made of it. *C.*

This 'Tradition' is mentioned in Holinshed's *History* (1577) and in Camden's *Britannia* (1586) where other authors who have discussed it are listed. Edmund Gibson, who translated and edited Camden in 1695, added the names of writers who had 'favoured this groundless fancy', p. ii and *n*; cp. also pp. 206–7 for further discussion by Camden of the question. C. was surprisingly mistaken in believing that no earlier use had been made of the theory in poetry, for several of his favourite poets has used it. Spenser, *Faerie Queene* II x 5, 5 and 8–9, wrote of Britain: 'Ne was it Island then . . . / . . . and of some thought / By the sea to haue bene from the *Celticke* maynland brought'; cp. IV xi 16, 3–4 (in a different connection, however): 'Out of his *Albion* did on dry-foot pas / Into old Gall, that now is cleeped *France* . . .'; Drayton, *Poly-Olbion* xviii 718–20: 'To make the channel wide that then he forced was, / Whereas (some say) before he used on foot to pass' (the allusion is amplified in a note by Selden and a list of antiquarian authorities added); Waller, *Panegyric to my Lord Protector* 25–7, speculated 'Whether this portion of the world were rent, / By the rude ocean, from the continent; / Or thus created . . .' There is a similar allusion in Thomson, *Liberty* iv 460–3: 'the rushing flood, / Urged by almighty power, this favoured isle / Turned flashing from the continent aside, / Indented shore to shore responsive still.'

68. *hoary*] The first sense given by Johnson is 'White; whitish', without associations of age. Under 'Hoar' (= white), Johnson cites Thomson, 'Island of bliss, all assaults / Baffling, like thy hoar cliffs the loud sea-wave'.

72. *wolfish*] Abounding in wolves, rather than wolf-like. Cp. Pope, *Imitations of Horace, Ep.* II i 328–9: 'Loud as the Wolves on Orcas' stormy steep, / Howl to the roarings of the Northern deep.' Of 'Orcas' Pope noted: 'The farthest Northern Promontory of Scotland, opposite to the Orcades [i.e. Orkeneys].' Mitford, in Dyce's 1827 edn, cited Joseph Hall, *Satires* IV v 27: 'the wolfish western isle'.

Till all the banded West at once 'gan rise,
A wide wild storm even Nature's self confounding,
75   Withering her giant sons with strange uncouth
surprise.
This pillared earth so firm and wide,
By winds and inward labours torn,
In thunders dread was pushed aside,
And down the shouldering billows borne.

73. *banded West*] Woodhouse, 'Collins and the Creative Imagination',
p. 105 *n* (see p. 413 above), refers once again to Nashe, *Pierce Penniless* (cp.
Fear 16–19 and *Mercy* 14–16). Referring to spirits who operate through
storm and earthquake, Nashe states that 'by help of Alrynach, a spirit of the
West, they will raise storms, cause earthquakes, whirlwinds, rain, hail, or
snow. . . . The spirits of the air will mix themselves with thunder and light-
ning', *Works*, ed. R. B. McKerrow (1904–08) i 231. Cp. 'the banded Powers
of *Satan*', *Par. Lost* vi 85. Milton uses 'banded' similarly elsewhere.
74. Spenser describes the winds, which 'tosse the deepes, and teare the
firmament, / And all the world confound with wide vprore', *Faerie Queene*
IV ix 23, 7–8.
75. *giant sons*] C. is no doubt referring to the giants described by Geoffrey
of Monmouth, Holinshed, Camden and others, as the first inhabitants of
Britain. Spenser, *Faerie Queene* II x 7, also describes the 'saluage nation . . . /
Of hideous Giants' who inhabited Albion; and Drayton, *Poly-Olbion* xix
137–8, refers to huge bones found in Essex as evidence that 'in her height of
youth, the lusty fruitful earth / Brought forth her big-limb'd brood, even
giants in their birth.' For the phrase used by C., cp. 'Earths Giant Sons', *Par.
Lost* i 778 and 'giant sons of earth', Thomson, *Autumn* 803. Cp. also Dryden,
Palamon and Arcite iii 302–3: 'Terrour is thine, and wild Amazement flung /
From out thy Chariot, withers ev'n the Strong'. Spenser often uses 'un-
couth' for sights which amaze or cause wonder.
76–9. Camden, ed. Gibson (1695) pp. 206–7, discusses the different ways in
which the land joining Britain and Gaul could have been swept away,
'split by the general deluge, or by the breaking in of the waves, or some
earth-quake. . . . that Islands, by earth-quakes and the rushing in of waters,
have been broke off from the Continent, is a point plainly evident from
Authors of the best credit'. Cp. *Par. Lost* vi 195–7: 'as if on Earth / Winds
under ground or waters forcing way / Sidelong, had push't a Mountain from
his seat . . .'
76. Spenser, *Hymne of Heavenly Beautie* 36: 'th' Earth, on adamantine
pillers founded'. Milton has 'the pillar'd firmament', *Comus* 598 and 'the
pillard frame of Heaven', *Par. Regained* iv 455.
79. Spenser, *Ruines of Rome* 213: 'Eftsoones of thousand billowes shouldred
narre'; Drayton, *Barons Wars* vi 24, 3, describes a river which 'shoul-
dreth down his mound'; and Fairfax's *Tasso* XV xli 3–4: 'And how the seas

80 And see, like gems, her laughing train,
      The little isles on every side,
Mona, once hid from those who search the main,
      Where thousand elfin shapes abide,
And Wight who checks the westering tide,

betwixt those isles in-throng, / And how they shouldered land from land
away.'
80–1. Milton, *Comus* 21–3: 'the Sea-girt Iles / That like to rich, and various
gemms inlay / The unadorned boosom of the Deep.'
82. There is a Tradition in the Isle of *Man*, that a Mermaid becoming en-
amour'd of a young Man of extraordinary Beauty, took an Opportunity of
meeting him one day as he walked on the Shore, and open'd her Passion to
him, but was receiv'd with a Coldness, occasion'd by his Horror and
Surprize at her Appearance. This however was so misconstrued by the Sea-
Lady, that in revenge for his Treatment of her, she punish'd the whole Island,
by covering it with a Mist, so that all who attempted to carry on any Com-
merce with it, either never arriv'd at it, but wander'd up and down the Sea,
or were on a sudden wreck'd upon its Cliffs. *C.*
    Although more commonly identified as Anglesey, the Mona mentioned
by Latin authors was also taken by some to be the Isle of Man. Henry Row-
lands, *Mona Antiqua Restaurata* (Dublin, 1723) p. 78, refers to recent anti-
quarian arguments on this point, Rowlands himself arriving at the conclusion
that the druids at different times called both islands Mona. No exact source
for C.'s story has been identified, although it seems most probable that he
deliberately adapted a passage in George Waldron, *A Description of the
Isle of Man* in his *Works* (1731) Pt. ii, 176–7 (2nd edn 1744, and accord-
ingly accessible to C.), which tells of a mermaid's love for a young man, who
was alarmed at her advances. But according to Waldron, her revenge was
to throw a stone at him, the mere touch of which resulted in his death a few
days later. C. has altered the story so as to be able to fuse with it a separate
tradition described by Waldron, pp. 100–1: 'Some Hundred Years, say
they, before the Coming of our Saviour, the Isle of *Man* was inhabited by a
certain Species called *Fairies*, and that every thing was carried on in a kind
of supernatural manner; that a blue Mist hanging continually over the Land,
prevented the Ships that passed by, from having any Suspicion there was an
Island.' William Sacheverell, *An Account of the Isle of Man* (1702) p. i, also
refers to 'Magical Arts', which had long concealed the island with 'Mists and
Vapours'.
83. Cp. Waldron (1731) pp. 126: 'they maintain that these little People
have still their Residence among them: They call them *the good People*, and
say they live in Wilds and Forests, and on Mountains.' Waldron goes on to
tell many stories of the Manx fairies. Langhorne, *1765* p. 166, remarked
that Anglesey and Man were now 'the only places where there is the least
chance of finding a faery'.
84. Cp. 'the westering wheel' of the evening star, *Lycidas* 31.

85   For thee consenting heaven has each bestowed,
      A fair attendant on her sovereign pride:
      To thee this blest divorce she owed,
      For thou hast made her vales thy loved, thy last abode!

                    SECOND EPODE

      Then too, 'tis said, an hoary pile
90   Midst the green navel of our isle,
      Thy shrine in some religious wood,
      O soul-enforcing goddess stood!
      There oft the painted native's feet
      Were wont thy form celestial meet:
95   Though now with hopeless toil we trace
      Time's backward rolls to find its place;
      Whether the fiery-tressed Dane,
      Or Roman's self o'erturned the fane,
      Or in what heaven-left age it fell,

89–92. Early writers on the druids inevitably engaged in speculation about their 'temples'. C. may have had in mind something like the intrepid reconstruction of the 'great *Druidical* Grove or Temple', which Henry Rowlands believed to have existed at the druid headquarters on Anglesey, *Mona Antiqua Restaurata* (1723) pp. 91–2. But C. may also have remembered Thomson, *Liberty* iv 626–31: 'Bold were those Britons, who, the careless sons / Of nature, roamed the forest-bounds, at once / Their verdant city, high-embowering fane, / And the gay circle of their woodland wars: / For by the Druid taught, that death but shifts / The vital scene, they that prime fear despised.' Thomson goes on to describe Roman and Danish invasions. Rowlands also has much to say about the battles between the Romans and the druids.

90. Homer, *Odyssey* i 50–51: 'the navel of the sea, a woodland isle'. Drayton refers to certain counties as 'the navel' of England, *Poly-Olbion* xxiii 147; and cp. also Milton, *Comus* 520: 'Within the navil of this hideous Wood'.

92. 'soule enchanting might', Spenser, *Hymne in Honour of Beautie* 14.

93–4. Dryden, *Astraea Redux* 46–7: 'They own'd a lawless salvage Libertie, / Like that our painted Ancestours so priz'd'.

95–6. *rolls*] The word may have been suggested by a sentence in Camden, *Britannia*, ed. Gibson (1695) p. iv, admitting the difficulty of identifying the first inhabitants of Britain: 'Nor indeed could it otherwise be, considering under how much rubbish the revolutions of so many past ages have buried Truth'.

97. Milton, *Psalm cxxxvi* 29, has 'Golden-tressed'. There are several 'fiery-' formations in Spenser and Milton.

100   'Twere hard for modern song to tell.
        Yet still, if truth those beams infuse,
        Which guide at once and charm the muse,
        Beyond yon braided clouds that lie
        Paving the light-embroidered sky,
105   Amidst the bright pavilioned plains,
        The beauteous model still remains.
        There happier than in islands blest
        Or bowers by spring or Hebe dressed,
        The chiefs who fill our Albion's story,
110   In warlike weeds, retired in glory,
        Hear their consorted Druids sing
        Their triumphs to the immortal string.
        How may the poet now unfold
        What never tongue or numbers told?
115   How learn delighted and amazed,

100. Milton, *Comus* 44–5: 'in Tale or Song / From old, or modern Bard'.
103–4. Mitford (in Dyce's edn, 1827) cites Dekker, *Wonder of a Kingdom* III
i 18: 'I'll pave my great hall with a floor of clouds.'
104. 'bright embroidered', Spenser, *Faerie Queene* V iii 33, 7; and 'violet
embroidered vale', *Comus* 233.
105. *Par. Lost* v 650, has 'Pavilions numberless' on the plain of Heaven, and
xi 215, 'The field Pavilion'd'.
107. C. may be referring back to the scolion he had quoted earlier (see
ll. 7–12 and *n*), in which Harmodius and Aristogeiton are said to be living in
the Blessed Isles. But Camden, *Britannia*, ed. Gibson (1695) p. iii, mentions the
theories of some writers that the Fortunate or Blessed Isles of classical myth-
ology were in fact Britain, 'the master-piece of Nature . . . . The most accurate
model which she proposed to her self, to beautifie the other parts of the
Universe.' Henry Rowlands, *Mona Antiqua Restaurata* (1723) pp. 71–3,
solemnly discusses the possibility of Anglesey and the Isle of Man having
been the Blessed Isles, at the period when they were inhabited by the druids,
'a Company of divinely inspir'd Souls, abounding with instructive Docu-
ments of Virtue, and profound Discoveries of Nature.' C.'s similar collo-
cation of Blessed Isles and druids (l. 111) may seem more than coincidental.
108. Hebe] The handmaiden of the gods and the goddess of youth.
110. Spenser, *Faerie Queene* V vi 23, 7: 'Those warlike weedes'.
111–12. Camden, *Britannia*, ed. Gibson (1695) pp. iv–v, xiii–xvi, describes
the function of the druids in celebrating 'all gallant and remarkable adven-
tures'. In this he follows Caesar, *Gallic War* VI xiv, where the druids are
described as both bards and priests. See also Milton, *Lycidas* 53 and *Manso*
42–4. Cp. *Faerie Queene* II xii 70, 8: 'there consorted in one harmonee';
and Milton, *At a Solemn Music* 13: 'immortal Harps of golden wires'.

What hands unknown that fabric raised?
Even now before his favoured eyes,
In Gothic pride it seems to rise!
Yet Græcia's graceful orders join
120   Majestic through the mixed design.
The secret builder knew to choose
Each sphere-found gem of richest hues;
Whate'er heaven's purer mould contains,
When nearer suns emblaze its veins;
125   There on the walls the patriot's sight
May ever hang with fresh delight,
And, graved with some prophetic rage,
Read Albion's fame through every age.
    Ye forms divine, ye laureate band,
130   That near her inmost altar stand!
Now soothe her, to her blissful train
Blithe Concord's social form to gain:
Concord, whose myrtle wand can steep

116–20. Liberty, in Thomson's *Liberty* iv 117–8, describes her Temple in
Britain as 'my fabric' and cp. also v 374–8: 'To softer prospect turn we now
the view, / To laurelled science, arts and public works, / That lend my
finished fabric comely pride, / Grandeur and grace.' Similarly, Akenside,
Pleasures of Imagination ii 43–4, refers to 'freedom's ample fabric, fixed at
length / For endless years on Albion's happy shore'. C.'s mixture of Grecian
and Gothic architecture differs from that of earlier poets in superficially
similar descriptions (Pope, *Temple of Fame* 75 ff and 119 ff; Thomson,
Liberty iii 508–11). Although 'Gothic' often retained its meaning of aes-
thetically barbarous and tasteless at this period, it had long been associated
in political contexts with constitutional and democratic forms of govern-
ment and so used sympathetically especially by the Whigs; see S. Kliger,
'The "Goths" in England', *Modern Philology* xliii (1945) 107–17. The word
has this connotation as used by C. here but it was also being transferred to
aesthetic discussion in the first part of the eighteenth century, as a taste for
'irregular fancy' became acceptable. During the 1740s, in any case, Gothic
architecture itself was being made fashionable, especially through the works
of Batty Langley, *Ancient Architecture Restored* (1742) and *Gothick Architecture
Improved* (1747).

122. 'Sphear-born', Milton, *At a Solemn Music* 2.

123. mould] Soil, ground.

124. emblaze] Set in a blaze. Cp. *Comus* 732–3: 'th'unsought diamonds /
Would so emblaze the forhead of the Deep'.

127. graved] Engraved.

133–4. Milton, *Nativity Ode* 51–2, describing Peace: 'And waving wide her
mirtle wand, / She strikes a universall Peace through Sea and Land.'

Even Anger's blood-shot eyes in sleep:
135 Before whose breathing bosom's balm
Rage drops his steel and storms grow calm;
Her let our sires and matrons hoar
Welcome to Britain's ravaged shore,
Our youths, enamoured of the fair,
140 Play with the tangles of her hair;
Till in one loud applauding sound,
The nations shout to her around:
'O how supremely art thou blest,
Thou, lady, thou shalt rule the West!'

133–6 Cp. *Mercy* 17–22 (p. 441); and Pindar, *Pythian Odes* i 5–12, quoted in note to Gray, *Progress of Poesy* 13 (p. 163 above).
135. *Par. Lost* ii 400, 402: 'the soft delicious Air / ... /Shall breath her balme'.
137. C. is remembering such phrases in Spenser as 'a matrone graue and hore' and 'An aged sire with head all frory hore,' *Faerie Queene* I x 3, 5 and III viii 30, 3.
140. *Lycidas* 68–9: 'To sport with *Amaryllis* in the shade, / Or with the tangles of *Neaera's* hair.'
141–2. Pope, *Imitations of Horace, Ep.* II i 330: 'Such is the shout, the long-applauding note.'
143. Pope, *Essay on Man* ii 270: 'Supremely blest, the poet in his muse'.
144. Perhaps a reminiscence of *Faerie Queene* I ii 22, 8: 'He that the wide West vnder his rule has.'

14 Ode, to a Lady on the Death of Colonel Ross in the Action of Fontenoy

Written between 11 May 1745 and the end of that month, if the original title of the poem can be accepted as C.'s own. It was first printed anonymously in Robert Dodsley's periodical (edited by Mark Akenside), *The Museum: Or the Literary and Historical Register* i 215–17, on 7 June 1746 and was there entitled: 'Ode to a Lady, On the Death of Col. Charles Ross, in the Action at Fontenoy. Written May, 1745.' The allied forces had been defeated at Fontenoy on 11 May 1745. Among those listed as having died in the battle in the *Gentleman's Mag.* xv (1745) 276, is 'Capt. Ross, a fine young gentleman, member for the shire of Ross'. A letter from Col. John Munro after the battle, in *Culloden Papers* (1815) p. 200, describes Ross's death: 'Poor Charles Ross of Balnagown was shot with a musket ball through the belly, I believe early in the action; my Servants found him in a Ditch, and I

sent him away to our head Quarters, where he died that night.' Charles
Ross, second son of George, 13th Lord Ross, born in 1721, had become
owner of the estate of Balnagown in 1732, had been commissioned in the
Scots Guards in about 1740 and had become M.P. for the County of Ross in
1741. He had set off for Flanders not long after Feb. 1743 (not 1742, as stated
by P. L. Carver, who gives detailed information about Ross in *Notes and
Queries* clxxvii (1939) 220–2 and *The Life of a Poet* (1967) pp. 75–7). As
Carver suggests, the facts that C. was mistaken about Ross's rank and that
Ross had been abroad since 1743 make it unlikely that C. was personally
acquainted with him.

When the poem was included in the *Odes* in Dec. 1746, the date of com-
position and Ross's christian name were omitted from the title and two new
stanzas were introduced (ll. 37–48). In part they contain an expansion of an
idea in the original stanza 4, which was now rewritten, and they also
compliment William, Duke of Cumberland, the hero of Culloden in
April 1746, who, it was hoped, would soon return to Flanders to avenge the
defeat of Fontenoy. Further revision occurred when the poem appeared in
the 2nd edn of Dodsley's *Collection* (Dec. 1748) i 327–9. C. had now once
more removed the added stanzas 7 and 8, no doubt as a result of Cumber-
land's defeat by the French at Laeffelt in July 1747, and the title (the same as in
The Museum) and punctuation suggest that the original text in *The Museum*
was used as the basis of that in Dodsley's *Collection*. But instead of returning
to the original text of stanza 4, C. now made further revisions. Additional
textual variants in a MS., which precedes all printed texts, seen by Thomas
Warton and described by him in a letter printed in *The Reaper* No. 26 and
reprinted in Nathan Drake's *The Gleaner* (1811) iv 477, are given in the
notes.

In the same letter, Warton confidently identified the 'Lady' to whom the
poem is addressed as 'Miss Elizabeth Goddard, who then lived at or near
Harting, in Sussex'. Unless Warton had grounds for the identification which
he does not give here, it seems likely that he arrived at it by combining an
allusion to Harting within the poem itself (l. 58) with a statement in a letter
written to him by his brother Joseph in May 1746. This letter is that which
describes the original plan for the joint publication of the odes of C. and
Joseph Warton, quoted by Wooll, *Memoirs of Joseph Warton* (1806) pp. 14–
15. Warton added: 'You will see a very pretty one of Collins's, on the death
of Colonel Ross before Tournay. It is addressed to a lady who was Ross's
intimate acquaintance, and who by the way is Miss Bett Goddard.' The fact
that nothing definite is known about Miss Goddard has not prevented a
web of speculation and confident assertion from collecting around her. She
has been further identified as the 'young lady' to whom C. was 'extremely
attached', but who 'did not return his passion with equal ardour', described
by William Seward, *Supplement to Anecdotes of Some Distinguished Persons*
(1797) p. 125. The version of l. 49 seen by Thomas Warton has been taken
to confirm C.'s own attachment to the lady to whom this poem is addressed
but this is slender evidence for such a conclusion. Thomas Warton seems also

to have been responsible for the statement that Miss Goddard was an inhabitant of Harting, a village in Sussex, mentioned by C. in l. 58. This may have been no more than a hasty deduction on Warton's part and it is by no means clear that C. is stating that the lady he is addressing lived in Harting. It would be more plausible to suppose that he mentions Harting as a place of some obscurity, known both to himself and the lady, but not necessarily her dwelling-place. If she actually lived there, why should C. seem to think it remarkable that Harting should learn of Ross's death? No Elizabeth Goddard has been identified as living in Harting. In some pages which mingle useful information with wild speculation, H. D. Gordon, *History of Harting* (1877) pp. 166–8, mentions that Goddard was a name found in the village in the 17th century but his additional information that members of the Collins family lived there provides a more reasonable explanation of C.'s allusion to the village. As Gordon points out, Harting is midway between Chichester and Winchester on a route which must have been familiar to C. His fellow-Wykehamist, Lord Tankerville, lived at Up-Park in Harting until 1745 and the Vicar of Harting was Thomas Durnford who later married C.'s sister Anne as his second wife. C.'s contemporary at Oxford, Gilbert White of Selborne, also had an early connection with Harting and was a landowner there from the 1750s: see H. D. Gordon, pp. 206–8.

The most reasonable interpretation of the scanty evidence is that Miss Goddard had been a visitor to Up-Park or some other great house in the district. Such a theory, though it is not clear from what sources it was derived, was outlined by Sir Harris Nicolas in the Aldine edn of C., (1830) pp. xxxviii: 'The lady is supposed to have been Miss Elizabeth Goddard, the intended bride of Colonel Ross, to whom he addressed his beautiful Ode on the death of that officer at the battle of Fontenoy, at which time she was on a visit to the family of the Earl of Tankerville, who then resided at Up-Park, near Chichester, a place that overlooks the little village of Harting, mentioned in the Ode.' That Ross was engaged to Miss Goddard seems more likely than that he was her uncle, as asserted by J. S. Cunningham, *William Collins: Drafts and Fragments* (1956) p. 31, who has provided no evidence to support this statement. Similarly, Cunningham's assumption that the young lady who is the subject of the draft poem, 'No longer ask me, gentle friends' (see p. 548 below), is once more Elizabeth Goddard, however attractive, must be approached cautiously, since there is no evidence to confirm it. But if the identification is correct, it would support the theory that Miss Goddard was merely a visitor to Harting.

P. L. Carver, *The Life of a Poet* (1967) p. 135, notes that the poem was reprinted from *1746* in *The British Mag.* vol. i, at Edinburgh in July 1747.

The text followed here is that of *1746* which includes the two added stanzas not present in *The Museum* and dropped again in 1748, on the assumption that their omission then was the result of political rather than literary considerations. Variants are also given from the MS seen by Thomas Warton.

1

While, lost to all his former mirth,
Britannia's Genius bends to earth
    And mourns the fatal day;
While stained with blood he strives to tear
5   Unseemly from his sea-green hair
    The wreaths of cheerful May;

2

The thoughts which musing Pity pays
And fond Remembrance loves to raise,
    Your faithful hours attend:
10 Still Fancy, to herself unkind,
Awakes to grief the softened mind,
    And points the bleeding friend.

¶ 14.1. *lost to*] Deprived of.

2–6. These lines and 37–42 below are strongly reminiscent of a couplet in a poem by Thomas Warton Senior, 'The Regal Dream' (written 1715), not published until Joseph Warton edited his *Poems* in 1748, p. 218. C. may have seen this poem already, however, through Joseph: '*Britannia's* self abandon'd to Despair, / Her azure Mantle tore, and sea-green Hair'; there seems also to be a vague echo of Milton, *Nativity Ode* 186–8: 'The parting Genius is with sighing sent, / With flowre-inwov'n tresses torn / The Nimphs in twilight shade of tangled thickets mourn.'

3. Faerie Queene I vi 38, 2: 'This fatall day, that shall I euer rew'.

4. stained with blood] sunk in grief *Warton.*

4–6. Pope, *Essay on Man* iv 295–6: 'Now Europe's laurels on their brows behold, / But stain'd with blood'.

5. sea-green] C. may have adopted this word from Dryden, who is fond of it, as appropriate to a marine deity, no doubt referring to Britain's reliance on sea-power. Cp. Dryden, *First Bk. of Ovid's Art of Love* 256: 'Flows the swift Tigris with his sea-green hair'; and *Aeneid* x 299: 'the Sea-green God appears'. But see ll. 2–6 *n* above.

7–8. Pope, *Epistles to Several Persons* ii 250: 'To raise the Thought and touch the Heart, be thine!'

7. 'musing meditation', Milton, *Comus* 386.

11. Pope, *Eloisa to Abelard* 248: 'And wake to all the griefs I left behind'; and 'softened heart', *Faerie Queene* IV i 1, 7 and 'softened spirit', *Hymne of Heavenly Love* 253.

12. Cp. *Epistle to Hanmer* 120 (p. 398), for this use of 'points'.

3

By rapid Scheldt's descending wave
His country's vows shall bless the grave,
15   Where'er the youth is laid:
That sacred spot the village hind
With every sweetest turf shall bind,
    And Peace protect the shade.

4

Blest youth, regardful of thy doom,
20 Aerial hands shall build thy tomb,
    With shadowy trophies crowned:

13. In fact, the Scheldt flows through almost completely flat country.
Cp. Goldsmith, *The Traveller* 2: 'lazy Scheldt' (p. 632 below).
13–24. Cp. *Song from Cymbeline* 1–4 and *Ode, Written in the Beginning of 1746*, and notes (pp. 401, 437).
19–24. In The Museum this stanza reads:

Ev'n now, regardful of his Doom,
Applauding *Honour* haunts his Tomb,
    With shadowy Trophies crown'd:
Whilst *Freedom's* Form beside her roves
Majestic thro' the twilight Groves,
    And calls her Heroes round.

(In l. 5 of this stanza 'twilight groves' derives from Milton, *Il Penseroso* 133 and Pope, *Eloisa to Abelard* 163; perhaps via J. Warton, *Ode to Evening* 4.)

The version seen in MS by Warton followed this text, with 'regardless' for 'regardful', almost certainly Warton's error. In *1746* C. introduced 'Aerial hands' into the stanza, perhaps taken from the *Ode, Written in the Beginning of 1746* and expanded the personification of Freedom into the added stanzas 7–8. When these stanzas were once more dropped in the 1748 text (see headnote), Freedom disappears from the poem completely. C. may have decided not to revert to the original *Museum* text of stanza 4 because its pair of personifications were now too close to the *Ode, Written in the Beginning of 1746* 9–12, where Freedom and Honour also appear, no doubt in imitation of the earlier poem. In Dodsley's *Collection* (2nd edn) 1748, stanza 4 reads:

O'er him whose doom thy virtues grieve,
Aërial forms shall sit at eve
    And bend the pensive head!
And, fall'n to save his injur'd land,
Imperial Honor's awful hand
    Shall point his lonely bed!

Cp. with l. 2 of this stanza, J. Warton, *Ode to Fancy* 127–8: 'On which thou

Whilst Honour bathed in tears shall rove
To sigh thy name through every grove
And call his heroes round.

5

25 The warlike dead of every age,
Who fill the fair recording page,
Shall leave their sainted rest:
And, half-reclining on his spear,
Each wondering chief by turns appear
30   To hail the blooming guest.

6

Old Edward's sons, unknown to yield,
Shall crowd from Crecy's laurelled field,
And gaze with fixed delight:
Again for Britain's wrongs they feel,
35 Again they snatch the gleamy steel,
And wish the avenging fight.

lov'st to sit at eve, / Musing o'er your darling's grave'; and with l. 3, *Lycidas*
147: 'Cowslips wan that hang the pensive hed'.
22. 'bath'd in Tears', Dryden, *Aeneid* ii 353.
25–36. Cp. *Aeneid* vi 477–88, on the region of the underworld set apart for
those renowned in war, where the warriors crowd round Aeneas. With this
scene C. seems to have merged the later description, vi 637–65, of the 'Bliss-
ful Groves', where the warriors retain their arms and military ardour. As in
C.'s version, those admitted to this happy scene include those who were
wounded fighting for their country and again they surround the visiting
Aeneas.
26. *fair recording page*] i.e. of history, or the Muse of History: cp. *The Passions*
108 (p. 485 below); and Thomson, *Liberty* iii 33: 'The brightest witness of
recording fame'.
31. *unknown*] untaught *Warton.*   *unknown to yield*] A variant of a common
heroic phrase, 'unknowing how to yield'. Cp. *cedere nescii*, Horace, *Odes I*
vi 6; 'Conquered, yet unknowing how to yield', Dryden, *Aeneid* xi 472;
'unknowing how to yield', *Palamon and Arcite* iii 309, and Pope, *Elegy to
an Unfortunate Lady* 42. C.'s suggestion that more than one of Edward III's
sons fought at Creçy in 1346 is erroneous. Only the Black Prince, the eldest,
did so: the others were too young and in any case never acquired military
fame. The Battle of Creçy was fought almost exactly 400 years before the
first publication of this poem, on 26 Aug. 1346. Pope, *Windsor Forest* 305,
refers to 'Cressi's glorious Field'.

7

But lo! where, sunk in deep despair,
Her garments torn, her bosom bare,
   Impatient Freedom lies!
40 Her matted tresses madly spread,
To every sod which wraps the dead
   She turns her joyless eyes.

8

Ne'er shall she leave that lowly ground,
Till notes of triumph bursting round
45   Proclaim her reign restored;
Till William seek the sad retreat
And, bleeding at her sacred feet,
   Present the sated sword.

9

If, weak to soothe so soft an heart,
50 These pictured glories nought impart

37–48. These stanzas were added to the poem in *1746*, as a compliment to
William, Duke of Cumberland (l. 46), the hero of Culloden in April 1746,
but were removed in 1748. The various changes in stanza 4 were made
to accommodate this insertion and then its eventual removal. The
two stanzas must therefore have been written between May and Dec. 1746.
The British forces returned to Flanders in June 1746 and it was at first ex-
pected that Cumberland would join them; but the *General Evening Post*
(29–31 July 1746) reported that 'The Talk of his Royal Highness the Duke
of Cumberland's going to Flanders this Campaign is dropt.' The campaign
was suspended in Oct. 1746. In Dec. 1746 Cumberland was sent over to
persuade the Dutch to renew the campaign against the French. The stanzas
were presumably dropped in 1748 because of the defeat of the allies under
Cumberland at Laeffelt in July 1747.

37–40. Spenser, *Faerie Queene* II i 13, 5–9: 'Where sate a gentle Lady all
alone, / With garments rent, and haire discheueled, / Wringing her hands,
and making piteous mone; / Her swollen eyes were much disfigured, /
And her faire face with teares was fowly blubbered.' Cp. also II ii 27, 2–3:
'The faire *Medina* with her tresses torne, / And naked brest'.

39. impatient] 'Vehemently agitated by some painful passion' (Johnson).

41. wraps] Cp. *Ode, Written at the Beginning of 1746* 10 n (p. 437).

44. Pope, *Ode on St Cecilia's Day* 16: 'Exulting in Triumph now swell the
bold Notes'.

49. If drawn by all a lover's art *Warton.* This may be thought to indicate
that C. saw himself as the 'lover' of Miss Goddard, although the expression
– and the sentiment in the context – is curious.

To dry thy constant tear;
If yet, in Sorrow's distant eye,
Exposed and pale thou see'st him lie,
Wild War insulting near;

10

55 Where'er from time thou court'st relief,
The Muse shall still, with social grief,
Her gentlest promise keep:
Even humble Harting's cottaged vale
Shall learn the sad repeated tale,
60   And bid her shepherds weep.

53–4. Dryden, *Alexander's Feast* 82–3: 'On the bare Earth expos'd He lyes, /
With not a Friend to close his Eyes.'
54. insulting] Scornfully triumphing.
58. cottaged] This is the first use of the word in this sense given by *OED*.
58. Harting is a village near Midhurst in Sussex. For the possibility that Miss
Goddard lived there, see headnote. But G.'s use of 'Even' suggests that,
while Harting was known to Miss Goddard, she did not live there, but that
C. himself knew the village well.
59. 'the repeated air / Of sad *Electra's* Poet', Milton, *Sonnet viii* 12–13.

15 Ode to Evening

Written between May and Dec. 1746, if weight can be placed on the poem's
apparent relationship to compositions by the Warton brothers. It seems
probable that the form and content of the poem were both influenced by
C.'s meeting with Joseph Warton at Guildford Races in May 1746 (see
general headnote to *Odes*). It has often been pointed out that C.'s poem
follows metrically Milton's unrhymed translation of Horace's 'Pyrrha' ode,
Bk I v, to which Thomas Warton, in his edn of Milton's *Poems upon
Several Occasions* (1785) p. 369 *n*, appended a comment by his brother
Joseph: 'In this measure, my friend and school-fellow Mr. William Collins
wrote his admired Ode to EVENING; and I know he had a design of writing
many more Odes without rhyme.' But the distinctive metre and unrhymed
stanza were in fact probably suggested to C. by its use by the Wartons
themselves, though they must have derived it from Milton. The odes shown
by Joseph Warton to C. in May 1746 would have included the 'Ode to a
Fountain' which employs it and which was printed in Joseph's *Odes* in
Dec. 1746, although it was actually written by Thomas Warton (see Joseph's

letter to Thomas in general headnote). The poem was replaced in the 2nd edn of Warton's *Odes* by 'The Happy Life' in the same metre. Another poem in this metre and stanzaic form, 'To Taste', appears in the *Poems* of Thomas Warton Senior (1748) pp. 180–3.

In the footnote to Milton's poem quoted above, Thomas Warton added to his brother's comment: 'Dr. J. WARTON might have added, that his own ODE to EVENING was written before that of his friend Collins.' There are some resemblances between the two poems, although C. seems to have been much more influenced by Warton's *Ode to Fancy*. If C. did, consciously or unconsciously, imitate Warton and if he did not see Warton's odes until May 1746, his own *Ode to Evening* must be dated after this meeting.

After appearing in the *Odes* in Dec. 1746, the poem was reprinted with some alterations in the 2nd edn of Dodsley's *Collection* (1748) i 331–2; and this text was followed exactly (except for a misprint) when the poem appeared in *The Union: Or Select Scots and English Poems* (1753) pp. 39–41, a collection edited anonymously by Thomas Warton and actually printed at Oxford, although Edinburgh appears on the title-page. The Dodsley text of 1748 has been followed here. The poem was not printed in distinct stanzas until the *Poetical Calendar* xii 55–7, in 1763, an arrangement followed by Langhorne in 1765, and the original continuous form is retained here.

There are perceptive comments on this poem in Merle E. Brown's article, 'On William Collins' "Ode to Evening"', *Essays in Criticism* xi (1961) 136–53, although it is over-ingenious at times, as is Henry Pettit's 'Collins' "Ode to Evening" and the Critics', *Studies in English Literature 1500–1900* iv (1964) 361–9. Another important discussion of the poem, as well as its relation to the fragment, 'Ye genii who, in secret state', is A. D. McKillop's 'Collins's *Ode to Evening*–Background and Structure', *Tennessee Studies in Literature* v (1960) 73–83. McKillop quotes an early comment on this *Ode* which appeared in the *Universal Magazine* xxii (Jan. 1758) 1–4, in an essay entitled 'Observations on Poetry and Painting; and the Superiority of the former above the latter'. But this essay is only an expanded adaptation (presumably by the author himself) of a passage in John Gilbert Cooper's *Letters Concerning Taste* (1755) pp. 43–51. Cooper, a friend of C., had written, pp. 49–50: 'the following Scene, in Mr. COLLIN's Ode to the Evening, being animated by proper Allegorical Personages, and colour'd highly with incidental Expression, warms the breast with a sympathetic Glow of retired Thoughtfulness.' Cooper then quoted ll. 21–8 and added a footnote: 'See a Collection of Odes publish'd a few Years ago by Mr. *William Collins*, whose neglected Genius will hereafter be both an Honour and a Disgrace to our Nation.' (This note did not appear in 1758.) Later (*Letters* p. 103), Cooper asked, 'Has HORACE any moral Ode equal to Mr. NUGENT's *Ode to MANKIND*, or any descriptive one to Mr. COLLINS's *Ode to the* EVENING?' The introduction of Nugent's name (see Goldsmith, *Haunch of Venison*, p. 696 below) somewhat devalues the praise of C.

     If aught of oaten stop or pastoral song
     May hope, chaste Eve, to soothe thy modest ear,
          Like thy own solemn springs,
          Thy springs and dying gales,
5   O nymph reserved, while now the bright-haired sun
     Sits in yon western tent, whose cloudy skirts,
          With brede ethereal wove,
          O'erhang his wavy bed;

¶ *15.1. If aught*] A Spenserian phrase. The rest of the line imitates *Comus* 345:
'Or sound of pastoral reed with oaten stops'.

2. May hope, O pensive *Eve*, to sooth thine Ear *1746*. C. may have made the
alteration in 1748 because of the repetition of 'pensive' in l. 27; and also
because of an echo of Thomas Warton, *Pleasures of Melancholy* (1747) 10–11:
'while murmurs indistinct / Of distant billows soothe thy pensive ear'.
Warton's poem was written in 1745 and C. may well have seen it before
publication.

3–4. Pope, *Eloisa to Abelard* 157–60: 'The wandring streams that shine
between the hills, / The grots that eccho to the tinkling rills, / The dying
gales that pant upon the trees, / The lakes that quiver to the curling breeze';
and Akenside, *Pleasures of Imagination* iii 471–2: 'at eve, / Soft-murm'ring
streams and gales of gentlest breath'.

3. solemn] brawling *1746*. Cp. *As You Like It* II i 32: 'The brook that brawls
along this wood'; and Thomson, *Winter* 69: 'the brawling brook'. B. A.
Wright, *Notes and Queries* cciii (1958) 222, points out that C.'s use of 'springs'
to mean 'brooks' is unusual, although it derives easily enough from the
usual meaning of 'source' of a stream or river.

5. 'bright-hair'd *Vesta*', *Il Penseroso* 23.

5–6. skirts] A common poeticism for the edge of a cloud. Cp. Spenser,
Faerie Queene V ix 28, 4, 6: 'a cloud ... / ... / Whose skirts were bordred
with bright sunny beams'; Milton, *Par. Lost* v 187: 'Till the Sun paint your
fleecie skirts with Gold' and xi 878: 'fluid skirts of that same watrie Cloud'.
Pope parodies the expression, *Dunciad* iii 254 and cp. also Thomson,
Autumn 961 and Akenside, *Pleasures of Imagination* iii 295.

6. Cp. Milton's description of 'still evening', *Par. Lost* iv 596–7, which
includes the sun 'Arraying with reflected Purple and Gold / The Clouds that
on his Western Throne attend'; and 'yon Western Cloud', xi 205.

7. brede] Braid. Cp. *OED*, sb.³ 3: 'Applied by the poets to things that show
or suggest interweaving of colours, or embroidery, *esp.* to the prismatic
colouring of the rainbow.' Akenside, *Pleasures of Imagination* ii 118–19,
describes the 'brede of colours' in the rainbow, perhaps in imitation of
J. Philips, *Cyder* (1708) ii 298–9: 'the watry Brede, with thousand Shews /
Of Painture vary'd'.

8. wavy] Dryden, *Lucretius* i 10, has the 'wavy breast' of the ocean. On this
kind of formation (cp. 'paly', l. 22), see G. Tillotson, *Essays in Criticism and
Research* (1942) pp. 127–9.   *bed*] The image inevitably recalls Milton,

Now air is hushed, save where the weak-eyed bat
10   With short shrill shriek flits by on leathern wing,
          Or where the beetle winds
          His small but sullen horn,
As oft he rises midst the twilight path,
Against the pilgrim borne in heedless hum:
15   Now teach me, maid composed,
          To breathe some softened strain,
Whose numbers stealing through thy darkening vale
May not unseemly with its stillness suit;
          As musing slow, I hail
20   Thy genial loved return!
For when thy folding star arising shows

Nativity Ode 229–31: 'So when the Sun in bed, / Curtain'd with cloudy
red, / Pillows his chin upon an Orient wave . . .'
9. For the 'silence . . . save where' formula, see Gray, *Elegy* 5–8 *n* and 9–12 *n*
(p. 119 above).
9–14. Macbeth III iii 40–3: 'Ere the bat hath flown / His cloistered flight; ere
to black Hecate's summons / The shard-borne beetle with his drowsy hums /
Hath rung night's yawning peal . . .' Cp. also John Gilbert Cooper, *The
Power of Harmony* (Nov. 1745) 43–4: 'the stillness of the grey-ey'd Eve, /
Broke only by the beetle's drowsy hum'; and T. Warton, *Song Imitated from
A Midsummer Night's Dream* 11: 'the beetle's sullen hum' (see 'Lost and
Doubtful Poems' p. 564 below).
10. The 'leathern wing' of the bat is conventional: e.g. 'The lether-winged
Bat', *Faerie Queene* II xii 36, 6; and the bat's 'leathern wings' in Shakespeare,
Midsummer Night's Dream II ii 4; Pope, *Odyssey* xii 514; Gay, *Shepherd's Week*,
'Wednesday' 117; and the single line that survives of C.'s juvenile *Battle
of the School Books* (see p. 559).
11–12. Lycidas 28: 'What time the Gray-fly winds her sultry horn'.
13. 'twilight meadows', Milton, *Comus* 844, and 'twilight groves', *Il
Penseroso* 133.
14. pilgrim] Traveller or wanderer.
16–17. Pope, *Rape of the Lock* ii 49–50: 'While melting Musick steals upon
the Sky, / And soften'd Sounds along the Waters die.'
16. breathe] So used of musical utterance by Milton, *Comus* 245, and *Il
Penseroso* 151.
17. 'the darkening plain', J. Warton, *Ode to Evening* 28.
21. 'the unfolding star', *Measure for Measure* IV ii 218; and 'The Star that
bids the Shepherd fold', Milton, *Comus* 93.
21–2. Milton, *Nativity Ode* 240–2: 'Heav'ns youngest teemed Star, / Hath
fixt her polisht Car, / Her sleeping Lord with Handmaid Lamp attending';
and *Par. Lost* viii 519–20: 'bid haste the Eevning Starr / On his Hill top, to
light the bridal Lamp.'

His paly circlet, at his warning lamp
The fragrant Hours, and elves
Who slept in flowers the day,
25 And many a nymph who wreathes her brows with
sedge,
And sheds the freshening dew, and, lovelier still,
The Pensive Pleasures sweet,
Prepare thy shadowy car.
Then lead, calm vot'ress, where some sheety lake
30 Cheers the lone heath, or some time-hallowed pile,

22. Milton has the 'bright Circlet' of the Morning Star, *Par. Lost* v 169.
23–4. Cp. T. Warton, *Song Imitated from A Midsummer Night's Dream* (see
'Lost and Doubtful Poems', p. 564 below) 2–3: 'Within a cowslip's blos-
som deep, / The lovely Queen of Elves is laid'.
24. *flowers*] Buds *1746*. (C. may have made the change because buds are of
course closed until they become flowers: but the result of the alteration is a
rhyme with 'Hours' in the previous line.)
28. Cp. the 'gilded Car of Day', *Comus* 95, and 'Carr of Night', *Par. Lost*
ix 65. J. H. Hagstrum, *The Sister Arts* (Chicago, 1958) p. 278, compares
Thomson's description of the coming of dawn, represented as the preparation
of Aurora's car, *Summer* 113–29, which he describes as a literal transcription
of Guido's famous fresco *Aurora*, and suggests that C. had a similar pictorial
intention here.
29–32. *1746 has:*

> Then let me rove some wild and heathy Scene,
> Or find some Ruin 'midst its dreary Dells,
>> Whose Walls more awful nod
>> By thy religious Gleams.

C. probably decided to drop 'wild' in the first line because of the repe-
tition in l. 36. Cp. Pope, *Epistle to Jervas* 30: 'Or seek some ruin's formidable
shade'; and Milton, *Il Penseroso* 160: 'a dimm religious light'. The am-
biguous syntax of the substituted lines has aroused some argument. See
Times Lit. Supp. 1928, pp. 188, 221, 243, 272, and Garrod, 1928, pp. 48–50.
In the earliest text, the 'gleams' belonged to Evening herself ('thy religious
Gleams') and on these grounds the emendation of 'its' (l. 32) to 'thy' has
been urged. Other commentators take 'its' to refer to the lake in l. 29, and
a correspondent in the *Times Lit. Supp.* 1930, p. 991, has pointed out that
Keats, imitating these lines in *Endymion* ii 833 ('A sleeping lake, whose cool
and level gleam' etc) had thus interpreted it. But 'its' more probably refers
to Evening's 'car' (l. 28), an interpretation which permits the easiest tran-
sition from the earlier text.
29. Cp. Milton, *Comus* 188–9: 'the gray-hooded Eev'n / Like a sad Votarist
in Palmers weed'.   *sheety*] This is the earliest example recorded in the
OED.

> Or upland fallows grey,
> Reflect its last cool gleam.
> But when chill blustering winds or driving rain
> Forbid my willing feet, be mine the hut
> 35   That from the mountain's side
> Views wilds and swelling floods,
> And hamlets brown, and dim-discovered spires,
> And hears their simple bell, and marks o'er all
> Thy dewy fingers draw
> 40   The gradual dusky veil.
> While Spring shall pour his showers, as oft he wont,

31. 'Fallows Gray' and 'up-land Hamlets', Milton, *L'Allegro* 71, 92.

32. For the 'gleam', cp. the passage from Thomson's *Summer*, cited in ll. 36–40 *n.*

33–4. Cp. Thomson, *Winter* 425–6, 429: 'while without / The ceaseless winds blow ice, be my retreat / . . . / A rural, sheltered, solitary scene.'

33. But when] Or if *1746.*   *blustering winds*] A formula found in Spenser, Fairfax's *Tasso*, and Milton, *Par. Lost* ii 286.

34. Forbid] Prevent *1746.*   Cp. 'with wearied wings, and willing feet', *Par. Lost* iii 73.

35–6. J. Warton, *Ode to Fancy* 22–5: 'Say, in what deep and pathless vale, / Or on what hoary mountain's side, / 'Midst falls of water you reside, / 'Midst broken rocks, a rugged scene.'   *swelling*] Often used by Spenser of the sea or rivers; and cp. 'the swelling flood', Fairfax's *Tasso* XVII lxxi, 1.

36–40. Thomson's descriptions which may have influenced C. include *Spring* 952–6: 'o'er hill and dale, and wood and lawn, / And verdant field, and darkening heath between, / And villages embosomed soft in trees, / And spiry towns by surging columns marked / Of household smoke, your eye excursive roams'; and *Summer* 1684–5, 1687–93: 'Evening yields / The world to Night . . . / While wavering woods, and villages, and streams, / And rocks, and mountain-tops that long retained / The ascending gleam are all one swimming scene, / Uncertain if beheld.'

37. 'up-land Hamlets', Milton, *L'Allegro* 92; and see l. 31 above. Cp. 'dim-discovered', Thomson, *Summer* 946.

39. 'morning's dewy fingers', Akenside, *Pleasures of Imagination* iii 247; and cp. *Ode, Written at the Beginning of 1746* 3 (p. 437).

40. 'The cloudy curtain of refreshing eve', Akenside, *Pleasures of Imagination* ii 504.

41–52. C. appears to have modelled this sequence of the seasons on a passage in J. Warton's *Ode to Fancy* 107–16: 'When young-ey'd Spring profusely throws / From her green lap the pink and rose, / When the soft turtle of the dale / To Summer tells her tender tale, / When Autumn cooling caverns seeks, / And stains with wine his jolly cheeks, / When Winter, like poor pilgrim old, / Shakes his silver beard with cold, / At every season let my ear / Thy solemn whispers, Fancy, hear.'

And bathe thy breathing tresses, meekest Eve!
While Summer loves to sport
Beneath thy lingering light;
45 While sallow Autumn fills thy lap with leaves,
Or Winter, yelling through the troublous air,
Affrights thy shrinking train,
And rudely rends thy robes;
So long, sure-found beneath the sylvan shed,
50 Shall Fancy, Friendship, Science, rose-lipped Health,
Thy gentlest influence own,
And hymn thy favourite name!

42. *breathing*] Emitting fragrance.
46-9. C. uses a number of characteristically Spenserian words in these lines: troublous (= stormy), yelling, affrights, regardful.
48. *Faerie Queene* II i 11, 5: 'Her looser golden lockes he rudely rent'; and IV i 21, 4: 'rent robes'.
49. *sure-found . . . shed*] regardful of thy quiet Rule *1746*. Cp. 'the Silvan Lodge', *Par. Lost* v 376.
50. *rose-lipped Health*] smiling *Peace 1746*. (C. may have thought that Peace was not an appropriate characteristic of Evening after his description of Winter.) Cp. 'rose-lipp'd cherubim', *Othello* IV ii 63; and 'Joy, rose-lipt Dryad', T. Warton Senior, 'Retirement: An Ode', in *Poems* (1748) p. 13.
52. *hymn*] love *1746*.

16 Ode to Peace

The most likely date of composition is between June 1746 and the following Dec. when C.'s *Odes* were published. The poem desires rather than celebrates peace and, as the last stanza makes clear, it desires peace with honour. Such a wish would not have been appropriate to the Young Pretender's invasion, so the poem probably refers to the war with France. British troops, recalled from Flanders to deal with the rebellion in Aug. 1745, returned there in June 1746 and it is reasonable to assume that the poem was written in a mood that combined optimism after Culloden with weariness over the war on the Continent. The mood was not simply a private one. By mid-Aug. 1746 the newspapers were reporting that peace talks between the powers involved in the War of the Austrian Succession were to be held at Breda (e.g. *General Evening Post*, 14–16 Aug. 1746) and it was not until the late autumn that the abortive negotiations were abandoned. See *Gentleman's Mag.* xvi (Sept., Oct. and Nov. 1746) 499, 559, 615. A similar desire for Peace or Concord is expressed in the *Ode to Liberty*, which appears on other grounds to have been written in Sept. or Oct. 1746 (see headnote).

O thou, who bad'st thy turtles bear
Swift from his grasp thy golden hair,
    And sought'st thy native skies:
When War, by vultures drawn from far,
5   To Britain bent his iron car,
    And bade his storms arise!

2

Tired of his rude tyrannic sway,
Our youth shall fix some festive day,
    His sullen shrines to burn:
10 But thou who hear'st the turning spheres,
What sounds may charm thy partial ears,
    And gain thy blest return!

3

O Peace, thy injured robes upbind,
O rise, and leave not one behind
15   Of all thy beamy train:
The British lion, goddess sweet,
Lies stretched on earth to kiss thy feet,
    And own thy holier reign.

¶ 16.*1–6.* Cp. the myth of Astraea, the Goddess of Justice, who lived among
men on earth in the Golden Age, but withdrew to the sky, because of the
wickedness of later ages (Ovid, *Metamorphoses* i 150). C.'s first two stanzas
echo Milton's description of 'meek-eyd Peace', 'softly sliding / Down
through the turning sphear / . . . / With Turtle wing the amorous clouds
dividing', in *Nativity Ode* 45–50.
4–5. Dryden, *Palamon and Arcite* i 109–10: 'the God of War / Was drawn
triumphant on his Iron Carr'; and Thomson, *Nuptial Song Intended for
Sophonisba* 27–8: 'the furious god of war / Has crushed us with his iron car'.
10. turning spheres] See the lines from Milton's *Nativity Ode*, cited in ll. 1–6 *n.*
C. refers to the music of the spheres, which could be detected only by the
pure.
11. Cp. *Par. Lost* i 787: 'with jocond Music charm his ear'; and Pope, *Eloisa
to Abelard* 126: 'With other beauties charm my partial eyes'.
13. Spenser uses 'upbind' and 'upbound' several times.
15. beamy] Shining, radiant.
16–18. C. may be deliberately alluding to the similar behaviour of the 'British
lion' in *Faerie Queene* I iii 6, 1–3, which begins by threatening Una, but
'In stead thereof he kist her wearie feet, / And lickt her lilly hands with
fawning tong, / As he her wronged innocence did weet.'

4

Let others court thy transient smile,
20   But come to grace thy western isle,
      By warlike Honour led!
And, while around her ports rejoice,
While all her sons adore thy choice,
      With him for ever wed!

17 The Manners. An Ode

Completed not earlier than 1745, as is clear from C.'s reference to Le Sage's death in ll. 67–70 and his note stating that Le Sage had died in 1745. The French writer did not in fact die until 1747 but C. had obviously heard a mistaken rumour of it (see l. 67 *n*) and there is no need to doubt his own statement that this had been in 1745. C. chose to characterize Le Sage by the rather untypical story of Blanche introduced into his *Gil Blas* (see ll. 69–70 *n*), a fact which may help further with the dating, since the story could have been brought to C.'s attention by James Thomson's use of it as the basis of his tragedy *Tancred and Sigismunda*, first produced on 18 March 1745.

    Such a date of composition, based on the allusion to Le Sage, is later than the traditional one, first suggested by Langhorne, *1765* p. 174: 'From the subject and sentiments of this ode, it seems not improbable that the author wrote it about the time when he left the University; when weary with the pursuit of academical studies, he no longer confined himself to the search of theoretical knowledge, but commenced the *scholar of humanity*, to study nature in her works, and man in society.' If the poem is interpreted as a literal farewell to academic studies, as has often been the case, then it would have to be dated in the first few months of 1744, and the lines on Le Sage considered a later interpolation. C. had probably left Oxford for London by the time the 2nd edn of his *Epistle to Hanmer* (see headnote) had appeared in May and he was certainly there by July 1744. John Mulso, *Letters to Gilbert White*, ed. R. Holt White, p. 3, wrote on 18 July 1744, 'I saw Collins in Town, he is entirely an Author, & hardly speaks out of Rule.' A variety of reasons have been given for his leaving Oxford, including his disappointment over failing to obtain a Fellowship, increasing debts, a quarrel with his cousin, Dr Payne of Magdalen, and the death of his mother on 6 July 1744: cp. *The Gleaner*, ed. Nathan Drake (1811) iv 481 and *Gentleman's Mag.* xciii (1823), Pt ii 334. Potentially more relevant to the content of this poem may be Gilbert White's account of C. at Oxford, *Gentleman's Mag.* li (1781) 11: 'As he brought with him, for so the whole turn of his conversation discovered, too high an opinion of his school acquisitions, and a sovereign contempt for all academic studies and discipline, he never looked with any complacency on his situation in the University, but was always complaining of the dulness of a college life.'

There is nothing in the poem itself, however, that demands so literal a reading nor is it necessary to tie it to any specific occasion in C.'s life. He is abandoning primarily a kind of philosophical study, which did not have to be literally academic in character, and turning to the world of reality and to the empirical study of humanity, only too aware, however, that he will be lured soon enough into 'Art's enchanted school'. But Art, unlike the philosophy he has abandoned, does reflect nature and describe human manners. C. uses the term 'manners' in this poem in explicit connection with literature, in the sense, often used by literary critics, of the portraiture of character, disposition and temperament (perhaps deriving from Aristotle's ἦθος in the *Poetics*). Cp. Dryden, 'The Grounds of Criticism in Tragedy', in *Of Dramatic Poesy and Other Critical Essays*, ed. George Watson (1962) i 248–53, a long discussion beginning: 'The manners in a poem are understood to be those inclinations, whether natural or acquired, which move and carry us to actions, good, bad, or indifferent, in a play; or which incline the persons to such or such actions. . . . The manners arise from many causes; and are either distinguished by complexion, as choleric and phlegmatic, or by the differences of age or sex, of climates, or quality of the persons, or their present condition: they are likewise to be gathered from the several virtues, vices, or passions'.

Later, in his 'Preface to Fables Ancient and Modern' (Watson, ii 278), Dryden defines the manners as 'the passions and, in a larger sense, the descriptions of persons, and their very habits.' C. had a precedent for a contrast of philosophy and manners in Shaftesbury, *Characteristicks* (5th edn, 1732) i 286–7, who writes of '*Philosophy* in some famous Schools' that: 'There can be nothing more ridiculous than to expect that *Manners* or *Understanding* shou'd sprout from such a Stock. It pretends indeed some relation to *Manners*, as being definitive of the Natures, Essences, and Propertys of Spirits; and some relation to *Reason*, as describing the Shapes and Forms of certain Instruments imploy'd in the reasoning Art. But had the craftiest of Men, for many Ages together, been imploy'd in finding out a method to confound *Reason*, and degrade the *Understanding* of Mankind; they cou'd not perhaps have succeeded better, than by the Establishment of such a *Mock-Science*.'

> Farewell, for clearer ken designed,
> The dim-discovered tracts of mind:
> Truths which, from action's paths retired,
> My silent search in vain required!

¶ 17.1. Cp. *Par. Lost* xi 379–80: 'The Hemisphere of Earth in cleerest Ken / Stretcht out'.
2. *dim-discovered*] Cp. *Evening* 37 *n* (p. 466).

5 No more my sail that deep explores,
   No more I search those magic shores,
   What regions part the world of soul,
   Or whence thy streams, Opinion, roll:
   If e'er I round such fairy field,
10 Some power impart the spear and shield
   At which the wizard Passions fly,
   By which the giant Follies die!
   Farewell the porch, whose roof is seen
   Arched with the enlivening olive's green:
15 Where Science, pranked in tissued vest,
   By Reason, Pride, and Fancy dressed,

5-6. C. probably alludes to Pope, *Essay on Criticism* 643-6, on Aristotle:
'Such once were *Criticks*, such the Happy *Few*, / *Athens* and *Rome* in better
Ages knew. / The mighty *Stagyrite* first left the Shore, / Spread all his Sails,
and durst the Deeps explore.'

7. *part*] Presumably a verb, meaning to separate (from the material world).
C. may be remembering *Il Penseroso* 88-92: 'unsphear / The spirit of *Plato*
to unfold / What Worlds, or what vast Regions hold / The immortal mind
that hath forsook / Her mansion in this fleshly nook . . .'

9. *round*] Travel round, make a complete circuit of. Cp. 'the low Sun / . . .
Had rounded still th' *Horizon*', *Par. Lost* x 682-4.

10-12. Blunden (1929) p. 174, comments: 'Collins amusingly compares
himself among the philosophers to the heroes of the chap-books, Thomas
Thumb the Great, Sir Thomas Hickathrift, Knight, and above all, Jack the
Giant-Killer'. But it is unlikely that C. is being so self-derisive: the phrase
'Spear and Shield' is a Spenserian formula used of the function and power of
knighthood e.g. *Faerie Queene* II viii 14, 6; III ii 6, 4; III iii 31, 8; III iv 1, 4, etc.
C. could have in mind more specifically Britomart's magic spear and Prince
Arthur's magic shield: cp., concerning the former, *Faerie Queene* III iii 60,
8-9: 'Both speare she tooke, and shield, which hong by it: / Both speare
and shield of great powre, for her purpose fit.'

13-18. *the porch*] 'A public ambulatory in the agora of ancient Athens, to
which Zeno the philosopher and his disciples resorted; hence the Stoic school
of philosophy' (*OED*). The term was often used more loosely. Cp. Akenside,
Pleasures of Imagination ii 738-40: 'the muse's haunt, / The marble porch
where wisdom wont to talk / With Socrates or Tully'. C.'s reference to
Plato in l. 18 suggests that he had Greek philosophy in general in mind.

13-14. Milton has the 'arched roof', *Nativity Ode* 175; *Par. Lost* i 726;
Samson 1634. Cp. also *Faerie Queene* II xii 54, 1-2: 'So fashioned a Porch with
rare deuice, / Archt ouer head with an embracing vine . . .'

Comes like a bride so trim arrayed,
To wed with Doubt in Plato's shade!
   Youth of the quick uncheated sight,
20 Thy walks, Observance, more invite!
O thou, who lov'st that ampler range,
Where life's wide prospects round thee change,
And with her mingling sons allied,
Throw'st the prattling page aside:
25 To me in converse sweet impart
To read in man the native heart,
To learn, where science sure is found,
From Nature as she lives around:
And gazing oft her mirror true,
30 By turns each shifting image view!
Till meddling Art's officious lore
Reverse the lessons taught before,
Alluring from a safer rule
To dream in her enchanted school;
35 Thou Heaven, whate'er of great we boast,

14, 18. The olive was sacred to Athena, the patron deity of Athens. Cp. *Par. Regained* iv 244–5: 'See there the Olive Grove of *Academe*, / *Plato*'s retirement'; and Akenside, *Odes* (1745) p. 12: 'Plato's godlike tongue / Resounding thro' the olive shade'.

15–16. Cp. *Comus* 759: 'false rules pranckt in reasons garb'.   *tissued*] Originally, 'woven with gold and silver thread'. Tissue was at first used of rich cloth of this sort and only later of cloth of a delicate or gauzy texture. *Science*] Knowledge in general.

17. 'in trim aray', Spenser, *Faerie Queene* III xii 6, 9; *Prothalamion* 85.

20. Observance] Observation.

21. Par. Lost xi 380: 'Stretcht out to amplest reach of prospect'; and Pope, *Essay on Man* i 207: 'Far as Creation's ample range extends'.

23. mingling] mingled *1765*.

25. 'sweet Converse', *Par. Lost* ix 909.

26–30. Pope, *Essay on Man* iv 391–3: 'That urg'd by thee, I turn'd the tuneful art / From sounds to things, from fancy to the heart; / For Wit's false mirror held up Nature's light'.

33. Alluring from] Alluring him from *1746, corrected in errata.   Alluring from*] i.e. away from the safer instruction of 'nature as she lives around' to the understanding of human manners through art, by the agency of Fancy.

35–6. H. W. Garrod (1928) p. 47, urged the emendation of 'Thou' and 'Hast' at the beginning of these lines, to 'Tho'' and 'Has' (adopted in the Oxford text, 3rd edn (1937)) on the grounds that these lines contain

Hast blest this social science most.
  Retiring hence to thoughtful cell,
  As Fancy breathes her potent spell,
  Not vain she finds the charmful task;
40 In pageant quaint, in motley mask,
  Behold before her musing eyes
  The countless Manners round her rise;
  While ever varying as they pass,
  To some Contempt applies her glass:
45 With these the white-robed Maids combine,
  And those the laughing Satyrs join!
  But who is he whom now she views,
  In robe of wild contending hues?

a qualification of the earlier account of Art which needs clarifying. But
C.'s criticism of Art in l. 31 (meddling, officious) can be read as affec-
tionate and the emendation is unnecessary. Cp. *The Passions* 104.

37–58. C. seems to have in mind Thomson, *Winter* 609–16: 'But when
with these the serious thought is foiled, / We, shifting for relief, would play
the shapes / Of frolic fancy; and incessant form / Those rapid pictures, that
assembled train / Of fleet ideas, never joined before, / Whence lively wit
excites to gay surprise, / Or folly-painting humour, grave himself, / Calls
laughter forth, deep-shaking every nerve.'

37–9. she] Apparently 'Art' of l. 31, i.e. the artistic or creative imagination.
C. echoes *Par. Lost* v 108–11, where Reason 'then retires / Into her private
Cell when Nature rests. / Oft in her absence mimic Fansie wakes / To imitate
her . . .'; and viii 460–1: 'the Cell / Of Fancie'.   *breathes . . . spell*] Cp.
Milton, *Nativity Ode* 179–80: 'or breathed spell, / Inspire's the pale-ey'd
Priest from the prophetic cell'.

39. charmful] Delightful, but retaining also something of the original magical
connotations of 'charm'.

40–1. Milton, *L'Allegro* 128–30: 'With mask, and antique Pageantry, /
Such sights as youthfull Poets dream / On Summer eeves by haunted stream.'

42. Pope, *Essay on Man* i 13–14: 'Eye Nature's walks, shoot Folly as it flies, /
And catch the Manners living as they rise'; Pope's image of sportsmen en-
tangling birds in a net is hardly present in C.'s imitation.

44. 'Kind Self-conceit to some her glass applies', Pope, *Dunciad* iv 533.

45–6. C. appears to imitate Parnell, *To Mr. Pope* 27–8, characterizing Pope's
poetry: 'The Graces stand in sight; a Satyr train / Peep o'er their heads, and
laugh behind the scene.' C.'s 'white-robed Maids' are probably also the
Graces. Cp. 'white-robed Truth', Milton, *On the Death of a Fair Infant* 54;
and 'white-roab'd Innocence', Pope, *Messiah* 20.

47–8. Pope, *Dunciad* i 81–2: 'She, tinsel'd o'er in robes of varying hues, /
With self-applause her wild creation views.'

Thou by the Passions nursed, I greet
50   The comic sock that binds thy feet!
O Humour, thou whose name is known
To Britain's favoured isle alone:
Me too amidst thy band admit,
There where the young-eyed healthful Wit,
55   (Whose jewels in his crispèd hair

49. Thou] Garrod (1928) p. 47, suggested an emendation to 'Tho'' (adopted in the Oxford edn) on the grounds that 'It is not the Comedy of Humours, but Collins himself, who has been nursed by the Passions.' But there was no absurdity in C.'s description of Humour as nursed by the Passions. He does not mean that Humour expresses, or is the product of, powerful emotions, but that Humour (still combining something of the older sense of a person's temperament with the later comic sense) involves an understanding of individual human 'passions' or 'humours' (and is in this way distinct from 'wit'). Cp. Dryden, *Of Dramatic Poesy*, ed. G. Watson, i 73: 'Among the English ... by humour is meant some extravagant habit, passion, or affection, particular ... to some one person, by the oddness of which he is immediately distinguished from the rest of men; which being lively and naturally represented, most frequently begets that malicious pleasure in the audience which is testified by laughter.' Earlier, i 56, Dryden had said that 'the soul of poesy ... is imitation of humour and passions'.

50. The comic sock] A light shoe worn by comic actors on the ancient Greek and Roman stage and hence, as opposed to the tragic buskin, symbolic of comedy: cp. '*Jonsons* learned Sock', *L'Allegro* 132.

51-2. Some of C.'s editors have objected to this assertion, which was, however, a commonplace in the eighteenth century. Sir William Temple, 'Of Poetry' (1690), in *Critical Essays of the 17th Century*, ed. J. E. Spingarn, iii 103, refers to 'a Vein Natural perhaps to our Country, and which with us is called Humour, a Word peculiar to our Language too, and hard to be expressed in any other', and goes on to discuss the reasons for this circumstance. Congreve, 'Concerning Humour in Comedy' (1696), (Spingarn, iii 252) similarly says, 'I look upon Humour to be almost of English Growth; at least, it does not seem to have found such Encrease on any other Soil'. Cp. also Spingarn's Introduction, i lx–lxii, for further discussion of this belief. Johnson questioned it in *Adventurer* No. 84 (25 Aug. 1753) and it appears as one of Dick Minim's critical clichés in *Idler* No. 60 (9 June 1759).

53. Milton, *L'Allegro* 38: 'Mirth, admit me of thy crue'.

54. 'young-eyed cherubins', *Merchant of Venice* V i 62.

55. crispèd] Curling. Cp. *Faerie Queene* II iii 30, 1: 'Her yellow lockes crisped, like a golden wyre'; and Fairfax's *Tasso* I xliii 1: 'crisped Locks and fair'.

55-6. It seems likely that C. was aware of a recent and fairly elaborate work on the subject he is treating here, Corbyn Morris's *Essay towards Fixing the True Standards of Wit, Humour, Raillery, Satire, and Ridicule* (1744). Morris,

Are placed each other's beams to share,
Whom no delights from thee divide)
In laughter loosed attends thy side!
   By old Miletus who so long
60 Has ceased his love-inwoven song;
By all you taught the Tuscan maids,
In changed Italia's modern shades;
By him, whose Knight's distinguished name
Refined a nation's lust of fame,
65 Whose tales even now, with echoes sweet,

p. 23, repeats the familiar belief that humour is peculiarly an English pos-
session. He attempts throughout his essay to differentiate Wit and Humour,
describing the former in terms of light reminiscent of C.'s imagery here.
Morris, p. 2, refers to 'the high *Brilliancy*, and *Sparkling* of WIT'; and, p. 11,
asserts that the highest wit results from the sudden and direct realization of
the relationship of two objects: 'It is then adorn'd with the Charms of
Propriety, *Clearness* and *Illustration*; It dispels the Darkness around an Object,
and presents it distinctly and perfectly to our View; chearing us with its
Lustre, and at the same time informing us with its *Light*.' See also ll. 63–6 and
n below.

58. In laughter loosed] C. probably alludes to Virgil, *Georgics* ii 386: *risuque
soluto*. Cp. *L'Allegro* 32: 'And Laughter holding both his sides'.

59–60. Miletus] Alluding to the *Milesian* Tales, some of the earliest Romances.
C.

    C. evidently confuses the author of these tales with the city where he
lived. The lost Milesian Tales were written by Aristides of Miletus (a writer
of the 2nd century B.C.) and are assumed to have been short stories of love
and adventure. C. probably read about them in Temple's 'Of Poetry',
Spingarn, iii 90: 'The next Succession of Poetry in Prose seems to have
been in the *Miletian* Tales, which were a sort of little Pastoral Romances;
and though much in request in old *Greece* and *Rome*, yet we have no Ex-
amples that I know of them'.

60. love-inwoven] Cp. 'flowre-inwov'n tresses', Milton, *Nativity Ode* 187.

61–2. C. presumably refers to Giovanni Boccaccio (1313–75), who lived in
Florence for much of his life.

63–6. him] Cervantes. C.

    Miguel de Cervantes (1547–1616) wrote the first part of *Don Quixote*
(1605) at Villadolid in Castile. The Moors had conquered Spain in the
Middle Ages. There is some discussion of the humour of *Don Quixote* in
Corbyn Morris's *Essay* (1744) pp. 38–41. See ll. 55–6 and *n* above.

64. C. evidently accepted the common early 18th-century view that *Don
Quixote* was written to attack the abuses of chivalry and false honour: e.g.
Charles Jarvis's translation (1742), I vii, xxii–xxiii.

65. Milton, *Comus* 230: 'Sweet Echo, sweetest nymph'; and 'Sweet Echo',
Pope, *Winter* 41.

     Castilia's Moorish hills repeat;
     Or him, whom Seine's blue nymphs deplore,
     In watchet weeds on Gallia's shore,
     Who drew the sad Sicilian maid,
70   By virtues in her sire betrayed:
     O Nature boon, from whom proceed

67. *him*] Monsieur *Le Sage*, Author of the incomparable Adventures of *Gil Blas de Santillane*, who died in *Paris* in the Year 1745. *C.*

Alain René Le Sage (1667–1747) died two years later than C. states, at Boulogne not Paris. No source for C.'s error has been discovered but Le Sage's total retirement from society and his removal from Paris to Boulogne in the last years of his life make the mistake understandable. It is possible that in some report which reached C. his death was confused with that of his son, René André Le Sage, an actor, who died in 1743.

68. *watchet*] Light blue. The use of 'blue' in the previous line suggests that C. did not know the word's meaning but was merely imitating Spenser, *Faerie Queene* III iv 40, 5: 'watchet mantles'; IV xi 27, 2: 'a robe of watchet hew'; *Elegie for Astrophel* 3: 'The skie like glasse of watchet hew'; or Drayton, *Poly-Olbion* v 13: 'a watchet weed'.

69–70. C. refers to Le Sage's *Gil Blas* (1715–35) IV iv, a story interpolated into the main narrative. Blanche ('the sad Sicilian maid'), in love with the King of Sicily, was forced to marry another man through her father's mistaken sense of duty (cp. l. 70). Her jealous husband, mortally wounded by the King, stabbed her as she held him in her arms. Mrs Barbauld, 1797, p. xxxvi, objected: 'LE SAGE should not have been characterized by the story of *Blanche*, which, though beautiful, is not in his peculiar stile of excellence, and has more to do with the high passions than with *Manners*.' C.'s reference to Blanche's story may be explained by the fact that it had twice been exploited recently by other writers: by James Thomson, who took the story as the basis of his tragedy *Tancred and Sigismunda*, first performed on 18 March 1745, *Gentleman's Mag.* xv 168; and by an anonymous writer, whose *Henry and Blanche: Or, The Revengeful Marriage*, is dated 1745, but is included in the new books of Feb. 1746 in the *Gentleman's Mag.* xvi 112.

71–4. C. appears to have in mind a passage in Akenside, *Pleasures of Imagination* iii 358–68: 'For not th' expanse / Of living lakes in summer's noontide calm, / Reflects the bord'ring shade and sun-bright heav'ns / With fairer semblance; not the sculptur'd gold / More faithful keeps the graver's lively trace, / Than he whose birth the sister-pow'rs of art / Propitious view'd, and from his genial star / Shed influence to the seeds of fancy kind; / Than his attemper'd bosom must preserve / The seal of nature. There alone unchang'd, / Her form remains.'

71. *boon*] Bounteous, benign. Cp. 'Nature boon', *Par. Lost* iv 242; 'boon nature', Philips, *Cyder* (1708) ii 442; and Thomson, *Liberty* ii 98: 'All that boon nature could luxuriant pour'.

> Each forceful thought, each prompted deed;
> If but from thee I hope to feel,
> On all my heart imprint thy seal!
> 75 Let some retreating Cynic find
> Those oft-turned scrolls I leave behind:
> The Sports and I this hour agree
> To rove thy scene-full world with thee!

75. *retreating*] Retiring from the world. C. refers to the Cynic school of philosophers, founded by Antisthenes, a pupil of Socrates, characterized by contempt for ease, wealth and enjoyment. Its most famous and ascetic representative at a later date was Diogenes.
76. *scrolls*] The philosophy dismissed in ll. 1–18.
77–8. Cp. the lines from *L'Allegro* 31–2, 35–40, which have been in C.'s mind throughout the poem: 'Sport that wrincled Care derides, / And Laughter holding both his sides / . . . / And in thy right hand lead with thee, / The Mountain Nymph, sweet Liberty; / And if I give thee honour due, / Mirth, admite me of thy crue / To live with her, and live with thee, / In unreproved pleasures free.'
78. *scene-full*] This is the only example of the word given in *OED*.

18 The Passions. An Ode for Music

There is no evidence for dating this poem, apart from a possible debt (see l. 86 *n*) to Akenside's *Pleasures of Imagination* (Jan. 1744), but there is no internal reason for supposing that it was written earlier than the other odes in *1746*, i.e. before 1745.

As C.'s title suggests, the poem was written with a musical setting in mind. It was in fact eventually performed to a setting by William Hayes (1705–77), Professor of Music in the University, at Oxford on 2 July 1750. The occasion was Encaenia, the commemoration of the benefactors of the University. A detailed account of this 'solemnity' in the *Gentleman's Mag.* xx (July 1750) 328, describes the procession to the Sheldonian Theatre and mentions that, after an oration, the ceremony was concluded with 'an ode set for music'; see *London Mag.* xix (1750) 330, for a similar account. Thomas Warton may have been connected with the choice of C.'s *Ode* for this occasion. By his own account, he saw C. frequently in 1750 (*The Reaper*, reprinted in *The Gleaner* (1811) iv 475), and his own *Ode for Music*, again set by Hayes, was performed at Encaenia in the following year. Hayes's vocal and instrumental score for C.'s ode is now in the Bodleian Library, Oxford (MS. Mus. d. 120–1). Of this setting William Seward, *Supplement to the Anecdotes of Some Distinguished Persons* (1797) p. 123, wrote: 'The music . . . was excellently well adapted to the words. The chorusses were very full and majestic, and the airs gave completely the spirit of the Passions which they were intended to imitate.' Seward then printed a letter from C. to Dr Hayes, dated 8 Nov. 1750, which began: 'Mr. Blackstone, of Winchester, some time since informed me of the honour you had done me at Oxford last summer; for which I return you my sincere thanks. I have another more perfect copy of the Ode; which, had I known of your obliging design, I would have communicated to you. Inform me by a line, if you should think one of my better judgement acceptable.' C. then went on to mention that he could also send Hayes another ode, on 'the Music of the Grecian Theatre' (see p. 554 below); and he asked for a copy of Hayes's setting of *The Passions*.

C.'s gratitude may have been tempered somewhat when he eventually saw the score, since his original ending had been altered for the purposes of the setting. His own text was interrupted at l. 93 and was followed by 21 ll. added by the Earl of Litchfield, Chancellor of the University. See H. O. White, 'The Letters of William Collins', *Review of English Studies* iii (1927) 16. This text was printed in a small quarto pamphlet of 10 pages, entitled *The Passions, An Ode. Written by Mr. Collins. Set to Musick by Dr. Hayes. Performed At the Theatre in Oxford, July 2, 1750.* (It contains one variant, 'different' for 'differing' in l. 55.) There is an 8-page issue of the pamphlet in the British Museum with different variants, although there is no reason to suppose that they have any authority ('round' for 'around', l. 4; 'Bublings, runnels' for 'Bubbling runnels', l. 63; 'lik'd' for 'loved', l. 84). (I am grateful to Mr Michael Gearin-Tosh for drawing my attention to this pamphlet and for making available to me his detailed collations of these separate edns of *The Passions*.) The pamphlet was reprinted at Winchester in the 8-page format, presumably for another undated performance organized by C.'s friends (apart from obvious misprints, this text has the following variants: 'different' for 'differing', l. 55; 'sprightliest' for 'sprightlier', l.69; 'Satyrs' for 'Satyrs and', l. 76; 'shade' for 'shades', l. 87). A further edn of the pamphlet was published at Gloucester in 1760, as a result of another performance of Hayes's setting there; see Daniel Lysons, *History of the Origin and Progress of the Meeting of the Three Choirs of Gloucester, Worcester and Hereford* (Gloucester, 1812) p. 190, and A. D. McKillop, *Times Lit. Supp.* 1936, p. 204.

C., who was 'passionately fond of music', according to Gilbert White, *Gentleman's Mag.* li (1781) 11, would have been pleased by the fact that there were at least two other musical compositions inspired by his poem before the end of the century. Benjamin Cooke (1734–93) wrote a more ambitious setting than Hayes's in 1784; and James Sanderson (1769–1841) composed a set of instrumental interludes for *The Passions* in 1789. The poem enjoyed another kind of popularity: a writer in the *Gentleman's Mag.* lii (1782) 22, refers to the 'frequent public recitals' of the poem as 'a mark of its universally acknowledged excellence'. Dickens's account of Mr Wopsle's rendering of the poem (*Great Expectations*, ch. vii) is well known; Mr J. C. Maxwell has also drawn my attention to references to its currency in early nineteenth-century America in Van Wyck Brooks, *The World of Washington*

Irving (London, 1945) pp. 63, 116, and to an allusion at the beginning of ch. x of James Fenimore Cooper's *The Water Witch* (1830).

In a note to his edn of Milton's *Poems on Several Occasions* (1785) 369 *n*, Thomas Warton asserted that a poem by his brother Joseph, 'entitled the ASSEMBLY OF THE PASSIONS' was written 'before Collins's favourite Ode on that subject.' J. S. Cunningham, *Durham University Journal* xlvi (1953) 22–4, has shown from the Warton MSS that Joseph's plan for writing his *Assembly of the Passions* was dated 1740. John Wooll, in his *Memoirs of Joseph Warton* (1806) pp. 10–13, quotes a 'sketch, laid out by him as a subject for verse', which Joseph wrote at the age of 18, which may well be the work described by Thomas Warton as a poem and which begins: 'The Subjects of Reason having lately rebelled against him, he summons them to his court, that they may pay their obedience to him; whilst he sits on his throne, attended by the Virtues, his handmaids.' The Passions which appear are Fear, Superstition, Anger, Cruelty, Revenge, Joy, Mirth, Pleasure, Sorrow, Courage, Cowardice, Emulation, Fame, Hope, Pity, Despair, Love, Friendship, Truth, Jealousy, Hatred, Doubt, Honour, Ambition, Esteem, Flattery, Envy, Contempt, Justice and Temperance. These pictorial descriptions of the passions may have influenced C. in minor ways. Wooll comments: 'When the intimacy between Collins and Warton is recollected, it is no improbable surmise that the above sketch furnished the former with the idea of writing an Ode on the Passions.'

Blunden mentions 'An Enquiry into the Nature of the Passions, and the Manner in which they are represented by the Tragick Poets', in *The Museum* (29 Aug. 1747) iii 437–42, and suggests that it may be by C.; but the essay is largely devoted to a discussion of *Othello*, and has nothing in common with C.'s poem. Such discussions of the passions were in fact frequent at this period and it must also be remembered that C. was writing in a recognized genre, the purpose of which was to exploit the passions. The title of C.'s poem explicitly relates it to the musical ode, in which the poet was expected to provide a 'scenario' to demonstrate the imitative powers of music and, in particular, its power to arouse and soothe the passions. (Cp. Dryden, *Song for St Cecilia's Day* 16: 'What Passion cannot MUSICK raise and quell!'). The genre was most powerfully represented by the odes written to celebrate St Cecilia's Day, with which C.'s poem associates itself in its closing lines. In such poems, various passions were described and contrasted, the prime example being Dryden's *Alexander's Feast*, which influenced C. structurally and verbally, although he elaborates on Dryden's portrayal of five passions linked by the narrative of Timotheus and his lyre. Another feature of the genre which obviously influenced C. was the attempted rhythmic imitation of the passion described, which the licensed irregularity of the form permitted. See James Hutton, 'Some English Poems in Praise of Music', *English Miscellany* ii (1951) 1–63, on the 'effects' of music in ancient and Renaissance theory; Brewster Rogerson, 'The Art of Painting the Passions', *Journal of the History of Ideas* xiv (1953) 68–94; and Robert M. Myers, 'Neo-Classical Criticism of the Ode for Music', *PMLA* lxii (1947) 399–421.

When Music, heavenly maid, was young,
While yet in early Greece she sung,
The Passions oft to hear her shell
Thronged around her magic cell,
5   Exulting, trembling, raging, fainting,
Possessed beyond the muse's painting;
By turns they felt the glowing mind,
Disturbed, delighted, raised, refined.
Till once, 'tis said, when all were fired,
10 Filled with fury, rapt, inspired,
From the supporting myrtles round
They snatched her instruments of sound,
And as they oft had heard apart
Sweet lessons of her forceful art,
15 Each, for madness ruled the hour,
Would prove his own expressive power.

First Fear his hand, its skill to try,
    Amid the chords bewildered laid,
And back recoiled, he knew not why,
20   Even at the sound himself had made.

Next Anger rushed, his eyes on fire,

¶ 18.*1–6*. C.'s starting-point was probably Dryden, *Song for St Cecilia's Day* 16–20: 'What Passion cannot MUSICK raise and quell! / When *Jubal* struck the corded Shell, / His list'ning Brethren stood around / And wond'ring, on their Faces fell / To worship that Celestial Sound.'

3. Cp. *Pity* 42 *n* (p. 418).

5. Pope, *Dying Christian to his Soul* 3: 'Trembling, hoping, ling'ring, flying'.

9–10. Pope, *Eloisa to Abelard* 201–2: 'But let heav'n seize it, all at once 'tis fir'd, / Not touch'd, but rapt, not waken'd, but inspir'd!'

13. apart] Separately. (The spelling in *1746* is 'a-part').

16. expressive power] The power of manifesting or representing qualities or feelings.

17–20. The idea of Fear or Dread being terrified at itself or its own activities can be traced back in English at least to Sackville's Induction to *A Mirror for Magistrates* 232–8; and cp. the opening lines of a sonnet by Sir Philip Sidney, *Poems*, ed. W. A. Ringler (Oxford, 1962) p. 145: 'A Satyre once did runne away for dread, / With sound of horne, which he himselfe did blow, / Fearing and feared thus from himselfe he fled, / Deeming strange evill in that he did not know.'

21–2. The eyes of Spenser's Wrath, *Faerie Queene* I iv 33, 5, 'did hurle forth sparkles fiery red'; and cp. also his description of Furor, II iv 15, 5–6: 'His burning eyen, whom bloudie strakes did staine, / Stared full wide, and threw forth sparkes of fire.'

In lightnings owned his secret stings,
In one rude clash he struck the lyre,
And swept with hurried hand the strings.

25   With woeful measures wan Despair
     Low sullen sounds his grief beguiled,
  A solemn, strange and mingled air,
     'Twas sad by fits, by starts 'twas wild.

  But thou, O Hope, with eyes so fair,
30   What was thy delightful measure?
  Still it whispered promised pleasure,
     And bade the lovely scenes at distance hail!
  Still would her touch the strain prolong,
     And from the rocks, the woods, the vale,
35   She called on Echo still through all the song;
     And, where her sweetest theme she chose,
  A soft responsive voice was heard at every close,
And Hope enchanted smiled, and waved her golden hair.

  And longer had she sung—but with a frown,
40   Revenge impatient rose;

22. Pope refers to the 'Lightnings' of the eyes in *Rape of the Lock* i 144, iii 155, v 76, perhaps in imitation of Cowley, *Davideis* Bk. i, as suggested by Tillotson. But the figure appears in Spenser, *Faerie Queene* V v 30, 3, Fairfax's *Tasso* III xxii 1, and Milton, *Par. Lost* vi 849. Cp. 'secret sting', *Faerie Queene* III viii 25, 2; *Samson Agonistes* 1007; Dryden, *Lucretius Bk. III* 53, and *Sigismunda and Guiscardo* 36.

24. 'loudly sweep the string', *Lycidas* 17.

26. *Faerie Queene* I v 17, 7–8: 'sweet musicke . . . / Him to beguile of griefe and agony'. Bronson pointed out that 'sounds' must either be in apposition to 'measures' (l. 25) or is governed by 'with' understood. Langhorne had sensed the difficulty but merely placed an evasive dash at the end of l. 25 in 1765.

27. *mingled*] A favourite word of C.'s for music: cp. ll. 64 and 114.

30. *delightful*] delighted 1765.

33–7. For 'prolong . . . echo . . . close', C. is indebted to his memory of Milton, *Nativity Ode* 99–100: 'The Air such pleasure loth to lose, / With thousand echo's still prolongs each heav'nly close.' For 'responsive' cp. *Par. Lost* iv 682–3: 'Celestial voices to the midnight air, / Sole, or responsive each to others note.'

38. Cp. Spenser's description of Hope, *Faerie Queene* III xii 13, 1–5: 'With him went *Hope* in rancke, a handsome Mayd, / Of chearefull looke and louely to behold; / In silken samite she was light arayd, / And her faire lockes were wouen vp in gold; / She alway smyld . . .'

40–2. Dryden, *Theodore and Honoria* 285–8: 'Then on the Crowd he cast a

He threw his blood-stained sword in thunder down,
    And with a withering look,
    The war-denouncing trumpet took,
  And blew a blast so loud and dread,
45 Were ne'er prophetic sounds so full of woe.
      And ever and anon he beat
      The doubling drum with furious heat;
  And though sometimes each dreary pause between,
    Dejected Pity at his side
50   Her soul-subduing voice applied,
  Yet still he kept his wild unaltered mien,
While each strained ball of sight seemed bursting from
    his head.

Thy numbers, Jealousy, to nought were fixed,
    Sad proof of thy distressful state,
55 Of differing themes the veering song was mixed,
    And now it courted Love, now raving called on
      Hate.

furious Look, / And wither'd all their Strength before he strook: / Back on
your Lives: let be, said he, my Prey, / And let my Vengeance take the des-
tin'd way.'

43. denouncing] Announcing. Milton uses it so, *Par. Lost* x 210, 853, 962, and
xi 811. Cp. also Gay, *Fables* I xxv, 4: 'Denouncing war to all thy race';
and Dryden, *Aeneid* vi 1090: 'And threatening Oracles denounce the War'.

45. This line is unrhymed.

46. This part of the description of Revenge borrows from Dryden's two
odes for music. The trumpet and drum derive from the *Song for St Cecilia's
Day* 25–30: 'The TRUMPETS loud Clangor / Excites us to Arms / With shrill
Notes of Anger / And mortal Alarms. / The double double double beat / Of
the thundring DRUM'. (The last two lines occur again in *Song ii* from *King
Arthur*.) The contrast of warlike emotions and pity is derived from *Alexander's
Feast* 69–74: 'The Master saw the Madness rise; / His glowing Cheeks, his
ardent Eyes; / And while He Heav'n and Earth defy'd, / Chang'd his hand,
and check'd his Pride. / He chose a Mournful Muse / Soft Pity to infuse'.

47. 'furious heat', *Faerie Queene* II viii 27, 6; V v 47, 8; V xi 13, 3; and
Shepheardes Calender, 'Feb.' 193.

50. OED gives an earlier example of 'soul-subduing', in J. Beaumont,
Psyche (1648) XVIII cxl.   *applied*] Used of music by Spenser, *Faerie
Queene* II xii 32, 2; III i 40, 3, etc; and Milton, *Par. Lost* iv 264. Cp. also
Pope, *Ode on St Cecilia's Day* 25: 'Music her soft, assuasive Voice applies.'

51. 'unalter'd brow', *Par. Regained* i 493.

54. Pope, *Eloisa to Abelard* 172: 'Sad proof how well a lover can obey!'

56. Eloisa to Abelard 197–8: 'Ere such a soul regains its peaceful state, / How
often must it love, how often hate!'

With eyes up-raised, as one inspired,
Pale Melancholy sat retired,
And from her wild sequestered seat,
60   In notes by distance made more sweet,
Poured through the mellow horn her pensive soul:
    And dashing soft from rocks around,
    Bubbling runnels joined the sound;
Through glades and glooms the mingled measure stole,
65   Or o'er some haunted stream with fond delay,
        Round an holy calm diffusing,
        Love of peace and lonely musing,
In hollow murmurs died away.

But O how altered was its sprightlier tone!
70   When Cheerfulness, a nymph of healthiest hue,
    Her bow across her shoulder flung,
    Her buskins gemmed with morning dew,

57-8. Cp. Milton's description of Melancholy, *Il Penseroso* 38-40: 'With eev'n step, and musing gate, / And looks commercing with the skies, / Thy rapt soul sitting in thine eyes.'

59. 'dark sequester'd nook', Milton, *Comus* 500.

62-6: Thomson, *Spring* 909-14: 'There along the dale / With woods o'er-hung, and shagged with mossy rocks / Whence on each hand the gushing waters play, / And down the rough cascade white-dashing fall / Or gleam in lengthened vista through the trees, / You silent steal . . . .'

63. 'bubbling roundell', *Faerie Queene* III iv 33, 7; and Fairfax's *Tasso* XII lxvii 1-2: 'With murmur loud down from the mountain's side / A little runnel tumbled near the place.'

64-8. C. may have been imitating Pope, *Ode on St Cecilia's Day* 18-21: 'Till, by degrees, remote and small, / The Strains decay, / And melt away / In a dying, dying Fall.'

64. Spenser is fond of the phrase 'gloomy glade', *Faerie Queene* I vii 4, 4; II vii 3, 1, etc.

65. 'haunted stream', Milton, *L'Allegro*, 130; Thomson, *Summer* 12; J. Warton, *Ode to Fancy* 41; 'haunted shades and tuneful streams', Akenside, *Odes* (1745) p. 32.

66-7. Milton's Melancholy is asked to 'joyn with thee calm Peace, and Quiet', *Il Penseroso* 45.

68. *Faerie Queene* I viii 11, 9: 'The neighbour woods around with hollow murmur ring.'

70-2. Spenser personifies Cheerfulness in *Faerie Queene* IV x 50, 6-9, but C.'s description is closer to Spenser's Belphoebe, II iii 27-29. Such passages, however, describing healthy maidens usually based on Diana with buskins and bow, are relatively common. Cp. Dryden, *Palamon and Arcite* ii 646-8, and *Meleager and Atalanta* 65-73; and Pope, *Windsor Forest* 169-70.

Blew an inspiring air, that dale and thicket rung,
　　The hunter's call to faun and dryad known!
75　The oak-crowned sisters and their chaste-eyed queen,
　　Satyrs and sylvan boys were seen,
　　Peeping from forth their alleys green;
　Brown Exercise rejoiced to hear,
　And Sport leapt up and seized his beechen spear.

80　Last came Joy's ecstatic trial,
　　He with viny crown advancing,
　　First to the lively pipe his hand addressed,
　But soon he saw the brisk awakening viol,
　　Whose sweet entrancing voice he loved the best.
85　　They would have thought, who heard the strain,
　　They saw in Tempe's vale her native maids,
　　Amidst the festal sounding shades,
　To some unwearied minstrel dancing,
　　While as his flying fingers kissed the strings,
90　Love framed with Mirth a gay fantastic round:
　　Loose were her tresses seen, her zone unbound,
　　And he, amidst his frolic play,

75. *queen*] Diana, goddess of Chastity, often depicted as a huntress, and her attendant nymphs. Mitford compares a couplet from Nathaniel Baxter, *Sir Philip Sidney's Ourania*, 1606, sig. B2: 'Satyrs and Sylvans at the harmonie, / Sometime came darting from the darksome Grove.'

77. 'every alley green', *Comus* 311, and 'Allies green', *Par. Lost* iv 626; Thomson, *Spring* 517; and J. Warton, *Ode to Fancy* 70.

78. Exercise is personified in Parnell's eclogue *Health* but there is no resemblance.

80. *ecstatic trial*] i.e. trial of exalted feeling or intense emotion.

85. Garrod points out that this line is unrhymed and suggests that a line is missing, an unnecessary hypothesis.

86. The vale of Tempe lies between Mts Olympus and Ossa. C. was probably indebted to Akenside, *Pleasures of Imagination* i 299–305: 'Fair Tempe! haunt belov'd of sylvan powers, / Of nymphs and fauns; where in the golden age / They play'd in secret on the shady brink / With ancient Pan: while round their choral steps / Young hours and genial gales with constant hand / Show'r'd blossoms, odours, show'r'd ambrosial dews, / And spring's Elysian bloom.'

89. Dryden, *Alexander's Feast* 22: 'With flying Fingers touch'd the Lyre'; and *Aeneid* vi 879: 'His flying Fingers, and harmonious Quill'. Johnson, under 'String', cites a passage from Rowe containing 'The master's flying fingers'.

90. Cp. 'In a light fantastick round', Milton, *Comus* 144.

92. *he*] Love (in l. 90). Cp. Milton, *L'Allegro* 18–19: 'The frolick Wind that breathes the Spring, / Zephir with Aurora playing . . .'

As if he would the charming air repay,
Shook thousand odours from his dewy wings.

95   O Music, sphere-descended maid,
Friend of pleasure, Wisdom's aid,
Why, goddess, why to us denied?
Lay'st thou thy ancient lyre aside?
As in that loved Athenian bower,
100   You learned an all-commanding power,
Thy mimic soul, O nymph endeared,
Can well recall what then it heard.
Where is thy native simple heart,
Devote to virtue, fancy, art?
105   Arise as in that elder time,
Warm, energic, chaste, sublime!
Thy wonders in that god-like age
Fill thy recording Sister's page—
'Tis said, and I believe the tale,
110   Thy humblest reed could more prevail,
Had more of strength, diviner rage,
Than all which charms this laggard age,
Even all at once together found,
Caecilia's mingled world of sound—
115   O bid our vain endeavors cease,
Revive the just designs of Greece,
Return in all thy simple state!
Confirm the tales her sons relate!

94. Cp. *Faerie Queene* I v 2, 4, where Phoebus, 'Came dauncing forth, shaking his deawie haire'; Fairfax's *Tasso* I xiv 8: 'And shook his wings with rory May dews wet'. In *Par. Lost* v 286–7, Raphael 'shook his Plumes, that Heav'nly fragrance filld / The circuit wide'; in *Par. Regained* ii 364–5, the winds '*Arabian* odors fann'd / From their soft wings'. So too Pope, *Eloisa to Abelard* 218: 'And wings of Seraphs shed divine perfumes.'
95. Milton, *At a Solemn Music* 2: 'Sphear-born harmonious Sisters, Voice, and Vers'.
100. 'all-commanding might', Milton, *Psalm cxxxvi* 25.
101. *mimic*] Endowed with the power of imitation. Cp. 'mimic Fansie', *Par. Lost* v 110.   *endeared*] Beloved.
103. *native . . . heart*] Cp. *Manners* 26 (p. 472).
104. *devote*] C. probably derives this form of the past participle from Milton.
105. 'elder time', Spenser, *Shepheardes Calender*, 'Dec.' 73.
106. *energic*] Energetic, powerful.
108. *recording Sister*] Clio, the Muse of History.
114. C. refers to St Cecilia, the patron saint of music.

19 Ode Occasioned by the Death
of Mr Thomson

Written between 27 Aug. 1748 and June 1749. James Thomson, the author
of *The Seasons*, died at Richmond on 27 Aug. 1748 and was buried in the
parish church two days later. C.'s *Ode* was published in a folio pamphlet in
June 1749 (*Gentleman's Mag.* xix 288) by R. Manby and H. S. Cox: Manby
was the bookseller for whom C. had earlier undertaken to contribute to the
Biographia Britannica, another of his abortive projects according to John
Ragsdale (*The Gleaner*, ed. N. Drake (1811) iv 483). Patrick Murdoch, in
his 'Life' of Thomson, prefixed to his edn of Thomson's *Works* (1762)
I xvi, wrote: 'Only one gentleman, Mr. *Collins*, who had lived some time
at *Richmond*, but forsook it when Mr. *Thomson* died, wrote an Ode to his
memory.' Murdoch went on to praise 'the dirge-like melancholy it breathes,
and the warmth of affection that seems to have dictated it', and reprinted
the poem (I xxi–xxiii). Murdoch's statement was not strictly accurate, since
Robert Shiels published *Musidorus: A Poem, Sacred to the Memory of Mr.
James Thomson* in 1748, and the *Scots Mag.* printed two anonymous sets of
verse: 'On the Death of the celebrated Mr. James Thomson' in Sept. 1748
(also in the *Gentleman's Mag.* xviii 423, in the same month) and 'On the
Death of Mr. Thomson' in Oct. 1748, x 441, 486. Thomas Warton also
wrote an unpublished 'Monody' on Thomson, dated 27 Oct. 1748, an
incomplete MS of which is among the Warton papers in Trinity College,
Oxford.

C. appears to have been intimate with Thomson and was living at Rich-
mond himself by 1747. Common friends of the two men, according to John
Ragsdale, who also lived at Richmond (*The Gleaner* (1811) iv 483–4), were
Garrick, Quin, Dr John Armstrong and Andrew Millar the bookseller, who
published the poetry of both men. It was C. who introduced Joseph Warton
to Thomson, according to Warton's own account, *Works of Pope* (1797) iv
10 *n*: 'Thomson was well acquainted with the Greek Tragedies, on which I
heard him talk learnedly, when I was once introduced to him by my
friend Mr. W. Colling [*sic*].' Warton mentions another conversation
between Thomson and C. in the same work (i 61n; see headnote to *Persian
Eclogues*, p. 370). It was presumably through Thomson or his friend David
Mallet that C. met the works of the Scottish traveller, Martin Martin,
which he was to use in his *Ode on the Popular Superstitions of the Highlands*
(see headnote, p. 500).

C.'s *Ode* is dedicated to George Lyttelton, later first Baron Lyttelton
(1709–73), who had been secretary to the Prince of Wales 1737–44 and
became a Lord of the Treasury in 1744. He was a generous patron of
literature and was Thomson's chief friend and patron during the 1740s.
Lyttelton was one of Thomson's executors and it was through his influence
that the posthumous tragedy *Coriolanus* was performed in Jan. 1749 at

Covent Garden for the benefit of the family. Thomson describes Lyttelton in *The Castle of Indolence* I lxv–lxvi, and the description of Thomson himself in it, I lxviii, has been attributed to him. It may be mentioned here that the stanzas in *The Castle of Indolence* I lvii–lix, which have been taken to refer to C. at least since W. Moy Thomas's edn of C., 1858, pp. xxiii–xxiv, are now considered to describe Thomson's friend the minor poet William Paterson. See A. D. McKillop, *The Castle of Indolence* (1961) pp. 192–3.

Between its first publication and its inclusion in Murdoch's 'Life' of Thomson, the *Ode* appeared in Thomas Warton's *The Union* (1753) pp. 108–10 (2nd edn, 1759), and in *The Art of Poetry on a New Plan*, probably edited by John Newbery, with assistance from Goldsmith, (1762) ii 68–9, where it is described as 'of the pastoral and elegiac kind, and both picturesque and pathetic'. C.'s *Ode* was admired by the young Wordsworth, who imitates and echoes it in his *Remembrance of Collins Composed upon the Thames Near Richmond* (1789).

C.'s epigraph on the title-page was taken from Virgil, *Eclogues* v 74–5 and 52: 'These rites shall be thine for ever, both when we pay our yearly vows to the Nymphs, and when we purify our fields'; and 'Me, too, Daphnis loved'.

C.'s explanation that the 'scene' of the poem is the Thames near Richmond has been elaborated by E. M. W. Tillyard in his essay on the poem in *A Review of English Literature* i (July 1960) 30–8 (reprinted in *Essays Literary and Educational* (1962) pp. 89–98). Tillyard traces the double progression in the poem of the movement of the boat on the river and of the coming of nightfall. The other main topic in recent discussions of the poem has been C.'s use of the word 'Druid' in the first and last lines of the poem. Mrs Barbauld, 1797, p. xliii, objected strongly to it: 'there is no propriety in calling THOMSON a Druid or a pilgrim [l. 12], characters totally foreign to his own. To the sanguinary and superstitious Druid, whose rites were wrapped up in mystery, it was peculiarly improper to compare a Poet whose religion was simple as truth, sublime as nature, and liberal as the spirit of philosophy.' But most of C.'s early readers would probably assume that C. meant no more than that Thomson wrote brilliantly about nature. Langhorne, *1765* p. 184, found 'the appellations of "Druid" and "meek nature's child" . . . happily characteristic'; and Dyce, 1827, pp. 196–7, defended C. against Mrs Barbauld on the grounds that he was referring to the 'rural scenes' described in Thomson's poetry. J. M. S. Tompkins, 'In Yonder Grave a Druid Lies', *Review of English Studies* xxii (1946) 1–16, defends C.'s usage on more rigorous grounds, claiming that C. saw in Thomson a modern manifestation of the idealized druid described by such antiquarians as Stukeley, Carte and Toland, i.e. as a poet-priest of nature, a patriot glorifying liberty, a devout enthusiast of a benevolent Creative Spirit, a hymnmaker, and a student and teacher of natural philosophy. See also A. D. Mc Killop's remarks on this article, *Philological Quarterly* xxvi (1947) 113–14. Some of these aspects of the druids no doubt existed in C.'s mind only as vague associations, but he probably chose to call Thomson a druid to allude both to his powers as a poet of nature in *The Seasons* and to his celebration of British liberty in his poem of that name. C. himself had earlier associated the druids with both liberty and nature in his *Ode to Liberty* 89–112 (pp. 451–2 above). A. L. Owen, *The Famous Druids* (Oxford, 1962) pp. 172–8, has recently drawn attention to Thomson's use of a 'Druid-wight' in *The Castle of Indolence* II xxxiii, as the vehicle of his own philosophy, which Owen finds comparable to that traditionally attributed to the druids, although he ends with the conclusion that C. may have meant merely to identify Thomson as 'a poet-philosopher of Nature'.

TO
GEORGE LYTTELTON, Esq;
THIS
ODE
IS INSCRIBED BY
THE AUTHOR

ADVERTISEMENT

The scene of the following stanzas is supposed to lie on the Thames near Richmond.

Haec tibi semper erunt, et cum solennia vota
reddemus Nymphis, et cum lustrabimus agros.

—— —— Amavit nos quoque Daphnis.
VIRG. Bucol. Eclog. v [74–5, 52]

I

In yonder grave a Druid lies,
Where slowly winds the stealing wave!

¶ 19.1. Fawkes and Woty, the editors of the *Poetical Calendar* xii (1763) 104, emended 'grave' to 'grove'. The traditional association of druids with 'groves' and the repetition of 'grave' 3 ll. later make the emendation attractive, but there is no other evidence to justify it. R. A. Wilmott, 1854, pp. 68–9, however, accepted it on the grounds that Thomson's grave could not be seen from the river: '[it] is not viewed, but remembered. The boat glides up the river, the oar is suspended for a moment, and the eye is turned to the spot, behind the elms and chestnuts, where the Bard lies buried. The trees of Richmond, embowering the terrace-walks, and sloping down to the water-edge, are aptly described by "yonder grove". The designation of "Druid" is another proof.' For a similar discussion, see *Gentleman's Mag.* xix, New Series (1843), Pt i 494, 603. But the repetition of 'grave' in the last line of the poem, deliberately parallel, makes the possibility of a misprint very small.

The year's best sweets shall duteous rise
 To deck its poet's sylvan grave!

II

5   In yon deep bed of whispering reeds
 His airy harp shall now be laid,
That he, whose heart in sorrow bleeds,
 May love through life the soothing shade.

III

Then maids and youths shall linger here,
10   And, while its sounds at distance swell,
Shall sadly seem in Pity's ear
 To hear the woodland pilgrim's knell.

IV

Remembrance oft shall haunt the shore
 When Thames in summer wreaths is dressed,
15   And oft suspend the dashing oar
 To bid his gentle spirit rest!

V

And oft as Ease and Health retire

3–4. C. calls Thomson the 'year's' poet, because he had celebrated its various
aspects in *The Seasons*. Cp. *Song from Cymbeline* 3–4 and *n*, and *Ode,
Written in the Beginning of 1746* 3–4 and *n* (pp. 401, 437, above); and cp. also
Pope, *Elegy to an Unfortunate Lady* 63, 65–6: 'Yet shall thy grave with rising
flow'rs be drest / . . . / There shall the morn her earliest tears bestow, /
There the first roses of the year shall blow.'
6. *airy harp*] The Harp of *Aeolus*, of which see a Description in the *Castle of
Indolence*. C.
The Aeolian Harp is a stringed instrument which produces musical
sounds when placed in a current of air. Thomson had referred to it
in *The Castle of Indolence* (1748) I xl–xli; and he had also written *An Ode on
Aeolus's Harp*, first published in Dodsley's *Collection* in 1748. In Newbery's
Art of English Poetry on a New Plan (1762) ii 68, the words 'invented by Mr.
Oswald' are added to C.'s note after '*Aeolus*'. For the supposed invention of
the instrument by James Oswald, a music publisher, with Thomson's
assistance, see *The Castle of Indolence*, ed. A. D. McKillop (Lawrence, Kansas,
1961) pp. 206–9, and Roger Lonsdale, *Dr. Charles Burney* (1965) p. 29.
9. Cp. *Song from Cymbeline* 1–2 (p. 401).
10. *its*] The sounds of the Aeolian Harp, fluctuating with the rise and fall of
the breeze.
17–18. Pope, *Windsor Forest* 237, 239–41: 'Happy next him who to these
Shades retires / . . . / Whom humbler Joys of home-felt Quiet please, /

To breezy lawn or forest deep,
The friend shall view yon whitening spire,
20   And mid the varied landscape weep.

VI

But thou, who own'st that earthy bed,
Ah! what will every dirge avail?
Or tears, which Love and Pity shed
That mourn beneath the gliding sail!

VII

25   Yet lives there one, whose heedless eye
Shall scorn thy pale shrine glimmering near?
With him, sweet bard, may Fancy die,
And Joy desert the blooming year.

VIII

But thou, lorn stream, whose sullen tide
30   No sedge-crowned Sisters now attend,
Now waft me from the green hill's side,
Whose cold turf hides the buried friend!

Successive Study, Exercise and Ease. / He gathers Health from Herbs the Forest yields . . .'
18–19. Thomson, *Spring* 522–4: 'Now meets the bending sky, the river now / Dimpling along, the breezy ruffled lake, / The forest darkening round, the glittering spire.'
19. spire] *Richmond*-Church. *C.*
   Thomson was buried in the parish church of St Mary Magdalene, Richmond, on 29 Aug. 1748. It is not known whether any stone or monument to the poet was immediately erected over the vault where he was buried, in spite of C.'s reference to his 'shrine' (l. 26). Richard Crisp, *Richmond and Its Inhabitants* (1866) p. 198, suggests that such a stone or memorial had been erected soon after his burial but that it had been destroyed later in the century when the pew accommodation was being increased.
21. earthy] earthly *1765.*
29–30. Bronson takes 'now' as meaning 'nowadays' (as opposed to the 'poetical days of yore'); but C.'s meaning is surely that, since the death of Thomson, the 'sedge-crowned Sisters' or Naiads have deserted the Thames. Cp. Pope, *Windsor Forest* 346–7: 'The gulphy *Lee* his sedgy Tresses rears: / And sullen *Mole,* that hides his diving Flood.' Pope was echoing Milton's 'sullen *Mole*' and 'Sedgie *Lee*', *At a Vacation Exercise* 95, 97. Cp. also 'Come, *Meles,* hither turn thy sedge-crown'd Head', Thomas Warton Senior, *Poems* (1748) p. 203.
29. lorn] Forlorn or deserted; as in Spenser, *Shepheardes Calender,* 'Jan.' 62: 'And am forlorne, (alas why am I lorne?)'.
31. 'waft the haples youth', *Lycidas* 164.

IX

And see, the fairy valleys fade,
    Dun Night has veiled the solemn view!
35   –Yet once again, dear parted shade,
    Meek Nature's child, again adieu!

X

The genial meads, assigned to bless
    Thy life, shall mourn thy early doom,
    Their hinds and shepherd-girls shall dress
40   With simple hands thy rural tomb.

XI

Long, long, thy stone and pointed clay
    Shall melt the musing Briton's eyes:
    'O! vales and wild woods', shall he say,
    'In yonder grave your Druid lies!'

33–4. Thomson, *Autumn* 950–2: 'But see the fading many-coloured woods, /
Shade deepening over shade, the country round / Imbrown; a crowded
umbrage, dusk and dun'; cp. also 'dun shades', *Comus* 127; and 'on this side
Night / In the dun Air', *Par. Lost* iii 71–2; and 'Nights Hemisphere had
veild the Horizon round', *Par. Lost* ix 52.

39–40. Pope, *Winter* 19–20: 'Sing, while beside the shaded Tomb I mourn, /
And with fresh Bays her Rural Shrine adorn.' Cp. also *Song from Cymbeline*
1–4 (p. 401 above).

41. See 19 *n* above.   *pointed*] Tillyard, in the essay mentioned in the head-
note, has suggested that this meant 'pointed out'; but A. Henderson,
Review of English Literature i (Oct. 1960) 65, argues that the 'pointed clay'
is the brickwork of Thomson's tomb, 'pointed' being used in the sense of
'point' as given in the *OED*: 'To fill in the lines of the joints of (brickwork)
with mortar or cement'. This interpretation makes sense but is curiously par-
ticular in a rather generalized description. Other senses are possible: 'pointed'
could refer to the shape of Thomson's monument as visualized by C.; and
Milton's sonnet *On Shakespear* 3–4, has been compared: 'Or that his hallow'd
reliques should be hid / Under a Star-ypointing *Pyramid*'. But Tillyard's
interpretation remains the most likely, fitting in as it does with C.'s sustained
use of the imaginary spectator throughout the poem. Pope, *Odyssey* xxiv
105–6, has: 'Where all, from age to age, who pass the coast / May point
Achilles' tomb, and hail the mighty ghost.' And C. himself uses the verb in
this sense in *Epistle to Hanmer* 120, and *Ode to a Lady* 12 (pp. 398, 457).

42. Pope, *Elegy to an Unfortunate Lady* 77–8: 'Ev'n he, whose soul now melts
in mournful lays, / Shall shortly want the gen'rous tear he pays.'

20 An Ode on the Popular Superstitions of the Highlands of Scotland, Considered as the Subject of Poetry

[ODE TO A FRIEND ON HIS RETURN &c.]

Written between Nov. 1749 and early 1750. The dating rests entirely on the fact that the poem was addressed to John Home (1722–1808), a Scottish clergyman and later a celebrated playwright, and presented to him during a visit to London shortly before his return to Scotland. For this reason, as will be seen below, the poem was dated 1749 by those involved in its first publication; but three incompletely dated letters from Home to Carlyle, written during his visit to London, indicate that while he was a recent arrival on 6 Nov. 1749, he was apparently still there early in 1750; see *Works of John Home*, ed. Henry Mackenzie (Edinburgh, 1822) i 133, 136–7, and L. M. Knapp, *Tobias Smollett* (Princeton, 1949) pp. 77, 89. During his stay in London, the purpose of which was to persuade Garrick to accept his tragedy *Agis* (see l. 4 *n*), Home looked up an old friend, Thomas Barrow (see ll. 5–8 *n*) and through him was introduced to C., the connection no doubt being that Barrow lived in C.'s native town of Chichester. According to Alexander Carlyle's account, quoted below, Home and C. paid Barrow a visit at Chichester (Carlyle's reference to Winchester is an error), and this common friend was therefore mentioned in the poem C. presented to Home on his departure for Scotland. There is no evidence of any later contact between C. and Home, who became famous after the resounding success of his play *Douglas* (1756), by which time C. himself was considered insane. Henry Mackenzie, who was involved in the first publication of C.'s *Ode* and was later Home's biographer, stated in his *Anecdotes and Egotisms*, ed. H. W. Thompson (1927) p. 166, that he had 'never . . . heard Mr. Home speak of Collins (probably from his thinking it an unpleasant subject), nor among Mr. Home's papers were any letters or notes from Collins or concerning him.'

Nothing more is known of the *Ode* in C.'s lifetime than that it was seen by the Warton brothers when they visited the poet at Chichester in Sept. 1754. It was at last published almost 40 years after it had been written and almost 30 years after C.'s death. The chain of events leading to its discovery began in 1781, when Samuel Johnson in his biography of C. (*Lives of the Poets*, ed. G. B. Hill, (1905) iii 340) referred to the visit to C. in 1754 by the Warton brothers about which he had been told by Joseph Warton. C. had shown them on that occasion 'an ode inscribed to Mr. John Home, on the superstitions of the Highlands; which they thought superior to his other works, but which no search has yet found.' Further information provided by Thomas Warton in 1783 about the visit to C. will be given below. Johnson's reference to the *Ode* caught the attention of Dr Alexander Carlyle (1722–1805), a Scottish Presbyterian Minister and a friend of John Home, who remembered that he had had the MS of such an ode in his possession many years earlier. After searching among his papers, Carlyle discovered a defective draft of the poem, which he eventually read at a meeting of the Literary Class of the newly formed Royal Society of Edinburgh on 19 April 1784. When the first volume of the *Transactions of the Royal Society of Edinburgh* was published in March 1788 it contained the *Ode* (in Part II, 63–75), prefaced by an introductory note and two letters concerning its discovery.

Alexander Fraser Tytler (1747–1813), later Lord Woodhouselee, had been appointed by a Committee of the Edinburgh Royal Society to obtain from Carlyle 'every degree of information which he could give' about the *Ode*. Carlyle then sent Tytler C.'s MS and described its history and his discovery of it as follows:

'THE manuscript is in Mr COLLINS's handwriting, and fell into my hands among the papers of a friend of mine and Mr JOHN HOME's, who died as long ago as the year 1754. Soon after I found the poem, I shewed it to Mr HOME, who told me that it had been addressed to him by Mr COLLINS, on his leaving London in the year 1749: That it was hastily composed and incorrect; but that he would one day find leisure to look it over with care. Mr COLLINS and Mr HOME had been made acquainted by Mr JOHN BARROW, (the *cordial youth* mentioned in the first stanza), who had been, for some time, at the university of Edinburgh; had been a volunteer, along with Mr HOME, in the year 1746; had been taken prisoner with him at the battle of Falkirk, and had escaped, together with him and five or six other gentlemen, from the castle of Down. Mr BARROW resided in 1749 at Winchester, where Mr COLLINS and Mr HOME were, for a week or two, together on a visit. Mr BARROW was paymaster in America, in the war that commenced in 1756, and died in that country.

'I THOUGHT no more of the poem, till a few years ago, when, on reading Dr JOHNSON's life of COLLINS, I conjectured that it might be the very copy of verses which he mentions, which he says was much prized by some of his friends, and for the loss of which he expresses regret. I sought for it among my papers; and perceiving that a stanza and a half were wanting, I made the most diligent search I could for them, but in vain. Whether or not this great chasm was in the poem when it first came into my hands, is more than I can remember, at this distance of time.'

Much the same account was given by Carlyle in an undated letter to an unknown friend, one copy of which is mentioned by P. L. Carver, *Notes and Queries* clxxvii (1939) 258–9, and the other quoted in the *Times Lit. Supp.* 1943, p. 312. (The second of these copies is now in the National

Library of Scotland.) In this letter Carlyle states that the *Ode* was 'hastily wrote on John Home's leaving Chichester . . . in the year 1749', thus making clear that the reference to Winchester in the later printed account was an error. In this letter Carlyle planned to publish the *Ode* himself 'next Winter', but in another fragment of a letter in the John Lee Collection in the National Library of Scotland the *Ode* is to be introduced to the world through the Royal Society of Edinburgh. Carlyle added that he himself did not like the poem's 'Spencerian [*sic*] stanza' and regretted that 'the finest stanza in the Poem has too strong a resemblance to the description of the Man perishing in the Snow in Thomson's *Winter*' (see ll. 95–8 *n*). Carlyle's reference to the Spenserian stanza is curious, especially as Thomas Warton, before the rediscovery of the MS, described it as written 'in the octave stanza' (see below). Both men were recording hurried impressions, of course, and C.'s unusual stanzaic form obviously struck both at first as a pair of 8- or 9-line stanzas.

A letter from Alexander Tytler to John Robison, the General Secretary of the Royal Society of Edinburgh, accompanied Carlyle's in the *Transactions*. It describes in detail C.'s MS that Carlyle had sent him, and the additions made by Henry Mackenzie and Carlyle to make it fit for publication:

'It is evidently the *prima cura* of the poem, as you will perceive from the alterations in the manuscript, by deleting many lines and words, and substituting others, which are written above them. In particular, the greatest part of the twelfth stanza is new-modelled in that manner. These variations I have marked in notes on the copy which is inclosed, and I think they should be printed. . . .

'THIS ode is, beyond all doubt, the poem alluded to in the life of COLLINS by JOHNSON . . . . COLLINS himself, it appears from this passage [the account of the Wartons' visit to C. in 1754], had kept a copy of the poem, which, considering the unhappy circumstances that attended his last illness, it is no wonder was mislaid or lost; and, but for that fortunate hint given by JOHNSON, it appears from Dr CARLYLE's letter, that the original manuscript would, in all probability, have undergone the same fate.

'STRUCK with the singular beauty of this poem, of which, I believe, no man of taste will say that Dr WARTON and his brother have over-rated the merit, I could not help regretting the mutilated form in which it appeared; and, in talking on that subject to my friend Mr HENRY MACKENZIE of the Exchequer, (a gentleman well known to the literary world by many ingenious productions) I proposed to him the task of supplying the fifth stanza, and the half of the sixth, which were entirely lost. How well he has executed that task, the public will judge; who, unless warned by the inverted commas that distinguish the supplemental verses, would probably never have discovered the chasm. Several hemistichs, and words left blank by Mr COLLINS, had before been very happily supplied by Dr CARLYLE. These are likewise marked by inverted commas. They are a proof that this poem, as Dr CARLYLE has remarked, was hastily composed; but this circumstance evinces, at the same time, the vigour of the author's imagination, and the ready command he possessed of harmonious numbers.'

Mackenzie himself, *Anecdotes and Egotisms*, ed. H. W. Thompson (1927) p. 166, described his effort to fill the gap as 'an almost extempore production, written in the same evening in which Mr. Tytler asked me to write it'. In the letter to Tytler, dated 23 Dec. 1785 (quoted in the article by Miss Lamont cited below), which accompanied his attempt to 'fill up the Blank in *Collins*'s Ode', Mackenzie explained that he had 'endeavoured to keep up a congenial Wildness of Imagery, with which indeed I have, from my Infancy, been well acquainted'. He urged Tytler to make any alterations he thought fit.

The publication of the long-lost *Ode* aroused considerable interest, the general reaction being perhaps typified by Anna Seward, the poetess of Lichfield, who was delighted that it had 'so lately emerged from the oblivion into which it had fallen' (17 June 1788), *Letters* (1811) ii 138. The *Ode* was widely reprinted or quoted in the newspapers and magazines (e.g. *Edinburgh Mag.* vii (March 1788) 203–10; *European Mag.* xiii (April 1788) 241–6; *Gazeteer*, 4 April 1788; *London Chronicle*, 1–3 and 3–5 April 1788; and *Annual Register* xxx (1788) 170–7). William Erskine published three additional stanzas of his own, dealing with various superstititions which C. had neglected, in the *Edinburgh Mag.* vii (April 1788) 307. According to A. S. P. Woodhouse, *Times Lit. Supp.* 1930, p. 838, the *Ode* was collected in the first American edn of C.'s poems at Philadelphia, 1788.

A rather more complicated issue was raised by a letter in the *St James's Chronicle* for 12–15 April 1788, signed 'Verax', which emphasized the fact that the text in the Edinburgh *Transactions* 'appears to have been taken from a mutilated and incorrect Copy. That a more complete and even a *perfect* Copy once existed, may be proved from the following Anecdotes:–About five Years ago, Mr. John Hymers, a Fellow of Queen's College, Oxford, circulated Proposals for printing the Works of Mr. Collins, with a *Life* and *Notes*. Mr. Wharton gave Mr. Hymers some curious Particulars relating to the Life of Collins. I have seen Mr. Hymers's Papers, who is since dead, from which I send you this short Extract. "In 1754, I and my Brother Dr. Wharton, visited Collins at Chichester, where he lived in the Cathedral Cloysters with his Sister. Here he shewed us an Ode to Mr. Home, on his Return from England to Scotland in 1749, full of the most striking superstitious Imagery. It was in his own Hand-writing, without a single Interpolation or *Hiatus*; and had every Appearance of the Authour's last Revisal, and of a Copy carefully and completely finished for the Press. I offered to take it with me to Town, &c." On the whole we may conclude, that the Edinburgh Copy is nothing more than a foul and early Draught of this Composition.'

What is mysterious about 'Verax''s letter is that what would otherwise appear to be the full text of Thomas Warton's letter to the Rev. John Hymers was later printed in *The Reaper* No. 26, one of a series of occasional essays which appeared in the *York Chronicle*, on 16 Feb. 1797, later collected by Nathan Drake, *The Gleaner* (1811) iv 475–8. In Warton's account of the *Ode* in this version there is no description of the state of the MS he saw:

'Here he shewed us an Ode to Mr. John Home, on his leaving England for Scotland, in the octave stanza, very long, and beginning, "Home, thou return'st from Thames!" I remember there was a beautiful description of the spectre of a man drowned in the night, or in the language of the old Scotch superstitions – seized by the angry spirit of the waters, appearing to his wife with pale blue cheek, &c. Mr. Home has no copy of it.'

The only explanation of the difference between these two versions of Warton's letter to Hymers must be that 'Verax' in fact knew of the existence of the real letter, had probably seen it and that, for purposes of his own, he interpolated into his quotation from it a passage on the state of the MS seen by the Wartons in C.'s possession in 1754. Why was 'Verax' so anxious to stress the fact that the Edinburgh text was based on a defective draft and that the copy seen by the Wartons in 1754 was 'carefully and completely finished for the Press'? In May 1788 another text of the poem was published at London by J. Bell. This version, 'Never before printed', it was claimed, was the complete and final version seen in 1754 by the Wartons, to whom, indeed, this edn was dedicated. The 'discovery' of this MS was described in the Preface: 'A Gentleman who, for the present, chooses not to publish his name, discovered last summer the following admirable Ode, among some old papers, in the concealed drawers of a bureau, left him, among other articles, by a relation.' The fact that 'a Scotch clergyman' had recently discovered and published a 'very imperfect' text of the poem was, in the view of the Preface, no more than a curious coincidence. The Preface was followed by a Dedication to the Warton brothers, which declared: 'Your mentioning it to Dr. JOHNSON, as it was the means that led to the imperfect first draught, so it likewise was the happy means of bringing the PERFECT copy to light.'

Since this London text of the Ode has been accepted as genuine by many later editors, some attention should perhaps be devoted to it. In particular, the immediate contemporary reaction must be stressed. A critic, in the English Review xi 347–50, observed in May 1788: 'The time of this anonymous gentleman's publication renders his story suspicious; and the internal proof drawn from his edition of the ode will condemn him before every literary tribunal.' The reviewer demonstrated the inferiority of the supposedly 'original' stanzas v and vi to the rest of the poem (as well as to Mackenzie's attempt to fill the gap) and concluded: 'More attention has been paid to this publication than it deserves; but it is to more than its literary demerits that it owes that attention. We consider literary imposition in a serious light; and a cheat is not less so because he is a bungler in his profession.' A writer in the Critical Review lxvi 318–19, in Oct. 1788, was suspicious of, but also puzzled by, the London text of the Ode. Arthur Murphy, the dramatist, in the Monthly Review lxxix 555, in Dec. 1788, politely but firmly refused to accept its authenticity: 'it is to be lamented that the evidence of its authenticity is with-held from the Public. Surely the gentleman, who found it in 'the drawers of a bureau,' should allow his name to be published, and give us the satisfaction of knowing whether it was in the hand-writing of Mr.

Collins; which is, certainly, a material question. The lines that supply the chasm in the whole of the 5th and half of the 6th stanza, introduce the execution of Charles the First, the rebellion in 1745, the battles of Preston-Pans, Falkirk, and Culloden; but the style does not seem, to us, to be in the manner of Collins.'

The 'gentleman' who had accidentally discovered the MS did not publish his name or make any further statement about the poem; and yet, in spite of the objections of the professional reviewers and in spite of the crudeness of the long insertion in the middle of the poem, Bell's edn was reprinted in 1789 and soon became the standard text, remaining such for more than a century in spite of occasional protests. Thus Bell's text was included in the 1790 edn of Johnson's *English Poets* (vol. lviii) and, with some misgivings, in Robert Anderson's *British Poets* (vol. ix) in 1794. Benjamin Strutt in his edn of C. published at Colchester in 1796 broke with the new orthodoxy by printing his own attempts to fill the gaps in the text, but Bell elsewhere prevailed, partly, no doubt, for no better reason than that his text was much more easily accessible than that published at Edinburgh in a learned journal. In some cases editorial theory and practice varied. Alexander Chalmers found it necessary in his *General Biographical Dictionary* (1813) x 79 *n*, 'to guard the Reader against a spurious edition' of the *Ode* published in London, but it was Bell's text which had appeared in 1810 in Chalmers's *Works of the British Poets* xiii 206–8. Similarly Sir Egerton Brydges, in the 'Essay on the Genius and Poems of Collins', prefixed to the Aldine edn, 1830, p. lv, wrote of the supposedly 'recovered' stanzas in Bell's edn: 'I have no more doubt that they are *spurious* than that I did not write them myself. . . There is not one line among these interpolated stanzas which it is possible that Collins could have written.' Nevertheless, the Aldine edn printed Bell's text, even if it noted some variants from the Edinburgh text. Alexander Dyce, one of the best of the earlier editors of C., surprisingly accepted Bell's text in his edn of 1827, p. 203, asserting that 'all doubts seem at last to have subsided'. Dyce was rudely awoken from this belief by a letter from William Wordsworth, to whom he had sent a copy of his edn. Wordsworth's impassioned letter to Dyce of 29 Oct. 1828, *Letters of William and Dorothy Wordsworth, The Later Years*, ed. E. de Selincourt (1939) i 313–6, remains one of the most cogent demonstrations of the spurious nature of Bell's edn. Writing again to Dyce on 12 Jan. 1829, Wordsworth added (*Letters* i 345–6): 'You are at perfect liberty to declare that you have rejected Bell's Copy in consequence of my opinion of it—and I feel much satisfaction in being the Instrument of rescuing the memory of Collins from this Disgrace.'

Nevertheless, Bell's text remained the standard one throughout the nineteenth century. W. Moy Thomas, in his influential 1858 edn, p. xxvi, accepted it with some hesitation on the grounds that the Wartons, to whom it was dedicated, had never repudiated it. A more eccentric solution was provided by the *The Universal Library* (1854) vol ii, which included in the same text both the stanzas supplied by Mackenzie and those inserted in the Bell edn. Finally, however, W. C. Bronson (1898) rejected Bell's text as having any independent authority whatsoever, and he has been followed by most later editors. Bell has, however, retained a few adherents. Edmund Blunden in his edn of 1929, p. 175, expressed his faith in the honesty of the anonymous London editor of the poem, and as a result the spurious passages can still be solemnly discussed as if they were by C., e.g. by J. M. Cohen in *The Listener* lxii (1959) 62–3.

The spurious nature of Bell's edn seems clear on the internal evidence alone; but there is also external information which, if not conclusive, certainly points to forgery. This appears in a letter from Francis Horner to Thomas Thomson, 29 Nov. 1815 (*Memoirs and Correspondence of Francis Horner, M.P.*, ed. L. Horner (1843) ii 276):

'I have made out the history of those supplementary stanzas in Collins's Ode on the Superstitions of the Highlands, which puzzled us. Mackintosh, who told me the story, would not mention the man's name; but it was a very low northern littérateur, who, about five and twenty years ago, published at Cadell's [sic] shop a new edition of that ode, as from another manuscript, with all the blanks and vacancies supplied. The additions were one and all a forgery of his own, of which he boasted to Mackintosh. The man is dead. This piece of literary history ought to be made known; for the forgery has not only crept into the edition of Collins which I shewed you, and that is part of a general collection, but also into the large body of the English poets published by Chalmers.'

Horner's informant was Sir James Mackintosh (1765–1832), the distinguished philosopher, historian and lawyer, than whom one could hardly have a more reliable witness.

Bell's text is virtually no more than that of the Edinburgh *Transactions*, with alternative readings for every gap supplied by Carlyle and Mackenzie. As Wordsworth put it in his letter to Dyce of 29 Oct. 1828, the only differences between the two texts were in 'the supplemental part, and a few alterations made as should seem for alteration's sake, and a hemisstich and word or two supplied'. Wherever Carlyle had suggested that a stanza seemed to lack a line according to the general rhyme-scheme, the London edn dutifully supplied it. The punctuation of the Edinburgh edn is virtually reproduced intact. The London edn does include a few readings differing from C. himself (as opposed to Carlyle and Mackenzie), but these seem to be only what Wordsworth called 'alterations . . . for alteration's sake': e.g. 'where' for 'whose' (l. 13); 'brawny' for 'bony' (l. 51); 'skill' for 'style' (l. 138); 'scented' for 'sainted', (l. 164); 'murmuring' for 'num'rous' (l. 202); and a few other variants which are probably no more than misprints. As for the quality of the inserted stanzas, their feebleness has often been pointed out and may be checked in the footnotes. There is in fact no evidence to suggest that the London edn of 1788 was not the imposture–in some ways an impressively elaborate one–as which it was immediately recognized in some responsible quarters. The 'Verax' letter was presumably part of the conspiracy, its apparent involvement of the Wartons in the affair being the masterstroke. As for the Wartons themselves, they were elderly men by this time, and their silence can be ascribed either to their uncertainty as to just what text they had seen in 1754, or to unwillingness to be involved in any hoax or literary controversy (Thomas Warton had taken part in the Chatterton controversy in 1782; see his *Enquiry* into the authenticity of the Rowley poems), or to complete indifference. It need not be interpreted as approval.

The MS of the *Ode*, after its publication in 1788, once more disappeared. No more predictable than Carlyle's original discovery of it was its rediscovery in the summer of 1967 by Miss Claire Lamont. The MS, together with a transcript of it by Carlyle and other papers of Alexander Fraser Tytler, who supervised its publication in 1788, had descended in the Tytler family into the possession of Col. A. E. Cameron of Aldourie Castle, Invernessshire, where it was identified by Miss Lamont. Her account of the MS and a full transcript of it were published in *Review of English Studies* xix (1968) 137–47; but I am indebted to Miss Lamont for the opportunity of discussing her discovery with her in full before her article was published.

The MS is entitled merely 'Ode to a Friend on his Return &c', possibly because C. was hurriedly copying an earlier draft which gave the title in full or because Home, the recipient of the MS, might be expected to know his own circumstances at the time. The title given to the poem in 1788, by which it has been known for 180 years, has been retained here to avoid confusion. Carlyle or Tytler, perhaps to emphasize that this was the missing poem mentioned by Johnson in his *Life* of C., probably derived their title from his reference to 'the superstitions of the Highlands'. The MS is written on 9 leaves of small quarto paper, which seem to have been removed from a notebook. The stanzas of the *Ode* are clearly numbered, thus disposing of all theories about the possible mis-ordering of certain stanzas. Of stanza 5 only the numeral appears, at the bottom of a page. This stanza and the first half of stanza 6 appeared on the following leaf which was already missing when Carlyle first described the MS. In general the text published in 1788 was accurate, recording as it did many of C.'s alterations. In addition to differences in spelling and punctuation, there are 12 significant variants, two footnotes by C. himself which were expanded by his editor in 1788, and a number of additional substitutions and deletions which can now be recorded in full. Of the variants, several appear to have been mere mistranscriptions but a few may have been intended as 'improvements'. In some cases C.'s Edinburgh editors seemed to have removed instances of his 'Scottish' diction (see below) as inappropriate.

Apart from his natural interest in the poem's subject, C. was no doubt stimulated to write this *Ode* by his meetings with John Home and some of the specific superstitions with which he deals may have been suggested in conversations with him. C.'s *Ode* in return may have had its influence on Home, who, on his return to Scotland, wrote his most successful play *Douglas*, which was partly based on the ballad of *Gil Morrice*, very much the sort of material C. had recommended to his friend. It may be added that

Home later on helped to stimulate and encourage James Macpherson, the 'translator' of Ossian, to collect and publish his Gaelic fabrications, and his enthusiasm in this direction may have been encouraged by C.'s *Ode*: see Alice E. Gipson, *John Home* (New Haven, 1916) pp. 25–7; and R. G. Thomas, 'John Home, Lord Bute and Ossian', *Modern Language Review* li (1956) 73–5.

Apart from the assistance of Home, about which nothing definite can be known, the most important of C.'s sources was Martin Martin's *Description of the Western Islands of Scotland* (1703), a 2nd edn of which, 'very much Corrected', appeared in 1716. (Quotations in the notes are from this 2nd edn.) Samuel Johnson had read Martin's book when young, and a copy of it was to accompany him and Boswell to the Western Isles in 1773 (*Life of Johnson*, i 450, v 13 and *n*). Other friends of C. who knew the book and were inspired poetically by it were James Thomson and David Mallet, who also used Martin's earlier work, *A Voyage to St Kilda* (1698). A new edn of this work had been published in March 1749 (see ll. 155–71 *n*). Carlyle or Tytler pointed to Martin Martin as C.'s general source as early as the notes to the first appearance of the *Ode* in the Edinburgh *Transactions*; but it was left to Wordsworth to point out a specific verbal debt, *Letters: The Later Years*, ed. E. de Selincourt (1939) i 315–16, 473; see also A. S. P. Woodhouse, 'Collins and Martin Martin', *Times Lit. Supp.* 1928, p. 1011.

Another 'Scottish' aspect of the poem, though a limited one, is its diction, to which C. attempts spasmodically to give a Northern colouring. Bernard Groom, *The Diction of Poetry from Spenser to Bridges* (Toronto, 1956) p. 152, has written that in this *Ode* C. tries 'to launch a flight of imagination on the wings of rare words. . . . The novel feature is the number of Northern words, little known in Southern English.' Groom's belief that these words were little known in Southern English is, however, hardly accurate, because, as is indicated in the footnotes, many of them occur in the enormously popular 'Scotch' poetry written or collected by Allan Ramsay and are glossed in edns of his poems and miscellanies, all easily accessible to C., who was original not so much in using this kind of diction as in using it in an English poem of so ambitious a character.

Apart from the 1749 edn of Martin Martin's *Voyage to St Kilda*, two other recently published books require mention since C. refers to them within the poem. William Hamilton of Bangour's *Poems* (Dec. 1748) may have been brought to C.'s notice by John Home, but he could also have seen Hamilton's most famous poem, 'The Braes of Yarrow', to which he alludes in l. 214, in some earlier miscellanies. Of greater importance for C.'s poem was the publication in Oct. 1749 of a new edn of Fairfax's translation of Tasso (see ll. 191–203 and *n*), a work greatly admired by C. (see his *Epistle to the Editor of Fairfax*, advertised but never published, under 'Lost or Doubtful Poems', p. 565 below). C.'s long tribute to Tasso and Fairfax was no doubt stimulated by this new edn, the appearance of which helps to confirm the dating of the poem.

For C.'s ambiguous attitude to the superstitions which he recommends to

Home, see the intelligent analysis by Patricia M. Spacks, *The Insistence of Horror* (Cambridge, Mass., 1962) pp. 70–4.

The text followed here is that of C.'s MS. Variants from the familar text in the *Transactions* of 1788 (cited as *1788*) have been recorded. The interpolations of Carlyle and Mackenzie have not normally been included, unless they are of particular interest. Some of Tytler's explanatory notes which appeared in *1788* have also been recorded. A problematical aspect of the MS is the stanzaic pattern. C. moved the position of 'Mid' and 'Shall' at the beginning of ll. 3–4 in the MS as if to indicate that these middle lines of the opening quatrain were to be inset to correspond to the rhyme scheme. The two following quatrains alternate in accordance with the rhyme scheme: the last five lines of the first stanza are apparently intended to progress systematically inwards and then out. C. may have meant to clarify the pattern in this opening stanza and merely have forgotten to do so in the remaining stanzas. Several of the remaining stanzas are similarly inset in their opening quatrains but in others no consistent pattern can be detected. In the remaining lines of the various stanzas no regular pattern occurs, although simple alternation is most common. This no doubt helps to explain why C. seems not to have noticed that in the later stanzas he was dropping lines required by his original rhyme scheme. The extensive rewriting which occurs in the MS in stanza 12 makes the basic pattern no easier to observe. Accordingly, C.'s most common pattern has been adopted in the text below.

I

H[ome], thou return'st from Thames, whose Naiads long
    Have seen thee lingering, with a fond delay,
      Mid those soft friends whose hearts, some future day,
    Shall melt, perhaps, to hear thy tragic song.
5 Go, not unmindful of that cordial youth,

¶ 20.*1. Home*] For John Home see headnote and l. *4 n.*

4. tragic song] C. presumably refers to Home's tragedy *Agis*, which he had brought to London late in 1749 but which was rejected by Garrick to whom it had been offered. *Agis* was first performed in Feb. 1758 at Covent Garden, after the success of Home's *Douglas* (completed in 1754, first performed at Edinburgh in Dec. 1756). There is no evidence to suggest that Home started *Douglas* until his return to Scotland, so that suggested borrowings from this play by C. are unlikely, whereas it is not unreasonable to suppose that Home may have echoed C.'s poem.

5–8. cordial youth] As explained in Carlyle's letter to Tytler (see headnote), C. refers to Thomas Barrow (d. 1780), who had been a medical student at Edinburgh and had fought with the Edinburgh volunteers against the rebels at Falkirk in Jan. 1746. The only Englishman in the party, he had been captured along with John Home and had then escaped with him and others

Whom, long endeared, thou leav'st by Lavant's side;
Together let us wish him lasting truth,
    And joy untainted with his destined bride.
Go! nor regardless, while these numbers boast
10   My short-lived bliss, forget my social name;
But think far off how, on the southern coast,
    I met thy friendship with an equal flame!
Fresh to that soil thou turn'st, whose every vale
    Shall prompt the poet and his song demand:
15   To thee thy copious subjects ne'er shall fail;

from the Castle of Doune in which they had been imprisoned, Barrow dislocating his ankle and breaking several ribs in the process. The episode is described in John Home's *History of the Rebellion in the Year 1745* (1802) pp. 187–91; see also *Works of John Home*, ed. H. Mackenzie (Edinburgh, 1822) i 5–6, 126; iii 161, 172. It was natural that Home should seek out Barrow during his visit to London and Carlyle, *Autobiography* (1861) p. 231, records that Home's disappointment at the rejection of *Agis* was partly consoled by the 'warm approbation' of Barrow and other friends. Barrow was evidently now living at Chichester, where C. had no doubt met him and it was Barrow, as Carlyle states more than once, who introduced Home to C., 'with whom he grew very intimate'. Carlyle's letter to Tytler states that Barrow was living in Winchester when Home and C. saw him, but C.'s reference to 'Lavant's side' (l. 6) indicates that this was a mistake for Chichester. The undated fragment of a letter from Carlyle (see headnote) which gives much the same information as that to Tytler, correctly states that the *Ode* was written 'on John Home's leaving Chichester', *Times Lit. Supp.* 1943, p. 312; for a copy of the same letter, see P. L. Carver, *Notes and Queries*, clxxvii (1939) 258–9. Carver quotes other evidence to prove that Barrow was living at Chichester at this period (see l. 8 *n*) and suggests that C. would have reason to visit his native town on legal business late in 1749. Thomas Barrow was appointed Deputy-Paymaster of the forces in North America in April 1757, was back in England in 1769 but died in New York in 1780.
6. *Scored through in MS, with* Whose *written above* Whom, *but no further substitution made. As C. seems to have intended to revise the line rather than omit it, his first version is retained, as in 1788.*
Lavant] The river running through Chichester.
8. Barrow married Mary Downer at Chichester on 2 April 1753; a daughter was born to them in June 1757 also at Chichester. Mrs Barrow was buried at Chichester in 1814, aged 87 (see P. L. Carver, *The Life of a Poet* (1967) pp. 151–3).
12. 'equal their flame', Dryden, *Iphis and Ianthe* 81; and 'His Flame was equal', *Sigismonda and Guiscardo* 471; and Pope, *Windsor Forest* 9: '*These*, were my Breast inspir'd with equal Flame'.
14. *prompt*] Inspire.

Thou need'st but take the pencil to thy hand,
And paint what all believe who own thy genial land.

2

There must thou wake perforce thy Doric quill,
    'Tis Fancy's land to which thou sett'st thy feet;
20   Where still, 'tis said, the fairy people meet
Beneath each birken shade on mead or hill.
There each trim lass that skims the milky store
    To the swart tribes their creamy bowl allots;
By night they sip it round the cottage-door,
25   While airy minstrels warble jocund notes.

16. pencil] Paintbrush (*Lat.* penicillum). Cp. *Faerie Queene* III Pr. ii, 2: 'Nor
life-resembling pencill can it paint'.
17. own] Acknowledge as having power over oneself.
18. Doric] Rustic. Cp. Fairfax's *Tasso* VI xxxix 7: 'my slender quill'; and
Milton, *Lycidas* 188–9: 'He touch'd the tender stops of various Quills, /
With eager thought warbling his *Dorick* lay'; also Thomson, *Autumn* 890:
'Whose pastoral banks first heard my Doric reed'. By 'quill' C. means,
like Milton, a musical reed or pipe, rather than the plectrum for plucking a
musical instrument, which has been suggested.
20–1. Dryden, *Wife of Bath's Tale* 3–4: 'The King of Elfs and little Fairy
Queen / Gamboll'd on Heaths, and danc'd on ev'ry Green.'
21. birken] A northern form of 'birchen', composed of birches; 'birks' for
birch-trees is included in the Glossary in Allan Ramsay's *Poems* (1731).
22–5. Cp. Martin Martin, *Description of the Western Islands of Scotland* (2nd
edn, 1716) p. 391, on the Shetland Islands: 'It is not long since every Family
of any considerable Substance in those Islands, was haunted by a Spirit they
called *Browny*, which did several sorts of Work; and this was the reason
why they gave him Offerings of the various Products of the Place: thus
some when they churn'd their Milk, or brew'd, pour'd some Milk and
Wort through the Hole of a Stone, called *Browny*'s Stone.' Earlier Martin,
p. 335, provided what is probably C.'s source for l. 25: 'These Spirits us'd
also to form Sounds in the Air, resembling those of a Harp, Pipe, Crowing of
a Cock, and of the grinding of Querns: and sometimes they have heard
Voices in the Air by Night, singing *Irish* Songs; the Words of which Songs
some of my Acquaintance still retain.' But C. had English traditions on which
to draw: cp. Milton, *L'Allegro* 105–6: 'Tells how the drudging *Goblin*
swet, / To ern his Cream-bowle duly set'; and Dryden, *Wife of Bath's Tale*
20–21: 'The Dairy-Maid expects no Fairy Guest, / To skim the Bowls and
after pay the Feast.' Cp. also Milton, *Comus* 436: 'No goblin, or swart faëry
of the mine'.
22. 'milky store', Dryden, *Georgics* iii 482.
25. airy] viewless *written above deleted*.

There every herd, by sad experience, knows
    How, winged with fate, their elf-shot arrows fly,
When the sick ewe her summer food foregoes,
    Or, stretched on earth, the heart-smit heifers lie.
30 Such airy beings awe the untutored swain:
    Nor thou, though learned, his homelier thoughts
        neglect;
Let thy sweet muse the rural faith sustain:
    These are the themes of simple, sure effect,
That add new conquests to her boundless reign,
35   And fill with double force her heart-commanding
        strain.

3

Even yet preserved, how often may'st thou hear,
    Where to the pole the Boreal mountains run,
Taught by the father to his listening son
Strange lays, whose power had charmed a Spenser's
    ear.
40 At every pause, before thy mind possessed,
    Old Runic bards shall seem to rise around

26–9. Allan Ramsay, *Patie and Roger* 42, has the phrase 'Three elf-shot were', which he explains in a note which was probably C.'s source for these lines. Cp. Ramsay's *Poems* (1731) i 139 *n*: 'Bewitch'd, shot by fairies, country people tell odd tales of this distemper amongst cows. When elf-shot, the cow falls down suddenly dead, no part of the skin is pierced, but often a little triangular flat stone is found near the beast, as they report, which is call'd the elf's arrow.'

27. 'wing'd with Fate', Dryden, *Threnodia Augustalis* 49, and *Aeneid* x 466.

28–9. Cp. Spenser, *Shepheardes Calender*, 'Nov.' 133: 'The feeble flocks in field refuse their former foode'; and Pope, *Winter* 37–8: 'the Flocks refuse their verdant Food, / The thirsty Heifers shun the gliding Flood'.

29. 'Heart-strook', *Par. Lost* xi 264.

30. C. is merging memories of the 'untutor'd mind' of Pope's 'poor Indian', *Essay on Man* i 99, with Thomson, *Castle of Indolence* I xxx, of 'a shepherd of the Hebrid Isles': 'aerial beings sometimes deign / To stand embodied to our senses plain'.

34. Dryden, *Lucretius* i 25: 'Extends thy uncontroul'd and boundless reign'.

37. Boreal] Northern.

39. Cp. *Peace* 11 and *n* (p. 468).

41. C.'s use of 'Runic' here to apply to ancient Scottish poetry is the first instance recorded in the *OED*. C. has transferred it from its more normal reference to ancient Scandinavian language and literature. In Olaus Wormius' *Danica Literatura Antiquissima* (1636), the running title is 'Literatura Runica', but C.'s source was probably Sir William Temple's essay,

With uncouth lyres, in many-coloured vest,
   Their matted hair with boughs fantastic crowned:
   Whether thou bidd'st the well-taught hind repeat
45   The choral dirge that mourns some chieftain brave,
When every shrieking maid her bosom beat,
   And strewed with choicest herbs his scented grave;
   Or whether, sitting in the shepherd's shiel,
   Thou hear'st some sounding tale of war's alarms;
50   When at the bugle's call, with fire and steel,
   The sturdy clans poured forth their bonny swarms,
And hostile brothers met to prove each other's arms.

4

'Tis thine to sing how, framing hideous spells,
   In Skye's lone isle the gifted wizard seer,

'Of Poetry' (1690), *Critical Essays of the 17th Century*, ed. J. E. Spingarn (1908–9) iii 93–6, which discusses Runic poetry. Cp. in particular Temple's description of the main themes of the Gothic 'Runers': 'the Records of Bold and Martial Actions, and the Praises of Valiant Men that had Fought Successfully or Dyed Bravely; and these Songs or Ballads were usually sung at Feasts, or in Circles of Young or Idle Persons, and served to inflame the Humour of War, of Slaughter, and of Spoils among them.' There are also two 'Runic Odes' in the *Poems* (1748) of Thomas Warton Senior, pp. 157–9, where reference is made to Temple's essay. Cp. also *Lycidas* 53: 'Where your old *Bards*, the famous *Druids* ly'.

43. Pope, *Dunciad* iv 398: 'A tribe, with weeds and shells fantastic crown'd'.
44. repeat] *Written above* relate *deleted in MS.*
47. Shakespeare often uses 'strew' and 'strewed' for the scattering of flowers on graves: cp. *Cymbeline* IV ii 287: 'These herblets . . . which we upon you strew'; also Milton, *Lycidas* 151: 'To strew the Laureat Herse where *Lycid* lies'.
48. shiel] a Kind of Hut built ev'ry summer for the convenience of milking the Cattle *C.'s MS note; expanded in 1788 to* A kind of hut, built for a summer habitation to the herdsmen, when the cattle are sent to graze in distant pastures.
   C. could have come across the word in Allan Ramsay's *Robert, Richy and Sandy* 127: 'Come to my shiel, there let's forget our care.'
51. The] e *written above the* ey *of* They.   *bonny*] bony *1788.*
52. prove] Test, make a trial of; a Spenserian phrase e.g. *Faerie Queene* I x 66, 9: 'And proue thy puissaunt armes'.
53. framing] Composing, contriving.
54–5. Martin Martin, *Western Isles* pp. 150–1, gives a description of the notable caves on the island of Skye.
54. Pope, *Rape of the Lock* iv 154: 'In some lone Isle, or distant *Northern* Land'.

55   Lodged in the wintry cave with
        Or in the depth of Uist's dark forests dwells;
        How they, whose sight such dreary dreams engross,
        With their own visions oft astonished droop,
        When o'er the watery strath or quaggy moss
60   They see the gliding ghosts unbodied troop.

56. depth] *Written above* gloom *deleted in MS.*   *Uist*] Ust *MS.*
    C.'s reference to Uist may be due to Martin Martin's description, p. 85, of
a valley on South Uist called Glenslyte: 'The Natives . . . are possessed with
a firm Belief that this Valley is haunted by Spirits, who by the Inhabitants
are call'd the great Men'.
57–69. Martin Martin, *Western Isles* pp. 300–35, gives many examples of the
gift of 'Second-Sight', the abnormal faculty of perceiving apparitions or
phantoms, usually sinister, connected with disastrous events about to take
place. The phenomenon was comically treated in Smollett's *Humphry
Clinker* (1771), letters of 12 and 15 September; but Boswell and Johnson
during their tour of the Hebrides were open-minded about it and anxious
to acquire evidence. Cp. *Life of Johnson* v 159–60, 163–4, 227, 320, 358, 390–1,
407. Martin Martin's description of 'Second-Sight', p. 300, begins: 'The
Second-Sight is a singular Faculty of Seeing an otherwise invisible Object,
without any previous Means us'd by the Person that sees it for that end; the
Vision makes such a lively impression upon the Seers, that they neither see
nor think of any thing else, except the Vision, as long as it continues: and
then they appear pensive or jovial, according to the Object which was
represented to them.'
58. astonished] *Written above* afflicted *deleted in MS.*   *droop*] Are depressed
spiritually. C. has nothing to say about the 'jovial' effects of the second-
sight mentioned by Martin.
59. strath] A stretch of flat land by water. Cp. Ramsay, *The Poet's Wish* 9–10:
'Nor those fair straths that water'd are / With Tay and Tweed's smooth
streams'.   *moss*] A Scottish or northern word for a bog or swamp. Cp.
the ballad *Hardiknute*, as extended by Allan Ramsay, stanza xv: 'And he
has ridden owre muir and moss, / Owre hills and mony a glen . . .'
60. In this line C. combines phrases associated with ghosts from his three
favourite poets. Cp. 'gliding ghosts', *Julius Caesar* I iii 63; 'Every one lets
forth his sprite, / In the churchway paths to glide', *Midsummer Night's
Dream* V i 388–9; and in the same play, III ii 381–2, 'Ghosts, wandering
here and there, / Troop home to churchyards'. Milton twice used 'troop' for
ghosts or evil spirits, *Comus* 603, and *Nativity Ode* 232–4: 'The flocking
shadows pale, / Troop to th'infernall jail, / Each fetter'd Ghost slips to his
severall grave.' Spenser, *Shepheardes Calender*, 'Nov.' 166, has: 'Her soule
vnbodied of the burdenous corpse'; and Death is described as 'a shade',
Faerie Queene VII vii 46, 5, 'vnbodied, vnsoul'd, vnheard, vnseene'.

Or if in sports, or on the festive green,
    Their   glance some fated youth descry,
Who, now perhaps in lusty vigour seen
    And rosy health, shall soon lamented die.
65 For them the viewless forms of air obey,
    Their bidding heed and at their beck repair.
They know what spirit brews the stormful day,
    And heartless, oft like moody madness stare
To see the phantom train their secret work prepare.

[Stanza 5 missing.]

6

[8 lines missing.]

95 What though far off, from some dark dell espied,

61–4. Martin Martin gives several instances of premonitions of the death of healthy persons, e.g. pp. 320–1.

65. viewless] Invisible. Cp. 'viewless winds', *Measure for Measure* III i 124; and 'Light as the viewless air', Pope, *Odyssey* vi 25.

65–6. Martin Martin had in fact made it clear that the seers were passive media rather than malevolent agents, e.g. p. 309: 'generally illiterate, and well-meaning People, and altogether void of design'.

66. heed] *Written above* mark *deleted in MS.*   Cp. *Par. Regained* ii 238, of Satan and his spirits: 'To be at hand, and at his beck appear'.

67. spirit] *Written over* Fiend *deleted.*   Cp. Pope, *Rape of the Lock* ii 85, of the sylphs: 'Or brew fierce Tempests on the wintry Main'.

68. heartless] Dismayed. Cp. Spenser, *Colin Clout* 228: 'hartlesse quite and full of inward feare'; and *Virgil's Gnat* 297: 'All suddenly dismaid, and hartles quight'.   *moody madness*] This may be a rare instance of C.'s echoing Gray: cp. *Eton Ode* 79 (p. 62 above).

95. For the missing leaf of the MS, containing stanza 5 and half of stanza 6, see headnote. Seven of the eleven complete stanzas of the poem have 17 ll. (the second has 18, the last three have 16), so that it is reasonable to assume, since 9 ll. of stanza 6 remain, that 25 ll. are missing. What would in that case have been the original numbering after the gap has therefore been retained. The poem continues at l. 95, in the middle of a description of a man deluded by wildfire into the clutches of the kelpie (see l. 137). In the text in the Edinburgh *Transactions*, the 'chasm' was filled by Henry Mackenzie, at the request of Tytler (see headnote). The interpolated lines in Bell's London edn, so often reprinted as C.'s in the nineteenth century are worth reproducing, partly to aid recognition of them, and also to support the argument in the headnote that C. did not write them:

v

To monarchs dear, some hundred miles astray,
    Oft have they seen Fate give the fatal blow!

His glimmering mazes cheer the excursive sight,
Yet turn, ye wanderers, turn your steps aside,
   Nor choose the guidance of that faithless light!
For watchful, lurking mid the unrustling reed,

The Seer, in *Sky*, shriek'd as the blood did flow,
When headless *Charles* warm on the scaffold lay!
As *Boreas* threw his *young Aurora* forth,
   In the first year of the first *George's* reign,
And battles rag'd in welkin of the North,
   They mourn'd in air, fell, fell Rebellion, slain!
And as, of late, they joy'd in *Preston's* fight,
   Saw at sad *Falkirk*, all their hopes near crown'd!
They rav'd! divining, thro' their *Second Sight*,
   Pale, red *Culloden*, where these hopes were drown'd!
Illustrious *William*! *Britain's* guardian name!
   One *William* sav'd us from a tyrant's stroke;
He for a sceptre, gain'd heroic fame,
   But thou, more glorious, Slavery's chain hast broke,
To reign a private man, and bow to Freedom's yoke!

vi

These, too, thou'lt sing! for well thy magic Muse
   Can to the topmost heav'n of grandeur soar!
   Or stoop to wail the swain that is no more!
Ah, homely swains! your homeward steps ne'er loose;
   Let not dank *Will* mislead you to the heath:
Dancing in mirky night, o'er fen and lake,
   He glows, to draw you downward to your death,
In his bewitch'd, low, marshy, willow brake!

These lines do not deserve or really need annotation, but the allusion in ll.
5–6 to the famous *aurora borealis* of 6 March 1716 may be mentioned, as well
as the praise of the Duke of Cumberland in the last 5 ll. of stanza v. It is
very unlikely that C. would pay such a tribute as late as 1749–50.
95–8. The description of wildfire may have been suggested by similar
passages in *Par. Lost* ix 634–42, and Thomson, *Autumn* 45–59. C.'s description
as a whole (ll. 95–137) recalls Thomson's description of a man lost in a
snowstorm, *Winter* 276–321: the resemblance was noted at once by Carlyle
(see letter quoted in headnote).
98. *choose*] trust *1788*.
96. *excursive*] Wandering, deviating. Cp. 'your eye excursive roams',
Thomson, *Spring* 953.
99. *unrustling*] The first usage recorded by the *OED*.

100   At those mirk hours the wily monster lies,
    And listens oft to hear the passing steed,
    And frequent round him rolls his sullen eyes,
If chance his savage wrath may some weak wretch
    surprise.

7

Ah, luckless swain, o'er all unblest indeed!
105   Whom late bewildered in the dank, dark fen,
    Far from his flocks and smoking hamlet then!
To that sad spot his
    On him enraged the fiend, in angry mood,
    Shall never look with pity's kind concern,
110   But instant, furious, rouse the whelming flood
    O'er its drowned banks, forbidding all return.
Or, if he meditate his wished escape
    To some dim hill that seems uprising near,

100. mirk] Written above sad in MS. The word is a variant of 'murk', dialect for 'dark'. Once again, C. may have found the word in Ramsay, *Gentle Shepherd* IV ii: 'Mirk despair'; but 'mirkest night' occurs in Fairfax's *Tasso* XVI lxviii, 1. *the monster]* The 'kaelpie' or kelpie, as made clear at l. 137. Tytler's note reads: 'A name given in Scotland to a supposed spirit of the waters.' The *OED*, in which C.'s usage here is the first instance given, describes it as 'The Lowland Scottish name of a fabled water-spirit or demon assuming various shapes, but usually appearing in that of a horse; it is reputed to haunt lakes and rivers, and to take delight in, or even to bring about, the drowning of travellers and others'. There are several references to the kelpie in Burns's poetry and letters. No particular printed source describing the monster earlier than 1749 has been identified: it is likely that C. learned about it chiefly through conversation with John Home himself, who refers to it as 'The angry Spirit of the water' in his *Douglas* III i.
102. Par. Lost i 56: 'round he throws his baleful eyes'.
103. 'Weak wretch', *Faerie Queene* II i 52, 8, and II iv 17, 6.
108. 'angry mood', *Faerie Queene* IV vi 29, 8; Fairfax's *Tasso* VII liii 6, XII l 1 and XX lviii 8; and Dryden, *Eclogues* ix 8; *Aeneid* i 159, 219 and xii 500.
109. Cp. *Epistle to Hanmer* 25 (p. 391).
110. rouse] raise *1788.* Cp. 'the whelming tide', Milton, *Lycidas* 157, and Dryden, *Eclogues* viii 80. *instant]* For the poetic use of this form adverbially, cp. *Hamlet* I v 94, and Milton, *Par. Lost* vi 549: 'Instant without disturb they took Allarm.'
111. banks] bank *1788. drowned]* Flooded.
112. meditate] Plan or design mentally.

To his faint eye the grim and grisly shape
115   In all its terrors clad shall wild appear.
Meantime the waterys urge shall round him rise,
Poured sudden forth from every swelling source.
What now remains but tears and hopeless sighs?
His fear-shook limbs have lost their youthly force,
120   And down the waves he floats, a pale and breathless
corse.

8

For him, in vain, his anxious wife shall wait,
Or wander forth to meet him on his way;
For him, in vain, at to-fall of the day,
His bairns shall linger at the unclosing gate

114. Spenser is fond of combining 'grim' and 'grisly', e.g. *Faerie Queene*
VII vii 46, 2: '*Death* with most grim and griesly visage seene'.
115. Cp. Gray, *Ode to Adversity* 35 and *n* (p. 73 above), although it was not
published until 1753.
117. Faerie Queene VI i 21, 1–2: 'a water streame, whose swelling sourse /
Shall driue a Mill'; and VI xi 34, 3.
119. youthly] *The first letters written over one or two illegible letters of another
word.*   The meaning is 'youthful,' as often in Spenser.
fear-shook] The only instance recorded by the *OED*.
120. Cp. 'flote upon his watry bear' and 'His goary visage down the stream
was sent', *Lycidas* 12 and 62.
121–4. Thomson, *Winter* 311–17, at the end of the passage referred to above
in l. 95 *n*: 'In vain for him the officious wife prepares / The fire fair-blazing
and the vestment warm; / In vain his little children, peeping out / Into the
mingling storm, demand their sire / With tears of artless innocence. Alas! /
Nor wife nor children more shall he behold, / Nor friends, nor sacred home.'
Cp. also Gray's *Elegy* 21–4, and the sources listed there (p. 121 above).
123. to-fall] The close. This is the first usage recorded in *OED*, but C. almost
certainly was imitating William Hamilton of Bangour's 'The Braes of
Yarrow' 79: 'e'er the toofall of the night'. See l. 214 *n* below.
124. bairns] babes *1788.*   *unclosing*] *Written above* Cottage *deleted in MS.*
125–37. This passage has been compared to Ovid, *Metamorphoses* xi 654–9,
describing Alcyone's vision of the dead Ceyx: *luridus, exanimi similis, sine
vestibus ullis,/coniugis ante torum miserae stetit: uda videtur/barba viri, madidisque
gravis fluere unda capillis./tum lecto incumbens fletu super ora profuso/haec ait:
'agnoscis Ceyca, miserrima coniunx/an mea mutata est facies nece?'* (Wan like
the dead, he stands before the couch of his hapless wife. His beard is wet, and
water drips from his sodden hair. Then with streaming eyes he bends over
her couch and says: 'Do you recognize your Ceyx, O most wretched wife?
or is my face changed in death?')

125 Ah, ne'er shall he return! Alone, if night
    Her travelled limbs in broken slumbers steep,
  With dropping willows dressed, his mournful sprite
    Shall visit sad, perhaps, her silent sleep:
  Then he, perhaps, with moist and watery hand,
130   Shall fondly seem to press her shuddering cheek,
  And with his blue swoll'n face before her stand,
    And, shivering cold, these piteous accents speak:
  'Pursue, dear wife, thy daily toils pursue
    At dawn or dusk, industrious as before;
135 Nor e'er of me one hapless thought renew,
    While I lie weltering on the osiered shore,
  Drowned by the Kaelpie's wrath, nor e'er shall aid
    thee more.'

9

  Unbounded is thy range; with varied style
    Thy Muse may, like those feathery tribes which
    spring
140   From their rude rocks, extend her skirting wing
  Round the moist marge of each cold Hebrid isle,
  To that hoar pile which still its ruin shows:

125. Alone] Only, solely.

126. travelled] Travailed, wearied; cp. 'travell'd steps', *Par. Lost* iii 501.

127. dropping] *Written over part of an illegible word, perhaps beginning* Sh.

For the meaning 'dripping', cp. Pope, *Winter* 31: 'Now hung with Pearls the dropping Trees appear.'

128. perhaps] perchance *1788*. (The change was no doubt made to avoid repetition of the word in l. 129.)

130. fondly] *Written above the line for insertion.*   *shuddering*] *Written above* cold and shuddring *deleted in* MS.   Cp. *Comus* 802–3: 'a cold shuddring dew / Dips me all o're'.

131. Dryden, *Georgics* i 607: 'his Cheeks are swoln with livid blue'.

133–7. C. has placed before each of these lines in the *MS* what appears to be a question mark, although it may have been intended to indicate direct speech.

133. Pursue] *Written above* Proceed *deleted in* MS.

136. weltering] Tossed about by waves. Cp. *Par. Lost* i 78, and *Lycidas* 13: 'and welter to the parching wind'.

137. Kaelpie] See l. 100 *n.*

139–40. Spenser, *Shepheardes Calender*, 'Oct.' 43–4: 'There may thy Muse display her fluttryng wing, / And stretch herselfe at large from East to West.'

142–5. Cp. Martin Martin, *Western Islands* p. 19, on the Flannan Islands, which he describes as 'places of inherent Sanctity': 'The Island of

In whose small vaults a pigmy-folk is found,
Whose bones the delver with his spade upthrows,
145   And culls them, wondering, from the hallowed
         ground!
Or thither, where beneath the showery west
The mighty kings of three fair realms are laid;
Once foes, perhaps, together now they rest.
No slaves revere them and no wars invade:
150   Yet frequent now, at midnight's solemn hour,
The rifted mounds their yawning cells unfold,
And forth the monarchs stalk with sovereign power
In pageant robes, and wreathed with sheeny gold,
And on their twilight tombs aerial council hold.

Pigmies, or, as the Natives call it, *The Island of Little Men*, is but of small
extent. There has been many small Bones dug out of the Ground here,
resembling those of Human Kind more than any other. This gave ground
to a Tradition which the Natives have of a very Low-statur'd People living
once here, call'd *Lusbirdan*, i.e. *Pigmies*.' Later Martin, p. 82, mentioned
similar discoveries at Bael-nin-Killach on Benbecula: 'The Natives have
lately discover'd a Stone Vault on the East-side the Town, in which there
are abundance of small Bones, which have occasion'd many uncertain
Conjectures; some said they were the Bones of Birds, others judg'd them
rather to be the Bones of Pigmies.' Martin added that Sir Normand Mack-
leod said 'that they must be the Bones of Infants born by the Nuns there'.
143–5. Pope, *Windsor Forest* 301–2: 'Or raise old Warriors whose ador'd
Remains / In weeping Vaults her hallow'd Earth contains!'
146–7. C.'s source is Martin Martin's description of St. Ouran's Church on
Iona, *Western Isles* p. 261: 'On the South-side of the Church, mention'd
above, is the Burial-place in which the Kings and Chiefs of Tribes are buried,
and over them a Shrine; there was an Inscription, giving an account of
each particular Tomb, but Time has worn them off. The middlemost had
written on it, *The Tombs of the Kings of* Scotland; of which forty eight lie
there. Upon that on the right hand was written, *The Tombs of the Kings of*
Ireland; of which four were buried here. And upon that on the left hand was
written, *The Kings of* Norway; of which eight were buried here.'
151. rifted] *Written above* Yawning *deleted in MS.*   Cp. Milton, *Comus* 518:
'And rifted Rocks whose entrance leads to hell'; and Pope, *Messiah* 71:
'rifted Rocks'.
152–3. Faerie Queene II ii 40, 4: 'her soueraigne powre, and scepter shene';
'sheen' also occurs in Fairfax's *Tasso*. This may have suggested C.'s use of
'sheeny', but cp. 'the wall / Of sheenie Heav'n', Milton, *On the Death of
a Fair Infant* 47–8.
153. pageant robes] Cp. *Simplicity* 9 and *n* (p. 424).
154. Cp. the various versions of C.'s *Ode to a Lady* 19–24 (p. 458).

10

155   But O, o'er all, forget not Kilda's race,
        On whose bleak rocks, which brave the wasting
            tides,
        Fair Nature's daughter, Virtue, yet abides!
        Go, just as they, their blameless manners trace!
        Then to my ear transmit some gentle song
160   Of those whose lives are yet sincere and plain,

155–71. Martin Martin describes St Kilda in his *Western Isles* pp. 280–9, but he had published a separate account, *A Voyage to St Kilda, The remotest of all the Hebrides*, in 1698, which was republished in March 1749 and so was easily accessible to C. In any case it had been mentioned and quoted in David Mallet's *Amyntor and Theodora* pp. v–vii, which is set in St Kilda, in May 1747; and James Thomson had also celebrated St Kilda in *Autumn* 862–78, 892–902. A 3rd edn of Martin's *Voyage to St Kilda* was published in 1749 and a 4th in 1753. References are to the 2nd edn, 1749, the most likely to be used by C. See A. S. P. Woodhouse, 'Collins and Martin Martin', *Times Lit. Supp.* 1928, p. 1011, who argues that C. somewhat exaggerates the stoical endurance of the islanders and the hardships they have to undergo.
156, 161. Martin, *St Kilda* p. 9, describes the island as 'naturally fenc'd with one continued Face of a Rock of great height, except a part of the Bay, which lies to the *South-East*, and is generally well fenced with a raging Sea'.
157–60, 167–9. Martin's *St Kilda* has a strong primitivistic purpose underlying its account of the lives of the inhabitants of the island, celebrating their simple virtues in contrast to the vices of sophisticated civilization. Mallet's *Amyntor and Theodora* had imitated this and C. follows suit. Martin wrote, pp. 67–8:
'The Inhabitants of St. *Kilda* are much happier than the Generality of Mankind, as being almost the only People in the World who feel the Sweetness of true Liberty: What the Condition of the People in the golden Age is feigned by the Poets to be, that theirs really is; I mean, in Innocency and Simplicity, Purity, mutual Love, and cordial Friendship, free from solicitous Cares, and anxious Covetousness; from Envy, Deceit, and Dissimulation; from Ambition and Pride, and the Consequences that attend them. They are altogether ignorant of the Vices of Foreigners, and governed by the Dictates of Reason and Christianity, as it was first delivered to them by those heroick Souls, whose Zeal moved them to undergo Danger and Trouble to plant Religion here in one of the remotest Corners of the World.
'There is this only wanting to make them the happiest People in this habitable Globe, *viz.* That they themselves do not know how happy they are, and how much they are above the Avarice and Slavery of the rest of Mankind. Their Way of living makes them contemn Gold and Silver, as below the Dignity of human Nature; they live by the Munificence of

Their bounded walks the ragged cliffs along,
    And all their prospect but the wintry main.
With sparing temperance, at the needful time,
    They drain the sainted spring or, hunger-pressed,
165   Along the Atlantic rock undreading climb,
    And of its eggs despoil the solan's nest.
Thus blest in primal innocence they live,
    Sufficed and happy with that frugal fare
Which tasteful toil and hourly danger give.
170   Hard is their shallow soil,   and bare;
    Nor ever vernal bee was heard to murmur there!

Heaven, and have no designs upon one another, but such as are purely
suggested by Justice and Benevolence.'

161. ragged] rugged *1788.*   For the meaning of 'ragged' as 'irregular,
jagged', cp. 'ragged cliffs', *Faerie Queene* I v 38, 6; and *III Henry VI* V iv 27
and Milton, *L'Allegro* 9. See also *Persian Eclogues* iv 19 (p. 383 above).

164. sainted spring] Martin, *St Kilda* pp. 13–14, describes several springs and
wells on the island. C.'s use of 'sainted' suggests that he was thinking of
'St. *Kilder*'s Well'; but C. may also have been thinking of '*the Well of Youth*'
which 'is only accessible by the Inhabitants, no Stranger daring to climb the
steep Rock'.   *hunger-pressed*] C.'s coinage according to the *OED*, although
such formations are common: cp. 'hunger-bit', *Par. Regained* ii 416.

165. undreading] The first instance of the word given in the *OED* is dated
1745, in Eliza Heywood's *Female Spectator* iii 171.

165–6. Martin more than once (pp. 20–1, 25–8, 55) describes the methods
used by the inhabitants to capture the solan geese or gannets or to rob their
nests of eggs. Cp. *St Kilda* p. 55: 'The Inhabitants, I must tell you, run no
small Danger in the Quest of the Fowls and Eggs, insomuch, that I fear it
would be thought an *Hyperbole* to relate the Inaccessibleness, Steepness,
and Height of those formidable Rocks which they venture to climb.'

168. Sufficed] *Written above* Content *deleted in MS.*   Martin, *St Kilda* pp.
58–9, describes the 'frugal' food and drink of the inhabitants of the island.

169. give] *The margin of the MS is here torn and only the downstroke of the
first letter is visible; Carlyle's transcript and 1788 read* give *and the word was
probably clearly legible then.*   *tasteful*] A curious usage, apparently com-
bining senses of 'agreeable' and 'conducive to appetite'.

170. Carlyle supplied and bleak *after* soil, *without indicating that it was an in-
sertion. The MS is torn at the end of the line but* ba *is visible and Carlyle could
no doubt read* bare.   Martin, *St Kilda* pp. 14–15, describes the island as 'one
hard Rock . . . all thinly cover'd with black or brown Earth, not above a
Foot, some Places half a Foot deep, except the Top of the Hills'; but adds
that 'The Soil is very grateful to the Labourer'.

171. murmur] *Only* mu *is now visible because of the tear in the MS but
Carlyle gives the present reading.*   Cp. Martin, *St Kilda* p. 17: 'There is no Sort
of Trees, no, not the least Shrub grows here, nor ever a Bee seen at any Time.'

II

Nor need'st thou blush that such false themes engage
   Thy gentle mind, of fairer stores possessed;
   For not alone they touch the village breast,
175 But filled in elder time the historic page.
   There Shakespeare's self, with every garland crowned,
   In musing hour his Wayward Sisters found,
     And with their terrors dressed the magic scene.
   From them he sung, when mid his bold design,
180   Before the Scot afflicted and aghast,
   The shadowy kings of Banquo's fated line,
     Through the dark cave in gleamy pageant passed
   Proceed, nor quit the tales which, simply told,
   Could once so well my answering bosom pierce;

This is the debt to Martin which was noted by Wordsworth (see headnote).
172. C's use of 'false' seems hardly appropriate after a description of the
simple virtues of the inhabitants of St Kilda. He is referring to the super-
natural and superstitious subjects he had discussed earlier. The awkwardness
of this transition may be considered evidence that stanza 10 was a
relatively late interpolation; but the recent discovery of C.'s MS disposes
finally of speculations that Carlyle had misplaced the stanza. See the editorial
note in *The Poets of Great Britain* (1807) liii 170; Blunden (1929) pp. 129–30
interchanged stanzas 9 and 10.
172–5. Pope, *To Mr. Addison* 49–50: 'Nor blush, these studies thy regard
engaged; / These pleas'd the Fathers of poetic rage.'
173. gentle mind] A Spenserian phrase, *Faerie Queene* V xi 64, 1; VI iii 1, 2, etc.
175. Cp. *Passions* 105 and *n* (p. 485).
176. This stanza is more incorrect in its structure than any of the foregoing.
There is apparently a line wanting between this and the subsequent one,
In musing hour, &c. The deficient line ought to have rhymed with *scene.*
Tytler.
    The last three stanzas each have 16 ll., compared with the 17 ll. of all
but the second, which has 18. Because of this relative consistency at the end
of the poem, it is perhaps unnecessary to believe that lines are missing.
Wayward Sisters] The Witches in *Macbeth*; 'wayward' means having the
supernatural power of dealing with fate or destiny. The word is spelt
'weyward' and 'weyard' in *Macbeth*.
*179, 181. The tear in the MS removed a few letters at the beginning of these
lines.*
179. Pope, *Essay on Criticism* 136: 'Convinc'd, amaz'd, he checks the bold
Design.'
181–2. Cp. *Macbeth* IV i.
183–4. These lines may mean that C. had learned of some of the Highland
superstitions he has described through conversation with Home.
184. Fairfax's *Tasso* VII xx 6: 'Shall feel sad Pity pierce his gentle mind'.

185   Proceed, in forceful sounds and colours bold
        The native legends of thy land rehearse;
        To such adapt thy lyre and suit thy powerful verse.

12

        In scenes like these, which, daring to depart
            From sober Truth, are still to Nature true,
190   And call forth fresh delights to Fancy's view,
        The heroic Muse employed her Tasso's art!
        How have I trembled when, at Tancred's stroke,

188–91. C.'s justification of the supernatural appears to imitate Dryden's in 'Of Heroic Poetry: An Essay' (in *Of Dramatic Poesy and Other Essays*, ed. G. Watson, i 160–1), a possibility which is strengthened by Dryden's reference to 'the Enchanted Wood in Tasso': 'For my part, I am of opinion that neither Homer, Virgil, Statius, Ariosto, Tasso, nor our English Spenser could have formed their poems half so beautiful without those gods and spirits, and those enthusiastic parts of poetry which compose the most noble parts of all their writings. And I will ask any man who loves heroic poetry ... if the ghost of Polydorus in Virgil, the Enchanted Wood in Tasso, and the Bower of Bliss in Spenser (which he borrows from that admirable Italian) could have been omitted without taking from their works some of the greatest beauties in them .... an heroic poet is not tied to a bare representation of what is true, or exceeding probable: but ... he may let himself loose to visionary objects, and to the representation of such things as depending not on sense, and therefore not to be comprehended by knowledge, may give him a freer scope for imagination.'

Addison wrote similarly of Shakespeare in *Spectator* No. 419 (1 July 1712): 'There is something so wild and yet so solemn in the speeches of his Ghosts, Fairies, Witches, and the like Imaginary Persons, that we cannot forbear thinking them natural, tho' we have no Rule by which to judge of them, and must confess, if there are such Beings in the World, it looks highly probable they should talk and act as he has represented them.'

190. delights] delight *1788.*   Cp. Pope, *Essay on Criticism* 666: 'And call new Beauties forth from ev'ry Line.'

191–203. C. refers to Tasso's *Gerusalemme Liberata* (three versions, 1576–93), and in particular to the translation by Edward Fairfax published in 1600. See headnote for the new edn of this translation published in Oct. 1749, shortly before C. wrote this poem.

192–5. These lines are written above the following deleted in the MS:

> How have I trembled, when at Tancred's side
> Like him I stalkd and all his Passions felt
> Where Charmd by Ismen thro' the Forrest wide
> Barkd in Each Plant a talking Spirit dwelt!

For Tancred's adventure in the Enchanted Wood, see Fairfax, *Tasso's*

Its gushing blood the gaping cypress poured;
When each live plant with mortal accents spoke,
195 And the wild blast upheaved the vanished sword!
How have I sat, where piped the pensive wind,
To hear his harp by British Fairfax strung.
Prevailing poet, whose undoubting mind
Believed the magic wonders which he sung!
200 Hence at each sound imagination glows;
Hence his warm lay with softest sweetness flows;

Jerusalem Delivered: Or Godfrey of Bulloign, 4th edn (1749) XIII xxxix–xlix.
The enchantment is part of the magician Ismeno's attempt to demoralize
the Christian knights. The trees are inhabited by evil spirits, which pretend
to be the souls of dead warriors. In his second version of these lines C. referred
more precisely to three particular passages. Cp. Fairfax XIII xli 1–4: 'He
drew his Sword at last, and gave the Tree / A mighty Blow, that made a
gaping Wound; / Out of the Rift red Streams he trickling see, / That all
be-bled the verdant Plain around'; XIII xlix 1–2: 'each tree through all
that wood, / Hath sense, hath life, hath speech, like human kind'; and XIII
xlvi 5–6: 'A whirling Wind his Sword heav'd up aloft, / And through the
Forest bare it quite away.'
193. Its gushing] *Written above* The Cypress *deleted in MS.*   Cp. *Faerie
Queene* I viii 16, 6: 'A sea of bloud gusht from the gaping wound.'
196. where] when *1788.*   Cp. Milton, *Il Penseroso* 126: 'While rocking
Winds are Piping loud.'
198. Prevailing] Potent.
199. This assertion is hardly confirmed by Tasso's invocation to the 'heav'nly
Muse', Fairfax, I ii 5–8: 'Inspire Life in my Wit, my Thoughts up-raise, /
My Verse ennoble, and forgive the Thing, / If Fictions light I mix with Truth
divine, / And fill these Lines with other Praise, than thine.'
200–03. These lines are written above the following deleted in the MS:

Hence with Each Strain
Hence sure to Charm his Early Numbers flow
Tho faithfull [*written above* strong yet] sweet, tho' strong, of simple kind.
Hence with Each Theme he bids the bosom glow
While his warm lays an easy passage find
Pour'd thro' Each inmost nerve,

C. evidently realised that he was imitating too closely in these lines the
celebrated quatrain in Denham's *Cooper's Hill* 188–91.
200. Once again this stanza has only 16 ll.: according to the rhyme scheme,
the 'missing' line should appear after this line.
201–3. Cp. 'melting sweetnesse', *Faerie Queene* III Prol. iv, 7; and 'sweetly
melting softness', Akenside, *Pleasures of Imagination* ii 709; also Gray,
Progress of Poesy 8 and *n* (see p. 162 above).
201. softest] est *is written above* ness *deleted in MS.*

Melting it flows, pure, numerous, strong and clear,
And fills the impassioned heart and lulls the
harmonious ear.

13

All hail, ye scenes that o'er my soul prevail,
205   Ye   firths and lakes which, far away,
Are by smooth Annan filled, or pastoral Tay,
Or Don's romantic springs, at distance, hail!
The time shall come when I perhaps may tread
Your lowly glens, o'erhung with spreading broom,
210   Or o'er your stretching heaths by Fancy led:
Then will I dress once more the faded bower,
Where Jonson sat in Drummond's   shade;
Or crop from Tiviot's dale each

202. numerous] Harmonious, musical. Cp. 'Prose or numerous Verse',
Par. Lost v 150.

203. and lulls] *Written above* and win *in MS, which is not deleted by C., although
the revised grammar requires the singular verb*; and wins *1788*.   Cp. Milton,
L'Allegro 148–9: 'Such streins as would have won the ear / Of *Pluto*'.

205. firths] friths *1788*.   The meaning is 'the estuary of a river or an arm
of the sea'.

206. Are] *Written over* By *in MS*.   Cp. '*Medway* smooth', Milton, *At a
Vacation Exercise* 100, and 'smooth Severn', *Comus* 825.

209. glens] This word is no doubt part of the 'Scottish' diction C. uses inter-
mittently throughout the poem, but he could have found it also in Spenser,
Shepheardes Calender, 'Apr.' 26 and *Faerie Queene* III vii 6, 1. But see also
the lines from Ramsay, l. 59 *n* above.

212. Drummond] Drummond of Hawthornden See Heads of Conversation
&c. *C.'s MS note*.

Tytler in *1788* noted: 'BEN JOHNSON undertook a journey to Scotland a-
foot in 1619, to visit the poet DRUMMOND, at his seat of Hawthornden, near
Edinburgh. DRUMMOND has preserved in his works, some very curious
heads of their conversation.' William Drummond's notes on his conversa-
tions with Ben Jonson were first published in his *Works*, Edinburgh, 1711,
pp. 224–7.

213. Tiviot's dale] The valley of the river Teviot in Roxburghshire. C. is
probably alluding to the Border Ballads, set in this area, and in particular
to the celebrated *Chevy Chase*, as quoted by Addison, *Spectator* No. 74
(25 May 1711): 'All men of pleasant Tividale, / Fast by the river Tweed' etc.

213–14. Both these lines left imperfect. . . . This last stanza bears more marks
of hastiness of composition than any of the rest. Besides the blanks which
are supplied by Dr CARLYLE, there is apparently an entire line wanting after
the seventh line of the stanza. The deficient line ought to have rhymed with
broom. *Tytler*.

And mourn on Yarrow banks

215 Meantime, ye powers, that on the plains which bore
The cordial youth, on Lothian's plains attend,
Where'er he dwell, on hill or lowly muir,
To him I lose your kind protection lend,
And, touched with love like mine, preserve my
absent friend.

214. *Yarrow*] Yarrow's *1788*.   C. evidently refers to the ballad by William
Hamilton of Bangour (1704–54), 'The Braes of Yarrow'. Carlyle's attempt
to fill the blank – 'the widow'd maid' – indicates that this was also his
conclusion, since Hamilton's poem is a young bride's lament for her hus-
band, slain by her family on her wedding day. C. could have found the poem
in one of the collections of Scottish poetry which appeared in the early
eighteenth century, e.g. Ramsay's *The Tea-Table*, vol ii [?1726]; and William
Thomson's *Orpheus Caledonius* (1733) ii 34–9. But it is more likely that C.'s
reference to the poem was connected with the publication in Dec. 1748 at
Glasgow of the first collected edn of Hamilton's poems, to which Home
could have drawn his attention. There was a 2nd edn in 1749. C.'s frag-
mentary reference to Hamilton's poem is apparently unique in one respect.
According to N. S. Bushnell, *William Hamilton of Bangour* (Aberdeen, 1957)
p. 29, no reference to his most famous poem had been recorded during his
lifetime. Cp. also C.'s use of the rare word 'to-fall' in l. 123, almost certainly
imitated from 'The Braes of Yarrow' 79.
216. *cordial youth*] C. now uses the phrase of Home, having applied it to
Barrow in l. 5.   *Lothian*] Edinburgh is in Lothian.
217. *muir*] A variant of 'moor'. See the lines from Ramsay quoted in l. 59 *n*.
219. Pope, *Epistle to Arbuthnot* 415: 'May Heav'n, to bless those days,
preserve my Friend'.   *touched*] Affected emotionally (in a stronger sense
than the modern).
After this line C. has written 'The End' in the MS.

DRAFTS AND FRAGMENTS

These ten incomplete drafts of poems, together with a poem only partly in C.'s handwriting and some other papers in his hand, were discovered among the Warton Papers in the library of Trinity College, Oxford and first printed as *Drafts and Fragments of Verse*, ed. J. S. Cunningham, in 1956. They can be identified with some confidence as those 'few fragments of some other odes [by C.], but too loose and imperfect for publication, yet containing traces of high imagery', which Thomas Warton stated in about 1783 were in the possession of his brother Joseph (*The Gleaner*, ed. Nathan Drake (1811) iv 477-8). As Cunningham suggests, C. may have given them to Joseph in Sept. 1754, when the Wartons visited C. at Chichester and saw various poems in MS.

Cunningham did not attempt to date the fragments or to arrange them in their order of composition. Although it is impossible to do so with any precision, it seems clear from the evidence, internal and circumstantial, that most of the fragments were written between C.'s arrival in London from Oxford in the spring or summer of 1744 and the publication of his *Odes* in Dec. 1746. Five of them are in the epistolary couplets, often heavily dependent on Pope for inspiration, which he did not use in his published verse after the 2nd edn of his *Epistle to Hanmer* in May 1744. Those addressed to James Harris and Jacob Tonson suggest a young writer anxious to establish useful literary relationships in the capital. Others explore rather tentatively aesthetic ideas which were to develop and become more personal in his later poetry. Several fragments reveal an interest in painting and its relationship with poetry which corresponds once more to a section in the *Epistle to Hanmer*: in C.'s later poetry the visual aspect was to remain of great importance but by then his interest in painting had become a way of perceiving rather than a topic of explicit interest in itself, as in these early poems. The stanzaic poem, 'No longer ask me, gentle friends', seems almost certainly autobiographical in character and, although it has been too facilely linked with the only known relationship with a woman in C.'s life, it may well belong to the period of the *Ode, to a Lady* (May 1745), which was addressed to Elizabeth Goddard. The stanzas 'To Simplicity' clearly precede the printed ode on the same subject; and the poem, 'Ye genii who, in secret state', contains a foreshadowing of a passage in the *Ode to Evening*. Only the fragment of an ode for music, which can probably be related to a lost 'Ode on the Music of the Grecian Theatre', appears to be later than the 1746 *Odes*, and may be as late as the autumn of 1750. For further details see headnotes to the individual poems.

Cunningham gives a careful transcription of the MSS, the text of which is here modernised, since C.'s punctuation is virtually non-existent. The MSS contain many corrections, the exact nature of which is noted by Cunningham. In the notes given here, earlier readings are noted, but the precise manner in which C. deleted them–e.g. by writing over them or on the line

above-has not been indicated. In a few instances Cunningham's transcription
has been corrected and a more precise description of the *lacunae* in the text
provided, when this seems significant. When the evidence suggests that C.
intended at some later stage to complete a fragmentary couplet or stanza,
the lines have been numbered accordingly. But the numbering ignores
gaps of uncertain length.

21 [Lines on Restoration Drama]

There is no definite evidence for dating this fragment, although, as Cunning-
ham and McKillop have agreed, it is natural to connect it with C.'s *Epistle
to Hanmer*, if not formally at least in period of composition. This would date
it late in 1743 or early in 1744 and C.'s use of couplets and imitation at
points of Pope support the hypothesis. In his *Epistle to Hanmer* C. had written
of English drama in the age of Shakespeare, Fletcher and Jonson and had
also referred to the slightly later French neo-classical drama. In these lines
he deals with English drama after the Restoration, condemning its 'froth
and foppery of wit' and its exploitation of theatrical machinery, and
deploring the disappearance in this age of 'nature's passions', except in the
plays of his old hero, Thomas Otway. C. blames the French for the condition
of the English theatre in this period and unfairly makes Sir William Dav-
enant the main agent of their influence. These lines are written on two sides
of a folio leaf: 1–18 are written on the recto with 19–26 on the verso; 27–32
are headed '2' and written vertically in the margin of the recto; 33–44 are
headed '3' and written upside down on the verso. It has been assumed here
that these numbers indicate the intended order of these sections and that they
are to be read continuously.

> Yet this wild pomp, so much in vain pursued,
> The courtly Davenant in our Thames renewed.
> For who can trace through time's o'erclouded maze
> The dawning stage of old Eliza's days?
> 5   What critic search its rise, or changes know,

¶ 21.*1–2.* Charles II issued a patent to Sir William Davenant in the summer
of 1660, allowing him to organize a company of actors and open a theatre.
Davenant was an influential figure in the development of two characteristic
dramatic forms of the Restoration: the heroic play and the English opera,
including operatic adaptations of Shakespeare.
1. pomp] scene *deleted.*
2. Thames] Isle *deleted.*   *courtly*] C. was fond of this epithet (see l. 13 below
and his *Lines to Tonson* 11). He may have been imitating Pope's 'Courtly
Talbot', *Epistle to Arbuthnot* 139.

With all the force of Holinshed or Stow?
Yet all may gain, from many a worthless page,
Some lights of Charles and his luxurious age.
Then, thanks to those who sent him forth to roam,
10 Or, equal weakness, brought the monarch home,
The taste of France, her manners and her style
(The fool's gay models), deluged all our isle.
Those courtly wits, which spoke the nation's voice,
In Paris learned their judgement and their choice.
15 Vain were the thoughts which nature's passions speak:
Thy woes, Monimia, impotent and weak!
Vain all the truth of just dramatic tales:
Naught pleased Augustus but what pleased Versailles!
His hand of power, outstretched with princely care,
20 From his low state upraised the instructive player;
And even in palaces, for never age
Was graced like Richelieu's, placed his regal stage.
To those proud halls, where Burgundy had vied

6. C. refers to Holinshed's *Chronicles* (1578) and Stowe's *Summarie of Englyshe Chronicles* (1565) and *Annales* (1580), as the works of laboriously detailed historians. Pope had linked their names more derisively in *Satires of Dr Donne* iv 131, following Donne himself. In C.'s MS the names of the two historians are asterisked, but the note at the bottom of the page also asterisked refers to ll. 15–16.

8. Similarly Pope, *Imitations of Horace, Ep.* II i 140, refers to '*Luxury* with *Charles* restor'd'.   *lights*] Information or instruction.

13. *Those courtly*] That Court of *deleted*.   Cp. Pope, *Epilogue to the Satires* ii 171: 'Let Courtly Wits to Wits afford supply.'

14. *In ... learned their*] From ... took its *deleted*.

15–16. C.'s footnote refers to these lines: 'Otway despis'd as a Writer while Dav'nant was in repute.' Monimia is the heroine of Otway's tragedy *The Orphan* (1680). For C.'s admiration for Otway see *Pity* 16–18 and *n* (p. 416).

18–26. C. makes a rather abrupt transition to an attack on the French theatre, which he saw as responsible for the condition of the Restoration stage. In l. 18 Augustus evidently refers to Charles II and Versailles to Louis XIV. 'His' in l. 19 must again refer to Louis.

19, 24. The repetition of 'princely' emphasizes that this is essentially only a draft. Cp. 'just' in ll. 17, 28, 42.

21–2. Cardinal Richelieu (1585–1642) employed several authors, including Molière, to write plays under his direction and himself wrote a tragi-comedy. It was produced in a hall of the Palais-Royal specially built for the purpose, where Molière's company acted after 1661.

22. *placed*] built *deleted*.

23–6. C. refers to the Hôtel de Bourgogne, an ancient residence of the Dukes of Burgundy in Paris, in the neighbourhood of Les Halles. The company

With all his Gallic peers in princely pride,
25 The Muse succeeded like some splendid heir
And placed her chiefs and favoured heroes there!
And could that theatre, believe you, trust
To those weak guides, the decent and the just?
Ah, no! Could aught delight that modish pit?
30 'Twas but the froth and foppery of wit.
True nature ceased; and in her place were seen
That pride of pantomime, the rich machine.
There, when some god, or spirit poised in air,
Surprised the scented beau or masking fair,
35 Think! with what thunder, in so just a cause,
The mob of coxcombs swelled their loud applause!
These witlings heeded nature less than they
That rule thy taste, the critics of today:
Yet all could talk how Betterton was dressed
40 And gave that queen their praise who curtsied best.
Thus Folly lasted long at Truth's expense,
Spite of just nature or reluctant sense.
Ask you what broke at last her idle reign?
Wit's easy villain could not laugh in vain.

of actors known as the *Confrérie de la Passion* moved to this site in 1548 and it remained in use as a theatre until the end of the eighteenth century. C. misleadingly gives the impression that the theatre was a stately home commandeered for the actors in the mid-seventeenth century.

31-3. C. has in mind the spectacular mechanical effects responsible for much of the popularity of the Restoration opera initiated by Davenant. Such machinery enabled gods and spirits to descend in clouds or float across the stage.

35-6. Pope, *Imitations of Horace, Ep.* II i 326, similarly describes and condemns the taste for theatrical spectacle, at which 'all the Thunder of the Pit ascends'.

37. Pope, *Essay on Criticism* 40: 'Those half-learn'd Witlings, num'rous in our Isle'.

39. talk] tell *deleted.*

39-40. C. is imitating Pope, *Imitations of Horace, Ep.* II i 330-7 (cp. 35-6 *n* above), where he satirizes the applause for 'Quin's high plume, or Oldfield's petticoat' and other theatrical finery, before a word of the play in question has been spoken. Thomas Betterton (1635-1710), probably the best-known Restoration actor, was associated with Davenant early in his career.

41. Thus Folly] Such Follies *deleted.   long at*] till *deleted.*

43. The 'Ask you' formula is imitated from Pope, *Epistles to Several Persons* 206, iii 119.

22 [Lines of Composite Authorship]

The first 24 ll. are written in an unknown hand and only the remaining lines
in C.'s hand. Cunningham remarks that 'its occasion is obscure' and sug-
gests that it belongs to C.'s days at Winchester. But the poem clearly concerns
the cost of theatrical production and scenery, a topic which is more likely
to have concerned C. during his early years in London, 1744–45, when he
himself entertained theatrical ambitions.

But why, you'll say to me, this   song?
Can these proud aims to private life belong?
Fair instances your verse unbidden brings,
The ambitious names of ministers and kings.
5   Am I that statesman whom a realm obeys?
What ready tributes will my mandate raise?
Or like the pontiff can my word command
Exacted sums from every pliant land,
That all of which the men of leisure read,
10   This taste and splendour, must from me proceed?
Tell me, if wits reprove or fortune frown,
Where is my hope but in the uncertain town.
Yet ere you urge, weigh well the mighty task:
Behold what sums one poet's dramas ask.
15   When Shakespeare shifts the place so oft to view,
Must each gay scene be beautiful and new?
Come, you who trade in ornament, appear,
Come, join your aids through all the busy year;
Plan, build and paint through each laborious day,
20   And let us once produce this finished play.
Yes, the proud cost allows some short suspense:
I grant the terrors of that word 'expence'.
Did taste at once for full perfection call,
That sole objection might determine all.
25   But such just elegance not gained at ease,
Scarce wished and seen, may come by slow degrees
Today   may one fair grace restore,
And some kind season add one beauty more.

¶ 22.7. *can*] will *deleted.*
15. *place*] scene *deleted.*
19. *each*] every *deleted.*
26. *Scarce*] *written above* Just.

And with these aims of elegant desire,
30 The critic's unities, 'tis sure, conspire;
And though no scenes suffice to deck the wild,
        round their works on whom the Muse has
    smiled,
Some scenes may still the fair design admit,
Chaste scenes which Addison or Philips writ.
35 Is but our just delight in one increased,
'Tis something gained to decency at least;
And what thy judgement first by nature planned,
May find completion from some future hand.
        &c.
The pomp. . . .

29. With these amendments, what some yet admire *deleted.*
31. *no . . . deck*] your Arts can not attend *deleted.*
32. whom the Muse by Art untutor'd smild *deleted. The first word of the line has been torn away.*
34. C. no doubt had in mind Addison's *Cato* (1713) and Ambrose Philips's *The Distressed Mother* (1712).
37. *thy*] *Cunningham reads* my.

23 [Lines Addressed to James Harris]

Written later than May 1744, probably not long afterwards. The MS is inscribed by Joseph Warton: 'This addrest by *Collins* to Mr. Harris of Sarum.' James Harris (1709–80), a native of Salisbury where he was a prominent patron of music, is best known as the author of *Hermes* (1751), an enquiry into the origins of language. But C.'s lines refer to–and were probably written soon after the publication of–Harris's *Three Treatises. The First Concerning Art. The Second Concerning Music, Painting, and Poetry. The Third Concerning Happiness. By J. H.* This work appeared in May 1744 (*Gentleman's Mag.* xiv (1744) 288), at about the time C. arrived in London. C.'s use of couplets suggests that these lines were written at this period. They bear out Gilbert White's statement (in *Gentleman's Mag.* li (1781) 11) that C. was 'passionately fond of music'. There is no other evidence of contact between C. and Harris.

These would I sing: O art for ever dear,
Whose charms so oft have caught my raptured ear,

¶ 23.1. *These*] The lines begin one-third of the way down a folio sheet. C. may have left space to describe 'These' at some later time. The 'art' in question is music.

O teach me thou, if my unpolished lays
Are all too rude to speak thy gentle praise,
5   O teach me softer sounds of sweeter kind,

Then let the Muse and Picture each contend,
This plan her tale and that her colours blend:
With me, though both their kindred charms combine,
10   No power shall emulate or equal thine!

And thou, the gentlest patron, born to grace
And add new brightness even to Ashley's race,
Intent like him in Plato's polished style
To fix fair Science in our careless isle:
15   Whether through Wilton's pictured halls you stray,

3. teach me] Scorn not *deleted* (*Cunningham incorrectly reads* learn not).
4. Spenser, *Faerie Queene* I xii 23, 4: 'My ragged rimes are all too rude and bace.'
5. O teach] O Smile *deleted above.*   Cp. *Evening* 15–16 (p. 464).
6. Left blank by C.
7–10. These lines were probably suggested by the second of Harris's *Three Treatises*, which was devoted to a comparison of the powers of Music, Poetry and Painting. Harris finally asserted the superiority of Poetry to the other two arts, but discussed at length's Music's power of raising 'various Affections' and concluded that Poetry and Music were most efficacious when combined. See *Three Treatises* pp. 95–103.
9. With me, though both] Ev'n these would I resign *deleted above.*
10. After this line C. has deleted the following couplet:

Ye too who living own'd her genial rule
The Sons and Daughters of her happy school

Cunningham leaves a blank in the text corresponding to this couplet and numbered the remaining lines of the poem accordingly. But C. leaves a longer gap than a single couplet at this point and it is not clear how many, if any, lines are missing. The numbering of the lines therefore ignores the gap.
11–12. James Harris (1709–80) was the nephew of Anthony Ashley Cooper, third Earl of Shaftesbury (1671–1713), author of the influential *Characteristicks of Men, Manners, Opinions, Times* (1711).
13–14. C. alludes to the use by both Shaftesbury and Harris of the form of the Platonic dialogue.
13. Intent] Whether *deleted.*
14. To fix] Few form *deleted.*   *careless*] Unconcerned, indifferent.
15. See Harris's *Three Treatises* p. 4: the dialogue occurs during the return

Or o'er some speaking marble waste the day,
Or weigh each sound, its various power to learn,
Come, son of Harmony, O hither turn!
Led by thy hand, Philosophy will deign
20 To own me, meanest of her votive train.
O, I will listen as thy lips impart
Why all my soul obeys her powerful art;
Why at her bidding, or by strange surprise
Or waked by fond degrees, my passions rise;
25 How well-formed reeds my sure attention gain
And what the lyre's well-measured strings contain.
The mighty masters too, unpraised so long,
Shall not be lost, if thou assist my song,
They who, with Pindar's in one age bestowed,
30 Clothed the sweet words which in their numbers
    flowed;
And Rome's and Adria's sons, if thou but strive
To guard their names, shall in my name survive.

from a walk to see the Earl of Pembroke's seat at Wilton. Harris observes
that 'The Beauties of Gardening, Architecture, Painting, and Sculpture
belonging to that Seat, were the Subject of great Entertainment to my
Friend'.

18. son of Harmony] Sweet Philosopher *deleted*.
19. Philosophy] *Written by C. in a larger hand.*
20. own] take *and* aid *deleted*.
21. as thy lips impart] will thy tongue reveals *deleted* (*Cunningham reads* well
but C. seems to have written will *as a mistake for* while), *with as above when
deleted.*
22. her] i.e. Music once more, rather than Philosophy in 19–20.
23–4. Pope, *Essay on Criticism* 223: 'behold with strange Surprize' and
374–5: 'Hear how *Timotheus*' vary'd Lays surprize, / And bid Alternate
Passions fall and rise!'
24. waked] gradual *deleted*.
26. Milton, *Sonnet to Lawes* 1: 'tuneful and well-measur'd Song'.
28. assist] inspire *deleted*.
31. Adria] Latin for the Adriatic sea (used by Milton, *Par. Lost* i 520). Perhaps
used by C. to mean Venice.

24 [Lines Addressed to Jacob Tonson]

There is no definite evidence for dating these lines but they were probably
written not long after C.'s arrival in London in 1744, when he was trying to
establish himself in literary circles there. One concern at least of C.'s poem

seems to be to remind Tonson of what his family owed to the great poets whose works it had published, perhaps as a prelude to offering the publisher some of his own poetry. C.'s use of couplets, his echoes of Pope, as well as his apparent respect for Waller and the poetic values he embodies (see ll.11–18) all suggest an early date, perhaps (if the first line is to be taken literally) the winter of either 1743/44 or 1744/45.

The lines are clearly addressed to a member of the Tonson family. The famous publishing business had been founded by Jacob Tonson (1656?–1736), the 'jovial Jacob' of l. 2, who had published the works of such writers as Dryden, Congreve, Addison, Pope and many other famous Augustan names. The elder Tonson retired in 1720 and the business was continued by his nephew, also Jacob, until his death in 1735. Thereafter the business passed to a third Jacob (d. 1767) and Richard (d. 1772) Tonson, great-nephews of the original Jacob. As J. S. Cunningham has pointed out, C.'s lines must be addressed to one of these two, although he leaves the question open. But since Richard Tonson 'interfered but little with the concerns of the trade' (J. Nichols, Literary Anecdotes i 298), it seems certain that C. would only be interested in addressing Jacob, who was still an active publisher and the possessor of the Kit-Cat portraits referred to in the opening lines.

The original Jacob Tonson had been the secretary of a political and social club, which included most of the leading Whig noblemen, writers and M.P.s, and which at first met at a tavern near Temple Bar owned by Christopher Cat. The Kit-Cat Club had moved by 1703 to a room specially built on to Tonson's house at Barn Elms in Surrey, and it continued to meet there at least until 1717 and possibly later. One of the members, the Duke of Somerset, commissioned Kneller to paint all the members for Tonson and these celebrated paintings, 42 in number, are now in the National Portrait Gallery; see Lord Killanin, Sir Godfrey Kneller and his Times (1948) pp. 76–83. A letter from Samuel Croxhall to the elder Tonson, 10 March 1733, states that the younger Tonson has 'made a room for the Kit Cats &c' at Barn Elms and the younger Tonson's will confirms that he made a special gallery for them (Sarah Clapp, Jacob Tonson in Ten Letters By and About Him (Austin, Texas, 1948) p. 20). This is the 'academic room' referred to by C., when Barn Elms was in the possession of the third Jacob Tonson. C.'s references to the Kit-Cat portraits confirm that his poem is addressed to Jacob and not Richard Tonson, since the latter lived at Water-Oakley near Windsor, and did not come into the possession of the portraits until after the death of Jacob in 1767 (see J. Nichols, Literary Anecdotes i 298).

> While you perhaps exclude the wintry gloom
> In jovial Jacob's academic room,

¶ 24.1. *exclude the wintry gloom*] Ev'n now your hours consume *deleted*. *A first version of the line has also been deleted*: When oft in ease at lov'd Barn Elms you trace.

2. *jovial Jacob*] Jacob Tonson the Elder, referred to by Pope, *Dunciad* i 57,

There pleased by turns in breathing paint to trace
The wit's gay air or poet's genial face,
5   Say, happy Tonson, say what great design
(For warmest gratitude must sure be thine),
What due return employs thy musing heart
For all the happiness their works impart;
What taste-directed monument, which they
10   Might own with smiles and thou with honour pay.
Even from the days when courtly Waller sung
And tuned with polished sounds our barbarous tongue,
Ere yet the verse to full perfection brought
With nicer music clothed the poet's thought,
15   The muse whose song bespoke securest fame
Made fair alliance with thy favoured name.
Dealt from thy press, the maid of elder days

as 'genial Jacob'. The 'academic room' is, of course, that in which the
Kit-Cat portraits were hung (see headnote).

3. Pope, *Epistle to Jervas* 55: 'Yet still her charms in breathing paint engage'.

8. happiness] Pleas[ure] *deleted*.

9. What taste-] Some tastefu[l] *deleted*.

10. Might] May *deleted*.

11. Even from] From those *deleted*.   *courtly*] Poli[shed] *deleted*.   Cp. C.'s
draft *Lines on Restoration Drama* 2 and *n* (p. 524 above).

11–14. This is the orthodox Augustan view of Waller's rôle in English literary
history and it demands an early dating of these lines. Contrast *Poetical Character*
68–9 (p. 435). Francis Atterbury's Preface to *The Second Part of Mr. Waller's
Poems* (1690), often reproduced in eighteenth-century edns of Waller,
states: 'The Tongue came into his hands, like a rough Diamond; he polish'd
it first, and to that degree that all Artists since him have admired the Work-
manship, without pretending to mend it. . . . He undoubtedly stands first
in the List of Refiners. . . . We are no less beholding to him for the new turn
of Verse, which he brought in, and the improvement he made in our
Numbers . . .' etc.

13. yet the verse to] yet the chaste Expression *deleted*.

14. nicer] More delicate, refined.   Cp. Pope, *Essay on Criticism* 318: 'Ex-
pression is the *Dress* of *Thought*'.

17. maid of elder days] Distant Lovers Eyes *deleted*.

17–20. A. D. McKillop has pointed out, *Philological Quarterly* xxxvi (1957)
354, that Henry Herringman was the principal publisher of both Waller
and Cowley to the end of the 17th century, although Tonson's name appears
with that of another publisher on an edn of Cowley in 1681. He suggests
that C. may have had in mind Tonson's apparent acquisition of the copy-
rights of Waller and Cowley from the Herringman estate in about 1705,
since his name appears on the title-page of an edn of Waller in that year
and he published edns of Waller regularly thereafter; and he also pub-

>   Lisped the soft lines to Sacharissa's praise;
>   Or the gay youth, for livelier spirits known,
> 20 By Cowley's pointed thought improved his own.
>   Even all the easy sons of song, who gained
>   A poet's name when Charles and pleasure reigned,
>   All from thy race a lasting praise derived:
>   Not by their toil the careless bards survived.
> 25 You wisely saved the race who,   gay,
>   But sought to wear the myrtles of a day.
>   At soft Barn Elms (let every critic join)
>   You more than all enjoy each flowing line.
>   Yours is the price, whate'er their merits claim,
> 30 Heir of their verse and guardian of their fame!
>   move
>   luxury and love!

lished edns of Cowley in 1707 and 1711. McKillop's main suggestion may be correct, but Tonson's connection with the publication of both poets is more complex. After the appearance of Francis Atterbury's edn of Waller in 1690, the poet's son asked Tonson to publish a corrected text of certain works; this appeared in the same year entitled *The Maid's Tragedy Altered. With Some Other Pieces. By Edmund Waller, Esq; Not Before Printed in the several Editions of his Poems;* see Sarah Clapp, *Jacob Tonson in Ten Letters to and about Him* (1948) p. 14. This collection was incorporated in the 1694 issue of Herringman's 6th edn of Waller's *Poems*, Tonson's name being added as bookseller to the main titlepage. Similarly Tonson's name appears as a bookseller on the titlepages of the 8th and 9th edns (1693 and 1700) of Cowley's *Works*, as well as on edns of individual works by Cowley in 1681 and 1693. It seems likely that C. was merely trying to demonstrate how far back in English literary history Tonson's career extended by linking his name with Waller and Cowley.

18. Sacharissa] The name by which Waller addressed Lady Dorothea Sidney in his poetry.

19. for] by *deleted.*

20. Pope, *Imitations of Horace, Ep.* II i 75–6: 'Who now reads Cowley? if he pleases yet, / His moral pleases, not his pointed wit.'

21–6. These lines must refer to the important anthology, featuring most of the poets of the Restoration, published by Tonson in six parts between 1684 and 1709 with different titles, but usually referred to as *Miscellany Poems.* The first four parts were edited by Dryden. There were new edns of all six parts in 1716 and 1727.

21–2. Pope, *Imitations of Horace, Ep.* II i 107–8: 'the Wits of either Charles's days, / The Mob of Gentlemen who wrote with Ease.'

24. by their toil] from themselves *deleted.*

29. price] Reward or honour, obtained by merit.

31–2. C. has left these lines blank except for the concluding words.

25 [Lines Addressed to a Fastidious Critic]

There is no definite evidence for dating this fragment, but it is unlikely to have been written before May 1743 or much later than the end of 1744. The earlier limiting date is suggested by the allusion in l. 14 to Roger de Piles' 'balance of painters', first translated into English in that month. Otherwise, both form and content of these lines suggest that they belong to C.'s first months in London. Apart from the use of couplets, not found in his published poetry after the *Epistle to Hanmer*, his conventional exposition of the parallelism of painting and poetry, his apparent respect for Addison, Rowe and Waller, his suspicion of his addressee's desire to be 'a chaste Athenian' and enthusiasm for 'old models', and his caution about the possibility of original genius in the modern writer or artist, all point to an early stage in the formation of C.'s thinking about literature and practice as a poet. Allusions to Dodsley and Hayman (ll. 29–31) may be linked with the facts that Dodsley had published the 2nd edn of C.'s *Epistle to Hanmer* in May 1744 and that Hayman had illustrated Hanmer's recently published edn of Shakespeare.

The fragment falls into three sections and C.'s difficulty in linking them into a coherent argument is emphasized by the gaps in the text at the crucial points. Basically, these lines are an attempt to answer a young and over-fastidious critic of poetry and painting, who dislikes the modern arts, particularly their imitative character, which C. seems at this point to consider inevitable.

> Yes, 'tis but Angelo's or Shakespeare's name:
> The striking beauties are in each the same.
> The s

> 5 Were Horace dumb, who knows even Fresnoy's art

¶ 25.*1–8.* C. is expounding that belief in the parallelism of the arts of poetry and painting which had become common by the later seventeenth century, largely on the authority of the tag from Horace, *Ars Poetica* 361: *ut pictura poesis,* so often quoted out of context. See l. 5 n.

1. Angelo] Michelangelo.

3–4. C. wrote no more of l. 3 and left l. 4 blank, presumably intending to complete the couplet later.

5. were Horace dumb] i.e. had he never written his *Ars Poetica. De Arte Graphica,* a Latin poem by the French painter and critic Charles Alphonse du Fresnoy (1611–65), had been published in 1668. It was translated into English by Dryden in 1695 as *The Art of Painting . . . . Together with an Original Preface containing a Parallel betwixt Painting and Poetry.* Du Fresnoy's treatise on

Might guide the muse in some   part;
Or searchful Vinci, who his precepts drew
For Tuscan pencils, form the poet too!

From these fair arts,
10   Obtain some fair ef
Nor fear to talk of numbers or of oil,
Though not quite formed like Addison or Boyle.
Defect[s] in each abound and more, you say,
Than sage de Piles instructs us how to weigh;

painting was intended to correspond to Horace's *Ars Poetica* and it begins
by quoting *ut pictura poesis* in its first line. Dryden translates the opening
as follows: 'Painting and Poesy are two Sisters, which are so like in all things,
that they mutually lend to each other both their Name and Office. One is
call'd a dumb Poesy, and the other a speaking Picture.' In his Preface Dryden
stated: 'Bossu has not given more exact rules for the epic poem, nor Dacier
for tragedy, in his late excellent translation of Aristotle, and his notes upon
him, than our Fresnoy has made for painting.'

7–8. Leonardo da Vinci's *Trattato della Pittura* was first published in Paris in
1651 and first translated into English in 1721 as *A Treatise on Painting*. In
describing Leonardo as 'searchful' C. may have been influenced by the
translation of Roger de Piles' *The Art of Painting, With the Lives and Characters
of above 300 of the most Eminent Painters* (2nd edn, 1744) p. 104, which states
that Leonardo was 'incessantly busy'd in reflections about his art, and spar'd
for no care or study to arrive at perfection in it'.

7. precepts] Lessons *deleted.*

8. pencils] Paintbrushes. See *Popular Superstitions* 16 *n* (p. 503). The space of
two lines is left blank in the MS.

9. which trust our Critic Friends *deleted after* Arts

10. Left blank after Ef, *presumably intended to be* Effects, *as Cunningham suggests.*

12. Addison or Boyle] Referred to as eminent arbiters of taste in literature
and the visual arts. Pope dedicated the fourth of his *Epistles to Several Persons*,
'Of the Use of Riches', to Richard Boyle, 3rd Earl of Burlington and 4th
Earl of Cork (1695–1753), the enthusiastic admirer of Palladio who had a
considerable influence on Georgian architecture.

14. Roger de Piles (1635–1709), a voluminous writer on art, had published
a commentary on Du Fresnoy's *De Arte Graphica* in 1668 and, in addition to
many other works, a *Dissertation sur la balance des peintres* (1708). C.'s use of
the word 'weigh' makes clear that he is referring to this work, perhaps
because of the publication in May 1743 of a translation from de Piles, *The
Principles of Painting . . . To which is Added, The Balance of Painters . . . now
first Translated into English* (see *Gentleman's Mag.* xiii 280). The 'balance'
consists of an attempt to tabulate the different merits of various painters in

15 Defects which, glanced on those who finely feel,
    All Thornhill's colours would in vain conceal,
    Or all the golden lines, howe'er they flow,
    Through each soft drama of unfruitful Rowe.
    These too you sometimes praise, to censure loth,
20 But fix the name of mannerist on both.
    And should my friend, who knew not Anna's age,
    So nicely judge the canvas or the page?
    Still should his thought, on some old model placed,
    Reject the Briton with so nice a taste?
25 From each some forceful character demand,
            but peculiar to his happy hand?
    Some sovereign mark of genius all his own,

    Ah, where on Thames shall gentle Dodsley find
30 The verse contrived for so correct a mind?
    Or how shall Hayman, trembling as you gaze,
    Obtain one breath of such unwilling praise?
    Go then, in all unsatisfied, complain
    Of Time's mistake in Waller's desperate strain,

a quasi-scientific manner, by assigning marks to different aspects of their work.
16. Sir James Thornhill (1675–1734) painted the cupola of St Paul's and provided other decorative paintings for Greenwich Hospital, Blenheim Palace and Moor Park.
18. C. presumably calls Nicholas Rowe (1674–1718), poet laureate and dramatist, 'unfruitful', because of his relatively premature death. Rowe wrote eight plays between 1700 and 1715, which C. may also have considered a small output.
26. In the first part of the line a word, perhaps bold, cancels another, perhaps But.
28. Left blank by C.
29. on Thames] Eugenia where deleted.
Robert Dodsley (1703–64), the publisher, whose name appeared on the 2nd edn of C.'s Epistle to Hanmer.
31. Francis Hayman (1708–76), the painter, who provided the illustrations for Sir Thomas Hanmer's edn of Shakespeare.
33. then] Rather deleted.
34–5. C. has a footnote:
                Waller to a very young Lady
                Why came I so untimely forth
                Into a world wᶜʰ wanting thee
C. refers to Waller's To my Young Lady Lucy Sidney st. i: 'Why came I so untimely forth / Into a world which, wanting thee, / Could entertain us with no worth / Or shadow of felicity? / That time should me so far remove / From that which I was born to love.'

35   For ah, 'untimely cam'st thou forth', indeed,
      With whom originals alone succeed!
      Go as thou wilt, require the bliss denied,
      To call back art and live ere Carlo died;
      But oh, in song the public voice obey,
40   There let each author   his   day.
      Abroad be candid, reason as you will,
      And be at home a chaste Athenian still!
        For each correct design the critic kind
      Look back through age to Homer's godlike mind;
45   But Blackhall's self might doubt if all of art
      Were self-produced in one exhaustless heart.

36. originals] Works of literature or art which are not imitations.
38. Carlo] Carlo Maratta or Maratti (1625–1713), the Italian painter.
41. candid] 'Free from malice; not desirous to find faults' (Johnson). To illustrate the word Johnson misquotes Pope, *Essay on Criticism* 233–4, substituting 'candid' for 'perfect' and 'piece' for 'Work': 'A candid judge will read each piece of wit / With the same spirit that its authour writ.' Cp. also *Essay on Man* i 15: 'Laugh where we must, be candid where we can'.
43–4. Pope, *Essay on Criticism* 134–6: 'But when t'examine ev'ry Part he came, / *Nature* and *Homer* were, he found, the *same*: / Convinc'd, amaz'd, he checks the bold Design'.
45. Blackhall] As Cunningham has suggested, this must be an error for 'Blackwell', as the reference to Homer in the previous line makes clear that C. has in mind Thomas Blackwell's *Enquiry into the Life and Writings of Homer* (1735), a notable investigation into the nature of original genius. Blackwell, p. 2, poses the 'hitherto unresolved' question: 'By what Fate or Disposition of things it has happened, that None have equalled him in *Epic-Poetry* for two thousand seven hundred Years, the Time since he wrote; Nor any, that we know, ever surpassed him before.'

26 [Lines Addressed to a Friend about to Visit Italy]

There is no definite evidence for dating this fragmentary draft. Cunningham's suggestion that it is related to the missing *Epistle to the Editor of Fairfax* (see 'Lost and Doubtful Poems') is unconvincing, as the reference to Fairfax's translation of Tasso is only incidental and C. was clearly interested in Fairfax before the publication of the new edn of his translation in the autumn of 1749; see his letter to J. G. Cooper, 10 Nov. 1747, in H. O. White, 'The Letters of William Collins', *Review of English Studies* iii (1927) 14. A. D. McKillop, *Philological Quarterly* xxxvi (1957) 354, points out that the lines

on medals resemble a passage in Addison's *Dialogue Upon Ancient Medals,*
in *Works,* ed. A. Guthkelch (1914) ii 284–6. But there is nothing in C.'s frag-
ment which could not have been derived from Pope's *To Mr. Addison
Occasion'd By His Dialogue on Medals.* The direct influence of Pope and
C.'s use of couplets point to a date of composition not long after his arrival
in London in 1744. There is an *Ode to a Gentleman upon his Travels thro'
Italy* in Joseph Warton's *Odes* (Dec. 1746), and it is possible that C. was
addressing the same person.

> On each new scene the sons of   vertù
> Shall give fresh objects to thy   view,
> Bring the graved gem or offer as you pass
> The imperial medal and historic brass.
> 5 Then o'er its narrow surface may'st thou trace
> The genuine spirit of some hero's face;
> Or see, minutely touched, the powerful charms
> Of some proud fair that set whole realms in arms;
> The patriot's story with his look compare
> 10 And know the poet by his genial air.
>
> Nor, for they boast no pure Augustan vein,
> Reject her poets with a cold disdain.
> Oh, think in what sweet lays, how sweetly strong,
> Our Fairfax warbles Tasso's forceful song;
> 15 How Spenser too, whose lays you oft resume,
> Wove their gay   in his fantastic loom;

¶ 26.4. Pope, *To Mr. Addison* 55–8: 'In living medals see her wars enroll'd,
And vanquish'd realms supply recording gold? / Here, rising bold, the
Patriot's honest face; / There Warriors frowning in historic brass . . .'
5. bending *deleted after* Then.   narrow] little *deleted.*
5–8. Pope, *To Mr. Addison* 25: 'A narrow orb each crouded conquest
keeps'; 33–4: 'In one short view subjected to your eye / Gods, Emp'rors,
Heroes, Sages, Beauties, lie'; and 46–7: 'Touch'd by thy hand, again Rome's
glories shine, / Her Gods, and god-like Heroes rise to view.'
8. *whole realms*] the world *deleted.*
9. *patriot's*] Sage's *deleted.*   *story*] Writing *deleted.*   *look*] form *deleted.*
10. Cp. the reference to the 'poet's genial face', *Lines to Jacob Tonson* 4
(p. 532).
11. C. presumably intended to provide a transition in the blank space pre-
ceeding this line from the subject of ancient medals to Italian poetry which
follows.
13. *Oh, think*] Remember *deleted.*
13–14. See C.'s other characterization both of Tasso and Fairfax's translation
in *Popular Superstitions,* esp. 200–03 (pp. 517–8 above).
15. *too*] oft *deleted.*
16. Colours *deleted after* gay.

That Cinthio prompted oft even Shakespeare's flame,
And Milton valued even Marino's name!

17. That Cinthio] How Shakespear's *deleted*.   Shakespeare's debt to Giraldi
Cinthio's *Hecatommithi* (1566) for the plot of *Othello* and other plays had
been pointed out by Dryden, Preface to 'An Evening's Love' (1671), in
Of Dramatic Poesy and other Critical Essays, ed. G. Watson (1962) i 154;
and Gerard Langbaine, *Account of the English Dramatic Poets* (1691) p. 461.
18. Cunningham notes that Milton refers to Marino in his Latin poem *Mansus*
9, 51.

27 [Stanzas on a Female Painter]

There is no definite evidence for dating this poem, although the opening
description of moonlight might be taken to link it with 'Ye genii who, in
secret state', a resemblance which would place it (presumably early)
in the period July 1744–Dec. 1746. It must seem unlikely that the poem
concerns a real person: the opening appears to describe a purely fictitious
setting and it is probable that C. is combining his interest in painting (re-
vealed in several of these drafts and fragments as well as in his *Epistle to
Hanmer*) with an imitation of Pope's *Elegy to the Memory of an Unfortunate
Lady*, which it resembles in various details (see l. 48 *n*) and in more general
ways: e.g. the opening moonlit setting and the later resignation to the inevit-
ability of being forgotten.

The poem is written on two quarto leaves: ll. 1–12 appear on p. 1, the
verso of which is blank; p. 3 continues with ll. 13–28, with ll. 29–36 written
vertically at the side, which may indicate that they were a later addition;
p. 4 has ll. 37 ff.

The moon with dewy lustre bright
    Her mild ethereal radiance gave,
On paly cloisters gleamed her light,
    Or trembled o'er the unresting wave.

¶ *27.1. lustre*] radiance *deleted*.
2. radiance] lustre *deleted*.   C. may have been trying to revise away from
Pope, *Spring* 74: 'The Sun's mild Lustre warms the vital Air.'
3. paly] For this variant of 'pale' see *Evening* 22 (p. 465). Cp. also Milton,
Il Penseroso 156: 'To walk the studious Cloysters pale'. (Eighteenth-century
editors were uncertain whether 'pale' was an adjective or noun (= 'enclo-
sure'): see T. Warton's edn of Milton's *Poems*, 1785). *Comus* 223, 225 has:
'a sable cloud / . . . casts a gleam over this tufted Grove'.
4. Pope, *Rape of the Lock* ii 48: 'The Sun-beams trembling on the floating
Tydes'; and *Imitations of Horace, Sat.* II vi 191: 'Tell how the Moon-beam
trembling falls'.

5   'Twas midnight's hour–

Long o'er the spires and glimmering towers,
10   The whispering flood and silvery sky,
As one whom musing grief devours,
She glanced by turns her silent eye!

Like hers, the fair Lavinia's hand
Once mixed the pallet's varied store;
15 Blest maid, whom once Italia's land
In years of better glory bore!

Like her, O death, O ruthless power,
O grief of heart remembered well,
In lovely youth's untimely hour
20   Like her soft Tintoretta fell:

5. 'at midnight hour', *Il Penseroso* 85. C. left the remainder of the stanza
blank.

12. *silent eye*] Perhaps an imitation of Virgil on Dido, *Aeneid* iv 363–4:
huc illuc solvens oculos, totumque pererrat / luminibus tacitus (turning her eyes to
and fro, and with silent glances scans the whole mass).

13–16. Cunningham offers two identifications of 'Lavinia': Titian's daughter,
Lavinia, 'who did not paint but who served him as a model', and who, he
suggests, 'fits the context better than the painter Fontana, whose Christian
name was Lavinia, but who lived to be quite old.' But, as McKillop pointed
out, the age of 'Lavinia' is not in question, only the fact that she was a
painter, like the subject of this elegy. For this reason it seems clear that C.
was referring to Lavinia Fontana (1552–1614), a successful Italian portrait
painter, the daughter of Prospero Fontana (1512–97), also a painter. Lavinia
is mentioned in Felibien's *Entretiens* (1705) iii 91 (see ll. 20–4 *n*).

16. After this line C. left a blank space sufficient for about a stanza: this
is ignored in the numbering of lines.

20–4. Cunningham identifies 'Tintoretta' as Marietta, the daughter of
Tintoretto, although he is incorrect, as McKillop points out, in suggesting
that the name was a coinage of C.'s. McKillop refers to the following
passage from André Felibien, *Entretiens Sur Les Vies . . . Des Plus Excellens
Peintres* (London 1705) iii 129:

'[Tintoret] avoit une fille nommée MARIETTA TINTORETTA qui peignit

Even she, whose science Philip sought
  To share his throne, an envied bride,
Like thee deplored, ah, fatal thought,
  By every art lamented died.

25 Thy draft, where Love his hand employed,
  Shall only please a short-lived day
And, timeless like thyself destroyed,
  In each revolving year decay.

Yet soft and melting flowed thy line,
30 As every Grace had lent her aid,
Bid each mild light unglaring shine
  And soft imbrowned each melting shade.

parfaitement bien, particulierement des portraits. L'Empereur Maximilien,
Philippe II. Roi d'Espagne, & l'Archiduc Ferdinand, tâcherent de l'avoir
auprés d'eux, parce qu'elle avoit beaucoup de bonnes qualitez. Mais son
pere qui l'aimoit passionnément, ne voulut jamais consentir qu'elle s'éloignât
de lui, aimant mieux la marier à Venise à un Joüaillier nommé Mario Aug-
usta, que de la voir dans une meilleure fortune qui l'auroit privé de sa présence.
Elle mourut dans la fleur de son age* l'an 1590. au grand déplaisir de son
pere qui en souffrir une douleur extrême. [n] *Agée de 30. ans.'
 This passage explains C.'s references to 'Philip' and to the 'envied bride'.
The statement that she died lamented by 'every art' may refer to Marietta's
musical accomplishments, unmentioned by Felibien, but alluded to in the
translation of Roger de Piles, *Art of Painting* (1744) p. 173 (in an article on
her which does not, however, contain all the information given by Felibien):
'She delighted in musick, and played well on several instruments'.
20. Like cancels The. 'Soft' or 'softest' recur in ll. 33, 36, 38 below.
24. Adorned with *deleted before* By.
25–42. Cp. with these stanzas, Pope's account of the effect of time on paint-
ing, *Essay on Criticism* 484–94.
25. Thy draught where Love his] Yet thy sweet draught *and* Gentle *deleted*.
draught] drawing. Cp. Dryden, *To the Memory of Mrs. Killigrew* 106–7:
'Her Pencil drew, what e're her Soul design'd, / And oft the happy Draught
surpass'd the Image in her Mind.'
27. timeless] Unseasonably, prematurely, rather than 'Not subject to, or
unaffected by, time'. Cp. Milton, *On the Death of a Fair Infant* 2: 'Soft
silken Primrose fading timelesslie.'
29. Cp. *Popular Superstitions* 201–2 (pp. 517–8).
31. unglaring] Apparently one of C.'s negative coinages (see *Popular Super-
stitions* 99).
32. soft imbrowned] softly shed *deleted*. Cp. *Par. Lost* iv 245–6: 'the unpierc't
shade / Imbround the noontide Bowrs'; and Dryden, *To Sir Godfrey
Kneller* 178: 'Mellow your Colours, and imbrown the Teint'.

And when thy tints, ah, fruitless care!
    With softest skill compounded lay,
35   The flaunting bowers where spring repairs
    Were not more bloomy sweet than they!

The child of them who now adore
    Thy tender tints and godlike flame,
Pass some few years on Adria's shore,
40   Shall only know thy gentle name;

Or, when his eyes shall strive in vain
    Thy fairy pencil's stroke to trace,
The faded draft shall scarce retain
    Some lifeless line or mangled grace.

33. when *cancels* thy.
35. 'flaunting Hony-suckle', *Comus* 545.
39. Adria] The Adriatic. Cp. 'Lines Addressed to James Harris' 31 (p. 530).
42. fairy] Mingling *deleted.*
44. C. left space for two more stanzas of which he wrote only the first and last lines, deleting the first: 'What tho' thy touch, belov'd of Art' and 'And but thy Grave be all forgot'. These two lines confirm that C., consciously or not, was imitating Pope's *Elegy to the Memory of an Unfortunate Lady*, in ll. 55–61 of which the 'What tho'' rhetorical question occurs three times and the last line of which like C.'s contains 'forgot': 'The Muse forgot, and thou belov'd no more!'

28 'Ye genii who, in secret state'

Probably written later than July 1744 and before Dec. 1746. The earlier date, which can be urged only tentatively, depends on the possibility of an echo of Thomson (see l. 24 *n*). The later date depends on the assumption that this poem preceded C.'s *Ode to Evening*, published in the *Odes* of Dec. 1746, and, particularly in its later stanzas, represents an early version of part of that poem. For a discussion of this relationship see A. D. McKillop, 'Collins's *Ode to Evening*–Background and Structure', *Tennessee Studies in Literature* v (1960) 73–83. C. begins with an impressive variation on the popular retirement theme, urging a retreat from the city to the country, and then, as McKillop points out, takes the poet through the ideal day of Milton's *L'Allegro* and *Il Penseroso* and James Thomson's *Summer*, describing the different times of day by reference to three famous landscape painters. He ends, however, by asserting the impossibility of achieving an adequate description of moonlight (not simply 'the delicate evening light', as stated by Cunningham) in either poetry or painting.

Ye genii who, in secret state
   Far from the wheaten field,
At some thronged city's antique gate
   Your unseen sceptres wield;

5 Ye powers that such high office share
   O'er all the restless earth,
Who see each day descend with care
   Or lost in senseless mirth;

Take them, who know not how to prize
10   The walks to wisdom dear,
The gradual fruits and varying skies
   That paint the gradual year;

Take all that to the silent sod
   Prefer the sounding street,
15 And let your echoing squares be trod
   By their unresting feet.

But me, by   springlets laid
   That through the woodland chide,
Let elms and oaks, that lent their shade
20   To hoary druids, hide.

Let me, where'er wild nature leads
   My sight, enamoured look
And choose my hymning pipe from reeds
   That roughen o'er the brook.

¶ 28.*1–4. genii*] Tutelary or controlling spirits. Their 'unseen sceptres' recalls 'th' unseen Genius of the Wood', *Il Penseroso* 154. Addison, in his *Dialogues upon Ancient Medals* (*Works*, ed. A. C. Guthkelch (1914) ii 285) after describing some of the figures depicted on the medals, states: 'To these you may add the Genies of nations, provinces, cities, high-ways, and the like Allegorical Beings.'
5. Take all who for the *deleted above.*
7. day] Sun *deleted.*
11–12. gradual] Slowly progressive, ripening.
12. See Gray, *Progress of Poesy* 90 *n* (p. 173 above).
17. springlets] Not recorded by *OED* in the sense of a small spring before Scott's *Marmion* (1808).
18. Dryden, *Eclogues* v 131–2: 'winding Streams . . . / . . . the scarce-cover'd Pebbles gently chide.'
19. Oak trees were sacred to the druids.
24. roughen] This intransitive sense, meaning 'to become wild or unculti-vated', is rare and the only comparable case quoted by the *OED* occurs in

25   Sometimes, when morning o'er [the] plain
      Her radiant mantle throws,
  I'll mark the clouds where sweet Lorraine
      His orient colours chose;

  Or, when the sun to noontide climbs,
30   I'll hide me from his view
  By such green plats and cheerful limes
    As   Rysdael drew.

Thomson, *Spring* 642–3: 'The grassy dale, / Or roughening waste'. Thomson uses the verb again in *Spring* 959–60: 'the broken landscape, by degrees / Ascending roughens into rigid hills'. Both passages were added by Thomson in the revised edn of *The Seasons* published in July 1744. If C. was imitating Thomson's distinctive usage here, this would provide one limiting date for the composition of this poem.

25. C. accidentally omitted 'the' before 'plain' (cp. l. 41).

25–8. C.'s characterization of the art of Claude Lorraine (1600–82), the immensely popular landscape painter, in these lines and again in 41–4, reflects his age's particular admiration for Claude's ability to depict light and especially the sun in the early morning and evening. See E. W. Manwaring, *Italian Landscape in Eighteenth Century England* (1925; new impression, 1965) pp. 35–44, 95.

25–6. Cp. *Par. Lost* iv 609, where the moon 'o're the dark her Silver Mantle threw'; and cp. ll. 41–2.

28. orient] A vague but common usage, meaning shining or radiant. Cp. 'Orient Colours', *Par. Lost* i 546; and *ibid* xi 204–5: 'Morning light / More orient in yon Western Cloud'.

29–30. Milton, *Il Penseroso* 131–2, 141: 'And when the Sun begins to fling / His flaring beams . . . . / Hide me from Day's garish eie.'

29. to] at *deleted*.

31–2. Jacob van Ruisdael or Rysdael (*c.* 1629–82), Holland's greatest landscape painter, was admired rather less by the eighteenth century than were the painters of Italian landscape, being considered a more literal imitator of nature. See Manwaring, p. v.

31. plat] A small patch of ground, a plot. Cp. 'This Flouerie Plat', *Par. Lost* ix 456 and 'a Plat of rising ground', *Il Penseroso* 73.

33–48. Cp. *Evening* 29–40 (pp. 465–6).

33–40. Salvator Rosa (1615–73) satisfied the eighteenth century's longing for the 'sublime and wild' in landscape painting and his name was endlessly contrasted with Claude. See Manwaring, pp. 44–56, and 95, where the Salvatorial landscape is characterized as showing 'precipices and great rock masses of fantastic form, cascades, torrents, desolate ruins, caves, trees dense of growth, or blasted trunks, and shattered boughs.'

Then on some heath, all wild and bare,
    With more delight I'll stand
35 Than he who sees with wondering air
    The works of Rosa's hand:

There where some rock's deep cavern gapes
    Or in some tawny dell,
I'll seem to see the wizard shapes
40   That from his pencil fell.

But when soft evening o'er the plain
    Her gleamy mantle throws,
I'll mark the clouds whence sweet Lorraine
    His   colours chose;

45 Or from the vale I'll lift my sight
    To some
Where'er the sun withdraws his light,
    The dying lustre falls.

Such   will I keep
50 Till
The modest moon again shall peep
    Above some eastern hill.

All tints that ever picture used
    Are lifeless, dull and mean,
55 To paint her dewy light diffused

What art can paint the modest ray,
    So sober, chaste and cool,

---

33. all wild and bare] of all unseen *deleted.* This earlier reading echoes *Il Penseroso* 65: 'I walk unseen' etc.

34. With more delight] in cooler hours *deleted.*

38. Or] Oer *deleted.* *tawny*] Yellowy-brown.

39. wizard] Magic. Cp. *Lycidas* 55: 'wisard stream'.

41–4. See ll. 25–8, esp. 25–6 n. Cp. Dryden, *Wife of Bath's Tale* 214: 'The Moon was up and shot a gleamy Light.'

48–55. Cp. *Stanzas on a Female Painter* 1–5 (p. 539 above).

54. lifeless] languid *deleted.*

56. Left blank by C.

57. the] yon *deleted.*

57–8. Cp. Pope, *Epistles to Several Persons* ii 254: 'All mild ascends the Moon's more sober light'.

As round yon cliffs it seems to play
60   Or skirts yon glimmering pool?

The tender gleam her orb affords
    No poet can declare,
Although he choose the softest words
    That e'er were sighed in air.

59. *round*] on *deleted.*
62. Pope, *Essay on Criticism* 141: 'Some Beauties yet, no Precepts can declare.'

29 To Simplicity

Written not later than Dec. 1746 and probably after the summer of 1744.
The evidence for dating this poem is the same as for the *Ode to Simplicity*
(see headnote), of which it must be considered an early version. The poem
which C. eventually published is, however, more than a mere revision of
this draft, since, in spite of some shared phrases, the later poem is organized
in a radically different way. John Butt, *Review of English Studies* xi (1958)
220–2, remarked that C.'s practice in the later *Odes* was to discover a
'fit embodiment for his allegoric abstractions, implying their nature (for
example) by the attitudes they strike, by the garb they wear, and by the
places they haunt. In the draft . . . there is but the faintest anticipation of this
practice, and perhaps that is why it was discarded.'
    The unfinished nature of the draft is indicated by C.'s repetition of such
words as 'chaste' and 'modest' (see notes to ll. 4 and 25), 'soft' and 'sweet'
or 'sweetest'; and by his apparent uncertainty as to the identity of the per-
sonification he is addressing (l. 9 *n*). In the MS the stanzas are numbered 1
to 7.

O Fancy, altered maid,
    Who now, too long betrayed,
To toys and pageant wedd'st thy cheated heart,
    Yet once with chastest thought
5   Far nobler triumphs sought,
Thrice gentle guide of each exalted art!

    Too

No more, sweet maid, the enfeebling dreams prolong.

¶ 29.*1–3.* Cp. the published *Ode to Simplicity* 7–9 (p. 424).
4. *chastest*] Cp. the recurrence of 'chaste' and 'chastest' in ll. 21, 31 and 39.
7–8. *weakly* deleted after *Too and l. 8 left blank.*
9. C. appears to be uncertain as to which personification he is addressing. He
has begun the poem by addressing Fancy and here may merely be urging

> *10*   Return, sweet maid, at length
>   In all thy ancient strength
> And bid our Britain hear thy Grecian song.
>
>   For thee, of loveliest name,
>   That land shall ever claim
> *15* And laid an infant on her favoured shore,
>   Soft bees of Hybla's vale
>   To age attests the tale
> To feed thy youth   their s   store.
>
>   From that   hour
> *20*   Thou knew'st the gentle power
> To charm her matrons chaste and virtuous youth;
>   For Wisdom learned to please
>   By thy persuasive ease
> And simplest sweetness more ennobled Truth.
>
> *25*   Nor modest Picture less
>   Declined the wild excess,
> Which frequent now distracts her wild design:
>   The modest Graces laid
>   Each soft, unboastful shade,
> *30* While feeling Nature drew the impassioned line!
>
>   O chaste, unboastful guide,
>   O'er all my heart preside
> And, midst my cave in breathing marble wrought,
>   In sober musing near

Fancy to return to her ancient simplicity. But later in the poem he seems to be addressing Simplicity herself, as the title would lead one to expect and as he does in his later version of the poem.

12. Similarly Akenside, *Pleasures of Imagination* i 604, tries to 'tune to Attic themes the British lyre'; and J. Warton, *Ode to Fancy* 148: 'O bid Britannia rival Greece!'

15–18. Cp. *Simplicity* 13–15 (pp. 424–5).

16. Soft] The *deleted.*

18. To feed thy youth] Around thy couch *deleted above.*

22. For Wisdom] From thy *deleted.*

25. modest] The word recurs in ll. 28 and 42.

27. now] too *deleted.*

29, 31. unboastful] See headnote to *Simplicity* and l. 12 *n* (pp. 423–4).

31. Come Gentle Goddess Sweet *deleted above.*

33. midst my cave] ever near my view *deleted.*

34. With lightest Attic lawn *deleted.* Cp. Milton's Melancholy, *Il Penseroso*

35   With Attic robe appear
       And charm my sight and prompt my temperate
          thought.

       And when soft maids and swains
       Reward my native strains
       With flowers that chastest bloom and sweetest breathe,
40   I, loveliest nymph divine,
       Will own the merits thine
       And round thy temples bind the modest wreath.

32 and 38, 'Sober, stedfast, and demure' and 'With eev'n step, and musing gate'.
35. *With*] On all *deleted*.   Cp. *Simplicity* 11 (p. 424).
36. Cp. *Simplicity* 47 and 51 (p. 427).
39. Cp. *Simplicity* 28 (p. 426).
40. *loveliest*] Sweetest *deleted*.

30 'No longer ask me, gentle friends'

The dating of this poem cannot be conclusive and depends entirely on two new tentative identifications of persons referred to by C. If stanza 5 refers to James Hammond's *Love Elegies*, the poem was written later than Dec. 1742. If the poetess, to whom the poem as a whole may well be addressed and who is described in the last 3 stanzas, is Elizabeth Carter (see l. 49 *n*), the date would have to be later, probably not earlier than 1746, and this would depend on the assumption that C. had seen some of Miss Carter's poetry before publication.

Such a dating would not be incompatible with the assumption of Cunningham and McKillop that this poem should be connected with C.'s *Ode, to a Lady*, written in May 1745. As in the last stanza of that poem, C. associates himself with a Sussex village. But it is less easy to accept the automatic assumption that the Delia beloved by C. in the present poem must be identified with the Elizabeth Goddard addressed in the *Ode, to a Lady*. Cunningham and McKillop both assume that C. was in love with Miss Goddard and that she lived in the village of Harting in Sussex: in the headnote to the *Ode, to a Lady*, caution is expressed about the first premise and the second is shown to be unlikely. As applied to the present poem, the belief that Miss Goddard lived in Harting has resulted in a misreading, since it seems clear enough that, like Miss Goddard, C.'s Delia was only a visitor to Sussex. C. first saw her either in Chichester (l. 43) or in the village of Harting, with which he himself had some connection: the reference to 'village friends' in the first version of the opening line may confirm this, or may be mere pastoral routine. C. himself then went to see Delia by 'Resnel's banks', where Otway spent his childhood (stanza 4). Otway was born in the village of Trotton, a few miles from Harting, but during his childhood his father became Vicar of Wool-bedding, three miles away, and C. may equally have had this second village in mind. It is noteworthy that Charles Mill, a member of the Mill family who occupied the manor house at Woolbedding throughout the century, was C.'s contemporary at Winchester, entering as a Scholar in 1734: see T. F. Kirby, *Winchester Scholars* (1888) p. 239. Delia may have been staying with the Mill family or in some similar mansion in the district. What is surely clear, however, is that she did not live there: she lived at some point along the Medway in Kent (see l. 44 *n*), so that she was divided from C. geographically as well as socially (see first version of ll. 21–4). C. ends his poem with protracted compliments to a poetess, who, if not Elizabeth Carter, is remarkably similar to her in a number of ways, in the hope that she might assist his pursuit of Delia. Unfortunately the identification of the poetess does not assist the identification of Delia, since Elizabeth Carter cannot be shown to have had a friend named Elizabeth Goddard or one in the habit of visiting Sussex villages. Whoever Delia was, it is not impossible that William Seward was referring to her in his *Supplement to the Anecdotes of Some Distinguished Persons* (1797) p. 125: 'Collins was extremely attached to a young lady who was born the day before him, and who did not return his passion with equal ardour. He said, on that occasion, "that he came into the world a day after the *fair*."'

In the MS the stanzas are numbered '1' to '9 and last'.

No longer ask me, gentle friends,
   Why heaves my constant sigh,
Or why my eye for ever bends
   To yon fair eastern sky.
5 Why view the clouds that onward roll?
   Ah, who can fate command?
While here I sit, my wandering soul
   Is in a distant land.

Did ye not hear of Delia's name,
10   When on a fatal day
O'er yonder northern hills she came
   And brought an earlier May?

¶ 30.*1. gentle*] Village *deleted.*
7. wandering] far off *written above.*
9. Cp. l. 60 (both versions) where Delia is also called Laura and Amanda.

Or if the month her bloomy store
By gentle custom brought,
15   She ne'er was half so sweet before
To my delighted thought.

She found me in my southern vale,
All in her converse blest:
My   heart began to fail
20   Within my youngling breast.
I thought when as her
To me of lowly birth,
There lived not aught so good and kind
On all the smiling earth.

25   To Resnel's banks, again to greet
Her gentle eyes, I strayed,
Where once a bard with infant feet
Among the willows played:

13–16. First version deleted:

She came and to my simple Mind
Improv'd the blossom'd Year
For She, Ye swains of all her kind
Is Damon's only Dear.

13. Or if the] Perhaps *deleted.*
17. Cp. *Popular Superstitions* 11, for C.'s reference to Chichester as 'on the southern coast' (p. 502).
18. And scarce one thought exprest *deleted.*
20. youngling] Inexperienced.
21–4. First version deleted:

I thought to mark her gentle Mind
Tho born of lofty birth
And when She left my Cot methought
She mark'd my starting Tear

25. I saw her next by Resnel's side *deleted.*
The reference to Otway later in this stanza suggests that C. is referring to the playwright's birthplace at Trotton in Sussex, where the Resnel was presumably a stream. As Cunningham has noted: 'No stream of this name is now known in the area. Harting Brook joins the Rother at Trotton, and a small stream rising at Elsted flows into the brook just before its junction with the main stream.' But see headnote for the possibility that C. was referring to nearby Woolbedding.
27. once a bard] Otway first *deleted.*   For C.'s admiration for, and sense of kinship with, Thomas Otway see *Pity* 16–18 *n* (p. 416).

His tender thoughts subdue the fair
30   And melt the soft and young,
But mine I know were softer there
    Than ever poet sung.

I showed her there the songs of one
    Who, done to death by pride,
35   Though Virtue's friend and Fancy's son,
    In love unpitied died.
I hoped when to that shepherd's truth
    Her pity should attend,
She would not leave another youth
40   To meet his luckless end.

Now tell me, you who hear me sing
    And prompt the tender theme,
How far is Lavant's little spring
    From Medway's mightier stream.

29. The thoughts which fill his tender scene *deleted.*

30. *And melt*] Subdue *deleted.* After this line C. first left a line blank and wrote 'I hung' as the rhyme in l. 32; he then drafted ll. 31–2 as below.

31. *Written above* And Yet my own were fond I ween *with the first four words deleted and with* But there *also deleted.*

32. *Than*] As *deleted.*

33–6. This unhappy 'shepherd' may have been invented by C., but it is possible that he was alluding to a contemporary poet, whose verse had achieved some fame soon after his death in the early 1740s. James Hammond (1710–42) died at the age of thirty-two, as it was widely believed at the time, from unrequited love for Catherine or Kitty Dashwood, who later became a Woman of the Bedchamber to Queen Charlotte. Hammond's *Love Elegies. Written in the Year 1732* were published, with a preface by Lord Chesterfield, in Dec. 1742, though with the title-page dated 1743. Hammond's fate as a lover and the nature of his poetry correspond precisely and uniquely with what C. says of his 'shepherd'.

35. Milton, *L'Allegro* 133: 'sweetest *Shakespear* fancies childe'.

41–2. *First version, l. 2 of which is deleted:*

    But Ye who know what bounds divide
    Our Shores or rightliest deem

43. C.'s footnote, 'Dic quibus in terris &c', refers to two riddles of which these are the first words, in Virgil, *Eclogues* iii 104–7, and probably to the first in particular: 'Tell me in what lands—and you shall be my great Apollo—Heaven's space is but three ells broad.' The explanation may be the view of the sky from the bottom of a well or cavern.

    is . . . little spring] remov'd is . . . side *deleted.*

45 Confined within my native dells,
        The world I little know,
    But in some tufted mead she dwells,
        Where'er those waters flow.

    There too resorts a maid, renowned
50   For framing ditties sweet:

44–8. These lines make it clear that, whoever Delia was, she did not live in Harting or Trotton, but at some point along the Medway in Kent. The Medway rises in Forest Ridges in Sussex, quickly flowing east to enter Kent near Ashurst, then passing north-east to Tonbridge, Maidstone, Rochester, Chatham and joining the Thames at Sheerness.

47. tufted] Adorned with tufts or clumps of trees or bushes. Cp. 'tufted Trees', *L'Allegro* 78; 'tufted Grove', *Comus* 225.

49. An attempt to identify this poetess may be foolhardy but, as is the case with the poetical 'shepherd' in the 5th stanza, enough information is given or hinted at to justify a tentative suggestion. The lady in question is 're-nowned' for her poetry; does not live with Delia on the Medway but 'resorts' there and is her friend; and she has written the complaint of a 'greenwood nymph', of 'Melancholy's gloomy power' and of the joys of Wisdom. No connection between C. and Elizabeth Carter (1717–1806), the friend of Richardson, Johnson and other literary figures, is recorded, but she was enjoying some literary reputation by the 1740s and may well have met C. through Johnson who already knew her. Her home was in Deal, but she also spent much of her time in these years with friends in Canterbury and London and must have known many of the leading families in Kent. Her poetry was being published from the late 1730s and it includes an *Ode to Melancholy*, printed in Nov. 1739 in the *Gentleman's Mag.* ix 599 and an *Ode on Wisdom*, which was in MS circulation at least by 1746, since, after appear-ing in Richardson's *Clarissa* without her consent in 1747, it was reprinted in the *Gentleman's Mag.* in Dec. 1747, xvii 585, with a note stating that it had been in the editor's hands for a year. As for the 'greenwood nymph', Miss Carter's *To Dr. Walwyn On his Design of Cutting Down a Shady Walk*, written in 1745 according to Pennington (see below), is the complaint of 'A weeping Hamadryad' for 'Her fate-devoted trees'. The similarities between Elizabeth Carter and C.'s poetess may be coincidental but they remain striking. In any case, even if this identification is admitted, it does not assist the identification of C.'s Delia, since Miss Carter does not appear to have known an Elizabeth Goddard and none of her numerous female friends, mentioned in Mathew Pennington's *Memoirs of Mrs. Elizabeth Carter* (1807), appears to have had a connection with the Sussex villages of Harting, Trotton or Woolbedding where C. met his Delia.

49. There too resorts] And near her Wonnes *suggested above.*

50. Spenser, *Colin Clout* 385: 'to frame an euerlasting dittie'.

I heard her lips
   Her gentle lays repeat.
They told how sweetly in her bower
   A greenwood nymph complained,
55 Of Melancholy's gloomy power,
   And joys from Wisdom gained.

Sweet sung that muse and fair befall
   Her life, whose happy art,
What other bards might envy all,
60   Can touch my Laura's heart.

53–6. *C. had great difficulty with these lines. After ll. 49–52 as in the present
text, he first wrote the four lines given in 61–4 n; then the following deleted
attempts to begin another stanza:*

  a From Wisdom whom she taught to please
  b She sootly sung how once she heard
      A Green-wood Nymph complain,
  c 'Twas she that sung how soft and sweet
      A Green
  d To Wisdom first whose Love she gain'd
      The duteous Verse she paid

*Interlined with these efforts are the opening lines of the drafted stanza which
follows next:*

    Ennobling Wisdom first she ownd
      And hail'd the Sacred Powr
    Then like a Green wood Nymph bemoan'd

    Of Melancholy last She tried
    To make the Virtues known
    Ah Why? That Theme with Love allied
      Belong'd to me Alone!

(*In l. 3 of this stanza* bemoan'd *is written above* complaind *and in l. 4*
Of *is written above* And.) *Finally C. wrote ll. 53–6 as in the main text here,
headed 7, with each line queried in the margin.*
53. *They told how*] The lays where of *deleted.*
55. 'gloomie power', *Par. Lost* iii 242.
56. *joys*] wreaths *deleted.*
57. *Sweet sung that muse*] Yet sweet the Song *deleted and* sung *written above*
flowd *deleted.*   *fair befall*] A Shakespearean phrase, e.g. 'Now fair befall
thee and thy noble house', *Richard III* I iii 282.
60. *my Laura's*] Amanda's *deleted.*

Sweet oaten reeds for her I'll make
  And chaplets for her hair,
If she, for friendly pity's sake,
  Will whisper Damon there.

65 Her strain shall dim, if aught succeeds
  From my applauding tongue,
Whate'er within her native meads
  The tuneful Thyrsis sung:
Less to my love shall he be dear,
70   Although he earliest paid
Full many a soft and tender tear
  To luckless Collins's shade!

61–4. First version at the end of stanza 7 (see ll 53–6 n):

I'll henceforth make with   Art
  Some Garland for her Hair
That She who charms my Delia's heart
  May plead for Damon there!

That She who charms *is written above* Her Verse may touch *deleted*; May *is written above* And *deleted*.

  There are four cancelled lines in the margin of stanza 8:

I will not soil with praise the lay
  Which soothly none can blame
But count the Songs let all who may
  Divine the Writers name

61. 'Oten reedes', Spenser, *Shepheardes Calender*, 'Oct.' 8 and 56; 'Dec.' 14; *Colin Clout* 13, etc.
65. dim] Overshadow.   *aught*] mine *deleted*.

31 [Lines on the Music of the Grecian Theatre]

Written almost certainly in or about Nov. 1750. This dating depends on the assumption that these lines are part–possibly all that was written–of a poem mentioned by C. in a letter to Dr William Hayes, Professor of Music at Oxford, on 8 Nov. 1750 (W. Seward, *Supplement to the Anecdotes of Some Distinguished Persons* (1797) pp. 123–4). Having mentioned Hayes's setting of *The Passions* and offered to send an improved version of that poem, C. continued:

'I could send you one written on a nobler subject; and which, tho' I have been persuaded to bring it forth in London, I think more calculated for an audience in the University. The subject is *the Music of the Grecian Theatre*; in which I have, I hope naturally, introduced the various characters with which the chorus was concerned, as Œdipus, Medea, Electra, Orestes, &c. &c.

The composition too is probably more correct, as I have chosen the ancient Tragedies for my models, and only copied the most affecting passages in them.'

Nothing else has ever been discovered about the poem and it would be characteristic of C. to have described it as complete to Hayes, when he had in fact completed only the opening lines. The description of the fragment as 'Recitative Accompanied' makes it clear that it is part of an ode for music and the subject was clearly going to be Greek music. Ptolemy appears to be introduced so as to enable C. to begin the poem by imitating the opening of the most famous of English musical odes, Dryden's *Alexander's Feast*. There is nothing in the style or structure of the fragment to contradict the dating suggested above, which makes it C.'s last known composition.

Recitative Accompanied

When glorious Ptolemy, by merit raised,
    Successive sat on Egypt's radiant throne,
Bright Ptolemy, on whom while Athens gazed,
    She almost wished the monarch once her own:
5 Then virtue owned one royal heart,
    For, loathing war, humanely wise,
For all the sacred sons of art,
    He bade the dome of science rise.
The Muses knew the festal day
10   And, called by power, obsequant came
With all their lyres and chaplets gay:
They gave the fabric its immortal name.

¶ *31.1 ff.* C. evidently refers to Ptolemy Soter, the founder of the dynasty of Macedonian kings of Egypt. Ptolemy I (*c.* 377/6–283/2 B.C.), originally one of Alexander's generals, became satrap of Egypt in 323 B.C. and declared himself king in 304. He was a patron of letters and founded the great Library and the Museum in Alexandria (see l. 12 and *n*). Cp. *Par. Lost* ii 5–6: 'By merit rais'd / To that bad eminence'.

2. Obtained his old Ægyptian Throne deleted.   successive] Presumably 'successful', the older sense, rather than 'by order of succession'.

6. humanely] too genrous and too *deleted*.

8. dome] Building (Latin *domus*).

10. obsequant] Apparently the obsolete 'obsequent', meaning 'obedient, compliant'. Cunningham mistakenly read 'Obsequiant'.

12. They gave] Assign'd *deleted*.   C.'s footnote identifies the 'fabric' as 'The

High o'er the rest in golden pride,
The monarch sat and, at his side,
15   His favourite bards, his Grecian choir,
Who, while the roofs responsive rung,
To many a fife and many a tinkling lyre,
Amid the shouting tribes in sweet succession sung.

Μουσεῖον', the great Museum at Alexandria founded by Ptolemy to house
a hundred research workers from all over the Mediterranean. C.'s account
of its musical activities appears to be his own invention.
13–14. Dryden, *Alexander's Feast* 3–6: 'Aloft in awful State / The God-like
Heroe sate / On his Imperial Throne: / His valiant Peers were plac'd
around'.
17. Cowley, *The Complaint* st. vii: 'The tinkling strings of thy loose
minstrelsy'.

LOST AND DOUBTFUL POEMS

32 A Battle of the School Books

In a short article on C. in his series 'Drossiana' (*European Mag.* xxviii, Dec. 1795, 377), William Seward wrote: 'A singular line of this great Poet, in a juvenile Poem which he made when he was twelve years old, on a Battle of the School Books at Winchester, is remembered, "And every Gradus flapped his leathern wing."' Seward presumably obtained this line from one of the Warton brothers, probably Joseph, who was C.'s friend and contemporary at Winchester. The phrase 'leathern wing' recurs in *Evening* 10. See the note there (p. 464 above) for earlier appearances of this phrase, which disprove 'how early Collins had turned to Shakespeare' (Ainsworth, p. 6).

33 On the Royal Nuptials

A note by Thomas Park, communicated by John Mitford to Alexander Dyce and discussed by him in his edn of C., 1827, p. 42*, has been responsible for much unnecessary expense of editorial energy. Park noted that in the 'Register' of recently published books in the *Gentleman's Mag.* iv 167, in March 1734, occur the following entries:

18. On the Royal Nuptials. An Irregular Ode. By Mr *Philips*, price 1s.
19. A Poem on the same Occasion. By *Wm Collins*. Printed for *J. Roberts*, pr. 6d.

The second item has never been identified, but, though C.'s *Persian Eclogues* were later published by J. Roberts (in 1742), it must appear improbable that C. should have written such a poem at the age of twelve. I. A. Williams, *Seven Eighteenth Century Bibliographies* (1924) p. 107, has suggested what must be the correct solution to the problem: that 'Collins' is a misprint for 'Collier'. A William Collier did write a similar poem, *A Congratulatory Poem on his Majesty's Happy Return to England* (1732), which was published by J. Roberts.

34 Hercules

This poem is attributed to C. in *The Crypt, Or, Receptacle for Things Past: An Antiquarian, Literary, and Miscellaneous Journal* ii (1828) 56–8, in the following article on 'W. Collins's Unpublished Poetry', written presumably by the editor, Peter Hall:

'The M.S. of the following Poem (on a subject of most interesting applicability to certain braggadocios) was formerly in the possession of the great

Thomas Warton, to whom it probably passed from his brother, the school-fellow and friend of Collins. In that family...it has always passed as a youth-ful production of the "Cicestrian Bard;" it bears the appearance of a school exercise, written out for the Master's inspection. If such it be, however, and the date of 1747 be that of the original composition, all claim to it on the part of *the* poet Collins must give way, as he quitted Winchester for Oxford, in 1740. Under this difficulty, an application was lately made to the Bishop of Hereford, the present Warden of Winchester College, by whose kindness we have obtained a list of every boy of that name admitted into the School within seventeen years of the above date; and we do not hesitate to decide, that to none of them is there any reasonable probability for attributing the verses in question. Whether, therefore, it be, or be not, a school per-formance, the date must be rather assigned to the time when the transcript was made, and the tradition in favour of William Collins be permitted, in lack of more substantial authority, to predominate.'

The poem is entitled 'Hercules' and is dated 'Collins, Jun. 1747'. In 1939, P. L. Carver, *Notes and Queries* clxxvii 272, revealed that the same poem appears in the *Gentleman's Mag.* viii 45, in Jan. 1738 (entitled 'On Hercules' and in an identical text) and urged that the attribution to C. was thus streng-thened, since it would then have been written, as Hall had suggested, in C.'s years at Winchester. Carver has repeated the argument in *The Life of a Poet* (1967) pp. 15–17. The supposed association of the lost MS with the Warton family no doubt prevents the attribution from being dismissed out of hand but further evidence is surely needed to demonstrate that C., at the age of just sixteen, could or would have written this dull satirical poem, 34 ll. long in anapaestic couplets, demonstrating admittedly a knowledge of schoolbook classical mythology, but ending with a laborious version of the hoary cuckold / horns joke.

35 To Miss Aurelia C———r, on her Weeping at her Sister's Wedding

This poem, 8 ll. long, signed 'Amasius', was first printed in the *Gentleman's Mag.* ix 41, in Jan. 1739 and was first attributed to C. in the *Poetical Calendar* xii 107, in Dec. 1763, in the life of C. contributed by his schoolfellow at Winchester, James Hampton: 'The following epigram, made by him while at Winchester-school, discovers a genius, and turn of expression, very rarely to be met with in juvenile compositions.'

Hampton's personal knowledge of C. might be thought to give this attribution some authority, but the matter is complicated by a letter written by Samuel Johnson to John Nichols, the publisher, early in 1780, when he was engaged on his *Lives of the Poets (Letters*, ed. R. W. Chapman (1952) ii 332–3): 'Dr. Warton tells me that Collins's first piece is in the G:M: for August, 1739. In August there is no such thing. *Amasius* was at that time the poetical name of Dr *Swan* who translated Sydenham. Where to find Collins I know not.' Johnson had been working for the *Gentleman's Mag.* in 1739 when this poem appeared in it and there is no reason to doubt his confident belief that 'Amasius' had been the pseudonym of Dr John Swan, the editor of Thomas Sydenham's *Works* (1742). Moreover, there are many other poems signed by 'Amasius' in the *Gentleman's Mag.* between 1739 and 1743, including a total of nine in 1739, and it is impossible to believe that C. was also responsible for these mediocre pieces. However, in spite of his letter to Nichols, Johnson states in his 'Life' of C. (*Lives of the Poets*, ed. G. B. Hill (1905) iii 342) that C. 'first courted the notice of the public by some verses to a *Lady weeping*, published in *The Gentleman's Magazine*'; and at the end of the 'Life' this poem was actually quoted. This apparent admission of the poem into the canon was followed by most later eighteenth and nineteenth century editors.

The situation is confused, but some such explanation as the following is probably correct. Johnson's original source of information was Joseph Warton, who probably told him no more than what Johnson states in the body of his 'Life' of C.: that C.'s first published poem was to a lady weeping and that it had appeared in the *Gentleman's Mag.*, though Warton may have added erroneously that it was published in Aug. 1739. Warton probably had in mind the 'Sonnet' (see p. 365 above) that C. contributed to the same magazine in Oct. 1739, which also deals with a 'lady weeping'. Johnson himself, as his letter to Nichols suggests, may have left the matter there, but Nichols or some other hand, discovering the present poem in the magazine for Jan. 1739 or else finding it attributed to C. in the *Poetical Calendar*, may well have added it at the end of Johnson's biography. The matter is still far from clear, but the fact that the lines are signed 'Amasius' seems to prevent their acceptance as C.'s.

36 On the Use and Abuse of Poetry

This fragment was printed by Joseph Warton in his *Essay on the Writings and Genius of Pope* (1756) i 60–1, after a discussion of Pope's *Ode on St Cecilia's Day*:

'I have lately seen a manuscript ode, entitled, "On the Use and Abuse of Poetry," in which Orpheus is considered in another, and a higher light, according to ancient mythology, as the first legislator and civilizer of mankind. I shall here insert a stanza of it, containing part of what relates to this subject.

ANTISTROPHE. II.
Such was wise Orpheus' moral song,
The lonely cliffs and caves among;
From hollow oak, or mountain-den,
He drew the naked, gazing men,
Or where in turf-built sheds, or rushy bowers,
They shiver'd in cold wintry showers,
    Or sunk in heapy snows;
Then sudden, while his melting music stole
With powerful magic o'er each softening soul,
Society, and law, and sacred order rose.

EPODE II.
Father of peace and arts! he first the city built;
No more the neighbour's blood was by his neighbour spilt;
    He taught to till, and separate the lands;
He fix'd the roving youths in Hymen's myrtle bands;
    Whence dear domestic life began,
    And all the charities that soften'd man:
    The babes that in their father's faces smil'd,
    With lisping blandishments their rage beguil'd,
        And tender thoughts inspir'd! — &c.

'I am not permitted to transcribe any more, and therefore return to POPE again.'

Edmund Blunden, in his edn of C. (1929) p. 179, believed that 'it is all but certain that Collins is the author of this fragment', on the strength of the fact that C. gave the Wartons various fragments of poems during their visit to Chichester in Sept. 1754; and also on stylistic 'consonances with Collins's known work'. It is now known that the fragments of poems in Trinity College, Oxford, which are presumably those given by C. to the Wartons, do not include these lines; and it may also be asked why C. should not have permitted Warton to transcribe more of the poem. Similarly, although some of the diction and phrasing of the lines resembles passages in C.'s poetry, these are in fact echoes shared by many poets of the period. In general the flat clarity of the lines is free from C.'s characteristic obscurity and vagueness on the one hand, and imaginative boldness on the other.

37 The Bell of Arragon

In his short memoir of C. (printed as *The Reaper*, No. 26, in the *York Chronicle* (16 Feb. 1797) and reprinted by Nathan Drake in *The Gleaner* (1811) iv 476–7) Thomas Warton recalled that when he and his brother visited C. at Chichester in Sept. 1754, he showed them, in addition to his *Ode on the Popular Superstitions of the Highlands*, 'another ode, of two or three four-lined stanzas, called the Bell of Arragon; on a tradition that, anciently, just before a king of Spain died, the great bell of the cathedral of Sarragossa, in Arragon, tolled spontaneously. It began thus:

> The bell of Arragon, they say,
> Spontaneous speaks the fatal day, &c.

Soon afterwards were these lines:—

> Whatever dark aerial power,
> Commission'd, haunts the gloomy tower.

The last stanza consisted of a moral transition to his own death and knell, which he called "some simpler bell."'

Nothing further is known about this poem. Nathan Drake himself, the preserver of this account, attempted to reconstruct the lost poem from these fragments many years later in *Mornings in Spring* (1828) ii 337–8.

38 On a Quack Doctor

William Seward printed this poem in the *Whitehall Evening Post*, early in July 1794 (see *The Journal of William Bagshaw Stevens*, ed. G. Galbraith (Oxford, 1965) p. 166), and again among the anecdotes of C. in his *Supplement to the Anecdotes of Some Distinguished Persons* (1797) p. 125:

'This great Poet did not often wander into the gayer and lively scenes of his art. The following Verses by him, on a Quack Doctor of Chichester, are still remembered in that city:

> Seventh son of Doctor John,
> Physician and Chirurgeon,
> Who hath travelled wide and far,
> Man-Midwife to a Man of War,
> In Chichester hath ta'en a house,
> Hippocrates, Hippocratous.'

In the *Whitehall Evening Post* Seward had stated that C. wrote the poem on the doctor's window. Although there is no further evidence to confirm this attribution, which does not perhaps advance C.'s reputation as a poet, a passage in John Ragsdale's letter about C. in *The Gleaner* iv 480, may confirm the possibility that C. should have composed such trivia and that they should still be circulating many years after his death: 'I had formerly several scraps of his poetry, which were suddenly written on particular occasions; these I lent among our acquaintance, who were never civil enough to return them; and being then engaged in extensive business, I forgot to ask for them, and they are lost; all I have remaining of his are about twenty lines, which would require a little history to be understood, being written on trifling subjects.' Seward seems to have heard the lines in question, however, in Chichester rather than from C.'s London friends.

W. Moy Thomas (1858) p. lix, refers, in explanation of the first line of the poem, to a popular proverb which 'assigns, as an hereditary right to all seventh sons, the names of Septimus, and the profession of a surgeon'.

39 A Song

Imitated from the Midsummer Night's Dream of Shakespeare– Act II Scene V [actually Act II Scene ii]

This poem, which first appeared in Dodsley's *The Museum* (16 Aug. 1746) i 425, was claimed for C. by I. A. Williams in *The London Mercury* in May 1923 and again in his *Seven Eighteenth-Century Bibliographies* (1924) pp. 102–4, on the grounds of its stylistic resemblances to C.'s poetry in general, and to his technique of drawing on Shakespearean material in particular. Williams suggests that the poem was 'probably rejected by him because he afterwards used so many of its phrases and thoughts in more important poems'. But Joseph Warton attributed the poem to his brother Thomas, as is revealed by Alexander Chalmers in his *British Poets* (1810) xviii 76, where he states that his own attribution of it to Thomas Warton is 'authenticated by Dr. Warton's autograph in his copy of the museum *penes me*'. (Chalmers presumably bought this copy of *The Museum* at the sale of Joseph Warton's books in 1801.) Williams preferred to believe that Warton or Chalmers was mistaken; or that if Thomas Warton 'did write it he must certainly have known Collins's *Odes* almost by heart before their publication'. The logic of this statement is not obvious. The poem was published in *The Museum* four months before C.'s *Odes* appeared: it is just as likely that C. was influenced by it as that the reverse process took place.

The resemblances between this poem and C.'s known work are in any case by no means as striking as Williams suggests. In some cases the *Song* and C. probably shared a common source: 'love-lorn' (*Song* 13; *Simplicity* 16) occurs in *Comus* 234, for example. Williams's methods could be used to prove that the *Song* was written by at least two other known contributors to *The Museum*. He notes the resemblance between the beetle's 'sullen hum' (*Song* 11) and the beetle's 'heedless hum' in *Evening* 14; but John Gilbert Cooper, in *The Power of Harmony* (1745) p. 44, has 'the beetle's drowsy hum'. Again, the reference to the owl's 'orgies' (*Song* 8) can be paralleled by two lines from Akenside's *Odes* (1745), 'An Allusion to Horace' 31–2: 'Nor where the raven, where the owl / By night their hateful orgies howl.' Chalmers's attribution to Thomas Warton needs a more thorough refutation than Williams provided before it can be set aside.

40 On Our Late Taste in Music

First attributed to C. by Sir Harris Nicolas in the 'Memoir' of C. prefixed to the Aldine edn of his poems, 1830, p. xxxviii: 'From the coincidence between Collins's love of, and addresses to, Music, his residence at Oxford, and from internal evidence, Some Verses on Our Late Taste in Music, which appeared in the Gentleman's Magazine for 1740 [in Oct x 520], and there said to be "by a Gentleman of Oxford," are printed in this edition of Collins's works, not, however, as positively his, but as being so likely to be written by him, as to justify their being brought to the notice of his readers.' Although included in some edns of C.'s poetry until the beginning of the present century, there is little in this attack on the taste for foreign music to suggest that C. may have written it.

41 An Epistle to the Editor of Fairfax his Translation of Tasso's Jerusalem Delivered

In 'A Lost Poem of Collins' (*Times Lit. Supp.* 1928, p. 965) A. D. McKillop first drew attention to two newspaper advertisements which mention this poem. The *Whitehall Evening Post*, 1–3 Feb. 1750, announced that 'An Epistle to the Editor of Fairfax his Translation of Tasso. By Mr. William Collins' would be published 'In a few Days', by R. Manby and H. S. Cox, the publishers of C.'s *Ode Occasioned by the Death of Mr. Thomson* in 1749. The *General Advertiser*, Tuesday, 27 March 1750, advertised the poem once more, promising it for 'Saturday next'. But no copy of the poem has ever been discovered and it must be assumed that it was never published and probably never written.

The new edn (described as the 'Fourth', although this ignores an edition in 1726) of Edward Fairfax's translation (1600) of Tasso had been published in Oct. 1749, entitled *Tasso's Jerusalem Delivered: or Godfrey of Bulloign. An Heroic Poem. Done into English, In the Reign of Queen Elizabeth, By Edward Fairfax, Gent.* Its editor, to whom C. was to have addressed his poem, has not been identified. C.'s interest in Tasso and Fairfax preceded the appearance of this edn, for he refers in a letter to John Gilbert Cooper, 10 Nov. 1747, to 'some manuscripts of Fairfax which I can procure'. He praises both poets in his fragmentary 'Lines to a Friend about to Visit Italy' 13–14, and in stanza 12 of his *Ode on the Popular Superstitions of the Highlands*, probably written only a few weeks before the missing *Epistle* was first advertised. McKillop also links with the *Epistle* the reference to Tasso in the *Ode to Horror* (see headnote to the *Odes*), the parody of C. and the Wartons which appeared in *The Student* in 1751. This is plausible, but it should be remembered that Joseph Warton also referred to Tasso in his poetry, e.g., *Ode to a Gentleman upon his Travels thro' Italy* 57.

42 An Ode to the People of Great Britain

In Imitation of the Sixth Ode of Horace

This poem, which originally appeared in *The Museum* (24 May 1746) 179–82, is attributed to C. by Blunden (1929) pp. 145–50, on internal evidence. It was in fact written by Robert Lowth: see *Memoirs of the Life and Writings of the Right Rev. Robert Lowth* (1787) p. 18; Lowth's *Sermons and Other Remains*, ed. Peter Hall, 1834, pp. 472–86, 491–3; Southey, *Specimens of the later English Poets* (1807) iii 279–84.

43 Prologue to *Venice Preserved*

Acted by some Young Gentlemen at Winchester School

This prologue, which was printed in *The Museum* (10 May 1746) i 133–4, is also attributed to C. by Blunden (1929) pp. 150–1, on internal evidence, with the suggestion that Joseph Warton wrote the accompanying Epilogue. But C. is unlikely to have been involved in such a production and would certainly not be the only Wykehamist conscious of the fact that Otway had attended the school. The language and imagery do not particularly 'indicate his authorship', as Blunden asserts.

44 Prologues and Epilogue to *Douglas*

Prologue to Home's *Douglas*; Prologue to *Douglas* spoken at Edinburgh; Epilogue to *Douglas*

Blunden (1929) pp. 151–5, suggests that C. may have helped John Home with these two prologues and the epilogue, but the suggestion seems groundless. They must have been written in 1756 and 1757, when C. had been in obscurity at Chichester for several years in a state of supposed lunacy. There is no evidence of any contact between C. and Home after early 1750 (see headnote to *Popular Superstitions*, p. 492 above). Some slight resemblances to phrases and ideas in C.'s poetry proves no more than that these pieces were also written in the mid-eighteenth century.

THE POEMS OF
OLIVER GOLDSMITH

THE POEMS

1730?   (*10 Nov.*) Born, probably at Pallas, Co. Westmeath, second
         son of the Rev. Charles G., who shortly afterwards becomes
         curate-in-charge of the parish of Kilkenny West and moves
         to the house in Lissoy where G. spends his childhood. [The
         year was torn away in the entry of G.'s birth in the family
         bible: 1729, 1730 and 1731 have been proposed. See K. C.
         Balderston, *Times Lit. Supp.* 7 March 1929, pp. 185–6,
         and *Philological Quarterly* x (1931) 201–2; R. S. Crane,
         Philological Quarterly ix (1930) 190–1; and A. Friedman,
         Notes and Queries cxcvi (1951) 388–9.]

c. 1737–45 Educated at the Diocesan School at Elphin and at schools
         at Athlone near Lissoy and Edgeworthstown, Co. Longford.

1745   (*11 June*) Admitted as sizar to Trinity College, Dublin.

1747   Death of his father.
         (*21 May*) Publicly admonished for his part in a student riot.

1750   (*Feb.*) Graduated B.A.

1750–52 Fails to obtain ordination in the Church and becomes tutor
         to a family named Flinn in Co. Roscommon. Makes abortive
         journeys to Cork (probably intending to emigrate to America)
         and to Dublin (intending to study law in London, supported
         by his relations).

1752   (*Sept.*) Enters University of Edinburgh to study medicine,
         with financial assistance from his relations.

1754   (*c. 10 Feb.*) Leaves Edinburgh to study medicine at Leyden
         University, where he remains until early 1755.

1755   Travels across Flanders to Paris, ostensibly to pursue medical
         studies, and probably through Germany and Switzerland
         to Padua, Venice and Florence, returning to England across
         France.
         (*Summer*) Begins writing *The Traveller.*

1756   (*c. 1 Feb.*) Lands at Dover and travels to London.

1756–57 Works in various positions: as assistant to an apothecary, as a
         physician in Southwark (it is probably at this period, if ever,
         that G. applies for a medical degree from Trinity College,

571

Dublin), perhaps as a proof-reader in Samuel Richardson's printing-house, and as usher at a boys' school at Peckham, Surrey, run by the Rev. John Milner.

1757   (*April–Sept.*) Contributes articles to the *Monthly Review*, living at this time with Ralph Griffiths, the editor and proprietor.

1758   (*Feb.*) His translation of Jean Marteilhe's *Mémoires d'un Protestant* published, probably while he is temporarily back at Peckham in charge of the school.
(*Aug.*) Promised post of civilian physician with the East India Company on the coast of Coromandel, India.
(*21 Dec.*) Fails to obtain post as hospital-mate on a ship to India, which would cover cost of his journey.

1759   (*Jan.*) Starts contributing to Smollett's *Critical Review*.
(*March*) Abandons plan of travelling to Coromandel when news of French victories in India reaches England.
(*2 April*) Publishes *An Enquiry into the Present State of Learning in Europe*. From this period he is known as 'Dr Goldsmith' and his widening literary acquaintance probably soon includes Percy, Smollett, Murphy, Burke, Young and Johnson.
(*6 Oct.–24 Nov.*) Writes *The Bee*.

1759–60   Contributes essays to the *Busy Body*, the *Weekly Mag.*, the *Royal Mag.*, the *British Mag.* and *Lady's Mag.*

1760   (*24 Jan.*) Starts to contribute his 'Chinese Letters' to John Newbery's *Public Ledger*, a series which continues until 14 Aug. 1761.
(*Summer*) Moves from Green Arbour Court to No. 6 Wine Office Court, off Fleet St.

1761   (*31 May*) Percy describes a meeting with G. and Johnson. G. probably meets Joshua Reynolds at this period.

1762   (*Jan.–June*) Contributes essays to *Lloyd's Evening Post*, including in June 'The Revolution in Low Life', concerned with depopulation.
(*1 May*) The 'Chinese Letters' published in book form as *The Citizen of the World*, an event marking the virtual end of G.'s journalistic period and the start of his career as compiler and hack-writer, mainly for Newbery.
(*14 Oct.*) *The Life of Richard Nash* published.
(*28 Oct.*) Newbery sells Collins, a bookseller in Salisbury, a third share in *The Vicar of Wakefield*, which he had bought

from G., arrested by bailiffs, through Johnson. Late in the year, G. moves to Canonbury House, Islington, to live with Newbery.

1764   (*c. Feb.*) A founder member of The Club, with Johnson, Reynolds, Burke, Garrick and others.

(*26 June*) Publishes *An History of England in a Series of Letters from a Nobleman to his Son.*

(*c. Sept.*) Moves to No. 2 Garden Court in the Temple.

(*31 Oct.*) Sells his oratorio libretto *The Captivity* to Newbery and Dodsley.

(*19 Dec.*) Publishes *The Traveller, or A Prospect of Society.*

1765   (*3 June*) Publishes his *Essays*, collected from earlier publications.

(*c. June*) Moves to No. 3 King's Bench Walk in the Temple.

1766   (*27 March*) *The Vicar of Wakefield* published at Salisbury.

(*Dec.*) Publishes an anthology, *Poems for Young Ladies*, dated 1767.

1767   Becomes increasingly friendly at this period with Reynolds and his circle, including Mrs Horneck, a widow, and her two daughters.

(*April*) Publishes an anthology, *The Beauties of English Poesy.*

(*Spring*) Completes his comedy, *The Good Natured Man.*

(*Dec.*) Death of John Newbery.

1768   (*29 Jan.*) First performance of *The Good Natured Man*, produced by Colman at Covent Garden.

(*May*) Death of his brother, Henry.

(*Spring*) Makes his last removal, to No. 2 Brick Court in the Temple; and with a friend, Edward Bott, acquires a cottage at Edgware.

1769   (*Feb.*) Contracts to write 'a new Natural History of Animals, &c' for Griffin.

(*18 May*) *The Roman History* published.

(*13 June*) Contracts to write a history of England for Davies.

(*Dec.*) Appointed Professor of Ancient History at the Royal Academy.

1770   (*26 May*) *The Deserted Village* published by Griffin.

(*June*) His *Life of Parnell* prefixed to an edition of Parnell's *Poems.*

(*July–late Aug. or early Sept.*) Journey to Paris with the Hornecks.

(*Autumn*) Writes *The Haunch of Venison*, addressed to Lord Clare with whom he is friendly at this period.

1771   (*Summer*) Stays in a cottage with a farmer near Hyde, working on his *History of England* and a new comedy.
(*6 Aug.*) His *History of England . . . to the Death of George II* published.

1772   (*20 Feb.*) Performance of his *Threnodia Augustalis*.
(*March*) Stays at the cottage at Hyde.
(*Aug.*) Seriously ill with a bladder infection.

1773   (*Jan.–March*) Contributes to the *Westminster Mag.*, including essays on the theatre.
(*15 March*) *She Stoops to Conquer* produced by Colman at Covent Garden.
(*Late March*) Assaults Thomas Evans, a newspaper proprietor, over an item linking his name with one of the Misses Horneck.
(*22 June*) Completes the first volume of his *Grecian History*.

1774   (*Jan. or Feb.*) Meeting of the club at the St James's Coffee-House, at which Garrick's satiric epitaph on G. provokes *Retaliation*, unfinished at his death.
(*25 March*) Seriously ill with kidney trouble and fever.
(*4 April*) Dies at the Temple, where he was buried five days later.
(*19 April*) *Retaliation* posthumously published.
(*15 July*) The *Grecian History* posthumously published.
(*1 July*) *History of the Earth, and Animated Nature* posthumously published.
(*2 July*) Abridgement of the *History of England* posthumously published.

1776   Monument by Nollekens with Johnson's Latin epitaph erected in Westminster Abbey.
The Haunch of Venison posthumously published.

Abbreviations

EDITIONS OF GOLDSMITH'S POEMS AND OTHER WORKS

Citizen	*The Citizen of the World,* 2 vols, 1762.
Vicar	*The Vicar of Wakefield,* 2 vols, Salisbury, 1766.
1775	*The Miscellaneous Works . . . Containing All his Essays and Poems,* 1775 (published by W. Griffin).
1777	*Poems and Plays,* ed. Edmond Malone, Dublin, 1777
1780	*The Poetical and Dramatic Works,* 2 vols, 1780 (published by T. Evans).
Works, 1801	*The Miscellaneous Works,* 4 vols, 1801 (vol. i contains Thomas Percy's 'Life').
Prior, *Works*	*The Miscellaneous Works,* ed. Sir James Prior, 4 vols, 1837.
Corney	*The Poetical Works,* ed. Bolton Corney, 1845.
Cunningham	*The Works,* ed. Peter Cunningham, 4 vols, 1854.
Gibbs	*The Works,* ed. J. W. M. Gibbs, 5 vols, 1884–86.
Dobson	*The Complete Poetical Works,* ed. Austin Dobson, Oxford, 1906.
New Essays	*New Essays by Oliver Goldsmith,* ed. Ronald S. Crane, Chicago, 1927.
Letters	*The Collected Letters,* ed. Katharine C. Balderston, Cambridge, 1928.
Friedman	*The Collected Works,* ed. Arthur Friedman, 5 vols, Oxford, 1966.

OTHER WORKS

Forster	John Forster, *The Life and Adventures of Oliver Goldsmith,* 1848; 6th edn, 2 vols, 1877.
Boswell, *Life of Johnson*	James Boswell, *The Life of Johnson,* ed. G. B. Hill and L. F. Powell, 6 vols, Oxford, 1934–50.

Nichols, *Illustrations*	John Nichols, *Illustrations of the Literary History of the Eighteenth Century*, 8 vols, 1817–58.
Prior, *Life*	Sir James Prior, *The Life of Oliver Goldsmith, M.B.*, 2 vols, 1837.
Temple Scott	Temple Scott, *Oliver Goldsmith Bibliographically and Biographically Considered*, New York, 1928.
Wardle	Ralph M. Wardle, *Oliver Goldsmith*, Lawrence, Kansas, 1957.

1 [Prologue of Laberius]

This imitation of Macrobius was first printed in G.'s *Enquiry into the Present State of Learning* pp. 176–7, published in April 1759, in the chapter 'Of the Stage'. This work may have been complete by Aug. 1758, in which month G. described it as 'now printing in London' (*Letters* pp. 34–5), but this could have been merely a device to encourage subscribers to the book. G. introduced these lines as follows:

'MACROBIUS has preserved a prologue, spoken and written by the poet Laberius, a Roman knight, whom Caesar forced upon the stage, written with great elegance and spirit, which shews what opinion the Romans in general entertained of the profession of an actor.'

Decimus Laberius (106–43 B.C.) was the first important writer of mimes in Latin and did much to raise the literary status of the form. A Roman knight, he did not act himself but, at the age of sixty, he was forced by Caesar to appear on the stage in competition with the young writer and actor of mimes, the freedman Publilius Syrus. An account of this occasion and the prologue he spoke are given by Macrobius, *Saturnalia* II vii. G. imitated ll. 1–15 of the prologue. As Corney suggested, G. may have found the prologue in the writings of Charles Rollin: e.g. the English translation of his popular *Method of Teaching and Studying the Belles Lettres* (1734) i 269. Dryden had referred to it in *Of Dramatic Poesy*, ed. G. Watson (1962) i 78.

G. had quoted the prologue in 1759 to buttress his attack on the arrogance of actors and managers. In the 2nd edn of the *Enquiry* in 1774, he drastically cut his severer observations on the stage, which had supposedly offended Garrick, and omitted the prologue. It was first collected in *1777* p. 3.

Prior (*Life* i 92) believed that the imitation should be dated about 1748, when G. was at Trinity College, Dublin, and was known to have produced 'original compositions of a light description, or translations from the classics'. But G. is just as likely to have translated the prologue for his specific purpose of attacking the contemporary theatre.

Necessitas cujus cursus transversi impetum, &c.

> What! no way left to shun the inglorious stage,
> And save from infamy my sinking age!
> Scarce half alive, oppressed with many a year,
> What in the name of dotage drives me here?
> 5 A time there was, when glory was my guide,
> Nor force nor fraud could turn my steps aside;
> Unawed by power and unappalled by fear,
> With honest thrift I held my honour dear:
> But this vile hour disperses all my store,
> 10 And all my hoard of honour is no more.

For ah! too partial to my life's decline,
Caesar persuades, submission must be mine;
Him I obey, whom heaven itself obeys,
Hopeless of pleasing, yet inclined to please.
15 Here then at once, I welcome every shame,
And cancel at threescore a life of fame;
No more my titles shall my children tell,
The old buffoon will fit my name as well;
This day beyond its term my fate extends,
20 For life is ended when our honour ends.

2 On a Beautiful Youth Struck Blind with Lightning

First printed in *The Bee* No. i, on 6 Oct. 1759. G. described it as 'Imitated
from the SPANISH' but this source has not been identified. Printed with it
was a Latin epigram, also turning on blindness, described as 'Another. In
the same spirit'. Often reprinted and imitated in the eighteenth century
(e.g. *A Collection of Epigrams* (1727) pp. ccxxi-ccxxii; *Memoirs of the Society
of Grub Street* (1737) ii 38; *Gentleman's Mag* xv (1745) 101, 159, 213, 327;
J. Warton, *Essay on Pope* (1756) pp. 289–90), this Latin epigram was written
by the sixteenth-century Italian poet Girolamo Amalteo: see *Trium Fratrum
Amaltheorum Carmina* (Amsterdam, 1689) p. 35, and many other edns.

G.'s English epigram was reprinted in the *British Mag.* i 381, in June
1760, entitled 'On a beautiful Child, who lost his sight in the small-pox'
and with minor variants: ''Twas sure' for 'Sure 'twas' (l. 1) and 'mercy'
for 'pity' (l. 2). Since G. definitely contributed essays to this magazine
during 1760, it is possible that he himself was responsible for these changes.
The epigram was first collected in *1780* i 119.

Sure 'twas by Providence designed,
Rather in pity than in hate,
That he should be like Cupid blind,
To save him from Narcissus' fate.

3 The Gift
To Iris, in Bow-Street, Covent-Garden

First printed in *The Bee* No. ii, 13 Oct. 1759. It is an imitation of *Etrène à
Iris* by Bernard de la Monnoye, found in *Ménagiana*, 3rd edn, 1715, iii
397–8 and his *Poesies* (1716) p. 53:

Pour témoignage de ma flame
Iris, du meilleur de mon ame,
Je vous donne à ce nouvel an
Non pas dentelle ni ruban,
Non pas essence, ni pommade,
Quelques boites de marmelade,
Un manchon, des gans, un bouquet,
Non pas heures, ni chapelet,
Quoi donc? Attendez, je vous donne,
O fille plus belle que bonne,
Qui m,avez toûjours refusé
Le point si souvent proposé.
Je vous donne: Ah! le puis-je dire?
Oui, c'est trop souffrir le martire,
Il est tems de s'émanciper,
Patience va m'échaper,
Fussiez-vous cent fois plus aimable,
Belle Iris, je vous donne . . . au Diable.

By giving Iris an address in Bow St, Covent Garden, not far from the theatre which had been opened in 1732, G. may have intended to suggest that Iris was an actress. A number of actors and actresses lived there at this period. But see also Francis Grose, *Classical Dictionary of the Vulgar Tongue*, ed. Eric Partridge (1963) p. 99, on Covent Garden: 'In its environs are many brothels, and, not long ago, the lodgings of the second order of ladies of easy virtue was either there, or in the purlieus of Drury Lane.'

The poem was reprinted and attributed to G. in *A Collection of the Most Esteemed Pieces of Poetry* (1767) p. 56 (2nd edn, 1770). It was first collected in *1777* pp. 67–8.

Say, cruel Iris, pretty rake,
    Dear mercenary beauty,
What annual offering shall I make,
    Expressive of my duty?

5 My heart, a victim to thine eyes,
    Should I at once deliver,
Say, would the angry fair one prize
    The gift, who slights the giver?

A bill, a jewel, watch, or toy,
10   My rivals give–and let 'em.
If gems, or gold, impart a joy,
    I'll give them–when I get 'em.

I'll give–but not the full-blown rose,
    Or rose-bud more in fashion;

15   Such short-lived offerings but disclose
    A transitory passion.

    I'll give thee something yet unpaid,
      Not less sincere than civil:
    I'll give thee–Ah! too charming maid,
20   I'll give thee–To the devil.

4 A Sonnet

First printed in *The Bee* No. iii, 20 Oct. 1759. Bolton Corney in 1845 identified it as an imitation of a poem by Denis Sanguin de Saint-Pavin (d. 1670), which G. may have seen in the 1759 edn of Saint-Pavin published at Amsterdam:

    Iris tremble qu'au premier jour
    L'himen, plus puissant que l'amour,
    N'enleve ses tresors sans qu'elle ose s'en plaindre.
      Elle a negligé mes avis;
      Si la belle les eust suivis,
    Elle n'auroit plus rien à craindre.

G.'s imitation was first collected in *1780* i 120, with an alteration to l.5 for which the authority remains uncertain. The text of *The Bee* is followed here.

    Weeping, murmuring, complaining,
      Lost to every gay delight,
    Myra, too sincere for feigning,
      Fears the approaching bridal night.

5   Yet why this killing, soft dejection?
      Why dim thy beauty with a tear?
    Had Myra followed my direction,
      She long had wanted cause to fear.

¶ 4.5–6. *Yet why this killing, soft dejection? | Why*]Yet why impair thy bright perfection? / Or *1780*.

5 An Elegy on that Glory of her Sex, Mrs Mary Blaize

G.'s model in this poem (and also in *On the Death of the Right Hon.* ✱✱✱ and *Elegy on the Death of a Mad Dog*) was a poem of 50 stanzas, in each of which

Plate 4 Oliver Goldsmith painted by
Sir Joshua Reynolds, probably in 1770

the last line deflates by its banality the lines that have preceded it, in La Monnoye's *Ménagiana* (3rd edn, 1715) iii 384–91 and *Poesies* (1716) pp. 91–102 (see *The Gift*, p. 578 above, for G.'s earlier imitation of La Monnoye). The hero of the French poem is *le fameux la Galisse, homme imaginaire*; but La Monnoye's inspiration is said to have been a quatrain composed soon after the battle of Pavia in 1525, in which the famous Jacques de Chabannes, Seigneur de La Palice, had been killed: *Monsieur de La Palice est mort, / Mort devant Pavie; / Un quart d'heure avant sa mort, / Il était encore en vie.*

As Dobson pointed out, G. obviously enjoyed this method of satirizing the banalities of contemporary elegiac verse, which he deplored in a review of Langhorne's *Adonis* in the *Critical Review* vii (1759) 263 and in the *Citizen* (1762) ii 162–5 (later renumbered Letter 106). But G.'s poems can hardly be read as parodies of Gray's *Elegy*, as Dobson suggested, as they bear no resemblance to that poem or its imitations.

G.'s poem was first printed in *The Bee* No. iv, 27 Oct. 1759. It was reprinted, attributed to G., in *A Companion for a Leisure Hour: being Fugitive Pieces, in Prose and Verse. By Several Gentlemen* in 1769; first collected in 1777 pp. 80–1.

Good people all, with one accord,
    Lament for Madam BLAIZE,
Who never wanted a good word –
    From those who spoke her praise.

5 The needy seldom passed her door,
    And always found her kind;
She freely lent to all the poor, –
    Who left a pledge behind.

She strove the neighbourhood to please,
10   With manners wondrous winning,
And never followed wicked ways, –
    Unless when she was sinning.

At church, in silks and satins new,
    With hoop of monstrous size,
15 She never slumbered in her pew, –
    But when she shut her eyes.

Her love was sought, I do aver,
    By twenty beaux and more;

¶ 5.16. La Monnoye, *Le Fameux La Galisse* 141–4: *On ne le vit jamais las, / Ni sujet à la paresse. / Tandis qu'il ne dormoit pas, / On tient qu'il veilloit sans cesse.*

> The king himself has followed her, –
> 20   *When she has walked before.*
>
> But now her wealth and finery fled,
>   Her hangers-on cut short all;
> The doctors found, when she was dead, –
>   *Her last disorder mortal.*
>
> 25   Let us lament, in sorrow sore,
>   For Kent-Street well may say,
> That had she lived a twelve-month more, –
>   *She had not died to-day.*

20. *Le Fameux La Galisse* 69–72: *On dit que dans ses amours | Il fut caressé des belles, | Qui le suivirent toûjours | Tant qu'il marcha devant elles.*
24. *Le Fameux La Gallisse* 189–92: *Il fut par un triste sort | Blessé d'une main cruelle. | On croit, puis qu'il en est mort, | Que la plaie étoit mortelle.*
26. G. had practised medicine at Bankside, Southwark, in 1756, and was thus familiar with Kent St which traversed Southwark. It was notoriously inhabited by beggars. G. had referred to it in *The Bee* No. iii (20 Oct. 1759), a week before he published this poem: 'You then, O ye beggars of my acquaintance, whether in rags or lace; whether in Kent-street or the Mall ...'

6 The Double Transformation: A Tale

First printed in *The Weekly Magazine: or, Gentleman and Lady's Polite Companion* No. ii, pp. 47–50, on 5 Jan. 1760. Only one copy of this periodical is known, see Arthur Friedman, 'Goldsmith and the *Weekly Magazine*', *Modern Philology* xxxii (1934–5) 281–99. In this version the poem, entitled 'The Double Metamorphosis: a Tale', contained 130 ll., with the prefatory note: 'We know not whom to thank for the following exquisite piece of humour; all we can say is, that every future favour of our anonymous correspondent will meet with as much gratitude from us, as it will esteem from the public.' G. omitted 14 ll. when he reprinted it with the altered title in *Essays* (1765) pp. 229–33, as No. xxvi; it was again revised and a further 12 ll. omitted in the 2nd edn of *Essays* (1766) pp. 241–5, where it was renumbered xxviii. Collected in 1775 pp. 189–92.

Prior (*Life* i 93) suggested that the poem was composed about 1748, when G. was at Trinity College, Dublin, because of 3 ll. which G. omitted in the final form of the poem (see l. 18 *n*):

> And told the tales oft told before,
> Of bailiffs pump'd, and proctors bit,
> At college how he shew'd his wit. ...

G. may have remembered his part in a notorious riot at Trinity College in May 1747, for which he was 'publicly admonished' (see Wardle p. 35), but such a reference hardly amounts to evidence for dating the poem.

G. appears to have been imitating such poems, dealing lightly in octosyllabics with marriage, as Swift's *Phillis, or the Progress of Love, The Progress of Marriage* and *Strephon and Chloe* (only the moral of this last is really comparable), and Prior's *Hans Carvel*, which G. later included in his *Beauties of English Poesy* (1767).

The text is that of the last revised version in the *Essays*, 2nd edn.

> Secluded from domestic strife,
> Jack Book-worm led a college life;
> A fellowship at twenty-five
> Made him the happiest man alive;
> 5   He drank his glass and cracked his joke,
> And freshmen wondered as he spoke.
>   Such pleasures, unallayed with care,
> Could any accident impair?
> Could Cupid's shaft at length transfix
> 10   Our swain, arrived at thirty-six?
> O had the archer ne'er come down
> To ravage in a country town!
> Or Flavia been content to stop
> At triumphs in a Fleet-Street shop.
> 15   O had her eyes forgot to blaze!
> Or Jack had wanted eyes to gaze.
> O——but let exclamation cease,
> Her presence banished all his peace.

¶ 6.2. *Book-worm*] Book wit *1760.*   *led*] liv'd *1760, 1765.*
6. *Followed in 1760 by:*

> He rak'd and toasted, dived or shone:
> And even was thought a knowing one.
> Without politeness aim'd at breeding,
> And laugh'd at pedantry and reading;
> Thus sad or sober, gay or mellow,
> Jack was a *college pretty fellow.*

1765 retained ll. 3–4 of this passage.
10. *Our swain*] Poor Jack *1760.*
13. *Flavia*] Hetty *1760.*
18. *Followed in 1760 by:*

> Our altered Parson now began,
> To be a perfect ladies man;
> Made sonnets, lisp'd his sermons o'er,
> And told the tales he told before,

So with decorum all things carried;
20 Miss frowned, and blushed, and then was–married.
Need we expose to vulgar sight
The raptures of the bridal night?
Need we intrude on hallowed ground,
Or draw the curtains closed around?
25 Let it suffice that each had charms;
He clasped a goddess in his arms;
And, though she felt his usage rough,
Yet in a man 'twas well enough.
The honey-moon like lightning flew,
30 The second brought its transports too.
A third, a fourth, were not amiss,
The fifth was friendship mixed with bliss:
But, when a twelvemonth passed away,
Jack found his goddess made of clay;

Of bailiffs pump'd, and proctors bit,
At college how he shew'd his wit;
And as the fair one still approv'd,
He fell in love–or thought he lov'd.
They laugh'd, they talk'd with giddy glee,
Miss had her jokes as well as he:
In short, their love was passing wonder,
They tallied as if torn asunder;

1765 retained ll. 1–8 of this passage.

tallied] Johnson defines 'To tally' as 'To fit; to suit; to cut out, so as to answer anything'; and cites Prior: 'Nor sister either had, nor brother; / They seemed just tallied for each other.'

20. frowned, and blushed] psha'd and frown'd *1760.*

24. Or] And *1760.*

25. Let it suffice] Suffice to say *1760.*

26. He] Jack *1760.*

27. usage] visage *1760, 1765.* Although the later reading makes good sense, the change may have been accidental: 'visage' would ironically anticipate the conclusion of the poem.

28. Followed in 1760 by:

And here direction might prevail,
To interrupt the tedious tale;
Poetic justice bids it rest,
And leave 'em both completely blest:
Yet more importunate than they,
Truth bids me on, and I obey.

In the first line direction *was probably a misprint for* discretion.
29. honey-moon] honey month *1760.*

35 Found half the charms that decked her face
Arose from powder, shreds or lace;
But still the worst remained behind,
That very face had robbed her mind.
        Skilled in no other arts was she,
40 But dressing, patching, repartee;
And, just as humour rose or fell,
By turns a slattern or a belle:
'Tis true she dressed with modern grace,
Half naked at a ball or race;
45 But when at home, at board or bed,
Five greasy nightcaps wrapped her head.
Could so much beauty condescend
To be a dull domestic friend?
Could any curtain-lectures bring
50 To decency so fine a thing?
In short, by night 'twas fits or fretting;
By day 'twas gadding or coquetting.
Fond to be seen, she kept a bevy
Of powdered coxcombs at her levy;
55 The squire and captain took their stations,
And twenty other near relations;
Jack sucked his pipe and often broke
A sigh in suffocating smoke;

39–40. Prior, *Hans Carvel* 7–8: 'For in all Visits who but She, / To Argue, or to Repartée'; and Swift, *The Furniture of a Woman's Mind* 11–12: 'Has ev'ry Repartee in Store, / She spoke ten Thousand Times before'.
44. Cp. *Citizen* (1762) i 10 (Letter 3): 'I have seen a lady who seem'd to shudder at a breeze in her own apartment, appear half naked in the streets.'
46. Nightcaps were commonly worn as a precaution against a cold in the head. Cp. *Citizen* (1762) ii 107 (renumbered Letter 90): 'An admiral, who could have opposed a broadside without shrinking, shall sit whole days in his chamber, mobbed up in double night-caps, shuddering at the intrusive breeze'; and *Essays* (2nd edn, 1766) p. 238, No. xxvii, which describes the Common Councilman's wife 'mobbed up in flannel night caps, and trembling at a breath of air"
49. curtain-lectures] 'A reproof given by a wife to her husband in bed' (Johnson) and so used by Swift, *His Grace's Answer to Jonathan* 37–8: 'Your Spouse shall there no longer hector / You need not fear a Curtain-Lecture.' But G. reverses the role of husband and wife.
53. Fond to be seen, she] Now tawdry Madam *1760, 1765 (both having new paragraph).*
58. Followed in 1760, 1765 by:

            She in her turn became perplexing,
            And found substantial bliss in vexing.

While all their hours were passed between
60   Insulting repartee or spleen.
     Thus as her faults each day were known,
He thinks her features coarser grown;
He fancies every vice she shows
Or thins her lip or points her nose:
65   Whenever rage or envy rise,
How wide her mouth, how wild her eyes!
He knows not how, but so it is,
Her face is grown a knowing phiz;
And, though her fops are wondrous civil,
70   He thinks her ugly as the devil.
     Now, to perplex the ravelled noose,
As each a different way pursues,
While sullen or loquacious strife
Promised to hold them on for life,
75   That dire disease, whose ruthless power
Withers the beauty's transient flower,
Lo! the small-pox with horrid glare
Levelled its terrors at the fair;
And, rifling every youthful grace,
80   Left but the remnant of a face.
     The glass, grown hateful to her sight,
Reflected now a perfect fright:
Each former art she vainly tries
To bring back lustre to her eyes.
85   In vain she tries her paste and creams,
To smooth her skin or hide its seams;
Her country beaux and city cousins,

59. *While all their hours were*] Thus every hour was *1760, 1765*.
61. Each day the more her faults are known *1760, 1765* (*with* were *for* are).
68. *knowing phiz*] 'knowing' combines senses of 'cunning' and 'affectedly fashionable'; 'phiz' was a common colloquial contraction of 'physiognomy'
71. *Now*] Thus *1760, 1765*.   G.'s spelling of 'noose' ('nooze') in all three texts indicates that the rhyme 'pursues' was exact.
72. *As*] While *1760, 1765*.
73. *sullen*] sulky *1760*
77. *with*] whose *1765, 1766*. The grammar requires the original reading of *1760*.
85. *paste*] pastes *1760, 1765*.
86. *seams*] Cp. Swift, *Cassinus and Peter* 48–9: 'Say, has the small or greater Pox / Sunk down her Nose, or seam'd her Face?'; and *Citizen* (1762) i 198 (renumbered Letter 46): 'an hateful phyz, quilted into a thousand seams by the hand of deformity'. This letter similarly describes a 'first-rate beauty' ravaged by small-pox and the deformity paralleled with moral defects.

Lovers no more, flew off by dozens:
The squire himself was seen to yield,
90 And even the captain quit the field.
Poor Madam, now condemned to hack
The rest of life with anxious Jack,
Perceiving others fairly flown,
Attempted pleasing him alone.
95 Jack soon was dazzled to behold
Her present face surpass the old;
With modesty her cheeks are dyed,
Humility displaces pride;
For tawdry finery is seen
100 A person ever neatly clean:
No more presuming on her sway,
She learns good-nature every day;
Serenely gay and strict in duty,
Jack finds his wife a perfect beauty.

91. *hack*] Lead a commonplace, everyday life (from 'hackney', a worn out horse for ordinary riding).

7 [The Description of an Author's Bedchamber]

Written between Jan. 1759 and May 1760. A version of these lines appears in a letter from G. to his brother Henry, *c.* 13 Jan. 1759, introduced as follows (*Letters* pp. 63–4):

'you should have given me your opinion of the design of the heroicomical poem which I sent you. You remember I intended to introduce the hero of the Poem as lying in a paltry alehouse you may take the following specimen of the manner; which I flatter myself is quite original. The room in which he lies may be described somewhat like this way.'

G. then quoted a passage corresponding to ll. 7–18 of the version below but went on to introduce 4 ll. later dropped:

'And Now immagine after his soliloquy the landlord to make his appearance in order to Dun him for the reckoning,

Not with that face so servile and so gay
That welcomes every stranger that can pay,
With sulky eye he smoak'd the patient man
Then pull'd his breeches tight, and thus began, &c.

All this is taken you see from Nature.'

G. seems to have written no more of his 'heroicomical poem' but he expanded and revised these lines in one of his 'Chinese Letters', which appeared in the *Public Ledger* for 2 May 1760, reprinted in the *Citizen* (1762) i 121 (Letter 30 in later edns). The letter describes a club of authors to which an impoverished poet reads part of 'an heroic poem, which he had composed the day before', introducing it as follows (there are minor differences in the text of the *Ledger*):

'"Gentlemen," says he, "the present piece is not one of your common epic poems, which come from the press like paper kites in summer; there are none of your Turnuses or Didos in it; it is an heroical description of nature. I only beg you'll endeavour to make your souls unison with mine, and hear with the same enthusiasm with which I have written. The poem begins with the description of an author's bed-chamber: the picture was sketched in my own apartment; for you must know, gentlemen, that I am myself the heroe." Then putting himself into the attitude of an orator, with all the emphasis of voice and action, he proceeded . . .'

The poet was so moved by the last line of the passage 'that he was unable to proceed. "There, gentlemen," cries he, "there is a description for you; Rablais's bed-chamber is but a fool to it . . . . There is sound and sense, and truth, and nature in the trifling compass of ten little syllables."'

Some details from the description were to be used yet again by G. in *The Deserted Village* 227–36 (see pp. 685–6).

It has been suggested that G. was indebted to some extent to Hogarth's engraving of *The Distrest Poet* in these lines: what seems more certain is that there is a strong autobiographical content in them. A friend who visited G. in March 1759, two months after G. sent his first version of the lines to Henry, found him in 'a wretched dirty room, in which there was but one chair' in 'poor and uncomfortable' lodgings (*Works*, 1801, i 60–1). Further parallels between the poem and G.'s situation at this period are indicated in the notes. Characteristically in his *Present State of Learning* pp. 139–40, published in April 1759, G. rebuked those who sneer at a poet's poverty ('We keep him poor, and yet revile his poverty').

The poem was first collected in *1777* p. 11. Variants from the passage included in G.'s letter of Jan. 1759 are given as *1759*.

> Where the Red Lion flaring o'er the way
> Invites each passing stranger that can pay;
> Where Calvert's butt and Parsons' black champagne

¶ *7.3.* Calvert and Parsons were prominent brewers at this period (cp. a return of the beer brewed by the chief London brewers 1759–60 in *Works*, ed. Gibbs, iv 413*n*), well known for their 'entire butt' beer or porter. Cp. 'the beer was extremely good, entire butt, I presume', in 'Essay on Various Clubs', *The Busy-Body* (13 Oct. 1759). G. refers again in his 'Adventures of a Strolling Player', *Essays* (1765) No. xxi, to 'Calvert's butt', which the strolling player considered 'out-tastes champagne'. Smollett mentions 'Calvert's entire butt beer' in *Humphry Clinker*, letter dated 10 June.

Regale the drabs and bloods of Drury-Lane;
5   There in a lonely room, from bailiffs snug,
The Muse found Scroggen stretched beneath a rug;
A window patched with paper lent a ray,
That dimly showed the state in which he lay;
The sanded floor that grits beneath the tread;
10   The humid wall with paltry pictures spread:
The royal game of goose was there in view,
And the twelve rules the royal martyr drew;

4. Drury Lane was a noted haunt of prostitutes at this period: cp. Steele, *Tatler* No. 46; Gay, *Trivia* iii 259 ff.; and Pope, *Second Satire of Donne* 64: 'Paltry and proud, as drabs in Drury-lane', which G. seems to echo (cp. 'paltry' in l. 10). See also the quotation from Francis Grose in headnote to *The Gift* (p. 579).
8. dimly] feebly *1759*.
9. grits] The earliest such usage as a verb recorded in *OED*.
10. Beau Tibbs likewise had 'several paltry, unframed pictures' on his walls, *Citizen* (1762) i 241 (later numbered Letter 54).
11. The game of goose was there exposd to view *1759*.
The royal game of goose] A medieval French game in origin, still popular in the eighteenth century and later. Joseph Strutt, *Sports and Pastimes of the English People* (1801) pp. 249–50, describes it as 'a childish diversion, usually introduced at Christmas time'. It was played with counters on a board divided into 63 compartments, the aim being to reach the 63rd by the throwing of a dice. According to Strutt, a goose was depicted in every fourth and fifth compartment in succession and a player doubled his throw if he landed on it. Forfeits were paid for landing on other compartments, such as an inn, a bridge and a fountain.
12. These rules, supposedly found in Charles I's study after his death, appeared beneath a popular woodcut of his execution. The rules were: 1. Urge no healths. 2. Profane no divine ordinances. 3. Touch no state matters. 4. Reveal no secrets. 5. Pick no quarrels. 6. Make no comparisons. 7. Maintain no ill opinions. 8. Keep no bad company. 9. Encourage no vice. 10. Make no long meals. 11. Repeat no grievances. 12. Lay no wagers.
12–14. Cp. *A Memoir of Thomas Bewick written by himself*, ed. M. Weekley (1961) pp. 194–5. Bewick (1753–1828) describes the prints 'so common to be seen when I was a boy in every cottage and farm house throughout the country . . . These prints, which were sold at a very low price, were commonly illustrative of some memorable exploits, or were, perhaps, the portraits of eminent men, who had distinguished themselves in the service of their country, or in their patriotic exertions to serve mankind. Besides these, there were a great variety of other designs, often with songs added to them of a moral, patriotic, or a rural tendency . . . . A constant one in every house was "King Charles' Twelve Good Rules". Amongst others were representations of remarkable victories at sea, and battles on land, often

> The Seasons framed with listing found a place,
> And brave Prince William showed his lamp-black face:
> *15* The morn was cold, he views with keen desire
> The rusty grate unconscious of a fire;
> With beer and milk arrears the frieze was scored,
> And five cracked teacups dressed the chimney board.
> A nightcap decked his brows instead of bay,
> *20* A cap by night—a stocking all the day!

accompanied with portraits of those who commanded, and others who had borne a conspicuous part in these contests with the enemy . . . In cottages everywhere were to be seen the "Sailor's Farewell" and his "Happy Return", "Youthful Sports", and the "Feats of Manhood", "The Bold Archers Shooting at a Mark", "The Four Seasons", etc.' At least four sets of 'Seasons' in mezzotint were published about the year 1759: cp. *Letters* p. 64.

13. listing] A border or edging made of a strip of cloth. G. wrote to Mrs Jane Lawder, 15 Aug. 1758 (*Letters* p. 45), that he was going to decorate his room with 'maxims of frugality . . . and my lanlady's daughter shall frame them with the parings of my black waistcoat.'

14. brave Prince William] Prussia's Monarch *1759*.

Bewick (see *n* to ll. 12–14 above) mentioned that 'views or representations of the battle of Zorndorff', at which Frederick the Great defeated a Russian army in 1758, were popular. In *Essays* (1765) No. viii, G. mentions an ale-house-keeper who changed his sign depicting the Queen of Hungary 'for the King of Prussia, who may probably be changed, in turn, for the next great man that shall be set up for vulgar admiration'. But G.'s intention in replacing Frederick in the text by William Augustus, Duke of Cumberland (1721–65) must have been different. The Duke became a national hero after his victory at Culloden in 1746: his features became a popular tavern sign and pictures of him were sold in every street: cp. E. Charteris, *William Augustus, Duke of Cumberland* (1913) p. 281. But he had retired in disgrace from public life in 1757 and G. must have been stressing the old-fashioned decoration of the room. He evidently refers to one of the silhouettes popular at this date.

16. The] A *1759*.

17. With beer and milk arrears] An unpaid reck'ning on *1759*.

17. Cp. G.'s letter to Robert Bryanton, 14 Aug. 1758 (*Letters* pp. 40–1), where he describes himself as 'in a garret writing for bread, and expecting to be dunned for a milk score!' As Dobson pointed out, this had already happened to Hogarth's *Distrest Poet*.   *frieze*] The mantelpiece.

20. Swift, *Cassinus and Peter* 11–12: 'He seem'd as just crept out of Bed; / One greasy Stocking round his Head'.

8 On Seeing Mrs **** Perform in the Character of ****

First printed in a 'Chinese Letter' in the *Public Ledger* of 21 Oct. 1760, reprinted without alteration in *Citizen* (1762) ii 87–8 (later renumbered Letter 85). The parody is introduced as follows: 'There are even a numerous set of poets who help to keep up the contention, and write for the stage. Mistake me not, I don't mean pieces to be acted upon it, but panegyrical verses on the performers, for that is the most universal method of writing for the stage at present. It is the business of the stage poet therefore to watch the appearance of every new player at his own house, and so come out next day with a flaunting copy of newspaper verses. In these nature and the actor may be set to run races, the player always coming off victorious; or nature may mistake him for herself; or old Shakespear may put on his winding-sheet and pay him a visit; or the tuneful nine may strike up their harps in his praise; or should it happen to be an actress, Venus, the beauteous queen of love, and the naked graces, are ever in waiting: the lady must be herself a goddess bred and born; she must—but you shall have a specimen of one of these poems, which may convey a more precise idea.'

> To you, bright fair, the nine address their lays,
> And tune my feeble voice to sing thy praise.
> The heartfelt power of every charm divine,
> Who can withstand their all-commanding shine?
> 5 See how she moves along with every grace,
> While soul-brought tears steal down each shining face.
> She speaks, 'tis rapture all and nameless bliss;
> Ye gods, what transport e'er compared to this.
> As when in Paphian groves the Queen of Love
> 10 With fond complaint addressed the listening Jove,
> 'Twas joy and endless blisses all around,
> And rocks forgot their hardness at the sound.
> Then first, at last even Jove was taken in,
> And felt her charms, without disguise, within.

9 On the Death of the Right Honourable ***

First printed in a 'Chinese Letter' in the *Public Ledger* of 4 March 1761, reprinted without alteration in *Citizen* (1762) ii 164–5 (later renumbered Letter 106). *Citizen* (1762) i 39–40 (Letter 12) has similar remarks on epitaphs. This is the second of G.'s imitations of La Monnoye's *Le fameux*

La Galisse (see headnote to *Elegy on Mrs Blaize*, pp. 580–1). The 'Chinese Letter' attacking vacuous panegyrics of the great introduces the poem as follows:

'I am sometimes induced to pity the poet, whose trade is thus to make Demigods and Heroes for a dinner. There is not in nature a more dismal figure than a man who sits down to premeditated flattery; every stanza he writes tacitly reproaches the meanness of his occupation, till at last his stupidity becomes more stupid, and his dullness more diminutive.

'I am amazed therefore that none have yet found out the secret of flattering the worthless, and yet of preserving a safe conscience. I have often wished for some method by which a man might do himself and his deceased patron justice, without being under the hateful reproach of self-conviction. After long lucubration, I have hit upon such an expedient; and send you the specimen of a poem upon the decease of a great man, in which the flattery is perfectly fine, and yet the poet perfectly innocent.'

> Ye Muses, pour the pitying tear
> For Pollio snatched away;
> O had he lived another year!
> *He had not died today.*
>
> 5 O, were he born to bless mankind,
> In virtuous times of yore,
> Heroes themselves had fallen behind!
> *Whene'er he went before.*
>
> How sad the groves and plains appear,
> 10 And sympathetic sheep;
> Even pitying hills would drop a tear!
> *If hills could learn to weep.*
>
> His bounty in exalted strain
> Each bard might well display;
> 15 Since none implored relief in vain!
> *That went relieved away.*
>
> And hark! I hear the tuneful throng
> His obsequies forbid.
> He still shall live, shall live as long!
> 20 *As ever dead man did.*

10 [Translation of a
South American Ode]

First printed in a 'Chinese Letter' in the *Public Ledger* of 13 May 1761, reprinted unaltered in *Citizen* (1762) ii 209 (later renumbered Letter 116).

The present title first appeared as an explanatory footnote in the *Citizen*: the source has not been identified. The poem occurs in a conversation on love and is quoted by a young woman to support her argument that love is a 'natural' rather than an 'artificial passion':

'No nation, however unpolished, is remarkable for innocence, that is not famous for passion; it has flourished in the coldest, as well as the warmest regions. Even in the sultry wilds of southern America the lover is not satisfied with possessing his mistress's person without having her mind.'

> In all my Enna's beauties blest,
> Amidst profusion still I pine;
> For though she gives me up her breast,
> Its panting tenant is not mine.

11 An Elegy on the Death of a Mad Dog

Probably written between the summer of 1760 and the autumn of 1762. London was seized with something of a panic about mad-dog bites during the summer of 1760, which G. derided in his 'Chinese Letters' in the *Public Ledger*, reprinted in *Citizen* (1762) i 118, ii 11, 15–21, ii 47–8, renumbered Letters 29, 68, 69, 75. Many cures for such bites were discussed in the *Public Ledger* and in the *Gentleman's Mag.*, which reprinted one of G.'s 'Chinese Letters' on the subject in Aug. 1760 (xxx 353–4). Cp. also *New Essays*, ed. Crane, p. 73, and *Vicar* ch. xx. It would be natural to relate G.'s *Elegy* to this panic in 1760; but his reference to Islington in l. 5 may be connected with his own residence there towards the end of 1762. In any case, it can presumably be assumed that the *Elegy* was included in the MS of *Vicar* which G. completed in the autumn of 1762 when he sold it to Newbery.

The *Elegy* imitates for 3 stanzas La Monnoye's *Le fameux la Galisse* (see headnote to *Elegy on Mrs Blaize*, pp. 580–1 above). Its context in *Vicar* indicates that G. was once again satirizing contemporary elegies. The Vicar's youngest son Bill offers to sing for his father:

'Which song do you chuse, *the Dying Swan*, or the *Elegy on the death of a mad dog?*' 'The elegy, child, by all means,' said I; 'I never heard that yet: and Deborah, my life, grief you know is dry, let us have a bottle of the best gooseberry wine, to keep up our spirits. I have wept so much at all sorts of elegies of late, that without an enlivening glass I am sure this will overcome me; and Sophy, love, take your guitar, and thrum in with the boy a little.'

The *Elegy* was first printed in *Vicar* i 175–6, Ch. xvii, published 27 March 1766. One change was made in the 2nd edn, the text followed here.

Good people all, of every sort,
  Give ear unto my song;
And if you find it wondrous short,
  It cannot hold you long.

5 In Islington there was a man,
  Of whom the world might say
That still a godly race he ran,
  Whene'er he went to pray.

A kind and gentle heart he had,
10 To comfort friends and foes;
The naked every day he clad,
  When he put on his clothes.

And in that town a dog was found,
  As many dogs there be,
15 Both mongrel, puppy, whelp and hound,
  And curs of low degree.

This dog and man at first were friends;
  But when a pique began,
The dog, to gain some private ends,
20 Went mad and bit the man.

Around from all the neighbouring streets
  The wondering neighbours ran,
And swore the dog had lost his wits,
  To bite so good a man.

25 The wound it seemed both sore and sad
  To every Christian eye;
And while they swore the dog was mad,
  They swore the man would die.

But soon a wonder came to light,
30 That showed the rogues they lied:
The man recovered of the bite,
  The dog it was that died.

¶ 11.5. G. himself lived in Canonbury House, Islington, with the publisher
John Newbery from the end of 1762 until 1764.
19. *some*] his *ed 1*.
31–2. G.'s source may have been Voltaire's *Épigramme imitée de l'Anthologie*
in *Oeuvres Complètes*, ed. Moland (1877) x 568: *L'autre jour, au fond d'un*

vallon, | Un serpent piqua Jean Fréron. | Que pensez-vous qu'il arriva? | Ce fut le serpent qui creva. But Voltaire's source was an epigram by Demodocus in the *Greek Anthology* xi 237: 'An evil viper once bit a Cappadocian; but it died itself, having tasted the venomous blood.' A Latin translation (*Vipera Cappadocem malè sana momordit; at ipsa | Gustato periit sanguine Cappadocis*) appeared in *Epigrammatum Delectus Ex omnibus Tum Veteribus, tum Recentioribus Poetis* (Paris, 1659) VI xxviii. G. could have known one of the many English edns of this work, e.g. 32nd edn, described as *In usum Scholae Etonensis* (London, 1762) p. 163.

12 Song from
The Vicar of Wakefield

Presumably written before the autumn of 1762 when the MS of *Vicar* was sold to Newbery. The *Song* was first printed when the novel was published on 27 March 1766, ii 78, ch. xxiv. It is sung to the rest of the Primrose family by the ruined Olivia, sitting on the 'honey-suckle bank' where she 'first met her seducer'. Dobson objected to the 'impropriety, and even inhumanity' of making the wretched girl sing such a song but G. and his audience, like the Primrose family, enjoyed the mood of soothing melancholy which it induced:

'Her mother too, upon this occasion, felt a pleasing distress, and wept, and loved her daughter as before. "Do, my pretty Olivia," cried she, "let us have that little melancholy air your pappa was so fond of, your sister Sophy has already obliged us. Do child, it will please your old father." She complied in a manner so exquisitely pathetic as moved me.' Dobson describes an accusation in the *St James's Gazette*, 28 Jan. 1889, that G. had merely translated a poem by 'Ségur' (1719); but this source has not been identified and the charge seems to have been a hoax. Friedman mentions a musical setting in *Vocal Music, or the Songster's Companion* (c. 1775).

The text is that of the 1st edn of *Vicar*.

When lovely woman stoops to folly,
    And finds too late that men betray,
What charm can soothe her melancholy,
    What art can wash her guilt away?

5 The only art her guilt to cover,
    To hide her shame from every eye,
To give repentance to her lover,
    And wring his bosom–is to die.

13 Edwin and Angelina

Written by Feb. 1764, perhaps as early as 1761, and it may well have been included in the MS of *Vicar* which G. sold in the autumn of 1762. The dating has been carefully investigated by A. Friedman, 'The Time of Composition of Goldsmith's *Edwin and Angelina*' in *Restoration and Eighteenth Century Studies*, ed. C. Camden (Chicago, 1963) pp. 155–9 and *Works* iv 191–7. Friedman argues from textual evidence that a version of G.'s ballad was already in the novel in 1762 but this cannot be definitely established. The other dates mentioned are suggested by statements by G. and Percy following the publication in the *St James's Chronicle* of 18–21 July 1767 of a letter signed 'Detector' (usually identified as William Kenrick), which accused G. of having virtually plagiarized *Edwin and Angelina* from Percy's 'The Friar of Orders Grey' in *Reliques of Ancient English Poetry* (1765) i 226–30, although it fell 'as short of Mr. Percy's ballad as the insipidity of negus is to the genuine flavour of Champagne'. G. replied in the same newspaper of 23–25 July 1767:

'Another Correspondent of yours accuses me of having taken a Ballad, I published some Time ago from one by the ingenious Mr. Percy. I do not think there is any great Resemblance between the two Pieces in Question. If there be any, his Ballad is taken from mine. I read it to Mr. Percy some Years ago, and he (as we both considered these Things as Trifles at best) told me, with his usual Good Humour, the next Time I saw him, that he had taken my Plan to form the Fragments of Shakespeare into a Ballad of his own. He then read me his little Cento, if I may so call it, and I highly approved it. Such petty Anecdotes as these are scarce worth printing, and were it not for the busy Disposition of your Correspondents, the Publick should never have known that he owes me the Hint of his Ballad, or that I am obliged to his Friendship and Learning for Communications of a much more important Nature.'

Percy himself was not satisfied with this account of his own debt to G. In his *Reliques* (3rd edn, 1775) i 250, he admitted that G.'s ballad had been written before 'The Friar of Orders Grey' but claimed that both poems were in fact indebted to another ballad, 'Gentle Heardsman', 'which the Doctor had much admired in manuscript, and has finely improved'. In a note to this ballad, *Reliques* ii 81, Percy tried to demonstrate G.'s debt and he repeated this account of the relationship of the three poems in his 'Life' of G., *Works*, 1801, i 74–6.

Both Percy and G. agree that *Edwin and Angelina* preceded 'The Friar of Orders Grey' which, as Friedman notes, had been written by 12 Feb. 1764. Similarly Percy sent a copy of 'Gentle Heardsman' to Thomas Warton in May 1761 and since he and G. met several times in May and June 1761 it may be assumed that it was at about this time that G. also saw the ballad. Percy's claim that G. was influenced by it appears to be justified (cp. ll.

129–44n). It may be worth noting that in ll. 31–2 G. quotes a line from Young's *Night Thoughts*, which he had also used in a 'Chinese Letter', first published in the *Public Ledger* on 22 Aug. 1760. This suggests that the 'Letter' and the ballad were written at not widely separated times. Two other scraps of information about the early history of the poem have survived. Francis Newbery, the son of G.'s publisher, remembered G. reading stanzas from the ballad to him, in the period between 1762 and 1764 when G. was living with the Newberys at Canonbury House, Islington. At best, this would only confirm the fact that the poem must have been written by early 1764. See C. Welsh, *A Bookseller of the Last Century* (1885) p. 46. Sir John Hawkins, *Life of Johnson* (2nd edn, 1787) p. 420n, stated of *Edwin and Angelina*, 'That this beautiful poem now exists, we owe to Dr. Chapman a physician now resident at Sudbury. Soon after he had wrote it, Goldsmith shewed it to the Doctor, and was by him hardly dissuaded from throwing it into the fire.' There is no way to check or date this incident, unless Hawkins was inaccurately referring to Dr John Chapman (1704–84), archdeacon of Sudbury from 1741.

The poem was first printed in an undated edn, entitled *Edwin and Angelina. A Ballad. By Mr. Goldsmith. Printed for the Amusement of the Countess of Northumberland*. Percy, in *Works*, 1801, i 74, stated that this edn was printed in 1765 and dedicated to the Countess because she 'had shown a partiality for poems of this kind, by patronizing the "Reliques of Ancient English Poetry," published in the same year.' The *Reliques* were published on 11 Feb. 1765, so that the private edn must be later than that date; and, as Friedman has suggested, it is likely that it appeared no later than the end of the year, when G. no doubt knew that the poem would be appearing in *Vicar*, published in March 1766. According to Sir John Hawkins, *Life of Johnson* (1787) pp. 418–9, G. met the Earl of Northumberland through Robert Nugent, later Lord Clare (see headnote to *The Haunch of Venison*, p. 696 below), not long after the publication of *The Traveller*, which both men admired. Hawkins goes on to tell a curious tale of G.'s refusal to accept the patronage of Northumberland. The private printing of *Edwin and Angelina* and the dedication to the Countess, who appointed Percy her chaplain and tutor to her son soon after the publication of his *Reliques*, may indicate that G. eventually regretted his failure to take advantage of Northumberland's patronage; but there is no evidence to suggest that the Countess responded in any way. Only one copy of the private edn of 1765 is now known to have survived. It belonged to Isaac Reed who inscribed it in 1775: 'Of this Ballad which is different from the Copy printed in Goldsmith's Works a few copies only were printed.' This copy later belonged to Richard Heber and the Murray family, was described in the biographies of G. by Prior and Forster and was finally sold at Sotheby's on 11 June 1963 for £1400. It is now in the Free Library of Philadelphia, who have published a facsimile of it.

The poem, now entitled merely 'A Ballad', appeared again in *Vicar*, published on 27 March 1766, in a text which showed many differences from the privately printed version and which may in fact not have been revised since G. sold the MS of the novel in 1762. It appears in ch. viii, in the course of an attack by Mr Burchell on contemporary English poetry, which 'is nothing at present but a combination of luxuriant images, without plot or connexion; a string of epithets that improve the sound, without carrying on the sense'. The ballad was accordingly introduced as being, 'whatever. . . its other defects, . . . at least free from those I have mentioned'. In the 2nd edn published in late May 1766 further changes were made, the result being a conflated text in which some of the readings of the 1st edn were evidently corrected from the privately printed text of 1765 and some entirely new readings were introduced. The text as printed in edns of *Vicar* was not to be changed again, but later in 1766 G. seems to have revised the poem yet again for his anthology *Poems for Young Ladies* pp. 91–8 (dated 1767 but published on 15 Dec. 1766); this text is close to that of the privately printed text of 1765 but introduces some readings from the texts in the novel as well as some of its own. Not long before his death G. told Cradock, *Literary and Miscellaneous Memoirs* (1828) iv 286, that *Edwin and Angelina* 'cannot be amended'. Viewed chronologically, G.'s revisions of the poem make this statement rather puzzling: it can only be assumed that the text in the 2nd edn of *Vicar* comes closest to representing his final wishes, in spite of the text in the *Poems for Young Ladies*. (It may be noted that the reprint of this work by E. Johnson in 1785 adopts the text of *Vicar*.) The poem was also reprinted in *A Collection of the Most Esteemed Pieces of Poetry* (1767) pp. 49–55 (2nd edn, 1770). During the nineteenth century the poem was often entitled *The Hermit*, which seems first to have been used in 1777. In *Vicar* it is entitled 'A Ballad' and elsewhere has its present title during G.'s lifetime. The text printed here is that of the 2nd edn of *Vicar*, which cannot be considered definitive, although it is perhaps the most carefully revised version. Variants from the private edn of 1765, the 1st edn of *Vicar* and *Poems for Young Ladies*, are given in the notes as *1765*, *1766a* and *1767* respectively. For an additional stanza first printed by Percy in 1801, see l. 117*n*.

G.'s ballad was singled out for the 'warmest praise' by the reviewer of *Vicar* in the *Critical Review* xxi (June 1766) 440: 'It is an exquisite little piece, written in that measure which is perhaps the most pleasing of any in our language, versified with inimitable beauty, and breathing the very soul of love and sentiment.' By 1790, Vicesimus Knox (*Winter Evenings: or, Lucubrations on Life and Letters*, 2nd edn, i 447) could call it 'one of the most popular pieces in the language; perhaps it stands next in the favour of the people to Gray's delightful Elegy'.

In 1797 G. was accused in *The Quiz, By a Society of Gentlemen* pp. 92–108, of having furtively translated *Edwin and Angelina* from a poem in an old French novel, *Les Deux Habitans de Lozanne* (1606). This accusation was discussed in the *Monthly Review* xxiv (Sept. 1797) 113–7, rejected by Percy in the same journal, pp. 239–40, in Oct. 1797 and finally disproved in the following July, when it was shown that G.'s supposed source was a French translation of the poem published in 1792. See Prior, *Life* ii 89–94.

'Turn, gentle hermit of the dale,
    And guide my lonely way,
To where yon taper cheers the vale
    With hospitable ray.

5   'For here forlorn and lost I tread,
        With fainting steps and slow;
    Where wilds immeasurably spread,
        Seem lengthening as I go.'

    'Forbear, my son,' the hermit cries,
10   'To tempt the dangerous gloom;
    For yonder faithless phantom flies
        To lure thee to thy doom.

    'Here to the houseless child of want
        My door is open still;
15 And though my portion is but scant,
        I give it with good will.

    'Then turn tonight, and freely share
        Whate'er my cell bestows;
    My rushy couch and frugal fare,
20   My blessing and repose.

    'No flocks that range the valley free
        To slaughter I condemn:
    Taught by that power that pities me,
        I learn to pity them.

25 'But from the mountain's grassy side
        A guiltless feast I bring;
    A scrip with herbs and fruits supplied,
        And water from the spring.

¶ 13.1–3. 1765 and 1767 have:

                Deign, saint-like tenant of the dale,
                    To guide my nightly way
                To yonder fire, that chears the vale

5. forlorn and lost] deserted, as 1765; 1767.
7. Where wilds] The wild 1765; 1767.
8. Seem] Seems 1765; 1767.
9. hermit cries] sage replies 1765; 1767.
10. dangerous] lonely 1765; 1767.
11. faithless phantom] phantom only 1766a.

'Then, pilgrim, turn, thy cares forgo;
30   All earth-born cares are wrong:
Man wants but little here below,
    Nor wants that little long.'

Soft as the dew from heaven descends,
    His gentle accents fell:
35   The modest stranger lowly bends,
    And follows to the cell.

Far in a wilderness obscure
    The lonely mansion lay;
A refuge to the neighbouring poor
40   And strangers led astray.

No stores beneath its humble thatch
    Required a master's care;
The wicket, opening with a latch,
    Received the harmless pair.

45   And now, when busy crowds retire
    To take their evening rest,
The hermit trimmed his little fire,
    And cheered his pensive guest:

And spread his vegetable store,
50   And gaily pressed and smiled;

---

29. pilgrim, turn] turn to-night *1765*; trav'ller turn *1767*.
30. All] For *1766a; 1767*.
31–2. G. quotes Young, *Night Thoughts* iv 119: 'Man wants but Little; nor that Little, long.' That G. was alluding to Young and not plagiarizing is clear from *1765* and *1767*, where these two lines are in quotation marks. In the texts in *Vicar* quotation marks are first used for conversation in the poem and those round these two lines were abandoned, perhaps by mistake. G. also echoed Young's lines in *Citizen* (1762) ii 9 (later numbered Letter 67): 'the running brook, the herbs of the field can amply satisfy nature; man wants but little, nor that little long.'
35. modest] grateful *1766a*.
37. in a wilderness] shelter'd in a glade *1766a*.
38. lonely] modest *1766a*.
39. the neighbouring] th'unshelter'd *1765; 1767*.
43. The wicket,] The door just *1766a*; But the door, *1767*.
45. busy] worldly *1766a*.
46. take their evening] revels or to *1766a*.
47. little] pleasant *1767*.

And, skilled in legendary lore,
  The lingering hours beguiled.

Around in sympathetic mirth
  Its tricks the kitten tries;
55 The cricket chirrups in the hearth;
  The crackling faggot flies.

But nothing could a charm impart
  To soothe the stranger's woe;
For grief was heavy at his heart,
60   And tears began to flow.

His rising cares the hermit spied,
  With answering care oppressed;
'And whence, unhappy youth,' he cried,
  'The sorrows of thy breast?

65 'From better habitations spurned,
  Reluctant dost thou rove;
Or grieve for friendship unreturned,
  Or unregarded love?

'Alas! the joys that fortune brings
70   Are trifling, and decay;
And those who prize the paltry things,
  More trifling still than they.

'And what is friendship but a name,
  A charm that lulls to sleep;
75 A shade that follows wealth or fame,
  But leaves the wretch to weep?

'And love is still an emptier sound,
  The modern fair one's jest:

53. *Around*] While round *1765; 1767.*
57–60. *1765 and 1767 have:*
    But nothing mirthful could assuage
      The pensive stranger's woe,
    For grief had seiz'd his early age,
      And tears would often flow.
69–72. *Not in 1765.*
73. *And . . . friendship*] Say, what is friendship? *1765; 1767.*
77. *love . . . emptier*] what is love? an empty *1765; 1767.*
78. *modern*] haughty *1766a.*

On earth unseen, or only found
80   To warm the turtle's nest.

'For shame, fond youth, thy sorrows hush,
    And spurn the sex,' he said:
But, while he spoke, a rising blush
    His love-lorn guest betrayed.

85   Surprised, he sees new beauties rise,
    Swift mantling to the view;
Like colours o'er the morning skies,
    As bright, as transient too.

The bashful look, the rising breast,
90   Alternate spread alarms:
The lovely stranger stands confessed
    A maid in all her charms.

'And, ah! forgive a stranger rude,
    A wretch forlorn,' she cried;
95   'Whose feet unhallowed thus intrude
    Where heaven and you reside.

'But let a maid thy pity share,
    Whom love has taught to stray;
Who seeks for rest, but finds despair
100   Companion of her way.

'My father lived beside the Tyne,
    A wealthy lord was he;

---

84. His love-lorn] The bashful *1766a.*
85. Surprised, he sees new] He sees unnumber'd *1766a.*   *beauties*] beauty
1767.
86. Swift mantling] Expanding *1765; 1766a; 1767.*
87. colours o'er] clouds that deck *1766a.*
89. The bashful look, the rising] Her looks, her lips, her panting *1766a.*
94. wretch] thing *1765; 1767.*
97–9. 1765 and 1767 (with A for An) have:
         Forgive, and let thy pious care
         An heart's distress allay,
         That seeks repose,
100. her] the *1765; 1767.*
101–3. 1765 and 1767 have:
         My father liv'd, of high degree
         Remote beside the Tyne,
         And as he had but only me,

And all his wealth was marked as mine,
   He had but only me.

105   'To win me from his tender arms
         Unnumbered suitors came;
      Who praised me for imputed charms,
         And felt or feigned a flame.

      'Each hour a mercenary crowd
110   With richest proffers strove:
      Among the rest young Edwin bowed,
         But never talked of love.

      'In humble, simplest habit clad,
         No wealth nor power had he;
115   Wisdom and worth were all he had,
         But these were all to me.

      'The blossom opening to the day,
         The dews of heaven refined,

104. *He . . . me*] Whate'er he had was mine *1765*; His opulence was mine
1767.
107–8. *1765 and 1767 have*:
         Their chief pretence my flatter'd charms,
            My wealth perhaps their aim.
109. *hour a mercenary*] morn the gay phantastic *1766a*; hour the mercenary
1765; 1767.
110. *richest*] glitt'ring *1765; 1767*.
112. *But . . . of*] Who offer'd only *1765; 1767*.
115. *Wisdom . . . were*] A constant heart was *1766a*.
116. *But*] And *1765. these were*] that was *1766a*.
117. Percy wrote to Cadell and Davies on 6 April 1798 (Nichols, *Literary
Illustrations* viii 673) that he had acquired 'a new and beautiful stanza of the
Hermit, which will render all former editions of that poem incomplete and
defective'. In *Works*, 1801, i 76, he explained that the stanza was preserved
by 'Richard Archdal, Esq. late a member of the Irish parliament, to whom
it was presented by the author himself'. The stanza, which was first printed
at this point in the *Works* ii 25, is:
         And when, beside me in the dale,
            He carol'd lays of love,
         His breath lent fragrance to the gale,
            And music to the grove.
Prior (*Works*, 1837, iv 41) stated without authority that the stanza 'was
written some years after the rest of the poem'.
117–28. *1765 and 1767 (with* e'en *for* even *in l.* 119 *and* hapless be *for* woe
betide *in l.* 125) *have instead*:

Could nought of purity display,
120   To emulate his mind.

'The dew, the blossom on the tree,
    With charms inconstant shine;
Their charms were his, but woe to me,
    Their constancy was mine.

125   'For still I tried each fickle art,
    Importunate and vain:
And while his passion touched my heart,
    I triumphed in his pain.

'Till quite dejected with my scorn,
130   He left me to my pride;
And sought a solitude forlorn,
    In secret, where he died.

Whene'er he spoke amidst the train,
    How would my heart attend!
And still delighted even to pain,
    How sigh for such a friend!

And when a little rest I sought
    In sleep's refreshing arms,
How have I mended what he taught,
    And lent him fancied charms!

Yet still (and woe betide the hour)
    I spurn'd him from my side,
And still with ill dissembled power,
    Repaid his love with pride.

125–40. Cp. 'Gentle Herdsman, tell to me' 33–52, in Percy's *Reliques* ii 74: 'When thus I saw he loved me well, / I grewe so proude his paine to see, / That I, who did not know myselfe, / Thought scorne of such a youth as hee. // And grew soe coy and nice to please, / As womens lookes are often soe, / He might not kisse, nor hand forsooth, / Unlesse I willed him soe to doe. // Thus being wearyed with delayes, / To see I pityed not his greeffe, / He gott him to a secrett place, / And there he dyed without releeffe. // And for his sake these weedes I weare, / And sacrifice my tender age; / And every day Ile begg my bread, / To undergoe this pilgrimage. // Thus every day I fast and praye, / And ever will doe till I dye; / And gett me to some secrett place, / For soe did hee, and soe will I.'
130. my pride] deplore *1765; 1767.*
132. And ne'er was heard of more. *1765; 1767.*

'But mine the sorrow, mine the fault,
    And well my life shall pay;
135 I'll seek the solitude he sought,
    And stretch me where he lay.

'And there forlorn, despairing, hid,
    I'll lay me down and die:
'Twas so for me that Edwin did,
140   And so for him will I.'

'Forbid it, heaven!' the hermit cried,
    And clasped her to his breast:
The wondering fair one turned to chide,
    'Twas Edwin's self that pressed.

145 'Turn, Angelina, ever dear,
    My charmer, turn to see
Thy own, thy long-lost Edwin here,
    Restored to love and thee.

'Thus let me hold thee to my heart,
150   And every care resign;
And shall we never, never part,
    My life—my all that's mine?

'No, never from this hour to part,
    We'll live and love so true;

133–4. 1765 and 1767 have:
            Then since he perish'd by my fault,
              This pilgrimage I pay,
137. forlorn, despairing] in shelt'ring thickets *1765; 1767 (with* thicket *for*
thickets).
138. lay . . . and] linger till I *1765; 1767.*
139. so . . . that Edwin] thus . . . my lover *1765; 1767.*
141. 'Forbid it, heaven!'] Thou shalt not thus, *1765; 1766a;*, *1767.*
143. The wondering] Th'astonish'd *1765; 1767.*
144. 1765 and 1767 have an additional stanza after this line:
            For now no longer could he hide
              What first to hide he strove,
            His looks resume their youthful pride,
              And flush with honest love.
152. My life] O thou *1766a;* My thou *1767.*
154–5. 1765 and 1767 have:
            Our love shall still be new,
            And the last sigh that rends thy heart

155   The sigh that rends thy constant heart
         Shall break thy Edwin's too.'

*156. 1765 and 1767 (with streams and for sylvan in the first line and o'er for
again in the last) have two additional stanzas at the end:*

                Here amidst sylvan bow'rs we'll rove,
                From lawn to woodland stray,
                Blest as the songsters of the grove,
                And innocent as they.

                To all that want, and all that wail,
                   Our pity shall be given,
                And when this life of love shall fail,
                   We'll love it again in heav'n.

In the Reed copy of *1765* 'it' in the last line is deleted.

14 The Captivity: an Oratorio

Written not later than 31 Oct. 1764. Some nineteenth-century editors of
G. date the oratorio 1761: this suggestion, for which no evidence has been
produced, seems to be found first in the limited edn of the work published
by Pickering in 1836 and was repeated in the Aldine edn, by Gibbs in 1885,
and by Wardle in 1957. Neither MS of the work is dated. On 31 Oct. 1764
G. signed a receipt (now inlaid in the Dodsley MS) for 10 guineas from James
Dodsley 'for an Oratorio which Mr. Newbery and he are to share'. Prior
(*Life* ii 1–2) believed G. wrote it during 1764, being inspired to do so by the ex-
ample of Christopher Smart's *Hannah*, set by Worgan, performed in April
1764, and by his friendship with the composer William Boyce, who, he
may have hoped, would provide him with a setting. These suggestions
are only surmise, but 1764 must still seem a more likely date than 1761.
G.'s libretto is mere hackwork and it is unlikely that he would have kept
by him for three years a work which can have been written for no other
purpose than financial gain. It is also worth noting that there was some-
thing of a vogue for oratorios during 1764. In the April *Monthly Review*
xxx 325, William Kenrick dealt with three oratorios: *Israel in Babylon* and
Nabul, as well as Smart's *Hannah*.
   G. made a copy of *The Captivity* for both Dodsley and Newbery but
neither printed the work. Two songs (see ll. 23–30, 131–8), in versions
differing from either MS, were printed with *The Haunch of Venison* in
1776. The two songs were collected in *1777* p. 78, and printed in G.'s
works thereafter. Percy was aware of the existence of the full libretto,
although he did not apparently feel that its publication was worth while and
it was not included in *Works*, 1801. George Steevens referred in a letter to

Percy, 3 Sept. 1797, to 'a late discovery . . . of a dramatic piece in [G.'s]
own handwriting; it turned up among the papers of the late Mr. Dodsley. . . .
It is now setting to music by an eminent composer, and great expectations
are formed of its success' (Prior, *Life* ii 9). Prior mentions a setting of the
work by the composer R. J. S. Stevens (1757–1836) but it seems never to
have been performed. The MS of this setting is in the British Museum. It
was set again by the Irish composer George Torrance (1835–1907) in 1864.
   The MS prepared by G. for Newbery was the first to be printed, in the
1820 edn of the *Miscellaneous Works* ii 451–70. This MS was auctioned in
1835, belonged to William Upcott and is now in the Pierpont Morgan
Library, New York. The Dodsley MS was owned by John Murray the
publisher and remained in the family until it was sold at Sotheby's on 11
June 1963 for £1,800. It is now in the Free Library of Philadelphia. Prior,
Works, 1837, iv 79–95, claimed to be printing the Dodsley MS for the first
time, although he in fact retained a number of readings from the Newbery
MS: in this rather misleading process of conflation he was later followed
by Gibbs and Dobson. The Dodsley MS was first 'faithfully printed from
the valuable manuscript of Mr. Murray of Albemarle-street' by Bolton
Corney in 1845. Cunningham in 1854 followed Corney more closely than
later editors but retained some readings from the Newbery MS. Most
editors have assumed that the Dodsley MS represented a later text: the
evidence is, in fact, contradictory, as will be clear from the corrections to
the Newbery MS given here in the notes. Although these corrections are
predominantly towards the readings of the Dodsley MS, in some cases G.
alters readings which are retained in the Dodsley MS. As occurs more than
once with poems by G., it is not easy to see consistency and purpose in many
of his alterations. For detailed speculation about the relationship of the
MSS, see Friedman, *Works* iv 209–13: his suggestion that the MSS are
'probably independent revisions of a manuscript now lost' seems the most
likely solution of the problem. The text given here is that of the Dodsley
MS with variants from the Newbery MS. Deletions and corrections from
both MSS are recorded when they are of any significance. Two minor
adjustments have been made. The spelling 'Recitativo', used twice by
G., has been altered to the more frequent 'Recitative'. The musical direc-
tions ('Air', 'Recitative' etc) which in the MS sometimes precede and some-
times follow the identification of the singer have been consistently placed
after the singer. Variants in the 'Songs' as printed with *The Haunch of
Venison* have also been noted (as *1776*).
   The action of the oratorio takes place in 539 B.C., when Cyrus, King of
Persia, conquered Babylon and ended the captivity of the Jews, which
followed the destruction of Jerusalem in 587 B.C. G. telescopes the action
to some extent, notably in delaying the death of King Zedekiah, which is
usually taken to have occurred not long after the fall of Jerusalem. See ll.
213 14 and 223–6n.

ACT I Scene I

Israelites sitting on the Banks of the Euphrates

FIRST PROPHET

Recitative

Ye captive tribes, that hourly work and weep
Where flows Euphrates murmuring to the deep,
Suspend awhile the task, the tear suspend,
And turn to God, your father and your friend.
5 Insulted, chained, and all the world a foe,
Our God alone is all we boast below.

CHORUS OF ISRAELITES

Our God is all we boast below,
To him we turn our eyes;
And every added weight of woe
10 Shall make our homage rise.

And though no temple richly dressed
Nor sacrifice is here,
We'll make his temple in our breast,
And offer up a tear.

SECOND PROPHET

Recitative

15 That strain once more; it bids remembrance rise,
And calls my long-lost country to mine eyes.
Ye fields of Sharon, dressed in flowery pride,
Ye plains where Jordan rolls its glassy tide,
Ye hills of Lebanon with cedars crowned,
20 Ye Gilead groves that fling perfumes around,
These hills how sweet! those plains how wondrous
fair,

¶ 14.3. *a while the task, the tear*] your woes awhile, the task *Newbery*.
5. *a*] our *Newbery*.
7–14. In *Newbery* this 'Chorus' is an 'Air' divided between the 1st and 2nd
prophets and the 1st stanza is then repeated by the chorus.
12. *is*] are *Newbery*.
15–22. In *Newbery* the 'Recitative' is sung by an 'Israelitish Woman'.
16. *calls*] brings *Newbery*.
17. *fields*] *in Dodsley altered to* groves *then back to* fields.
18. *Jordan*] Kidron *Newbery*.
21–2. How sweet those groves, that plain how wondrous fair, / How doubly
sweet *Newbery*.

But sweeter still, when Heaven was with us there!

Air

O memory, thou fond deceiver,
Still importunate and vain;
25 To former joys recurring ever,
And turning all the past to pain;

Hence, deceiver, most distressing,
Seek the happy and the free:
They who want each other blessing,
30 Ever want a friend in thee.

FIRST PROPHET
Recitative

Yet, why repine? What, though by bonds confined,
Should bonds enslave the vigour of the mind?
Have we not cause for triumph when we see
Ourselves alone from idol-worship free?
35 Are not this very day those rites begun,
Where prostrate error hails the rising sun?
Do not our tyrant lords this day ordain
For superstition's rites and mirth profane?
And should we mourn? should coward virtue fly,
40 When impious folly rears her front on high?
No; rather let us triumph still the more,
And as our fortune sinks, our wishes soar.

27–30. *1776 has:*

Thou, like the world, th'opprest oppressing,
Thy smiles increase the wretch's woe;
And he who wants each other blessing,
In thee must ever find a foe.

27. *deceiver*] intruder *Newbery.*
28. *Seek*] *so Newbery, with* Fly *to deleted.*
29. *They who want*] The wretch who wants *Newbery.*
30. *want*] wants *Newbery.*
31–42. Given to 2nd Prophet in *Newbery.*
31. *repine*] complain *Newbery.*
32. *enslave*] repress *Newbery.*
35. *days . . . rites*] morn . . . feasts *Newbery.*
36. *folly*] error *Newbery.*
38. *superstition's*] superstitious *Newbery.*
40. *impious . . . rears . . . front*] vaunting . . . lifts . . . head *Newbery.*
42. *wishes*] spirits *Newbery.*

Air

The triumphs that on vice attend
Shall ever in confusion end;
45   The good man suffers but to gain,
And every virtue springs from pain:

As aromatic plants bestow
No spicy fragrance while they grow;
But crushed, or trodden to the ground,
50   Diffuse their balmy sweets around.

SECOND PROPHET

Recitative

But hush, my sons, our tyrant lords are near;
The sound of barbarous mirth offends mine ear;
Triumphant music floats along the vale;
Near, nearer still, it gathers on the gale;
55   The growing note their near approach declares;
Desist, my sons, nor mix the strain with theirs.

Enter Chaldean Priests attended

FIRST PRIEST

Air

Come on, my companions, the triumph display;
   Let rapture the minutes employ;
The sun calls us out on this festival day,
60   And our monarch partakes of our joy.

Like the sun, our great monarch all pleasure supplies,
   Both similar blessings bestow;
The sun with his splendour illumines the skies,
   And our monarch enlivens below.

---

48. *while*] *written over* as *Newbery.*   *grow*] *written after* blow *deleted Dodsley.*
51–6. Given to 1st Prophet in *Newbery.*
52. *sound . . . mirth offends*] sounds . . . pleasure strikes *Newbery.*
53. *vale*] *altered from* gale *Newbery.*
55. *note*] sound *over* notes *deleted Newbery.*   *near*] swift *Newbery.*
60. *of our*] in the *Newbery.*
61–4. Given to 2nd Priest in *Newbery.*
61. *pleasure*] rapture *Newbery.*   *supplies*] *written above* bestows *deleted Dodsley.*

CHALDEAN WOMAN

Air

65 Haste, ye sprightly sons of pleasure;
Love presents its brightest treasure,
    Leave all other sports for me.

CHALDEAN ATTENDANT

Or rather, love's delights despising,
Haste to raptures ever rising:
70   Wine shall bless the brave and free.

SECOND PRIEST

Wine and beauty thus inviting,
Each to different joys exciting,
    Whither shall my choice incline?

FIRST PRIEST

I'll waste no longer thought in choosing;
75 But, neither love nor wine refusing,
    I'll make them both together mine.

Recitative

But whence, when joy should brighten o'er the land,
This sullen gloom in Judah's captive band?
Ye sons of Judah, why the lute unstrung?
80 Or why those harps on yonder willows hung?
Come, leave your griefs and join our warbling choir,
For who like you can wake the sleeping lyre?

SECOND PROPHET

Bowed down with chains, the scorn of all mankind,

66. *its brightest*] the fairest *Newbery.*
67. *sports*] joys *Newbery.*
71–82. In *Newbery* the two priests perform in reverse order, but the 1st Priest retains the 'Recitative'.
75. *love nor wine*] this nor that *Newbery.*
80. *Newbery adds after this line:*
        Come, take the lyre and pour the strain along
        The day demands it, sing us Sion's song.
81. *Come, leave*] Dismiss *Newbery.*
82. *wake*] *written over* strike *Newbery.*
82. Followed in *Newbery* by the 'Air' from 151–8.
83. *Bowed down with chains*] Chained as we are *Newbery* (*with the Dodsley reading deleted*).

To want, to toil and every ill consigned,
85 Is this a time to bid us raise the strain,
And mix in rites that Heaven regards with pain?
No, never! May this hand forget each art
That speeds the powers of music to the heart,
Ere I forget the land that gave me birth,
90 Or join with sounds profane its sacred mirth.

FIRST PRIEST

Insulting slaves! if gentler methods fail,
The whips and angry tortures shall prevail.
[*Exeunt Chaldeans*

FIRST PROPHET

Why, let them come, one good remains to cheer;
We fear the Lord, and know no other fear.

CHORUS

95 Can whips or tortures hurt the mind
On God's supporting breast reclined?
Stand fast, and let our tyrants see
That fortitude is victory.

End of the First Act

ACT II

Scene as before

CHORUS OF ISRAELITES

O Peace of mind, thou lovely guest,

---

86. *And*] Or *Newbery.*   *rites*] *written after* sound *deleted Dodsley.*
88. *speeds the powers of music to the*] wakes to finest joys the human *Newbery.*
90. *with*] to *Newbery.*
91–2. *Given to* 2nd Priest *in Newbery, which reads:* 'Rebellious slaves, if soft persuasion fail, / More formidable terrors' *etc.*
92. *The Chaldeans exeunt after* l. 94 *in Newbery.*
94. *know no*] scorn all *Newbery.*
95. *whips . . . hurt*] chains . . . bend *Newbery.*
96. *In Newbery this reading replaces* That leans on heaven for all felicity *deleted.*
97. *see*] find *deleted Newbery.*
98. *In Newbery this reading replaces* Our sufferings are victory *deleted.*
99–104. *Given to* 1st Prophet *as an* 'Air' *in Newbery.*
99. *thou lovely*] angelic *Newbery.*

100 Thou softest soother of the breast,
    Dispense thy balmy store.
    Wing all our thoughts to reach the skies,
    Till earth, diminished to our eyes,
    Shall vanish as we soar.

FIRST PRIEST

Recitative

105 No more. Too long has justice been delayed,
    The king's commands must fully be obeyed;
    Compliance with his will your peace secures,
    Praise but our gods and every good is yours.
    But if, rebellious to his high command,
110 You spurn the favours offered from his hand,
    Think, timely think, what ills remain behind;
    Reflect, nor tempt to rage the royal mind.

SECOND PRIEST

Air

    Fierce is the whirlwind howling
    O'er Afric's sandy plain,
115 And fierce the tempest rolling
    Along the furrowed main:

    But storms that fly
    To rend the sky,
    Every ill presaging,
120 Less dreadful show
    To worlds below
    Than angry monarchs raging.

ISRAELITISH WOMAN

Recitative

    Ah, me! what angry terrors round us grow;
    How shrinks my soul to meet the threatened blow!
125 Ye prophets, skilled in Heaven's eternal truth,

100. softest soother] soft companion Newbery with best deleted.
103. diminished to] receding from Newbery.
111. ills remain] terrors are Newbery.
113–22. Given to 1st Priest in Newbery.
113, 115. tempest and whirlwind are interchanged in Newbery.
114, 116. These lines are interchanged in Newbery.
119. Every] altered from And every Newbery.

Forgive my sex's fears, forgive my youth!
If, shrinking thus, when frowning power appears,
I wish for life and yield me to my fears.
Let us one hour, one little hour obey;
130   Tomorrow's tears may wash our stains away.

Air

To the last moment of his breath
On hope the wretch relies;
And even the pang preceding death
Bids expectation rise.

135   Hope, like the gleaming taper's light,
Adorns and cheers our way;
And still, as darker grows the night,
Emits a brighter ray.

SECOND PRIEST

Recitative

Why this delay? at length for joy prepare;
140   I read your looks and see compliance there.
Come raise the strain and grasp the full-toned lyre:
The time, the theme, the place and all conspire.

127–28. Not in Newbery.
129. Let us one hour] Ah let us one *Newbery.*
130. our stains] the stain *Newbery.*
131–3. 1776 has:

The Wretch condemn'd with life to part,
    Still, still on Hope relies;
And ev'ry pang that rends the heart . . . . etc.

In Newbery G. began by transcribing the first two lines and And *of the third as in Dodsley, and then deleted them and transcribed a version with the variants given below.*
131. Fatigued with life, yet loath to part *Newbery.*
133. And every blow that sinks the heart *Newbery.*
134. expectation] *deleted in Newbery and* the deluder *written above.*
135. gleaming taper's] tapers gleamy *Newbery*; glim'ring tapers *1776.*
136. and cheers our] the wretch's *Newbery, with* gloomy *deleted; and* chears the *1776.*
141. Newbery has Come on, *and bid the warbling rapture rise followed by* Our Monarchs fame the noblest theme supplies / Begin ye captive bands and strike the lyre.

CHALDEAN WOMAN

Air

See the ruddy morning smiling,
Hear the grove to bliss beguiling;
145 Zephyrs through the valley playing,
Streams along the meadow straying.

FIRST PRIEST

While these a constant revel keep,
Shall reason only bid me weep?
Hence, intruder! we'll pursue
150 Nature, a better guide than you.

SECOND PRIEST

Air

Every moment, as it flows,
Some peculiar pleasure owes;
Then let us, providently wise,
Seize the debtor as it flies.

155 Think not tomorrow can repay
The pleasures that we lose today;
Tomorrow's most unbounded store
Can but pay its proper score.

FIRST PRIEST

Recitative

But hush! see, foremost of the captive choir,
160 The master-prophet grasps his full-toned lyre.
Mark where he sits, with executing art,

145. valley] woo[d]land *Newbery.*
146. meadow] valley *Newbery.*
148. bid me] teach to *Newbery.*
151–8. In Newbery these lines follow l. 82.
153. Then let us] Come then *Newbery, altered from* Then let us.
154. as] ere *Newbery.*
156. pleasures . . . lose] debt of pleasure lost today *Newbery. In Dodsley that* we lose *is written over* we have lost *deleted. Two earlier attempts at the line are deleted in Newbery:* pleasures we have lost *and* debt that we have lost.
157. Tomorrow's most unbounded] Alass to morrow's richest *Newbery.*
159–86. Given to 2nd Priest in Newbery.
159. hush] hold *Newbery.*

Feels for each tone and speeds it to the heart.
See, inspiration fills his rising form,
Awful as clouds that nurse the growing storm;
165   And now his voice, accordant to the string,
Prepares our monarch's victories to sing.

FIRST PROPHET
Air

From north, from south, from east, from west,
Conspiring foes shall come;
Tremble, thou vice-polluted breast;
170   Blasphemers, all be dumb.

The tempest gathers all around,
On Babylon it lies;
Down with her! down, down to the ground;
She sinks, she groans, she dies.

SECOND PROPHET

175   Down with her, Lord, to lick the dust,
Ere yonder setting sun;
Serve her as she hath served the just.
'Tis fixed—it shall be done.

FIRST PRIEST
Recitative

Enough! when slaves thus insolent presume,
180   The king himself shall judge and fix their doom.
Short-sighted wretches, have not you, and all,
Beheld our power in Zedekiah's fall?
To yonder gloomy dungeon turn your eyes;
See where dethroned your captive monarch lies.
185   Deprived of sight and rankling in his chain,
He calls on death to terminate his pain.
Yet know, ye slaves, that still remain behind
More ponderous chains and dungeons more confined.

162. After this line Newbery has And now his *deleted.*
163. inspiration . . . rising] how prophetic rapture fill his *Newbery.*
168. foes shall] nations *Newbery.*
172. lies] *so both MSS with* falls *deleted.*
176. Ere yonder] Before yon *Newbery.*
179. Enough] *written over* No *Dodsley;* No more *Newbery.*
181. Short-sighted] Unthinking *Newbery.*
186. See where he mourns his friends and children slain *Newbery.*

CHORUS

190   Arise, all-potent Ruler, rise,
             And vindicate the people's cause;
             Till every tongue in every land
             Shall offer up unfeigned applause.

End of the Second Act

ACT III

Scene as before

FIRST PRIEST

Recitative

             Yes, my companions, Heaven's decrees are past,
             And our fixed empire shall for ever last;
195   In vain the maddening prophet threatens woe,
             In vain rebellion aims her secret blow;
             Still shall our fame and growing power be spread,
             And still our vengeance crush the guilty's head.

Air

             Coeval with man
200   Our empire began,
             And never shall fall
             Till ruin shakes all;
             With the ruin of all
             Shall Babylon fall.

SECOND PROPHET

Recitative

205   'Tis thus that pride triumphant rears the head:
             A little while and all her power is fled.
             But ha! what means yon sadly plaintive train,

190. *the*] thy *altered from* the *Newbery.*
197. *fame*] name *Newbery.*
198. *vengeance . . . guilty*] justice . . . traitors *Newbery.*
202. *shakes*] *so Newbery with* crowns *deleted.*
203. *With the ruin of*] When ruin shakes *Newbery with* Crowns *deleted.*
204. *Shall*] Then shall *Newbery.*
205. *that pride*] the proud *Newbery.   rears the*] rear the *Newbery altered from*
rears her.
206. *her*] their *Newbery.*

That this way slowly bends along the plain?
And now, methinks, a pallid corse they bear
210   To yonder bank, and rest the body there.
Alas! too well mine eyes observant trace
The last remains of Judah's royal race:
Our monarch falls and now our fears are o'er:
The wretched Zedekiah is no more!

Air

215   Ye wretches who, by fortune's hate,
In want and sorrow groan,
Come ponder his severer fate,
And learn to bless your own.

Ye sons, from fortune's lap supplied,
220   Awhile the bliss suspend;
Like yours his life began in pride,
Like his your lives may end.

SECOND PROPHET

Behold his squalid corse with sorrow worn,
His wretched limbs with ponderous fetters torn;
225   Those eyeless orbs that shock with ghastly glare,

208. this way] onward *Newbery.*
209. methinks . . . corse] behold to yonder bank *Newbery.*
210. To yonder bank] A pallid corse *Newbery.*
211. observant] indignant *Newbery.*
213–14, 223–6. Zedekiah, who became the last King of Judah in 597 B.C.,
might have reigned peacefully as a vassal of Babylon, but revolted and
provoked Nebuchadnezzar to the destruction of Jerusalem and the temple,
and the captivity of the Jews in 587 B.C. He himself broke out of Jerusalem
with his household during the siege but he was captured in the Jordan valley,
was brought before Nebuchadnezzar, saw his sons killed and was blinded.
He is thought to have died not long after, although G. delays his death to the
end of the captivity. See *2 Kings* xxv and *2 Chronicles* xxxvi.
213. Our monarch . . . now] Fallen is our King, and all *Newbery.*
214. The wretched] Unhappy *Newbery, with* And wretched, The wretched
and Ill-fated *deleted.*
219–22. Given to 1st Prophet in *Newbery.*
219. You vain whom youth and pleasure guide *Newbery.*
222. may] shall *Newbery.*
223–30. Given to 1st Prophet in *Newbery.*
223. squalid] wretched *Newbery.*
224. wretched . . . with] squalid . . . by *Newbery.*
225. eyeless] *written above* sightless *deleted Dodsley.*

Those ill-becoming robes and matted hair.
And shall not Heaven for this its terrors show,
And deal its angry vengeance on the foe?
How long, how long, Almighty Lord of all,
230   Shall wrath vindictive threaten ere it fall?

ISRAELITISH WOMAN

Air

As panting flies the hunted hind,
Where brooks refreshing stray,
And rivers through the valley wind,
That stop the hunter's way:

235   Thus we, O Lord, alike distressed,
For streams of mercy long;
Those streams which cheer the sore oppressed,
And overwhelm the strong.

FIRST PROPHET

Recitative

But whence that shout? Good Heavens! amazement
all!
240   See yonder tower just nodding to the fall:
See where an army covers all the ground,
Saps the strong wall and pours destruction round.
The ruin smokes, destruction pours along;
How low the great, how feeble are the strong!
245   The foe prevails, the lofty walls recline:
O God of hosts, the victory is thine!

226. *ill-becoming robes and*] unbecoming rags, that *Newbery.*
227. *its terrors show*] avenge the foe *Newbery.*
228. Grasp the red bolt, and lay the guilty low *Newbery.*
229. *Lord*] God *Newbery.*
233. *And*] *written above* Where *deleted Newbery.*
235. *distressed*] *written after* opprest deprest *deleted Newbery.*
237. *Those*] *deleted in Newbery.*
241. *See where*] Behold *Newbery.*
242. *Saps . . . and*] 'Tis Cyrus here that *Newbery, written above* They sap the
wall, *and deleted.*
243-4. Transferred to follow l. 252 in *Newbery.*
243. *destruction*] the torrent *Newbery.*
244. *great*] proud *Newbery.*
245. *The foe . . . walls*] And now behold the battlements *Newbery.*

CHORUS OF ISRAELITES

Down with her, Lord, to lick the dust;
Let vengeance be begun:
Serve her as she hath served the just,
250   And let thy will be done.

FIRST PRIEST

All, all is lost. The Syrian army fails;
Cyrus, the conqueror of the world, prevails.
Save us, O Lord! to thee, though late, we pray,
And give repentance but an hour's delay.

Air

255   Thrice happy, who in happy hour
To Heaven their praise bestow,
And own his all-consuming power
Before they feel the blow!

FIRST PROPHET

Recitative

Now, now's our time! ye wretches bold and blind,
260   Brave but to God and cowards to mankind,
Too late you seek that power unsought before,
Your wealth, your pride, your empire, are no more.

Air

O Lucifer, thou son of morn,
Alike of Heaven and man the foe;
265   Heaven, men and all

247. *her*] them *Newbery.*
248. *Let*] Thy *Newbery.*
249. *her as she hath*] them as they have *Newbery.*
250. *And let*] *followed by* O Lord *deleted Newbery.*
251. *The Syrian army fails*] *written above* O whither shall we fly *deleted Newbery.*
252. Followed in *Newbery* by ll. 243–4.
255–8. Given to both Priests in *Newbery.*
256. *Heaven*] God *Newbery.*
259–67. Given to 2nd Prophet in *Newbery.*
259. *ye wretches bold and blind*] *written above* ye haughty sons of earth *deleted Newbery.*
261. *Too late . . . power*] Ye seek in vain the Lord *Newbery.*
262. *pride . . . empire*] lives . . . kingdom *Newbery.*
264. *Alike of Heaven . . . foe*] Of heaven alike . . . foe *Newbery, with* Heavens bold Usurper mankind's foe *deleted.*

Now press thy fall,
And sink thee lowest of the low.

SECOND PRIEST

O Babylon, how art thou fallen,
Thy fall more dreadful from delay!
270   Thy streets forlorn
To wilds shall turn,
Where toads shall pant and vultures prey.

FIRST PROPHET

Recitative

Such be her fate. But listen, from afar
The clarion's note proclaims the finished war!
275   Cyrus, our great restorer, is at hand,
And this way leads his formidable band.
Now, give your songs of Sion to the wind,
And hail the benefactor of mankind:
He comes pursuant to divine decree,
280   To chain the strong and set the captive free.

CHORUS OF YOUTHS

Rise to raptures past expressing,
Sweeter from remembered woes;
Cyrus comes, our wrongs redressing,
Comes to give the world repose.

CHORUS OF VIRGINS

285   Cyrus comes, the world redressing,
Love and pleasure in his train;
Comes to heighten every blessing,
Comes to soften every pain.

CHORUS OF YOUTHS AND VIRGINS

Hail to him with mercy reigning,
290   Skilled in every peaceful art,

268–72. Given to 1st Prophet in *Newbery.*
272. *toads shall pant*] *written above* foxes haunt *deleted Newbery.*
273–80. Given to 2nd Prophet in *Newbery.*
273. *listen*] hark how *Newbery.*
275. *Cyrus . . . restorer*] Our great restorer Cyrus *Newbery.*
277. *Now*] Give *written above* now *deleted Newbery.*
281. *raptures*] transports *Newbery.*
282. *from*] by *Newbery.*
289–92. Described as 'Semichorus' in *Newbery.*

> Who from bonds our limbs unchaining,
> Only binds the willing heart.

LAST CHORUS

> But chief to Thee, our God, our father, friend,
> Let praise be given to all eternity;
> 295 O Thou, without beginning, without end,
> Let us, and all, begin and end in Thee!

FINIS

293. our father] defender *Newbery.*

15 The Traveller, or A Prospect of Society

Written between the summer of 1755 and Dec. 1764, when it was published. G.'s dedicatory letter to his brother Henry, prefixed to the poem, states that 'a part of this poem was formerly written to you from Switzerland.' G. travelled on the Continent between Feb. 1755 and Feb. 1756 and was in Switzerland in the summer of 1755. According to William Cooke, *European Mag.* xxiv (1793) 93, G. sent 'about two hundred lines' to Henry; but Prior, *Life* i 186–7, reported in 1837 that: 'All traces of this sketch . . . consisting of about seventy or eighty lines according to current report among his relatives, are now lost; being considered probably of no further value when the poem had been published.'

Speculation about the character of whatever G. wrote in 1755 is no doubt pointless. Perhaps G. began by writing purely descriptive verse and, as his political thinking developed over the next few years, then came to realize that the poem could also embody his views on national character, the monarchy and depopulation. The combination of description and political theorizing may, as has been suggested, have been inspired by Addison's *A Letter from Italy* (1703) of which G. was to remark in *The Beauties of English Poesy* (1767) I 111, that 'There is in it a strain of political thinking that was, at that time, new in our poetry'. A parallel has also been seen between G.'s poem and Sir Richard Blackmore's *The Nature of Man* (1711), which may have influenced Gray's *Education and Government*. But G. is more likely to have been influenced by Montesquieu's *L'Esprit des Loix* (1748) or by the discussion of the effect of climate on national character which followed its publication. G. was certainly reflecting on the problem by 1760, if R. S. Crane's attributions in *New Essays* are correct. Crane (p. xxxix) showed that the themes and attitudes of *The Traveller*, as well as anticipations of particular passages, can be found in a state of 'preliminary crystallization' in a number of essays G. may have written at this time, notably 'The Effect which

Climates have upon Men, and other Animals', *British Mag.* (May 1760);
and 'A Comparative View of Races and Nations', *Royal Mag.* (June to
Sept. 1760): see *Works* ed. Friedman, iii 66–86, 112–14. In addition to these
discussions of national psychology, 'The Revolution in Low Life' (*Lloyd's
Evening Post*, 14–16 June 1762; in *Works*, iii 195–8) also anticipates the gloomy
political and social thinking at the end of the poem. Parallels given in the
notes to the poem will illustrate how in other essays, in the *Citizen of the
World* and *A History of England in a Series of Letters* (1764), G. worked out
the ideas which were to appear in his poem if they were not simultaneous
with it.

There is virtually no definite information about the progress of the poem.
Percy, who first met G. in 1759, implies in a rather vague passage in his
'Life' of G. (*Works*, 1801, i 63–4) that G. wrote most of it while living
with the Newberys at Canonbury House in Islington between the end of
1762 and 1764. After describing G.'s less important writings of this period,
Percy states: 'But the production, which he meant should establish his
fame, and on which he bestowed his choicest hours, was his admirable
poem, "The Traveller" .... While he was composing this with the
greatest care, and finishing it in his highest and best manner, he scribbled
with all possible dispatch some of the above, and other slight publications, for
his present subsistence.' In his 'Autobiography' Francis Newbery the son
of G.'s publisher, remembered G. reading him 'favourite portions' of *The
Traveller* at Canonbury House (C. Welsh, *A Bookseller of the Last Century*
(1885) p. 46). Percy (*Works*, 1801, i 113), also stated that 'nothing could
exceed the patient and incessant revisal, which he bestowed' on his two
major poems: 'To save himself the trouble of transcription, he wrote the
lines in his first copy very wide, and would so fill up the intermediate
space with reiterated corrections, that scarcely a word of his first effusions
was left unaltered.' A point on which there is general agreement is that
Johnson, in one way or another, was instrumental in persuading G. to
complete and publish the poem. In some ways, however, the evidence is
contradictory. William Cooke (*European Mag.* xxiv (1793) 93) stated that
the first version of the poem 'lay by the Doctor some years, without any
determined idea of publishing, till persuaded to it by his friend Dr. Johnson,
who gave him some general hints towards enlarging it'. Cooke may refer
to the additions made in proof (see below) and may not in fact be contra-
dicting another account, referring perhaps to an earlier stage in composition.
Prior (*Life* ii 18) relying on information supplied by Dr McVeagh McDonnell
from Thomas English, stated that 'the original outline, said by his contem-
poraries to have been more extensive than now appears, was contracted and
filled up; and in this state though still imperfect and without the title (that
of "The Philosophical Wanderer" was first suggested) being positively
fixed, it was submitted to Dr. Johnson'.

Johnson's identifiable contribution to *The Traveller* cannot be discussed
without some reference to a bibliographical phenomenon of some impor-
tance in the development of the poem. In 1902 Bertram Dobell discovered

four quarto half-sheets (now in the British Museum) which constitute a unique early printed version of the poem, and contain 310 of the 416 ll. which were to appear in the 1st edn (73–92 and 103–400), with the title *A Prospect of Society*. The most striking fact about this version of the poem is that it contains what is substantially the text of *The Traveller* in nine regressing sections: ll. 1–42 of *A Prospect* correspond to ll. 353–400 of *The Traveller* and so on. This important feature of the poem was not apparent to Dobell when he edited *A Prospect of Society* in 1902. The first and attractively simply explanation of the regressing text was offered by Sir Arthur Quiller-Couch in a review of Dobell's edn in *The Daily News*, 31 March 1902 (quoted by Dobell in later issues of his edn and reprinted in *From a Cornish Window* (1906) pp. 86–92). He noticed that *A Prospect* was 'merely an early draft of *The Traveller* printed backwards in fairly regular sections' and suggested that G. had absentmindedly placed each page of his MS on top of the preceding one as he transcribed it and had never rearranged them for the press. But the nine regressing sections vary in length from 28 to 42 ll, and it is hard to imagine such a variation per page in the MS. R. S. Crane. in the *Cambridge Bibliography of English Literature* ii 641–2, suggested that the disarrangement occurred in the printing-house and this explanation has been elaborately investigated by W. B. Todd, 'Quadruple Imposition: An Account of Goldsmith's *Traveller*', *Studies in Bibliography* vii (1955) 103–11. Todd argues that the accidental reversal of the text occurred in the galley proofs and that the first three of the four surviving sheets of *A Prospect* represent what is to have been the 1st edn of the poem. L. W. Hanson, *The Library*, 5th series, x (1955) 297–8, suggests that *A Prospect* is no more than a bungled proof of *The Traveller*, before the title was changed and many additions and alterations had been made, to which Todd replied, *The Library* xi (1956) 123–4. In support of his view that *A Prospect of Society*, though accidentally reversed, is otherwise the final form of a complete poem, Todd reconstructed it in an edn published at Cambridge in 1954 and reprinted by the Bibliographical Society of the University of Virginia in 1956. Variant readings from this text are given in the notes.

All Johnson's identifiable contributions to the poem are later than the printing of *A Prospect*, although this does not mean that he may not have advised G. earlier. After the publication of *The Traveller* it was widely believed for a time that Johnson had written much if not all of it for G., and more than one of his friends questioned him on this matter. Boswell (*Life of Johnson* ii 5–6) described his attempt to 'settle, with authentick precision, what has long floated in publick report, as to Johnson's being himself the authour of a considerable part of that poem. Much, no doubt, both of the sentiments and expression, were derived from conversation with him; and it was certainly submitted to his friendly revision.' As early as 1780 Boswell tried to get Johnson to specify the lines he had written (*Life* iii 48); but he did not succeed until 1783, as the inscription on his own copy of *The Traveller* indicates; see the facsimile in *The R. B. Adam Library relating to Dr Johnson* (1929) ii 19: 'In Spring 1783 Dr. Johnson at my desire marked with a pencil the lines in this admirable Poem which he furnished viz l. 18 on p. 23 [l. 420] and from the 3 line on the last page to the end except the last couplet but one [ll. 429–34, 437–8]. "These (he said) are all of which I can be sure."' Johnson was noticeably cautious on this occasion; he once told Reynolds that he contributed twice as many lines to the poem. Reynolds recorded, *Portraits by Sir Joshua Reynolds*, ed. F. W. Hilles (1952) p. 77, that 'I pointed at some lines in *The Traveller* which I told him I was sure he writ. . . . But he only said, "Sir, I did write them, but that you may not imagine that I have wrote more than I really have, the utmost that I have wrote in that poem, to the best of my recollection, is not more than eighteen lines." It must be observed there was then an opinion about town that Dr. Johnson wrote the whole poem for his friend, who was then in a manner an unknown writer.' It is possible, therefore, that another 9 ll. by Johnson have still to be identified. Since the 9 he did claim were all added after *A Prospect* had been printed, it may perhaps be assumed that his specific contributions did not begin until this point and that the other 9 ll. are to be found among those added or altered in the first edn proper. A writer in the *Times Lit. Supp.*, 28 Jan. 1955, p. 64, has suggested that ll. 279–80, 401–4, all added in the 1st edn, show Johnson's hand, but the question must remain open.

The poem, under its new title *The Traveller, or A Prospect of Society*, was published by Newbery in quarto, price 1s 6d, on 19 Dec. 1764. There are four states of the 1st edn, two dated 1764 and two 1765. In the first state, the Dedication was merely: 'This Poem is inscribed to the Rev. Henry Goldsmith, M.A. by his most affectionate brother, Oliver Goldsmith.' In the second state the Dedication was expanded to 6 paragraphs and G.'s name for the first time was placed on the title-page of one of his works. No variants in the text of the poem occur within the 1st edn, differences in the four states of the edn affecting only the preliminaries, (for bibliographical details see the article by Todd cited above, pp. 110–11). A long extract from the poem was printed in the *London Chronicle*, 18–20 Dec. 1764, p. 589, being introduced with the comment that it showed 'a degree of poetical merit beyond what we have seen for several years'. Johnson himself went further, in the *Critical Review* xviii (Dec. 1764) 462, where he described the poem as 'a production to which, since the death of Pope, it will not be easy to find any thing equal'. (He made a similar remark to Boswell later, *Life* ii 5.) In the same month the *Gentleman's Mag.* xxxiv 594, was equally cordial, and, after some minor objections, John Langhorne in the *Monthly Review* xxxii (Jan. 1765) 47–55, ended by commending it 'as a work of very considerable merit'. It received further praise in the *St James's Chronicle*, 7–9 Feb. 1765. A 2nd edn, with some revisions, appeared on 14 March 1765, the 4th on 6 Aug. 1765 and six more in G.'s lifetime. The 6th edn contained G.'s final corrections and alterations. For the identification of an 8th edn, advertised on 29 Feb. 1772 but dated 1770, see A. Friedman, *Studies in Bibliography* xiii (1960) 234–5.

G. was paid 20 guineas for *The Traveller*, but a second payment of the same sum and for the same poem, that is recorded in Newbery's papers in 1766, suggests that the publisher shared some of his profits with the poet: see Temple Scott, p. 139. No doubt as important to G. was the new celebrity which resulted from the success of the poem. Its effect on his reputation may have been exaggerated (see R. S. Crane's corrective account of G.'s reputation before *The Traveller*, in *Life of Johnson* iii 502), but it did establish him for the first time as an eminent man of letters. His talents had usually been underestimated because of his clumsiness in 'polite society' where he seems to have been regarded as little more than a literary hack. This no doubt explains the widespread belief that Johnson had written the poem for him. See, for example, a conversation recorded by Boswell (*Life of Johnson* iii 252): 'Goldsmith being mentioned, Johnson observed, that it was long before his merit came to be acknowledged. That he once complained to him, in ludicrous terms of distress, 'Whenever I write any thing, the publick *make a point* to know nothing about it;' but that his 'Traveller' brought him into high reputation'. Johnson went on to explain that 'the partiality of his friends was all against him. It was with difficulty we could give him a hearing. Goldsmith had no settled notions upon any subject; so he talked always at random. It seemed to be his intention to blurt out whatever was in his mind, and see what would become of it . . . I remember Chamier, after talking with him for some time, said, "Well, I do believe he wrote this poem himself: and, let me tell you, that is believing a great deal."' (For the continuation of this conversation, see l. 1*n*.) According to Reynolds (*Portraits* p. 44), 'His *Traveller* produced an eagerness unparalleled to see the author'; and Mrs Cholmondeley, after hearing Johnson read the poem aloud, declared, 'I never more shall think Dr. Goldsmith ugly', *Johnsonian Miscellanies*, ed. G. B. Hill, ii 268. Edmond Malone recorded that Mark Akenside was 'very liberal' in praise of the poem and maintained from the first that Johnson could not have written it (Sir James Prior, *Life of Malone* (1860) p. 413–14). William Cooke, *European Mag.* xxiv (1793) 93, stated that *The Traveller* 'not only established him as an Author of celebrity among the Booksellers, but introduced him to several of the literati and men of eminence'. In a later article in the same volume (p. 171), Cooke tells a ludicrous story of G.'s patronizing airs with the Irish playwright Hugh Kelly because of his dinner engagements with Burke, Dr Nugent and Topham Beauclerck, invitations representative of his new social success. It was apparently as a result of the publication of *The Traveller* that G. became acquainted with Robert Nugent, later Lord Clare (see *The Haunch of Venison*, p. 696), and, according to Hawkins, *Life of Johnson* (1787) pp. 418–19, he was then offered the patronage of the Earl of Northumberland (see *Edwin and Angelina*, p. 597).

T. S. Eliot has remarked that G.'s originality as a poet lay in his 'having the old and the new in such just proportion that there is no conflict; he is Augustan and also sentimental and rural without discordance'. Eliot added of G.'s imitation of Pope's form that 'to be original with the *minimum* of alteration is sometimes more distinguished than to be original with the *maximum* of alteration' (Introduction to the Haslewood Books edn of

Johnson's *London* and *The Vanity of Human Wishes*, 1930). It is clear from the comments of G.'s early reviewers that *The Traveller* was welcomed as a return to the Augustan tradition after the experiments and excesses of English poetry since the death of Pope in 1745. G.'s own critical writings indicate his dislike of the poetry of most of his bolder contemporaries and his conviction that English poetry had declined sharply in recent years (see the Dedication below). *The Traveller* is in fact a late example of a favourite Augustan genre, the Horatian verse-epistle, which had received its classic expression in Pope's *Moral Essays* (or *Epistles to Several Persons* 1731–5) and *Essay on Man* (1733–4).

G. was probably influenced by one particular kind of verse epistle of which several earlier examples are found, the verse letter from abroad. His own poem in tone, content and in the occasional phrase often resembles Lord Lyttelton's epistles written to friends in England during his travels on the Continent, which contrast the political state of various nations with English liberty. His epistle *To the Rev Dr Ayscough* (written 1728) discusses France; his *Epistle to Mr Pope* (1730) deals with Italy; and *To My Lord Hervey* (written 1730) describes his discovery on his return to England of the happiness which he had sought in vain abroad: his conclusion, close to G.'s, is that 'In our own breasts the source of Pleasure lies'. These epistles were published together in Dodsley's *Collection* in 1748. An earlier example of the same kind of poem, which probably influenced both Lyttelton and G., is Addison's *Letter from Italy* (1703).

In another aspect *The Traveller* can be related to the genre of the topographical poem, really introduced into English poetry by Denham's *Cooper's Hill*. Although G.'s poem is at times intended to be a literally panoramic poem, its survey of various nations is essentially imaginative and its true concern is with moral landscapes. G.'s interest in the character of these nations is related to the problem of the connection between climate and character which occupied many writers during the 1740s and the following decades: see Montesquieu's *L'Esprit des Loix* (1748), Gray's *Alliance of Education and Government* (1748–9), and François Espiard de La Borde, *The Spirit of Nations. Translated from the French* (1753). G. also reflects the increasing primitivistic interest in the virtues of simple, rugged peoples, as contrasted with the decadent sophistication of civilized life, found, for example, in the discussion of Italy, Switzerland and England in Thomson's *Liberty* (1735–6), which considers the relationship between political liberty and other virtues in a nation, with a primitivistic emphasis on the virtues of the Swiss (for the background to Thomson's thought see notes to ll. 105–64 and 165–238). But it is characteristic of G. that he carefully balances the good and the bad to be found under each of the governments he considers. The hardy virtues of the Swiss are given their due but not a sentimental, primitivistic celebration: G. balances against their virtues the limitations of sensibility and imagination imposed by their surroundings.

The balanced, antithetical nature of the discussion, weighing up the good and the bad in each nation, the part played by Nature on the one hand and

Art on the other (ll. 81–8), relates G. to his Augustan predecessors; and it is reflected in the careful balance and design of the poem as a whole (cp. Macaulay's comment: 'No philosophical poem, ancient or modern, has a plan so noble, and at the same time so simple', *Encyclopaedia Britannica* (8th edn, 1856, s.v. 'Goldsmith'). Again, the didactic tone, the abstract and conventional poetic diction and the tendency to epigram emphasize the poem's Augustan affiliations. What is new is the introduction at the beginning and end of the poem of the poet's own predicament and sensibility as matters of interest and importance in such a poem. The traditional objective concerns of the poem are presented within a highly subjective framework. But the individual search for private happiness, which is the basic theme of the poem, is not made to carry the whole weight. It is allowed to merge with the more familiar search for happiness in a particular society and the discussion of human happiness in general, a subject which links the poem with yet another earlier poem, Pope's *Essay on Man*, Bk iv of which, a discussion of human happiness, G. frequently echoes. Accordingly the personal sense of loss and deprivation in the poem is countered by an assertion of the importance of the general happiness of mankind and of the benevolence of the Creation.

The poem's versification reveals the same proportion of old and new. For a detailed discussion, see Wallace C. Brown, *The Triumph of Form* (Chapel Hill, 1948) pp. 148–53. G. is somewhat less strict than Pope in closing his couplets, and his sentences tend to be longer and more meditative: but there is still little enjambement, the rhymes are emphatically masculine and the syntax predominantly parallel, expressing contrasts and parallels in thought (e.g. ll. 113–18, 127–30, 297–312). G.'s main contribution to the couplet lies in his use of word repetition, which Pope had reserved for the emotional climax or conclusion of an epistle, but which G. uses freely for general emphatic effects (ll. 313–16), structural unity (ll. 177–80), lyrical effects (ll. 11–22, 335–8) and contrasts in movement, to which metre and alliteration also contribute (ll. 321–4). Johnson's lines in the poem, stoic in mood and Augustan in style, contrast markedly with G.'s more sentimental manner.

The text followed here is that of the 6th edn, which contains G.'s final revisions. Variants are recorded from *A Prospect of Society*, the 1st and 2nd edns, with a few variants from edns later than the 6th, which almost certainly have no authority.

TO THE REV. HENRY GOLDSMITH

Dear Sir,
    I am sensible that the friendship between us can

¶ 15. *Dedication*. References to *ed 1* in the textual notes do not include the first state in which the Dedication consisted of one sentence only. See headnote.

d. 1. The Rev Henry Goldsmith (d. 1768), G.'s elder brother, is described

acquire no new force from the ceremonies of a dedication;
5 and perhaps it demands an excuse thus to prefix your
name to my attempts, which you decline giving with
your own. But as a part of this poem was formerly
written to you from Switzerland, the whole can now,
with propriety, be only inscribed to you. It will also
10 throw a light upon many parts of it, when the reader
understands that it is addressed to a man, who, despising
fame and fortune, has retired early to happiness and
obscurity, with an income of forty pounds a year.

I now perceive, my dear brother, the wisdom of your
15 humble choice. You have entered upon a sacred office,
where the harvest is great and the labourers are but
few; while you have left the field of ambition, where the
labourers are many and the harvest not worth carrying
away. But of all kinds of ambition, what from the re-
20 finement of the times, from differing systems of criticism
and from the divisions of party, that which pursues
poetical fame is the wildest.

Poetry makes a principal amusement among un-
polished nations; but in a country verging to the ex-
25 tremes of refinement, painting and music come in for a
share. As these offer the feeble mind a less laborious
entertainment, they at first rival poetry and at length

by his sister, Mrs Hodson (*Letters* p. 162), as 'remarkable for his polite
Learning . . . he marrying at nineteen a Lady he liked left the College &
retired to the Country and at his fathers Death possessed his Living [of
Kilkenny West, near Lissoy]'.

d. *13. forty pounds a year*] Cp. *Deserted Village* 141–2 (p. 682).

d. *16–19.* Cp. *Present State of Learning* (1759) p. 104: 'The harvest of wit is
gathered in, and little is left for him, except to glean what others have
thought unworthy their bringing away.'

d. *19–21. what from . . . party*] as things are now circumstanced, perhaps *edd*
1–5.

d. *20. different*] differing *ed* 7.

d. *22. wildest*] *ed 1 adds*: What from the encreased refinement of the times,
from the diversity of judgements produced by opposing systems of criti-
cism, and from the more prevalent divisions of opinion influenced by party,
the strongest and happiest efforts can expect to please but in a very narrow
circle. Though the poet was as sure of his aim as the imperial archer of anti-
quity, who boasted that he never missed the heart; yet would many of his
shafts now fly at random, for the heart is too often in the wrong place. *Edd*
2–5 omit the final sentence.

d. *26. As these*] And as they *edd 1–5.*

supplant her; they engross all that favour once shown to
her, and though but younger sisters, seize upon the
30   elder's birthright.

Yet, however this art may be neglected by the power-
ful, it is still in greater danger from the mistaken efforts
of the learned to improve it. What criticisms have we
not heard of late in favour of blank verse and Pindaric
35   odes, choruses, anapaests and iambics, alliterative care
and happy negligence. Every absurdity has now a
champion to defend it, and as he is generally much in
the wrong, so he has always much to say; for error is
ever talkative.

40   But there is an enemy to this art still more dangerous,
I mean party. Party entirely distorts the judgment and
destroys the taste. When the mind is once infected with
this disease, it can only find pleasure in what contributes
to increase the distemper. Like the tiger, that seldom
45   desists from pursuing man after having once preyed
upon human flesh, the reader, who has once gratified
his appetite with calumny, makes, ever after, the most
agreeable feast upon murdered reputation. Such
readers generally admire some half-witted thing, who

d. 28–9. that favour . . . her] favour to themselves edd 1–5.
d. 31–9. G. was consistently unsympathetic to the formal alternatives to the
Augustan couplet with which contemporary poets were experimenting. In
his Present State of Learning p. 148, he had blamed criticism for misleading the
poet: 'There is scarce an error of which our present writers are guilty, that
does not arise from this source. From this proceeds the affected obscurity of
our odes, the tuneless flow of our blank verse, the pompous epithet, laboured
diction, and every other deviation from common sense, which procures
the poet the applause of the connoisseur'. He referred again to 'the unmusical
flow of blank verse', in The Bee No. vii, 17 Nov. 1759. G.'s objections to
Pindaric odes are expounded in his review of Gray's Odes in the Monthly
Review in Sept. 1757 (Works ed. Friedman, i 112–7). G. also parodied Gray's
Bard in 'The Indigent Philosopher' in Lloyd's Evening Post, 29 Jan.–1 Feb.
1762 (Works iii 190), introduced as 'a blank Pindaric Ode . . . of my own
making; consisting of Strophe, Antistrophe, Trochaics, Iambics, Sapphics,
Pentameters, Exameters, and a Chorus.' In 'The Futility of Criticism' in
the Weekly Mag. 12 Jan. 1760 (Works iii 53), G. discusses alliteration as one
of the fashionable 'modes' of his day.
d. 38–9. say; . . . talkative.] say. ed 1.
d. 42–3. When . . . disease, it] A mind capable of relishing general beauty,
when once infected with this disease, edd 1–5.
d. 49–53. Prior, Life ii 54, quotes an article in the St James's Chronicle (7–9
Feb. 1765) which interprets this passage as 'a Reflection on the Memory of

50 wants to be thought a bold man, having lost the character
of a wise one. Him they dignify with the name of poet;
his tawdry lampoons are called satires, his turbulence is
said to be force, and his frenzy fire.

What reception a poem may find, which has neither
55 abuse, party nor blank verse to support it, I cannot tell,
nor am I solicitous to know. My aims are right. Without
espousing the cause of any party, I have attempted to
moderate the rage of all. I have endeavoured to show
that there may be equal happiness in states, that are
60 differently governed from our own; that every state has
a particular principle of happiness, and that this principle
in each may be carried to a mischievous excess. There
are few can judge better than yourself how far these
positions are illustrated in this poem.

65   I am, dear Sir,
              Your most affectionate brother,
                    OLIVER GOLDSMITH.

the late Mr. Churchill, whose Talents as a Poet were so greatly and so
deservedly admired, that, during his short Reign, his Merit, in great Measure,
eclipsed that of others; and we think it no mean Acknowledgement of the
Excellencies of this Poem to say, that "like the Stars, they appear the more
brilliant now the Sun of our Poetry is gone down."' Charles Churchill had
died on 4 Nov. 1764 at the age of 33, after establishing himself as a vigorous
satirist with *The Rosciad* (1761) and a series of other poems.

d. 52. tawdry lampoons] lampoons *edd 1–5.*

d. 56. solicitous] much solicitous *edd 1–5.*

d. 59. states, that are] other states though *edd 1–5.*

d. 60. every] each *edd 1–5.*

d. 61. particular] peculiar *edd 1–5.*

d. 62. each] each state, and in our own in particular *edd 1–5.*

d. 65. dear Sir] Sir *edd 1–5.*

1–72. There is no version of these lines in *Prospect.*

1. According to Boswell (*Life of Johnson* iii 252–3) Johnson stated in 1778
that Chamier once asked G. 'what he meant by *slow*' in this line. 'Did he
mean tardiness of locomotion? Goldsmith, who would say something with-
out consideration, answered, "Yes." I was sitting by, and said, "No, Sir;
you do not mean tardiness of locomotion; you mean, that sluggishness of
mind which comes upon a man in solitude." Chamier believed then that I
had written the line as much as if he had seen me write it.' But *slow* may
be taken to mean both slow-moving *and* correspondingly melancholy.

Mitford cites Ovid, *Metamorphoses* xiv 217: *Solus, inops, exspes, leto
poenaeque relictus* (alone, helpless and hopeless, abandoned to death and

Remote, unfriended, melancholy, slow,
Or by the lazy Scheldt or wandering Po;
Or onward, where the rude Carinthian boor
Against the houseless stranger shuts the door;
5 Or where Campania's plain forsaken lies,
A weary waste expanding to the skies:
Where'er I roam, whatever realms to see,
My heart untravelled fondly turns to thee;
Still to my brother turns with ceaseless pain,
10 And drags at each remove a lengthening chain.

Eternal blessings crown my earliest friend,
And round his dwelling guardian saints attend:
Blest be that spot, where cheerful guests retire
To pause from toil, and trim their evening fire;

suffering); and *Ibis* 113: *Exsul, inops erres, alienaque limina lustres* (Mayst thou wander an exile and destitute, and haunt the doors of others).

2. Scheldt] A river rising near Catelet in N. France and flowing through Belgium to Antwerp.   *Po*] The largest river in Italy, dominating the North and including parts of Switzerland and Austria in its basin.

3. Carinthia] An Alpine province in South Austria, which was a Habsburg duchy in G.'s time. Prior (*Life* i 192) states that G., 'being once questioned by Mr. Hickey on the justice of the censure passed upon a people whom other travellers praised for being as good if not better than their neighbours . . . gave as a reason his being once after a fatiguing day's walk, obliged to quit a house he had entered for shelter, and pass part or the whole of the night in seeking another.'

5. Campania] The Roman Campagna. Cp. Addison, *Remarks on Several Parts of Italy* (1705; in *Miscellaneous Works*, ed. A. C. Guthkelch, (1914) ii 91–2) on 'the present desolation of *Italy* . . . . one can scarce imagine how so plentiful a soil should become so miserably unpeopled in comparison of what it once was. We may reckon, by a very moderate computation, more inhabitants in the *Campania* of old *Rome*, than are now in all *Italy*.' Cp. also Thomson, *Liberty* i 123–43.

6. expanding] expanded *edd 1–5*.

7. realms] realm *edd 2–5*.

10. And] Or *edd 2–5*.   Cp. *Citizen* (1762) i 5 (Letter 3): 'The farther I travel I feel the pain of separation with stronger force, those ties that bind me to my native country, and you, are still unbroken. By every remove, I only drag a greater length of chain.' Mitford cites Dryden, *All for Love* II i: 'My life on't, he still drags a chain along, / That needs must clog his flight'; and cp. Dryden, *Secret Love* V i: '[my heart] is still your prisoner, it only draws a longer chain after it.' Cp. also Racine, *Andromaque* I i 43–4: *Tu vis mon désespoir; et tu m'as vu depuis / Traîner de mers en mers ma chaîne et mes ennuis.*

15 Blest that abode, where want and pain repair,
And every stranger finds a ready chair;
Blest be those feasts with simple plenty crowned,
Where all the ruddy family around
Laugh at the jests or pranks that never fail,
20 Or sigh with pity at some mournful tale,
Or press the bashful stranger to his food,
And learn the luxury of doing good.

But me, not destined such delights to share,
My prime of life in wandering spent and care,
25 Impelled, with steps unceasing, to pursue
Some fleeting good, that mocks me with the view;
That, like the circle bounding earth and skies,
Allures from far, yet, as I follow, flies;
My fortune leads to traverse realms alone,
30 And find no spot of all the world my own.

Even now, where Alpine solitudes ascend,
I sit me down a pensive hour to spend;
And, placed on high above the storm's career,
Look downward where an hundred realms appear;
35 Lakes, forests, cities, plains extending wide,
The pomp of kings, the shepherd's humbler pride.

When thus Creation's charms around combine,

17. with . . . crowned] where mirth and peace abound *edd 1–5*.
22. Prior compares Garth, *Claremont* 148–9, of the druids: 'Hard was their lodging, homely was their food, / For all their luxury was doing good.'
24. prime of life] G. was probably 25 when he went abroad.
25–8. Cp. *The Bee* No i, 'Letter from a Traveller': 'When will my wanderings be at an end? When will my restless disposition give me leave to enjoy the present hour? When at Lyons, I thought all happiness lay beyond the Alps; when in Italy, I found myself still in want of something, and expected to leave solicitude behind me by going into Romelia, and now you find me turning back, still expecting ease every where but where I am'; *Citizen* (1762) ii 37 (Letter 73): 'hope . . . dresses out the distant prospect in fancied beauty, some happiness in long perspective still beckons me to pursue' etc; and *Vicar* ch. xxix: 'death, the only friend of the wretched, for a little while mocks the weary traveller with the view, and like his horizon, still flies before him'.
30. Prior, *Written . . . in the Beginning of Robe's Geography* 5–7: 'My destined Miles I shall have gone, / By THAMES or MAESE, by PO or RHONE, / And found no Foot of Earth my own'.
35. extending] extended *edd 1–5*.

Amidst the store should thankless pride repine?
Say, should the philosophic mind disdain
40   That good, which makes each humbler bosom vain?
Let school-taught pride dissemble all it can,
These little things are great to little man;
And wiser he, whose sympathetic mind
Exults in all the good of all mankind.
45   Ye glittering towns, with wealth and splendour
        crowned,
Ye fields, where summer spreads profusion round,
Ye lakes, whose vessels catch the busy gale,
Ye bending swains, that dress the flowery vale,
For me your tributary stores combine;
50   Creation's heir, the world, the world is mine.

As some lone miser visiting his store,
Bends at his treasure, counts, re-counts it o'er;
Hoards after hoards his rising raptures fill,
Yet still he sighs, for hoards are wanting still:
55   Thus to my breast alternate passions rise,
Pleased with each good that heaven to man supplies:
Yet oft a sigh prevails and sorrows fall,
To see the hoard of human bliss so small;
And oft I wish, amidst the scene, to find
60   Some spot to real happiness consigned,
Where my worn soul, each wandering hope at rest,
May gather bliss to see my fellows blest.

But where to find that happiest spot below,

38–40. *In ed 1 only:*
    Amidst the store, 'twere thankless to repine.
    'Twere affectation all, and school-taught pride,
    To spurn the splendid things by heaven supply'd.
45. Thomson has 'glittering towns' in a similar passage, *Summer* 1440.
49–50. Pope, *Essay on Man* i 131–2: 'Ask for what end the heav'nly bodies shine, / Earth for whose use? Pride answers, "'Tis for mine"' *etc.*
50. Creation's tenant, all the world is mine *edd 2–5.*
55. Pope, *Essay on Criticism* 375: 'And bid Alternate Passions fall and rise'.
58. *hoard*] sum *edd 1–5.*
60. The phrasing in which G. describes his search for a 'spot' which guarantees 'happiness' (and cp. the 'happiest spot' of ll. 63 and 66) recalls Pope's conclusion on the matter, *Essay on Man* iv 15: 'Fix'd to no spot is Happiness sincere'.
62. Cp. Pope, *Essay on Man* iii 300: 'And, in proportion as it blesses, blest'.
63. *But*] Yet *edd 1–5.* Cp. Pope, *Essay on Man* iv 1–8, on Happiness,

Who can direct, when all pretend to know?
65 The shuddering tenant of the frigid zone
Boldly proclaims that happiest spot his own,
Extols the treasures of his stormy seas,
And his long nights of revelry and ease;
The naked negro, panting at the line,
70 Boasts of his golden sands and palmy wine,
Basks in the glare or stems the tepid wave,
And thanks his gods for all the good they gave.
Such is the patriot's boast, where'er we roam,
His first, best country ever is at home.
75 And yet, perhaps, if countries we compare,
And estimate the blessings which they share,
Though patriots flatter, still shall wisdom find
An equal portion dealt to all mankind,
As different good, by Art or Nature given,
80 To different nations makes their blessings even.

('Which still so near us, yet beyond us lies'): 'Say, in what mortal soil thou deign'st to grow?'
66. proclaims . . . spot] asserts that country for ed 1.
68. his long] live-long ed 1.   nights] night edd 2–5.
69. negro] Savage edd 2–5.   line] The Equator.
71. Cp. Gray, Agrippina 106–7 and n (p. 37 above).
72. Dryden, Alexander's Feast 106: 'Take the Good the Gods provide thee.'
73. Such is] Nor less Prospect, edd 1–5.
75–7. Prospect and ed 1 have:
             And yet, perhaps, if states with states we scan,
             Or estimate their bliss on Reason's plan,
             Though patriots flatter, and though fools contend,
78. We still shall find the doubtful scale depend Prospect; We still shall find uncertainty suspend ed 1.
      Pope's conclusion, Essay on Man iv 15, 53–4, 61–2, 69 etc. is similar and cp. Johnson's promise to his reader in the Preface to his translation of A Voyage to Abyssinia. By Father Jerome Lobo (1735) p. viii: 'He will discover, what will always be discover'd by a diligent and impartial Enquirer, that wherever Human Nature is to be found, there is a mixture of Vice and Virtue, a contest of Passion and Reason, and that the Creator doth not appear Partial in his Distributions, but has balanced in most Countries their particular Inconveniences by particular Favours.'
79–80. Prospect and ed 1 have:
             Find that each good, by Art or Nature given,
             To these or those, but makes the balance even.
Ed 1 only has an additional couplet:
             Find that the bliss of all is much the same,
             And patrioric [sic] boasting reason's shame.

Nature, a mother kind alike to all,
Still grants her bliss at Labour's earnest call;
With food as well the peasant is supplied
On Idra's cliffs as Arno's shelvy side;
85 And though the rocky-crested summits frown,
These rocks, by custom, turn to beds of down.
From Art more various are the blessings sent:
Wealth, commerce, honour, liberty, content.
Yet these each other's power so strong contest,
90 That either seems destructive of the rest.
Where wealth and freedom reign, contentment fails,
And honour sinks where commerce long prevails.
Hence every state, to one loved blessing prone,
Conforms and models life to that alone.
95 Each to the favourite happiness attends,
And spurns the plan that aims at other ends;
Till, carried to excess in each domain,
This favourite good begets peculiar pain.

82. bliss . . . earnest] blessings at Industry's *Prospect.*
83–4. Not in Prospect and ed 1.
84. cliffs] cliff *edd 2–5.*   *Idra*] It has been suggested that G. meant Lake
Idro in N. Italy; Idra, a village in Sweden; or Idra or Hydra, an Aegean
island; but he probably refers to Idria, a mining town in Carniola, Austria,
in a narrow Alpine valley, famous for its quicksilver mines. In *Animated
Nature* (1774) i 79, he mentions the mines and spells the name Idra once
more. The same spelling occurs in a description of the mines in *Gentleman's
Mag.* xxxvii (1767) 251.   *Arno*] Italian river, running to the sea via
Arezzo, Florence and Pisa.   *shelvy*] Referring presumably to the terraces
on which vines and crops are grown. But Shakespeare uses it differently:
cp. *Merry Wives* III v 15: 'The shore was shelvy and shallow.'
85. the rocky-crested summits] the rigid clime or rough rocks *Prospect*; rough
rocks or gloomy summits *ed 1.*
86. Othello I iii 230–2: 'The tyrant custom . . . / Hath made the flinty and
steel couch of war / My thrice-driven bed of down.'
88. commerce, honour, liberty] splendours, freedom, honor, and *Prospect*;
splendours, honour, liberty *edd 1–5.*
90. destructive] subversive *Prospect.*
91–2. Not in Prospect and edd 1–5.
94. Conforms . . . life] Chiefly conforms itself *Prospect.*
95–104. Not in Prospect.
98. peculiar] Appropriate.

But let us try these truths with closer eyes,
100   And trace them through the prospect as it lies:
Here for a while my proper cares resigned,
Here let me sit in sorrow for mankind,
Like yon neglected shrub at random cast,
That shades the steep and sighs at every blast.

105   Far to the right, where Apennine ascends,
Bright as the summer, Italy extends;
Its uplands sloping deck the mountain's side,
Woods over woods in gay theatric pride;
While oft some temple's mouldering tops between
110   With venerable grandeur mark the scene.

Could Nature's bounty satisfy the breast,
The sons of Italy were surely blest.
Whatever fruits in different climes are found,
That proudly rise or humbly court the ground;
115   Whatever blooms in torrid tracts appear,

99. *try*] view *ed 1.*
99–100. Cp. *Works* ed. Friedman, iii 69: 'Come then, and let us take a view of this earth in which providence has placed us; let us at least examine the outlines of the universal plan; let us survey the various customs of the inhabitants.' In the poem G. imagines himself seated at a point in the Alps from which he can literally see the first three nations he discusses, Italy, Switzerland and France.
101. *proper*] Own, personal.
105–64. G.'s account of Italy belongs to a tradition of political writing–which included Burnet, Addison and Thomson–on that country, which stressed the physical and moral degradation caused by its tyrannic government: see A. D. McKillop, *The Background of Thomson's Liberty* (1951) pp. 26–40.
105. *Apennine*] The Apennine mountains, the backbone of Italy.
107. *Its*] Her *Prospect, edd 1–5.*
108. *Paradise Lost* iv 140–2: 'A Silvan Scene, and as the ranks ascend / Shade above shade, a woodie Theatre / Of stateliest view'; and Pope, *Epistles to Several Persons* iv 60: 'Or scoops in circling theatres the Vale.'
109. *tops*] top *edd 1–5.*
110. *mark*] marks *Prospect, edd 1–5.*
111. With this description of the luxurious fertility of Italy cp. Addison's *Letter from Italy* 55–68, and the later part of the poem which contrasts rugged Britain's love of liberty with Italian subjection to tyranny.
113. *are*] were *edd 5–6.* (The change in *ed 5* seems to have been an error: the context demands the present tense.)

Whose bright succession decks the varied year;
Whatever sweets salute the northern sky
With vernal lives that blossom but to die;
These here disporting own the kindred soil,
120 Nor ask luxuriance from the planter's toil;
While sea-born gales their gelid wings expand
To winnow fragrance round the smiling land.

But small the bliss that sense alone bestows,
And sensual bliss is all the nation knows.
125 In florid beauty groves and fields appear,
Man seems the only growth that dwindles here.
Contrasted faults through all his manners reign:
Though poor, luxurious; though submissive, vain;
Though grave, yet trifling; zealous, yet untrue;
130 And even in penance planning sins anew.
All evils here contaminate the mind,
That opulence departed leaves behind;
For wealth was theirs, nor far removed the date,
When commerce proudly flourished through the state;
135 At her command the palace learned to rise,
Again the long-fall'n column sought the skies;

116. That dress in bright succession round the year *Prospect*.
118. *lives*] leaves *Prospect*.
121. *gelid*] Normally means 'extremely cold' but here 'refreshingly cool' seems more appropriate (cp. *gelidis convallibus Haemi*, Virgil, *Georgics* ii 488).
122. *winnow*] 'To fan; to beat as with wings' (Johnson). Cp. *Paradise Lost* v 269–70: 'Now on the polar windes, then with quick Fann / Winnows the buxom Air.'
124. *the*] this *edd 1–5*.   Cp. *Citizen* (1762) i 263 (renumbered Letter 59) where G. refers to the Italians as 'a people whose only happiness lies in sensual refinement.'
125. In rich luxuriance plants and flowers appear *Prospect*.
126. *Man seems*] Men seem *Prospect, edd 1–5*.
127–30. Cp. Lord Lyttelton, *To the Rev Dr Ayscough* 80–1, on the French: 'Whose people vain in want, in bondage blest, / Though plundered, gay; industrious, though oppressed'.
127. *his*] their *Prospect, edd 1–5*.
131. *evils here contaminate*] ills are here to pejorate *Prospect*.
133. *nor*] not *edd 8–9* (presumably in error, cp. l. 348).
134–8. Thomson, *Autumn* 134–40, similarly describes the effect on the arts (in England) of commerce and industry.
134. *commerce*] Notably at Genoa and Venice.

The canvas glowed beyond even Nature warm,
The pregnant quarry teemed with human form;
Till, more unsteady than the southern gale,
140   Commerce on other shores displayed her sail;
While nought remained of all that riches gave,
But towns unmanned and lords without a slave;
And late the nation found, with fruitless skill,
Its former strength was but plethoric ill.

145   Yet still the loss of wealth is here supplied
By arts, the splendid wrecks of former pride;
From these the feeble heart and long-fall'n mind
An easy compensation seem to find.
Here may be seen, in bloodless pomp arrayed,

137. beyond even Nature] with animation *Prospect*.   Cp. Addison, *Letter from Italy* 98, of Raphael: 'So warm with life his blended colours glow.' Cunningham also cites Pope, *Imitations of Horace, Ep.* II i 147–8: 'Then Marble soften'd into life grew warm, / And yielding Metal flow'd to human form'.

139. Till] But *Prospect, edd 1–5.*   *unsteady*] unstable *Prospect*.

140. Commerce . . . displayed] Soon Commerce turn'd on other shores *Prospect, edd 1–5.*   G. has in mind the discovery of America and of a route to the East via the Cape of Good Hope, which resulted in the decline of Venice and Genoa in mercantile importance.

141–2. Not in Prospect or ed 1.

143–4. Omitted from edd 2–5.

144. Its . . . but] Their . . . now *Prospect, ed 1.*   Johnson defines a 'plethora' as 'The state in which the vessels are fuller of humours than is agreeable to a natural state of health.' Cp. *Citizen* (1762) i 98 (renumbered Letter 25): 'In short, the state resembled one of those bodies bloated with disease, whose bulk is only a symptom of its wretchedness.' Cp. also *Deserted Village* 389–94 (p. 693).

145–6. Yet, though to fortune lost, there still abide / Some splendid arts, the wrecks *Prospect*; *and ed 1, with* here *for* there.

147. these] which *Prospect, ed 1.*

148. seem] seems *Prospect*.

149. bloodless pomp] G. echoes Pope's description of the Lord Mayor's procession, *Dunciad* i 87: 'Pomps without guilt, of bloodless swords and maces'.

149–58. For the Italian academies flourishing at this time, see Vernon Lee [Viola Paget], 'The Arcadian Academy' in *Studies of the 18th Century in Italy* (1880) pp. 7–64; and F. A. Pottle, 'Boswell as Icarus', *Restoration and 18th Century Literature*, ed. C. Camden (1963), pp. 389–406. G. wrote derisively of them several times: e.g. *Present State of Learning* (1759) pp. 50–1: 'Happy country, where the pastoral age begins to revive! Where the wits even of Rome are united into a rural groupe of nymphs and swains, under

150 The pasteboard triumph and the cavalcade;
Processions formed for piety and love,
A mistress or a saint in every grove.
By sports like these are all their cares beguiled,
The sports of children satisfy the child;
155 Each nobler aim, repressed by long control,

the appellation of modern Arcadians. Where in the midst of porticos, processions, and cavalcades, abbes turn'd into shepherds, and shepherdesses without sheep, indulge their innocent *divertimenti.*' There is similar mockery in *The Bee* No. vi, 10 Nov. 1759 and in an essay on the Coronation in the *Public Ledger*, 10 Sept. 1761 (*Works* ed. Friedman, iii 170–1): 'A city when at length debauched into a love of processions and cavalcades, for such passions encrease by indulgence, loses all its manly severity, and every incentive to true glory'; and *ibid* 171: 'a kingdom may be compared to a single individual in this respect, and when no arts are encouraged but the arts of luxury, every mind will be set upon trifles, the inhabitants must necessarily degenerate, till all at last, like the modern Italians, they seem castrated at a single blow. When I turn my eyes to modern Italy, that country of cavalcade, pageant, and frippery, their excesses in this respect, in some measure excite my pitty and contempt. Their passion for finery is in general in a reciprocal proportion to the beggary of the state. To think of cities laying out immense sums in adorning a temple of pasteboard, while their very walls are actually falling to ruin.'
153–4. Cp. the story told by Reynolds to Mrs Gwyn (Prior, *Life* ii 33): 'Either Reynolds, or a mutual friend who immediately communicated the story to him, calling at the lodgings of the Poet opened the door without ceremony, and discovered him not in meditation, or in the throes of poetic birth, but in the boyish office of teaching a favourite dog to sit upright upon its haunches, or as is commonly said, to beg. Occasionally he glanced his eye over his desk, and occasionally shook his finger at the unwilling pupil in order to make him retain his position; while on the page before him was written that couplet [ll. 153–4], with the ink of the second line still wet, from the description of Italy'. G.'s visitor bantered him and the poet admitted at once 'that the amusement in which he had been engaged had given birth to the idea'.
153. By] At *Prospect.*
154. Edd 1–5 add:

> At sports like these, while foreign arms advance,
> In passive ease they leave the world to chance.

So *Prospect, with* They proudly swell, and leave *in the second line.*
155. Each nobler aim repressed by] When strenuous aims have suffer'd *Prospect*; When struggling Virtue sinks by *ed 1*; When noble aims have suffer'd *edd 2–5.*

Now sinks at last or feebly mans the soul;
While low delights, succeeding fast behind,
In happier meanness occupy the mind:
As in those domes, where Caesars once bore sway,
160 Defaced by time and tottering in decay,
There in the ruin, heedless of the dead,
The shelter-seeking peasant builds his shed,
And, wondering man could want the larger pile,
Exults, and owns his cottage with a smile.

165   My soul, turn from them; turn we to survey
Where rougher climes a nobler race display,
Where the bleak Swiss their stormy mansions tread,
And force a churlish soil for scanty bread.
No product here the barren hills afford,
170 But man and steel, the soldier and his sword;
No vernal blooms their torpid rocks array,
But winter lingering chills the lap of May;
No zephyr fondly sues the mountain's breast,
But meteors glare and stormy glooms invest.

175   Yet still, even here, content can spread a charm,

156. *Now sinks*] They leave *Prospect*; She leaves *ed 1*; They sink *edd 2–5*.
mans] man *Prospect*, *edd 2–5*.
159. *domes*] Buildings.
160. *Defaced . . . tottering*] But now by time dismantled *Prospect*.
161. *There in*] Amidst *Prospect*, *edd 1–5*.
165–238. See A. D. McKillop, *The Background of Thomson's Seasons* (1942)
pp. 122–4, for the character of the Swiss in the primitivistic literary tradition.
To some extent G. adopts the primitivist theory that 'the great compen-
sation for simple people in barren places is liberty', but any tendency to
over-idealization is checked by his theory that good and evil are balanced
in every condition.
169–70. Swiss mercenaries were employed by other nations for many
centuries.
171. *blooms . . . array*] bloom . . . display *Prospect*.
171. *torpid*] Barren, unproductive.
172. *lap of May*] Cp. Gray, *Progress of Poesy* 84 *n* (p. 172).
173. *sues*] sooths *Prospect*, *edd 1–5*.   *sues*] Woos or courts.   *the moun-
tain's breast*] Cp. Milton, *L'Allegro* 73: 'Mountains on whose barren brest'.
174. *stormy glooms*] frowning storms *Prospect*.   *invest*] Enclose.
175–8. G. had written similarly of the Lapps in 'A Comparative View of
Races and Nations' in the *Royal Mag.* in June 1760 (*Works*, ed. Friedman, iii
70): 'Heaven seems to adapt the inhabitants to the miserable region in which
they are placed . . . these poor people, happy in their native stupidity, are

Redress the clime and all its rage disarm.
Though poor the peasant's hut, his feasts though small,
He sees his little lot the lot of all;
Sees no contiguous palace rear its head
180   To shame the meanness of his humble shed;
No costly lord the sumptuous banquet deal
To make him loathe his vegetable meal;
But calm, and bred in ignorance and toil,
Each wish contracting, fits him to the soil.
185   Cheerful at morn he wakes from short repose,
Breasts the keen air and carols as he goes;
With patient angle trolls the finny deep,
Or drives his venturous ploughshare to the steep;
Or seeks the den where snow-tracks mark the way,
190   And drags the struggling savage into day.
At night returning, every labour sped,
He sits him down the monarch of a shed;
Smiles by his cheerful fire and round surveys
His children's looks, that brighten at the blaze;
195   While his loved partner, boastful of her hoard,
Displays her cleanly platter on the board;
And haply too some pilgrim, thither led,
With many a tale repays the nightly bed.

perfectly satisfied, enjoy the uncertain meal with a voracious pleasure, and desire no more; for they know no better.'
176. Cp. *Deserted Village* 422 (p. 694).
179. Cp. *Deserted Village* 303–4 (p. 688).
180. shed] Any humble dwelling (cp. 192, 203).
181. costly] Lavish.
182. Cp. *Edwin and Angelina* 49 (p. 600).
186. Breasts] Quoted in later edns of his *Dictionary* by Johnson to illustrate this verb, 'To meet in front'. It was often emended without authority to 'Breathes' in late eighteenth and nineteenth century edns.
187. angle] Fishing rod.   *troll*] 'To fish for a pike with a rod which has a pulley towards the bottom, which I suppose gives occasion to the term' (Johnson). So Gay, *Rural Sports* i 264, 'troll for pikes'.
190. savage] Wild animal. Cp. Gray, *Education and Government* 93 (p. 99). For a similar usage by G., cp. *Citizen* (1762) i 113, (Letter 28).
191. sped] Achieved, completed.
196. her] the *Prospect, edd 1–5.*
197. Cp. *Deserted Village* 155–8 (p. 683).
198. nightly] For the night. Cp. *Othello* IV iii 16: 'nightly wearing'.

Thus every good his native wilds impart
200 Imprints the patriot passion on his heart,
And even those ills, that round his mansion rise,
Enhance the bliss his scanty fund supplies.
Dear is that shed to which his soul conforms,
And dear that hill which lifts him to the storms;
205 And as a child, when scaring sounds molest,
Clings close and closer to the mother's breast,
So the loud torrent and the whirlwind's roar
But bind him to his native mountains more.

Such are the charms to barren states assigned;
210 Their wants but few, their wishes all confined.
Yet let them only share the praises due:
If few their wants, their pleasures are but few;
For every want that stimulates the breast,
Becomes a source of pleasure when redressed.
215 Whence from such lands each pleasing science flies,

200. on] at *Prospect*.
201–2. Not in Prospect and ed 1.
203. conforms] 'To reduce to the like appearance, shape, or manner, with something else' (Johnson). Cp. G. on the Lapps in 'A Comparative View of Races and Nations' (see ll. 175–8*n*), *Works* ed. Friedman, iii 70–1: 'This is a picture of nature, conforming to the hard rules of necessity. Knowledge would only serve to make them miserable, only shew them the horrors of their situation, without lending them a clue to escape. They seem made for the climate they inhabit; a climate which they love, and they only can love. Here, amidst rocks, in winter covered with snow, and in summer with moss, they lead a life of contented solitude'.
205. child] babe, *Prospect, edd 1–5.*
209. Such] These *Prospect, edd 1–5.*
210. but] are *Prospect, edd 1–5.*
213–14. G. believed that 'luxury' was inevitable and beneficial in so far as it had a civilizing influence on man. To this extent he defends it as here and, most elaborately, in *Citizen*, Letter 11. Cp. *Citizen* (1762) i 35: 'The more various our artificial necessities, the wider is our circle of pleasure; for all pleasure consists in obviating necessities as they rise; luxury, therefore, as it encreases our wants, encreases our capacity for happiness.' For G.'s very different views on pernicious luxury, cp. *Deserted Village* 385 *n*. G. adapted this couplet in *Animated Nature* (1774) ii 123: 'Every want thus becomes a means of pleasure, in the redressing; and the animal that has more desires, may be said to be capable of the greatest variety of happiness.'
213. For] Since *Prospect, edd 1–5.*
214. source . . . redressed] means . . . possess *Prospect.*
215. Whence] Hence *Prospect, edd 1–5.*

That first excites desire and then supplies;
Unknown to them, when sensual pleasures cloy,
To fill the languid pause with finer joy;
Unknown those powers that raise the soul to flame,
220   Catch every nerve and vibrate through the frame.
Their level life is but a smouldering fire,
Unquenched by want, unfanned by strong desire;
Unfit for raptures, or, if raptures cheer
On some high festival of once a year,
225   In wild excess the vulgar breast takes fire,
Till, buried in debauch, the bliss expire.

But not their joys alone thus coarsely flow:
Their morals, like their pleasures, are but low.
For, as refinement stops, from sire to son
230   Unaltered, unimproved the manners run;
And love's and friendship's finely pointed dart
Fall blunted from each indurated heart.
Some sterner virtues o'er the mountain's breast
May sit, like falcons cowering on the nest;
235   But all the gentler morals, such as play
Through life's more cultured walks and charm the way,
These far dispersed on timorous pinions fly,
To sport and flutter in a kinder sky.

222. *Unquenched . . . unfanned*] Nor quench'd . . . nor fan'd *Prospect, edd 1–5*.
228. Cp. 'A Comparative View of Races and Nations' (*Works* ed. Friedman, iii 73): 'They are denied the refinements of sense, and it is impossible therefore to introduce philosophy among them . . . luxury ever preceded wisdom, or, in other words, every country must be luxurious before it can make any progress in human knowledge. Sensuality first finds out the pleasure, and wisdom comments on the discovery.' The same conclusion is reached in *Citizen*, Letters 11 and 82.   *low*] Crude, unsophisticated.
230. *Unaltered . . . manners*] Manners in one unmending track will *Prospect. the*] their *edd 1–5*.
231–2. With the *dart / heart* rhyme cp. Johnson, *London* 168–9 and *Vanity* 151–2.
231. *love's*] love *Prospect*.
232. *indurated*] Hardened.
236. *the*] our *Prospect, edd 1–5*.   In his *Life of Gray* Johnson objected to such recent formations as 'the *cultured* plain', etc. (*Lives of the Poets*, ed. G. B. Hill (1905) iii 434).
237. *dispersed*] disperse *Prospect*.
238. Cp. *Rape of the Lock* i 66: 'And sport and flutter in the Fields of Air'.

To kinder skies, where gentler manners reign,
240   I turn; and France displays her bright domain.
Gay sprightly land of mirth and social ease,
Pleased with thyself, whom all the world can please,
How often have I led thy sportive choir,
With tuneless pipe, beside the murmuring Loire?
245   Where shading elms along the margin grew,
And freshened from the wave the zephyr flew;
And haply, though my harsh touch faltering still
But mocked all tune and marred the dancer's skill,
Yet would the village praise my wondrous power,
250   And dance, forgetful of the noontide hour.
Alike all ages. Dames of ancient days
Have led their children through the mirthful maze,
And the gay grandsire, skilled in gestic lore,
Has frisked beneath the burthen of threescore.

255   So blest a life these thoughtless realms display,
Thus idly busy rolls their world away:
Theirs are those arts that mind to mind endear,

239ff. For other views by G. on France, see *Present State of Learning,* chs. vii
and viii; and *Citizen* (1762) ii 56–9 (renumbered Letter 78).
240. I] We *Prospect, edd 1–5. and]* where *Prospect.*
241. Gay] Thou *Prospect.*
243–54. These lines have always been taken as autobiographical. Cp. George
Primrose in *Vicar* ch. xx: 'I passed among the harmless peasants of Flanders,
and among such of the French as were poor enough to be very merry; for
I ever found them sprightly in proportion to their wants. Whenever I
approached a peasant's house towards night-fall, I played one of my most
merry tunes, and that procured me not only a lodging, but subsistence for
the next day.' Hawkins, *Life of Johnson* (1787) p. 417, describes G.'s pride in
his flute-playing but asserted that he could play 'as many of the vulgar do,
merely by ear'.
244. beside the murmuring] along the sliding *Prospect.*
Spenser has 'tunelesse harpe', *Amoretti* xliv 9.
245. along] beside *Prospect.*
246. wave . . . flew] waves . . . blew *Prospect.*
253. gestic] 'Of or pertaining to bodily movement, esp. dancing' (*OED,*
which gives this as the first instance). G. seems to have formed the word from
the obsolete 'gest' (from Latin *gestus,* 'bearing' or 'carriage'), meaning
'movement of a limb, an action or gesture'. Early erroneous explanations
of its meaning were 'legendary, historical', e.g. Todd's edn of Johnson's
Dictionary (1818).
256. busy] strenuous *Prospect. idly busy]* With this oxymoron cp. Pope,
Elegy to an Unfortunate Lady 81: 'Life's idle business'; and *Satires of Donne*
iv 203: 'The busy, idle Blockheads of the Ball'.

For honour forms the social temper here.
Honour, that praise which real merit gains,
260   Or even imaginary worth obtains,
Here passes current; paid from hand to hand,
It shifts in splendid traffic round the land:
From courts to camps, to cottages it strays,
And all are taught an avarice of praise;
265   They please, are pleased, they give to get esteem,
Till, seeming blest, they grow to what they seem.

But while this softer art their bliss supplies,
It gives their follies also room to rise;
For praise too dearly loved or warmly sought
270   Enfeebles all internal strength of thought;
And the weak soul, within itself unblest,
Leans for all pleasure on another's breast.
Hence ostentation here, with tawdry art,
Pants for the vulgar praise which fools impart;
275   Here vanity assumes her pert grimace,
And trims her robes of frieze with copper lace;
Here beggar pride defrauds her daily cheer,
To boast one splendid banquet once a year;
The mind still turns where shifting fashion draws,

262. in] its *Prospect.*
264. Dobson compares Horace, *Ars Poetica* 324: *praeter laudem nullius avaris* (they craved naught but glory).
265. Pope, *Imitations of Horace, Sat.* II vi 139: 'Each willing to be pleas'd, and please.'
274. Pope, *Epistles to Several Persons* i 119: 'All see 'tis Vice, and itch o vulgar praise.'
275. her] the *Prospect.*
276. frieze] A coarse, warm cloth, i.e. one on which ornate decoration, even if sham, is inappropriate. G. seems to have remembered and combined two passages in Swift, *To Dr Delany* 41–4: 'But as a poor pretending Beau / Because he fain would make a Show, / Nor can afford to buy gold Lace, / Takes up with Copper in the Place'; and *Verses said to be written on the Union* 8: 'Like a rich Coat with Skirts of Frize'. G. is no doubt thinking of copper-lace in his references to 'copper-tailed actresses' in *Citizen* (1762) ii 60, 90 (renumbered Letters 76, 82).
277. cheer] Food.
278. banquet] dish for *Prospect.*
279–80. Prospect has:
    And scarce a man is found, who rightly weighs
    The solid transports of internal praise.
Cp. Pope, *Essay on Man* iv 254–5, and *Vicar* ch. iii: 'His mind had leaned upon

280 Nor weighs the solid worth of self-applause.

     To men of other minds my fancy flies,
     Embosomed in the deep where Holland lies.
     Methinks her patient sons before me stand,
     Where the broad ocean leans against the land,
285 And, sedulous to stop the coming tide,
     Lift the tall rampire's artificial pride.
     Onward, methinks, and diligently slow,
     The firm-connected bulwark seems to grow;
     Spreads its long arms amidst the watery roar,
290 Scoops out an empire and usurps the shore;
     While the pent ocean, rising o'er the pile,
     Sees an amphibious world beneath him smile:
     The slow canal, the yellow-blossomed vale,
     The willow-tufted bank, the gliding sail,
295 The crowded mart, the cultivated plain,
     A new creation rescued from his reign.

     Thus, while around the wave-subjected soil
     Impels the native to repeated toil,

their adulation, and that support taken away, he could find no pleasure in the applause of his heart, which he had never learnt to reverence.'
281–96. Cp. *Animated Nature* i 276: 'the whole kingdom of Holland seems to be a conquest upon the sea, and in a manner rescued from its bosom. The surface of the earth, in this country, is below the level of the bed of the sea; and I remember, upon approaching the coast, to have looked down upon it from the sea, as into a valley.'
281. fancy] G. has to resort to imagination, because he cannot actually see Holland from his mountain-top, as he had the first three nations he described.
284. Mitford compares Dryden, *Annus Mirabilis* 654: 'And view the Ocean leaning on the sky.'
286. rampire] Rampart. This archaic spelling had been frequently used by Dryden in his translation of the *Aeneid*.
287–90. The order of these two couplets is reversed in Prospect and ed 1.
288. grow] go *Prospect, edd 1–5.*
289. Spreads its long] That spreads its *Prospect and ed 1.*   *watery roar*] swelling main *Prospect.*
290. And scoops an empire from the watry reign *Prospect.*
291. the pent ocean] ocean pent, and *Prospect, ed 1.*
294. Sir William Temple, *Observations upon the United Provinces of the Netherlands* (1673) p. 127, mentions 'the infinity of Sails that are seen every where coursing up and down' on the canals.
295. Plains, forests, towns, in gay profusion drest *Prospect.*   *cultivated plain*] Cp. l. 236 n.
296. rescued . . . reign] ravish'd . . . breast *Prospect.*

Industrious habits in each bosom reign,
300 And industry begets a love of gain.
Hence all the good from opulence that springs,
With all those ills superfluous treasure brings,
Are here displayed. Their much-loved wealth imparts
Convenience, plenty, elegance and arts;
305 But view them closer, craft and fraud appear,
Even liberty itself is bartered here.
At gold's superior charms all freedom flies,
The needy sell it and the rich man buys;
A land of tyrants and a den of slaves,
310 Here wretches seek dishonourable graves,
And calmly bent, to servitude conform,
Dull as their lakes that slumber in the storm.

Heavens! how unlike their Belgic sires of old!

299. bosom reign] breast obtain *Prospect, ed 1.*

300. G. refers to 'the avarice of Holland' in *Citizen* (1762) i 16, 245, ii 212–6 (Letters 5, 55, 117).

301–6. These lines summarize G.'s attitude to 'luxury': cp. ll. 213–14 *n.*

305. view them closer] turn the medal *Prospect.*

306. Friedman cites the *Literary Mag.* for Feb. 1758 on Holland: 'No longer do we see there the industrious citizen planning schemes to defend his own liberty and the liberty of Europe, but the servile money-meditating miser, who desires riches to dissipate in luxury, and whose luxuries make him needy.'

309. Cp. *Citizen* (1762) i 147 (Letter 35): 'Into what a state of misery are the modern Persians fallen! A nation once famous for setting the world an example of freedom, is now become a land of tyrants, and a den of slaves.' G. borrowed the phrase from Johnson's 'Introduction to the Political State of Great-Britain', *Literary Mag.* i (1756) 4. Cp. also 'The Revolution in Low Life' in *Works* ed. Friedman, iii 197: 'Venice, Genoa, and Holland, are little better at present than retreats for tyrants and prisons for slaves.'

310. Julius Caesar I ii 137–8: 'And peep about / To find ourselves dishonourable graves.'

311. calmly . . . servitude] calm beneath their injuries *Prospect.*

312. that slumber in the] quiescent in a *Prospect;* that sleep beneath the *edd 1–5.*

313–15. Cp. G.'s compilation, *A Political View of the Result of the Present War with America* (1760–1; printed by Prior, 1837, as *Preface and Introduction to the Seven Years' War*), in *Works* ed. Gibbs, v 8–9, on the Dutch: 'That people, once brave, enthusiasts in the cause of freedom, and able to make their state formidable to their neighbours, are, by a long continuance of peace, divided into faction, set upon private interest, and neither able nor willing to usurp its rights or revenge oppression. This may serve as a memorable instance of what may be the result of a total inattention to war, and

Rough, poor, content, ungovernably bold;
315 War in each breast and freedom on each brow;
How much unlike the sons of Britain now!

Fired at the sound, my genius spreads her wing,
And flies where Britain courts the western spring;
Where lawns extend that scorn Arcadian pride,
320 And brighter streams than famed Hydaspis glide.
There all around the gentlest breezes stray,
There gentle music melts on every spray;
Creation's mildest charms are there combined,
Extremes are only in the master's mind.
325 Stern o'er each bosom reason holds her state,

an utter extirpation of martial ardour. Insulted by the French, threatened by
the English, and almost universally despised by the rest of Europe–how
unlike the brave peasants their ancestors, who spread terror into either
India, and always declared themselves the allies of those who drew the
sword in defence of freedom!' G. may also have had in mind Temple,
Observations upon the Netherlands pp. 154–5: 'The two Characters that are
left by the old *Roman* Writers, of the ancient *Batavi* or *Hollanders*, are, That
they were both the bravest among the *German* Nations, and the most ob-
stinate lovers and defenders of their Liberty'. Temple believed that this valour
had 'but lately decayed; That is, since the whole application of their Natives
had been turn'd to Commerce and Trade, and the vein of their Domestique
lives so much to Parsimony'.

317–24. Cp. the eulogies of Britain in 'A Comparative View of Races and
Nations', *Works* ed. Friedman, iii 67–8, and *Citizen* (1762) ii 196 (Letter
114).

317. Fired] Flush'd *Prospect.*

318. courts] broods *Prospect, ed 1.*

319. scorn] spurn *Prospect.*   *lawns*] At this period, any open space between
woods.

320. Hydaspis] Campaspe *Prospect.*   The Hydaspes is a river in the Punjab in
India, now named the Jhilum. It is mentioned by Horace, *Odes* I xxii 8, as
fabulosus Hydaspes, which G. seems to remember; and by Virgil, *Georgics*
iv 211; *Paradise Lost* iii 435; and Swift, *On Poetry; a Rhapsody* 421.

321–2. Johnson, *London* 220–1: 'There ev'ry bush with nature's musick
rings, / There ev'ry breeze bears health upon its wings'.

325–34. During his tour of the Hebrides with Boswell, Johnson once repeated
these lines 'with such energy, that the tear started into his eye' (*Life* v 344)
With G.'s remarks on the English character, cp. *Citizen* (1762) ii 111–14
(renumbered Letter 91), subtitled 'The influence of climate and soil upon
the tempers and dispositions of the English'.

325–6. Cp. the 4th essay of G.'s 'Comparative View of Races and Nations'
(*Works* ed. Friedman, iii 85), on the English: 'this superiority of reason is

With daring aims irregularly great;
Pride in their port, defiance in their eye,
I see the lords of human kind pass by,
Intent on high designs, a thoughtful band,
330   By forms unfashioned, fresh from Nature's hand;
Fierce in their native hardiness of soul,
True to imagined right, above control,
While even the peasant boasts these rights to scan,
And learns to venerate himself as man.

335   Thine, Freedom, thine the blessings pictured here,
Thine are those charms that dazzle and endear;
Too blest, indeed, were such without alloy,
But fostered even by Freedom, ills annoy:
That independence Britons prize too high,
340   Keeps man from man and breaks the social tie;
The self-dependent lordlings stand alone,
All claims that bind and sweeten life unknown;
Here by the bonds of nature feebly held,

only the consequence of their freedom; they pursue truth wherever it may
lead, regardless of the result', etc; G. also mentions the superiority of the
English in reasoning in *Citizen* (1762) ii 226–9 (renumbered Letter 121).
327. Pride in their] With haughty *Prospect*.
327. Cp. *Citizen* (1762) i 10–11 (Letter 4) on the English:, Pride seems the
source not only of their national vices, but of their national virtues also';
and cp. *ibid* i 16 (Letter 5).
327–8. The order of these two lines is reversed in Prospect and ed 1.
328. human kind pass] mankind pass me *Prospect*.   Cp. *Aeneid* i 282:
Romanos, rerum dominos (Romans, lords of the world).
331. their] a *Prospect and ed 1.*   *hardiness*] hardihood *Prospect*.
332. above] whate'er *Prospect*.
333–4. Cp. *Citizen* (1762) i 11 (Letter 4): 'The lowest mechanic however
[in England] looks upon it as his duty to be a watchful guardian of his
country's freedom, and often uses a language that might seem haughty,
even in the mouth of the great emperor who traces his ancestry to the moon.'
335. Cp. G.'s allusion to 'the passion for liberty, now implanted among the
English' in 'A Comparative View of Races and Nations' (*Works* ed.
Friedman, iii 85).
337. Too blest] Happy *Prospect*.
338. fostered . . . Freedom] even from Freedom issuing *Prospect*.
340. breaks] cuts *Prospect*.
341–2. Not in Prospect and ed 1.
342. claims . . . sweeten] kindred claims that soften *edd 2–5*.
343. Here . . . feebly] There, though by circling deeps together *Prospect; and
ed 1, with* See *for* There.

Minds combat minds, repelling and repelled.
345 Ferments arise, imprisoned factions roar,
Repressed ambition struggles round her shore,
Till over-wrought, the general system feels
Its motions stopped or frenzy fire the wheels.

Nor this the worst. As nature's ties decay,
350 As duty, love and honour fail to sway,
Fictitious bonds, the bonds of wealth and law,
Still gather strength and force unwilling awe.
Hence all obedience bows to these alone,
And talent sinks and merit weeps unknown;
355 Till time may come when, stripped of all her charms,
The land of scholars and the nurse of arms,
Where noble stems transmit the patriot flame,
Where kings have toiled and poets wrote for fame,
One sink of level avarice shall lie,
360 And scholars, soldiers, kings unhonoured die.

Yet think not, thus when Freedom's ills I state,
I mean to flatter kings or court the great.
Ye powers of truth, that bid my soul aspire,

345. Cp. *Citizen*, Letter 121, on 'the disadvantages of a government acting from the immediate influence of reason': 'It is extremely difficult to induce a number of free beings to co-operate for their mutual benefit; every possible advantage will necessarily be sought, and every attempt to procure it must be attended with a new fermentation'. Cp. also Pope, *Windsor Forest* 421: 'There *Faction* roar, *Rebellion* bite her Chain'.
347. Till] While *Prospect, edd 1–5.*
348. stopped] stop *edd 8–9. fire*] fires *edd 1–5.*
349. this the worst] rest their ills *Prospect. nature's ties*] social bonds *Prospect, edd 1–5.*
353. obedience bows] distinction's paid *Prospect.*
354. And talent sinks . . . weeps] Talent must sink . . . weep *Prospect.*
356. The . . . the] That . . . that *Prospect, edd 1–5.* Cp. *Richard II* II i 51–2: 'This nurse, this teeming womb of kings, / Fear'd by their breed.'
357. noble . . . patriot] ancestry avows the noble *Prospect. flame*] claim *Prospect, edd 2–5.*
358. Where kings have toiled] And statesmen toil *Prospect;* And monarchs toil *edd 1–5. wrote*] pant *Prospect, ed 1;* paint *edd 2–5.*
360. scholars, soldiers,] even the worth of *Prospect.*
363–4. Cp. Pope, *Elegy to an Unfortunate Lady* 11–12: 'Why bade ye else ye Pow'rs! her soul aspire / Above the vulgar flight of low desire?'
363–80. For these lines Prospect has only:

Far from my bosom drive the low desire;
365   And thou, fair Freedom, taught alike to feel
The rabble's rage and tyrant's angry steel;
Thou transitory flower, alike undone
By proud contempt or favour's fostering sun,
Still may thy blooms the changeful clime endure,
370   I only would repress them to secure:
For just experience tells, in every soil,
That those who think must govern those that toil;
And all that Freedom's highest aims can reach
Is but to lay proportioned loads on each.
375   Hence, should one order disproportioned grow,
Its double weight must ruin all below.

O then how blind to all that truth requires,
Who think it freedom when a part aspires!
Calm is my soul nor apt to rise in arms,
380   Except when fast-approaching danger warms:
But when contending chiefs blockade the throne,

Think not I mean to sap my country's good;
I would not, heaven be witness! if I could.

Ed 1 has only:

Perish the wish; for, inly satisfy'd,
Above their pomps I hold my ragged pride.

368. proud] cold *edd 2–5.*
371–2. Cp. *Citizen* (1762) ii 143 (renumbered Letter 100), where G. refers to 'those natural or political subordinations which subsist in every society, for in such, tho' dependance is exacted from the inferior, yet the obligation on either side is mutual'; and ii 145 (renumbered Letter 101): 'In every society some men are born to teach, and others to receive instruction; some to work, and others to enjoy in idleness the fruits of their industry; some to govern, and others to obey. Every people, how free soever, must be contented to give up part of their liberty and judgment to those who govern, in exchange for their hopes of security'. There is a similar argument in *Vicar* ch. xix. G. must often have heard Johnson expressing such views, as is clear from Boswell's *Life.*
372. Pope, *Essay on Man* iii 196: 'Thus let the wiser make the rest obey.'
374. Followed in edd 2–5 by:

Much on the low, the rest, as rank supplies,
Should in columnar diminution rise;

375. Hence] While *edd 2–5.*
377–8. Cp. Pope, *Essay on Man* iv 93–4: 'Oh blind to truth, and God's whole scheme below, / Who fancy' etc.
381. contending . . . blockade] I see contention hem *Prospect.*
381–92. As late as 1773 Boswell records G. as saying, 'I'm for Monarchy

> Contracting regal power to stretch their own;
> When I behold a factious band agree
> To call it freedom, when themselves are free;
> 385 Each wanton judge new penal statutes draw,
> Laws grind the poor and rich men rule the law;
> The wealth of climes, where savage nations roam,

to keep us equal' (*Private Papers of James Boswell* (1928–34) vi 130). This argument often appears in G.'s writings. Cp. *Citizen* (1762) i 216–8, 244 (renumbered Letters 50, 56); *History of England in a Series of Letters* (1764) ii 16; *Vicar* ch. xix; *History of England* (1771) Preface, I vii–viii, III 248–9. For a very similar statement of the view that the interests of the middle classes and the monarchy against the aristocracy are identical, cp. Charles Churchill, *The Farewell* 361–8, published in June 1764, a few months before *The Traveller*: 'Let not a mob of tyrants seize the helm, / Nor titled upstarts league to rob the realm; / Let not, whatever other ills assail, / A damned aristocracy prevail. / If, all too short, our course of Freedom run, / 'Tis thy good pleasure we should be undone, / Let us, some comfort in our griefs to bring, / Be slaves to one, and be that one a King.'

381–2. Cp. *History of England* (1771) iv 390, on the early years of George III's reign: 'The strength of the crown was every day declining, while an aristocracy filled up every avenue to the throne, intent only on emoluments, not the duties of office.'

382. Contracting regal . . . their] Abridging kingly . . . her *Prospect.*

383–4. Cp. *Citizen* (1762) i 218 (renumbered Letter 50), where G. says of the Roman senators that they flattered the people 'with a shew of freedom, while themselves only were free'.

385–6. Cp. *Citizen* (1762) ii 65–6 (Letter 80), where G. asserts that 'a mercenary magistrate . . . desires to see penal laws encreased, since he too frequently has it in his power to turn them into instruments of exortion; in such hands the more laws, the wider means, not of satisfying justice, but of satiating avarice.' Earlier (ii 64), he wrote that 'numerous penal laws grind every rank of people, and chiefly those least able to resist oppression, the poor.' Cp. *Vicar* ch. xix, where Dr Primrose refers to 'Holland, Genoa, or Venice, where the laws govern the poor, and the rich govern the law'; and ch. xxvii: 'It is among the citizens of a refined community that penal laws, which are in the hand of the rich, are laid upon the poor.' In *History of England* (1771) iv 83, he was to argue, as here, that monarchy was the only guarantee against what was otherwise 'the insufficiency of any laws to protect the subject, when a majority of the powerful shall think proper to dispense with them'.

385. Each . . . statutes] Senates in blood the code of justic[e] *Prospect.*

386. rich men rule] opulence *Prospect.*

387–8. G. seems to have had in mind Clive's recent victories in India. Cp. *History of England* (1771) iv 382, where he writes of the English there, 'They were gratified in their avarice to its extremest wish; and that wealth which

Pillaged from slaves to purchase slaves at home;
Fear, pity, justice, indignation start,
390   Tear off reserve and bare my swelling heart;
Till half a patriot, half a coward grown,
I fly from petty tyrants to the throne.

Yes, brother, curse with me that baleful hour,
When first ambition struck at regal power;
395   And thus polluting honour in its source,
Gave wealth to sway the mind with double force.
Have we not seen, round Britain's peopled shore,
Her useful sons exchanged for useless ore?
Seen all her triumphs but destruction haste,

they had plundered from slaves in India, they were resolved to employ in
making slaves at home.'
389–90. Prospect has:

I can't forbear, but all my passions start
To tear the barb that grides *etc.*

391–2. Cp. *Citizen* (1762) i 244 (renumbered Letter 56) on Sweden: 'The
deluded people will however at last perceive the miseries of an aristocratical
government; they will perceive that the administration of a society of men
is ever more painful than that of one only. They will fly from this most
oppressive of all forms, where one single member is capable of controlling
the whole, to take refuge under the throne which will ever be attentive to
their complaints.'
391. Till . . . patriot] I can't forbear: but, *Prospect.*
392. fly . . . petty] wish to shrink from *Prospect.*
393. brother . . . baleful] my lov'd brother, cursed be that *Prospect.*
394. struck at regal] toil'd for foreign *Prospect.*
395–6. Not in Prospect.
397–9. Prospect has: When Britons learnt to swell beyond their shore, /
And barter useful men for useless ore, / To shine with splendors that *etc.*
397–8. G. deplored such an exchange in 'Some Thoughts Preliminary to
the General Peace' in the *Weekly Mag.* in Dec. 1759 (*Works* ed. Friedman,
iii 33), attacking the 'sordid' opinion that England should export 'thousands
of our best and most useful inhabitants, that we may be furnished with
tobacco and raw silk; send our honest tradesmen and brave soldiers to
people those desolate regions, that our merchants may furnish Europe with
tobacco and raw silk.' There is a similar passage in *Citizen* (1762) i 58–62
(Letter 17), again attacking emigration to the colonies. Cp. *Deserted Village*
385–6 (p. 693).
399–400. Cp. *The Busy Body* No. vi (20 Oct. 1759): 'A country at war re-
sembles a flambeaux; the brighter it burns, the sooner it is often wasted';
and the essay in the *Weekly Mag.* cited in the preceding note (*Works* ed.
Friedman, iii 32): 'A country may be very wretched and very successful,

400   Like flaring tapers brightening as they waste;
       Seen opulence, her grandeur to maintain,
       Lead stern depopulation in her train,
       And over fields where scattered hamlets rose,
       In barren solitary pomp repose?
405   Have we not seen at pleasure's lordly call,
       The smiling long-frequented village fall?
       Beheld the duteous son, the sire decayed,
       The modest matron and the blushing maid,
       Forced from their homes, a melancholy train,
410   To traverse climes beyond the western main;
       Where wild Oswego spreads her swamps around,
       And Niagara stuns with thundering sound?

       Even now, perhaps, as there some pilgrim strays
       Through tangled forests and through dangerous ways;
415   Where beasts with man divided empire claim,
       And the brown Indian marks with murderous aim;

resembling a lighted taper, which the brighter it blazes, only consumes the faster.'

401–4. Not in Prospect.

401–12. For G.'s conviction that rural depopulation had become common in England see headnote to *The Deserted Village* (p. 669) and the poem itself *passim.* A number of details echo 'The Revolution in Low Life', in *Lloyd's Evening Post* (June 1762), *Works* ed. Friedman, iii 195–7, in which G. had already described a 'happy community' forced to leave their 'abode of felicity, of which they and their ancestors had been in possession time immemorial' because 'a Merchant of immense fortune in London, who had lately purchased the estate on which they lived, intended to lay the whole out in a seat of pleasure for himself'. Among those 'driven out to meet poverty and hardship among strangers' were the 'modest matron' who 'followed her husband in tears', while 'the beautiful daughter parted for ever from her Lover'.

406. The ... village] An hundred villages in ruin *Prospect.*

411. Oswego] A river in Canada running between Lakes Oneida and Ontario. G. refers to 'the desarts of Oswego' and 'the wilds of Niagara' in *History of England in a Series of Letters* (1764) ii 203–4. Fort Oswego was captured by the French in 1756 and recaptured in 1759. A plan of the Fort is given in *Gentleman's Mag.* xxvii (1757) 79.

412. Niagara] G. clearly stressed the third syllable. Fort Niagara was surrendered by the French on 25 July 1759, *Gentleman's Mag.* xxix (1759) 436–7.

414. tangled] tangling *Prospect.*

415. Where ... man] Through woods, where beasts *Prospect.*

416. marks with murderous] takes a deadly *Prospect, edd 1–5.*

There, while above the giddy tempest flies,
And all around distressful yells arise,
The pensive exile, bending with his woe,
420 To stop too fearful and too faint to go,
Casts a long look where England's glories shine,
And bids his bosom sympathize with mine.

Vain, very vain, my weary search to find
That bliss which only centres in the mind:
425 Why have I strayed from pleasure and repose,
To seek a good each government bestows?
In every government, though terrors reign,
Though tyrant kings or tyrant laws restrain,
How small, of all that human hearts endure,
430 That part which laws or kings can cause or cure.
Still to ourselves in every place consigned,
Our own felicity we make or find:
With secret course, which no loud storms annoy,
Glides the smooth current of domestic joy.
435 The lifted axe, the agonising wheel,
Luke's iron crown and Damien's bed of steel,

417. *giddy*] forceful *Prospect*.
418. *yells arise*] yellings rise *Prospect*.
419. *pensive . . . with*] famish'd exile bends beneath *Prospect*.
420. *To stop . . . faint*] And faintly fainter, fainter seems *Prospect*. Johnson wrote the revised line (see headnote).
421. *long*] fond *Prospect*, edd 1–5.   *England's glories shine*] Britain's shores recline *Prospect*.   *long*] 'Longing; desirous; or perhaps long continued, from the disposition to continue looking at anything desired' (Johnson, giving instances from Sidney and Dryden).
422. *bids his bosom*] gives his grief to *Prospect*.
423–39. Not in *Prospect*.
429–34, 437–8. These characteristic lines contributed by Johnson (see headnote) can be paralleled in many of his other writings. Cp. *Vanity of Human Wishes* 359–68; *Life of Savage*, in *Lives of the Poets*, ed. G. B. Hill (1905) ii 379–80; Boswell, *Life of Johnson* i 381: 'The good or ill success of battles and embassies extends itself to a very small part of domestick life: we all have good and evil, which we feel more sensibly than our petty part of publick miscarriage or prosperity'; *ibid* ii 60: 'all that is to be valued, or indeed can be enjoyed by individuals, is *private* liberty'; and *ibid* ii 170: 'I would not give half a guinea to live under one form of government rather than another. It is of no moment to the happiness of an individual.'
436. *Luke's iron crown*] György Dozsa or Dosa (d. 1514) was a Szekler squire and soldier of fortune who organized a crusade against the Turks in 1513, which turned into a peasant rising. He was eventually captured and, pre-

> To men remote from power but rarely known,
> Leave reason, faith and conscience all our own.

sumably because the peasants had proclaimed him king, was made to sit on a red-hot iron throne, with a red-hot iron crown on his head and a red-hot sceptre in his hand. G. may have used the name of his brother Luke, who was also involved in the rising, for metrical reasons or, as Prior suggests, because he wished to avoid any possible allusion to George III. Corney in 1845 emended to 'Zeck's', since Boswell (*Life of Johnson* ii 5–6) had pointed out that the surname of the brothers was given as Zeck in the account of the rebellion in *Respublica et Status Regni Hungariae* (1634) p. 136. Forster (*Life* i 370) explained that the brothers merely 'belonged to one of the native races of Transylvania called Szeklers or Zecklers'. The allusion was obscure to G.'s readers. Thomas Davies, the bookseller, asked G. for an explanation on behalf of the Rev. James Grainger, to whom he wrote on 26 Jan. 1771, *Letters between the Rev. James Grainger and the Most Eminent Literary Men of his Time* (1805) pp. 52–3 : 'Dr. Goldsmith referred to a book called "Geographie curieuse," for an explanation of Luke's Iron Crown . . . The ringleader was punished in a most shocking and brutal manner, so as not to be read without horror. He had an iron throne, crown, &c. made for him; his veins were opened, and his brother Luke was obliged to drink his blood as it flowed from him. The name of this unhappy wretch was George, who bore his punishment without shrinking.' G.'s source was P. L. Berkenmeyer, *Le Curieux Antiquaire, ou Réceuil Géographique et Historique* (Leyden, 1729) ii 673.

Damien's bed of steel] Robert-François Damiens (1715–57) was barbarously tortured and executed for attempting to assassinate Louis XV on 5 Jan. 1757. The attempt and his execution are described in the *Gentleman's Mag.* xxvii (1757) 40, 87–8, 151, where his name is spelt 'Damien' as by G. According to Larousse, *Grand Dictionnaire Universel du XIXe Siècle* vi 47, Damiens was placed in a tower in the Conciergerie and *fut fixé sur un lit, et tous ses membres furent sanglés, retenus au moyen de courroies passées dans des anneaux scellés autour de lui.* Davies, in the letter to Grainger quoted above, states: 'The Doctor says, he meant by Damien's iron [*sic*] the *rack*; but I believe that the newspapers informed us that he was confined in a high tower, and actually obliged to lie upon an iron bed.'

16 A New Simile. In the Manner of Swift

First printed in *Essays* pp. 234–6, as No. xxvii, on 3 June 1765. In the Preface to *Essays* G. stated that its contents had 'already appeared at different times, and in different publications', but no earlier publication of this poem has yet been traced. Friedman (*Works* iv 372n) suggests that it could have appeared in 1760 in a 5th number of the *Weekly Magazine*, which was advertised in the press but no copy of which has survived. The only grounds for this suggestion might be the possible connection of the poem with *The Double Transformation* (see headnote and below).

Although G. claims to be imitating Swift, his model was clearly Thomas Sheridan's *A New Simile for the Ladies* (1732); the confusion no doubt occurred because Sheridan's verses, with Swift's reply, *An Answer to a Scandalous Poem* (1732), were printed together in 1733 and reprinted in Swift's *Works* after 1738. See Swift's *Poems*, ed. H. Williams (1937) ii 612–6.

The poem was slightly revised in 1766 for the 2nd edn of *Essays* pp. 246–8, where it was renumbered No. xxix. It was first collected in *1775* pp. 192–4. In both edns of *Essays* the poem is signed 'J.B.' The only explanation so far proposed is that by Gibbs (*Works* ii 89) who suggests that these initials stood for 'Jack Bookworm' in *The Double Transformation*, the poem which immediately preceded *A New Simile* in the *Essays*.

The text is that of the revised 2nd edn of *Essays*.

Long had I sought in vain to find
A likeness for the scribbling kind;
The modern scribbling kind, who write
In wit and sense and nature's spite:
5   Till reading, I forget what day on,
A chapter out of Tooke's Pantheon,
I think I met with something there
To suit my purpose to a hair.
But let us not proceed too furious,
10   First please to turn to god Mercurius;
You'll find him pictured at full length
In book the second, page the tenth:
The stress of all my proofs on him I lay,
And now proceed we to our simile.

¶ *6.1. Long had I sought in vain*] I long had rack'd my brains *1765*.
Cp. Sheridan, *A New Simile* 1–2: 'I often try'd in vain to find / A *Simile* for Woman-kind.'
6. G. refers to Andrew Tooke's *The Pantheon, Representing the Fabulous Histories of the Heathen Gods and Most Illustrious Heroes*, translated from the French of François Antoine Pomey, S.J., first published in 1698, which had reached a 35th edn by 1824. This popular schoolbook was illustrated with copper-plates, including that referred to throughout this poem, but G.'s reference in l. 12 is dictated by the rhyme. Cp. Tooke's description of Mercury in the 18th edn (1753) pp. 51 ff: '"Who is that young Man, with a cheerful Countenance, an honest Look, and lively Eyes; who is so fair without Paint; having Wings fixed to his Hat and his Shoes, and a Rod in his Hand, which is wing'd, and bound about by a couple of Serpents?'–'It is the Image of *Mercury*, as the *Egyptians* paint him . . . .'" Cp. Swift, *My Lady's Lamentation* 149–50: 'And pore ev'ry day on / That nasty Pantheon.'

15   Imprimis, pray observe his hat,
Wings upon either side—mark that.
Well! what is it from thence we gather?
Why these denote a brain of feather.
A brain of feather! very right,
20   With wit that's flighty, learning light;
Such as to modern bard's decreed:
A just comparison,—proceed.

In the next place, his feet peruse,
Wings grow again from both his shoes;
25   Designed, no doubt, their part to bear,
And waft his godship through the air;
And here my simile unites,
For in a modern poet's flights,
I'm sure it may be justly said,
30   His feet are useful as his head.

Lastly, vouchsafe to observe his hand,
Filled with a snake-encircled wand;
By classic authors termed caduceus,
And highly famed for several uses.
35   To wit—most wondrously endued,
No poppy water half so good;
For let folks only get a touch,
Its soporific virtue's such,
Though ne'er so much awake before,
40   That quickly they begin to snore.
Add too, what certain writers tell,
With this he drives men's souls to hell.

33. *caduceus*] Mercury's rod, emblematic of his divination and his power over the living and the dead, with a touch of which he could bring sleep to mortals.

36. *poppy water*] A popular soporific made by boiling poppies.

41–2. Cp. *Pantheon*, 18th edn, pp. 52–3: 'He attended upon dying Persons to unloose their Souls from the Chains of the Body, and to carry them to Hell. He also revived, and placed into new Bodies, those Souls which had compleated their full Time in the *Elysian* Fields.' Cp. Virgil, *Aeneid* iv 238–44 and Horace, *Odes* I x 17–19: *tu pias laetis animas reponis / sedibus virgaque levem coerces / aurea turbam* ('tis thou does bring the pious souls to their abodes of bliss, marshalling the shadowy throng with golden wand). But G. may have had in mind, here and in ll. 51–2, Swift's *The Virtues of Sid Hamet the Magician's Rod* 35–42, a satire on Sidney Godolphin: 'The *Rod* of *Hermes* was renown'd / For Charms above and under Ground; / To sleep could Mortal Eye-lids fix / And drive departed Souls to *Styx*. / That *Rod*

Now to apply, begin we then:
His wand's a modern author's pen;
45   The serpents round about it twined
Denote him of the reptile kind;
Denote the rage with which he writes,
His frothy slaver, venomed bites;
An equal semblance still to keep,
50   Alike too both conduce to sleep.
This difference only, as the god
Drove souls to Tartarus with his rod,
With his goosequill the scribbling elf,
Instead of others, damns himself.

55   And here my simile almost tripped,
Yet grant a word by way of postscript.
Moreover, Mercury had a failing:
Well! what of that? out with it—stealing;
In which all modern bards agree,
60   Being each as great a thief as he:
But even this deity's existence
Shall lend my simile assistance.
Our modern bards! why what a pox
Are they but senseless stones and blocks?

was just a Type of *Sid's*, / Which, o'er a *British* Senate's Lids, / Could *scatter Opium* full as well, / And drive as many *Souls to Hell*.'
58. Cp. *Pantheon*, 18th edn, pp. 53–4: 'In the Art of Thieving he certainly excelled all the Sharpers that ever were, or will be; for he is the very Prince and God of Thieves'; and Horace, *Odes* I x 7–8: *callidum, quicquid placuit, iocoso* / *condere furto* (clever, too, to hide in sportive stealth, whate'er thy fancy chose).
59. *all modern*] our scribling *1765*.
63–4. G. may be referring to the *hermae* or statues of Mercury described in the *Pantheon* pp. 56–7.

17 Verses in Reply to an Invitation to Dinner at Dr. Baker's

Written on 20 Jan. 1767. These lines appear to have been preserved by Catherine Horneck (the 'Little Comedy' of l. 17), who married Henry William Bunbury, the comic artist, in 1771. They were first printed in 1837 by

Prior, *Works* iv 132-3, by permission of Catherine's son, Major-General Sir Henry Bunbury, Bart. (The title described Baker as 'Sir George', although he had not yet been knighted: the title given above has been adjusted accordingly.) Prior dated them 'about the year 1769' and this date was accepted until the compliment to Reynolds and Angelica Kauffman mentioned in the last couplet was identified. Horace Walpole preserved a cutting of the verses from the *Public Advertiser* to which G. refers, with some notes on Angelica Kauffman, and dated them 20 Jan. 1767. See Walpole's *Anecdotes of Painting in England, Volume V*, ed. F. W. Hilles and P. B. Daghlian (New Haven, 1937) pp. 45-6. The verses in the *Advertiser* were preceded by a short letter:

'To the Printer of the Public Advertiser.

Sir,

By inserting the following lines in your paper, you will oblige one, who is proud to subscribe himself

An Admirer of Merit.

> While fair Angelica, with matchless grace,
> Paints Conway's lovely form, and Stanhope's face,
> Our hearts to beauty willing homage pay,
> We praise, admire, and gaze our souls away.
> But when the likeness she has done for thee,
> O, Reynolds, with astonishment we see;
> Forc'd to submit with all our pride, we own
> Such strength, such harmony, excell'd by none,
> And thou art rivall'd by thyself alone.'

Walpole also preserved a Latin imitation of these lines and another poem in praise of Angelica, both printed in the same paper a few days later. Her portrait of Reynolds was painted in the late summer and autumn of 1766.

G.'s lines were written in reply to a last-minute invitation to dinner at the house of Dr George Baker (not yet 'Sir George Baker' as stated in Prior's title in 1837), which was also to be attended by the other members of Reynold's circle (many of them Devonians like Reynolds himself) in which G. was an intimate at this time. G. was probably imitating the postscript, in similar shortlined verse, to Swift's verse letter to Sheridan, 14 Dec. 1719, (*Poems*, ed. Williams, iii 1014-15).

A MS of the verses, 'made probably by either Mrs Horneck or one of her daughters', was in the Elkins collection described by Temple Scott, pp. 229-31. The text followed here is that printed by Prior.

'This *is* a poem! This *is* a copy of verses!'

> Your mandate I got,
> You may all go to pot;
> Had your senses been right,
> You'd have sent before night;

662
REPLY TO AN INVITATION

5   As I hope to be saved,
     I put off being shaved;
     For I could not make bold,
     While the matter was cold,
     To meddle in suds,
10   Or to·put on my duds;
     So tell Horneck and Nesbitt,
     And Baker and his bit,
     And Kauffmann beside,
     And the Jessamy bride,
15   With the rest of the crew,
     The Reynoldses two,
     Little Comedy's face,

¶ *11.10. duds*] Clothes.

11. Horneck] Mrs Hannah Horneck (d. 1803), widow of Capt. Kane William Horneck of the Royal Engineers and mother of Mary, Catherine and Charles Horneck. Like Reynolds, through whom G. met them, the Hornecks were of Devonshire origin. G. accompanied them to France in 1770.   *Nesbitt*] Mrs Susannah Nesbitt (d. 1789), a sister of Henry Thrale the brewer, had married Arnold Nesbitt in 1758. He was M.P. for Cricklade and described by Mrs Thrale as 'a Gentleman of considerable Family in Ireland but bred a Merchant in the City of London', *Thraliana*, ed. K. C. Balderston (1942) i 300. He was insolvent at his death in 1779; Mrs Nesbitt married again in 1782.

12. Baker] Dr (later Sir) George Baker (1722–1809), Reynolds's physician and from 1776 physician to George III. Like many of the circle, Baker was a Devonian.

13. Kauffmann] Angelica Kauffman (1741–1807), the most celebrated woman painter of her time, born in Switzerland, came to England in 1766. Later in 1767 she married Count Horn, an impostor, and was legally separated from him less than three months later. Horace Walpole, in the notes referred to in the headnote, stated that she 'lodged in Suffolk street. She was pretty, sung well, and had a good character. She painted in oil; genteely but lightly, and her portraits were not very exact resemblances.'

14. Jessamy bride] Mary Horneck (*c.* 1752–1840), the elder of the sisters. A scurrilous newspaper attack in 1773 suggested that G. was in love with her (Wardle, pp. 241–2). She married Col. F. E. Gwyn in 1779. Reynolds painted her portrait. 'Jessamy' appears to mean something like 'fashionable'. A 'Jessamy' was a dandy or fop: cp. *The Adventurer* No. 100 (20 Oct. 1753).

16. Reynoldses two] Sir Joshua (1723–92), the celebrated painter, and his sister Frances (1729–1807), also a painter of some ability.

17. Little Comedy] Catherine Horneck (d. 1799), the younger of the Horneck sisters, who married Henry William Bunbury in 1771. Like her sister, she was painted by Reynolds.

And the Captain in lace,
(By the bye you may tell him,
20   I have something to sell him;
Of use I insist,
When he comes to enlist.
Your worships must know
That a few days ago,
25   An order went out,
For the foot guards so stout
To wear tails in high taste,
Twelve inches at least:
Now I've got him a scale
30   To measure each tail,
To lengthen a short tail,
And a long one to curtail).
       Yet how can I when vexed,
Thus stray from my text?
35   Tell each other to rue
Your Devonshire crew,
For sending so late
To one of my state.
But 'tis Reynolds's way
40   From wisdom to stray,
And Angelica's whim
To be frolic like him,
But, alas! your good worships, how could they be wiser,
When both have been spoiled in today's *Advertiser*?

OLIVER GOLDSMITH.

18. Captain in lace] Charles Horneck (d. 1804), brother of the girls, must have been about 15 at this time. He purchased an ensignship in the 3rd Regt. of the Foot Guards in March 1768 (cp. l. 22) and eventually became a general. An engraving and satirical account of him as 'Captn. H———, or the Military Macaroni' appeared in *The Macaroni and Theatrical Magazine* in Oct. 1772, pp. 1–5, which describes him as being extremely spoiled by his widowed mother.

43–4. For the poem in the *Public Advertiser* see headnote.

18 Epitaph on Edward Purdon

Written in March or April 1767. Edward Purdon, a fellow-student with G. at Trinity College, Dublin, had enlisted as a private soldier before becoming a professional writer in London. He published a translation of Voltaire's *Henriade* in 1759, which G. is supposed to have revised, and is also thought to have edited *The Busy Body* to which G. contributed in 1759. For these ascriptions and for G.'s assistance to Purdon in his poverty, see Prior, *Life* i 62, 305–8, 336, 369.

Purdon's death on 27 March 1767 was noticed in the *Gentleman's Mag.*: 'Mr Purdon, suddenly, in Smithfield, famous for his literary abilities.' Forster, *Life* (6th edn, 1877) ii 60, quotes the MS notes on a collection of songs and poems (then owned by Bolton Corney), which had belonged to William Ballantyne, a fellow-member with G. of a club which met at the Globe-Tavern in Fleet St, also known as the Wednesday Club. Ballantyne recorded that G. 'made this epitaph in his way from his chambers in the Temple to the Wednesday evening's club at the Globe. *I think he will never come back*, I believe he said. I was sitting by him, and he repeated it more than twice. *I think he will never come back.*'

The epigram was first collected in *1777* p. 79 and also appeared in 1777 in the 8th edn of *Retaliation* p. 32*: see headnote to *The Clown's Reply*, (p. 764). But it had already been printed in mysterious circumstances in the *Weekly Magazine, or Edinburgh Amusement* xxi 224, for 12 Aug. 1773, which included under the 'Deaths' for 19 July 1773: 'In Ireland, Mr Edward Purdon, formerly of Trinity-college, Dublin. He was well known from a variety of translations, compilations, &c. The following *extempore* was written on his death by a correspondent.' This text contains one variant from *1777* (followed here), 'ever' for 'wish to' in l. 4.

In any case, the epigram was hardly original. Cp. the old French epitaph on *La Mort du Sieur Etienne: Il est au bout de ses travaux | Il a passé le Sieur Etienne; | En ce monde il eut tant de maux, | Qu'on ne croit pas qu'il revienne.* G. may also have been indebted to Pope's 'mock epitaph' on John Gay: 'Well then, poor G—— lies under ground! / So there's an end of honest *Jack.* / So little Justice here he found, / 'Tis ten to one he'll ne'er come back.'

> Here lies poor Ned Purdon, from misery freed,
> Who long was a bookseller's hack;
> He led such a damnable life in this world,—
> I don't think he'll wish to come back.

19 Epilogue to *The Good Natured Man*

Written towards the end of Jan. 1768. G.'s first comedy, *The Good Natured Man*, was performed at Covent Garden on 29 Jan. 1768, with a solemn prologue by Johnson and this epilogue by G. himself. Both were reprinted

3333333

in the *St James's Chronicle*, 30 Jan.–2 Feb. 1768 and the *Public Advertiser* on 3 Feb. 1768, but with ll. 17–18 omitted from the epilogue; and again in the *Gentleman's Mag.* for Feb. 1768, xxxviii 86–7. The play was published by Wm Griffin on 5 Feb. and went through several impressions during 1768, in spite of its only moderate success on the stage. G. now added the following note to the epilogue: 'The Author, in expectation of an Epilogue from a Friend at Oxford, deferred writing one himself till the very last hour. What is here offered, owes all its success to the graceful manner of the Actress who spoke it.' The text is that printed with the play (to which one change was made in the 4th impression: see l. 34 *n*), with variants from the *St James's Chronicle*.

> As puffing quacks some caitiff wretch procure
> To swear the pill or drop has wrought a cure;
> Thus on the stage our playwrights still depend
> For Epilogues and Prologues on some friend,
> 5 Who knows each art of coaxing up the town,
> And make full many a bitter pill go down.
> Conscious of this, our bard has gone about,
> And teased each rhyming friend to help him out.
> 'An Epilogue–things can't go on without it;
> 10 It could not fail, would you but set about it.'
> 'Young man,' cries one–a bard laid up in clover–
> 'Alas, young man, my writing days are over;
> Let boys play tricks and kick the straw, not I:
> Your brother Doctor there, perhaps, may try.'
> 15 'What I? dear Sir,' the Doctor interposes,
> 'What, plant my thistle, Sir, among his roses!
> No, no, I've other contests to maintain;

¶ 19.1. *puffing*] Advertising with exaggerated or falsified praise. An advertisement such as G. has in mind occurs in the *London Chronicle*, 8–10 Jan. 1767, in which a witness swears before the Mayor to the efficacy of 'Dr. Bateman's Pectoral Drops'. For G.'s views on quacks see *Citizen* (1762) i 90–3, ii 10–15 (later renumbered Letters 24, 68).
4. Epilogues and Prologues] Epilogue, or Prologue *St James's Chron.*
6. make] makes *St James's Chron.*
14. brother Doctor] Gibbs suggests that G. may have had in mind Dr George Baker (see *Reply to an Invitation* 12 *n*, p. 662), who later held various offices at the College of Physicians and who had some reputation as a writer of light verse.
16. his] your *St James's Chron.*   Cp. Swift, *Verses said to be written on the Union* 9–10: 'As if a Man in making Posies / Should bundle Thistles up with Roses.' *17–18. Omitted in St James's Chron.*

The Royal College of Physicians was situated on the east side of Warwick Lane from 1674 to 1866. The *Gentleman's Mag.* xxxvii (1767) 476–7, reports

Tonight I head our troops at Warwick Lane.
Go, ask your manager.' 'Who, me? Your pardon;
20 Those things are not our forte at Covent Garden.'
Our author's friends, thus placed at happy distance,
Give him good words indeed, but no assistance.
As some unhappy wight, at some new play,
At the pit door stands elbowing a way,
25 While oft, with many a smile and many a shrug,
He eyes the centre, where his friends sit snug;
His simpering friends, with pleasure in their eyes,
Sink as he sinks and as he rises rise;
He nods, they nod; he cringes, they grimace;
30 But not a soul will budge to give him place.
Since then, unhelped, our bard must now conform
'To bide the pelting of this pitiless storm',
Blame where you must, be candid where you can,
And be each critic the Good Natured Man.

that on 23 Sept. 1767, a number of Licentiates of the College broke into a meeting and dinner of the Fellows by force and 'broke several of the windows with their canes, which caused great confusion'. The same magazine in Oct. 1767 (xxxvii 492) explained that the conflict had been caused by the decision of the Fellows to exclude from future Fellowships 'such of the Licentiates as had at any time practised Surgery . . . the Licentiates were alarmed and offended at this stigma fixed on a number of their members'. The legal argument dragged on until June 1771, when judgement was at last given in favour of the College (*Gentleman's Mag*. xli 283). Bonnell Thornton published a mock-heroic account of the struggle in *The Battle of the Wigs* in March 1768 and the *Gentleman's Mag*. for that month, pp. 132–3, describes an anonymous *Siege of the Castle of Aesculapius, an heroic Comedy, as it is acted in Warwick-lane*.
19. Go] No *St James's Chron*.
19–20. The manager of Covent Garden Theatre 1767–74 was George Colman the elder (1732–94), who was himself a dramatist and who wrote a number of prologues and epilogues for the plays of others. His refusal here, however, may be an oblique reference to the facility in writing such pieces of the manager of the rival theatre, David Garrick.
20. forte] Friedman misreads G's 'fort' as 'sort'.
21–2. In St James's Chron. these lines follow l. 30.
28–9. Perhaps a reminiscence of Pope, *Dunciad* iv 427–8: 'It fled, I follow'd; now in hope, now pain; / It stopt, I stopt; it mov'd, I mov'd again.'
32. G. quotes *King Lear* III iv 29: 'Whereso'er you are, / That bide the pelting of this pitiless storm.'
33. Cp. Pope, *Essay on Man* i 15: 'Laugh where we must, be candid where we can'.
34. According to W. B. Todd, 'The First Editions of *The Good Natur'd Man*

and *She Stoops to Conquer*', *Studies in Bibliography* xi (1958) 135–6, it was in the 4th and 5th impressions of the play (i.e. in the 2nd of the 'New Editions' and the so-called 'Fifth Edition') that the last line was altered to the present reading. In the first three impressions it reads 'And view with favour, the Good-natur'd Man'.

20 Epilogue to *The Sister*: *A Comedy*

Written between 12 and 18 Feb. 1768, when *The Sister*, by Mrs Charlotte Lennox (1720–1804), was performed at Covent Garden. On Sunday 12 Feb. 1769 George Colman, the manager of Covent Garden, wrote to Mrs Lennox, mentioning his own prologue and the fact that G.'s promised epilogue for the play had not yet been delivered. Colman therefore asked Mrs Lennox to write her own epilogue by the following Wednesday, but G. had evidently fulfilled his promise by the night of the performance. For Colman's letter, see D. E. Isles, *Times Lit. Supp.* 5 Aug. 1965, p. 685.

Mrs Lennox was best known for her novel *The Female Quixote* (1752). *The Sister* was dramatised from another of her novels, *Henrietta* (1758). She was a friend of many of the leading literary figures of the day including Johnson. In Boswell's *Life of Johnson* iv 10, there is a curious account by Bennet Langton of a conversation in which G. told Johnson that, when Mrs Lennox brought out a play (possibly *The Sister*, her first), he had been asked to go and hiss it, by someone who had been offended by her criticism of Shakespeare in her *Shakespeare Illustrated* (1753–4). If the play was *The Sister*, it is understandable that G. declined to do so.

The Sister had only one performance: 'The audience expressed their disapprobation of it with so much clamour and appearance of prejudice, that she would not suffer an attempt to exhibit it a second time', *Gentleman's Mag.* xxxix (April 1769) 199. See also Colman's letter to Mrs Lennox of 20 Feb. 1769, quoted in the article by D. E. Isles cited above. However, according to *Lloyd's Evening Post*, 17–20 Feb. 1769, both prologue and epilogue were 'received with uncommon applause from the very considerable share of merit they possessed'; and the *Gazetteer*, 20 Feb. 1769, praised Mrs Bulkley's speaking of the epilogue. G.'s epilogue was reprinted three times (without variants other than misprints) in newspapers before the play was printed in full on 3 March 1769. *The Sister* was more favourably received in this form and it enjoyed a 2nd edn. Isaac Reed, *Biographia Dramatica* (1782) ii 346, thought that it was 'written with a considerable degree of good sense and elegance' and added that G.'s epilogue was possibly 'the best that has appeared in the course of the last thirty years'. It was first collected in *1777* pp. 69–70. The text is that of the 1st edn of *The Sister*.

What! five long acts – and all to make us wiser!
Our authoress sure has wanted an adviser.
Had she consulted *me*, she should have made

Her moral play a speaking masquerade,
5   Warmed up each bustling scene and, in her rage,
Have emptied all the green-room on the stage.
My life on't, this had kept her play from sinking,
Have pleased our eyes and saved the pain of thinking.
Well, since she thus has shown her want of skill,
10   What if I give a masquerade? I will.
But how? ay, there's the rub! (*pausing*) – I've got my
        cue:
The world's a masquerade! the maskers, you, you, you.
        [*To Boxes, Pit, and Gallery.*
Lud! what a group the motley scene discloses!
False wits, false wives, false virgins and false spouses:
15   Statesmen with bridles on; and, close beside 'em,
Patriots, in party-coloured suits, that ride 'em.
There Hebes, turned of fifty, try once more
To raise a flame in Cupids of threescore.
These in their turn, with appetites as keen,
20   Deserting fifty, fasten on fifteen.
Miss, not yet full fifteen, with fire uncommon,
Flings down her sampler, and takes up the woman:
The little urchin smiles and spreads her lure,
And tries to kill ere she's got power to cure.
25   Thus 'tis with all – their chief and constant care
Is to seem everything but what they are.
Yon broad, bold, angry spark, I fix my eye on,
Who seems to have robbed his vizor from the lion,
Who frowns, and talks, and swears, with round parade,
30   Looking, as who should say, *Damme! who's afraid?*
        [*Mimicking.*
Strip but his vizor off, and sure I am
You'll find his lionship a very lamb.

¶ 20.11. *ay, there's the rub*] From *Hamlet* III i 65.
16. *patriots*] Cp. Johnson's two meanings of 'patriot', the second introduced into the 4th edn of the *Dictionary* in 1773: '1. One whose ruling passion is the love of his country. 2. It is sometimes used for a factious disturber of the government.'   *party-coloured*] G. plays on the political sense and the normal meaning, 'Having diversity of colours.' He probably derived the pun from Pope, *Dunciad* iv 538: 'Int'rest that waves on Party-coloured wings.'
17. *Hebe*] Daughter of Zeus and Hera, the handmaiden of the gods, associated with perpetual youth.
27. *spark*] 'A lively, showy, splendid, gay man. It is commonly used in contempt' (Johnson).
28. *vizor*] A mask. G. is still describing the 'masquerade' of the world.

Yon politician, famous in debate,
Perhaps, to vulgar eyes, bestrides the state;
35   Yet, when he deigns his real shape to assume,
He turns old woman and bestrides a broom.
Yon patriot, too, who presses on your sight,
And seems to every gazer all in white,
If with a bribe his candour you attack,
40   He bows, turns round, and whip–the man's a black!
Yon critic, too–but whither do I run?
If I proceed, our bard will be undone!
Well then, a truce, since she requests it too:
Do you spare her, and I'll for once spare you.

34. Julius Caesar I ii 135–6: 'he doth bestride the narrow world / Like
Colossus.'
40. whip] Suddenly, in a trice.

21 The Deserted Village

Probably written between 1768 and 1770. But R. S. Crane's ascription to
G. (in *Times Lit. Supp.* 8 Sept. 1927, p. 607; and *New Essays* (1927)
pp. 116–24) of an essay entitled 'The Revolution in Low Life', first printed
in *Lloyd's Evening Post*, 14–16 June 1762, made it clear that G. had been
concerned about the problems of rural depopulation long before the publi-
cation of *The Deserted Village*. This essay anticipates the basic situation of the
poem as well as many of G.'s reflections on it. Depopulation is discussed in
The Traveller 397–422, in 1764; and in his dedication to Reynolds of *The
Deserted Village*, G. forestalled charges that he was exaggerating the prob-
lem by stating that 'I have taken all possible pains, in my country excursions,
for these four or five years past, to be certain of what I allege'. G. had therefore
been reflecting on the problem of 'luxury' and its consequences for a
decade before the publication of the poem; but the available evidence
suggests that he did not actually begin writing it until about 1768. Hawkins,
Life of Johnson (2nd edn, 1787) p. 420, asserts that G. 'was two years about it',
a statement confirmed in William Cooke's more detailed account of its
composition, *European Mag.* xxiv (1793) 171–2:

'He was by his own confession, four or five years collecting materials in all
his country excursions for this poem, and was actually engaged in the con-
struction of it above two years. His manner of writing poetry was this: he
first sketched a part of his design in prose, in which he threw out his ideas as
they occurred to him; he then sat carefully down to versify them, correct
them, and add such other ideas as he thought better fitted to the subject. He
sometimes would exceed his prose design, by writing several verses im-
promptu, but these he would take uncommon pains afterwards to revise,
lest they should be found unconnected with his main design.

'The Writer of these Memoirs called upon the Doctor the second morning after he had begun "The Deserted Village," and to him he communicated the plan of his poem. "Some of my friends," continued he, "differ with me on this plan, and think this depopulation of villages does not exist–but I am myself satisfied of the fact. I remember it in my own country, and have seen it in this." He then read what he had done of it that morning [ll. 5–14]. "Come," says he, "let me tell you, this is no bad morning's work; and now, my dear boy, if you are not better engaged, I should be glad to enjoy a *Shoe-maker's* holiday with you."'

Two events possibly connected with the nostalgia and the description of rural innocence which permeate the poem may also confirm this dating. By May 1768 G. had taken a cottage near Edgware, some 8 miles from London (his 'Shoemaker's Paradise'); and in the same month his brother Henry died.

It is clear from G.'s own remarks that he considered the problem of rural depopulation to be common to England and his own native country; and the reference to 'England's griefs' in l. 57 suggests that he wished the poem to be taken as referring specifically to England. The positive identification of the village in question would not have seemed desirable and perhaps not even possible by G. himself, but elaborate efforts have been made to identify it with Lissoy, where G. spent his childhood. The most assiduous of these attempts to identify the people and places mentioned by G., which began with members of his own family, are a letter from Dr Annesley Strean (Henry Goldsmith's successor at Lissoy) to Edward Mangin, dated 31 Dec. 1807, printed in Mangin's *An Essay on Light Reading* (1808) pp. 136–50; and R. H. Newell's edn of G.'s *Poetical Works . . . with Remarks attempting to ascertain, chiefly from Local Observation, the actual Scene of the Deserted Village* (1811). (The illustrations no doubt have some biographical interest.) See also Prior, *Life* i 18–19, ii 255–60; J. F. Waller's edn of G.'s *Poems*, 1865, p. 194n; and K. C. Balderston, *Percy's Memoir of G.* (1926) p. 19. A repeated claim for Lissoy is the story that Genl. Robert Naper or Napier, during G.'s childhood, purchased the estates round the village and began to enclose an area 'of nine miles in circumference', causing hundreds to move to other parts of the country or to emigrate to America. The parallels with Lissoy may help to confirm what might in any case be apparent enough– that the poem contains some highly idealized memories of G.'s childhood– but G.'s conscious and urgent point was that depopulation was to be found not far from complacent London. The village which was about to be 'deserted' in the early essay attributed to G., 'The Revolution in Low Life' (1762; see above), was 'distant about fifty miles from town' (*Works* ed. Friedman, iii 195). A specific English parallel is mentioned in some 'Anecdotes' of G. in the *Universal Mag.* lxvii (Aug. 1780) 84 (reprinted in the *Public Advertiser*, 29 Sept. 1780). The writer states that G. wrote *The Deserted Village* 'in rural stillness and solitude' and adds that 'In one of his country excursions he resided near the house of a great West-Indian, in the neighbourhood of which several cottages were destroyed, in order to enlarge, or rather to polish the prospect. This circumstance the Doctor often mentioned to evince the truth of his reasoning, and to this he particularly alludes in [ll. 65–6].' The same writer adds: 'With whatever facility the Doctor might write in prose, or in the lighter species of poetry, his Deserted Village was a very laboured composition. He himself declared, that he never wrote more than four lines of it a day, and the four which begin the poem have been in as many states of variation as would cover the side of a half-sheet of paper.' Two typically vague local traditions as to the identification of Auburn may be mentioned in conclusion. A tradition that G. wrote it at Springfield, Essex, dates back to at least 1818 (Notes and Queries, 3 Aug. and 12 Oct. 1878, 5th series, x 88, 294); and another tradition that G. was referring to Sir Robert Walpole's great house at Houghton in Norfolk is mentioned in Norfolk Archaeology viii (1879) 255–7. See K. J. Fielding, English xii (1958) 130–2.

The last 4 ll. of the poem were written by Johnson, as was established by Boswell who wrote on his copy: 'The four last lines were marked at my desire by Dr. Johnson spring 1783 as all that he wrote of this admirable Poem': see Catalogue of the R.B. Adam Library (1929), facsimile opposite ii 19. Johnson seems to have preferred The Traveller: 'his "Traveller" is a very fine performance; ay, and so is his "Deserted Village," were it not sometimes too much the echo of his "Traveller"', Boswell, Life of Johnson ii 236.

There is some uncertainty as to the amount G. received for the poem. Samuel Glover, in the Universal Mag. liv 254, for May 1774, a few weeks after G.'s death, states that G. received 100 guineas for it; but that when a friend expressed surprise at the sum, G. admitted that he had been uneasy about it himself and returned it; 'and left it entirely to the Bookseller to pay him according to the profits produced by the sale of the piece, which turned out very considerable.' Glover repeated the story in his Life of G., which appeared in July 1774. The story was considered dubious by Percy (Works, 1801, i 85) and Prior (Life ii 280–1), but had been described as 'strictly true' by Cooke, European Mag. xxiv (1793) 171: 'His way of computation was this, "that it was near five shillings a couplet, which was more than any bookseller could afford, or, indeed, more than any modern poetry was worth." The Poet, however, lost nothing by his generosity, as his bookseller (the late Mr. Griffin, Catharine-street, Strand) paid him the remainder of the hundred pounds, which the rapid sale of the poem soon enabled him to do.' Hawkins, Life of Johnson (2nd edn, 1787) p. 420, states that G. already owed Griffin about £200: soon after the publication of The Deserted Village, 'Griffin declared, that it had discharged the whole of his debt'. But it is worth noting that, as Miss Balderston, Letters p. 65n, points out, when G. was asked why he had not expressed his views on depopulation in a prose pamphlet, he replied, 'It is not worth my while. A good poem will bring me a hundred guineas, but the pamphlet would bring me nothing', J. H. Ward, Life and Times of Bishop White (1892) p. 24. Whether or not Glover's story is correct, this may be the sum G. received.

The imminent publication of the poem was announced in the *Public Advertiser*, 16 and 17 Nov. 1769, but it did not in fact appear until 26 May 1770, on which day the same paper announced that it would be published 'This Day at Twelve', price 2s in quarto, by Wm Griffin. The poem was an immediate success: a 2nd edn was published on 7 June 1770, a 3rd on 13 June, a 4th on 28 June, a 5th on 9 Aug. and a 6th on 4 Oct. At the end of the nineteenth century it was often stated that a number of duodecimo issues of the poem, dated 1770, were published before Griffin's first quarto edn as 'trial issues' or for private circulation. In various forms the theory persisted until W. B. Todd, 'The "Private Issues" of *The Deserted Village*', *Studies in Bibliography* vi (1954) 25–44, showed that all such issues and all other unauthorised edns of the poem before 1784 derived from Griffin's quartos.

The reviewers of G.'s poem were all troubled to some extent by its description of rural depopulation and its attack on commerce and 'luxury'; but such disagreement did not affect opinions of its poetic merit. The *Critical Review* xxix 435–43 attacked G.'s arguments but praised his descriptive powers generously; John Hawkesworth in the *Monthly Review* xlii 440–5, had similar objections but concluded that 'as a picture of fancy' it 'has great beauty'; and the critic (possibly Hawkesworth again) in the *Gentleman's Mag.* xl 271–3, while accepting only a modified version of G.'s social views, assured the reader that 'if he has not vitiated his taste, till, like a sick girl, he prefers ashes and chalk to beef and mutton, we can promise him more pleasure than he has received from poetry since the days of Pope'. A similar response can be finally illustrated from the *Town and Country Mag.* ii 268, which found the poem 'a most beautiful structure, though we think it is built upon a very sandy foundation; or rather, it is a rainbow castle in the air, raised and adorned solely by the strength of the author's imagination; for we cannot believe, that this country is depopulating, or that commerce is destructive of the real strength and greatness of a nation'. The interest aroused by the poem is illustrated by Prior's statement (*Life* ii 270) that 17 letters about it appeared in the *St James's Chronicle* within a few months. For another attack on G.'s views see Thomas Comber, *Free and Candid Correspondence on the Farmer's Letters* (1770); and for some moderate support, John Robinson's *The Village Oppressed* (1771) p. iv. Although G. admits in his Dedication that several of his 'best and wisest friends' disagreed with his views, the causes and effects of emigration were becoming 'a common topick of discourse' at this time: cp. Boswell, *Life of Johnson* iii 231–2, v 27, and *Gentleman's Mag.* xliii (1773) 467–8.

In *The Deserted Village* the blending of traditional form, content and style with a new sensibility and rhetoric already evident in *The Traveller* is taken a stage further. Formally related in some ways to the topographical poem (for the development of the genre, see R. A. Aubin, *Topographical Poetry in Eighteenth Century England*, New York, 1936), *The Deserted Village*, while purporting to describe a particular place, is more meditative than descriptive. The element of incidental reflection present in earlier poems describing particular buildings, villages or towns is given a new importance and a new economic and sociological character by G. But the descriptive and humani-tarian concerns of the poem are not simply objective: characteristically, they are presented as the essential product of the experience, memory and emotion of the poet himself. (The reviews quoted above make it clear that a gap between the subjective and objective truth of the poem was detected at once by G.'s readers.) G. takes the depopulation of Auburn to be represen-tative of various social ills about which he can be indignant in general terms as the poem proceeds. But the original impulse is presented as deeply per-sonal. Auburn in its happier days is remembered from the poet's own youth: he is lamenting the lost innocence and happiness of his own childhood as well as of the village. The desolate village of the present is described by the 'poet' who had himself planned to end his days there.

Even in the personal and emotional sections of the poem, traditional affiliations can be detected: the praise of retirement from the great world to the peace of the village for which the poet had hoped (ll. 97–112) is reinforced by memories of the ever-potent praise of the innocence of rural life in Virgil's *Georgics* ii 458ff, which also underlies the contrast of city and country in the rest of the poem. The poet listening to the happy sounds of village life (ll. 113–26) is a descendant of the poet in Milton's *L'Allegro* and *Il Penseroso*. In addition, the 'character' studies at the centre of the poem (ll. 137–216) can be related to earlier 'characters' in Dryden and Pope, although the satire is softened by G.'s humour and sensibility, by the innocence and virtue of the subjects and the sad, personal affection of the poet. What is characteris-tically G.'s own is the nostalgic evocation of the lost innocence of the village, and the blend of the various elements–descriptive, didactic, elegiac and lyrical–which contribute to the poem. The familiar world of pastoral elegy is renewed and made acceptable by its involvement in the poet's own ex-perience, by its role as representative of the passing of a way of life and a certain kind of society, and by its place in G.'s view of society as a whole.

Just as the formal genres to which the poem is related are adapted to express G.'s new subjectivity and sensibility, his couplets, still basically similar to Pope's, reveal a further development towards an emotional and musical lyricism, which is opposed in effect to the earlier, rational, witty, didactic mode. For a full discussion see Wallace C. Brown, *The Triumph of Form* (Chapel Hill, 1948) pp. 153–60. G.'s lyrical tendencies are especially mani-fested in a development of that repetition of words, phrases and syntactic patterns, already noted in *The Traveller*, with an effect which at times is almost incantatory, e.g. ll. 31–7, 83–96. One result of this process can be thinness of intellectual content and it has been noted how much work such words as 'sweet', 'smiling', 'past', 'fled', their synonyms and associated words, have to do in the poem; but the same technique of echoing repeti-tions, when reinforced by alliteration, assonance, firm syntax and G.'s increasing metrical skill (e.g. in ll. 51–6) can achieve at best a rhetorical elevation of some force.

Most of the recent discussion of the poem has been concerned, if rather more subtly, with the problems which worried its first critics: the nature and accuracy of its social commentary. Much has been done to relate the poem to G.'s views on society, especially on 'luxury', in his other writings and to demonstrate that instead of, or as well as, containing elements of purely personal idealised fantasy, the poem carries a coherent political (Tory) philosophy, directed against the newly rich commercial classes. See in particular R. S. Crane's introduction to *New Essays* (1927); R. W. Seitz, 'The Irish Background of Goldsmith's Social and Political Thought', *PMLA* lii (1937) 405–11; H. J. Bell, '*The Deserted Village*, and Goldsmith's Social Doctrines', *PMLA* lix (1944) 747–72; and Earl Miner, 'The Making of *The Deserted Village*', *Huntington Library Quarterly* xxii (1958–9) 125–41. See also R. Quintana, '*The Deserted Village*: Its Logical and Rhetorical Elements', *College English* xxvi (1964) 204–14.

The textual history of *The Deserted Village*, by comparison with *The Traveller*, is uncomplicated. A number of slight changes were made in the 2nd edn and final revisions were made in the 4th edn. For a detailed bibliographical discussion see A. Friedman, *Studies in Bibliography* xiii (1960) 143–7. Friedman does not mention, however, an issue of the 2nd edn identical with the 1st except for the title-page. There is a copy in the Bodleian Library. *Ed 2* in the textual notes, however, refers to the revised edn.

DEDICATION

TO SIR JOSHUA REYNOLDS

DEAR SIR,

     I can have no expectations in an address of this kind,
5 either to add to your reputation, or to establish my own. You can gain nothing from my admiration, as I am ignorant of that art in which you are said to excel; and I may lose much by the severity of your judgement, as few have a juster taste in poetry than you. Setting
10 interest therefore aside, to which I never paid much attention, I must be indulged at present in following my affections. The only dedication I ever made was to my brother, because I loved him better than most other men. He is since dead. Permit me to inscribe this poem to
15 you.
     How far you may be pleased with the versification and mere mechanical parts of this attempt, I don't pretend to enquire; but I know you will object (and indeed several of our best and wisest friends concur in the opinion) that
20 the depopulation it deplores is no where to be seen, and the disorders it laments are only to be found in the poet's

¶ 21. *Dedication.* 12–14. G. had dedicated *The Traveller* to his brother Henry, who had died in 1768.

own imagination. To this I can scarce make any other
answer than that I sincerely believe what I have written;
that I have taken all possible pains, in my country
25 excursions, for these four or five years past, to be certain
of what I allege; and that all my views and enquiries
have led me to believe those miseries real, which I here
attempt to display. But this is not the place to enter into
an enquiry, whether the country be depopulating, or
30 not; the discussion would take up much room, and I
should prove myself, at best, an indifferent politician,
to tire the reader with a long preface, when I want his
unfatigued attention to a long poem.

In regretting the depopulation of the country, I
35 inveigh against the increase of our luxuries; and here
also I expect the shout of modern politicians against me.
For twenty or thirty years past, it has been the fashion
to consider luxury as one of the greatest national advan-
tages; and all the wisdom of antiquity in that particular,
40 as erroneous. Still however, I must remain a professed
ancient on that head, and continue to think those
luxuries prejudicial to states, by which so many vices
are introduced, and so many kingdoms have been un-
done. Indeed so much has been poured out of late on the
45 other side of the question, that, merely for the sake of
novelty and variety, one would sometimes wish to be in
the right.

I am,
Dear Sir,
Your sincere friend,
and ardent admirer,

OLIVER GOLDSMITH.

Sweet Auburn, loveliest village of the plain,
Where health and plenty cheered the labouring swain,
Where smiling spring its earliest visit paid,
And parting summer's lingering blooms delayed:
5   Dear lovely bowers of innocence and ease,

---

d. 39. For the 'wisdom of antiquity' on this subject see the article by H. J.
Bell cited in the headnote, pp. 767–82.
1. Auburn] The origin of the name of G.'s village has exercised commen-
tators. Usually cited is an Auburn or Albourne in Wilts., 8 miles N.E. of
Marlborough. Forster, *Life* ii 206, says that G. obtained the name from
Bennet Langton: there is a village named Auburn, near Boothby in Lincoln-
shire, the county where Langton had his seat.

Seats of my youth, when every sport could please,
How often have I loitered o'er thy green,
Where humble happiness endeared each scene;
How often have I paused on every charm,
10   The sheltered cot, the cultivated farm,
The never-failing brook, the busy mill,
The decent church that topped the neighbouring hill,
The hawthorn bush, with seats beneath the shade,
For talking age and whispering lovers made.
15   How often have I blessed the coming day,
When toil remitting lent its turn to play,
And all the village train, from labour free,
Led up their sports beneath the spreading tree,
While many a pastime circled in the shade,
20   The young contending as the old surveyed;
And many a gambol frolicked o'er the ground,
And sleights of art and feats of strength went round.
And still as each repeated pleasure tired,
Succeeding sports the mirthful band inspired;
25   The dancing pair that simply sought renown,
By holding out to tire each other down;
The swain mistrustless of his smutted face,
While secret laughter tittered round the place;

---

11. All such features of G.'s village as the brook and mill throughout the poem, are 'identified' at Lissoy in the works by Newell and Prior mentioned in the headnote.

15. Those who are anxious to site G.'s village in Ireland argue that the 'coming day' is an Irish Catholic Sunday, on which dancing and the other amusements were common, rather than an English fair. Friedman suggests that G. refers to the traditional English holidays mentioned by him elsewhere, e.g. *Vicar* ch. iv, and 'The Revolution in Low Life' (*Works* iii 195). But G. seems to be describing a summer holiday, rather than Christmas, St Valentine's Day, Shrovetide, April 1 or Michaelmas Eve, described in these passages.

17. *train*] G. is curiously fond of this common poetical diction for 'retinue': cp. ll. 63, 81, 135, 149, 252, 320, 337.

18. *led up*] Led off, began. Cp. *Vicar* ch. ix: 'Mr. Thornhill and my eldest daughter led up the ball.'

25. *simply*] Naïvely (rather than *merely*).

27. *smutted face*] The result no doubt of some game in which the victim innocently imitates the actions of another, unaware that his hands have been covered in dirt or soot: e.g. the action to be imitated is that of rubbing one's fingers on the bottom of a plate and then on one's face. In the victim's case the bottom of the plate is covered with lampblack or something similar.

The bashful virgin's sidelong looks of love,
30 The matron's glance that would those looks reprove.
These were thy charms, sweet village; sports like these,
With sweet succession, taught even toil to please;
These round thy bowers their cheerful influence shed,
These were thy charms—But all these charms are fled.

35   Sweet smiling village, loveliest of the lawn,
Thy sports are fled and all thy charms withdrawn;
Amidst thy bowers the tyrant's hand is seen,
And desolation saddens all thy green:
One only master grasps the whole domain,
40 And half a tillage stints thy smiling plain:
No more thy glassy brook reflects the day,
But, choked with sedges, works its weedy way.
Along thy glades, a solitary guest,
The hollow-sounding bittern guards its nest;
45 Amidst thy desert walks the lapwing flies,
And tires their echoes with unvaried cries.
Sunk are thy bowers in shapeless ruin all,
And the long grass o'ertops the mouldering wall;
And trembling, shrinking from the spoiler's hand,
50 Far, far away, thy children leave the land.

29. Thomson, *Winter* 625: 'The kiss, snatched hasty from the sidelong maid'
(G. imitates this passage again later, see l. 122*n*), and *Summer* 1280: 'In side-
long glances from her downcast eye.'
39. In 'The Revolution in Low Life', 'a merchant of immense fortune in
London' has acquired the estate on which the villagers live and intends 'to
lay the whole out in a seat of pleasure for himself'. Cp. also the 'great
West-Indian' mentioned in the 'Anecdotes of G.', *Universal Mag.* (1780)
quoted in the headnote.
40. *tillage*] Tilled or ploughed land, as distinct from pasturage.
44. Cp. *Animated Nature* (1774) vi 1–2, on the noises of water fowl: 'Of all
those sounds, there is none so dismally hollow as the booming of the bittern.
It is impossible for words to give those who have not heard this evening-call
an adequate idea of its solemnity. It is like the interrupted bellowing of a
bull, but hollower and louder, and is heard at a mile's distance, as if issuing
from some formidable being that resided at the bottom of the waters.'
Cf. also vi 4: 'I remember in the place where I was a boy with what terror
this bird's note affected the whole village; they considered it as the presage of
some sad event; and generally found or made one to succeed it.' G. mentions
in this passage Thomson's reference to the bittern, *Spring* 21–3.
45. G. refers to the 'whining of the lapwing', *Animated Nature* vi 1.

Ill fares the land, to hastening ills a prey,
Where wealth accumulates and men decay:
Princes and lords may flourish or may fade;
A breath can make them, as a breath has made;
55 But a bold peasantry, their country's pride,
When once destroyed, can never be supplied.

A time there was, ere England's griefs began,
When every rood of ground maintained its man;
For him light labour spread her wholesome store,
60 Just gave what life required, but gave no more:
His best companions, innocence and health;
And his best riches, ignorance of wealth.

But times are altered; trade's unfeeling train
Usurp the land and dispossess the swain;
65 Along the lawn, where scattered hamlets rose,
Unwieldy wealth and cumbrous pomp repose;
And every want to opulence allied,
And every pang that folly pays to pride.
These gentle hours that plenty bade to bloom,
70 Those calm desires that asked but little room,
Those healthful sports that graced the peaceful scene,
Lived in each look and brightened all the green;
These, far departing, seek a kinder shore,

53–4. Prior compares De Caux de Montlebert, *L'Horloge de Sable, figure du monde* 11–12: *C'est un verre qui luit, / Qu'un souffle peut détruire, et qu'un souffle a produit.* This poem is printed in *Bibliotheque Poëtique* (Paris, 1745) iv 337, with which there is other evidence to suggest G. was familiar. See 93–6 *n.* But a more obvious source could have been Pope, *Imitations of Horace, Ep.* II i 300–1: 'Who pants for glory finds but short repose, / A breath revives him, or a breath o'erthrows.'
55–6. G. had made this point repeatedly elsewhere. Cp. *Citizen* (1762) i 62 (Letter 17), where he argues that colonialism involves the loss of 'the laborious and enterprising, of such men as can be serviceable to their country at home, of men who ought to be regarded as the sinews of the people'; and in 'The Revolution in Low Life' (*Works* ed. Friedman, iii 196) those who are being forced abroad 'should be considered as the strength and ornament of their country'. Cp. also *The Traveller* 397–8 and *n* (p. 654).
57–8. In the article cited in the headnote, H. J. Bell points out that a number of classical authors had compared with contemporary luxury the days when a mere two *iugera* of land would support a family: e.g. Juvenal, *Satires* xiv 140–9, 166–77; and Pliny, *Naturalis Historia* xviii 7.
67. *opulence*] luxury *ed 1.*

And rural mirth and manners are no more.

75 Sweet Auburn! parent of the blissful hour,
Thy glades forlorn confess the tyrant's power.
Here as I take my solitary rounds,
Amidst thy tangling walks and ruined grounds,
And, many a year elapsed, return to view
80 Where once the cottage stood, the hawthorn grew,
Remembrance wakes with all her busy train,
Swells at my breast and turns the past to pain.

In all my wanderings round this world of care,
In all my griefs—and God has given my share—
85 I still had hopes my latest hours to crown,
Amidst these humble bowers to lay me down;
To husband out life's taper at the close,
And keep the flame from wasting by repose.
I still had hopes, for pride attends us still,
90 Amidst the swains to show my book-learned skill,
Around my fire an evening group to draw,
And tell of all I felt and all I saw;
And, as a hare, whom hounds and horns pursue,

74. *manners*] Customs.
80. *Followed in edd 1–3 by*:
    Here, as with doubtful, pensive steps I range,
    Trace every scene, and wonder at the change,
84. Cp. Collins, *Persian Eclogues* ii 21–2: 'Ye mute companions of my toils, that bear, / In all my griefs, a more than equal share!'
82–96. Cp. *Citizen* (1762) ii 153 (renumbered Letter 103): 'There is something so seducing in that spot in which we first had existence, that nothing but it can please; whatever vicissitudes we experience in life, however we toil, or wheresoever we wander, our fatigued wishes still recur to home for tranquillity, we long to die in that spot which gave us birth, and in that pleasing expectation opiate every calamity.' Cp. also an essay in the *Royal Mag.* ii (1760) which contains resemblances to this passage (*Works* ed. Friedman, iii 66–71).
87–8. *Edd 1–3 have*: My anxious days to husband near the close, / And keep life's flame *etc*.
93–6. Cp. Racan (1589–1670), *Douceurs de la vie champêtre*, st. vii, printed in *Bibliotheque Poëtique* (1745) ii 10: *Il suit aucunes fois un cerf par les foulées, / Dans ses vieilles forêts du peuple reculées, / Et qui même du jour ignorent le flambeau: / Aucunes fois des chiens il suit les voix confuses; / Et voit enfin le liévre après toutes ses ruses, / Du lieu de sa naissance en faire son tombeau.* Cp. also Dryden, *To My Honour'd Kinsman, John Driden* 62–5: 'The Hare, in Pastures or in Plains is found, / Emblem of Humane Life, who runs the

Pants to the place from whence at first she flew,
95 I still had hopes, my long vexations past,
Here to return – and die at home at last.

O blest retirement, friend to life's decline,
Retreats from care, that never must be mine,
How happy he who crowns in shades like these
100 A youth of labour with an age of ease;
Who quits a world where strong temptations try
And, since 'tis hard to combat, learns to fly.
For him no wretches, born to work and weep,
Explore the mine or tempt the dangerous deep;
105 No surly porter stands in guilty state
To spurn imploring famine from the gate;
But on he moves to meet his latter end,
Angels around befriending virtue's friend;
Bends to the grave with unperceived decay,
110 While resignation gently slopes the way;
And, all his prospects brightening to the last,
His Heaven commences ere the world be past!

Round; / And, after all his wand'ring Ways are done, / His Circle fills, and
ends where he begun . . .'
97–112. This passage contains a number of echoes of Virgil's celebration of
rural life, *Georgics* ii 458ff. Cp. also Pope, *Windsor Forest* 237–40.
99. happy] blest is *ed 1.*
102. Cp. *The Bee* No. ii, 13 Oct. 1759: 'by struggling with misfortunes, we
are sure to receive some wounds in the conflict. The only method to come
off victorious, is by running away.'
104. tempt] Common poetical diction for 'venture on', from Latin (cp.
Collins, *Persian Eclogues* ii 36n); enfeebled by having to follow 'temptations'
in l. 101 above.
105. Cp. *Citizen* (1762) i 123 (renumbered Letter 30): 'I never see a noble-
man's door half opened that some surly porter or footman does not stand
full in the breach.'
106. the] his *ed 1.*
109. Bends] Sinks *ed 1.*   Cp. Dryden, *State of Innocence* V i: 'Still quitting
ground, by unperceiv'd decay, / And steal myself from life, and melt away';
Johnson, *Vanity of Human Wishes* 292–3: 'An age that melts with un-
perceiv'd decay, / And glides in modest Innocence away'; and *Irene* II vii
91: 'And varied Life steal unperceiv'd away.'
110. Reynolds painted a picture of 'An Old Man' in 1771, which he entitled
'Resignation' when it was engraved by Thomas Watson in 1772. It was
inscribed: 'This attempt to express a Character in *The Deserted Village*, is
dedicated to Dr. Goldsmith, by his sincere Friend and admirer, JOSHUA
REYNOLDS.'

Sweet was the sound, when oft at evening's close
Up yonder hill the village murmur rose;
115   There, as I passed with careless steps and slow,
The mingling notes came softened from below;
The swain responsive as the milkmaid sung,
The sober herd that lowed to meet their young;
The noisy geese that gabbled o'er the pool,
120   The playful children just let loose from school;
The watchdog's voice that bayed the whispering wind,
And the loud laugh that spoke the vacant mind;
These all in sweet confusion sought the shade,
And filled each pause the nightingale had made.
125   But now the sounds of population fail,
No cheerful murmurs fluctuate in the gale,
No busy steps the grassgrown foot-way tread,
For all the bloomy flush of life is fled.
All but yon widowed, solitary thing
130   That feebly bends beside the plashy spring;
She, wretched matron, forced, in age, for bread,
To strip the brook with mantling cresses spread,
To pick her wintry faggot from the thorn,
To seek her nightly shed and weep till morn;

114. hill] Identified by those anxious to find a Lissoy original with 'the little mount before Lishoy gate' from which could be seen 'the most pleasing horizon in nature', mentioned by G. in a letter in Dec. 1757 (*Letters* p. 30).

115. Cp. Gray, *Ode for Music* 36n (p. 270).

116. Cp. Pope, *Rape of the Lock* ii 50: 'And soften'd Sounds along the Waters die'.

117. Cp. Gray, *Ode on the Spring* 6n (p. 49).

122. vacant] Untroubled by thought, carefree (as in 'vacant hilarity', *Vicar* ch. v); G. was probably echoing Thomson, *Winter* 622–4: 'Rustic mirth goes round— / The simple joke that takes the shepherd's heart, / Easily pleased; the long loud laugh sincere'. Cf. l. 29n above.

123. sweet] soft *edd 1–3* (changed because of 'softened' in l. 116, though he had used 'Sweet' in l. 113).

124. Cp. *Animated Nature* v 327–8, on the nightingale: 'Her note is soft, various, and interrupted; she seldom holds it without a pause above the time that one can count twenty. The nightingale's pausing song would be the proper epithet for this bird's music with us'. G. says that this bird is 'totally unknown' in Ireland, a blow for the Lissoyans, who however claim that the robin is the 'Irish nightingale'.

128. For] But *edd 1–3.*

129–36. G.'s cress-gatherer is identified as a Catherine Giraghty of Lissoy by Strean, Newell and Prior.

130. plashy] Abounding in pools, marshy.

135 She only left of all the harmless train,
       The sad historian of the pensive plain.

       Near yonder copse, where once the garden smiled,
       And still where many a garden flower grows wild;
       There, where a few torn shrubs the place disclose,
140 The village preacher's modest mansion rose.
       A man he was to all the country dear,
       And passing rich with forty pounds a year;
       Remote from towns he ran his godly race,
       Nor e'er had changed, nor wished to change, his
              place;
145 Unpractised he to fawn, or seek for power,
       By doctrines fashioned to the varying hour;
       Far other aims his heart had learned to prize,
       More skilled to raise the wretched than to rise.
       His house was known to all the vagrant train,
150 He chid their wanderings, but relieved their pain;
       The long-remembered beggar was his guest,

140. The 'village preacher' has inevitably been identified with G.'s father, the Rev. Charles G. and his brother, the Rev. Henry G., both of whom held the living of Kilkenny West near Lissoy, as well as with his uncle, Thomas Contarine, Prebend of Oran. Mrs Hodson, G.'s sister, wrote that, 'as to the Charactor of his father none c^d draw it better than himself in the Village Preacher in his Deserted Village which is none [= known] to be a just Picture of that Worthy man', (*Letters* p. 162).

142. passing] Exceedingly. G. described his brother Henry, in the Dedication to *The Traveller*, as 'a man, who, despising fame and fortune, has retired early to happiness and obscurity, with an income of forty pounds a year'. This was also the salary of Henry's successor (Mangin, p. 140). The sum is quoted as proper for modest contentment in an article attributed to G. in the *Critical Review* in 1760 (*Works* ed. Friedman, i 227). Cp. Swift, *A Libel on Doctor Delany* 133–4: 'Or, some remote inferior *Post*, / With forty Pounds a Year at most.' Dr Primrose's first living brought him £35 a year, his second only £15 (*Vicar* chs. ii, iii). Parson Adams's (*Joseph Andrews* ch. iii) was £23.

144. place] Appointment, or (in this case) living.

145. Unpractised] Unskilful *edd 1–3* (no doubt caused by the change in l. 148).

148. skilled] bent *edd 1–3*. (G. probably realised that the purely physical connotations of 'bent' made the line ludicrous.)

149. Cp. Prior, *Life* ii 268–9, who suggests that G. is describing the relatively 'privileged' beggars of Ireland, who were provided for by no Poor Laws and therefore had to be maintained by the 'poorer and middling classes of people', rather than English beggars.

Whose beard descending swept his aged breast;
The ruined spendthrift, now no longer proud,
Claimed kindred there and had his claims allowed;
155   The broken soldier, kindly bade to stay,
Sat by his fire and talked the night away;
Wept o'er his wounds or tales of sorrow done,
Shouldered his crutch and showed how fields were won.
Pleased with his guests, the good man learned to glow,
160   And quite forgot their vices in their woe;
Careless their merits or their faults to scan,
His pity gave ere charity began.

      Thus to relieve the wretched was his pride,
And even his failings leaned to virtue's side;
165   But in his duty prompt at every call,
He watched and wept, he prayed and felt, for all.
And, as a bird each fond endearment tries
To tempt its new-fledged offspring to the skies,
He tried each art, reproved each dull delay,
170   Allured to brighter worlds and led the way.

      Beside the bed where parting life was laid,
And sorrow, guilt, and pain by turns dismayed,
The reverend champion stood. At his control,
Despair and anguish fled the struggling soul;
175   Comfort came down the trembling wretch to raise,
And his last faltering accents whispered praise.

      At church, with meek and unaffected grace,
His looks adorned the venerable place;
Truth from his lips prevailed with double sway,
180   And fools, who came to scoff, remained to pray.
The service past, around the pious man,

152. Mitford compares Joseph Hall, *Virgidemiarum* IV i 168: 'Stay till my beard shall sweep mine aged breast'.
155. Cp. the 'old broken soldiers' mentioned in *Vicar* ch. iii.
159–60. Pope, *Elegy to an Unfortunate Lady* 45–6: 'So perish all, whose breast ne'er learned to glow / For others' good, or melt at others' woe.'
170. Tickell, *On the Death of Mr Addison* 42: 'And saints who taught, and led, the way to Heaven'; and Dryden, *Character of a Good Parson* 19–20: 'For, letting down the golden Chain from high, / He drew his Audience upward to the Sky'.
180. Dryden, *Britannia Rediviva* 4: 'And sent us back to Praise, who came to Pray.'

With steady zeal, each honest rustic ran;
Even children followed with endearing wile,
And plucked his gown, to share the good man's smile.
185 His ready smile a parent's warmth expressed,
Their welfare pleased him and their cares distressed;
To them his heart, his love, his griefs were given,
But all his serious thoughts had rest in Heaven.
As some tall cliff, that lifts its awful form,
190 Swells from the vale and midway leaves the storm,
Though round its breast the rolling clouds are spread,
Eternal sunshine settles on its head.

Beside yon straggling fence that skirts the way,
With blossomed furze unprofitably gay,
195 There, in his noisy mansion, skilled to rule,
The village master taught his little school;
A man severe he was and stern to view;
I knew him well, and every truant knew;
Well had the boding tremblers learned to trace
200 The day's disasters in his morning face;
Full well they laughed, with counterfeited glee,
At all his jokes, for many a joke had he;

182. steady] ready *ed 1* (changed to avoid the repetition in l. 185).
189–92. Cp. *Animated Nature* i 144–5: 'Upon emerging from this war of the elements, he ascends into a purer and serener region, where vegetation is entirely ceased; where the precipices, composed entirely of rocks, rise perpendicularly above him; while he views beneath him all the combat of the elements; clouds at his feet; and thunders darting upwards from their bosoms below.' G.'s source for this description was *A Voyage to South-America . . . by Don George Juan, and Don Antonio de Ulloa* (1758) i 231. Cp. also Young, *Night Thoughts* ii (*ad fin*): 'As some tall tower, or lofty mountain's brow / Detains the sun illustrious from its height; / While rising vapours and descending shades / With damps and darkness drown the spacious vale . . .' Parallels in Lucan, Statius, Claudian, Chapelain, Chaulieu have also been suggested.
192. Pope, *Eloisa to Abelard* 209: 'Eternal sun-shine of thy spotless mind'.
196. village master] Supposedly to be identified with G.'s master at Lissoy, Thomas Byrne. Cp. Mangin (pp. 141–2); Prior, *Life* ii 266–7; and the narrative of Mrs Hodson, G.'s sister, who wrote of the master that, 'tho he was severe on the D^r yet he was his greatest favourite & from him I realy beleive he first Learnd to despise fortune & feel more for every creature he saw in distress then for him self', (*Letters* p. 164).
199–204. Dobson cites *Spectator* No. 49, where 'Eubulus' has a similar effect on his 'little Diurnal Audience' in the coffee-house, although he is imitated for disinterested motives.

Full well the busy whisper, circling round,
Conveyed the dismal tidings when he frowned;
205 Yet he was kind, or, if severe in aught,
The love he bore to learning was in fault;
The village all declared how much he knew;
'Twas certain he could write and cipher too;
Lands he could measure, terms and tides presage,
210 And even the story ran that he could gauge.
In arguing too, the parson owned his skill,
For even though vanquished, he could argue still;
While words of learned length and thundering sound
Amazed the gazing rustics ranged around,
215 And still they gazed, and still the wonder grew,
That one small head could carry all he knew.

But past is all his fame. The very spot,
Where many a time he triumphed, is forgot.
Near yonder thorn, that lifts its head on high,
220 Where once the signpost caught the passing eye,
Low lies that house where nutbrown draughts inspired,
Where greybeard mirth and smiling toil retired,
Where village statesmen talked with looks profound,
And news much older than their ale went round.
225 Imagination fondly stoops to trace
The parlour splendours of that festive place;
The white-washed wall, the nicely sanded floor,
The varnished clock that clicked behind the door;
The chest contrived a double debt to pay,
230 A bed by night, a chest of drawers by day;
The pictures placed for ornament and use,
The twelve good rules, the royal game of goose;

205–6. The 'aught/fault' rhyme was correct in the eighteenth century.
Johnson in his *Dictionary* quotes a 'fault/thought' rhyme from Dryden and
it occurs in Pope, *Essay on Criticism* 422–3. Cp. also *Edwin and Angelina* st.
xxxv and *Retaliation* 73–4 (p. 605 and p. 752 below).
208. cipher] 'To practise arithmetic' (Johnson), used especially of elementary
education.
209. terms] Term or quarter days, when rents, wages, and other dues were
paid and tenancies begun and ended.   *tides*] Moveable feasts of the year.
210. gauge] Calculate the capacity of some such vessel as a cask, usually with
a gauging rod. A gauger was an exciseman: so Fielding, *Joseph Andrews* I
xvi: 'the exciseman descended into the cellar to gauge the vessels.'
227 36. A reworking of *Description of an Author's Bedchamber* 9–20 (see p. 589).
232. For the 'twelve good rules' and 'game of goose', see *Description of an
Author's Bedchamber* 11n and 12n.

The hearth, except when winter chilled the day,
With aspen boughs and flowers and fennel gay;
235   While broken teacups, wisely kept for show,
Ranged o'er the chimney, glistened in a row.

Vain, transitory splendours! Could not all
Reprieve the tottering mansion from its fall!
Obscure it sinks, nor shall it more impart
240   An hour's importance to the poor man's heart;
Thither no more the peasant shall repair
To sweet oblivion of his daily care;
No more the farmer's news, the barber's tale,
No more the woodman's ballad shall prevail;
245   No more the smith his dusky brow shall clear,
Relax his ponderous strength and lean to hear;
The host himself no longer shall be found
Careful to see the mantling bliss go round;
Nor the coy maid, half willing to be pressed,
250   Shall kiss the cup to pass it to the rest.

Yes! let the rich deride, the proud disdain,
These simple blessings of the lowly train;
To me more dear, congenial to my heart,
One native charm than all the gloss of art;
255   Spontaneous joys, where nature has its play,
The soul adopts and owns their firstborn sway;
Lightly they frolic o'er the vacant mind,

235-6. Swift, *Baucis and Philemon* 113-14: 'The Porrengers that in a Row /
Hung high and made a glitt'ring Show'.
248. *mantling*] Frothing. Cp. Gray, *Descent of Odin* 43 (p. 225).
249-50. Friedman compares G.'s 'History of Miss Stanton', *British Mag.* i
(July 1760) (*Works* iii 130): 'the earthen mug went round. Miss touched the
cup, the stranger pledged the parson'.
251-2. Cp. Gray, *Elegy* 29-32 (pp. 122-3).
251-64. G. contrasts 'Artificial pleasure' unfavourably with simple and
healthy rural pleasures in an essay, 'A Lady of Fashion in the Times of Anna
Bullen compared with one of Modern Times', in the *Lady's Mag.* in Oct.
1760, in *Works* ed. Friedman, iii 149: 'The midnight masquerade, the pro-
longed brag party, the five hours labour of the toilet are only the pleasures of
fashion and caprice, and will last no longer than till some more fashionable
folly comes to take their place. Happy they who pursue pleasure as far as
Nature directs, and no farther; pleasure rightly understood, and prudently
followed, is but another name for virtue!'
257. Cp. 122 and *n* above.

Unenvied, unmolested, unconfined:
But the long pomp, the midnight masquerade,
260 With all the freaks of wanton wealth arrayed,
In these, ere triflers half their wish obtain,
The toiling pleasure sickens into pain;
And, even while fashion's brightest arts decoy,
The heart distrusting asks, if this be joy.

265   Ye friends to truth, ye statesmen, who survey
The rich man's joys increase, the poor's decay,
'Tis yours to judge how wide the limits stand
Between a splendid and an happy land.
Proud swells the tide with loads of freighted ore,
270 And shouting Folly hails them from her shore;
Hoards, even beyond the miser's wish abound,
And rich men flock from all the world around.
Yet count our gains. This wealth is but a name
That leaves our useful products still the same.

258. The use of three negative past participles to the line is in Milton's manner,
Par. Lost ii 185, v 896.
259. Cp. Pope, Rape of the Lock i 72: 'In Courtly Balls, and Midnight
Masquerades'.
261–4. Cp. Thomson, Autumn 1253–6, condemning 'those fantastic joys /
That still amuse the wanton, still deceive; / A face of pleasure, but a heart of
pain; / Their hollow moments undelighted all.'
266. Cp. 'The Revolution in Low Life', in Works ed. Friedman, iii 197:
'Wherever the traveller turns, while he sees one part of the inhabitants of
the country becoming immensely rich, he sees the other growing miserably
poor, and the happy equality of condition now entirely removed.'
262. Cp. Pope, Essay on Man iv 45–6: 'Abstract what others feel, what others
think, / All pleasures sicken'.
267–8. Cp. Citizen (1762) i 98 (Letter 25): 'too much commerce may injure
a nation as well as too little; and ... there is a wide difference between a
conquering and a flourishing empire.'
273–86. Cp. 'The Revolution in Low Life', in Works ed. Friedman, iii 197–8:
'Let others felicitate their country upon the encrease of foreign commerce and
the extension of our foreign conquests; but for my part this new introduction
of wealth gives me but very little satisfaction. Foreign commerce, as it can
be managed only by a few, tends proportionally to enrich only a few . . . .
A country, thus parcelled out among the rich alone, is of all others the most
miserable . . . . A country, therefore, where the inhabitants are thus divided
into the very rich and very poor, is, indeed, of all others the most helpless;
without courage and without strength; neither enjoying peace within itself,
and, after a time, unable to resist foreign invasion.'

275   Not so the loss. The man of wealth and pride
        Takes up a space that many poor supplied;
        Space for his lake, his park's extended bounds,
        Space for his horses, equipage and hounds;
        The robe that wraps his limbs in silken sloth
280   Has robbed the neighbouring field of half their growth;
        His seat, where solitary sports are seen,
        Indignant spurns the cottage from the green;
        Around the world each needful product flies,
        For all the luxuries the world supplies:
285   While thus the land, adorned for pleasure all,
        In barren splendour feebly waits the fall.

        As some fair female unadorned and plain,
        Secure to please while youth confirms her reign,
        Slights every borrowed charm that dress supplies,
290   Nor shares with art the triumph of her eyes;
        But when those charms are passed, for charms are frail,
        When time advances and when lovers fail,
        She then shines forth, solicitous to bless,
        In all the glaring impotence of dress:
295   Thus fares the land, by luxury betrayed,
        In nature's simplest charms at first arrayed;
        But verging to decline, its splendours rise,
        Its vistas strike, its palaces surprise;
        While scourged by famine from the smiling land,
300   The mournful peasant leads his humble band;
        And while he sinks, without one arm to save,
        The country blooms–a garden and a grave.

        Where then, ah where, shall poverty reside,
        To scape the pressure of contiguous pride?
305   If to some common's fenceless limits strayed,

275–86. Horace, *Odes* II xv 1–5: *Iam pauca aratro iugera regiae / moles relinquent, undique latius / extenta visentur Lucrino / stagna lacu, platanusque caelebs // evincet ulmos* (A short time and our princely piles will leave but few acres to the plough; on all sides will be seen our fishponds spreading wider than the Lucrine Lake, and the lonely plane-tree will drive out the elm). For the influence on G. of classical protests against the growth of private estates, see the article by H. J. Bell cited in headnote; and cp. G.'s ref. to 'the wisdom of antiquity' in the Dedication.

294. Cp. Prior, *Solomon* i 95: 'Our vile Attire, and Impotence of Pride'.

305–8. G. seems here definitely to refer to the effect of the enclosure of common land (ll. 39–50 might be similarly interpreted). In general, however, G. is not concerned with what now appear to be the major economic shifts

He drives his flock to pick the scanty blade,
Those fenceless fields the sons of wealth divide,
And even the bare-worn common is denied.

    If to the city sped – What waits him there?
310 To see profusion that he must not share;
To see ten thousand baneful arts combined
To pamper luxury and thin mankind;
To see those joys the sons of pleasure know
Extorted from his fellow creature's woe.
315 Here, while the courtier glitters in brocade,
There the pale artist plies the sickly trade;
Here, while the proud their long-drawn pomps display,
There the black gibbet glooms beside the way.
The dome where Pleasure holds her midnight reign
320 Here, richly decked, admits the gorgeous train;
Tumultuous grandeur crowds the blazing square,
The rattling chariots clash, the torches glare.
Sure scenes like these no troubles e'er annoy!
Sure these denote one universal joy!
325 Are these thy serious thoughts? – Ah, turn thine eyes

of the age – the industrial or agricultural revolution, the shift of population
to the cities – but rather with the acquisition of land by the rich commercial
class for their pleasure gardens, which G. sees as expressing most clearly the
bourgeois capitalism he was deploring.
309–25. Some details of this description of city pleasures are influenced by
a similar passage on the 'sons of riot' in Thomson, *Winter* 630–45.
310. Cp. *Animated Nature* iii 42–3: 'In countries where a greater inequality of
conditions prevail, the shepherd is generally some poor wretch who attends
a flock from which he is to derive no benefits, and only guards those
luxuries which he is not fated to share.'
313. those joys] each joy *ed* 1.
316. artist] Artisan.
318. Public executions at Tyburn were not abolished until 1783 and in
other parts of the country they continued well into the nineteenth century.
For G.'s views on capital punishment, see *Vicar* ch. xxvii.
   glooms] Frowns, lowers. Cp. the transitive use of the verb in l. 363 below.
319. dome] Simply a building (Lat. *domus*).
321–2. Cp. Johnson, *London* 182–3: 'th'affrighted crowd's tumultuous
cries / Roll thro' the streets, and thunder to the skies.'
325–36. Cp. a passage which appears first in *The Bee* No. iv, 27 Oct. 1759
in 'A City Night-Piece' and later in *Citizen* (1762) ii 211 (later renumbered
Letter 117): 'These poor shivering females have once seen happier days, and
been flattered into beauty. They have been prostituted to the gay luxurious
villain, and are now turned out to meet the severity of winter. Perhaps, now

Where the poor, houseless, shivering female lies.
She once, perhaps, in village plenty blest,
Has wept at tales of innocence distressed;
Her modest looks the cottage might adorn,
330   Sweet as the primrose peeps beneath the thorn;
Now lost to all; her friends, her virtue fled,
Near her betrayer's door she lays her head,
And, pinched with cold and shrinking from the shower,
With heavy heart deplores that luckless hour,
335   When idly first, ambitious of the town,
She left her wheel and robes of country brown.

Do thine, sweet Auburn, thine, the loveliest train,
Do thy fair tribes participate her pain?
Even now, perhaps, by cold and hunger led,
340   At proud men's doors they ask a little bread!

Ah, no. To distant climes, a dreary scene,
Where half the convex world intrudes between,
Through torrid tracts with fainting steps they go,
Where wild Altama murmurs to their woe.

lying at the doors of their betrayers, they sue to wretches whose hearts
are insensible, or debauchees who may curse, but will not relieve them.'
338. participate] The transitive use is found into the nineteenth century.
341. G.'s description of what awaited the emigrant differs markedly from
those of earlier poets. Johnson (*Lives of the Poets*, ed. G. B. Hill, ii 393–4)
condemned the poet who 'guides the unhappy fugitive from want and
persecution to plenty, quiet, and security, and seats him in scenes of peaceful
solitude, and undisturbed repose'. But he himself had done just that in *London*
(1738) 170–5. Cp. also J. Warton, *The Enthusiast* (1744) 233–52.
343. Through] To *edd 1–3*.
344. Altama] The Altamaha, a river in the state of Georgia, in North America.
G. may not be purporting to describe Georgia in particular and his descrip-
tion in some ways seems more like South than North America. But G. was
friendly with General Oglethorpe, who had obtained the charter for the
foundation of the state in 1732 and was probably familiar with certain
aspects of its early history which were appropriate to his poem. Cp. William
Burke, *Account of the European Settlements in America* (3rd edn, 1760) ii 264:
'In pursuance of the original design, the trustees [of Georgia] resolved to
encourage poor people to settle in the province, which had been committed
to their care; and to this purpose found them in necessaries to transport them
into a country, of which they had previously published a most exaggerated
and flattering description. In reality the country differs little from South

345 Far different there from all that charmed before
    The various terrors of that horrid shore:
    Those blazing suns that dart a downward ray,
    And fiercely shed intolerable day;
    Those matted woods where birds forget to sing,
350 But silent bats in drowsy clusters cling;
    Those poisonous fields with rank luxuriance crowned,
    Where the dark scorpion gathers death around;
    Where at each step the stranger fears to wake
    The rattling terrors of the vengeful snake;
355 Where crouching tigers wait their hapless prey,

Carolina, but that the summers are yet hotter, and the soil in the general of a poorer kind.'

For the details of his description, G. could have had many sources. But Burke (ii 273) also describes the powerful tribes of Indians bordering on Georgia: cp. l. 356; and see l. 355n.

348. intolerable day] Cp. Dryden, *Palamon and Arcite* iii 81: 'So fierce they flashed intolerable day'; and Thomson, *Summer* (1727) 627, has 'intolerable day' in a passage on the tropics dropped in 1744.

349. For the silent birds see J. R. Moore, 'Goldsmith's Degenerate Song-Birds: an Eighteenth Century Fallacy in Ornithology', *Isis* xxxiv (1943) 324–7, which discusses the widespread belief at this period, emanating from the French naturalist Buffon, that all American species, including man, had degenerated.

355. tigers] G. has often been derided for introducing tigers into Georgia. But *Animated Nature* ii 332, iii 244, makes it clear that G. meant, not the jaguar which is not found north of Texas, but the 'Red Tiger' or cougar. In calling it a tiger G. was following Buffon, according to whom the term was applied in America to some dozen animals. See E. D. Seeber, 'Goldsmith's American Tigers', *Modern Language Quarterly* vi (1945) 417–19. G. also describes the 'American tiger' or 'cougar' in his introduction to Brookes's *Natural History* (1763), in *Works* ed. Friedman, v 246. 'Tigers' in Georgia are mentioned in *A Voyage to Georgia. By a Young Gentleman* (2nd edn, 1737) p. 13; and W. Burke, *Account of the European Settlements in America* (3rd edn, 1760) ii 211, refers to 'a sort of panther or tiger' found in Virginia.

355–62. Mitford compares Sir William Temple, 'Upon the Approach of the Shore at Harwich', *Works*, 1720, i 320: 'Their vast and frightful Woods seem only made / To cover cruel Deeds, and give a Shade / To Savage Beasts, who on the weaker prey, / Or human Savages more wild than they. / Thy pleasant Thickets, and thy shady Groves, / Only relieve the Heats, and cover Loves, / Shelt'ring no other Thefts or Cruelties, / But those of killing or beguiling Eyes.' But cp. also Waller, *Upon the Death of My Lady Rich* 3–4: 'Prove all a desert, and none there make stay, / But savage beasts, or men as wild as they'.

And savage men more murderous still than they;
While oft in whirls the mad tornado flies,
Mingling the ravaged landscape with the skies.
Far different these from every former scene,
360   The cooling brook, the grassy-vested green,
The breezy covert of the warbling grove,
That only sheltered thefts of harmless love.

Good Heaven! what sorrows gloomed that parting
day,
That called them from their native walks away;
365   When the poor exiles, every pleasure past,
Hung round their bowers and fondly looked their last,
And took a long farewell and wished in vain
For seats like these beyond the western main;
And shuddering still to face the distant deep,
370   Returned and wept, and still returned to weep.
The good old sire the first prepared to go
To new-found worlds, and wept for others' woe;
But for himself, in conscious virtue brave,
He only wished for worlds beyond the grave.
375   His lovely daughter, lovelier in her tears,
The fond companion of his helpless years,
Silent went next, neglectful of her charms,
And left a lover's for a father's arms.
With louder plaints the mother spoke her woes,
380   And blessed the cot where every pleasure rose;
And kissed her thoughtless babes with many a tear,
And clasped them close, in sorrow doubly dear;
Whilst her fond husband strove to lend relief
In all the silent manliness of grief.

363. *gloomed*] Made gloomy or melancholy. Cp. Young, *Night Thoughts* ii
358: 'A night that glooms us in the noontide ray.'
373. Cp. Pope, *Prologue to Cato* 3: 'mankind, in conscious virtue bold'.
375–84. Cp. 'The Revolution in Low Life', in *Works* ed. Friedman, iii 196,
describing the departure of the villagers: 'The modest matron followed her
husband in tears, and often looked back at the little mansion where she had
passed her life in innocence, and to which she was never more to return;
while the beautiful daughter parted for ever from her Lover, who was now
become too poor to maintain her as his wife.' Cp. also *The Traveller* 405–9
(p. 655); and H. J. Bell cites Horace, *Odes* II xviii 26–8, on the effect of the
rich man's palace: *pellitur paternos / in sinu ferens deos / et uxor et vir sordidosque
natos* (Man and wife are driven forth bearing in their arms their household
gods and ragged children).
378. *a father's*] her father's *edd 1–3*.
384. *silent*] decent *edd 1–3*.

385   O luxury! thou cursed by Heaven's decree,
How ill exchanged are things like these for thee!
How do thy potions with insidious joy
Diffuse their pleasures only to destroy!
Kingdoms, by thee to sickly greatness grown,
390   Boast of a florid vigour not their own.
At every draught more large and large they grow,
A bloated mass of rank unwieldy woe;
Till sapped their strength and every part unsound,
Down, down they sink and spread a ruin round.

395   Even now the devastation is begun,
And half the business of destruction done;
Even now, methinks, as pondering here I stand,
I see the rural virtues leave the land.
Down where yon anchoring vessel spreads the sail,
400   That idly waiting flaps with every gale,
Downward they move, a melancholy band,
Pass from the shore and darken all the strand.
Contented toil and hospitable care,
And kind connubial tenderness are there;
405   And piety, with wishes placed above,
And steady loyalty and faithful love.
And thou, sweet Poetry, thou loveliest maid,

385. G. at times apparently defends 'luxury' in his prose writings but is not necessarily contradicting himself. Like other eighteenth-century writers on the subject he made a distinction between innocent and pernicious luxury and consistently attacked the latter, which he identified as profusion, excessive sensuality, extravagance and oppression by the rich. Cf. for his different approaches to the subject, *Citizen*, Letters 11 and 82; *The Bee* No. v, 'On political Frugality'; *Works* ed. Friedman, iii 73; and *The Traveller* 213–14 and *n* (p. 643).

386. Cp. *Citizen* (1762) i 62 (Letter 17): 'England, therefore, must make an exchange of her best and bravest subjects for raw silk, hemp, and tobacco; her hardy veterans and honest tradesmen, must be truck'd for a box of snuff or a silk petticoat.' Cp. also *The Traveller* 397–8 (p. 654 above).

389–94. Cp. *The Traveller* 144*n* for the image (p. 639).

398. A resemblance to George Herbert, *The Church Militant* 235–6, is probably coincidental: 'Religion stands on tip-toe in our land, / Ready to pass to the American strand.'

402. Cp. Dryden, *Absalom and Achitophel* 272: 'Cov'ring the Beach, and blackning all the *Strand*'.

403–6. These are the 'rural virtues' England is losing.

407–16. For the association of poetry with national virtues, cp. Thomson, *Liberty*; Collins, *Ode to Liberty*; Gray, *Progress of Poesy*. Friedman cites G.'s

> Still first to fly where sensual joys invade;
> Unfit, in these degenerate times of shame,
> *410* To catch the heart or strike for honest fame;
> Dear charming nymph, neglected and decried,
> My shame in crowds, my solitary pride;
> Thou source of all my bliss and all my woe,
> That found'st me poor at first and keep'st me so;
> *415* Thou guide by which the nobler arts excel,
> Thou nurse of every virtue, fare thee well!
> Farewell, and oh, where'er thy voice be tried,
> On Torno's cliffs or Pambamarca's side,
> Whether where equinoctial fervours glow,
> *420* Or winter wraps the polar world in snow,
> Still let thy voice, prevailing over time,
> Redress the rigours of the inclement clime;
> Aid slighted truth; with thy persuasive strain
> Teach erring man to spurn the rage of gain;
> *425* Teach him that states of native strength possessed,
> Though very poor, may still be very blest;
> That trade's proud empire hastes to swift decay,
> As ocean sweeps the laboured mole away;
> While self-dependent power can time defy,
> *430* As rocks resist the billows and the sky.

Roman History (1769) i 249: the Romans 'now began to have a relish for poetry, the first liberal art which rises in every civilized nation, and the first also that decays.'

410. Prior (*Life* ii 432*n*) notes that G. is fond of this usage and cites *Grecian History* (1774) i 166, 'strike for' victory; and *Vicar* ch. xx, 'strike for a subscription'.

418. Torno] The Swedish river Tornea or Torne, and the town and lake of the same name, on the Gulf of Bothnia. This, rather than the identification with Torno, a village on Lake Como in N. Italy, is proved both by G.'s desire here for an antithesis and by the fact that the Académie des Sciences of Paris made expeditions in the 1730s to both Torno and Quito, a town in Ecuador (then in Peru), near which is the mountain of Pambamarca, also mentioned in this line. Friedman cites J. B. Le Blanc, *Letters on the English and French Nations* (1747) i 173, on the 'academicians, who are actually measuring a degree of the earth, some in the scorching heat of *Quito*, others on the benumbing ice of *Torno*'. G. refers to the expedition to Quito in *Citizen* (1762) ii 74 (Letter 82) and an essay in the *Royal Mag.* in July 1760 (*Works* iii 73). In *Animated Nature* i 383, G. also quotes a description of Pambamarca from Ulloa, *Voyage to South America* (1758) i 473.

419. equinoctial fervours] The intense heat at the Equator.

427–30. Written by Johnson (see headnote).

22 Epitaph [on Thomas Parnell]

This *Epitaph* cannot be definitely dated but has usually been connected with the *Life* of Parnell which G. wrote for the edn of his poems published by Tom Davies in June 1770. It is not clear why G. should have written an epitaph for a poet who died in 1718; but it is worth noting that, in his *Life* p.v, G. states that his father and uncle had both been acquainted with Parnell. The *Epitaph* may also be related to an undated incident at Reynolds's, recorded by Miss Frances Reynolds, *Johnsonian Miscellanies*, ed. G. B. Hill (1897) ii 293–4. G. had asked Johnson to write an epitaph for Parnell and Johnson almost immediately recited one in extempore latin:

'Every person that understood latin seem'd much pleased with it. But Dr. Goldsmith, for what reason I know not, paid him no compliment, and only said on hearing it, "Ay, but this is in latin." "'Tis in latin, to be sure," reply'd Dr. Johnson. I do not remember what follow'd, but I could not forget the striking proof that Dr. Johnson gave of his abilities on this occasion, nor of Dr. Goldsmith's unwillingness to be pleased with it, apparently confused, and not knowing what to say. I did not hear him express any desire to have the epitaph in english, either before or after Dr. Johnson composed it. However he soon after wrote one himself in english, and it is, I believe, inscribed on Dr. Parnel's Tomb.'

No such use of G.'s epitaph as suggested by Miss Reynolds has been found and she may also have been mistaken in thinking that G. had yet to write it. G. may well have been intending to produce the epitaph as if it had been improvised and then been disconcerted to find that Johnson was using Latin for the purpose.

The *Epitaph* was first published with *The Haunch of Venison* in 1776, p. 9, and first collected in 1777 p. 68.

> This tomb, inscribed to gentle Parnell's name,
> May speak our gratitude, but not his fame.
> What heart but feels his sweetly-moral lay,
> That leads to truth through pleasure's flowery way?
> 5   Celestial themes confessed his tuneful aid;
> And Heaven, that lent him genius, was repaid.
> Needless to him the tribute we bestow,
> The transitory breath of fame below:
> More lasting rapture from his works shall rise,
> 10 While converts thank their poet in the skies.

23 The Haunch of Venison.
A Poetical Epistle to Lord Clare

Written not earlier than 24 Oct. 1770 and probably not later than Jan. 1771. The dating rests primarily on G.'s references to newspaper writers (see ll. 77–8 n), one of whom began contributing on 24 Oct. 1770, another ceasing to appear after mid-Jan. 1771. G. may also refer to another periodical essay published late in Jan. 1771. Other allusions in the poem – to Dorothy Monroe (l. 24) and to the trial of the Duke of Cumberland on 5 July 1770 (l. 60) – confirm that the poem must have been written in this period, as do the facts of G.'s friendship with Lord Clare. G. was in the country with Clare on 27 Oct. 1770 (see below) so that it is unlikely that the poem was written before Nov.

G. appears to have met Robert Nugent (1702–88), to whom the poem is addressed, in about 1765, soon after the publication of The Traveller. Nugent, who became Viscount Clare and Baron Nugent in 1766 and Earl Nugent in 1776, had been a M.P. since 1741, was Vice-Treasurer for Ireland 1760–65 and 1768–82, and President of the Board of Trade 1766–68. He had had poetic aspirations, having published Odes and Epistles in 1739 and contributed to Dodsley's Collection in 1748. G. printed his 'Epistle to a Lady' in his Beauties of English Poesy (1767) i 51–7; and see also l. 24n. Richard Glover, Memoirs of a Celebrated Literary and Political Character (1813) p. 47, described him as a 'jovial and voluptuous Irishman, who had left Popery for the Protestant religion, money, and widows'. See also Claud Nugent, Memoir of Robert, Earl Nugent (1898). G. seems to have been most intimate with Lord Clare during 1770 and 1771: he was in the country with him on 27 Oct. 1770, stayed at Bath with him in March 1771 and spent much of the following summer with him either at Bath or at his country seat at Gosfield, Essex. Early in July 1771 it was said of G. that he 'now generally lives with his countryman, Lord Clare'. See Wardle, pp. 213–16. The poem no doubt acknowledges the receipt of a real gift of venison, although, as parallels in the notes indicate, G. was influenced by Swift's The Grand Question Debated, which apparently suggested the metre and some details of phrasing; and by Boileau's third Satire, which was itself a partial imitation of Horace, Satires II viii. In Boileau's poem, the poet is trapped into a meal with an acquaintance whom he has long been avoiding. Two of the poet's friends who had promised to attend fail to appear and are replaced by a pair of simpletons. Most of the poem is devoted to describing several courses of offensive food and the conversation; it ends in a brawl, enabling the poet to escape.

The poem was first published by G. Kearsley and J. Ridley in 1776, two years after G.'s death, with 'a Head of the Author, Drawn by Henry Bunbury, Esq; and Etched by Bretherton'. As Henry Bunbury had married Catherine Horneck, the poem may have been printed from a copy of the poem preserved by the Horneck family. It had presumably circulated in

MS and at some stage G. revised it, making alterations and additions. (In the second state of this edn, in which the text is unaltered, the booksellers' names are in reverse order on the title-page.) Later in 1776, a 2nd edn with 'Additions and Corrections' was published, which, in all but a few minor details, follows the autograph MS now in the Berg Collection of the New York Public Library, having been sold at Sotheby's on 14 Nov. 1929. The text is that of the 2nd edn. except when the MS supports readings in the 1st edn.

> Thanks, my Lord, for your venison, for finer or fatter
> Never ranged in a forest or smoked on a platter;
> The haunch was a picture for painters to study,
> The fat was so white and the lean was so ruddy.
> 5 Though my stomach was sharp, I could scarce help regretting
> To spoil such a delicate picture by eating;
> I had thoughts in my chamber to place it in view,
> To be shown to my friends as a piece of *virtù*;
> As in some Irish houses, where things are so so,
> 10 One gammon of bacon hangs up for a show:
> But for eating a rasher of what they take pride in,
> They'd as soon think of eating the pan it is fried in.
> But hold—let us pause—Don't I hear you pronounce
> This tale of the bacon a damnable bounce?
> 15 Well, suppose it a bounce, sure a poet may try,
> By a bounce now and then, to get courage to fly.
>   But, my Lord, it's no bounce: I protest in my turn,
> It's a truth—and your Lordship may ask Mr Byrne.

¶ 23.2. *on*] MS, *ed 1*; in *ed 2*.

4. *fat . . . lean*] white . . . red *ed 1*.

5–6. *Not in ed 1*.

5. *sharp*] Hungry.

7. *chamber*] MS, *ed 1*; chambers *ed 2*.   *place*] hang *ed 1*.

10. G. described the same custom in Germany, Poland and Switzerland in *Animated Nature* (1774) iii 9, which he was writing at about this time: 'A piece of beef hung up there, is considered as an elegant piece of furniture, which, though seldom touched, at least argues the possessor's opulence and ease. But it is very different, for some years past, in this country, where our lower rustics at least are utterly unable to purchase meat any part of the year, and by them even butter is considered as an article of extravagance.'

13. *us*] MS, *ed 1*; me *ed 2*.

14. *bounce*] A boastful lie.

18. *Byrne*] Burn MS; Burne *ed 1*. A note in *Works* (1801) ii 92, describes him as 'Lord Clare's nephew'. He was further identified by J. F. Waller, *Works*

To go on with my tale – as I gazed on the haunch,
20   I thought of a friend that was trusty and staunch;
So I cut it and sent it to Reynolds undressed,
To paint it or eat it, just as he liked best.
Of the neck and the breast I had next to dispose;
'Twas a neck and a breast that might rival Monroe's:
25   But in parting with these I was puzzled again,
With the how, and the who, and the where and the when.
There's Howard, and Coley, and Haworth, and Hiff,
I think they love venison – I know they love beef.

of G. (1865) as 'Michael Byrne, Esq. of Cabinteely, in the county of Dublin; son of Robert Byrne and Clare, sister of Lord Clare'.

21. Reynolds] G.'s friend Sir Joshua.

24. Monroe's | *ed 1*; Monros *MS*; M—r—se *ed 2*.   Dorothy Monroe was niece of Henry, 4th Viscount Loftus and 1st Earl of Ely (1709–83). Her beauty is mentioned in the satirical *Baratariana* (Dublin, 1772) pp. 175–6, where she appears as Dorothea del Monroso and her aunt's scheme to marry her to Lord Townshend, Lord-Lieutenant of Ireland is described. Townshend's wife died early in Sept. 1770 and the letter in *Baratariana* (attributed to Langrishe, Flood and Grattan) was originally published on 6 April 1771. G. no doubt knew of Dorothy Monroe through Lord Clare, who was a friend of Townshend and wrote a poem on the death of his wife, *Town and Country Mag.* ii (Sept. 1770) 496. Townshend himself referred to her beauty in his poem 'To Dr Andrews', published in John Almon's *Fugitive Miscellany* (1774) pp. 9–10. The same work (pp. 16–18) reprints Clare's poem on Lady Townshend. The reference to Dorothy Monroe supports other evidence suggesting that the poem should be dated in late 1770 or early 1771.

27. MS gives these names in full. Ed 1 has There's COLEY, and WILLIAMS, and HOWARD, and HIFF–.

The identification of these impoverished writers has proved difficult. 'Hiff' is certainly Paul Hiffernan (1719–77), an Irish miscellaneous author who settled in London. Isaac Reed, *Biographia Dramatica* (1782) i 221–2, describes his conduct as 'unworthy of the lowest and most contemptible of the vulgar. His conversation was highly offensive to decency and good manners, and his whole behaviour discovered a mind over which the opinions of mankind had no influence.' There are some strange anecdotes of him in the *European Mag.* xxv (1794) 110–15, 179–84. 'Howard' has been identified as Henry Howard, who published *The Choice Spirit's Museum. A Collection of Songs* (1765) and as Gorges Edmond Howard (1715–86), an Irish miscellaneous author. But there is nothing to link G. with either. 'Coley' has been identified with George Colman, the manager of Covent Garden, but the context makes this very unlikely. Haworth and Williams cannot be identified with any likelihood.

There's my countryman Higgins—Oh! let him alone,
30 For making a blunder or picking a bone.
But hang it—to poets who seldom can eat,
Your very good mutton's a very good treat;
Such dainties to them, their health it might hurt,
It's like sending them ruffles, when wanting a shirt.
35   While thus I debated, in reverie centred,
An acquaintance, a friend as he called himself, entered;
An under-bred, fine-spoken fellow was he,
And he smiled as he looked at the venison and me.
'What have we got here?—Ay, this is good eating!
40 Your own, I suppose—or is it in waiting?'
'Why, whose should it be?' cried I with a flounce,
'I get these things often;'—but that was a bounce.
'Some lords, my acquaintance, that settle the nation,
Are pleased to be kind—but I hate ostentation.'
45   'If that be the case, then,' cried, he, very gay,
'I'm glad I have taken this house in my way.
Tomorrow you take a poor dinner with me;

29–30. Not in ed 1.

29. Higgins] Possibly the Capt. Higgins involved in G.'s quarrel with Thomas Evans over the publication of Kenrick's offensive letter in *The London Packet*, 24 March 1773: see Wardle, p. 242.

33. them . . . hurt] them! It would look like a flirt *ed 1*.   *flirt*] A jest or gibe.

34. It's . . . them] Like sending 'em *ed 1*.   The comparison seems to originate with Samuel Sorbière: see *Sorberiana* (Paris, 1694), the prefatory 'Memoires', sig ★★2: 'Sorbiere s'en plaignoit aussi fort agreablement en disant, *qu'il avoit plus de besoin d'une charretée de pain que d'un bassin de confitures: On envoie*, ajoûtoit-il, *des manchettes à un homme qui n'a point de chemise: qu'on m'envoie du pain pour manger le beurre qu'on me donne*'. It is imitated in Tom Brown's *Laconics: Or, New Maxims of State and Conversation* (1701) p. 100; and G. himself had used it not long before writing this poem in a letter *c.* 10 Jan. 1770 (*Letters* p. 84): 'Honours to one in my situation are something like ruffles to a man that wants a shirt.'

37–8. A fine-spoken Custom-house Officer he, / Who smil'd as he gaz'd on *ed 1*.

39. Ay] *MS, ed 1*; Why *ed 2*.

40. is it] *MS, ed 1*; it is *ed 2*.

41. be] be, Sir *ed 1*.   *flounce*] A sudden movement, expressing impatience or disdain.

43–4. Not in ed 1.

47–9. Cp. Boileau, *Sat.* iii 20, 25–8: *Ah! Monsieur, m'a-t-il dit, je vous attends demain* / . . . / *Molière avec Tartuffe y doit joüer son rôle: / Et Lambert,*

No words—I insist on't—precisely at three.
We'll have Johnson and Burke, all the wits will be
    there;
50 My acquaintance is slight or I'd ask my Lord Clare.
And now that I think on't, as I am a sinner,
We wanted this venison to make out the dinner.
What say you—a pasty? it shall and it must,
And my wife, little Kisty, is famous for crust.
55 Here, porter!—this venison with me to Mile-End;
No stirring—I beg—my dear friend—my dear friend!'
Thus snatching his hat, he brushed off like the wind,
And the porter and eatables followed behind.
    Left alone to reflect, having emptied my shelf,
60 'And nobody with me at sea but myself';
Though I could not help thinking my gentleman hasty,
Yet Johnson and Burke and a good venison pasty
Were things that I never disliked in my life,
Though clogged with a coxcomb and Kisty his wife.
65 So next day, in due splendour to make my approach,
I drove to his door in my own hackney coach.
    When come to the place where we all were to dine
(A chair-lumbered closet just twelve feet by nine),

qui plus est, m'a donné sa parole. / C'est tout dire en un mot, et vous le
connaissez. / Quoi! Lambert?—Oui, Lambert.—A demain. C'est assez.
48. three] The normal time for dinner at this period, although it was already
fashionable to dine as late as five.
49–50. In ed 1 these lines follow l. 54.
52. out] up ed 1.
53. I'll take no denial—you shall, and you must ed 1.   Cp. Swift, The Grand
Question Debated 26: 'It must, and it shall be a Barrack, my Life.'
54, 64. Kisty] Kitty edd 1 and 2.
55. Mile-End] Mile-End Old Town and New Town were hamlets in the
parish of Stepney, still only a village near London at this date.
56. No words, my dear GOLDSMITH! my very good Friend! ed 1. Cp. Swift,
The Grand Question Debated 77–8: 'Good Morrow, good Captain,—I'll
wait on you down,— / You shan't stir a Foot—You'll think me a Clown.'
57. snatching] seizing ed 1.   brushed off] Johnson defines to 'brush' as 'To
move with haste: a ludicrous word, applied to men.'
60. This phrase occurs in one of the letters from Henry Frederick, Duke of
Cumberland to Lady Grosvenor, produced as evidence during his trial for
adultery with her in July 1770. In the third of these semiliterate letters, the
Duke describes a dream that Lady Grosvenor was with him, 'but alas when
I woke I found it all dillusion nobody by me by myself at Sea'; see The Trial
of His R.H. the D. of C. July 5th, 1770, For Criminal Conversation with Lady

My friend bid me welcome, but struck me quite dumb
70 With tidings that Johnson and Burke could not come.
'For I knew it,' he cried, 'both eternally fail,
The one with his speeches, the other with Thrale;
But no matter, I'll warrant we'll make up the party
With two full as clever and ten times as hearty.
75 The one is a Scotchman, the other a Jew,
They both of them merry and authors like you;
The one writes the *Snarler*, the other the *Scourge*;

Harriet G------r (6th edn, 1770) p. 14. Dobson quotes a ballad in the
Public Advertiser, 1 Aug. 1770, which also introduces the phrase.
69–70. Similarly in Boileau, *Sat.* iii 31–4, the poet's host expains that Molière
and Lambert cannot come. *Deux nobles campagnards, grands lecteurs de
romans* correspond to G.'s Scotsman and Jew in l. 75.
69. *bid*] *MS, ed 1*; bade *ed 2*.
70. *could*] *MS, ed 1*; would *ed 2*.
71. *For*] And *ed 1*.
72. *with his speeches*] at the House *ed 1*.   *the other*] *MS, ed 1*; and t'other
ed 2.   For G.'s opinion of Burke as a parliamentarian, see *Retaliation* 29–42
(pp. 748–50). Johnson had met Henry Thrale, a wealthy brewer, and his wife
in 1765 and at this period was spending about half his time at their elegant
house at Streatham. William Strahan once complained to Boswell that
Johnson 'was in a great measure absorbed from the society of his old friends'
as a result, *Life of Johnson* iii 225.
73. *no . . . we'll*] I warrant for me, we shall *ed 1*.
76. Who dabble and write in the Papers–like you *ed 1*.
77–8. No use of the pseudonym 'Snarler' at this period has been discovered
and G. may have invented it; but the remaining three names were actually
used to sign letters to the *Public Advertiser* and other newspapers during 1770
and 1771. This fact is of importance in dating the poem. Friedman finds
letters signed by 'Scourge' in the *Public Advertiser* between 8 Aug. 1770
and 5 June 1771 (a later appearance, however, occurs on 6 Aug. 1771), in
the *Gazetteer* between 31 Dec. 1770 and 13 March 1771 and in the *General
Evening Post*, 4–6 June 1771. Since G. actually refers to 'the Scourge', he
may have had in mind an anti-government periodical essay so titled, pub-
lished as far as is known only on 23 and 30 Jan. 1771 (both numbers are in
the Bodleian). This would date his allusion more precisely. 'Cinna' is a
frequent correspondent in the *Public Advertiser* from July 1770, the last
contribution noted by Friedman being on 12 Jan. 1771. 'Panurge' appears in
the *Public Advertiser* between 24 Oct. 1770 and 20 March 1771. The letters
of 'Cinna' and 'Panurge', supporting the government and Lord Sandwich,
the first Lord of the Admiralty, in particular, have been attributed to Dr
James Scott (1733–1814), a Cambridge clergyman better known for letters
to the *Public Advertiser* in 1765 signed 'Anti-Sejanus'. In April 1771 he was

Some think he writes *Cinna*—he owns to *Panurge*.'
While thus he described them by trade and by name,
80   They entered and dinner was served as they came.
    At the top a fried liver and bacon was seen,
    At the bottom was tripe in a swinging tureen;
    At the sides there was spinach and pudding made hot;
    In the middle a place where the pasty—was not.
85   Now, my Lord, as for tripe, it's my utter aversion,
    And your bacon I hate like a Turk or a Persian;
    So there I sat stuck, like a horse in a pound,
    While the bacon and liver went merrily round.
    But what vexed me most was that damned Scottish
        rogue,
90   With his long-winded speeches and smiles and his
        brogue.
    'And Madam,' quoth he, 'may this bit be my poison,
    A prettier dinner I never set eyes on;
    Pray a slice of your liver, though may I be cursed,
    But I've eat of your tripe till I'm ready to burst.'
95   'The tripe,' quoth the Jew, with his chocolate cheek,

presented to a living in Northumberland through Sandwich's influence.
See Prior, *Life* ii 277; and Horace Walpole, *Memoirs of the Reign of George III*,
ed G. F. Russell Barker (1894) ii 191. Basil Montagu told Prior, *Life* ii 278,
that Scott had unsuccessfully attempted to persuade G. to write for the
government some years earlier.
81–6. Boileau gives a similar, if more detailed, description of the various
dishes.
81. was] MS, ed *1*; were ed *2*.
82. swinging] 'Great; huge. A low word' (Johnson).
84. pasty] Ven'son ed *1*; pudding *deleted in MS.*
87–8. Not in ed 1.   *pound*] An enclosure for straying animals.
89. damned] MS, ed *1*; d—'d ed *2*.
90. and smiles] MS, ed *1*; his smiles ed *2*.
91. quoth] says ed *1. In MS* quite as *has been deleted before* may this.   Cp. Swift,
The Grand Question Debated 141–2: 'And Madam, says he, if such Dinners
you give, / You'll never want *Parsons* as long as you live'.   *my poison*]
A favourite phrase of G. Cp. *Citizen* (1762) i 11–12 (Letter 4): 'Before I
would stoop to slavery, may this be my poison (and he held the goblet in
his hand) may this be my poison—but I would sooner list for a soldier.' It
occurs also in *She Stoops to Conquer* I ii and see *Works* ed. Friedman, iii 18,
137.
92. A . . . never] If a . . . ever ed *1*.
93. though] but ed *1*.
95. The] Your ed *1*.   with . . . cheek] if the truth I may speak ed *1*.
chocolate] Chocolate-coloured.

'I could dine on this tripe seven days in the week:
I like these here dinners so pretty and small;
But your friend there, the Doctor, eats nothing at all.'
'O ho,' quoth my friend, 'he'll come on in a trice,
100 He's keeping a corner for something that's nice:
There's a pasty'–'A pasty!' repeated the Jew,
'I don't care if I keep a corner for't too.'
'What the de'il, mon, a pasty!' re-echoed the Scot,
'Though splitting, I'd still keep a corner for thot.'
105 'We'll all keep a corner,' the lady cried out;
'We'll all keep a corner,' was echoed about.
While thus we resolved and the pasty delayed,
With looks that quite petrified, entered the maid;
A visage so sad and so pale with affright
110 Waked Priam by drawing his curtains by night.
But we quickly found out–for who could mistake her?–
That she came with some terrible news from the baker:
And so it fell out, for that negligent sloven
Had shut out the pasty on shutting his oven.
115 Sad Philomel thus–but let similes drop–
And now that I think on't, the story may stop.
To be plain, my good Lord, it's but labour misplaced
To send such good verses to one of your taste;
You've got an odd something–a kind of discerning–

96. *dine on*] eat of *ed 1*.
98. Cp. the host in Boileau, *Sat.* iii 116: *Qu'avez vous donc, dit-il, que vous ne mangez point?* etc.
99. *ho*] MS, *ed 1*; Oh *ed 2*.
101. *repeated the Jew*] returned the *Scot ed 1*.
102. *for't too*] for *thot ed 1*.   Dobson cites Swift, *Polite Conversation* (*Prose Works*, ed. Herbert Davis, iv 173): 'Come, you have kept a Corner of your Stomach for a Bit of Venison-Pasty.'
103–4 Not in *ed 1*.
104. *I'd*] I'll *edd 1 and 2*.   *thot*] that *MS, ed 2*. (G. obviously intended the humorous rhyme as in l. 102 of *ed 1*; but in revising the lines, or merely in transcribing them, he appears to have overlooked it.)
108. *that . . . petrified*] quite astonishing *ed 1*. MS omits *that* perhaps *accidentally*. Cp. *II Henry IV* I i 70–3: 'Even such a man, so faint, so spiritless, / So dull, so dead in look, so woe-begone, / Drew Priam's curtains in the dead of night, / And would have told him half his Troy was burnt.'
110. *by*] MS, *ed 1*; in *ed 2*.
111. *we quickly*] too soon we *ed 1*.
117. *it's*] 'tis *ed 1*.

120   A relish – a taste – sickened over by learning;
     At least, it's your temper, it's very well known,
     That you think very slightly of all that's your own:
     So, perhaps, in your habits of thinking amiss,
     You may make a mistake and think slightly of this.

120. relish] 'sense; power of perceiving excellence; taste' (Johnson). Cp.
Hamlet III i 85: 'sicklied o'er with the pale cast of thought'.
121. it's very] *MS*; 'tis very *ed 1*; as very *ed 2*.

24 Prologue to *Zobeide*

Probably written in early Dec. 1771. *Zobeide*, a tragedy by Joseph Cradock
(1742–1826) adapted from Voltaire's unfinished *Les Scythes*, was first
performed at Covent Garden on 11 Dec. 1771. Cradock was a wealthy
musical and literary dilettante especially addicted to amateur theatricals.
He recalled in his *Literary and Miscellaneous Memoirs* (1828) i 224, that he
probably first met G. through Richard Yates the actor: 'The doctor after-
wards favoured me with a Prologue for my tragedy of Zobeide, probably
in consequence of some application made by the Yates' family.' The pass-
age also includes the undated note from G. which accompanied the
prologue: 'Mr. Goldsmith presents his best respects to Mr. Cradock, has sent
him the Prologue, such as it is. He cannot take time to make it better. He
begs he will give Mr. Yates the proper instructions; and so, even so, he
commits him to fortune, and the public.' Cradock adds that the prologue
was not in fact spoken by Yates since his wife, Mary Anne Yates, was
playing the heroine: 'A comic Prologue, by the husband, in the char-
acter of a Sailor, would have ill-suited with the lofty dignity of the first
tragic Actress.'
   G.'s prologue is a particularly well-sustained exploitation of a common
comparison in prologues: that of 'the author to a sailor tempting the dramatic
seas in his frail bark of a play'. See Mary E. Knapp, *Prologues and Epilogues
of the 18th Century*, New Haven, 1961, p. 115. After the first performance,
the *Middlesex Journal* (12–14 Dec. 1771) reported that 'Upon the whole,
there is merit in the Prologue, and the town was too just to withold the tribute
of approbation'; and the *Critical Review* xxxii (Dec. 1771) 464, praised it,
together with Arthur Murphy's epilogue to the play, as 'not excelled by
many on the English stage'.
   The prologue is attributed to G. in the 1st edn of the play, published on
19 Dec. 1771 (it reached a 3rd edn in 1772). It appeared also in several news-
papers and in the *Scots Mag.* xxxiii (Dec. 1771) 655, in a text which has
several variants, cited here from the *Scots Mag.* Other variants from the text
printed with the 1st edn of the play, followed here, are given from the

autograph MS of the prologue, sent by G. to Cradock with the note quoted
above, which was preserved in the Nichols family until sold at Sotheby's
on 18 Nov. 1929. It was sold there again on 9 Nov. 1965 for £2200. The
MS contains a couplet not printed with the play. Sotheby's catalogue for the
first of the sales gives a facsimile of ll. 1–30 of the MS. The prologue was first
collected in *1780* i 109–11.

> In these bold times, when Learning's sons explore
> The distant climate and the savage shore;
> When wise astronomers to India steer,
> And quit for Venus many a brighter here;
> 5 While botanists, all cold to smiles and dimpling,
> Forsake the fair and patiently–go simpling;
> When every bosom swells with wondrous scenes,
> Priests, cannibals and hoity-toity queens:
> Our bard into the general spirit enters,
> 10 And fits his little frigate for adventures:
> With Scythian stores and trinkets deeply laden,
> He this way steers his course in hopes of trading—

¶ 24.1–5. G. refers to Capt. Cook's expedition in the *Endeavour* to Tahiti
to observe the transit of Venus across the sun in June 1769. The expedition
left on 7 Aug. 1768 and returned in mid-July 1771. The botanists who
accompanied Cook, Joseph (later Sir Joseph) Banks (1743–1820) and Daniel
Solander (1736–82), assistant librarian at the British Museum, stole much of
the glory. By the time *Zobeide* was produced Banks and Solander were
planning a new botanical expedition to Iceland. They had been presented
to the King and Banks had received the degree of D.C.L. at Oxford on
21 Nov. 1771. Lady Mary Coke wrote in her journal: 'The most talked of at
present are Messrs. Banks and Solander', H. C. Cameron, *Sir Joseph Banks*
(1952) p. 45.
4. And . . . Venus] For that Venus quitting *deleted in MS.*
5. While] When *deleted in MS.*
6. simpling] On 21 March 1772 Johnson, on being asked what 'share of glory'
Banks and Solander were entitled to for their part in Cook's expedition,
replied: 'Why, Sir, it was properly for botany that they went out: I believe
they thought only of culling of simples', *Life of Johnson* ii 148. Johnson was
quoting *Romeo and Juliet* V i 40, which G. may also have had in mind.
7–8. Omitted from Scots Mag.
7. When] While MS.
8. Francis Grose, *Classical Dictionary of the Vulgar Tongue*, ed. Partridge,
p. 190, gives 'A hoity-toity wench; a giddy, thoughtless, romping girl',
but G. probably had the surviving sense of 'haughty, petulant, huffy' in
mind.
11. Voltaire's tragedy which Cradock was adapting was set in Scythia.

Yet ere he lands he's ordered me before,
To make an observation on the shore.
15   Where are we driven? our reckoning sure is lost!
This seems a barren and a dangerous coast.
Lord, what a sultry climate am I under!
Yon ill-foreboding cloud seems big with thunder.
                                                  (*Upper Gallery*)
There mangroves spread, and larger than I've seen 'em—
                                                  (*Pit*)
20   Here trees of stately size—and turtles in 'em—
                                                  (*Balconies*)
Here ill-conditioned oranges abound——   (*Stage*)
And apples (*takes up one and tastes it*), *bitter* apples
      strew the ground.
The place is uninhabited, I fear;
I heard a hissing—there are serpents here!
25   O there the natives are—a dreadful race!
The men have tails, the women paint the face!
No doubt they're all barbarians.—Yes, 'tis so.
I'll try to make palaver with them though;
                                                  (*making signs*)
'Tis best, however, keeping at a distance.
30   Good savages, our captain craves assistance;
Our ship's well stored;—in yonder creek we've laid her;

---

16. barren] rocky *Scots Mag.*

18–21. For G.'s differentiation of the habitués of box, pit and gallery see
Citizen (1762) i 77–8 (Letter 21). Such allusions to the different sections of the
audience were common in prologues and epilogues: see H. W. Pedicord,
The Theatrical Public in the Time of Garrick (New York, 1954) pp. 19–20.

20. turtles] monkies *MS*; billing turtles *Scots Mag.*   *balconies*] to the
pidgeon holes *MS*. (The 'pigeon holes' were the seats in the top row of the
gallery.)

21–3. Rotten oranges and apples were often flung onto the stage as missiles.
A German visitor to Drury Lane as late as 1791 wrote: 'The best plan is to
keep your face turned towards the stage, and thus quietly submit to the hail
of oranges on your back'; cp. H. W. Pedicord, *op cit*, p. 45.

23. Th'inhabitants are cannibals, I fear *Scots Mag.*

24. there] Yes—there *MS, with* Yes *deleted.*

25. dreadful] savage *MS.*

25–30. Scots Mag. has only: O there the people are—best keep my distance; /
Our Captain, gentle natives, craves assistance;

28. palaver] Not in Johnson's *Dictionary*; derived from Portuguese *palavra*,
word or speech; originally slang used by Portuguese sailors for a parley with
African or other uncivilised natives and thence picked up by English sailors.

> His honour is no mercenary trader;
> This is his first adventure; lend him aid,
> Or you may chance to spoil a thriving trade.
> 35 His goods, he hopes, are prime and brought from far,
> Equally fit for gallantry and war.
> What! no reply to promises so ample?
> I'd best step back—and order up a sample.

32. After this line MS adds: To make you finer [better *deleted*] is his sole
endeavour / He seeks no benefit content with favour
32. Cradock gave the profits of *Zobeide* to Mrs Yates (*Literary and Miscel-
laneous Memoirs* (1828) iv 211).
34. Or you . . . spoil] And we . . . drive *Scots Mag.*

25 [Translations in *An History of the Earth, and Animated Nature*]

Written between 1769 and 1771 or 1772. These two translations appear in
G.'s *History of the Earth, and Animated Nature* iii 6 and v 312, published post-
humously on 1 July 1774. Since G. had undertaken this work by Feb. 1769
(Wardle, p. 191) and it was 'about half finished' in Sept. 1771 (*Letters* p. 105),
he may be supposed to have been working on vol. iii during 1770 and vol. v
at the end of 1771 or early 1772.

The couplet is introduced as follows: 'there are numberless other animals
that appear to ruminate; not only birds, but fishes, and insects. . . . The
salmon also is said to be of this number: and, if we may believe Ovid, the
scarus likewise; of which he says . . .' In a footnote G. quotes *Halieuticon*
118–19: *At contra herbosa pisces laxantur arena, / Ut scarus epastas solus qui
ruminat escas.*

The second translation is thus introduced: 'Addison, in some beautiful
Latin lines, inserted in the Spectator [No. 412], is entirely of the opinion
that birds observe a strict chastity of manners, and never admit the caresses
of a different tribe.' The Latin verses are assumed to be Addison's because
corrections in his hand to several lines appear in the first draft of the essay,
in the Houghton Library, Harvard; see J. Dykes Campbell, *Some Portions
of Essays Contributed to the Spectator by Mr. Joseph Addison* (Glasgow,
1864). They had already been translated in the 1744 edn of the *Spectator*.
Addison had introduced them as follows: 'Thus we see that every different
Species of sensible Creatures has its different Notions of Beauty, and that
each of them is most affected with the Beauties of its Kind. This is no where
more remarkable than in Birds of the same Shape and Proportion, where we

often see the Male determined in his Courtship by the single Grain or Tincture of a Feather, and never discovering any Charms but in the Colour of its Species.'

i

Of all the fish that graze beneath the flood,
He only ruminates his former food.

ii

Chaste are their instincts, faithful is their fire,
No foreign beauty tempts to false desire:
The snow-white vesture and the glittering crown,
The simple plumage or the glossy down,
5 Prompt not their love. The patriot bird pursues
His well-acquainted tints and kindred hues.
Hence through their tribes no mixed, polluted flame,
No monster-breed to mark the groves with shame:
But the chaste blackbird, to its partner true,
10 Thinks black alone is beauty's favourite hue;
The nightingale, with mutual passion blest,
Sings to its mate and nightly charms the nest;
While the dark owl to court his partner flies,
And owns his offspring in their yellow eyes.

26 Threnodia Augustalis

Written between 10 and 14 Feb. 1772 and performed at a memorial concert for Augusta, Princess Dowager of Wales and mother of George III, who had died on 8 Feb. 1772. The concert was devised by Mrs Theresa Cornelys (1723–97), owner of the fashionable Great Room in Carlisle House, Soho Square. After a decade as a highly successful organiser of subscription balls, masquerades and concerts, Mrs Cornelys was now being subjected to strong rivalry and a prosecution for debt. By Nov. 1772, in fact, she was bankrupt. There is an air of desperation about her efforts to profit from the death of Princess Augusta, while concealing her mercenary motives as far as possible. A detailed account of her negotiations with G., through the printer William Woodfall, is given by Miss Balderston, *Letters* pp. xxxiii–xxxvii. Woodfall wrote to G. on 10 Feb. describing the sort of poem required and his efforts to engage performers and a composer. Mrs Cornelys wished the 'Entertainment' to be in two parts, 'with a view of relieving the Performers and preserving the Auditors from Dulness from too great a length of solemnity'.

¶ 26. *Title*. G. was probably imitating Dryden's *Threnodia Augustalis* (1685), on the death of Charles II.

Two speakers, three singers, a chorus and band were to be employed but 'if it appears to Dr. G. that more or less may be proper for the occasion, and his opinion does not occasion an Expence inadequate to the ultimate view of Profit on the side of Mrs. Cornelys, it will be adopted. Secrecy as to the name of the Author shall be inviolably preserved.' G. had apparently finished the poem by 14 Feb. when Woodfall wrote to arrange a meeting with the composer Mattia Vento, a Neapolitan who had come to London c. 1763. Woodfall's letter again stressed the secrecy in which the plan was enveloped and a furtiveness on the part of Mrs. Cornelys which G. seems to have accepted without a qualm: 'if you see Mr. Vento you will on no account mention that Mrs. Cornelys is concerned in the Affair, particular and most cogent Reasons demand this Secrecy; the Story now stands that I am directed by some Persons of Consequence to procure the performance at some great Room in Westminster at the instance of several of the 1st Nobility . . . many very urgent Causes make it necessary that Mrs. Cornelys should not be known to act in it or have any Concern with it.'

According to the *Public Advertiser*, the poem was published by Woodfall at midday on 20 Feb. 1772, price one shilling, and a porter was 'employed to sell the books at the door of the house' at the performance that evening. Although the poem was anonymous, the papers reported that it was written by 'a gentleman of acknowledged literary merit' (Prior, *Life* ii 339). But G. was understandably unwilling to own a hastily written piece not without plagiarisms. The 'Advertisement' that he prefixed explains his own attitude: 'The following may more properly be termed a Compilation than a Poem. It was prepared for the Composer in little more than two days: and may therefore rather be considered as an industrious Effort of Gratitude than of Genius. In justice to the Composer it may likewise be right to inform the public, that the Music was adapted in a period of time equally short.' There is no evidence to suggest that G. had any personal reason for 'gratitude' to the Princess. As he stresses in the poem, she had given away a great deal to charity; but, in fact, the belief that she had some control over George III's political conduct, probably unfounded in her later years, had made her unpopular. She had been attacked in the press and, according to Walpole (described, however, as her 'arch-maligner'), her body was followed to the grave with insults from the mob, (*Last Journals* i 17). Cp. W. H. Wilkins, 'Augusta: Princess of Wales', *The Nineteenth Century and After* liv (1903) 660–76.

A description of the actual performance on 20 Feb. 1772 has survived. The poem was spoken by Mr Lee and Mrs Bellamy and sung by Messrs Champnes and Dyne and Miss Jameson, with a chorus of twelve. Mrs Harris wrote to her son James, the British Minister at Berlin, on 25 Feb. 1772 (*Letters of the 1st Earl of Malmesbury* (1870) i 253–4): 'Madame Cornelly [*sic*] gave a most odd entertainment, a kind of funeral elegy on the death of the Princess. A large kind of frame was made round the glasses and in various parts of the room with lamps stuck in it, and black crape strained over the lamps to make the light solemn. At the upper end of the room was a black canopy, under which was a white tomb with 'Augusta' writ on it; on one side stood a man, the other side a woman, who sang forth the praises of the Princess; a most ridiculous whim of the woman's. Window curtains all black, &c.'

The literary world received the poem with polite indifference. The *Monthly Review* xlvi (March 1772) 260, called it 'a decent performance'; the *Critical Review* xxxiii (Feb. 1772) 173, noted its lack of 'original merit' but concluded: 'As a compilation, however, the several parts are well applied to the occasion, and properly arranged; and both the additions and alterations are conceived in a strain of tender sentiment.'

Because of its anonymity the poem was not collected with G.'s other works for almost forty years; but Miss Balderston (*Letters* p. xxxiii) was incorrect in stating that it was unknown to Percy, George Steevens and others who helped to prepare the 1801 edn of G.'s *Works*. Steevens pointed out its existence to Percy in a letter in Sept. 1797 (Prior, *Life* ii 9–10) but it was not printed until 1810. G. had given a copy to Joseph Cradock (*Literary and Miscellaneous Memoirs* (1828) i 224–5), which via John Nichols eventually reached Alexander Chalmers, who printed it in 1810 in his *Works of the English Poets* xvi 509–12. (There seems no reason to suppose, as Gibbs does, that this was a MS and not a copy of the printed pamphlet.) Chalmers's verdict on the piece is not unfair: 'If it adds little to [G.'s] fame, it exhibits a curious instance of the facility with which he gratified his employers on a very short notice.'

Only four copies of the original pamphlet are known to have survived. There were copies in the Spoor and Elkins Collections and the Huth-Widener copy is now at Harvard. Isaac Reed's copy, used by Prior for his edn, was sold at Sotheby's on 11 June 1963 with four other works by G. for £1450. Reed had written on it: 'This Poem was written or as he says compiled by Dr. Oliver Goldsmith. It is very scarce and ought to be in his works. When Evans collected his pieces [1780] this was not to be procured.'

The text followed here is that of the original pamphlet, the full title of which is 'Threnodia Augustalis Sacred To The Memory Of Her late Royal Highness The Princess Dowager of Wales, Spoken and Sung in the Great Room at *Soho-Square*, on *Thursday* the 20th of *February*'.

OVERTURE—A SOLEMN DIRGE

Air. Trio

Arise, ye sons of worth, arise,
And waken every note of woe;
When truth and virtue reach the skies,
'Tis ours to weep the want below.

CHORUS

5   When truth and virtue reach the skies,
'Tis ours to weep the want below.

MAN SPEAKER

The praise attending pomp and power,
The incense given to kings,
Are but the trappings of an hour,
10 Mere transitory things!
The base bestow them; but the good agree
To spurn the venal gifts as flattery.
But when to pomp and power are joined
An equal dignity of mind;
15 When titles are the smallest claim;
When wealth and rank and noble blood,
But aid the power of doing good,
Then all their trophies last—and flattery turns to fame!
Blest spirit thou, whose fame, just born to bloom,
20 Shall spread and flourish from the tomb,
How hast thou left mankind for heaven!
Even now reproach and faction mourn,
And, wondering how their rage was born,
Request to be forgiven.
25 Alas! they never had thy hate:
Unmoved in conscious rectitude
Thy towering mind self-centred stood,
Nor wanted man's opinion to be great.
In vain, to charm thy ravished sight,
30 A thousand gifts would fortune send;
In vain, to drive thee from the right,
A thousand sorrows urged thy end:
Like some well-fashioned arch thy patience stood,
And purchased strength from its increasing load.
35 Pain met thee like a friend that set thee free;
Affliction still is virtue's opportunity!
Virtue on herself relying,
Every passion hushed to rest,
Loses every pain of dying
40 In the hopes of being blest.
Every added pang she suffers
Some increasing good bestows,
And every shock that malice offers
Only rocks her to repose.

SONG, BY A MAN
Affettuoso

45 Virtue on herself relying,
Every passion hushed to rest,
Loses every pain of dying

In the hopes of being blessed.
Every added pang she suffers
50   Some increasing good bestows,
Every shock that malice offers
Only rocks her to repose.

WOMAN SPEAKER

Yet, ah! what terrors frowned upon her fate:
Death with its formidable band,
55   Fever and pain and pale consumptive care,
Determined took their stand.
Nor did the cruel ravagers design
To finish all their efforts at a blow;
But, mischievously slow,
60   They robbed the relic and defaced the shrine.
With unavailing grief,
Despairing of relief,
Her weeping children round
Beheld each hour
65   Death's growing power,
And trembled as he frowned.
As helpless friends who view from shore
The labouring ship and hear the tempest roar,
While winds and waves their wishes cross;
70   They stood, while hope and comfort fail,
Not to assist, but to bewail
The inevitable loss.
Relentless tyrant, at thy call
How do the good, the virtuous fall!
75   Truth, beauty, worth, and all that most engage,
But wake thy vengeance and provoke thy rage.

SONG, BY A MAN
Basso. Staccato. Spiritoso

When vice my dart and scythe supply,
How great a king of terrors I!
If folly, fraud, your hearts engage,
80   Tremble, ye mortals, at my rage!

Fall, round me fall, ye little things,
Ye statesmen, warriors, poets, kings;
If virtue fail her counsel sage,
Tremble, ye mortals, at my rage!

77–8. Parnell, *A Nightpiece on Death* 61–2: 'When men my darts and scythe supply, / How great a King of Fears am I!'

MAN SPEAKER

85   Yet let that wisdom, urged by her example,
Teach us to estimate what all must suffer;
Let us prize death as the best gift of nature,
As a safe inn, where weary travellers,
When they have journeyed through a world of cares,
90   May put off life and be at rest for ever.
Groans, weeping friends, indeed, and gloomy sables
May oft distract us with their sad solemnity:
The preparation is the executioner.
Death, when unmasked, shows me a friendly face,
95   And is a terror only at a distance;
For as the line of life conducts me on
To Death's great court, the prospect seems more fair.
'Tis nature's kind retreat, that's always open
To take us in when we have drained the cup
100   Of life, or worn our days to wretchedness.
In that secure, serene retreat,
Where all the humble, all the great,
Promiscuously recline;
Where wildly huddled to the eye,
105   The beggar's pouch and prince's purple lie,
May every bliss be thine.
And ah! blest spirit, wheresoe'er thy flight,
Through rolling worlds or fields of liquid light,
May cherubs welcome their expected guest;
110   May saints with songs receive thee to their rest;
May peace that claimed while here thy warmest love,
May blissful, endless peace be thine above.

SONG, BY A WOMAN

Amoroso

Lovely, lasting Peace below,
Comforter of every woe,
115   Heavenly born and bred on high
To crown the favourites of the sky:
Lovely, lasting Peace, appear.

91–2. Friedman compares a passage on how 'people of distinction in England'
die, in *Citizen of the World* (Letter 12) but G. is imitating Lee, *Lucius Junius
Brutus* IV ii: 'Groans, and Convulsions, and discolour'd Faces, / Friends
weeping round us, Blacks and Obsequies, / Make [Death] a dreadful
thing: the Pomp of Death / Is far more terrible than Death it self.'
98. Cp. Johnson, *Vanity of Human Wishes* 364: 'Counts death kind Nature's
signal of retreat'.

This world itself, if thou art here,
Is once again with Eden blessed,
120 And man contains it in his breast.

WOMAN SPEAKER

Our vows are heard! Long, long to mortal eyes,
Her soul was fitting to its kindred skies:
Celestial-like her bounty fell,
Where modest want and patient sorrow dwell.
125 Want passed for merit at her door,
Unseen the modest were supplied,
Her constant pity fed the poor,
Then only poor, indeed, the day she died.
And oh, for this! while sculpture decks thy shrine,
130 And art exhausts profusion round,
The tribute of a tear be mine,
A simple song, a sigh profound.
There Faith shall come, a pilgrim gray,
To bless the tomb that wraps thy clay;
135 And calm Religion shall repair
To dwell a weeping hermit there.
Truth, Fortitude and Friendship shall agree
To blend their virtues while they think of thee.

AIR. CHORUS
Pomposo

Let us, let all the world agree
140 To profit by resembling thee.

END OF THE FIRST PART

PART II

OVERTURE PASTORALE

MAN SPEAKER

Fast by that shore where Thames' translucent stream
Reflects new glories on his breast,

126–8. Friedman cites the *Gazetteer*, 11 Feb. 1772: 'Her late R.H. the P. of
Wales expended annually six thousand pounds in private charities; and
that in so secret a manner, that forty, fifty, or one hundred pounds have been
dropt into the bosoms of families in distress, without their ever knowing
from whence the gift came.'
133–6. Cp. Collins, *Ode Written . . . in 1746* 9–12 (p. 437 above).
141–2. Cp. Pope, *Rape of the Lock* iii 1–2.

Where, splendid as the youthful poet's dream,
He forms a scene beyond Elysium blest;
145 Where sculptured elegance and native grace
Unite to stamp the beauties of the place;
While sweetly blending still are seen
The wavy lawn, the sloping green;
While novelty, with cautious cunning,
150 Through every maze of fancy running,
From China borrows aid to deck the scene;
There, sorrowing by the river's glassy bed,
Forlorn, a rural bard complained,
All whom Augusta's bounty fed,
155 All whom her clemency sustained.
The good old sire, unconscious of decay,
The modest matron, clad in homespun gray,
The military boy, the orphaned maid,
The shattered veteran, now first dismayed:
160 These sadly join beside the murmuring deep,
And, as they view the towers of Kew,
Call on their mistress, now no more, and weep.

CHORUS

Affettuoso. Largo

Ye shady walks, ye waving greens,
Ye nodding towers, ye fairy scenes,
165 Let all your echoes now deplore
That she who formed your beauties is no more.

MAN SPEAKER

First of the train the patient rustic came,
Whose callous hand had formed the scene,
Bending at once with sorrow and with age,
170 With many a tear and many a sigh between:
'And where,' he cried, 'shall now my babes have
        bread,
Or how shall age support its feeble fire?
No lord will take me now, my vigour fled,
Nor can my strength perform what they require;

143. Milton, *L'Allegro* 129: 'Such sights as youthful Poets dream'.
149–51, 161. Sir William Chambers, who was largely responsible for the
current vogue for 'the Chinese' in architecture and gardening, had improved
the palace and gardens at Kew for the Princess Augusta.
156 ff. Cp. *Traveller* 407–9 (p. 655) and *Deserted Village* 371 ff (p. 692).
168. *callous*] Hardened (of the skin).

175 Each grudging master keeps the labourer bare;
A sleek and idle race is all their care.
My noble mistress thought not so:
Her bounty, like the morning dew,
Unseen, though constant, used to flow;
180 And as my strength decayed, her bounty grew.'

WOMAN SPEAKER

In decent dress and coarsely clean,
The pious matron next was seen;
Clasped in her hand a godly book was borne,
By use and daily meditation worn;
185 That decent dress, this holy guide,
Augusta's care had well supplied.
'And ah!' she cries, all woe-begone,
'What now remains for me?
Oh! where shall weeping want repair,
190 To ask for charity?
Too late in life for me to ask,
And shame prevents the deed,
And tardy, tardy are the times
To succour, should I need.
195 But all my wants, before I spoke,
Were to my mistress known;
She still relieved nor sought my praise,
Contented with her own.
But every day her name I'll bless,
200 My morning prayer, my evening song,
I'll praise her while my life shall last,
A life that cannot last me long.'

SONG, BY A WOMAN

Each day, each hour, her name I'll bless,
My morning and my evening song;
205 And when in death my vows shall cease,
My children shall the note prolong.

MAN SPEAKER

The hardy veteran after struck the sight,
Scarred, mangled, maimed in every part,
Lopped of his limbs in many a gallant fight,
210 In nought entire—except his heart.
Mute for a while and sullenly distressed,
At last the impetuous sorrow fired his breast.

'Wild is the whirlwind rolling
O'er Afric's sandy plain,
215 And wild the tempest howling
Along the billowed main:
But every danger felt before,
The raging deep, the whirlwind's roar,
Less dreadful struck me with dismay
220 Than what I feel this fatal day.
Oh, let me fly a land that spurns the brave,
Oswego's dreary shores shall be my grave;
I'll seek that less inhospitable coast,
And lay my body where my limbs were lost.'

SONG, BY A MAN
Basso. Spiritoso.

225 Old Edward's sons, unknown to yield,
Shall crowd from Crecy's laurelled field,
To do thy memory right;
For thine and Britain's wrongs they feel,
Again they snatch the gleamy steel,
230 And wish the avenging fight.

WOMAN SPEAKER

In innocence and youth complaining,
Next appeared a lovely maid,
Affliction o'er each feature reigning,
Kindly came in beauty's aid;
235 Every grace that grief dispenses,
Every glance that warms the soul,
In sweet succession charmed the senses,
While pity harmonized the whole.
'The garland of beauty'—'tis thus she would say—
240 'No more shall my crook or my temples adorn;
I'll not wear a garland—Augusta's away—
I'll not wear a garland until she return.
But alas! that return I never shall see;
The echoes of Thames shall my sorrows proclaim;
245 There promised a lover to come—but, O me!
'Twas death, 'twas the death of my mistress that came.
But ever, for ever, her image shall last;
I'll strip all the spring of its earliest bloom;

213–16. Cp. *The Captivity* 113–16 (p. 613 above).
222. Cp. *Traveller* 411 (p. 655 above).
225–30. Cp. Collins, *Ode to a Lady* 31–6 (p. 459 above).

On her grave shall the cowslip and primrose be cast,
250   And the new-blossomed thorn shall whiten her tomb.'

SONG, BY A WOMAN
Pastorale

With garlands of beauty the queen of the May
No more will her crook or her temples adorn;
For who'd wear a garland when she is away,
When she is removed and shall never return?

255   On the grave of Augusta these garlands be placed;
We'll rifle the spring of its earliest bloom,
And there shall the cowslip and primrose be cast,
And the new-blossomed thorn shall whiten her tomb.

CHORUS
Altro Modo

On the grave of Augusta this garland be placed;
260   We'll rifle the spring of its earliest bloom,
And there shall the cowslip and primrose be cast,
And the tears of her country shall water her tomb.

256, 260. Cp. Collins, *Song from Cymbeline* 3–4 (p. 401 above).

27 Song from
She Stoops to Conquer

Written before 15 March 1773, when the play was first performed. This song occurs in the second scene, which is set in 'An Alehouse Room. Several shabby Fellows with punch and tobacco. TONY at the head of the table, a little higher than the rest, a mallet in his hand.' *The Three Pigeons*, on which G. puns in the song, is the name of the alehouse. Dobson suggests that the approval expressed by the 'shabby fellows' of the song's 'gentility'–'O damn anything that's *low*, I cannot bear it'–was intended to satirise those who had objected to the 'low' scene with the bailiffs in *The Good Natured Man* in 1768. No changes were made to the text in the various impressions of the play.

Let school-masters puzzle their brain,
     With grammar and nonsense and learning;
Good liquor, I stoutly maintain,
     Gives *genus* a better discerning.

¶ *27.4. genus*] A term used in grammar and logic (cp. Tony's use of it as a mere

5   Let them brag of their heathenish gods,
        Their Lethes, their Styxes and Stygians:
     Their Quis and their Quaes and their Quods,
        They're all but a parcel of pigeons.
                     Toroddle, toroddle, toroll.

     When Methodist preachers come down
10   A-preaching that drinking is sinful,
     I'll wager the rascals a crown
        They always preach best with a skinful.
     But when you come down with your pence
        For a slice of their scurvy religion,
15   I'll leave it to all men of sense,
        But you, my good friend, are the pigeon.
                     Toroddle, toroddle, toroll.

     Then come, put the jorum about,
        And let us be merry and clever;
     Our hearts and our liquors are stout;
20   Here's the Three Jolly Pigeons for ever.
     Let some cry up woodcock or hare,
        Your bustards, your ducks and your widgeons;
     But of all the birds in the air,
        Here's a health to the Three Jolly Pigeons.
                     Toroddle, toroddle, toroll.

catchword in *She Stoops* III i); but G. may also be attempting a mild pun on
'genius'.
6–7. Tony is dismissing classical learning (the rivers and inhabitants of the
underworld) and Latin grammar.
8. *pigeons*] Simpletons, dupes, those who let themselves be swindled.
9. *Methodist*] G. more than once ridicules the absurdities of extreme 'en-
thusiasts'. Cp. *The Bee* no. vii; *Citizen* (1762) ii 182–6 (Letter III); *Essays*
(1765) no. xvii. For G.'s interest in Wesleyanism and its influence on him,
see C. G. Osgood, *Modern Philology* v (1907) 242–5.
16. See l. 8 *n* above.
17. *jorum*] A large drinking bowl, used especially for punch.
18. *clever*] Cp. *First Rejected Epilogue* 25 and *n* (p. 723).

28 [Song Intended for
She Stoops to Conquer]

Written before March 1773. The song was preserved by James Boswell,
who published it in the *London Mag.* xliii 295 in June 1774, two months after
G.'s death. Boswell prefixed the following letter:

To the Editor of the London Magazine

Sir,

I send you a small production of the late Dr. *Goldsmith*, which has never been published, and which might perhaps have been totally lost had I not secured it. He intended it as a song in the character of Miss *Hardcastle*, in his admirable comedy, *She stoops to conquer*; but it was left out, as Mrs. *Bulkeley* who played the part did not sing. He sung it himself in private companies very agreeably. The tune is a pretty Irish air, called *The Humours of Balamagairy*, to which, he told me, he found it very difficult to adapt words; but he has succeeded happily in these few lines. As I could sing the tune, and was fond of them, he was so good as to give me them about a year ago, just as I was leaving London, and bidding him adieu for that season, little apprehending that it was a last farewell. I preserve this little relick in his own handwriting with an affectionate care. I am, Sir,

Your humble Servant,
JAMES BOSWELL.

Boswell had heard G. sing this song, as well as Tony Lumpkin's song from the same play, on 13 April 1773, when he dined with G. and Johnson at General Oglethorpe's. Boswell called on G. on 10 May 1773, the day on which he left London, and presumably persuaded him to give him a copy of the song. This MS, in G.'s hand and with Boswell's inscription, is in the Boswell Papers at Yale. A facsimile was printed in the *Private Papers of James Boswell*, ed. G. Scott and F. A. Pottle (1928–34), ix 114 (see also vi 118 and ix 109–11); and again in *Boswell for the Defence*, ed. W. K. Wimsatt and F. A. Pottle (1960) p. 218. See also *Life of Johnson* ii 219, 260. The Irish air to which G. wrote his words dates from the early 17th century, and is also known as 'Old Langoler': see M. Sands, *Music and Letters* xxxii (1951) 149.

The song was first collected, with Boswell's letter, in *1780* i 107–8. No variants are found between the MS and printed texts.

> Ah, me! when shall I marry me?
>   Lovers are plenty but fail to relieve me.
> He, fond youth, that could carry me,
>   Offers to love but means to deceive me.
>
> 5 But I will rally and combat the ruiner:
>   Not a look, not a smile shall my passion discover.
> She that gives all to the false one pursuing her,
>   Makes but a penitent, loses a lover.

29 [First Rejected Epilogue to *She Stoops to Conquer*]

G. wrote three epilogues for *She Stoops to Conquer* between *c.* 4 and 14 March 1773. A letter to Cradock (*Letters* pp. 118–20, corrected here against the MS sold at Sotheby's on 7 Nov. 1951), written a day or two after the first performance of the comedy at Covent Garden on 15 March 1773, explains what had become a complicated situation. Garrick had provided a prologue and Arthur Murphy had been asked to supply an epilogue:

'Murphy sent me rather the outline of an Epilogue than an Epilogue, which was to be sung by Mrs.Catley, and which she approved. Mrs. Bulkley hearing this, insisted on throwing up her part, unless, according to the custom of the theatre, she were permitted to speak the Epilogue. In this embarrassment I thought of making a quarrelling Epilogue between Catley and her, debating who should speak the Epilogue, but this Mrs. Catley refused, after I had taken the trouble of drawing it out. I was then at a loss indeed; an Epilogue was to be made, and for none but Mrs. Bulkley. I made one, and Colman thought it too bad to be spoken; I was obliged therefore to try a fourth time, and I made a very mawkish thing, as you'll shortly see.'

Cradock, who had read the play in MS, had also sent G. an epilogue, which he himself described as 'a mere Jeu d'esprit . . . not intended to be spoken'; it was printed in an abridged form with the play, see *Letters* pp. xxxviii–xl.

Arthur Murphy explained his inability to write the epilogue, because of his business as a lawyer at Aylesbury Assizes on the Norfolk Circuit, in a letter of 2 March 1773; see J. P. Emery, *Philological Quarterly* xvii (1938) 88–90. Murphy merely outlined a suggested plan for an epilogue which would describe love in different countries by means of a characteristic recitative and air for the Italian, French, English, Irish and Scotch nations. G. may have drafted an epilogue on this plan, as he refers to the final epilogue as the 'fourth'. In any case, he obviously tried to salvage parts of this original scheme in the 'quarreling' epilogue which follows, after Mrs Bulkley, as the senior actress, had insisted on her right to speak the epilogue. This attempt to placate Mrs Bulkley merely offended Anne Catley, originally cast as Miss Neville, who eventually withdrew, her place in the cast being taken by Mrs Kniveton. This epilogue had accordingly to be abandoned.

G. gave the MS of this epilogue in his own hand to Thomas Percy, with other papers in April 1773; see J. Nichols, *Literary Illustrations* viii 672, and Miss Balderston, *Percy's Memoir of G.* p. 17. Through Percy it was first printed in *Works*, 1801, ii 82–6, although Percy did not know for what play it had been intended. Friedman (*Works* iv 391) suggests that this was the MS in the possession of Dr William Farr and his family at least until the mid-19th century, according to Prior (*Life* i 153 and *Works*, 1838, iv 154). But Prior explicitly states that G. himself presented that MS to Farr, which may have been the one sold in 1900 and in 1926 in the possession of J. A. Spoor; see Miss Balderston, *Census of G.'s MSS* pp. 43–4. There is also a MS copy of the epilogue in the Percy papers in the British Museum, Add. MS. 42515 ff. 81–2, on paper watermarked 1797. A few variants from this MS have been recorded. The text followed here is that of *Works*, 1801.

Enter Mrs Bulkley, who curtsies very low as beginning to speak. Then enter Miss Catley, who stands full before her and curtsies to the audience.

MRS BULKLEY

Hold, Ma'am, your pardon. What's your business
    here?

MISS CATLEY

The Epilogue.

MRS BULKLEY

    The Epilogue?

MISS CATLEY

                    Yes, the Epilogue, my dear.

MRS BULKLEY

Sure you mistake, Ma'am. The Epilogue, *I* bring it.

MISS CATLEY

Excuse me, Ma'am. The Author bid *me* sing it.

Recitative

5   Ye beaux and belles, that form this splendid ring,
    Suspend your conversation while I sing.

MRS BULKLEY

Why, sure the girl's beside herself: an Epilogue of
    singing,
A hopeful end indeed to such a blest beginning.
Besides, a singer in a comic set!
10 Excuse me, Ma'am, I know the etiquette.

MISS CATLEY

What if we leave it to the house?

MRS BULKLEY

                    The house!–Agreed.

MISS CATLEY

                          Agreed.

MRS BULKLEY

And she, whose party's largest, shall proceed.
And first, I hope, you'll readily agree
I've all the critics and the wits for me.

15   They, I am sure, will answer my commands:
     Ye candid-judging few, hold up your hands.
     What, no return? I find too late, I fear,
     That modern judges seldom enter here.

MISS CATLEY

     I'm for a different set. – Old men, whose trade is
20   Still to gallant and dangle with the ladies;

Recitative

     Who mump their passion and who, grimly smiling,
     Still thus address the fair with voice beguiling:

Air – Cotillon

     Turn, my fairest, turn, if ever
       Strephon caught thy ravished eye.
25   Pity take on your swain so clever,
       Who without your aid must die.
     Yes, I shall die, hu, hu, hu, hu!
     Yes, I must die, ho, ho, ho, ho!

                                 Da capo

MRS BULKLEY

     Let all the old pay homage to your merit:
30   Give me the young, the gay, the men of spirit.
     Ye travelled tribe, ye macaroni train,

¶ *29.19–20.* G. repeatedly ridiculed elderly 'battered beaus' in *Citizen* (1762) i 29, 112; ii 98, 207 (Letters 9, 27, 88, 116).
20. dangle] F. Grose, *Classical Dictionary of the Vulgar Tongue*, ed. E. Partridge, p. 117, gives the meaning 'To follow a woman without asking the question'.
21. mump] Mumble, mutter.
25. clever] G. uses it in the 'Song' from *She Stoops* 18 (see p. 719) to mean 'good-natured, amiable'; but here it might also mean 'handsome'.
27. hu, hu, hu, hu] ha ha ha ha *MS*.
31. macaroni train] The foplings who flourished *c.* 1765–80. See the article on the 'Origin of the Word Macaroni' in *The Macaroni and Theatrical Mag.* (Oct. 1772) p. 1, which explains that the food of that name began to be imported in the mid-1760s 'by our *Connoscenti* in eating' at Almack's Club, who became known as the 'Macaronies': 'and, as the meeting was composed of the younger and gayer part of our nobility and gentry, who, at the same time that they gave into the luxuries of eating, went equally into the extravagancies of dress; the word Macaroni then changed its meaning to that of a person who exceeded the ordinary bounds of fashion; and is now justly used as a term of reproach to all ranks of people, indifferently, who fall into this absurdity.' Caricature prints of wellknown

Of French friseurs and nosegays justly vain,
Who take a trip to Paris once a year
To dress and look like awkward Frenchmen here:
35   Lend me your hands.—Oh! fatal news to tell:
Their hands are only lent to the Heinel.

MISS CATLEY

Ay, take your travellers, travellers indeed!
Give me my bonny Scots that travel from the Tweed.
Where are the chiels? Ah! Ah, I well discern
40   The smiling looks of each bewitching bairn.

Air—A bonny young lad is my Jockey.

I'll sing to amuse you by night and by day,
And be unco merry when you are but gay;
When you with your bagpipes are ready to play,
My voice shall be ready to carol away
45   With Sandy, and Sawney and Jockey,
          With Sawney, and Jarvie and Jockey.

MRS BULKLEY

Ye gamesters, who, so eager in pursuit,
Make but of all your fortune one *va toute*;
Ye jockey tribe, whose stock of words are few,

personalities as various kinds of 'macaroni' were popular. Young Marlow in
She Stoops IV i, says 'I shall be stuck up in carricatura in all the print-shops.
The *Dullissimo Maccaroni.*'
32. friseurs] Hairdressers.   *nosegays*] Perfumes.
36. Anna-Frederica Heinel (1752–1808) was dancing at the King's Theatre
during March 1773. According to Dr Burney, *History of Music* (1789) iv
498, her 'grace and execution' were 'so perfect as to eclipse all other
excellence' in the operas in which she performed. He added that her 'extra-
ordinary merit had an extraordinary recompence: for besides the £600
salary allowed her by the Hon. Mr. Hobart as manager [of the opera-house],
she was complimented with a *regallo* of six hundred more from the Macc-
aroni Club.'
38. Scots that travel] Scot, that travels *MS*.
39. Ah! Ah] Oh oh *MS*.
45. Sawney, like Sandy, is a Scotch diminutive of Alexander, as is Jockey of
Jock or John and Jarvie of Jarvis or Jervis. These names often appear in the
'Scotch' songs sung, for example, at the Vauxhall Gardens during the
1770s.
46. Jarvie] Jamie *MS*.
49. *jockey*] Often used of anyone concerned with horses, not merely their
riders; and, from the cunning character attributed to horse-dealers, 'a
crafty or fraudulent bargainer or cheat' (*OED*).

50 'I hold the odds.–Done, done, with you, with you';
Ye barristers, so fluent with grimace,
'My Lord,–your Lordship misconceives the case';
Doctors, who cough and answer every misfortuner,
'I wish I'd been called in a little sooner':
55 Assist my cause with hands and voices hearty;
Come, end the contest here and aid my party.

MISS CATLEY

Air—Baleinamony

Ye brave Irish lads, hark away to the crack,
Assist me, I pray, in this woeful attack;
For sure I don't wrong you, you seldom are slack,
60 When the ladies are calling, to blush and hang back.
For you're always polite and attentive,
Still to amuse us inventive,
And death is your only preventive:
Your hands and your voices for me.

MRS BULKLEY

65 Well, Madam, what if, after all this sparring,
We both agree, like friends, to end our jarring?

MISS CATLEY

And that our friendship may remain unbroken,
What if we leave the Epilogue unspoken?

MRS BULKLEY

Agreed.

MISS CATLEY

Agreed.

MRS BULKLEY

And now with late repentance,
70 Un-epilogued the poet waits his sentence.
Condemn the stubborn fool who can't submit
To thrive by flattery, though he starves by wit.

[*Exeunt.*

53. *misfortuner*] importuner MS.
54. *wish*] wish'd *MS.*
57. *crack*] A boast or exaggeration. Cp. *She Stoops* Act IV: 'That's a damned confounded crack.'
62. *us*] as MS.

30 [Second Rejected Epilogue to *She Stoops to Conquer*]

Written early in March 1773, probably between 9 and 14 March (see l. 48 *n*).
For the full background see headnote to the *First Rejected Epilogue* (p. 720
above). This epilogue is G.'s first attempt to write one for Mrs Bulkley
alone, after Anne Catley's refusal to participate in the dialogue: 'An
Epilogue was to be made, and for none but Mrs. Bulkley. I made one, and
Colman thought it too bad to be spoken.' George Colman was the manager
of Covent Garden theatre and his objection obliged G. to abandon this
epilogue.

Like the *First Rejected Epilogue*, this was given by G. to Percy in a packet of
letters and other papers in April 1773, although it differed in being 'in the
handwriting of the actor who was to recite it' (Nichols, *Literary Illustrations*
viii 672). This may be the copy in the Percy papers in the British Museum
(Add. MS 42515 ff. 83–4). Through Percy it was first printed in *Works*,
1801, ii 87–8: it was entitled merely 'An Epilogue, Intended for Mrs.
Bulkley', for, as a footnote admitted, 'for what comedy it was intended is
not remembered'. Prior (*Life* ii 7–9) prints an exchange of letters between
George Steevens and Percy about the possible purpose of the epilogue,
which Steevens thought might have been produced by G. as 'a piece of
sale-work, for the service of a chance customer, or for his own future use'.

Because part of it was reworked by G. for his final attempt, Percy in 1801
made extensive alterations to this epilogue, the MS of which was not in
G.'s hand, when it was printed. He transposed, changed and omitted
lines as he thought fit. The MS was first printed in full by Miss Balderston
(*Letters* pp. xliv–xlvi). Percy had reduced the text from 58 to 42 ll, printing
only ll. 1–18, 43–4, 47–8, 19–20 (altered), 23–30 and 49–58 in that order.
The text of the MS is followed here with variants from the 1801 text.

There is a place, so Ariosto sings,
A treasury for lost and missing things.
Lost human wits have places there assigned them,
And they, who lose their senses, there may find them.

¶ 30.*1–6.* In Ariosto's *Orlando Furioso* xxxiv 68 ff, Astolfo travels to the
moon to look for Orlando's lost wits and finds (in Harington's translation,
1634) 'A mighty masse of things strangely confused, / Things that on earth
were lost, or were abused.' On the moon, 'man's wit' which has been lost
through love, ambition etc., is preserved in jars. G. may have been influenced
by Pope's *Rape of the Lock* v 113–6, where the debt to Ariosto is acknowledged
in a note: 'Some thought it mounted to the Lunar Sphere, / Since all things
lost on Earth, are treasur'd there. / There Heroes' Wits are kept in pondrous
Vases, / And Beaus' in *Snuff-boxes* and *Tweezer-Cases*.'

5   But where's this place, this storehouse of the age?
       The moon, says he: but I affirm the stage.
       At least in many things, I think I see
       His lunar and our mimic world agree.
       Both shine at night, for, but at Foote's alone,
10   We scarce exhibit till the sun goes down.
       Both prone to change, no settled limits fix;
       'Tis said the folks of both are lunatics.
       But in this parallel my best pretence is
       That mortals visit both to find their senses.
15   To this strange spot, rakes, macaronies, cits,
       Come thronging to collect their scattered wits.
       The gay coquette, who ogles all the day,
       Comes here by night and goes a prude away.
       The gamester too who, eager in pursuit,
20   Makes but of all his fortune one *va toute*,
       Whose mind is barren and whose words are few—
       'I take the odds'; 'Done, done, with you, and you'—
       Comes here to saunter, having made his bets,
       Finds his lost senses out and pays his debts.
25   The Mohawk too, with angry phrases stored—

9–10. This couplet is crossed out in MS.

9. The London theatres at this period opened their doors at 5 p.m. and raised the curtain at 6 p.m. Early in March 1773 Samuel Foote (1720–77), actor, mimic and dramatist, was presenting his *Primitive Puppet Show* at the Haymarket Theatre, the doors opening at 12 a.m. and the performance beginning at 1 p.m. See the *Public Advertiser*, 8 March 1773.

12. '*Tis said*] And sure *1801*.

15. *macaronies*] See the *First Rejected Epilogue* 31 *n*. Johnson defines a 'cit' as 'a pert, low townsman'.

18. *by*] at *1801*.

19–22. G. has reworked the first epilogue, ll. 47–50. *1801* alters the first couplet and omits the second as follows: 'The gamester too, whose wits all high or low, / Oft risques his fortune on one desperate throw'.

25. *Mohawk (or Mohock)*] 'The name of a cruel nation of America given to ruffians who infested, or rather were imagined to infest, the streets of London' (Johnson). The Mohawks were a supposedly cannibalistic tribe of Red Indians, whose name was transferred in the early eighteenth century to brutal aristocratic rakes, whose activities are described in the *Spectator* Nos. 324, 327. See also Swift, *Journal to Stella*, March 1712 *passim*; Gay, *Trivia* iii 326; and a letter of Lady Wentworth, 14 March 1712, in the *Wentworth Papers* (1883) pp. 277–8, describing vividly the 'barbarous tricks' of this 'gang of devils'. The name may have been suggested by the title of one of four Indian kings, the Emperor of the Mohocks, who visited England in 1710. By G.'s day it was no doubt used of a much less violent sort of rake.

As 'damme, Sir,' and 'Sir, I wear a sword'–
Here lessoned for a while and hence retreating,
Goes out, affronts his man and takes a beating.
Here come the sons of scandal and of news,
30   But find no sense–for they had none to lose.
The poet too comes hither to be wiser,
And so for once I'll be the man's adviser.
What could he hope in this lord-loving age,
Without a brace of lords upon the stage?
35   In robes and stars unless the bard adorn us,
You grow familiar, lose respect and scorn us.
Then not one passion, fury, sentiment:
Sure his poetic fire is wholly spent!
Oh, how I love to hear applauses shower
40   On my fixed attitude of half an hour;
              (*Stands in an attitude*)
And then with whining, staring, struggling, slapping,
To force their feelings and provoke their clapping.
Hither the affected city dame advancing,

29–42. These lines are crossed out in MS.

31–58. These lines show that part of G.'s purpose in *She Stoops* was to
undermine the current vogue of mawkish 'sentimental' comedy with its
facile morality. In Jan. 1773 he had contributed to the *Westminster Mag.*
'An Essay on the Theatre; or, A Comparison between Laughing and Senti-
mental Comedy', in which he had argued that humour was being driven
from the stage. The proper subject of comedy was 'Human Absurdity'.
'When Comedy . . . ascends to produce the Characters of Princes or Generals
upon the Stage, it is out of its walk, since Low Life and Middle Life are en-
tirely its object.' To write 'Sentimental' comedy, 'It is only sufficient to
raise the Characters a little; to deck out the Hero with a Ribband, or give the
Heroine a Title; then to put an Insipid Dialogue, without Character or
Humour, into their mouths, give them mighty good hearts, very fine
cloaths, furnish a new sett of Scenes, make a Pathetic Scene or two, with a
sprinkling of tender melancholy Conversation through the whole, and there
is no doubt but all the Ladies will cry, and all the Gentlemen applaud.' Cp.
also G.'s preface to *The Good Natured Man* and dedication to *She Stoops*. G.
was supported in his attack on sentimental comedy by Samuel Foote, whose
Primitive Puppet Show (see l. 9 *n.*) was performing a parody of one, en-
titled *The Handsome Housemaid; or, Piety in Pattens*.

31–42. Omitted in 1801.

39–42. For G.'s dislike of the traditional shrugs and attitudes of acting see
his essays on the theatre in *The Bee* Nos. i and ii; *Citizen* (1762) ii 62 (Letter
79); *Essays* No. xxi; *Vicar* chs. xviii, xx.

      Who sighs for operas and dotes on dancing,
45   Who hums a favourite air and, spreading wide,
      Swings round the room, the Heinel of Cheapside,
      Taught by our art her ridicule to pause on,
      Quits *Che faro* and calls for *Nancy Dawson.*
      Of all the tribe here wanting an adviser,
50   Our author's the least likely to grow wiser.
      Has he not seen how you your favours place
      On sentimental queens and lords in lace?
      Without a star, a coronet or Garter,
      How can the piece expect or hope for quarter?
55   No high-life scenes, no sentiment, the creature
      Still stoops among the low to copy nature.
      Yes, he's far gone. And yet some pity mix:
      The English laws forbid to punish lunatics.

44–8. G. reworked these lines in the final epilogue, 25–8. Percy omitted 45–6 and altered 48, placing 43–4 and 47–8 after l. 18.
46. Cp. *First Rejected Epilogue* 36 *n.*
48. Che faro] the *Ballet 1801.*   The famous aria 'Che farò senza Euridice', from Gluck's opera *Orfeo* (1764), was first performed in its original form at the King's Theatre on 9 March 1773, a fact which may help to date this epilogue's composition. Nancy Dawson (1730?–1767) was a celebrated figure dancer at Sadler's Wells and Covent Garden, who became famous in 1759 for her dancing the hornpipe in *The Beggar's Opera.* G. probably refers to a popular air named after her.
51. favours] favour *1801.*
56. G. seems to have changed the title of his play from *The Mistakes of a Night* to *She Stoops to Conquer* at the last moment, perhaps as late as 14 March, and this line appears to have given him the hint. See *Letters* pp. xlvii–xlviii.
57. mix] fix *1801.*

31 Epilogue to
She Stoops to Conquer

Possibly written as late as Sunday, 14 March 1773, the day before the first performance of the comedy at Covent Garden. (For the full background and G.'s two previous attempts to write an epilogue see headnote to *First Rejected Epilogue*, p. 720). It was on the Sunday that Younger, the stage manager, acknowledged the receipt of the new epilogue and of the play's new title: 'Mrs. Bulkley has got a fair Copy of the Epilogue & he will take care in the Morning that the Licenser shall have another, & also the additional

Title to the Play.' On the Monday morning Mrs Bulkley asked G. to call on her, 'she being perfect in the Epilogue, & very desirous of the Doctor's hearing it' (*Letters* pp. xlvi–xlviii).

That this epilogue was written in haste is indicated by G.'s efforts to rework as much as possible of his previous attempt. With Shakespeare's 'Seven Ages of Man' as framework, G. seems also, as Miss Balderston pointed out (*Letters* p. xlviii), to have taken up the basis of the epilogue written by Joseph Cradock (see headnote to *First Rejected Epilogue*, p. 721 above). Cradock described Tony Lumpkin and Bet Bouncer in London exchanging their country manners for the affectations of the town. In G.'s epilogue, Kate Hardcastle, still posing as the barmaid as in the play, does the same, but in a manner which corresponds to nothing in her character or the rest of the play. G. himself thought it 'a very mawkish thing' and his view was shared by others. The *St James's Chronicle*, 13–16 March 1773, reviewing the play, stated: 'The Prologue (spoken by Mr. Woodward) is Mr. Garrick's, and is excellent. The Epilogue (spoken by Mrs. Bulkley) is Mr. Goldsmith's, and is not so good.' But the *Morning Chronicle* (16 March 1773) considered that 'The Epilogue had wit and humour, and was delivered with great spirit by Mrs. Bulkley.' An engraved portrait of Mrs Bulkley speaking this epilogue is given in *A Collection of Prologues and Epilogues*, ed. Acton Griffith, 1779.

In some early texts, e.g. *London Chronicle* (18–20 March 1773), *Public Advertiser* (19 March 1773), and *Macaroni and Theatrical Mag.* (March 1773) p. 278, ll. 25–6 are omitted, and the couplet may have been added after the first performance of the play. The text followed here is that of the 1st edn of the play, with variants from the *London Chronicle*.

> Well, having stooped to conquer with success,
> And gained a husband without aid from dress,
> Still, as a barmaid, I could wish it too,
> As I have conquered him, to conquer you:
> 5 And let me say, for all your resolution,
> That pretty barmaids have done execution.
> Our life is all a play, composed to please:
> 'We have our exits and our entrances.'
> The first act shows the simple country maid,
> 10 Harmless and young, of everything afraid,
> Blushes when hired and, with unmeaning action,

¶ 31.1. Cp. *Second Rejected Epilogue* 56n (p. 729).
6. *execution*] For this metaphorical usage of the effect of personal charm, cp. Farquhar, *Beaux Stratagem* II ii: 'You are so well dressed . . . that I fancy you may do execution in a country church'; and *Vicar* ch i: 'Sophia's features were not so striking at first; but often did more certain execution.'
8. Adapted from *As You Like It* II vii 141: 'They have their exits and their entrances'.

'I hopes as how to give you satisfaction.'
Her second act displays a livelier scene—
The unblushing barmaid of a country inn,
15 Who whisks about the house, at market caters,
Talks loud, coquets the guests and scolds the waiters.
Next the scene shifts to town, and there she soars,
The chop-house toast of ogling connoisseurs.
On squires and cits she there displays her arts,
20 And on the gridiron broils her lovers' hearts:
And as she smiles, her triumphs to complete,
Even Common-Councilmen forget to eat.
The fourth act shows her wedded to the squire,
And Madam now begins to hold it higher;
25 Pretends to taste, at operas cries *caro*,
And quits her *Nancy Dawson* for *Che faro*,
Dotes upon dancing and, in all her pride,
Swims round the room, the Heinel of Cheapside;
Ogles and leers with artificial skill,
30 Till, having lost in age the power to kill,
She sits all night at cards and ogles at spadille.
Such, through our lives, the eventful history—
The fifth and last act still remains for me.

15. caters] Buys food.
17. soars] spars *London Chron.*
18. chop-house] 'A mean house of entertainment, where provision ready dressed is sold' (Johnson). The 'variety of characters' to be found in a chop-house is well described in *The Connoisseur* xix (6 June 1754): 'at Betty's, and the chop-houses about the inns of court, a pretty maid is as inviting as the provisions. In these common refectories you may always find the jemmy attorney's clerk, the prim curate, the walking physician, the captain upon half pay, the shabby valet de chambre upon board wages, and the foreign count or marquis in dishabille, who has refused to dine with a duke or an ambassador.'
22. The Common Council was the administrative body of a corporate town or city. G. more than once ridicules the Common-Councilman's vulgarity and self-importance. Cp. *Essays* (2nd edn, 1766), Nos. xxvi and xxvii, supposedly written by a Common-Councilman.
26. Cp. *Second Rejected Epilogue 48 n* (p. 729).
28. Cp. *First Rejected Epilogue 36 n* (p. 724).
29. Ogles] Cp. *Citizen* (1762) i 78 (Letter 21): 'Gentlemen and ladies ogled each other through spectacles; for my companion observed, that blindness was of late become fashionable.'
31. spadille] The ace of spades in the game of ombre, in which the two black aces were always trumps, the ace of spades ranking higher. Cp. *Rape of the Lock* iii 49: 'Spadillio first, unconquerable Lord!'.

> The barmaid now for your protection prays,
> 35   Turns female barrister and pleads for Bayes.

34–5. G. falls back on one of the most venerable comparisons in prologues
and epilogues, with the speaker as an advocate, the author as a criminal and
the audience as jury.
35. Bayes] The chief character in the Duke of Buckingham's *The Rehearsal*
(1672), originally a satiric caricature of Dryden, became a generic name for
the dramatist, as here. But G. follows up his play on 'barmaid' and 'bar-
rister' with a pun on 'bays', as the traditional crown awarded to the poet.

32 Epilogue, Spoken by Mr Lee Lewes, In the Character of Harlequin, at his Benefit

Written in late April or early May 1773. Charles Lee Lewes (1740–1803)
was the original Young Marlow of *She Stoops to Conquer*. Previously he had
been best known as a pantomime Harlequin but, according to William
Cooke, *European Mag.* xxiv (1793) 173, he was persuaded by Shuter, the
comedian, to ask for a part in G.'s comedy, 'which Dr. Goldsmith at first
agreed to with some reluctance, but after one or two rehearsals so altered
his opinion, that he declared it was the second best performance in the piece'.
In gratitude for the success he made of the part, G. wrote for Lewes this
epilogue to be spoken on the benefit night which, as one of Covent Garden's
leading performers, he was granted towards the end of the season. (There
seems to have been some trouble over the date of Lewes's benefit. Jane
Green, who had played Mrs Hardcastle in *She Stoops*, wrote to G. on 6 April
1773 complaining that Lewes had tried to appropriate her benefit night;
see Wardle, p. 316 n 49.) Lewes spoke it on Friday, 7 May 1773. The *Public
Advertiser* for that day announced that, after the performance of Rowe's
Lady Jane Grey, 'a new Occasional EPILOGUE (written by Dr. Goldsmith,)
will be spoken by Mr. LEWES. To which will be added, HARLEQUIN SORCERER'.
Lewis Theobald's *Harlequin Sorcerer, with the Loves of Pluto and Proserpine* had
first been performed in 1725 but the fact that it contained 'a great deal of
very fine machinery . . . brought crowded houses to the manager of Covent-
Garden Theatre for several seasons after its revival in [1752]' (*Biographia
Dramatica* (1782) ii 146). It is to this sort of infernal machinery that G. re-
fers in ll. 15–18. He had expressed his distaste for pantomime as early as
1754, *Letters* p. 23.
    Lewes repeated the epilogue at Covent Garden after a performance of
She Stoops to Conquer on 28 April 1774, a little more than three weeks after
G.'s death. It was printed for the first time in the *London Chronicle*, (28–30

April 1774, p. 416, and reprinted with minor changes, in the *Universal Mag.* liv (May 1774) 261. Some obvious errors in this text were corrected in *1780* i 112–14, which has been followed here.

> Hold! Prompter, hold! a word before your nonsense;
> I'd speak a word or two to ease my conscience.
> My pride forbids it ever should be said
> My heels eclipsed the honours of my head;
> 5 That I found humour in a piebald vest,
> Or ever thought that jumping was a jest.
>   [*Takes off his mask*
> Whence and what art thou, visionary birth?
> Nature disowns and reason scorns thy mirth,
> In thy black aspect every passion sleeps,
> 10 The joy that dimples and the woe that weeps.
> How hast thou filled the scene with all thy brood,
> Of fools pursuing and of fools pursued!
> Whose ins and outs no ray of sense discloses,
> Whose only plot it is to break our noses;
> 15 Whilst from below the trap-door demons rise,
> And from above the dangling deities.
> And shall I mix in this unhallowed crew?
> May rosined lightning blast me, if I do!
> No–I will act, I'll vindicate the stage:

¶ *32.2. I'd*] I'll *London Chron.*

3–6. Harlequin was usually dressed in a tight costume with a criss-cross design in various colours and wore a half-mask. The English Harlequin, a personal creation of John Rich *c.* 1725, was virtually mute and spent most of his time on the stage in miming, acrobatic dancing, leaping and tumbling.

6. In the stage direction London Chron. reads Taking *for* Takes.

7. visionary birth] Unreal creation, existing only in fantasy.

15–18. Much of the appeal of the pantomimes featuring Harlequin lay in the elaborate machinery they used, which lowered characters on to the stage or raised them through trap-doors. *The Adventurer* No. 3, 14 Nov. 1752, describes a mock pantomime entitled *Harlequin Hercules*: 'Though this is the most applauded scene in many of our favourite Pantomimes, I don't doubt but my HELL will outdo whatever has been hitherto attempted of the kind, whether in its gloomy decoration, its horrors, its flames, or its devils.' The writer also refers to the 'refluent flood of burning rosin', used for the representation of fire or lightning on the stage. *Harlequin Sorcerer* itself (see headnote), 1752 edn, pp. 18–19, represents in Scene III: 'A Chamber; Harlequin reposing himself on a Couch; Thunder and Lightning; several Demons arise; seize and bear away *Harlequin* in Triumph'; and in Scene IV, 'A Machine descends with PLUTO and PROSERPINE, and fixes on the Stage.'

19. I will] I'll *London Chron.*

20   Shakespeare himself shall feel my tragic rage.
'Off! off! vile trappings!': a new passion reigns!
The maddening monarch revels in my veins.
Oh! for a Richard's voice to catch the theme:
'Give me another horse! bind up my wounds!–soft–
        'twas but a dream.'

25   Aye, 'twas but a dream, for now there's no retreating:
If I cease Harlequin, I cease from eating.
'Twas thus that Aesop's stag, a creature blameless,
Yet something vain, like one that shall be nameless,
Once on the margin of a fountain stood,

30   And cavilled at his image in the flood.
'The deuce confound,' he cries, 'these drumstick
        shanks,
They never have my gratitude nor thanks;
They're perfectly disgraceful! strike me dead!
But for a head, yes, yes, I have a head.

35   How piercing is that eye! how sleek that brow!
My horns! I'm told horns are the fashion now.'
Whilst thus he spoke, astonished, to his view,
Near, and more near, the hounds and huntsmen drew.
'Hoicks! hark forward!' came thundering from
        behind,

21. *King Lear* III iv 113: 'Off, off, you lendings! Come, unbutton here.'
24. *Richard III* V iii 177–8: 'Give me another horse: bind up my wounds. /
Soft! I did but dream.'
25. *'twas but*] it was *London Chron.*
27–46. G. adapted the end of the fable and lost some of its point. Cp. Sir
Roger L'Estrange's translation (3rd edn, 1699) p. 45 (Fable xliii): 'As a *Stag*
was Drinking upon the Bank of a Clear Stream, he saw his Image in the
Water, and Enter'd upon This Contemplation upon't. Well! says he, if
These Pityful Shanks of mine were but Answerable to this Branching Head,
I can but think how I should Defy all my Enemies. The Words were hardly
out of his Mouth, but he Discover'd a Pack of Dogs coming full Cry towards
him. Away he Scours cross the Fields, Casts off the Dogs, and Gains a Wood;
but Pressing through a Thicket, the Bushes held him by the Horns, till
the Hounds came in, and Pluck'd him Down. The last Thing he said was
This. What an Unhappy Fool was I, to Take my Friends for my Enemies, and
my Enemies for my Friends! I Trusted to my *Head*, that has Betray'd me,
and I found fault with my *Legs*, that would otherwise have brought me off.'
32. *never*] neither *London Chron.*
34. *yes, yes*] yes *London Chron.*; Oh, yes *Universal Mag.*
36. And, my horns! I'm told that horns are all the fashion now *London Chron.*
horns] No doubt the usual pun on the cuckold's horns.

40 He bounds aloft, outstrips the fleeting wind:
    He quits the woods and tries the beaten ways;
    He starts, he pants, he takes the circling maze.
    At length his silly head, so prized before,
    Is taught his former folly to deplore;
45 Whilst his strong limbs conspire to set him free,
    And at one bound he saves himself, like me.
                    [*Taking a jump through the stage door*

40. Pope, *Dunciad* ii 62: 'He left huge Lintot, and out-strip'd the wind'.
41. *beaten*] beating *London Chron.*
42. Pope, *Windsor Forest* 122: 'And trace the Mazes of the circling Hare'.
44. *his*] its *London Chron.*

33 Letter in Verse and Prose to Mrs Bunbury

Written about 25 Dec. 1773, as was shown by Miss Balderston from internal evidence, *Letters* p. 128 *n*. The letter is a reply to an invitation from Mrs Catherine Horneck Bunbury (see headnote to *Reply to an Invitation to Dinner*, p. 600 above, and 17 *n*) to spend New Year 1774 at the family seat of the Bunburys at Great Barton in Suffolk. G. alludes throughout to Mrs Bunbury's verse invitation, reproduced here from the contemporary MS copy printed in *Letters* pp. 128–9 *n*:

> I hope my good Doctor you soon will be here
> And your spring velvet coat very smart will appear
> To open our ball the first day of the year.
> And bring with you a wig that is modish and gay
> To dance with the girls that are makers of Hay;
> Tho of Hay we don't often hear talk in these times,
> Yet it serves very well towards making of rhimes.
> My sister will laugh at my rhimes about Hay,
> Yet this I am sure I may venture to say,
> That we all here do wish and intreat and desire
> You will straightway come hither and sit by our fire.
> And if you will like in the evening to game
> We'll all play at Loo where you'll surely get fame
> By winning our money away in a trice,
> As my sister and I will give you advice.
> Or if you shoot, Sir, we'll lend you a gun,
> And Druid t'oblige will after Birds run.
> But if you like better to hunt o'er the ground[s]
> Mr B[unbur]y'll lend you [so]me [ve]ry good Hounds.

But these simple sports to a fine London Beau
Who doubtless is thinking of fashion and show
And whose interested friends all wish to detain,
As they know very well what pleasure they gain
By keeping one with them they so much admire
And whose cheerful company always desire,
Yet to leave these pleasures if he condescends
He will greatly oblige his very good friends.

G.'s verses concentrate on Mrs Bunbury's suggestion that they play Loo
at Barton. Awareness of what had become a serious weakness underlies
G.'s humorous derision of his lack of success at cards. He was a reckless
gambler for a man of a limited and uncertain income. Robert Day re-
membered in 1831 that G., 'in losing his money . . . never lost his temper.
In a run of bad luck and worse play, he would fling his cards upon the floor
and exclaim "*Bye-fore* George I ought for ever to renounce thee, fickle,
faithless, Fortune"'; see Prior, *Life* ii 357–8. Cradock, *Literary and Mis-
cellaneous Memoirs* (1828) i 232, stated that G.'s greatest fault was that 'if he
had thirty pounds in his pocket he would go into certain companies in the
country, and in hopes of doubling the sum, would generally return to town
without any part of it'. Before going to Barton at New Year 1774, G.
borrowed £60 from Garrick.

G.'s letter was first printed in 1837 by Prior, *Works* iv 148–51, where it
was dated 1772; it was reprinted by the owner of the MS, Sir Henry
Bunbury in *Correspondence of Sir Thomas Hanmer* (1838) pp. 379–83, where
a date of 1773 or 1774 is suggested. Both these texts omit the final couplet
(see 67–8 n). The present text is that of the original MS in the Pierpont Morgan
Library, New York, first printed in *Letters* pp. 128–36. The introductory
prose, a necessary context for G.'s verses, is also given, in a modernised text.

Madam.

I read your letter with all that allowance which critical
candour could require, but after all find so much to object to,
and so much to raise my indignation, that I cannot help giving
it a serious reply. I am not so ignorant, madam, as not to see
there are many sarcasms contained in it, and solecisms also.
(Solecism is a word that comes from the town of Soleis in Attica
among the Greeks, built by Solon, and applied as we use the
word Kidderminster for curtains, from a town also of that name;
– but this is learning you have no taste for.) I say, madam, there
are sarcasms in it and solecisms also. But not to seem an ill-
natured critic, I'll take leave to quote your own words and give
you my remarks upon them as they occur. You begin as follows:

I hope my good Doctor you soon will be here
And your spring velvet coat very smart will appear
To open our ball the first day of the year.

Pray, madam, where did you ever find the epithet 'good,' applied to the title of Doctor? Had you called me 'learned Doctor,' or 'grave Doctor,' or 'noble Doctor,' it might be allowable, because these belong to the profession. But, not to cavil at trifles, you talk of my 'spring velvet coat,' and advise me to wear it the first day in the year, that is, in the middle of winter. A spring velvet in the middle of winter!!! That would be a solecism indeed. And yet, to increase the inconsistence, in another part of your letter you call me a beau. Now, on one side or other, you must be wrong. If I'm a beau, I can never think of wearing a spring velvet in winter: and if I am not a beau, why then, that explains itself. But let me go on to your two next strange lines:

> And bring with you a wig that is modish and gay
> To dance with the girls that are makers of hay.

The absurdity of making hay at Christmas you yourself seem sensible of: you say your sister will laugh; and so indeed she well may. The Latins have an expression for a contemptuous kind of laughter, 'Naso contemnere adunco'; that is, to laugh with a crooked nose. She may laugh at you in the manner of the ancients if she thinks fit. But now I come to the most extraordinary of all extraordinary propositions, which is, to take your and your sister's advice in playing at Loo. The presumption of the offer raises my indignation beyond the bounds of prose; it inspires me at once with verse and resentment. I take advice! and from who? You shall hear.

> First let me suppose, what may shortly be true,
> The company set, and the word to be Loo;
> All smirking and pleasant and big with adventure,
> And ogling the stake which is fixed in the centre.
> 5 Round and round go the cards, while I inwardly
>   damn

¶ 33.2. Loo or Lanterloo was a popular eighteenth-century card-game, played on the lines of whist with trumps. Any number could participate, the object being to take the pool by winning the largest number of tricks. There were two leading varieties, 3-card and 5-card Loo. In 5-card Loo, which was evidently played at Barton (see l. 24), the knave of clubs, known as Pam, is made a sort of paramount trump, with precedence even over the ace of the trump suit (cf. l. 6). The player who wins no tricks is 'looed' i.e. he forfeits his contribution to the pool, and contributes to the pool for the next round (see ll. 8, 26, 32). See Angelo John Lewis, *Hoffmann's Cyclopaedia of Card and Table Games* (1891) p. 122.

At never once finding a visit from Pam.
I lay down my stake, apparently cool,
While the harpies about me all pocket the pool.
I fret in my gizzard, yet, cautious and sly,
10 I wish all my friends may be bolder than I.
Yet still they sit snug, not a creature will aim
By losing their money to venture at fame.
'Tis in vain that at niggardly caution I scold,
'Tis in vain that I flatter the brave and the bold:
15 All play in their own way and think me an ass.
'What does Mrs Bunbury?' 'I, sir? I pass.'
'Pray what does Miss Horneck? Take courage, come
      do.'
'Who, I? let me see, sir, why I must pass too.'
Mr Bunbury frets, and I fret like the devil,
20 To see them so cowardly, lucky and civil.
Yet still I sit snug and continue to sigh on,
Till made by my losses as bold as a lion,
I venture at all, while my avarice regards
The whole pool as my own. 'Come, give me five
      cards.'
25 'Well done!' cry the ladies; 'Ah, Doctor, that's good!
The pool's very rich. Ah! the Doctor is Loo'd!'
Thus foiled in my courage, on all sides perplexed,
I ask for advice from the lady that's next:
'Pray, ma'am, be so good as to give your advice;
30 Don't you think the best way is to venture for't twice?'
'I advise,' cries the lady, 'to try it, I own.
Ah! the Doctor is Loo'd! Come, Doctor, put down.'
Thus, playing and playing, I still grow more eager,
And so bold and so bold, I'm at last a bold beggar.
35 Now, ladies, I ask, if law-matters you're skilled in,

6. *After this line two lines are crossed out:* I lay down my stake, I double that
too, / While some harpy beside me picks up the whole.
See l. 2 n above; and cp. the 'mighty Pam' in Pope, *Rape of the Lock* iii 61.
9. *in my gizzard*] *Written above an undecipherable deletion.*   *fret in my gizzard*]
A common eighteenth-century phrase meaning 'To worry oneself'.
12. G. refers to the line in Mrs Bunbury's invitation: 'We'll all play at Loo
where you'll surely get fame.'
16–17. The Horneck sisters, Catherine Bunbury and Mary Horneck (see
Reply to an Invitation 14 n, p. 662 above).
19. *Mr Bunbury*] Henry William Bunbury (1750–1811), the artist and cari-
caturist, who married Catherine Horneck in 1771.
24, 26. See l. 2 n.

Whether crimes such as yours should not come before
    Fielding?
For giving advice that is not worth a straw
May well be called picking of pockets in law;
And picking of pockets, with which I now charge ye,
40 Is, by quinto Elizabeth, Death without Clergy.
What justice, when both to the Old Bailey brought!
By the gods, I'll enjoy it; though 'tis but in thought!
Both are placed at the bar with all proper decorum,
With bunches of fennel and nosegays before 'em;
45 Both cover their faces with mobs and all that,
But the judge bids them angrily take off their hat.
When uncovered, a buzz of enquiry runs round:
'Pray what are their crimes?'–'They've been pilfering
    found.'
'But, pray, whom have they pilfered?'–'A Doctor,
    I hear.'
50 'What, yon solemn-faced, odd-looking man that stands
    near?'
'The same.'–'What a pity! how does it surprise one!
Two handsomer culprits I never set eyes on!'
Then their friends all come round me with cringing
    and leering,
To melt me to pity and soften my swearing.

36. Fielding] Sir John Fielding (d. 1780), the famous Bow Street magistrate and blind half-brother of Henry Fielding the novelist, whom he succeeded as Justice of the Peace for Westminster on Henry's death in 1754.

40. Dobson points out that the Act in question is really 8 Eliz. cap. iv, under which 'Cutpurses or Pyckpurses' who stole more than 12d. 'privately from a man's person' were condemned to 'suffer Death in suche a maner and fourme as they should if they were no Clarkes' i.e. debarred from benefit of clergy. Balderston relates G.'s 'familiarity' with the law as instanced here to the tradition that he applied for the Gresham lectureship in Civil Law in 1767: see Wardle, p. 180.

44. During the session at the Old Bailey in May 1750 the Court became infected with gaol-fever, which killed 'Judges, Counsel, and others to the number of forty without making allowance for those of a lower rank whose death may not have been heard of', *Johnson's England*, ed. A. S. Turbeville (1933) ii 279. The *Gentleman's Mag.* xx (1750) 235, describes the precautions taken against a repetition of the infection and lists the prominent men who had died through it. One precaution was that such herbs as G. mentions here were placed in the prisoner's dock.

45. mobs] Mob-caps, the ordinary indoor headdress for women in the eighteenth century, which concealed the hair.

50. What, yon solemn-faced, odd] Yon handsome fac'd well *deleted in MS.*

55   First Sir Charles advances with phrases well strung:
     'Consider, dear Doctor, the girls are but young.'
     'The younger the worse,' I return him again;
     'It shows that their habits are all dyed in grain.'
     'But then they're so handsome, one's bosom it grieves.'
60   'What signifies handsome, when people are thieves?'
     'But where is your justice? Their cases are hard.'
     'What signifies justice? I want the reward.
     There's the parish of Edmonton offers forty pound;
     there's the parish of St Leonard, Shoreditch, offers forty
65   pound; there's the parish of Tyburn, from the Hog-
     in-the-Pound to St Giles's watch-house, offers forty
     pounds, I shall have all that if I convict them.'

     'But consider their case: it may yet be your own!
     And see how they kneel: is your heart made of stone?'
70   This moves, so at last I agree to relent,
     For ten pounds in hand and ten pounds to be spent.
     The judge takes the hint, having seen what we drive at,
     And lets them both off with correction in private.

I challenge you all to answer this: I tell you, you cannot. It
cuts deep. But now for the rest of the letter: and next—but I
want room—so I believe I shall battle the rest out at Barton
some day next week. I don't value you all.

55. *Sir Charles*] Sir Thomas Charles Bunbury (d. 1821), M.P., Henry Bun-
bury's elder brother, who had succeeded to the baronetcy in 1764. Barton
passed to Catherine's son Henry on his death. G. seems to require two
syllables in 'Charles'.
71. *in hand*] In ready money.
72–3. Sir Henry Bunbury must have seen some dire innuendo ('correction'
meaning 'flogging'?) in this couplet which was omitted in the texts published
by Prior and himself. A writer in *The Academy* xxvi (22 Nov. 1884) 342,
announced that they existed in a copy of the lines made *c.* 1819 for James
Northcote, in the Plymouth Public Library. (This text has 'dismisses them
both' for 'lets them both off'.) Gibbs, *ibid* xxvi (6 Dec. 1884) 377, rejected
the couplet (cp. *Works*, 1885, v 410–11), but it appears in the original MS,
printed by Miss Balderston in 1928. She notes that the couplet is carefully
deleted in another contemporary copy in the Langton papers formerly in
the Elkins Collection, now in the Free Library of Philadelphia.
67. *After* judge *a word is deleted, possibly* too, *as suggested by Friedman.*

34 Retaliation

Begun not earlier than mid-Jan. 1774 and unfinished at G.'s death on 4 April 1774. The various accounts of the circumstances in which this poem was written agree that it was instigated by events at a meeting of an informal club of G.'s friends at the St James's Coffee-House. Most of its members are commemorated in the poem itself: several were also members of Johnson's Literary Club, with which it should not, however, be confused. The most reliable account of the origins of *Retaliation* was first printed by Cunningham in 1854, *Works* i 78, from a MS signed by Garrick and found among his papers, and lent to Cunningham by the book-collector George Daniel. It seems to have been intended as a preface to a collection of the various poems which provoked and were provoked by G.'s *Retaliation*:

'As the cause of writing the following printed poem called *Retaliation* has not yet been fully explained, a person concerned in the business begs leave to give the following just and minute account of the whole affair.

'At a meeting of a company of gentlemen, who were well known to each other, and diverting themselves, among many other things, with the peculiar oddities of Dr. Goldsmith, who never would allow a superior in any art, from writing poetry down to dancing a hornpipe, the Dr. with great eagerness insisted upon trying his epigrammatic powers with Mr. Garrick, and each of them was to write the other's epitaph. Mr. Garrick immediately said that his epitaph was finished, and spoke the following distich extempore:—

> Here lies NOLLY Goldsmith, for shortness call'd Noll,
> Who wrote like an angel, but talk'd like poor Poll.

Goldsmith, upon the company's laughing very heartily, grew very thoughtful, and either would not, or could not, write anything at that time: however, he went to work, and some weeks after produced the following printed poem called *Retaliation*, which has been much admired, and gone through several editions. The publick in general have been mistaken in imagining that this poem was written in anger by the Doctor; it was just the contrary; the whole on all sides was done with the greatest good humour; and the following poems in manuscript were written by several of the gentlemen on purpose to provoke the Doctor to an answer, which came forth at last with great credit to him in *Retaliation*.'

Garrick gives a similar account in a MS note accompanying his couplet on G. now in the Berg Collection of the New York Public Library: 'The following distich was written by Mr G[arrick] upon a Challenge of Dr Goldsmith which could write the other's Epitaph the soonest.' After quoting his couplet, Garrick adds: 'N. B. Goldsmith could not or would not write upon G[arrick] Extempore, but produc'd some time after his Epitaphs now printed call'd Retaliation.'

Garrick's accounts are probably as accurate as any. If he makes it appear that the affair began as an essentially private contest between himself and G. his story does not rule out the possibility that the club as a whole was engaged in writing epitaphs on G. or even on each other, as is suggested in other accounts. Cp. the anonymous letter to Kearsley, the publisher, which was printed with the 1st edn of the poem in April 1774: 'Dr. Goldsmith belonged to a club of *beaux esprits*, where wit sparkled sometimes at the expense of good-nature. It was proposed to write epitaphs on the Doctor; his country, dialect and person furnished subjects of witticism. The Doctor was called on for *retaliation*, and at their next meeting produced the following poem, which I think adds one leaf to his immortal wreath.' Garrick's statement that it took G. 'some weeks' to produce the poem is more convincing than the anonymous assertion that he produced it 'at their next meeting'. According to Richard Cumberland (the subject of one of G.'s 'epitaphs'), *Memoirs* (1806) p. 271, the members of the club were all supposed to write epitaphs on each other, but his account of the evening contains many dubious details and has usually been distrusted. Two other accounts of the original meeting may be mentioned, but they add little. Joseph Cradock, *Literary and Miscellaneous Memoirs* (1828) i 228–30, remembered being taken to the club by Thomas Percy on the day in question but, after an account of the earlier conversation, added only that 'We sat very late; and the conversation that at last ensued, was the direct cause of my friend Goldsmith's poem, called "Retaliation".' There may be no first-hand knowledge behind William Cooke's story, *European Mag.* xxiv (1793) 259, that Garrick wrote his epitaph on G. 'after the Doctor had finished one of his rhodomontade stories' and that G. 'was stung to the heart at the laugh which this little *jeu d'esprit* occasioned'.

On the whole it seems likely that, although it was Garrick's couplet that in effect provoked G. to an answer, other members of the club wrote epitaphs on him. Only Garrick's has survived in full (for a facsimile of the couplet in his hand see Temple Scott, p. 322); but Cumberland (*Memoirs* p. 272) quotes a line of his own, and ll. 1–4 of Caleb Whitefoord's epitaph on G. are quoted in *The Whitefoord Papers*, ed. W. A. S. Hewins (Oxford, 1898) p. xxvii *n*, where it is stated that 'the remaining eight lines are unfit for publication'. Whitefoord's verse apology to Reynolds for this epitaph on G. and another on Cumberland is printed in *The New Foundling Hospital for Wit* (1784) ii 281–2. Distinct from these original epitaphs are two other categories of verses connected with *Retaliation*. Garrick's account mentions those written by members of the club 'to provoke the Doctor to an answer'. An example may be the verses addressed to G. by Dr Barnard, Dean of Derry, printed in *The New Foundling Hospital* (1784) ii 277. Stanzas ii and iii are:

> Draw not thy angel's quill for shame,
>   On one who cries peccavi!
> But rather seek for nobler game,
>   Go set thy wit at DAVY!

On him let all thy vengeance fall,
On me you but misplace it;
Remember how he call'd thee POLL,
But ah! he dares not face it.

A note explains that Garrick 'was absent when these were first read' at the club. G. may have already produced the lines in *Retaliation* on Barnard but not yet those on Garrick.

A separate category is that of poems written in answer to *Retaliation*. Cumberland's reply was printed in the *Gentleman's Mag.* xlviii (1778) 384; the MS of Barnard's reply, addressed to both G. and Cumberland, is in the Berg Collection; and Garrick wrote three further poems on G., two of which were printed in Davies's *Life of Garrick* (1780) ii 157, 160 and the third in the *Public Ledger* (see Forster, *Life* ii 410–11 *n*). Needless to say, in the various accounts mentioned above the three categories of verses connected with *Retaliation*, as well as the meetings at which they were read, have been confused, in some cases irretrievably. A final category should perhaps be added. Less than a week after the publication of *Retaliation*, 'L.O.' sent a verse character of Johnson to the *Public Advertiser*, 25 April 1774, on the grounds that 'It seems unaccountable that [G.] should have left out so conspicuous a Member of the Society, unless he thought it too hazardous'. An attempt to supply the character G. would have written of himself appeared in the *London Chronicle*, 7–9 July 1774.

Although it seems likely that G. began the poem in Jan. 1774, the events mentioned in l. 86 cannot be taken to date the earlier part of the poem with any precision. G. probably wrote it slowly and released portions of it as he wrote them. Some of the poem was no doubt written during March 1774, when G. spent much of his time in the country. Soon after his return to London at the end of the month, he became seriously ill and died on 4 April. As the poem breaks off in the middle of the epitaph on Reynolds, it is obviously unfinished. According to *An Impartial Character of the Late Dr. Goldsmith*, as quoted in the *London Chronicle*, 7–9 July 1774, G. intended to conclude the poem with a character of himself: 'for which, he had declared to some of his friends, he was determined to sit (as far as self could possibly be divested) to the most general opinion conceived of him by his acquaintance'. This assertion was later repeated by Malone, *Works of Reynolds* (1797) I liii *n*. It may be noted also that G. wrote no epitaph of Ridge, who is mentioned in the opening lines. The evidence suggests that parts of the poem had already been circulated and even read to the other members of the club. Cp. William Cooke, *European Mag.* xxiv (1793) 174:

'When he had gone on as far as the character of Sir Joshua Reynolds in the poem, which was the *last Character*, I believe *of the Doctor's writing* [a reference to the epitaph on Whitefoord added to the 4th edn], he shewed it to Mr. Burke, of whose talents and friendship he always spoke in the highest degree, but required at the same time a solemn promise of secrecy. "Before I promise this," says Mr. Burke, "be explicit with me; have you shewn it to anybody else?" Here the Doctor paused for some time, but at length confessed he had given a copy of it to Mrs. Cholmondeley. "O then," replied Mr. Burke, "to avoid any possible imputation of betraying secrets I'll promise nothing, but leave it to yourself to confide in me."–Mr. Burke's suspicion was soon verified; the Doctor, it appeared, had given copies to others, who had given copies to others again, so that he was under a necessity of reading it himself a little after in full Club, where, though *some* praised it, and others *seemed* highly delighted with it, they still thought a publication of it not altogether so proper.'

For Hugh Boyd's story of his efforts to get G. to moderate his epitaphs on Burke himself and his kinsmen, see l. 29 *n.*

That G. did read at least part of *Retaliation* at the club seems to be clear from an undated letter from Cumberland to Garrick, quoted by Forster (*Life* ii 408), which describes a meeting at which Garrick was not present. The letter shows that other members of the club were still cheerfully producing 'epitaphs' and 'extempores' on each other. Of *Retaliation* Cumberland wrote: 'Doctor Goldsmith's Dinner [ll. 1–18] was very ingenious, but evidently written with haste and negligence. The Dishes were nothing to the purpose, but they were followed by epitaphs that had humour, some satire, and more panegyric.' Cumberland also refers to the extempore addressed to himself and G. by Barnard (quoted by Forster in a note; for the MS see above), which makes clear what might not otherwise not be apparent, that G. was still alive. The shrewdness and occasional astringency of G.'s portraits of his friends obviously surprised those who were in the habit of affectionately mocking his awkwardness, vanity and social ineptness. Reynolds, *Portraits*, ed. F. W. Hilles, p. 52, recorded that 'Even his friends did not think him capable of marking with so much sagacity and precision the predominant and striking features of their characters as he did in the epitaphs'. Cooke added to the account quoted above that G. was treated with more 'civility and seeming affection' after this revelation of his powers: 'Our Poet was not unobserving of all this, and though he meant not immediately at least to publish *Retaliation*, he kept it, as he expressed himself so to a friend, "as a rod in pickle upon any future occasion".' As G. can have had only a few more weeks to live at this stage, it must seem unlikely that the poem had time to alter drastically his relationships with his friends, even if he was treated with new respect.

Retaliation was published, little more than two weeks after G.'s death, on 19 April 1774 by G. Kearsley, in a quarto priced 1s 6d. The full title was *Retaliation: A Poem. By Doctor Goldsmith. Including Epitaphs on the Most Distinguished Wits of this Metropolis*. It was prefaced by a letter to Kearsley from the unidentified person responsible for its publication. According to Cumberland, the decision to publish the poem was taken after G.'s death at a meeting of the club at the St James's Coffee-House but there is no other evidence to support this and the poem could clearly have been sent to press by anyone who had received one of the several copies in circulation. That it was being circulated is confirmed by the statements of Cooke quoted above and by the first sentence of the letter to Kearsley: 'I am unable to account for the mystery with which the poem I send you has been handed about.'

Four edns of the poem were published in two months and a seventh had appeared before the end of 1774. An engraved vignette of G. by Basire after Reynolds appears on the title-page of the 1st edn, the second state of which is dated 18 April 1774. An item (not an advertisement) in the *Public Advertiser* (19 April 1774) states that 'Those who have purchased Dr. Goldsmith's last Poem of Retaliation, &c. may be furnished with explanatory Notes and Observations, gratis, by the Publisher, at No. 46, Fleet-street'. These notes were printed on an additional half-sheet, which is found with many copies of the 1st edn and which also included a 5-line list of errata, some of which are corrected in later issues. A 'New' or 2nd edn was announced on 21 April 1774 in the *Public Advertiser*: a copy of this edn in the Bodleian lacks the engraving on the title-page and is followed by the original half-sheet of notes with the 5-line list of errata, all but one of which are corrected in the text. But in its more normal state this edn has the half-sheet of notes incorporated into the book and replaces the original errata-ist with the following note from the publisher: 'Some gentlemen of the Doctor's acquaintance having made a few alterations, under the title of *Corrections*, and printed them in a News-paper, they are here subjoined for the inspection of our Readers. [For these 'Corrections', see notes to ll. 34, 87, 100 and 115.] G. Kearsley, the Publisher, thinks it his duty to declare, that Doctor Goldsmith wrote the Poem as it is here printed, a few errors of the press excepted, which are taken notice of at the bottom of this page.' A new 7-line list of errata follows.

In the 3rd edn the title was slightly changed to read *Some of the Most Distinguished* etc. and the notes, some of which had been altered, were distributed as footnotes to the poem. The notes are here given as they appear in this edn, except for additional information given in the notes to the 1st edn and subsequently omitted, here included in square brackets. Some copies of the 4th edn show no further change; but in others a 'Postscript' is added, introducing what purports to be an additional epitaph by G. on Caleb Whitefoord. Its authenticity was soon questioned and the fact that Whitefoord is not mentioned in the opening lines of the poem, the length and unusually friendly tone of the 'epitaph', with the fact that Whitefoord never produced the MS he claimed to possess, have led to the conclusion that he wrote it himself. More additional verses to *Retaliation*, which seem also to be the work of Whitefoord, have recently come to light: see *Correspondence of Burke*, ed. L. S. Sutherland (1960) ii 535–7; see also D. Wecter, *Times Lit. Supp.* 12 Feb. 1938, p. 108.

The text followed here is that of the 3rd edn, which incorporates the corrections made in the *errata* of the 1st and 2nd edns.

TO

MR KEARSLEY,

BOOKSELLER, IN FLEET STREET.

Sir,

5   I am unable to account for the mystery with which the poem I send you has been handed about. – In some part of Doctor Goldsmith's works he confesses himself so unable to resist the hungry attacks of wretched compilers that he contents himself with the demand of the fat man

10   who, when at sea and the crew in great want of provisions, was pitched on by the sailors as the properest subject to supply their wants: he found the necessity of acquiescence, at the same time making the most reasonable demand of the first cut off himself for himself. When the

15   Doctor in his lifetime was forced by these Anthropophagi to such capitulations, what respect can we now expect from them? Will they not dine on his memory? To rescue him from this insult, I send you an authentic copy of the last poetic production of this great and good

20   man, of which I recommend an early publication, to prevent spurious editions being ushered into the world. – Dr. Goldsmith belonged to a club of *beaux esprits*, where wit sparkled sometimes at the expense of good-nature. It was proposed to write epitaphs on the Doctor; his

25   country, dialect and person furnished subjects of witticism. The Doctor was called on for *retaliation*, and at their next meeting produced the following poem, which I think adds one leaf to his immortal wreath.

Of old, when Scarron his companions invited,
Each guest brought his dish and the feast was united.
If our landlord supplies us with beef and with fish,
Let each guest bring himself and he brings the best
    dish:

¶ 34. *Letter 6–14.* See the Preface to *Essays* (1765).
1–2. Scarron] Paul Scarron (1610–60), the French poet and comic writer, intimate with the most brilliant society of his time. G. was translating his *Roman Comique* at this time. G.'s source for these two lines may be Charlotte Lennox's *Memoirs for the History of Madame de Maintenon and of the*

5 Our Dean shall be venison, just fresh from the plains;
   Our Burke shall be tongue, with a garnish of brains;
   Our Will shall be wild-fowl, of excellent flavour,
   And Dick with his pepper shall heighten their savour;
   Our Cumberland's sweet-bread its place shall obtain,
10 And Douglas is pudding, substantial and plain;
   Our Garrick's a salad, for in him we see

Last Age (1757, i 136–7, which describes Scarron's supper parties, 'where
pleasure and vivacity reigned uncontrolled. . . . Every one either ordered or
sent his particular dish.'
3. 'The Master of the St. James's Coffee-house, where the Doctor, and the
Friends he has characterized in this Poem, held an occasional Club' (*ed 3*).
This coffee-house, near the corner of St James's St and St James's Palace, was
established in 1705 and often mentioned in the *Tatler* and *Spectator*. From
1767 to 1776 the lease was held by Thomas Stapylton: see B. Lillywhite,
London Coffee Houses (1963) pp. 500–4.
5–16. G. tries to characterize his friends by both the nature and the name of
the dishes to which he compares them.
5. *Dean*] 'Doctor Barnard, Dean of Derry in Ireland, author of many
ingenious pieces [, particularly a reply to Macpherson's Antiquities of Great
Britain and Ireland]' (*ed 3, ed 1*.) See l. 23 *n*.
6. *Burke*] 'Mr. Edmund Burke, member for Wendover, and one of the
greatest orators in this kingdom' (*ed 3*). See l. 29 *n*.
7. *Will*] 'Mr. William Burke, late secretary to General Conway, and member
for Bedwin [, Wiltshire]' (*ed 3, ed 1*). See l. 43 *n*.
8. *Dick*] 'Mr. Richard Burke, collector of Granada, no less remarkable in
the walks of wit and humour than his brother Edmund Burke is justly
distinguished in all the branches of useful and polite literature' (*ed 3*). See
l. 51 *n*.
9. *Cumberland*] '[Doctor Richard Cumberland,] Author of the West Indian,
Fashionable Lover, the Brothers, and other dramatic pieces' (*ed 1, ed 3*). See
l. 61 *n*.
10. *Douglas is*] Douglass's *ed 1* (*corrected in errata to ed 2.*)   *Douglas*] 'Doctor
Douglas, Canon of Windsor, an ingenious Scotch gentleman, who has no
less distinguished himself as a *Citizen of the World*, than a *sound Critic* in
detecting several literary mistakes (or rather *forgeries*) of his countrymen;
particularly Lauder on Milton, and *Bower's History of the Popes*' (*ed 3*). See
l. 79 *n*.
11. *Garrick*] 'David Garrick, Esq; joint Patentee and acting Manager of the
Theatre-Royal, Drury-lane. For the *other parts* of his character, *vide* the
Poem' (*ed 3*). See l. 93 *n*.

Oil, vinegar, sugar and saltness agree;
To make out the dinner, full certain I am
That Ridge is anchovy and Reynolds is lamb;
15   That Hickey's a capon and, by the same rule,
Magnanimous Goldsmith a gooseberry fool.
At a dinner so various, at such a repast,
Who'd not be a glutton and stick to the last?
Here, waiter! more wine, let me sit while I'm able,
20   Till all my companions sink under the table;
Then, with chaos and blunders encircling my head,
Let me ponder and tell what I think of the dead.

Here lies the good Dean, reunited to earth,
Who mixed reason with pleasure and wisdom with
          mirth.
25   If he had any faults, he has left us in doubt:
At least, in six weeks I could not find 'em out;
Yet some have declared, and it can't be denied 'em,
That sly-boots was cursedly cunning to hide 'em.

Here lies our good Edmund, whose genius was such,

14. Ridge] 'Counsellor John Ridge, a gentleman belonging to the Irish bar, the *relish* of whose agreeable and pointed conversation is admitted, by all his acquaintance, to be very properly compared to the above sauce' (*ed 3*). Ridge (*c.* 1728–76) was Edmund Burke's lawyer, and one of his most trusted friends, in Ireland; entered Trin. Coll. Dublin 1743, Middle Temple 1753, called to the Irish Bar 1762. Burke described him in a letter of 19 Feb. 1772 (*Correspondence* ii 301), as 'an old, loved, and honour friend of mine—one capable of filling the highest stations with reputation, and of giving Credit to any station by his excellent parts and uncommon integrity'.
Reynolds] 'Sir Joshua Reynolds, President of the Royal Academy' (*ed 3*). See l. 137 *n*.
15. Hickey] 'An eminent Attorney, whose hospitality and good-humour have acquired him, in this Club, the title of "honest Tom Hickey"' (*ed 3*). See l. 125 *n*.
23. Dean] Thomas Barnard (1728–1806), Dean of Derry 1769, who later held various bishoprics in Ireland and became a member of Johnson's Literary Club in Dec. 1775.
29. Edmund] Edmund Burke (1729–97), M.P. for Wendover, the greatest parliamentary orator of his time.
29–60. L. D. Campbell, in his 'Life' of Boyd prefixed to the *Misc. Works of Hugh Boyd* (1800) i 187–8, states that Boyd visited G. while he was working on *Retaliation* and heard him read the poem; but 'fearful lest the severity with which he had drawn the characters of the Burkes, would not only put an end to the friendship which subsisted between them and Goldsmith, but likewise disturb the harmony which prevailed in the Club, induced

30   We scarcely can praise it or blame it too much;
        Who, born for the universe, narrowed his mind,
        And to party gave up what was meant for mankind;
        Though fraught with all learning, yet straining his
           throat
        To persuade Tommy Townshend to lend him a vote;
35   Who, too deep for his hearers, still went on refining,
        And thought of convincing, while they thought of
           dining;

him to soften several expressions, and intirely to cast anew the character of William Burke'. The Burkes are said to have been partly responsible for the mismanagement of the estate of G.'s friends the Hornecks; see Sir Henry Bunbury, *Corresp. of Sir Thomas Hanmer* (1838) p. 400; and D. Wecter, *Times Lit. Supp.*, 12 Feb. 1938, suggests that this may explain G.'s resentment against them.

31–2. The justice of this couplet has often been debated. G. no doubt had in mind Burke's early literary achievements, especially his *Enquiry into the Sublime and Beautiful*. Boswell (*Life of Johnson* i 472) also quotes this couplet in connection with Burke's supposed intention of writing a refutation of Bishop Berkeley, abandoned because of his political career. He entered Parliament in Dec. 1765 and spent much of his career in opposition. The famous speech on American taxation which he was to make a few weeks after G. wrote these lines, in April 1774, was certainly not dictated by considerations of 'party'.

33. yet] kept *ed 1 (corrected in errata to ed 2).*

34. Townshend] 'Mr. T. Townsend [Junior], Member for Whitchurch [, Hampshire]' (*ed 3, ed 1*). Thomas Townshend (1733–1800) was M.P. for Whitchurch 1754–83; Joint-Paymaster 1767–8; Baron Sydney 1783, Visct. Sydney 1789. Boswell, *Life of Johnson* iv 318, suggests that an attack by Townshend on the pension granted to Johnson, to which Burke retaliated, explained Townshend's appearance here. Townshend attacked Johnson twice in the House of Commons, on 14 March 1770 and on 16 Feb. 1774, but in neither case did Burke reply. But the second attack, made while G. was writing *Retaliation*, may explain the reference. Boswell also states that 'in the original copy of Goldsmith's character of Mr. Burke, in his 'Retaliation', another person's name stood in the couplet where Mr. Townshend is now introduced'. The publisher's note at the end of the 'New' or 2nd edn mentions that various changes in the text have been printed by G.'s 'friends' in a newspaper as truer to his intentions: they include 'for *Tommy Townsend*, they have inserted *Dicky Whitworth*'. Richard Whitworth (1734–1811) was M.P. for Stafford.

36. Burke was an orator rather than a debater: he spoke with unrivalled eloquence and amplitude in the House of Commons, sometimes for as long as three or four hours, but his speeches when published usually had greater impact than when spoken. His enemies often ostentatiously went to dinner

Though equal to all things, for all things unfit;
Too nice for a statesman, too proud for a wit;
For a patriot, too cool; for a drudge, disobedient;
40 And too fond of the *right* to pursue the *expedient*.
In short, 'twas his fate, unemployed or in place, sir,
To eat mutton cold and cut blocks with a razor.

Here lies honest William, whose heart was a mint,
While the owner ne'er knew half the good that was
in't;
45 The pupil of impulse, it forced him along,
His conduct still right, with his argument wrong;
Still aiming at honour, yet fearing to roam;
The coachman was tipsy, the chariot drove home.
Would you ask for his merits? alas! he had none:
50 What was good was spontaneous, his faults were his
own.

Here lies honest Richard, whose fate I must sigh at;

when he began to speak and some members of his own party thought that
he spoke at too great a length. According to Johnson, 'It was commonly
observed, he spoke too often in parliament', Boswell, *Life* ii 131.
37. *unfit*] he's fit *ed 1, first state (corrected in errata to ed 1)*.
41. *place*] play *ed 1 (corrected in errata to ed 1)*.
42. *cut blocks with a razor*] 'A metaphor describing absurdly incongruous and
futile application of abilities or means' (*OED*).
43. William Burke (1730–98), a kinsman of Edmund Burke, although
Edmund himself was unsure of the precise relationship. He was an under-
secretary for state 1755–58, M.P. for Great Bedwin 1766–74 and held a
variety of political posts. He wrote a number of political pamphlets and spent
most of his later years in India. G.'s remarks on him are strikingly confirmed
by a sketch of his character by Edmund Burke, in a notebook quoted by
Dixon Wecter, *Edmund Burke and his Kinsmen* (Boulder, Colorado, 1939)
p. 10, which describes him as having 'a mind endued with the most quick
poinant and delicate feelings that I ever knew. Love, Grief, Joy, hatred,
are with him sudden & violent; they come on like fits, nothing can oppose
them whilst they last'. His 'understanding . . . is strong & Quick but it is
not steady, he looks at many things like a man who stands in a boat he sees
them in their proper colours, he sees them plainly, but he does not always
keep them long enough in his Eye in the same posture to make the most
usefull Judgement on them.'
51. Richard Burke (1703–94), Edmund's younger brother, had become
Collector of Customs in Grenada in May 1763. He was well known for his
wild manner. Fanny Burney, *Diary and Letters* (1904–5) v 90, described him
as 'the comic, humorous, bold, queer brother of *the* Mr. Burke'. Boswell

Alas, that such frolic should now be so quiet!
What spirits were his, what wit and what whim!
Now breaking a jest and now breaking a limb;
55   Now wrangling and grumbling to keep up the ball,
Now teasing and vexing, yet laughing at all!
In short, so provoking a devil was Dick,
That we wished him full ten times a day at Old Nick;
But, missing his mirth and agreeable vein,
60   As often we wished to have Dick back again.

Here Cumberland lies, having acted his parts,
The Terence of England, the mender of hearts;

found him 'vulgar and fierce' in 1781 and 'rough and wild in his manner'
in 1788.

54. 'This gentleman having slightly fractured one of his arms and legs, at
different times, the Doctor has rallied him on those accidents, as a kind of
retributive justice for breaking his jests upon other people' (*ed 3*). Richard
Burke broke his arm in the summer of 1762 and his leg, by a fall in the street,
in about Feb. 1767: see *Correspondence of E. Burke*, ed. T. W. Copeland
(1958) i 145, 307–8.

55. keep up the ball] Keep the conversation from flagging.

61. Richard Cumberland (1732–1811), author of such plays as *The Brothers*
(1769), *The West Indian* (1771) and *The Fashionable Lover* (1772). See headnote
for his account of the origin of *Retaliation*. He is believed to have been sat-
irised in Sheridan's *The Critic* (produced 1779) as Sir Fretful Plagiary. G.'s
portrait of him may be affectionate but he also greatly disliked the senti-
mental comedy he describes here, of which Cumberland was a notable
exponent. That sharp criticism underlies the polite tone is clear from a
comparison with G.'s views as expressed in *Second Rejected Epilogue for
She Stoops to Conquer* 31 *n* (p. 728).

62. G.'s comparison of Cumberland to Terence is not casual. The common-
place contrast between Terence and Plautus corresponds to the difference
G. was anxious to point between 'sentimental' comedy and his own 'laugh-
ing' comedy. Terence's comedy is more serious, less exaggerated, less
robust. Cp. Thomas Cooke's preface to his translation of *Terence's Comedies*
(2nd edn, 1755) pp. 38–9: ' *Terence's* Superiority to *Plautus*' is 'in the genteel
and delicate'. His comedy is 'not without Wit and Humour, cloathed with
Purity and Delicacy. *Plautus* is often mean and immodest, *Terence* never:
and Meanness and Immodesty are generally the Fruits of low and vulgar
Souls'. The comparison no doubt pleased Cumberland but made G.'s
point about his limitations clear. For G.'s views on sentimental comedy, see
his 'Essay on the Theatre', in the *Westminster Mag.* for 1773 (*Works* ed.
Friedman, iii 209–13), where he also mentions Terence's approach to the
tragic: 'he is even reproached by Caesar for wanting the *vis comica*.' See also
R. Quintana, 'Oliver Goldsmith as a Critic of the Drama', *Studies in
English Literature 1500–1900*, v (1965) 435–54.

       A flattering painter, who made it his care
       To draw men as they ought to be, not as they are.
65   His gallants are all faultless, his women divine,
       And comedy wonders at being so fine;
       Like a tragedy queen he has dizened her out,
       Or rather like tragedy giving a rout.
       His fools have their follies so lost in a crowd
70   Of virtues and feelings, that folly grows proud;
       And coxcombs, alike in their failings alone,
       Adopting his portraits, are pleased with their own.
       Say, where has our poet this malady caught,
       Or wherefore his characters thus without fault?
75   Say, was it that vainly directing his view
       To find out men's virtues, and finding them few,
       Quite sick of pursuing each troublesome elf,
       He grew lazy at last and drew from himself?

       Here Douglas retires, from his toils to relax,
80   The scourge of impostors, the terror of quacks.
       Come, all ye quack bards and ye quacking divines,
       Come and dance on the spot where your tyrant
              reclines.
       When satire and censure encircled his throne,
       I feared for your safety, I feared for my own;
85   But now he is gone and we want a detector,
       Our Dodds shall be pious, our Kenricks shall lecture;

67. *dizened*] Bedizen: 'To dress; to deck; to rig out. A low word' (Johnson).
Cp. Swift, *The Grand Question Debated* 102: 'For sure, I had *dizen'd* you out
like a *Queen*'.
68. *rout*] A fashionable assembly, the large evening party or reception which
came into vogue in the mid-eighteenth century.
69. *lost*] left ed 1 (*corrected in errata to ed. 2*).
69–70. A comparable accusation, though on different grounds, had been
made against Restoration comedy. Cp. Dryden, *Epilogue to the Man of
Mode* 7–8, of Etherege: 'Sir *Fopling* is a Fool so nicely writ, / The Ladies
wou'd mistake him for a Wit'; and Pope, *Imitations of Horace, Ep.* I i 287:
'Tell me if Congreve's Fools are Fools indeed?'
73. *where*] when ed 1 (*corrected in errata to ed 1*).
79. Dr John Douglas (1721–1807), Canon of Windsor 1762, Bishop of
Carlisle 1787 and of Salisbury 1791, was a member of Johnson's Club. See
below for his detections of 'impostors'.
83. *When*] Where ed 1.
86. *Dodds*] 'The Rev. Dr. Dodd' (*ed 3*). William Dodd (1729–77) was a
popular preacher, a writer of edifying books and an editor of and writer for
the *Christian Mag.*, 1760–67. He became tutor to Philip Stanhope, godson

Macpherson write bombast and call it a style,
Our Townshend make speeches, and I shall compile;
New Lauders and Bowers the Tweed shall cross over,

and heir of Lord Chesterfield. Various scandals became attached to his
name *c.* 1770 and he was depicted in the *Town and Country Mag.* in May 1773
as the 'Macaroni' parson. Dodd was struck off the list of royal chaplains
when his wife was found to have anonymously approached the wife of
Lord Chancellor Apsley in an attempt to obtain for him the promise of the
living of St George's, Hanover Square. Dodd wrote to the papers a letter
dated 10 Feb. 1774 protesting his innocence and G. apparently refers to this,
although he would also have had in mind the scandalous 'Memoirs of the
Macaroni Preacher and Mrs. R——n', cited by Friedman, which appeared
in the *Town and Country Mag.* v (1773) 681–3 (actually published 24 Jan.
1774). He was executed in 1777, in spite of Johnson's efforts to save him, for
forging Chesterfield's signature on a bond; see Boswell, *Life of Johnson* iii
139–48.

Kenricks] 'Mr. Kenrick lately read lectures at the Devil Tavern, under
the Title of "The School of Shakespeare"' (*ed 3*). William Kenrick
1725?–79) was no friend of G. (see headnote to *Edwin and Angelina*, p. 596
above). He was a miscellaneous writer who once planned an edn of
Shakespeare but eventually only lectured on the plays. See *Gentleman's Mag.*
xliv (1774) 44, under 19 Jan. 1774: 'This evening a novel kind of entertain-
ment was exhibited by Dr. Kenrick in the Great Room at the Devil Tavern,
Temple bar: being an attempt to exhibit the beauties of Shakespear, both
by speaking, action, and explanation, in which he is said to have succeeded
to admiration.'

87. Macpherson] 'James Macpherson, Esq; who lately, from the mere *force
of his style*, wrote down the first poet of all antiquity' (*ed 3*). James Mac-
pherson (1736–96), the alleged translator of the Ossianic poems in the
previous decade, published a prose translation of the *Iliad* in March 1773,
which was generally ridiculed. In *ed 2* the publisher's note recording the
variants published in a newspaper by G.'s 'friends' includes the substitution
of 'Blockheads' for 'Macpherson' in this line.

88. Townshend] See 34 *n.* *compile*] Cp. the 'Advertisement' to *Threnodia
Augustalis* (p. 709).

89. William Lauder (d. 1771) published in 1749 his *Essay on Milton's Use and
Imitation of the Moderns* (partly published in the *Gentleman's Mag.* from Jan.
1747 on), with a preface by Johnson. Purporting to demonstrate Milton's
borrowings from modern Latin authors, Lauder had merely attributed to
them a later Latin translation of *Paradise Lost*. This was demonstrated by
Douglas in his *Milton Vindicated from the Charge of Plagiarism* (1750). Johnson
forced Lauder to confess his guilt in *A Letter to the Rev. Mr. Douglas* (1751).

Archibald Bower (1686–1766), another Scot, published a *History of the
Popes* in 7 vols, 1748–66. Formerly a Roman Catholic, Bower professed in
this work to have conformed to the Church of England but in four pamphlets

90   No countryman living their tricks to discover;
    Detection her taper shall quench to a spark
    And Scotchman meet Scotchman and cheat in the
        dark.

    Here lies David Garrick, describe me who can,
    An abridgment of all that was pleasant in man;
95   As an actor, confessed without rival to shine:
    As a wit, if not first, in the very first line;
    Yet, with talents like these and an excellent heart,
    The man had his failings, a dupe to his art.
    Like an ill-judging beauty, his colours he spread
100   And beplastered with rouge his own natural red.
    On the stage he was natural, simple, affecting:
    'Twas only that, when he was off, he was acting.
    With no reason on earth to go out of his way,
    He turned and he varied full ten times a day.
105   Though secure of our hearts, yet confoundedly sick,
    If they were not his own by finessing and trick,
    He cast off his friends, as a huntsman his pack,
    For he knew when he pleased he could whistle them
        back.
    Of praise a mere glutton, he swallowed what came,
110   And the puff of a dunce, he mistook it for fame;
    Till his relish grown callous, almost to disease,
    Who peppered the highest was surest to please.
    But let us be candid and speak out our mind:
    If dunces applauded, he paid them in kind.
115   Ye Kenricks, ye Kellys and Woodfalls so grave,

in 1756–58 Douglas revealed that Bower was still a Catholic and still in contact with the Jesuits. Some 22 pamphlets were provoked by the controversy. Garrick at one time thought of parodying Bower on the stage (see Davies, *Life of Garrick* i 270–4). Churchill had attacked Lauder (praising Douglas) in *The Ghost* (1762) ii 221–32, and Bower in *Independence* (1764) 135–8.

92. Dobson cites Dryden and Lee, *Oedipus* Act IV: 'But gods meet gods and jostle in the dark' (repeated by Farquhar in *Love and a Bottle* Act III).

93. David Garrick (1717–79), joint patentee and the manager of Drury Lane Theatre.

99. *ill-judging*] ill judge in *ed 1* (*corrected in ed. 2 errata*).

100. The publisher's note in *ed 2* states that for 'natural red', G.'s 'friends' have published in the press the alteration to 'better red'.

111. *relish*] Sense of taste.

115. For Kenrick see l. 86 *n*. Garrick instituted a suit for libel against Kenrick in July 1772 and in the following Nov. Kenrick made an abject apology

What a commerce was yours, while you got and you
        gave!
How did Grub-street re-echo the shouts that you
        raised,
While he was be-Rosciused and you were be-praised!
But peace to his spirit, wherever it flies,
120 To act as an angel and mix with the skies:
Those poets, who owe their best fame to his skill,

and suppressed the offending play, *Love in the Suds*. But there is a compli-
ment to Garrick in Kenrick's *Introduction to the School of Shakespeare* (1774)
pp. 13–14.

Kellys] 'Hugh Kelly, Esq; Author of False Delicacy, Word to the Wise,
Clementina, School for Wives, &c. &c.' (*ed 3*). Kelly (1739–77) was a
prominent exponent of the 'sentimental' comedy deplored by G. *False
Delicacy* (1768), produced by Garrick at Drury Lane shortly before *The
Good Natured Man* at Covent Garden, was a much greater success and
as a result G. broke off his friendship with Kelly. His envy had been stimu-
lated again by the success of Kelly's *School for Wives*, produced by Garrick
at Drury Lane in Dec. 1773. It was said to have 'almost killed him'. But
Garrick was at this time trying to help G.: see Wardle, pp. 267–9. For Kelly
at G.'s funeral, see Prior, *Life* ii 361.

Woodfalls] 'Mr. William Woodfall, Printer of the Morning Chronicle' (*ed
3*). William Woodfall (1746–1803), actor, journalist, parliamentary reporter
and dramatic critic, worked with various newspapers, including the *Public
Advertiser, London Packet* and *Morning Chronicle*. According to his obituary
notice in the *Gentleman's Mag.* lxxiii (1803) pt. ii 792, 'He was so passionately
fond of theatrical representations as never to have missed the first perfor-
mance of a new piece for the last 40 years; and the publick had so good an
opinion of his taste, that his criticisms were decisive of the fall or fortune
of the piece and the performer.' His relations with Garrick were not always
entirely amicable; see J. Boaden, *Private Corresp. of Garrick* (1831–2) i 583–5.
The publisher's note to *ed 2* states that G.'s 'friends' have substituted in the
press 'Glover' for 'Woodfall' in this line, adding of Glover that he was 'A
Surgeon of distinguished abilities, and an agreeable companion; very in-
timate with, and much esteemed by, the late Doctor Goldsmith.' The reading
G——r appears in an extract from *Retaliation* in the *Gentleman's Mag.* xliv
184, in April 1774. Glover wrote a short life of G. published soon after his
death.

118. be-Rosciused] berossia'd *ed 1* (*corrected to* berosciad *in errata to ed 1 and to
the present reading in errata to ed 2*). Roscius was the most famous comic
actor of his day in Rome. Churchill's satire on the acting profession was
The Rosciad (1761).

121–4. Garrick had been largely responsible for the revived theatrical
vogue for Shakespeare which began in the 1740s; and he had also produced
the plays of Ben Jonson and of Beaumont and Fletcher. Cp. *Vicar* ch. xviii:

Shall still be his flatterers, go where he will.
Old Shakespeare, receive him, with praise and with
    love,
And Beaumonts and Bens be his Kellys above.

125   Here Hickey reclines, a most blunt, pleasant
        creature,
    And slander itself must allow him good-nature:
    He cherished his friend and he relished a bumper;
    Yet one fault he had, and that one was a thumper.
    Perhaps you may ask if the man was a miser?
130   I answer, no, no, for he always was wiser.
    Too courteous, perhaps, or obligingly flat?
    His very worst foe can't accuse him of that.
    Perhaps he confided in men as they go,
    And so was too foolishly honest? Ah no!
135   Then what was his failing? come, tell it, and burn ye!
    He was—could he help it?—a special attorney.

'Dryden and Row's manner, Sir, are quite out of fashion; our taste has gone back a whole century, Fletcher, Ben Johnson, and all the plays of Shakespear, are the only things that go down.'

125. *Hickey*] Joseph Hickey (*c.* 1714–94): 'His profession, the Doctor tells us, is that of an attorney, but whether he meant the words an echo to the sense or not, he has told us so in, perhaps, the only indifferent couplet of the whole Poem. To soften this censure, however, in some respect, the English Reader is to be told, that the phrase of "burn ye," in [l. 135], tho' it may seem *forced* to rhyme to "attorney," is a familiar method of salutation in Ireland amongst the lower classes of the people' (*ed 1, omitted in ed 3*). According to the *Gentleman's Mag.* lxiv (1794) 769, 'He had passed an enviable life in the society of the first literary characters for nearly half a century; and, if not a wit himself, was lively, pleasant, and intelligent; so that, if he did not add to the splendor, he did not cloud the brilliant circle into which he was admitted.' Hickey, who was father of William Hickey, the diarist, was Edmund Burke's solicitor and friend and he also acted for Reynolds on occasion. Burke describes him as 'an eminent Sollicitor' in April 1773 (*Correspondence* ii 432).
128. *thumper*] Anything strikingly big.
129. *the*] that *ed. 1*.
131. *flat*] Insipid (of manners).
133. *men as they go*] Men as they ordinarily are.
135. *his*] omitted in ed 1 and added in errata.
136. *special attorney*] Attorneys were officers of the Common Law Courts, as opposed to the solicitors of the Court of Chancery. Johnson quotes Cowel: '*Attorney special* or *particular* is he that is employed in one or more causes particularly specified. There are also, in respect of the divers courts, *attorneys at large*, and *attorneys special*, belonging to this or that court only.'

Here Reynolds is laid and, to tell you my mind,
He has not left a better or wiser behind:
His pencil was striking, resistless and grand;
140 His manners were gentle, complying and bland;
Still born to improve us in every part,
His pencil our faces, his manners our heart;
To coxcombs averse, yet most civilly steering,
When they judged without skill he was still hard of
    hearing;
145 When they talked of their Raphaels, Correggios and
    stuff,
He shifted his trumpet and only took snuff.

In *The Bee* No. v, 3 Nov. 1759, G. refers to the 'pawnbroker, the attorney, and other pests of society'. He shared this prejudice against attorneys with Johnson; see Boswell, *Life* ii 126 and *n*, iv 313 and 538.
137. Sir Joshua Reynolds, shortly to be G.'s executor.
138. better or wiser] wiser or better *ed 3*.
140. bland] Malone, *Works of Reynolds* (1797) I liii, says this word was 'eminently happy, and characteristick of [Reynolds's] easy and placid manners'.
143. steering] staring *ed 1 (corrected in errata to ed 2)*.
144–6. 'Sir Joshua Reynolds is so remarkably deaf as to be under the necessity of using an ear trumpet in company; he is, at the same time, equally remarkable for taking a great quantity of snuff: his manner in both of which, taken in the point of time described, must be allowed, by those who have been witnesses of such a scene, to be as happily given upon *paper*, as that great Artist himself, perhaps, could have exhibited upon *canvas*' (*ed 3*). Reynold's deafness was attributed to a severe cold he caught while studying Raphael in the Vatican. He ear-trumpet appears in his self-portrait of 1775 and his snuff-box, according to Dobson, was exhibited with other relics at the Grosvenor Gallery in 1883–4.
145. Cp. Swift, *The Grand Question Debated* 159: 'Your *Noveds*, and *Blutraks*, and *Omurs* and Stuff' (i.e. Ovids, Plutarchs and Homers).
146. Malone, *Works of Reynolds* (1797) I liii *n*, states: 'These were the last lines the author wrote. He had written half a line more of this character, when he was seized with the nervous fever which carried him in a few days to the grave. He intended to have concluded with his own character.' (G. would also, no doubt, have written an epitaph on Ridge, mentioned in the opening lines; and as he deals with his friends in alphabetical order, Ridge would have occurred here.) According to Prior, *Life* ii 499, the incomplete half-line was 'By flattery unspoiled'.
    Nineteenth-century editors printed at this point the following 'Postscript' on Caleb Whitefoord (1734–1810), added to the second issue of the 4th edn of the poem. See headnote for doubts about the authenticity of these lines, which may, however, deserve to be preserved. Whitefoord was a wine-merchant, author of political squibs and humorous pieces, and later a

diplomatist. His celebrated 'Cross-readings' and other pieces, referred to in these lines, were often reprinted and had some famous admirers, including Goldsmith: see Boswell, *Life of Johnson* iv 322; Walpole, *Correspondence* x 237–8; Northcote, *Life of Reynolds* (1813) p. 128; J. T. Smith, *Nollekens and his Times* (1828) i 336–7; *New Foundling Hospital for Wit* (1768) pp. 127–9 and (1784) ii 224–42.

'After the Fourth Edition of this Poem was printed, the Publisher received an Epitaph on Mr. (*a*) Whitefoord, from a friend of the late Doctor Goldsmith inclosed in a letter, of which the following is an abstract.

'I have in my possession a sheet of paper, containing near forty lines in the Doctor's own handwriting: there are many scattered, broken verses, on Sir Jos. Reynolds, Counsellor Ridge, Mr. (*b*) Beauclerk, and Mr. Whitefoord. The Epitaph on the last-mentioned gentleman is the only one that is finished, and therefore I have copied it, that you may add it to the next edition. It is a striking proof of Doctor Goldsmith's good-nature. I saw this sheet of paper in the Doctor's room, five or six days before he died; and, as I had got all the other Epitaphs, I asked him if I might take it. "*In truth you may, my Boy,* (replied he) *for it will be of no use to me where I am going.*"'

Here Whitefoord reclines, and deny it who can,
Though he *merrily* liv'd, he is now a (*c*) *grave* man;
Rare compound of oddity, frolic and fun!
Who relish'd a joke, and rejoic'd in a pun;
Whose temper was generous, open, sincere;
A stranger to flatt'ry, a stranger to fear;
Who scatter'd around wit and humour at will,
Whose daily *bons mots* half a column might fill:
A Scotchman from pride and from prejudice free,
A scholar, yet surely no pedant was he.

What pity, alas! that so lib'ral a mind
Should so long be to news-paper-essays confin'd!
Who perhaps to the summit of science could soar,
Yet content "if the table he set on a roar;"
Whose talents to fill any station were fit,
Yet happy if (*d*) *Woodfall* confess'd him a wit.

Ye news-paper witlings! ye pert scribbling folks!
Who copied his squibs, and re-echoed his jokes,
Ye tame imitators, ye servile herd come,
Still follow your master, and visit his tomb:
To deck it, bring with you festoons of the vine,
And copious libations bestow on his shrine;
Then strew all around it (you can do no less)
(*e*) *Cross-readings*, *Ship-news*, and *Mistakes* of the *Press*.

> Merry Whitefoord, farewel! for *thy* sake I admit
> That a Scot may have humour, I had almost said wit:
> This debt to thy mem'ry I cannot refuse,
> 'Thou best humour'd man with the worst humour'd muse!'

(*a*) Mr. Caleb Whitefoord, Author of many humorous Essays.

(*b*) Topham Beauclerk, Esq; well known in the polite world as a scholar, a man of wit, and a fine gentleman.

(*c*) Mr. W. is so notorious a punster, that Doctor Goldsmith used to say, it was impossible to keep him company, without being *infected* with the *itch* of *punning*.

(*d*) Mr. H. S. Woodfall, Printer of the Public Advertiser.

(*e*) Mr. Whiteford [*sic*] has frequently indulged the town with humorous pieces under those titles in the Public Advertiser.

POEMS OF DOUBTFUL AUTHENTICITY

35 'Theseus did see, as poets say'

These lines occur in the narrative of G.'s life sent by his sister, Catherine Hodson, to Bishop Percy not later than 15 July 1776; understandably they were not used in G.'s *Works*, 1801. If, as Mrs Hodson believed, G. was aged seven at the time, the lines were written about 1737. They were first printed with Mrs Hodson's narrative in 1928 in *Letters* pp. 163–4, from the Percy papers (British Museum, Add. MS 42516 ff. 20–26). The eccentric spelling and punctuation of Mrs Hodson's account has been modernised:

'There was company at his father's at that time he was turned of seven. They were attended at tea by a little boy, who was desired to hand the kettle but, the handle being too hot, the boy took up the skirt of his coat to put between him and it. But unfortunately the ladies perceived something which made them laugh immoderately, whether from the awkwardness of the turn or anything that might be seen there I can't say. But the Doctor immediately perceived their cause of laughter and informed his father, who promised him a reward of gingerbread to write something on it; and as it was one of his earliest productions that can be recollected, though perhaps not fit for the public, I shall insert it here.'

> Theseus did see, as poets say,
> Dark Hell and its abysses,
> But had not half so sharp an eye
> As our young charming misses.
>
> 5   For they could through boys' breeches peep
> And view whate'er he had there.
> It seemed to blush and they all laughed
> Because the face was all bare.
>
> They laughed at that which sometimes else
> 10   Might give them greatest pleasure.
> How quickly they could see the thing
> Which was their darling treasure.

36 [A Couplet on Aesop]

Like the preceding poem, this couplet was preserved by Mrs Hodson and sent to Percy, through whom it was first printed in the *Works*, 1801, i 5; but Percy polished Mrs Hodson's narrative and altered the first line of the couplet to read 'Our herald hath proclaim'd this saying'. In this form the couplet was first collected with G.'s poems by Corney in 1845 but Mrs

Hodson's original account was not printed in full until 1928, *Letters* pp. 165–6. If G. was aged nine at the time, the couplet was composed in about 1739.

'One evening, for a large company of young people at his uncle's, a young gentleman played the fiddle, who thought himself a greater wit and humourist than anyone else did. The company insisted upon the D[octo]r dancing a hornpipe, which he refuse[d] a long time but, on the commands of his uncle, he exhibited. He was then nine years old and had lately had the small-pox, which left very deep red marks and he really cut an ugly figure. However, he was a very good subject for the wit of our fiddling gentleman, who cried out in rapture, 'There was Aesop! How like Aesop he was! The very man by G—!' The D[octor] still danced for more than an hour till he fatigued our wit sufficiently, who still kept on the comparison of Aesop with a very hearty laugh at so bright a thought, when the D[octor] stopped short and repeated these lines:

> The herald proclaimed out then, saying,
> 'See Aesop dancing and his monkey playing.'

'The laugh turned against our wit and the D[octor] was embraced by his uncle and got some sweetmeats, which was always his reward.'

37 The Clown's Reply

Dated 'Edinburgh, 1753', although no authority is given, in *1777* p. 79, where it was apparently first printed. It was also added during 1777 to a new issue of the 8th edn of *Retaliation* (i.e. the 8th edn of 1776 with a new title-page, contents leaf and 8 inserted pages), on inserted page 32*. Friedman, *Works* iv 410 *n*, suggests that this printing had priority over the Dublin edn, but the reverse seems more likely, in view of the clumsy manner of the insertion. If correctly attributed to G., it is the only poem to survive from his period at Edinburgh University, whose medical school he had entered in Oct. 1752. It may well reflect G.'s social uneasiness in the aristocratic circles to which he occasionally had access at this period. Cp. G.'s letter to his uncle Thomas Contarine, *c*. Dec. 1753 (*Letters* p. 17): 'I have spent more than a fortnight every second day at the Duke of Hamilton's, but it seems they like me more as a *jester* than as a companion; so I disdained so servile an employment; 't was unworthy my calling as a physician.' For later examples of G.'s scorn of flattery of the great, see *Citizen* (1762) i 106–7, 132–3 (Letters 27 and 32).

> John Trott was desired by two witty peers
> To tell them the reason why asses had ears.

¶ *37.1. John Trott*] Commonly used for 'a man of slow or uncultured intellect, a bumpkin, a clown' (*OED*). It is the name of Sir Fopling Flutter's

> 'An't please you,' quoth John, 'I'm not given to
>   letters,
> Nor dare I pretend to know more than my betters;
> 5 Howe'er from this time I shall ne'er see your graces,
> As I hope to be saved! without thinking on asses.'

one English servant in Etherege's *The Man of Mode*. Steele used it to sign
two letters in *Spectator* Nos. 296, 314; and it appears in the epilogue to
Samuel Foote's *Englishman in Paris* in the same year as G.'s poem.
6. Dobson cites Swift, *Polite Conversation* (*Prose Works*, ed. Herbert Davis,
iv (1957) 182): 'I believe, I shall never see a Goose again, without thinking
on Mr. *Neverout*.'

38 The Logicians Refuted

Announced as forthcoming in No ii, this poem was first printed in *The Busy
Body* No v, 18 Oct. 1759, where it was preceded by an attribution to Swift:
'The following Poem written by Dr. SWIFT, is communicated to the Public
by the BUSY BODY, to whom it was presented by a Nobleman of distinguished
Learning and Taste.' It was printed as Swift's in Faulkner's Dublin edn of
1762 and in later edns of Swift into the nineteenth century, including
Scott's edns of 1814 and 1824. But it had also been collected as G.'s in
1780 i 115–17, and appears in all later edns. Sir Harold Williams, *Poems
of Swift* (2nd edn, 1958) iii 1141, accepts the attribution to G., who is known
to have made other contributions to *The Busy Body*. The poem is a careful,
if rather wooden, vehicle of attitudes held by Swift, whom G. deliberately
imitated in 'A New Simile'; but, apart from the reference to Smiglesius,
there is no real internal evidence to confirm the attribution in *1780*. The
poem may not be by either Swift or Goldsmith.
    The text followed here is that of *The Busy Body*.

> Logicians have but ill defined
> As rational, the human kind;
> Reason, they say, belongs to man,
> But let them prove it if they can.

¶ 38.1. *ff* In the old-fashioned textbooks in logic still used in the eighteenth
century, a frequent definition is *Homo est animal rationale*. Swift had explored
and inverted this and similar maxims in *Gulliver's Travels*, particularly Bk iv.
See R. S. Crane, 'The Houyhnhnms, the Yahoos, and the History of Ideas',
in *Reason and Imagination*, ed J. A. Mazzeo (1962) pp. 245–6. For other pro-
tests by Swift against the definition see his letters to Pope of 29 Sept. and 26
Nov. 1725. There is some similarity in these opening lines to the end of
Swift's *The Beasts Confession to the Priest* 215–20, which also plays with a
Latin definition of man used in logic.

5   Wise Aristotle and Smiglesius,
By ratiocinations specious,
Have strove to prove with great precision,
With definition and division,
Homo est ratione praeditum;
10 But for my soul I cannot credit 'em.
And must in spite of them maintain
That man and all his ways are vain;
And that this boasted lord of nature
Is both a weak and erring creature;
15 That instinct is a surer guide
Than reason-boasting mortals' pride;
And that brute beasts are far before 'em,
Deus est anima brutorum.
Who ever knew an honest brute
20 At law his neighbour prosecute,
Bring action for assault and battery,
Or friend beguile with lies and flattery?
O'er plains they ramble unconfined,
No politics disturb their mind;
25 They eat their meals and take their sport,
Nor know who's in or out at court;

5. With his own experience no doubt in mind, G. wrote of Parnell, in his life of the poet prefixed to his *Poems* (1770) p. iii, that 'his imagination might have been too warm to relish the cold logic of Burgersdicius, or the dreary subtleties of Smiglesius; but it is certain, that as a classical scholar, few could equal him'. Martin Smiglesius, S.J. (d. 1618) was a theologian and logician whose *Logica* was still used in G.'s time at Trinity College, Dublin. See Constantia Maxwell, *History of TCD* (Dublin, 1946) p. 149.

8. *division*] In logic, the distinction of the various meanings of a term.

18. Dobson compares *Spectator* No. 121 (19 July 1711), where Addison discusses the view that instinct is 'the immediate Direction of Providence': 'A modern Philosopher, quoted by Monsieur *Bayle* in his Learned Dissertation on the Souls of Brutes, delivers the same Opinion, tho' in a bolder form of words, where he says *Deus est Anima Brutorum*, God himself is the Soul of Brutes.' Cp. Pierre Bayle's *Historical and Critical Dictionary* (English translation, 1710) iv 2614a, article 'Rorarius', which collects a mass of discussion of whether animals have souls. Bernard is quoted as saying, 'I think I have read somewhere this Assertion, *Deus est Anima Brutorum*.'

19 *ff*. The remainder of the poem is reminiscent of Gulliver's list of the civilized corruptions not found among the Houyhnhnms, ch x. Cf., for example, with l. 35 Swift's 'No lords, fiddlers, judges, or dancing-masters'.

26. *King Lear* V iii 14–15: 'Talk of court news . . . / Who loses and who wins, who's in, who's out.'

They never to the levee go
To treat as dearest friend a foe;
They never importune his grace,
30 Nor ever cringe to men in place;
Nor undertake a dirty job,
Nor draw the quill to write for B—b.
Fraught with invective they ne'er go
To folks at Pater-Noster-Row;
35 No judges, fiddlers, dancing-masters,
No pickpockets or poetasters,
Are known to honest quadrupeds;
No single brute his fellows leads.
Brutes never meet in bloody fray,
40 Nor cut each others' throats for pay.
Of beasts, it is confessed, the ape
Comes nearest us in human shape;
Like man he imitates each fashion,
And malice is his ruling passion;
45 But both in malice and grimaces
A courtier any ape surpasses.
Behold him, humbly cringing, wait
Upon a minister of state;
View him soon after to inferiors
50 Aping the conduct of superiors:
He promises with equal air,
And to perform takes equal care.
He in his turn finds imitators;
At court, the porters, lacqueys, waiters,
55 Their master's manners still contract,
And footmen, lords and dukes can act.
Thus at the court both great and small
Behave alike, for all ape all.

32. B—b] Bob, or Sir Robert Walpole, Prime Minister 1715–42, frequently
so nicknamed by Swift: cp. *Poems*, ed. Williams, ii 503, 531–3, 560.
34. *Pater-Noster-Row*] A street off St Paul's Churchyard, largely inhabited
by booksellers. G. himself had lived there with Ralph Griffiths, editor of
the *Monthly Review*, in 1757.
41ff. Dobson points out that Gay was particularly given to comparing
courtiers to apes or proving that they were baser, e.g. *Fables*, I xiv, xxxiii,
II iii; but the comparison is much older, e.g., Spenser's *Mother Hubbard's
Tale*.
54–6. Steele had written on this subject in *Spectator* No. 88, which inspired
Townley's farce *High Life below Stairs*, performed shortly after the publica-
tion of this poem on 31 Oct. 1759. But G. criticised the play adversely in

The Bee No. v, 3 Nov. 1759. The same subject is treated in Le Sage's *Gil Blas* III iv, more than once imitated by the English novelists of the period, e.g. Fielding, *Joseph Andrews* II xiii.

39 On the Taking of Quebec

General Wolfe had been killed during the taking of Quebec on 13 Sept. 1759, news of which reached England on the evening of 16 Oct. In his *History of England, in a Series of Letters from a Nobleman to his Son* (1764) ii 241, G. wrote of Wolfe's death: 'Perhaps the loss of such a man was greater to the nation than the conquering of all Canada was advantageous; but it is the misfortune of humanity, that we can never know true greatness till that moment when we are going to lose it'; G. wrote in a similar strain in his *History of England* (1771) iv 400. He told Percy in 1773 that 'General Wolfe was allied to the Goldsmith Family', K. C. Balderston, *Percy's Memoir of G.* (1926) p. 13; Prior (*Life* i 6) confirms that Wolfe's mother's maiden name was Goldsmith.

The poem was first printed in *The Busy Body* No. vii, 22 Oct. 1759, the text followed here. It was first collected in *1780* i 118, the only authority for the attribution to G., which is not notably supported by the undistinguished nature of the poem itself, an inflated panegyric of the sort G. most disliked.

Amidst the clamour of exulting joys,
　Which triumph forces from the patriot heart,
Grief dares to mingle her soul-piercing voice,
　And quells the raptures which from pleasures start.

5　O Wolfe, to thee a streaming flood of woe
　Sighing we pay, and think even conquest dear;
Quebec in vain shall teach our breast to glow,
　Whilst thy sad fate extorts the heart-wrung tear.

Alive, the foe thy dreadful vigour fled,
10　And saw thee fall with joy-pronouncing eyes;
Yet they shall know thou conquerest, though dead!
　Since from thy tomb a thousand heroes rise.

40 The Barber's Boy's Epigram

Written by G., if it is his, by 24 Nov. 1762, when the letter in which it appears, signed A. B., was printed in *Lloyd's Evening Post*. This letter was a reply to a review in Robert Lloyd's *St James's Mag.* i 124–9, in Oct. 1762, of G.'s *Life of Richard Nash*. It was first attributed to G. by Friedman (*Works* iii 392–4). The reviewer had ridiculed G.'s treatment of James Quin the actor and his attribution to him of a letter, referred to in the following *Epigram. To the Editor of Nash's Life*, printed after the review:

> Think'st thou that Quin, whose parts and wit
>   Might any station grace,
> Could e'er such ribbald stuff have writ,
>   Or wish'd for Nash's place?
>
> With scorn we read thy senseless trash,
>   And see thy toothless grin,
> For Quin no more cou'd sink to Nash,
>   Than thou can'st rise to Quin.

These lines were quoted in A.B.'s letter defending G. in *Lloyd's Evening Post* three and a half weeks later, which continued: 'This he thought very ingenious; but a Barber's boy, who shaved me this morning, was of a contrary opinion, and said, though he knew the Author, and was well assured he was a fortnight about it, 'twas but a poor piece of business. Then begging pen and ink he sate down and wrote the following answer . . .' Then follows 'The Barber's Boy's Epigram, in the Style and Spirit of the above', the blank in the first line no doubt to be filled by Lloyd. Friedman's main argument for attributing the letter to G. himself rests on the fact that a paragraph from it reappeared with only minor changes as a footnote to the 2nd edn of the *Life of Nash* early in Dec. 1762; on G.'s known connection with *Lloyd's Evening Post* in 1762; and on some parallels with his known writings. These, and lesser considerations, are expounded in full in Friedman's appendix cited above.

> Laborious ———, why all this spleen?
>   With satire why so free?
> He who can't rise to mighty Quin
>   May dwindle down to *thee*.

41 [Riddle for Mary Nugent]

Perhaps written in 1773. It is addressed to Mary, daughter of Robert Nugent, Lord Clare (see headnote to *Haunch of Venison*, p. 696) and was communicated in 1849 by her younger son to Forster, *Life* (6th edn, 1877) ii 329–30 *n*. The accompanying letter describes G.'s friendship with the child, whom he met either at Gosfield or Nugent's house in Great George St, Westminster, and tells how Mary tied G.'s wig to the back of his chair while he was asleep, an incident which he used in the first scene of *She Stoops to Conquer*. If, as is stated in the letter, G. wrote the couplet 'by way of an amends to her for having immortalised her in Tony Lumpkin, as a riddle on her name', it must have been written after March 1773, when the play was first performed.

> The clothes we love best and the half of an agent
>   Is the name of a lady, to whom I'm obadient.

Index of First Lines

771